CW01548216

Atharva-Veda-Saṁhitā

Atharva-Veda-Saṁhitā

Translated into English
With Critical and Exegetical Commentary by
WILLIAM DWIGHT WHITNEY

Revised and Edited by
CHARLES ROCKWELL LANMAN

Second Half
Books VIII to XIX

MOTILAL BANARSIDASS PUBLISHERS
PRIVATE LIMITED • DELHI

Reprint : Delhi, 1962, 1971, 1984, 1993, 1996, 2001, ***2011***
First Published: Cambridge, Mass., 1905

© MOTILAL BANARSIDASS PUBLISHERS PRIVATE LIMITED
All Rights Reserved

ISBN : 978-81-208-1083-9 (Cloth)
ISBN : 978-81-208-1084-6 (Paper)
ISBN : 978-81-208-1085-3 (Set)

MOTILAL BANARSIDASS
41 U.A. Bungalow Road, Jawahar Nagar, Delhi 110 007
8 Mahalaxmi Chamber, 22 Bhulabhai Desai Road, Mumbai 400 026
203 Royapettah High Road, Mylapore, Chennai 600 004
236, 9th Main III Block, Jayanagar, Bangalore 560 011
Sanas Plaza, 1302 Baji Rao Road, Pune 411 002
8 Camac Street, Kolkata 700 017
Ashok Rajpath, Patna 800 004
Chowk, Varanasi 221 001

Printed in India

By Jainendra Prakash Jain at Shri Jainendra Press,
A-45, Naraina, Phase-I, New Delhi 110 028
and Published by Narendra Prakash Jain for
Motilal Banarsidass Publishers Private Limited,
Bungalow Road, Delhi 110 007

Book VIII.

⌊The second grand division of the Atharvan collection comprehends books viii.–xii. It consists wholly of hymns of more than twenty verses, and contains all the hymns of that length except such as for especial reasons were placed in the later books. Leaving out of account the later books, there are forty-five such hymns; and these have been divided into five books, of which the first four, books viii., ix., x., and xi., have ten hymns each, while the remaining five hymns make up the twelfth book. Disregarding ix. 6 and xi. 3 (*paryāya*-hymns), it may be noted that books viii.–xi. contain all the hymns of from twenty to fifty verses to be found in the first two grand divisions, and that book xii. contains all of more than that number in the same divisions. "Of any other principle of arrangement dependent on the length of the different hymns, no trace is to be observed," says Whitney. For the divisions of book viii., see below. The whole book has been translated by Victor Henry, *Les livres VIII et IX de l'Atharva-véda traduits et commentés*, Paris, 1894. The commentary ("of Sāyaṇa") breaks off at the end of hymn 6 and we have no more of it till the beginning of book xi. But in lieu of the missing introductions, Shankar Pandurang Pandit gives introductions of his own, modelled on those of the *bhāṣya*, and drawn from the same sources, the Kāuçika, the Keçavī, etc.⌋

⌊The Major Anukramaṇī, at the beginning of § 2 of its treatment of book viii., says that, 'up to the end of book xi., the *artha-sūktas* constitute the norm and the *paryāyas*, beginning with *virāḍ vā* (viii. 10. 1), the exception': *yāvad ekādaçakāṇḍāntam artha-sūkta-prakṛtis, tāvad vihāya paryāyān virāḍvā-prabhṛtīn iti.* And in fact, all through books viii.–xii., and even to the end of book xviii., every *arthasūkta* is by one ms. or another designated as an *arthasūkta* (xviii. 2 is an exception, solitary and doubtless casual). — In this place it may be well to enumerate the *paryāya*-hymns (including those also of the next division) and to print an account of the way in which the mss. present them. The account (barring slight changes) is by Mr. Whitney, and is written on a loose slip of paper found in his Collation-book at viii. 10. 1.⌋

⌊The **paryāya-hymns** are eight in number and are scattered over seven different books. Specifically, and with the number of *paryāyas* in each, they are as follows: viii. 10 (with 6 *paryāyas*); ix. 6 (with 6); ix. 7 (with 1); xi. 3 (with 3); xii. 5 (with 7); xiii. 4 (with 6); book xv. (18 *paryāyas*); book xvi. (9 *paryāyas*).⌋

They are called *paryāya-sūktas* in distinction from those among which they occur and which are named *artha-sūktas*. The separate portions of which they are composed are called each a *paryāya* ⌊or also *paryāya-sūkta*⌋. Each ⌊*paryāya* taken separately⌋ is in the mss. numbered as to its verses separately; but they ⌊the *paryāyas* of a given group taken together⌋ so evidently constitute each a whole, as shown by the sense and likewise by the manner in which the Anukramaṇīs treat them, that we ⌊R. and W.⌋ regarded it as beyond question that they should be numbered continuously, to save a citation by more than three numbers. ⌊In this connection should be consulted SPP's "Critical Notice," prefixed to vol. i., p. 19 ff.⌋ ⌊See pages cxxxiii–vii.⌋

Each *paryāya* has its own summing up at the end: if a numbered division corresponding to an *ṛc* is composed of more than one divided portion, it is called a *gaṇa*, and its subdivisions *avasāna-ṛcas* or *gaṇā 'vasāna-ṛcas*. Thus the first division ⌊of viii. 10⌋ is summed up as follows: *paryāyaḥ* 1, *gaṇāḥ* 6, *gaṇāvasānarcaḥ* 13; and it is by the latter number that the Anukr. treats it. Similarly the third *paryāya* ⌊of viii. 10⌋ is summed up as *paryāya-sūktam* 1, *gaṇāḥ* 4, *gaṇāvasānarcaḥ* 8. ⌊Cf. the summation at the end of viii. 10.⌋

In xii. 5 the divisions are called *vacanāni* or *vacanā 'vasāna-ṛcas*. In *paryāyas* 5 and 6 of xiii. 4 a distinction is made between *avasānarcaḥ* and *gaṇāvasānarcaḥ*, those which have the refrain receiving the latter designation.

The divisions of books xv. and xvi. are likewise *paryāyas*, and their subdivisions are styled *avasānarcaḥ* or *gaṇāvasānarcaḥ* in the same manner.

⌊The *anuvāka*-division of each of the ten-hymned books viii.–xi. is into five *anuvākas* of two hymns each; and that of book xii. (consisting of five long hymns) is also into five *anuvākas*, but these are of one hymn each, so that here the *anuvāka*-division and the hymn-division coincide. The comm. divides the *anuvākas* into hymns in a manner nearly like that described for book vii. (see p. 388): that is, his "hymns" are mechanical decads of verses, with an overplus or shortage in the last "decad" when the total for the *hymn* (not — as in book vii. — for the *anuvāka*) is not an exact multiple of ten. A tabular conspectus for book viii. follows:

Anuvākas	1		2		3		4		5	
Hymns	1	2	3	4	5	6	7	8	9	10
Verses	21	28	26	25	22	26	28	24	26	33 ¶
Decad-div.	10 + 11	10 + 10 + 8	10 + 10 + 6	10 + 10 + 5	10 + 12	10 + 10 + 6	10 + 10 + 8	10 + 14	10 + 10 + 6	6 P

Here ¶ means "paragraph of a *paryāya*" (such as is numbered as a "verse" in the Berlin edition) and P means "*paryāya*." The last line shows the "decad"-division. These divisions are shown also in the Berlin edition. Of these "decads," *anuvākas* 1, 2, 3, and 4 contain respectively 5, 6, 5, and 5 (in all, 21 "decads"); while *anuvāka* 5 has 3 "decads" and 6 *paryāyas*. The sum is 24 "decad"-*sūktas* and 6 *paryāya-sūktas* or 30 *sūktas*. Cf. again the summation at the end of hymn 10.⌋

1. For some one's continued life.

[*Brahman. — ekaviṅçakam. ārṣy (ārtvy?) āyuṣyam. trāiṣṭubham: 1. purobṛhatī triṣṭubh; 2, 3, 17–21. anuṣṭubh; 4, 9, 15, 16. prastārapañkti; 7. 3-p. virāḍ gāyatrī; 8. virāṭ pathyābṛhatī; 12. 3-av. 5-p. jagatī; 13. 3-p. bhuriñ mahābṛhatī; 14. 1-av. 2-p. sāmnī bhurig bṛhatī.*]

Found also in Pāipp. xvi., with verse 17 after 20. ⌊Partly prose, "verse" 14.⌋

⌊Hymns 1 and 2 together are used with others in Kāuç. in the *upanayana* (55. 17) with touching the student's navel, and again with others in rites for long life (58. 3, 11).

The comm. cites them from Nakṣ. K. 23 in a *mahāçānti*. They are reckoned by Kāuç. to the *āyuṣya gaṇa* (note to 54. 11). For vs. 10, see below.⌋

Translated: Muir, v. 444; Ludwig, p. 495; Henry, 1, 35; Griffith, i. 385; Bloomfield, 53, 569.

1. To the ender Death [be] homage. Let thy breaths, expirations, rest here. Let this man be here with his life (*ásu*), in the portion of the sun, in the world of the immortal.

Ppp. puts our second pāda last.

2. Up hath Bhaga taken him, up Soma rich in shoots ⌊hath taken⌋ him, up the heavenly Maruts ⌊have taken⌋ him, up have Indra-and-Agni, for his welfare.

Or *añçumant* means 'rich in rays,' Soma having its secondary sense of 'moon': both were probably in the author's mind.

3. Here [be] thy life, here breath, here life-time, here thy mind; we bear thee up from the fetters of perdition with divine speech.

4. Step up from here, O man, fall not down, loosening down the fetter (*páḍbīça*) of death; be not severed from this world, from the sight (*saṁdṙç*) of fire, of the sun.

The mss., as usual, vary between *páḍvīçam* and *páḍb-*, and SPP. adopts the former; the comm. has the latter.

5. Let the wind, Mātariçvan, be cleansing for thee; for thee let the waters rain immortal things; may the sun burn weal for thy body; let death compassionate thee; do not thou perish.

Pavatām 'be cleansing' might properly enough be rendered simply 'blow.'

6. Up-going [be] thine, O man, not down-going; length of life (*jīvā́tu*), ability, I make for thee; for do thou ascend this immortal easy-running chariot, then shalt thou in advanced age (?*jírvi*) speak to the council (*vidátha*).

Both here and at xiv. 1. 21, our mss. on the whole read decidedly *jīrvis* (only P.M. have *jivrīs*, Bp. *jīvis*, here), and SPP. reports all his authorities without exception as giving it, so that it is without question the true AV. reading (as against RV. *jīvri*); the comm. reads *ajirvis*, and glosses it with *ajīrṇas*, and Ludwig renders 'lebenskräftig.'

7. Let not thy mind go thither; let it not be lost (*tiró-bhū*); do not neglect (*pra-mad*) the living, go not after the Fathers; let all the gods defend thee here.

8. Do not regard (*ā-dhī*) the departed, who lead [one] to the distance; ascend out of darkness, come to light; we take hold on thy hands.

Ppp. begins **c** with *ud ā roha*, which makes the pāda a good *triṣṭubh;* the omission of *e 'hi* would rectify it to an *anuṣṭubh*. The comm. omits *e 'hi*. Ppp. also reads *hastam* in **d**. ⌊With **b**, cf. v. 30. 12 **b**.⌋

9. Let not the dark and the brindled one, sent forth, [seize] thee, that are Yama's dogs, road-defenders; come thou hitherward; do not hesitate; stand not there with mind averted.

Ppp. reads *mā 'va* for *mā vi* in **c**. The comm. omits *préṣitāu* in **a**; he ⌊twice⌋ supplies *bādhatām* as the missing verb in **a**.

10. Do not follow that road; that is a frightful one — the one thou hast not gone before, that I speak of; to that darkness, O man, do not go forth; [there is] fear in the distance, safety for thee hitherward.

⌊Kāuç. reckons the vs. to the *abhaya gaṇa*, note to 16. 8.⌋ Ppp. mutilates *tamas* in **c** to *tam*. The comm. reads *purastāt* in **d**. ⌊For *iyátha*, see *Gram.* § 801 d.⌋

11. Let the fires that are within the waters defend thee; let that defend thee which human beings kindle; let Vāiçvānara, Jātavedas defend [thee]; let not [the fire] of heaven consume thee along with the lightning.

Our text should read in **d** *mā́ prá dhāk;* the omission of *prá* is an error of the press. Ppp. reads *mā pra dahāt.*

12. Let not the flesh-eating [fire] plot against thee; move far from the destroying (*sáṁkasuka*) one; let heaven defend, let earth defend thee; let both sun and moon defend thee; let the atmosphere defend from the gods' missile.

Most of the mss. (not our Bp.P.M.I.) read *rákṣatām* in **d**, which SPP. accordingly (following all his authorities) retains, though the accent is not defensible. ⌊I can find no note to the effect that P.M.I. leave *rakṣatām* unaccented.⌋ Ppp. puts pādas **a**, **b** after **c**, **d**. The comm. reads *saṁkusukāt* in **b**.

13. Let both the knower and the attender defend thee; let both the sleepless one and the unslumbering one defend thee; let both the guardian and the wakeful one protect thee.

In *bodhá* and *pratībodhá*, in **a**, the radical sense is perhaps more that of 'wake.' The comm. understands six rishis bearing these several appellations to be intended. ⌊Cf. the closely related v. 30. 10, above; also MGS. ii. 15. 1 a, b, c, d, and the Index to their *pratīkas*.⌋ A similar formula is found also in K. xxxvii. 10; compare further PGS. iii. 4. 17. Ppp. reads *anavadrāṇiç ca* in **b**. ⌊In **b**, the first *ca* might be dropped, without hurting the meter.⌋

14. Let these defend thee; let these guard thee; to these [be] homage! to these hail!

After *gopāyantu*, Ppp. inserts *te tvāṁ hasassāyatu.*

15. Let Vāyu, Indra, Dhātar, the preserving Savitar, assign thee unto converse with the living; let not breath, strength, leave thee; we call after thy life.

The *pada*-text has *samoúde* in **a**, and the translation follows this (cf. *vyoúṣi* from root *vas*), as being on the whole probably the understanding of the text-makers; if they

16. What enveloping (*paridhā́na*) garment thou hast, what inner wrap (*nīví*) thou makest for thyself, that we make propitious unto thy body; be it not harsh to thy touch.

SPP. reads, "with all his authorities," *ádrūkṣṇam* in **d**. Our mss. might doubtless all be understood in the same way, but some of them look more like *-ḍū-* or *-dū-*; *-rū-*, which our text unfortunately gives, is not found in any; neither *rūkṣṇa* nor *drūkṣṇa* appears to be met with elsewhere; the comm. glosses with *arūkṣam;* he also reads *açnute* for *astu te* at the end. Ppp. has *'dukṣaṇam.* ⌊Vait. (10.6) employs the vs. in the *paçubandha* on draping the sacrificial post.⌋

17. In that with a dangerous (? *marcáyant*) very sharp (*sutejás*) razor thou, a hair-dresser, shearest hair and beard, adorning the face, do not thou steal away our life-time.

The translation given implies in **c** the reading *çúmbhan*, which, it can hardly be questioned, is the true one, although it is read by only one ms. (our W.) and by Ppp.; the rest of our mss. all have, and our edition with them, *çúmbhaṁ*. SPP. accepts the unintelligible *çúbham*, with the comm., and with, as he reports, the majority of his authorities, the rest reading, like ours, *çúmbhaṁ;* the comm. explains *çubham* with *dīptaṁ tejasvi* and has to supply after it *kuru* to make any sense. Ppp. further reads *-çmaçrū* in **b**, and *māi 'nam* for *mā nas* in **c**. According to the distinct direction of the Prāt. (ii. 76), we ought to read *ā́yuṣ prá* in **d**, and its authority is sufficient to establish that as the true text, against both the editions; half SPP's authorities give it, though only one of ours (R.); on such a point the mss. are often at odds, and their evidence of little weight. The verse occurs also in several Gṛhya-Sūtras, AGS. (i. 17. 16); PGS. (ii. 1. 19), and HGS. (i. 9. 16); all read *supeçasā* in **a**; in **b**, HGS. has *vaptar*, PGS. *vapati*, AGS. and PGS. *keçān;* in **c**, the two latter have *çunddhi çiras*, HGS. *varcayā mukham;* in **d**, AGS. and PGS. give *asya* for *nas;* all have *āyuḥ pra.* ⌊Found also MP. ii. 1. 7: see also MGS. i. 21. 7 and p. 153.⌋ ⌊Cf. Oldenberg, IFA. vi. 184.⌋

18. Propitious to thee be rice and barley, free from *balā́sa*, causing no burning (?); these drive off the *yákṣma;* these free from distress.

Compare Grohmann in *Ind. Stud.* ix. 399. The comm. does not connect *abalāsāú* with *balā́sa*, but regards it as *a-bala-asa*, and glosses it with *çārīrabalasyā 'kṣeptārāu. Adomadhāú* (cf. *adomadám*, vi. 63. 1, and note) is very obscure; Ppp. reads instead *adhomadhāu;* the comm. *adomadhū*, glossing it with *upayogānantaram madhurāu.* Ppp. reads *yatas* for *etāu* in both **c** and **d**, and follows it in **d** by *muñcata mā 'ṅhasaḥ.*

19. What thou eatest (*aç*), what thou drinkest, of grain, milk of the plowing — what should be eaten, what should not be eaten — all food I make for thee poisonless.

The comm. reads strangely *kṛchrāt* instead of *kṛṣyās* in **b**.

20. Both to day and to night, to them both we commit thee. Defend ye this man for me from the *arā́yas* that seek to devour [him].

Some of SPP's authorities, also the comm. and Ppp., read *dadhmasi* at end of **b**. Ppp. further has *rāyebhyas* at beginning of **c**, and *nas* (for *me*) in **d**. The comm. explains *arāyebhyas* as = *adhanebhyo dhanāpahartṛbhyo vā.*

21. A hundred, a myriad years, two periods (*yugá*), three, four, we make for thee; let Indra-and-Agni, let all the gods, approve thee, not showing enmity.

The second half-verse is i. 35. 4 **c**, **d**. The 'periods' here are not at all likely to be those of the later chronology, though the comm. naturally thinks them so. ⌊Alternatively, he makes *yugé* = 'generations.'⌋ Ppp. has *santu* for *kṛṇmas* in **b**, and omits *te* in **c**. The *pada*-mss. read *té : ánu* instead of *te : ánu :* compare under i. 35. 4. ⌊We had a "*satahpañkti*" at vi. 20. 3.⌋

22. Unto autumn, unto winter, unto spring, unto summer, we commit thee; [be] the rains pleasant to thee, in which the herbs grow.

Ppp. has again *dadhmasi* in **b**.

23. Death is master of bipeds; death is master of quadrupeds; from that death, lord of kine, I bear thee up; ⌊so⌋ do thou not be afraid.

Ppp. reads for **d** *ud dharāmi sa mā mṛta* ⌊intending *mṛthās?*⌋.

24. Thou, unharmed one, shalt not die; thou shalt not die, be not afraid; [men] die not there, nor go to lowest darkness.

Ppp. gives in **c** *pra mīyante* — a better reading, as rectifying the meter. ⌊Pāda **b** occurs as vs. 1 **a** of a *khila* to RV. i. 191, with the two clauses inverted.⌋

25. Every one, verily, lives there — ox, horse, man, beast — where this charm (*bráhman*) is performed, a defense (*paridhí*) unto living.

The verse has a correspondent in TA. (vi. 11. 12), but with a different first pāda: TA. makes it *ná vāí tátra prá mīyate* (nearly as our 24 **c** in Ppp.).

26. Let it protect thee from thy fellows, from witchcraft, from thy kinsmen; be thou undying, immortal, surviving; let not thy life-breaths (*ásu*) leave thy body.

Ppp. reads *sugantubhyas* at end of **b**.

27. The deaths that are a hundred and one, the perditions (*nāṣṭrā́*) that are to be over-passed — from that let the gods free thee, from Agni Vāiçvānara.

Ppp. reads in **b** *nāṣṭrātta* (*-tu*?) *jīvyāḥ*. ⌊See note to iii. 11. 5 for "101 deaths."⌋

28. Agni's body art thou, successful (*pārayiṣṇú*); demon-slayer art thou, rival-slayer, likewise expeller of disease, a remedy *pūtúdru* by name.

Pūtúdru is (OB.) *Acacia catechu* or *Pinus deodora;* the comm. reads *pūtadru* and does not attempt ⌊on p. 587⌋ to identify it.* The mss. vary between *-ṇú* and *-ṇús* at end of **a**; our edition reads *-ṇús* (with our P.M.E.s.m.); SPP. adopts *-ṇú*, with the great majority of his authorities; the comm. has *-ṇus;* Ppp., as noticed above, lacks this verse. There is little to choose in point of acceptability between the two readings. *⌊As noted in the introd., the use of the hymn is followed in Kāuç. 58. 15 by the binding on of *pūtu-dāru* (so Bl's text, with the variant *pūta-*; in citing the text, at p. 568, comm. has *pūti-*). This is explained by Daç. Kar. as an "amulet of deodar," *devadāru-maṇi;* and so Dār. and Keç. to 8. 15, and comm. p. 567 end.⌋

⌊The first *anuvāka*, 2 hymns and 49 verses, ends here. The quoted Anukr. (cf. end of h. 1) says *ādyasahitam.*⌋

3. To Agni: against sorcerers and demons.

[*Cātana.—ṣaḍvinçam. āgneyam. trāiṣṭubham: 7, 12, 14, 15, 17, 21. bhurij; 25. 5-p. bṛhatīgarbhā jagatī; 22, 23. anuṣṭubh; 26. gāyatrī.*]

Found also in Pāipp. xvi. (in the verse-order 1–4, 6, 5, 7–14, 18, 15, 17, 16, 19–22, 24, 26, 25, 23). The first 23 verses are (in slightly different order*) vss. 1–23 of RV. x. 87, and most of them are found in no other text. ⌊Cf. Oldenberg, *Die Hymnen des RV.* i. 246.⌋ *⌊Namely, with 4 after 6, with 17 and 18 inverted, and with 12 between 21 and 22.⌋

⌊Kāuç. reckons the hymn to the *cātana* hymns (8. 25). The comm. says (p. 587, l. 18 ff.) that the whole *anuvāka*, that is hymn 4 as well as 3, is to be used in a variety of practices, which he details. In the *vaçāçamana* ceremony (44. 16), after the victim's "breath has been stopped" with ii. 34. 5, the performer takes his place at her right and mutters this hymn. Vs. 22 (not 21) is identical with vii. 71. 1, which was prescribed at 2. 10 for use in the *parvan* sacrifices, to accompany the carrying of fire thrice about the offering. Moreover, verses of this hymn are used in four expiatory rites as follows: vss. 15–18 accompany an oblation (112. 1) made when the cows give bloody milk; vs. 26 is used with vi. 63. 4 if spontaneous combustion occurs (46. 23); and the same vs. is used (130. 3) when there appears a bright glow without any fire; and yet again (131. 3), when the fire puffs (*çvasati*). Finally, the same vs. is used by Vāit. (6. 11) in the *agnyādheya* (with vi. 19. 2 etc.) with an offering to Agni Çuci.⌋

Translated: Henry, 7, 43; Griffith, i. 392.

1. I pour ghee upon (*ā-ghṛ*) the vigorous (*vājín*) demon-slayer; I go for broadest protection to the friend; Agni, sharpened, [is] kindled with acts of skill (? *krátu*); let him by day, let him by night, protect us from harm.

This verse is found further in TS. (i. 2. 14[6]); neither RV. nor TS. offers a variant reading.

2. Do thou, of iron tusks, O Jātavedas, kindled, touch the sorcerers with thy flame (*arcís*); take hold of the false-worshipers with thy tongue; cutting off (?) the flesh-eaters, shut them in thy mouth.

The comm. reads *dhṛṣṭvā* in **d**, paraphrasing it only with *dharṣitvā*. RV. has *vṛktví*, which is most probably to be referred to root *vṛj*. Ppp. has *datsvā* (for *dhatsva*).

3. Apply both thy tusks, thou that hast them in both jaws (*ubhayāvín*), the lower one and the upper, being harmful, sharpened; also in the atmosphere go about, O Agni; put together thy grinders upon the sorcerers.

RV. reads *dáṅṣṭrā* at end of **a**, and *rājan* for *agne* at end of **c**. Ppp. has *dehy* ⌊in **a**, apparently⌋ and *api* for *abhi* in **d**.

4. O Agni, split the skin of the sorcerer; let the harmful thunderbolt smite him with flame (*háras*); crush his joints, O Jātavedas; let the flesh-eating, flesh-craving ⌊one⌋ divide him.

RV. (vs. 5; its vs. 4 is our 6) reads *vṛknám* for *enam* at the end. The comm. understands 'a wolf or the like' in **d**, and takes *vi-ci* as 'scatter about, dragging him to and fro to eat him.' It more probably refers to the flesh-eating Agni.

5. Wherever now, O Jātavedas, thou seest a sorcerer standing, O Agni, or also moving, also flying in the atmosphere, him [as] archer, pierce with a shaft, being sharpened.

RV. (vs. 6) has a quite different **c**, *yád vā 'ntárikṣe pathíbhiḥ pátantam*. Ppp. (vs. 6) reads in **d** *viddhi çarvā*. Many mss. (including our Bp.W.E.O.T.) have *sárvā* in **d**.

6. By sacrifices, O Agni, straightening (*sam-nam*) thine arrows, by speech smearing their tips with thunderbolts — with them pierce in the heart the sorcerers; break back (*pratīcás*) their arms.

'By sacrifices,' 'by speech' — i.e. in virtue of our offerings and praise. RV. (vs. 4) offers no variant; Ppp. (vs. 5) reads *çalyam* in **b**.

7. Both those that are seized do thou win (*spṛ*), O Jātavedas, and also the sorcerers that have seized with spears; do thou, O Agni, first, greatly gleaming, smite [him] down; let the variegated raw-flesh-eating *kṣvíñkās* eat him.

This verse differs somewhat, and inconsistently, from RV., which has *ā́labdham* in **a**, and, without *utá*, *ālebhānā́t . . . yātudhā́nāt* in **b**, giving the clear sense 'win away him that is seized from the sorcerer that has seized him,' and agreeing with the sing. *tám* in **d**. The AV. version yields no acceptable meaning; and most of the *saṁhitā*-mss. read *ā́rabdhāṁ* in **a** (including our P.M.W.I.: some of the others not noted), as if the word were after all a singular. The comm. reads *kṣvañkās* in **d**, and explains it simply as *pakṣiviçeṣās*. He gives a most absurd version of **a, b**: 'protect (us) who have begun (to praise thee) and (slay) with spears the sorcerers who have made a noise'! ⌊Comm. seems to read *rebhāṇān* and to take it from root *ribh*: cf. note to vs. 21.⌋ Ppp. has our version of **a, b**, except that it reads *utā* "*lab*- in **a**, and omits *uta* in **b** ⌊i.e., if I understand R., it appears to begin **b** with *ārebhāṇāṅ*⌋.

8. Proclaim thou here which that [is], O Agni — the sorcerer that is doing this; him take hold of with the fuel, O youngest [god]; subject him to the eye of the men-watcher.

RV. inserts another *yás* at beginning of **b**, and Ppp. has the same. The comm. reads *kṛṇoṣi* (explaining it ⌊alternatively⌋ as = *kṛṇoti*) at end of **b**, and *yaviṣṭhya* at end of **c**. ⌊Better, perhaps, in **a**, 'Proclaim which one he [is]' etc.⌋

9. With sharp eye, O Agni, defend thou the sacrifice; conduct it forward to the Vasus, O forethoughtful one; thee that art harmful, greatly gleaming against the demons, let not the sorcerers injure, O men-watcher.

Ppp. reads *hiṅsrā* at beginning of **c**. The comm. appears to regard *abhiçoçucānam* as a compound.

10. A men-watcher, do thou look around for the demon among the people (*vikṣú*); crush back his three points (*ágra*); crush, O Agni, his ribs with flame (*háras*); cut up threefold the root of the sorcerer.

The comm. attempts no explanation of the 'three points,' but simply glosses *agra* with *uparibhāga*.

11. Let the sorcerer thrice come within thy reach (? *prásiti*), who, O Agni, slays truth (*ṛtá*) with untruth; roaring [at] him with thy flame (*arcís*), O Jātavedas, do thou put him down (*ni-yuj*) before the eyes of the singer.

Our *ní yuñdhi* at the end is a weakened corruption of RV. *ní vṛñdhi*, which is read also by Ppp., the comm., and one of SPP's authorities. SPP. reads *yuñgdhi*, not heeding the rule of the Prāt. (ii. 20) to the contrary. ⌊Cf. his *bhañgdhi* in vs. 6. And in his "Corrections" to vol. ii., he is at pains thrice to correct *vṛñdhi* of p. 71–2 to *vṛñgdhi*.⌋ The majority of the mss. (including all ours save D.R.p.m.K.) accent *ágne* in **b**; both editions, of course, emend to *agne*. The comm. paraphrases *prásitim* with *jvālām*; he does not deign to add any explanation to *sphūrjáyan*. The occurrence of *enam* in **d** seems to require us to regard *tám* as object of *sphūrjáyan*.

12. What, O Agni, the pair utter in curses today, what harshness (*tṛṣṭá*) of speech the reciters (*rebhá*) produce: the shaft that is born of fury of the mind — with that pierce thou the sorcerers in the heart.

'That' in **d** is fem., as if referring to the 'shaft' alone; and the comm. regards **a** and **b** as describing faults caused by the sorcerers, which Agni is to requite — which is doubtless the true connection. *Mithunā* is explained as = *strīpuṅsāu*, and *çapātas* as = *parasparam ākroçatas*. The verse is RV. vs. 13, its vs. 12 being found much further on, as our vs. 21. Ppp. again reads *viddhi* for *vidhya* in **d**.

13. Crush away the sorcerers with heat; crush away, O Agni, the demon with flame (*háras*); crush away with burning (*arcís*) the false-worshipers; crush away the greatly gleaming ones that feed on lives (? *asutṛ́p*).

RV. (vs. 14) is quite different in **d**: *párā 'sutṛ́po abhí çóçucānaḥ*. The comm. paraphrases *asutṛpas* with *paraprāṇāir ātmānaṁ tarpayantaḥ*.

14. Let the gods crush away today the wicked one (*vṛjiná*); let [his] curses sent forth go back upon him; let shafts strike (*ṛch*) in the vitals him who steals by [magic] speech; let the sorcerer come within every one's reach.

RV. (vs. 15) reads *tṛṣṭā́s* (for *sṛṣṭā́s*) at end of **b**, and the comm. and one of SPP's authorities have the same. The comm. this time paraphrases *prásitim* with *prakarṣeṇa abhibhavitrīṁ hetim*, adding as alternative *agner jvālām*.

15. The sorcerer that smears himself (*sam-añj*) with the flesh of men, who with that of horses, with cattle, who bears [off] the milk of the inviolable [cow], O Agni — their heads cut thou into with flame.

Ppp. reads *bharata* in **c**. ⌊The *áçveyena* of Aufrecht's RV.[2] seems to be a misprint.⌋

16. Let the sorcerers bear [off] poison of the kine; let them of evil courses fall under the wrath of Aditi; let god Savitar abandon them; let them lose their share of the herbs.

'Lose': lit. 'have it conquered from them.' RV. (vs. 18: RV. inverts the order of our vss. 16 and 17) reads *pibantu* for *bharantām* (with Ppp.) in **a**, has the proper passive form *vṛçcyantām* in **b** (Ppp. has *mṛddhyantām*), and leaves *enān* unlingualized in **c**; the lingualization in our text is by Prāt. iii. 80, where the commentary quotes this passage.

17. Yearly [is] the milk of the ruddy [cow]; of that let not the sorcerer partake (*aç*), O men-watcher; whatever one [of them], O Agni, would fain enjoy (*tṛp*) the beestings, him do thou pierce back in the vitals with thy burning (*arcís*).

Our *pada*-text divides wrongly *mā́ : āçīt* in **b**; RV. has the true reading, *mā́ : açīt*. RV. also has *mármaṇ* at the end, making the *triṣṭubh* verse regular. Ppp. once more reads *vidhi* (not *viddhi* this time) for *vidhya* in **d**, and *marman* after it.

18. From of old, O Agni, thou killest the sorcerers; the demons have not conquered thee in fights; burn up the flesh-eaters together with their dupes (? *mūrá*); let them not be freed from thy heavenly missile.

We had this verse above, as v. 29. 11. The only variant in the version of RV. (vs. 19) is that, in **c**, *sahámūrān* is put after *ánu daha*; ⌊so also SV. i. 80, which has besides *kayā́das* for *kravyā́das*⌋. The comm. regards *-mūrān* as for *-mūlān*, and renders it *mūlasahitān* 'together with their roots,' and it is perhaps one of the cases contemplated by Prāt. i. 66 — at least, the commentary there quotes this passage as one of the instances of substitution of *r* for *l*; and it is very likely that the tradition is right.

19. Do thou, O Agni, from below, from above, do thou defend us from behind and from in front; let those [flames] of thine, unaging, extremely hot, greatly paining, burn against the evil-plotter.

RV. (vs. 20) reads *údaktāt* at end of **a**, and *té* for *tyé* in **c**; in the latter case, the comm. does the same; he supplies *sphuliñgās* as the missing noun in **c**, **d**. An accent-mark has dropped out in our edition under the *-du-* of *paçcā́d utá* in **b**.

20. From behind, in front, below, and above, do thou, O Agni, a poet, protect us about with poesy; [as] friend a friend, [as] unaging in order to old age, [as] an immortal mortals, do thou [protect] us, O Agni.

RV. (vs. 21) reads again *údaktāt* for *utó 'ttarā́t* in **a**, also *rājan* for *agne* at end of **b**, and *sákhe* at beginning of **c**; and it combines *-mṇé 'gne* between **c** and **d**. The comm. has *martyān* in **d**.

21. Set thou in the reciter, O Agni, that eye with which thou seest the hoof-breaking sorcerers; Atharvan-like, with brightness of the gods, scorch (*uṣ*) down the truth-damaging fool (*acít*).

The obscure epithet in **b** is divided in *pada*-text *çapha°ārújaḥ* (RV. *-jam*, and later *yātudhā́nam*). The comm. is in part obscure: *çaphārujaḥ çaphavat çaphāḥ : nakhā ity arthaḥ;* but he adds as alternative *atha vā paçurūpadhāriṇāṁ çaphā api* had seen in the word anything of the root *mud*, they would have divided *sa○múde;* and yet it is very likely that it is a corruption for *sam○múde;* the comm. glosses it with *sammodāya*, as if the reading were *sammúde*. No variant from Ppp. is noted.

The comm. divides our 15–17 into two long verses, ending 15 with *kathā́ syāḥ*. His intention seems to be to make just twenty verses of the hymn.

16. Let not the jaw-snapping (?) grinder (*jambhá*), let not the darkness find thee, let not the tongue-wrencher (?); how shouldst thou be one that perisheth? up let the Ādityas, the Vasus bear thee, up let Indra-and-Agni, for thy welfare.

The translation implies a bold emendation of the unintelligible *jihvā́ ā́ barhīs* to *jihvābarhás*, formed like *muṣkābarhás* ⌊at iii. 9. 2⌋; Ludwig has a kindred conjecture, *ā́ barhīs* (aor.). The comm. thinks of a demon's tongue stretched to the size of a *barhis*. The rendering of *saṁhanu* agrees with that of the Petersburg Lexicon, and with the comm's first gloss, *saṁhatadanta;* he adds as an alternative *saṁhatahanur jambho 'sthūladantaḥ*. ⌊But cf. v. 28. 13 and note.⌋ Ppp. reads, for **b**, *mā jihvacaryaḥ prasuyuṣ kathāsya*.

17. Up hath heaven, up hath earth, up hath Prajāpati caught thee; up out of death have the herbs, with Soma for their king, made thee pass.

Put after vs. 20 in Ppp., as noted above.

18. Be this man just here, O gods; let him not go yonder from hence; him by what is of thousand-fold might do we make pass up out of death.

19. I have made thee pass up out of death; let the vigor-givers blow together; let not the women of disheveled locks, let not the evil-wailers, wail for thee.

The 'evil-wailers,' perhaps professional lamenters of death or other misfortune, appear again at xi. 2. 11. The comm., in **a**, has *apīparan*, which SPP., without sufficient reason, is inclined to regard as the original reading. For the fuller use of 'blow together,' see 2. 4 below. ⌊For *agha-rúd*, see Bloomfield, AJP. xi. 339; Caland, *Todtengebräuche*, Note 106*. See also his note 517.⌋

20. I have taken, I have found thee; thou hast come back renewed; whole-limbed one! I have found thy whole sight, and thy whole life-time.

The verse is RV. x. 161. 5, which has another *tvā* after *ā́ 'hārṣam* in **a**, and the voc. *punarnava* ⌊with unlingualized *n*⌋ at end of **b**, with both of which variants the comm. agrees, while Ppp. also gives the former. ⌊For the lingualized *ṇ*, see Prāt. iii. 82.⌋

21. It hath shone out for thee; it hath become light; darkness hath departed from thee; away from thee we set down death [and] perdition, away the *yákṣma*.

The comm. also recognizes *vy avāt* as coming from root *vas* 'shine,' glossing it with *vyāucchat:* compare *tasmāi vyāuchat* PB. xvi. 1. 1. ⌊For the form, cf. *Gram.* § 890 a and § 167.⌋

⌊The first *artha-sūkta*, so called (see above, p. 472, top), ends here. The quoted Anukr. says *ekaviṅçakam ihā "dyam ucyate*. It adds, further, *sūktaçaç ca gaṇanā pravartate.*⌋

⌊See p. cxl.⌋

2. To prolong some one's life.

[*Brahman.* — *aṣṭāvin̄çakam. ārṣy* (*ārtvy* ?) *āyuṣyam. trāiṣṭubham* *: *1, 2, 7. bhurij; 3. āstārapan̄kti; 4. prastārapan̄kti; 6. pathyāpan̄kti; 8. purastāj jyotiṣmatī jagatī; 9. 5-p. jagatī; 11. viṣṭārapan̄kti; 12. purastādbṛhatī; 14. 3-av. 6-p. jagatī; 15. pathyāpan̄kti; 19. upariṣṭādbṛhatī; 21. satahpan̄kti; 26. āstārapan̄kti; 22, 28. purastādbṛhatī; 5, 10, 16–18, 20, 23–25, 27. anuṣṭubh* (*17. tripāt*).]

Found also in Pāipp. xvi., all but the last verse, and with 9 before 8. *⌊Verse 13 appears to be the one upon the strength of which the Anukr. declares the hymn to be *trāiṣṭubham* (its remaining 27 vss. being exceptions !); and even this is no real *triṣṭubh*. It counts indeed 44 (8 + 12 : 12 + 12) and might be called *purastāj jyotiṣmatī*.⌋

⌊Vāit. uses only vs. 16: see under 16. — The uses by Kāuç. are many. For the uses of this hymn with h. 1, see introd. to h. 1. Further, in the name-giving ceremony, it is used (58. 14) with pouring a continuous stream of water on the youth's right hand; and this is followed (58. 15) by the binding on of an amulet of deodar (see note to vs. 28 below); and the use of vs. 16 is especially prescribed (58. 17: the text of the sūtra in the comm. differs from that of Bl.) to accompany the putting a new garment upon him. Vss. 12–13 are prescribed (97. 3) in case of family quarrels (see also note to vs. 9 below); vs. 14 (comm., 14–15) is used in the tonsure ceremony (54. 17); and again vs. 14 (comm., 14–15), on the child's first going out of the house (58. 18). Vs. 17 was previously prescribed for the same tonsure ceremony (53. 19: the comm. reads *kṣuram abhyukṣya triḥ pramārṣṭi*) on sprinkling and wiping the razor; and the same vs. is substituted for vi. 68. 3 by the Daça Karmāṇi in the same ceremony (53. 17 note); furthermore, it is used at the beginning of the ceremony of the reception of the Vedic student (55. 3). Vs. 18 (comm., 18–19) is used on the first feeding of the child (with rice and barley: 58. 19); and vss. 20 and 22 on his "committal" (58. 20, 21) respectively "to day and night" and "to the seasons." — Bloomfield (note to 58. 17) cites a passage describing the four "committals": 1. to heaven and earth, with vss. 14–15; 2. to rice and barley, with vss. 18–19; 3. to day and night, with vs. 20; 4. to the seasons, with vs. 22. — Finally, the comm. regards vs. 15 as intended, with v. 1. 7 etc., at Kāuç. 46. 1–3, in the rite against false accusation.⌋

Translated: Muir, v. 447; Ludwig, p. 496; Henry, 4, 39; Griffith, i. 388; Bloomfield, 55, 573.

1. Take thou hold on this bundle (?) of immortality; unsevered length of life be thine; I bring back thy life, [thy] life-time; go not to the welkin (*rájas*), to darkness; do not perish.

SPP. with all his authorities save one (which has *snú-*) reads *çnúṣṭim* in **a**, and this must doubtless be regarded as the true AV. text: compare iii. 17. 2. The comm. glosses it here with *prasnuti* 'a dripping forth,' and then explains *amṛtasya çnuṣṭi* as the stream of water which, according to one direction in Kāuç. (58. 14), is to be poured out while the hymn is recited. He glosses *rajas* with *rāga*, and explains it and *tamas* as the two familiar *guṇas* so called: it is, indeed, a little startling to find the two names here side by side.

2. Come thou hitherward unto the light of the living; I take thee in order to life for a hundred autumns; loosening down the fetters of death, imprecation, I set for thee further a longer life-time.

Some of SPP's mss. accent falsely *abhyèhi* in **a**. Ppp. transposes the order of **c** and **d**, and reads *lokam* for *arvāñ* in **a**.

3. From the wind have I found thy breath, from the sun I thy sight; what is thy mind, that I maintain in thee; be in concord with thy limbs; speak with thy tongue, not babbling.

The comm. reads in **d** *viçvāñgāis* and *ālapan*.

4. I blow together upon thee with the breath of bipeds [and] quadrupeds as upon [new-] born fire; homage, O death, to thy sight, homage to thy breath have I made.

5. Let this man live; let him not die; him we send together; I make a remedy for him; death, do not slay the man.

The majority of the mss. (including all ours save Bp.O.) leave *mṛtyo* in **d** accentless. ⌊Both editions read *mṛ́tyo*.⌋

6. The lively, by-no-means-harming, living herb, the preserving, overpowering, powerful, do I call hither, for this man's freedom from harm.

⌊Pādas **a** and **b** are repeated at viii. 7. 6.⌋ The accent of the two participles *jīvantī́m* and *trāyamāṇā́m* seems to mark them as appellatives rather than proper participles. *Naghāriṣá*, like *naghamārá*, seems a fusion of the phrase *na ghā* (or *gha*) *riṣyati* etc.; the *pada*-mss. chance mostly to agree in the frequent error of reading *ṛ* for *ri* (*naghaoṛṣā́m;* Bp. *oriṣā́m*); the comm. reads and explains *nagharuṣām*, taking *-gha-* as representing root *han: yasyāḥ kopo 'pi na ghātakaḥ;* he regards the plant intended as the *pāṭhā* (*Clypea hernandifolia*). Ppp. reads *naghāriṣaṁ*, adds *arundhatīm* after *sahasvatīm* in **d**, and has *hvaye* for *huve*. The long *ī* in *óṣadhīm* is expressly taught by Prāt. iii. 6; *naghāriṣām* is mentioned in the introduction to the fourth chapter (add. note 4, at II. 7).

7. Bless thou [him]; do not take hold; let him loose; even being thine, let him be one of completed years (?) here; O Bhava-and-Çarva, be ye gracious; yield protection; driving away difficulty, bestow ye life-time.

The obscure *-hāyas* in **b** is translated here as if akin with *hāyana* ⌊cf. vs. 8 **d**⌋; the comm. glosses *sarvahāyas* with *sarvagati;* the Petersburg Lexicons conjecture 'having complete liveliness or power.' For *sán*, the comm. reads *sam* ⌊and joins it with *sṛjá*, supplying *prāṇāis*⌋.

8. Bless thou this man, O death; pity him; let him go up from here; unharmed, whole-limbed, well-hearing, hundred-yeared by old age, let him attain enjoyment with himself.

Ppp. reads *him* for *'yam* in **b**, and combines in **d–e** *-hāyanā "tm-*. The comm. paraphrases *ātmánā* in **d** with *ananyāpekṣaḥ san*. ⌊Read as 8 + 11 : 8 + 8 + 8.⌋

9. Let the missile of the gods avoid thee; I make thee pass from the welkin (*rájas*); I have made thee pass up out of death; removing afar the flesh-eating Agni, I set for thee an enclosure in order to living.

The comm. reads in c *nirāuham;* SPP. follows grammatical rule and reads *-haṅ jīv-* this time ⌊cf. note to 1. 19. 4⌋ because all his *saṁhitā*-mss. happen to agree in doing so; some of ours, however, do not. The comm. explains *rájasas* in b as *mūrchālakṣaṇād āvaraṇāt.* ⌊At 97. 6, Kāuç. gives in full, for use in case of a family quarrel (cf. above, introd.), a verse whose first half agrees entirely with the second half of this.⌋

10. The down-going in the welkin, not to be ventured down upon, which is thine, O death — from that road defending this man, we make *bráhman* a covering (*vármaṇ*) for him.

The comm. reads in b *anavadhr̥ṣyam;* root *dhr̥ṣ + ava* is found only in these two derivatives. For *rajasám* ⌊cf. *Gram.* § 1209 b⌋ Ppp. has *rajasas;* the comm. simply paraphrases the former by *rajomayam.* One or two of the *pada*-mss. (including our Bp.) leave *mr̥tyo* unaccented in b; Ppp. elides *'nav-* after it; and, in c, combines *pathāi 'maṁ* (satisfying the meter).

11. I make for thee breath-and-expiration, old age as [mode of] death, long life-time, welfare; all the messengers of Yama, sent forth by Vivasvant's son, moving about, I drive away.

Ppp. reads in b *jarāmr̥tyum,* and, in d, *caratā "rān* (i.e. *carata ārād?*) *apa.*

12. Afar niggardliness, perdition, away seizure (*gráhi*), the flesh-eating *piçācás,* every demon that is of evil nature — that we smite away, as it were into darkness.

Or 'like darkness.' The comm. reads in b *purogrāhim,* and, in d, *eva* for *iva.* Ppp. has *tavāi 'va* for *tat tama iva.* 'Afar' and 'away' in a, b anticipate as it were the 'we smite away' of d.

13. Thy breath I win from immortal Agni, from long-lived Jātavedas, that thou mayest take no harm, mayest be immortal in alliance [with him]: that I make for thee; let that prove successful for thee.

A number of the mss. (including our Bp.E.D.) read *r̥ṣyās* in c. Ppp. has *vanave* for *vanve* in b, and *yatrā* at beginning of c.

14. Let heaven-and-earth be propitious to thee, not distressing, conferring fortune (? *abhiçrī́*); let the sun burn weal unto thee; let the wind blow weal to thy heart; let the heavenly waters, rich in fatness (*páyas*), flow propitious upon thee.

Ppp. combines *sūryā "tapatu* in c, reads *kṣaranti* in e, and adds further at the end *çivās te santv oṣadhīḥ.* The comm. gives *adhiçriyāu* in b, glossing it with *prāptaçrīke çrīprade.*

15. Propitious to thee be the herbs; I have caught thee up from the lower unto the upper earth; there let both the Ādityas, sun and moon, defend thee.

Ppp. reads *ā 'hāriṣam* in b, and *ati* for *abhi* in c, and combines *-masā ubhā* at the end.

sambhavanti: tāir ārujantī'ti çaphārujaḥ: i.e. 'breaking things with their hoofs.' The irregularity of meter allows us to suspect the tradition of the word. The comm. also strangely explains *rebhe* as *çabdaṁ kurvate rakṣase!* ⌊Root *ribh:* cf. note to vs. 7.⌋ Ppp. reads in **d** *aditi* for *acitam.*

The verse is RV. vs. 12, where it is decidedly better in place.

22. Thee the devout, O Agni, powerful one, would we fain put about us [as] a stronghold, [thee] of daring color, day by day, slayer of the destructive one.

We have had this verse above, as vii. 71. 1; for its different correspondences and variants, see the note at that place; ⌊but Ppp. here ends with *bhaṅgurāvatām*⌋. The comm., though he notes it as 'explained above,' goes on to give a new explanation, curiously accordant with and yet not a little different from the other; the most important point of difference is that, in explaining *pari dhīmahi,* he there gave us our choice between *parito dhārayāmaḥ* and *paridhiṁ kurmaḥ,* while here he gives us our choice between the latter and *dhyāyemahi.* The real reason of the repetition probably is that he this time reads at the end *bhaṅgurāvatām,* with RV. ⌊and Ppp.⌋, while before he had no variant from our AV. text. ⌊Here and in vs. 23, W. queries his version of *bhaṅg-* as he did at vii. 71, which see.⌋

23. With poison smite thou back the destructive ones, the demoniacs, O Agni, with keen brightness (*çocís*), with heat-pointed flames (*arcí*).

RV. in **b** lingualizes the particle to *ṣma,* and reads *daha* for *jahi;* and it ends **d** with *ṛṣṭíbhis* instead of the anomalous *arcíbhis.* Ppp. has in **c** *çukreṇa* instead of *tigména.*

The RV. hymn ends with four *anuṣṭubh* verses, of which only the first two find place thus in our text.

24. With great light Agni shineth out; he maketh all things manifest by his greatness; he forceth away the ill-conditioned ungodly wiles; he sharpeneth his two horns to gore the demons.

All the authorities read at the end *viníkṣve,* and even the comm. is with them, calling the *v* a Vedic accretion (*vakāropajanaç chāndasaḥ*). RV., in the corresponding verse (v. 2. 9: repeated without variant in TS. i. 2. 14⁷), has *viníkṣe,* which our edition reads by emendation, SPP. retaining the totally inadmissible *v,* which seems to have blundered into the word out of *ví nikṣva* in the following verse. RV. (and TS.) has before it *rákṣase* (sing.).

25. The two horns that thou hast, O Jātavedas, unaging, of keen thrust, sharpened by devotion (*bráhman*) — with them do thou gore, O Jātavedas, the attacking enemy (*durhā́rd*), the advancing *kimīdín* with thy flame (*arcís*).

At the end of this verse, *nikṣva* seems to have been taken for a 2d sing. middle; but it is doubtless a corruption* for *nikṣa,* the root showing an *a*-stem elsewhere. Ppp. avoids the error by reading *nṛcakṣaḥ;* and also *yātudhānam* for *arciṣā* before it, which gets rid of yet another difficulty of construction, though it makes the irregular meter yet worse. In our edition, in **d**, the accent-mark which should stand under the *do* of *jātavedo* has slipped out of place to the left, under *ve.* *⌊We must assume that the corruption is an old one if the *v* of *viníkṣve* is to be ascribed to it. Since the forms from stem *nikṣa-* are so few (in 3 AV. verses), perhaps we might after all assume that this is a root-class imperative, *nikṣ-ṣva.*⌋

26. Agni drives off the demons, he of bright brightness, immortal, bright, purifying, laudable.

This verse is RV. vii. 15. 10, and is found also in TB. (ii. 4. 1[6]) and MS. (iv. 11. 5); the text is the same in all. ⌊Ritual uses, above.⌋

⌊Here ends the third *artha-sūkta* and the quoted Anukr. says *tṛtīyaṁ tu.*⌋

4. Against sorcerers and demons: to Indra and Soma.

[*Cātana.—pañcaviṅçakam. mantroktadevatyam. jāgatam: 8–14, 16, 17, 19, 22, 24. triṣṭubh; 20, 23. bhurij; 25. anuṣṭubh.*]

Found also in Pāipp. xvi. (with exchange of order between 4 and 5, and between 19 and 20). It is, with no change of order of verses, and with only few and insignificant variants, RV. vii. 104; not a verse occurs further in any other text, so far as known. ⌊No ritual use of the hymn is prescribed either by Kāuç. or by Vāit. But the comm. regards this hymn as used with the preceding one in a variety of practices: see h. 3.⌋

Translated: by the RV. translators; and as AV. hymn by Henry, 10, 47; Griffith, i. 396.

1. O Indra-and-Soma, burn the demon, oppress (*ubj*) [him]; put (*arpay-*) down, ye two bulls, them that thrive in darkness; crush away, scorch down the fools (*acít*); slay, push, pin (*çā*) down the devourers.

Tamovṛ́dh may be (so Ludwig) 'increaser of darkness.' The comm. has nothing better than *hiṅs* to suggest for *ubj.*

2. O Indra-and-Soma, against ⌊*abhí*⌋ the evil-plotter, the evil, let heat boil all up ⌊*sam-yas*⌋ like a fiery pot; assign unavoidable hate unto the brahman-hating, flesh-eating *kimīdín* of terrible aspect.

The construction and meaning of the first half-verse are doubtful; the comm. glosses *yayastu* with simple *gacchatu.* RV. has *agnivā́n* instead of *-mā́n* in **b**. In our edition, the accent-sign which should stand under *gni* in this word has slipped to the right, under *mān.* ⌊Here W. seems to take *sam* as intensive and to render its force by "all up." Neither in BR. nor in the *Index* is it joined with *yas*: but cf. *saṁ-yāsa.*⌋

3. O Indra-and-Soma, pierce ye the evil-doers within their hiding-place (*vavrá*), in untenable darkness, whence there shall not come up again any one soever of them; be that your furious might unto over-powering.

RV. reads at beginning of **c** *yáthā nā́ 'taḥ pún-*. In our edition read *duṣkṛ́to* in **a**.

4. O Indra-and-Soma, cause to roll (*vṛt*) from the sky the deadly weapon, from the earth also, a shattering for the evil-plotter; shape out from the mountains (*párvata*) the noisy one, wherewith ye burn down the increasing demon.

The comm. glosses *svaryà* with *svaraṇārha.* Ppp. has the easier reading *pra haratam* for *vartayatam* in **a**.

5. O Indra-and-Soma, cause [it] to roll forth from the sky; with fire-heated, stone-smiting, unaging heat-weapons do ye pierce the devourers in the abyss; let them go to silence.

Ppp. reads *divas* for *yuvam* in **b**; the comm. has in **d** *niḥsvaram*, which would be a good reading, but is against the *pada*-texts of both RV. and AV. (*ni○svarám*).

6. O Indra-and-Soma, be there about you on all sides this prayer (*matí*), as a girth [about] two vigorous (*vājín*) horses, the invocation (*hótrā*) that I send forth to you with wisdom; these acts of worship (*bráhman*) quicken ye like two lords of men.

RV. reads in **d** *nṛpátī 'va*, as the meter demands, and so do our P.M.W.R.T.K. and part of SPP's authorities, also the comm., and Ppp., and this is, almost beyond question, the true text; but SPP. adopts in his edition *nṛpátī iva*, with the remainder (a majority) of his *saṁhitā* authorities. The *pada*-reading is probably *nṛpátī ivé 'ti nṛpátī○iva*, as all the *pada*-mss. except our Bp. (both copies) appear to read, and as the RV. *pada* reads; but we should altogether expect *nṛpátī 'vé 'ti nṛpátī○iva*, as Bp. reads. The anomaly of the addition of *íti* after *iva* instead of after *nṛpátī* (first time) is noted in Prāt. i. 82 c; the Prāt. takes no notice of the exceptional combination *nṛpatī 'va* — which is, to be sure, an argument against its right to stand in the *saṁhitā*-text: see note to Prāt. iii. 33. The retention of dental *n* in *hinómi* after *pari* is prescribed by Prat. iii. 88. Ppp. reads instead *pra hiṇomi.* ⌊Cf. Geldner, *Ved. Stud.* ii. 134.⌋

7. Remember ye with [your] rapid courses; smite the haters, the destructive demoniacs; O Indra-and-Soma, let there not be ease (*sugá*) for the evil-doer, the hater that at any time vexes me.

RV. reads, in **d**, *nas* for *mā*, and *druhā́* for *druhús*. Ppp. ends with (for *abhi* . . .) *api kā cid uḍ ūhuḥ*. The retention of dental *s* in *práti smar-* is by Prāt. ii. 102; the passage is there quoted in the commentary. Our comm. glosses *tujayadbhis* with *balavadbhis*, and attenuates the difficult *prati smaretham* to *prati gacchatam*.

8. Whoever reviles with untrue speeches me walking with simple mind — like waters grasped with the fist, let the speaker of what is not be [himself] non-existent, O Indra.

The comm. glosses *abhicáṣṭe* with *abhiçāpaṁ karoti*. The long initial vowel of *ā́satas* (p. *ásataḥ*) is by Prāt. iii. 21, iv. 90; the passage is there quoted.

9. They who distract (*vi-hṛ*) with [their] courses him of simple intent, or who spoil at their will (*svadhā́bhis*) what is excellent — let Soma either deliver them up to the serpent, or let him set them in the lap of perdition.

The comm. declares *svadhā* in **b** an *annanāma*, and renders *svadhābhis* by *annāir nimittabhūtāiḥ*, 'for food'! An accent-mark is wanting in our text over the *ya* of *dūṣáyanti* in **b**.

10. Whoever, O Agni, tries to harm our taste of drink, of horses, of kine, whoever of our bodies — let the enemy, the thief, the theft-committer, go to want (*dabhrá*); let him be degraded with self and with posterity.

RV. reads in **b** *yó áçvānāṁ yó gávām*, and the comm. does the same. ⌊But SPP. reports that Sāyaṇa's text reads **b** thus: *ye aç. ye g. yas t.*⌋ A number of our mss. (P.M.W.R.K.) read *ví* for *ní* at beginning of **d**, but SPP. reports no such variant among his authorities. The form *ṣá* after *ní* here is not quoted in the Prāt. commentary. ⌊Join *nas* rather with the genitives of **a** and **b**?⌋

11. Be he far away, with self and with posterity, be he beneath all the three earths, let his glory dry up, ye gods, who by day and who by night tries to harm me.

RV. reads in **d** *nas* instead of *mā*.

12. It is easy of understanding for a knowing man (*jána*) [that] true and untrue words (*vácas*) are at variance; of them what is true, whichever is more right, that Soma verily favors; he smites the untrue.

Ppp. reads *paspṛçāte* at end of **b**.

13. Soma by no means furthers the wicked [man], nor the *kshatríya* who maintains [anything] falsely; he smites the demon; he smites the speaker of untruth; both lie within reach of Indra.

14. If I am one of false gods, or if I put upon (? *api-ūh*) the gods what is vain, O Agni — why art thou angry with us, O Jātavedas? let them of hateful speech obtain (*sac*) misery of thee.

RV. reads *ā́sa* instead of *ásmi* at end of **a**. The comm. renders *te* in **d** as if it were *té;* for the difficult *apy-ūhé* he gives simply *vahāmi* (*moghaṁ vyarthaṁ devān stotavyān yaṣṭavyāṅç ca apyūhe vahāmi*).

15. May I die today if I am a sorcerer, or if I have burnt (*tap*) a man's lifetime; then let him be divided from ten heroes who vainly says to me "thou sorcerer."

The comm. glosses *vīrāis* with *putrāis*, which is probably its virtual meaning: 'may he lose ten heroic sons.' Our *pada*-text differs from that of RV. by dividing *daçá°bhiḥ* in **c**. Ppp. reads *pāuruṣasya* in **b**.

16. Whoever to me that am no sorcerer (*áyātu*) says "thou sorcerer," or whatever demoniac says "I am pure (*çúci*)" — let Indra smite him with a great deadly weapon; may he fall lowest of every creature.

Áyātu doubtless literally 'that have no *yātú* or familiar demon' (though the proper accent in such case would be *ayātú*), opposite of *yātumánt* 'possessing such a *yātú*,' or *yātudhā́na* 'holding or containing such.'

17. She who goes forth in the night like an owl (?), hateful, hiding herself away — may she fall down into an endless hole (*vavrá*); let the [pressing-] stones smite the demoniacs with [their] noises.

RV. again (as in 7 **d**) reads *druhā́* for *druhús* in **b**; also *vavrā́n anantā́n áva* in **c**. Ppp. reads *dūhas* in **b**; and the comm. has *upa* instead of *apa*. He glosses *khargálā* with *ulūkī*.

18. Scatter yourselves, O Maruts, among the people (*vikṣú*); seek, seize, crush (*sam-piṣ*) the demoniacs, who, becoming birds, fly in the nights, or who have put defilements (*rípas*) on the heavenly sacrifice.

RV. has *bhūtví* in **c**. SPP. reads *íȝcchata* in **a**, because the great majority of his authorities give it. This is contrary to the established usage of both RV. and AV. (but in accordance with that of SV.), although in nearly every such case a part of the mss. lengthen the vowel; part of ours do the same here, as elsewhere. The comm. glosses *ripas* with *hiṅsās;* and *dadhire* with *dhārayanti!*

19. Cause the stone to roll forth from the sky, O Indra; [it,] sharpened by Soma, do thou wholly sharpen, O liberal one; from before, from away, from below, from above, do thou smite upon the demoniacs with a mountain.

RV. reads in **a** *áçm-* after *divó*, and some of SPP's authorities do the same. RV. has also *prā́ktād ápāktād* and *údaktād* in **c**; the directions admit also of being understood as from east, west, south, and north.

20. Here fly these dog-sorcerers (*çváyātu*); Indra the unharmable they the harm-seeking seek to harm; the mighty one (*çakrá*) sharpens his deadly weapon for the treacherous ones (*píçuna*); now may he let fly (*sṛj*) the thunderbolt at the sorcerers (*yātumánt*).

The epithets like *çváyātu* in this verse and below in vs. 22 seem by their accent (and by comparison with *yātumánt* and *yātudhā́na*) to signify strictly 'one having a dog (etc.) for his familiar demon.' The comm. glosses with *çvarūpadhāriṇaḥ çvasahitā* [*vā*]. Ppp. combines at end of **b** *-vo adābhyam.*

21. Indra was the crusher-away of the familiar demons (*yātú*), of the oblation-disturbers, of them who strive to win upon [it]; let the mighty one (*çakrá*) attack them that are demoniacs as an ax the woods, splitting [them] like vessels.

RV. reads *eti* in **d**, and no small share of the AV. mss. (the majority of SPP's) do the same (including our P.s.m.I.D.R.p.m.Kp.); both editions give *etu.* The AV. *pada*-text, like the RV., divides and accents in **b** *abhí: āovívāsatām.* The Petersburg Lexicons treat the *abhi* as if in direct combination with the participle; and they translate 'approach with hostile intent,' which is highly arbitrary. The comm. gives no aid, rendering simply *abhimukhaṁ gacchatām.* Ppp. reads in **b** *-matīnām.* ⌊W. would probably have changed "crusher-away" to "demolisher" on the revision.⌋

22. The owl-sorcerer, the owlet-(?)sorcerer smite thou, the dog-sorcerer and the cuckoo-sorcerer, the eagle-(? *suparṇá-*)sorcerer and the vulture-sorcerer — do thou destroy (*pra-mṛṇ*) the demon, O Indra, as if with a mill-stone.

As to the renderings of these various names for sorcerers, see under vs. 20. For *çuçulūka-* Ppp. has *çulūka-*, the comm. *çiçulūka-*. The translation of it is a mere guess, to avoid transferring the word.

23. Let not the sorcerous demon reach us; let the *kimīdíns* that are paired fade away; let the earth protect us from earthly distress, let the atmosphere protect us from heavenly.

RV. reads, in **a**, **b**, *yātumā́vatām ápo 'chatu mithunā́ yā́ kimīdínā.* Ppp. has *kimīdinām.* The comm. glosses *apo 'chantu* with simple *apa gacchantu.* The *pada*-division of *yāt-* in **a** is *yātu॰mā́vat* both in AV. and in RV.; the word is the subject of Prāt. iv. 8.

24. O Indra, smite the man sorcerer, likewise the woman ⌊who is⌋ prevailing with magic (*māyā́*); let the neckless false-worshipers vanish (? *ṛd*); let them not see the sun moving upward.

The obscure *ṛdantu* in **c** is glossed by the comm. with *naçyantu;* Ppp. reads *rujanta* instead. *Çā́çadānām* the comm. explains as = *hiṅsatīm.*

25. Look thou on; look abroad; O Soma, Indra also, watch ye; hurl ye the deadly weapon at the demons, the thunderbolt at the sorcerers (*yātumánt*).

⌊Here ends the second *anuvāka*, with 2 hymns and 51 verses. The quoted Anukr. says *turīyam āhur iha pañcaviṅçakam.*⌋

5. Against witchcraft etc.: with an amulet.

[*Çukra. — dvāviṅçam. kṛtyādūṣaṇadevatyam uta mantroktadevatyam. ānuṣṭubham: 1. upariṣṭādbṛhatī; 2. 3-p. virāḍgāyatrī; 3. 4-p. bhurigjagatī; 5. saṁstārapañkti bhurij; 6. upariṣṭādbṛhatī; 7, 8. kakummatī; 9. 4-p. puraskṛti jagatī; 10. triṣṭubh; 11. pathyāpañkti; 14. 3-av. 6-p. jagatī; 15. purastādbṛhatī; 19. jagatīgarbhā triṣṭubh; 20. virāḍgarbhā* prastārapañkti; 21. parāvirāṭ triṣṭubh; 22. 3-av. 7-p. virāḍgarbhā bhurik çakvarī.*]

Found also (except vs. 18) in Pāipp. xvi. *⌊The Berlin ms. reads *-garbhā "stāra-*, which is more nearly right.⌋

⌊Kāuç. uses the hymn, with iii. 5 etc., to accompany the binding on of an amulet in a rite (19. 22) for general prosperity; and again, with ii. 11 etc., in a rite (39. 7) against witchcraft. It is reckoned (note to 19. 1) to the *puṣṭika mantras.* To the *svastyayana gaṇa* (note to 25. 36) are reckoned vs. 18 (not 15: and probably not xix. 20. 4, which has the same *pratīka* as 18) and its fellow vs. 19; and to the *abhaya gaṇa* (note to 16. 8), vs. 22. The comm. cites from Nakṣ. Kalpa (19) the use of the hymn in a *mahāçānti* called *rāudrī.* Vāit. passes the hymn unnoticed.⌋

Translated: Henry, 14, 50; Griffith, i. 400; Bloomfield, 79, 575.

1. This reverting amulet, a hero, is bound on a hero; heroic, rival-slaying, true hero, a very propitious protection.

The comm. calls the amulet *tilakavṛkṣanirmita,* thus ⌊cf. comm. to vss. 4, 8⌋ identifying *tilaka* and *srāktya.* Ppp. omits our **b** and the first words of our **c**, reading as its **b** *sapatnahas suvīraḥ:* then *paripāṇaḥ* etc.

2. This amulet, rival-slaying, having excellent heroes, powerful, vigorous, overpowering, formidable, a hero, goes to meet the witchcrafts, spoiling [them].

Ppp. reads *etu* in **c**.

3. With this amulet Indra smote Vritra; with this he, being filled with wisdom, ruined the Asuras; with this he conquered both, heaven-and-earth here; with this he conquered the four directions.

Ppp. reads, for **c**, *anena dyāvāpṛthivī ubhe ajayat.*

4. This amulet of *sraktyá*, back-turning, reverting, forcible, remover of scorners, controlling — let it protect us on all sides.

Ppp. reads *maṇis* again for *vaçī* in **c**; also *viçvatas* at the end.

5. This Agni says, this also Soma says, this Brihaspati, Savitar, Indra; let these gods, my representatives (*puróhita*), drive the witchcrafts backward with the reverters.

In this verse and the next, Ppp. has the better reading *pratisareṇa* for *-rāis* in **d**. The first half-verse is found again below as xix. 24. 8 **c**, **d**. ⌊Cf. also MS. i. 5. 3. The first pāda recurs at xvi. 9. 2.⌋

6. I interpose heaven-and-earth, also the day, also the sun; let these gods, my representatives, drive the witchcrafts backward with the reverters.

'Interpose' — i.e. between me and what I dread. Ppp. *pratisareṇa* in **d**, as noted above; also, for **b**, *utāi 'va brahmaṇaspatim;* and, at beginning of **c**, *te te devāṣ pu-*.

7. The people who make the amulet of *sraktyá* their defenses — like the sun ascending the sky, it, controlling, drives away the witchcrafts.

Ppp. puts *iva* after *divam* in **c**.

8. By the amulet of *sraktyá*, as by a seer (*ṛ́ṣi*) full of wisdom, I have conquered all fighters; I smite away the scorners, the demoniacs.

9. The witchcrafts that are of the Añgirases, the witchcrafts that are of the Asuras, the witchcrafts that are self-made, and those that are brought by others — let these, of both kinds, go away to the distances, across ninety navigable [streams].

'Self-made' (*svayaṁkṛta*), doubtless 'made by ourselves'; the comm. so understands. 'Navigable' — i.e. not to be crossed without the help of a boat. SPP's mss. do not punctuate between **b** and **c**, but the comm. does so, like our edition. Ppp. combines *kṛtyā "ñgirasīr*, has for **b** *yāḥ kṛtyā "surīr uta* (the addition rectifying the meter), and combines in **f** *nāvyā 'ti;* and in **c** it puts *yās* after *kṛtyās*.

10. On this man let the gods bind the amulet [as] defense: [namely,] Indra, Vishṇu, Savitar, Rudra, Agni, Prajāpati, Parameshṭhin, Virāj, Vāiçvānara, and all the seers.

⌊For a somewhat similar combination of names, cf. iv. 11. 7.⌋

11. Thou art the chief (*uttamá*) of herbs, as the ox of moving creatures (*jágat*), as the tiger of wild beasts (*çvápad*); whom we sought, him have we found, a watcher near at hand (?).

The mark of division in this verse is badly placed in our edition; it should be after *çvápadām iva*, as in the mss. ⌊and SPP's edition⌋. SPP. reads at the end, with all the mss., *ántitam;* the comm. this time (cf. the note to vi. 4. 2) gives us our choice between taking it as one word (= *atyantasaṁnihitam*) or two (= *tam eva antike*); Ppp. avoids the difficulty by reading instead *adhruvam*. To me the emendation to *ánti tám* seems unacceptable. The comm. reads before it *pratispāçinam*. Prāt. iii. 10 notes the double form *çvápad* and *çvā́pad*. The first three pādas are found again below as xix. 39. 4 **a**, **b**, **c**; the irregular *uttamás* instead of *uttamā́* seems due to the influence of the two masculine nouns in the double comparison.

12. He verily becomes a tiger, likewise a lion, likewise a bull, likewise a lessener of rivals, who bears this amulet.

'Lessener' —lit'ly 'one who makes lean'; but, though all the mss. and both editions have *-kárçana*, it can hardly be otherwise than a misreading for *-kárṣaṇa*, which the comm. gives. Ppp. has a wholly different **c**, *sarvā diço vi rājati* (as our 13 **c**), and so deprives us of its witness.

13. Not Apsarases smite him, not Gandharvas, not mortals; he reigns over (*vi-rāj*) all the quarters who bears this amulet.

14. Kaçyapa created thee; Kaçyapa collected thee; Indra bore thee in human wise (?); bearing [thee], he conquered in the conflict (?); the amulet, of thousand-fold might, the gods made their defense.

The obscure *mā́nuṣe*, in **c**, the comm. explains as ⌊a collective⌋ = *mānuṣeṣu madhye;* he reads in **d** *saṁçreṣaṇe*, which is much more acceptable; one is inclined also to conjecture *saṁçreṣṭṇo 'jayat*. Ppp. brings no help, only reading *abadhnata* for *akṛṇvata* at the end.

⌊The comm. reckons our **e**, **f** as a separate verse, the 5th of his "decad," thus making this "decad" come out with 13 vss. (instead of 22 – 10 = 12, as in the Berlin ed.).⌋

15. Whoever with witchcrafts, whoever with consecrations, whoever with sacrifices desires to slay thee — him do thou, O Indra, smite back with the hundred-jointed thunderbolt.

The omission of the second *yás tvā* would rectify the meter of **a**.

16. Let this back-turning, forcible, all-conquering amulet verily defend [our] progeny and riches, a very propitious protection.

Ppp. reads *sahasvān* instead of *ojasvān* in **b**. Our text should, for consistency, read *ójasvānt s-*.

17. Freedom from rivals for us below, freedom from rivals for us above, freedom from rivals for us behind, O Indra, light in front make thou, O hero.

Or the directions may be understood as south, north, west, and east. Ppp. has, for **c**, *indra piçācaṁ naṣ paçcāt*.

18. A defense for me [be] heaven-and-earth, a defense the day, a defense the sun, a defense for me both Indra and Agni; a defense let Dhātar assign (*dhā*) to me.

Compare AÇS. i. 2. 1 ⌊and ĀpÇS. xiv. 26. 1⌋ with **a**, **b**; both substitute *agnis* for *ahar*. The verse, as noted above, is wanting in Ppp. The comm. omits *me* in **c**. The first half-verse occurs again as xix. 20. 4 **a**, **b**.

19. Indra-and-Agni's abundant formidable defense, which not all the gods together pierce through — let that, being great, save my body on all sides, that I may be long-lived, attaining old age.

With **d** compare VS. xxxiv. 52 **d**, which differs from it only by reading at the end the irregular form *ásam*. Ppp. has *te* for *me* in **c**, and *asat* in **d** ⌊though the pronoun calls for *asas*⌋.

20. The divine amulet hath ascended me, in order to great unharmedness; enter ye together unto this post (? *methí*), body-protecting, thrice-defending, in order to vigor (*ójas*).

Ppp. reads *tvā* instead of *mā* in **a**, and *enyam* instead of *methim* in **c**. The comm. questions whether *mahyāi* in **b** means *mahatyāi* or *mahyam!* The difficult and doubtful second half-verse puzzles him (as us) greatly: first he regards 'men' as addressed (*he narāḥ*), and takes *methi* as 'a stirrer-up, a destroyer of enemies,' or alternatively as a post in a threshing floor (*methī khale yatho 'cchirā vartata evam ayam api 'ti;* or, secondly, the gods are addressed, and *methi* means an amulet representing such a post (*methīsthānīyam maṇim*).

21. In this let Indra deposit manliness; this, O gods, enter ye together unto, in order to long life-time of a hundred autumns; that he may be long-lived, attaining old age.

⌊With **d**, cf. MP. ii. 1. 3 d.⌋

22. Giver of welfare, lord of the people, Vritra-slayer, masterful remover of scorners, let Indra bind ⌊for thee⌋ the amulet, [he] that has conquered, is unconquered, soma-drinking, fearless-making bull; let him defend thee on all sides, by day and by night on all sides.

The majority of mss. (nearly all SPP's) put no pause at the end of **d** (after *aparājitaḥ*). The first two pādas are nearly the same with i. 21. 1 **a**, **b**, above (and with other texts: see the note to that verse). Ppp. omits **a**, **b**, and reads (better) *sarvadā* instead of *sarvatas* at end of **f**. ⌊An accent-mark is lacking under the *so* of *somapā́ḥ*.⌋

⌊Here ends the fifth *artha-sūkta*. The quoted Anukr. says *pañcame*.⌋

⌊Here also ends the eighteenth *prapāṭhaka*.⌋

6. To guard a pregnant woman from demons.

[*Mātṛnāman. — ṣaḍviṅçam. mātṛnāmādevatyam uta mantroktadevatyam. ānuṣṭubham: 2. purastādbṛhatī; 10. 3-av. 6-p. jagatī; 11, 12, 14, 16. pathyāpañkti; 15. 3-av. 7-p. çakvarī brāhmaṇaspatyā; 17. tathā jagatī.*]

Found also in Pāipp. xvi., ⌊but with vs. 8 before 7, vs. 15 between 11 and 12, and vs. 24 between 13 and 14⌋.

⌊The hymn is reckoned by Kāuç. (8. 24), with ii. 2 (which see) and vi. 111, to the *mātṛnāmāni*. It is employed in the *sīmanta* rite (35. 20) in the eighth month of a woman's pregnancy with binding on an amulet "as specified in the text" (cf. vs. 20):

Dār. and Keç. and comm. (p. 636[1], p. 648[8]) say an amulet of white and yellow mustard; the Ath. Paddh. seems to prescribe a "talisman in the form of a doll made of red and yellow mustard plants" (?) and reaching from the woman's neck to her navel. In Dārila's note on the same passage (35.20), vs. 18 is specially cited for the same rite. The hymn is not noticed by Vāit.⌋

Translated: Weber, *Ind. Stud.* v. 251; Ludwig, p. 523; Henry, 17, 54; Griffith, i. 403.

1. The two spouse-finders which thy mother rubbed up for thee when born (fem.) — for them ⌊*tátra*⌋ let not the ill-named one be greedy, the *alíṅça* nor the *vatsápa* (calf-drinker *or* -protector?).

Weber (and Zimmer after him: p. 321) conjectures that the two 'winners of a husband' are the breasts, and that the reference is to the ceremonious washing of the young child. The numerous names of evil beings in the hymn are in good part unknown elsewhere and untranslatable; of some of them tentative versions can be added in parenthesis. The comm. reads *alīças* in **d**, and explains it as *ali* + *īça* ⌊taking *ali* as diseases (or deities representing them) that fly about like bees⌋.

2. *Palāla* (straw) and *anupalāla* (after-straw), *çárku*, *kóka* (cuckoo), *malimlucá* (robber), *palíjaka*, the entwiner (*āçréṣa*), the wrap-garmented, the bear-necked, the winking one.

Ppp. reads *çulkam* for *çarkum* in **a**; in **b**, *malīmṛtaṁ palītakam;* in **c**, *açleṣam*, and adds ⌊cf. vss. 5, 23⌋ at the end *muṣkayor apa hanmasi* 'we smite away in the *pudenda*,' which gives a construction to the accusatives of which our text is alone made up. The comm. gives in **b** *palīcakam;* he supplies *nāçayāmi* to govern the accusatives.

3. Approach (*sam-vṛt*) thou not; creep thou not on; creep not down between the thighs; I make for her a remedy, the *bajá*, expeller of the ill-named.

Ppp. reads *javam* instead of *bajam* in **d**. The comm. identifies *baja* with the white mustard (*çvetasarṣapa*) ⌊see introd.⌋.

4. Both the ill-named and the well-named — both seek approach (*saṁvṛ́t*); the niggards (*aráya*) we smite away; let the well-named seek what is woman's (*strāíṇa*).

Ppp. reads *icchatām* at end of **b**, and omits the second half-verse. The comm. explains *strāiṇam* as *striyāḥ sambandhy aṅgaṁ strīsamūhaṁ vā;* he takes *-nāman* from root *nam*. The *ṇ* of *durṇāman* is prescribed by Prāt. iii. 84.

5. The *ásura* that is black, hairy, tuft-born, also snouted (*túṇḍika*) — the niggards we smite away from her pudenda, from her buttocks (*bháṅsas*).

Ppp. reads, in **c**, **d**, *asyā bhaṅsaso muṣkayor apa* ⌊cf. vss. 2, 23⌋.

6. The after-snuffling, fore-feeling, and the much-licking flesh-eater, the niggards, the dog-*kiṣkins*, hath the brown *bajá* made to disappear.

Ppp. reads, for **c**, *rāyaç çukaṣkiṇaṁ;* the comm. has *ca kiṣkiṇas* (for *çvakiṣ-*); and he explains *kiṣkin* to mean either 'uttering the sound *kiṣ kiṣ*,' or 'constantly injuring' (from the root *kiṣk*).

7. He who lies with (*ni-pad*) thee in sleep, having become [like] a brother and like a father — them, eunuch-formed, tiara-decked (*tirīṭín*), let the *bajá* force (*sah*) from here.

Tirīṭin = 'womanish,' as wearing a distinctive woman's head-dress; the comm., however, paraphrases the word with *antardhānenā 'ṭataḥ*, as if from *tiraḥ-aṭin!* Ppp. puts the verse after vs. 8, and reads *suptāṁ* for *svapne* in **a**, and, in **c**, **d**, *vajas taṁ . . . klībarūpaṁ kirīṭinam.* ⌊Cf. RV. x. 162. 5–6 with our vss. 7–8.⌋

8. He who surprises (*tsar*) thee sleeping, who tries to harm thee waking — them the circling (*pari-kram*) sun hath made to vanish away like a shadow.

Both translators understand the second half-verse to mean 'them hath the *baja* made to vanish, as the sun the shadow,' and the comm. takes it in the same way; but, though that may be the virtual sense, it is not what the line actually says. Ppp. reads, in **a**, *suptāṁ chinatti*, with *ca* for *tvā* in **b**. The comm. has *carati* instead of *tsarati* in **a**. Nearly all our mss. (all save D.R.) read *jā̆gratim* at end of **b**, but SPP. strangely reports no such variant from any of his authorities.

9. Whoever makes this woman one having a dead child (*-vatsá*), or a miscarriage, him, O herb, do thou make disappear, lustful ⌊accusative⌋ for her, slippery.

The last pāda is very obscure and doubtful, and quite otherwise understood by the translators; the version given follows the Petersburg Lexicon. The comm. interprets *kamalam* by *garbhadvāram*, and *añjivam* by *abhivyaktimad mlakṣaṇopetaṁ vā*, and supplies to them *kuru*. Ppp. reads instead *kamalavaṁ dyuvam;* it also reverses the order of *mṛtávatsām* and *ávatokām* in **a**, **b**. *Añjivám* (p. *añji○vám*) is quoted under Prāt. iv. 18 as an example of a word made with a *taddhita*-suffix beginning with *v*.

10. They who dance around the dwellings (*çā́lā*) in the evening, making donkey-noises — they that [are] *kusū́las* (granaries) and *kukṣilás* (paunchy), exalted (*kakubhá*), *karúmas, srímas* — these, O herb, with thy smell do thou make to disappear scattered.

One or two of our mss. (as of SPP's) read *strimāḥ* (I.) or *sṛmāḥ* (W.) at end of **d**, or omit the *visarga* before it (M.s.m.W.O.). Ppp. reads, for **c**, **d**, *kuçūlā yaç ca kukṣulā kakubhā svarasā* (*-ramā?*) *sumā;* the comm., for the last two words, has *kharumāḥ çrumāḥ;* he interprets *kusūlās* as *kusūlākṛtayas*, *kukṣilās* as *bṛhatkukṣayas*, and *kakubhās* as *arjunavṛkṣavad bhayaṁkarākṛtayas.* ⌊Over "exalted" W. has interlined "humped?" As for *srīma*, cf. *sṛma* in OB.⌋

11. The *kukúndhas*, the *kukū́rabhas*, that bear skins (*kṛ́tti*), pelts (? *dūrçá*), dancing on like impotent men, that make a noise in the forest — them we make disappear from here.

Ppp. reads *kakundhāṣ karūrabhāṣ kṛtyāir duriçāni bibhrati: klīvāi 'va pr. ghoṣāṁ ye kurvate vane.* The comm. has *kṛkandhāḥ kukūravāḥ kṛtyāir dūṣyāṇi.*

12. They who do not endure yonder sun, burning down from the sky, the niggards, buck-clothed, ill-smelling, red-mouthed, the *mákakas*, we make to disappear.

Ppp. reads in **c** *rāyāṁ vastavāsino*, and, in **e**, *mṛṣakān* for *makakān*. In *bastavāsin*, Weber understands *-vāsin* as 'smelling,' the Petersburg Lexicons (also Ludwig alternatively) as 'bleating' (for *-vāçin*); the comm. *avicarmavasanān*. ⌊For the verse-sequence in Ppp., see above.⌋

13. They who, putting their excessive self on the shoulder, carry [it], thrusters-forth of women's hips — O Indra, make the demons disappear.

The comm. has several different explanations of the first half-verse, the translators as many more; a literal rendering seems admissible enough. Ppp. reads for **b** *ahiṁ mādhāya bibhrati.*

14. They who go before a woman, bearing horns (pl.) in the hand, stayers in the oven, laughing out, who make light in the tuft — them we make to disappear from here.

All our mss., and nearly all those of SPP., read *badhvàs* in **a**, and our edition follows them. SPP. gives in his text *vadhvàs*, with the commentator. In **c**, he adopts *āpākeṣṭhā́s*, with a small minority of his mss., and directly against Prāt. ii. 94, which prescribes *-sthā́s*. One would like to emend to *apāk-* 'standing aloof.'

15. Of whom the front-feet are behind, the heels in front, the faces in front, who are threshing-floor-born, dung-smoke-born, who are *úruṇḍas* and *maṭmaṭás*, pot-testicled, *ayāçús* (impotent ?) — these from her, O Brahmaṇaspati, do thou make to disappear by attention (? *pratībodhá*).

Ppp. reads in **c** *çākadh-*, in **d** *ye ca mayyajā*, and in **e** combines *-ṣkā 'yāç-*. Some of our mss. (Bp.P.M.W.), as of SPP's, read *múkhāḥ* at end of **b**. The comm. has, for **d**, *aruṇḍā ye ca muṭmuṭāḥ;* he explains *ayāçavas* by *ayo vāyur vāyuvad āçugāminaḥ.*

16. With eyes cast about, not looking forward (? *ápracaṅkaça*), womenless be the eunuchs; make to fall down, O remedy, him who, not her husband, tries to approach this woman that has a husband.

The comm. reads in **a** *pracaṅkaçās*, and strangely explains it ⌊alternatively⌋ as = *prakṣīṇorupradeçās;* for *paṇḍagās* in **b** he has *pannagās* (*pādena na gacchantaḥ*); for *pādaya* in **c**, *pātaya*. Ppp. gives in **e** *svapati.*

17. The bristling, hermit-haired, grinding up, much handling one, hastening up, copper-colored, snouted (? *tuṇḍéla*) and *çáluḍa*, pierce thou forth with the foot, with the heel, as a kicking cow a pot.

Doubtless the concluding word should be *spandanā́*, as given by SPP., in accordance, as he claims, with all but two of his authorities. The mss. are always so careless and untrustworthy in their distinction of *sp* and *sy* that it must be the sense rather than their testimony that decides in any case which is the true reading. Ppp. appears to have *syandanā.* The combination *upéṣantam* (p. *upa॰éṣantam:* Ppp. *upeçantam*) is according to Prāt. iii. 52; the passage is quoted in the commentary to that rule; the comm. ⌊and his text⌋ read here *upāiṣ-*. The comm. also has *çālaḍam* (Ppp. *çālūḍham*) in **d**, and takes *prá vidhya* (Ppp. *pravṛddhi*) in **e** as *pravídhya*, gerund. Further, he has *prāsyāt* instead of *pārṣṇyā*, and, at the end, *spandanāt.* His verse-division is different from ours, as he reckons **e**, **f** to vs. 18. He explains *marīmṛçam* in **b** as = *punaḥpunar mṛçantam.* Ppp. has, for *udumbalaṁ tuṇḍelam, adaraṁ sulatuṇḍenam.*

18. Whoever shall handle thy embryo, or shall make it born dead — let the brown one, with formidable bow, make him pierced to the heart.

The comm. explains *prati mṛçāt* by *pīḍayet*. The *ā* of *hṛdayāvídham*, and its non-division in *pada*-text, are the subject of Prāt. iii. 3, iv. 68. ⌊Delete the accent mark under *tu* in d.⌋

19. They who suddenly make die those that are born, [who] lie by the bearing [women] — the Gandharvas, woman-seekers (?), let the brown one drive, as the wind a cloud.

Ppp. begins *ye sto j-*, and ends *abhrāi vātāi 'va rājatu*. The comm. explains *amnojātān* as = *ardhotpannān*. The Prāt., ii. 52, expressly prescribes that the final of *amnáḥ* is not ⌊convertible into⌋ *r* — which seems a plain acknowledgment that at a later period the word was treated as being *amnár*.

20. Let [her] maintain what is left (?); what is set, let not that fall down; let the two formidable remedies, to be borne in the under garment, defend thine embryo.

Parisṛṣṭam in a is very hard to deal with, both on account of the meaning and because combinations of root *sṛj* with *pari* are hardly met with; the Pet. Lexicon suggests emendation to *-çriṣṭam*; as both Ppp. and the comm. have *-çiṣṭam*, I have taken the liberty of so translating. The comm. paraphrases it by *homādiviniyogāvaçiṣṭaṁ sarṣapadvayam* ⌊see the introduction⌋ and makes it the object of *dhārayatu*. Ppp. also reads *yujyatam* for *yad dhitam* in b, and, at the end, *nivabhāryayāu*. ⌊Whitney queries for a: 'Let what is wreathed about (*pari-sṛj*) maintain.' This might refer to bandages swathed around, to support the abdomen. In b, *hitám* would refer to the embryo (cf. *dhātā dadhātu* etc.), and *áva pādi* to untimely delivery (cf. i. 11. 4–6).⌋

21. From the rim-nosed, the *taṅgalvà*, the shady (? *cháyaka*) and naked, from the *kimīdín*, let the brown one protect thee about for progeny, for husband.

Or *cháyaka* may come from root *chā*, and so signify 'tearing' or the like; the comm. reads instead *sāyakāt*. Ppp. has at the beginning *pavāinasā taṅ-*.

22. From the two-mouthed, the four-eyed, the five-footed, the fingerless one, from the much twining twiner (*vṛnta*) that creeps forth upon [one], do thou protect [her] about.

All the *pada*-mss. most absurdly divide *anamogureḥ* at end of b; SPP. properly emends to *anaṅguréḥ*, but why "with Sāyaṇa" is not evident; Ppp. reads *anaṅguleḥ;* and further has, in c, *vṛddhād adhi pra-*. SPP. seems to regard the comm. as reading *abhiprasarpataḥ*.

23. They who eat raw meat, and who the flesh of men, the hairy ones [that] devour embryos — them we make to disappear from here.

Ppp. combines at the beginning *yā"mam*, and has in place of our d *'rāyān* ⌊combined *keçavārāyān*⌋ *asyā bhaṅsaso muṣkayor apa hanmasi* (as in its version of our 5 c, d — cf. 2). The *pada*-reading *keçaovā́ḥ* is quoted in the commentary to Prāt. iv. 18.

24. They that creep away from the sun, as a daughter-in-law away from her father-in-law — let both *bajá* and *piñgá* pierce in into their heart.

Pari in **a**, though compounded with the verb, has the value of a strengthener of the ablative sense of *sū́ryāt*, as *ádhi* in **b** of that of *çváçurāt.* ⌊Cf. Geldner, *Ved. Stud.* i. 270.⌋

25. *Piñgá*, defend thou [the child] in process of birth; let them not make the male female; let not the egg-eaters injure the embryos; drive thou the *kimīdíns* from here.

In **b**, lit'ly 'not make the man a woman.' Ppp. puts the *mā* after *pumāṅsam.*

26. Childlessness, still-birth, also crying, guilt (*aghá*), barrenness (? *āvayá*) — that do thou attach to [our] enemy (*ápriya*), as if having made a garland from a tree.

Ppp. reads, in **a**, **b**, *mārtavatsam āmābhrogham agham ānayam.* The comm. has, for *agham āvayam*, *aghavāvayam*, and paraphrases it with *aghānām pāpānāṁ tatphala-bhūtānāṁ duḥkhānāṁ vā 'sakṛd vayanam.* It is curious that both *ā-vayam* and *mārta-vatsam* are quoted in the commentary to Prāt. iv. 18, as if their second member were 'a *taddhita* beginning with *v.*' — ⌊Cf. MB. i. 1. 14; MP. i. 4. 11.⌋

⌊Here ends the third *anuvāka*, with 2 hymns and 48 verses. It is also the end of the sixth *artha-sūkta*, which begins with *yāú te.* The quoted Anukr. says *yāu te.*⌋

From this point on, the commentary is wanting until the beginning of book xi.

7. To the plants: for some one's restoration to health.

[*Atharvan. — aṣṭāviṅçakam.* bhāiṣajyāyuṣyam uta mantroktāuṣadhidevatākam. ānuṣṭubham : 2. upariṣṭād bhurig bṛhatī ; 3. purauṣṇih ; 4. 5-p. parānuṣṭub atijagatī ; 5, 6. pathyāpañkti (6. virāḍgarbhā bhurij) ; 9. 2-p. ārcī bhurig anuṣṭubh ; 10. pathyāpañkti ; 12. 5-p. virāḍ atiçakvarī ; 14. upariṣṭān nicṛd bṛhatī ;* † *25. pathyāpañkti ; 26. nicṛt ; 28. bhurij.*]

Found also in Pāipp. xvi. ⌊with verses 16–19 in the order 16, 18, 19, 17⌋. *⌊The mss. have *sāṣṭāviṅçakam.*⌋ †⌊The Anukr. omits the definition of vss. 15 (*triṣṭubh*) and 24 (*6-p. jagatī*).⌋

⌊Used by Kāuç. in a remedial rite (26. 33, 40, note), "with a gilt and lacquered amulet made [cf. introd. to AV. ii. 9] of splinters of ten kinds of trees" (Keç., p. 327[22]), against all diseases. In the *puṁsavana*, vs. 27 accompanies (note to 35. 6) the giving of food to the pregnant woman. Vāit. prescribes the hymn for use in the *sāutrāmaṇī* rite (30. 6) when the priest mixes herbs with the *surā.*⌋

Translated: Ludwig, p. 504; Henry, 20, 58; Griffith, i. 408; Bloomfield, 41, 578.

1. Those that are brown, and that are bright (*çukrá*), the red and the spotted, the swarthy, the black herbs — all [of them] do we address (*acha-ā-vad*).

2. Let them save (*trā*) this man from the *yákṣma* sent by the gods — the plants of which heaven has been the father, earth the mother, ocean the root.

The second half-verse was found above, as iii. 23. 6 **a**, **b**. This time it is also in Ppp. In **c**, *dyāúṣ* is read by W.I.R.T. We should expect *pū́ruṣam* in **a**.

3. Waters [were] the beginning, heavenly herbs; they have made disappear from every limb thy sinful (*enasyà*) *yákṣma*.

The first pāda is a fragment, in meter and in construction; the omission of *ágram* would fairly rectify both. As in sundry other like cases, most of the mss. read at the end *anīnaçam* (or *-çaṁ*); only P.M.W. have *-çan*.

4. The spreading, the bushy, the one-spathed, the extending herbs do I address; those rich in shoots, jointed (*kāṇḍín*), that have spreading branches (*víçākha*); I call for thee the plants that belong to all the gods, formidable, giving life to men.

Víçākha might also signify 'branchless.' Ppp. reads in **a–b** *ekaçṛṅgāṣ pradhanvatīr*.

5. What power [is] yours, ye powerful ones, [what] heroism and what strength [is] yours, therewith, O herbs, free ye this man from this *yákṣma;* now (*átho*) do I make a remedy.

The last pāda is wanting in Ppp.

6. The lively, by-no-means-harming, living herb, the non-obstructing, up-guiding, flourishing (?*puṣyá*) one, rich in sweets, do I call hither, for this man's freedom from harm.

Compare 2. 6, with which this agrees in the first two pādas and in most of the last two. The mss. again are much at variance as to the reading of *naghāriṣā́m;* Bp.P. M.p.m.E.p.m.O. read ⌊Bp. with *-ghă-*⌋ *naghārṣā́m*. ⌊Ppp. reads *naghāriṣām* (as does Berlin ed.) and omits *iha* and pāda **e**.⌋ The omission of the obscure *puṣyā́m* would rectify the meter; the Pet. Lexx. regard the word as proper name of a plant.

7. Let the forethoughtful ones come hither, allies (*medín*) of my spell (*vácas*), that we may make this man pass forth out of difficulty.

Read *medínīr* in **b** (two accent-signs slipped out of place leftward).

8. Food of fire, embryo of the waters, they that grow up renewed, fixed, thousand-named — be they remedial [when] brought.

9. Wrapped in *ávakā*, water-natured, let the herbs, sharp-horned, thrust away difficulty.

Literally, 'having the *avakā* as fœtal envelop.'

10. Releasing, free from Varuṇa, formidable, that are poison-spoiling, also *balā́sa*-dispelling, and that are witchcraft-spoiling — let those herbs come hither.

'Free from Varuṇa': i.e., doubtless, 'freeing from the bonds of Varuṇa,' with which he visits guilt on the guilty. Ppp. reads in **c–d** *balāsanāçinī rakṣonāçanīṣ kṛtyād-*. Read in our text *kṛtyādū́ṣaṇīç* (for *-yad-*) in **d**.

11. Let the purchased, very powerful plants that are praised save in this village cow, horse, man, beast.

Ppp. prefixes an additional pāda to each half-verse: *çivās te santv oṣadhir apak-*; and *apā sarasvatī jyeṣṭhaṁ trāy-*.

12. Rich in sweets the root, rich in sweets the tip of them, rich in sweets was the middle of the plants; rich in sweets the leaf, rich in sweets the flower of them; partaking of sweet, a drink of nectar (*amṛ́ta*), let them milk out ghee, food, with milk (*gó-*) as chief (*-purogavá*).

The mss. (except D. and R.s.m.?) agree in the unmotived accent *babhūva* at end of **b**. Ppp. has instead *balena;* also, for *sambhaktās*, *sambhūtās* 'originated,' which is easier.

13. However many [may be] these herbs upon the earth, let them, thousand-leafed, free me from death, from distress.

All the mss. leave *oṣadhīs* unaccented at end of **b**; and most (all save P.M.D.R.T.) accent *-parṇyás* at end of **c**. ⌊Cf. Caland, KZ. xxxi. 265.⌋

14. Let the tigerish amulet of plants, saving, protecting from imprecation, smite far away from us diseases [and] all demons.

The *pada*-text reads *sárvā* (not *sárvāḥ*) in **c**, and the translation follows it. Ppp. has *vyāghro* in **a**, and *asmāt* at the end. *Adhi* in **d** is redundant in respect both to sense and to meter.

15. As at the roaring of a lion do they quake; as at fire do they tremble at [the herbs when] brought; let the *yákṣma* of kine, of men, go driven by the plants beyond navigable streams.

The usual expression is 'beyond ninety-nine' such streams. Ppp. reads *oṣadhīnām* for *saṁ vijante* in **a**. ⌊Over "quake" W. interlines "shrink with fear." He would probably have changed it to "they are all in a tremble," as in v. 21. 4, 6.⌋

16. The herbs, becoming freed from Agni Vāiçvānara — go ye stretching over the earth, [ye] whose king is the forest-tree.

We should expect vocatives instead of nominatives in the first line.

17. They who, belonging to the Angirases, grow on mountains and on plains — let those herbs, rich in milk, propitious, be weal to our heart.

In Ppp. this verse follows our vs. 19. ⌊Ppp. inserts after **b** *vīrudho viçvabheṣajīs*, and continues *tā no mayasvatīç çivāḥ : o. s. ç. h.*⌋

18. Both what plants I know, and what I see with the eye, the unknown and what we are acquainted with, and those in which we know what is brought together —

That is, probably, their collected or concentrated virtue. Ppp. reads in **c** *janīmasi* for *jānīmaç ca.* ⌊We might render *ájñātās* by 'what we are not acquainted with,' to correspond with W's version of *jānīmás.*⌋

19. Let all the entire herbs note (*budh*) my spell (*vácas*), that we may make this man pass forth out of difficulty.

Ppp. omits the second half-verse; it is identical with 7 **c**, **d**, above.

20. The *açvatthá*, the *darbhá*, *sóma* king of plants, immortal oblation — rice and barley [are] remedial, immortal sons of heaven.

Ppp. reads *yavasya bheṣajo* in **c**.

21. Ye rise up (*ud-hā*); it thunders, it roars at [you], O herbs! when, O ye children of the spotted one, Parjanya favors you with seed.

With the second half-verse is to be compared RV. v. 83.4 **c**, **d**. *Pṛçnimātṛ* is elsewhere epithet only of the Maruts. The accent *abhikrándati* is unmotived ⌊unless, indeed, with Henry, we bring it, with *standyati*, under the domain of *yadā́*⌋.

22. Of this *amṛ́ta* we make this man to drink the strength; now do I make a remedy, that he may be one of a hundred years (*-hāyaná*).

W. and O.s.m. read *pārayāmasi* at end of **b**; Ppp. has *phalayāmasi*.

23. The boar knows the plant; the mongoos knows the remedial [herb]; what ones the serpents, the Gandharvas know, those I call to aid for him.

One or two of our mss. (Bp.M. ⌊only one, Bp., if I understand W's Collation-book⌋) read *vīrúdhām* at end of **a**. Ppp. puts *sarpās* after *gandharvās* in **c**, and has for **d** *tā ihā "yantv oṣadhīḥ*.

24. What [herbs] of the Añgirases the eagles [know], what heavenly ones the *ragháṭs* know, what ones the birds, the swans know, and what all the winged ones, what herbs the wild beasts know — those I call to aid for him.

Raghāṭ (which *divyā́s* 'heavenly' might also qualify) is elsewhere unknown; Ppp. reads instead *vagh-*; the major Pet. Lex. suggests emendation ⌊apparently withdrawn in the minor: see *raghāṭ*⌋ to *raghávas* 'swift'; Ludwig conjectures 'bees.' Ppp. also combines *suparṇā "ñg-* in **a**. ⌊Render *hansā́s* by the prosaic 'geese,' since the poetic tone of the AV. is not so elevated as to make that version intolerable. Cf. JAOS. xix., 2d half, p. 154.⌋

25. Of how many herbs the inviolable kine partake (*pra-aç*), of how many the goats and sheep, let so many herbs, being brought, extend protection to thee.

Ppp. exchanges the second halves of vss. 25 and 26, and makes *ābhṛtās* and *oṣadhīs* change places.

26. In how many ⌊herbs⌋ human physicians (*bhiṣáj*) know a remedy, so many, all-remedial, do I bring unto thee.

Ppp. ⌊see under vs. 25⌋ reads at the end *iti* for *abhi*.

27. Rich in flowers, rich in shoots (*prasū́-*), rich in fruits, also those lacking fruits — like joint mothers, let them milk unto this man in order to his freedom from harm.

Ppp. combines *saṁmātarāi 'va* in **c**. The first pāda is nearly identical with RV. x. 97.3 **b**.

28. I have taken thee up out of what has five *çalas*, and also out of what has ten *çalas*, also out of Yama's fetter, out of all offense against the gods.

The Pet. Lexx. explain *-çala* as 'a certain measure of distance,' but that sense does not in the least suit the connection, either here or in TB. i. 5. 10[1]. Ppp. reads *ahāriṣam* in **a**, ⌊*ut tvā* for *atho* in **c**,⌋ and, for **d**, *oṣadhībhir apīparam*. The second half-verse is identical with vi. 96. 2 **c**, **d**, above ⌊and nearly identical with RV. x. 97. 16 **c**, **d**⌋.

⌊Here ends the seventh *artha-sūkta*, with 28 verses. The quoted Anukr. says *sa saptamaṁ vṛddhiviṅçatim ṛco 'ṣṭa cā 'parāḥ* (unclear).⌋

8. To conquer enemies.

[*Bhṛgvañgiras.—caturviṅçam. āindram uta vānaspatyam. parasenāhananam. ānuṣṭubham: 2, 3. bṛhatī (2. upariṣṭāt; 3. virāj); 4. bṛhatīpurastātprastārapañkti; 6. āstārapañkti; 7. viparītapādalakṣmā 4-p. atijagatī; 8–10. upariṣṭādbṛhatī; 11. pathyābṛhatī; 12. bhurij; 19, 20. purastādbṛhatī (19. virāj; 20. nicṛt); 21. triṣṭubh; 22. 4-p. çakvarī; 23. upariṣṭādbṛhatī; 24. 3-av. triṣṭubuṣṇiggarbhā parāçakvarī 5-p. jagatī.*]

Found also in Pāipp. xvi.; ⌊but the order of vss. 3 and 4 is inverted; likewise that of vss. 6 and 7⌋. ⌊"Verses" 22–24 are prose, in Brāhmaṇa style.—Whitney's treatment of this hymn is doubtless only a rough first draft, which he would have revised thoroughly had his life been spared. The understanding of this hymn is so peculiarly dependent upon an understanding of the ritual that I have felt obliged to present the latter with exceptional fulness—without attempting, however, to revise W's version into entire accordance therewith.⌋

⌊Vāit. does not notice the hymn. Its principal use by Kāuç. is in the army rites of the 16th *kaṇḍikā*. In the previous one (15. 11), vs. 22 is used with v. 2. 6 etc. when the king mounts a new chariot. And at 73. 5, among the citations for the morning and evening oblations, is one that bears a marked resemblance to our vs. 14.⌋

⌊The text of the "army rites" (16. 9–20), cites expressly vss. 1, 2, and parts of 24, and is indeed largely made up of the names of the objects mentioned in the hymn (see below). Not only Dārila, but also Keçava (Bl., p. 314[28 ff.]), and the introd. which SPP. gives (p. 658–9) in lieu of the lost comm., all present instructive details.⌋

⌊With vs. 1, the sorcerer twirls a fire-drill (16. 9) made of *açvattha* and *badhaka* sticks (16. 11: cf. vss. 3, 4). Thereupon, while reciting the first half of vs. 2, he lays down some "old rope" (*jīrṇa-rajju*, Dār.: apparently to serve as tinder?) "in the place where the sparks [from the fire-drill] fall" (so Dār. and Keç.). When the smoke appears, he exorcises it with the words

dhūmám parādṛ́çyā 'mítrā hṛtsú ā́ dadhatām bhayám.

This is the second half of our verse 2, with *agním* left out. When the flame breaks out (*agniṁ jātam*), he addresses it with

agním parādṛ́çyā 'mítrā hṛtsú ā́ dadhatām bhayám.

This is the same half-verse, with *dhūmám* left out. See Keç., p. 314[31 ff.], SPP., p. 658[18-19].—This now is the fire for the "army rites."⌋

⌊Upon it, with use of h. 8, is placed successively (16. 14) fuel of *açvattha*, *badhaka*, *tājad-bhañga* ('castor-oil plant'), *āhva* ('*palāça*'), *khadira*, and *çara* ('reeds'). These things are all mentioned in vss. 3–4; Dārila's list (n. to 48. 1) agrees entirely with this: cf. also Bl., p. xliv.—Next follows the bestrewing of the tracks of the hostile army with various symbolical objects, to wit: first (16. 15), "the fetters aforesaid" (at 14. 28) of hemp and of muñja-grass smeared with *iñgiḍa;* then (16. 16–17), "traps [?*kūṭa:* see n. to vs. 16] of *açvattha*," "hempen nets," and "stakes of *badhaka*." Various expressions in the hymn may be taken either as allusions to these objects or else as suggesting their use: such are the "fetters" of vss. 10, 16; the "trap" of vs. 16; the "net" of vss. 4–8 and 18; the "net-stakes" of vss. 5, 12.⌋

⌊Finally, with "hail to these" (*svā́hāi 'bhyás* of vs. 24), the sorcerer makes, with his right hand, for his friends (16. 18) an oblation in the fire kindled with the drill of *badhaka;* and with "wail to those" (*durā́hā 'mī́bhyas* of vs. 24), he makes, with his left, in the same fire an oblation of the uncanny *iñgiḍa* for the destruction of the army of his enemies (16. 19). Then, setting up a branch of red *açvattha* to the north of his fire, he winds it with threads of blue and red with the last pāda of vs. 24, and moves it to the south (16. 20).⌋

⌊In counter-sorcery, *iñgiḍa* is the regular surrogate for ghee (Kāuç. 47. 3). In the rites accompanying iii. 6 (the hymn is notably affiliated with ours in respect of substance and expression: cf. "fetters," *açvattha, khadira;* cf. also viii. 8. 3 **a** with iii. 6. 2 **a**; 10 **a, b** with 5 **a, b**; 19 **c** with 7 **c**), it is used (48. 4) for smearing the threads or symbolical fetters; similarly at 14. 28, above; and again (with vi. 75: Kāuç. 48. 31) with a leaf of red *açvattha.*⌋

⌊A most interesting critical result is won from the study of the ritual use of our hymn, to wit: that here (vs. 2 **c**) we have an instance in which both alternatives (*dhūmám* and *agním*) of an *ūha* have been adopted into the received text. This has given it a semblance of metrical blemish (Henry, Bloomfield, and Whitney all suggest the excision of *amítrāḥ*), the true meaning of which has been missed by the Occidental exegetes. SPP. (as above) understands Keçava's introd. to Kāuç. 14 aright and explains it clearly, p. 658[18]. — It may be noted that Ppp. unintelligently, with its *agniṁ dhāmaṁ* (intending *dhūmaṁ*), has both alternatives, but in the wrong order.⌋

Translated: Muir, v. 88 (vss. 5–8); Ludwig, p. 527; Henry, 23, 61; Griffith, i. 412; Bloomfield, 117, 582.

1. Let Indra the shaker shake (*math*) [them], he the mighty hero, stronghold-splitter, in order that we may slay by thousands the armies of our enemies.

Quoted in Kāuç. 16. 9 ⌊see introd.⌋.

2. Let the putrid rope, breathing on [it], make yonder army putrid; seeing afar smoke, fire, let our enemies set fear in their hearts.

Ppp. reads *agniṁ dhāmaṁ* in **c**. The different parts of the verse are quoted in Kāuç. 16. 10, 12, 13, where the 'putrid rope' appears to be understood as an actual rope which is burnt, and of which the 'smoke' and 'fire' are to frighten the foe. It is perhaps quite as likely that the ceremony is founded on a crass misinterpretation of the verse, and that the 'rope' is a poisonous serpent (as conjectured by Ludwig). The omission of *amítrās* in **d** would rectify the meter. ⌊With regard to the last and to the whole verse, see the introd.⌋

3. Crush yonder men out, O *açvatthá;* devour (*khād*) them speedily, O *khadirá;* let them be suddenly ⌊*tājád*⌋ broken ⌊*bhañj*⌋ like hemp ⌊*bháñga*⌋; let the slayer (*vádhaka*) slay (*han*) them with deadly weapons (*vadhá*).

The translation implies the emendation (which is made in our text) of *ajiram* (p. *khadira∘ajiram!*) to *-rám,** and the treatment of *tājā́t* and *bháñgas* (p. *tājádbháñ-gaḥ∘iva!*) as two separate words. Ppp. reads in **b** *khadirā 'ciram,* and in **c** combines

-bhañgāi 'va; for **d** it has *bṛhajjālena saṁcitāḥ* ⌊cf. our 4 **d**⌋. Kāuç. (16. 14) takes *tājadbhañga* as a single word, and its comm. explains it as the castor-oil plant (*eraṇḍa*). ⌊In *çṛṇīhi* I see an allusion to the sorcerer's favorite "reeds" (*çará*) of vs. 4. Griffith notes the power of the *açvattha* to rend asunder the masonry etc. in whose crevices its seed has germinated. The other word-plays, including that on *vádhaka badhaka* (cf. *bādhaka* and root *bādh*), are evident. See also introd.⌋ *⌊So also SPP. with several of his authorities.⌋

4. Let the rough-called one make yonder men rough (*paruṣá*); let the slayer slay them with deadly weapons; let them be broken quickly like a reed (*çará*), tied together with a great net.

Ppp. combines *çare 'va* in **c**,* and has at the end (as in 3 **d**) *saṁcitās;* it puts the verse before our vs. 3. The Pet. Lexx. conjecture *paruṣāhvá* to be 'a kind of reed.' ⌊For the materials of the sorcery, and the "net," cf. introd.⌋ *⌊As the meter requires; why then does not the Anukr. call the vs. a *purastādbṛhatī* and have done with it?⌋

5. The atmosphere was the net; the great quarters [were] the net-stakes; therewith encircling [them], the mighty one (*çakrá*) scattered away the army of the barbarians (*dásyu*).

Ppp. has an easier but virtually equivalent version of **c**, **d**: *tenā 'bhidhāya senām indro dasyūn apā 'vapat.* Vss. 5–8 are translated by Muir (v. 88). ⌊"Net-stakes": cf. introd. — For "encircling" W. first had "girding"; *abhi-dhā* carries the idea of bridling, curbing, or restraining: cf. vss. 7, 8, 9 and note to iii. 11. 8.⌋

6. Since great [is] the net of the great mighty one, the vigorous (*vājínīvant*) — therewith do thou crowd (*ubj*) down upon all [our] foes, that no one soever of them may be released.

Ppp. adds to our first half-verse (with *rocanāvatas* for *vāj-* in **b**) the second half-verse of our 7 (omitting *nyarbudaṁ* and reading at the end *senām*), then putting the whole after 7. All the mss. accent *múcyātāi*, which, though supported by the usage of sundry Vedic texts (including even RV.), was emended in our edition to agree with the Atharvan accentuation elsewhere. ⌊Henry would read *móci*, of which he holds *mucyā́tāi* to be a gloss.⌋

7. Great, O Indra, hero (*çū́ra*), is the net of thee that art great, that art worth a thousand, that hast hundred-fold heroism; therewith encircling the army of the barbarians, the mighty one slew a hundred, a thousand, ten thousand, a hundred million.

The translation follows Ppp. (see under the preceding verse) in reading *senām* at the end. Instead of our **c**, **d**, Ppp. has *tena ny ubja maghavann amitrāñ çaçvatībhyaḥ.*

8. This great world was the net of the great mighty one; by that net of Indra do I encircle all yon men with darkness.

9. Debility, formidable ill-success, and mishap that is not to be exorcised away (*an-apavācaná*), toil, and weariness, and confusion — with these do I encircle all yon men.

10. To death do I deliver those yonder; with fetters of death [are] they bound (*sā*); the sad messengers that are death's — them I lead them to meet, having bound (*bandh*) [them].

Ppp. reads *khālās* for *aghalās* in **c**, and at the end *baddhān*. All our mss. agree in giving the abbreviated form *badhvā́*. ⌊"Fetters": cf. introd.⌋

11. Lead ye them, O messengers of death; O messengers of Yama, restrain (*apa-umbh*) [them]; be they slain to more than thousands; let Bhava's club (? *matyà*) shatter them.

Ppp. reads for **a** *mṛtyudūtā amuṁ nayata;* **d** is corrupt, but apparently is the same with our **d**.

12. The Perfectibles (*sādhyá*) go lifting with force one net-stake, the Rudras one, the Vasus one; by the Ādityas one is lifted.

Ppp. has for second half-verse: *rudrā dvitīyaṁ vasavas tṛtīyam ādityāir ekā udyatā.*

13. Let all the gods from above go crowding with force; let the Añgirases go slaying midway the great army.

Ppp. has at the end *vadhāis* instead of *mahīm.*

14. The forest trees, them of the forest trees, the herbs and the plants, what is biped, what is quadruped I despatch (*iṣ*), that they may slay yonder army.

'Them of the forest trees,' *vānaspatyān*, acc. pl. masc.; the lexicographers explain the word to mean 'fruit tree with conspicuous flowers.' At the end both of this verse and of the next, Ppp. reads *hatāṁ*. Bp. reads *dvi॰pát* in **c**. ⌊For the citation in Kāuç. 73. 5, see introd.⌋

15. The Gandharvas and Apsarases, the serpents, the gods, the pure-folks, the Fathers, those seen, those unseen I despatch, that they may slay yonder army.

Ppp. makes *devān* and *sarpān* change places ⌊and reads *hatāṁ* again at the end⌋. ⌊Muir, v. 296, cites MBh. ii. 11. 45 = 461, where the Fathers are divided into seven troops, four of embodied and three of bodiless.⌋

16. Here are spread the fetters of death, which stepping into thou art not released; let this horn (*kū́ṭa*) slay of yonder army by thousands.

Ppp. gives for **a** *mṛtyupaçā yama* ⌊that is, *ime?*⌋ *yuktā.* Kāuç. (16. 16) speaks of '*kūṭas* of *açvattha*[-wood] and nets of hemp.' ⌊Geldner, *Ved. Stud.* i. 139, renders the vs. and takes *kū́ṭa* as "trap"; SPP., p. 659[13], says *niṣādānām prāṇibandhanam;* Bl., p. 119 (see esp. p. 585), "hammer."⌋

17. The hot drink (*gharmá*) [is] kindled with fire, this thousand-slaying oblation (*hóma*); both Bhava and the spotted-armed one — O Çarva, slay ye (two) yonder army.

All the mss. read *bhávas* at beginning of **c**; our edition emends to *bhavás*. The common construction *bhaváç ca . . . çárva . . . hatam* (cf. the next verse) is much disturbed by the addition of *pṛ́çnibāhus*, which the second *ca* forbids to take as a mere epithet. Ppp. reads *sahasraçaḥ* and *hatām* at the end of the two lines respectively.

18. Let them go unto death's burning (?), unto hunger, debility, the deadly weapon, fear; by snare (*ákṣu*) and net, O Çarva, [do thou] and Indra slay yonder army.

Only P. and R.s.m. have *óṣam*, all the rest *ā́ṣam*, which must accordingly be regarded as the traditional text, though unintelligible. Further emendation to *oṣám* 'quickly' is hardly advisable. Ppp. has *oṣam*. Ppp. also differs much in **c**, **d**: *indrasyā 'kṣamālābhyāṁ sarva senām amūṁ hatām*. Part of our mss. also (W.O.D.T.) read *sárva* in **d**. ⌊Geldner discusses *ákṣu*, *Ved. Stud.* i. 136.⌋

19. Flee (*tras*) forth, O enemies, being conquered; run, ⌊being⌋ thrust by the charm (*bráhman*); of them yonder, thrust forth by Brihaspati, let none soever be freed.

The second half-verse is nearly repeated as xi. 10. 19 **c**, **d**, below. The *pada*-mss. absurdly read *nuttā́* (not *nuttā́ḥ*) in **b**. *Amitrās* is metrically redundant in **a**. ⌊Rather 11 + 8 : 8 + 8.⌋ The *pada*-reading of *bṛ́haspáti○pranuttānām* ⌊cf. iii. 6. 7⌋ is by Prāt. iii. 76, iv. 77, the commentary quoting it under each rule.

20. Let their weapons (*ā́yudha*) fall down; let them not be able to fit the arrow; then, of them fearing much let arrows strike in the vitals.

Ppp. reads *çiṣaṁ* for *çakan* in **d**.

21. Together let heaven-and-earth yell at them; together let the atmosphere, along with the deities; let them not find a knower, nor a foundation; mutually destroying one another let them go unto death.

The second half-verse is identical with vi. 32. 3 **c**, **d**, above. Ppp. puts *enāṅ* before *kroçatām*, and adds *ubhe* at the end of **a**.

22. The four quarters [are] the she-mules of the god-chariot; the sacrificial cakes [are] the hoofs, the atmosphere the seat (? *uddhí*), heaven-and-earth the two sides, the seasons the reins, the intermediate directions the attendants, speech the rim (? *pártirathya*).

Ppp. reads *çaphā 'ntarikṣa buddhiḥ* and omits the clause *antardeçāḥ kiṁkarāḥ*. The verse is quoted in Kāuç. 15. 11 ⌊see introd.⌋.

23. The year (*saṁvatsará*) is the chariot, the complete year (*parivatsará*) the chariot-lap, *virā́j* the pole (*īṣā́*), Agni the chariot-mouth, Indra the left-stander, the moon the charioteer.

Ppp. reads, for the first part of the paragraph, *ahorātre cakre māma ārāt saṁvatsaro adhiṣṭhānam: virāḍ* etc. *Savyaṣṭhā́s* (p. *savya○sthā́ḥ*) is a subject of Prāt. ii. 95. ⌊As for the "years," see n. to vi. 55. 3.⌋

24. On this side conquer thou; on this side conquer away, conquer completely, conquer; hail! let these here conquer, let those yonder be

conquered; hail ⌊*svā́hā*⌋ to these! wail (*durā́hā*) to those! with the blue-red one I stretch down upon them yonder.

That is, probably, with Çiva's aid I bring the net down upon them. ⌊Ppp. omits all after the first *svā́hā*.⌋ Parts of the verse are quoted in Kāuç. 16. 18–20: 'with "hail to these" he makes a libation for his friends; with "wail to those" [he pours] with the left hand *iñgiḍa* on the [staff] of *badhaka;* having stuck in a branch of red *açvattha* north of the fire, having surrounded it with two blue and red threads, he pulls it up toward the right with "with the blue-red one"': evidently artificial adaptations of ceremonies to the words of the text. ⌊For the whole matter, see introd.⌋

⌊Here ends the fourth *anuvāka*, with 2 hymns and 52 verses. Here also ends the eighth *artha-sūkta*, which begins with *indro manthatu*. The quoted Anukr. says *indro manthatu*.⌋

9. Mystic: extolling the virā́j.

[*Atharvan.—ṣaḍvinçam. kāçyapeyam uta sarvārṣaṁ chāndasam. trāiṣṭubham: 2, 3. pañkti (3. āstārapañkti); 4, 5, 23, 25, [26]. anuṣṭubh; 8, 11, 12, 22. jagatī; 9. bhurij; 14. 4-p. atijagatī.*]

Found also (except vss. 19, 20) in Pāipp. xvi. ⌊with vs. 23 after vs. 24⌋. The Kāuç. takes no notice of the hymn; ⌊but the Vāit. (33. 8) allows the use of 21 vss. (from vs. 6 to the end) in the *sattra* sacrifice at the celebrant's option⌋.

Translated: Ludwig, p. 439; Henry, 26, 65; Griffith, i. 416.—See also Muir, v. 370.

1. Whence [were] those two born? which side (*árdha*) was that? out of what world? out of which earth? the two young (*vatsá*) of the *virā́j* rose out of the sea (*salilá*); of those I ask thee: by whether [of them was] she milked?

The 'which' is both times *katama*, implying the existence of more than two; but Ppp. has instead *katarasyāḥ pṛthivyāḥ*.

2. He who caused the sea to resound (*krand*) with greatness, making a threefold lair (*yóni*) as he lay, the desire-milking young of the *virā́j;* he made his bodies secret (*gúhā*) in the distance.

Ppp. combines *yo 'krand-* at the beginning, and reads in **b** *tyabhijaṁ çayānaṁ*.

3. What three great ones (*bṛhát*, n) there are, the fourth of which [one] disjoins [as] speech—the priest (*brahmán*) may know it by penance, the inspired one, in which one (*ékam*) is joined, in which one [is joined].

Ppp. reads *catvāri* instead of *trīṇi* in **a**. *Caturthám* 'fourth' might also be subject of 'disjoins.' Compare ix. 10. 27 (RV. i. 164. 45).

4. Forth out of *bṛhát* [as] sixth five sāmans [were] fashioned; *bṛhát* was fashioned out of *bṛhatī́;* out of what was *bṛhatī́* made?

Ppp. reads *ṣaṣṭhaḥ* instead of *-ṭhāt*.

5. *Bṛhatī́* the measure (*mā́trā*) was fashioned forth out of measure [as] a mother; illusion (*māyā́*) was born from illusion, Mātalī out of illusion.

The desire to play upon the root *mā* 'measure, fashion,' is the leading motive in the making of this verse. The *pada*-text gives the absurd reading *māyā́ḥ* at beginning of **c**; Ppp. reads after it *hi* instead of *ha*.

6. Vāiçvānara's counterpart [is] the sky above, as far as Agni forced (*bādh*) apart the two firmaments; from that sixth yonder come the *stómas;* up from here they go unto the sixth of the day.

For *ā́ 'múto*, in **c**, Ppp. reads *āmico*. The remainder of the hymn, from this verse on, is by Vāit. 33. 8 allowed to be introduced at pleasure in the *navarātra* ceremony.

7. We these six seers ask thee, O Kaçyapa, for thou didst join what is joined and what is to be joined; they call (*ah*) *virā́j* the father of the *bráhman;* distribute (? *vi-dhā*) it to us [thy] friends according to [our] numbers.

Ppp. reads *pṛchāmi ṛṣ-* in **a**.

8. After whom, when removed, the sacrifices remove (*pra-cyu*), [whom], when attending, they attend on (*upa-sthā*), in whose course (*vratá*) ⌊and ?⌋ impulse the monster (? *yakṣá*) stirs — that, O seers, is the *virā́j* in the highest firmament.

9. Breathless, she goes by the breath of breathing ones (f.); *virā́j* goes unto *svarā́j* from behind; *virā́j* that touches, that is adapted to, everything — some see her, some see her not.

No ms. ⌊of ours⌋ inserts *t* between *-rā́ṭ* and *sva-* in **b** ⌊but four of SPP's do so⌋, as required by Prāt. ii. 8 (under which this is one of the passages quoted). In **d** we ought properly to have emended to *tve . . . tve* (accentless); all the mss. accent the two words, against the uniform usage elsewhere; and the *pada*-mss. commit the further blunder of giving both times *tvé íti*, as if the word were the Vedic locative of the 2d pers. pronoun (as in v. 2. 3).

10. Who understandeth (*pra-vid*) the pair-ness of *virā́j?* who the seasons, who the ordering (*kálpa*) of her? who her steps (*kráma*), how many times milked out (*vi-duh*)? who her abode (*dhā́man*), how many times dawnings (*vyùṣṭi*)?

The version is much more literal than intelligent, especially at the end, where we expect rather *vyùṣṭam* than *-ṭīs*. 'Pair-ness,' *mithunatvám*, means especially the condition of being a pair of opposite sexes.

11. This same is she that first shone forth; among these other ones (f.) she goes about having entered; great mightinesses [are] within her; the woman, the new-going generatrix, hath conquered.

This verse occurred above, as iii. 10. 4. It is found also in other texts in connection with the four verses which follow it here. Ppp. has ⌊in **a**, **b**⌋ the same readings as in iii. 10. ⌊4 **a**, **b**⌋; ⌊and, here also, it inverts the order of **c** and **d**⌋.

12. The two meter-winged dawns, greatly adorning themselves, move on together toward the same lair (*yóni*); spouses of the sun, they move on together, understanding, having ensigns, unaging, having abundant seed.

The Pet. Lexx. give the first word in the form *chándaspakṣa*, although Prāt. ii. 62 expressly requires *-aḥpa-*, and all the mss. read it except Bp., which has *-aspa-*. The verse is found also in TS. iv. 3. 11[1], MS. ii. 13. 10, K. xxxix. 10. Both TS. and MS. have at the beginning *chándasvatī;* MS. reads *uṣásāu*, and at the end *-retasāu;* at end of **b**, MS. gives *anusáṁcarete* and TS. *ánu saṁcárantī;* both have *ví* for *sám* in **c**, and TS. *ketúṁ kṛṇvāné* for *ketumátī* in **d**. Ppp. reads *carati* in **c**.

13. Three (f.) have come along the road of righteousness; three heats (*gharmá*) have come after the seed; one (f.) enlivens the progeny, one the refreshment (*ū́rj*); one defends the realm of the godly ones.

The verse follows the preceding in the other three texts also. TS.MS. rectify the meter of **b** by reading *gharmā́sas*, and for *rétaṣ* MS. has *rétasā* and TS. *jyótiṣā;* TS. gives *rákṣati* for *jínvati* in **c**; and for *rāṣṭrám* in **d** TS. has *vratám* and MS. *kṣatrám*.

14. She that was fourth set Agni-and-Soma; the seers arranging the (two) wings of the sacrifice — *gāyatrī́, triṣṭúbh, jágatī, anuṣṭúbh, bṛhad-arkī́*, bringing heaven (*svàr*) for the sacrificer.

The meter-names in the second half-verse are all in the accusative, possibly as coördinate with 'wings' in **b**; but comparison with the other texts indicates that the verse is very corrupt. The translation implies emendation of *adadhus* to *adadhāt* in **a**; it would not be absolutely impossible to take 'the seers' as subject in **a**, and 'her that was fourth' as joint object with 'Agni-and-Soma.' Of the other texts (as above), TS. begins with *catuṣṭomó abhavad*, and MS. with *catuṣṭomám adadhād;* both rectify the meter of **a** by omitting *ā́sīt;* in **b** both have *ṛṣayas* as vocative, and after it *bhávantī*, and MS. has *pakṣā́* (for *-ṣāú*) before it; in **c**, MS. has *virā́jam* for *anuṣṭúbham;* in **d**, TS. begins with *bṛhád arkám*, MS. with *arkám* alone; and both follow it with *yuñjā-nā́ḥ svàr* (TS., of course, *súvar*) *ā́ 'bharann idám*. Ppp's only variant is *bṛhadarkīr* in **d**.

15. Five milkings after five dawnings; five seasons after the five-named cow; five quarters arranged by the fifteenth — those (f.) ⌊are⌋ one-headed toward one world.

'The fifteenth' (masc. or neut. sing.) might mean also 'fifteen-fold, of fifteen parts,' etc. The verse is found in the three other texts (as above), but in TS.MS. (also in K.?) separated at some distance from those that here precede; also in PGS. iii. 3. 5: all read *samānámūrdhnīs* instead of *ékamū-* in **d**.

16. Six [are] born the beings first-born of righteousness; six *sā́mans* carry the six-day (?) [sacrifice]; after the six-yoked plough (*sī́ra*) severally a *sā́man;* six they call (*ah*) the heavens and earths, six the wide [spaces].

The translation implies in **b** the reading *ṣaḍahám;* this is given in our text, against the authority of our *pada*-mss. ⌊which have *ṣáṭ : ahám*⌋; the *saṁhitā*-mss. (except O.p.m.) have *ṣaḍ-*. All the latter read in **a** *-já ṛtásya* (p. *prathama○jā́ : ṛtásya* ⌊cf. JAOS. x. 451⌋.

17. Six they call the cold, and six the hot months; tell ye us the season, which one [is] in excess (*átirikta*); seven eagles (*suparṇá*), poets, sat down; seven meters after seven consecrations.

None of the mss. read *çītā́nt ṣád* in **a**, as demanded by Prāt. ii. 9. In **d** the construction of the two nouns is reversible.

18. Seven [are] the offerings (*hóma*), the fuels seven, the sweet things (*mádhu*, n.) seven, the seasons seven; seven sacrificial butters (*ā́jya*) went about the existent thing (*bhūtá*); those (f.) are seven-vultured, so have we heard.

The version is as literal as possible; to modify it would imply an understanding of it. The nearest fem. word for 'those' in **d** to relate to is 'fuels' in **a**. All the *saṁhitā*-mss. combine *saptá rtávo* in **b**. Ppp. reads in **b** *nu* for *ha*, and has instead of our **c**, **d**: *sapta jyāyāṁ paruhūta gāyaṁ saptahotā ṛtudayajetitās sapta gṛdhrā iti çuçravā 'haṁ*. Nearly all the mss. (all of ours save E.) read *āyam* (the *saṁhitā*-mss. *-aṁ*) at end of **c**.

19. Seven [are] the meters increasing (*-úttara*) by four, the one set upon the other: how do the praises (*stóma*) stand firm in them? how are they set in the praises?

The gender of *anyás* at beginning of **b** speaks strongly for a compound like the later *anyo 'nya*; but the double accent and the *pada*-reading (*anyáḥ : anyásmin*) are against it. The *pada*-text divides *ā́rpitāni* (*ā○árp-*) at end of **b**, but not at end of **d**. The verse is wanting in Ppp.

20. How did *gāyatrī́* permeate (*vi-āp*) the triple [*stóma*]? how is *triṣṭúbh* adapted to that of fifteen? how *jágatī* to that of thirty-three? how [is] *anuṣṭúbh* that of twenty-one?

This verse, like the preceding, is wanting in Ppp.; and they are in a manner interruptions of the progress of the hymn.

21. Eight [are] born the beings first-born of righteousness; eight, O Indra, are the priests (*ṛtvíj*) who are of the gods; Aditi has eight wombs (*yóni*), eight sons; the oblation (*havyám*) goes unto the eighth night.

With **a** compare 16 **a** above; here as there all the *saṁhitā*-mss. combine *-já rtásya*, as in **b** all combine *indra rtv-*. Ppp. reads from the beginning: *aṣṭāu dhāmāni prathamajaṁ tasyā 'ṣṭe 'ndra ṛtv-*; and, in **d**, *api* for *abhi*.

22. Thus thinking what is better have I come hither; in your friendship I am auspicious (*çéva*); being of the same birth, your skill is propitious; it (m.), understanding, goes about to you all (f.).

The adjectives in **a**, **b** are fem., seeming to indicate that the *virāj* is regarded as speaking. Ppp. has *ā 'gaṁ* at end of **a**, and *nas* for *vas* both times in **c**, **d**. 'It' in **d** apparently refers to 'skill.'

23. Eight of Indra, six of Yama, seven of the seers, seven-fold; waters, men (*manuṣyà*), herbs — them five followed (*sac*) after.

The nouns in **c** are accusatives, and are apparently summed up in 'them' (*tā́n*). All the mss. this time read with our text *yamásya ṛ́ṣ-* in **a–b**. Ppp. puts the verse after our 24.

24. Since the heifer milked solely (*kévalī*) for Indra [his] will (*váça*), the beestings, [when] first milked, then [she] gratified in four ways the four — gods, men, Asuras, and seers.

Ppp. reads at the end *atha ṛṣīn;* all our mss. save O. make the combination *utá ŕṣīn* as in the printed text.

25. What now [is] the ox (*gó*), who the sole seer, what the abode (*dhā́man*), what the blessings (*āçís*)? the monster on the earth [is] simple (*ekavŕt*); the sole season — which now is that?

Ppp. reads *sāma* for *dhāma* in **b**. All our mss. combine *ekarṣís* in **a**, but all *ekartús* (also Ppp.) in **d**. It is necessary here and in the next verse to render *gāús* 'ox,' because the accompanying adjectives are masculine. 'Which' in **d** is the superlative *katamá*. ⌊Over "simple" W. has interlined "single."⌋

26. One [is] the ox, one the sole seer, one the abode, singly the blessings; the monster on the earth [is] single; the sole season is not in excess.

Again Ppp. reads *sāma* for *dhāma*, and all the mss. (with Ppp.) have *ekarṣís* but *ekartús*.

⌊Here ends the ninth *artha-sūkta*. It begins with *kútaḥ*. The quoted Anukr. here says *kutaḥ*.⌋

10. Extolling the virā́j.

[*Atharvācārya.* — *ṣaṭ paryāyā virāḍdevatyās.*]

This curious piece of prose is (with the exception of paragraphs here and there) found also in Pāipp. xvi. ⌊Pāipp. has the order 22, 24, 23, 26, 25.⌋ ⌊This is the first of the *paryāya-sūktas*. For the *paryāya*-hymns in general, see introduction to book viii., pages 471–2, above.⌋

⌊Neither Kāuç. nor Vāit. makes use of the hymn; but one of the "committals" in the *upanayana* (Kāuç. 56. 13) is to *mārtyuṁjaya mārtyava;* cf. vs. 23.⌋

Translated: Henry, 29, 71; Griffith, i. 421. — See also Muir, v. 370.

[**Paryāya I.** — *trayodaçakam. 1. 3-p. ārcī pañkti;* **a** *of 2–7. yājuṣī jagatī;* **b** *of 2, 5. sāmny anuṣṭubh;* **b** *of 3. ārcy anuṣṭubh;* **b** *of 4, 7. virāḍgāyatrī;* **b** *of 6. sāmnī bṛhatī.*]

1. *Virā́j* verily was this [universe] in the beginning; of her when born everything was afraid, [thinking] "this one indeed will become this [universe]."

Ppp. reads *'jāyata* for *āsīt*, and, after *tasyās*, *jātāyā 'bibhed eka sarvam: yam eve 'dam bhaviṣyati na vayam iti.*

2. She ascended (*ut-kram*); she descended (*ni-kram*) in the householder's fire (*gā́rhapatya*); house-sacrificing (*gṛhamedhín*) house-holder ⌊*gṛhápati*⌋ becometh he who knoweth thus.

This paragraph and the one following are wanting in Ppp.

3. She ascended; she descended in the fire of offering (*āhavanīya*): to his god-invocation the gods go, dear to the gods becometh he who knoweth thus.

The introductory clause *só 'd akrāmat*, which belongs to the paragraphs from here on to 29 inclusive (8–17 counting in this respect as a single paragraph), is omitted by the mss., according to their custom, almost without exception, until the last paragraph, 29, where all give it; it is restored throughout in our edition. R. alone gives it in this paragraph.

4. She ascended; she descended in the southern ⌊*dákṣiṇa*⌋ fire: justified (? *-ṛtá*) by the offering, fit for sacrificial gifts ⌊*dakṣiṇíya*⌋, fit for refuge (*vā́sateya*) becometh he who knoweth thus.

Our *pada*-mss. divide *yajñártas* into *yajñaॱṛ́taḥ*, which is evidently wrong, for *yajñáॱṛtaḥ* ⌊as indeed two of SPP's read⌋; and the quotation of the word under Prāt. iii. 64 also indicates that the latter is the true accent. Ppp. reads instead *yajñāntas*, and omits after it *dakṣiṇīyas*.

5. She ascended; she descended in the assembly (*sabhā́*): [men] go to his assembly, fit for the assembly becometh he who knoweth thus.

6. She ascended; she descended in the gathering (*sámiti*): [men] go to his gathering, fit for gatherings becometh he who knoweth thus.

This superfluous equivalent of § 5 is wanting in Ppp.

7. She ascended; she descended in address (? *āmántraṇa*); [men] go to his address, fit for address becometh he who knoweth thus.

By the connection, *āmántraṇa* ought to involve the idea of a locality. Instead of ⌊line 2?⌋, Ppp. repeats *yajñānto vāsateyo bhavati* etc. from § 4.

[**Paryāya II.** — *daçakam. 8, 16. sāmny anuṣṭubh (8. 3-p.); 9. uṣṇiggarbhā 4-p. upariṣṭādvirāḍ bṛhatī; 10. 1-p. yājuṣī gāyatrī; 11* [?], *14. sāmnī pañkti (11. 1-p.); 12. virāḍ gāyatrī; 13. ārcy anuṣṭubh; 15. āsurī gāyatrī; 17. sāmnī bṛhatī.*]

8. She ascended; she stood striding (? *víkrāntā*) fourfold in the atmosphere.

The phrase 'she ascended' is prefixed by only one or two of the mss. (P.s.m.R.), but is implied in the metrical description of the Anukr.

9. Of her gods and men said: "she verily knoweth that upon which we of both classes may subsist; let us call to her."

Ppp. reads at the end *hvayāmahi* (without *iti*).

10. They called to her:

11. "O refreshment, come! O *svadhā́*, come! O pleasantness, come! O thou rich in cheer (*írā*), come!"

Ppp. combines *svadhe 'hi* and *sūnṛte 'hi*, and omits *iti* at the end (as in § 9).

12. Of her Indra was the young (*vatsá*), *gāyatrī́* the halter, cloud the udder;

Ppp. begins *tasyā 'gnir vat-*. Accent in our text, with all the mss., *ā́sīt*.

13. Both *bṛhát* and *rathantará* were two teats; both *yajñāyajñíya* and *vāmadevyá* [were] two.

Ppp. prefixes a *tasyās* at the beginning. Accent again in our text *ā́stām*, with all the mss.

14. Herbs did the gods milk [from her] by *rathantará*, expansion (*vyácas*) by *bṛhát;*

15. Waters by *vāmadevyá*, the sacrifice by *yajñāyajñíya*.

16. Herbs doth *rathantará* milk, expansion doth *bṛhát*,

17. Waters doth *vāmadevyá*, the sacrifice doth *yajñāyajñíya*, for him who knoweth thus.

For the last two paragraphs, Ppp. reads: *te vāi virājāḥ kāmadhuga stanā kāmaṁ-kāmaṁ yajamānan maha yaḥ.*

[**Paryāya III.** —*aṣṭāu.* **a** *of 18. 4-p. virāḍ anuṣṭubh;* **b** *of 18. ārcī triṣṭubh;* **a** *of 19–21. 4-p. prājāpatyā pañkti;* **b** *of 19–21. ārcī bṛhatī.*]

18. She ascended; she came to the forest trees; the forest trees slew her; she in a year came into being; therefore what is cut of the forest trees grows over in a year; cut off (*vraçc*) is his unfriendly foe (*bhrā́tṛvya*) who knoweth thus.

Only P.s.m. and R. give here the first phrase, and only R. in the three following paragraphs. Ppp. puts *vanaspatīnām* after *saṁvatsare.* ⌊For *vṛçcáte*, see note to vi. 136. 3.⌋

19. She ascended; she came to the Fathers; the Fathers slew her; she in a month came into being; therefore to the Fathers they give in a month the monthly [oblation]; he understandeth the road that goes to the Fathers who knoweth thus.

Again Ppp. puts *pitṛbhyas* after *māsi* ⌊R's collation, *masi*⌋, and then reads *dadhatas svadhāvān pitṛṣu bhavati pitṛyāṇaṁ* etc. O.R. accent *jānā́ti.*

20. She ascended; she came to the gods; the gods slew her; she in a half-month came into being; therefore for the gods they make *váṣaṭ* in a half-month: he understandeth the road that goes to the gods who knoweth thus.

Ppp. reads *tasmād ardhamāse devebhyo juhoti: juhoty agnihotraṁ pra devay-.* O.R. again accent *jānā́ti.*

21. She ascended; she came to men (*manuṣyà*); men slew her; she at once (*sadyás*) came into being; therefore on both days they present (*upa-hṛ*) to men; in his house do they present who knoweth thus.

'Present,' i.e. 'food'; 'on both days' is a queer expression for 'every day.' Ppp. is corrupt, but perhaps means *ahar-ahar manuṣyāṇām upa h-.*

[**Paryāyas IV. and V.** — *dve ṣoḍaçake.* **a** *of 22, 23, 26, 29. 4-p. sāmnī jagatī;* **b** *of 22–24, 28, 29. sāmnī bṛhatī;* **c** *of 22, 26. sāmny uṣṇih;* **d** *of 22, 23, 26, 29. ārcy anuṣṭubh;* **c** *of 23. āsurī gāyatrī;* **a** *of 24, 25, 28. 4-p. uṣṇih;* **c** *of 24. prājāpatyā 'nuṣṭubh;* **d** *of 24, 25, 27. ārcī triṣṭubh;* **b** *of 25, 26. sāmny uṣṇih;* **c** *of 25, 27, 28. virāḍ gāyatrī;* **a** *of 27. 4-p. prājāpatyā jagatī;* **b** *of 27. sāmnī triṣṭubh;* **d** *of 28. 3-p. brāhmī bhurig gāyatrī;* **c** *of 29. sāmny anuṣṭubh.*]

22. She ascended; she came to the Asuras; the Asuras called to her: O illusion (*māyā́*), come! of her Virochana son of Prahrāda was young (*vatsá*), the metal-(*áyas-*)vessel [was] vessel; her Dvimūrdhan son of Ṛitu milked; from her he milked illusion; that illusion the Asuras subsist upon; one to be subsisted on becometh he who knoweth thus.

R. alone gives the first phrase in §§ 22–28. In this and the following paragraphs to 29 inclusive, the text should accent *ā́sīt,* with all the mss. Ppp. reads *vāirocanas* instead of *vir-*. Single points in these paragraphs find correspondences in MS. iv. (p. 21, l. 14 ff.; p. 36, l. 8 ff.) and in TB. ii. 2.9[6] ff. ⌊cf. i. 5.9[1]⌋.

23. She ascended; she came to the Fathers; the Fathers called to her: O *svadhā́,* come! of her king Yama was young, the silver-vessel [was] vessel; her Antaka son of Mṛityu milked; from her he milked *svadhā́;* that *svadhā́* the Fathers subsist upon: one to be subsisted upon becometh he who knoweth thus.

The *saṁhitā*-mss. vary a good deal over *mārtyavò 'dhok:* P.M. read *mārtvyò,* R. *mārtvyó,* E.O.K. *mārtyavó,* T. *mārtyávo;* ⌊cf. introd.⌋. Ppp. has instead *ādityo;* and it omits *rājā* after *yamas;* it puts the paragraph after our 24.

24. She ascended; she came to men (*manuṣyà*); men called to her: O rich in cheer, come! of her Manu son of Vivasvant was young, earth [was] vessel; her Pṛithī son of Vena milked; from her he milked both cultivation (*kṛṣí*) and grain; upon those two, both cultivation and grain, men subsist; successful by what is cultivated (*kṛṣṭá-*), one to be subsisted upon, becometh he who knoweth thus.

Té at beginning of **d** is rendered in accordance with the paragraphs that precede and follow; but the *pada*-text reads *té* simply (not *té íti*), as if it qualified *manuṣyàs.* Ppp. reads *pṛthus* for *pṛthī.* An accent-mark has dropped out in our edition under the *va* of *irāvaty* in **a**.

25. She ascended; she came to the seven seers; the seven seers called to her: O rich in *bráhman,* come! of her king Soma was young, meter [was] vessel; her Brihaspati son of Añgiras milked; from her he milked both *bráhman* and penance; upon that, both *bráhman* and penance, the seven seers subsist; possessed of *bráhman*-splendor, one to be subsisted upon, becometh he who knoweth thus.

Ppp. puts this paragraph after our 26, and omits *rājā* after *somas* in **b**.

26. She ascended; she came to the gods; the gods called to her: O refreshment, come! of her Indra was young, the bowl [was] vessel;

her god Savitar milked; from her he milked refreshment; upon that refreshment the gods subsist; one to be subsisted upon becometh he who knoweth thus.

Ppp. reads *dārupātram* instead of *camasas* in **b**, and omits *devas* in **c**.

27. She ascended; she came to the Gandharvas and Apsarases; the Gandharvas and Apsarases called to her: O thou of sweet (*púṇya*) odor, come! of her Chitraratha son of Sūryavarchas was young, the blue-lotus leaf [was] vessel; her Vasuruchi son of Sūryavarchas milked; from her he milked sweet odor; upon that sweet odor the Gandharvas and Apsarases subsist; of sweet odor, one to be subsisted upon, becometh he who knoweth thus.

Ppp. has *kāuvero vāiçravaṇo* ⌊cf. our 28 **b**⌋ and *dārupātraṁ* in **b**, and *rājatanābhiḥ kāuverako* ⌊cf. our 28 **c**⌋ in **c**. Restore in our text the lost accent-mark under the *ti* of *jīvanti* in **d**.

28. She ascended; she came to the other-folks; the other-folks called to her: O concealment (*tirodhā́*), come! of her Kubera son of Viçravaṇa was young, the raw vessel [was] vessel; her Rajatanābhi son of Kubera milked; from her he milked concealment; upon that concealment the other-folks subsist: he concealeth all evil, becometh one to be subsisted upon, who knoweth thus.

Ppp. gives everywhere *puṇyajana* instead of *itarajana* ⌊twice: third occurrence not noted⌋, and reads in **b** *vasuruciḥ sūryavarcaso* and *puṣkaraparṇaṁ* ⌊cf. our 27 **b**⌋. P.p.m. and K. read *kúveras* in **b**, and Bp.K. read *kāverakás* in **c**.

29. She ascended; she came to the serpents; the serpents called to her: O poisonous one, come! of her Takshaka descendant of Viçāla was young, the gourd-vessel [was] vessel; her Dhṛitarāshṭra son of Īrāvant milked; from her he milked poison; upon that poison the serpents subsist; one to be subsisted upon becometh he who knoweth thus.

All the mss. give the first phrase in this verse, where it is for the last time repeated. *Āirā°vatáḥ* is quoted under Prāt. iv. 55 as an example of a word divided in the *pada*-text notwithstanding its secondary formation with initial *vṛddhi*. Ppp. reads *viṣābhayas* for *vāiçāleyas* in **b**, and combines *-rāṣṭrāi* "*rāv-* in **c** ⌊R's collation has *-rǎṣṭrāirāv-*⌋.

[**Paryāya VI.** — *catuṣkas. 30. 2-p. virāḍ gāyatrī; 31. 2-p. sāmnī triṣṭubh; 32. 2-p. prājāpatyā 'nuṣṭubh; 33. 2-p. ārcy uṣṇih.*]

30. Then for whomsoever that knoweth thus one shall pour out with a gourd, he should reject [it].

A gourd, apparently, being a too simple vessel to be respectful. ⌊The connection of the gourd with serpents (vss. 29, 32, 33), would seem to be the reason for rejection, as Dr. Ryder suggests.⌋ The readings of Ppp. in this division of the hymn are "confused but apparently essentially accordant" with those of our text. Read *tád* for *yád* at the beginning in our text.

31. Should he not reject [it], he should reject [it] by [thinking]: with the mind I reject thee.

32. In that he rejects [it], he thus rejects poison.

33. Poison is poured out after the unfriendly foe of him who knoweth thus.

⌊The quotations from the Old Anukr. for the *paryāya-sūkta* are given piecemeal at the end of each *paryāya*. For brevity they may here be given together: I. *trayodaça;* II. *daça;* III. *aṣṭāu ca;* IV. *tataḥ ṣoḍaça;* V. *ṣoḍaça;* VI. *catuṣkas.*⌋

⌊SPP., "Critical Notice," vol. i., p. 19, prints them in full in their metrical form:

trayodaça daçā 'ṣṭāu cā tataḥ ṣoḍaça ṣoḍaça:
virāḍvāyāṁ catuṣkas tu; ṣaṭ paryāyās tu niçcitāḥ:

'In the [hymn beginning] "*virāḍ vā*" (*vāi*), [the last *paryāya* is] one of four [*avasāna-rcas*]; while the *paryāyas* count six.'⌋

⌊The summations of *gaṇas* and (*gaṇa-*)*avasāna-rcas* are as follows: I. *g.*, 6; *av.*, 13; II. *av.*, 10; III. *g.*, 4; *av.*, 8; IV. *g.*, 4; *av.*, 16; V. *g.*, 4; *av.*, 16; VI. *av.*, 4.—Total of *av.*, 67.⌋

⌊Here ends the fifth *anuvāka*, with 2 hymns and 59 verses: that is 1 *artha-sūkta* of 26 verses and 1 *paryāya-sūkta* with 6 *paryāyas* and 33 verses.⌋

⌊Some mss. sum up the hymns and verses correctly. Thus D. reckons 30 *sūktas* (that is 24 of the decad-divisions of our hymns 1–9, plus 6 *paryāya-sūktas* of our h. 10) with 226 verses (i.e. in our hymns 1–9) plus 67 *avasāna-rcas*. Similarly ms. I. makes 30 hymns; but 259 verses (i.e. 226, plus the 33 of our h. 10).⌋

⌊Here ends the nineteenth *prapāṭhaka.*⌋

Book IX.

⌊This ninth book is the second of the second grand division of the Atharvan collection. For a general statement as to the make-up of the books of this division, see page 471. The Old Anukramaṇī describes the length of hymns 1, 3, and 5 by stating in each case the excess over 20 verses — perhaps assuming 20 as the normal length. The whole book has been translated by Victor Henry, *Les livres VIII et IX de l'Atharva-véda traduits et commentés*, Paris, 1894. The *bhāṣya* is lacking for this book.⌋

⌊**Paryāya-hymns**: for details respecting them, see pages 471–2. The *paryāya*-hymns of this book are hymn 6 (with 6 *paryāyas*) and hymn 7 (with 1 *paryāya*).⌋

⌊The *anuvāka*-division of the book (as is explained on page 472 also) is into five *anuvākas* of two hymns each. The "decad"-division likewise is as described on page 472. A tabular conspectus for book ix. follows:

Anuvākas	1		2		3		4		5	
Hymns	1	2	3	4	5	6	7	8	9	10
Verses	24	25	31	24	38	62¶	26¶	22	22	28
Decad-div.	10 + 14	10 + 10 + 5	10 + 10 + 11	10 + 14	10 + 10 + 10 + 8	6P	1P	10 + 12	10 + 12	10 + 10 + 8

Here ¶ means "paragraph of a *paryāya*" (such as is numbered as a "verse" in the Berlin edition) and P means "*paryāya*." The last line shows the "decad"-division. These divisions are shown also in both editions. Of these "decads," *anuvākas* 1, 2, 3, 4, and 5 contain respectively 5, 5, 4, 2, and 5 (in all, 21 "decads"); while *anuvākas* 3 and 4 have respectively 6 *paryāyas* and 1. The sum is 21 "decad"-*sūktas* and 7 *paryāya-sūktas* or 28 *sūktas*.⌋

---

1. To the honey-whip etc.

[*Átharvan. — caturviṅçarcam. madhudevatyam; āçvinam. trāiṣṭubham: 2. triṣṭubgarbhā pañkti; 3. parānuṣṭubh; 6, 7. mahābṛhatī (6. atiçākvaragarbhā; 7. atijāgatagarbhā); 8. bṛhatīgarbhā saṁstārapañkti; 9. parābṛhatī prastārapañkti; 10. paroṣṇik pañkti; 11–13, 15, 16, 18, 19. anuṣṭubh; 14. purauṣṇih; 17. upariṣṭādvirāḍ bṛhatī; 20. bhurig viṣṭārapañkti; 21. 1-av. 2-p. ārcy anuṣṭubh; 22. 3-p. brāhmī purauṣṇih; 23. 2-p. ārcī pañkti; 24. 3-av. 6-p. aṣṭi.*]

⌊Partly prose — 14 **a** and 21 to the end.⌋ Found also ⌊with vs. 3 before 2, vs. 7 before 6, and vs. 18 before 16⌋ in Pāipp. xvi.; ⌊but according to a note in W's Collation-book, vss. 1–24 occur in Pāipp. at folios 226 a, 108 a, 69 b, i.e. in several different *kāṇḍas!* ⌋. The hymn is called the *madhusūkta* 'honey-hymn' in Vāit. 16. 12, and is prescribed to be recited to accompany the mixing of soma with milk in a part of the *agniṣṭoma* ceremony. It is reckoned to the *varcasya gaṇa* (see note to Kāuç. 12. 10); and (always in company with iii. 16; vi. 69) is directed in Kāuç. 10. 24*; 12. 15; 13. 6 to be recited in various ceremonies. ⌊See also notes to vss. 13, 18.⌋ *⌊vi. 125. 2 and ix. 1. 1 and xix. 3. 1 have the same *pratīka* (*divaspṛthivyās*). SPP. understands the comm. at iii. 16 and at vi. 69 as intending ix. 1 by *divaspṛthivyās;* but the comm. at xix. 3 understands xix. 3 as intended (cf. Whitney's introduction to xix. 3). — The "honeyed whip," *mádhumatī káçā*, of the Açvins is mentioned in the RV. (i. 22. 3; 157. 4). Oldenberg, *Rel. des Veda*, p. 209, thinks it refers to the morning dew. Cf. Macdonell, *Ved. Mythol.*, p. 49, 54.⌋

Translated: Henry, 81, 115; Griffith, i. 427; Bloomfield, 229, 587.

1. Verily from sky, from earth, from atmosphere, from ocean, from fire, from wind was born the honey-whip; noting (*cāy*) it, [as] putting on immortality, all creatures (*prajā́*) rejoice to meet it with their hearts.

The irregularities of meter in **a** and **c** may be rectified ⌊very unsatisfactorily⌋ by combining *pṛthivyā́ 'nt-* (as Ppp. actually reads) and resolving *cāyitu-ā́*. *Divás p-* is prescribed by Prāt. ii. 68.

2. Great, all-formed [is] the milk of it; also they call thee the seed of ocean; whence the granting honey-whip cometh, thither breath, thither immortality (*amṛ́ta*) hath entered in.

Ppp. puts *payas* in **a** after *viçvarūpam* ⌊and combines *payo 'syās*⌋ and puts *tvā* in **b** after *uta;* and it reads at the end *diviṣṭaṁ*. It also gives the verse after our vs. 3. The metrical definition of the Anukr. is wrong, since a fair *triṣṭubh* is restorable by a little resolution (*viçu-a*, *pṛ-āṇas*).

3. Men, manifoldly meditating (*mīmāṅs-*) severally see its movement (*caritá*) on the earth; verily from fire, from wind was born the honey-whip, the formidable daughter (*naptí*) of the Maruts.

Pāda **c** is identical with 1 **b**, pādas **c**, **d** with 10 **c**, **d**. Ppp. reads at end of **a** *pṛthivyāṣ;* at end of **d**, *ugrā anapatiḥ* (also in vs. 10).

4. Mother of the Ādityas, daughter of the Vasus, breath of creatures (*prajā́*), navel of immortality (*amṛ́ta*), gold-colored, dripping with ghee (*ghṛtā́cī*), the honey-whip moves among mortals [as] a great brightness (*bhárga*).

Bp.p.m., Bp.²T. read *gárbhas* in **d**, and our edition follows them, doubtless erroneously. ⌊All of SPP's authorities give *bhárgas*.⌋ With **a**, **b** compare RV. viii. 101 (90). 15 **a**, **b** ⌊and MB. ii. 8. 15 **a**, **b**⌋. The Anukr. does not heed the redundant syllable in **c**. ⌊Correct *gárbhaç* to *bhárgaç*.⌋

5. The gods generated the whip of honey; of it there came to be an all-formed embryo; this, when born [and] tender, its mother fills; it, [when] born, looks abroad on all existences.

Ppp. has at the end *bhuvanā 'bhi vaste.*

6. Who knows (*pra-vid*) that, who understands (*cit*) that which [is] the unexhausted soma-holding vessel of the heart of it? The priest (*brahmán*) of excellent wisdom — he may revel in it.

'Of it' (**b**) is fem., and so relates to the 'honey-whip'; 'in it,' at the end, relates to the 'vessel.' *Akṣitas* (Ppp. *akṣatas*) at the end of **b** is plainly an intrusive addition to the pāda; the Anukr., wrongly reckoning the initial *a* of *asyās* as unelided, counts 15 syllables in the pāda, and calls both this and the next verse by the unusual and indefinite name *mahābṛhatī*.

7. He knows those two, he understands them that [are] its two unexhausted, thousand-streaming breasts; they milk out refreshment (*ū́rj*), unresisting.

'Its,' i.e. of the 'honey-whip.' Ppp. reads again *akṣatāu* in **b**, and it puts this verse before our vs. 6.

8. She that, crying much, great, vigor-bestowing, loud-noised, goes unto her course (?*vratá*), bellowing at three *gharmás* — she lows a lowing, she abounds (*pī*) with milk (*páyas*).

'Crying loudly,' lit. 'making to excess the sound *hiṅg*'; 'abounds with milk,' perhaps rather 'gives milk in streams.' The verse is very obscure; it is in part identical with 10.6 below (= RV. i. 164. 28). Its irregular meter (11 + 10 [11 ?]: 9 + 11 = 41 syllables) is very ill defined by the Anukr. ⌊which seems to scan as 11 + 9 : 9 + 11⌋.

9. Whom, when fattened, the waters wait upon, the mighty (*çākvará*) bulls that are self-ruling, they rain, they cause to rain, for him who knows this, his desire, refreshment, waters.

'Whom' is fem.; 'they' (**c**) is masc., = the bulls. Parts of this verse and the following one are lost in Ppp. The Anukr. ⌊seems to scan as 11 + 11 : 9 + 9⌋.

10. Thunder [is] thy voice, O Prajāpati; a bull, thou castest (*kṣip*) vehemence (?*çúṣma*) over the earth; verily from fire, from wind was born the honey-whip, the formidable daughter of the Maruts.

The latter half-verse we had above, as 3 **c**, **d**; the former half-verse is repeated below, as 20 **a**, **b** ⌊with *divi* for *ádhi* at the end⌋. ⌊Bloomfield thinks *çuṣma* is 'lightning': ZDMG. xlviii. 566.⌋ O. reads at the beginning *stanayitnúṣ ṭe*. The metrical description of the Anukr. means only that the syllables are 40 in all (10 + 12 : 11 + 7), and that one pāda contains seven.

11. As at the early pressing soma is loved (*priyá*) of the Açvins, so, O Açvins, let splendor be maintained in my self.

12. As at the second pressing soma is loved of Indra-and-Agni, so, O Indra-and-Agni, let splendor be maintained in my self.

13. As at the third pressing soma is loved of the Ṛibhus, so, O Ṛibhus, let splendor be maintained in my self.

This group of three verses is specially quoted at Vāit. 21.7 to accompany an offering of *ājya*. It is one of the passages forming the *varcasya gaṇa* (see note to Kāuç. 13.1);

and at Kāuç. 139. 15 it is prescribed to be used, with many others, in the ceremony of initiation of a Vedic student. The verses are not metrical, though the Anukr. calls them *anuṣṭubh* (as having 31 and 32 syllables). In 12 **a** the accent-mark under *ye* has dropped out.

14. May I generate honey; may I win honey; rich in milk, O Agni, have I come; unite me here with splendor.

The second part of the verse we have had above as vii. 89. 1 **c**, **d**. The edition reads, with all the mss., *vaṅçiṣīya*, but it should be emended to *vaṅsiṣīya* (root *van*); cf. the similar misreading at xvi. 9. 4. Ppp. reads *madhu janiṣī manu mambikīyaḥ;* and it combines *agnā "gamaṁ*. By reckoning the first part of the passage as metrical (which it is not) the Anukr. counts out a good *purauṣṇih*.

15. Unite me, O Agni, with splendor, with progeny, with life-time; may the gods know me as such; may Indra know, together with the seers.

We had the verse above, as vii. 89. 2.

16. As the honey-makers bring together honey upon honey, so, O Açvins, let splendor be maintained in my self.

Ppp. reads, for the second half-verse, *evā me 'çvinā balam ojaç ca dhriyatām :* cf. our 17 **c**, **d**. The line is, like the corresponding parts of 11–13, not metrical as it stands.

17. As the flies (*mákṣā*) smear down here honey upon honey, so, O Açvins, let my splendor, brilliancy, strength, and force be maintained.

In **a**, delete the superfluous accent-mark under *dhu*. Ppp. has quite another version of **a**, **b**: *yathā makṣā mayuntyujaṁ dakṣiṇām adhi:* and it omits *balam ojas* in **d**. The omission of any one of the three nouns in our **d** would rectify the meter.

18. What honey on hills (*girí*), on mountains, what in kine, in horses, in strong drink (*súrā*) as poured out, what honey [is] there, [be] that in me.

With this verse and the next are to be compared vi. 69. 1, 2 ⌊where the use by Vāit. is given⌋. Ppp. has only *yadi giriṣyavipāṁ citviṣī* in place of this verse, and puts it before our 16.

19. O ye Açvins, lords of beauty! anoint me with the honey of bees (*sāraghá*), that I may speak splendid words among the people.

This verse differs only by one word from vi. 69. 2.

20. Thunder [is] thy voice, O Prajāpati; a bull, thou castest vehemence on the earth, on the sky; upon that live all cattle; with this it lavishes (*pṛ*) food (*iṣ*) [and] refreshment.

The first half-verse is the same with 10 **a**, **b**, saving *diví* for *ádhi* at the end. 'That' in **c** is fem. (*tā́m*), and might refer either to 'voice' or to 'earth'; 'this' is masc. (or neut., *téna*), and might refer either to 'vehemence' or to 'sky'; while 'it' is again fem. The obscurity of the verse baffles interpretation. The Pet. Lex. suggests 'seed' as a possible rendering of *çúṣma* ('vehemence'). The metrical description of the

Anukr. is, as usual in such an irregular case (10 + 12 : 11 + 9 [11?] = 42), quite worthless. Ppp. omits the first pāda, reads *divas* for *divi* at the end of the second, and goes on thus: *madhoṣ kaçayoṣ pṛthivīm anakṣi tāṁ dātāraṁ paçava upa jīvanti : sarve tena vo çeṣam ūrjaṁ bibharti.*

21. Earth [is] the staff, atmosphere the embryo, sky the whip, lightning the snapper (? *prakaçá*), of gold the globule (*bindú*).

The Pet. Lex. conjectures "Peitschenriemen" for *prakaçá*. Ppp. leaves the initial of *antarikṣam* unelided, and for *prakaças* has *prakāçā madhokaçā ci ghṛtācī.*

22. He who knows the seven honeys of the whip becomes rich in honey: the Brahman, and the king, and the milch-cow, and the draft-ox, and rice, and barley; honey the seventh.

One does not see why the Anukr. calls the passage *brāhmī purauṣṇih* ⌊that is $\frac{6}{4}$ of 12 : 8 + 8 = 18 : 12 + 12 = 42⌋ rather than simply *brāhmī uṣṇih* ⌊$\frac{6}{4}$ of 8 + 8 : 12 = 12 + 12 : 18 = 42⌋; it is the only example of either name in the treatise. ⌊The not very sufficient reason for the preference would seem to be the position of the *avasāna*, which divides the "vs." as 18 : 24 and not as 24 : 18.⌋ ⌊Ppp. has in **a** *madhukaçāyās* for *kaç-* and *sapta madhumatīm* for *madhumān bhavati;* then follows *madhumato lokāṅ jayati* (cf. vs. 23).⌋

23. Rich in honey he becomes; rich in honey becomes his provision (*āhāryà*); worlds rich in honey he conquers, who knows thus.

24. When it thunders in a clear sky, that is Prajāpati himself becoming manifest to his creatures; therefore I stand with the sacred cord over the right shoulder, saying: O Prajāpati, take notice (*anu-budh*) of me: creatures [take notice], Prajāpati takes notice of him who knows thus.

In order to make an *aṣṭi* (64 syll.) of this piece of prose, we have to restore *ánu* and separate *íti* in **d**, and to resolve *ánu enam* in **e**; and to make six pādas the last line has to be violently divided; the *pada*-text intimates a division after the second *ánu*. ⌊Ppp. in **a–b** has a *tat* also before *prajāpatis* and in **e** it reads *prajā budhyante* for *prajāp- budhyate.*⌋

⌊The hymn begins with *divás* and the quoted Anukr. says "*divaç*" *ca catur-uttarāḥ* (referring to a plus of 4 over the normal 20).⌋

2. To Kāma: for various blessings.

[*Atharvan.—pañcaviṅçakam. kāmadevatyam. trāiṣṭubham: 5. atijagatī; 7. jagatī; 8. 2-p. ārcī pañkti; 11, 20, 23. bhurij; 12. anuṣṭubh; 13. 2-p. ārcy anuṣṭubh; 14, 15, 17, 18, 21, 22. jagatī; 16. 4-p. çakvarīgarbhā parājagatī.*]

⌊Partly prose — "vs." 13.⌋ Found also (except vs. 4) in Pāipp. xvi. ⌊with vs. 16 before 12 and vs. 24 before 20⌋. The hymn (vs. 1) is prescribed in Vāit. 24. 10 to be recited, with homage to Kāma, in a part of the Agniṣṭoma ceremony; and in Kāuç. 49. 1 it (vs. 1) accompanies the release of a bull in a witchcraft ceremony.

Translated: Muir, v. 404 (nearly all); Ludwig, p. 519; Scherman, *Philosophische Hymnen*, p. 76 (part); Henry, 84, 118; Griffith, i. 430; Bloomfield, 220, 591.—Cf. Hillebrandt, *Veda-Chrestomathie*, p. 40.

1. The rival-slaying bull Kāma do I desire to aid (?*çikṣ*) with ghee, with oblation, with sacrificial butter; do thou, praised with great heroism, make my rivals to fall downward.

Kāma, lit. 'desire, love,' is so thoroughly personified throughout the hymn that the word is better transferred than translated.

2. What of my mind or my sight is not agreeable (*priyá*), what of me gnaws, does not enjoy (*abhi-nand*), that evil-dreaming do I fasten on my rival; praising Kāma, may I shoot up.

The sense of **a**, **b** is very doubtful; without **b** added, **a** would naturally mean 'what is not agreeable to my mind or sight'; the Pet. Lex. proposes to help the difficulty rather by emending **b** to *yasmād bībhatse yac ca nā 'bhinande.* This verse and the following one are included in the *duḥsvapnanāçana gaṇa:* see note to Kāuç. 46. 9. There is an irregularity in every pāda, but the Anukr. does not heed them. Ppp. has, for **b**, *yan me hṛdaye nā 'bhinandanti;* and, for **d**, *kāmaṁ juṣṭa hānudaṁ bhideyam* — thus giving us no help. ⌊Pischel treats the vs., *Ved. Stud.* ii. 61. Aufrecht, KZ. xxxiv. 459, sees here a root *bhas* 'verdriessen, taedere.'⌋

3. Evil-dreaming, O Kāma, and difficulty, O Kāma, want of progeny, homelessness, ruin do thou, formidable, masterful, fasten on him who shall seek to devise (*cikits-*) distresses for us.

Ppp. combines *yo 'smabhyam* in **d**.

4. Thrust, O Kāma; thrust forth, O Kāma; let them who are my rivals go to ruin; of them, thrust to lowest darknesses, do thou, O Agni, burn out the abodes (*vā́stu*).

The Anukr. takes no notice of the deficiency of two syllables in **d**, which in 9 **d** is made up by the addition of *anu.* In Vāit. 4. 5 the verse is strangely used to accompany the separation of two sacrificial ladles; in Kāuç. 48. 5 it accompanies the driving away of something with a branch.

5. That daughter of thine, O Kāma, is called a milch-cow, what utterance (*vā́c*) the poets name *virā́j;* with that do thou avoid them that are my rivals; let breath, cattle, life avoid them.

Or **a** might be 'that milch-cow is called thy daughter.' O. reads *páry eṇān* in **d**; but the passage is quoted under Prāt. iii. 80 as one in which the lingualization of *n* does not take place.

6. With the strength of Kāma, of Indra, of king Varuṇa, of Vishṇu, with the impulse of Savitar ('the impeller'), with the priestship (*hotrá*) of Agni I thrust forth my rivals, as a skilful pole-man (?*çambín*) a boat on the waters (*udaká*).

Çambín occurs nowhere else, and the meaning of *çámba* is doubtful. Ppp. reads in **c** *piçācān* instead of *sapatnān.*

7. Let Kāma, my valiant (*vājín*) formidable overseer, make for me freedom from rivals; let the all-gods be my refuge; let all the gods come to this call of mine.

'All' is *viçve* in **c**, and *sárve* in **d**. The verse is called *jagatī* by the Anukr., though only **d** is a *jagatī* pāda ⌊and that only by count⌋. Ppp. combines at the end of **d** *māi 'mam* ⌊and thus suggests the true metrical rendering of **d** as a *triṣṭubh*: similarly at ix. 3. 15⌋.

8. Enjoying this sacrificial butter rich in ghee, do ye, with Kāma as chief (*-jyéṣṭha*), revel here, making for me freedom from rivals.

Ppp. reads *ghṛtam id* in **a**, and *kṛṇvantu* in **c**. The verse is a perfectly good *virāṇnāmagāyatrī*, but the Anukr. calls it an *ārcī pañkti*, as if it had 30 syllables.

9. Becoming, O Kāma, in alliance (*sarátham*) with Indra-and-Agni, may ye make my rivals to fall downward; of them, fallen to lowest darknesses, do thou, O Agni, burn along out the abodes.

With **c**, **d** compare 4 **c**, **d** above. The first half-verse presents various anomalies: *sarátham* demands an instrumental case; we should expect rather a plural verb (but compare vi. 104. 3 **a**, **b**); and it should be accented after *hí*. Emending *indrāgní* to *índreṇa*, and reading *pādáyāthas*, would make everything right.

10. Slay thou, O Kāma, those that are my rivals; make them fall down to blind darknesses; be they all senseless (?*nírindriya*), sapless; let them not live any day soever.

Ppp. combines *sapatnā 'ndhā* in **a**–**b**, combines and reads *nirindriyā 'ravāḥ* in **c**, and has for **d** *yathā nu jīvāt katamac* ⌊*-maç*?⌋ *cane 'ṣāṁ*.

11. Kāma hath slain (*vadh*) them that are my rivals; he hath made for me wide space, prosperity; let the four directions bow to me; let the six wide ones ⌊fem.⌋ bring ghee to me.

The third pāda was found above as v. 3. 1 **c**. It is unusual for the Anukr. to note as *bhurij* a *triṣṭubh* containing a *jagatī*-pāda. ⌊Cf. Bergaigne, *Rel. Véd.* ii. 122.⌋

12. Let them float away downward, like a boat severed from its mooring; of them, thrust forth by missiles, there is no return again.

The verse is nearly identical with iii. 6. 7 above. ⌊Ppp. reads in **c** *sāyakaṣ pra-*.⌋

13. Agni [is] a repeller (?*yáva*), Indra a repeller, Soma a repeller; let the repelling (?*yavayávan*) gods repel (*yu*) him.

⌊Prose.⌋ This translation is altogether questionable. Perhaps the verse accompanies a ceremony in which barley (*yáva*) is used, a play on words being intended between *yáva* 'barley' and the root *yu* 'repel' · *yavayā́van* would then be 'going in barley.' Ppp. has for second half *yavayanty amum āmuṣyāyaṇam amuṣyāṣ putraṁ jīvalokaṁ mṛtalokaṁ katā 'mum*. It is strange that the Anukr. does not note the paragraph as *dvyavasānā*.

14. With his heroes not safe ⌊*á-sarvavīra*⌋ let him go on, thrust forth, to be hated of friends, to be avoided of his own kin; on earth also stay (*ava-sā*) thunderbolts; may the formidable god massacre your rivals.

The sense of **c** is obscure; *vidyútas* might also be object of the verb: 'they let loose thunderbolts.' Ppp. puts *dveṣyas* after *mitrāṇām* in **b**. The Anukr. calls the verse a *jagatī*, although it is a *triṣṭubh* with one *jagatī*-pāda (like 11). ⌊W. usually renders *sárvavīra* by 'with all [his, our, etc.] heroes.'⌋

15. This great [earth], both stirred and unstirred, bears the lightning and all the thunders; let the Āditya, arising with property, with brilliancy, thrust downward my rivals, he the powerful one.

The first half-verse is wholly obscure, and the version given commits the grammatical solecism of taking *vidyút* as neut. accus. But for the last *ca*, *vidyut* might be taken as subject of the sentence. The verse has a *triṣṭubh*-pāda (**a**), of which the Anukr. makes no account.

16. What sufficient (*udbhú*) triply-guarding defense thou hast, O Kāma, worship (*bráhman*) as extended protection (*vármam*), made unpierceable, with that do thou avoid them that are my rivals; let breath, cattle, life avoid them.

The last half-verse is ⌊nearly⌋ identical with 5 **c**, **d** above, and O. again reads *eṇān* in **d**. Ppp. puts the verse next before our 12. The description of the meter by the Anukr. is unintelligible, since we have (12 + 14 : 12 + 14) 52 syllables, or an *atijagatī*; perhaps *parājagatī* is a misreading for this.

17. Wherewith the gods thrust forth the Asuras, wherewith Indra conducted the barbarians (*dásyu*) to lowest darkness, therewith do thou, O Kāma, thrust forth far from this world those who are my rivals.

Ppp. reads at end of **b** *tamo 'pabādhe*, and at end of **d** *sarvān* for *dūram*. The verse (11 + 13 : 11 + 11 = 46) is a queer sort of "*jagatī*."

18. As the gods thrust forth the Asuras, as Indra drove (*bādh*) the barbarians to lowest darkness, so do thou, O Kāma, thrust forth far from this world those who are my rivals.

Ppp. has again *tamo 'pabādhe*, but this time *dūram*. The "*jagatī*" meter is like that of vs. 17.

19. Kāma was first born; not the gods, the Fathers, nor mortals attained (*āp*) him; to them art thou superior (*jyáyāṅs*), always great; to thee as such, O Kāma, do I pay homage.

Ppp. reads in **a**, **b** *prathamo nā 'nyat puro nāi 'naṁ devāsaṣ pitaro no 'ta martyāḥ*; and it combines in **d** *namāi 't*. The verse (9⌊10?⌋ + 10 : 12 + 11 = 42) is a queer "*triṣṭubh*."

20. How great in width are heaven-and-earth; how far the waters flowed, how far fire — to them art thou etc. etc.

With **a** is identical iv. 6. 2 **a**. Some *saṁhitā*-mss. read *sisyadúr* in **b** (O.s.m.R.). ⌊I find no note of R.⌋ The meter is described by the Anukr. in accordance with that of vs. 11.

21. How great are the divergent (*víṣvañc*) quarters [and] directions; how great the regions (*áçā*), on-lookers of the sky — to them art thou etc. etc.

The verse lacks two syllables of being a real *jagatī*.

22. How many the humble-bees (*bhṛ́ñga*), the bats, the *kurūrus;* how many have been the *vághās*, the tree-creepers—to them art thou etc. etc.

The verse is a *jagatī* in number of syllables (12 + 13 : 12 + 11 = 48). Bp. accents *jatváḥ* in **a**.

23. Superior art thou to him that winks, that stands; superior to the ocean art thou, O Kāma, fury—to them art thou etc. etc.

24. Verily no wind soever attains (*āp*) Kāma, not fire, sun, also not moon; to them art thou etc. etc.

Ppp. puts this verse before our 20, and reads for **c, d** *na vāpaç cana kāmam āpur nā 'horātrāṇi nihatāni yanti na vāi puṇyajāç* ⌊intending *puṇyajanāç ?*⌋ *cana kāmam āpur na gandharvāpsaraso na sarpāḥ.* The Anukr. accounts the verse simply a *triṣṭubh* ⌊perhaps counting **b** as 10 and balancing it with the 12 of **c**⌋.

25. What propitious excellent bodies thou hast, O Kāma, with which what thou choosest becometh real, with them do thou enter wholly into us; make evil devices (*dhī*) enter away elsewhere.

The combination *tā́bhiṣ ṭvám* is an example under Prāt. ii. 84, and is quoted in the commentary there. Ppp. reads *vṛṇīte* at end of **b**, *upa-* for *abhi-* in **c**, and *upa* for *apa* in **d**. The Anukr. pays no heed to the extra syllable in **d**. The verse is quoted in Kāuç. 24. 29 in the *āgrahāyaṇī* ceremony, to accompany the act of lying down (apparently merely on account of the occurrence of *-saṁ-viç* in **c**).

⌊The quoted Anukr. here says *kāmasūktaḥ.*⌋

⌊Here ends the first *anuvāka*, with 2 hymns and 49 verses.⌋

3. To accompany the releasing of a house.

[*Bhṛgvañgiras.—ekatriṅçatkam. çālādevatyam. ānuṣṭubham: 6. pathyāpañkti; 7. paroṣṇih; 15. 3-av. 5-p. atiçakvarī; 17. prastārapañkti; 21. āstārapañkti; 25, 31. 3-p. prājāpatyā bṛhatī; 26. sāmnı triṣṭubh; 27–30. pratiṣṭhānāmagāyatrī; 25–31. 1-av. 3-p.*]

⌊Partly prose—25 to end.⌋ Found also in Pāipp. xvi. (in the verse-order 1–3, 5, 4, 6–10, 14, 16, 11, 12, 13, 15, 17, 21, 18, 20, 19, 24, 23, 22, 25–31). The hymn is not noticed in Vāit.; but several verses (1, 15, 18, 22, 24) are quoted in Kāuç. 66. 22–30, in connection with an inauguration-ceremony (*savayajña*) in which a house (a toy house?) is an object given.

Translated: Ludwig, p. 464; Zimmer, p. 151 (vss. 1–24); Grill, 60, 188 (vss. 1–24); Henry, 87, 121; Griffith, i. 434; Bloomfield, 193, 595.—Cf. also Oldenberg, IFA. vi. 179.

1. Of the props (*upamít*), of the supports (*pratimít*), and also of the connectors (?*parimít*) of the dwelling (*çā́lā*) that possesses all choice things, we unfasten the tied (*naddhá*) [parts].

Ppp. reads *upamitaṣ pratimito 'tho parimitaç ca yaç çālāyā viçvavārāyā te naddhān vi cṛtāmasi.*

2. What of thee is tied, O thou that possessest all choice things, what fetter and knot is made, that with a spell (*vā́c*) I make fall apart, as Brihaspati [did] Bala.

All the mss. read *balám* (not *valám*) in **c**, as also Ppp. (*bṛhaspatiṁ vahaṁ balam*). Our Bp. has in **d** *srañçayāmi : tvát.* The Anukr. seems to imply the abbreviation of *iva* to *'va* in **c**.

3. He stretched (*ā-yam*), he combined (*sam-bṛh*), he made thy knots firm (*dṛḍhá*); with Indra we unfasten [them], as a knowing slaughterer the joints.

4. Of thy beams (*vañçá*), ties (*náhana*), and binding (*prāṇāhá*) grass, of thy sides (*pakṣá*), O thou that possessest all choice things, we unfasten the tied [parts].

Vañçá is properly a bamboo beam. *Prāṇāhá* (unchanged in *pada*-text) seems to occur only here, nor is root *nah* elsewhere combined with *pra;* I have ventured to render it as an adj., as *tṛ́ṇa* appears to call for a descriptive epithet. Ppp. reads *naddhān vi* in **d**.

5. Of the clamps (*saṁdañçá*), of the *paladás*, and of the embracer (*páriṣvañjalya*) — now of the mistress of the building do we unfasten the tied [parts].

Ppp. reads, in **a**, **b**, *palidānāṁ pariṣvañcanadasya ca;* and, for **c**, *sarvā mānasya patni te;* it also puts the verse before our 4.

6. What hanging vessels (?*çikyà*) they bound on to thee within for enjoyment, those we unfasten for thee; be thou, [when] set up, O mistress of the building, propitious to our self (*tanū́*).

Çikyà may be an ornamental hanging appendage of some kind.* All the mss. read *mā́nasya patni* in **d**; our edition emends to *mān-*. The *pada*-text has *úddhitā*, undivided, in **e** (as at xviii. 2. 34, and *uddhitḥ* at viii. 8. 22); the case ought to fall under Prāt. iv. 62, but root *dhā* is not mentioned there, though we find *han* superfluously included. Ppp. reads *yāni te antaç cikyāny āmedho 'ntyāya kaṁ;* and, for **d**, *sarvā mānasya patnyā.*

*⌊As to decorations of this kind, see John Griffiths, *The Paintings in the Buddhist Cave-Temples of Ajantâ*, London, 1896, plates 6, 10, and 13; cf. also Karpūra-mañjarī, iii. 27, ed. Konow, and my note thereon at p. 289. W. has interlined "slings" as an alternative rendering of *çikyà*.⌋

7. Oblation-holder (*havirdhā́na*), fire-place (*agniçā́la*), wives' site [and] seat; seat of the gods art thou, O heavenly dwelling.

The *paroṣṇih* is regular, save for the common variant of a *triṣṭubh* instead of a *jagatī*-pāda at the end.

8. The thousand-eyed net (*ákṣu*), stretched out as *opaçá* on the division-line (*viṣūvánt*), tied down, put on, do we with worship (*bráhman*) unfasten.

Abhihita in **c** doubtless contains the suggestion of *abhidhānī* 'a halter.' Geldner (*Ved. Stud.* i. 136) wants to make of *akṣu* a 'stake' or 'pillar.' *Viṣūvant* probably means the 'parting of the hair, crown' (so Zimmer), here the ridge of the roof. Ppp. begins with *yakṣmopiçam*, and has in **c** the easier reading *apinaddham apihitam*.

9. He who, O dwelling, accepts thee, and he by whom thou art built — let both those, O mistress of the building, live to attain old age.

The *mā́nasya* of the mss. in **c** is again emended in our edition to *mān-*. Ppp. rectifies the meter of **a** by reading *yaç citrā (ca tvā?) pr-*. The Anukr. pays no heed to the irregularity of the verse (9 + 8 : 8 + 7).

10. Do thou, made firm, tied, adorned (*pari-kṛ*), go to him yonder — thou whose every limb, whose every joint we unfasten.

O. reads in **a** *amútrāi 'ṇam*. *Páriṣkṛtā* is unaltered in the *pada*-text, as prescribed by Prāt. iv. 58. *Enam* probably indicates the "acceptor" (9 **a**, 15). Ppp. reads in **b** *tridhā* for *dṛḍhā*, and begins **c** with *tasyās*. ⌊As to *amútra*, cf. Oldenberg, IFA. vi. 179.⌋

11. He who fixed (*ni-mi*) thee, O dwelling, [who] brought together the forest trees — unto progeny, O dwelling, he, [as a] most exalted Prajāpati, made thee.

Ppp. reads *pūrvas* for *çāle* in **a**.

12. Homage to him, homage to the giver, and to the lord of the dwelling we pay; homage to the forth-moving (*pra-car*) fire, and to thy spirit (? *púruṣa*) [be] homage.

Ppp. reads in **b** *kṛṇmasi*.

13. Homage to kine, to horses, whatever is born (*vi-jā*) in the dwelling; thou rich in births (*vijā-*), rich in progeny, we unfasten thy fetters.

Ppp. lacks, probably by an oversight, the second half-verse.

14. Thou coverest within the fire, the men together with the cattle (*paçú*); thou rich in births, rich in progeny, we unfasten thy fetters.

15. Between both heaven and earth what expanse [there is], therewith do I accept this dwelling of thine; the atmosphere that pervades (*vimā́na*) space (*rájas*), that do I make a paunch (*udára*) for treasures; therewith I accept the house for this man.

This verse in Kāuç. 66. 28 accompanies the "acceptance" of the house in question. The Anukr. calls it an *atiçakvarī*, though it contains only 57 syllables (12 + 12 : 11 + 11 : 11) instead of 60. Ppp. reads at end of **b** *tāi 'māṁ* (an abbreviation which is here acceptable, as making a good *triṣṭubh*-pāda ⌊such was the case at ix. 2. 7 also⌋), and in **e** *yac chālāṁ* for *tena ç-*.

16. Rich in refreshment, rich in milk, fixed (*ni-mi*), built upon the earth, bearing all food, O dwelling, do not thou injure those accepting [thee].

17. Wrapped (*ā-vṛ*) with grass, clothing itself in *paladás*, the dwelling, place of rest (*nivéçanī*) of living creatures, like the night — built on the earth thou standest, like a she-elephant, having feet.

That is, apparently, heavy and big on the four corner posts, like an elephant (female because 'dwelling' is feminine) on its feet. With **b** compare xii. 1. 6 **b**. The verse as a *prastārapañkti* (11 + 12 : 8 + 8) has no irregularity which the Anukr. is wont to heed.

18. Of thy rush-work (*íṭa*) I unfasten what was tied on, uncovering; [thee] pressed together by Varuṇa let Mitra in the morning open out.

The verse in Kāuç. 66. 24 accompanies the letting down (*ava-sṛ*) of the door. ⌊Bergaigne has a note on the vs., *Rel. Véd.* iii. 122.⌋

19. The dwelling fixed with worship (*bráhman*), fixed, built by the poets — let Indra-and-Agni, immortal, defend the dwelling, the seat for soma (*somyá*).

P. reads *nírmitām* in **b**, and *sāumyám* in **d**. Ppp. has a quite different version: *catussraktim̐ paricakrām̐* for **a**; *viçvāna bibhratī çālām* (cf. our 16 **c**) *amṛto sāumyam̐ sadaḥ* for **c**, **d**.

20. A nest (*kuláya*) upon a nest, a vessel (*kóça*) pressed together in a vessel — there a mortal is born (*vi-jā*), from whom all is generated (*pra-jā*).

Ppp. has *martyas* in **c**.

21. [The dwelling] which is fixed with two sides, with four sides, which with six sides — the eight-sided, the ten-sided dwelling, the mistress of the building, Agni lies in like an embryo.

The *pada*-text reads *aṣṭā°pakṣām* in **c**, by Prāt. iii. 2; iv. 94. ⌊As to *pakṣa*, cf. iii. 7. 3.⌋ The verse is a good *pan̄kti*, involving only the resolution *mánasi-a* in **d**, but the Anukr. absurdly treats it as of four pādas; and, in accordance with this, the *pada*-mss. mark a pāda division after *çálām*.

22. I go forward, O dwelling, turned toward thee, uninjuring, that art turned toward me; for within [are] fire and waters, the first door of right (*ṛtá*).

Ppp. reads at the end *prathamobhā*. The mss. all have *ca ṛtásya* in **c–d**. The verse is quoted in Kāuç. 66. 25, accompanying the action of 'going forward with (*ādāya*) water-pot [and] fire.'

23. I bring forward these waters, free from *yákṣma*, dispellers of *yákṣma*; I set forth unto the houses, together with immortal fire.

We had this verse above, as iii. 12. 9. Ppp. (which omitted it as part of that hymn) reads in **a** *harāmi*, and in **c** *abhi* (for *upa*).

24. Fasten thou not on us the fetter; a heavy burden, become thou light; like a woman (*vadhū́*), O dwelling, we carry thee where we will.

Quoted in Kāuç. 66. 30. ⌊Cf. again Oldenberg, IFA. vi. 179. — Over "woman" W. interlines "bride?"⌋

25. From the eastern quarter, homage to the greatness of the dwelling! hail to the gods that are to be hailed!

⌊Ppp. puts *svāhā devebhyaḥ svāhyebhyaḥ* before *prācyāḥ*: and has a similar order in the following vss.⌋

26. From the southern quarter, homage etc. etc.

27. From the western quarter, homage etc. etc.

28. From the northern quarter, homage etc. etc.

29. From the firm quarter, homage etc. etc.

30. From the upward quarter, homage etc. etc.

31. From every quarter, homage etc. etc.

In the last verse *diçódiçaḥ* should have been printed without space before the repetition, as is our usage elsewhere.

⌊After this hymn, which exceeds the norm by 11 verses, the quotation from the Old Anukr. is *ekādaçāi 'vo "'pamitām" iti syuḥ.*⌋

4. Accompanying the gift of a bull.

[*Brahman.—caturvinçakam. ārṣabham. trāiṣṭubham: 8. bhurij; 6, 10, 24. jagatī; 11–17, 19, 20, 23. anuṣṭubh; 18. upariṣṭād bṛhatī; 21. āstārapañkti.*]

Found also in Pāipp. xvi. (in the verse-order 1–3, 5, 4, 6, 8, 7, 9, 10–13, 15, 14, 16–22, 24, 23). Not noticed in Vāit., and not in Kāuç. in a way to cast any light whatever upon it; the hymn is quoted in Kāuç. 24. 19 (with vi. 111) in the ceremony of turning a bull loose, and vs. 24 separately in the same ceremony in Kāuç. 24. 21; also vs. 1 in 66. 18 in connection with a bull; the hymn is reckoned (see note to Kāuç. 19. 1) among the *puṣṭika mantras*.

Translated: Henry, 90, 128; Griffith, i. 438.—For some of the vss. the reader may consult Hillebrandt, *Ved. Myth.* i. 330, 516, 382, 358, 525.

1. The bright bull of a thousand, rich in milk, bearing all forms in his bellies, desiring to accomplish (?*çikṣ*) what is excellent for his giver, the sacrificer—he, the ruddy one of Brihaspati, hath stretched ⌊*ā-tan*⌋ the line (*tántu*).

That is, doubtless, 'has extended *or* performed the sacrifice.'

2. He who in the beginning became the counterpart (*pratimā́*) of the waters, prevailing (*prabhū́*) for everything, like the divine earth, father of young (*vatsá*), lord of the inviolable [kine]—let him set (*kṛ*) us in thousandfold prosperity.

3. A male (*púmāñs*), [yet] pregnant, big (*sthávira*), rich in milk, the bull bears a trunk (*kábandha*) of good (*vásu*); him, sacrificed to Indra, let Agni Jātavedas carry by the roads traveled by the gods.

W. reads in **b** *vásoṣ ká-*.

4. Father of calves, lord of the inviolable [kine], also father of great gulfs (*gárgara*); calf, afterbirth, fresh milk, beestings, curd, ghee—that [is] his seed.

The verse occurs also in TS. (iii. 3. 9²), MS. (ii. 5. 10), and K. (xiii. 9). In **b**, MS. reads *utā́ 'yám* for *átho;* for **d**, TS. has *āmíkṣā mástu ghṛtám asya rétaḥ*, and MS. the same, save *yóniḥ* for *rétaḥ*.

5. The gods' portion [was] that load, the sap of waters, of plants, of ghee; the mighty one (*çakrá*) chose a drink of soma; a great stone became what [was his] body.

This verse also is found in TS. and MS. (as above), in both texts preceding our vs. 4 (in MS. one other verse intervenes, our xviii. 4. 28). Both have, for **a**, *devā́nām eṣá upanāhá āsīt;* for **b**, TS. has *apā́ṁ gárbha óṣadhīṣu nyàktaḥ*, and MS. *apā́m pátir vṛṣabhá óṣadhīnām;* in **c**, both have *drapsám* for *bhakṣám* and *pūṣā́* for *çakráḥ;* in **d**, after *abhavat*, MS. has *yát tád ā́sīt*, and TS. *tád eṣām*.

6. Thou bearest a vessel filled with soma, shaper (*tváṣṭṛ*) of forms, generator of cattle; propitious to thee be these pudenda (?*prajanū́*) that are here; to us, O ax, confirm those that are yonder.

Ppp. reads at the beginning *somasya;* its second half-verse is unintelligible. The verse is with no propriety called a *jagatī* (11 + 11 : 13 + 12 = 47).

7. Sacrificial butter he bears; ghee [is] his seed; thousandfold prosperity — that they call the sacrifice; the bull, clothing himself in Indra's form — let him, O gods, come propitious to us, being given.

Ppp. reads in **b** *sahasrapoṣas*, and in **d** '*smā* and *çivāi* "*tu*.

8. Indra's force, Varuṇa's two arms, the Açvins' two shoulders, of the Maruts this hump; they who are wise, poets, who are skilful (*manīṣín*), call him Brihaspati brought together.

The verse has two *jagatī*-pādas, though called by the Anukr. simply *bhurij*. Read at the end of **b** *kakút*.

9. Rich in milk, thou stretchest unto the people (*víç*) of the gods; thee they call Indra, thee Sarasvant; he gives a thousand [kine] with one face who makes offering (*ā-hu*) of a bull to a Brahman.

⌊Cf. Oldenberg, IFA. vi. 183.⌋

10. Brihaspati, Savitar bestowed on thee vigor (*váyas*); from Tvashṭar, from Vāyu was brought forth thy soul (*ātmán*); with mind in the atmosphere I make offering (*hu*) of thee; let heaven-and-earth both be thy *barhís*.

Ppp. reads *manas* for *vayas* in **a**. The Anukr. calls the verse *jagatī*, though two of its pādas are *triṣṭubh*.

11. He who goes speaking out greatly among the kine, like Indra among the gods — of that bull let the worshiper (*brahmán*) praise together the members excellently.

All our mss. (save O.) read, like the edition, *tásya ṛṣa-* in **c**, although the passage is quoted as example under the Prāt. rule (iii. 46) that *a* or *ā* + *ṛ* make *ar*. Ppp. reads in **a** *āindrī* '*va*. The *paddhati* (note to Kāuç. 24. 19) has the verse whispered in the right ear of the released bull.

12. His sides were Anumati's; his flanks (?*anūvṛ́j*) were Bhaga's; of his knees (*aṣṭhīvánt*) Mitra said: those are wholly mine.

All the nouns are duals. The Anukr. takes no notice of the redundant syllable in **c**. ⌊Henry would emend thus: *-vántābrav-*, i.e. *-vántā abrav-*.⌋ Ppp. reads at the beginning *pārçvay āstām*.

13. His rump was the Ādityas'; his two thighs were Brihaspati's; his tail [was] the heavenly wind's; therewith he shakes the herbs.

Ppp. reads in **b** *çroṇīy āstām*.

14. His intestines (*gúdā*) were Sinīvālī's; they called his skin Sūryā's; they called his feet (pl.) the upstander's (*utthātṛ́*), when they prepared (*kalpay-*) the bull.

The *pada*-text reads, like the *saṁhitā*, *utthātúḥ*, by Prāt. iv. 62. Ppp. combines *gudā "saṁ;* it also makes our 14 **c**, **d** and 15 **c**, **d** exchange places. ⌊Ppp. puts *yat* before *ṛṣabham*, and for *akalpayan* it has *vika* . . . (gap).⌋

15. His breast (*kroḍá*) was Jāmiçaṅsa's; his vessel [was] maintained as Soma's, when all the gods, coming together, distributed (*vi-kalpay-*) the bull.

We had *jāmiçaṅsa* above (ii. 10. 1) as 'imprecation of sisters'; the word does not occur elsewhere. What part of the bull is his 'vessel' is obscure. The first pāda has a redundant syllable.

16. Those dew-claws (*kúṣṭhikā*) [were] Saramā's; they assigned the hoofs to the tortoises (*kūrmá*); the content of his bowels they maintained for the worms, the *çavartás*.

The mss. are divided between *çavarta* (P.s.m.I.O.R.p.m.T.D.Kp.) and *çvavarta* (Bp.E.R.s.m.); while M. and P.p.m. have *çvaçavarta*, and W. *çaçavarta*. The occurrence of *çavartá* in TS. (v. 7. 23[1]: also in connection with *ūbadhya*) determined the reading of our text. But our *pada*-text divides the word (Bp. *çva∘vartá;* D.Kp. *ça∘v-*), which favors the reading *çva-*, since it implies a combination of the two recognizably independent words *çvan* and *varta*, 'occurring in dogs,' or something of the sort. Ppp. apparently has *çivaratrebhyo*. ⌊Roth suggests that *çavarta* may be for *çavavarta* 'Aaswurm, Made.'⌋

17. With his horns he pushes the demon; with his eye he slays ruin; with his ears he hears what is excellent — he who is the inviolable lord of kine.

Ppp. reads in **a**, **b** *rakṣa riṣad rātī*. The Prāt. (ii. 70) notes that the reading in **d** is not *yás pát-*. Some of the mss. (Bp.I.K.) accent *aghnyàs*.

18. With a hundred-fold sacrifice he sacrifices; the fires burn him not; all the gods quicken him, who makes offering of a bull to a Brahman.

The last pāda is the same with 9 **d**. Ppp. has *sarve* instead of *viçve* in **c**.

19. Having given a bull to Brahmans, one makes his mind wider; he beholds (*ava-paç*) prosperity of the inviolable [kine] in his own stall.

Ppp. reads in **a** *brāhmaṇāya vr̥ṣabhaṁ*, and in **d** *vi paçyatu*. In **a**, we have to combine (as not very rarely elsewhere) *-bhya r̥ṣ-*.

20. Let there be kine, let there be progeny, also let there be own strength; let the gods approve all that for the giver of a bull.

Ppp. puts *tat* after *sarvam* in **c**.

21. Let this burly (*pípāna*) one, a very Indra, bestow conspicuous wealth; let this one [bestow] a well-milking cow, constantly with calf; let him yield (*duh*) inspired will beyond the sky.

Ppp. has very different readings, which in part are less unacceptable than those of our text: for **a**, **b**, *ayaṁ pipānā indriyaṁ gayāṁ bibharti tejanī:* in **d**, *vipaçyataṁ puro divaḥ*. ⌊For *pípāna*, cf. Bloomfield, AJP. xii. 443.⌋

22. Of reddish form, clouded (?*nabhasá*), vigor-giving, vehemence of Indra, all-formed, he hath come to us, assigning to us life-time and progeny; and with abundances of wealth let him attach himself to (*abhi-sac*) us.

The last half-verse agrees nearly with xviii. 4. 62 **c**, **d**, where *dádhatas* and *sacadhvam* make better meter. It is not impossible to resolve *asmábhi-am* in **c**, but *sacantām*, which some of the mss. read (P.p.m.W.D.), is forbidden by the sense. Ppp. has a wholly different line: *prajām asmabhyaṁ dadhato rayiṁ ca dīrghāyutvāya çataçāradāya*. ⌊Bloomfield translates the verse at ZDMG. xlviii. 566, but overlooks the accent of *nabhasó:* cf. *támas-ā* and *tamasā́* (*saṁhitā*-form at xi. 9. 22).⌋

23. Here in this stall, O closeness (*upapárcana*), be thou close unto us; unto [us] what seed the bull has; unto [us], O Indra, thy heroism.

This is a variant of RV. vi. 28. 8 (with which TB. ii. 8. 8[12] and LÇS. iii. 3. 4 precisely agree); RV. has, for **a**, **b**, *úpe 'dám upapárcanam āsú góṣū́ 'pa pr̥cyatām*, with *rétasi* for *yád rétas* in **c**, and *vīryè* at the end: a very different sense; the Pet. Lexx. understand *upa-pr̥c* as signifying here sexual union. We have to combine irregularly *goṣṭho 'pa* in order to rectify the meter of **b**; the Anukr. does not heed the irregularity.

24. This young male we set toward you here; with him go ye (fem.) playing according to your wills; abandon us not with birth, ye well-portioned ones; and with abundances of wealth attach yourselves to us.

The last pāda is the same with xviii. 4. 62 **d**. The verse is found, in much more acceptable form, in TS. (iii. 3. 9[1], followed, after one intervening verse, by our vss. 5, 4 above) and PGS. (iii. 9. 6, disagreeing with TS. in only one word); they read, for **a**, *etáṁ yúvānam pári* (but PGS. *patiṁ*) *vo dadāmi* (omitting *atra*); in **b**, *priyéṇa* for *váçāṅ ánu;* in **c**, *çāpta* for *hāsiṣṭa;* and, for **d**, *rāyás póṣeṇa sám iṣā́ madema* (nearly our iii. 15. 8 **c**). Ppp. agrees with our text, only combining *dadhmo 'tra* in **a**. But for the accent of *janúṣā* (in TS. also), we might render, with Stenzler, 'ye who are by birth well-portioned.' Bp.R.p.m. have at end of **c** *subhagās*. The Anukr. weakly calls the verse (12 + 12 : 11 + 11) a *jagatī*, in spite of the *triṣṭubh* cadence of its first pāda. It is quoted in Kāuç. 24. 21, to accompany the sending away of an older bull and the release of a new one. ⌊See also note to Kāuç. 25. 24.⌋

⌊Here ends the second *anuvāka* with 2 hymns and 55 verses. The quoted Anukr. says "*sāhasre*."⌋

5. With the offering of a goat and five rice-dishes.

[*Bhṛgu.—aṣṭātriṅçat. mantroktājam pañcāudanadevatyam. trāiṣṭubham: 3. 4-p. purotiçakvarī jagatī; 4, 10. jagatī; 14, 17, 27–30. anuṣṭubh (30. kakummatī); 16. 3-p. anuṣṭubh; 18, 37. 3-p. virāḍ gāyatrī; 23. purauṣṇih; 24. 5-p. anuṣṭubuṣṇiggarbho 'pariṣṭādbārhatā virāḍ jagatī; 20–22. ?; 26. 5-p. anuṣṭubuṣṇiggarbho 'pariṣṭādbārhatā bhurij; 31. 7-p. aṣṭi; 32–35. 10-p. prakṛti; 36. 10-p. ākṛti; 38. 1-av. 2-p. sāmnī triṣṭubh.*]

⌊Partly prose — "vss." 16, 20–22, 31–36; also considerable parts of 23–30.⌋ Found for the most part also in Pāipp., but not all together, nor even all in the same book; the greater part of the vss. (1, 3–6, 8, 7, 11, 9, 12, 10, 13–15, 19–21, 23, 24, 2) occur in xvi.; vss. 16, 17, 37 (part) in iii.; vss. 27, 28 in viii.; vss. 24–26, 31–36 are represented by similar, but briefer and very corrupt material, in xvi.; vss. 18, 22, 37 (part), 38 are wanting ⌊apparently also 29–30⌋. Three of the verses are quoted in Vāit., and more in Kāuç.: see under the verses.

Translated: Muir, v. 304–6 (parts); Ludwig, p. 435; Henry, 93, 133; Griffith, i. 442.

1. Conduct him hither; take hold; let him go, foreknowing, unto the world of the well-doing; crossing the great darknesses variously, let the goat step unto the third firmament (*nā́ka*).

Ppp. has, in **c**, *vipaçyaṁ* for *mahānti*: cf. our 3 **c**. The first six verses of the hymn are quoted in their order in Kāuç. 64. 6–16 (vs. 1 also in 64. 27) in connection with the bringing in, slaughtering, and cooking of a goat; vss. 1 and 2 also in Vāit. 10. 14, 15, in connection with the sacrifice of an animal. This verse is called by the Anukr. simply a *triṣṭubh*, although its first half is very irregular (8 + 13).

2. I lead thee about as portion for Indra, as patron (*sūrí*) for the sacrificer at this sacrifice; whoever hate us, them take hold after; innocent (*ánāgas*) [are] the sacrificer's heroes.

The verse in Ppp. (as noted above) follows what corresponds to our vs. 24, and has, for **a**, **b**, *ind. bh. çamitā kṛṇotvaṁ yajña yajñapatiç ca sūriḥ;* and, for **d**, *ariṣṭā vīrā yajamānāç ca sarve.*

3. Away from his foot wash thou down the evil walk that he walked (*car*); with cleansed hoofs let him step on, foreknowing; crossing the darknesses, variously looking abroad let the goat step unto the third firmament.

Or *padás* in **a** may be accus. pl.; the redundancy of the pāda, in sense and meter, is an indication of intrusion; but the mode of its reduction to proper shape is not obvious, and Ppp. gives no help. Ppp. has, instead of our **c**, **d**, *te jyotiṣmantaṁ sukṛtāl lokam īpsan tṛtīye nāke adhi vikramasva.*

4. Cut along this skin with the dark [metal], O slaughterer, joint by joint with the knife (*así*); do not plot against [him]; do not be hostile to [him]; prepare him joint-wise; set him up apart in the third firmament.

Ppp. has, for **d**, *sukṛtām madhye adhi vi çraye 'mam.* The Anukr. weakly calls the verse a *jagatī*, although it is a *triṣṭubh* with three redundant syllables (doubtless *çyāména* or *viçastar*) in **a**. The *pada*-text divides *paruḥ-çaḥ*, by Prāt. iv. 19.

5. With a verse I set the kettle upon the fire; pour thou on the water; set him down; set [him] about with fire, ye quellers; when cooked, let him go where is the world of the well-doing.

Ppp. has instead, for **a**, *bhūmyāṁ bhūmim adhi dhārayāmi;* and, in **b**, *abhi* for *ava*. The successive parts of the verse are quoted in Kāuç. 64. 11-15, to accompany corresponding acts. The Anukr. does not heed the redundant syllable in **d**.

6. Step up from here, if thou hast been completely heated, from the heated pot on to the third firmament; thou, a fire, hast come into being out of fire; conquer [thy way] unto that world of light.

The translation of **a** implies the emendation to *átapthās*, which seems very probable; nearly all the mss. read *ataptās* (only E. *áta-*, P.M. *ataptas*), which the edition has altered to *átaptas*. Of the reading in Ppp. I have no note; Ppp. reads for **d** *jyotiṣmo acha sukṛtāṁ yatra lokaḥ;* our **d** is found (nearly) as its 8 **d**.

7. The goat [is] Agni, and they call the goat light; they say that the goat is to be given by one living to a priest (*brahmán*); the goat, given in this world by one having faith, smites far away the darknesses.

For the first two words Ppp. reads *ajam evā 'gnim;* in **b**, it puts *jīvatā* after *brahmaṇe*. The redundant syllable in **b** is not noticed by the Anukr. ⌊See note under 8.⌋

8. Having five rice-dishes, let him step out five-fold, about to step unto the three lights; go thou forth to the midst of the well-doing that have made offerings; spread out (*vi-çri*) upon the third firmament.

The last pāda is the same with xviii. 4. 3 **e**; Ppp. has instead *jyotiṣmantam abhi lokaṁ jayā 'smāi*, with which compare our 6 **d**. The Anukr. passes in silence the irregularities of the second pāda. ⌊Cf. Oldenberg, ZDMG. l. 449.⌋

9. Ascend, O goat, to where is the world of the well-doing; like an expelled *çarabhá* mayest thou move (*eṣ*) across difficult places; given, with five rice-dishes, to a priest (*brahmán*), he shall rejoice the giver with rejoicing.

Ppp. reads *kramasva* instead of *roha* in **a**, and reads *çalabhas* 'locust,' which is more sensible, in **b**; our **d** is its 10 **d**, with *dhātāram* instead of *dā-*. The Anukr. treats the second pāda as regular, and it can, indeed, be read by violence into 11 syllables.

10. The goat sets him that has given it on the three-firmamented, three-heavened, three-backed back of the firmament; being given with five rice-dishes to a priest, thou art a single milch-cow, all-formed, wish-yielding.

Ppp. reads in **b** *sukṛtāṁ loke* for *nākasya pṛṣṭhe;* and our **d** is its 9 **d**, with the intrusive *dhenus* left out. The verse, in spite of its irregularity, is by the Anukr. reckoned simply a *jagatī* (11 + 12 : 11 + 12[13?]).

11. This third light of yours, O Fathers, the goat with five rice-dishes one gives to a priest; the goat, given in this world by one having faith, smites far away the darknesses.

The second half-verse is identical with 7 **c**, **d** above. Ppp. has, for **d**, *pañcodano brahmaṇe dīyamānaḥ* (our 9 **c**, 10 **c**).

12. Desiring to obtain the world of the well-doing that have made offerings, one gives to a priest a goat with five rice-dishes; do thou conquer complete attainment (*vyā̀pti*) unto that world; be he, accepted, propitious to us.

Ppp. begins *pra jyotiṣmantaṁ sukṛtāṁ lok-*; and reads **c**, **d** thus: *sa vyāpo neṅṣ abhi lokaṁ jayā 'sme çivo 'smabhyaṁ pratigṛhyate 'dhi.*

13. The goat verily was born from the heat of the fire, wise, of the wise (*vípra*), of power, he the inspired one; what is offered, is bestowed, is conferred (*abhípūrta*), accompanied with *váṣaṭ* — that let the gods prepare in due season (*ṛtuçás*).

The first pāda is identical with iv. 14. 1 **a**. Ludwig (also p. 370) proposes to emend in **c** to *gūrtam abhigūrtam*. Part of the mss. blunderingly accent *ṛtuçàs* in **d**. Ppp. has in **b** *vayodhā* instead of *vipaçcit*, and in **c** puts *pūrtam* before *iṣṭam*. The last two pādas are irregular, but the Anukr. takes no notice of it. ⌊Pāda **c** is a good *jagatī;* and **d**, a good *triṣṭubh*, if we read *devā́sas*, or (with Henry) *tád íd.*⌋

14. A home-woven garment he may give, also gold as sacrificial gift; so he fully obtains the worlds that are heavenly and that are earthly.

15. Unto thee, O goat, let these streams of soma (*somyá*) go, divine, ghee-backed, honey-dripping; establish thou earth and sky, upon the seven-rayed back of the firmament.

The mss. in general (not P.M.) accent *ája* in **a**. They are rather evenly divided between *ádhi* and *'dhi* in **d** (W.I.O.R.T.K. have *'dhi*). Compare with **a**, **b** the refrain to iv. 34. 5–7. Ppp. reads for **a**: *etās tvā dadhārā 'cchamayanti viçvatās somyaṁ;* ⌊*somyaṁ* would seem to be the beginning of Ppp's **b**;⌋ in **c**, **d**, for *uta . . . pṛṣṭhe*, it gives *divaṁ sadasva nāke tiṣṭhāsy*. Pādas **b**, **c** are metrically irregular, but the Anukr. does not heed it.

16. A goat art thou; O goat, heaven-going (*svar-gá*) art thou; by thee the Aṅgirases foreknew [their] world; that pure (*púṇya*) world would I fain foreknow.

⌊Prose.⌋ The translation of **a** is according to the accent of the vocative *ája;* there may be a play on words between *ajá* 'goat' and *ajá* 'unborn': 'unborn art thou, O goat' (emending to *aja*). Ppp. reads for **c** *taṁ lokam anu pra jñeṣma.* ⌊This vs. and the next are in its iii.⌋ The definition of the meter by the Anukr. seems senseless (7 [8 ?] + 11 : 8 = 26). The third pāda is VS. xx. 25 **c**.

17. Wherewith thou carriest a thousand; wherewith, O Agni, [the offering of] one's whole possession — therewith carry thou this our offering to go to heaven (*svàr*) among the gods.

The verse is found also in VS. (xv. 55), TS. (iv. 7. 13[4]; v. 7. 7[3]), MS. (ii. 12. 4), and K. (xl. 12 ⌊but Schroeder under the MS. passage refers to K. xviii. 18⌋). VS. and MS. put *sahásram* after *váhasi* in **a**, and VS. reads ⌊*yéna* in **a**, and⌋ *naya* for *vaha* in **c**;

TS. has in iv. for **d** *devayā̃no yá uttamáḥ* (in v. it agrees throughout with our text). Ppp. begins with *yena vā sah-*. Vāit. quotes the verse in 29. 9, 23. ⌊MS. has *yéna.*⌋

18. The cooked goat, having five rice-dishes, driving off perdition, sets [one] in the heavenly (*svargá*) world; with it may we conquer worlds that possess suns.

As noted above, the verse is wanting in Ppp.

19. [The goat] which one deposited with the Brahman, and which among the people (*vikṣú*); what scattered drops (*viprúṣ*) [there are] of the rice-dishes, of the goat — all that of ours, O Agni, do thou later know in the world of the well-done, at the meeting of the ways.

20. The goat verily strode out here (*idám*) in the beginning; this [earth] became its breast, the sky its back, the atmosphere its middle, the quarters its (two) sides, the (two) oceans its paunches;

⌊Prose — 20, 21, and 22.⌋

21. Both truth and right its eyes, all truth [and] faith its breath, the *virā́j* its head; this verily is an unlimited offering, namely (*yát*) the goat with five rice-dishes.

The second *satyam* in vs. 21 is doubtless a corrupt reading, and the Ppp. version indicates that we should have instead *rūpám* ('the universe its form,' instead of 'all truth'). Ppp. reads, for the two verses: *ajaṣ pañcāudano vy akramata tasyo 'ra iyam abhavad udaram antarikṣam: dyāuṣ ṭe pṛṣṭhaṁ diçaṣ pārçve: diçaç cā 'tidiçaç ca çṛñge satyaṁ ca ṛtaṁ ca cakṣuṣī viçvarūpaṁ çraddhā* etc. All the *saṁhitā*-mss. read *ca rtáṁ* (instead of *ca ṛtáṁ*) near the beginning of vs. 21. The text of the Anukr. is apparently defective, leaving out the metrical definition of vss. 20–22 and vs. 25.

22. An unlimited offering does he obtain, an unlimited world does he take possession of (*ava-rudh*), who gives a goat with five rice-dishes, with the light of sacrificial gifts.

Wanting in Ppp., as noted above.

23. He should not split its bones; he should not suck out its marrow; taking it all together, he should cause it to enter here and here.

Or, 'should cause this and this to enter'; the sense is obscure. Ppp. reads in **c** *sarvāṇi* for *sarvaṁ enam*. By calling the verse a *purauṣṇih*, the Anukr. intends that its first two pādas be read as one, of 12 syllables. The Kāuç. quotes (66. 31, 32; next after quotations of verses from hymn 3) both halves of the verse, the latter to accompany the act of piercing an object and scattering it into a pit filled with water.

24. This and this verily becomes its form; therewith one makes it come together; food, greatness, refreshment it yields (*duh*) to him who gives a goat with five rice-dishes, with the light of sacrificial gifts.

Ppp. reads for the second half-verse *svadhāṁ ūrjam akṣatiṁ maho 'smāi duhe: ya evaṁ viduṣo 'jaṁ pañcāudanaṁ dadāti;* and, as above noted, our vs. 2 then follows. The metrical description of the Anukr. (closely accordant with that of vs. 26, though the real construction of the verses is very different) implies the artificial division of the refrain (as in vs. 28 and other verses below) into two pādas, of 7 and 9 syllables, and counts 46 syllables in all; the natural number is 45 (12 + 8 : 10 + 15 = 45).

25. Five gold ornaments (*rukmá*), five new garments, five milch-cows milking his desire come to be his who gives a goat with etc. etc.

This verse, of which at least the first pāda is metrical (11 + 13 : 15 = 39) is left undescribed in the Anukr. It (or vs. 26, both having the same *pratīka*) is quoted in Kāuç. 64. 25. ⌊More nearly, 'Five milch-cows become wish-milking for him who,' that is, 'yield or grant to him his wishes who' etc.⌋

26. Five gold ornaments become light for him; his garments become a defense for his body, he attains the heavenly (*svargá*) world, who gives a goat with etc. etc.

Here are plainly four pādas, of which the first three are metrical, with the refrain added (11 + 11 : 8 + 15); the definition of the Anukr. seems to imply 11 + 10 : 8 + 7 + 9 = 45 syllables, or a *bhurik triṣṭubh*.

27. Whoever (fem.) having gained a former husband, then gains another later one — if (*ca*) they (dual) shall give a goat with five rice-dishes, they shall not be separated.

The mss., as usual in such cases, read *vitvā́* in **a**; and all but Bp. strangely accent *anyàm* in **b**. Ppp. reads *pacatas* for *dadātas* in **d**. ⌊This vs. and the next are in Ppp's viii.⌋

28. Her later husband comes to have the same world with his remarried spouse who (masc.) gives a goat with five rice-dishes, with the light of sacrificial gifts.

The Anukr. treats the prose refrain of vss. 22, 24–26 as a half *anuṣṭubh* in the second line of this verse. Ppp. reads instead *ajaṅ ca pañcāudanaṅ dadat.*

29. A milch-cow having one calf after another, a draft-ox, a pillow, a garment, gold, having given, those go to the highest heaven (*dív*).

The Anukr. takes no notice of the redundant syllable in **b**. ⌊Perhaps it balances the redundancy of **b** with the deficiency of **c**.⌋

30. Self, father, son, grandson, grandfather, wife, generatrix, mother, those who are dear — them I call upon.

Nor does the Anukr. heed the deficient syllables in **b** of this verse. ⌊We might render *jánitrīm mātáram* by 'the mother that bore [me].'⌋

31. Whoever knows the season "torrid" (*nāídāgha*) by name — that verily is the season "torrid" by name, namely (*yát*) the goat with five rice-dishes; he indeed burns out the fortune of his unfriendly foe (*bhrā́tṛvya*), he thrives (*bhū*) by himself, who gives a goat with five rice-dishes, with the light of sacrificial gifts.

In this and the following verses the mss. read *nā́ma rtúm* etc. throughout. The natural division is into four pādas instead of seven, and ⌊the paragraph, read as prose, has⌋ only 61 syllables instead of 64 (=*aṣṭi*); but the three missing syllables can easily be made out by resolutions. One would expect *nı́ dahati*, to correspond with *nāı́dāgha.* Read in **b** *yád ajáḥ* (an accent-sign slipped out of place).

32. Whoever knows the season "making" by name, each making fortune of his unfriendly foe he takes to himself; that verily is the season "making" by name, namely the goat with five rice-dishes; he indeed etc. etc.

33. Whoever knows the season "gathering" by name, each gathering fortune of his unfriendly foe he takes to himself; that verily is the season "gathering" by name, namely the goat etc. etc.

34. Whoever knows the season "fattening" by name, each fattening fortune of his unfriendly foe he takes to himself; that verily is the season "fattening" by name, namely the goat etc. etc.

35. Whoever knows the season "up-going" by name, each up-going fortune of his unfriendly foe he takes to himself; that verily is the season "up-going" by name, namely the goat etc. etc.

These four verses agree in number of syllables, and the name given them by the Anukr. (*prakṛti*) demands 84; this number it is possible to make out by resolutions of *saṁdhi*, though the natural reading gives only 80 (10 + 20 : 15 : 20 + 15 = 80). *Saṁyatī́m*∘*saṁyatīm* in vs. 33 **b** is quoted by the commentary under Prāt. iv. 44, as an example of a repeated separable word which gives up in *pada*-text its individual separation in favor of that between the repetitions. Read in 32 **c** *yád ajáḥ* (an accent-sign gone), and supply an omitted mark of punctuation after *datte* in 33.

36. Whoever knows the season "overcoming" (*abhibhū́*) by name, each overcoming fortune of his unfriendly foe he takes to himself; that verily is the season "overcoming" by name, namely the goat etc. etc.

This verse has six more syllables than the preceding ones, and the Anukr. gives it a name (*ākṛti*) applying properly to 88 syllables. In **c** read *eṣá* for *eṣā́*.

37. Cook ye the goat and the five rice-dishes; let all the quarters, like-minded, united (*sadhryàñc*), with the intermediate directions, accept that of thee.

All the mss. (except D.) read at the end *tá* (*pada*-text *té*) before *etám*; our edition emends to *ta*; the word could better be spared altogether. Ppp. has (in iii.) only the first pāda. The Anukr. describes the verse as if this pāda as well as the other two were metrical.

38. Let them defend this of thine for thee; to them I offer (*hu*) sacrificial butter, this oblation.

'Them' is fem., designating the 'quarters' of vs. 37. The translation omits a *te*; it may be regarded as an ethical dative, anticipating the distincter *túbhyam* 'for thee' that follows.

⌊This hymn begins with *ā́ naya*; and, with its 38 vss., exceeds the norm by 18. The quoted Anukr. says *aṣṭādaçā* " "*naya*."⌋

⌊The twentieth *prapāṭhaka* ends here. As in the cases of the tenth and eighteenth (ending at v. 7 and viii. 5), the *prapāṭhaka*-division here fails to coincide with the *anuvāka*-division.⌋

6. Exalting the entertainment of guests.

[*Brahman.* — *ṣaṭ paryāyāḥ.* *ātithyā uta vidyādevatyāḥ.*]

This whole prose hymn is found in Pāipp. xvi., except a few verses, as noted below. It is not quoted by either Kāuç. or Vāit. In the Prāt., on the other hand, it has more than its fair share of notice. ⌊With regard to the *paryāya*-hymns in general, see pp. 471–2.⌋

Translated: Henry, 98, 137; Griffith, i. 448.

[**Paryāya I.** — *saptadaçarcaḥ.* *1. 3-p. gāyatrī; 2. 3-p. ārṣī gāyatrī; 3, 7. sāmnī triṣṭubh; 4, 9. ārcy anuṣṭubh; 5. āsurī gāyatrī; 6. 3-p. sāmnī jagatī; 8. yājuṣī triṣṭubh; 10. sāmnī bhurig bṛhatī; 11, 14–16. sāmny anuṣṭubh; 12. virāḍ gāyatrī; 13. sāmnī nicṛt pañkti; 17. 3-p. virāḍ bhurig gāyatrī.*]

1. Whoever may know the obvious (*pratyákṣa*) *bráhman*, whose joints are the preparations (*sambhārá*), whose spine the verses (*ṛ́c*);

Ppp. reads, instead of our **a**, as follows: *yo vā ekaṁ brahmā 'nuṣṭhā vidyāt sadya mahadvate*, making an *anuṣṭubh* of the verse. The Anukr. is corrupt at this point, one ms. appearing to call the verse *nāgī nāma tripād gāyatrī;* one sees no reason why.

2. Whose hairs the chants (*sā́man*), [whose] heart the sacrificial formula (*yájus*) is called, [whose] litter (*paristáraṇa*) the oblation.

Ppp. reads *chandāṅsi* for *sāmāni* in **a**, and puts **c** before **b**. The unlingualized *st* of *paristáraṇam* is noted under Prāt. ii. 105. The 'obvious *bráhman*,' or '*bráhman* in visible presence,' thus wondrously made up, is doubtless the guest, all attentions to whom the hymn proceeds to glorify by identifying them with sacred acts.

3. When in truth the lord of guests meets with his eyes the guests, he looks at a sacrificing to the gods.

Ppp. reads at the beginning *yad atithipatiḥ preṣyate.* The verse has one syllable too many for a regular *sāmnī triṣṭubh;* but the system of nomenclature affords no ⌊simple⌋ name for one of 23 syllables.

4. When he greets them, he enters upon consecration; when he offers (*yāc*) water, he brings forward the [sacrificial] waters.

Prá ṇayati is quoted as an example under Prāt. iii. 79. We have to read *yā́cati apáḥ* to make out the defined meter.

5. Just what waters are brought in at the sacrifice, those are the very ones.

Praṇīyánte also is quoted under Prāt. iii. 79.

6. When they fetch a gratification (*tárpaṇa*) — that is just the same as an animal for Agni-and-Soma that is bound [for sacrifice].

Ppp. adds after this verse *yat khātam āharanti puroḍāçā eva te.*

7. In that they prepare lodgings, they so prepare the seat (*sádas*) and oblation-holders (*havirdhā́na*).

8. In that they strew [a couch], that is a *barhís.*

Ppp. omits the second clause of vs. 7, and reads *pari-* for *upa-* in 8; it omits 9 here: see under 10, below.

9. In that they fetch a coverlet (? *upariçayaná*), thereby one gains possession of the heavenly (*svargá*) world.

Upariçayaná, lit. 'above-lying,' occurs only here; ⌊but cf. *upariçaya*, OB. iv. 296 c⌋. The minor Pet. Lex. renders it 'an elevated couch.' The verse lacks a syllable.

10. In that they fetch mattress and pillow, those are the enclosures (*paridhí*).

That is, the sticks laid about the altar-fire to shut it in. In this verse, the extra syllable is noted by the Anukr. Ppp. reads *-barhaṇāni* and *paridhe 'va te;* and it adds its version of 9: *yat parṣeṇam* (*pariçayanam?*) *āharanti svar-* etc.

11. In that they fetch ointment and unguent, that is sacrificial butter.

The *pada*-reading *āñjana*◦*abhyañjaná* is quoted under Prāt. iv. 42, as example of words that lose their own individual division in favor of separation from each other. Ppp. omits *āñjana*. The Anukr. reads 16 syllables, which may be obtained in more than one way (most probably *-ranti āj-*).

12. In that they fetch a morsel (*khādá*) before the serving-up (*pariveṣá*), that is the two sacrificial cakes.

Khādá is perhaps a special bit or bite, anticipatory of the proper meal. The verse is wanting in Ppp.

13. In that they call the food-maker (*açanakṛ́t*), they so call the maker of oblations.

Some of the mss. read *haviḥkṛ́tam*.

14. The grains of rice, of barley, that are scattered out — those are soma-shoots (*aṅçú*).

The Anukr. requires *-yante aṅç-* to be read, although the passage is quoted under Prāt. i. 69 as an example of the elision of initial *a* with the transfer of its nasalization to the eliding *e*. Ppp. reads at the end *aṅçava eva te 'nūpyante*.

15. The mortar and pestles — those are the pressing-stones.

The Anukr. expects us to read *yā́ni ul-*. Ppp. omits *yāni* and reads *-musalam*, which is easier; it also omits *eva te* at the end.

16. The sieve ⌊*çū́rpa*⌋ is the soma-strainer (*pavítra*); the chaff is the pomace (*ṛjīṣá*); the waters are those of pressing.

That is, ⌊the waters are⌋ those used in facilitating the pressing of the Soma. ⌊Is not *çū́rpa* rather 'winnowing-basket'?⌋ The 'pomace' is the refuse stalks from which the soma has been pressed. ⌊All of SPP's and of W's *pada*-mss. seem to agree in reading *ṛjīṣā́* as fem.⌋ Ppp. reads *rajīṣaḥ*. It omits *abhiṣavaṇīr āpaḥ* here: but see vs. 17.

17. The spoon is the sacrificial spoon, the stirring-stick the spit (? *nékṣaṇa*), the kettles the wooden vessels, the drinking-vessels those of Vāyu, this [earth] itself the black antelope's skin.

Ppp. reads *-kalaças kumbhīm eva kṛṣṇājinaṁ vāyavyāni pātrāṇi;* and it also has *abhiṣavaṇīr āpaḥ* in this verse, after *āyavanam*, instead of in vs. 16. The Anukr. defines the verse as if it were metrical, and intends us to read it as 10 + 16 + 8 = 34 syllables.

[**Paryāya II.** — *trayodaça. 18. virāṭ purastādbṛhatī; 19, 29. sāmnī triṣṭubh; 20. āsury anuṣṭubh; 21. sāmny uṣṇih; 22, 28. sāmnī bṛhatī (28. bhurij); 23. ārcy anuṣṭubh; 24. 3-p. svarāḍ anuṣṭubh;* 25. āsurī gāyatrī;† 26. sāmny anuṣṭubh; 27. 3-p. ārcī triṣṭubh; 30. 3-p. ārcī pañkti.*] *⌊Berlin ms.: *5-p. virāṭ purastādbṛhatī.*⌋ †⌊Berlin ms.: *sāmny anuṣṭubh.*⌋

18. The lord of guests verily makes for himself a sacrificer's *bráhmaṇa* in that he looks at the [portions] to be partaken of, saying "is this larger, or this?"

Several of the mss. (O.R.D.) accent at the end *bhū́yā́s* (D. *bhū́yā́ḥ* 3), which is the far preferable reading; *bhū́yās* (read by I.) could be borne, since in RV. and AV. the usage does not seem yet established that the protracted final syllable is acute, in addition to whatever accent the word may have on other syllables ⌊*Skt. Gram.* § 78⌋; but *bhūyās*, as our edition reads, in accordance with nearly all the mss. compared up to the time of its publication, is nothing but a blunder. The protracted words are quoted in Prāt. i. 105. The verse counts naturally 18 + 8 + 8 = 34 syllables (the second and third pādas being really metrical). ⌊Scan rather 10 + 8 + 8 + 8 with the Anukr.⌋ Ppp. reads *kṛṇute* and *avekṣata*.

19. In that he says "take up the larger one," he thereby makes his breath longer (*várṣīyāṅs*).

Ppp. has a quite different text: *yad āha bhūyo 'ddhara te prajāṁ cāi 'va paçūṅç ca vardhayate . . .* (?) *prāṇaṁ kṛṇute: yat saṁpṛchati kāmam eva tenā 'va rundhe: kāmo ha pṛṣṭo yājāti: yad udakam upasiñcaty apa eva tenā 'va rundhe.* ⌊Then follows 20.⌋

20. [In that] he presents [it], he brings libations near.

21. Of them, brought near, the guest makes libations in himself; —

22. With his hand as sacrificial spoon, at his breath as stake, with the sound of swallowing as utterance of *váṣaṭ*.

'The sound of swallowing,' lit. the sound *sruk*. Ppp. reads in 21 *ātmani j-* for *ātmán j-* and has in 22 *çulkāreṇa vaṣaṭkāreṇa srucā hastena*.

23. These same guests, both loved (*priyá*) and unloved, [as] priests (*ṛtvíj*), make [one] go to the heavenly world.

This verse is wanting here in Ppp.; but it is inserted below, just before our vs. 49 ⌊and without variant except *cārtvijas*, which may be a slip of Roth's pen for *cartvijas*⌋.

24. He who, knowing thus, shall partake, not hating, he shall not partake the food of one hating, not of one that is doubted, nor of one doubting (?).

We must emend at the end either to *mīmāṅsamānasya* or to *mīmāṅsyámānasya;* the translation assumes the former. Bp.[1] reads *vidyā́t* for *vidvā́n*, and it would be a welcome improvement; the same reads the first time *açnīyā́t*, which seems necessary if *vidvā́n* and not *vidyā́t* is read, and which is implied in the translation. Ppp. has instead *tasmān na dviṣann adyān na dviṣato 'nnam adyān na mīm-*. The two mss. of the Anukr. describe the verse differently but equivalently, both requiring 34 syllables (which implies restoration of *'nnam* to *ánnam*).

25. Verily every such one has his sin devoured, whose food they partake of.

26. Verily every such one has his sin undevoured whose food they partake not of.

'Devoured,' doubtless 'destroyed, removed' by the eating of the guests. Ppp. reads for vs. 26 *sarvā upaço jagdhapāpmānaṁ yasyā 'nnam açnāti*. One of the Anukr. mss. (but doubtless by a misreading ⌊?⌋) calls 25 as well as 26 a *sāmny anuṣṭubh* ⌊16 syllables⌋. ⌊Vss. 25 and 26 have each 15 (*āsurī gāyatrī*).⌋ Read in 25 *jagdhá-* (an accent-sign slipped out).

27. Verily he who presents [the food] hath always his pressing-stones harnessed, his cleanser wet, his sacrifice extended, his ceremony of offering assumed.

Ppp. reads *sutasomas* instead of *yuktagrāvā*, and puts *vitatādhvaras* as last of the four epithets; it also sets the whole paragraph after our 28.

28. To Prajāpati, verily, is his offering extended who presents.

29. He who presents verily strides Prajāpati's strides after [him].

This verse is wanting in Ppp.

30. [The fire] that is the guests', that is the fire of libations (*āhavanī́ya*); the one in the dwelling (*véçman*), that is the householder's fire (*gā́rhapatya*); the one in which they cook, that is the southern fire (*dakṣiṇāgní*).

Ppp. reads *sā "havanīyo yo 'nnakaraṇasya* ⌊intending *-karaṇas sa ?*⌋ *dakṣiṇāgnir yo veç- sa gār-*. The metrical definition of the Anukr. requires us to restore at the beginning *yó átith-*.

[**Paryāya III.** — *navakaḥ. 31–36, 39. 3-p. pipīlikamadhyā gāyatrī; 37. sāmnī bṛhatī; 38. pipīlikamadhyo 'ṣṇih.*]

31. Verily both what is sacrificed and what is bestowed of the houses doth he partake of who partakes before a guest.

That is, doubtless, 'doth he eat up, devour, destroy.' Ppp. omits *gṛhāṇām*, and puts next vss. 34 and 33, omitting 35 and 39 ⌊and 32 and 36 also⌋. The Anukr. describes the paragraphs as if they were metrical, and defines them as if the text read *pū́rvo átither*.

32. Verily both the milk and the sap of the houses doth he etc. etc.

33. Verily both the refreshment and the fatness of the houses doth he etc. etc.

Ppp. reads *payas* instead of *sphātim*.

34. Verily both the progeny and the cattle of the houses doth he etc. etc.

35. Verily both the fame and the glory of the houses doth he etc. etc.

36. Verily both the fortune (*çrī́*) and the alliance (?*saṁvíd*) of the houses doth he etc. etc.

The Pet. Lexx. interpret *saṁvíd* as 'possessions.'

37. He verily is a guest, namely (*yát*) one versed in sacred learning (*çrótriya*); before him one should not partake.

The meaning intended ought to be that a guest is the equivalent of such a sage; but the literal sense is as translated. The verse lacks one syllable (unless we read *ná açnīyāt*) of being full measure.

38. When the guest hath partaken he should partake, in order to the soulfulness of the sacrifice, in order to the integrity of the sacrifice; that is the [proper] course.

The verse is an *uṣṇih* only as containing (if we resolve *açitā́vati át-*) 28 syllables (11 + 14 + 3). The *pada*-text reads *açitáovati.* Ppp. has *açitāvaty açnīyāt tad vrataṁ yajñasyā 'vichedāya yajñasya guptaye yajñasya sātmatvāya.* ⌊Cf. Oldenberg, IFA. vi. 184: also *Skt. Gram.* § 960.⌋

39. That verily is specially sweet which comes from the cow (*adhigavá*), either milk (*kṣīrá*) or flesh; that he should not partake of.

That is, doubtless, he should leave it for his guest. The verse is wanting in Ppp. The so-called *gāyatrī* is to be thus divided: 7 + 11 + 6 = 24.

[**Paryāya IV.** — *daçakaḥ.* **a** *of 40–43. prājāpatyā 'nuṣṭubh;* **a** *of 44. bhurij;* **b** *of 40–43. 3-p. gāyatrī;* **b** *of 44. 4-p. prastārapañkti.*]

40. He who, thus knowing, pouring out milk, presents [it] — as much as, having sacrificed with a very successful *agniṣṭomá,* one gets possession of, of so much thereby does he get possession.

The mss. are divided between reckoning ten verses (with the Anukr. ⌊cf. the quotations etc. at the end of the hymn⌋) in this section, or only five, with two parts to each; the latter method was adopted in our edition as the better. The second part in the first five verses, though doubtless meant only as prose, divides into three subdivisions of eight syllables each, like a real *gāyatrī.* Ppp. begins all the verses with *yat,* instead of *sa ya evaṁ vidvān,* and reads in 40 **b** *yā. ag. sapṛṣṭhene 'ṣṭvā 'varundhe.*

41. He who, thus knowing, pouring out butter (*sarpís*), presents [it] — as much as, having sacrificed with a very successful *atirātrá,* one gets etc. etc.

Ppp. reads in **b** *āhnena samṛddhena* for *atirātreṇa.*

42. He who, thus knowing, pouring out honey, offers [it] — as much as, having sacrificed with a very successful session-sitting, one gets etc. etc.

Ppp. reads in **b** *rātreṇa samṛddhena.* The Anukr. expects, of course, the resolution *mádhu up-.*

43. He who, thus knowing, pouring out meat, presents [it] — as much as, having sacrificed with a very successful twelve-day sacrifice, one gets etc. etc.

44. He who, thus knowing, pouring out water, presents [it] — he arrives at (*gam*) firm standing in order to the generating of progeny; he becomes loved of progeny — he who, thus knowing, pouring out water, presents [it].

The second part of the verse, though not metrical, ⌊seems to be scanned as 11 + 11 + 8 + 8 by the Anukr. (which, with the mss., reckons *pratiṣṭhā́m* to the second pāda !)⌋. Ppp. reads in **b** *gachati sarvam āyur eti: na punar ā jarasaṣ pra mīyate ya* etc.

[**Paryāya V.** — *daçakaḥ.* *45* **a.** *sāmny uṣṇih;* *45* **b.** *purauṣṇih;* *45* **c**, *48* **c.** *sāmnī bhurig bṛhatī;* *46* **a**, *47* **a**, *48* **b.** *sāmny anuṣṭubh;* *46* **b.** *3-p. nicṛd viṣamā nāma gāyatrī;* *47* **b.** *3-p. virāḍ viṣamā nāma gāyatrī;* *48* **a.** *3-p. virāḍ anuṣṭubh.*]

45. For him the dawn utters *hiṅg;* Savitar preludes (*pra-stu*); Brihaspati with refreshment (*ūrjáyā*) sings the *udgīthá;* Tvashṭar with prosperity responds (*prati-hṛ*); all the gods [are] the conclusion (*nidhána*): the conclusion of thrift, of progeny, of cattle becometh he who knoweth thus.

Here and in the following verses ⌊cf. PB. iv. 9. 9⌋ are had in view the five successive parts or divisions of a *sāman*, of which the *udgītha* is the central and principal: cf. Chānd. Upan. ii. 2 ff. In this section also the majority of the mss. divide and number in accordance with our edition; the rest, with the Anukr., number the subdivisions successively. Our edition assumes the subdivision *nidhánam bhū́tyāḥ* to be repeated at the end of each of the four paragraphs; the Anukr. ⌊counting 10 (not 12) *avasāna-rcas:* cf. p. 546 below⌋ is against this; as for the mss., their testimony is nothing, since they all, in any case, write such an addition only the first time and the last, omitting all intermediate occurrences; it is altogether probable that the edition is right. The artificial description by the Anukr. of **b** as an *uṣṇih*, implies resolving *ūrjáyā úd*, and either *púṣṭi-ā* or *víçu-e.* Ppp. adds *vāi* after *tasmāi*, and *bhūtyā* after *savitā*, and reads *ūrjā* for *ūrjayā.*

46. For him the rising sun utters *hiṅg;* cow-gathering time (*saṁgavá*) preludes; noon sings the *udgīthá;* afternoon responds; the setting [sun is] the conclusion: the conclusion of etc. etc.

Ppp. combines *madhyandino 'd.* The ⌊*nicṛt*⌋ "dissimilar *gāyatrī,*" **b**, divides as 8 + 9 + 6 = 23.

47. For him the cloud, forming (*bhū*), utters *hiṅg;* thundering, it preludes; lightening, it responds; raining, it sings the *udgīthá;* holding up, it is the conclusion: the conclusion of etc. etc.

Ppp. reads *vidyotamānaḥ pra stāuti stanayann ud gāyati aparāhṇa prati harati astaṁyaṁ nidhanam.* The "dissimilar *gāyatrī,*" **b**, is this time 10 + 6 + 6 = 22. Bp.Bp.²p.m.D. read *várṣam*, and several of the *saṁhitā*-mss. *várṣaṁn* instead of *-ṣann.* Cf. Chānd. Upan. ii. 3.

48. [When] he meets the guests with his eyes, he utters *hiṅg;* [when] he greets [them], he preludes; [when] he offers water, he sings the *udgīthá;* [when] he presents [food], he responds; the remnant (*úchiṣṭa*) [of the food] is the conclusion: the conclusion of etc. etc.

Ppp. seems again to mix in matter from vs. 46, reading *yācaty udakavaty aparāhṇa* * *prati harati.* ⌊See also note to vs. 23.⌋ The first subdivision makes the 30 syllables required by the Anukr. if we give syllabic value (*-ti*) to the thrice-occurring verb-ending *-ty*; and similarly we get 16 for **b.** *⌊The phonetic resemblance of *udakavati* to *ud gāyati* (cf. note to ii. 13. 3) and of *aparāhṇa* to *upa harati* is obviously the occasion for the confusion.⌋

[**Paryāya VI.** — *caturdaçakaḥ. 49. āsurī gāyatrī; 50. samny anuṣṭubh; 51, 53. 3-p. ārcī pañkti; 52. 1-p. prājāpatyā gāyatrī; 54–59. ārcī bṛhatī; 60. 1-p. āsurī jagatī; 61. yājuṣī triṣṭubh; 62. 1-p. āsury uṣṇih.*]

49. When (*yát*) he calls the distributor, then he is just summoning (*ā-çrāvay-*).

That is, he is virtually an *adhvaryu* summoning the *agnīdh* to do his duty. The verse is made an *āsurī gāyatrī* by resolving *-ty* twice. Ppp. inserts before this verse our vs. 23 above; and it omits *eva tat.*

50. When [the distributor] assents, then he is just answering the summons.

That is, as an *agnīdh.* Again, to justify the definition of the Anukr., we must read *prati-ā́çrāvayati evá.* ⌊A hyphen is missing after the *pra* of *pratyā́çr-.*⌋ Ppp. again omits *eva tat* at the end.

51. When the servers, with drinking-vessels in their hands, both the former and the latter, go forward, they are just cup-bearing priests.

Bp. gives the false accentuation *camasāodh-* (instead of *-sáoadh*). Ppp. reads *yat pariveṣṭārā 'vasatām prabhibhyante cam-.* To make 30 syllables, we must resolve *ca ápare* (or else *camasá-adh-*).

52. Of them, none soever is not an invoker (*áhotṛ*).

Ppp. reads *vāi* instead of *na;* and then it adds as follows: *yat prātar upaharati prātassavanam eva tat: yad yavo 'paharati mādhyandinam eva tat savanam: yat sāyam upaharati tṛtīyam eva tad yad atithipatir avabhṛtham eva tat prāhvayanti;* and it omits our vs. 53; ⌊R. does not expressly note such omission⌋.

53. Verily when the lord of guests goes up unto the houses serving the guests, then he is even going down unto the purificatory bath (*avabhṛ́tha*).

⌊Ppp. omits *eva tat.*⌋

54. When he apportions [them], he is apportioning sacrificial fees; when he follows [them], then he is even shifting the place of sacrifice (*ud-ava-sā*).

⌊Ppp. omits *eva tat.*⌋ ⌊Cf. Oldenberg, IFA. vi. 183.⌋

55. He ⌊the guest?⌋, being invited (*úpahūta*), feeds (*bhakṣay-*) on the earth; in him ⌊locative⌋, invited ⌊nominative⌋, [he ⌊the host?⌋ feeds on] what of every form [there is] on the earth.

⌊Whitney's first "on" is intended as a rendering of the locative relation of "earth"; his second "on" goes with "feeds." He has tried to indicate this by putting the first after the parenthesis and the second within the brackets. The inherent ambiguity of the English combination is such that I do not know how to remove it for the non-Sanskritist save by an express statement.⌋

The sense of this and the following verses is very obscure; it is here translated as if the guest were the subject of the first *bhakṣayati*, and the entertainer (in recompense for the entertainment given) of the second ⌊*bhakṣayati* (supplied)⌋. Ppp. adds *pṛthivyāṁ tat pṛthivyām ā bhāti svargo loko bhavati ya evaṁ veda*. Only vs. 56 has the full number of syllables (27) belonging to an *ārcī bṛhatī*; 55, 58, 59 have only 26 syllables (a number for which the system affords no separate name), and 57 has only 24.

56. He, being invited, feeds in the atmosphere; in him, invited, [he feeds on] what of every form [there is] in the atmosphere.

Ppp. adds *antarikṣe patanty antarikṣā "bhāti* ⌊*svargo* etc.⌋.

57. He, being invited, feeds in the sky (*dív*); in him, invited, [he feeds on] what of every form [there is] in the sky.

Ppp. adds *divi tapati divy ā bhāti* ⌊*svargo* etc.⌋.

58. He, being invited, feeds among the gods; in him, invited, [he feeds on] what of every form [there is] among the gods.

Ppp. adds *deveṣu patati* ⌊intending *tapati?*⌋ *deveṣu bhāti* ⌊*svargo* etc.⌋.

59. He, being invited, feeds in the worlds; in him, invited, [he feeds on] what of every form [there is] in the worlds.

Ppp. adds *lokeṣu patati lokeṣu bhāti* ⌊*svargo loko bhavati ya evaṁ veda*⌋.

60. He, whoever invited, —

61. Obtains this world, obtains yon [world].

The translation implies emendation in 60 to *úpahūta-upahūtaḥ* (as repeated word); it seems impossible to give the verse a meaning as it stands. Vss. 60–62 are wanting in Ppp. The metrical definition of 61 demands the resolution *-ti amúm*.

62. Worlds rich in light conquereth he who knoweth thus.

⌊The quotations from the Old Anukr. for the six *paryāyas* may here be given together: I. *yo vidyāyāṁ daça sapta ca pūrvaḥ syāt;* II. *dvitīyaḥ syāt trayodaça;* III. *tṛtīyo navako dṛṣṭaḥ;* IV. and V. *tasmād dvāu daçakāu parāu;* VI. *ṣaṣṭhaṁ tu caturdaçakam āhuḥ*. — Cf. SPP's "Critical Notice," vol. i., p. 20, where they are printed in metrical form.⌋

⌊The summations of *gaṇas* and (*gaṇa-*) *avasānarcas* may be given as follows: I. *av.*, 17; II. *av.*, 13; III. *av.*, 9; IV. *g.*, 5; *av.*, 10*; V. [*g.*, 4;] *av.* 10†; VI. *av.* 14. — Total of *av.*, 73.⌋ *⌊Cf. note to vs. 40.⌋ †⌊Cf. note to vs. 45.⌋

⌊Here ends the third *anuvāka*, with 2 hymns and 100 verses: that is 1 *artha-sūkta* of 38 verses and 1 *paryāya-sūkta* with 6 *paryāyas* and 62 verses.⌋

7. Extolling the ox.

[*Brahman.—ekaḥ* [*paryāyaḥ*]. *ṣaḍviñçaḥ. gavyaḥ.*]

⌊Prose.⌋ Found for the most part (for details, see under the verses) in Pāipp. xvi. also. Not noticed in Vāit., but quoted (vs. 1) in Kāuç. 66. 19, next after hymn 4 of this book. ⌊For the *paryāya*-hymns in general, see pages 471–2.⌋

Translated: Henry, 103, 139; Griffith, i. 453.

[**Paryāya I.**—*ṣaḍviñçaḥ. 1. ārcī bṛhatī; 2. ārcy uṣṇih; 3, 5. ārcy anuṣṭubh; 4, 14, 15, 16. sāmnī bṛhatī; 6, 8. āsurī gāyatrī; 7. 3-p. pipīlikamadhyā nicṛd gāyatrī; 9, 13. sāmnī gāyatrī; 10. purauṣṇih; 11, 12, 17, 25. sāmny uṣṇih; 18, 22. 1-p. āsurī jagatī; 19. 1-p. āsurī pañkti; 20. yājuṣī jagatī; 21. āsury anuṣṭubh; 23. 1-p. āsurī bṛhatī; 24. sāmnī bhurig bṛhatī; 26. sāmnī triṣṭubh.* (*ihā 'nuktapādā* ⌊*7, 18, 19, 22, 23*⌋ *dvipadāḥ.*)] ⌊☞ See p. 1045.⌋

1. Prajāpati and the most exalted one are his two horns, Indra his head, Agni his forehead, Yama his neck-joint.

The copula and the possessive, wherever read, are supplied in the translation. Ppp. omits *yamaḥ kṛkāṭam*. The verse has only 26 syllables (instead of 27).

2. King Soma his brain, the sky his upper jaw, the earth his lower jaw.

Ppp. inserts, after *mastiṣkas, satyaṁ cakṣur ṛtaṁ çrotre prāṇāpānāu nāmivate*, and reads *adharā* for *-rahanuḥ*, adding after it *agnir āsyaṁ*. We are required to resolve *pṛthivī adh-*.

3. Lightning his tongue, the Maruts his teeth, the Revatīs his neck, the Kṛittikās his shoulders (*skandhā́s*), the hot drink (*gharmá*) his withers (*váha*).

Váha is properly the "carrying" part, that on which the yoke rests. The Revatīs and Kṛttikās, two asterisms, in Pisces and Taurus respectively; their connection with the parts to which they are assigned is, as in nearly all the other cases in this hymn, of the most purely imaginary and meaningless kind. Ppp. has only as far as *dantāṣ*, following it with *pavamānaṣ prāṇaḥ*. Read in our text *grīvā́ḥ* (*visarga*-sign omitted). The *pada*-text has *kṛ́ttikāḥ*, and some of the mss., as usual, retain the *ḥ* before the following *sk*. The verse has but 23 syllables (unless we analyze *jihu-ā́*).

4. Vāyu his all (*viçvam*), the heavenly world his *kṛṣṇadrá*, the whirlwind (?*niveṣyà*) his separator (?*vidhā́raṇī*).

The words here in part (and in the last clause the distinction of subject and predicate) are wholly obscure. The *pada*-text divides *kṛṣṇa°drám* ('black-runner'?). Many of the mss. (E.O.D.R.T.K.) accent *niveṣyā́ḥ*. Ppp. reads *viçvaṁ vāyuṣ kaṇṭhas svargo lokaṣ kṛṣṇadra vyadriṇī vivaçvaḥ;* and then it adds the omitted part of our vs. 3 except *vahaḥ* at the end.

5. The falcon his breast (*kroḍá*), the atmosphere his belly (?*pājasyà*), Brihaspati his hump, the *bṛhatī́s* his vertebræ.

The sense of *bṛhatī* here is doubtful. Ppp. reads *pājasyaṁ* and inserts our vs. 7 after it ⌊continuing with *bṛhasp-*⌋. The required number of 24 syllables is made out by reading *kroḍó ant-* and *pājasi-am*.

6. The spouses of the gods his side-bones (*pṛṣṭí*), the attendants (*upasád*) his ribs (*párçu*).

The distinction between *pṛṣṭí* and *párçu* is not clear.

7. Both Mitra and Varuṇa his (two) shoulders (*áṅsa*), both Tvashṭar and Aryaman his (two) shanks (*doṣán*), the great god his fore-legs.

By Ppp. the verse is inserted in our vs. 5, as there noted. The verse has 23 syllables, but is not 'ant-waisted,' as it divides 8 + 9 + 6.

8. Indrāṇī his buttock, Vāyu his tail (*púcha*), the purifying [soma] his whisk (*vā́lās*).

Some of the mss. (Bp.[2] s.m.E.I.O.D.R.T.Kp.) read *bā́lāḥ*, which is preferable, since all the other passages have it. Ppp. omits, making our vs. 9 follow our 6.

9. Both the Brahman-caste (*bráhman*) and the Kshatriya-caste (*kṣatrá*) his (two) hips, force his (two) thighs.

10. Both Dhātar and Savitar his (two) knee-joints (*aṣṭhīvánt*), the Gandharvas his calves (*jáṅghā*), the Apsarases his dew-claws (*kúṣṭhikā*), Aditi his hoofs.

Ppp. combines *gandharvā 'ps-*. The so-called *purauṣṇih* divides 10 + 12 + 5 = 27 syllables.

11. Thought (*cétas*) his heart, wisdom his liver, ceremony (*vratá*) his *purītát*.

The *pada*-text divides *puri°tát*, but one can only wonder why. After *medhā*, Ppp. inserts *harimā cittam*.

12. Hunger his paunch, cheer (*írā*) his rectum (?*vaniṣṭhú*), the mountains his *plāçís*.

Ppp. reads at the end *prāça*, for *plāçayaḥ*, and adds next vss. 16, 17.

13. Anger his kidneys, fury his testicles, progeny his virile member.

The verse follows our vs. 17 in Ppp.

14. The stream (*nadī́*) his birth-giver (?*sūtrī́*), the lords of rain his teats, thunder his udder.

Ppp. prefixes *samudro vastir*, and puts *varṣasya patayas stanās* after *ūdhas*, then adding 15 without interpunction.

15. The all-expansive his hide, the herbs his hairs, the asterisms his form.

Ppp. reads *carma oṣadhayo romāṇi*, and follows with our vs. 18.

16. The god-folks his intestines, human beings his entrails, eaters (?*atrá*) his belly (*udára*).

Ppp. reads *manuṣyā "ntrāṇy ātrā ud-*, putting the verse after our 12. In order to make out 18 syllables, we have to resolve *-ṣṭ-ā āntrā́ṇi at-*.

17. The demons his blood, the other-folks the contents of his bowels.

Ppp. inverts the order of the two clauses, and reads *ūvadhyam*.

18. The cloud his fat, the conclusion (? *nidhána*) his marrow.

In Ppp. this verse follows our 15, and there is added *bhūtyāṣ prajāyāṣ paçūnāṁ bhavati ya evaṁ veda*.

19. [He is] Agni when sitting, the two Açvins when arisen;

This verse is wanting in Ppp. The metrical definition requires restoration of the *a* of *açvínā*.

20. Indra when standing eastward, Yama when standing southward;

21. Dhātar when standing westward, Savitar when standing northward;

The metrical definition requires the resolution *dhātā́ údañ*. Read *savitā́* (an accent-sign slipped out of place).

22. King Soma when having obtained grass;

The *pada*-mss. have the false accent *pra°ā́ptaḥ* (for *prá°āptaḥ*). ⌊Ppp. reads *tṛṇān prāptas somo rājā.*⌋

23. Mitra when looking, delight (*ānandá*) when turned this way;

Ppp. unites this verse with the preceding, and inverts the order of the two clauses of this verse, reading *rājā "nṛtā "nandaḥ īkṣamāṇo mitrāvaruṇo.*

24. Belonging to all the gods when being yoked, Prajāpati when yoked, everything (*sárvam*) when released.

Ppp. reads *vāiçvānaras* instead of *vāiçvadevas*.

25. That verily is all-formed, of every form, of kine-form.

Ppp. reads *vorūpam* for *viçvárūpam*; ⌊it seems to omit *sarvarūpaṁ gorūpam*⌋.

26. Cattle all-formed, of every form come unto (*upa-sthā*) him who knoweth thus.

Ppp. reads *upāi 'naṁ rūpaṁṇvataṣ paçavaḥ* ⌊intending *rūpavantaṣ*⌋.

⌊The quoted Anukr. says *ṣaḍviṅço brāhmaṇo gavaḥ*. The *avasānarcas* are summed up as 26.⌋

8. Against various diseases.

[*Bhṛgvaṅgiras.* — *dvāviṅçakam.* ⌊*anena*⌋ *sarvaçīrṣāmayādyāmayam* ⌊*apākarot*⌋. *ānuṣṭubham* : *12. anuṣṭubgarbhā kakummatī 4-p. uṣṇih* ; *15. virāḍ anuṣṭubh* ; *21. virāṭ pathyābṛhatī* ; *22. pathyāpaṅkti.*]

Found also (except vs. 4) in Pāipp. xvi. Not noticed in Vāit., but quoted (vs. 1) in Kāuç. 32. 18, in a remedial ceremony. ⌊The last two verses are specified (32. 19) as used "with worship of the sun."⌋

Translated: Zimmer, p. 378; Henry, 105, 141; Griffith, i. 455; Bloomfield, 45, 600.

1. Headache, head-ailment, earache, anæmia (? *vilohitá*), every head-disease of thine, do we expel out [of thee] by incantation (*nir-mantray-*).

Ppp. reads in **a** *çīrṣaktyaṁ*, and in **b** *tṛtīyakam* for *vilohitam*. ⌊For *çīrṣakti*, see references under i. 12. 3.⌋

2. From thy (two) ears, from thy *káñkūṣas*, the earache, the *visálpaka*, every head-disease etc. etc.

As to *visalpakam*, instead of the *visalyakam* of the edition, see under vi. 127. 1. For the obscure *kañkūṣa* Ppp. has *kaṅkukha*, and for **b** it reads *çuktivalçaṁ vilohitam*.

3. For reason of which the *yákṣma* removes from ears, from mouth — every head-disease etc. etc.

Ppp. reads in **b** *nāsatā* "*syata* ⌊intending *-tas -tas*⌋.

4. Whatever one makes a man dumb (? *pramóta*), makes [him] blind — every head-disease etc. etc.

'Dumb' for *pramóta* is Zimmer's conjecture; the word is wholly obscure, and form, accent, and meter make it suspicious; one is tempted to conjecture *prámohitam;* but *muh* with prefix *pra* is not a Vedic combination. The Anukr. takes no notice of the defective pāda.

5. Limb-splitting, limb-wasting, and *visálpaka* of all the limbs — every head-disease etc. etc.

Ppp. reads instead, for **a**, **b**, *çīrṣarogam añgarogaṁ viçvāñgīnaṁ viçalyakam.* ⌊As to *visálp-*, see under vi. 127. 1.⌋ With **a** is to be compared v. 30. 9 **a**.

6. Of whom the fearful aspect makes a man tremble — the *takmán* of every autumn we expel out [of thee] by incantation.

Ppp. reads *pāuruṣam* in **b**, and, for **c**, **d**, *takmānaṁ çītaṁ rūraṁ ca taṁ tve nir man-*: cf. v. 22. 10, 13.

7. The *yákṣma* that creeps along the thighs, that goes also to the groins, from thy limbs within we expel etc. etc.

Ppp. reads in **c** *balāsam* for *yakṣmaṁ te* ⌊cf. our 8 **c** and under 9⌋.

8. If it is born out of desire, of aversion, of the heart — the *balā́sa* from thy heart, thy limbs we expel etc. etc.

9. Yellowness from thy limbs, *apvā́* from thy belly within, the *yákṣma*-maker from thy self within we expel etc. etc.

The *pada*-text reads in **c** *yakṣmaḥ॰dhā́m.* The Prāt. takes no notice of the irregular form of the first member of the compound, as it does, superfluously (ii. 56), of the contrary treatment of *çepas* in *çepa॰harṣaṇīm.* In Ppp. our third pāda becomes the second, and for third we have nearly our 7 **c**: *yakṣmaṁ te sarvam añgebhyo.*

10. Let the *balā́sa* become ash, let it become sickening urine; the poison of all *yákṣmas* have I exorcised from thee.

11. Forth at the orifice let it run out, the *kā́hābāha*, from thy belly; the poison of all etc. etc.

⌊Literally 'to the orifice'; Henry "vers le trou," i.e. "par l'anus."⌋ The Pet. Lexx. plausibly conjecture *kāhābāha* to be an imitative term for rumbling in the bowels; it may also possibly be understood as used adverbially, like *bāl* in i. 3. Ppp. has a quite different reading for **b**: *kahāvalaṁ tvaṅdarā.*

12. Out of thy belly, lung, navel, heart, the poison of all etc. etc.

Ppp. rectifies the meter of **a** by inserting *pari* before *klomnas*, and makes **c**, **d** agree with our 9 **c**, **d**. The Anukr. brings out an *uṣṇih* (28 syll.) by unnaturally refusing to make the resolutions *nābhi-ās* and *tu-at* ⌊and scanning as 6 + 7 : 8 + 7⌋.

13. They that break apart the crown, rushers against the head (*mūrdhán*) — not injuring, free from disease, let them run out, out at the orifice.

The 'they' in this and the following verses (13–18) is fem. The Pet. Lexx. take *arṣaṇī́* in **b** as an independent noun (it is found only here), and conjecture it to mean 'pricking pains.'

14. They that rush unto the heart, that stretch along the vertebræ — not injuring etc. etc.

Prāt. iii. 47 prescribes the form *uparṣánti* (instead of *upārṣánti*: p. *upa∘ṛṣánti*) in this and the two following verses. Ppp. reads every time *upadiçanti.*

15. They that rush unto the two sides, that stab (*nikṣ*) along the ribs — not injuring etc. etc.

The Anukr. intends *pārçvé* to be read unresolved.

16. They that rush on crosswise, rushers in thy belly (*vakṣáṇā*) — not injuring etc. etc.

Ppp. reads in **b** *vakṣaṇābhyaḥ*, and omits the following *te.*

17. They that creep along the intestines, and confound the entrails — not injuring etc. etc.

Ppp. reads in **b** *yāpayanti* for *mohayanti.* ⌊Roth most ingeniously suggests that the Ppp. reading may mean *āntrā ni-y-āmayanti.* Or is *yāpayanti* to be taken in a sense quite like our English 'cause (the bowels) to move,' i.e. 'produce diarrhœa'?⌋

18. They that suck out the marrow, and break apart the joints — not injuring etc. etc.

Ppp. reads in **a** *anusarpanti* for *nirdhayanti.* We are to resolve *maj-jñ-o* to fill out the measure.

19. They that intoxicate (*maday-*) the limbs, the *yákṣmas*, thy gripers — the poison of all *yákṣmas* have I exorcised from thee.

Ppp. reads in **b** *ropaṇā saha.* Some of our mss. (P.M.O.p.m.) read *yé 'ñgāni.*

20. Of the *visalpá*, of the *vidradhá*, or of the *vātīkārá*, of the *alají* — the poison etc. etc.

Ppp. again reads *viçalyasya* ⌊cf. under vi. 127. 1⌋; also, in **b**, *vātīkālasya.*

21. Forth from thy feet, knees, hips, buttock, spine, nape the pangs, from thy head the disease have I made disappear.

Ppp. reads, after *te*, *gulphābhyāṁ jañghābhyāṁ jānubhyām ūrubhyāṁ çro. p. bh.*; it reads *ānūkyāt* in **c**, and inserts before *çīrṣṇas*, *grīvābhyas skandhebhyas.* It is apparently the intrusion of *arṣaṇī́s* that spoils the meter in our **c**.

22. Together the bones (*kapā́la*) of thy head, and the discussor (*vidhú*) of thy heart — arising, O Āditya, thou with thy rays hast made disappear the disease of the head, hast pacified the limb-splitter.

The first two pādas seem independent; an unfinished construction. The *pada*-text reads *vi°dhúḥ* in **b**, as if it recognized in the word the root *dhū + vi;* this is not implausible, and the translation follows it (the simple "beat" of the Pet. Lexx. seems quite unacceptable; it might be 'palpitation'). But Ppp. reads instead *vidus*, and so do a part of our mss., namely, W.O.s.m.D.Kp. ⌊W. interlines a query over "discussor," which word he coins and uses in the sense 'shaker asunder.' "Discuss" in this sense is "obsolete except in surgical use."⌋ Ppp. further has, for our **c** etc.: *udyat sūryādityo an̄gāni roma nakhāni sarvāṇi sadanāni nīnaçat.*

⌊The fourth *anuvāka*, with 2 hymns and 48 verses, ends here. The quoted Anukr. says *navadaçā 'pare ca.*⌋

9. Mystic.

[*Brahman. — dvāvinçakam. vāmīyam ādityadevatyam adhyātmakaram. trāiṣṭubham: 12, 14, 16, 18. jagatī.*]

This hymn and the following (except a few verses of the latter) are one Rig-Veda hymn, namely, i. 164, and but a small part of them occur in any other Vedic text. Both are found in Pāipp. xvi., in somewhat changed verse-order, as will be noted under the different verses below. Vāit. takes no notice of this hymn; in Kāuç. it (vs. 1) is quoted in 18. 25, with various others, in a ceremony for prosperity; and the *gaṇamālā* (see note to Kāuç. 18. 25) reckons it as belonging to the *salila gaṇa.*

Translated: as RV. hymn, by Ludwig, no. 951; and Grassmann, ii. p. 456–460; also by M. Haug, under the title, *Vedische Räthselfragen und Räthselsprüche, Sb. der philos.-philol. Classe der k. bairischen Ak. der Wiss.*, Bd. II., Heft 3, für 1875, München, 1876 (the essay, says Whitney, "casts extremely little light upon its labored obscurities"); further, with an elaborate comment touching the significance of its philosophic content, by Deussen, *Geschichte*, i. 1. 105–119; parts also by Muir, v. (see Index, p. 484), and Hillebrandt, *Ved. Mythol.*, i. (see Index, p. 542); and under the title, *Zwei Sprüche über Leib und Seele*, ZDMG. xlvi. 759 f., Roth explains two verses answering to our ix. 10. 8 and 16. Under the title, *Das Räthsel vom Jahre*, ZDMG. xlviii. 353, E. Windisch discusses the RV. verse answering to our vs. 12.

Translated, moreover, as AV. hymn, by Henry, 107, 143; Griffith, i. 458. The critical remarks of Oldenberg, IFA. vi. 180–183, may also be consulted. — Further, von Schroeder, *Der Rigveda bei den Kaṭhas*, WZKM. xii. 282, reports variants for certain vss. of the RV. hymn which correspond to our vss. ix. 9. 9, 12, 17, 22 and ix. 10. 16. — Finally, A. Wünsche's essay, *Das Rätsel vom Jahr und seinen Zeitabschnitten in der Weltlitteratur*, may be cited in this connection; it is found in *Zeitschrift für vergl. Litteraturgeschichte*, N.F., ix. 425–456.

1. Of this pleasant (*vāmá*) hoary invoker — of him the brother is the midmost stone (? *áçna*); his third brother [is] ghee-backed; there I saw the lord of the people who hath seven sons.

The three brothers are explained as the three forms of Agni, in heaven, in the atmosphere (lightning), and on earth (sacrificial fire); the 'seven sons' are most probably his many flames. ⌊The collocation of *madhyamó* with *bhrā́tā* would seem more natural, considering the phrase *tṛtī́yo bhrā́tā.*⌋

2. Seven harness (*yuj*) a one-wheeled chariot; one horse, having seven names, draws (*vah*) [it]; of three naves [is] the wheel, unwasting, unassailed, whereon stand all these existences.

Doubtless the sun. The verse is repeated as xiii. 3. 18. It occurs also in TA. iii. 11. 8, with *anarvām̐ yene 'mā v. bhuvanāni t.* in **c**, **d** (the accent of the verse is too corrupt to heed).

3. The seven that stand on this chariot — seven horses draw it, seven-wheeled; seven sisters shout at [it] together, where are set down the seven names of the kine.

RV. reads *navante* in **c**, and *nā́ma* in **d**.

4. Who saw it first in process of birth, as the boneless one bears (*bhṛ*) him that has bones? where forsooth the earth's life (*ásu*), blood, soul? who shall go to ask that of him who knows?

'Bears,' not in the sense of 'gives birth to,' but of 'carries' or 'supports' or the like.

5. Let him who truly knows ⌊here⌋ tell (*brū*) the set-down track of this pleasant bird; the kine extract (*duh*) milk from his head; clothing themselves in a wrap, they have drunk water with the foot.

Explained as relating to the clouds and the sun. The verse is vs. 7 in RV., and also in Ppp.; the latter reads *çīrṣṇā* in **c**.

6. Simple, not discerning (*vi-jñā*) with the mind, I ask about the thus set-down tracks of the gods; over the yearling (? *baṣkáya*) calf have the poets stretched out seven lines (*tántu*) for weaving.

7. I, not understanding (*cit*), ask here the understanding poets, I unknowing (*vid*), them that know; he who propped asunder these six spaces (*rájas*), in the form of the goat (? *ajá*) — was that also alone?

The sense of the last pāda is utterly obscure, and the version given only tentative; *ajá* is perhaps here really the 'unborn one,' as the translators render it. RV. reads in **a** *ácikitvāñ cik-*, and, in **b**, *vidmáne*, for which our *vidvánas* is apparently a mere corruption.

8. The mother portioned the father in righteousness, for with meditation (*dhītí*), with mind, came together in the beginning she, repugnant, womb-sapped, pierced; paying homage, verily, they went unto encouragement.

The version is in part only mechanical. Ppp. combines *ṛtā "babh-* in **a**, and reads *jajñe* at end of **b**.

9. The mother was yoked to the pole of the sacrificial gift; the embryo stood among the wiles (? *vṛjanī́*); the calf bleated, looked after the cow of all forms, in the three distances (*yójana*).

⌊Kaṭha variants, WZKM. xii. 282, *vṛjanéṣv antáḥ* and *yojáneṣu.* — Cf. IFA. vi. 180, as noted above.⌋

10. The one, bearing three mothers [and] three fathers, stood upright; verily they do not exhaust him; on the back of yon sky the all-knowing ones talk a speech not found by all.

RV. reads *glāpayanti* at end of **b** ⌊and the translation follows that reading⌋, and, for **d**, *viçvavídaṁ vā́cam ávíçvaminvām*. The *pada*-text reads *glapayanta;* Prāt. iv. 93 notes the case. Ppp. agrees with RV. in *glāpayanti* and *viçvavidam*.

11. On the five-spoked circumvolving wheel on which stood all existences — its axle, much-burdened, is not heated; even from of old it is not severed with the nave.

RV. and Ppp. count this verse as 13, our version inverting the order of 11–13. In **b**, RV. reads *tásminn ā́ tasthur bh. v.*, and Ppp. *samārohanti bh. v.;* and RV. has *çīryate* for *chidyate* in **d**.

12. The five-footed father, of twelve shapes (*-ā́kṛti*), they call rich in ground (*purīṣín*) in the far (*pára*) half of the sky; then these others call [him] set (*árpita*) in the lower outlook that is seven-wheeled, six-spoked.

RV. and Ppp. have the easier and better reading *vicakṣaṇám* in **c**, and Ppp. reads before it *upari*. ⌊The Kaṭha reading also is *úpari*, WZKM. xii. 282.⌋ Read in **b** *páre* (an accent sign slipped out of place). ⌊See Roth, KZ. xxvi. 66, and Windisch as cited in the introduction; cf. also IFA. vi. 181, as noted above.⌋

13. The twelve-spoked wheel — for that is not to be worn out — revolves greatly about the sky of righteousness; there, O Agni, stood the sons, paired, seven hundred and twenty.

Here the 'twelve' and the 'seven hundred and twenty' are plainly the months, and the days and nights, of the year of 360 days. The verse, as noted above, is vs. 11 in RV. and Ppp. The more proper reading in **b** would be *várvartti*.

14. The unwasting wheel, with rim, rolls about; ten harnessed ones draw upon the outstretched one (fem.); the sun's eye goes surrounded with the welkin (*rájas*), in which stood all existences.

Ppp. has *vrajanti* for *vahanti* in **b**, and, for **d** *yasminn ārpitā bhuvanāny ārpitā;* RV. has *tásminn ā́rpitā* for our *yásminn ātasthúḥ*. The Anukr. calls the verse simply a *jagatī*, though only two of its pādas have 12 syllables.

15. Them, being women, they declared (*ah*) to me to be men; he who hath eyes may see, [but] the blind will not distinguish (*vi-cit*); the son that is a poet, he verily understood (*ā-cit*); whoever knows those things apart, he shall be [his] father's father.

RV. and Ppp. put this verse after our vs. 16. It is found also in TA. i. 11.4, with *tā́ u* in **a**, *imā́s* in **c** for *īm ā́*, and *savitúḥ p-* in **d**. Some of our mss. (P.s.m.O.K.T.) read *pitúḥ p-* in **d**; we had the phrase once before, at ii. 1.2, and the combination falls under Prāt. ii. 73. We might expect, in **d**, *tā́ḥ*, referring to *strī́yaḥ*, but the *pada*-texts have *tā́*, as neuter pl.

16. Of those born together the seventh they call sole-born; six, they say, are twins, god-born seers; the sacrifices (? *iṣṭá*) of them, distributed according to their abodes, quake in their station, being altered (*vi-kṛ*) in respect to form.

Iṣṭā́ni in **c** might equally mean 'things desired.' *Sthātré* in **d** is most probably loc. of *-trá*, since, if from *sthātṛ́*, we should expect instead the ablative. ⌊The vs. recurs at TA. i. 3. 1 with *udyamā́s* for *íd yamā́s.*⌋

17. Below the distant (*pára*), thus beyond the lower, bearing (*bhṛ*) her calf with her foot, the cow hath stood up; whitherwards, to what quarter (*árdha*) hath she forsooth gone away? where giveth she birth? for [it is] not in this herd.

The Anukr. takes no notice of the redundant syllable in **a**; we may suppose *pará enā́-* to be combined to *parāt 'nā́-*. ⌊The verse is repeated below as xiii. 1. 41. RV. ends with *antáḥ* for *asmín.* The Kaṭha variant *párākāt* for *párāgāt* (WZKM. xii. 282) shows an exchange of surd and sonant, the reverse of that noted at ii. 13. 3.⌋

18. Below the distant whoever knows his father, below the distant, thus beyond the lower — who, playing the poet, shall proclaim [him] here? from whence [is] heavenly mind produced?

RV. and Ppp. read, in **a, b**, *yó asyā 'nuvéda pará enā́-*, rectifying the meter and lightening the construction. Only the first two pādas have any "*jagatī*" character, and they are very irregular. But by giving this name the Anukr. shows that it reads our version; in RV. and Ppp. the verse is a pure *triṣṭubh.* Read in **d** *kúto* (for *kṛ́to*).

19. Them that are hitherward they call off-ward; them, again, that are off-ward they call hitherward; what things, O Soma, thou and Indra have done, those they draw, harnessed as it were with the pole of the welkin.

The verse is found also in JB. i. 279, with no various readings that are not evident corruptions. The 'them' of **a, b** is masc., probably the same with the 'they' of **d** (*yuktā́ḥ*, p.). Ppp. reads *niyuktā* instead of *na yuktā.*

20. Two eagles (*suparṇá*), joint companions, embrace the same tree; of them the one eats the sweet berry; the other looks on all the time, not partaking.

Ppp. reads in **a** *suyujā.* Here and in the next verse, as everywhere else, some of our mss. read *píṣpalam.* ⌊The vs. plays a rôle in the Upanishads: cf. Çvet. iv. 6; Muṇḍ. iii. 1. 1. Hillebrandt, *Ved. Mythol.*, i. 466, 399, treats this and the following vss.⌋

21. On what tree the honey-eating eagles all settle and give birth — what they call the sweet berry in the top of it, that cannot he attain who knoweth not [his] father.

RV. has *íd āhuḥ* instead of *yád āhúḥ* in **c**, and so also Ppp. (but *āhuṣ*). In RV. this verse follows after our vs. 22. There is a redundant syllable in **c** of which the Anukr. takes no notice (and the pāda is also capable of being crowded together into eleven syllables).

22. Where the eagles, with counsel (*vidátha*), sound incessantly (*ánimeṣam*) unto the draught of *amṛ́ta*, — thus the shepherd of all existence, he the wise one entered there into me that am simple.

RV. reads *bhāgám* for *bhakṣám* in **a**. For *enā́* in **c**, RV. has *inás*, and Ppp. *yo no;* ⌊Ppp's *yo no* seems to be an attempt to make sense out of the rare and probably unintelligible *inó*⌋. ⌊The Kaṭha variant (WZKM. xii. 282) is *ánimiṣam.*⌋

⌊The quoted Anukr. says *navadaçe ca.*⌋

10. Mystic.

[*Brahman.* — *aṣṭāviṅçakam. govirāḍadhyātmadāivatyam* (*23. māitrāvaruṇī*). *trāiṣṭubham: 1, 7, 14, 17, 18. jagatī; 21. 5-p. atiçakvarī; 24. 4-p. puraskṛtir bhurig atijagatī; 2, 26, 27. bhurij.*]

This hymn is in RV. a continuation of the preceding; but our vss. 9 and 23 are not found in the RV. with the rest (9 is RV. x. 55. 5 and 23 is RV. i. 152. 3); ⌊while of 19, only **d** is found in RV., making, with the odd fifth pāda of our vs. 21, the first half of RV. i. 164. 42 (42 **a**, **b** = 21 **e** + 19 **d**); and our 24 (prose) does not occur in the RV. at all⌋. The first 23 verses are found also in Pāipp. xvi. The hymn is not quoted in Kāuç. (except as vs. 20 is also vii. 73. 11); but a few verses (9, 13, 14) are cited in Vāit.

Translated: as AV. hymn, by Henry, 110, 150; Griffith, i. 464. — For other translations etc. see the introduction to hymn 9.

1. That the *gāyatrī́*-verse is set (*ā-dhā*) in the *gāyatrī́*-verse, or that they fashioned the *triṣṭúbh*-verse out of the *triṣṭúbh*-verse, or that the *jágatī* step is set in the *jágatī* (*jágat*) — whoever know that, they have attained immortality.

RV. ⌊vs. 23⌋ and Ppp. read in **b** *trāíṣṭubhād vā trāíṣṭubham.*

2. By the *gāyatrī́*-verse he measures off the song (*arká*), by the song the chant (*sā́man*), by the *triṣṭúbh*-verse the hymn (*vāká*), by the hymn of two feet [or] of four feet the hymn; by the syllable they measure the seven tunes (*vā́ṇi*).

The words 'song,' 'hymn,' 'tune' are used rather loosely in rendering here.

3. By the *jágatī* he established (*skabh*) the river in the sky; in the *rathaṁtará* he beheld (*pari-paç*) the sun; they call the three kindlers (*samídh*) the *gāyatrī́*-verse's; it was superior to them by bulk, by greatness.

The translation of the last pāda is not without uncertainties; *tátas* is here understood as *quasi*-object of *prá ririce.* RV. ⌊vs. 25⌋ reads in **a** *astabhāyat.*

4. I invite that well-milking milch-cow; a skilful-handed milker also shall milk her; may the impeller impel us the best impulse; the hot drink is kindled about: that may he kindly proclaim.

We had this verse above as vii. 73. 7. The only variant in RV. ⌊vs. 26⌋ is the better *vocam* at the end. ⌊Oldenberg discusses verses 4–7, IFA. vi. 182.⌋

5. Lowing, mistress of good things, seeking her calf with her mind, hath she come unto [it]; let this inviolable one yield milk for the Açvins; let her increase unto great good-fortune.

This verse, again, is vii. 73.8, above, excepting that the latter reads *nyā̆gan* at end of **b**. Our *pada*-text has here *abhi°āgāt*, while that of RV. ⌊vs. 27⌋ gives *abhí : ā́ : agāt;* both yield the same *saṁhitā*-reading.

6. The cow lowed toward the winking calf; she uttered *hiṅg* at [its] head, in order to lowing; bellowing the mouth (? *sṛ́kvan*) unto the hot drink, she lows a lowing, she abounds with milk.

Compare 1.8, above; the second line is nearly identical in the two verses. It is quite differently rendered by the translators at one and another point, being very obscure. For *abhí* in **a**, RV. reads *ánu*, Ppp. *apa*.

7. This one here twangs, by whom the cow is surrounded; she lows a lowing, being set (*çritá*) on the sparkler (*dhvasáni*); since she put down mortals by her thoughts (*cittí*), becoming the lightning, she threw (*ūh*) back the wrap.

Both RV. ⌊vs. 29⌋ and Ppp. read *mártyam* in **c**.

8. Breathing lies the swift moving thing, living, stirring, fixed, in the midst of the abodes (*pastyā̀*); the living one moves at the will (? *svadhā́bhis*) of the dead one; the immortal one [is] of like source with the mortal.

The verse is excessively obscure, and Hillebrandt's translation of the second half, and reference to the moon (*Ved. Mythol.*, pp. 336, 498), very forced and implausible. The verse lacks a syllable in **a** (and the *pada*-text sets its mark of pāda-division after *éjat*); perhaps we are to resolve *-ga-ātu*. Ppp. puts the verse after our vs. 9. ⌊RV., vs. 30, shows no variant. Roth's most interesting interpretation (ZDMG. xlvi. 759) makes of the verse a riddle whose answer is "the body and the soul." He emends to *ánanac* in **a**. Böhtlingk, *Berichte der sächsischen Gesell.*, 1893, xlv. 88, reviews Roth's interpretation.⌋

9. The shaker-apart (? *vidhú*) that runs on the back of the sea, being young, the hoary one swallowed; see thou the poesy of the heavenly one with greatness; today he died, yesterday he received breath (*sam-an*).

This verse is RV. x. 55.5; also SV. i. 325 etc.; TA. iv. 20. 1; MS. iv. 9. 12. All alike read *sámane bahūnā́m* for *salilásya pṛṣṭhé* (MS., except in its *pada*-text, has other slight differences which are palpable blunders). *Vidhú* is (as at 8. 22, above) divided in *pada*-text *vi°dhú*. It doubtless designates here the moon, however it may have won the right to do so. Ludwig and Hillebrandt (*Ved. Mythol.* i. 465) translate **d** 'today (he died yesterday) he has come to life'; but this is in the highest degree forced, and may be pronounced even inadmissible. Ppp. reads *vidyudūdrāṇā* at the beginning. ⌊See *Kaṭha-hss.*, p. 82.⌋ The verse is quoted in Vāit. 40.7; 41. 12.

10. He who made him knows not of him; [he is] verily out of sight now of him who saw him; he, enveloped within his mother's womb, with his much progeny, entered into perdition (*nírṛti*).

The translation follows the RV. reading, *nírṛtim*, in **d**, since the nom. *-tis* seems unconstruable. Both RV. ⌊vs. 32⌋ and Ppp. put the verse after our vs. 11, and the latter reads *so 'sya* in **a**. Haug interprets the lightning to be intended.

11. I saw the shepherd, not lying down, moving both hither and thither upon his roads; he, clothing himself in the collecting, he in the dispersing ones, rolls greatly on among existences.

Doubtless the sun. The verse ⌊RV. vs. 31⌋ is found a second time in RV. as x. 177. 3; and also at VS. xxxvii. 17; TA. iv. 7. 1; MS. iv. 9. 6; AA. ii. 1. 6⁶⁻¹⁰ — all accenting in **a** *ánipadyamānam*, which is alone acceptable. ⌊Our **d** recurs, with *sá* prefixed, at x. 2. 7 **c**. If we read *varīvartti* there, we ought also to do so here.⌋ ⌊Cf. *Kaṭha-hss.*, p. 101.⌋

12. The heaven our father, generator, navel here; this great earth our connection, mother; the womb (*yóni*) within the (two) outstretched cups (*camū́*); here the father hath set (*ā-dhā*) the daughter's embryo.

'Navel,' i.e. 'central point, place of union.' RV. ⌊vs. 33⌋ reads *me* for *nas* in **a** and **b**.

13. I ask of thee the extreme (*pára*) end of the earth; I ask the seed of the male (*vṛ́ṣan*) horse; I ask the navel of all existence; I ask the highest (*paramá*) firmament (*vyòman*) of speech.

RV. ⌊vs. 34⌋ exchanges the place of **b** and **c**, and rectifies the meter by inserting another *tvā* before *vṛ́ṣṇo*, and reading *pṛchā́mi yátra bhúvanasya nā́bhiḥ*. Ppp. follows RV. in the former case, but in the latter has *pṛchāmi tvām̐ bh. n.;* it makes ⌊as between **b** and **c**⌋ the same inversion of order as RV.; and it begins **d** with *vācaṣ pṛchāmi*. The Anukr. takes no notice of the irregularity of our meter. The verse, with the following one, is found also in other texts: VS. xxiii. 61, 62; TS. vii. 4. 18²; LÇS. ix. 10. 13, 14. VS. reads in both verses precisely as RV., and LÇS. differs from it only by having *pṛchāmas* instead of *-mi* four times in vs. 13. TS. has for 13 **b** *pṛchā́mi tvā bhúvanasya nā́bhim*. The two verses are quoted in Vāit. 37. 3.

14. This sacrificial hearth is the extreme end of the earth; this soma is the seed of the male horse; this sacrifice is the navel of all existence; this priest (*brahmán*) is the highest firmament of speech.

RV. ⌊vs. 35⌋ (also VS. LÇS.: see above) and Ppp. read for **b**, **c**: *ayám̐ yajñó bhúv. nā́.: ayám̐ sómo* etc. (our **b**). TS. has *védim āhuḥ páram ántam pṛthivyā́ yajñám āhur bhúvanasya nā́bhim: sómam āhur vṛ́. áç. ré. brahmā́ 'vá vācáḥ* etc. The Anukr. absurdly calls the verse a *jagatī* on account of the two redundant syllables in the AV. version of **c**.

15. I do not distinguish what this is that I am; I go secret, fastened together with mind; when the first-born of righteousness hath come to me, then indeed I attain a share of this speech.

Ppp. agrees with RV. ⌊vs. 37⌋ in putting this verse ⌊and the next⌋ after our vs. 17. The RV. *pada*-text has in **c** *ā́: ágan* ⌊so Müller's five editions and Aufrecht's first: Aufrecht's second, *ā́ : agan*⌋; our *ā°ágan* is better. Ppp. reads *balinā* for *manasā* in **b**.

16. Offward, forward goes, seized by *svadhā́*, the immortal one, of like source with the mortal; the two, constantly going separate apart — the one they noted, the other they noted not.

Haug and Hillebrandt (*Ved. Mythol.*, i. 336, note) both understand *svadhā* here as meaning the offering to the manes, but their conjectural interpretations of the verse are totally discordant. ⌊The vs. is RV. vs. 38 without variant. See the interpretations of Roth and of Böhtlingk as cited under vs. 8 above. — The Kaṭha variant (WZKM. xii. 282) is *ápräñ* for *ápāñ*. — The vs. is found at AA. ii. 1. 8.⌋

17. Seven half-embryos, the seed of existence, stand in front (? *pradíçā*), in Vishṇu's distribution; they, by thoughts (*dhītí*), by mind, they, inspired, surround on all sides the surrounders.

Or, 'being surrounders.' As noted above, the verse in RV. ⌊vs. 36⌋ and Ppp. stands before our vs. 15. Both 17 and 18 are defective as *jagatīs*. ⌊Cf. Oldenberg, IFA. vi. 184; also Henry, *Actes du dixième Congrès intern. des Orientalistes*, Section I, Inde, p. 45–50, "Cruelle énigme."⌋

18. In the syllable of the verse (*ṛ́c*) in the highest firmament, on which all the gods sat down: he who knoweth not that, what will he do with the verse? they who know that sit together yonder.

RV. ⌊vs. 39⌋ reads *imé* instead of *amī́* in **d**. O. combines *vidúṣ ṭé* just before it. The verse is found also in TB. iii. 10. 9[14] and TA. ii. 11. 1 — in both, with the RV. reading. Its *pratīka* occurs also in GB. i. 22. Read *véda* in **c**.

19. Shaping (*kalpay-*) with measure the step of the verse, they shaped by the half-verse all that stirs; the *bráhman* of three feet, many-formed, spread out (*vi-sthā*); by that do the four quarters live.

The comm. to the Prāt. (ii. 93) quotes *ví taṣṭhe* at end of **c** as an example of the *s* of *sthā* lingualized after *ví* even though the reduplication intervenes; and that establishes *ví taṣṭhe* as the true reading. The majority of the *saṁhitā*-mss. have it; but W.E.O. give *caṣṭe;* Ppp. also has *parirūpaṁ vi caṣṭe*. Only the fourth pāda is found in RV., being i. 164. 42 **b** (we have 42 **a** as our 21 **e**); the same occurs below as xi. 5. 12 **d**.

20. Mayest thou be well-portioned, feeding in excellent meadows; so also may we be well-portioned; eat thou grass, O inviolable one, at all times; drink clear water, moving hither.

We had this verse ⌊RV. vs. 40⌋ above, as vii. 73. 11.

21. The cow verily lowed, fashioning the seas; one-footed, two-footed [is] she, four-footed; having become eight-footed, nine-footed, thousand-syllabled, a series (*pañtí*) of existence; out from her flow apart the oceans.

The five pādas are vs. 41, and 42 **a**, of the RV. hymn; which, however, reads *gāurī́s* for *gāúr íd* in **a**, and *paramé vyòman* for *bhúvanasya pañtīḥ* in **d**. The RV. vs. 41 occurs also in TB. ii. 4. 6[11] ⌊and it is there followed by the RV. vs. 42 entire⌋ and TA. i. 9. 4, with the RV. readings, excepting *gāurī́* at the beginning ⌊and *tásyām* in TB. for *tásyās*⌋. Our pādas **b–e**, again, are repeated as xiii. 1. 42 below. The verse (12 + 12 : 12 + 11 + 11 = 58) lacks two syllables of being a proper *atiçakvarī* (60 syllables).

22. Black the descent, the yellow eagles, clothing themselves in waters, fly up to the sky; they have come hither from the seat of righteousness; then, forsooth, with ghee they deluged the earth.

The verse occurs also above as vi. 22. 1, and pādas **a–c** below in xiii. 3. 9. For parallel passages etc. see the note to vi. 22. 1. It is RV. i. 164. 47, the last verse of the RV. hymn that is included in the AV. text here (RV. vss. 43–46 are our 25–28 below), although of the remaining five RV. vss. all but one (51) are found in other parts of our text.

23. She that is footless goes first of them (fem.) that have feet: who understood (*ā-cit*) that of you, O Mitra and Varuṇa? the embryo brings (*ā-bhṛ*) the burden of her; she (?) fills (?*pṛ*) truth, protects (*ni-pā*) untruth.

The last pāda is especially obscure: he? or she? or it? and which root *pṛ*, 'fill' or 'pass'? The verse is RV. i. 152. 3, where we read *tārīt* instead of *pāti* at the end, and *asya* for *asyās* at end of **c**. Ppp. also has *tārīt*, but, instead of *ā́ cid asyāḥ* (or *asya*), it reads *ād ṛtasya*.

24. *Virā́j* [is] speech, *virā́j* earth, *virā́j* atmosphere, *virā́j* Prajāpati; *virā́j* became death, the over-king of the perfectibles (*sādhyá*); in his control are what was, what is to be; let him put in my control what was, what is to be.

⌊Prose.⌋ This verse, with all that follows it, is wanting in Ppp. The Anukr. reckons the whole first part to the pause as one pāda (20 syllables, a *kṛti*-pāda); the *pada*-text understands it as two, dividing after *pṛthivī*.

25. The dung-made smoke I saw from far, with the dividing one, thus beyond the lower; the heroes cooked a spotted ox (*ukṣán*); those were the first ordinances.

The construction and sense of **b** are very obscure. The verse is 43 of RV. i. 164, and the remaining three follow in order. ⌊Henry, *Mém. de la Soc. de linguistique*, ix. 247, cites the vs.⌋

26. Three hairy ones look out seasonably; in the (a?) year one of them shears itself; another looks upon all with might (*çácībhis*); of one is seen the rush, not the form.

The RV. version ⌊vs. 44⌋ has in **c** *víçvam éko abhí caṣṭe;* our *abhicáṣṭe* is a regular case of antithetical accent. The RV. *pada*-text does not divide *saṁvatsare*. Haug interprets the verse of the three forms of Agni; Hillebrandt (*Ved. Mythol.*, i. p. 472), of the moon (!?), sun, and wind.

27. Speech [is] four measured out quarters (*padá*); those are known by Brahmans who are skilful; three, deposited in secret, they do not set in motion (*iñgay-*); a fourth of speech human beings speak.

This verse is found, without variant, in TB. (ii. 8. 8⁵) and ÇB. (iv. 1. 3¹⁷), as well as in RV. ⌊vs. 45⌋. Our Bp.²D.Kp. read *ná : iñgayanti* in **c**.

28. They call [him] Indra, Mitra, Varuṇa, Agni; likewise he [is] the heavenly winged eagle; what is one the sages (*vípra*) name (*vad*) variously; they call [him] Agni, Yama, Mātariçvan.

Our *pada*-text differs from that of RV. ⌊vs. 46⌋ by dividing *bahuºdhā́*.

⌊The fifth *anuvāka*, with 2 hymns and 50 verses, ends here.⌋

⌊One of our mss., P., sums up the book as of 8 *artha-sūktas* [their vss. number 214] and 7 *paryāya-sūktas* [hymns 6 and 7: their ¶'s number 62 + 26 = 88] or "15 *sūktas* of both kinds" reckoned together. Cf. the introduction, p. 517. The same ms., P., sums up the *avasānarcas* [of hymns 6 and 7] as 99 [73 + 26] and the "verses of both kinds" as 313 [that is 214 + 99]; but codex I. gives 302 [that is 214 + 88].⌋

⌊The twenty-first *prapāṭhaka* ends here.⌋

Book X.

⌊This tenth book is the third of the second grand division of the Atharvan collection. For a general statement as to the make-up of the books of this division, reference should again be made to page 471. The Old Anukramaṇī describes the length of hymns 1, 2, 5, 6, 7, 8, and 10 by giving the overplus of each hymn over 30 verses. The assumed normal length in the case of book ix. seems to be 20 verses. The whole book has been translated by Victor Henry, *Les livres X, XI, et XII de l'Atharva-véda traduits et commentés*, Paris, 1896. The *bhāṣya* again is lacking. There are no *paryāya*-hymns in this book.⌋

⌊The *anuvāka*-division of the book (as noted above, page 472) is into five *anuvākas* of two hymns each. The "decad"-division likewise is as described on page 472. A tabular conspectus for this book also may be acceptable:

Anuvākas	1		2		3		4		5	
Hymns	1	2	3	4	5	6	7	8	9	10
Verses	32	33	25	26	50	35	44	44	27	34
Decad-div.	10+10+12	10+10+13	10+10+5	10+10+6	5 tens	3 tens+5	3 tens+14	3 tens+14	10+10+7	10+10+14

Sum of verses, 350. The sum of "decad"-*sūktas* is 35. In this book, therefore, the average length of the "decad"-*sūktas* is precisely 10 verses.⌋

---

1. Against witchcraft and its practisers.

[*Pratyañgirasa.* — *dvātriṅçat. kṛtyādūṣaṇadevatyam. ānuṣṭubham: 1. mahābṛhatī; 2. virāṇ nāma gāyatrī; 9. pathyāpañkti; 12. pañkti; 13. urobṛhatī; 15. 4-p. virāḍ jagatī; 17, 20, 24. prastārapañkti (20. virāj); 16, 18. triṣṭubh; 19. 4-p. jagatī; 22. 1-av. 2-p. ārcy uṣṇih; 23. 3-p. bhurig viṣamā gāyatrī; 28. 3-p. gāyatrī; 29. madhyejyotiṣmatī jagatī; 32. dvyanuṣṭubgarbhā 5-p. atijagatī.*]

Found also in Pāipp. xvi. The hymn (vs. 1) is quoted in Kāuç. 39. 7, with several others, in a ceremony against witchcraft, and several of its verses or parts of verses elsewhere. The Vāit. uses only one half-verse (21 **c, d**).

Translated: Ludwig, p. 520; Henry, **1**, 39; Griffith, ii. 1; Bloomfield, 72, 602.

1. She whom the adepts (*cikitsú*) prepare, all-formed, hand-made, like a bride at a wedding — let her go far off; we push her away.

'She,' because *kṛtyā* 'witchcraft' is feminine. The name, *mahābṛhatī*, given to the verse, is improperly applied, ⌊if we understand it as defined by RV. Prāt. xvi. 48: here is meant rather that defined as of three *jāgata* pādas (12 + 12 : 11) at *Ind. Stud.* viii. 243⌋.

2. Having a head, having a nose, having ears, put together, all-formed, by the witchcraft-maker — let her go far off; we push her away.

The addition of a *ca* at the end of **a** would rectify the meter, and justify the Anukr. The *pada*-reading *çīrṣaṇ॰vátī* is by Prāt. iv. 99, and the word is quoted there in the comment as an example. Ppp. puts the adjectives in the accus., and reads, instead of our **c**: *pratyak pra hiṇmasi yaç cakāra tum ṛcchatu:* cf. vs. 5 **c** and v. 14. 11 **c**.

3. Çūdra-made, king-made, woman-made, made by Brahmans (*brahmán*), like a wife expelled (*nuttá*) by her husband, let her go to her maker, as connection.

Either 'as her' or 'as his connection'; Ppp. decides for the former, reading *bandhum* ⌊for our *bándhu*⌋. ⌊W's alternative seems to be: *bándhum* must be in apposition with *kartā́ram;* but *bándhv* (p. *bándhu*) must be a neuter (as at v. 13. 7) and so in apposition with the subject-nominative, *kṛtyā́* understood.⌋

4. With this herb have I spoiled all witchcrafts — what one they have made in the field, what in the kine, or what in thy men.

This is a repetition of iv. 18. 5, above. The Anukr. here, as there, takes no notice of the defective last pāda.

5. Let evil be to the evil-doer, a curse to the curser; backward we send [her] forth back, that she may slay the witchcraft-maker.

Ppp. reads for **a** *kṛtyās santu kṛtyākṛte*, and, for **c**, **d** *pratyak pratipravartaya yaç cakāra tum ṛcchatu.* To read in our **c** *hiṇmasi* (as Ppp. in vs. 2 **c**) would rectify the meter, of whose irregularity the Anukr. takes no notice. The *pada*-reading *prati॰prahiṇmaḥ* is by Prāt. iv. 95; the word is quoted there in the comment as example.

6. Opposed [is] the Āñgirasa, our appointed (*puróhita*) overseer; do thou, having turned the witchcrafts in the opposite direction, slay yonder witchcraft-makers.

Ppp. is corrupt, mixing up our verses 6 and 7. It combines *pratīcīnā "ñgi-* in 6 **a**.

7. He who said to thee "go forth," against the current, up-stream, him, O witchcraft, do thou return against; seek not us who are innocent.

Of this verse is legible in Ppp. *udāyyam* in **b**; as for our mss., they cannot be relied upon in the least to distinguish *pya* and *yya*, but the majority rather favor *udāyyàm*, while P. reads *-āryyàm*, D. *-ājyàm* (?), W. *-āhyam.* Neither word has been found anywhere else, but doubtless *udāpyàm* is the true form.

8. He who put together thy joints, as an *ṛbhú* [those] of a chariot with skill (*dhī́*), unto him go thou; there is thy going; this person is unknown to thee.

All the *saṁhitā*-mss. read *-va rbhur* in **b**.

9. They who, having made, took hold of thee, cunning sorcerers — this is a healthful (*çambhú*) spoiler of witchcraft, counteracting, reverting; therewith do we bathe thee.

The address changes, as often elsewhere, from the witchcraft to the bewitched person. Ppp. reads, in **c**, *vidma* for *çambhu*, and, in **d**, *pratisaram*. Our text ought to read in **c** *çambhv ìdám*, although all the mss. happen to agree here in lengthening the *i*.

10. In that we have come upon the ill-portioned one (fem.), bathed forth, whose young (*-vatsá*) is dead — let all ill (*pāpá*) go away from me; let property come unto (*upa-sthā*) me.

The *pada*-mss. have in **b** *upa॰eyimá*, and combination to *upeyimá* falls under the rule Prāt. iii. 38, although the *ā* contained in *eyimá* (= *ā-īyimá*) does not appear ⌊as *ā*⌋ in the *pada*-text. ⌊Ppp. ends **a** corruptly with *pṛṣṇipathāṁ*.⌋

11. In that they have taken (*grah*) the name of thee giving to the Fathers, or at the sacrifice — let these plants free thee from all ill that is designed (? *saṁdeçyà*).

It might be also (in **a**, **b**) 'those giving to the Fathers have taken the name of thee' (Ludwig, 'thy Fathers'). *Saṁdeçyà* is very obscure. The first half-verse is wholly corrupt in Ppp.

12. From sin against the gods, against the Fathers, from name-taking, that is designed, that is devised against [any one], let the plants free thee by their energy (*vīryà*), with spell (*bráhman*), with verses, with milk of the seers.

'Milk' (*páyas*) in the last pāda looks like a corrupt reading, but Ppp. appears to have the same; Bp.E. accent *payasā́*. ⌊As for the combinations of *-ā ṛ-*, see note to Prāt. iii. 46.⌋ Several mss. (Bp.O.p.m.R.T.K.) read *pitryàt* in **a**. The verse, which ought to be called an *anuṣṭubgarbhā triṣṭubh* (11 + 8 : 11 + 11 = 41), is very foolishly described by the Anukr. as a *pañkti*, because it contains nearly (and can easily be reduced to precisely) 40 syllables.

13. As the wind sets in motion the dust from the earth and the cloud (*abhrá*) from the atmosphere, so from me may everything of evil nature go away, pushed by the spell (*bráhman*).

14. Step away, making much noise, like an unfastened she-ass; attain thy makers, pushed hence by an energetic spell.

Some of the mss. (O.p.m.K.) read *kartrén* in **c**, as in other such cases.

15. Saying "this is the road, O witchcraft," we conduct thee; thee that wast sent forth against [us] we send forth back again; by that [road] go against [them], breaking, like a draft-cow with a cart, all-formed, wearing a wreath (? *kurūṭín*).

The last word is found only here, and has to be rendered conjecturally (with the Pet. Lexx.). All the *saṁhitā*-mss. ⌊or rather, most of them: see also note to Prāt. iii. 35⌋ combine *kṛtyé 'ti* ⌊and thus indeed the meter requires us to pronounce⌋; but our edition restores the more correct reading ⌊*kṛtya íti*⌋, since the Prāt. does not countenance the irregularity; we should expect to find it with *vandane 'va* (in ii. 56). Ppp. reads at the beginning *ayaṁ panthā 'pinayāmi tvā kṛtye prahitāṁ prati* etc.; in **c** ⌊or rather **c–d**⌋, *tuñjaty anasvinī 'va*. In the Anukr. it seems as if *catuṣpadā* must be a misreading for *pañcapadā* (11 + 11 : 8 + 8 + 8 = 46): but compare vs. 19.

16. Offward is light for thee, hitherward is no road for thee; make thy goings elsewhere than [toward] us; go thou by a distant [road] beyond ninety difficult navigable streams; do not wound thyself; go away.

One would like to emend *kṣaniṣṭhās* in **d**, perhaps to *kṣamiṣṭhās* 'be patient' i.e. 'linger'; Ppp. has instead *ghāniṣṭhāṣ*, which unfortunately gives no help. Ppp. also combines *nāvyā 'ti* in **c**; and the description of the Anukr. appears to sanction it.

17. As the wind the trees, do thou crush (*mṛ*) down, cause to fall; do not leave of them cow, horse, man; turning back, O witchcraft, from here to thy makers, awaken them unto childlessness.

Here, in **c**, even a majority of the mss. (W.I.O.D.T.K.) read *kartrén*. Ppp. combines at the beginning *vāte 'va*, as the meter demands, and as the Anukr. assumes; *úchiṣāi 'ṣām* is doubtless also the real reading in **b**.

18. What [witchcraft] they buried for thee in the *barhís*, what in the cemetery, [what] witchcraft or secret spell (*valagá*) in the field, or practised against thee in the householders' fire — they, being wiser, [against thee] who art simple, innocent.

Ppp. helps both meter and sense by inserting *cakrus* before *barhiṣi* in **a**; it also arranges *kṛtyāṁ kṣetre* in **b**, combines *dhīratarā 'nāg-* at the end, and adds, to complete the verse, *tam* ⌊so Roth's Collation! for *tām ?*⌋ *ito nāçayāmasi*. The Anukr. notices neither the deficiency in **a** nor the redundancy in **d**.

19. We have found out (*anu-vid*) the hostile sneaking magic (? *kártra*) that was applied, perceived (? *anu-budh*), buried: let that go whence it was brought; there let it roll about like a horse; let it slay the progeny of the witchcraft-maker.

Ppp. reads in **c** *āgatam* for *ābhṛtam*, and combines in **d** *açve 'va*, as called for by the meter. The Anukr. is as bad in its treatment of this verse as of 15.

20. There are knives of good metal in our house; we know thy joints, O witchcraft, how many they are; just stand up; go away from here; unknown one, what seekest thou here?

That is, 'thou who art no acquaintance of ours.' The Anukr. is much more scrupulous than usual in calling the verse (12 + 11 : 8 + 8 = 39) *virāj* ⌊scanning **a** perhaps as 11⌋. Ppp. begins with *svayasā*. The third pāda is quoted in Kāuç. 39. 19.

21. Thy neck-bones (*grīvā́*), O witchcraft, and thy (two) feet I will cut up; run thou out; let Indra-and-Agni defend us, they who are of progeny rich in progeny.

Prajā́vatī at the end looks like a corruption of *prajā́patī*, which Ppp. reads ⌊R's collation has *prajapatī*⌋. Ppp. also has in **c** *enāṁ vṛçcatā*. But Kāuç., which quotes the last half-verse in full in 5. 2, reads *prajāvatī*. The same half-verse appears also by *pratīka* in Vāit. 8. 6 (unless Vāit. takes it rather from Kāuç.).

22. King Soma [is] our over-ruler and favorer (*mṛḍitṛ́*); let the lords of being favor us.

The verse properly contains 22 syllables (11 + 11), and should therefore be called a *sāmnī triṣṭubh*. Ppp. reads in **b** *ṛtasya naṣ*.

23. Let Bhava-and-Çarva hurl (*as*) at the evil-doer, the witchcraft-maker, the ill-doer, the missile of the gods, the lightning.

Ppp. reads in **a** *pāpakṛtvane* ⌊which is metrically much better⌋. The definition of the verse by the Anukr. is very stupid; it is plainly two *triṣṭubh* pādas, with an intruded word of three syllables (either *duṣkṛ́te* or *vidyútam;* either could be spared). The mss. insert a cesura-mark after *kṛtyākṛ́te*.

24. If thou camest [as] biped, as quadruped, put together by the witchcraft-maker, all-formed, do thou, becoming octoped, go away again from here, O misfortune!

The verse has the same structure as 20. The *pada*-text here and in vs. 28 reads *ā○iyátha*.

25. Anointed, smeared, well-adorned, bearing all difficulty, go thou away; recognize (*jñā*), O witchcraft, thy maker, as a daughter her own father.

The definition of this verse appears to be omitted in the Anukr., as we can hardly be meant to take it for an *anuṣṭubh*. The first pāda is capable of being crowded together into 8 syllables, or expanded into 12 (either procedure being about equally strained), making the verse either an *urobṛhatī* or a *prastārapañkti*. It is quoted in Kāuç. 39. 18.

26. Go away, O witchcraft; stand not; lead, as it were, the track of one pierced; it is a deer, thou a deer-hunter; it is unable to put thee down.

'Lead,' in **b**, appears to be used in the sense of 'follow'; the 'track' is doubtless that of the maker: ⌊cf. note to xi. 2. 13⌋. The *pada*-text divides *mṛga○yúḥ:* cf. Prāt. iii. 18.

27. Also the after one (*ápara*) slays with an arrow, fitting it (?), the one shooting (*-āsin*) in front; also of the front one, smiting down, the after one smites down in return.

This obscure and probably corrupt verse gets no help from Ppp., which merely reads *uto* for *uta* in **c**. The Pet. Lex. suggests emendation of *-dā́ya* to *-dhā́ya* in **b**, and the translation implies the change.

28. Hear thou, verily, these words of mine; then go whence thou camest, to meet him who made thee.

Ppp. reads at the end *punaḥ* for *prati*.

29. The slaying of an innocent person is indeed fearful, O witchcraft; slay thou not our cow, horse, man; wheresoever thou art set down, from there we make thee stand up; become thou lighter than a leaf.

The *pada*-text has in **d** *út : sthāp-*; the example of the omitted *s* is quoted under Prāt. ii. 18. The verse (10 + 10 : 8 + 8 + 8 = 44) is very badly defined by the Anukr. Ppp. reads in **a** *-hatyam* and *bhīmam*.

30. If ye are covered (*ā-vṛ*) with darkness, like those who are girt (*abhi-dhā*) with a net — having torn up (*sam-lup*) all witchcrafts from here, we send them forth again to the maker.

The *pada*-text strangely reads *ā́॰vṛtā* in **a**, instead of *-tāḥ*.

31. The progeny of the witchcraft-maker, of him of secret spells, of him that devises against [others], O witchcraft, do thou kill; do not leave [them alive]; slay yonder witchcraft-makers.

Ppp. uses the singular in **d**.

32. As the sun is freed out of darkness, [and] quits the night and the ensigns of the dawn, so do I quit all evil-natured magic made by the witchcraft-maker, as an elephant the difficult haze (?*rájas*).

Ppp. puts *tamasas* before *mucyate* in **a**, reads *ketum* at end of **b**, and omits **d** altogether. The verse (12 + 11 : 8 + 8 + 11 = 50) lacks two syllables of being a full *atijagatī* (52). The *pratīka* (*yathā sūrya*) is quoted in Kāuç. 39. 26; but the comm. regards vii. 13. 1, and not this, as the verse intended.

⌊The quoted Anukr. says *dve* (i.e. 2 above the norm of 30).⌋

2. The wonderful structure of man.

[*Nārāyaṇa. — trayastrin̄çat. pārṣṇisūktam; pāuruṣam; brahmaprakāçisūktam* (*31, 32. sākṣātparabrahmaprakāçinyāu*). *ānuṣṭubham: 1–4, 7, 8. triṣṭubh; 6, 11. jagatī; 28. bhurig bṛhatī.*]

Found also (except vss. 8, 18, 23, 28) in Pāipp. xvi. (in the verse-order 1–7, 26, 27, 9–12, 17, 15, 13, 14, 16, 22, 19, 24, 25, 20, 21, 30, 29, 31, 32, 33). Quoted (vs. 1) in Vāit. 37. 19, together with the other *puruṣasūkta* (xix. 6), in the *puruṣamedha* or human sacrifice; not noticed in Kāuç.

Translated: Muir, v. 375 (nearly all); Ludwig, p. 398; Scherman, *Philosophische Hymnen*, p. 41 (nearly all); Deussen, *Geschichte*, i. 1. 265; Henry, 5, 45; Griffith, ii. 6.

1. By whom were brought the two heels of a man (*púruṣa*)? by whom was his flesh put together? by whom his two ankle-joints (*gulphá*)? by whom his cunning (*péçana*) fingers? by whom his apertures? by whom his (two) *uchlakhás* in the midst? who [put together] his footing (*pratiṣṭhā́*)?

The *pada*-text divides *ut॰çlakhāú*, as if there were such a word as *çlakha*. Ppp. reads, instead of *keno 'chlakhāu*, *keno 'cchinaṁ ko*; also, in **a**, *pārṣṇīy ābhṛte pāuruṣasya*; and, in **c**, *peçinīṣ*. *Péçana* is more literally 'arranging, adorning.'

2. From what, now, did they make a man's two ankle-joints below, his two knee-joints above? separating (?*nir-ṛ*) his two back-thighs (*jáṅghā*), where, forsooth, did they set them in? the two joints of his knees — who indeed understands (*cit*) that?

Nirṛtya is a difficult and doubtful expression here. Ppp. reads *nirṛtijaṅghe ni dadhuḥ;* also, in **d**, *saṁdhīm ū ca jānā*. In **b** it has again *pāuruṣasya*.

3. There is joined, fourfold (*cátuṣṭaya*), with closed (*sáṁhita-*) ends, above the two knees, the pliant (*çithirá*) trunk; what the hips are, the thighs — who indeed produced (*jan*) that, by which the body (*kúsindha*) became very firm?

Ppp. reads *saṁhatantaṁ* in **a**, and *sudhṛtam* in **d**.

4. How many gods [and] which were they, who gathered (*ci*) the breast, the neck-bones of man? how many disposed the two teats? who the two collar-bones (? *kaphoḍá*)? how many gathered the shoulder-bones (pl.)? how many the ribs?

Ppp. has again *pāuruṣasya* in **b**. In **c** it reads *ni dadhuṣ kaṣ kapolāu*. The mss. are extremely discordant as to the form of the word which our edition gives as *kaphāuḍāú;* that is the reading of Bp.W.D.; P.M.R.s.m. have *kapheḍāú*, I. *kaphāujhāú*, E.O.R.p.m.T.K. *kaphoḍāú* (which accordingly has the most authority in its favor ⌊all SPP's mss. read so⌋); several *saṁhitā*-mss. (P.M.T.O.p.m.R.s.m.) have *káṣ* before it. The meaning given is, of course, conjectural only; 'collar-bone' is Ludwig's guess, and seems to suit the connection (though that is a rather weak ground of preference) better than the '*perhaps* elbow' of the Pet. Lexx. The Anukr. takes no notice of the lacking syllable in **a**.

5. Who brought together his two arms, saying "he must perform heroism"? what god then set on his two shoulders upon the body (*kúsindha*)?

⌊Ppp. has *kṛṇavān* for *karavāt* in **b**, and, for **d**, *kvasindhād adhādadhi.*⌋

6. Who bored out the seven apertures in his head — these ears, the nostrils, the eyes, the mouth? in the might of whose conquest (*vijayá*) in many places quadrupeds [and] bipeds go their way.

Bp. reads at the end *yā́man*. Ppp. puts *nāsike* after *cakṣaṇī*, and reads in **c** *vijāyasya mahamani*, and at the end *yomūn*. The Anukr. does not heed that **d** is a *triṣṭubh* pāda.

7. Since in his jaws he put his ample (*purūcī*) tongue, then attached (*adhi-çri*) [to it] great voice; he rolls greatly on among existences, clothing himself in the waters: who indeed understands that?

With **c** is to be compared ix. 10. 11 **d**; the irregularity of the pāda is not noticed by the Anukr. Ppp. reads instead of **c**: *sa ā varīvarti mahinā vyomaṁ : avasānaṣ kata cit pra veda*. Our text ought to read *varīvartti*.

8. Which was that god who [produced] his brain, his forehead, his hindhead (? *kakā́ṭikā*), who first his skull, who, having gathered a gathering in man's jaws, ascended to heaven?

D. reads *cityám* in **c**; all the mss. agree in *ruroha*, although *ruróha* is obviously required. ⌊Otherwise Henry.⌋ The verse, as noted above, is wanting in Ppp.

9. Numerous things dear and not dear, sleep, oppressions and wearinesses, delights and pleasures — from where does formidable man bring (*vah*) them?

Ppp. reads in **b** *-tandriyaḥ*, and in **d** again *pāur-*.

10. Whence now in man [come] mishap, ruin, perdition, misery, accomplishment, success, non-failure? whence thought (*matí*), uprisings (*úditi*)?

The minor Pet. Lex. suggests for *úditi* 'end, disappearance.' Ppp. reads in **b** *kuto 'dhi pur-*. *Vṛddhis* instead of *ávy-* would improve both sense and meter.

11. Who disposed in him waters, moving apart, much moving, produced for river-running, strong (*tīvrá*), ruddy, red, dark and turbid, upward, downward, crosswise in man?

Ppp. reads in **a** *āpo dadhāt*, and in **c** combines (as the meter requires us to read) *tīvrā 'ruṇā*. The verse (8 + 8 + 7 : 11 + 11 = 45) is very stupidly defined as *jagatī* by the Anukr.

12. Who set form in him? who both bulk (*mahmán*) and name? who [set] in him progress (*gātú*)? who display (*ketú*)? who [set] behaviors (*carítra*) in man?

Ppp. again *pāuruṣe* at the end.

13. Who wove in him breath? who expiration and respiration (*vyāná*)? what god attached (*adhi-çri*) conspiration (*samāná*) to man here?

Ppp. reads *adadhāt* for *avayat* in **a**, and again *pāuruṣe*.

14. What one god set sacrifice in man here? who [set] in him truth? who untruth? whence [comes] death? whence the immortal?

Ppp. reads, for **b** etc., *eko 'gre adhi pāuruṣe : ko anṛtaṁ ko mṛtyuṁ ko amṛtaṁ dadhāu*.

15. Who put about him clothing (*vā́sas*)? who prepared (*kalpay-*) his life-time? who extended to him strength? who prepared his swiftness?

Ppp. reads for **a** *ko vāsasā pari dadhāt*, and elides *ko 'syā-* in **d**.

16. With what did he stretch the waters along? with what did he make the day to shine? with what did he kindle (*anu-idh*) the dawn? with what did he give the coming-on of evening?

The *pada*-text reads *ā́paḥ* (as in 11 **a**) in **a**. Ppp. elides *'nv* after it. ⌊For *āindha*, cf. *Gram.* § 684 c.⌋

17. Who put in him seed, saying "let his line be extended"? who conveyed into him wisdom? who gave (*dhā*) [him] music? who dances?

Ppp. has, for **a**, *ko 'smin reto 'dadhāt;* at end of **b**, *itaḥ ;* for **d**, *ko vāçāṁ ko anṛtaṁ dadhāu*.

18. With what did he cover this earth? with what did he surround the sky? by what is man a match for (*abhí*) mountains in greatness? by what, for deeds?

This verse, as noted above, is wanting in Ppp.

19. With what does he go after Parjanya? with what [after] the out-looking Soma? with what [after] both sacrifice and faith? by whom was mind put in him?

Ppp. reads *āpnoti* for *anv eti*, and has for **c**, **d** our 20 **c**, **d** (but *puruṣaḥ* in **c**).

20. Wherewith does he obtain one learned in revelation (*çrótriya*)? wherewith this most exalted one? wherewith does man [obtain] this Agni? wherewith did he measure (make?) the year?

Ppp. has for **b** our 19 **b** again; also *puruṣaḥ* in **c**.

21. The *bráhman* obtains one learned in revelation, the *bráhman* this most exalted one; the *bráhman* [as] man this Agni; the *bráhman* measured the year.

Here and in vss. 23 and 25 an instrumental is distinctly and strongly called for, instead of the nominative *bráhma;* yet to call *bráhma* an instr., and translate it as such, does not seem possible. ⌊Cf. Caland, KZ. xxxi. 261.⌋ Ppp. reads, for **c**, **d**, *brahma yajñasya çraddhā ca brahmā 'smi ca hataṁ manaḥ.*

22. Wherewith does he dwell upon (?*anu-kṣi*) the gods? wherewith [upon] the people of the god-folk? wherewith this other asterism? whereby is authority (*kṣatrá*) called real (*sát*)?

The sense here is very obscure, and the rendering mechanical. ⌊Griffith suggests that the point may lie in using *nakṣatram* as if it were *na kṣatram*, 'non-power,' in opposition to *kṣatram* in **d**.⌋ Ppp. has, for **b**, *kena devīr ajanayad diçaḥ*. The meter requires in **a** *kṣyati*, as the forms are written in some texts. The Anukr. takes no notice of the irregularity.

23. The *bráhman* dwells upon the gods, the *bráhman* [upon] the people of the god-folk; the *bráhman* this other asterism; the *bráhman* is called real authority.

This verse is wanting in Ppp.

24. By whom is this earth disposed? by whom the sky set above? by whom this atmosphere, the expanse, set aloft and across?

Ppp. reads, for **a**, *kene 'daṁ bhūmir nihataḥ.*

25. By the *bráhman* is the earth disposed; the *bráhman* [is] the sky set above, the *bráhman* this atmosphere, the expanse, set aloft and across.

Ppp. reads, for **a**, **b**, *brahmaṇā bhūmir niyatā brahma dyām uttarāṁ dadhāu*, thus relieving in **b** the difficulty as to the construction of *brahma*. ⌊Cf. note to vs. 21.⌋

26. Atharvan, having sewed together his head, and also (*yát*) his heart — aloft from the brain the purifying one sent [them] forth, out of the head.

'The purifying one' (*pávamāna*) is soma; it is perhaps identified here with Atharvan; but the whole sense is extremely obscure. Ppp. reads at the end *çīrṣṇaḥ*.

27. Verily that head of Atharvan [is] a god-vessel, pressed together; breath defends that, the head, food, also mind.

For *samubjita*, as said of a *koça*, compare ix. 3. 20 above. Ppp. reads *prāṇo 'bhi* in **c**, and *çrīm* for *çiras* in **d**. The three nouns in **d** might be nom. instead of accus.

28. Was he now created upward (*ūrdhvá*)? [or] was he now created crosswise? did man grow unto (*ā-bhū*) all the quarters? — he who knoweth the *bráhman's* stronghold, from which man is [so] called.

The meaning of the protracted final syllables here is unquestionable, although it has been overlooked by both Muir and Ludwig. The cases of protraction call out much treatment from the Prāt.: see the rules i. 70, 97, 105; iv. 6, 120, 121, and the notes upon them. The mss. differ in regard to accenting or leaving unaccented the final syllable of **b**; nor is the usage of either RV. or AV. sufficiently settled to determine which reading ought to be preferred. *Puruṣa* in this verse and the sequel seems to approach its later meaning of 'supernal Person or Spirit.' There is no apparent connection between the two halves of the verse: for the second, see vs. 30. The whole verse is wanting in Ppp. The Anukr. should have called it a *prastārapañkti; bhurig bṛhatī* is purely mechanical (10 + 11 : 8 + 8 = 37).

29. Whoever indeed knoweth that *bráhman's* stronghold, covered with *amṛ́ta* — unto him both the *bráhman* and the Brahmans have given sight, breath, progeny.

The verse is found also in TA. (i. 27. 3), which reads *purīm* at end of **b**, *brahmā* for *brāhmāç* in **b**, and *āyuḥ kīrtim* for *cakṣuḥ prāṇam* in **d** (the accentuation is corrupt and worthless through the whole verse). Ppp. has also in **d** *āyus* for *cakṣuḥ*, and at the end *dadhuḥ*.

30. Him verily sight doth not desert, nor breath, before old age, who knoweth the *bráhman's* stronghold (*púr*), from which man (*púruṣa*) is [so] called.

The latter half-verse is identical with 28 **c**, **d**. Ppp. reads *puraḥ* at end of **b**, and *yasmāt* in **d**.

31. Eight-wheeled, nine-doored, is the impregnable stronghold of the gods; in that is a golden vessel, heaven-going (*svargá*), covered with light.

The verse is found also in TA. (i. 27. 2–3), which reads *hiraṇmayas* in **c**, and inserts *lokás* after *svargás* in **d**. ⌊Reminiscences of this verse are seen in x. 8. 43 **a**, **b**.⌋

32. In that golden vessel, three-spoked, having three supports — what soul-possessing monster (*yakṣá*) there is in it, that verily the knowers of the *bráhman* know.

Ppp. reads in **b** *tridive* for *tryare*, and, in **c**, *antar* for *yakṣam*. ⌊Pādas **c**, **d** recur at x. 8. 43 **c**, **d**.⌋

33. The *bráhman* entered into the resplendent, yellow, golden, unconquered stronghold, that was all surrounded with glory.

The verse is found also in TA. (i. 27. 3–4), which again reads *hiraṇmayīm*, and *brahmā́ viveça* ⌊so both ed's⌋ (the accent has no authority, as it is full of faults in this vicinity; but the comm. explains *brahmā́* as = *prajāpatiḥ*: which also does not go for much). ⌊TA. has further *vi-* for *pra-* at the beginning and ends with *-jitā* (which the comm. explains as *-jitām*).⌋ Ppp. likewise has *hiraṇmayīm*; and further, in **d** *viveçā ca parājitaḥ*.

⌊The quoted Anukr. says for this second hymn *tisraḥ* (i.e. 3 above the norm of 30). — Here ends the first *anuvāka*, with 2 hymns and 65 verses.⌋

3. With an amulet of varaṇá.

[*Atharvan.* — *pañcaviṅçakam. mantroktavaraṇadevatyam uta vānaspatyaṁ; cāndramasam. ānuṣṭubham: 2, 3, 6. bhurik triṣṭubh; 8, 13, 14. pathyāpañkti; 11, 16. bhurij; 15, 17–25. 6-p. jagatī.*]

Found also in Pāipp. xvi. (in the verse-order 1–7, 9, 8, 10–13, 15, 14, 16, 17, 19, 22, 21, 20, 18, 24; 23 and 25 are wanting). Quoted (vs. 1) in Kāuç. 19. 22, with three other hymns, in connection with the binding on of amulets for welfare. Not noticed in Vāit.

Translated: Zimmer, p. 60 (17 vss.); Henry, 9, 53; Griffith, ii. 11; Bloomfield, 81, 605.

1. This *varaṇá* [is] my rival-destroying, virile (*vṛ́ṣan*) amulet; with it do thou take hold of thy foes, slaughter thy injurers (*durasy-*).

The *varaṇa* is a tree, the *Cratæva Roxburghii* found throughout India. The name comes doubtless from the root *vṛ* 'cover, protect, ward off'; and the hymn is full of allusions to a connection with that root; ⌊cf. the play in iv. 7. 1 and vi. 85. 1⌋. Ppp. reads throughout *varuṇa*, which is also in later Skt. recognized as a form of the tree-name.

2. Crush them, slaughter, take hold; be the amulet thy forerunner in front; the gods by the *varaṇá* warded off the hostile practice (*abhyācārá*) of the Asuras from one morrow to another.

The comm. to Prāt. iii. 80 quotes the beginning of the verse as example of *eṇa* after *pra*. It is unnecessary to view, with the Anukr., the verse as redundant. Ppp. combines *te 'stu* in **b**.

3. This amulet, the *varaṇá*, all-healing, thousand-eyed, yellow, golden — it shall make thy foes go downward; do thou, in front, damage them that hate thee.

Ppp. reads *hiraṇmayaḥ* at end of **b**, and *yas* for *sa* at beginning of **c**. The verse is rather *svarāj* than *bhurij*.

4. This *varaṇá* [shall ward off] the witchcraft extended for thee; this shall shield thee against fear arising from men, this against all evil.

Ppp. preserves unity of construction through the verse, by reading, for **b**, **c**: *pāuruṣeyam ayaṁ vadham: ayaṁ te sarvaṁ pāpmānaṁ.*

5. The *varaṇá,* this divine forest-tree, shall ward off; the *yákṣma* that has entered into this man — that have the gods warded off.

We had this verse above, as vi. 85. 1. The Anukr. takes no notice in either place of the deficient syllable in **a**. Ppp. reads here, for **b**, *idaṁ devo bṛhaspatiḥ;* and, for **c**, *yakṣmā pratiṣṭhā yo 'smin;* ⌊and then *tam u* etc.⌋.

6. If, having slept, thou shalt see an evil dream; if a wild beast (*mṛgá*) shall run a disagreeable course — from overmuch (?*pari-*) sneezing, from the evil utterance of a bird (*çakúni*), this amulet, the *varaṇá,* shall shield thee.

The translation implies in **b** emendation of *yáti* to *yádi,* which seems unavoidable. Ppp., however, appears to have *yati;* it reads further in **b** *mṛgaçrutaṁ* and *ajuṣṭaṁ,* in **c** *paricchavā,* ⌊and in **d** *vārayātāi*⌋. The verse is included in the *duḥsvapna-nāçana gaṇa:* see note to Kāuç. 46. 9.

7. From the niggard, from perdition, from sorcery, also from fear, from the more violent deadly weapon of death, the *varaṇá* shall shield thee.

Ppp. reads, for **d**, *tvaṁ varuṇo vāraya.*

8. What sin my mother, what my father, and what my own brothers, what we ourselves have done, from that shall this divine forest-tree shield us.

Ppp. reads *tasmāt* for *tatas* in **d**, and, for **e**, *idaṁ deva bṛhaspatiḥ:* compare its version of 5 **b**.

9. Driven (*vyath*) forth by the *varaṇá,* my enemies (*bhrā́tṛvya*) [who are my] kinsmen have gone unto unlighted (? *asū́rta*) space (*rájas*); let them go to lowest darkness.

⌊Bloomfield discusses *asū́rta,* JAOS. xvi., p. clxii = PAOS. Dec. 1894.⌋

10. Unharmed [am] I, with unharmed kine, long-lived, having all my men; let this amulet, the *varaṇá,* protect me, being such, from every quarter.

Ppp. reads in **b** *-pāuruṣaḥ* (as usual, where *pūr-* and not *pur-* is meant).

11. This *varaṇá* on my breast, king, divine forest-tree — let it drive (*bādh*) away my foes, as Indra the barbarians, the Asuras.

The verse is quoted in the schol. to Kāuç. 10. 2. Ppp. combines *varuṇo 'rasi,* as the meter requires, but as the Anukr. takes pains not to authorize. Ppp. also exchanges the second halves of vss. 11 and 12.

12. I bear this *varaṇá* being long-lived, one of a hundred autumns; may it assign to me both kingdom and authority, to me cattle and force.

Ppp., as noted above, reads for the second half of this verse our 11 **c**, **d**, and *vice versa.*

13. As the wind breaks with force the trees, the forest-trees, so do thou break my rivals, those born before and after; let the *varaṇá* defend thee.

Ppp. reads *jīrṇān* for *vṛkṣān* in **b**; and, in **c**, *-tnāṅs tvaṁ bhañdhi.* ⌊With **d**, cf. the Ppp. vs. cited under iii. 6. 2.⌋

14. As both wind and fire devour (*psā*) the trees, the forest-trees, so do thou devour my rivals, those born etc. etc.

Ppp. again relieves the redundancy of expression by reading *sarvān* instead of *vṛkṣān* in **b**; also it has in **c** *-tnāṅs tvam* for *-tnān me.*

15. As, destroyed by the wind, the trees lie prostrate (*nyàrpita*), so do thou destroy, prostrate my rivals, those born etc. etc.

Ppp. is quite corrupt in this verse, but does not appear to offer any variant. *Prá kṣiṇīhi* properly ought to be divided in our text.

16. Them, O *varaṇá*, do thou cut off (*pra-chid*), before what is appointed (*diṣṭá*), before [the end of] their life-time — them who strive to damage him in respect to cattle, and who are intent to damage his kingdom.

Ppp. reads, for **b**, *purā dṛṣṭān parā "yuṣaḥ.* ⌊In **c**, pronounce *yāt 'nam.*⌋

17. As the sun shines exceedingly, as in it brilliancy is set, so let the *varaṇá* amulet fix (*ni-yam*) in me fame [and] growth; let it sprinkle me with brilliancy; let it anoint me with glory.

Part of the mss. (P.M.D.) accent *asmín* in **b**. Ppp. reads, for **c** etc., *evā sapatnāṅs tvaṁ sarvān ati bhāhi syaçvo varuṇas tvā 'bhi rakṣatu.* ⌊Either Mr. Whitney took *me* as locative (*Gram.* § 492 a); or else his 'in me' is an inadvertence for 'for me.'⌋

18. As glory [is] in the moon, and in the men-beholding Āditya, so let the *varaṇá* amulet etc. etc.

From here on, Ppp. has the same refrain ⌊as the Berlin text⌋, only reading at the end *mām.*

19. As glory [is] in the earth, as in this Jātavedas, so let the *varaṇá* amulet etc. etc.

20. As glory [is] in the maiden, as in this constructed (*sámbhṛta*) chariot, so let the *varaṇá* amulet etc. etc.

21. As glory [is] in Soma-drink, as in honey-mixture [is] glory, so let the *varaṇá* amulet etc. etc.

22. As glory [is] in the *agnihotrá*, as in the *váṣaṭ*-utterance [is] glory, so let the *varaṇá* amulet etc. etc.

All the mss. save P.M.O. have *yaço 'gnihotre* in **a**, and this is accordingly the better-supported reading.

23. As glory [is] set in the sacrificer, as in this sacrifice, so let the *varaṇá* amulet etc. etc.

Wanting in Ppp., as above noted.

24. As glory [is] in Prajāpati, as in this most exalted one, so let the *varaṇá* amulet etc. etc.

Ppp. reads *jātavedasi* instead of *parameṣṭhini.*

25. As in the gods [is] immortality (*amṛ́ta*), as in them is set truth, so let the *varaṇá* amulet etc. etc.

⌊The quoted Anukr. seems to say "*varaṇāu*" (intending *varaṇo ?*).⌋

4. Against snakes and their poison.

[*Garutman.* — *ṣaḍviṅçati. takṣakadāivatam. ānuṣṭubham: 1. pathyāpañkti; 2. 3-p. yavamadhyā gāyatrī; 3, 4. pathyābṛhatī; 8. uṣṇiggarbhā parātriṣṭubh; 12. bhurig gāyatrī; 16. 3-p. pratiṣṭhā gāyatrī; 21. kakummatī; 23. triṣṭubh; 26. 3-av. 6-p. bṛhatīgarbhā kakummatī bhurik triṣṭubh.*]

Found also in Pāipp. xvi. (with one or two changes of order: see below). Not noticed in Vāit. Quoted (vs. 1), as addressed to Takṣaka (king of the serpent-divinities), in Kāuç. 32. 20, and also 139. 8, in the ceremonies of beginning Vedic study (see further under vss. 25, 26).

Translated: Ludwig, p. 502; Henry, 11, 56; Griffith, ii. 14; Bloomfield, 152, 605.

1. Indra's [was] the first chariot, the gods' the after chariot, Varuna's the third one; the snakes' chariot, the furthest one (?), hath run against the pillar: then may it come to harm (?).

There are very questionable points here; the translation of **d** implies emendation of *apamā́* (p. *apa°mā́*) to *apamás;* yet *apa-mā́* might perhaps be understood adverbially (like *upamā́*, p. *upa°mā́:* twice in RV.). Ppp. reads *upama* here. The translation of the last clause implies the reading *áthā riṣat*, which is given by several mss. (P.M.I.K.) and by Ppp., and which the meter favors; but such variants as *ariṣat* for *arṣat* are found elsewhere, and the ms. authority is decidedly in favor of *arṣat*, as the *pada*-texts read (but Kp. *ardvyat*, by a curious blunder) — if only we knew what to make of it. No indicative form not an aorist can be coördinated with *ārat.*

2. *Darbhá*-grass, brightness, young shoot (? *tarū́ṇaka*); horse's tail-tuft, rough-one's tail-tuft; chariot's seat (? *bándhura*).

The translation, of course, is only mechanical. ⌊Henry, *Mém. de la Soc. de Ling.*, ix. 238, corrects an error of his version.⌋ We should have expected the Anukr. at least to add *bhurij* to its definition of the verse as a *gāyatrī* (8 + 11 : 6 = 25). O. (and E. in margin) read *puruṣasya* in **b**.

3. Smite down, O white one, with the foot, both the fore and the hind; like water-floated wood, sapless [is] the snakes' poison, fierce water (*vā́r*).

Ppp. puts the verse after our 4, and reads at the end *vār id ugram.* Part of our mss. (T.D.K.) read *vā́r*, accented, in both verses, and that seems most likely to be the true reading; the translation adopts it. ⌊Pischel takes it as "halte auf," *Ved. Stud.*,

ii. 75.⌋ The first half-verse is read in several *gṛhya-sūtras* (AGS. ii. 3. 3; PGS. ii. 14. 4; ÇGS. iv. 18; HGS. ii. 16. 8), as part of a verse in a charm against serpents; they all begin with *apa* instead of *ava*. ⌊Cf. also MGS. ii. 7. 1 a.⌋ The verse (8 + 8 : 8 + 8 + 3) would be more properly called *upariṣṭād bṛhatī*. ⌊Cf. xviii. 1. 32 n.⌋

4. The *araṁghuṣá*, having immerged, having emerged, said again: like water-floated wood, sapless is the snake's poison, fierce water.

The *pada*-text divides *aram○ghuṣáḥ* in **a**, and the Pet. Lexx. conjecture the meaning accordingly to be 'loud-sounding.' ⌊Pischel discusses the vs., *Ved. Stud.*, ii. 74.⌋ Ppp. is corrupt at the beginning, but seems to read *udañghojyonmajya punar* etc.; ⌊again it ends with *vār id ugram*⌋.

5. Pāidva slays the *kasarṇīla* (snake), Pāidva the whitish and the black; Pāidva hath split altogether the head of the *ratharví*, of the *pṛdākū́*.

Pāidva 'of Pedu' is the white snake-destroying horse given by the Açvins to Pedu (RV. i. 117–119). ⌊Cf. Bergaigne, *Rel. Véd.* ii. 451.⌋ For *kasarṇīlam* Ppp. reads *kvaṣarṣṇīlam*, and, for *ratharvyās*, *rathavrihā*. The exceptional accent of *pṛdākvā́ḥ* is noted in the comm. to Prāt. iii. 60. The *pada*-text divides neither *kasarṇī́la* nor *ratharví*.

6. Go forth first, O Pāidva; we come after thee; cast thou out the snakes from the road by which we come.

7. Here was Pāidva born; this [is] his going-away; these [are] the tracks of the snake-slaying vigorous steed.

⌊For the difficult and debatable form *ahighnyo*, BR. and W. assume a stem *ahighní*. This is probably to be considered, not as a feminine formation (cf. my *Noun-Inflection*, JAOS. x., p. 384), but rather as a masculine, like the masc. proper names *Tíraçcī́* (l.c., p. 367 end), or, better, like the masculines *ahī́*, *āpathī́*, *prāvī́*, *starī́* etc. (about a dozen of them, l.c., p. 369, middle: genitive *ahyò* etc.). In the latter case we might regard the printed accent *ahighnyó*, when contrasted with the *ahyò* of the RV., as characteristic of the AV. (cf. l.c., p. 369 top): but both W's and SPP's authorities are here uncertain as to the accent: the majority have *ahighnyó*, p. *ahi○ghnyáḥ*; K. and three of SPP's have *ahighnyò*; while W's D. and SPP's P.² have *áhi○ghnyaḥ*. — Or have we, after all, to assume a stem *ahighnī* (cf. *sahasraghnī*, xi. 2. 12), of which this would be a genitive like *ary-ás*? — One wonders why the reading is not simply *ahighnó*; but not a ms., either of W's or of SPP's, gives that reading. — Cf. *atighnyàs*, xi. 7. 16.⌋

8. What is shut together may it not open; what is opened may it not shut together; in this field [are] two snakes, both a female and a male; those [are] both sapless.

The first half-verse we had above as vi. 56. 1 **c**, **d** ⌊see note for suggested emendation⌋, also applied to a snake. The curiously irregular verse (7 + 7 : 8 [7 ?] + 11 = 33) is strangely defined by the Anukr.

9. Sapless here [are] the snakes, they that are near and they that are far; with a club (*ghaná*) I slay the stinger (*vṛ́çcika*), with a staff the snake that has come.

The second half-verse is found in a suppl. to RV. i. 191; see Aufrecht's RV.[2], p. 672; instead of *ahim* is there read *aham*. Ppp. reads *ye 'nti te ca* in **b**; and all our mss. ⌊save D., which has *áti*⌋ leave *anti* unaccented (it is emended to *ánti* in our text), as if by some carelessness *yé 'nti* had been changed to *yé anti;* it is one of the strangest of the many strange blunders of the AV. text. ⌊One might think that this vs. or one much like it was had in mind by Karṇa in his address to Çalya, MBh. viii. 40. 33 = 1848.⌋

10. This is the remedy of both, of the ill-horse (*aghāçvá*) and of the constrictor; the mischievous (*aghāy-*) snake hath Indra, the snake hath Pāidva put in my power (*randhay-*).

The Anukr. takes no notice of any deficiency in **b**; it can only be supplied by the violent resolution *su-aj-*. Ppp. rectifies the meter by the better reading *vṛçcikasya ca* ⌊cf. our 15 **c**, **d**, below⌋.

11. We reverence Pāidva, the staunch one, of staunch abode (*-dhā́man*); here behind sit *pṛ́dākus*, plotting forth.

Ppp. combines at the end *-dhyatā "sate*. The Anukr. treats **b** as regular, thus sanctioning the resolution *-dhā-ma-naḥ*.

12. Of lost lives, of lost poison [are they], slain by the thunderbolt-bearing Indra; Indra hath slain, we have slain.

13. Slain [are] the cross-lined ones, crushed down the *pṛ́dākus;* slay thou the whitish [snake] that makes a great hood, the black snake, in the *darbhá*-grasses.

'Hood,' *dárvi*, lit. 'spoon.' Ppp. reads in **c** *kanikradam*. ⌊The first half recurs as the second of vs. 20.⌋

14. The little girl of the Kirātas, she the little one, digs a remedy, with golden shovels, upon the ridges (*sā́nu*) of the mountains.

15. Hither hath come the young physician, slayer of the spotted ones, unconquered; he verily is a grinder-up of both, the constrictor and the stinger.

16. Indra hath put the snake in my power, [also] both Mitra and Varuṇa, and Vāta ('wind') and Parjanya, both of them.

The name given by the Anukr. to the verse is of uncertain value; it is possible to read the last pāda either as 8 or as 6 syllables. Ppp. reads in **a** *me 'hīn ajambhayat*. Many of our mss. (P.I.O.R.T.K.) ⌊and the majority of SPP's⌋ read in **c** *-janyò 'bhā́*, but it is contrary to all rule and analogy; ⌊and W's Bp. and SPP's *pada*-text give *-janyà ubhā́*⌋.

17. Indra hath put the snake in my power, the *pṛ́dāku* and the she-*pṛdākū́*, the constrictor, the cross-lined one, the *kasarṇīla*, the *dáçonasi*.

The accent *pṛdākvám* (instead of *-kvàm*) is read by all the mss., and hence by our text; but it is incontestably wrong. The Anukr. takes no notice of the lacking syllable in **c**. Ppp. reads ⌊for **a**⌋ *pāidvo me 'hīn ajambhayat*, and ⌊for **d**⌋ *kuçirṇīlaṁ naçonaçīṁ*.

18. Indra hath slain first thy progenitor, O snake; of them, being shattered, what forsooth can be their sap?

Ppp. reads *vas* instead of *u* in **c**.

19. Since I have grasped together their heads, as a fisherman the *kárvara*; having gone away to the middle of the river, I have washed out the snake's poison.

The mss. do not in general distinguish *ṣṭ* and *ṣṭh*, and *pāuñjiṣṭa* would be equally correct here. Ppp. reads *pāuñjiṣṭhī 'va*.

20. The poison of all snakes let the rivers carry away; slain [are] the cross-lined ones, crushed down the *pṛ́dākus*.

21. I choose as it were the filaments of herbs successfully; I conduct as it were mares; O snake, let thy poison come out.

Apparently processes analogous to that of extracting the poison are referred to. The *pada*-division *sādhu°yā́* is prescribed by Prāt. iv. 30. There seems to be no reason why the Anukr. should call the verse *kakummatī*.

22. What poison is in fire, in the sun, what in the earth, in herbs, *kāndā*-poison, *kanáknaka* — let thy poison come out; let it come.

Ppp. has *karikradam* ⌊cf. vs. 13⌋ instead of *kanaknakam*, and at the end *vahī* ⌊intending *ahe?*⌋ instead of *viṣam*; and it puts next our vs. 25.

23. Whichever of the snakes [are] fire-born, herb-born, whichever came hither (*ā-bhū*) [as] water-born lightnings; those of which the kinds are variously great — to those serpents would we pay worship with reverence.

Ppp. reads, for **b** etc., *ye abhrajā vidyutā "babhūvuḥ : tāsāṁ jātāni bahudhā bahūni tebhyaḥ sarvebhyo* etc.

24. Thou art a girl, *tāúdī* by name; verily thou art by name ghee-like (*ghṛtā́cī*); I take beneath thy poison-spoiling track.

That is, possibly, 'I put it beneath me, walk in it.' The obscure *tāudī* (ultimately from *tud* 'thrust'?) is read also by Ppp., which combines *vā 'si* in **b**, and has the easier reading *pados* for *padam* in **c**.

25. Remove thou [it] from every limb; make [it] avoid the heart; then, what keenness (*téjas*) the poison has, let that go downward for thee.

Ppp. reads *hṛdayo* in **b**, and combines *tejo av-* in **c**, **d**. The verse is quoted in Kāuç. 32. 23.

26. He (it?) hath come to be afar; he hath obstructed the poison; he hath mixed poison in poison; Agni hath put out the snake's poison; Soma hath conducted [it] out; the poison hath gone after the biter; the snake hath died.

Ppp. reads (corruptly) *āre 'bhūd viṣam aro viṣe viṣam aprayāg api : agnir aher nir adhād viṣaṁ somo ānṛṇāiḥ dviṣam ahīr amṛtaḥ*. Kāuç. prescribes the use of the verse in 32. 24. ⌊With the ideas of **b** and **e**, cf. vii. 88. 1. With reference to the auto-toxic action of snake-venoms, see note to v. 13. 4.⌋

⌊Here ends the second *anuvāka*, with 2 hymns and 51 verses. The quoted Anukr. says "*indrasya prathamaḥ*" (see vs. 1).⌋

5. Preparation and use of water-thunderbolts.

⌊The hymn is mingled prose and verse: 22–24, 42–43, 45–50, and parts of 7–14 and 36–41 are metrical. Cf. Whitney, *Index*, p. 5.⌋ This hymn, which by the mss. is given and numbered as one,* without any intimation of a subdivision, is by the Anukr. divided into four † parts, which are even ascribed to different authors. ⌊Part A = verses 1–24; B = 25–35; C = 37–41; D = 42–50.⌋ Verses 1–41, or the first three divisions, are found also in Pāipp. xvi.; part of the last division (vss. 45, 42 **c**, **d**, 43, 44, in this order), in Pāipp. i. — ⌊"Water-thunderbolts" appears to me to be nothing more than a highfalutin name, well befitting the black magic of this hymn, for handfuls of water hurled with much hocus-pocus.⌋

*⌊Bp. does indeed begin anew at vs. 41 (not vs. 42 !) to number the verses as 1 etc.⌋

†⌊Just where vs. 36 belongs — if it does not form a division by itself — is not clear; it goes well as an ending to the group of vss. 25–35 and is cited with them (Keçava, p. 352[31]: *iti dvādaçabhiḥ*). On the other hand, the Anukr. expressly defines division B as *ekādaça;* and the corrupt *mārtvī* or *mārtvi* of the Anukr. seems to contain an ascription of authorship for vs. 36. Dr. Ryder suggests that *Mārīca* may be intended (cf. vii. 62, 63; x. 10). See my arrangement of the Anukr. extracts just before vs. 25.⌋

⌊A carefully digested report of the ritual uses of this hymn, even now that Caland has done so much to elucidate them, would require more detailed study than I can at present give to it. Vāit. takes no notice of the hymn. The principal uses are treated in Kāuç. 49. I give them, following Caland, *Altindisches Zauberritual*, p. 171 f. — With the first halves of vss. 1–6 the performer washes the jar for the water; with the second halves of vss. 1–6 he begins to make use of (*yunakti*) the water (49. 3, 4). With vss. 7–14 he heats a part of it (see Keçava, p. 352[19]); and with the seven vss. 15–21 and with vs. 42 and vs. 50 he hurls "water-bolts" (49. 13). This last is done seven times (Caland, p. 172, n. 6): namely, to the east, with vss. 15, 42, 50; to the south, with vss. 16, 42, 50; to the west, with vss. 17, 42, 50; and so on, to the north, nadir, center, and zenith. — With vss. 25–36 he makes his Viṣṇu-strides (49. 14) against the foe. — Other citations under the verses.⌋

Translated: Henry, 14, 62; Griffith, ii. 18.

[A. (vss. 1–24). *Sindhudvīpa. — caturviṅçati. āpyam uta cāndramasam. ānuṣṭubham: 1–5. 3-p. puro'bhikṛti kakummatīgarbhā pañkti; 6. 4-p. jagatīgarbhā jagatī; 7–14. 3-av. 5-p. viparītapādalakṣmī bṛhatī (11, 14. pathyāpañkti); 15–21. 4-av. 10-p. trāiṣṭubhagarbhā 'tidhṛti (19, 20. kṛti); 24. 3-p. virāḍ gāyatrī.*]

1. Indra's force are ye; Indra's power are ye; Indra's strength are ye; Indra's heroism are ye; Indra's manliness are ye; unto a conquering junction (*yóga*) with *brahman*-junctions I join you.

The *pada*-text marks a pāda-division after each *stha;* but the Anukr. lumps all ⌊up to the *avasāna*-mark⌋ together as an *abhikṛti*-pāda (25 syll.), and reckons the whole verse (25 : 6 + 8 = 39) mechanically as a *pañkti*, because it contains nearly 40 syllables. Ppp. has in succession *balam*, *nṛmṇam*, *çuklam*, *vīryam*, and in **c**, *indrayogāis*.

⌊Render: 'for a use conducive to victory, with uses of incantation [*or* with masterly uses] [*or* with Brahman uses] I use you.' In *brahma-* I am inclined to see a triple *çleṣa*, the second sense being like that in the title *Brahma-jāla-sutta* (of the Dīgha-nikāya), 'the boss-net, the master-net.' In the first and second senses, *brahma-* is pertinent: not so in the sense of Brahman, in which last, however, it serves well enough for a point of departure for *kṣatram*, considering what black magic this is.⌋

2. Indra's force etc. etc.; unto a conquering junction, with *kṣatrá*-junctions I join you.

The connection of vss. 1 and 2 indicates that *bráhman* and *kṣatrá*, as often elsewhere, typify the Brahman and Kshatriya classes or castes.

3. Indra's force etc. etc.; unto a conquering junction, with Indra-junctions I join you.

Ppp. reads in **c** *annayogāis*.

4. Indra's force etc. etc.; unto a conquering junction, with Soma-junctions I join you.

Ppp. has this time *brahmayogāis*.

5. Indra's force etc. etc.; unto a conquering junction, with water-junctions I join you.

Ppp. reads *apām̆ yogāis*.

6. Indra's force etc. etc.; unto a conquering junction; let all existences wait upon (*upa-sthā*) me; joined to me are ye, O waters.

The Anukr. quotes this verse by the first words that are peculiar to it, viz. *viçvāni mā*, but its description applies to the whole (25 : 6 + 11 + 6 = 48); probably *jagatī-garbhā* is an oversight for *triṣṭubgarbhā*. The Kāuç. quotes the common *pratīka* of the six verses at 49. 3, in a witchcraft-ceremony; and their common second part (*jiṣṇave yogāya*) at 49. 4, to accompany the 'joining of waters' (*ity apo yunakti*). According to the editor of Kāuç., vss. 6 and 7 are quoted also in 49. 24, 25; but it does not appear why the 'sixth' and 'seventh' verses of this hymn should be intended. ⌊Caland, p. 173, in fact understands xiii. 3. 6, 7 as intended.⌋ According to the comm. to Kāuç. 47. 31, these verses, with vss. 15–21, 42, 50, accompany the hurling of 'water-thunderbolts' (*udavajra*: cf. vs. 50 below), whatever those may be; it is perhaps their preparation that is the subject of these verses; in Kāuç. 49. 13, only vss. 15–21, 42, 50 are quoted together, in connection with the same ⌊cf. the introduction⌋. ⌊See above, p. lxxvi.⌋

7. Agni's portion are ye, sperm (? *çukrám*) of the waters, O heavenly waters; put ye splendor in us; with the ordinance (*dhāman*) of Prajāpati I set you for this world.

Ppp. reads *devīr āpo*.

8. Indra's portion are ye, sperm of the etc. etc.

9. Soma's portion are ye, sperm of the etc. etc.

10. Varuṇa's portion are ye, sperm of the etc. etc.

11. Mitra-and-Varuṇa's portion are ye, sperm of the etc. etc.

12. Yama's portion are ye, sperm of the etc. etc.

13. The Fathers' portion are ye, sperm of the etc. etc.

14. God Savitar's portion are ye, sperm of the etc. etc.

In these verses, Pāipp. makes 9 and 10, also 11 and 12, change places. After our 13 it inserts two more verses, beginning *bṛhaspater* and *prajāpater;* and in our 14 it omits *devasya*, and reads *çuklaṁ devīr āpo.* To read *dhattana* for *dhatta* ⌊and pronounce *dhāmanā*⌋ would make a regular *anuṣṭubh* of the refrain. The Anukr., as usual, gives no real description of the agglomeration, but calls 11 and 14 *pañkti* because they count up 40 syllables (9 : 8 + 7 : 8 + 8 = 40), and the others *bṛhatī* because they have nearly 36 syllables. As to the alleged quotation of vs. 7 in Kāuç. 49. 25, see above, note to vs. 6.

15. What of you, O waters, is the portion of waters within the waters, of the nature of sacrificial formula, sacrificing to the gods, that now I let go; that let me not wash down against myself; that do we let go against him who hates us, whom we hate; him may I slay (*vadh*), him may I lay low, with this spell (*bráhman*), with this act, with this weapon (*mení*).

⌊Render **c**: 'therewith (i.e. *apām bhāgena* = *udavajreṇa*) do we let fly against (*abhy-ati-sṛj*) him *or* do we shoot against him who' etc.; i.e. *ati-sṛj* is used intransitively and "him" is governed by the *abhi-*.⌋ ⌊Pādas **b**, **c** are repeated below as xvi. 1. 4, 5.⌋ At the beginning of **c** read *téna* (accent-sign slipped out of place).

16. What of you, O waters, is the wave of the waters within the waters, etc. etc.

17. What of you, O waters, is the young (*vatsá*) of the waters within the waters, etc. etc.

18. What of you, O waters, is the bull of the waters within the waters etc. etc.

19. What of you, O waters, is the golden embryo of the waters within the waters, etc. etc.

20. What of you, O waters, is the heavenly spotted stone of the waters within the waters, etc. etc.

21. What of you, O waters, are the fires of the waters within the waters, of the nature of sacrificial formula, sacrificing to the gods, them now I let go; them let me not wash down against myself; them we let go against him who hates us, etc. etc.

⌊For **c**: 'with them do we let fly against him who' etc., as in vs. 15.⌋ In vss. 17–21, after *apām*, Ppp. reads *bindur*, *vego*, *vatso*, *gāvo*, *garbho* respectively. For the quotations in Kāuç. of the common *pratīka* of vss. 15–21, together with those of vss. 42 and 50, ⌊see the introduction⌋. In all the verses it is possible only by violence to make out the structure called for by the Anukramaṇī. ⌊Delete the accent-mark over *agnáyo.*⌋

22. What untruth soever we have spoken since a three years' period, — let the waters protect me from all that difficulty, from distress.

We had the second half-verse as vii. 64. 1 **c**, **d**; and Ppp. has again the same variants as there; it also reads in **a** *āikahāyanāt*. The word *trāihāyaṇāt* (p. *trāihāyanāt*) is noted in Prāt. iv. 83. The verse is quoted in Kāuç. 46. 50 in a *prāyaçcitta* ceremony ⌊Keç.: for lying or cheating⌋; and it is reckoned (see note to Kāuç. 32. 27) as belonging to the *aṅholiṅga gaṇa*. The Anukr. does not heed the redundant syllable in **a**.

23. I send you forth to the ocean; go ye unto your own lair; uninjured, of completed years (?); and let nothing whatever ail (*am*) us.

The third pāda apparently belongs to 'us,' though out of construction. ⌊As to *-hāyas*, cf. viii. 2. 7, note, and Bergaigne, *Rel. Véd.*, iii. 287.⌋ The last pāda occurred above, as vi. 57. 3 **b**. The first two pādas, with the first word of the third, are found also in several sūtras: ÇÇS. iv. 11. 6; LÇS. ii. 1. 7; PGS. i. 3. 14; AÇS. iii. 11. 6; Āp. xiii. 18. 1; iv. 14. 4; the first three read in **b** *abhi gacchata*, the others *api gacchata* (and Āp. iv. 14. 4 has *acchidraḥ* instead of *ariṣṭāḥ*); the end of the verse is entirely different from ours, and more or less discordant in the various works. ⌊See also MGS. ii. 11. 18 and the Index, p. 157.⌋ Kāuç. quotes the verse at 6. 17, in a *parvan* ceremony; and with vs. 24, at 136. 6. Ppp. reads in **a** *vo 'pasṛjāmi* ⌊and inverts the order of vss. 23 and 24⌋.

24. Free from defilement (*-riprá*) [are] the waters; [let them carry] away from us defilement, forth from us sin, mishap (*duritá*), they of good aspect; let them carry forth evil dreaming, forth filth.

The verse is in part repeated below, as xvi. 1. 10, 11.

[B¹. (vss. 25–35). *Kāuçika. — ekādaça. viṣṇukramadevatyā uta pratimantroktadevatyāḥ. 25–35. 3-av. 6-p. yathākṣaraṁ çakvaryatiçakvarī.*]

[B². (vs. 36). *Mārtvī* (?). —*5-p. atiçākvarātijāgatagarbhā 'ṣṭi.* See introduction.]

25. Vishṇu's stride art thou, rival-slaying, earth-sharpened (*-sáṁçita*), Agni-brightened; after earth I stride out; from earth we disportion him who hates us, whom we hate; let him not live; him let breath quit.

The Pāipp. version of sections B. and C. agrees with that of our text with only trifling differences; the details are not furnished. It is not difficult to read this and the following verses of B. into *çakvarī* and *atiçakvarī* verses, as required by the Anukr. (this, for example, as 10 + 10 : 9 + 8 : 9 + 10 = 56). The whole section, apparently, is quoted by its common *pratīka* in Kāuç. 6. 14, to accompany the taking of the Viṣṇu strides in a *parvan* ceremony; and again in 49. 14 ⌊after hurling the water-bolts: cf. introd.⌋. ⌊Cf. vii. 31. 1 **d**.⌋

26. Vishṇu's stride art thou, rival-slaying, atmosphere-sharpened, Vāyu-brightened; after atmosphere I stride out; from atmosphere we disportion him who etc. etc.

27. Vishṇu's stride art thou, rival-slaying, sky-sharpened, sun-brightened; after the sky I stride out; from the sky we disportion him who etc. etc.

A single ms. (R.) reads *dyāuḥsaṁçitaḥ*.

28. Vishṇu's stride art thou, rival-slaying, quarter-sharpened, mind-brightened; after the quarters I stride out; from the quarters we disportion him who etc. etc.

29. Vishṇu's stride art thou, rival-slaying, region-sharpened, wind-brightened; after the regions I stride out; from the regions we disportion him who etc. etc.

30. Vishṇu's stride art thou, rival-slaying, verse-(*ṛc-*)sharpened, chant-(*sā́man-*)brightened; after the verses I stride out; from the verses we disportion him who etc. etc.

Some of the mss. (E.s.m.R.K.) read in **a** *-hā ṛks-*.

31. Vishṇu's stride art thou, rival-slaying, sacrifice-sharpened, *bráhman*-brightened; after the sacrifice I stride out; from the sacrifice we disportion him who etc. etc.

32. Vishṇu's stride art thou, rival-slaying, herb-sharpened, *sóma*-brightened; after the herbs I stride out; from the herbs we disportion him who etc. etc.

Read in **b** *krame* (an accent-sign slipped out of place).

33. Vishṇu's stride art thou, rival-slaying, water-sharpened, Varuṇa-brightened; after the waters I stride out; from the waters we disportion him who etc. etc.

Read *apó* at beginning of **b** (an accent-sign slipped out of place).

34. Vishṇu's stride art thou, rival-slaying, plowing-sharpened, food-brightened; after plowing I stride out; from plowing we disportion him who etc. etc.

35. Vishṇu's stride art thou, rival-slaying, breath-sharpened, man-(*púruṣa-*)brightened; after breath I stride out; from breath we disportion him who etc. etc.

⌊Correct the edition: read *-saṁçitaḥ* for *-saçitaḥ*.⌋

36. Ours [is] what is conquered, ours what has shot up; I have withstood (*abhi-sthā*) all fighters, niggards; now do I involve (*ni-veṣṭ*) the splendor, brightness, breath, life-time of him of such-and-such lineage, son of such-and-such mother; now do I make him fall (*pad*) downward.

⌊As to the place of this vs. in the general divisions of the hymn and its possible ascription to Mārīca, see the introd. and the Anukr. excerpts above.⌋ With this vs. compare xvi. 8. 1; ⌊also the *mantra* cited at Kāuç. 47. 22⌋. The vs. reads naturally as 62 syllables (11 + 11 : 15 + 13 + 12 = 62), but can be brought by forced resolutions up to a full *aṣṭi* (64 syll.). *Abhy asthām* is by Prāt. ii. 92.

[C. (vss. 37–41). *Brahman.* — *pañca. pratimantroktadevatyāḥ. 37. virāṭ purastādbṛhatī; 38. purauṣṇih; 39, 41. ārṣī gāyatrī; 40. virād viṣamā gāyatrī.*]

37. I turn after the sun's turn (*āvṛ́t*), after his turn to the right; let it yield (*yam*) me property; [let] it [yield] me Brahman-splendor.

The verse is quoted in Kāuç. 6. 15, in a *parvan* ceremony, accompanying a turn to the right (vss. 25–35 were quoted in the next preceding rule). ⌊Cf. also MB. i. 6. 19, where the comm. cites also GGS. ii. 10. 27.⌋

38. I turn toward the quarters full of light; let them yield me property, let them etc. etc.

The metrical description of the Anukr. does not fit the verse (11 : 8 + 8) quite accurately. The resolution *abhi-ā́v-* is implied in all these verses.

39. I turn toward the seven seers; let them yield etc. etc.

40. I turn toward the *bráhman;* let it yield etc. etc.

41. I turn toward the Brahmans; let them yield etc. etc.

[D. (vss. 42–50). *Vihavya. — navarcam. prājāpatyam. ānuṣṭubham : 44. 3-p. gāyatragarbhā nuṣṭubh* (?); *50. triṣṭubh.*]

42. Whom we hunt, him will we lay low with deadly weapons; by our spell (*bráhman*) have we made him fall (*pad*) into the opened mouth of the most exalted one.

Only the latter half-verse is found in Ppp. ⌊namely, in i.⌋. The *pada*-text in **d** reads *bráhmaṇā : ā́ : apīp-*. The quotation of the verse, with vss. 15–21, 50, in Kāuç. was noted above, ⌊see introd.⌋.

43. The missile hath closed upon him with the two tusks of Vāiçvānara; let this offering (*ā́huti*) devour him, the very powerful divine fuel.

Ppp. reads *saṁvatsarasya* instead of *vāiçvānarasya.*

44. King Varuṇa's bond art thou; do thou bind so-and-so, of such-and-such lineage, son of such-and-such mother, in food, in breath.

There is apparently something wrong, perhaps an omission, in the text of the Anukr. at this point; it reads *tripād gāyatragarbhā st anuṣṭubh*, and then passes to vs. 50, taking no notice of vss. 48, 49 (which are redundant *triṣṭubhs :* but see the note to vs. 49), ⌊nor of vs. 47⌋. Our present verse (prose) reads most naturally as 10 : 12 + 7 = 29 syllables.

45. What food of thine, O Lord of earth (*bhū́*), dwells upon the earth (*pṛthivī́*) — of that, O lord of earth, do thou furnish unto us, O Prajāpati.

The Anukr. implies the contraction of *kṣiyati* in **b** to *ksyati* (cf. above, 2. 22, 23). Ppp. ⌊in i.⌋ puts this verse before our vs. 42.

46. The heavenly waters have I honored; with sap have we been mingled; rich in milk, O Agni, have I come; unite me here with splendor.

47. Unite me, O Agni, with splendor, with progeny, with life-time; may the gods know me as such; may Indra know, together with the seers.

These two verses we had above, as vii. 89. 1, 2. Neither they nor the two that follow are found in Ppp. here.

48. What, O Agni, the pair utter in curses today, what harshness of speech the reciters produce: the shaft that is born of fury of the mind — with that pierce thou the sorcerers in the heart.

49. Crush away the sorcerers with heat; crush away, O Agni, the demon with flame; crush away with burning the false worshipers; crush away the greatly gleaming ones that feed on lives.

These two verses are viii. 3. 12, 13. As usual in such a case, only the first words are given here in the mss. (both *pada* and *saṁhitā*): thus, *yád agna íti dvé.* Unfortunately it was overlooked by us that *yád agne* begins not only viii. 3. 12, but also vii. 61. 1; and, though both passages fit about equally ill into the connection here, yet the meter of vii. 61. 1, 2, being *anuṣṭubh*, implies a less oversight on the part of the Anukr., and, on the whole, the chance is in favor of the latter passage (vii. 61. 1, 2) being the one here intended. If in any one of the mss. accessible to us since the publication of the text there occurs anything to settle the question, it has been overlooked by us. ⌊SPP. fills out the *pratīka* with viii. 3. 12, 13; but herein he may merely have followed the Berlin edition.⌋

50. I, knowing, hurl at this man, to split his head, the four-pointed (*-bhṛṣṭí*) thunderbolt of the waters; let it crush all his limbs: to this on my part let all the gods assent.

The Anukr., strictly understood, implies the resolution *va-jṛ-am* in **a**. For the quotations of the verse, with other verses of the hymn, by Kāuç., see above ⌊introduction⌋.

⌊The hymn exceeds the norm by 20 verses and the quoted Anukr. says *viṅçatiḥ.*⌋

⌊Here ends the twenty-second *prapāṭhaka.*⌋

6. With an amulet.

[*Bṛhaspati. — pañcatriṅçat. mantroktaphālamaṇidevatyam uta vānaspatyam.* ⌊*3. āpyā.*⌋ *ānuṣṭubham: 1, 4, 21. gāyatrī; 5. 6-p. jagatī; 6. 7-p. virāṭ çakvarī; 7–10. 3-av. 8-p. aṣṭi (10. 9-p. dhṛti); 11, 20, 23–27. pathyāpañkti; 12–17. 3-av. 7-p. çakvarī; 31. 3-av. 6-p. jagatī; 35. 5-p. tryanuṣṭubgarbhā jagatī.*]

Found also in great part (not vss. 18, 19, 23, 24, 26, 27, 29, 30, 33, 35) in Pāipp. xvi. A number of verses and parts of verses are prescribed in Kāuç. 19 ⌊and its schol.⌋ to be used in various acts of a ceremony for prosperity, and a few in other connections. Verses 1 and 3 are also used in Vāit. ⌊For details, see under the several verses.⌋

Translated: Henry, 18, 65; Griffith, ii. 21; Bloomfield, 84, 608.

1. The head of the niggardly (*arātīyú*) cousin, of the evil-hearted hater, I cut off with force.

The hymn (vs. 1) is quoted in Kāuç. 19. 22, with 3 and a couple of yet earlier hymns. At 8. 12, also, the verse is used in connection with the preparation of the *darbha*-sickle. Further, it is reckoned (note to Kāuç. 19. 1) as a *puṣṭika mantra*. In Vāit. 10. 2, it accompanies the cutting of a sacrificial post.

2. This amulet, born of the plow-share, shall make defense (*várman*) for me; it hath come to me filled with stir-about, with sap, together with splendor.

Ppp. reads *tṛptas* instead of *pūrṇas* in **c**. ⌊Pāda **b** is cited with vss. 1, 4 **c**, 6 **b** in the schol. to Kāuç. 19. 23.⌋

3. In that the skilful smith (*tákṣan*) hath smitten thee away with the hand by a knife, from that let the lively, bright (*çúci*) waters purify thee, that art bright.

Ppp. has in **b** *vāçyā*, which is the more proper form of the word. But *vāsyā* is read also in the Āp. (vii. 9. 9) version of the verse, which further has *te* for *tvā* in **a**, and, for **c**, **d**, *āpas tat sarvaṁ jīvalāḥ çundhantu çucayaḥ çucim*. In Kāuç. 8. 13 and Vāit. 10. 3, the verse is used to accompany the washing off of an instrument or post.

4. Let this golden-garlanded amulet, bestowing (*dhā*) faith, sacrifice, greatness, dwell a guest in our house.

⌊For Dārila's citation of **c**, see under vs. 2.⌋

5. To it we distribute (*kṣad*) ghee, strong drink, honey, food after food; for us, as a father for his sons, let it provide (*cikits-*) what is better and better, more and more, morrow after morrow — the amulet, coming from the gods.

Ppp. omits the fifth pāda. By a curious blunder, most of our mss. (all save I.O.D.) leave *surām* in **a** unaccented; ⌊and so do four of SPP's⌋.

6. What amulet, plow-share, ghee-dripping, the formidable *khadirá*, Brihaspati bound on, in order to force — that Agni fastened on; it yields (*duh*) to him sacrificial butter, more and more, morrow after morrow; with that do thou slay thy haters.

The series of epithets in **b**, **c** is an obscure one; perhaps 'made of *khadira*-wood and shaped like a plow-share,' is meant; the comm. to Kāuç. 19. 23 says *khādiryāç cibukāyāḥ kartavyaḥ*. Ppp. reads after **d** *ājyāya rasāya kam: so 'smā ājyaṁ duhe*. There is no reason why the Anukr. should call the verse *virāj*.

7. What amulet etc. etc. — that Indra fastened on, in order to force, to heroism; it yields to him strength, more and more etc. etc.

8. What amulet etc. etc. — that Soma fastened on, in order to great hearing (*çrótra*) [and] sight (*cákṣas*); it yields to him splendor, more and more etc. etc.

9. What amulet etc. etc. — that the sun fastened on; therewith he conquered these quarters; it yields to him growth (*bhūti*), more and more etc. etc.

Ppp. has Soma in this verse, and the sun in the preceding one; and here it reads *varcas* for *bhūtim*; for 8 **e** it has *draviṇāya rasāya kam*; and, for *varcas*, *mahit* (?).

10. What amulet etc. etc. — bearing that amulet, the moon conquered the strongholds of the Asuras, the golden [strongholds] of the Dānavas; it yields to him fortune, more and more etc. etc.

Ppp. reads *tejas* for *çriyam*.

11. What amulet Brihaspati bound on for the swift wind, that yields him vigor (*vājina*), more and more etc. etc.

A number of our mss. (I.O.R.D.) read *vājînam* in **c**. ⌊So do the great majority of SPP's, and he adopts it in his text. But four of his read *vā́jinam*.⌋ In this batch of verses (11–17) Ppp. has sundry unimportant exchanges and variants; the details are not given.

12. What amulet Brihaspati bound on for the swift wind, with that amulet the Açvins defend this plowing (*kṛṣí*); it yields for the two physicians greatness, more and more etc. etc.

13. What amulet Brihaspati bound on for the swift wind, Savitar, bearing that amulet, conquered with it this heaven (*svàr*); it yields to him pleasantness (*sūnṛ́tā*), more and more etc. etc.

14. What amulet Brihaspati bound on for the swift wind, bearing that amulet the waters run always unexhausted; it yields to them immortality (*amṛ́ta*), more and more etc. etc.

15. What amulet Brihaspati bound on for the swift wind, that healthful amulet king Varuṇa fastened on; it yields to him truth, more and more etc. etc.

16. What amulet Brihaspati bound on for the swift wind, bearing that amulet, the gods conquered by fight all worlds; it yields to them conquest, more and more etc. etc.

The *pada*-text resolves *yudhā́jayan* erroneously into *yudhā́ ájayan* (instead of *aj-*).

17. What amulet Brihaspati bound on for the swift wind, that healthful amulet here the deities fastened on; it yields to them everything, more and more etc. etc.

Part of our mss. (Bp.P.W.I.D.K.) ⌊and a great majority of SPP's⌋ read *amuñcata* in **d**. | The error has doubtless crept in by confusion with the oft repeated *abadhnata* below and perhaps with the *amuñcata* of vs. 15. Cf. my note to vi. 74. 2.⌋

18. The seasons bound it on; they of the seasons bound it on; the year, having bound it on, defends all existence.

As noted above, this verse and the one following are wanting in Ppp.

19. The intermediate quarters bound on; the directions bound it on; the amulet created by Prajāpati hath made my haters beneath me (*ádhara*).

20. The Atharvans bound on; the descendants of Atharvan bound on; allied (*medín*) with them, the Aṅgirases split the strongholds of the barbarians; with it do thou slay thy haters.

21. Dhātar fastened it on; he disposed (*vi-kḷp*) [all] existence; with it do thou slay thy haters.

Ppp. reads in **b** *subhūtāny akalpayat*.

22. What [amulet] Brihaspati bound on for the gods, a destruction of Asuras — that amulet hath come here to me, together with sap, with splendor.

Ppp. reads in **b** *-kṣatim*, and substitutes for **c**, **d** our 23 **c**, **d** (23, 24, 26, 27, 29, 30, 33, 35 being wanting in Ppp.).

23. What [amulet] etc. etc., together with kine, with goats and sheep, together with food, with progeny.

24. What [amulet] etc. etc., together with rice and barley, together with greatness, growth.

25. What [amulet] etc. etc., with a stream of honey, of ghee, together with sweet drink — the amulet.

26. What [amulet] etc. etc., together with refreshment, with milk, together with property, with fortune.

27. What [amulet] etc. etc., together with brightness, with brilliance, together with glory, with fame.

The mss. vary greatly as to the accent of *kīrtyā*, only D. having the correct *kīrtyā́*; P.M.T. have *kī́rtyā*, the rest *kīrtyā̀*. ⌊Cf. JAOS. x. 381. Correct the Berlin edition, and also that of SPP., who has *kīrtyā̀*, against the majority of his authorities.⌋

28. What [amulet] etc. etc., together with all growths.

Ppp. reads *ojasā tejasā saha*.

29. This amulet here let the deities give to me in order to prosperity — the overpowering, dominion-increasing, rival-damaging amulet.

This verse and the one following are quoted in Kāuç. 19. 25, in connection with earlier quotations from this same hymn; ⌊the second pāda of this verse further in the schol. to 19. 22⌋.

30. Together with *bráhman*, with brightness, I fasten on myself the propitious one; free from rivals, rival-slaying, it hath made my rivals beneath me.

Besides the quotation in Kāuç. 19. 25 (see just above), this verse is used in the comm. to Kāuç. 26. 40. *Muñcāsi* in **b** is a misprint for *muñcāmi*.

31. Let this god-born amulet make me superior to my hater; whose milked-out milk these three worlds worship, let that amulet mount here upon me, in order to supremacy, at the head.

That is, probably, 'mount upon my head.' According to Prāt. ii. 65, we ought to read *maṇíṣ kṛ-*; ⌊this is the reading of three of SPP's mss., but of none of W's so far as noted: both texts give *maṇíḥ*⌋. The pāda *sa mā 'yam adhi rohatu* (31 **e**, 32 **c**) is quoted in the comm. to Kāuç. 19. 25. The Anukr. takes no notice of the redundant syllable in **a**. Ppp. reads, for **e**, *sa tvā 'yam abhi rakṣatu*.

32. What gods, Fathers, men, always subsist upon, let that amulet mount here upon me, in order to supremacy, at the head.

The Anukr. passes without notice the redundant syllable in **a**.

33. As seed in a cultivated field (*urvárā*) grows up in what is dragged with the plow-share, so in me let progeny, cattle, food upon food, grow up.

The Anukr. seems to read **c**, **d** as 9 + 7 syllables.

34. On whom, O sacrifice-increasing amulet, I have fastened thee, propitious, him do thou quicken unto supremacy, O amulet of a hundred sacrificial gifts.

⌊Cf. Bloomfield, AJP. xvii. 409.⌋

35. This fuel, laid on together, do thou, O Agni, enjoying, welcome with oblations; in him may we find favor, welfare, progeny, sight, cattle — in Jātavedas kindled with worship (*bráhman*).

Some of our mss. (R.T.p.m.D.) read *agne* without accent, and this is decidedly preferable, since a pāda-division before *juṣāṇás* gives an *anuṣṭubh* pāda followed by a *triṣṭubh*, while one after the same word gives a *triṣṭubh* followed by an irregular combination of syllables. The *pada*-text puts its mark of pāda-division after *juṣāṇas*, to correspond with its accentuation of *ágne*. ⌊Of SPP's authorities, only four have *agne* against nine with *ágne*, and his text adopts the latter reading.⌋ The concluding division is hopelessly unmetrical. The Anukr. intends us to divide 8 + 11 (or 11 + 8) : 8 + 8 + 11 = 46, a *virāḍ jagatī*. The verse is thrice quoted in Kāuç. (2.41; 19.24; 137.30) to accompany the piling of fuel on the fire. It is wanting in Ppp.

⌊The quoted Anukr. says for this sixth hymn *pañca* (i.e. 5 over 30). — Here ends the third *anuvāka*, with 2 hymns and 85 verses.⌋

7. Mystic: on the skambhá or frame of creation.

[*Atharvan* (*kṣudra*). — *catuçcatvāriñçat. mantroktaskambhādhyātmadevatyam. trāiṣṭubham* *: *1. virāḍ jagatī; 2, 8. bhurij; 7, 13. parosṇih; 10, 14, 16, 18, 19. upariṣṭād bṛhatī; 11, 12, 15, 20, 22, 39. upariṣṭājjyotirjagatī; 17. 3-av. 6-p. jagatī; 21. bṛhatīgarbhā 'nuṣṭubh; 23–30, 37, 40. anuṣṭubh; 31. madhyejyotirjagatī; 32, 34, 36. upariṣṭādvirāḍ bṛhatī; 33. paravirāḍ anuṣṭubh; 35. 4-p. jagatī; 38, 42, 43. triṣṭubh* *; 41. ārṣī 3-p. gāyatrī; 44. ārcy anuṣṭubh* (?) †.]

Found also (except vss. 13, 42 44) in Pāipp. xvii. (with slight differences of order, noted under the verses). Neither Kāuç. nor Vāit. takes any notice of the hymn. — *⌊If the hymn is *trāiṣṭubham*, why are these verses specified? see note to 38.⌋ †⌊As to the Anukr's description of this verse, see under the verse.⌋

Translated: Muir, v. 380–384 (vss. 1–41); Ludwig, p. 400; Scherman, p. 50 (vss. 1–41: with comment); Deussen, *Geschichte*, i. 1. 310 (sympathetic interpretation and useful introduction); Henry, 22, 68; Griffith, ii. 26. — As to the appearance of Brahm as a new conception, as a *Wunderding* (*yakṣá*: vs. 38), cf. the Kena Upanishad, § 3, vss. 14–25, and Deussen's introduction, *Sechzig Upanishad's*, p. 204. — The hymn is nearly related to the following one (8), and, with many a riddle and paradox, they both lead up to the fundamental conception of the Upanishads (see last verse of hymn 8), the idea of the Ātman. — In the new volume of the *Ved. Stud.*, iii. 126 ff., Geldner discusses *yakṣá* at length.

1. In what member of him is penance situated? in what member of him is right (*ṛtá*) deposited? where is situated [his] vow (*vratá*), where his faith? in what member of him is truth established?

Ppp. combines in **a** *tapo 'sya*. In **b**, the *pada*-text reads *asya : ádhi : ā́ohitam*. There is no reason for calling the verse *virāj*.

2. From what member of him flames Agni? from what member blows (*pū*) Mātariçvan? from what member doth the moon measure out, measuring the member of great Skambha?

Skambha, lit. 'prop, support, pillar,' strangely used in this hymn as frame of the universe or half-personified as its soul. Ppp. reads in **d** *skambhasya mahan mim-*. ⌊Read *vimímāno* in **d**?⌋

3. In what member of him is situated the earth? in what member is situated the atmosphere? in what member is the sky set? in what member is situated what is beyond the sky?

This is one of the five verses (3–6, 9) which are left by the Anukr. to fall under the general description of the hymn as *trāiṣṭubham*. All of them are more or less redundant; this, for example, is as much *bhurij* as vs. 2, which was so described. Ppp. puts the verse before our 2.

4. Whither desiring to attain does Agni flame aloft? whither desiring to attain blows Mātariçvan? whither desiring to attain, the turns (*āvṛ́t*) go, that Skambha tell [me]: which forsooth is he?

Here we have two syllables in excess, unnoticed by the Anukr. Many of the mss. accent *svìt* in **d**.

5. Whither go the half-months, whither the months, in concord with the year? whither the seasons go, whither they of the seasons, that Skambha tell [me]: which forsooth is he?

Again two unnoticed redundant syllables.

6. Whither desiring to attain run in concord the two maidens (*yuvatí*) of diverse form, day-and-night? whither desiring to attain, the waters go, that Skambha tell [me]: which forsooth is he?

Here it is only the last pāda that is one syllable in excess. Ppp. puts the verse before our 5.

7. In what, having established [them], Prajāpati maintained all the worlds, that Skambha tell [me]: which forsooth is he?

Many of our mss. appear to read *stabdhā́* in **a**, but it is doubtless only carelessness in writing. Here again, as above and in the verses below where the refrain is written out, part of the mss. accent *svìt*.

8. What that was highest, lowest, and what that was midmost Prajāpati created, of all forms — by how much did Skambha enter there? what did not enter, how much was that?

Or (in **d**) 'what he did not enter.' The Anukr. this time notices the redundant syllable (in **a**).

9. By how much did Skambha enter the existent? how much of him lies along that which will exist? what one member he made thousandfold, by how much did Skambha enter there?

The Anukr. again passes without notice the redundant syllable in **c**.

10. Where men know both worlds and receptacles (*kóça*), waters, *bráhman*, within which [are] both the non-existent and the existent — that Skambha tell [me]: which forsooth is he?

A part of this verse has disappeared in Ppp. ⌊The *pada* reads *ā́paḥ* and *antáḥ*.⌋

11. Where penance, striding forth, maintains the higher vow (*vratá*), where both right and faith, waters, *bráhman*, are set together, that Skambha etc. etc.

The verse (8 + 8 : 8 + 8 + 12 = 44) is, with those that agree with it, strangely named by the Anukr. ⌊Ppp. exchanges the places of *vratam* and *ṛtam* in **b**, **c**, and of *āpas* and *brahma* in **d**.⌋

12. In whom earth, atmosphere, in whom sky is set, where fire, moon, sun, wind stand fixed (*ā́rpita*), that Skambha etc. etc.

⌊The *pada*-text has *ā́rpitāḥ*, which SPP., with many of his *saṁhitā*-mss., adopts as *saṁhitā*-reading also; Ppp. has *-tā*.⌋

13. In whose member all the thirty-three gods are set together, that Skambha etc. etc.

Wanting in Ppp., as noted above.

14. Where the first-born seers, the verses, the chant, the sacrificial formula, the great one (*mahī́*); in whom the sole seer is fixed — that Skambha etc. etc.

Mahī́ usually designates the earth; what in this connection it should be meant to apply to is doubtful. All the *saṁhitā*-mss. combine *ekarṣír* (Ppp. *eka ṛṣir*), but most of them, with the Anukr., *yátra ṛ́ṣ-* in **a**. Ppp. reads *bhūtakṛtas* for *prathamajās*.

15 Where both immortality (*amṛ́ta*) and death are set together in man (*púruṣa*), of whom the ocean, the veins (*nāḍī́*) are set together in man, that Skambha etc. etc.

Ppp. reads, for **b**, *puruṣaç ca samāhitāḥ*, and puts the verse after our 16. Read in **a** *mṛtyúç ca* (an accent-sign slipped out of place).

16. Of whom the four directions are (*sthā*) the teeming (?*prapyasá*) veins, where the sacrifice hath strode forth, that Skambha etc. etc.

Prathamā́s at end of **b** in our edition seems to be a misprint for *prathasā́s*, intended as a correction of *prapyasā́s*, which last, however, is distinctly read by all our mss.* (p. *pra°pyasā́ḥ*); for the formation, compare *-bhyasa* from root *bhī* (through a secondary root *bhyas*). *⌊Except P., which has *prathasā́s*; SPP. puts *-mā́s* into his text against his fifteen authorities, which give *prapyasā́s*.⌋

17 Whoever know the *bráhman* in man, they know the most exalted one; whoever knows the most exalted one, and whoever knows Prajāpati, whoever know the chief *brā́hmaṇa*, they know also accordingly (*anu-saṁ-vid*) the Skambha.

For both **b** and **f**, Ppp. reads *te skambham arasaṁ viduḥ* (intending *anusaṁviduḥ* ?).

18. Whose head [was] Vāiçvānara, [whose] eye the Añgirases were, whose members the familiar demons (*yātú*) — that Skambha tell [me]: which forsooth is he?

19. Of whom they call *bráhman* the mouth, the honey-whip the tongue also, of whom they call *virā́j* the udder — that Skambha etc. etc.

Ppp. reads for **c** *virājaṁ yasyo "dhā "hus.*

20. From whom they fashioned off the verses, from whom they scraped off the sacrificial formula, of whom the chants [are] the hairs (*lóman*), the Atharvans-and-Añgirases the mouth — that Skambha etc. etc.

⌊Ppp. combines *ṛco 'pāt-* in **a**, and has *chandāṅsy asya* for *sāmāni yasya* in **c**.⌋

21. The branch of the non-existent, standing forth, people know as in a manner the highest thing; also the lower ones who worship (*upa-ās*) thy branch think [it?] the existent thing.

The translation of this highly obscure verse is only mechanical, and as literal as possible. Ppp. has only the first half. The definition of the Anukr. is a strange one; the verse is only a *bhurig anuṣṭubh* (in virtue of the *iva*, which properly is to be reduced to *va*, making a regular *anuṣṭubh*).

22. Where both the Ādityas and the Rudras and the Vasus are set together; where both what is and what is to be, [and] all the worlds are established — that Skambha tell [me]: which forsooth is he?

23. Of whom the thirty-three gods always defend the treasure (*nidhí*): that treasure, which, O gods, ye defend, who at present knoweth?

24. Where the *bráhman*-knowing gods worship the chief *bráhman* — whoso verily knoweth them eye to eye (*pratyákṣam*), he may be a Brahman (*brahmán*), a knower.

Perhaps an acceptable emendation in **d** would be *bráhma*: i.e. 'he may be (may be regarded as) one knowing the *bráhman*': cf. ÇB. xiv. 6. 9[11]. Ppp. reads, for **c**, **d**, *yo vāi tad brahmaṇo veda taṁ vāi brahmavido viduḥ*. Read in **a** *devā́* (an accent-sign dropped out).

25. Great (*bṛhánt*) by name [are] those gods who were born out of the non-existent; that one member of Skambha people call non-existent beyond.

The second half-verse is capable of other interpretations; Ludwig emends *parás* to *purā́*; Muir, tacitly, to *páram*; Scherman translates it 'afterwards' (*nachher*); Ppp. reads instead *puras*. One of our mss. reads in **b** *'satas p-*; ⌊and so does SPP. without report of variant⌋.

26. Where the *skambhá*, generating forth, rolled out the ancient one, that one member of the *skambhá* they know also accordingly [as] the ancient one.

Or, 'know etc. that ancient one as one member of the *skambha*.' Ppp. again (as in 17 **b**, **f**) *arasaṁ viduḥ* in **d**. Read in our edition *prajanáyan* in **a**.

27. In whose member the thirty-three gods shared severally the limbs (*gā́tra*) — those thirty-three gods verily only (*éka*) the *bráhman*-knowers know.

Or (so Muir), 'some *bráhman*-knowers.' Ppp. reads in **b** *gātrāṇi bhejire.*

28. People know the golden-embryo [as] highest, not to be overcrowed (*anatyudyá*); the *skambhá* in the beginning poured forth that gold within the world.

Ppp. puts this verse after our 30.

29. In the *skambhá* the worlds, in the *skambhá* penance, in the *skambhá* right is set; thee, O *skambhá*, I know plainly [as] set all together in Indra.

The mss. are much at variance in regard to *skámbha* in **c**; all save W. (the poorest and least trustworthy of all) end the word with *m*, and O.s.m.D. accent *skambhám.* That *skámbha* is really intended can hardly admit of question; Ppp. appears to read it.

30. In Indra the worlds, in Indra penance, in Indra right is set; thee, O Indra, I know plainly [as] all established in the *skambhá.*

The translation implies emendation in **c** of *índram* to *índra*. Of course, it is possible to render *índram* here, and *skambhám* in 29 **c**, but where the whole sense is so mystically obscure alterations help little.

31. Name with name he calls aloud, before the sun, before the dawn; as first the goat (? *ajá*) came into being, he went unto that autocracy beyond which there is nothing else existent.

Ppp. reads *johavīmi* in **a**, and *jagāma* (for *iyāya*) in **d**. The translators all understand *ajás* here as 'the unborn one,' and with more reason than in most places elsewhere. The description given by the Anukr. of the very irregular verse (8 + 8 : 10 + 10 + 11 = 47) is altogether ill-fitting.

32. Of whom earth is model (*pramá*) and atmosphere belly; who made the sky his head — to that chief *bráhman* be homage.

In this and the two following verses and vs. 36 we have the anomaly that *bráhman*, neuter, is apparently referred to by the masculine relative *yás* (in accordance with which the genitive *yásya* is also doubtless to be understood as masculine); perhaps we ought to render the last pāda thus: 'to him, [who is] the chief *bráhman*,' etc. ⌊Cf. Deussen, p. 312.⌋ The verse is shorter by two syllables than verses 34 and 36, with which the Anukr. reckons it, and, on the other hand, agrees with 33, to which the Anukr. gives a different name.

33. Of whom the sun is eye, and the moon that grows new again; who made Agni his mouth — to that chief *bráhman* be homage.

Ppp. combines *cakrā "syaṁ* in **c**. As to the meter, see the note to vs. 32. ⌊The Anukr. seems to mean that this is an *anuṣṭubh* of which the last pāda is one of 10 syllables (*virāj*).⌋

34. Of whom the wind [was] breath-and-expiration, [of whom] the Añgirases were the eye; who made the quarters fore-knowing (?*prajñā́na*) — to that chief *bráhman* be homage.

Ppp. gets rid of the obscure *prajñānīs* by reading for **c** *divaṁ yaç cakre mūrdhā-naṁ*. The Anukr. describes correctly vss. 34 and 36.

35. The *skambhá* sustains both heaven-and-earth here; the *skambhá* sustains the wide atmosphere; the *skambhá* sustains the six wide directions; into the *skambhá* hath entered this whole existence (*bhúvana*).

The *pada*-text has (as translated) *skambhé* in **d**. Ppp. puts the verse after our 36, and reads in **a** *pṛthivīṁ dyām utā 'mūṁ*, and in **d** combines *skambhāi 'daṁ*. The Anukr. takes no notice of the irregularity of the verse (14 + 11 : 11 + 13 = 49). ⌊Bergaigne, *Rel. Véd.*, ii. 122, would separate *pradiças* from *urvīs*.⌋

36. Who, born from toil, from penance, completely attained all worlds; who made soma all his own — to that chief *bráhman* be homage.

The sense of 'own' in **c** is given by the middle verb-form.

37. How does the wind not cease (*il*)? how does the mind not rest (*ram*)? why (*kím*) do the waters, seeking to attain truth, at no time soever cease?

Ppp. reads for **d** *pra cakramati sarvadā*. ⌊Scherman, p. 54: 'warum kommen fürwahr die strebenden Wasser niemals zur Ruhe?'⌋

38. A great monster (*yakṣá*) in the midst of the creation (*bhúvana*), strode (?*krāntá*) in penance on the back of the sea — in it are set (*çri*) whatever gods there are, like the branches of a tree roundabout the trunk.

The first pāda is repeated below, as 8. 15 **c**. Ppp. combines in **d** to *paritāi 'va*. Notwithstanding the lack of a syllable in **a**, the Anukr. ⌊balancing **a** with redundant **d**?⌋ calls the verse simply a *triṣṭubh*; the hymn is so long that it has apparently been forgotten that the whole was called *trāiṣṭubha*, and that therefore no *triṣṭubh* needs a further specification. Since there are more regular *anuṣṭubh*-verses than *triṣṭubh* also, we should expect rather the designation *ānuṣṭubham* for the hymn. Read at end of **a** *mádhye* (an accent-sign dropped out). ⌊With regard to Brahm as a "wonder" (*yakṣá*), see introduction.⌋

39. Unto which with the two hands, with the two feet, with speech, with hearing, with sight; unto which the gods continually render (*pra-yam*) tribute, unmeasured in the measured out — that *skambhá* tell [me]: which forsooth is he?

Notwithstanding the discordance of case, *vímite* is perhaps coördinate with *yásmāi*. Ppp. omits the first two pādas. The dual and the repetition of *yásmāi* make it probable that we have to supply in them 'one renders tribute,' or the like. The Anukr. takes no notice of the redundant syllable in **d**.

40. Smitten away is his darkness; he is separated from evil; in him are all the three lights that are in Prajāpati.

41. He who knows the golden reed (*vetasá*) standing in the sea — he verily is in secret Prajāpati.

All the mss. have in **c** *gúhya pr-*; perhaps *gúhā* was the original reading; our text has emended to *gúhyaḥ*.

The remaining verses are wanting in Ppp.; they appear to constitute no original part of the hymn. They are also not translated by Muir and Scherman.

42. A certain pair of maidens, of diverse form, weave, betaking themselves to it, the six-pegged web; the one draws forth the threads (*tántu*), the other sets [them]; they wrest not off (*apa-vṛj*), they go not to an end.

Ápa vṛñjāte perhaps means only 'break off, finish.' ⌊*Ná gamāto*, 'they shall not go' etc.⌋ A nearly related verse is found in TB. (ii. 5. 5[3]): *dvé svásārāu vayatas tántram etát sanātánam̐ vítatam̐ ṣáṇmayūkham: ávā 'nyā́ṅs tántūn kiráto dhattó anyā́n nā́ 'pa vṛjyā́te* (? both text and comm. have in the Calc. ed. *nā́ṣapṛjyā́te* ⌊and in the Poona ed. *nā́vapṛjyā́te*⌋) *ná gamāte ántam;* this is a preferable version especially of **c**. We have to resolve *tan-tṛ-am* in order to make a full *triṣṭubh*. ⌊The TB. comment makes the verse refer to day and night: cf. RV. i. 113. 3.⌋

43. Of them, as of two women dancing about, I do not distinguish (*vi-jñā*) which is beyond; a man (*púmāñs*), weaves it, ties [it] up; a man hath borne it about upon the firmament (*nā́ka*).

The last two pādas, with 44, correspond to RV. x. 130. 2, which reads: *púmān̐ enam̐ tanuta út kṛṇatti púmān ví tatne ádhi nā́ke asmín: imé mayū́khā úpa sedur ū sádaḥ sā́māni cakrus tásarāṇy ótave.* Our *úd gṛṇatti* is only a corruption, but simulates a form from root *grath*, and is rendered accordingly. ⌊For the exchange of surd and sonant, cf. Roth, ZDMG. xlviii. 110 and note to ii. 13. 3.⌋ The true scanning in **a** is doubtless *-yanti-or 'va;* ⌊better *-tior iva*, with *jagatī* cadence?⌋.

44. These pegs propped up the sky; the chants they made shuttles for weaving.

See the note to the preceding verse. Both here and in 42 **b** some of the mss. read *mayūṣa*. Bp. reads at the end *yā́tave*. The Anukr. says of the verse *ime mayūkhā ity ekāvasānā pañcapadā nicṛt padapañktir* ⌊i.e. 5 + 5 + 5 + 5 + 4 = 24⌋ *ārcy anuṣṭub dvipadā vā* ⌊i.e. 12 + 12 = 24⌋ *pañcapadā nicṛt padapañktir iti.* ⌊The last three or four words seem to be mere repetition.⌋

⌊The quoted Anukr. says *caturdaça* (i.e. 14 over 30).⌋

8. Mystic.

[*Kutsa. — catuçcatvāriñçat. adhyātmadevatyam. trāiṣṭubham: 1. upariṣṭādvirāḍ bṛhatī; 2. bṛhatīgarbhā 'nuṣṭubh; 5. bhurig anuṣṭubh; 6, 14, 19–21, 23, 25, 29, 31–34, 37, 38, 41, 43. anuṣṭubh; 7. parābṛhatī; 10. anuṣṭubgarbhā; 11. jagatī; 12. purobṛhatī triṣṭubgarbhā "rṣī pañkti; 15, 27. bhurig bṛhatī; 22. purauṣṇih; 26. dvyuṣṇiggarbhā 'nuṣṭubh; 30. bhurij; 39. bṛhatīgarbhā; 42. virāḍ gāyatrī.*]

Found in greater part (not vss. 1, 7, 15, 18, 30–44) in Pāipp. xvi. (in the verse-order 2, 8, 5, 9, 3, 4, 12, 6, 14, 29, 13, 11, 10, 16, 19–28, 17). Not noticed in Kāuç., and only one verse (42) used in Vāit.

Translated: Muir, v. 368 n., 386 (parts); Ludwig, p. 395; Scherman, p. 60 (parts); Deussen, *Geschichte*, i. 1.318 (cf. 310); Henry, 27, 75; Griffith, ii. 34. — Deussen's interpretation should on no account be overlooked. — Cf. the introduction to hymn 7.

1. He who is set over both what is and what is to be and everything, and whose alone is the heaven — to that chief *bráhman* be homage.

The concluding pāda is that of some of the verses of the preceding hymn (see vs. 32, above, and note).

2. By the *skambhá* these two stand fixed apart, both sky and earth; in the *skambhá* [is] all this that has soul, what [is] breathing and what winking.

The Anukr. is scrupulous enough not to sanction the irregular combination *skambhé 'dám* in **c**; why it calls the verse *br̥hatīgarbhā*, instead of simply *bhurij* (like vs. 5), it were hard to say.

3. Three offspring (*prajā́*) went an over-going; others settled (*ni-viç*) about the sun (? *arká*); great stood the traverser (*vimā́na*) of space (*rájas*); the yellow one (m.) entered into the yellow ones (f.).

The verse is RV. viii. 90 (101). 14, which reads, for **a**, *prajā́ ha tisró atyā́yam īyur;* at end of **b**, *viviçre;* for **c**, **d**, *br̥hád dha tasthāu bhúvaneṣv antáḥ pávamāno haritā́ ā́ viveça* (the last pāda is our 40 **d** below). AA. (ii. 1. 14) has the same version as RV. JB. (ii. 224) has a version agreeing in the main with RV., but beginning like ours, *tisro ha prajā*, ending **b** with *viviçyur*, beginning **c** with *br̥han* (but *br̥had* in a following brief exposition); in **c**, again, with our text, *rajaso vimānāi 'va* (in the exposition simply *vimāne*); in **d** as RV. The Anukr. takes no notice of the defective fourth pāda. Ppp. reads *na* (for *ha*) and *vimānaṁ* in **c**, and combines *prajā 'ty-*, and *anyā 'rkam*.

4. Twelve fellies, one wheel, three naves — who understands that? therein are inserted (*ā́hata*) three hundred and sixty pins (*çañkú*), pegs (? *khīla*) that are immovable.

The verse is also RV. i. 164. 48, which, however, has a very different second half: *tásmin sākáṁ triçatā́ ná çañkávo 'rpitā́ḥ ṣaṣṭír ná calācalā́saḥ*. The 'pins' or 'pegs' must be the equivalents of spokes. The three naves are probably seasons ⌊Hot, Wet, and Cold: cf. Bühler, *Epigraphia Indica*, ii. 262⌋, though the number is unusual. Ppp. reads *kelās* for *khīlās* in **d**. The Anukr. does not heed that **c** is a *jagatī* pāda. ⌊Kaṭha-reading *nā́bhyāni*, WZKM. xii. 282.⌋

5. This, O Savitar, do thou distinguish: six [are] twins, one [is] sole-born; they seek participation (*apitvá*) in him who of them is the sole sole-born.

The usual twelve months, two to a season, and the thirteenth occasional intercalary one, are doubtless meant. Ppp. reads in **b** *yomokas* (for *yamā ekas*). ⌊The *pada*-mss. of both W. and SPP. have *api॰tvám;* but in the *Index* W. assumes that *āpitvám* is the word. Both are well authenticated in BR.; but *apitvám* seems to fit best here (cf. ÇB. iv. 1. 3[11]).⌋

6. Being manifest (*āvís*), [it is] deposited in secret; the great track (*padá*), "aged" (*járat*) by name; there is set (*ā́rpita*) this all, [there is] established what stirs, what breathes.

7. One-wheeled it rolls, one-rimmed, thousand-syllabled, forth in front, down behind; with a half it has generated all existence; what its [other] half is — what has become of that?

This agrees nearly with xi. 4. 22 below, and Ppp. has it there, though not here. The sun is evidently meant, with half his course lost to view.

8. One carrying five carries the summit (*ágra*) of them; side-horses, harnessed, carry also along; what is not gone of it was seen, not what is gone; the higher thing [is] closer, the lower more distant.

⌊Or (c) 'of him' (*asya*).⌋ The sense is wholly obscure, and the version a mechanical one. *Pañcavāhī́* may be either fem. (of *-vāhá:* so *çatavāhī́* v. 17. 12) or masc. (of *-vāhin*); Pet. Lexx. say 'mit Fünfen bespannt.' Some of the mss. read *pṛ́ṣṭhayas* in **b**, as often in such cases. Ppp. has *asya* instead of *eṣām* at end of **a**.

9. A bowl (*camasá*) with orifice sideways, bottom-side up — in it is deposited glory of all forms; there sit together the seven seers, who have become the keepers of it, the great one.

The verse has a correspondent in ÇB. xiv. 5. 24 (BAU. ii. 2. 4). This reads at the beginning *arvā́gbilas;* in **c**, *tásya . . . tī́re* for *tát . . . sākám;* and, for **d**, *vā́g aṣṭamī́ bráhmaṇā saṁvidānā́.* The Brāhmaṇa itself explains the head as intended, the seven seers being the seven *prāṇas* or senses (the seven orifices of the head); this is extremely implausible. Ppp. reads at beginning of **c** *atrā "sata.*

10. The one which is applied (*yuj*) in front and which behind, which is applied in all cases and which in every case, by which the sacrifice is extended forward — that I ask of thee: which one of the verses is it?

The verse is quoted by *pratīka* in GB. i. 1. 22. All our *saṁhitā*-mss. save one (R.) ⌊and the great majority of SPP's⌋ read at the end *sá rcā́m* (Ppp. the same), and the words are quoted under Prāt. iii. 49 as example of that combination ⌊p. *sā́ ṛcā́m*⌋. The Anukr. does not heed that **b** is a *jagatī* pāda. Ppp. reads twice *yo 'ta* for *yā ca.*

11. What stirs, flies, and what stands, and what is breathing, not breathing, winking — that, all-formed, sustains the earth; that, combining, becomes one only.

One may conjecture *apānát* for *áprāṇat* in **b**. The Anukr. does not heed that two of the pādas are *triṣṭubh.* Ppp. reads at end of **b** *ca tiṣṭhat*, and, in **c**, *dyām utā 'muṁ* ⌊at 7. 35 it was fem.⌋ for *viçvarūpam.*

12. What is endless, stretched out on many sides; what is endless, and what has an end, ending together — these (two) the lord of the firmament keeps (*car*) separating (*vi-ci*), knowing what is and what shall be of it.

Ppp. reads *samakte* at end of **b**, *prajānan* at end of **c**, and *yadi* for *uta* in **d**. Probably earth and heaven are intended. The metrical definition of the Anukr. fits the verse (9 + 10 : 11 + 10 = 40) fairly.

13. Prajāpati goes about (*car*) within the womb; not being seen, he is manifoldly born (*vi-jā*); with a half he has generated all existence; what his [other] half is — which sign is that?

The third pāda is the same with 7 **c** above; the second half-verse is found below as xi. 4. 22 **c**, **d**; to the first half-verse corresponds VS. xxxi. 19 **a**, **b** and TA. iii. 13. 13 **a**, **b**: both reading *ájāyamānas* at beginning of **b**; ⌊so *Kaṭha-hss.*, p. 84⌋. Ppp. reads in **b** *prajāyate*, and, for **c**, **d**, *ardhene 'daṁ pari babhūva viçvaṁ etasyā 'rdhaṁ kim u taj jajāna*. The Anukr. takes no notice of the *jagatī* pāda **b**.

14. Him bearing water aloft, as a water-bearer (f.) with a vessel (*kumbhá*), all see with the eye, not all know with the mind.

Some mss. (P.M.I.) accent *vidúḥ* at the end.

15. In the distance it dwells with the full one, in the distance it is abandoned by the deficient one — the great monster (*yakṣá*) in the midst of existence; to it the kingdom-bearers bear tribute.

The verse, as noted above, is wanting in Ppp. ⌊Pāda **c** occurs as x. 7. 38 **a**: see note thereon and introd. to hymn 7.⌋

16. Whence the sun arises, and where he goes to rest — that same I think the chief (*jyeṣṭhá*); that nothing whatever surpasses.

The Kaṭha Up. ⌊iv. 9⌋ has a nearly corresponding verse: *yataç co 'd eti sūryo 'staṁ yatra ca gacchati: taṁ devāḥ sarve 'rpitās tad u nā 'ty eti kaç cana;* and the first half of this occurs also in ÇB. xiv. 4. 3[34] (BAU. i. 5. 23). The Anukr. omits to define the meter (*anuṣṭubh*) of the verse.

17. They who hitherward, in the middle, or also anciently, speak round about him who knows the Veda, they all speak around the sun (*ādityá*), Agni [as] second, and the threefold swan (*haṅsá*).

The verse is found also in TA. (ii. 15[8]), which omits *mádhye* and reads *purāṇé* in **a**, and *tṛtī́yam* (for *trivṛ́tam*) in **d**. ⌊Cf. *Kaṭha-hss.*, p. 63.⌋ Our *pada*-text ⌊as also SPP's⌋ reads near the beginning *arvā́ñ*, which is doubtless an error for *arvā́k* (though TA. reads *arvā́ñ utá*). Perhaps *védam* in **b** is to be rendered simply 'knowledge.' The Anukr. takes no notice of the two redundant syllables in **c**.

18. A thousand days' journey [are] expanded (*vi-yam*) the wings of him, of the yellow swan flying to heaven (*svargá*); he, putting all the gods in his breast, goes, viewing together all existences.

The verse is found again below as xiii. 2. 38; 3. 14. It is, as noted above, wanting here in Ppp.

19. By truth he burns aloft; by *bráhman* he looks abroad hitherward, by breath he breathes crosswise — he on whom rests (*çritá*) the chief thing.

20. Whoever indeed knows those two churning-sticks, with which is churned out what is good (*vásu*), he may think himself to know the chief thing; he may know the great *brā́hmaṇa* ⌊neut.⌋.

21. Footless came he into being in the beginning; he in the beginning brought the heaven (*svàr*); having become four-footed, enjoyable, he took to himself all enjoyment (*bhójana*).

Ppp. reads, for **b**, *so 'gre asurā 'bhavat*.

22. Enjoyable shall he become, likewise shall he eat much food, who shall worship (*upa-ās*) the everlasting god who gives superiority (*uttarávant*).

⌊After *bhógyo bhavat*, for which there are no variants, Bp. has a mark of pāda-division; but the Anukr. evidently scans as 12 : 8 + 8, eliding the *a* of *ánnam* after a *pragṛhya.*⌋ *Bhā́gyo* at the beginning is a misprint for *bhógyo*.

23. Everlasting they call him, also may he be at present ever-renewed; day and night are generated (*pra-jā*) in each other's forms.

The *pada*-text reads *anyáḥ : anyásya* in **d**, although the masc. *anyás* shows that the two words are virtually a compound, as later.

24. A hundred, a thousand, a myriad, a hundred million, an innumerable [number], is his own entered into him; that of him they slay, even as he looks on; therefore this god shines (*ruc*) thus.

Instead of *eṣa etat* at the end, Ppp. reads what appears to be *agha bhavat.* The version is as literal (and as unintelligent) as possible. The Anukr. takes no notice of the irregularity of the meter; it is possible, by violence, to count only 44 syllables in the verse.

25. One thing is more minute (*áṇu*) than a child (*bā́la*), also one is hardly (*né 'va*) seen; than that a more embracing deity, is she dear to me.

Ppp. reads, for **a**, *ārāgramātraṁ dadṛçe*, and begins **c** with *ataṣ pa-*, thus doing nothing to help our comprehension of the wholly obscure verse.

26. This beautiful one (f.) [is] unaging, an immortal in the house of a mortal; for whom she [was] made, he lies; he who made [her] grew old.

Ppp. reads *tasmāi* for *yasmāi* in **c**. ⌊The natural reading of **b** would be *mártyasya amṛ́tā gṛhé;* but⌋ the definition of the Anukr. forbids us to make ⌊it. Can a *sā́* have dropped out before *çáye sá?* Cf. note to iv. 5. 5.⌋

27. Thou art woman, thou [art] man, thou boy, or also girl; thou, when aged, totterest (*vañc*) with a staff; thou, when born, becomest facing all ways.

Ppp. politely puts *kumārī* first and *kumāras* second in **b**, and reads *jātam* in **d**. The verse is found, without variant, in Çvet. Up. iv. 3. It is so far correctly described by the Anukr. that it counts 37 syllables (7 + 10 : 9 + 11 = 37).

28. Both their father, or also their son; both the chief or also the meanest (*kaniṣṭhá*) of them; the one god, who has entered into the mind, born the first, and he within the womb.

The verse is also found, quoted as a *çloka*, in JUB. 85 (iii. 10. 12): *utāi 'ṣāṁ jāiṣṭha uta vā kaniṣṭha utāi 'ṣāṁ putra uta vā pitāi 'ṣām: eko ha devo manasi praviṣṭaḥ pūrvo ha jajñe sa u garbhe 'ntaḥ.* Ppp. reads, for **a**, **b**, *ute 'va jyeṣṭho 'ta vā kaniṣṭho 'tāi 'ṣa bhrāto 'ta vā pitāi 'ṣaḥ;* and, in **d**, *pūrvo jātaḥ.*

29. The full from the full he bends up (*ud-ac*); the full is poured with the full; also that may we know today, whence that is poured out.

This verse is akin with ⌊the oft-repeated⌋ one in ÇB. xiv. 8. 1 (BAU. v. 1): *pūrṇám adáḥ pūrṇám idám pūrṇā́t pūrṇám úd acyate* etc. What follows of the hymn is (as noted above) wanting in Ppp.

30. She, everlasting, born indeed of old, she, ancient, encompassed (*pari-bhū*) all; the great goddess of the dawn, shining forth, she looks forth by every one who winks.

The Anukr. calls the verse *bhurij* on account of the redundant syllable in **b**, not heeding the corresponding deficiency in **c**.

31. The deity, Avi by name, sits enveloped with right; by her form these trees [are] green, green-garlanded.

Or, 'by the form of her, the green-garlanded one' (so Ludwig). *Ávi* means 'sheep,' but is possibly here a derivative from the root *av* 'favor, aid.' All the *saṁhitā*-mss. combine in **a**, **b** *-ta rténa*.

32. Him that is near by he (?) deserts not; him that is near by he (?) sees not; see the wisdom (*kā́vya*) of the god: he died not, he grows not old.

There is nothing to determine the subject of the verbs in **a**, **b**; Ludwig renders 'she.'

33. The voices sent forth by the unpreceded one — they speak as they should (*yathāyathám*); where they go speaking, that [people] call the great *brā́hmaṇa* ⌊n.⌋.

34. Where both gods and men (*manuṣyà*) are set (*çritá*) as spokes in a nave — I ask thee of the flower (*púṣpa*) of the waters, where that by magic was placed.

The Anukr. takes no notice of the redundant syllable ⌊perhaps the first *ca?*⌋ in **a**.

35. They by whom the wind sent forth blows on, who give the five quarters together (*sadhryàñc*), the gods who thought themselves above (*ati-man*) the offering (*ā́huti*), conductors of the waters — which were they?

The first half-verse is found also in Ppp. ⌊xvi.⌋, but not in connection with the rest of the hymn. The Anukr. does not heed that **a** is defective by one syllable. Read in **b**, with all ⌊W's and SPP's⌋ mss., *dádante;* the form is from the same secondary root *dad* as the sing. *dadate* in 36 **c**. ⌊JUB. (i. 34) has this verse, putting it in the mouth of Pṛthu Vāinya, and its answer (vs. 36), with appended Brāhmaṇa-comment. It reads *samīcīḥ* for *sadhrīcīḥ* of our 35 **b**, and *āhutīs* in **c**.⌋

36. One of them clothes himself in this earth; one encompassed the atmosphere; he of them who is disposer (*vidhartṛ́*) gives the sky; some defend respectively all regions (*ā́çā*).

⌊JUB. (see under vs. 35) has *ekas* for *eṣām* of our **c** and *anye* for *eke* of our **d**.⌋

37. Whoso may know the stretched-out string in which these offspring (*prajā́*) are woven in, whoso may know the string of the string, he may know the great *brā́hmaṇa*.

38. I know the stretched-out string in which these offspring are woven in; the string of the string I know, likewise the great *bráhmaṇa.*

39. As between heaven-and-earth Agni went, burning on, all-consuming, where stood beyond they (f.) of one husband — where perchance was Mātariçvan then?

The *bṛhatī* of the Anukr. ⌊scanning 11 + 9 : 11 + 11⌋ is the second pāda, read with *āït* included as a part (the *pada*-text so marks the division) — which is, of course, artificial and wrong. ⌊Read as 12 + 8 : 11 + 11, pronouncing *-dāvías* and *kúe 'vā "sīn.*⌋ Ludwig's 'spouses of the only one' for *ékapatnīs* is against the accent.

40. Mātariçvan was entered into the waters; the gods were entered into the seas; great stood the traverser of space; the purifying one entered into the green ones.

The third pāda is identical with 3 **c** above, and the fourth with RV. viii. 90 (101). 14 **d**. 'The purifying one' is probably here the wind.

41. Higher, as it were, than the *gāyatrī,* upon the immortal (*amṛta*) he strode out; they who know completely chant with chant — where then was seen the goat?

Or, 'the unborn one' (*ajá:* so Ludwig); the verse is too utterly obscure to let us choose between them.

42. The reposer, the assembler of good things, like god Savitar, of true ordinances (*-dhárman*), he stood like Indra in the conflict for riches.

The verse corresponds with pādas **a**, **c**, **d** of RV. x. 139. 3 and of VS. xii. 66, TS. iv. 2. 5[4], MS. ii. 7. 12. RV. reads at the beginning *rāyó budhnáḥ* (for *nivéçanaḥ*); the other texts have at the end *pathīnā́m.* The verse is quoted in Vāit. 28. 28.

43. The lotus-flower of nine doors, covered with three strands (*guṇá*) — what soulful prodigy (*yakṣá*) is within it, that the *bráhman*-knowers know.

The 'nine doors' indicate that the human body with its nine orifices is intended; the three *guṇas* are probably the three temperaments familiar under that name later. The second half-verse was found above as 2. 32 **c**, **d** ⌊cf. vs. 31⌋. ⌊☞ See p. 1045.⌋

44. Free from desire, wise (*dhīra*), immortal, self-existent, satisfied with sap, not deficient in any respect — knowing that wise, unaging, young soul, one is not afraid of death.

⌊See Deussen, *Geschichte*, i. 1. 334: "die erste und älteste Stelle, die wir kennen, in der rückhaltlos der Ātman als Weltprincip proklamiert wird, AV. x. 8. 44." Cf. also p. 312, end. Muir, *Metrical Translations from Sanskrit Writers*, p. 1, gives a metrical paraphrase of the verse.⌋

⌊The quoted Anukr. says *caturdaça* (i.e. 14 above 30). The fourth *anuvāka*, with 2 hymns and 88 verses, ends here.⌋

9. With the offering of a cow and a hundred rice-dishes.

[*Atharvan.* — *saptaviṅçati. mantroktaçatāudanadevatyam. ānuṣṭubham: 1. triṣṭubh; 12. pathyāpañkti; 25. dvyuṣṇiggarbhā 'nuṣṭubh; 26. 5-p. bṛhatyanuṣṭubuṣṇiggarbhā jagatī; 27. 5-p. atijāgatānuṣṭubgarbhā çakvarī.*]

Found also in Pāipp. xvi. The hymn (vs. 1) is quoted in Kāuç. 65. 1 to accompany the closing of the mouth of a victim, and some of the verses (1-3, 26, 27) in other neighboring parts of the sūtra. In Vāit. is used a single verse (26).

Translated: Ludwig, p. 270 (in great part); Henry, 32, 83; Griffith, ii. 42.

1. Fasten thou up the mouths of the mischief-making ⌊ones⌋; bring (*arpay-*) this thunderbolt upon our rivals; given by Indra, first, with a hundred rice-dishes, cousin-slaying, the success (*gātú*) of the sacrificer.

It is a cow (f.) accompanied by a whole hundred of *odanas* or offerings of boiled rice, that is here the subject; we had in various places above a goat (m.) with five such additions. Ppp. reads in **d** *yajamānāya*. The Anukr. does not heed that the third pāda is *jagatī*.

2. Be thy skin the sacrificial hearth, [be] the hairs which [are] thine the *barhís*; this rein (*raçanā́*) hath seized thee; let this pressing-stone dance over thee.

The parts of this and the preceding verse are prescribed in Kāuc. 65. 1-3 to be used to accompany certain sacrificial acts to which they are adapted.

3. Be thy tail-tuft the sprinklers; let thy tongue do the cleansing, O inviolable one; do thou, having become clean, fit for sacrifice, go on to heaven, O thou of the hundred rice-dishes.

The form *bā́lās* (which Ppp. also reads) ⌊as against *vā́lās*⌋ is vouched for ⌊incidentally⌋ by the comm. to Prāt. i. 66 ⌊in its discussion of the exchange of *r* and *l*⌋. The verse is quoted in Kāuç. 65. 9. *Sam mārṣṭu* = 'serve as *sammārjana*.'

4. Whoso cooks her of the hundred rice-dishes, he is adapted to the fulfilment of wishes; for all his priests (*ṛtvíj*), being gratified, go as they should.

All the *saṁhitā*-mss. read in **c** *asya rtv-*.

5. He ascends the heavenly road (*svargá*), where is yon triple heaven of the heaven (*dív*), who, making [her] cake-naveled, gives her of the hundred rice-dishes.

The meaning and connection of **c** are not very clear. Ludwig renders "and makes her the middle point of the *apūpa*," which is against the accent; probably 'adding cakes numerous enough to cover her.' ⌊Is it not virtually equivalent to 'putting a cake on her navel,' as preparatory to sacrificing her?⌋ Ppp. has *hiraṇyajyotiṣam* instead of *apūpanābhim* (cf. the next verse). The resolution *kṛtu-ā́*, necessary to make the verse a regular *anuṣṭubh*, is rather harsh.

6. He obtains those worlds, [those] which are heavenly and ⌊those⌋ which are earthly, who, having made [her] lighted with gold, gives her of the hundred rice-dishes.

Ppp. reads for **b** *yeṣa devās samāsate*, and has *apūpanābhim* here in **c**, instead of in 5 **c**.

7. What people are thy quellers, O heavenly one ⌊f.⌋, and what thy cookers, they shall all guard thee: be not afraid of them, thou of the hundred rice-dishes.

Ppp. puts this verse before our 5.

8. The Vasus shall guard thee on the right, thee the Maruts on the left (*uttarā́t*), the Ādityas behind; do thou run beyond the Agnishṭoma.

That is, probably, exceed or surpass even this important ceremony.

9. The gods, the Fathers, men (*manuṣyà*), and they that are Gandharvas-and-Apsarases — they shall all guard thee; do thou run beyond the over-night sacrifice (*atirātrá*).

Ppp. reads *gandharvāpsaraso devā rudrāñgirasas tvā.* ⌊Cf. note to vs. 8.⌋

10. He obtains the atmosphere, the sky, the earth, the Ādityas, the Maruts, the quarters, all worlds, who gives her of the hundred rice-dishes.

11. Sprinkling forth ghee, well-portioned, the divine one will go to the gods; hurt not him who cooks thee, O inviolable one; go on to heaven, O thou of the hundred rice-dishes.

Ppp. reads in **b** *devāṅ devī.*

12. The gods that are stationed (*-sad*) in the sky, and that are stationed in the atmosphere, and these that are upon the earth — to them do thou always yield (*duh*) milk, butter, also honey.

Several of the mss., with a carelessness common in such cases, read *dhukṣa* in **d**. We have to resolve *deva-ā* in **a**, in order to make a normal pāda. Ppp. rectifies the meter of **a** by reading instead *pitaras* for *devās.* ⌊Ppp. combines *-ṣado 'ntar-* in **a–b.**⌋

13. What head is thine, what mouth is thine, what ears and what jaws are thine — let them yield to thy giver curd, milk, butter, also honey.

Ppp. reads *ye te çṛñge* for second half of **a**, and so for second part of **b** *yāu ca te akṣāu* ⌊cf. vs. 14⌋.

14. What lips are thine, what nostrils, what horns, and what thine eyes — let them yield etc. etc.

Ppp. reads instead *yat te mukhaṁ yā te jihvā ye dantā yā ca te hanū.*

15. What lungs are thine, what heart, the *purītát* with the throat — let them yield etc. etc.

Yás at the beginning is emended from *yát*, which all the mss. ⌊both W's and SPP's⌋ read.

16. What liver is thine, what two *mátasnās*, what entrail, and what thine intestines — let them yield etc. etc.

Ppp. reads in **b** *yā "ntrāṇi.*

17. What *plāçí* is thine, what rectum (? *vaniṣṭhú*), what (two) paunches, and what thy skin — let them yield etc. etc.

18. What marrow is thine, what bone, what flesh, and what blood — let them yield etc. etc.

Ppp. reads in **a** *yāny asthīni*, thus rectifying the meter. The Anukr. does not notice the lacking syllable in the pāda. *Yás* at the beginning is again emendation for the *yát* of all the mss. ⌊both W's and SPP's⌋.

19. What fore-legs (*bāhú*) are thine, what shanks (*doṣán*), what shoulders ⌊*áṅsa*⌋, and what thy hump — let them yield etc. etc.

Ppp. reads, after *bāhū*, *yāu te aṅsāu dūhanaṁ yā ca* etc.

20. What neck-bones (*grīvā́*) are thine, what shoulder-bones ⌊*skandhā́*⌋, what side-bones (*pṛṣṭí*), and what ribs (*párçu*) — let them yield etc. etc.

The Anukr. does not notice the lacking syllable in **a**.

21. What thighs are thine, knee-joints, what hips, and what thy rump — let them yield etc. etc.

22. What tail is thine, what thy tail-tuft, what udder, and what thy teats — let them yield etc. etc.

23. What hind-thighs are thine, what dew-claws, [what] pasterns (*ṛchára*), and what thy hoofs — let them yield etc. etc.

One of our mss. (O.) reads in **b** *ṛtsárās*, and Ppp. supports it by giving *kṛtsarās*. ⌊The reading *ṛtsárās* seems to be supported by E. as well as by O. and Ppp. Its phonetic relation to *ṛcchárās* resembles that of Pāli *ucchādana*, *jighacchā*, *bībhaccha* to Skt. *utsādana*, *jighatsā*, *bībhatsa* (Kuhn, *Pāli-gram.*, p. 52, gives *kucchā* = *kutsā*, *vaccha* = *vatsa*). Unless I err, our vulgate text here shows a Prākritism such as we have good right to assume also at iii. 12. 4, in case of the much-discussed *ucchántu*, which may be a mere vernacularized rendering of *ukṣántu* (cf. *tacchaka* = *takṣaka*, Kuhn, l.c.).⌋

24. What hide is thine, O thou of the hundred rice-dishes, what hairs, O inviolable one — let them yield etc. etc.

25. Let thy two breasts (*kroḍá*) be sacrificial cakes, smeared over with sacrificial butter; having made them wings, O divine one, do thou carry him who cooks thee to heaven (*dív*).

The Anukr. very strangely ignores the two resolutions in **b** and **c**, and reckons the pādas as 7 syllables each.

26. What in the mortar, on the pestle, and on the hide, or what rice-grain, [what] kernel in the winnowing-basket, or what the wind, Mātariçvan, blowing (*pū*), shook (*math*) — let Agni as *hótar* make that well-offered.

It is very much out of place to reckon five pādas (12 + 9 : 8 + 7 + 11 = 47) in this verse; but the *pada*-ms. supports the Anukr., by making a mark of pāda-division after *mātariçvā;* evidently either this word or *pávamānas* (rather the former) is an intrusion in **c**. ⌊The last pāda we had as vi. 71. 1 **d**.⌋ The verse is quoted in Vāit. 4. 9; also (with vi. 122, 123) in Kāuç. 63. 29, to accompany the closing libations. Ppp. reads in **b** *ye vā çūrpe taṇḍulāṣ kaṇāḥ.*

27. The heavenly waters, rich in honey, dripping with ghee, I seat in separate succession in the hands of the priests (*brahmán*); with what desire I now pour you on, let all that fall to my lot; may we be lords of wealth.

Ppp. begins **a** with *imā āpo madh-*, and **c** with *yatkāme 'dam.* Compare the verses vi. 122. 5 and xi. 1. 27, which are in part coincident with this; ⌊also MGS. i. 5. 4 and Index under *devīr āpo*⌋. The verse (rather than i. 4. 3, which has the same *pratīka*) is quoted in Kāuç. 65. 8, to accompany the setting of water pots. The metrical definition of the Anukr. suits well enough.

⌊The quoted Anukr. says "*aghāyatām*": cf. vs. 1.⌋

10. Extolling the cow (vaçā́).

[*Kaçyapa.—catustrin̄çat. mantroktavaçā́devatyam. ānuṣṭubham: 1. kakummatī; 5. skandhogrīvābṛhatī; 6, 8, 10. virāj; 23. bṛhatī; 24. upariṣṭādbṛhatī; 26. āstārapan̄kti; 27. çan̄kumatī; 29. 3-p. virāḍ gāyatrī; 31. uṣṇiggarbhā; 32. virāṭ pathyābṛhatī.*]

Found also in Pāipp. xvi. ⌊with the verse-sequence 15 **a**, **b**, 14 **c**, **d**, 13, 14 **a**, **b**, 15 **c**, **d**, 17, 16, 18; vs. 3 is lacking⌋. Not noticed in Vāit., and only once in Kāuç., at 66. 20, where vs. 1 (or the hymn ⌊rather the hymn⌋) is used, with xii. 4, to accompany the sprinkling of an offered cow.

Translated: Ludwig, p. 534; Deussen, *Geschichte*, i. 1. 234 (cf. p. 230 f., 233 f.); Henry, 35, 85; Griffith, ii. 45.

1. Homage to thee while being born, homage also to thee when born; to thy tail-tuft, hoofs, form, O inviolable one, be homage.

The Anukr. chooses to reject the common resolution *-bhi-as* (twice) in **c**.

2. Whoso may know the seven advances (?*pravát*), [and] may know the seven distances, whoso may know the head of the sacrifice—he may accept the cow (*vaçā́*).

Ppp. reads in **b** *veda* instead of *vidyāt.* The verse is quoted by *pratīka* in GB. i. 2. 16.

3. I know the seven advances, I know the seven distances; I know the head of the sacrifice, and the outlooking soma in her.

This verse, with a part of the preceding one, is wanting in Ppp. ⌊*Asyām*, sc. *vaçā́yām.*⌋

4. By whom the sky, by whom the earth, by whom these waters are guarded—the cow, of a thousand streams (*-dhā́rā*), we address with worship (*bráhman*).

We need to resolve *-dhāra-ām* in **c** in order to make out the full pāda which the Anukr. assumes.

5. A hundred metal dishes (*kaṅsá*), a hundred milkers, a hundred guardians, upon the back of her; the gods that breathe in her, they know the cow singly.

The verse (9 + 11 : 8 + 8 = 36) is a *bṛhatī* in number of syllables only.

6. Having the sacrifice for feet, cheer (*írā-*) for milk, *svadhā́* for breath, being *mahī́lukā*, the cow, having Parjanya for spouse, goes unto the gods with worship (*bráhman*).

Ppp. reads for **a**, **b** *yajñapatir ākṣīrāt svadhāprāṇā mahilokāḥ*, which does not solve the problem of the obscure word *mahī́lukā* (found nowhere else). There is no need of calling the verse *virāj*.

7. After thee entered Agni, after thee Soma, O cow; thine udder, O excellent one, is Parjanya; the lightnings are thy teats, O cow.

8. The waters thou yieldest (*duh*) first, the cultivated fields after, O cow; thou yieldest kingdom third, food, milk, O cow.

The permissible resolution *rāṣ-ṭr-ám* in **c** would obviate the necessity of reckoning the verse as *virāj*. Ppp. combines in **b** *urvarā 'parā*.

9. When, called by the Ādityas, thou didst approach, O righteous one, Indra made thee drink a thousand vessels (*pā́tra*) of soma, O cow.

By a notable inconsistency, the Anukr. reckons this verse as a complete *anuṣṭubh*, although it requires, to make it such, precisely the same resolution (*pā́-tr-ān*) as vs. 8.

10. When thou didst go following (*anvā́ñc*) Indra, then the bull called thee; therefore the Vṛitra-slayer, angry, took thy milk (*páyas*), milk (*kṣīrá*), O cow.

All the *saṁhitā*-mss. accent in **b** *-bhó 'hvayat*, and one *pada*-ms. (D.) has accordingly *áhvayat*. In like manner, all save R.p.m. have *kruddhó 'har-* in **d**. In both cases our edition emends to *ŏ*. In this verse also (as in 6, 8) the designation *virāj* is uncalled-for. Ppp. reads *uvūcī* in **a**, and *ād vṛṣabho* in **b**.

11. When the lord of riches, angry, took thy milk, O cow, then this the firmament (*nā́ka*) now keeps (*rakṣ*) in three vessels.

Ppp. reads, in **a–b**, *-patiḥ kṣīraṁ dehi bharad vaçe*.

12. In three vessels the heavenly cow took that soma, where Atharvan, consecrated, sat on a golden *barhís*.

Ppp. reads *hitaṁ* for *tam* in **a**, and *ādyevy abharad* in **b**.

13. Since she has united (*sam-gam*) with soma, and with all that has feet, the cow has stood upon the ocean, together with the Gandharvas, the *kalís*.

Before this verse, Ppp. sets one made up of our 15 **a**, **b** and 14 **c**, **d**. *Pada*-text in **c** *ádhi : asthāt*. ⌊As to *kali*, cf. Bergaigne, *Rel. Véd.* ii. 482.⌋ ⌊For *ágata*, see *Gram.* § 834 **b**.⌋

14. Since she has united with the wind, and with all winged ones the cow danced forth in the ocean, bearing the verses, the chants.

Ppp. combines (as above noted) our 15 **a**, **b** and 14 **c**, **d**, and then again our 14 **a**, **b** and 15 **c**, **d**, without other variant.

15. Since she has united with the sun, and with all sight, the cow has overlooked the ocean, bearing excellent lights.

Some of the mss. (P.M.E.) read in **c** *aty akṣad* (K. *akṣyad*).

16. As, O righteous one, thou didst stand decked (*abhi-vṛ*) with gold, the ocean, having become a horse, mounted (*adhi-skand*) thee, O cow.

Ppp. puts this verse after our 17.

17. There the excellent ones united, the cow, the directress, also the *svadhā́*, where Atharvan, consecrated, sat on a golden *barhís*.

The second half-verse is identical with 12 **c**, **d** above. Ppp. reads in **a** *gachanti*.

18. The cow is mother of the noble (*rājanyà*), the cow thy mother, O *svadhā́;* from the cow was born the weapon; from it was born intent (*cittá*).

The translation implies the obvious emendation of *yajñé* in **c** to *jajñé*, as at iv. 24. 6 ⌊see note thereto⌋.

19. The globule (*bindú*) went (*car*) up aloft, out of the summit (*kákuda*) of the *bráhman;* thence wast thou born, O cow; thence was the invoker born.

20. From thy mouth came (*bhū*) the songs (*gā́thā*), from thy nape-bones, O cow, [came] force; from thy belly (? *pājasyà*) was born the sacrifice, from thy teats the rays.

Ppp. reads in **a** *bhavanti* for *abhavan.*

21. From thy (two) fore-legs (*īrmá*) motion (*áyana*) was born, and from thy thighs (*sákthi*), O cow; from thine entrails were born eaters (*attrá*), out from thy belly (*udára*) the plants.

Ppp. reads at the beginning *ayurmābhyām*, and in **c** *yatrā jajñire.* ⌊For *atrā́s*, cf. note to i. 7. 3.⌋

22. When (*yát*), O cow, thou didst enter along the belly of Varuṇa, thence the priest (*brahmán*) called thee up; for he knew thy guidance (*netrá*).

23. All trembled at the embryo, while being born, of her who gives not birth (? *asūsū́*); for "the cow hath given birth," they say of her; shaped (m.) by charms (*bráhman*); for it is her connection.

Much here is obscure and doubtful. *Asūsū́* (not divided in p.) ought, by its accent, to be *asū-sū* 'giving birth to one who does not herself give birth' ⌊*Gram.* § 1147 c⌋. The connection of *kḷptás* with *vaçā́* is strange; the former belongs probably to *gárbhas* understood. The accent of *āhús* indicates that *hí* belongs with it, and not with *sasū́va*. The name *vaçā́* used for the cow throughout the hymn implies non-pregnancy. Ppp. reads at the end *brahmaṇā kl̥pta* ⌊R's Collation spells it *klipta*⌋ *uta bandhur asyāt.* ⌊The verse may be counted as 36 syllables; but the nearest approach to a natural scansion would seem to be 8 + 8 : 11 (*taām*) + 11.⌋ ⌊I will not attempt to revise W's treatment of this verse. Griffith and the other translators may be consulted.⌋

24. One combines (*sam-sr̥j*) the fighters who alone is in control (*vaçín*) of her; the sacrifices became energies (? *táras*); the cow became the eye of energies.

The Anukr. should have qualified the name of this *br̥hatī* by adding *virāj.* Ppp. combines at the beginning *yudhe 'kas s-*.

25. The cow accepted the sacrifice; the cow sustained the sun; within the cow entered the rice-dish together with the priest (*brahmán*).

Ppp. reads *yajñam* instead of *sūryam* in **b**. All the mss. have *brahmáṇā.*

26. The cow they call immortality (*amŕ̥ta*); the cow they worship (*upa-ās*) as death; the cow became this all — gods, men, Asuras, Fathers, seers.

Ppp. reads *āhur amr̥taṁ* in **a**. The definition of the meter by the Anukr. is bad; it ⌊seems to be 8 + 8 : 8 + 14⌋.

27. Whoso knoweth thus, he may accept the cow; for so doth the all-footed sacrifice yield milk (*duh*) to the giver, unresisting.

28. Three tongues glisten (*dīdī*) within the mouth of Varuṇa; of these, the one that shines (*rāj*) in the middle is the cow, hard of acceptance.

The mss., as is usual in such cases, are divided between *duḥpr-* and *duṣpr-* in **d**.

29. The seed of the cow was quartered: the waters a quarter, the *amŕ̥ta* a quarter, the sacrifice a quarter, the domestic animals a quarter.

30. The cow [is] the sky, the cow the earth, the cow Vishṇu, Prajāpati; the yield (*dugdhá*) of the cow did the Perfectibles (*sādhyá*) and they who are Vasus drink.

31. Having drunk the yield of the cow, the Perfectibles and they who are Vasus — they verily worship the milk (*páyas*) of her at the summit of the ruddy one.

Ppp. reads *ime* instead of *te vāi* at beginning of **c**. The definition of the meter by the Anukr. is bad, the verse being, by usual and easy resolutions, a regular *anuṣṭubh.*

32. Some milk her for soma; some worship ghee; they who gave the cow to the one knowing thus are gone to the triple heaven of the heaven.

The *pada*-mss., by an absurd blunder, read *yá* before *evám* into *yáḥ* instead of *yé.* It is apparently the intrusion of *vaçā́m* into **c** that makes the meter irregular. ⌊Pādas **a**, **b** are a reminiscence of RV. x. 154. 1 (= AV. xviii. 2. 14).⌋

33. Having given the cow to the Brahmans, one attains all worlds; for righteousness is set in her, also *bráhman,* likewise penance.

Ppp. reads in **a** *vaçā dattvā brāh-*, and in **c** *āhitam* instead of *ārpitam.*

34. On the cow the gods subsist; on the cow, men also; the cow became this all, so far as the sun looks abroad.

The Anukr. takes no notice of the redundant syllable in **a** (read, by irregular combination, *devó 'pa*).

⌊Here ends the fifth *anuvāka*, with 2 hymns and 61 verses. The quoted Anukr. says, referring to this last hymn, *catasraḥ* (i.e. 4 over 30).⌋

⌊One ms. (P.) sums up the verses aright as 350.⌋

⌊Here ends the twenty-third *prapāṭhaka*.⌋

Book XI.

⌊This eleventh book is the fourth book of the second grand division of the Atharvan collection. As to the general make-up of the books of this division, see page 471. The Old Anukramaṇī describes the length of hymns 6 and 8 by stating the excess of each over 20 verses. All of the book except hymns 3 and 8 has been translated by Bloomfield in *Sacred Books of the East*, vol. xlii.; and all of it by Victor Henry, *Les Livres X, XI et XII de l'Atharva-véda traduits et commentés*, Paris, 1896. Here again we have the *bhāṣya* for the entire book.⌋

⌊The ritual uses of this book are confined for the most part to the first hymn, nearly every verse of which is quoted in Kāuçika 60–63 and 65 in connection with the details of the *sava* sacrifice. Of the other nine hymns only sporadic citations are made by Kāuçika; and in the Vāitāna, only a single quotation (of 2.1) is made out of the whole book.⌋

⌊**Paryāya-hymns**: for details respecting them, see pages 471–2. The *paryāya*-hymn of this book is hymn 3, with 3 *paryāyas*.⌋

⌊**Discrepancies of hymn-numeration**, as between the two editions, in so far as they are occasioned by the counting of each *paryāya* as a separate hymn by the Bombay edition. The matter is discussed at this place because it is in this book, page 625, that Whitney has condemned the procedure of the Bombay edition. The facts are as follows:⌋ ⌊☞ See p. cxxxiv and p. 1013.⌋

⌊In book viii., the Bombay edition, counting separately each of the 6 *paryāyas* of our last hymn (h. 10), makes for that book a total of 15 hymns; but, since the discrepancy is confined to our last hymn, the plus of 5 does not affect the numeration of the preceding 9.⌋

⌊In book ix., the Bombay edition, counting separately each of the 6 *paryāyas* of our hymn 6 (its 6–11), has a plus of 5 for our h. 7 (its 12) and the following. Our h. 7 is also a *paryāya*-hymn; but since it has but 1 *paryāya*, the plus remains a constant from our h. 7 to the end. The total is again 15.⌋

⌊In book x. there is no *paryāya*-hymn to affect the numeration.⌋

⌊In book xi., the Bombay edition, counting the 3 *paryāyas* of our hymn 3 as its 3 and 4 and 5, has a plus of 2 for our 4 (its 6) and the following. Its total is therefore 12.⌋

⌊In book xii., the Bombay edition, counting separately each of the 7 *paryāyas* of our last hymn (h. 5), makes for that book a total of 11 hymns; but, since the discrepancy is confined to our last hymn, the plus of 6 does not affect the numeration of the preceding 4.⌋

⌊In book xiii., the Bombay edition, counting separately each of the 6 *paryāyas* of our last hymn (h. 4), makes for that book a total of 9 hymns; but the discrepancy is confined to our last hymn (as in books viii. and xii.), and the plus of 5 does not affect the numeration of the preceding 3.⌋

⌊Book xiv. contains no *paryāya*-hymn. Books xv. and xvi. consist wholly of *paryāyas*, the former of 18 and the latter of 9, and there is accordingly no practical discrepancy between the two editions.⌋

⌊In his Critical Notice (prefixed to vol. i.), pages 19–23, S. P. Pandit rests his procedure in this matter of numeration upon the authority of the Major Anukr. and of the Minor or Old Anukr. (*Pañcapaṭalikā*): see especially his page 23, end. His citations undoubtedly prove the right of each *paryāya* to be presented separately, and they are so presented in the Berlin edition. But the mss., in numbering the verses of each *paryāya*, begin anew each time with 1; perhaps this is required by the prescription of the Old Anukr. (Critical Notice, p. 23), *paryāyeṣv avasānānām ṛgbhis tulyo vidhir bhavet.* Accordingly, R. and W. may be wrong in numbering the verses of a group of *paryāyas* continuously (see above, p. 472, top). But I am not sure that independent verse-numbering for each *paryāya* forbids the grouping of several related *paryāyas* into one *sūkta*. This is the real point at issue between the two editions and I will not try to decide it.⌋

⌊I will say, however, that the uniformity of structure in books viii.–xi. as books of ten hymns each (see p. 471), which uniformity results from counting the *paryāyas* in groups, seems to support the procedure of R. and W. Moreover, as W. says (p. 472, top), the *paryāyas* of a given group taken together do "evidently constitute each ⌊group⌋ a whole"; and he is borne out by the comm. (at vol. iii., p. 562[22]), who speaks of the "rice-dish-triad," our xi. 3, as constituting one "subject-matter-hymn" (*artha-sūkta:* but not in its narrower technical sense).—It may be added that the Major Anukr., at the end of its 7th *paṭala* and of its treatment of our book xi., says *evaṁ ṣaṭ-triṅçad arthasūktāni:* that is right; for books viii.–xi. have, according to the Berlin count, (4 × 10 hymns =) 40 hymns, of which 4 hymns (our viii. 10, ix. 6, ix. 7, and xi. 3) are *paryāya-sūktas*, leaving 36 *artha-sūktas*. But this does not prove that our 4 *paryāya-sūktas* should not be counted as 16 (cf. p. 471, end).⌋

⌊The *anuvāka*-division of the book (as is explained on page 472) is into five *anuvākas* of two hymns each. The "decad"-division likewise is as described on page 472. A tabular conspectus for book xi. follows:

Anuvākas	1		2		3		4		5	
Hymns	1	2	3	4	5	6	7	8	9	10
Verses	37	31	56¶	26	26	23	27	34	26	27
Decad-div.	10+10+10+7	10+10+11	3P	10+10+6	10+10+6	10+13	10+10+7	10+10+14	10+10+6	10+10+7

Here ¶ means "paragraph of a *paryāya*" (such as is numbered as a "verse" in the Berlin edition) and P means "*paryāya*." The last line shows the "decad"-division. Of these "decads," *anuvākas* 1, 2, 3, 4, and 5 contain respectively 7, 3, 5, 6, and 6 (in all, 27 "decads"); while *anuvāka* 2 has 3 *paryāyas*. The sum is 27 "decad"-*sūktas* and 3 *paryāya-sūktas* or 30 *sūktas*.⌋

1. Accompanying a rice-dish offering.

[*Brahman.*—*saptatriṅçat. brāhmāudanikam. trāiṣṭubham : 1. anuṣṭubgarbhā bhurik pañkti ; 2. bṛhatīgarbhā virāj ; 3. 4-p. çākvaragarbhā jagatī ; 4. bhurij ; 5. bṛhatīgarbhā virāj ; 6. uṣṇih ; 8. virāḍgāyatrī ; 9. çākvarātijāgatagarbhā jagatī ; 10. virāṭ purotijagatī virāḍjagatī ; 11. jagatī ; 15, 16. bhurij ; 17. virāḍ jagatī ; 18. atijāgatagarbhā parātijāgatā virāḍ atijagatī ; 20. atijāgatagarbhā paraçākvarā 4-p. bhurig jagatī ; 21, 24–26, 29. virāḍjagatī (29. bhurij) ; 27. atijāgatagarbhā jagatī ; 31. bhurij : 35. 4-p. kakummaty uṣṇih ; 36. purovirāḍ vyāghrādiṣv avagantavyā* ; 37. virāḍ jagatī.*]

⌊Verse 35 is prose.⌋ Found also in Pāipp. xvi. (in the verse-order 1–10, 12, 11, 13–18, 22, 19, 20, 21, 23–37). Nearly every verse of the hymn is quoted in Kāuç. 60–63 and 65 in connection with the description of the *sava* offerings ; ⌊see Bloomfield, page 610 and the following for details so far as they are helpful⌋. ⌊Citations in other parts of Kāuç. are noted under the verses. The hymn is not noticed by Vāit. : see page 610.⌋ *⌊This curious addition to the Anukr., *vyāghrādiṣv avagantavyā*, recurs in the Anukr's treatment of xiv. 1.60 and of the **c** of xv. 5. 1–7. See note to xv. 5. 7.⌋

Translated : Henry, 97, 133 ; Griffith, ii. 51 ; Bloomfield, 179, 610.

1. O Agni, be thou born ; Aditi here, suppliant, cooks a *brahmán*-rice-dish, desiring sons ; the seven seers, being-makers — let them churn thee here together with progeny.

Aditi's cooking of a rice-dish in order to obtain progeny is repeatedly referred to in the Brāhmaṇas — probably by way of echo of this verse : compare TS. vi. 5. 6[1] ; TB. i. 1. 9[1] ; K. vii. 15 ; MS. i. 6. 12 ; ⌊ii. 1. 12 and references⌋ ; ⌊also AV. vi. 81. 3⌋ ; the comm. quotes the TS. passage in his explanation of the verse. He defines a *brahmāudana* as *brahmaṇe jagatsraṣṭre svāhākāreṇa deya odanaḥ*, and then adds : *yad vā brahmāudanasavākhye 'smin karmaṇi brāhmaṇānām bhojanāya bhāgatvena kalpita odano brahmāudanaḥ*.

2. Make ye smoke, O ye bulls, companions, ye that are aided by the unhateful (?), unto speech ; this Agni [is] fight-overpowering, having good heroes, by whom the gods overpowered the barbarians.

The second pāda is mechanically rendered, being quite corrupt, as appears ⌊from the meter and⌋ by comparison with the corresponding RV. verse (iii. 29. 9), which reads instead *ásredhanta itana vā́jam ácha*. The comm. explains *ádrogh-* as *adrohakāriṇāṁ sucaritrāṇāṁ yajamānānām avitā rakṣitā*, as if the *pada*-reading were *-avitā* instead of *-avitāḥ*. ⌊W's Collation-book gives *-avitāḥ* as *pada*-reading without note of variant ; and this is the reading also of two or three of SPP's mss. : but he admits *-avitā* into his *pada*-text, following one or two mss.⌋ RV. begins also *kṛṇóta*, and has *vṛṣaṇam* for *vṛṣaṇas* in **a** ; also *devā́sas* (rectifying the meter) in **d**. All the mss. ⌊save one or two⌋ read *asahanta*, unaccented, in **d**, but both editions make the necessary emendation to *ásahanta* — which, of course, RV. has. Ppp. is corrupt in **d**, reading *devā 'santa** ; after it *çatrūn*. *⌊A most interesting instance of haplography on the part of the AV. : cf. note to iv. 5. 5. Note the fourfold occurrence of the sound-combination *ăs* within the RV. pāda ; and that three of these are reduced by Ppp. to one.⌋

3. O Agni, thou hast been born unto great heroism, unto the cooking of the *brahmán*-rice-dish, O Jātavedas ; the seven seers, being-makers —

they have given thee birth; do thou confirm to this woman wealth with all heroes.

Ppp. reads *paktaye* in **b**, combines *saptarṣ-* in **c**, and has in **d** *asme* and *ni yachatām*.

4. Kindled, O Agni, be thou kindled with kindling (*samídh*); mayest thou bring hither, knowing, the worshipful gods; for them cooking (*çrā*) the oblation, O Jātavedas, make thou this man to ascend to the highest firmament (*nā́ka*).

Ppp. reads in **b** *viçvā devān*. In **a**, the comm. has *samiddhaḥ sa* for *sám idhyasva*. ⌊For **d**, cf. i. 9. 2, 4; vi. 63. 3.⌋

5. Threefold is set down the share that is yours of old — of gods, of Fathers, of mortals; know ye the portions (*áñça*); I share them out to you; that one that is the gods' shall set this woman across.

That is (at the end), as the comm. paraphrases it, *iṣṭaphalasya pāraṁ gamayati* 'bring her to the further shore (the completion) of desired result.' Ppp. reads *jātavedas* in **a** for *yaḥ purā vaḥ*, inserts *uta* before *martyānām* in **b**, and has in **d** *sāi 'vaṁ* for *sa imām*.

6. O Agni, powerful, overcoming, thou overcomest; put down (*ni-ubj*) [our] hating rivals; let this measure (*mā́trā*), being measured, and measured, make [thy] fellows tribute-bringers to thee.

The comm. does not try to give *ny ubja* a more distinctive meaning than *adhomukhān pātaya;* the obscure *mā́trā* he simply glosses by *nirmātrā* ⌊as instrumental sing. masc. (supplying *iyaṁ çālā* as subject); but the three translators take it as nom.⌋.

7. In company with thy fellows, be thou united with milk; urge her up unto great heroism; ascend aloft to the summit (*viṣṭáp*) of the firmament (*nā́ka*), which they call by the name heavenly world.

Addressed, according to the comm., to the sacrificer; the Kāuç. (61.20) makes it accompany the pouring of rice into the mortar. The comm. explains *ud ubja* as *ud gamaya unnataçiraskāṁ kuru*. Ppp. reads *sujātāiṣ* in **a**, and *viṣṭapas* in **c**.

8. Let this great one (*mahī́*) accept the hide, the divine earth, with favoring mind; then may we go to the world of the well-done.

This accompanies, as is plain, the spreading-out of the ox-hide upon the ground (so Kāuç. 60. 30). Ppp. reads in **b** *pṛthivyāi*, and, at the end, *sukṛtām u lokam*. The last pāda is the same with vi. 121. 1 **d**; vii. 83. 4 **d**.

9. Join thou on the hide these two allied stones; split apart the shoots (*añçú*) successfully for the sacrificer; smiting down, smite them that would fight her; bearing up thy progeny aloft, lift up.

The feminine participles in **c**, **d** indicate that the verse is addressed to the wife of the sacrificer, though the comm. understands the first half as for the priest. *Añçu* he regards as applied by a figure to the rice, as *grāvāṇāu* 'soma-pressing-stones,' means mortar and pestle. 'Smite down' and 'lift up' are the alternate movements of the pestle, each viewed as symbolical. *Imām* is redundant in **c** as regards both meter and sense;

perhaps it has blundered in here out of 11 **c**. Ppp. is corrupt in **c** and **d**, but can be seen to read *uddharantī* in **d**. The verse and its parts are quoted in Kāuç. 61. 18, 22, 24.

10. Seize in thy hand, O hero, the two joint-acting (*sakṛ́t*) stones; the worshipful gods have come to thy sacrifice; three boons, whichsoever thou choosest — those successes do I here make successful for thee.

The comm. and one or two of SPP's authorities read *sukṛ́tāu* in **a** (Ppp. *sayujā*); *sakṛ́t* is not elsewhere found used as an adjective. Ppp. further combines *hasta ā* into *hastā* in **a–b**, and reads *yajñeyā* and *ayus* in **b**. The comm. renders *te* in **b** as if it were *té*. ⌊The definition of the Anukr. may perhaps mean 'a *jagatī* of elevens (*virāḍ-jagatī*), which possesses a thirteen at the beginning, (and which is) deficient-by-two (*virāṭ*).'⌋

11. This [is] thy thought (? *dhītí*) and this thy place of birth; let Aditi, of hero-sons, seize thee; cleanse away them that would fight her; confirm to her wealth with all heroes.

Said, according to Kāuç. (61. 23), in connection with taking up the winnowing fan (*çūrpa*). The comm. explains *dhīti* as = *pāna*, taking it from the root *dhā* 'suck.' One would like to derive it from *dhā* 'put,' as 'place' or something similar. Ppp. reads at the end *ni yachāt*.

12. Sit ye in the wooden blower (? *upaçvasá*); be ye winnowed, worshipful ones, from the husks. By fortune (*çrī́*) may we surpass all [our] equals; I make [our] haters to fall under foot.

⌊The second half-verse recurs below, vs. 21.⌋ The majority of SPP's authorities, and some of ours (P.M.W.O.s.m.R.T.) read *dhruváye* ⌊Ppp. *druye*⌋ in **a**; also the comm., who explains it as = *dhruvāya sthirāya satyaphalāya karmaṇe; upaçvasé* ⌊Ppp. *upasvade*⌋ he absurdly takes for a verb: (*he taṇḍulā yuṣmān*) *upa samīpa āçvāsayāmi prabhūtān karomi!* ⌊The meaning '*das Blasen, Luftzug*,' is assigned to it in OB. iii. 257 b.⌋ ⌊Ppp. reads *pādayema* at the end of **d**.⌋ The verse accompanies (so Kāuç. 61. 29) the operation of winnowing. The comm. treats *yajñiyāsas* in **b** as nominative.

13. Go away, woman; come back quickly; the stall (*goṣṭhá*) of the waters hath ascended thee for bearing; seize then of them ⌊f.⌋ whichever shall be worshipful; having shared [them] out wisely, then leave the others.

The comm. explains *goṣṭha* by *jalarāçi;* it is rather, doubtless, the vessel in which the water is brought, on the shoulder or head (*adhi-ruh:* comm. *çirasi ā-ruh*). ⌊Cf. OB. iii. 261 b.⌋ The comm. reads *āsan* at end of **c**. Ppp. combines *yajñiā 'san* in **c**, and in **d** reads *vibhajya*, and *hvayīta* for *jahītāt*. SPP. reads in **b** *goṣṭhó 'dhy*, with the majority of his authorities.

14. These maidens (*yoṣít*) have come, adorning themselves; stand up, woman, take hold of the mighty one; well-spoused with husband, progeny-possessing with progeny; to thee hath come the sacrifice; receive thou the vessel (*kumbhá*).

The comm. explains the 'maidens' as the 'water-bringing women,' but they are evidently the waters (fem.) themselves: compare vss. 17, 27 below. The comm. reads *tava sam*, two separate words, in **b**; ⌊Roth, in his Notes, adds that Ppp. reads *tavas saṁ bharasva*⌋; the 'mighty one' is the 'vessel' of **d**. Verses 13–15 are quoted in Kāuç. (60. 25–29), but not in natural sequence with the verses that precede and follow.

15. The portion of refreshment (*ū́rj*) [is] set down which [is] yours of old; do thou, instructed by the seer, bring these waters; let this sacrifice be for you progress-gaining (*gātu-víd*), refuge-gaining, progeny-gaining, formidable, cattle-gaining, hero-gaining.

'Thou' in **b** is fem., the water-bearer, doubtless, of vs. 13. The 'yours' of **a** and the 'you' of **d** refer probably to those interested in the ceremony, though the comm. understands the former of the waters. Ppp. reads *nihatas* in **a**, combines and reads *-ṣṭā 'pā 'harāi 'tāḥ* in **b**, puts *nāthavid* before *gātuvid* in **c**, and elides *vo 'stu* in **d**.

16. O Agni, the worshipful pot hath ascended thee; bright (*çúci*), very hot, do thou heat it with heat; let those of the seers, those of the gods, gathering unto their share, very hot, heat this with the seasons.

The comm. understands the epithets in **b** as belonging to *carús*, which is doubtless wrong; those in **c** he understands of 'Brahmans' and 'attendants on Indra and the other gods'; without much question, the flames of Agni are intended. Ppp. reads in **c** *devā 'bhisaṁhatya*. The verse plainly accompanies the setting of the vessel for boiling on the fire: so Kāuç. 61. 31; also 2. 7.

17. Let these cleansed, purified, worshipful maidens, the waters, beauteous ones, creep down to the pot; they have given us abundant progeny, cattle; let the cooker of the rice-dish go to the world of the well-doers.

⌊Pāda **a** is identical with vs. 27 **a** and vi. 122. 5 **a**.⌋ The mss. are about equally divided in **c** between *bahulā́m* and *bahulā́n* (our I.T.K.Kp. have the latter; O. has *-lāṁn*); SPP. accepts the latter, we the former; the comm. has *-lān*; and he reads *pakvā* for *paktā* in **d** ⌊or **c**⌋. Ppp. has *dadat* for *adus* in **c**, and *eti* for *etu* in **d**. The verse concerns the pouring in of the water: so Kāuç. 61. 34–5, and 2. 8. — ⌊If we read *bahulā́ñç ca* in **c**, and in **d** *pakvāúdanasya* as a compound (against the *pada*-division, which reckons *paktā́* to **c**, and against the double accent) and *u* for *etu*, we get most acceptable sense and meter: *lokám* would be construed as coördinate with *paçū́n* and *pakvāúdanasya* as coördinate with *nas* (cf. xi. 8. 10 **c** and Speyer, *Vedische Syntax*, § 71, end). The heroic surgery implies no worse corruptions than we have often seen. But this is all mere suggestion.⌋

18. Cleansed with prayer (*bráhman*) and purified with ghee, shoots of Soma [are] these worshipful rice-grains; enter ye the waters; let the pot receive you; having cooked this, go ye to the world of the well-doers.

A few mss. (including our O.) read *etu* for *eta* in **d**. Ppp. has instead *eti*; further, in **a**, *utpūtās*, and, in **c**, *apa praviçyatu*. The verse accompanies the pouring of the rice-grains into the water: so Kāuç. 61. 36, and 2. 9. ⌊Read *somāñçávas?*⌋ ⌊The Anukr. seems to scan as 12 + 13 : 12 + 13 = 50; but the mark of pāda-division is after *carur*, not before it.⌋

19. Spread thyself broad, with great greatness, thousand-backed, in the world of the well-done: grandfathers, fathers, progeny, descendants (*upajā́*): I am thy fifteen-fold cooker.

Fifteen-fold ⌊cf. *Skt. Gram.* § 488⌋, probably, as representing so many generations, or degrees of kindred. The verse accompanies the boiling ⌊Kāuç. 61. 37: employed also in connection with other verses at 68. 27⌋, and alludes apparently to the swelling of the mess in the process. Ppp. combines *te 'smi* at the end. The mss. vary between *paktā́* and *paktvā́* in **d** (our T.K.Kp. have *-tā́*); SPP. gives *paktā́*, with the large majority of his authorities, and it is doubtless the true reading. The comm. has again *pakvā*. ⌊Correct the Berlin ed. to *paktā́*.⌋

20. Thousand-backed, hundred-streamed, unexhausted, [is] the *brahmán*-rice-dish, god-traveled, heaven-going; them yonder I assign to thee; lessen (?) thou them with progeny; be gracious then to me [as] bringer of tribute.

Kāuç. makes no use of this parenthetical verse of praise, prayer, and imprecation. The comm. and two of SPP's authorities read *reçaya* in **c**, and the comment to Prāt. iii. 94 (though reading *reṣayāi 'nān*) quotes it as an example of a palatal or lingual or dental mute interposed between *r* and *n*, which would seem to imply *recaya*.* The comm. glosses his *reçaya* with *leçaya alpīkuru*, and, as the expression looks as if meant for the opposite to that in vs. 21 **a**, the translation has been made accordingly. ⌊Ppp. reads *akṣato* at end of **a**.⌋ ⌊Where the Anukr. finds a pāda of 13 syllables I know not. — The one of 14 must be **c**: does *para* mean simply the second half-verse?⌋ *⌊That is, it implies the mute (*c*) rather than the sibilant (*ç*), the intervention of which was treated in the preceding rule, iii. 93.⌋

21. Go thou up to the sacrificial hearth; increase her with progeny; push [away] the demon; set her further forward; by fortune may we surpass all [our] equals; I make [our] haters to fall under foot.

The last half-verse is the same with vs. 12 **c**, **d** above. The whole evidently accompanies the bringing of the cooked dish to the place of offering: according to Kāuç. 61. 41, its removal from the fire. Ppp. reads *enam* at end of **a**, *pratiraṁ dhehy enam* at end of **b**, *paçyā* for *çriyā* in **c**, and *pādayema* ⌊cf. vs. 12⌋ at end of **d**.

22. Turn thou toward her together with cattle; be opposite to her together with the divinities; let not curse attain thee, nor witchcraft (*abhicārá*); bear rule (*vi-rāj*) in thine own field (*kṣétra*), free from disease.

The comm. reads *enān* in both **a** and **b**. ⌊All⌋ the *pada*-mss. read *anamīvā́ḥ* in **d** ⌊save SPP's J. *prima manu*: W's translation and the comm. imply *-vā́*, and this SPP. has adopted as his *pada*-reading⌋. Ppp. has in **a** *prajayā sahāi 'naṁ*, and, for **c**, **d**, a very different (and corrupt) text: *svargo lokam abhi saṁvihīnam āditya deva parame vyoma;* ⌊its **b** is corrupt⌋. According to Kāuç. 61. 42, with this verse the vessel is made to take a turn to the right. In **b** the duplication of *n* before *enām* is overlooked in nearly all the mss., and SPP. admits in his text the ungrammatical combination.

23. Fashioned by righteousness (*ṛtá*), set by mind, this was ordained in the beginning the sacrificial hearth of the *brahmán*-rice-dish; apply,

O woman, the cleansed shoulder-bearer (?); on that set the rice-dish of them of the gods.

SPP. reads in **c** *aṅsadrī́m*, with rather the larger number of authorities (of our mss. Bp.P.M.W.I.K.Kp.), though only *-dhrīm* seems to offer any etymology, and that an unsatisfactory one. The comm. has *aṅçadhrīm* 'portion-holder,' which is perhaps the true reading. The *pada*-text leaves the word undivided. The mss. of Kāuç. (61.44), it may be noted, also vary between *aṅsadhrīm* and *-drīm* in quoting the *pratīka* of the second half-verse. *Dāivyānām* would rectify the meter of **d**, but no ms. reads it, though two of SPP's, and the comm., give *devānām*. Ppp. reads in **a** *manaso hite 'yaṁ*, in **b** *nihaṅtā* for *vihitā*, in **c** *açadhriyaṁ*, emended by another hand to *-ddhiyaṁ*.

24. Aditi's hand, this second ladle (*srúc*), which the seven seers, being-makers, made — let that spoon, knowing the members of the rice-dish, collect it upon the sacrificial hearth.

The comm. reads in **a** *hastam* and *dvitīyam*, indicating that he regards the adjective as qualifying *hastām* rather than *srucam* — which may well be the case. Ppp. ⌊has *hastāṁ* and⌋ combines *saptarṣayas*.

25. Let them of the gods sit by thee, a cooked (*çṛtá*) oblation; having crept out of the fire, sit thou forward again to them; purified by soma, sit thou in the belly of the worshipers (*brahmán*); let not them of the seers, partakers (*prāçitṛ́*) of thee, suffer harm.

Ppp. begins *çrutaṁ tvā havir*, has for **b** *anusṛpyā 'gne punar enaṁ pra sṛpyas* (without any *avasāna*), reads in **c–d** *brāhmaṇā ārṣeyās*, and reads and combines *ma ṛṣaṁ* in **d**. The comm. ⌊with two of SPP's authorities⌋ reads *devās* at end of **a**, and treats *te* in **d** as *té*. Accompanies, according to Kāuç. 63. 3, the seating of 'four *ārṣeyas*, who know the *bhṛgvaṅgiras*' by the offering.

26. O king Soma, strew harmony for them, for whatsoever good Brahmans shall sit by thee; with good call, I call loudly to the *brahmán*-rice-dish the seers, them of the seers, born from penance (*tápas*).

In **a–b**, for *-bhyaḥ súbrāhmaṇās*, Ppp. reads *-bhyo brāhm-* ⌊intending perhaps *ábrāhmaṇās?* cf. vs. 32⌋; in **c** it has *ṛṣīṇām ṛṣayas tap-*, and *jātā* (so also the comm.) for *-tān;* ⌊and begins **d** with *brāhmāudane*⌋. The comm. understands *suhavā* in **d** as fem., and makes the sacrificer's wife the speaker. The verse is not quoted in Kāuç.; ⌊but Keçava cites it just before vs. 25 in 63. 3⌋.

27. These cleansed purified worshipful maidens I seat in separate succession in the hands of the priests (*brahmán*); with what desire I now pour you on, may Indra here with the Maruts grant me that.

⌊Pāda **a** = vs. 17 **a**.⌋ Nearly identical with vi. 122. 5, and slightly different from x. 9. 27. The verse is quoted by Kāuç. 63. 4; ⌊so the comm.: under vi. 122. 5 he made the sūtra apply to that verse⌋. Ppp. has a wholly different **a**: *iyam āpo madhumatī ghṛtaçcyuto;* ⌊it reads *brāhmaṇā* at beginning of **b**⌋; and combines *yatkāme 'dam* in **c**.

28. This my light (*jyótis*), immortal gold, cooked (*pakvá*) from the field, this my desire-milker; this riches I deposit in the Brahmans; I make a road to the Fathers that is heaven-going.

The construction of the nominatives in **a**, **b** is left undetermined in the translation, as it is in the text. ⌊Cf. Griffith's version and note, p. 55.⌋ Ppp. has *hiraṇmayaṁ* in **a**, and *yat svargāiḥ* at the end of **d**. The verse is quoted by Kāuç. at 62. 22 and 68. 27; and at 63. 5 Kāuç. cites **b** ⌊comm. **b** and **c**⌋ as accompanying a removal of something (*ity apakarṣati:* it is not clear what; ⌊the comm. thinks the rice-dish and reads *upa-* for *apa-*⌋).

29. Strew thou the husks in the fire, in Jātavedas; wipe off far away the chaff (?*kambū́kān*); this we have heard to be the share of the house-king; also we know the portion (*bhāgadhéya*) of Perdition (*nírṛti*).

Ppp. reads *upa mṛdhvayetām* for *apa mṛddhi dūram* in **b**. The comm. explains *kambūkān* as = *phalīkaraṇān*, and follows Kāuç. (63. 7) in regarding the 'wiping away' as done with the foot.

30. Know thou the toiling, cooking, soma-pressing one; make him to ascend the heaven-going road, by which he may ascend, arriving at the vigor that is beyond, to the highest firmament, to the furthest vault (*vyòman*).

'Know,' i.e. take note or be mindful of. The comm. takes the three participles in **a** as accus. pl. instead of gen. sing.; ⌊and reads accordingly *enān* at end of **b**⌋. Ppp. has, for **b**, *svargaṁ lokam adhi rohaye 'nam*, and omits **d**. The quotation in Kāuç. 63. 20 casts no light on the verse.

31. Wipe off, O serving priest (*adhvaryú*), this face of the bearing one (?*babhrí*); make thou, understanding it, room for the sacrificial butter; wipe off with ghee along all [its] members; I make a road to the Fathers that is heaven-going.

The real sense of the epithet *babhri* applied to the *odana* or rice-dish is obscure; the comm. explains it here with *bharaṇaçīlasya poṣakasya pakvasya odanasya*, 'supporting' or 'nourishing.' The comm. appears to read *vidvān* instead of *pravidvān* in **b**; Ppp. has *prajānan*. Ppp. has *yat* for *yas* in **d**. According to Kāuç. 62. 15, the verse accompanies the making of an *āpāna* (? the mss. vary as to the word) above (*upari*); which the comm. explains by *odanasyo 'pari gartaṁ kuryāt*, glossing *lokam* in **b** with *sthānaṁ gartarūpam;* what is meant is obscure.

32. O bearing one, [as] a demon, strew discord for them, for whatsoever non-Brahmans shall sit by thee; rich in ground (?*purīṣín*), spreading themselves forward, let not them of the seers, partakers of thee, suffer harm.

With the first half-verse compare vs. 26 **a**, **b**, above; the last pāda is the same with 25 **d**. The construction of *rákṣas* in **a** is doubtful; it might be vocative; the comm. combines it into a compound with *samadam;* and he treats *te*, as before, as if it were *té*. Ppp. reads at beginning of **b**, as our text in vs. 26, *subrāhmaṇās*. The verse is not quoted in Kāuç.

33. I set thee down, O rice-dish, among them of the seers; for them that are not of the seers there is no portion here; let Agni my guardian, and all the Maruts, let all the gods defend the cooked [offering].

'Is no portion for,' lit'ly 'is not also (*api*) of'—a common form of expression in the Brāhmaṇas. Ppp. reads *rakṣanti* in **d**. The verse is quoted with vs. 25 **c** in Kāuç. 65. 12.

34. The offering, yielding milk (*duh*), constantly full (*prápīna*), a male (*púmāṅs*) milch-cow, seat of wealth, immortality through offspring, and a long life-time—and may we sit by thee with abundance (pl.) of wealth.

The construction of the third pāda is very indeterminate; the words may be either nominative or accusative; they express in some way what the offering is to procure. To illustrate *prajāmṛtatvam*, the comm. quotes, quite appositely, TB. i. 5. 5⁶ and RV. v. 4. 10, 'by progeny, O Agni, may I obtain immortality.' *Prapīnam* he explains as = *pravṛddhodhaskam*, which is doubtless its true meaning. Ppp. reads in **d** *poṣam* for *poṣāis*. Neither this nor the following verse, nor vs. 37, is quoted in Kāuç. ⌊Cf. Henry's version, p. 102; and, for the awkward *ca*, his note, p. 139.⌋

35. Thou art a heaven-going bull; go to the seers, to them of the seers; sit in the world of the well-doing; there is there preparation (*saṁskṛtá*) for us both.

⌊Prose.⌋ Ppp. reads *ṛṣabhas* at the beginning, and *lokaṁ* for *loke* in **c**. With the second half-verse is to be compared TS. i. 4. 43², and MS. i. 3. 37 (end) and iv. 8. 2 (end), which read: *sukṛ́tāṁ loké sīdata tán naḥ saṁskṛtám;* and VS. iv. 34 has the last pāda, reading *tán* for *tátra*. The *pada*-texts do not divide *saṁskṛtam;* the case falls under rule iv. 58 of the AV. Prāt.

36. Gather thou together unto, go thou together forth after; O Agni, make ready (*kalpay-*) the roads traveled by the gods; by them, well-made, may we go after the offering, that stands upon the seven-rayed firmament.

All the mss. ⌊save one or two of SPP's⌋ leave *agne* unaccented, as if it belonged to **a**, and Bp. puts the double division-mark after it accordingly; SPP. reads with the ⌊majority of his⌋ mss.; we have made the necessary emendation to *ágne*. Ppp. reads at the beginning *samātanuṣva;* for **c** it has *yebhis sukṛtāir anu prajñeṣṭhaṅs sa yajñe*. The comm. regards **a** as addressed to the rice-dish, which is to 'gather up' all its members. The verse is quoted in Kāuç. 63. 9, but not in a way to cast any light upon it. TS. iv. 7. 13⁴ and MS. ii. 12. 4 are to be compared with the first half-verse, but they vary much from it and from one another.

37. With what light the gods went up to the sky, having cooked the *brahmán*-rice-dish, to the world of the well-done, with that may we go to the world of the well-done, ascending the heaven, unto the highest firmament.

The second half-verse is identical with iv. 14. 6 **c**, **d**, above ⌊see my note⌋. The comm. reads *jeṣma* in **c**, explaining it by *jayema* ⌊= *prāpnuyāma*⌋. Ppp. has, instead of this repetition, a new half-verse: *taṁ tvā pacāmi jyotiṣāṁ jyotir uttamaṁ sa nas tad dhehi sukṛtām u loke.*

⌊The quoted Anukr. here says *saptā 'nupūrveṇa çeṣāḥ syus triṅçateḥ parāḥ.*⌋

2. To Rudra, especially as Bhava and Çarva.

[*Atharvan. — ekatrin̄çat. mantroktarudradāivatam. trāiṣṭubham.* 1. parātijāgatā virāḍ jagatī; 2. anuṣṭubgarbhā 5-p. pathyājagatī; 3. 4-p. svarāḍ uṣṇih; 4, 5, 7, 13, 15, 16, 21. anuṣṭubh; 6. ārṣī gāyatrī; 8. mahābṛhatī; 9. ārṣī; 10. puro'kṛti 3-p. virāj; 11. 5-p. virāḍ jagatīgarbhā çakvarī; 12. bhurij; 14, 17, 18, 19, 23, 26, 27. virāḍ gāyatrī; 20. bhurig gāyatrī; 22. viṣamapādalakṣmyā 3-p. mahābṛhatī; 24, 29. jagatī; 25. 5-p. atiçakvarī; 30. 4-p. uṣṇih; 31. 3-av. viparītapādalakṣmyā 6-p.* ⌊*jagatī?*⌋.]

Found also in Pāipp. xvi. — *⌊Verses 9 and 28 are *triṣṭubh*, the remaining 29 being exceptions !⌋

⌊The *pratīka* coincides with that of xi. 6. 9, *bhavāçarvā́v idám brūmaḥ*, and that of iv. 28, *bhávāçarvāu manvé vām*: see introduction to the latter. The only quotation in Vāit. is at 29. 10, where the hymn accompanies an offering to Rudra: and it is accordingly reckoned to the *rāudra gaṇa* (note to Kāuç. 50. 13). Verse 31 is reckoned to the *abhaya gaṇa* (note to Kāuç. 16. 8). Further citations in Kāuç. are as follows: the hymn is used (129. 3) with an oblation in deprecating an evil omen; Dārila understands it as meant at 28. 8 (see introd. to iv. 28); Keçava and the comm. hold that it is to be used with a dozen other hymns in a rite (50. 13–14) for safety on a business journey; Keçava (not the comm.) takes it to be intended with v. 6 at 51. 7 in a rite for the safety of the cattle. — According to Caland's interpretation of *yuktayos* at 50. 17, it is to be used (with vi. 128) in the rite there prescribed for keeping snakes etc. from house and field; but perhaps iii. 26 and 27 are rather intended (see my introduction to iii. 26).⌋

Translated: Muir, iv. 334; Ludwig, p. 549; Henry, 103, 139; Griffith, ii. 57; Bloomfield, 155, 618. — Cf. also Bergaigne-Henry, *Manuel*, p. 157; and von Schroeder, *Tübinger Kaṭha-hss.*, p. 14–15, where the text corresponding to our verses 1–9 and 13 and 16 is given.

1. O Bhava-and-Çarva, be gracious; do not go against [us]; ye lords of beings, lords of cattle, homage to you! [the arrow] that is fitted, that is drawn, do not let fly; do not harm our bipeds nor quadrupeds.

The comm. first explains *mā́* in **a** as if it were *mā*, object of *abhí yātam*, and then, alternatively, in its proper sense. ⌊For *ā́yata*, see note to vi. 65. 1.⌋

2. Make ye not bodies for the dog, the jackal, for the buzzards (?*alíklava*), the vultures, and them that are black [and] greedy (*aviṣyú*); let thy flies, lord of cattle, let thy birds not find themselves at food.

'Bodies' (*çarīra*) must be taken here in the sense of 'dead bodies.' The accent of *kártam* is, though rather strange, not indefensible, as in the former of two parallel clauses; the comm. reads instead *kartum*. *Alíklava* is found only here and in 9. 9, and is rendered purely conjecturally; the comm. reads instead *aviklabebhyas*, and Ppp. *ariklavebhyas*. All the *pada*-mss. separate *mā́vidanta* at the end into *mā́ : avidanta*; SPP., in his *pada*-text, makes, with the comm., the necessary emendation to *vid-*. The construction and sense of **d** are obscure and doubtful; Ppp. has a wholly different reading: *viçase mā viçyantu*.

3. Unto thy noise (?*kránda*), [thy] breath, and what pangs (?*rópi*) are thine, O Bhava — homage we pay to thee that art thousand-eyed, O Rudra, immortal one.

The comm. glosses *krandāya* with *krandanāya çabdāya*, and *ropayas* with *ropayitryo mohayitryas tanvaḥ;* he reads at the end *amartyas*, explaining it as used for a dative.

4. We pay thee homage in front, above, also below; forth from the sphere of the sky, homage [be] to thine atmosphere.

The comm. explains *abhīvargá* as = *avakāçātmaka ākāçaḥ*. The verse is mostly wanting in Ppp.

5. To thy face, O lord of cattle; the eyes that thou hast, O Bhava; to [thy] skin, form, aspect, to thee standing opposite [be] homage.

Or 'to thy mouth,' instead of 'face.' The comm. paraphrases *pratīcīnāya* with *pratyagātmarūpiṇe*.

6. To thy members, belly, tongue, thy mouth, to thy teeth, smell, [be] homage.

Ppp. (omitting the first *te*) combines *añgebhyo 'darāya* and *jihvāyā "syāya* ⌊and reads *ca* for *te* at end of **b**⌋.

7. With the blue-locked archer, the thousand-eyed, vigorous, with Rudra, the half-smiter (?) — with him may we not come into collision (*sam-ṛ*).

Ardhaka-ghātin, in **c**, is met with only here, and is of obscure meaning; the comm. says *senāyā ardhaṁ hantuṁ çīlam asya*, i.e. 'able to destroy half an army at once.' No variant is reported from Ppp. ⌊in the Collation: but in his Notes, Roth does report *adhvaga-*⌋; the minor Pet. Lex. says "Ppp. *adhvaga-*," and itself conjectures *andhaka-*. ⌊Cf. the notes of Henry, Griffith, Bloomfield. The Kaṭha reading, however, should now be taken into account; and that has in fact *adhvaga-*: see *Kaṭha-hss.*, p. 155.⌋ Ppp. has at the end *samarāmasi*.

8. Let this Bhava avoid us on every side; as fire the waters, let Bhava avoid us; let him not plot against us; homage be to him.

Ppp. reads *āpāi 'vā 'gniṣ pari* in **b**, and combines *no abhi* in **c**. The comm. has in **c** the regular form *maṅsta;* but long *ā* in this tense occurs a couple of times in other texts also.

9. Four times ⌊*catúṣ*⌋ homage, eight times, to Bhava; ten times, O lord of cattle, be homage to thee; thine are shared out these five creatures (*paçú*) — cows, horses, men, sheep and goats.

All the mss. agree in the inconsistent readings *aṣṭakṛ́tvas* and *dáça kṛ́tvas* (cf. Prāt. iv. 27); SPP. regards the comm. as having *daçakṛtvas* as a compound, but I do not see on what ground. Ppp. reads in **d** *gāvo 'çvāṣ puruṣāṅd aj-*.

10. Thine are the four directions, thine the heaven, thine the earth, thine, O formidable one, this wide atmosphere, thine is all this that has life (*ātmán*), that is breathing upon (*ánu*) the earth.

Ppp. omits *tava pṛthivī*, thus rectifying the meter; and it has for **d** *yad ejad adhi bhūmyām*.

11. This wide vessel, holder of good things, is thine, within which are all these beings; do thou be gracious to us, O lord of cattle; homage to thee; away let the jackals, the portents (*abhibhā́*), the dogs go, away the weepers of evil with disheveled hair.

The comm. identifies the vessel (*koça*) with the *aṇḍakaṭāha*, the shell of the world-egg. He takes *abhibhā́s* as = *abhibhavitāras*, and epithet of *kroṣṭāras*, and *agharudas* as = *amañgalaṁ yathā bhavati tathā rodanaṁ kurvatyaḥ*; ⌊but see viii. 1. 19 and references⌋. ⌊The meter of **b** would be rectified by reading *víçvāni* in place of *imā́ víçvā.*⌋

12. Thou bearest a yellow golden bow, a thousand-slaying, hundred-weaponed, O tufted one; Rudra's arrow goes, a god-missile; to that be homage, in whichever direction from here.

SPP. reads in **b** *sahasraghnī́*, with the majority of his authorities; none of ours have it, but P.M.W. have *-ghnyā́m*, with two of SPP's mss., and with the comm. ⌊cf. note to x. 4. 7 and Henry's note⌋; Ppp. gives *-ghni*. The comm. has *çikhaṇḍi* at end of **b**.

13. He who, attacked (*abhi-yā*), hides himself, [who] tries to put thee down, O Rudra, him from behind thou pursuest, like the tracker (? *padanī́*) of one that is pierced.

With the last pāda compare x. 1. 26 **b**; the expression is apparently a familiar or proverbial one: ⌊cf. Manu viii. 44, 'as the hunter follows the track (*padaṁ nayati*) of a deer by the drops of blood'; also Dhammapada, vss. 179, 180⌋. Ppp. reads *ugra* instead of *rudra* in **b**.

14. Bhava-and-Rudra, allied, in concord, both go about, formidable, unto heroism; to them be homage, in whichever direction from here.

Ppp., instead of repeating vs. 12 **d**, reads *tayor bhūmim antarikṣaṁ svar dyāus tābhyāṁ namo bhavamatyāya* ⌊cf. vs. 19 **a**?⌋ *kṛṇva*. The comm. explains *vīryāya* ⌊alternatively⌋ by *svavīryaprakaṭanārtham*, which is doubtless correct.

15. Homage be to thee coming, homage be [to thee] going away; homage to thee, O Rudra, standing; to thee sitting also [be] homage.

SPP's text has in **a** *te 'stv*, with about half of his authorities. The verse is repeated as 4. 7, below, with *prāṇa* for *rudra* in **c**; Ppp. reads *prāṇa* in both places. The first half-verse is found in AÇS. i. 12. 34 and Āp. ix. 2. 9, in both with *rudra* for *astu* in **b**.

16. Homage in the evening, homage in the morning, homage by night, homage by day; to Bhava and to Çarva, to both have I paid homage.

17. With the thousand-eyed one, seeing across in front, with Rudra, hurling in many places, inspired one, may we not come in collision, as he goes about (*ī́ya-*) with the tongue.

The comm. paraphrases *atipaçyám* with *atiçayenā 'tikramya vā paçyati* (the word is omitted in both Pet. Lexx.), and connects *purastāt* either with it or with *asyantam*; *jihváyé "yamānam* he explains as *jihvāgreṇa kṛtsnaṁ jagad vyāpnuvantam bhakṣaṇārthaṁ lihantam*, which is rather absurd; perhaps *jihvayā* (so Ludwig) belongs rather to 'we': 'we, by what we say.'

18. We go forward (*pū́rva*) to meet him of dark horses, black, swarthy, killing, fearful, making to fall the chariot of the hairy one (*keçín*); homage be to him.

The comm. understands the connection as here given, making *keçín* the name of an Asura; Ludwig takes *ratham* as object of *pratī 'mas* and the other words as its epithets. ⌊Ppp. reads *çyāvāsyaṁ* at the beginning, and has, in **b**, *bhīmo* and *pārayantam.*⌋

19. Do not let fly at us the club (? *matyà*), the god-missile; be not angry at us, O lord of cattle; homage to thee; elsewhere than [over] us shake out the heavenly bough.

The bough, namely (so it would seem), from which the portents that fall from the sky appear to be shaken by a hostile divinity. The comm. reads *martyam* instead of *matyam* in **a**. He recognizes that *srās* (i.e. *srā*[*kṣ*]*s*) is from root *sṛj* ("= *vi sṛja*"). Ppp. has *srā m. devahitam* in **a**.

20. Do not harm us; bless us; avoid us; be not angry; let us not come into collision with thee.

Ppp. omits *nas* before *brūhi* in **a**, and has at the end *arāmasi* (as in vs. 7).

21. [Be] not [greedy] for our kine, our men; be not greedy for our goats and sheep; elsewhere, O formidable one, roll forth [thy missile]; smite the progeny of the mockers (*píyāru*).

The insertion in **c** seems unavoidable; the comm. ⌊in a passage restored by SPP.?⌋ supplies *tava hetim;* Ludwig, *deinen Pfeil.* ⌊Ppp. inserts '*çveṣu* before *goṣu.*⌋

22. Of whom the *takmán*, the *kā́sikā*, goes as one weapon, like the noise of a stallion horse, to him, leading out in succession, be homage.

The verse is very obscure, and the translation mechanical; Ppp. reads, in **a–b**, *ekā 'çvasya*, and this reading is followed; the comm. supplies, to *ekam*, *upakāriṇam puruṣam*, and makes it object of *eti* = *prāpnoti*. Ludwig understands *nirṇayate* as 'extracting arrows from the quiver.' ⌊As for *vṝṣaṇas*, cf. JAOS. x. 534, 524.⌋

23. He who stands propped up in the atmosphere, killing the non-sacrificing, the god-mockers — to him be homage with the ten clever ones (*çákvarī*).

The 'ten clever ones' are probably the fingers: cf. v. 28. 11; the comm. glosses the word with *aṅgulibhis*, as = *karmasu çaktābhiḥ*. Ppp. begins *yas tiṣṭhati viçvabhṛto antarikṣe 'yajvanaṣ pra-*.

24. To thee are assigned the forest animals ⌊*paçú*⌋, the wild beasts in the woods, the geese (*haṅsá*), eagles, hawks, birds; thine, O lord of cattle, is the monster (? *yakṣá*) within the waters; for thine increase flow the waters of the heaven.

Ppp. reads, for **b**, *tubhyaṁ vayāṅsi çakunāṣ patatriṇaḥ*, elides the *a* of *apsu* in **c**, and combines *divyā "po* in **d**. The comm. has *mṛdhe* at the end, explaining it as = *undanāya*. He takes *yakṣam* as = *pūjyaṁ svarūpam*, but does not give any reason why, etymological or other. ⌊Our **a** is nearly xii. 1. 49 **a** (with the same redundancy of a dissyllable), and **b** is precisely xii. 1. 51 **b**: for *paçavas*, cf. also iii. 31. 3, xi. 5. 21, and iii. 10. 6 note.⌋

25. The dolphins (*çiñçumā́ra*), boas (*ajagará*), *purīkáyas*, *jashás*, fishes, *rajasás*, at which thou hurlest: there is no distance for thee nor hindrance for thee, O Bhava; at once thou lookest over the whole earth; from the eastern thou smitest in the northern ocean.

Ppp. begins *siçumārā 'jagarāḥ purīṣayā jagā mat-*. The comm. has *pulīkayās* (like MS.); he takes *rajasā́* (p. *-sā́ḥ*) as if it were the instr. sing. *rájasā;* he passes *jaṣā́s* and *mátsyās* without mention, but defines *çiñçumāra* as 'a kind of crocodile (*nakra*)' and *ajagara* as 'a kind of serpent.' For *jaṣā́s*, some of the mss. (including our Bp.P.M.W.) have *jakhā́s*, one or two (including our I.) have *jaghā́s*, and one of SPP's *jhaṣā́s;* doubtless it is the sea-monster called later *jhaṣa*. Nearly all the mss. have *sárvān* in **d** (only our B. ⌊and D.Kp.?⌋ and two of SPP's *sárvāṁ*), and SPP's text accordingly admits it, though it seems an evident error, and the comm. reads *-vām*. Most of the *pada*-mss. resolve *pariṣṭhā́sti* into *-sthā́ : ásti* (instead of *asti*). We are surprised to find a 'northern' ocean spoken of, and set over against the 'eastern' one ⌊cf. xi. 5. 6⌋, but *úttara* cannot well mean anything else. Consistency requires the reading *-smint sam-* in **e**, but the *t* is accidentally omitted in our text, and SPP's also leaves it out.

26. Do not, O Rudra, unite (*sam-sṛj*) us with the *takmán*, not with poison, not with the fire of heaven; elsewhere than [on] us make that lightning fall.

The comm. again correctly paraphrases *saṁ srāḥ* with *saṁ sṛja*.

27. Bhava is master (*īç*) of the heaven, Bhava of the earth; Bhava has filled the wide atmosphere; to him be homage, in whichever direction from here.

All our mss., and nearly all SPP's, strangely read *tásyāi* at beginning of **c**, as if governed by the example of vs. 12 **d**. SPP. emends to *tásmāi* in his text, with the comm. and less than a quarter of his authorities; ⌊and the translation implies the change⌋. Ppp. has a different **c**: *tasya vā* (with *nā* written over it) *prāpad duchunā kā cane 'ha;* it also combines *bhavā "papra* ⌊*urv*⌋ in **b**.

28. O king Bhava, be gracious to the sacrificer, for thou hast become cattle-lord of cattle; whoever has faith, saying "the gods are," be thou gracious to his bipeds [and] quadrupeds.

29. Not our great one, and not our small, not our carrying one, and not those that will carry, not our father and mother do thou harm; our own self (*tanū́*), O Rudra, do not injure.

The verse occurs also as RV. i. 114. 7; VS. xvi. 15; TS. iv. 5. 10²; TA. x. 52, with *úkṣantam* and *ukṣitám* for *váhantam* and *vakṣyatás* in **b**; *vadhīs* for *hiṅsīs* and *mó 'tá mātáram* for *mātáraṁ ca* in **c**; and, for **d**, *mā́ naḥ priyā́s* (TS.TA. *priyā́ mā́ nas*) *tanvò rudra rīriṣaḥ*. The comm. has *vakṣatas* in **b**. ⌊Ppp. has, for **b**, *mā na kṣīyanta uta mā no akṣata*.⌋

30. To Rudra's howl-making, unhymned-swallowing (?), great-mouthed dogs I have paid this homage.

The obscure *asaṁsūktagilá* (Ppp. *-girebhyas*) is paraphrased by the comm. with *asamīcīnam açobhanavacanaṁ gṛṇanti bhāṣante.* How *asaṁsūkta* should come to mean 'unmasticated,' as given in the Pet. Lexx., does not appear. The translation given conjectures 'not having a hymn with it.' The comm. reads *elavak-* in **a**.

31. Homage to thy noisy ones, homage to thy hairy ones, homage to those to whom homage is paid, homage to the jointly-enjoying — homage, [namely], O god, to thine armies; welfare [be] to us, and fearlessness to us.

The adjectives are fem., as belonging to *senābhyas*. Ppp. disagrees with our text in the last two thirds of the verse, but is corrupt. The comm. reads *cana* at the end. ⌊The vs., as noted above, is quoted in the first *abhaya gaṇa* (note to 16. 8).⌋

⌊Here ends the first *anuvāka*, with 2 hymns and 68 verses. The quoted Anukr. says *tathāi 'va rāudre 'pi parās tu viṅçateḥ*, designating the hymn as a "Rudra-hymn."⌋

3. Extolling the rice-dish (odaná).

[*Atharvan.— trayaḥ paryāyāḥ.*]

⌊Prose, except vss. 19–22.⌋ A corresponding passage is found in Pāipp. xvi., but so different in detail that it would require to be given in full for comparison; and this has not been done.

SPP., without any good reason,* counts the three *paryāyas* or divisions of this hymn as so many independent hymns, thus not only defacing the structure of the book, but defeating all the references that had been made to it in lexicons and elsewhere.

*⌊Whether Whitney's condemnation of SPP's procedure is justified or not may be decided when all the facts are before us. Some of them have been put together by me, above, pages 610, 611, which see.⌋

⌊The hymn is not cited by Vāit.; nor in the text of Kāuç., unless vs. 31 is meant at 62. 8: but Keçava (p. 353[1]) cites it for use in witchcraft practices (so the comm.), and also (p. 365[2]) for use in the *bṛhaspati sava* (so comm.).⌋

Translated: Henry, 106, 145; Griffith, ii. 61.— Cf. especially Henry's introduction, p. 145. The rice-dish, hot and yellow and nourishing, is a symbol of the sun (cf. vs. 50); its ingredients and the utensils used in making it are identified with all sorts of things in the most grotesque manner of the Brāhmaṇas.

[**Paryāya I.** — *ekatriṅçat. bārhaspatyāudanadevatyam. 1, 14. āsurī gāyatrī; 2. 3-p. samaviṣamā gāyatrī; 3, 6, 10. āsurī paṅkti; 4, 8. sāmny anuṣṭubh; 5, 13, 15, 25. sāmny uṣṇih; 7, 19–22. prājāpatyā 'nuṣṭubh; 9, 17, 18. āsury anuṣṭubh; 11. bhurig ārcy anuṣṭubh; 12. yājuṣī jagatī; 16, 23. āsurī bṛhatī; 24. 3-p. prājāpatyā bṛhatī; 26. ārcy uṣṇih; 27. . . . .; [28, 29.] sāmnī bṛhatī (29. bhurij); 30. yājuṣī triṣṭubh; 31. alpaçaḥ (?) paṅktir uta yājuṣī.*]

1. Of this rice-dish Brihaspati is the head, Brahman the mouth (*múkha*).

The comm. combines in part two or three verses of the first *paryāya* together in giving his explanations.

2. Heaven-and-earth are the ears, sun-and-moon the eyes, the seven seers the breaths-and-expirations.

3. Sight (*cákṣus*) the pestle, desire (*kā́ma*) the mortar.

4. Diti the winnowing basket, Aditi the basket-holder; the wind winnowed (*apa-vic*).

5. Horses the corns (*káṇa*), kine the grains (*taṇḍulá*), flies the husks.

6. *Kábru* the hulls, the cloud the stalk (*çára*).

The comm. reads *kabhru*, and gives a forced etymology, from *ka* 'head' and *bhrū* 'brow'; he also has *çīras* for *çáras*, and this reading is found in some of the mss. (including our B.p.m.,E.s.m.,O.p.m. ⌊and some of SPP's⌋).

7. Dark metal its flesh, red its blood (*lóhita*).

That is, doubtless, iron and copper respectively.

8. Tin [its] ash, greens (? *háritam*) [its] color, blue lotus (*púṣkara*) its smell.

The comm. glosses *hárita* with *heman* 'gold.' ⌊Over "greens" W. has interlined "gold? (so BR.)." He rendered *hárita* by "the yellow one" at v. 28. 5, 9.⌋

9. The threshing-floor [its] receptacle, the two splints (*sphyá*) [its] shoulders, the two poles (*īṣā́*) [its] spines (*anūkyā̀*).

The comm. reads *sphāu*, and defines as *pravṛddhāu dhānyādhārasya çakaṭasyā 'vayavāu;* and he defines *anūkyè* as *aṅsayor madhyadehasya ca saṁdhī.* Bp. reads *īçé* for *īṣé.*

10. Entrails [its] neck-ropes (?*jatrú*), intestines [its] straps.

Jatrú is rendered with the commentary, who explains it as *anaḍudgrīvāṇāṁ çakaṭayojanārthā rajjavaḥ.*

11. This very earth is the vessel (*kumbhī́*) of the finishing (*rādh*) rice-dish, heaven the cover.

⌊W. interlines a query over "finishing." The comm. renders *rādh-* by *pacyamānasya.*⌋

12. The furrows [its] ribs, gravel the content of [its] bowels.

The comm. reads *ūvadhyam.*

13. Righteousness (*ṛtá*) [its] hand-washing, the brook (*kulyā̀*) [its] pouring-on.

In order to force a parallelism into it, the comm. explains *ṛta* as a 'name for water,' and as signifying 'all the water that is found in the world.' The Pet. Lex., on the other hand, conjectures 'family custom' for *kulyā̀;* it is translated above as if = *kulyā́*, as the comm. takes it.

14. With sacred verse (*ṛ́c*) is the vessel put on, with priesthood sent forth;

15. With sacredness (*bráhman*) seized about, with sacred chant (*sā́man*) carried about.

For the sake of the parallelism again, the comm. makes 'priesthood' indicate the Yajur-Veda, and 'sacredness' the Brahma-Veda of the Atharvans.

16. *Bṛhát* the stirring-stick, *rathaṁtará* the spoon.

The comm. paraphrases *āyavana* with *udake prakṣiptānāṁ taṇḍulānām miçraṇasādhanaṁ kāṣṭham.*

17. The seasons the cooks; they of the seasons kindle fire.

18. Heat (*gharmá*) burns upon the pot of five openings, the boiler (*ukhá*).

19. By the rice-dish of him who hath an offering (?) all worlds are to be obtained together.

The translation implies emendation of the unintelligible *yajñavacás* to *yajñavatas*, the Ppp. reading, as reported in the minor Pet. Lex. ⌊and Roth's notes⌋. The comm. explains the word as = *yajñāir agniṣṭomādibhiḥ prāptavyatveno 'cyamānaḥ.*

20. In which ⌊rice-dish⌋ are set (*çritá*), one below the other, the three, sea, sky, earth.

21. In the remnant (*úchiṣṭa*) of which took shape six times eighty gods.

The comm. paraphrases *akalpanta* by *samarthā vīryavanto 'bhavan.*

22. Thee here I ask of the rice-dish, what is its great greatness.

23. He who may know the greatness of the rice-dish —

24. May not say "[it is] little," not "[it is] without onpouring," nor "[it is] this thing soever."

Upasecana is explained by the comm. as 'milk, butter, curd, or the like, that is poured on' — we might render by 'sauce.'

25. As much as the giver may set his mind upon, that one should not overbid (*ati-vad*).

26. The theologues (*brahmavādín*) say: hast thou eaten (*pra-aç*) the rice-dish as it was retiring (*páranc*), or as it was coming on (*pratyáñc*)?

The *pluta-* or protracted syllables in this and the next verse are quoted in Prāt. i. 105, but nothing is said as to their accentuation, from which it seems most plausible to infer that the protraction made no difference in the accent; and though in the Brāhmaṇas a protracted syllable is always accented ⌊see *Gram.* § 78 a⌋, that is not the invariable rule in the Vedic texts (thus, only once among the three instances occurring in RV.). Here the mss. are greatly at variance. ⌊SPP's V. (a then living *çrotriya*) read *prā́çī3ḥ*; and by his ms. D^c the reading *prā́çīḥ3* is given *secunda manu*. Among our mss., O.R.Kp. (and E.?) give *prā́çīḥ3*. SPP. reports that 16 of his authorities agree in giving *pratyáñcā́3m*; and (apart from the presence or position of the *3*) this seems to be the reading of many of W's mss.⌋ SPP's text gives an accent to the protracted syllable in both cases in both vs. 26 and vs. 27. — ⌊SPP's *pada*-reading in vs. 26 is *prá : āçī3ḥ*, and in 27 it is *prá : ā́çī3ḥ*. An accented *ā́* in *āçī3ḥ* would require *pra°ā́çī3ḥ* (cf. vs. 28); but one does not see why the *ā* should be accented.⌋

27. Hast thou eaten the rice-dish, or the rice-dish thee?

The mss. again disagree as to the accent of *prāçī3s*, the majority (including our Bp.P.M.) having *prā́çī3s*; as *odaná* happens to have its natural accent on the final, there is no discordance as to *odanā́3ḥ*.

28. If thou hast eaten it retiring, thy breaths (*prāṇá*) will quit thee: so one says to him.

29. If thou hast eaten it coming on, thine expirations (*apāná*) will quit thee: so one says to him.

30. Not I, indeed, [have eaten] the rice-dish, nor the rice-dish me.

31. The rice-dish itself hath eaten the rice-dish.

[**Paryāya II.** — *dvāsaptati. mantroktadevatyam.* **a** *of 32, 38, 41,* **g** *of 32–49. sāmnī triṣṭubh;* **b** *of 32, 35, 42,* **c** *of 32–49,* **e** *of 33, 34, 44–48. 1-p. āsurī gāyatrī;* **d** *of 32, 41, 43, 47. dāivī jagatī;* **b** *of 38, 44, 46,* **e** *of 32, 35–43, 49. 1-p. āsury anuṣṭubh;* **f** *of 32–49. sāmny anuṣṭubh;* **a** *of 33–49.* ārcy anuṣṭubh;* **a** *of 37. sāmnī pañkti;* **b** *of 33, 36, 40, 47, 48. āsurī jagatī;* **b** *of 34, 37, 41, 43, 45. āsurī pañkti;* **d** *of 34. āsurī triṣṭubh;* **d** *of 35, 46, 48. yājuṣī gāyatrī;* **d** *of 36, 37, 40. dāivī pañkti;* **d** *of 38, 39. prājāpatyā gāyatrī;* **b** *of 39. āsury uṣṇih;* **d** *of 42, 45, 49. dāivī triṣṭubh;* **b** *of 49. 1-p. bhurik sāmnī bṛhatī.*†]

*⌊The text of the Anukr. reads *enam anyābhyāṁ çrotrābhyām* (= **a** of 33) *ity āditaḥ saptadaçā "rcyanuṣṭubhaḥ*. The definition applies (perhaps with occasional forcing) to 14 of the 17 first *avasānas* of vss. 33–49. As for the other 3, the **a** of 38 and the **a** of 41 are accurately defined above, in the first line of the Anukr. excerpts for this *paryāya;* and the **a** of 37, in the definition next following the asterisk.⌋

†⌊The definition of 33 **d**, 44 **d** (9 syllables) is omitted by the Anukr.⌋

The second *paryāya* of this hymn is reckoned in the Anukr. as of 72 divisions in 18 *gaṇas* or paragraphs; but the actual division in the mss. is into 126 such divisions (7 to each *gaṇa*), as given in both editions; and the metrical description of the Anukr. (as reported above) is also on that basis.

⌊**The division of this paryāya into 72 avasānas.** — In his Critical Notice, p. 20–21, at the beginning of his first volume, SPP. treats of this matter; and just after the end (p. 356) of the text of his third volume, he prints again this *paryāya*, but divided into 72 *avasānas* "according to the instructions contained in the Sarvānukramaṇikā" which he had printed in the Critical Notice, l.c.⌋

⌊The Major Anukr. calls the 18 main divisions of this *paryāya* (answering to the "verses" of the Berlin ed.) by the name of *daṇḍakas*. Since the *daṇḍakas* are all subdivided, they are also (see p. 472) called *gaṇas*. Each *daṇḍaka* falls into 7 subdivisions or *avasānas*, which may be designated as **a, b, c, d, e, f, g**. Each of these 7 is written out and counted for the first and last *daṇḍaka* (vss. 32 and 49, Berlin).⌋

⌊Similarly, in a sequence of refrains or *anuṣañgas*, the refrain is given and counted as an *avasāna* only for its first and last occurrence in that sequence. The third subdivision (or **c**: beginning *taṁ vā aham*) of each *daṇḍaka*, being unvaried throughout the *paryāya*, constitutes a sequence of 18 and is given and counted independently only for vss. 32 and 49; while for the 16 vss., 33–48, it is given (see SPP. in vol. iii.) and counted as one with **b**, thus making the *avasāna* to consist of **b–c**. — In like manner, the sixth subdivision (or **f**: beginning *eṣa vā odanaḥ*) and the seventh subdivision (or **g**: beginning *sarvāñga eva*), being unvaried throughout, constitute a sequence of 18 and are given and counted independently only for vss. 32 and 49; while for the other 16 vss. they are counted as one with **e**, thus making the *avasāna* to consist of **e–g**.⌋

⌊Furthermore, and on the other hand, subdivision **e** varies as to its beginning between *tenāi 'nam, tayāi 'nam*, and *tāir enam*, and *tābhyām enam:* but we find no unvaried sequences of more than two except *tenāi 'nam* etc. in the 5 vss., 39–43, and *tābhyām* *enam* etc. in the 5 vss., 44–48. For vss. 40, 41, 42, accordingly, and for vss. 45, 46, 47, as well, not only is **f–g** reckoned to **e**, but also **e–f–g** is reckoned as an *anuṣaṅga* to **d**, thus making the *avasāna* to consist of **d–g.**⌋

⌊For these six verses, therefore, arranged and counted as 3 *avasānas* (**a**, **b–c**, **d–g**), we have the reckoning 6 × 3 = 18. — For verses 32 and 49 (counted as **a**, **b**, **c**, **d**, **e**, **f**, **g**, as above noted), we have the reckoning 2 × 7 = 14. — And for the remaining ten verses, we have the arrangement and count, **a**, **b–c**, **d**, **e–g**, or 10 × 4 = 40. This gives us (18 + 14 + 40 =) 72, which is the count, not only of the Major Anukr., but of the Old Anukr. or *Pañcapaṭalikā* as well.⌋

32. If ⌊*ca*⌋ thou hast eaten it with another head than that (*tátas*) with which the ancient seers ate this, thy progeny, from the oldest down, will die: so one says to him; it verily I [have] not [eaten] coming hither (*arvā́ñc*), nor retiring, nor coming on; with Brihaspati [as] head, therewith have I eaten it, therewith have I made it go; this rice-dish, verily, is whole-limbed, whole-jointed, whole-bodied; whole-limbed, whole-jointed, whole-bodied becometh he who knoweth thus.

The *pada*-reading of *prā́çīs* in **a** is *pra॰ā́çīḥ*.

33. If thou hast eaten it with other ears than those ⌊*tátas*⌋ with which the ancient seers ate this, thou wilt become deaf: thus one says to him; it verily [have] I not [eaten] coming hither, nor retiring, nor coming on; with heaven-and-earth as ears, with them have I eaten it, with them have I made it go etc. etc.

34. If thou hast eaten it with other eyes than those with which the ancient seers ate this, thou wilt become blind: thus one says to him; it verily [have] I not [eaten] coming hither, nor retiring, nor coming on; with sun-and-moon as eyes, with them have I eaten it, with them etc. etc.

All the mss. read *sūryācandramasā́bhyām*, which SPP. has very properly retained in his text; ours was altered to agree with vi. 128. 3, but the alteration should have been the other way.

35. If thou hast eaten it with another mouth (*múkha*) than that with which the ancient seers ate this, thy progeny will die from in front (*mukhatás*): thus one says to him; it verily [have] I not [eaten] coming hither, nor retiring, nor coming on; with *bráhman* as mouth, therewith have I etc. etc.

36. If thou hast eaten it with another tongue than that with which the ancient seers ate this, thy tongue will die: thus one says to him; it verily [have] I not [eaten] coming hither, nor retiring, nor coming on; with Agni's tongue, therewith have I etc. etc.

37. If thou hast eaten it with other teeth than those with which the ancient seers ate this, thy teeth will fall out (*çad*): thus one says to him; it verily [have] I not [eaten] coming hither, nor retiring, nor coming on; with the seasons as teeth, therewith have I etc. etc.

The comm. reads *satsyanti* for *çatsyanti*.

38. If thou hast eaten it with other breaths-and-expirations than those with which the ancient seers ate this, breaths-and-expirations will quit thee: thus one says to him; it verily [have] I not [eaten] coming hither, nor retiring, nor coming on; with the seven seers as breaths-and-expirations, therewith have I etc. etc.

The mss., as usual, are divided between *saptarṣibhis* and *saptarṣi-* in this verse; SPP. adopts the former.

39. If thou hast eaten it with another bulk (*vyácas*) than that with which the ancient seers ate this, the king-*yákshma* will slay thee: thus one says to him; it verily [have] I not [eaten] coming hither, nor retiring, nor coming on; with the atmosphere as bulk, therewith have I etc. etc.

The comm. explains *vyacasā* by *vyāptimatā rūpeṇa*.

40. If thou hast eaten it with another back than that with which the ancient seers ate this, the lightning will slay thee: thus one says to him; it verily [have] I not [eaten] coming hither, nor retiring, nor coming on; with the sky as back, therewith have I etc. etc.

41. If thou hast eaten it with another breast than that with which the ancient seers ate this, thou wilt not prosper with plowing: thus one says to him; it verily [have] I not [eaten] coming hither, nor retiring, nor coming on; with the earth as breast, therewith have I etc. etc.

42. If thou hast eaten it with another belly than that with which the ancient seers ate this, the colic (? *udaradārá*) will slay thee: thus one says to him; it verily [have] I not [eaten] coming hither, nor retiring, nor coming on; with truth as belly, therewith have I etc. etc.

The comm. explains *udaradāra* as *udarasya daraṇātmako 'tīsārākhyo rogaḥ*, or diarrhœa.

43. If thou hast eaten it with another bladder than that with which the ancient seers ate this, thou wilt die in the waters: thus one says to him; it verily [have] I not [eaten] coming hither, nor retiring, nor coming on; with the ocean as bladder, therewith have I etc. etc.

44. If thou hast eaten it with other thighs than those with which the ancient seers ate this, thy thighs will die: thus one says to him; it verily [have] I not [eaten] coming hither, nor retiring, nor coming on; with the thighs of Mitra-and-Varuṇa, therewith have I etc. etc.

45. If thou hast eaten it with other knees (*aṣṭhīvánt*) than those with which the ancient seers ate this, thou wilt become lame: thus one says to him; it verily [have] I not [eaten] coming hither, nor retiring, nor coming on; with Tvashṭar's knees, therewith have I etc. etc.

46. If thou hast eaten it with other feet than those with which the ancient seers ate this, thou wilt be much-wandering: thus one says to

him; it verily [have] I not [eaten] coming hither, nor retiring, nor coming on; with the feet of the two Açvins, therewith have I etc. etc.

47. If thou hast eaten it with other front-feet than those with which the ancient seers ate this, a serpent will slay thee: thus one says to him; it verily [have] I not [eaten] coming hither, nor retiring, nor coming on; with Savitar's front-feet, therewith have I etc. etc.

Read in our text *savitúḥ* in **d** (an accent-mark slipped out of place).

48. If thou hast eaten it with other hands than those with which the ancient seers ate this, thou wilt slay a Brahman: thus one says to him; it verily [have] I not [eaten] coming hither, nor retiring, nor coming on; with the hands of righteousness (*ṛtá*), therewith have I etc. etc.

49. If thou hast eaten it with another firm standing (*pratiṣṭhā́*) than that with which the ancient seers ate this, without firm standing, without support (*āyátana*) wilt thou die: thus one says to him; it verily [have] I not [eaten] coming hither, nor retiring, nor coming on; standing firm in truth, therewith have I etc. etc.

All our *saṁhitā*-mss., and the majority of SPP's, have the false accent *apratiṣṭhānó 'nāy-* in **b**; both editions emend to *-ṣṭhānò*. Some of our mss. (B.P.M.) read *pratiṣṭhā́yā* in **d**, as if aiming at *pratiṣṭháyā*.

[**Paryāya III.** — *saptakaḥ. mantroktadevatyam. 50. āsury anuṣṭubh; 51. ārcy uṣṇih; 52. 3-p. bhurik sāmnī triṣṭubh; 53. āsurī bṛhatī; 54. 2-p. bhurik sāmnī bṛhatī; 55. sāmny uṣṇih; 56. prājāpatyā bṛhatī.*]

50. This — namely, the rice-dish — is indeed the summit (*viṣṭápa*) of the ruddy one (*bradhná*).

The comm. explains *bradhna* as *sūryamaṇḍalamadhyavartī "çvaraḥ*, and *viṣṭapa* as *viyati viṣṭabdham maṇḍalam*.

51. He cometh to have the ruddy one for his world, he resorteth (*çri*) to the summit of the ruddy one, who knoweth thus.

52. Out of this rice-dish Prajāpati verily fashioned thirty-three worlds.

53. In order to the knowledge (*prajñā́na*) of them he created the sacrifice.

54. He who becomes the on-looker (*upadraṣṭṛ́*) of one knowing thus stops [his own] breath.

Upadraṣṭṛ́ ought to have here some special and offensive sense; but what? All the mss. leave *bhavati* unaccented, and SPP's text follows them; ours makes the necessary emendation to *bhávati*. We might expect *runddhe*, middle, but the following verses show whose breath is meant.

55. If he does not stop [his own] breath, he is scathed a complete scathing.

The comm. explains *sarvajyānim* by *prajāpaçvādirūpasya sarvasyā 'bhimatasya vastunaḥ . . . hānir yathā bhavati tathā.* ⌊Cf. GB. i. 3. 13, p. 52[18]; LÇS. x. 17. 7.⌋

56. If he is not scathed a complete scathing, before old age breath quits him.

⌊The quotations from the Old Anukr. for the *paryāya-sūkta* are given piecemeal at the end of each *paryāya*. They may here be given together in their metrical form:

ekatrinçad bhavet pūrvas tasmād dvāsaptatiḥ paraḥ:
tṛtīyaḥ saptako dṛṣṭo "bṛhaspatiḥ çirasy" api:

'In the [hymn beginning] "*bṛhaspatiḥ çiraḥ*"' etc. — The summations of *gaṇas* and (*gaṇa-*)*avasāna-rcas* are as follows: I. *g.*, 0; *av.*, 31; II. *g.*, 18; *av.*, 72; III. *g.*, 0; *av.*, 7. Total of *av.*, 110. — The second *paryāya-sūkta* is called also a *gaṇa-sūkta.*⌋

4. Extolling the breath (prāṇá).

[*Bhārgava Vāidarbhi.* — *ṣaḍvinçakam. mantroktaprāṇadevatyam. ānuṣṭubham: 1. çankumatī; 8. pathyāpankti; 14. nicṛt; 15. bhurij; 20. anuṣṭubgarbhātriṣṭubh; 21. madhyejyotir jagatī; 22. triṣṭubh; 26. bṛhatīgarbhā.*]

Found also in Pāipp. xvi. The whole hymn (together with a considerable number of others) is quoted by its opening words in Kāuç. 55. 17; 58. 3, 11, but not in a way to cast the least light upon its meaning and value. ⌊The hymn is reckoned to the *āyuṣya gaṇa* (note to Kāuç. 54. 11); the comm. quotes further uses from Nakṣatrakalpa 19, Çāntikalpa 15, and a Pariçiṣṭa.⌋

Translated: Muir, v. 394 (the greater part); Scherman, p. 69 (nearly all); Deussen, *Geschichte*, i. 1. 301 (with a general introduction); Henry, 111, 147; Griffith, ii. 64; Bloomfield, 218, 622. — The hymn to Prāṇa, introduced into the second *praçna* of the Praçna Upanishad, contains reminiscences of this hymn: cf. vs. 19, and Deussen, *Upanishads*, p. 562.

1. Homage to breath (*prāṇá*) in whose control is this All, who hath been lord of all, in whom all stands firm.

2. Homage, O breath, to thy roaring, homage to thy thunder; homage, O breath, to thy lightning, homage to thee raining, O breath.

Ppp. reads in **c** *'stu* for *prāṇa*.

3. When breath with thunder roars at the herbs, they are impregnated (*pra-vī*), they receive embryos, then they are born many.

Ppp. makes up the material of our vss. 3 and 4 differently, giving first 4 **a, b** and 3 **c, d**, and then 3 **a, b** and 4 **c, d**. It reads *garbhaṁ* in **c**, and *vi jāyate* in **d**. The comm. paraphrases *pra vīyante* with *garbhaṁ gṛhṇanti* ⌊cf. xii. 4. 37⌋. ⌊For "many" one might better say 'in great numbers.'⌋

4. When, the season having come, breath roars at the herbs, then all is delighted, whatever is upon the earth.

In **d** in our text, *kiṁ* is a misprint for *kíṁ*. With **c, d** is to be compared the similar half-verse RV. v. 83. 9 **c, d**.

5. When breath hath rained with rain upon the great earth, then the cattle are delighted: "verily there will be greatness for us."

⌊Cf. vs. 17 below.⌋ Ppp. has, for **a, b**: *yadā prāṇo abhyakrandīd varṣeṇa stanayitnunā.* ⌊Pāda **d** doubtless means precisely the same thing as the English slang, 'that 'll be great for us!'⌋

6. The herbs, being rained on, have talked with breath: "verily thou hast extended our life-time; thou hast made us all fragrant."

Ppp. reads in **b** *avāciraṁ*, and in **c** *acīcarat.*

7. Homage be to thee coming, homage be to [thee] going away; homage to thee, O breath, standing; to thee sitting also [be] homage.

Compare 2. 15 above, which differs only in the vocative used. Ppp. puts the verse after our 8, and reads *te 'stu* in **a**, and *namo 'stu* in **b**; a few of SPP's authorities make the same combinations.

8. Homage to thee breathing, O breath; homage be to [thee] making expiration; homage to thee turned away, homage to thee turned toward [us]; to the whole of thee [be] this homage.

Ppp. reads in **b** *namo 'stu*, and makes *parācīnāya* and *pratīcīnāya* change places in **c**, **d**.

9. The dear body that is thine, O breath, and the dearer one that is thine, O breath, likewise what remedy is thine, assign thou of it to us in order to life (*jīvás*).

For *yó* in **b** (to be read *yā́ u*) the comm. has *yāu*, regarding it as dual.

10. Breath clothes (*anu-vas*) human beings (*prajā́*), as a father a dear son; breath is lord of all, both what breathes and what does not.

Ppp. combines *prajā 'nu* in **a**, and in **d** reads twice *yas* for *yat. Prāṇáti* in **d** remains undivided in *pada*-text by Prāt. iv. 57.

11. Breath [is] death, breath *takmán;* breath the gods worship (*upa-ās*); breath may set the truth-speaker in the highest world.

Ppp. has for **a** *prāṇo mṛtyuṣ prāṇo amṛtaṁ* ⌊cf. RV. x. 121. 2⌋, which is less devoid of sense; at the end it reads *lokaṁ dadhat.*

12. Breath is *virā́j*, breath the directress; breath all worship; breath is the sun, the moon; breath they call Prajāpati.

Ppp. reads *prāṇo sarvam* ⌊sandhi!⌋ for *prāṇaṁ sarve* in **b**, and its **c** is *prāṇo 'gniç candramās sūryaṣ.* The comm. explains *deṣṭrī* as = *svasvavyāpāreṣu sarveṣām prerayitrī paradevatā.*

13. Breath-and-expiration are rice-and-barley; breath is called the draft-ox; breath is set in barley; expiration is called rice.

Ppp. combines *prāṇā "hito* in **c**. Our P.M.W. read *yávena* for *yáve ha* in **c**.

14. A man breathes out (*ápānati*), breathes (*prā́ṇati*) within the womb; when, O breath, thou quickenest, then he is born again.

Ppp. reads, in **b** and beyond: *garbhe antaḥ : yā vā tvaṁ prāṇa jinvaḥ sa damba vāyase tvat.* The comm. has *atho* in **d**.

15. Breath they call Mātariçvan; breath is called the wind; in breath what has been and what will be, in breath is all established (*prátiṣṭhita*).

Ppp. has at the end *samāhitāḥ.*

16. They of the Atharvans, they of the Añgirases, they of the gods, also those born of men — the herbs are generated (*pra-jā*), when thou, O breath, quickenest.

Ppp. has *ca yās* instead of *uta* at end of **b**, and, for **c**, *sarvā pra modanty oṣadhīḥ*. The adjectives are feminine, denoting the herbs.

17. When breath hath rained with rain on the great earth, the herbs are generated, likewise whatever plants [there are].

Compare vs. 5 above, of which this is an imitation; Ppp. makes it yet closer, by reading *modante* for *jāyante* in **c**. Some of the *saṁhitā*-mss. read *jāyante 'tho* (losing the accent of *átho*) in **c–d**.

18. He who knoweth this of thee, O breath, and in whom thou art established — to him shall all bring tribute in yon highest world.

Ppp. separates *prāṇa idaṁ* in **a**.

19. As, O breath, all these human beings (*prajā́*) are tribute-bearers to thee, so shall they bring tribute to him who shall hear thee, O thou of good report (*suçrávas*).

Ppp. has for **d** *yas tvā çuçrāva çuçruvaḥ;* and the comm. also reads *çuçruvaḥ*. ⌊With this vs., cf. Praçna Upanishad, ii. 7.⌋

20. He moves, an embryo, within the divinities; having come into being (?*ā́bhūta*), having been (*bhūtá*), he is born again; he, having been, entered with might (*çácībhis*) what is to be, what will be, [as] a father a son.

The understanding of this very obscure verse is not helped by the comm., and Ppp. offers no variants. The comm. reads *bhūtam* instead of *bhavyam* in **c**. A part of the mss. read *viveça* (not *-çā*) in **d**.

21. The swan (*haṅsá*), ascending, does not extract (*ut-khid*) one foot from the sea; verily, if he should extract that, there would not be today nor tomorrow; there would not be night nor day; at no time soever would it dawn (*vi-vas*).

Ppp. reads *utpapadam* at end of **b**, and goes on thus: *imaṁ sa tuṁ utkhide ahnāivācya naḥ çyo na rātrī nna ha syā hnaṣ prajñā tu ki cana*. The comm. explains the verse first as relating to the sun, for which it appears to be really intended, and then as applied to breath, to which it may be conceived to belong as being for the microcosm what the sun is to the macrocosm. ⌊Cf. my note to viii. 7. 24. Here one would indeed be reluctant to translate *haṅsa* by 'goose.'⌋

22. The eight-wheeled [thing, neut.] rolls, having one rim, thousand-syllabled, forth in front, down behind; with a half it has generated all existence; what its [other] half [is] — which sign is that?

This verse also evidently belongs to the sun; with its mystic ascriptions are to be compared those of the partly corresponding verses x. 8. 7, 13. Ppp. ends instead with *kiṁ u tasya ketuḥ;* it also combines *vartate 'kanemi* in **a**. The comm. reads *paçcāt* at end of **b**, and two or three of the mss. (including our O.) do the same. 'In front' and 'behind' are, of course, = 'in the east' and 'in the west.' The *ā* of *aṣṭā́cakra*, and its retention in the *pada*-text (*aṣṭā́○cakram*) are by Prāt. iii. 2 and iv. 94.

23. He who is lord of this that has every (*víçva*) [kind of] birth, of every stirring thing — to thee being such, O breath, having a quick bow among the unexhausted (?*ányа*), be homage.

The very rare *ánya* is rendered, at a venture, with the Pet. Lexx. ⌊see BR. under *ányā*, and OB. i. 66 a, end⌋; ⌊and the parallelism of the next vs., with its *átandra*, favors this rendering⌋. The wholly obscure pāda in which it occurs is explained by the comm. to mean *prāṇiçarīreṣu kṣipraṁ gacchate vyāpnuvate:* he takes *ánya* from the root *an* 'breathe,' and *-dhanvan* from *dhav* 'go.' Ppp. has no variants to help us.

24. He who is lord of this that has all (*sárva*) [kinds of] birth, of all that stirs, unwearied, wise by *bráhman* — let breath go after (*anu-sthā*) me.

Ppp. has at the end the easier reading *mām abhi rakṣatu.* ⌊W. interlines "attend" as a rendering of *anu-sthā.*⌋

25. Upright among the sleeping he wakes; by no means (*nanú*) does he fall down horizontal (*tiryáñ*); no one soever has heard of his sleeping among the sleeping.

The comm. reads in **a** *jāgara* and understands it as impv. 2d sing. Ppp. has in **c** ⌊? or in **a**?⌋ *svapneṣu.* The combination of *suptám* and *asya* seems to make it necessary to take the former in the sense of *svapna*, or of *svāpa*, as the comm. glosses it. The activity of the breath while the other powers and senses of the body are asleep is a theme of wonder elsewhere also. For *suptéṣú* in **a**, read *suptéṣu* (an accent-mark slipped over the wrong syllable).

26. O breath, turn not about from me; not another than I shalt thou be; like the embryo of the waters, in order to life (*jīvás*), I bind thee to me, O breath.

The obscure second pāda is by the comm. explained to mean *mayā saha tādātmyāpanna eva vartase.* Some mss. (including our O.) accent *mát* both times, and SPP. follows them in his text: compare xii. 3. 46.

⌊The quoted Anukr. says "*prāṇāya.*"⌋

⌊Here ends the second *anuvāka*, with 2 hymns and 82 verses, according to the count of the Berlin edition: that is 1 *paryāya-sūkta* with 3 *paryāyas* and 56 verses and 1 *artha-sūkta* with 26 verses. But some mss. sum up the *anuvāka* as containing 136 "verses of both sorts," that is the 110 *avasāna-ṛcas* of our h. 3 (see p. 632, top, and p. 629, top) and the 26 *ṛcas* of our h. 4.⌋

⌊The following quotation from the Old Anukr. seems to be put after the end of h. 4 as pertaining to the *anuvāka: trayas "tasyāu 'dano" bhavet.* Does this mean that we have no right to count the "*tasyāudana*" as less than 3 hymns? Cf. p. 611, ¶ 4.⌋

5. Extolling the Vedic student (brahmacārín).

[*Brahman. — ṣaḍviṅçakam. mantroktabrahmacārīdevatyam. trāiṣṭubham: 1. puro'tijāgata-virāḍgarbhā; 2. 5-p. bṛhatīgarbhā virāṭ çakvarī*; 6. çākvaragarbhā 4-p. jagatī; 7. virāḍ-garbhā; 8. puro'tijāgatā virāḍ jagatī; 9. bṛhatīgarbhā; 10. bhurij; 11. jagatī; 12. çākvaragarbhā 4-p. virāḍ atijagatī; 13. jagatī; 15. purastājjyotis; 14, 16–22. anuṣṭubh; 23. purobārhatātijāgatagarbhā; 25. 1-av. ārcy uṣṇih; 26. madhyejyotir uṣṇiggarbhā.*]
*⌊The words *virāṭ çakvarī* are lacking in the London ms. and are supplied from the Berlin ms. The latter adds *parā urobṛhatī:* but vs. 3 is hardly metrical, and at any rate no *urobṛhatī.*⌋

Found also in Pāipp. xvi. (with slight differences of order, which will be pointed out under the verses). Not quoted either in the Kāuçika or in the Vāitāna Sūtra; ⌊but the schol. to Kāuç. 55.18 prescribe vs. 3 for use in the *upanayana*⌋. ⌊It is cited also at the beginning of GB. (i. 2. 1–8), the chapter on the *brahmacārin.*⌋

Translated: Muir, v. 400 (18 vss.); Ludwig, p. 452; Scherman, p. 84 (19 vss.); Deussen, *Geschichte*, i. 1. 277; Henry, 114, 150; Griffith, ii. 68; Bloomfield, 214, 626. — Cf. also Bergaigne-Henry, *Manuel*, p. 161; Hillebrandt, *Ved. Mythol.*, i. 471. Henry, p. ix of his preface to Books X–XII, cites this hymn in his discussion of *bráhman*, which he connects with root *bhrāj;* and Oldenberg reviews the matter in IFA. viii. 40–41. Deussen entitles the hymn "The Brahman-pupil as incarnation of Brahm," and gives a general interpretation of its content by way of introduction. This should be consulted. The rendering "Vedic-studentship" is too rigid to fit everywhere: cf. vs. 18, note.

1. The Vedic student goes on setting in motion (*iṣ*) both firmaments; in him the gods become like-minded; he maintains earth and heaven; he fills his teacher with fervor (*tápas*).

Ppp. has *yasmin* for *tasmin* in **b**; it rectifies the meter of **c** by reading at the end *dyām utā 'mūm;* it combines *sā "cāryam*, and ends the verse with *bibharti*. The comm. explains *piparti* with *pālayati* both here and in vs. 2.

2. The Fathers, the god-folk, all the gods individually assemble after the Vedic student; the Gandharvas went after him, thirty-three, three hundred, six thousand; he fills all the gods with fervor.

Ppp. puts the verse after 3, and reads, after *pitaras* in **a**, *manusyā devajanā gandharvā 'nusaṁyantu sarve: trayastriṅçataṁ triçataṁ ṣaṭsahasrān sarvān sa devāṅs tapasā bibharti.* None of the mss., nor either edition, reads *ṣaṭtsahasrāḥ*, as required by Prāt. ii. 8.

3. The teacher, taking [him] in charge (*upa-nī*), makes the Vedic student an embryo within; he bears him in his belly three nights; the gods gather unto him to see him when born.

Upa-nī probably already a technical term for 'receive as pupil, initiate.' ⌊Prescribed in the schol. to Kāuç. 55. 18, as noted above.⌋ ⌊The first line seems to be prose: see at end of Anukr.-extracts.⌋

4. This piece of fuel [is] earth, sky the second; also the atmosphere he fills with fuel; the Vedic student fills the worlds with fuel, girdle, toil, fervor.

Ppp. reads *mekhalāvī* for *-layā*, and at the end again ⌊for the third time⌋ *bibharti*. ⌊We have the converse variant at xiii. 1. 1.⌋

5. Prior born of the *bráhman*, the Vedic student, clothing himself with heat (*gharmá*), stood up with fervor; from him [was] born the *brā́hmaṇa*, the chief *bráhman*, and all the gods, together with immortality (*amṛ́ta*).

Ppp. reads *tapaso 'dhi tiṣṭhat* at end of **b**. Of **a** the meaning may probably be 'was born before the *bráhman*' (so the translators).

6. The Vedic student goes kindled with fuel, clothing himself in the black-antelope-skin, consecrated, long-bearded; he goes at once from the eastern to the northern ocean, having grasped the worlds, again and again violently shaping (?*ācarikṛ*) [them].

Ppp. reads in **b** *kārṣṇiṁ*, and in **c** *sadyet pūrvād*. The comm. has in **d** *saṁgṛhya;* he explains *muhur ācarikrat* by *atyartham ābhimukhyena karoti*. ⌊'Northern ocean': cf. note to xi. 2. 25.⌋

7. The Vedic student, generating the *bráhman*, the waters, the world, Prajāpati, the most exalted one, the *virā́j*, having become an embryo in the womb of immortality; having become Indra, he has shattered (*tṛh*) the Asuras.

Ppp. reads in **d** *amṛtān* instead of *asurān*. More than half of SPP's authorities read *bhūtvā amṛt-* uncombined in **c**.

8. The teacher fabricated both these envelops (*nábhas*), the wide, profound, [namely] earth and sky; them the Vedic student defends by fervor; in him the gods become like-minded.

The last pāda is identical with 1 **b** above. Ppp. is more original, reading for **c**, **d**: *tāu brahmacārī tapasā 'bhi rakṣati tayor devās sadamādam madanti;* it also omits *ime* in **a**; and it puts the verse after our vs. 9. The comm. ⌊and two of SPP's authorities⌋ read *tam* for *te* at beginning of **c**.

9. This broad (*pṛthivī́*) earth, and the sky, the Vedic student first brought [as] alms (*bhikṣā́*); having made them [both] fuel, he worships; in them are set (*ā́rpita*) all beings.

Ppp. omits the meter-disturbing *ā́* in **b**, and reads for **c**, *te brahma kṛtvā samidhā upāsata*. 'Worships': i.e., as the comm. explains, 'tends the fire with them.'

10. The one this side, the other beyond, the back of the sky, in secret [are] deposited ⌊*ni-dhā*⌋ the two treasures (*nidhí*) of the *brā́hmaṇa;* them the Vedic student defends by fervor; the whole of that he, knowing, makes *bráhman* for himself.

The construction and sense of the last pāda are very doubtful. For **c**, Ppp. has its version of our 8 **c** over again: *tāu brahmacārī tapasā 'bhi rakṣati;* it also combines *parā 'nyo* in **a**. ⌊To bring out the play of the original, one might render *nidhí* by 'deposits.'⌋

11. The one this side, the other hence, from earth, the two fires come together between these two envelops; upon them are set (*çri*) the firm rays; these the Vedic student stands upon by fervor.

For our obscure first pāda Ppp. substitutes a more translatable version: *arvāg anyo divas pṛṣṭhād ito 'nyaṣ pṛthivyāḥ;* and it reads *ati* for *'dhi* in **c**; and the comm. has also *ati*, combining it with the following to *atidṛḍhās.* ⌊The comm. also has *tām* (misprinted *tā:* see "Corrections") for *tān* in **d.**⌋

12. Roaring on, thundering, the ruddy white-goer has introduced (?*anu-bhṛ*) in the earth a great virile member; the Vedic student pours seed upon the surface (*sā́nu*), on the earth; by that live the four directions.

Extremely obscure, and there are no valuable variants. Ppp. has at the beginning *abhikrandann iruṇac chatiñgo;* the comm. reads *varuṇaḥ çyatiñgo*, explaining the latter word by *çyetavarṇaṁ jalapūrṇam megham prāptaḥ.* The last pāda is found elsewhere, as ix. 10. 19 **d**, RV. i. 164. 42 **b**.

⌊For consistency, the Berlin ed. should have *abhikrándant.*⌋ ⌊The Anukr. defines the vs. as of 50 syllables and appears to scan it as 13 + 11 : 11 + 14 = 49. The ms. puts the mark of pāda-division before *pṛthivyā́m.* This last is a most palpable gloss of *sā́nāu.* If we reject it, pādas **b**, **c**, **d** are good *triṣṭubhs.*⌋

13. In the fire, in the sun, in the moon, in Mātariçvan, in the waters, the Vedic student puts fuel; their gleams (*arcís*) go about separately in the cloud; their sacrificial butter (*ā́jya*) is man, rain, waters.

Ludwig conjectures "*purīṣam* fog" in **d** for *puruṣas.* Ppp. is too corrupt in **c**, **d** to be of service. 'Their' in **c**, **d** is *tā́sām* fem., apparently relating to *samidhas* 'sticks of fuel,' though we had only the singular in **b**; but the comm. regards it as 'of fire etc.,' the fem. being used because the last of the series (⌊the meter-disturbing⌋ *apsu* 'waters') was feminine — which is possible.

14. The teacher [was] death, Varuṇa, Soma, the herbs, milk; the thunder-clouds were warriors; by them [was] this heaven (*svàr*) brought.

This verse stands in Ppp. before our vs. 13; it reads at the beginning *parjanyas* instead of *ācāryas*, reads in **c** *jīmūtā "saṅ*, and in **d** *svar ābharam.* The comm., in order to put some sense into the identification of the teacher with death and Varuṇa, regards it as alluding to the instruction of Naciketas by Death (Kaṭha Upanishad, etc.) and of Bhṛgu by Varuṇa ⌊TA. ix. 1, etc.⌋. ⌊For **c**, **d**, Roth compares ÇB. xi. 8. 1[2].⌋

15. Varuṇa, having become teacher, makes his own (?*amā́*) the entire ghee; whatever he sought of Prajāpati, that the Vedic student furnished, a friend (*mitrá*) from his own self.

The translation implies *svā́t* as the proper *pada*-reading in **d**, and the comm. also understands this; but all the *pada*-mss. read *svā́n*, as if accus. pl. The end of this verse and the beginning of the next are unfortunately wanting in Ppp.; it reads at the beginning *amād idaṁ kṛṇ-.* The mss. put the *avasāna* after *prajā́patāu* instead of after *váruṇaḥ*, and SPP. divides accordingly ⌊see his note⌋: our division is changed in obedience to the requirements of the sense. Ludwig understands *mitrás* as signifying the god Mitra.

16. The teacher [is] the Vedic student; the Vedic student [is] Prajāpati; Prajāpati bears rule (*vi-rāj*); the *virā́j* became the controlling Indra.

17. By Vedic-studentship, by fervor, a king defends his kingdom; a teacher by Vedic-studentship (*brahmacárya*) seeks a Vedic student.

Ppp. reads *rakṣate* in **b**, and *ichati* in **d**.

18. By Vedic-studentship a girl wins (*vid*) a young husband; by Vedic-studentship a draft-ox, a horse strives to gain (*ji*) food.

Instead of *jigīṣati* at the end, SPP. reads *jigīrṣati* 'strives to swallow,' finding it in the comm., and in less than a quarter (four out of seventeen) of his authorities; none of ours give it, so far as noted. Ppp. suggests yet another and a better reading, namely *jihīrṣati* — if, as seems probable, that underlies its corruption *jāhiruṣati*. As between *jigīṣati* and *jigīrṣati*, the former seems preferable. ⌊These verses will seem much less inept if we give a less rigid interpretation to *brahmacarya*: see Deussen, p. 281, p. 278.⌋

19. By Vedic-studentship, by fervor, the gods smote away death; Indra by Vedic-studentship brought heaven (*svàr*) for the gods.

Ppp. reads *apā 'jayan* at end of **b** ⌊and *amṛtaṁ* for *devebhyaḥ* in **d**⌋.

20. The herbs, past and future, day and night, the forest tree, the year together with the seasons — they are born of the Vedic student.

All the *saṁhitā*-mss. chance to agree in **c** in reading *sahá rtúbhis*, which SPP. accordingly gives in his text. Ppp. also has it; and further *bhūtābhavyam* in **a**, and *brahmacāriṇā* at the end.

21. The earthly, the heavenly cattle, they of the forest, and they that are of the village, the wingless and they that are winged — they are born of the Vedic student.

Ppp. again reads at the end *-cāriṇā*. ⌊For *paçavas*, cf. xi. 2. 24 note.⌋

22. Individually do all that are of Prajāpati bear breaths in their bodies (*ātmán*); all these the *bráhman* defends, brought in the Vedic student.

Ppp. reads at end of **b** *bibhrate;* one would like to emend to *bíbhratas*. ⌊But cf. Deussen's interpretation, p. 282.⌋ Ppp. also has in **c** *sarvāṅs tān*.

23. That, sent forth (?*pariṣūtá*) of the gods, not mounted onto, goes about shining; from that [was] born the *brā́hmaṇa*, the chief *bráhman*, and all the gods, together with immortality.

The translation of the first half-verse is merely mechanical. The second is identical with 5 **c**, **d**, above. Ppp. puts the verse after our vs. 24, reads *puruhūtam* instead of the obscure *pariṣūtam* in **a**, and gives the verse a last half of its own: *tasmin sarve paçavas tatra yajñās tasminn annaṁ saha devatābhiḥ;* and this version of the second half-verse is given in GB. i. 2. 7. The comm. explains *pariṣūtam* as *parigṛhītam; ātmatayā sākṣātkṛtam*.

24. The Vedic student bears a shining *bráhman;* in that [are] woven together all the gods; [he] generating breath-and-expiration, then outbreathing (*vyāná*), speech, mind, heart, *bráhman*, wisdom.

Ppp. reads in **b** *asmin* for *tasmin;* its verse has for second half our 26 **c**, **d**, and our 24 **c**, **d** is added at the end of our 23, which, as above noticed, comes second of the two verses; it reads for **d** *cakṣuç çrotraṁ janayan brahma medhām.* ⌊The sequence is, therefore, 24 **a**, **b**, 26 **c**, **d**, 23, 24 **c**, **d**.⌋ The GB. cites *prāṇāpānāu janayan* as a *pratīka* at i. 2. 8.

25. Sight, hearing, glory put thou in us; food, seed, blood (*lóhita*), belly.

Ppp. begins differently: *vācaṁ çreṣṭhāṁ yaço 'smāsu.* ⌊Deussen renders *udáram* by 'Leibessegen.'⌋

26. Shaping (?) these things, the Vedic student stood performing penance (*tapas tapya-*) on the back of the sea (*salilá*), in the ocean; he, bathed, brown, ruddy (*piñgalá*), shines much on the earth.

The comm. explains 25 and 26 together, as if one verse. The translation implies the emendation, apparently unavoidable, of *kálpat* to *kálpan;* the comm. makes no scruple of glossing it with *kalpayan.*

⌊The quoted Anukr. says "*brahmacārī*" *ca.*⌋

⌊Here ends the twenty-fourth *prapāṭhaka.*⌋

6. To many different gods: for relief.

[*Çaṁtāti.* — *trayoviñçakam. cāndramasam uta mantroktadevatyam. ānuṣṭubham* *: *23. bṛhatīgarbhā.*] * ⌊The Anukr. omits the definition of 18 as *pathyāpañkti.*⌋

Found also (except vss. 3, 20, 23) in Pāipp. xv. (in considerably altered verse-order: 1, 2, 4, 6, 5, 7, 15, 8, 9, 14, 17, 10, 11, 19, 13, 12, 18, 16, 22, 21).

⌊The hymn is included by Kāuç. 9. 2, 4 in the *çānti gaṇas*, major and minor; and all of the hymn except vss. 7, 9, 22, 23 (those in which the word *añhas* is missing) is reckoned to the *añholiñga gaṇa* (note to 32. 27). The last verse is cited separately at 58. 25 in a rite for long life. The same verse is variously cited by the subordinate works and the schol.: see note to 9. 2; 42. 13 (student's return); 53. 8 (*godāna*); 55. 1 (*upanayana*); Keç. to 44. 5 (*vaçāçamana*). Verse 9 is reckoned to the *rāudra gaṇa*, note to 50. 13.⌋

Translated: Henry, 117, 155; Griffith, ii. 72; Bloomfield, 160, 628.

1. We address (*brū*) Agni, the forest trees, the herbs and the plants, Indra, Brihaspati, the sun: let them free us from distress.

The comm. questions whether to render *brūmas* by *stumas* or by *iṣṭaphalaṁ yācāmahe.*

2. We address king Varuṇa, Mitra, Vishṇu, likewise Bhaga; Añça, Vivasvant we address: let them free us from distress.

3. We address god Savitar, Dhātar and Pūshan; we address Tvashṭar at the head (*agriyá*): let them free us from distress.

MS. has nearly the same verse in ii. 7. 13, but with **a** like our 2 **a**.

4. The Gandharvas-and-Apsarases we address, the (two) Açvins, Brahmaṇaspati, the god that is Aryaman by name: let them free us from distress.

5. Day-and-night now we address, sun-and-moon both; all the Ādityas we address: let them free us from distress.

Ppp. combines, in **b**, *-masā ubhā*, and reads in **c** *ādityān sarvān.*

6. The wind we address, Parjanya, the atmosphere, also the quarters, and all regions we address: let them free us from distress.

7. Let day-and-night, likewise dawn, free me from what comes from a curse; let god Soma free me, whom they call the moon.

Ppp. reads at end of **b** *vṛṣā* for *uṣāḥ*, and in **c** *ādityas* for *devas.* ⌊Cf. Hillebrandt, *Ved. Mythol.*, i. 270.⌋

8. The earthly, the heavenly cattle, also the beasts (*mṛgá*) that are of the forest; we address the hawks (*çakúnta*), the birds (*pakṣín*): let them free us from distress.

Or, 'the winged hawks.' Ppp. has a better and more independent **a** (ours = 5. 21 **a**, above): *ye grāmyās sapta paçavaḥ* ⌊cf. iii. 10. 6 note⌋.

9. Bhava-and-Çarva now we address, Rudra and him that is lord of cattle; the arrows of them which we well know (*saṁ-vid*) — let those be ever propitious to us.

Ppp. reads in **b** *ugraṣ* for *rudram*, and, instead of **d**, the refrain *te no muñcantv aṅhasaḥ.* The comm. has *vidmas* for *-ma* in **c**. ⌊Pāda **d** is nearly repeated at vs. 22 **d**.⌋

10. We address the sky, the asterisms, the earth, the *yakṣás*, the mountains; the oceans, the rivers, the pools — let them free us from distress.

Ppp. reads in **b** *bhāumam.* The comm. explains *yakṣāṇi* as *pūjyāni tatrátyāni puṇyakṣetrāṇi.* MS. has the verse in ii. 7. 13, but reads *samudrā́n* and *veçantā́n* in **c**.

11. The seven seers now we address, the heavenly waters, Prajāpati; the Fathers with Yama as their chief (*çréṣṭha*) we address: let them free us from distress.

Most of the mss. (including all of ours that are noted) read *saptarṣín* in **a**, and SPP. gives it in his text; the comm. has *saptarṣīn.*

12. The gods that are seated in the sky, and that are seated in the atmosphere, the mighty ones (*çakrá*) that are set (*çri*) on the earth — let them free us from distress.

⌊We had **a**, **b** above at x. 9. 12. In **a** read *devā́so?*⌋

13. The Ādityas, the Rudras, the Vasus, the gods in heaven, the Atharvans, the Aṅgirases full of wisdom — let them free us from distress.

Perhaps **b** is rather 'the divine Atharvans in heaven'; Ppp. reads *devā dāivā atharvaṇaḥ.*

14. We address the sacrifice, the sacrificer, the verses (*ṛ́c*), the chants (*sā́man*), the remedies; the sacred formulas (*yájus*), the invocations we address: let them free us from distress.

Bheṣajā, which probably refers to material like that included in the Atharva-Veda, is explained by the comm. as *çāntikarāṇi vāmadevyādīni;* no hymns in our collection receive any such title in the Kāuçika.

15. The five kingdoms of plants, having Soma as their chief (*çréṣṭha*), we address; the *darbhá*, hemp, barley, *sáha* — let them free us from distress.

Ppp. rectifies the meter of **b** by reading *brūmasi;* in **c** it puts *bhañgas* before *darbhas*. The mss., as usual, differ as to the accent of *rājya;* several (including our O.) read *rā́jyāni*, and our R.s.m. has *rājyā̀ni*. The comm. calls *saha* simply 'a kind of herb.'

16. The niggards we address, the demons, the serpents, the pure-folk, the Fathers; the hundred-and-one deaths we address: let them free us from distress.

⌊With **b**, cf. viii. 8. 15, and 9. 24 below. Cf. note to iii. 11. 5 for the "hundred-and-one deaths." Cf. also Chāndogya Up., viii. 7[3], 9[3], 10[3], where Indra passes three thirty-two-year terms of studentship with Prajāpati and is then bidden (viii. 11[3]) to pass five years more, to make out the full tale of 101 years.⌋

17. The seasons we address, the lords of the seasons, the year-divisions and the winters, the summers, the years, the months: let them free us from distress.

The verse nearly agrees with iii. 10. 9. The comm. quotes from Tāitt. Brāh. ii. 6. 19 in explanation of what gods are lords of the several seasons. *Ārtavān* he defines as *tattadṛtuviçeṣasambandhinaḥ padārthān;* *hāyana* and *samā* are to him simply other names for 'year.'

18. Come, ye gods, from the south; from the west come up eastward; from the east, from the north, mighty, all the gods, coming together: let them free us from distress.

Ppp. rectifies the meter of **b** by adding *nas* at the end.

19. All the gods now we address, of true agreements, increasers of righteousness, together with all their spouses: let them free us from distress.

20. The collective gods now we address, of true agreements, increasers of righteousness, together with their collective spouses: let them free us from distress.

This verse (omitted in Ppp.) differs from the preceding only by twice reading *sarva* instead of *viçva*. The epithet *ṛtāvṛ́dh* may also signify 'increasing by righteousness.'

21. Existence we address, the lord of existences, and who is controller of existences; all existences, assembling — let them free us from distress.

Bhūtám at the beginning may be adjective, 'him who is.' Ppp. reads *patis* for *vaçī* at end of **b**, and, for **c**, *bhūtāni sarvā brūmas*.

22. They that are the five divine directions, that are the twelve divine seasons, that are the fangs of the year — let them be ever propitious to us.

All the *saṁhitā*-mss. happen to read together in **b** *dvā́daça rtávaḥ*, which SPP. adopts; Ppp. makes the same combination. ⌊Pāda **d** is nearly 9 **d** above.⌋

23. The immortal remedy, chariot-bought, which Mātalī knows — that Indra made enter into the waters; that remedy, O waters, give ye.

The *pada*-text reads *mā́talī* also. ⌊Concerning Mātalī, see Weber, *Sb.* 1895, p. 837.⌋ All the mss. accent *ā́po* in **d**, and it accordingly is read by both editions; but the sense requires the emendation to *āpo*, as translated; ⌊so the comm.: *he āpaḥ*⌋. The verse is so discordant with the rest of the hymn as to seem an addition made to it; ⌊it is not found in Ppp.⌋.

The comm. ⌊p. 123⌋ regards the verse as referred to in Vāit. 3. 13, quoting the whole *sūtra*, but with *mātalyā* instead of *pātrāṇy* at the beginning; the mss. of Vāit. read *mātalyā* or *mārttalyā*.

⌊Here ends the third *anuvāka*, with 2 hymns and 49 verses. The quoted Anukr. says *agnim-brūmake tisraḥ:* i.e. 'in the hymn *agnim brūmaḥ*, there are three [over twenty].'⌋

7. Extolling the remnant (úcchiṣṭa) of the offering.

[*Atharvan. — saptavinçati. mantroktochiṣṭādhyātmadāivatam. ānuṣṭubham* *: *6. puroṣṇigbārhataparā; 21. svarāj; 22. virāṭ pathyābṛhatī.*] *⌊The Anukr. omits the definition of vs. 11 as *pathyāpañkti.*⌋

Found also (except vs. 25) in Pāipp. xvi. ⌊The hymn is not cited in the text of Kāuç. nor of Vāit.⌋

Translated: Muir, v. 397 (part); Scherman, p. 87 (part); Deussen, *Geschichte*, i. 1. 305–310; Henry, 120, 156; Griffith, ii. 75; Bloomfield, 226, 629. — See Deussen's valuable introduction. He does not believe that *ucchiṣṭa* means 'remnant of the offering' in this hymn, but rather 'residuum in general,' the remainder that we get after subtracting from the universe all the forms of the world of phenomena.

1. In the remnant [are set] name and form, in the remnant [is] set the world; within the remnant both Indra and Agni, everything is set together.

The comm. connects the hymn with hymn 3, above, making the *ucchiṣṭa* the remnant of Aditi's rice-dish; he quotes Tāitt. Brāh. i. 1. 9[1], where it says "they gave her what remained" (*ucchesaṇa*) etc. Ppp. reads *rūpāṇi* for *rūpaṁ ca* in **b**.

2. In the remnant heaven-and-earth, all existence is set together; in the remnant the waters, the ocean, the moon, the wind is set.

Ppp. combines at the end *vātā "hitaḥ.*

3. In the remnant [are] the being one and the non-being one, both, death, vigor, Prajāpati; they of the world (*lāukyá*) are supported (*ā-yat*) on the remnant, both *vrá* and *drá;* also fortune (*çrī́*) in me.

Ppp. reads *'sañç* ⌊for *asañç*⌋ in **a**; in **d**, where we should welcome its aid in making sense, it is corrupt, reading *pṛçcadṛçcāvṛçcīr mayi;* it also combines *ucchiṣṭā "yattās* in c. The comm. has *āhitās* again instead of *āyattās* in c; he supplies *prajās* to *lāukyās;* and he explains *vras* as *vārako varuṇaḥ* and *dras* as *drāvako 'mṛtamayaḥ somaḥ*, and the last clause by *tatprasādāc chrīḥ sampad mayi viduṣy āhitā "sthitā bhavatu.*

4. Being fixed, fix thou, being stanch, *nyá*, the *bráhman*, the ten all-creators; as the wheel on all sides of the nave, the divinities [are] set (*çritá*) in the remnant.

Ppp. gives no variant in a; at the end it has *devatā hitāḥ* (i.e. "*hitāḥ?*). SPP., against the authority of all the *pada*-mss., combines *dṛṅhasthiras* into one word, merely because the comm. so explains it (*dṛṅhaṇena sthirīkṛto lokaḥ*) — which is no reason at all for such an absurdity. *Nyas* the comm. glosses with *netāras tatratyāḥ prāṇinaḥ*, which gives us no help.

5. The verse (*ṛ́c*), the chant (*sā́man*), the formula (*yájus*) [are] in the remnant, [also] the song (*udgīthá*), the introductory praise (*prástuta*), the praise (*stutá*); the sound *hiṅg* [is] in the remnant, the tone (*svára*), and the ring (? *meḍí*) of the chant; that in me.

The comm. gives alternative explanations of *svára* and *meḍí*, showing that their technical meaning was doubtful to him, as to us. Ppp. has for b *udgītaṣ prastutaṁ sthitam;* in d it has *mīḍhus* for *meḍis*. ⌊To the last clause the comm. supplies *bhavatu:* cf. vss. 12, 14.⌋

6. That relating to Indra-and-Agni, that to the purifying [Soma] (*pāvamāná*), the great-named ones (f., *mahā́nāmnīs*), the great ceremony (*mahāvratá*) — within the remnant are [all] the members of the sacrifice, like an embryo within a mother.

The *āindrāgna* and *pāvamāna* are explained by the comm. as two *sāmans;* for the *mahānāmnīs* he refers to Āit. Ār. iv. 1.

7. The *rājasū́ya* (royal consecration), the *vājapéya* (vigor-drinking), the *agniṣṭomá* (fire-praise), then the sacrifice (*adhvará*), the *arká* and *açvamedhá* (horse-sacrifice) [are] in the remnant, the one having a living *barhís*, most intoxicating.

Ppp. has in b the preferable reading *tato 'dhvaraḥ.*

8. The establishing of a fire, also the consecration, the desire-fulfiller, together with the meter (*chándas*); the removed (? *útsanna*) sacrifices, the sacrificial sessions (*sattrá*), are set together in the remnant.

All the *pada*-mss. read in b *kāma॰práḥ : chándasā:*, but no *saṁhitā*-ms. gives correspondingly *kāmapráç chán-*; they vary between *-prá chán-* (thus the majority) and *-práḥ chán-* (including our I.K.); both editions emend to *-práç chán-*; the comm. understands the two words as one compound. He also reads *utsannayajñās* as a compound in c, and takes it to mean sacrifices that have gone out of use and knowledge.

9. Both the fire-offering (*agnihotrá*) and faith, the *váshaṭ*-exclamation, the vow (*vratá*), penance, the sacrificial gift (*dákṣiṇā*), what is offered (*iṣṭá*) and what is bestowed (*pūrtá*) — are set together in the remnant.

Ppp. reads *'ti* instead of *'dhi* in **d**. The comm. explains *iṣṭá* as *çrutivihitaṁ yāgahomādi karma*, and *pūrtá* as *smṛtipurāṇābhihitaṁ vāpīkūpataṭākadevāyatanārāmādinirmāṇam.*

10. The one-night [sacrifice], the two-night, the same-day-purchase (*sadyaḥkrī́*), the purchasable (?*prakrī́*), the praiseworthy (*ukthyà*) — [it] is woven, deposited, in the remnant; the minute things of the sacrifice, by wisdom.

Ppp. betters the grammar of the last half-verse by reading for **d** *yajñasyā 'no nu vidyayā.* The comm. reads in **b** *sadyaskrīḥ; sadyaḥkrī* is especially prescribed by Prāt. ii. 62.

11. The four-night [sacrifice], the five-night, and the six-night, of both kinds, together, the one of sixteen (*ṣoḍaçín*), and the seven-night — from the remnant were born all the sacrifices that are put in immortality.

Ppp. combines *yajñā 'mṛte* near the end. The comm. understands by *ubhayas* in **b** the doubles of the numbers of nights given. *Ṣoḍaçin* is the subject of Prāt. iv. 51, and *catūrātra* (p. *catuḥ○rātraḥ*) of Prāt. iv. 80.

12. The response (*pratīhārá*), the conclusion (*nidhána*), both the all-conquering and the on-conquering (*abhijít*) one, the same-day and over-night ones [are] in the remnant, the twelve-day one: also that in me.

Ppp. has at the beginning *pratihāro.* ⌊The comm. joins the "also" to what precedes and says that "that in me" (supply *bhavatu*) is to be understood as a prayer: cf. vss. 5, 14.⌋

13. Pleasantness, compliance (*sáṁnati*), comfort (*kṣéma*), custom (?*svadhā́*), refreshment, immortality, power — in the remnant all occurring (*pratyáñc*) desires are satisfied with desire.

Ppp. reads at the end *tṛmpanti.* Most of the *pada*-mss. and many of the *saṁhitā*-mss. read simply *kṣéma* in **a** (including our Bp.O.D.R.K.Kp.).

14. The nine earths, oceans, skies, are set (*çritá*) in the remnant; the sun shines in the remnant; day-and-night: also that in me.

The *pada*-mss. in general read simply *çritā́* (or *çṛtā́*) in **b**. Two or three mss. (including our O.) read *'pi* in **d**. Ppp. reads in **a**, **b** *bhūmyāṁ samudrasyo 'chiṣṭe*, and has *ca* for *api* in **d**. ⌊The comm. treats the last words of the vs. as under vs. 12.⌋

15. The added oblation (*upahávya*), the dividing [day], and the sacrifices that are put in secret, the remnant bears, bearer of all, father of the generator.

Ppp. reads *divi çrutaḥ* ⌊intending *çritāḥ?*⌋ for *guhā hitāḥ* in **b**. The mss. are divided between *upahávyam* and *upahavyám;* the latter is read by our B.W.O.s.m. D.R.T.; and K. has *-havyàm.*

16. The remnant, father of the generator, of breath (*ásu*) the grandson, grandfather — he dwells, ruler of all, an overpowering (?*atighnyà*) bull upon the earth.

Ppp. reads in **b** *'sāu putraç ca*, which, without the *ca*, is an acceptable improvement.

17. Righteousness, truth, penance, kingship, toil, and virtue (*dhárma*) and deed (*kárman*), being (*bhūtá*), what will be, [is] in the remnant; heroism, fortune (*lakṣmī́*), strength in strength.

Ppp. has *dīkṣā* for *rāṣṭram* in **a**: a better reading. The comm. explains *ṛta* here by *manasā yathārthasaṁkalpanam* 'right conception'; *bale* at the end he makes = *balavati tasminn ucchiṣṭe.*

18. Success, force, design, dominion, kingship, the six wide [quarters], the year [is] in the remnant, *íḍā*, the orders (*prāiṣá*), the dips (*gráha*), the oblation.

Ppp. combines *ojā "kūtiḥ* in **a**. ⌊W. interlines 'potions' as an alternative for 'dips.'⌋

19. The four-priest (*cátur-hotṛ*) [sacrifices], the *āprī́s*, the seasonal [oblations], the *nivíds* — in the remnant [are] the sacrifices, the invocations, the victim-offerings (*paçubandhá*), then the offerings (*íṣṭi*).

Tádiṣṭayaḥ at the end in our edition is a misprint for *tád íṣṭayaḥ.*

20. Both the half-months and the months, the year-divisions (*ārtavá*) with the seasons; in the remnant [are] the noisy waters, the thunder, the great sound (? *çrúti*).

The comm. reads *çuci* in **d**, so we lack his conjecture as to the meaning of *çruti.*

21. Pebbles, gravel, stones, herbs, plants, grasses, clouds, lightnings, rain — in the remnant [are they] set together, set.

Ppp. combines *sikatā 'çm-* in **a**. ⌊Read *oṣadhīr?*⌋

22. Success (*ṛ́ddhi*), attainment, obtainment, permeation, greatness, prosperity ⌊*edhatú*⌋ — in the remnant over-attainment and growth (*bhū́ti*) [is] put in, put down, put.

Several of our mss. (P.M.W.I.O.) accent *vyā́pti* in **b**. All the mss. save one or two (including our B.) leave *edhatuḥ* unaccented, as if it were taken for a 3d dual perfect; both editions read *edhatúḥ*. The comm. strangely reads at the end *hitāḥ;* ⌊but the *pada*-text makes all three words of **d** singular⌋.

23. Both what breathes with breath and what sees with sight: from the remnant were born all the gods in heaven, heaven-resorters.

24. The verses (*ṛ́c*), the chants, the meters, the ancient (*purāṇá*), together with the formula (*yájus*): from the remnant were born etc. etc.

Ppp. reads, for *ṛcaḥ sāmāni*, *ṛgyajussāmāni*, and also prefixes to the verse our 27 **a**, **b** (combining *devāṣ pit-*).

25. Breath-and-expiration, sight, hearing, indestructibleness and destruction: from the remnant etc. etc.

The first half-verse is found below as 8. 4 **a**, **b**, 26 **a**, **b**. The verse, as noted above, is wanting in Ppp.

26. Delights, joys, enjoyments, and they that enjoy enjoyments — from the remnant etc. etc.

⌊The first half-verse recurs as 8. 24 **a**, **b**.⌋ ⌊In the Berlin ed., there should be a space between *módāḥ* and *pra-*.⌋

27. The gods, the Fathers, human beings, and they that are Gandharvas-and-Apsarases: from the remnant etc. etc.

⌊The quoted Anukr. says "*uchiṣṭe*."⌋

8. Mystic: especially on the constitution of man.

[*Kāurupathi. — catustrinçat. adhyātmamanyudāivatam. ānuṣṭubham: 33. pathyāpañkti.*]

Found also (except vss. 33, 34) in Pāipp. xvi. (in the verse-order 1–6, 8–10, 7, 12, 11, 13, 15, 14, 16–32). ⌊The hymn is noticed neither by Kāuç. nor by Vāit.⌋

Translated: Ludwig, p. 402; Scherman, p. 67 (8 vss.); Deussen, *Geschichte*, i. 1. 270–277 (with introduction and interpretation); Henry, 123, 160; Griffith, ii. 80.

1. When fury (*manyú*) brought his wife away from the house of contrivance (*saṁkalpá*), who were the groomsmen (*jánya*)? who the wooers (*vará*)? who also was chief wooer?

Ppp. combines in **c** *kā "san.* ⌊Its **c**, **d** = our 6 **c**, **d**.⌋

2. Penance and also action were within the great sea (*arṇavá*); those were the groomsmen, those the wooers; the *bráhman* was chief wooer.

The *pada*-mss. (save one of SPP's) divide *evā́stām* in **a** into *evá : ā́stām*, and the accent of the verb is perfectly defensible, though SPP. alters to *āstām*. Some of the mss. (including our Bp.P.M.E.) leave *mahati* unaccented: cf. vs. 6 **b**, and iii. 6. 3.

3. Ten gods were born together from gods of old; whoever may know them plainly, he verily may talk big to-day.

'May teach the unlimited *brahman*' is the comm's understanding of the last clause.

4. Breath-and-expiration, sight, hearing, indestructibleness and destruction, out-breathing and up-breathing, speech, mind — they verily brought design (*ā́kūti*).

The first half-verse occurs also as 7. 25 **a**, **b** above, and the first three pādas as vs. 26 **a**, **b**, **c** below. Ppp. combines *vā "kūtim* in **d**.

5. Unborn were the seasons, likewise Dhātar, Brihaspati, Indra-and-Agni, the two Açvins, at that time: whom did they worship (*upa-ās*) [as] chief?

The comm. reads at the end *āsate*.

6. Both penance, namely, and action were within the great sea; penance was born from action; that did they worship as chief.

The comm. again has *āsate* at the end. SPP. reads *ástām* in *pada*-text, this time with two of his mss. Some mss. again (cf. vs. 2) read *mahati* (so our Bp.E.; P.M. *mahaty árṇavé*).

7. The earth that was previous to this one (*itás*), which the sages (*addhātí*) indeed knew — whoever may know that by name, he may think himself knowing in ancient things.

The translation implies emendation of *tā́n* in **c** to *tā́m*, which SPP. gives in his text, with about half of his mss. Ppp's version is quite different; it reads for **a** *ye 'to bhūmiṣ pūrvā "sīt;* and, for **c**, **d**, *ke tasyan devā "sate kasmin sā 'dhi çrutaḥ* ⌊intending *tasyām* and *çritā?*⌋.

8. Whence was Indra, whence Soma, whence Agni born? whence did Tvashṭar come into being? whence was Dhātar born?

Ppp. has for **d** *dhātā sam abhavat kutaḥ.*

9. From Indra Indra, from Soma Soma, from Agni Agni was born; Tvashṭar was born from Tvashṭar; from Dhātar Dhātar was born.

Ppp. arranges in **d** *dhātā dhātur.*

10. The ten gods that were of old, born from gods — having given the world to [their] sons, in what world sit they?

Ppp. combines *tā "san* in **a**, and reads *puraḥ* for *purā* in **b**. ⌊For consistency, the Berlin ed. should have *dattvā́.*⌋

11. When he brought hair, bone, sinew, flesh, marrow, having made a body with feet, what world did he afterward enter?

The comm. reads *sam abharat* in **b**.

12. Whence brought he the hair, whence the sinew, whence the bones? the limbs, the joints, the marrow, the flesh who brought from whence?

Ppp. combines at the end *kutā "bharat.* The comm. appears again to read *sam abharat* at end of **b**. A few mss. (including our Bp.R.) read *snā́vaḥ* in **a**.

13. Pourers-together namely are those gods who brought together the bringings-together; having poured together the whole mortal, the gods entered man.

Ppp. reads *çaṅsatas* for *saṁsicas* in **a**, and *saṁsṛjya* for *saṁsicya* in **c**.

14. Thighs, feet, knee-joints, head, hands, also face, ribs, nipples (? *barjahyà*), sides: what seer put that together?

The comm. has nothing to say for *barjahyè* except 'the parts so called.' Ppp. reads instead *majjahye;* and it has *çroṇī* for *çiras* in **b**. It also makes our 14 **c**, **d** and 15 **c**, **d** exchange places.

15. Head, hands, also face, tongue and neck, vertebræ — all that, having enveloped with skin, the great putting-together put together.

Ppp. reads ⌊*bāhu* for *mukham* in **a** and has⌋ in **c** *tat sarvam.* The comm. paraphrases *saṁdhā* in **d** with *saṁdhānakartrī devatā.*

16. The great body which lay there, put together by the putting-together — who brought into it the color with which it shines (*ruc*) here today?

Ppp. reads *adadhat* for *açayat* in **a**, *mayi* for *mahat* in **b**, and *ko 'smin* in **d**. SPP. reports all his *pada*-mss. as having at the end *ā॰ábharat*, which he emends to *ā́ : abharat;* our *pada*-mss. give the latter.

17. All the gods assisted (?*upa-çikṣ*); that she who was a woman knew; she who was wife of control (?*váça*), mistress (*īçā́*), brought color into it.

Ppp. reads in **a** *upāsikṣan*, and *viṣasya* for *vaçasya* in **c**; the comm. (with two or three of SPP's mss.) has instead of the latter *viçvasya*. There are, failing help from sense, various questionable points in the construction.

18. When Tvashṭar bored through [him?] who [was] the superior father of Tvashṭar, having made the mortal a house, the gods entered into man.

Probably **c** is adjunct of *devā́s;* whether **b** is object of the verb in **a** is more doubtful. Ppp. gives no help. The comm. makes **b** define Tvaṣṭar himself, and understands the 'boring' of the openings for the senses, the eyes and ears etc. ⌊Ludwig renders **c**: "machten die götter den sterblichen zu [ihrem] hause."⌋

19. Sleep, weariness, misery (*nírṛti*), the deities named evils, old age, baldness, hoariness, entered the body afterward (*ánu*).

The comm. reads *tandrī* in **a**, and *khālityam* in **c**. *Anu* perhaps rather 'one after another.'

20. Theft, ill-doing, wrong, truth, sacrifice, great glory, both strength, dominion, and force, entered the body afterward.

Ppp. has the better reading *sahas* for *bṛhat* in **b**.

21. Both growth (*bhū́ti*) and diminution, generosities and niggardlinesses, both hungerings and all thirstings, entered the body afterward.

Ppp. combines *vā 'bhūtiç* in **a**.

22. Both revilings and non-revilings, both what [says] "come on" (*hánta*) and "no," faith, the sacrificial fee, and non-faith, entered the body afterward.

Ppp. combines *vā 'nindāç* in **a**. The majority of mss. (including our Bp.B.P.M.E. T.R.K.) read *dakṣiṇā́* in **c**; ⌊if I understand W's Collation Book, only Bp.T.K. among his mss. are noted as so reading;⌋ both editions give *dákṣiṇā*. The comm. explains the word as meaning *dhanasamṛddhi*. ⌊Cf. Oldenberg, ZDMG. l. 449.⌋

23. Both knowledges and ignorances, and what else is to be taught (*upa-diç*); the *bráhman* entered the body; the verses, the chant, also the formula.

Ppp. combines *vā 'vidyāç* in **a**, and reads for **c** *çarīraṁ sarve prā 'viçan* ⌊= our 25 **c**⌋. *Bráhman* perhaps is here the 'charm,' representing the Atharvan hymns.

24. Delights, joys, enjoyments, and they that enjoy enjoyments, laughter, sport, dances, entered the body afterward.

Ppp. reads for **a** *ānandā nandāṣ pramado.* The comm. reads *nur iṣṭās* in **c** ⌊see SPP's note, p. 163⌋. The first half-verse is identical with 7. 26 **a**, **b** above.

25. Both appeals (*ālāpá*) and pratings (*pralāpá*), and they who utter (*-lap*) addresses (*abhīlāpa-*) — all entered the body, joiners-on (*āyúj*), joiners-forth (*prayúj*), joiners.

Ppp. reads *prāyujas* in **d**. The comm. explains the last words as = *āyojanāni, prayojanāni*, and *yojanāni.* The first half-verse is as it were a change rung on 24 **a**, **b**.

26. Breath-and-expiration, sight, hearing, indestructibleness and destruction, out-breathing and up-breathing, speech, mind — they go about (*īya-*) with the body.

The first three pādas are the same with 4 **a**, **b**, **c**, above.

27. Both blessings (*āçís*) and precepts (*praçís*), demands (*saṁçís*) and explanations (*viçís*), thoughts, all devisings, entered the body afterward.

The comm. explains the difficult compounds of *-çis* as mechanically as those of *-yuj* in vs. 25 : *āçāsanāni, praçāsanāni, saṁçāsanāni, vividhāni çāsanāni.*

28. Both those of the blood and those of the bladder, the hasting and those that are pitiable, the secret, the clear, the thick waters — those they caused to settle in the repugnant one.

That is, apparently, in the body that was loth to receive them. SPP. reads unaccountably at the beginning *ā́steyīs*, against the great majority of his mss., the comm., and the sense. The reading has not been noted at all among our mss., but *sn* and *st* are very imperfectly distinguished in general by the scribes, and the latter may possibly have been intended by some among them. The comm. derives the word from *ā* + *snā*, instead of from *asan;* the form in which he gives it is *āsneyyas*. The second word he reads *vāsneyyas*, and derives it from *vā* 'or' + *snā!* Then he adds another derivation for both words, from *āsana* 'sitting,' and *vasna* 'price' respectively. He reads then *āpas* in **c**. Ppp. reads *çukriyā* in **c**.

29. Having made bone [their] fuel, then they caused eight waters to settle; having made seed [their] sacrificial butter, the gods entered man.

The first part of the verse is spoiled in Ppp. The comm. has the more regular accus. pl. *apas* in **b** (the *pada*-text *aṣṭá : ā́paḥ*, as required by the accent; the comm. in general pays no heed to accent). He acutely refers to Tāitt. Brāh. i. 1.9[4], where bone is identified with fuel, and seed with sacrificial butter.

30. What waters [there are], and what deities, what *virā́j*, with *bráhman; bráhman* entered the body; on (*ádhi*) the body [is] Prajāpati.

31. The sun, the wind, shared [respectively] the eye, the breath of man; then his other self the gods bestowed (*pra-yam*) on Agni.

'Shared' (*vī bhejire*, pl.) is ungrammatical as taken with the subject (which is only two-fold) given in the text. The comm. understands that the other 'senses' with their deities are viewed as included with these two. Ppp. reads *tathā* instead of *atha* in **c**.

32. Therefore, indeed, one who knows man ⌊*púruṣa*⌋ thinks "this is *bráhman*"; for all deities are seated in him, as cows in a cow-stall.

Our text should read at the end *ivā́ "sate* with SPP. and nearly all the mss. (our Bp.B. *ivā "sate*). Ppp. has a less naïve **d**: *çarīre 'dhi samāhitāḥ.*

33. By the first dying, it goes apart dividing threefold: yonder goes it with one [part]; yonder goes it with one; here with one it dwells (*? ni-sev*).

This verse and the one following are (as above noted) wanting in Ppp. The comm. reads *ni* for *vi* in **b**. He regards the two 'yonders' as pointing respectively to heaven and hell, and paraphrases *ni ṣevate* by *nitarāṁ sukhaduḥkhātmakān bhogān sevate.* ⌊He makes *jīvātmā* the subject: and a masculine subject seems required by *víṣvañ*, unless we read *nī* just after it.⌋

34. Within waters that are sluggish (*? stīmá*), old, is the body placed; within that is might (*? çáva, çávas ?*); thence is it called might.

There is perhaps in **c, d** a play upon the word *çávas*, which may mean either 'might' (as neut.) or (as masc.) 'corpse.' The comm. paraphrases it both times with *balātmakaḥ sūtrātmā* ⌊i.e. the *parameçvara*⌋. He explains *stīmāsu* as *anārdraṁ sarvaṁ jagad ārdraṁ kurvatīṣu.*

⌊Here ends the fourth *anuvāka*, with 2 hymns and 61 verses. The quoted Anukr. says with reference to this eighth hymn "*yan manyur*" *ity atra caturdaça ca:* that is 14 over 20.⌋

9. To conquer enemies: to Arbudi.

[*Kāñkāyana.—ṣaḍviṅçakam. mantroktārbudidevatyam. ānuṣṭubham: 1. 7-p. virāṭ çakvarī 3-av.; 3. paroṣṇih; 4. 3-av. uṣṇigbṛhatīgarbhā parātriṣṭup 6-p. atijagatī; 9, 11, 14, 23, 26. pathyāpañkti; 15, 22, 24, 25. 3-av. 7-p. çakvarī; 16. 3-av. 5-p. virāḍ upariṣṭājjyotis triṣṭubh; 17. 3-p. gāyatrī.*]

This and the following hymn are wanting in Pāipp., although bits of vss. 15–17 of this one are to be found in Pāipp. xvii. The opening words of the two are quoted together in Kāuç. 16. 21, in connection with rites for insuring success in war. ⌊The use of the two hymns forms a sequel to the rites described in the introduction to viii. 8, which see; and cf. under viii. 8. 24.⌋

Translated: Ludwig, p. 530; Henry, 126, 164; Griffith, ii. 84; Bloomfield, 123, 631.

1. What arms (*bāhú*) [there are], what arrows, and the powers (*vīryà*) of bows, swords (*así*), axes (*paraçú*), weapon, and what thought-and-design in the heart — all that, O Arbudi, do thou make our enemies to see; and do thou show forth specters (*udārá*).

The comm. refers to AB. vi. 1, where Arbuda is named and called a serpent-sage, and declares Arbudi and Nyarbudi to be his two sons. *Udārān* he explains as *udgatān antarikṣacarān rakṣaḥpiçācādīn mantrasāmarthyodbhāvitān*, or also as *sūryaraçmiprabhavā ulkādaya āntarikṣyā utpātāḥ*, specters or portents. ⌊Pāda **d**, below, vs. 13 **b**.⌋

2. Stand up, equip ye yourselves (*saṁ-nah*), O friends, god-folk; beheld concealed of you be [those] who are our friends, O Arbudi.

The occurrence of *mitrās* m. and *mitrāṇi* n. in the same verse is puzzling, also the conjunction of *saṁdṛṣṭa* and *gupta*, and of *vas* with the singular *arbude*. The comm. reads *saṁdṛṣṭās* and *guptās* in **c**. Our Bp. reads *yā́ḥ* in **d**. ⌊Pāda **a** = 26 **b** and 10. 1 **a**.⌋ ⌊W. interlines "protected?" over "concealed."⌋

3. Stand ye (two) up, take ye hold; with tying up, with tying together, gird ye the armies of our enemies, O Arbudi.

The dual verbs doubtless imply, as the comm. also points out, the inclusion of Nyarbudi in the address to Arbudi ⌊cf. vs. 11⌋. The comm. reads *senām* in **c**.

4. The God that is Arbudi by name, and the lord (*īçāna*) Nyarbudi, by whom the atmosphere is involved (*ā-vṛ*), and this great earth — by those (two) who are allied with Indra, I go after what is conquered with an army.

Probably 'I follow up with my army what is already conquered by them.' The two last pādas are by the comm. reckoned as the first line of the next verse.

5. Stand thou up, O god-folk, Arbudi, with the army; breaking (*bhañj*) the army of our enemies, envelop it with [thy] coils (*bhogá*).

The comm. explains *bhogébhis* as *ātmīyāiḥ sarpaçarīrāiḥ*.

6. Presenting to view, O Nyarbudi, the seven kinds of specters, with them all do thou stand up, when the butter is offered, with the army.

The *pada*-text reads in **a** *jātā́n : ni॰arbude;* but the reading is plainly false, and should be either *jātā́ : ni॰arbude*, or *jātā́ni : arbude;* either of these, considering that to the scribes *nya* and *nnya* are entirely equivalent and exchangeable (see my *Skt. Gr.* §§ 229, 232), would correctly represent the *saṁhitā*-reading. ⌊Cf. the reading of the comm. at 10. 21.⌋

7. Smiting herself, tear-faced, and crop-eared(?), let her yell, with disheveled hair, when the man is slain, bitten (?*rad*), O Arbudi, of thee.

'Her' — namely, the wife or sister or the like; more distinctly pointed to in the next verse. *Radita* ought to mean rather 'scraped' or 'scratched'; there seems to be no other example of it in the sense 'bitten': perhaps as a mere scratch from the fang of a serpent is enough to kill. The comm. takes *radita* as a noun (like *ruta*, *smita*, *citta*, etc.), = *dantāir vilekhane khādane sati*. Of *kṛdhukarṇī* the comm. says: *kṛdhv iti hrasvanāma : karṇābharaṇaparityāgena hrasvakarṇī*. The verse is translated (also vs. 14, and 10. 7) by Bloomfield, in AJP. xi. 340.

8. Drawing in her *karūkara*, seeking with her mind her son, husband, brother, also her people (*svá*) — in case of thy bite, O Arbudi.

The ending is the same with that of vs. 7, understood as the comm. takes it; we might also supply '[he being] bitten' etc. The Pet. Lex. renders *karūkara* 'vertebræ of the neck and spine': rather (in ÇB. xii. 2. 4[10, 14]), perhaps, 'a point or spinous process of a vertebra.' The comm. explains *karu* as an imitative word, and *karūkara* as meaning anything that makes the sound *karu*, and so designating *hastapādādy-avayavagataṁ saṁdhimad asthijātam;* and he goes on *loke hi bhayavaçād ubhayor hastayoḥ parasparāñgulinipīḍanena tādṛçaṁ çabdam utpādayanti*. This is far from relieving satisfactorily the obscurity. Most of our mss. accent *svā̀n* in **c**.

9. Let the buzzards, *jāṣkamadás*, vultures, falcons, winged ones, let the crows, the birds (*çakúni*), satisfy themselves — exhibiting among the enemies — in case of thy bite, O Arbudi.

We have here two refrain-phrases, neither of which stands in any grammatical connection with its surroundings (the pple. 'exhibiting' being nom. sing. masc.). The comm. reads in **a** *aliklabāḥ* and *yāḥ klamadāḥ;* and some of the mss. have *jāḥkam-* (so our B.O.s.m.).

10. Then let all wild beasts, let the fly, let the worm satisfy itself upon the carrion of men, bitten, O Arbudi, of thee.

Here the refrain stands again in grammatical connectic ı.

11. Take ye (two) hold, tear out (*sam-bṛh*) [their] breath-and-expiration, O Nyarbudi; let groaning (?*nivāçá*) noises assemble — exhibiting among the enemies — in case of thy bite, O Arbudi.

Again (as in vs. 3) the other serpent-deity is included in **a** in the invocation ⌊this time of Nyarbudi⌋. The comm. reads *vṛhatam* in **a**. He explains *nivāçās* as *nīcīnaṁ vāçyamānā ābhāṣyamāṇāḥ*.

12. Make thou [them] tremble; let them quake together; unite our enemies with fear; with broad-gripping arm-hooks pierce thou our enemies, O Nyarbudi.

The comm. reads in **c** *ūrugrāhāis* (which is not bad) and *bāhuvañkāis*, explaining the latter by *bāhunā vakrabandhanāiḥ*. Our P.M.W. read at the end *amítrāṇy arbude:* compare 6 **a**, above.

13. Let their arms be confounded, and what thought-and-design is in their heart; let not anything of them be left — in case of thy bite, O Arbudi.

The second pāda is the same with vs. 1 **d**, above.

14. Smiting themselves let them (f.) run together, smiting on the breast, the thighs (?*paṭāurá*), not anointing, with disheveled hair, wailing when the man is slain, bitten, O Arbudi, of thee.

Translated by Bloomfield, ib. (see vs. 7). I follow both translators in rendering *paṭāurá* by 'thigh,' although it is not too acceptable, considering the familiarity of *ūru* as name for 'thigh.' SPP. reads instead *paṭūrāú*, with a very small minority of his mss. (of ours, only B.s.m. has it), and with the comm. The latter defines it simply as *tat-* (i.e. *uraḥ*) *pradeçāu*. He makes *aghārin* from *agha* and root *ṛ*: *aghena bhartṛviyogajanitena duḥkhenā "rtāḥ!*

15. Dog-accompanied Apsarases, she-jackals (?*rūpakā*) also, O Arbudi, the *riçá*, licking much in the inner vessel, seeking what is ill-deposited — all these (f.), O Arbudi, do thou make our enemies to see, and do thou show forth specters; —

The conclusion is nearly the same with vs. 1 **e**, **f**, **g**, above, and is also repeated below ⌊vss. 22, 24⌋. The accent of *çvànvatīs* seems certainly wrong, but it is read by all the mss., and avouched by the commentary to Prāt. iii. 73. The translation of *rūpakā* is that of the minor Pet. Lex., apparently founded solely on an Avestan analogue; the comm. defines it as *māyāvaçāt kevalaṁ rūpamātreṇo 'palabhyamānāḥ senārūpakāḥ.* He reads *antaḥ* and *pātre* as two independent words, according to his custom of caring nothing for accent. For *riçām* ("tearing one, as designating some small animal," minor Pet. Lex.) he reads *vaçām* 'cow,' so that we lose any light he might have cast on the obscure description. Bp. reads *riṣā́m*. Prāt. iii. 75 and iv. 77 prescribe the *pada*-reading *durnihita-*.

16. Her that strides upon the *khaḍū́ra*, mutilated, wearing what is mutilated(?); the specters that are concealed, and what Gandharvas-and-Apsarases [there are], serpents, other-folk, demons;—

The comm. reads at the beginning *khadūre*, and explains it as *ākāçe dūradeçe;* our Bp.Kp. have *ṣaḍū́re*. Again neglecting the accent, he takes *adhi* and *cañkramām* as two independent words. He also reads *-vāçinīm* in **b**; *-vāsin* might be 'dwelling' (so understood by the Pet. Lexx. and Ludwig). Finally, he reckons the last (irregular) pāda to the following verse. ⌊Pāda **e** = 10. 1 **c.**⌋

17. The four-tusked ones, the black-toothed, the pot-testicled, the blood-faced; they that are self-frighting and frighting.

The first four epithets are accus. pl. masc.; probably, like the accus. fem. at beginning of vs. 16, objects of *prá darçaya* 'show forth' in vs. 15. The comm. explains *svabhyasās* and *udbhy-* by *svāyattabhītayo rākṣasāḥ* and *udgatabhītayaḥ.*

18. Do thou, O Arbudi, make to tremble yonder lines (*sic*) of our enemies; let both the conquering one and the conqueror, allied with Indra, conquer our enemies.

SPP. reads in his *saṁhitā*-text *jáyāñç ca* in **c**, with the large majority of his mss., and with part of ours (E.O.s.m.K.). The prolongation being so anomalous, and unsupported by the Prāt., I think *jáyañç ca* decidedly the more acceptable reading. The comm. gives it. He also has *çucas* for *sicas* in **b**. Read *amitrāñ* at end of **c**, with *anusvāra*-sign, not *anunāsika*. ⌊Pāda **b** = 10. 20 **b.**⌋

19. Let our enemy lie squelched, crushed, slain, O Nyarbudi; let tongues of fire, tufts of smoke, go conquering with the army.

The comm. reads in **a** *pravlīnas*, in accordance with the more usual form.

20. Of our enemies, pushed forth by it, O Arbudi, let Indra, lord of might (*çácīpáti*), slay each best man (*vára*); let no one soever of them be freed.

'By it'—i.e. by the army; the comm. reads instead *tvayā* 'by thee.' With **a, b** compare vi. 67. 2 **c, d.** ⌊Our **d** occurs several times: see note to iii. 19. 8.⌋

21. Let their hearts burst open (*ut-kas*), their breath pass up aloft; let dryness of mouth follow after our enemies, ⌊and⌋ not those who are friendly.

The comm. renders *ut kasantu* by *çarīrād udgacchantu*, and *ud īṣatu* equivalently.

22. Both they who are wise (*dhīra*) and they who are unwise, those going away and they who are deaf, they of darkness and they who are

hornless (*tūpará*), likewise those that smell of (?) the goat — all those (m.), O Arbudi, do thou make our enemies to see, and do thou show forth specters.

The meaning of *-abhivāsin* is wholly uncertain ⌊cf. Pāli *vāsita*⌋; the Pet. Lex. conjectures instead *-abhivāçin*, and the comm. reads *bastāvivāçin*, as from *basta* + *avi* + *vāçin*. He also, in defiance of *pada*-text and accent, renders *tamasā́s* as *támasā*. ⌊Cf. *nabhasá-s* (not *nábhas-as*), ix. 4. 22.⌋

23. Let both Arbudi and Trishandhi pierce through our enemies, in order that, O Indra, Vṛitra-slayer, lord of might, we may slay of them, of our enemies, by thousands.

Triṣandhi, lit. 'of three joints,' is conspicuous especially in the next hymn. The comm. explains it here as *kaçcit senāmohako devaḥ saṁdhitrayopetavajrāyudhābhimānī vā*.

24. The forest-trees, them of the forest-trees, herbs and plants, Gandharvas-and-Apsarases, serpents, gods, pure-folk (*puṇyajaná*), Fathers — all those, O Arbudi, do thou make our enemies to see, and do thou show forth specters.

The comm. identifies the 'pure-folk' with the *yakṣas*. ⌊With **c**, **d**, cf. viii. 8. 15, above.⌋ ⌊Cf. Kāuç. 73. 5.⌋

25. Mastery over you have the Maruts [gained], the heavenly Āditya, Brahmaṇaspati; mastery over you have both Indra and Agni, Dhātar, Mitra, Prajāpati; mastery over you have the seers gained (*kṛ*) — exhibiting among the enemies — in case of thy bite, O Arbudi.

One would like to emend *devás* to *devā́s* in **a**.

26. Masters (*īçāna*) of them all, stand ye up, equip yourselves, ye friends, god-folks; having wholly conquered in this conflict, scatter ye to your several worlds.

The mss. set the *avasāna* in this verse after *yūyám*, and SPP. very properly does the same. ⌊Our **b**, **c** = 2 **a**, **b**: **b** = 10. 1 **a**.⌋

⌊The quoted Anukr. says "*ye bāhavaḥ*": see vs. 1.⌋

10. To conquer enemies: to Trishandhi.

[*Bhṛgvañgiras. — saptaviñçati. mantroktatriṣandhidevatyam. ānuṣṭubham: 1. virāṭ pathyābṛhatī; 2. 3-av. 6-p. triṣṭubgarbhā 'tijagatī; 3. virāḍ āstārapañkti; 4. virāj; 8. virāṭ triṣṭubh; 9. purovirāṭ purastājjyotis triṣṭubh; 12. 5-p. pathyāpañkti; 13. 6-p. jagatī; 16. 3-av. 6-p. kakummaty anuṣṭuptriṣṭubgarbhā çakvarī; 17. pathyāpañkti; 21. 3-p. gāyatrī; 22. virāṭ purastādbṛhatī; 25. kakubh; 26. prastārapañkti.*]

Not found in Pāipp. ⌊For its use by Kāuç. in connection with hymn 9, see introduction to hymn 9.⌋

Translated: Ludwig, p. 531; Henry, 129, 169; Griffith, ii. 88; Bloomfield, 126, 637.

1. Stand ye up, equip yourselves, ye specters, together with ensigns; ye serpents, other-folks, demons, run after our enemies.

⌊Pāda **a** = 9. 2 **a**, 26 **b**; **c** = 9. 16 **e**.⌋

2. Your mastery I know, [your] kingdom, O Trishandhi, together with red ensigns; what in the atmosphere, what in the sky, and what men (*mānavá*) [are] on the earth, let those ill-named ones sit (? *upa-ās*) in the mind (*cétas*) of Trishandhi.

The translation implies *veda rā́jyam* in **a**, while all the *pada*-mss. treat the word as a compound (*vedaᵒrā́jyam*). The comm. takes *veda* as an independent word, but renders it as a 3d sing., with *triṣandhis* supplied as subject; and he understands the enemies as addressed by *vas* in **a**. He supplies *ketavas* to the three *ye*'s in **c**, **d**, regarding *mānavās* as adj., 'human.' And he cuts off the last two pādas, adding them instead to vs. 3, and reading at the beginning *trisandhe tve* ("= *tava*"); explaining *upāsatām* by *sambhajantām*, and making the following nouns its subject. For *durṇāmānas* he has *-nam* (as also our B.O.).

3. Iron-(*áyas-*)mouthed, needle-mouthed, likewise thorn-tree-(*vikaṅkaṭī-*)mouthed, let the flesh-eaters, of wind-swiftness, fasten on our enemies with the three-jointed (*tríṣandhi*) thunderbolt.

The comm. regards the epithets as signifying flesh-eating birds, and supplies ⌊alternatively⌋ 'sent forth' (*preritās*) to the concluding instrumentals.

4. O Jātavedas, Āditya, put thou between much human flesh; let this army of Trishandhi be well-placed in my control.

Most of SPP's *pada*-mss. give *sénāḥ* in **c**; no such reading has been noted among our mss. One would like to improve meter and sense together by emending *trī́ṣandhes* to *-dhinā*, understanding the 'army' to be the enemy's. *Antár dhehi* at the beginning may also mean 'hide'; and the comm. juggles the line into signifying, 'O Jātavedas, make the corpses of our enemies hide the sun'!

5. Stand thou up, O god-folk, O Arbudi, with the army; this tribute is offered (*ā-hu*) to you ⌊pl.⌋; the offering [is] dear to Trishandhi.

The comm. reads *āhutis* (for *-tas*) in **c**, and *āhutipriyā* as compound in **d**. ⌊In some copies the *i* of *priyā* is broken.⌋

6. Let the white-footed one tie together, this shaft (*çaravyà*), four-footed; O witchcraft, be thou for our enemies, together with the army of Trishandhi.

The comm. reads for *dyatu*, in **a**, *patatu*: cf. vs. 7 **a**. By *çitipadī* he understands a white-footed cow, called a *çaravyà* as being a *çarūṇām bāṇānāṁ samūhaḥ*.

7. Let the smoke-eyed (f.) one fall together, and the crop-eared one (f.) yell; it being conquered by the army of Trishandhi, let the ensigns be red.

The comm. supplies *parakīye bale* to *jité*; the *pada*-reading (simply *jité*) forbids us to regard the word as fem. dual. He takes the epithets in the first half-verse first as applying to the enemy's army, and then to the *kṛtyā* which is invoked against it. The verse is translated by Bloomfield, as noted above (see 9. 7), at AJP. xi. 340.

8. Let the winged ones descend, the birds, they that go about in the atmosphere, in the sky; let the wild beasts, the flies, take hold together; let the raw-flesh-eating vultures scratch at the human carrion.

The comm. explains *radantām* by *svatuṇḍāiḥ pādāiç ca vilikhantu.* ⌊Read *divi ca yé?*⌋

9. The agreement (*saṁdhā́*) which thou hast agreed on with Indra and with the *bráhman*, O Brihaspati, by that Indra-agreement do I call hither all the gods: conquer ye on this side, not on that!

The comm. (with two or three of SPP's authorities) reads *-adhattās* in **a**; and he treats *indra-saṁdhayā* as two independent words in **c**. *Saṁdhā́m* in **a** is clearly proved an intrusion by the meter.

10. Brihaspati of the Añgiras race, the seers sharpened by the *bráhman*, set up (*ā-çri*) in the sky the Asura-destroying weapon, Trishandhi.

One would like to emend *āñgirasás* to *áñgirasas* (as Ludwig translates). The comm. renders *ā́ 'çrayan* by *asevanta*, as if it were *ā́ 'çrayanta*.

11. By whom yonder sun, and Indra, both stand protected — Trishandhi the gods shared, in order to both force and strength.

12. All worlds did the gods completely conquer by means of that offering (*ā́huti*) — the thunderbolt which Brihaspati of the Añgiras race poured, an Asura-destroying weapon.

'Poured,' i.e. 'cast': a term used also elsewhere of the thunderbolt (BR. vii. 980).

13. The thunderbolt which Brihaspati of the Añgiras race poured, an Asura-destroying weapon — therewith do I blot out (*ni-lip*) yon army, O Brihaspati; I slay the enemies with force.

The comm. renders *ní limpāmi* by *nitarāṁ chinadmi.* He also has the strange reading *amūs* for *amūm* before *sénām*.

14. All the gods come over hither, who partake of [the offering] made with *váṣat;* enjoy ye this offering; conquer ye on this side, not on that!

15. Let all the gods come over hither; the offering [is] dear to Trishandhi; defend ye the great agreement by which in the beginning the Asuras were conquered.

The comm. appears to read in **a** *-yanti*, as in vs. 14 **a**, but he interprets it as an imperative this time.

16. Let Vāyu bend up the arrow-points of the enemies; let Indra break back their arms; let them not be able to set the arrow; let Āditya make their missile weapon (*astrá*) disappear; let the moon put (*yu*) them on the track of what is not gone.

The last clause is very doubtful and difficult: the comm. gives no aid, explaining with *aprāptasyā "jigamiṣataḥ çatroḥ . . . panthānam asmatprāptyupāyabhūtam mārgaṁ yutāṁ tataḥ pṛthakkurutām* (taking *yutām* from *yu* 'separate,' and adding) *tādṛçam mārgaṁ çatrur na paçyatv ity arthaḥ.* He divides the verse into two, making the second begin with *ādityá eṣām.*

17. If they have gone forward to the gods' strongholds, have made the *bráhman* their defenses; if (?*yát*) they have encouraged (?*upa-vac*) themselves, making a body-protection, a complete protection — all that do thou make sapless.

The verse occurred above as v. 8. 6, and the comm. declines to repeat his explanation there given — which, however, is not in our hands.

18. Causing to follow the *puróhita* with the flesh-eating [fire] and with death, O Trishandhi, go forth with the army; conquer the enemies; go forward.

The last pāda is identical with iii. 19. 8 **c**.

19. O Trishandhi, do thou envelop our enemies with darkness; of them yonder, thrust forth by the speckled butter, let none soever be freed.

The last half-verse is nearly identical with viii. 8. 19 **c**, **d**. ⌊For the stock-phrase **d**, see iii. 19. 8, note.⌋

20. Let the white-footed one (f.) fall upon (?*sam-pat*) yonder lines of our enemies; let yonder armies of our enemies be confounded today, O Nyarbudi.

The second pāda is identical with 9. 18 **b**; to be put in any connection with it, the words of the first pāda require to be rendered otherwise than in 6 **a**, 7 **a**, above. The comm. again reads *çucas* for *sicas*, as in the other passage ⌊9. 18: comm. p. 181[17]⌋.

21. Confounded [be] our enemies, O Nyarbudi; slay thou of them each best man (*vára*); slay [them] with this army.

The comm. strangely reads *amitrān* beside *mūḍhās*. ⌊The rationale of his variant is perhaps as in 9. 6 above (*nnya* = *nya*). The *pada*-text has *amitrāḥ*. But the comm. also takes *mūḍhāḥ* as = *mūḍhān*.⌋

22. Whoever is mailed, and who without mail, and what enemy is in march (?*ájman*); by bowstring-fetters, by mail-fetters, smitten by the march let him lie.

The mss. are in good part awkward about the combination *jm* (in *ajmani*, *ajmanā*), writing what looks like a *ṭm* or *pm*, but there is no real variant. The comm. explains *ájman* as *ajati gacchaty anene 'ty ajma rathādi yānam*. He gives *abhihitas*, a preferable reading, in **d**.

23. Who have defenses, who have no defenses, and the enemies who have defenses — all those, O Arbudi, being slain, let dogs eat on the ground.

The accent *yé 'varmā̆ṇaḥ*, though read by all the mss. ⌊save R.⌋, is wholly inadmissible, and should be emended to *yè 'v-*.

24. Who have chariots, who have no chariots, those without seats and they who have seats (*sādá*) — all those, being slain, let vultures, falcons, birds (*patatrín*) eat.

We may fairly question whether 'seat' means here 'seat on horseback.' The comm. explains *asādās* by *açvādiyānarahitāḥ padātayaḥ*, and *sādinas* by *açvārūḍhāḥ* 'mounted on horses.'

25. Let the army of our enemies lie with thousand corpses (*-kúṇapa*) in the conflict of weapons, pierced through, cut to pieces (?).

The obscure *kakajā́kṛtā* at the end is guessed by the comm. to mean *kutsitajananā vilolajananā vā kṛtā;* he attempts no etymology, but evidently sees in it the root *jā*. In **a** he has the strange reading *senām* for *çetām*.

26. Let the eagles (*suparṇá*) eat him, pierced to the vitals, crying loudly, lying crushed, the evil-minded one — what enemy of ours wishes to fight against this opposing offering.

The translation implies the emendation (which Ludwig's version also makes) of *suparṇāís* to *suparṇā́s* in **a**. The comm. takes it as qualifying *çarāis* understood and adjunct of *marmāvídham:* 'pierced etc. by well-feathered arrows.' In the irregular meter of the first line, the division is perhaps best made before *adantu;* a small minority of SPP's mss. so regard it, and accent *adántu* accordingly, and he follows them in his text; our Bp. puts its pāda-division after *adantu*, and, with one other ms., leaves the word without accent. ⌊See Henry's elaborate conjectures, p. 172: *marmāvídho róruvataḥ suparṇā́ gaṇāír adantu mṛditáṁ çáyānam*. The other versions imply *mármaviddham*, and Bloomfield expressly conjectures *marmaviddhám*, overlooking the accent; but the comm. to Prāt. iv. 68 quotes *marmāvídham* as an instance of non-separation in *pada*-text.⌋

27. [The offering] which the gods follow (*anu-sthā*), of which there is no failure — with that let Indra, Vṛitra-slayer, slay, with the three-jointed thunderbolt.

⌊Here ends the fifth *anuvāka*, with 2 hymns and 53 verses. The quoted Anukr. says, referring to this last hymn, *antyo viṅçatiḥ sapta cā 'parāḥ*.⌋

⌊The sum of the verses for hymns 1–2 and 4–10 is (68 + 189 =) 257. Reckoning hymn 3 (with the Berlin ed.) as of 56 vss., we get for the book (257 + 56 =) 313: and this is the summation given by codex I. On the other hand, reckoning hymn 3 as of (31 + 72 + 7 =) 110 vss. (see pp. 632, 628), we get for the book (257 + 110 =) 367. But the summation given by four of W's mss. (including P.W.B.) is 365. How to account for the discrepancy I do not see. One ms. sums up the last *anuvāka* as 51 (i.e. 26 + 25? — instead of 26 + 27 = 53) verses, and 10. 17 is indeed a *galita*-verse; but the Old Anukr. reckons hymn 10 as 27, not 25.⌋

⌊Three or four mss. sum up the *sūktas* "of both kinds" as 12.⌋

⌊Here ends the twenty-fifth *prapāṭhaka*.⌋

Book XII.

⌊This twelfth book is the fifth and last of the second grand division of the Atharvan collection. For a general statement as to the make-up of the books of this division, page 471 may again be consulted. The Old Anukramaṇī describes the length of the *artha-sūktas*, hymns 1, 2, 3, and 4, by giving the overplus of each hymn over 60 verses. The assumed normal lengths in the case of books ix., x., xi., and xii. seem to be respectively 20, 30, 20, and 60 verses. The whole book has been translated by Victor Henry, *Les livres X, XI et XII de l'Atharva-véda traduits et commentés*, Paris, 1896. The *bhāṣya* is again lacking. The fifth or last hymn is made up of 7 *paryāyas* (see pages 471–2), which, if they be counted separately, make the hymns number 11 instead of 5: see page 611, top.⌋

⌊The *anuvāka*-division of the book (as noted above, page 472) is into five *anuvākas* of one hymn each. The "decad"-division likewise is as described on page 472. A tabular conspectus for this book also may be added:

Anuvākas	1	2	3	4	5
Hymns	1	2	3	4	5
Verses	63	55	60	53	73¶
Decad-div.	5 tens + 13	5 tens + 5	6 tens	4 tens + 13	7 P

Here, as before, ¶ means "paragraph of a *paryāya*" (such as is numbered as a "verse" in the Berlin edition) and P means "*paryāya*." The last line shows the "decad"-division. Of these "decads," *anuvākas* 1, 2, 3, and 4 contain respectively 6, 6, 6, and 5 (in all, 23 "decads"); while *anuvāka* 5 has 7 *paryāyas*. The sum is 23 "decad"-*sūktas* and 7 *paryāya-sūktas* or 30 *sūktas*. Cf. the summation at the end of hymn 5.⌋

---

1. To the earth.

[*Atharvan.—triṣaṣṭiḥ. bhāumam. trāiṣṭubham: 2. bhurij; 4–6, 10, 38. 3-av. 6-p. jagatī; 7. prastārapañkti; 8, 11. 3-av. 6-p. virāḍ aṣṭi; 9. parānuṣṭubh; 12, 13, 15. 5-p. çakvarī (12, 13. 3-av.); 14. mahābṛhatī; 16, 21. 1-av. sāmnī triṣṭubh; 18. 3-av. 6-p. triṣṭubanuṣṭubgarbhā 'tiçakvarī; 19, 20. urobṛhatī (20. virāj); 22. 3-av. 6-p. virāḍ atijagatī; 23. 5-p. virāḍ atijagatī; 24. 5-p. anuṣṭubgarbhā jagatī; 25. 3-av. 7-p. uṣṇiganuṣṭubgarbhā çakvarī; 26–28, 33, 35, 39, 40, 50, 53, 54, 56, 59, 63. anuṣṭubh (53. purobārhatā); 30. virāḍ gāyatrī; 32. purastājjyotis; 34. 3-av. 6-p. triṣṭubbṛhatīgarbhā 'tijagatī; 36. viparītapādalakṣmī pañkti; 37. 3-av. 5-p. çakvarī; 41. 3-av. 6-p. kakummatī çakvarī; 42. svarāḍ anuṣṭubh; 43. virāḍ āstārapañkti; 44, 45, 49. jagatī; 46. 6-p. anuṣṭubgarbhā parāçakvarī; 47. 6-p. uṣṇiganuṣṭubgarbhā parātiçakvarī; 48. puro'nuṣṭubh; 51. 3-av. 6-p. anuṣṭubgarbhā kakummatī çakvarī; 52. 5-p. anuṣṭubgarbhā parātijagatī; 57. puro'tijāgatā jagatī; 58. purastādbṛhatī; 61. purobārhatā; 62. parāvirāj.*]

Found also in Pāipp. xvii. (excepting vss. 62, 63). Many of the verses are used by the Kāuç., as also the whole hymn (which is also by itself an *anuvāka*), under the name *bhāuma*, '[hymn] to earth': so at 38. 12, 16, in a ceremony for giving firmness to buildings; at 98. 3 (with vi. 87, 88), for safety from earthquake; and in 8. 23 it is (with iii. 12, vi. 73, 93) reckoned a *vāstoṣpatya* hymn. The first 7 verses (Kāuç. 24. 27) and the first 9 (? 24. 31, 35) are used in the *āgrahāyaṇī* ceremony. ⌊Further, cf. Keç. to 70. 8, 9.⌋ In Vāit., vss. 1, 13, 27, 30, and others are quoted. ⌊The whole hymn is prescribed in Nakṣ. Kalpa, 18, in a *mahāçānti* called *pārthivī:* see SPP. iii. 2025.⌋

Translated: by Charles Bruce, *Journal of the Royal Asiatic Society*, Old Series, xix. 321 ff. (with comparisons from Greek writers); Ludwig, p. 544; Henry, 179, 215; Griffith, ii. 93; Bloomfield, 199, 639.

1. Great (*bṛhánt*) truth, formidable right, consecration, penance, *bráhman*, sacrifice sustain the earth; let her for us, mistress of what is and what is to be — let the earth make for us wide room (*loká*); —

Found also in MS. (iv. 14. 11), which reads *yajñā́s* in **b**, and *bhúvanasya* (for *bhávyasya*) in **c**. The Anukr. does not heed that pāda **a** is *jagatī*. The verse (unless more of the hymn is meant to be included with it) is, according to Vāit. 12. 6, to be repeated by one who relieves on the ground the needs of nature. It is quoted by Kāuç. 24. 24 in the *āgrahāyaṇī* ceremony; also in the comm. to 24. 35 (cf. above); and it, with vs. 38, is reckoned (see note to Kāuç. 19. 1) among the *puṣṭika mantras*.

2. Unoppressedness in the midst of men (*mānavá*). Whose are the ascents (*udvát*), the advances (*pravát*), the much plain (*samá*); who bears the herbs of various virtue (*nā́nāvīrya*) — let the earth be spread out for us, be prosperous for us.

The mss. vary in **a** between *badhyatás* and *madhyatás* (Bp.P.M.I. have *ba-*), but only the latter can be right, and the translation adopts it; the former (which Ppp. also has, and *mānaveṣu*) seems to have come in under the influence of *-bādham*. ⌊Correct the edition.⌋ As the text stands, pāda **a** can only be an adjunct to vs. 1, and so Ppp. reckons it, and begins our **b** with *asyās*. But MS. (iv. 14. 11) reads *asambādhā́ yā́ madhyató mānavébhyo;* it also has *mahát* for *bahú* at end of **b**, and *nā́nārūpās* and *bibhárti* in **c**. This time the Anukr. notices that **b** has 12 syllables. Kāuç. 137. 16 quotes the verse ⌊in the preparation of the *vedi*⌋.

3. On whom [are] the ocean and the river (*síndhu*), the waters; on whom food, plowings, came into being; on whom quickens this that breathes, that stirs — let that earth (*bhū́mi*) set us in first drinking.

That is, doubtless, give us precedence over others (but MS. reads *pūrvapéyam:* see note to vs. 5). Ppp. reads for **b** *yasyāṁ devā 'mṛtam anvavindan;* and for second half-verse it has our 4 **c**, **d**, giving our 3 **c**, **d** as second half of vs. 5, with the easier reading *jīvati*, ⌊followed by⌋ *viçvam ejāt* in **c**. We should expect *kṛṣáyas* in **b**.

4. Whose, the earth's, [are] the four quarters; on whom food, plowings, came into being; who bears manifoldly what breathes, what stirs — let that earth (*bhū́mi*) set us among kine, also in inexhaustibleness (? *ánya*).

Ppp. reads in **a** *yasyām* and *pṛthivyām*, and in **b** *gṛṣṭayas* ⌊cf. note to ii. 13. 3⌋. As second half-verse it has our 5 **c**, **d**, giving our 4 **c**, **d** as 3 **c**, **d**, reading (after *bahudhā*) *prāṇine jāñgano bhūmir goṣv açveṣu pinve kṛṇotu*, thus relieving us of the difficult *ánye*. Kāuç. (137. 17) uses the verse next after vs. 2, in connection with making the sacrificial hearth four-cornered. The description given by the Anukr. of this and the two following verses is so wholly wrong that we cannot help suspecting a corrupt text. This verse is, if we make no resolutions in **d**, a regular *triṣṭubh*.

5. On whom the people of eld (*pūrvajaná*) formerly spread themselves (?*vi-kṛ*); on whom the gods overcame the Asuras; the station (? *viṣṭhá*) of kine, of horses, of birds (*váyas*) — let the earth assign us fortune (*bhága*), splendor.

Ppp. reads in **a** *nicakrire*, and in **b** *atyavartayan;* also in **c** (found as ⌊its⌋ 4 **c**) *vayasayya* ⌊?⌋. MS. has a verse made up of our 5 **a**, **b** (without variant), 4 **c** (accenting *bibhárti*), and 3 **d** (with *pūrvapéyam*). The verse is mixed *triṣṭubh* and *jagatī*. ⌊In Ppp. this verse precedes our 4. — The sequence of the half-verses of the Vulgate as they stand in Ppp. seems therefore to be as follows: 3 **a**, **b**, 4 **c**, **d**, 5 **a**, **b**, 3 **c**, **d**, 4 **a**, **b**, 5 **c**, **d**.⌋

6. All-bearing, good-holding, firm-standing, gold-backed (*-vákṣas*), reposer of moving things (*jágat*), bearing the universal (*vāiçvānará*) fire, let the earth (*bhūmi*), whose bull is Indra, set us in property.

The verse is found also in MS. (iv. 14. 11), which reads, in **a–b**, *purukṣúd dhíraṇyavarṇā jágataḥ pratiṣṭhā́;* and in **d** *drávinam* (the editor also admits in his text the bad reading *índra ṛṣabhā́*). It is quoted in Kāuç. 137. 28. ⌊I do not see why W. has preferred 'gold-backed' to 'gold-breasted' here and in vs. 26.⌋ ⌊By 'reposer' he means 'bringer-to-rest.'⌋

7. She the earth (*bhūmi pṛthivī*), whom the gods, sleepless, defend all the time without failure — let her yield (*duh*) to us honey, what is dear; then let her sprinkle us with splendor.

The verse is found also in MS. (iv. 14. 11), which reads in **c** *ghṛtám* instead of *priyám*.

8. She who in the beginning was sea (*salilá*) upon the ocean (*arṇavá*); whom the skilful (*manīṣín*) moved after with their devices (*māyā́*); the earth whose immortal heart covered with truth is in the highest firmament (*vyòman*) — let that earth (*bhūmi*) assign to us brilliancy, strength, in highest royalty.

The verse is properly $11+12:11+11:8+8=61$ syllables, and not very well described by the Anukr. The last two clauses perhaps have independent construction: '[assign] to us brilliancy [and] strength, [and] set [us] in highest royalty.'

9. On whom the circulating waters flow the same, night and day, without failure — let that earth (*bhūmi*), of many streams (*-dhárā*) yield (*duh*) us milk; then let her sprinkle [us] with splendor.

The Anukr. does not heed that **c** is a *jagatī* pāda. ⌊In Ppp., this verse precedes our 7.⌋

10. Whom the Açvins measured; on whom Vishṇu strode out; whom Indra, lord of might (*çácī-*), made free from enemies for himself — let that earth (*bhū́mi*) to us, a mother to a son, release (*vi-sṛj*) milk ⌊to me⌋.

Some of the mss. read in **d** *-trā́ṅ chácī-*, and Bp. has accordingly *-trā́n*. Ppp. also has *cakrā "tmane 'namitrāṅ cchacī-*; and, at the end, *naṣ payaḥ*. ⌊Ppp's repetition of *nas* is more tolerable than the harsh change from pl. to sing. which W. seems to have overlooked.⌋

11. Let thy hills (*girí*) [and] snowy mountains (*párvata*), let thy forest-land (*áraṇya*), O earth, be pleasant (*syoná*); upon the brown, black, red, all-formed, fixed (*dhruvá*) earth (*bhū́mi*), the earth guarded by Indra — I, unharassed, unsmitten, unwounded, have stood upon the earth.

Ppp. reads in **b** *āraṇyaṁ* corrected to *ar-*, and *naḥ* after *astu*; also in **c** *lohinīṁ*, and in **f** *adhi ṣṭhāṁ*, which is better. ⌊Roth's Collation has in fact *addhi*.⌋ The verse (11 + 11 : 11 + 11 : 8 + 8 = 60) should be called *atiçakvarī* rather than *virāḍ aṣṭi*. Verses 11 and 12 are reckoned to the *svastyayana gaṇa* (see note to Kāuç. 25. 36).

12. What is thy middle, O earth, and what thy navel, what refreshments (*ū́rj*) arose (*sam-bhū*) out of thy body — in them do thou set us; be purifying (*pū*) toward us; earth (*bhū́mi*) is mother, I am earth's son; Parjanya is father — let him save (fill? *pṛ*) us.

Ppp. reads at end of **a** *yaç ca nādyā*.

13. On what earth (*bhū́mi*) they enclose the sacrificial hearth; on what [earth] men of all works extend the sacrifice; on what earth are set up (*mi*) the sacrificial posts, erect, bright, before the oblation — let that earth (*bhū́mi*), increasing, make us increase.

Ppp. reads in **b** *viçvakarmaṇaḥ*, and in **d** reads and combines *çukrā "hutyā pur-*. All the mss. accent at the end *vardhamānā́*. In Vāit. 15. 8, the verse is used to accompany the enclosing of the sacrificial hearth. In virtue of one *jagatī* pāda (**b**), the verse is a full *çakvarī* (56 syll.).

14. Whoso shall hate us, O earth; whoso shall fight [us]; whoso shall vex [us] with mind, who with deadly weapon — him, O prior-acting earth (*bhū́mi*), do thou put in our power.

'Prior-acting,' i.e., apparently, 'getting the start of him'; we should expect a nom. rather than a vocative case. Ppp. reads instead *pūrvakṛtvane*; also, in **b**, *'bhimanyā tāindanamā dhanena*. Read in our text *pṛtanyā́d yò* (an accent-sign omitted); one of our mss. ⌊and five of SPP's authorities, and his text!⌋, however, read *yó*. According to the usual nomenclature of the Anukr., the verse is a *virāḍ gāyatrī* (11 + 11 : 12 = 34, hence *bhurij*). ⌊Dr. Ryder suggests that the *mahābṛhatī* here intended is one of 3 *jāgata* pādas (see *Ind. Stud.* viii. 243–4). Both this vs. and 17 may be scanned as 12 + 12 : 12 — cf. under vs. 17.⌋

15. Born from thee, mortals go about upon thee; thou bearest bipeds, thou quadrupeds; thine, O earth, are these five [races] of men, for whom, mortals, the rising sun extends with his rays immortal light.

Ppp. reads in **b** *ca* instead of the second *tvam*.

16. Let those creatures, without exception (*samagrá*), together yield fruit (*duh*) to us; the honey of speech, O earth, do thou assign unto me.

Té for *tā́s* at the beginning, allowing us to regard *prajā́s* as accus., would be a welcome emendation.

17. The all-producing (*-sū́*) mother of herbs, the fixed earth (*bhū́mi*), the earth maintained by ordinance, the auspicious, the pleasant, may we go about over always.

This verse (10 ⌊properly 11⌋ + 12 : 12 = 34 syll.) is overlooked by the Anukr.; it nearly accords in structure with vs. 14, above. ⌊Dr. Ryder observes that the dual (*mahābṛhatyāu*) of the Anukr.-text suggests the possible falling out of the *pratīka* of this verse. See under vs. 14.⌋ ⌊There is a play of words in *dhármaṇā dhṛtā́m* which cannot easily be reproduced in translation.⌋

18. Thou hast become great, a great station (*sadhástha*); great is thy trembling, stirring, quaking; great Indra defends thee unremittingly. Do thou, O earth (*bhū́mi*), make us to shine forth as in the aspect (*saṁdṛ́ç*) of gold; let no one soever hate us.

Ppp. reads *vīryeṇa* for *apramādam* in **c**, and from **e** ⌊*saṁdṛçi*⌋ passes directly on to our 19 **c** (*agnir antaṣ pur-* etc.): probably an accidental omission. The verse (12 + 11 : 11 : 8 + 8 + 8 = 58) lacks two syllables of a full *atiçakvarī*.

19. Agni is in the earth (*bhū́mi*), in the herbs; the waters bear Agni; Agni [is] in the stones (*áçman*); Agni is within men; in kine, in horses are Agnis.

This and the two following verses are quite out of connection here, and seem to be an intrusion. They are quoted together in Kāuç. 2. 41 as accompanying the feeding of the fire with fuel; in 120. 5, in a ceremony against the cleaving open of the ground; and in 137. 30 (each singly) to accompany the strewing of the sacrificial hearth in the *ājyatantra*. The first part of the verse (as noted above) is wanting in Ppp.

20. Agni sends heat from the sky; the wide atmosphere is god Agni's; mortals kindle Agni [as] oblation-bearer, ghee-lover.

Ppp. combines in **a** *divā "tapaty.*

21. Let the earth, fire-clad, black-kneed, make me sharpened, brilliant (*tviṣī́mant*).

This verse is quoted by *pratīka* in GB. i. 2. 9. As to the ritual uses of it and of vs. 20, see the note to vs. 19. Ppp. reads *tviṣīvantaṁ* in **b**.

22. On the earth (*bhū́mi*) they give to the gods the sacrifice, the oblation, duly prepared; on the earth (*bhū́mi*) mortal men (*manuṣyà*) live by *svadhā́*, by food; let that earth (*bhū́mi*) assign us breath, life-time; let earth make me one who attains old age.

The verse (8 + 8 : 8 + 8 : 11 + 11 = 54) should be called by the Anukr. *svarāj* instead of *virāj*. Ppp. reads in **a** *juhvati* instead of *dadati*.

23. What odor of thine, O earth, came into being, which the herbs, which the waters bear, which the Gandharvas and Apsarases shared — with that do thou make me odorous; let no one soever hate us.

Ppp. adds, after *bhejire*, *yas te gām açvam arhati;* and it reads for our **d** *tenā 'smān surabhīṣ kṛṇu*, and, in our **e**, *dvakṣata*. The verse (11 + 11 : 12 : 8 + 8 = 50) is as well described by the Anukr. as the latter's system admits. Verses 23–25 ⌊so the schol.⌋ are called in Kāuç. 13. 12 and 54. 5 *gandhapravādās* (likewise in the comm. to 24. 24); they are also reckoned as belonging to the second *varcasya gaṇa* (see note to Kāuç. 12. 10).

24. What odor of thine entered into the blue lotus; which they brought together at Sūryā's wedding — the immortals, O earth, [what] odor in the beginning — with that do thou make me odorous; let no one soever hate us.

Ppp. has again *tenā 'smān surabhīṣ kṛṇu*, and *dvakṣata*. ⌊To the definition of the⌋ verse (11 + 11 : 11 + 8 + 8 = 49) ⌊should be added "*bhurij*"⌋.

25. What odor of thine is in human beings (*púruṣa*); in women, in men, [what] portion, pleasure; what in horses, in heroes, what in wild animals and in elephants; what splendor, O earth (*bhū́mi*), in a maiden — with that do thou unite us also; let no one soever hate us.

Or, in **d**, *mṛgeṣu hastiṣu* may mean simply 'elephants' (lit. 'wild beasts having a hand'). Ppp. reads *yas te bhāume puruṣeṣu . . . rucir yo vadhūṣu : yo goṣv açveṣu yo mṛgeṣu : . . . yad bhāume abhi saṁ sṛja;* and in **g** *dvakṣata*. If the verse contains an *uṣṇih* pāda (namely **c**, the resolution *aç-u-eṣu* being rejected), it is *nicṛt* as a *çakvarī*.

26. Rock [is?] earth (*bhū́mi*), stone, dust; this earth (*bhū́mi*) [is] held together, held; to that earth, gold-backed (*-vákṣas*) have I paid homage.

Ppp reads, in **a–b**, *pāṅsv aryā bhūmi strtā dhṛtā*, and omits **c**, **d**. ⌊Cf. note to vs. 6.⌋

27. On whom stand always fixed the trees, the forest trees (*vānaspatyá*), the all-supporting earth that is held [together] do we address.

Ppp. reads for **d** *bhūmyāi hiraṇyavakṣasi dhṛtam acchāv-*. Vāit. 2. 8 quotes the verse to accompany the laying down of the enclosing sticks.

28. Arising (*ud-īr*), also sitting, standing, striding forth, with right and left feet, let us not stagger upon the earth.

The Anukr. seems to assume the resolution *-kṛ-ā-* in **b**. This verse and 33 below are quoted in Kāuç. 24. 33 to accompany the taking of three steps, while looking around, in the *āgrahāyaṇī* ceremony.

29. The cleansing (*vimṛ́gvan*) earth do I address, the patient (*kṣamá*) earth (*bhū́mi*), increasing by worship (*bráhman*); may we sit down, O earth (*bhū́mi*), upon thee, that bearest refreshment, prosperity (*puṣṭá*), food-portion, ghee.

Ppp. reads at the beginning *vimargvāya*, in **b** *vāvṛdhānaḥ*, in **c** *puṣṭiṁ*, in **d** *bhāume*. The verse is quoted four times in Kāuç.: in 3. 8; 24. 28; 137. 40, to accompany a sitting down in different ceremonies; and in 90. 15, when causing a guest to stand upon a cushion.

30. Let cleansed (*çuddhá*) waters flow for our body; what mucus (? *syédu*) is ours, that we deposit on him we love not (*ápriya*); with a purifier (*pavítra*), O earth, do I purify myself.

Part of the *pada*-mss. (Bp. ⌊and one of SPP's⌋) accent *mā́* in c. Ppp. has *mā́* for *nas* in a; and, in b, *yo me sehnur*. The verse is quoted in Kāuç. 58. 7 (and at second hand under 24. 24) in connection with rinsing the mouth after spitting; also in Vāit. 12. 6 in connection with easing nature.

31. What forward directions are thine, what upward, what are thine, O earth (*bhū́mi*), downward, and what behind, let those be pleasant to me going about; let me not fall down [when] supported (*çri*) on creation (*bhúvana*).

The verse is found also in MS. (iv. 14. 11), which reads, for b, *yā́ç ca bhūmy adharā́g yā́ç ca paçcā́*; also *çivā́s* for *syonā́s* in c. Ppp. has in b *bhāume 'dharād*, and in d *çuçriyāṇe*. This and the following verse are reckoned to the *svastyayana gaṇa*: see note to Kāuç. 25. 36.

32. Do not push (*nud*) us behind, nor in front, nor above and below; become thou welfare for us, O earth (*bhū́mi*); let not the waylayers find [us]; keep very far off the deadly weapon.

The directions 'forward' etc., in this and the preceding verse, are also equivalent, as elsewhere, to 'eastern' etc. Pāda d occurs below as xiv. 2. 11 a; e was found above as i. 20. 3 d etc. Ppp. reads *mā* for *nas* in a, omits b, reads in c *bhāume me kṛṇu*, and makes d and e change places, reading also *vāyas* for *varīyas* ⌊and *vidhan* for *vidan*⌋. The verse (11 + 8 : 8 + 8 + 8 = 43) is curiously defined by the Anukr.

33. How much of thee I look forth upon, O earth (*bhū́mi*), with the sun for ally (*medín*), so far let my sight not fail (*mī*), from one year (*sámā*) to another.

Ppp. has again *bhāume* in b. For the use of the verse in Kāuç., see note to vs. 28. It is quoted also in Vāit. 27. 7 as used by one gazing at the earth after mounting the sacrificial post. ⌊Pāda d we had at iii. 10. 1; 17. 4.⌋

34. In that, lying, I turn myself about upon the right [or] the left side, O earth (*bhū́mi*); in that we with our ribs lie stretched out upon thee that meetest us — do not in that case injure us, O earth (*bhū́mi*), thou underlier of everything.

'Underlier,' lit. 'counter-lier, one whose lying answers to that of another.' In a, b, perhaps rather 'in that I turn over toward [thee] the one or the other side' ⌊cf. vii. 100. 1⌋. Our Bp. puts its sign of pāda-division between c and d before instead of after *yát*, and the Anukr. supports it by counting a *bṛhatī* element in the verse (which is properly 8 + 11 : 8 + 8 : 8 + 8 = 51). The verse is prescribed in Kāuç. 24. 30, to accompany the act of turning over while lying down, in the *āgrahāyaṇī* ceremony. All the mss., with the edition, ⌊likewise SPP's mss. and ed.,⌋ accent *paryā́varte*; it should be *paryāvárte*. Ppp. puts the verse after 35, and reads *api* for *abhi* in b; and, for d, *pṛṣṭvā yad ṛdva çemahe*; and *bhāume* both times for *bhūme*.

35. What of thee, O earth (*bhū́mi*), I dig out, let that quickly grow over; let me not hit (*arpay-*) thy vitals nor thy heart, O cleansing one.

'Grow over,' i.e. heal up, like a wound. Ppp. has again *bhāume* in **a**; also *oṣaṁ* for *kṣipram* in **b**, and *arpitam* in **d**; this time (cf. vs. 29) it agrees with our text in the peculiar epithet *vimṛgvari*, lit. 'wiping off.' Kāuç. (46. 51) quotes the verse to accompany an act of digging in a *prāyaçcitta* ceremony; and again similarly at 137. 12.

36. Let thy hot season, O earth (*bhū́mi*), rainy season, autumn, winter, cool season, spring — let thine arranged seasons, years, let day-and-night, O earth, yield milk (*duh*) to us.

One would expect in **c** *hāyanā́s* 'belonging to or constituting the year'; and Ppp., combining *hāyanā 'hor-*, favors that reading. Ppp. has also again *bhāume* in **a**. The irregularity of the verse (8 + 11 : 10 + 11 = 40) indicates corruption; it is a *pañkti*, of course, only by the sum of syllables. It is quoted in Kāuç. 137. 9, as one approaches to measure out the sacrificial hearth. ⌊Cf. 137. 4, note.⌋

37. She who, cleansing one, trembling away the serpent; on whom were the fires that are within the waters, abandoning the god-insulting barbarians, choosing, she the earth, Indra [and] not Vṛitra, kept herself (*dhṛ*) for the mighty one (*çakrá*), the virile bull.

The first pāda is extremely obscure; it is here translated mechanically, as closely as possible to the text. Bruce understands at the beginning *yā́ : ā́pa* (instead of the *yā́ : ápa* of the *pada*-text); and that would be a natural and easy emendation, if only the resulting sense were more acceptable. Ludwig renders as if we read *sárpāt* ('trembling at the serpent'). The totally different reading of Ppp., *ya āpas sarpan yatamānā vimṛgvari*, indicates that the text is corrupt. Ppp. further reads in **b** *agnayo 'psv*, and stops the verse at *dadatī*, then adding our vs. 40. Our verse (12 + 11 : 11 + 11 : 11 = 56) adds up as a true *çakvarī*.

38. On whom are the seat and oblation-holder; on whom the sacrificial post (*yū́pa*) is planted; on whom worshipers (*brahmán*) praise (*arc*) with verses, with the chant, knowing the sacrificial formulas; on whom are joined the priests (*ṛtvíj*), for Indra to drink the soma; —

Ppp. reads in **e** *yujyante 'syām ṛtyavas s-*. The verse is quoted in Kāuç. 24. 37 to accompany an oblation ⌊and by Dārila to 24. 24, in the *āgrahāyaṇī* ceremony⌋. It is also reckoned with vs. 1 among the *puṣṭika mantras* (see note to Kāuç. 19. 1). In Vāit. 15. 4, this verse and the two following are prescribed to accompany the *subrahmaṇyā* recitation; in 10. 8, it is used at the setting up of the sacrificial post.

39. On whom the former being-making seers sang out (*ud-arc*) the kine — the seven pious ones (*vedhás*), by their session, together with sacrifice [and] penance; —

Ppp. reads *udānāt* for *udānṛcus* in **b**; all our mss. accent *úd ānṛcús*, but the edited text has emended to *udān-*. Vāit. 22. 1 gives the verse as prescribed by a certain authority to be used instead of iii. 14. 2, in driving out the kine from the place of sacrifice.

40. Let that earth (*bhū́mi*) appoint unto us what riches we desire; let Bhaga join on after; let Indra go [as our] forerunner.

For consistency, our text should read in **c** *-yuñtām*, as called for by Prāt. ii. 20 (see the note). As noticed above, this verse is in Ppp. joined on to 37 as a part of it; in its place, as conclusion of 39, is given here *sā naṣ paçūn viçvarūpān dadhātu jaradaṣṭiṁ mā pṛthivī kṛṇotu.* ⌊In **d** of our vs. 40, Ppp. reads *indro yātu.*⌋

41. On whom, the earth (*bhū́mi*), mortals sing [and] dance with loud noises (? *vyā̀ilaba*); on whom they fight; on whom speaks the shout (*ākrandá*), the drum — let that earth (*bhū́mi*) push forth our rivals; let earth make me free from rivals.

Yudhyánte should be emended to *yúdhyante.* The verse (8 + 8 : 8 + 8 : 11 + 11 = 54) has no *kakubh* element in it, but as *çakvarī* it is *virāj.* Ppp. puts the verse after our vs. 42, and reads for **b**: *janā martyā dvāilavā;* ⌊in **c** *yudhyante 'syām;*⌋ and, for **e**, **f**, *sā no bhūmiṣ pra dadhatāṁ sapatnāñ : yo no dveṣty adharaṁ taṁ kṛṇotu.*

42. On whom is food, rice-and-barley; whose are these five races (*kṛṣṭí*) — to the earth, whose spouse is Parjanya, fattened (*-médas*) by the rain, be homage.

With the irregular, but not infrequent, combination *yásye 'mā́ḥ* in **b**, the verse is a regular *anuṣṭubh;* for the epithet *svarāj* of the Anukr. there is no ⌊sufficient⌋ reason. Ppp. reads for **b** *yatre 'māṣ pañca gṛṣṭayaḥ*, and ends with *-medhase.* Kāuç. uses the verse at 24. 38 (next after vs. 38), and at 137. 24, with homage to the ⌊earth (*bhūmi*)⌋.

43. Whose are the god-made strongholds; in whose field [men] fall out (? *vi-kṛ*) — the earth, womb of everything, let Prajāpati make pleasant (*ráṇya*) to us, spot by spot.

⌊BR. render *viçvágarbha* by 'Alles im Schoosse tragend.'⌋ Ppp. reads *yasyāṁ* both times for *yasyāḥ;* also, at the end, *niṣ ṭaṇotu.* The Anukr. is more than usually scrupulous in calling the verse *virāj.* Read in **b** *vikurváte.*

44. Bearing treasure [and] good in many places hiddenly, let the earth give me jewel (*maṇí*), gold; giver of good, bestowing good things on us, let the divine one assign [them to us] with favoring mind.

Ppp. ⌊puts the verse after our 30, and⌋ reads at end of **b** *dadhātu naḥ.* Kāuç. quotes the verse at 24. 39, as used by one who desires jewels or gold. ⌊So Keç., p. 322: also SPP. (*maṇihiraṇyādikāmaḥ*) at p. 201[18]; but at 201[26] he cites the sūtra with Bl's reading (*maṇiṁ hir-*); cf. Caland, p. 66.⌋

45. Let the earth, bearing in many places people of different speech, of diverse customs (*-dhárman*), according to their homes, yield (*duh*) me a thousand streams of property, like a steady (*dhruvá*) unresisting milch-cow.

Ppp. reads in **a** *janaṁ yaṁ bibhratī bahuvācasaṁ*, and in **c** *nas* for *me.* The Anukr. does not heed that the last pāda in this verse, and the last two in vs. 44, are *triṣṭubh.* ⌊Keç., p. 322[31], couples this vs. with the preceding: cf. note to vs. 44.⌋

46. What stinging (*vṛçcika*) harsh-biting serpent of thine lies in secret, winter-harmed, torpid (? *bhṛmalá*); whatever worm, O earth, becoming lively, stirs in the early rainy season — let that, crawling, not crawl upon us; be thou gracious to us with that which is propitious.

Ppp. reads in **a** *vṛçcakas*, and for **b** ff. *hemantalabdho bhramalo* (!) *kṛmir lisaṁ pṛthivyāi prāvṛṣī yad ejati*. The treatment of *krimis* in **c** as neuter is very strange. ⌊Is it a collective neuter like *Gewürm?* cf. *Noun-Inflection*, JAOS. x. 570.⌋ In the description of the verse (11 + 12 : 7 + 8 + 8 + 8 = 54) by the Anukr. there is perhaps something omitted (or we are to read *virāṭ çakvarī* for *parāç-*). The verse is used according to Kāuç. 50. 17 (with ⌊iii. 26 (see introduction thereto) and 27 and⌋ vi. 56. 1) in the removal of vermin; also, according to 139. 8, with a number of other verses about serpents and the like; and it is reckoned to the *rāudra gaṇa* (note to Kāuç. 50. 13). In Vāit. 29. 10 it accompanies a libation to Rudra.

47. What many roads thou hast, for people to go upon, a track (*vártman*) for the chariot, and for the going of the cart, by which (pl.) men of both kinds, excellent and evil, go about — that road, free from enemies, free from robbers, may we conquer; be thou gracious to us with that which is propitious.

Ppp. reads *bahudhā* (for *bahavas*) in **a**, *yebhiç car-* at beginning of **c**, and *panthām* in **d**; and it omits the last pāda ⌊repeated from vs. 46⌋. The *pratīka* (*ye te panthānaḥ*), quoted in Kāuç. 50. 1, might refer either to this verse or to vii. 55. 1; the comm. to vii. 55 declares the latter to be intended.

48. Bearing the fool, bearer of what is heavy, enduring (*titikṣú*) the death (? *nidhána*) of the excellent and of the evil, the earth, in concord with the boar, opens itself to the wild (*mṛgá*) hog.

Ludwig understands *gurubhṛt* in **a** as 'bearer of the wise' (*guru* as antithesis of *malva*); the Pet. Lexx. translate *nidhána* as 'residence' (and so Bruce, 'abode'). Ppp. has at the beginning a very different text: *sarpaṁ bibhratī surabhir;* and it reads *sūkareṇa* in **c** and *varāhāya* in **d**.

49. What forest animals of thine, wild beasts set in the woods, lions, tigers, go about man-eating — the jackal (? *ulá*), the wolf, O earth, misfortune, the *ṛkṣīkā*, the demon, do thou force (*bādh*) away from us here.

The translation here given agrees with its predecessors in assuming emendation of *té* in **a** to *te*. Some of our mss. read in **c–d** *itá rakṣīkām;* and Bp. has after it *ṛ́kṣaḥ*. Ppp. gives *eta rakṣīkāṁ rakṣo 'pa bādhā mat;* and, at the beginning, *yatāraṇyāṣ paç-*; ⌊and *ulaṁ* in **c** like our text⌋. With **a** compare the nearly identical xi. 2. 24 **a**; in spite of their agreement, one can hardly help regarding *mṛgās* as an intruded word. The Anukr. apparently accepts the two redundant syllables as making up for the deficiency in **b** and **d**, since 14 + 11 : 12 + 11 = 48 syllables. ⌊As to the "man-eaters," cf. note to xv. 5. 7.⌋

50. What Gandharvas, Apsarases [there are], and what *arā́yas, kimīdíns:* the *piçācás*, all demons — them do thou keep away from us, O earth (*bhū́mi*).

Ppp. combines in **a** *gandharvā 'ps-*, and has at the end *bhāume yāvayaḥ*.

51. She to whom two-footed winged-ones fly together, swans, eagles, hawks, birds; on whom the wind, Mātariçvan, goes about, making clouds of dust (? *rájas*) and setting in motion the trees — flame (*arcís*) blows after the forth-blowing, the toward-blowing, of the wind.

The second pāda is identical with xi. 2. 24 **b**. *Upavā́m* is metrically an intrusion into **e**: with the pāda is to be compared RV. i. 148. 4 **c** (which, however, casts little light upon it). Ppp. reads in **c–d** *vātayate mātariçvā raj-*; and, in **e**, it omits *upavām*, and has at the end *arciṣe*. The Anukr. appears to divide the last redundant pāda into two, an *anuṣṭubh* (8) and a *kakubh* (6); the whole makes two syllables more than a proper *çakvarī* (11 + 11 : 11 + 11 : 8 + 6 = 58). ⌊Hopkins, JAOS. xx.² 217, thinks that fire caused by the friction of branches is here alluded to, and cites parallels. We may add *Indische Sprüche*, 3759, which is very clear.⌋

52. On whom the black and the ruddy, combined, [namely] day-and-night, [are] disposed upon the earth (*bhū́mi*); the broad (*pṛthivī́*) earth (*bhū́mi*), wrapped [and] covered with rain — let her kindly (*bhadráyā*) set us in each loved abode.

Ppp. reads *gṛṣṭam* for *kṛṣṇam* in **a**, reads and combines *saṁbhṛte 'horātre* in **a–b**, and reads *vṛtāvṛdhā* in **c**, and *dhāmnidhāmni* in **e**. In **c** is to be understood, with the *pada*-text, *vṛtā́ : ā́॰vṛtā*. An accent-mark under the final *tā* is needed in order to indicate the acute of *sā́* in the next line. The verse (11 + 12 : 12 + 8 + 8 = 51) is not well described by the Anukr. ⌊A *ca* with syllabic value, inserted after *kṛṣṇám*, would be an effective, albeit cheap, means of improving the meter of **a**.⌋ The verse is quoted in Kāuç. 24. 41 (next after various of the preceding verses), as accompanying a mouth-rinsing and head-splashing with rainwater; and pāda **c**, again, in 137. 23, with a sprinkling with water.

53. Both heaven and earth and atmosphere [have given] me this expanse; fire, sun, waters, and all the gods have together given me wisdom (*medhā́*).

The translation of **a**, **b** is doubtful; *vyácas* may be in apposition with *antárikṣam*, and the gift as in the second line. The Anukr. takes no notice of the irregular combination *me 'dam* in **a**, which is needed to make the verse a simple *anuṣṭubh*. Ppp. combines *māi 'daṁ*, and it has at the end *saṁ dadhāu*. Not this verse, but vi. 53. 1 (according to the comm. on the latter), is quoted in Kāuç. 10. 20, in a ceremony for wisdom; ⌊but Dārila understands our verse as the one intended⌋.

54. I am overpowering, superior by name on the earth (*bhū́mi*); I am subduing, all-overpowering, vanquishing in every region.

The treatment of the compounds of *sah* (p. also *abhīṣā́ṭ*, *viçvāṣā́ṭ*) is the subject of several rules in the Prāt. (ii. 82; iii. 1; iv. 70). ⌊Cf. above, iii. 18. 5.⌋ The verse is by Kāuç. 38. 30 prescribed to be repeated as one goes to an assembly (*pariṣad*).

55. When yonder, O divine one, spreading thyself forward, told by the gods, thou didst expand (*vi-sṛp*) to greatness, then entered into thee well-being; thou didst make fit the four directions.

Ppp. at the beginning puts *yat* before *adas;* it has in **b** *sṛṣṭā* instead of *uktā*, and *mahitvā* (which is better); and in **c** *ā vāmabhūtam av-*. The Anukr. does not heed the redundant syllable in **a**.

56. What villages, what forest, what assemblies, [are] upon the earth (*bhū́mi*), what hosts, gatherings—in them may we speak what is pleasant (*cā́ru*) to thee.

With the first half-verse may be compared VS. iii. 45 **a**, **b**. Ppp. reads for **a** *ye grāmyā yāny araṇyāni*, and for **c**, **d** *teṣv ahaṁ devi pṛthvi vibhyāsaṁ mayu satva ca.*

57. As a horse the dust, she has shaken apart those people who dwelt upon the earth since (*yā́t*) she was born—pleasing, going at the head, keeper of creation (*bhúvana*), container of forest trees, of herbs.

Ppp. reads at the beginning *açvī 'va*, and is corrupt throughout; ⌊but it reads *gṛbhir* like our text⌋. The Anukr. calls the first pāda an *atijagatī* rather than admit the abbreviated form *'va* for *iva*.

58. What I speak, rich in honey I speak it; what I view, that they win (? *van*) me; brilliant am I, possessed of swiftness; I smite down others that are violent (? *dódhat*).

The sense of **b** is obscure. Ppp. reads *vadantu* (for *vananti*); Bp. has *vadanti*, and O.s.m. (p.m.?) *vahanti*. Ppp. has at the end *dodhata*. Kāuç. quotes the verse at 24. 14 and 38. 29, each time adding *mantroktam* 'as expressed in the verse.' ⌊Ppp. puts this verse before our 57.⌋

59. Tranquil, fragrant, pleasant, with sweet drink in her udder, rich in milk, let earth (*bhū́mi*) bless me, earth together with milk.

Ppp. reads at the beginning *santivā* ⌊cf. iii. 30. 2, note⌋, and in **c** *no 'dhi* (in place of *adhi*). The verse is quoted in Kāuç. 24. 31, among many other verses from this hymn; ⌊further, by Dārila to 3. 4, and by Keç. to 70. 8, 9⌋.

60. Whom Viçvakarman sought after with oblation within the ocean, when she was entered into the mist (? *rájas*); an enjoyable vessel that was deposited in secret became manifest in enjoyment (*bhóga*) for them that have mothers.

Ppp. reads for **b** *yasyām āsann ugrayo* ⌊intending *agnayo?*⌋ *'psv antaḥ;* and, in **c**, **d**, *guhā çāir āvir bhor abhavan mātṛmadbhiḥ:* which casts no light on the strange and obscure meaning.

61. Thou art the scatterer (? *āvápana*) of people, [art] a wish-fulfilling (*kāmadúgha*) Aditi, spreading out; what of thee is deficient, may Prajāpati, first-born of righteousness, fill that up for thee.

The word *āvápana* seems to mean sometimes, and perhaps here, a (wide, shallow?) receptacle onto which things are strewn or scattered. Ppp. has at the beginning *viṁ* for *tvam*, and in **b** *viçvarūpā* for *paprathānā;* for **c**, **d** it reads *yat tāu "naṁ tat tāpūrayāti prajāpatiḥ prajābhis saṁvidānām;* and it ends the hymn here. The Anukr. refuses to admit two familiar resolutions in **a**, and gratuitously calls the pāda a *bārhata*

(9 syll.). The second half-verse is twice quoted in Kāuç. (46. 52; 137. 13) in connection with filling up a hole that has been dug (*iti saṁvapati*); and the verse, in 137. 14, with removing elsewhither the dirt taken out.

62. Let standers upon thee, free from disease, free from *yákṣma*, be produced (*prásūta*) for us, O earth; awakening to meet our long lifetime, may we be tribute-bearers to thee.

The sense of *upasthā́s* (p. *upa॰sthā́ḥ*) in **a** is doubtful; Ludwig renders 'laps,' as if *upásthās*; ⌊and so Bloomfield⌋; Bruce 'that shall dwell in thee.' The verse is quoted in Kāuç. 50. 10, in a ceremony for success. The description of the Anukr. is unintelligible, as the verse is a perfectly regular *triṣṭubh*.

63. O mother earth (*bhū́mi*), do thou kindly set me down well established; in concord with the heaven, O sage (*kávi*), do thou set me in fortune, in prosperity (*bhū́ti*).

The verse is used by Kāuç. (24. 27) in connection with vss. 1–7; also by the comm. to 58. 19 in the *annaprāçana* ceremony. Vāit. 27. 8 prescribes it on descending from the sacrificial post (cf. note to vs. 33). ⌊For *çriyā́m*, the only form of its kind in the AV., see JAOS. x. 389.⌋

⌊Here ends the first *anuvāka*, of 1 hymn and 63 verses. The quoted Anukr. says *bhāumas tryadhikā ṣaṣṭiḥ.*⌋

2. The flesh-eating and the householder's fires.

[*Bhṛgu.—pañcapañcāçat. āgneyam uta mantroktadevatyam; 21–33. mārtvyaḥ. trāiṣṭubham; 2, 5, 12–20, 34–36, 38–41, 43, 51, 54. anuṣṭubh (16. kakummatī parābṛhatī; 18. nicṛt; 40. purastātkakummatī); 3. āstārapañkti; 6. bhurig ārṣī pañkti; 7, 45. jagatī; 8, 48, 49. bhurij; 9. anuṣṭubgarbhā viparītapādalakṣmī pañkti; 37. purastādbṛhatī; 42. 3-p. 1-av. bhurig ārcī gāyatrī; 44. 1-av. 2-p. ārcī bṛhatī; 46. 1-av. 2-p. sāmnī triṣṭubh; 47. 5-p. bārhatavāirājagarbhā jagatī; 50. upariṣṭādvirāḍ bṛhatī; 52. purastādvirāḍ bṛhatī; 55. bṛhatīgarbhā.*]

⌊Partly prose—vss. 42, 44.⌋ Found also (except vss. 36, 52) in Pāipp. xvii., with slight differences of order, pointed out under the verses. The whole hymn (which is also an *anuvāka*) is quoted in Kāuç. 69. 7 (with vii. 62 and the *mahāçānti* hymns), in the ceremony of preparing the house-fire; and a large proportion of the verses in this and other ceremonies; a few also are used in the Vāit.; ⌊and the hymn is cited by Dārila on Kāuç. 43. 5⌋.

Translated: Ludwig, p. 479 (omitting here vss. 21–26, 30–31); Henry, 188, 227; Griffith, ii. 102.—The RV. correspondents of a number of the verses (7, 8, 21–25, 26, 30, 31) are discussed in my *Skt. Reader*, pages 380 ff., 388.

1. Ascend the reeds (*naḍá*); no place for thee is here; this lead is thy portion; come! what *yákṣma* is in kine, [what] *yákṣma* in men, in company with that do thou go forth downward.

This and vss. 11, 54, and 55 are quoted together in Kāuç. 71. 5, when putting fuel on the flesh-eating (*kravyā́d*) fire; also, in 71. 8, vss. 1–4, 42, 43, 15, 16 (with iii. 21. 8), with quenching it. Ppp. combines *te 'tra* in **a**.

2. By evil-plotter and ill-plotter, by actor and helper, both all *yákṣma* and death do we thereby drive out from here.

Ppp. reads in **c**, **d** *mṛtyūṅç ca sarvāṅs tene 'to yakṣmāṅç ca nir* etc. The first half-verse is like a half-verse in MS. iv. 14. 17; TA. ii. 4⁷: *duḥçaṅsānuçaṅsā́bhyāṁ ghanénā 'nughanéna ca* ⌊cf. *Kaṭha-hss.*, p. 72⌋.

3. Out from here do we drive death, perdition, out the niggard; whoso hates us, him, O non-flesh-eating Agni, do thou eat; whomso we hate, him do we impel to thee.

The *pada*-text has in **c**, *ádhi;* and most of the *saṁhitā*-mss. *ádhy agne*, in accordance with it, though one or two (Bs.E.) have *áddhy agne*, which is no various reading, but only an allowed equivalent. The case is like those in i. 22. 1 and v. 20. 12 above; the abbreviated reading *adhy* has been mistaken for *adhi* instead of *addhi*, and then accented accordingly. Bp. accents also *akravyaºát*. Our text emends to *addhy àgne akravyāt*, but should read instead *agne*, since there is no reason whatever for the accentuation *addhí*. A better reading would seem also to be *kravyāt*. Ppp. has *adhy agne kravyād;* but that, of course, might mean '*kravyāt*. Ppp. also has simply *aṁ* for *yam u* in **d**, omits the second *u*, and ends with *suvāmaḥ*. ⌊Ppp. reads *yakṣmas* for *dviṣmas* in **d**. So the Ppp. reading is *adhy agne kravyād aṁ yakṣmas taṁ te pra suvāmaḥ.*⌋

4. If the flesh-eating Agni, or if the tiger-like, hath entered this stall (*goṣṭhá*), being not at home (?), him, having made him to have beans for sacrificial butter, I send far forth; let him go unto the Agnis that have seat in the waters.

Part of the mss. (E.I.O.R.T.K.) have *vyāghrás* in **a**, and that is perhaps the true reading, since *-ghrya* seems to be found nowhere else. Ppp. reads in **b** *anyokā viveça*, and in **c** *tan mā-*. The Anukr. takes no notice of the redundant (*tám* intruded?) syllable in **c**. In Kāuç. 71. 6 the verse is used (with vss. 7 and 53) in making a libation of crushed beans with mother-of-pearl (? *çukti*) to the flesh-eating fire which is to be banished. ⌊The verse contains reminiscences of 7 and 8 below.⌋

5. If angry men put thee forth (*pra-kṛ*), with fury, a man having died, that, O Agni, is easy to be arranged by thee; we make thee flame up again.

Ppp. reads *kṛtvā* for *kruddhās* in **a**, *mite* for *mṛte* in **b**, and *ca* for *tat* in **c**. The Anukr. appears to sanction the resolution *cakṛ-ur* in **a**. The verse is quoted in Kāuç. 70. 6; also in Vāit. 5. 13, to accompany the removal of fire from the householder's to the other two fires.

6. The Ādityas, the Rudras, the Vasus [have set] thee again; again, O Agni, the priest (*brahmán*), conductor of good; Brahmaṇaspati hath set thee again, in order to length of life-time to a hundred autumns.

With the first half-verse is to be compared that of VS. xii. 44 (also in TS. iv. 2. 3⁵; MS. i. 7. 1), which inserts *sám indhatām* after *vásavas*, and reads, for **b**, *púnar brahmā́ṇo* (Ppp. also *brahmāṇo*) *vasunītha* (MS. *vasudhīte*) *yajñāḥ* ⌊MS. *agne*⌋. ⌊But see also WZKM. xi. 120.⌋ The verse (10 + 10 : 10 + 11 = 41; but **c** has really 11 syll.) is artificially described by the Anukr. It is made in Vāit. 28. 22 to accompany the laying of fuel in the *ukhya*.

7. If the flesh-eating Agni hath entered our house, seeing this other Jātavedas, him I take afar for the Fathers' sacrifice; let him kindle the hot drink (*gharmá*) in the highest station.

The verse is also RV. x. 16. 10, where is read *vas* for *nas* in **a**, *devám* for *dūrám* in **c**, and *invāt* for *indhām* in **d**. It is used in Kāuç. 71. 6 with vs. 4 (see note to latter).

8. I send far forth the flesh-eating Agni; let him go, carrying evil (*riprá-*), to Yama's subjects; here let this other Jātavedas carry the oblation, a god to the gods, foreknowing.

The verse is also RV. x. 16. 9 (and VS. xxxv. 19 ⌊with *yamarā́jyam*⌋): our text defaces the meter of **c**, **d** by omitting *evá* after *ihá* and inserting *devás*. ⌊Cf. MGS. ii. 1. 8 and p. 149.⌋ This and the two following verses are used in Kāuç. 71. 12 to accompany the removed fire. ⌊The same three vss. are quoted by the comm. to 81. 33.⌋

9. I, being sent, take the flesh-eating Agni, a death, making people fixed with the thunderbolt; I, knowing, separate (? *ni-çās*) him from the householder's fire; also in the world of the Fathers be he [their] portion.

Ppp. reads *iṣitaṁ* in **a**, and, in **d**, *lokaṁ paramo yotu*. The sense of **b** is so strange that we cannot but suspect a corrupt text. ⌊Roth would read *tṛṅhantam*, ZDMG. xlviii. 107.⌋ In **d**, nearly all the *saṁhitā*-mss. (all save Bs.E.) read *loké 'pi*, which is therefore probably the true text. The description by the Anukr. of this fairly regular *triṣṭubh* is very strange.

10. The flesh-eating Agni, active, praiseworthy, I send forth by the roads that the Fathers go; come thou not back by those that the gods go; be thou just there (*átra*); watch thou over the Fathers.

Ppp. reads, in **c–d**, *mā devayānāiṣ pathibhir ā gā 'trāi 'va*, which does not help the defective meter; of this the Anukr. takes no notice.

11. They kindle the devouring one (*sáṁkasuka*) in order to well-being, becoming cleansed, bright, purifying; he abandons evil (*riprá*), passes over sin; Agni, kindled, purifies with a good purifier.

Ppp. combines *ene 'ti* in **c**. The Anukr. does not heed that the first pāda is properly *jagatī*. The verse is quoted in Kāuç. 71. 5 (see note to vs. 1). ⌊Caland, WZKM. viii. 368, thinks that this verse (not xviii. 4. 41) is intended at Kāuç. 86. 18.⌋ ⌊Over "devouring," as rendering of *sáṁkasuka* (which occurs in vss. 11–14, 19, 40), W. has interlined 'crushing' in three instances.⌋

12. God Agni the devouring hath ascended the backs of the sky; being released out of sin, he hath released us from imprecation.

Some of our mss. (P.M.W.E.) read *nír éṇaso* in **c**. Ppp. reads, here and below, *saṁkusika-*.

13. On this devouring Agni do we wipe off evils; we have become fit for sacrifice, cleansed; may he prolong our life-times.

The verse is found also in Āp. ix. 3. 22 (following a verse resembling our vs. 14), which reads *saṁkusuke 'gnāu* in **a–b**. Our mss., as often in such cases, vary between *tāriṣat* and *tārṣat* at the end (Bs.E.D.R.K. have *tārṣat*). The verse is quoted (with vss. 19, 40) in Kāuç. 71. 16 and 86. 19, to accompany the act of washing off (*ity abhyavanejayati*).

14. The crushing ⌊*sáṁkasuka*⌋, the bursting (*víkasuka*), the destroying (*nirṛthá*) and the noiseless (? *nisvará*) — they, of like possessions (? *sávedas*), have made from far thy *yákṣma* to disappear afar.

The translation implies emendation at the end to *anīnaçan*, which seems altogether necessary. Yet MS. (iv. 14. 17) and TA. (ii. 4⁵) strangely have instead of it *acīcatam* (not *-tan*). ⌊But see *Kaṭha-hss.*, p. 72, where the Berlin ms. is reported as reading *cīcatan*. The TA. comm. renders *acīcatam* by *cātayantu.*⌋ In **b**, TA. reads *nisvanáḥ*, and MS. *nírṛto* and *nísvanaḥ;* in **c**, MS. has *'smad* (not *'smád!*) for *te*, and TA. *té ye 'smád* (but the *ye* perhaps a blunder of the edition *); both *ánāgasas* instead of *sávedasas* (which looks like a mere blunder, intended to have the sense of *saṁvidānā́s*). Then TA. has *sáṁkus-*, *víkus-*, in **a**, and with it agrees Āp. (ix. 3. 22, **a** and **b** only, with *vikiro yaç ca viṣkiraḥ* for **b**). Moreover, both MS. and TA. accent *yakṣmám.** Some of our mss. (Bp.I.K.) read *nirrathás* in **b**, but this is only an example of the frequent confusion of *ṛ* and *ra*. Ppp. has ⌊*vikasukas* in **a**, like our text⌋, *savedhasas* in **c**, and *ucidyavo* (for *anīnaçam*) at the end. *⌊The Poona ed., p. 126, gives *té 'smád*, but notes one ms. as having *te ye 'smad;* and it accents *yákṣmam.*⌋

15. The flesh-eating one that is in our horses, heroes, that is in our kine, goats-and-sheep, do we thrust out — the fire that obstructs the people.

Ppp. combines in **a** *no 'çv-*, and reads for **b** *yo goṣu yo 'jāviṣu;* ⌊and puts the verse after 16⌋. This verse and the one following are quoted with others (see note to vs. 1) in Kāuç. 71. 8.

16. Thee from inexhaustible (? *ányа*) men, kine, horses, thee the flesh-eating one do we thrust out — the fire that obstructs life.

Ludwig gets rid of the difficulty of *ánya* by taking it as *anyá* and the nouns in **a**, **b** as datives. Ppp. reads *ajñānā* for *anyebhyas tvā;* in **c** it puts *nis* after *kravyadam*. Some of our mss. (Bs.I.) combine *niṣ kr-* (*níḥ* and *kr-* should be separated in our edition). The Anukr. very unnecessarily scans the verse as 8 + 6 : 8 + 9, while it is easily read into a regular *anuṣṭubh*.

17. On what the gods wiped off, on what human beings (*manuṣyà*) also — on that having wiped off the drops of ghee (?), O Agni, do thou mount the sky.

All our mss. have *amṛjata* unaccented save one (E.), which has *ásṛjata*. ⌊All of SPP's have *amṛjata* save his J., which has, s.m., *ámṛjata.*⌋ *Ghṛtastā́vàs* in **c** is translated after the Pet. Lexx., but the rendering is in the highest degree doubtful, on account both of form and of sense. Probably the reading is corrupt. Ppp. gives no help, as most of vss. 17, 18 is lost out of the ms.; ⌊but their order appears to be inverted⌋. Our mss. seem to read *-stā́-* very plainly ⌊and SPP. reports no variant⌋, but that need not prevent our understanding instead *-snā́-*, if more acceptable.

18. Being kindled, O Agni, thou to whom oblations are made, go (*kram*) thou not away against us; shine just here by day, and that [we] long see the sun.

Or *dyavi*, in **c**, 'in the sky' (so Ludwig). The last pāda is also i. 6. 3 **d**. ⌊Cf. also note to vi. 19. 2.⌋ There is no good reason for calling the verse *nicṛt*.

19. Wipe ye off on the lead; wipe ye off on the reeds; and what on the consuming fire; likewise on the dark (*rāmā́*) ewe; headache on the pillow.

The rendering is very literal, and does not disguise the obscurity of the connection. Ppp. reads for **b** *agnis saṁkusikaç ca yaḥ*, which is more manageable: 'and on [that] which [is] the consuming fire': i.e. 'on the fire.' ⌊Caland, KZ. xxxiv. 457, comparing Avestan locutions, says that *agnāu saṁkasuke ca yat* is locative to *agniḥ saṁkasukaç ca yaḥ*: cf. vs. 40 and i. 30. 1.⌋ The verse is quoted in Kāuç. 71. 16; 86. 19, with vss. 13 and 40: see above, under vs. 13. The mss. in general, according to their wont, read in **a** *mṛdhvam* (but Bs. *mṛdhḍham*). ⌊For *çīrṣakti*, see ref's under i. 12. 3.⌋

20. Having settled what is foul upon the lead [and] headache upon the pillow, having wiped off on the black ewe, be ye cleansed, fit for sacrifice.

Compare xiv. 2. 67. ⌊Cf. MGS. ii. 1. 10.⌋

21. Go away, O death, along a distant road which is thine here, other than that the gods go upon; I speak to thee having sight, hearing; let these many heroes be here.

The verse (except **d**) is RV. x. 18. 1, and found also in VS. (xxxv. 7), TB. (iii. 7. 14[5]), and TA. (iii. 15. 2: vi. 7. 3). RV. has *svás* for our *eṣás* in **b**, and, for **d**, *mā́ naḥ prajā́ṁ rīriṣo mó 'tá vīrā́n*, and the other texts agree with it, save that VS. has *anyás* for *svás* in **b**. Ppp. omits *iha* in **d**. ⌊Cf. MB. i. 1. 15; also MGS. ii. 18. 2 m.⌋ The verse is used several times in Kāuç.: at 71. 11, 21; 72. 13; 86. 24.

22. These living ones have turned away from the dead; our invocation of the gods hath been auspicious (*bhadrā́*) today; we have gone forward unto dancing, unto laughter; may we, rich in heroes, address counsel.

The verse (again with exception of **d**) is RV. x. 18. 3, and found also in TA. (vi. 10. 2). The last pāda in the other texts is *drā́ghīya ā́yuḥ pratarā́ṁ* (TA. *-rā́ṁ*) *dádhānāḥ*; our **d** is identical with RV. i. 117. 25 **d**. TA.* has *ā́ 'vavartin* in **a**, and *agāmā* in **c**. ⌊With **b** cf. RV. x. 53. 3 **d**.⌋ The verse is used (with vs. 29) in Kāuç. 71. 18 and 86. 21. ⌊At vs. 30, W. wrote "speak to the counsel," and then interlined suggestion of "council."⌋ *⌊TA. has also *prā́ñjo* for *prā́ñco*.⌋

23. I set this enclosure for the living; let not another of them now go to that goal; living a hundred numerous autumns, let them set an obstacle to death with a mountain.

The verse is RV. x. 18. 4, and found also in VS. (xxxv. 15), TB. (iii. 7. 11[3]), TA. (vi. 10. 2), and Āp. (ix. 12. 4; xiv. 22. 3). RV. differs from our text only by reading *jīvantu* in **c**, and *antár* (for *tirás*) in **d**. VS. agrees throughout with RV.; TB. differs only by having (like AV.) *tirás* in **d** (*eṣā́n nu* in **b** is doubtless a misprint, as *mátyám* in **d** is a misprint for *mṛtyúm*: see the comm. ⌊the Poona ed., p. 1137, corrects them both⌋), and *árdham* in **b**. TA. reads *mā́ nó 'nu gād* and *árdham* in **b**, and *tirás* and *dadmahe* in **d**. Āp. agrees exactly with TB. the first time; but the second time it has *no nu* (or *'nu*) in **b**, and *dadhmahe* in **d**. ⌊Cf. MP. ii. 22. 24.⌋ Ppp. gives, in **c**, *jyok* for *çatam*, and combines *çaradaṣ pu-*. In Kāuç. 72. 17 the verse accompanies the setting down (of a stone) in the door; in 72. 2 the last pāda is recited while stepping over the stone.

24. Mount, choosing old age for life-time, pressing on, one after another, as many as ye be; you here let Tvashṭar, him of good births, in accord [with you], lead on to living your whole life-time.

The verse is (once more with exception of the last pāda) RV. x. 18. 6, and found also in TA. (vi. 10. 1). RV. reads *ṣṭhá* after *yáti* in **b**, and *ihá* for *tā́n vas* in **c**, and its **d** is *dīrghám ā́yuḥ karati jīvá se vaḥ*. TA. differs from RV. by having *gṛṇānā́s* in **a**, *surátnas* (for *sajóṣās*) in **c**, and *karatu* in **d**. Ppp. puts the verse after our 25, and combines in **a–b** *vṛṇānā 'nu*. The verse is used in Kāuç. 72. 13 with vss. 21, 32, 44, 55, and others from elsewhere.

25. As days take place (*bhū*) one after another, as seasons go along with seasons, as an after one does not desert (*hā*) a preceding — so, O creator (*dhā́tṛ*), arrange their life-times.

This verse is RV. x. 18. 5, found also in TA. (vi. 10. 1). For *sākám*, at end of **b**, RV. reads *sādhú*, and TA. *kḷptā́ḥ*.

26. The stony one flows (*rī*); take ye hold together; play the hero, pass over, O friends; quit here them that are of evil courses; may we pass up unto powers (? *vā́ja*) that are free from disease.

The verse is RV. x. 53. 8, and found also in VS. (xxxv. 10) and TA. (vi. 3. 2). RV. has *út tiṣṭhata* for *vīráyadhvam* in **b**, *jahāma* and (for *durévās*) *áçevās* in **c**, and *çivā́n vayám* (for *anamīvā́n*) in **d**. ⌊VS. agrees with RV. save that it accents *sákhāyaḥ* in **b** and reads, for **c**, *átra jahīmó 'çivā yé ásan*.⌋ TA. agrees in general with RV., but has *revatīs* ⌊unaccented⌋ for *rīyate* in **a**, and in **d** puts *út tarema* after *abhí vā́jān*. Vss. 26 and 27 are quoted in Kāuç. 71. 24 and 86. 27 to accompany the symbolical act of crossing over northward; and in Vāit. 12. 11 to accompany (at any time) the crossing of streams.

27. Stand up, pass over, O friends; the stony river here runs (*syand*); quit ye here them that are unpropitious; may we pass up unto propitious pleasant powers.

This variation of vs. 26 gives part of the RV. variants to that vs. ⌊For a discussion of the RV. verse, see notes to my *Skt. Reader*, p. 388.⌋ Ppp. makes **b** identical with 26 **a**. The use by Kāuç. was stated in the preceding note.

28. Take ye hold on that of all the gods in order to splendor, becoming cleansed, clear, purifying; stepping over difficult tracks, may we revel a hundred winters with all our heroes.

The first half-verse is identical with vi. 62. 3 **a**, **b**, save that the latter begins with *vāiçvānarī́m*. We have doubtless to supply *nā́vam* 'boat.' But Ppp. has *sūnṛtām* for *varcase* in **a**; and the comm. to Nirukta vi. 12 quotes the *pratīka* in this form, explaining *sūnṛtām* by *vācam* (Roth). According to Kāuç. 72. 6, it is a young heifer (*vatsatarī*) that is caused to be laid hold on.

29. By upward roads, full of wind, by distant (*pára*) ones, stepping over those that are lower (*ávara*), thrice seven times did the departed (*páreta*) seers bear back death with the track-obstructor.

Ppp. reads for **b** *apakrāmanto duritaṁ parehi.* In Kāuç. 71. 18 and 86. 21, this verse is quoted with vs. 22 'for the purpose expressed in the texts' (*mantroktam*); and in 71. 19 and in 86. 22 the second half-verse is quoted to accompany 'the effacement (*lup*) of the tracks to the streams.' ⌊W's "(*lup*)" was intended to express his doubt as to the warrantableness of Bloomfield's change of *lup* to *yup*. Caland expresses the same doubt, WZKM. viii. 369: cf. his *Todtengebräuche*, p. 120.⌋

30. Come ye, obstructing the track of death, assuming further on a longer life-time; sitting in your station, thrust ye [away] death; then may we, living, speak to the council.

The first half-verse is RV. x. 18. 2 **a**, **b**, and is found also in TA. (vi. 10. 2); for our *é 'ta*, RV. reads *yád āíta*, TA. *yád āima* (*āima* unaccented, unless there is a misprint ⌊Poona ed. rightly *āíma*, p. 444⌋); and TA. has *pratarā́m* in **b**. ⌊Cf. MGS. ii. 1. 13 and p. 153.⌋ The verse is quoted in Kāuç. 71. 20 and 86. 23 in connection with doing something to (symbolical) boats; and the second half-verse in Kāuç. 72. 10. Ppp. reads *pratiram* in **b**, and *jīvās* in **d**, thus in the latter pāda rectifying the meter. The Anukr. takes no notice of the irregularities in **a** and **d**, perhaps because they balance each other. ⌊As to *vidáthaṁ*, cf. note to vs. 22, and Bloomfield in JAOS. xix.[2] 14.⌋

31. Let these women, not widows, well-spoused, touch themselves with ointment, with butter; tearless, without disease, with good treasures (*-rátna*), let the wives ascend first to the place of union (*yóni*).

This verse is repeated below, as xviii. 3. 57. It is RV. x. 18. 7, and found also in TA. (vi. 10. 2). RV. has *viçantu*, and TA. *mṛçantām*, for our *spṛçantām* in **b**, and TA. *suçévās* for *surátnās* in **c**; RV. also combines *anaçrávo 'nam-* in **c**. Ppp. reads *saṁ viçanta* in **b**; and it adds another corresponding verse for the men: *ime vīrar avidhavās sujānayā narā "ñjanena sarpiṣā* etc. (**d**) *syonād yoner adhi talpaṁ vṛheyuḥ* ⌊intending *ruheyuḥ*⌋. With our verse, in Kāuç. 72. 11, grass shoots dipped in butter are handed to the women; and 72. 12 appears to quote the Ppp. verse (the *pratīka* is given as *ime jīvā avidhavāḥ sujāmayaḥ*) to accompany a similar act to the men.

32. I separate (*vy-ā-kṛ*) these two by oblation; I shape them apart with a spell (*bráhman*); I make for the Fathers unwasting *svadhā́;* I unite these with a long life-time.

Ppp. reads for **c** *sudhāṁ pitṛbhyo amṛtaṁ duhānā.* From Vāit. 6. 2 the separation would appear to be that of the other two fires when taken from the householder's fire; but Kāuç. 70. 10 has it repeated while one looks upon the householder's and the flesh-eating fires; the latter is most likely to be its true application. It is also quoted in Kāuç. 72. 13 with several other verses, from this hymn and elsewhere, as noted under vs. 24.

33. What Agni, O Fathers, hath entered into our hearts, an immortal into mortals, that god do I enclose in me; let him not hate us, nor let us [hate] him.

Ppp. reads in **b** *amartyas* for *amṛtas*, and, in **c**, *mahyaṁ taṁ prati gṛh-*. The verse is found also in TS. (v. 7. 9[1]) and MS. (i. 6. 1); both read, for **b**, *ámartyo mártyāñ āvivéça;* for **c**, **d**, TS. has *tám ātmán pári gṛhṇīmahe vayám mā́ só asmā́ñ avahā́ya párā gāt*, and MS. *tám ātmáni pári gṛhṇīmasī 'há néd eṣó asmā́n avahā́ya parā́yat.* The verse is quoted in Kāuç. 70. 15 for recitation while the hearts are touched.

34. Having turned away from the householder's fire, go ye forth to the right with the flesh-eating one; do ye what is dear to the Fathers, to self, what is dear to the priests (*brahmán*).

Ppp. reads, for **a**, **b**, *apāvartyā 'gniṁ gārhapatyaṁ kravyādā 'py etu dakṣiṇā;* and, in **d**, *kṛṇuta* (not *-tā*). Kāuç. 71. 4 quotes the verse, to accompany a corresponding action. ⌊Caland, *Todtengebräuche*, Note 417, would read *krávyādaḥ*, as voc.⌋

35. The flesh-eating Agni that is unremoved (*á-nir-ā-hita*), taking to himself the double-portioned riches of the oldest son, destroys [him] with ruin.

Ppp. begins with *vibhā-*; it omits our vs. 36.

36. What one plows, what one wins (*van*), and what one gains (*vid*) by pay (*vasná*) — all that is not a mortal's, if the flesh-eating one be unremoved.

As usual in such cases, in most of the mss. it is wholly doubtful whether *vastena* or *-sne-* or *-sre-* is intended in **b**; the true reading is *vasnéna.* The verse, as noted above, is wanting in Ppp. Bp. reads *ásti* at end of **c**.

37. He becomes unfit for sacrifice, of smitten splendor; not by him is the oblation to be eaten; [him] the flesh-eating one cuts off from plowing, kine, riches, whom it pursues.

Ppp. reads, in **a**, *ye agnayo* for *ayajñiyó;* and, in **c**, *kṛṣṭiṁ gāṁ dhanaṁ.* Bp. has in **b** *ná : énena.* The *bhavati* which spoils the meter of **a** is doubtless an intrusion ⌊although Ppp. also has it⌋.

38. A mortal, going down to mishap, speaks forth repeatedly with greedy ones (? *gṛ́dhya*); whom (pl.) the flesh-eating Agni, from near by, after-knowing, follows (? *vi-tāv*).

The translation is purely mechanical, the sense being wholly obscure. Nothing corresponding to *vitā́vati* is found anywhere else; the Pet. Lex. suggests emendation to *vidhāvati;* Ludwig, alternatively, to *vitāmyati* or *vitāmati.* Yet **c**, **d** are repeated below as 52 **c**, **d** (that verse is wanting in Ppp., which, however, has these two pādas in vs. 50). The much corrupted version of Ppp. gives no help as to the verse in general: *bahu krudhīṣ pra vadanty anti tarmato 'nveti ca : kravyādam agnir* ⌊intending *kravyād yam ag-*?⌋ *anuvidvān vibhāvati* (*vitāvati?*).

39. The houses are united with seizure (*grā́hi*) when a woman's husband dies; a knowing priest (*brahmán*) is to be sought, who shall remove the flesh-eating one.

Ppp. reads in **b** *yat strīyāṁ mriyate.* 'United' (in **a**), i.e. 'caused to be affected.'

40. What evil (*riprá*), pollution we have committed, and what ill-doing, from that let the waters cleanse me, and from the crushing Agni what.

The last clause seems a false construction, the true one being something like the version of Ppp.: *agnis saṁkusikaç ca yaḥ;* but Ludwig fills it out to "and [from that] which [arises] from Agni Saṁkasuka." ⌊As to the construction, see Caland as cited under vs. 19.⌋ ⌊As to *saṁkasuka*, cf. note to vs. 11.⌋ Ppp. further reads *duritaṁ* (for *çamalam*) in **a**; and it has *çundhantu* in **c** ⌊cf. note to vi. 115. 3 and the VS. variant there⌋. The Anukr. understands the verse as 6 + 8 : 8 + 8 = 30 syllables; but the *pada*-mss., less acceptably, mark the pāda division as occurring after *cakṛmá*. The verse is quoted in Kāuç. 71. 16 and 86. 19 in company with others, as noted under vs. 13.

41. These fore-knowing ones (f.) have turned hither upward from below by roads that the gods go upon; upon the back of the virile (*vṛṣabhá*) mountain the ancient streams (*sarít*) go about new.

'Waters' (*ā́pas*) is doubtless to be supplied with the adjectives in **a**, **b**. Ppp. combines *tā 'dharād* at the beginning, and reads *ṛṣabhasya* in **c**. It is doubtless by a blunder (*catasras* for *tisras*) that the Anukr. appears to reckon this regular *triṣṭubh* to the *anuṣṭubhs* of the hymn. The verse is quoted in Kāuç. 72. 3.

42. O non-flesh-eating Agni, push out the flesh-eating one; bring the god-sacrificing one.

The Anukr. scans this verse as 5 + 6 + 8 = 19 syllables, acknowledging the unelided *a* of *ákravyāt*, and separating *nuda ā́ dev-*. The prose *yajus* (as it really is) is quoted in Kāuç. 69. 8 as accompanying the bringing of a light from the frying-pan (*bhraṣṭra*), and in 71. 8 with other verses, as noted under vs. 1 above. ⌊The first half-verse is defaced in Ppp.⌋

43. The flesh-eating one entered into this man; he has gone after the flesh-eating one; having made two tigers severally, I take him, who is other than propitious.

Ppp. reads *pra viveça* in **a**, and *nānā 'ḥaṁ* in **c**. The verse is quoted, with others (see note to vs. 1), in Kāuç. 71. 8.

44. Concealment of the gods, defense (*paridhí*) of men (*manuṣyà*), the householder's fire is set (*çritá*) between both classes.

In accordance with the Anukr., the mss. interpose no stroke of interpunction in this verse, which plainly is not metrical, though the last 8 syllables read like an *anuṣṭubh* pāda. It is quoted, with others (see note to vs. 24), in Kāuç. 72. 13. Ppp. reads *ubhayād* in **c**. ⌊The medial *avasāna* is lacking in SPP. and should be deleted from the Berlin ed.⌋

45. Lengthen thou out, O Agni, the life-time of the living; let them who are dead go unto the world of the Fathers; do thou, a good householder's fire, burning away the niggard, assign to this man an ever better dawn.

Ppp. reads, for **a**, *jīvānām agneṣ pratar dīrgham āyuṣ*, and, in **c**, **d**, *arātīr uṣām-uṣāṁ çrayaṁ çrayasi dadhat.* Kāuç. and Vāit. quote as *pratīka* only the beginning of **c**;

this looks rather as if they made one verse of our 45 **c**, **d** and 46. In Kāuç. (71. 2) it accompanies setting down fuel on the householder's fire; in Vāit. (4. 8) it is used with one of the offerings of the sacrificer's wife. It (11 + 13 : 11 + 11 = 46) is very ill defined as simply a *jagatī*.

46. Overcoming, O Agni, all [our] rivals, do thou assign to us their refreshment [and] wealth.

The Anukr. agrees with the mss. in reckoning these two *triṣṭubh* pādas as a whole verse.

47. Take ye hold after this saving (*pápri*) carrier (*váhni*) Indra; he shall carry you out of difficulty [and] reproach; by him smite away the on-flying shaft; by him ward off (*pari-pā*) Rudra's hurled [missile].

Ppp. reads, for **b**, *sa yo vidvān vijahāti mṛtyum;* ⌊and its **d** is like ours⌋. The verse (13 + 11 : 11 + 11 = 46) is unintelligibly ill described by the Anukr. One of the four dissyllabic words in **a** is apparently an intrusion — perhaps most probably *índram*, since one does not see why Indra should make his appearance in this Agni hymn (but see vs. 54), and the epithet *vahni* belongs especially to Agni. In Kāuç. 72. 7 the verse is used (next after vs. 28) to accompany laying hold on a bull ⌊cf. introd. to iv. 22⌋.

48. Lay ye hold after the draft-ox [as] float (*plavá*); he shall carry you out of difficulty [and] reproach; mount this boat of Savitar; may we cross over misery by the six wide [directions].

This and the remaining verses of the hymn are given by Ppp. in the order 49–51, 54, 53, 55, 48 (52 being wanting). ⌊Cf. MGS. ii. 1. 14 and p. 146.⌋ In Kāuç. 72. 8, this verse and the next are used (next after vss. 28, 47) in laying hold on a couch (*talpa*); the third pāda in 71. 23 and 86. 26, in causing some one to embark on a (symbolical) boat containing gold and barley. There is no good reason for calling the verse *bhurij*.

49. Day-and-night thou goest after, bearing, standing comfortable (*kṣemyá*), prolonging [life], having good heroes; bearing, O couch, healthful (*ánātura*), well-minded ones (m.), do thou long be for us smelling of men (*púruṣagandhi*).

The description of the Anukr. seems to require us to resolve *-ra-ā-tre* in **a**. The use by Kāuç. was noticed under the preceding verse.

50. They fall under the wrath of the gods, they live always evilly, after whom the flesh-eating fire, from near by, like a horse, scatters reeds.

Ppp. reads in **a** *deveṣu*, and this is the usual and regular construction with *ā-vraçc*. Further, for **d** it has our 38 **d** and 52 **d**. The Anukr. gives *iva* two syllables in **d**. Our Bp. reads *antikā́n* (instead of *-kā́t*) here and in 38 **c** and 52 **c**. ⌊One could easily scan **d** as an *anuṣṭubh* pāda, *áçvevānvápate naḍám* (*Gram.* § 233 a), if it were worth scanning.⌋

51. Whoever, without faith, from desire of riches then sit together with the flesh-eating one, they verily feed the fire (*ā-dhā*) about the pot (*kumbhī́*) of others ⌊always⌋.

That is, doubtless, never have a fire of their own. The *pada*-text in **a-b** is *dhana*○*-kāmyā́ : ā́t : kravya*○*ádā;* Ppp. has a different reading, *-kāmyāṣ krav-*, thus getting rid of the difficult *ā́t*. ⌊The mark of pāda division is after *ā́t;* it should be before it.⌋ The Anukr. seems to authorize the resolution *ṣa-ām* in **c**.

52. He desires, as it were, to fly forth with his mind; repeatedly he returns again — they whom the flesh-eating Agni, from near by, after-knowing follows.

We had the obscure second half-verse above as 38 **c, d**. The verse is wanting in Ppp., as already noted. The substitution of *patati* for *pipatiṣati* would rectify the meter of **a**. ⌊Pāda **b** seems clearly to refer to rebirth: cf. Praçna Upanishad, i. 9.⌋

53. A black ewe [is] of cattle [thy] portion; lead, too, they call thy gold (? *candrá*), O flesh-eating one; ground beans ⌊are⌋ thy portion [as] oblation; seek (*sac*) thou the thicket of the forest-spirit (*araṇyānī́*).

Ppp. reads (better) *uta* for *api* in **b**. The verse is quoted in Kāuç. 71. 6 (with vss. 4 and 7: see note to vs. 4), and again in 71. 14, in connection with setting down the light (*dīpa*).

54. Having made offering of withered (? *járat*) cane (*iṣīkā*), of *tilpiñja*, of *dáṇḍana*, of reeds; having made fuel of this, Indra removed Yama's fire.

Various kinds of reed or cane are doubtless named in **a, b**. *Jarant* is lit. 'aged.' Ppp. reads in **c** *tān indre 'dhmaṁ*. The Anukr. does not note **c** as defective; we may resolve either *índr-a* or *kṛtu-ā́*. The verse is quoted (with vss. 1, 11, 55: see note to vs. 1) in Kāuç. 71. 5, to accompany the feeding of the flesh-eating fire.

55. Having sent in opposition an opposing (*pratyáñc*) song (*arká*), I, foreknowing, have entered abroad on the road; I have directed away the lifebreaths of them yonder; these here I unite with long life-time.

The first half-verse is difficult and doubtful. The use made of the verse by Kāuç. gives no help; it is quoted in 71. 5 as noted above, under vs. 54; and in 72. 13 with several other verses, as noted under vs. 24. Ppp. reads *ācakāra* at end of **b**. ⌊W. has overlooked the *hí* and the accent of the two perfects: perhaps, 'since I have entered [and] have directed . . . , [accordingly] I unite' etc. Henry, p. 238, inserts another *hí* after *amī́ṣām*.⌋

⌊Here ends the second *anuvāka*, with 1 hymn and 55 verses. The quoted Anukr. says "*naḍas*" *tu pañconā*.⌋

3. Cremation as a sacrifice.

[*Yama.—ṣaṣṭiḥ. mantroktasvargāudanāgnidevatyam. trāiṣṭubham: 1, 42, 43, 47. bhurij; 8, 12, 21, 22, 24. jagatī; 13. ? ; 17. svarāḍ ārṣī pañkti; 34. virāḍgarbhā; 39. anuṣṭub-garbhā; 44. parābṛhatī; 55–60. 3-av. 7-p. çañkumaty atijāgataçākvarātiçākvaradhārtya-garbhā 'tidhṛti* (*55, 57–60. kṛti; 56. virāṭ kṛti*).]

⌊Partly prose — namely parts of vss. 55–60.⌋ Found also ⌊except vs. 28⌋ in Pāipp. xvii. (with slight differences of verse-order, noted under the verses). Nearly all the verses of the hymn are used, according to Kāuç. 60–63, and on the whole in their natural order, and combined especially with xi. 1 (often a verse from each hymn being quoted in the same rule), in the *sava* ceremony; very few verses anywhere else. Vāit. quotes only 4 verses.

Translated: Henry, 195, 238; Griffith, ii. 110; Bloomfield, 185, 645.

1. Stand, a man (*púmāṅs*), upon men; go to the hide; call thither her who is dear to thee; of what age (? *yā́vant*) ye two first came together in the beginning, let that be your same age in Yama's realm.

Ppp. combines *puṅso adhi* and omits *ihi* in **a**. Kāuç. 60. 31 has the verse used when the sacrificer is made to stand upon the ox-hide which is to be his station during the ceremony. The various antecedents have been prepared to the accompaniment of the first verses of xi. 1.

2. So much [be] your sight, so many your powers (*vīryà*), so great your brilliancy (*téjas*), so many-fold your energies (*vā́jina*); Agni fastens on (*sac*) the body when [it is his] fuel (?); then, O paired ones (*mithuná*), shall ye come into being from what is cooked (*pakvá*).

The *pada*-text has *yadā́ : édhaḥ* in **c**, as translated. Ppp. reads before it *agniṁ çarīraṁ sajate*, and after it *atha;* and in **a**, **b** it makes *cakṣus* and *tejas* change places. ⌊In OB. v. 258, *pakvá* is defined as 'the charred remains and ashes of a corpse.' Pāda **d** recurs in vs. 9.⌋ ⌊W. makes a query on the margin: "the husband and wife burnt together?? and born anew and alike out of the cremation?"⌋

3. Together in this world, together on the [road] the gods travel, together also unite ye (du.) in the realms of Yama; purified by purifiers, call ye to yourselves whatever seed (*rétas*) came into being from you.

All the mss. agree in the unaccented *asmin* in **a**. The verse appears to be quoted (as 'third verse') in Kāuç. 60. 33, to accompany a calling upon their offspring (*apatya*).

4. Enter together, ye sons, into the waters, coming together, ye rich in life, unto this living one (m.); of them (f.) share ye the one which (m.) they call immortal, the rice-dish which your (du.) generatrix cooks.

The meaning and connection are very obscure. 'Of them' seems to refer to the waters (f.). Ppp. removes one difficulty by reading *vas* instead of *vām* in **d**; it has in **b** ⌊*-dhanyāt*⌋ *sametā* ⌊cf. vs. 25⌋. In Kāuç. 60. 35 the verse is used when the pair lie down together, accompanied by their offspring, after a vessel of water has been set on the hide.

5. What one your (du.) father cooks, and what one [your] mother, in order to release from evil (*riprá*) and from pollution of speech — that hundred-streamed, heaven-going rice-dish hath permeated (*vi-āp*) with greatness both firmaments (*nábhas*).

Ppp. reads at the beginning *yaṁ vaṣ pitā*.

6. Both firmaments, and worlds of both kinds, what heaven-going ones are conquered of the sacrificers — which one of them is chiefly (? *ágre*) full of light, full of honey, in that combine ye (du.) with your sons in old age.

Ppp. combines in **c** *yo 'gre*, and part of our mss. (P.M.W.T.) read the same.

7. Take ye (du.) hold upon each forward direction; to this world they that have faith attach themselves (*sac*); what of you that is cooked is served up in the fire, combine ye, O husband-and-wife, in order to its guarding.

The verse is nearly accordant with vi. 122. 3. 'Forward' (*prā́ñc*) is also 'eastern.' ⌊Note here again the sequence of the cardinal points (*pradakṣiṇa*), and cf. end of introd. to iii. 26.⌋ The Anukr. passes the irregularity of the second half-verse (11 + 11 : 10 + 12 = 44) without notice. Kāuç. 61. 1 quotes this verse alone; and 61. 2 quotes 7–10 as used while they follow around the vessel of water. Ppp. reads, for **c**, **d**, as follows: *mimāthāṁ pātṛ tad vāṁ pūrṇam astu çivāṁ pakvaṣ pitryāyaṇe 'ty* (*'bhy ?*) *āmayat*.

8. Attaining unto the southern quarter, turn ye (du.) about unto this vessel; in it shall Yama, in concord with the Fathers, assure abundant protection unto your cooked [offering].

'In it': i.e., as the gender shows, in the vessel. Some of our mss. make very bad work with *vām* in **c**, reading *vāyám* (P.M.W.), *vayám* (Bs.s.m.), *varā́m* (R.), *vāṁ yam* (T.). It is absurd of the Anukr. to reckon the verse (11 + 11 : 12 + 11 = 45) a *jagatī*.

9. This western of the quarters verily is a thing to be preferred, in which Soma is over-ruler and favorer; to it resort (*çri*) ye (du.); attach yourselves to the well-doers; then, O paired ones, shall ye come into being from what is cooked.

The last pāda is identical with 2 **d** above. But Ppp. reads instead *adhā pakvena saha saṁ bhavema*, which is nearly identical with vi. 119. 2 **d** and the concluding pāda of 55–60 below. The Anukr. takes no notice of the deficiency of the first pāda.

10. A superior realm, having superiority by progeny, may the northern of the quarters make our (pl.) apex (? *ágra*); a five-fold (*pā́ñta*) meter hath the man become; may we come into being together with all, having all their limbs.

Ppp. reads *paṅktiç chandaṣ* at the beginning of **c**. We have to resolve *pa-āñ-* in order to make a full pāda.

11. This fixed [quarter] is *virā́j*; homage be to it; let it be propitious to [my] sons and to me; do thou, O goddess Aditi, having all choice things, like an active herdsman defend our cooked [offering].

The verse is quoted in Kāuç. 61. 3, next after the four preceding ones.

12. Do thou embrace us, as a father his sons; let propitious winds blow here for us on the earth; what rice-dish the two deities cook here, let that know our penance and also truth.

Ppp. reads *çagdā* for *bhūmāu* in **b**, and *vittam* for *vettu* at the end. 'That' (*tát*) in **d** is neuter, and so not correlative to 'what' (*yám* m.) in **c**. P.M.W. read *svaja naḥ* at end of **a**. The verse lacks two syllables of being a good *jagatī*. ⌊The verse is quoted at Kāuç. 61. 4.⌋

13. Whenever the black bird, coming hither, hath sat upon the orifice, surprising (*tsar*) what is resolved (*vi-sañj*), or when the barbarian woman (*dāsī*) with wet hands smears over — cleanse, ye waters, the mortar [and] pestle.

Ppp. combines in **a** *çakune 'ha*, and reads in **c** *dāsī vā yad*, and in **d** ⌊cf. vss. 21 and 26 and note to vi. 115. 3⌋ *çundhatā "pah*. Kāuç. quotes the verse in 8. 14, and the comm. also under 2. 6, but they cast no light on the obscure first half-verse. The verse is a good *triṣṭubh*, yet the Anukr. attempts to give it some special description, of which the text is corrupt and unintelligible (*yad-yat kṛṣṇa ity āthā*).

14. Let this pressing-stone, broad-based, vigor-bestowing, purified by purifiers, smite away the demon; mount thou the hide; yield great protection; let not the husband-and-wife fall into evil proceeding from sons (*pāútra*).

Ppp. has at the end *gāthām*, with which, of course, *dampatī* would have to be understood as vocative, unaccented. Expressions like that in **d** are found in several of the Sūtras: in AGS. i. 13. 7, *mā 'ham pāutram aghaṁ ni yām* (should be *gām*, probably); in PGS. i. 5. 11, *yathe 'yaṁ strī pāutram aghaṁ na rodāt;* and the same in HGS. i. 19. 7, with *pāutram ānandam* as antithesis to it. The verse is quoted in Kāuç. 61. 18 (in connection with xi. 1. 9), to accompany the setting of mortar, pestle, and winnowing basket, after sprinkling, upon the hide.

15. The forest tree hath come to us together with the gods, forcing off the demon, the *piçācás;* he shall rise up (*ut-çri*), shall speak forth his voice; with him may we conquer all worlds.

Ppp. reads and combines *sāu 'cchrāyātāi* in **c**, and reads *api* for *abhi* in **d**. According to Kāuç. 61. 21, one sets up the pestle with this verse; in 125. 3 the verse is used with reference to the sacrificial post ⌊in case it puts forth fresh shoots⌋; and similarly in Vāit. 10. 8 ⌊in the *paçubandha*⌋.

16. Seven sacrifices (*médha*) the cattle enclosed — which ⌊*the relative pronoun*⌋ of them was full of light, and which was pining; to them thirty deities attach themselves; do thou (m.) conduct us (pl.) unto the heavenly (*svargá*) world.

Our Bp. reads *tā́m* in **c**, and a few of the *saṁhitā*-mss. (P.M.W.E.) agree with it; *tā́m* is certainly wrong, but *tám* would be an acceptable improvement. Ppp. has *medhasvān* instead of *jyotiṣmān* (and the latter must be taken as having the sense of the former); also *cakarṣa* in **b**, and *neṣi* in **d**. ⌊For *neṣa*, see *Gram.* § 896.⌋ The verse is quoted in Kāuç. 61. 13, to accompany the handling or stroking of something by the two spouses ⌊with their offspring⌋. Pāda **b** has a redundant syllable, unnoticed by the Anukr., unless we contract to *yāi 'ṣām*.

17. Unto the heavenly world shalt thou conduct us (pl.); may we be united with wife, with sons; I grasp [her (?)] hand; let her (?) come here after me; let not destruction pass us, nor the niggard.

The last pāda is nearly the same with vi. 124. 3 **d**; cf. also ii. 7. 4 **c**, **d**. Ppp. ends **d** with *no 'rātiḥ*. The verse is a good *triṣṭubh*, and its description by the Anukr. is absurd. Kāuç. 61. 14 uses the latter half-verse, not in a way to cast light on its meaning.

18. The seizure (*gráhi*), evil (*pāpmán*)—may we go beyond them (pl.); dissipate thou the darkness; mayest thou speak forth what is agreeable; made of forest tree, uplifted, do not injure; do not crush to pieces ⌊*vi-çṛ*⌋ the god-loving rice-grain.

Jihiṅsīr in **c** is a misprint for *jīhiṅsīr*, which all the ⌊i.e. W's⌋ mss. read. ⌊So read 9 of SPP's authorities: and 4 have *jáhiṅsīs;* but SPP. prints *jihiṅsīs*, accentless, with 3 of his mss. Perhaps the accent is to be regarded as antithetical.⌋ A part of our mss. (O.T.K.D.R.p.m.) read *çarīs* in **d**; Ppp. has *çarāis* ⌊see the references under vi. 32. 2⌋. The verse (with xi. 1. 9 **b**) accompanies in Kāuç. 61. 22 the pounding with the pestle.

19. About to become all-expanded, ghee-backed, go thou, of like origin (*sáyoni*), unto that world; hand thou (*upa-yam*) the rain-increased sieve; let that winnow away the husk, the chaff.

The first half-verse is identical with 53 **c**, **d** below. Some mss. (I.O.D.K.: also half of the Kāuç. mss.) read *palā́vām* in **d**. Ppp. has *vidvān* instead of *etaṁ* in **b**. With **c**, according to Kāuç. 61. 23, the *çūrpa* is grasped; with **a** (or the whole verse?), according to 24, it is raised; with **d**, according to 25, the sifting is done. The third pāda lacks a syllable, unless we may resolve *çu-úrpam*. ⌊For "sieve," here and in vs. 20, read rather "winnowing-basket"?⌋

20. The three worlds are commensurate with the *bráhmaṇa:* yon heaven, namely, earth, atmosphere; having seized the [soma-]stalks, take ye (du.) hold after; let them swell up (*ā-pyā*); let them come again to the sieve.

All our mss. (except D.) read *asāu*, unaccented, in **b**; emendation to *asā́u* was plainly necessary. All the *saṁhitā*-mss. (except E.) separate in **c** *gṛbhītvā́ anv-*, which, accordingly, might perhaps as well have been left, though the Prāt. does not recognize the case of irregular hiatus. Ppp. seems to combine the two words in the usual fashion; but it has *-rabhetām*; also, in **b**, *pṛthivyām ant-*. The verse is quoted in Kāuç. 61. 27 in connection with touching the winnowed grains (?); and, in 28, the last words of **d** (*punar* etc.), with scattering them, apparently, again on the sieve.

21. Manifoldly separate [are] the forms of cattle; thou becomest one-formed together with success; that red skin—that thrust thou [away]; the pressing-stone shall cleanse like a fuller (? *malagá*) the garments.

Or **b** may be 'thou comest into being one-formed with success.' *Malagá* occurs nowhere else; its use with *iva* makes it impossible to tell whether the *pada*-text would divide *mala॰gaḥ*. Ppp. reads *bhavati* in **b** and *malagāi 'va* in **d**. ⌊Again, as in vss. 13 and 26, it reads *çundhāti* for *çumbhāti:* cf. note to vi. 115. 3.⌋ The quotation in Kāuç. 61. 26 casts no light on the meaning. Our text ought to read *sáṁṛddhyā* at end of **b**. The verse is very ill named *jagatī* by the Anukr.; the treatment of *iva* in **d** as only one syllable makes a regular *triṣṭubh* of it.

22. Thee that art earth I make enter into earth; this like body of thee [is] separated; whatever of thee is burnt (? *dyuttá*), [or] scratched by driving (*árpaṇa*); with that do not leak; I cover that over by a spell (*bráhman*).

Ppp. reads, for **a**, *bhūmyām̐ bhūmim adhi dhārayāmi;* in **c**, *arpaṇam̐ ca;* in **d**, *çuçror apa tad*, thus restoring the meter. The verse (12 + 11 : 11 + 13 = 47) is very ill defined simply as a *jagatī*. In Kāuç. 61. 30, the verse accompanies the smearing of a vessel (*kumbhī*); in Vāit. 28. 12, the fashioning of a kettle.

23. Mayest thou welcome as a mother a son; I unite (*sam-dhā*) thee that art earth with the earth; a kettle, a vessel, do not stagger upon the sacrificial hearth, overhung by the implements of offering [and] by sacrificial butter.

The first pāda is apparently addressed to the earth, differently from the others. Ppp. puts the verse before our vs. 22, and reads in **c** *kumbhīr vedyām̐ sam̐ carantām̐*. One or two of our mss. (Bs.O.) read *uṣā́* in **c**.

24. Let Agni, cooking, defend thee on the east; let Indra, with the Maruts, defend on the south; may Varuṇa fix thee in the maintenance (*dharúṇa*) of the western [quarter]; on the north may Soma give thee together.

Ppp. corrects the meter of **b** by reading *rakṣāt;* and that of **d** by having *varuṇas* instead of *somas*. The verse is irregular, but by no means a *jagatī*. ⌊If we make *varuṇas* and *somas* exchange places, as suggested by Ppp., and read *rakṣāt* with Ppp., the vs. becomes a good *triṣṭubh*.⌋ In Kāuç. 61. 32 it is used when arranging the fire about the kettle.

25. Purified with purifiers, they purify themselves from the cloud; they go both to heaven and to earth [as their] worlds; them, lively, rich in life, firm-standing, poured into the vessel (*pā́tra*), let the fire kindle about.

Ppp. puts the verse after our vs. 26, and reads at end of **b** *dharmaṇā* (cf. RV. x. 16. 3 **b**), and in **c**, **d** *jīvadhānyāt sametā* ⌊cf. vs. 4⌋ *pātrā "siktāt*. The verse is defective by a syllable in **a**, but the Anukr. passes this without notice. Kāuç. 61. 34 quotes the verse to accompany putting into the strainer.

26. They come from the sky, they fasten on (*sac*) the earth; from the earth they fasten upon the atmosphere; being cleansed, they just cleanse themselves; let them conduct us to the heavenly world.

The accent of *çúmbhante* in **c** is unmotived. Ppp. reads ⌊cf. vss. 13 and 21 and note to vi. 115. 3⌋ *çundhanti*, which (or *çumbhanti*) is decidedly preferable. That the reading in **a** is *diváḥ p-* is noted in the comm. to Prāt. ii. 68.

27. Both as it were prevailing (*prabhú*) and also commensurate, also bright and clean, immortal — as such do ye, O waters, directed, helping, cook the rich-dish for the two spouses, ye of good refuge.

The translation implies in **d** emendation of *āpaḥ॰çīkṣantīḥ* to *ā́paḥ çīkṣ-*, the former seeming wholly unacceptable. Ppp. combines and reads *praçiṣṭā "pas sīkṣ-*. Our text reads with the mss.

28. The numbered drops (*stoká*) fasten on the earth, being commensurate with breaths-and-expirations, with herbs; being scattered on, unnumbered, of good color, the clean ones have obtained all cleanness.

This verse, as noted above, is wanting in Ppp. It is quoted in Kāuç. 61.36 to accompany the scattering in of the rice-grains after washing.

29. They struggle up (*ud-yudh*), they dance on, being heated; they hurl foam and abundant drops (*bindú*); like a woman that is in her season, seeing her husband, unite yourselves, O waters, with these rice-grains.

The translation assumes the emendation, made in our edited text, of *ṛ́tviyā yā́*, for the *ṛ́tviyāya* of all the mss. ⌊See SPP's note on this matter, p. 231. He says *ṛtviya* = *māithuna*.⌋ Ppp. reads *ṛtviyāvāis tāis taṇḍ-*. In Kāuç. 61.37 the verse accompanies the making of the water to boil.

30. Make thou them stand up, as they sit on the bottom; let them touch themselves all over with the waters; I have measured with vessels (*pā́tra*) the water that is here; measured are the rice-grains that are these directions.

The last pāda is translated as if *yádīmā́ḥ* (p. *yádi imā́ḥ*) were meant as equivalent to *yád imā́ḥ*, corresponding to the *yád etát* of **c**. Ppp. has *sṛjantām* at end of **b**.

⌊Here, at the end of a decad-division, ends the twenty-sixth *prapāṭhaka*.⌋

31. Reach thou forth the sickle (*párçu*), hasten, take [it] quickly; let them, not harming, cut (*dā*) the herbs at the joint; they of whom Soma compassed the kingship — let the plants be without wrath toward us.

One or two of our mss. read in **a** *páraçum* (M.W.; O. *párárçum*); and, as usual, some (O.D.R.) accent *rā́jyam* in **c**. Ppp. has *harantu* for *harāu 'ṣam* in **a**; and, in **c**, *somo yāsām*. *Amanyutāḥ* is undivided in the *pada*-text. In Kāuç. 61.38 the first pāda is used with handing over the sickle for gathering the *darbha*-grass; the second pāda,* in 61.39, with cutting it above the joints; and in 1.24, 25 both for a similar purpose; so also the first pāda (or the verse) in 8.11; and yet again both in the comm. to 137.4. *⌊Quoted as *oṣadhīr dāntu parvan* at i.25 and 61.39. According to Daç. Kar. (note to 137.4), the quotation *pra yacha parçum* covers a pāda and a half, that is, it includes the *ahiṅsantas* which is omitted in the quotation of **b**.⌋

32. Strew ye a new *barhís* for the rice-dish; be it dear to the heart, agreeable to the eye; on it let the gods [and] the divine ones (f.) settle (*viç*) together; sitting down (*ni-sad*), let them partake of this with the seasons.

The mss. read in **b** *priyā́m*, but our text makes the unavoidable emendation to *-yám*. Some of the mss. also are bothered over the unusual combination *lgva* in **b**: ⌊thus Bs. has *vaglàv astu;*⌋ R. *valgáv astu;* T. *valgvustu*. And again, in **d**, Bs. reads *-çnan ṛ́t-*, and O.s.m.R. *-çnanty ṛt-*. The verse accompanies in Kāuç. 61.40 the strewing of the *barhis*.

33. O forest tree, sit on the strewn *barhís*, being commensurate with the Agni-praises (*agniṣṭomá*), with the deities; like a form well made by an artisan (*tváṣṭṛ*) with a knife, so (*enā́*) let the eager ones be seen round about in the vessel (*pā́tra*).

Bp. and Bs.s.m. read *svádhiyā* at end of **c**. The anomalous hiatus *enā́* (p. *enā́*) *ehā́ḥ* is noted in Prāt. iii. 34. Ppp. reads *svadhityāināhyāṣ pari pātre dadṛçyām*, which is welcome as ridding us of the wholly unsupported form *dadṛçrām;* ⌊cf. *Gram.* § 813⌋. In Kāuç. 61. 43, the verse accompanies the setting of a vessel (*pātrī*) upon the *barhis;* in Vāit. 10. 7, the laying of the sacrificial post upon the same (the editor of Kāuç. regards it as quoted also in 15. 11, but the verse there intended must be rather vi. 125. 1).

34. In sixty autumns may he (?) seek unto the treasure-keepers; may he attain unto the sky with the cooked [offering]; may both fathers [and] sons live upon him; make thou this one to go unto the heaven-going end of the fire.

The last pāda admits of various other constructions. Both here and in vs. 41 (where pāda **a** is repeated) Bp. reads at the beginning *çaṣṭhyā́m*. In **c**, O.p.m.R. accent *jīvā́n*. Ppp. puts the verse after our vs. 35, and reads, for **a**, *ṣaṣṭyāṁ çaradbhyaṣ paridadhma enam;* for **c**, *upāi 'naṁ putrān pitaraç ca sīdām;* in **d**, *imam* for *etam*. There is no reason why the Anukr. should regard the verse as anything but a regular *triṣṭubh*. In Kāuç. 62. 9 it accompanies the setting down of the rice-dish westward from the fire.

35. A maintainer, maintain thyself in the maintenance of the earth; thee that art unmoved let the deities make to move (*cyu*); thee shall the two spouses, living, having living sons, cause to remove (*ud-vas*) out of the fire-holder.

Ppp. combines *-vyā 'cyutam* in **a–b**, omits the meter-disturbing (and probably intrusive) *tvā* of **c**, reads in **c** *-putrā*, and in **d** *ud vāsayāthaṣ p-*. The Anukr. takes no notice of the redundant syllable in our **c**. In Kāuç. 61. 41, the verse accompanies the removal of the vessel; in Vāit. 10. 9, the insertion of the end of the sacrificial post in the ground.

36. Thou hast come together unto all the worlds, having conquered; however many [be] the desires, thou hast made them wholly satisfied; plunge ye (du.) in — both the stirring-stick [and] the spoon; take thou him up upon one vessel.

This obscure verse wins no light from Kāuç. (62. 1), which says simply *iti mantroktam*, connecting it with xi. 1. 24. Some of our mss. (P.M.W.T.) read *abhí* for *ádhi* in **d**. We should expect in **c** *gāhetām*, as the nouns are not vocative. Ppp. reads in **a** *samāgān abhicikya*, and in **b** *kāmān samitāu purastāt*. ⌊See p. lxxxviii.⌋

37. Strew thou on, spread forward, smear over with ghee this vessel; as a lowing cow (*usrā́*) [toward] a young [calf] desiring the teat, do ye, O gods, utter the sound *hing* toward this one.

'Strew on': i.e., specifically, make an *upastaraṇa* or covering of butter. In Ppp. the second half-verse is wholly corrupt. The verse is quoted in Kāuç. 61. 45, as accompanying the operation described, and the next verse is added in 61. 46 when the operation is completed.

38. Thou hast strewn on, hast made that world; let the broad unequalled heavenly world (*svargá*) spread itself out; to it shall resort (*çri*) the mighty eagle; the gods shall reach him forth to the deities.

Ppp. begins with *apāskārāir*, and makes *çrayātāi* and *suparṇas* change places in **c**.

39. What in any case thy wife cooks beyond thee, or thy husband, O wife, in secret from thee, that do ye unite; that be yours together; agreeing (? *sampāday-*) together upon one world.

Kāuç. 62. 11 quotes the verse (*iti mantroktam*), but casts no light upon it. ⌊Has a second *pácati* fallen out after *jāye* ?⌋

40. How many of her fasten on (*sac*) the earth, what sons came forth into being from us (pl.) — all those do ye (du.) call to you in the vessel; knowing the navel, the young ones (*çíçu*) shall come together.

The mss. (excepting R.D.) leave *sacante* in **a** unaccented. Ppp. reads after it *'smat.* The verse, especially the first pāda, is obscure. 'Navel' = 'central point, place of union.' The Anukr. does not heed the deficiency of a syllable in **c**; it means us, perhaps, to resolve *ta-ā́n.*

41. What streams (*dhā́rā*) of good (*vásu*) [there are], fattened with honey, mixed with ghee, navels of immortality — all those doth the heaven-goer (? *svargá*) take possession of; in sixty autumns may he seek unto the treasure-keepers.

The last and obscurest pāda is identical with 34 **a**. The Anukr. perhaps accepts the redundant syllable of **b** and the deficient of **c** as balancing each other. The verse is used, with 44 below, in Kāuç. 62. 18, to accompany the further pouring in of juices. Ppp. reads *samaktās* for *prapīnās* in **a**, and *dhāmayas* at end of **b**, and combines *-pā 'bh-* in **d**.

42. He shall seek unto it, [as] treasure-keepers unto a treasure; let those who are others be not lords (*ánīçvara*) about; given by us, deposited, heaven-going, with three divisions it has ascended to three heavens (*svargá*).

Ppp. again combines in **a** *-pā 'bhy.* Kāuç. 62. 10 makes the verse accompany the division of the rice-dish into three parts. There is no reason for calling it *bhurij*, as the Anukr. does.

43. Let Agni burn the demon that is godless; let the flesh-eating *piçācá* not have a draught here; we thrust him, we bar him away from us; let the Ādityas, the Añgirases, fasten on him.

Doubtless we should emend to *rundhmas* in **c**. Ppp. reads in **d** *ādityā no añg-*, thus rectifying the meter. The Anukr. notices this time the redundance of the pāda. Doubtless, as often elsewhere, we are to contract to *ādityāt 'nam.* In Kāuç. 62. 14 the verse is made to accompany the carrying of fire around the offering. ⌊BR. render the force of *pra* by defining *pra-pā* as 'sich an's Trinken machen.'⌋

44. To the Ādityas, the Añgirases, I announce this honey mingled with ghee; with cleansed hands, not smiting down [anything of] the Brahman's, go ye (du.), O well-doers, unto this heavenly world (*svargá*).

The description by the Anukr. is quite wrong. The use by Kāuç. 62. 18 was noted above, under vs. 41. ⌊For the use of the genitive, W. has noted a reference to Delbrück's *Altindische Syntax*, p. 161.⌋

45. I have obtained this highest division of it, from which world the most exalted one obtained [it] completely; pour thou on the butter (*sarpís*); anoint with ghee; this is the portion of our Aṅgiras here.

Ppp. has in **a** a different order of words: *idaṁ kāṇḍam uttamaṁ prāpam asya.* The verse (with xi. 1. 31: the first half of each) is quoted in Kāuç. 62. 15, and again (the second half of each) in 62. 17, in connection with anointing the vessel with butter.

46. Unto truth, unto penance, and unto the deities, we deliver this deposit (*nidhí*), [this] treasure (*çevadhí*); let it not be lost (*ava-gā*) in our play, nor in the meeting; do not ye release it to another in preference to (*purā́*) me.

One or two of our mss. (R.D.) accent at the end *mát;* and the word is not found without accent unless here and at xi. 4. 26. ⌊SPP. reads *mát* with 8 of his authorities, against 7 that have *mat.*⌋ Ppp. reads in **b** *dadhmas.* This and the two following verses are quoted, with a number of others, in Kāuç. 68. 27, at a later point in the rice-dish ceremony. ⌊With **c**, cf. 52 **a**.⌋

47. I cook; I give; verily upon my action [and] deed (? *karúṇa*) the wife; a virgin (? *kāúmāra*) world hath been born, a son; take ye (du.) hold after vigor (*váyas*) that hath what is superior.

The translation here is purely mechanical. Ppp. puts the verse after our vs. 48, and reads in **a**, for *dadāmi*, *ud vadāmi* ⌊thus suggesting the probably correct restoration of the pāda (*aham u dadāmi*)⌋, and in **c** *putrās.* The verse (10 + 11 : 11 + 11 = 43) is very ill described by the Anukr.

48. No offense is here, nor support (? *ādhārá*), nor that one goes agreeing (*sam-am*) with friends; this vessel of ours is set down not empty; the cooked [dish] shall enter again him that cooked it.

This verse is little more intelligible than the preceding. Ppp. puts **c** after **d**, and reads at the end of **c** *astu* instead of *etat.* ⌊It is hardly worth while to discuss the accent of *ásti.*⌋

49. May we do what is dear to them that are dear; whosoever hate [us], let them go to darkness; milch-cow, draft-ox, each coming vigor (*váyas*) — let them thrust away the death that comes from men.

Or, 'that concerns, comes upon, men' (*pāúruṣeya*). The Anukr. seems to accept the two redundant syllables of **c** (*evá* an intrusion) as compensating for the deficiency in **a**. According to Kāuç. 62. 19, the verse is used of 'the milch-cow etc.' north of the fire.

50. The fires are in concord, one with another — he that fastens on the herbs, and he that [fastens on] the rivers; as many gods as send heat (*ā-tap*) in the sky — gold hath become the light of him that cooks.

Ppp. reads *sindhum* in **b**, and *dadhatu** (for *pacatas*) in **d**. In Kāuç. 62. 22, the verse (with xi. 1. 28) is made to accompany the laying on of a piece of gold; it is also quoted in 68. 27, with vss. 46–48, etc.: see note to vs. 46. The Anukr. does not notice the lack of a syllable in **a**. *⌊Intending *dadhato ?*⌋

51. This one of skins (*tvác*) hath come into being on man; not naked are all the animals (*paçú*) that are other; ye (du.) cause to wrap (*paridhā*) yourselves (*ātmán*) with authority (*kṣatrá*), a home-woven garment, the mouth of the rice-dish.

The translation is as literal as possible; but other constructions may be made in the second half-verse. Ppp. leaves the hiatus between **a** and **b**, *babhūva an-*; it combines *-gnās sarve* in **b**; and it reads in **c** *dhāpayeta*, with a division-line after it. Kāuç. 62. 23 makes the verse accompany the depositing of such a garment, with gold. ⌊Has the vs. anything to do with the legend, cited under ii. 13. 3, about the cow and her skin, which the gods took from man and gave to the cow?⌋

52. What [untruth] thou shalt speak at the dice, what at the meeting, or what untruth thou shalt speak from desire of gain — clothing yourselves (du.) in the same web (*tántu*), ye shall settle in it all pollution.

Ppp. rectifies the meter of **a** by reading *vadasi;* in **b** it has *dhane* instead of *vadās;* in **c** it gives *saha* for *abhi.* The Anukr. does not notice the deficiency in **a**. The verse is quoted in Kāuç. 63. 1 (next after vs. 51), with the explanation 'the two become dressed in the same garment.' ⌊With **a**, cf. 46 **c**.⌋

53. Win thou rain; go unto the gods; thou shalt make smoke fly up out of the skin; about to become all-expanded, ghee-backed, go thou, of like origin, unto that world.

The second half-verse is identical with 19 **a**, **b** above. Ppp. begins **b** with *tatas* instead of *tvacas;* and it has a different second half: *viçvavyacā viçvakarmā svargas sayoniṁ lokam upa yāhy ekam*, which seems less unintelligible. In Kāuç. 63. 5 the verse is quoted (together with xi. 1. 28 **b**) with the direction 'he draws off [the garment?].'

54. The heaven-goer hath variously changed his body, as he finds (? *vidé*) in himself one of another color; he hath conquered off the black one, purifying a shining one (*rúçat*); the one that is red, that I offer (*hu*) to thee in the fire.

The adjectives here are all fem., relating to 'body' (*tanū́*). The defective meter of **b** helps to make the isolated ⌊or rather, unusual?⌋ *vidé* ⌊see *Gram.* § 613⌋ suspicious; the Anukr. takes no notice of the deficiency. The first half-verse is corrupt in Ppp., so that the comparison gives us no help. In Kāuç. 63. 8 the verse accompanies the scattering on of other husks (*phalīkaraṇān*). ⌊For the form *ajāit*, see the references under vi. 32. 2.⌋

55. To the eastern quarter, to Agni as overlord, to the black [serpent] as defender, to Āditya having arrows, we commit thee here; guard ye him for us until our coming; may he lead on our appointed [life-time] here unto old age; let old age commit us unto death; then may we be united with the cooked [offering].

⌊Vss. 55–60 are partly unmetrical.⌋ We are surprised to find the pause before instead of after the phrase *etám pári dadmaḥ.* With the items in the first division of these verses are to be compared the corresponding ones in iii. 27. 1–6. The concluding pāda of the metrical refrain is identical with vi. 119. 2 **d**. The *pada*-reading at the end of the prose is *á : asmā́kam : ā́°etoḥ.* In every verse, Ppp. omits *tvā* before *diçé* (an improvement) and reads *dadhmas* for *dadmas.* In the refrain ⌊of every verse, apparently⌋, it has *dadhātv adhā* for *dadātv atha.* In this verse it combines *diçe agnaye.* The metrical description of the Anukr. is very puzzling; the part common to all the verses is 6 + 10 : 11 + 11 + 11 = 49 syllables; then the varying parts range ⌊with some resolutions⌋ from 25 to 31 syllables: all together, from 74 to 80 syllables; and *atidhṛti* is regularly 76, and *kṛti* 80; but the Anukr., after calling all *atidhṛti*, appears to call all but one *kṛti.* The verses are quoted in Kāuç. 63. 22, in connection with the rest of the hymn.

56. To the southern quarter, to Indra as overlord, to the cross-lined [serpent] as defender, to Yama having arrows, we commit thee here; guard ye etc. etc.

57. To the western quarter, to Varuṇa as overlord, to the *pṛ́dāku* as defender, to food having arrows, we commit thee here; guard ye etc. etc.

58. To the northern quarter, to Soma as overlord, to the constrictor as defender, to the thunderbolt having arrows, we commit thee here; guard ye etc. etc.

Our edition follows all the mss. in accenting *rakṣitré 'çányāi;* it should be, of course, *-trè.*

59. To the fixed quarter, to Vishṇu as overlord, to the spotted-necked [serpent] as defender, to the herbs having arrows, we commit thee here; guard ye etc. etc.

Ppp. reads *vīrudbhyas* for *oṣadhībhyas.*

60. To the upward quarter, to Brihaspati as overlord, to the white [serpent] as defender, to rain having arrows, we commit thee here; guard ye etc. etc.

⌊Here ends the third *anuvāka*, with 1 hymn and 60 verses. The quoted Anukr. says *svargaḥ ṣaṣṭiḥ*, i.e., 'the *svarga*[-hymn] is sixty.' The stem *svarga*, in one form or another, occurs a dozen times in the hymn.⌋

4. The cow (vaçā́) as belonging exclusively to the Brahmans.

[*Kaçyapa. — tripañcāçat. mantroktavaçādevatyam. ānuṣṭubham: 7. bhurij; 20. virāj; 32. uṣṇigbṛhatīgarbhā; 42. bṛhatīgarbhā.*]

Found also in Pāipp. xvii. (with slight differences of verse-order ⌊4, 6, 5, 8, 7, 9 and 17, 19, 18, 20⌋). Not noticed at all in Vāit., and in Kāuç. only once, in 66. 20, where, with x. 10, it (or the first verse) is to be spoken by the giver of a cow, after sprinkling etc.

Translated: Ludwig, p. 448; Henry, 203, 248; Griffith, ii. 120; Bloomfield, 174, 656.

1. I give [her] — thus should he say, if they have noticed (? *anu-budh*) her — [I give] the cow (*vaçā́*) to the priests (*brahmán*) that ask for her; that brings progeny, descendants.

Perhaps *ánu ábhutsata* is rather 'have recognized': i.e., have made her out to be the kind of cow that is called *vaçā́;* or there may be in it something of the meaning of *anu-jñā:* 'have approved, or taken a liking to.' ⌊Cf. MGS. i. 8. 6 and p. 150.⌋

2. He bargains away his progeny and becomes exhausted of cattle who is not willing to give the cow (*gó*) of the gods to the sons of seers that ask for her.

⌊Pādas **c**, **d** recur as 12 **a**, **b**.⌋

3. By a hornless one they are crushed for him; by a lame one he falls (? *ard*) into a pit; by a crippled one his houses are burned; by a one-eyed one his possessions are taken away (?).

The adjectives are feminine, and the sense doubtless is that as the result of giving such defective cows the thing threatened will happen. In **a**, probably the subject to be understood is *gṛhā́s*, as in **c**; **b** and **c** have perhaps become transposed — and, in that case, *svám* might be the subject also of *árdati*. ⌊Ppp. has *kāṭam*, like the Vulgate.⌋ The translation of **d** implies emendation (which seems advisable ⌊cf. W. in AJP. xiii. 302⌋) of *kāṇáyā* to *kāṇáyā́*: i.e. *kāṇáyā : ā́ : dīyate*. Ppp. has *jīyate* 'is harmed,' which would remove the difficulty. ⌊On *kūṭá*, see von Bradke, KZ. xxxiv. 157.⌋

4. Anæmia (*vilohitá*) from the station of the dung visits (*vid*) the master of kine; so is the agreement (?) of the cow; for door-damaging (?) art thou called.

Nearly everything in the second half-verse is doubtful. The majority of our mss. read *sáṁvidyam* (p. *sám॰vidyam*), but *sā́ṁ-* instead is given by M.s.m.O.s.m. and D.; and in R. *sā́ṁ-* is emended to *sāṁ-*. *Sā́ṁvidya* seems a much more probable form of stem. The Pet. Lexx. render 'possession,' which is very unsatisfactory. *Duradabhnā́* (also in vs. 19) seems pretty clearly the reading of nearly all our mss. in **c**, though it might, as usual in such cases, be *-bhrā́* in most; Bp. has (both times) apparently *-bhdnā*, and O. ⌊in vs. 4⌋ *-bdnā* or *-b-h-nā* (the *b* and *h* separate letters, as again below in xiii. 1. 25 **c**). The word is not divided in the *pada*-text. The translation given is ⌊suggested by⌋ that of the Pet. Lexx.; Ludwig renders here 'unbetrieglich' (undeceivable), but leaves the word untranslated in vs. 19. The second person *ucyáse* is quite unexpected; ⌊most of our⌋ *saṁhitā*-mss. read *hy ū́3cyáse;* ⌊and SPP's are much at variance⌋. ⌊As alternative rendering in **a**, **b**, W. notes 'from standing on her dung.'⌋ Ppp. reads, in **c**, **d**, *svāṁ vidyuṁ duritagrāhy uccase.*

5. From the station of the two feet of her, soaking (? *viklíndu*) namely visits [him]; unexpectedly (?) are they crushed who snuff at her with the mouth.

Here, too, much is obscure and doubtful. The first part might be: 'From the station of her ⌊or 'from standing on her,' as W. queries⌋, soaking of the feet visits [him],' as it is hard to see what two feet have to do with a cow. And in **d** *yā́s* can be either subject or object, and *jíghrati* either sing. or pl. I take *anāmanā́t* from root *man;* Ludwig renders it 'without becoming ill'; the Pet. Lexx. explain the word as meaning a kind of disease. Ppp. reads, in **a**, **b**, *asyā 'dhiṣṭhānād vikulaṁ dvin nāma.*

6. Whoever punches (*ā-sku*) the two ears of her, he falls under the wrath of the gods; if he thinks "I am making a mark," he makes his possessions less.

Ppp. begins *yo 'syāṣ karṇāv āskanoty*, and reads in **c** *lakṣmīṣ kurvīta.* ⌊Pāda **b** recurs as 12 **c**. For the construction, cf. 26 **d**, 47 **d**: and, *per contra*, 12 **d**, 34 **d**, and

51 c.⌋ We are to make the combination *kurve 'ti.* ⌊As to the marking of cattle's ears, cf. vi. 141. 2 and note, and Zimmer, p. 234. In a marginal note, W. compares MS. iv. 2. 9 (p. 315). The MS. passage and this vs. and the root *akṣ* are discussed by Delbrück, *Gurupūjākaumudī*, p. 48–49. — Ppp. puts the vs. between 4 and 5.⌋

7. If, for any one's advantage, any one cuts off the tail-tuft of her, then his colts die, and the wolf slays his calves.

Or (in **a**), 'for any advantage *or* use.' Ppp. makes 7 **c**, **d** and 8 **c**, **d** change places. It reads also *vālān* in **b**.

8. If of her, while being with her master, a crow hath vexed (*hīḍ*) the hair, then his boys die, [and] the *yákṣma* visits him unexpectedly (?).

As to *anāmanā́t*, see note to vs. 5. The first pāda apparently means 'in presence of her master,' and so, 'without his interference for her protection.' ⌊Ppp. combines *tataṣ k-* in **c**.⌋

9. If the lye, the dung of her a barbarian woman flings together, then is born what is deformed, what will not escape from that sin.

All our mss. appear to read distinctly *palpūl-* in **a**, yet they are never to be trusted to make the distinction between *lp* and *ly*. Apparently the word is used here for 'urine,' and the meaning is 'if such precious stuff is carelessly treated by a slave-woman (*dāsī*).' Ppp. reads *'pirūpaṁ* in **c**. We have to resolve *as-i-āḥ* to fill out the meter of **a**.

10. When being born, the cow (*vaçā́*) is born for (*abhí*) the gods together with the Brahmans; therefore she is to be given to the priests (*brahmán*); that people call the guarding (*gópana*) of one's possessions.

The *pada*-text makes the extraordinary division *gó○panam* ⌊for the sake of the play upon *go* 'cow'?⌋, as if the word were not a simple derivative from root *gup!* 'For' (*abhí*); more literally 'unto, into the possession of.'

11. They who come to the winning (*vaní*) of her, theirs is the god-made cow ⌊*vaçā́*⌋; they called it *bráhman*-scathing, if anyone keeps her to himself.

Pāda **b** seems to mean virtually 'she is by the gods made theirs.' Ppp. reads at the end (as also in vss. 21, 25) *nu priyāyate*, and *nipr-* is certainly very questionable, since no *nipriya* nor even root *prī* + *ni* occurs. The minor Pet. Lex. gives the word two totally different explanations, under *nipriyāy* and *priyāy* respectively.

12. Whoever is not willing to give the cow (*gó*) of the gods to the sons of seers that ask for her, he falls under the wrath of the gods and the fury of the Brahmans.

Ppp. reads, for **a**, **b**, *ya enāṁ yācadbhya ārṣeyebhyo nirucchati.* ⌊We had **a**, **b** above as 2 **c**, **d**, and **c** as 6 **b**.⌋

13. Whatever may be his use for the cow (*vaçā́-*), he should then seek another [cow]; she, ungiven, harms a man, if he is not willing to give her when asked for.

Ppp. has a quite different version of **a–c**: *yasyā 'nya syād vaçābhogo 'nyām icchetu barhiṣaḥ: hiṅsrā ṇi dhatsva gopatim*. We should expect *pūruṣam* at end of **c**, as elsewhere in such a position.

14. As a deposited treasure (*çevadhí*), so of the Brahmans is the cow (*vaçā́*); accordingly ⌊*etát*⌋ they come unto her, in whosesoever possession she is born.

15. They come thus unto their own property, namely the Brahmans unto the cow; as one might scathe them in any other respect (?), so is the keeping back of her.

The third pāda is unclear, and the bad meter makes the reading suspicious; yet Ppp. has the same, and varies only in combining *brāhmaṇā 'bhi* in **b**, and combining and reading *'syā 'dhirohaṇam* in **d**. Most of our mss. (all except D. and R.s.m.) have the false accent *brā́hmaṇās* in **b**; our text emends. The Anukr. takes no notice of the redundant syllable in **c**.

16. She may go about until ⌊*ā́*⌋ the space of three years, being of unrecognized (*vi-jñā*) speech (*-gada*); should he know the cow, O Nārada, then the Brahmans are to be sought.

This is obscure, but appears to mean that the cow may not betray herself as a *vaçā* for as much as three years; but, as soon as she is recognized as such, she must be delivered over to the Brahmans. The *pada*-text has in **a**, of course, *evá : ā́ : tr-*.

17. Whoever declares her to be not the cow, the deposited deposit of the gods, at him Bhava-and-Çarva, both, striding about, hurl the arrow.

18. Whoever knows not the udder of her, and likewise the teats of her, to him she yields milk with both, if he has been able to give the cow.

That is, probably, if her owner has sought no profit from her (cf. Ludwig). The first pāda is quoted under Prāt. ii. 52, as an example of *ūdho* (not *ūdhar*) before a sonant. A number of our mss. read *veda*, without accent.

19. Door-damaging (?) lies she on him, if he is not willing to give her when asked for; he does not succeed in the desires which, without having given her, he would fain accomplish (*cikīrṣa-*).

The translation implies the obviously necessary emendation of *yā́m* to *yā́n* in **d** ⌊so Ludwig⌋. As to *duradabhnā́* at the beginning, see the note to vs. 4. That the conjectural rendering is extremely unsatisfactory is plain. Ppp. has instead, for **a**, *duritavinapāçaye*; and, in **c**, **d**, apparently *kāmas sam ṛdhyate yam ad-*, thus supporting our emendation. ⌊In Ppp. this verse precedes our 18.⌋

20. The gods asked for the cow, having made the Brahman their mouth; the wrath (*héḍa*) of them all incurs (*ni-i*) the man (*mā́nuṣa*) who gives not.

The translation implies emendation in **b** to *brāhmaṇám*. Ppp. reads in **a** *yācanti*, which does not rectify the meter. ⌊Read *devā́so*?⌋

21. He incurs the wrath of cattle (*paçú*) who gives not the cow to the Brahmans — if a mortal keeps to himself the deposited portion of the gods.

The *saṁhitā*-mss. accent in **b** *brāhmaṇébhyo dadat*, and the *pada* correspondingly *adadat* (instead of *ádadat*). Our text makes the necessary emendation. Ppp. gives for **d** *ṛtāse nu priyāyate.* ⌊See note to 11, above.⌋

22. If a hundred other Brahmans should ask the cow of its master, yet (*átha*) the gods said of her: the cow is his who knoweth thus.

All our mss. save two (I. and [?] E.s.m.) read *etām* (without accent) in **c**; our text follows the two.

23. Whoever, not having given her to one who knoweth thus, then shall give the cow to others, hard to go upon for him in his station is the earth with its deity.

In **b** the *pada*-text has *anyébhyaḥ : adadat*, and the *saṁhitā*-mss. correspondingly *-bhyo dadad v-*; this is emended in our text to *-bhyó 'd-* (as if *ádadat*, as in vs. 21); but a decidedly better emendation would be to *-bhyo dádat*, as translated. Ppp. reads *anyasmāi d-*, which favors this understanding of the pāda; it also combines *tasmā 'dh-* in **c**.

24. The gods asked the cow [of him] in whose possession she was first (*ágre*) born; that same one may Nārada know; together with the gods he drove her away.

The connection of **c**, **d** is obscure, and tempts to conjectural emendations; Ludwig suggests *vidvā́n* for *vidyāt*: 'knowing her to be such, Nārada together with the gods drove her away (as theirs)'; this is quite acceptable. Ppp. reads at the end *udājitā̦*. One or two of our mss. (D.R.p.m.) accent *nāradáḥ*. The Anukr. takes no notice of the lack of a syllable in **a**. ⌊Read *devā́so* as in 20?⌋

25. The cow makes a man (*pū́ruṣa*) destitute of descendants, poor in cattle, if, when she is asked for by the Brahmans, then he keeps her to himself.

Ppp. reads in **b** *pāuruṣam*, and in **d** *nu priyāyata*. The Anukr. takes no notice of any deficiency in **c**; we may best resolve *br-āh-*. ⌊Read *brāhmaṇébhiç ?*⌋

26. For Agni-and-Soma, for Love (*kā́ma*), for Mitra and for Varuṇa — for these the Brahmans ask her; under their wrath falls he who gives not.

27. So long as the master of her should not himself overhear the verses (*ṛ́c*), so long may she go about among his kine (*gó*); she may not abide in his house after he has heard.

The translation implies the evidently necessary emendation of *vaçet* at the end to *vaset;* R., indeed, has the latter; ⌊and so have 8 of SPP's authorities, against 7 with *vaçet;*⌋ Ppp. is corrupt: *nā 'sya çrutā gṛhe sya.* The Anukr. takes no notice of any redundancy in **b**; but it can hardly expect us to make a pāda-division between *no* and *'paçṛṇuyāt.* The 'verses' are doubtless those with which the Brahmans come to claim their rightful property.

28. If any one, having overheard the verses of her, has then made her go about among his kine (*gó*), both the life-time and the growth of him do the gods, made wrathful, cut off (*vraçc*).

Nearly all our mss. (E. has *ácī-*) ⌊and all of SPP's⌋ leave *acīcarat* in **b** unaccented; and then, as if by way of compensation, they mostly (except Bs.s.m.D.R.) accent *vṛ́çcanti*.

29. The cow, going about variously, the deposited deposit of the gods, manifests her forms, when she desires to go (?) to her station (*sthā́man*).

That is, her rightful and appointed place. The translation implies in **b** the reading *kṛṇute* instead of *kṛṇuṣva*, although the former is found only in O.p.m.D.T. (*-uti*). ⌊Three of SPP's *pada*-mss. have *kṛṇute*.⌋ The comm. to Prāt. ii. 63 quotes *āviṣ kṛṇute rūpāṇi*, which is not found in the text unless here. The translation also implies at the end *jigāṅsati*. The Prāt. (i. 86) seems to imply the occurrence in the text of such forms, and the sense obviously calls for them here and in the next verse; see the note to Prāt. i. 86. Ppp. reads in **d** *yathā* for *yadā*.

30. She manifests herself when she desires to go to her station; then the cow ⌊*vaçā́*⌋ makes up her mind for the asking of the priests (*brahmán*).

That is, prepares herself to be asked for by them; *brahmábhyas*, dat. by attraction. ⌊Read again *jigāṅsati*: see note to vs. 29.⌋ Read in **d** *yācñyā́ya*, though the mss. mostly have *-ñcy-*, as they often blunder over such an unusual consonant-group. Ppp. reads *uto* for *atho* in **c**.

31. She plans (*sam-kḷp*) [it] with her mind; then she goes unto the gods; thence the priests (*brahmán*) go on to ask for the cow.

32. By offering of *svadhā́* to the Fathers, by sacrifice to the deities, by giving of the cow, the noble (*rājanyà*) does not incur (*gam*) the mother's wrath.

Ppp. reads *devebhyaḥ* at end of **b**. The description of the Anukr. very unnecessarily forbids us to resolve *-bhi-aḥ* in **b**.

33. The cow is mother of the noble; so came it (n.) into being in the beginning; they call it a non-abandonment (? *ánarpaṇa*) of her that she is presented to the priests (*brahmán*).

The Pet. Lexx. render the difficult *ánarpaṇa* by 'a not giving away'; Ludwig, by 'no restitution.' Ppp. combines *tasyā "hur* in **c**.

34. As one might snatch (? *ā-lup*) from the spoon sacrificial butter held forth for the fire, so he who gives not the cow ⌊*vaçā́*⌋ ⌊to the priests⌋ falls under the wrath of Agni.

Perhaps, 'as [the fire] might snatch,' etc. — seizing on the butter before it is duly offered. Ppp. reads for **a** *yad ājyaṁ pratijagrāha*, and in **d** omits *ā*, thus rectifying the meter. The Anukr. takes no notice of the redundant syllable in our text; we are doubtless to get rid of it by contracting to *agnáy' ā́*. ⌊Were emendation necessary, one might be tempted to suggest *agnā́v ā́*: but cf. note to vs. 6 **b**.⌋

35. With the sacrificial cake as calf, milking well, she draws near to him in the world; she yields (*duh*) to him all his desires — [namely,] the cow ⌊*vaçā́*⌋ to him who has presented her.

Ppp. reads, in **b**, *loke 'syo 'pa;* and, for **c**, *sahasmāi sarvān kāmān mahe.* The Anukr. takes no notice of the irregular meter in pādas **a** and **c**. All the *saṁhitā*-mss. accent *loké 'smā* in **b**; our text emends to *lokè*.

36. All his desires, in Yama's realm, does the cow ⌊*vaçā́*⌋ yield to him who has presented her; likewise they call hell the world of him who keeps her back when asked for.

The *pada*-text reads *nárakam*, and the difference of the two texts is noted in Prāt. iii. 21; iv. 90. Ppp. reads *tathā* for *atha* in **c**.

37. Being impregnated, the cow ⌊*vaçā́*⌋ goes about angry at her master: thinking me barren, let him be bound in the fetters of death.

38. And he who, thinking her barren, cooks the cow ⌊*vaçā́*⌋ at home (*amā́*)—his sons and sons' sons also does Brihaspati cause to be asked for.

Ppp. reads in **b**, for *amā ca*, the equivalent *gṛheṣu;* further, in **c**, **d**, *asya svaputrān pāutrāç cātayate bṛh-*. ⌊Over "at home" W. interlines "in private": see vs. 53.⌋

39. She sends down great heat, going about a cow (*gó*) among kine; further, to the master who has not given her the cow (*vaçā́*) milks poison.

In **b**, apparently, 'being treated as an ordinary cow.' The 'milks' in **d** does not necessarily mean that she gives actual milk. Ppp. reads *tato* in **c**, for *atho ha*, thus rectifying the meter; the Anukr. takes no notice of the redundancy of the pāda, caused by the apparently intrusive *ha*.

40. It is a thing dear to the cattle that she is presented to the priests (*brahmán*); further, that is a thing dear to the cow ⌊*vaçā́*⌋, that she be an oblation to the gods.

Lit. 'among the gods' (p. *deva°trā́*).

41. What cows the gods shaped out (*ut-kl̥p*), rising up from the sacrifice, of them Nārada selected for himself the fearful *vilipti*.

The root *kl̥p* (*kalpay-*) with *ud* occurs nowhere else. In **c**, P.M.W.I.E.p.m.R. read *viliptím*, which would be the more normal accus. of *-tí*, but the meter is against it. But the accent *-tyám* is entirely inadmissible; it must be emended to *-tyàm*; ⌊cf. JAOS. x. 379, 369⌋. What sort of a cow (*vaçā́*) is intended by *vilipti* (which ought to signify 'smeared over') is altogether obscure. Ppp. reads instead *vilapatiṁ*.

42. The gods questioned (*mīmāṅs-*) about her: is this a cow ⌊*vaçā́*⌋, or not a cow? Of her Nārada said: she is of cows the most truly cow (*vaçátama*).

The more proper reading in **b** would seem to be *ávaçā́3iti;* but all the *saṁhitā*-mss. read *ávaçé 'ti*, as in our text, although the *pada* gives the sign of protraction (*3*) also after *avaçā*, as it should be. But the Prāt. (i. 97) requires *-çé 'ti* simply: see the rules i. 97 and 105, and the notes to them. The verse (8 + 8 : 7 + 10) is very ill described by the Anukr. Ppp. reads in **a** *devā 'mīm-*; for **b**, *vaçe 'yāṁ ntavaçe 'ti*; and it omits *iti* at the end. ⌊For the use of the superlative in **d**, cf. the punning lampoon on the name of Gotama, *Indische Sprüche*², 4875.⌋

43. How many, pray (*nú*), Nārada, are the cows which thou knowest, born among men (*manuṣyà-*)? those I ask of thee who knowest; of which may a non-Brahman not partake (*aç*)?

Ppp. reads, for **c**, *katimā "sāṁ bhīmatamā* (like our vs. 45 **c**).

44. The *viliptī́*, O Brihaspati, and the cow ⌊*vaçā́*⌋ that has given birth to [such] a cow — of that one a non-Brahman who should hope for prosperity (*bhū́ti*) may not partake.

The translation implies at the beginning emendation to *viliptī́ yā́* (as in vs. 46); the proper reading might also be *viliptyàs*, nom. pl.; *-tyā́s* seems inadmissible; Ppp. reads *vilaptyā* (for *-ās*?). Ppp. has further *tā́sāṁ* for *tasyās* in **c**. *Sūtávaçā* is rendered according to the requirement of the accent; the Pet. Lexx. define as 'a cow remaining barren after the birth of one calf'; and the legends told in explanation of the name in TS. vi. 1. 3⁶ and MS. ii. 5. 4 support that understanding. ⌊Cf. Henry's translation, p. 208, and note, p. 256.⌋ Pāda **c** is redundant in this verse, as are also 46 **c** and 43 **d**; the Anukr. heeds none of these cases.

45. Homage be to thee, O Nārada; [be] the cow to him who at once knows it. Which one of them is the most fearful, not having given which, one would perish?

Ppp. reads in **a** *te 'stu*, and in **b** *vaçām*, which is easier (Ludwig translates ⌊as if the text were *vaçā́ḥ*⌋). In **d**, our text might better read *ádattvā*.

46. She that is *viliptī́*, O Brihaspati, further the cow that has given birth to [such] a cow — of that one a non-Brahman who should hope for prosperity may not partake.

Ppp. reads at the beginning *viluptiṁ bṛhaspataye yā ca sū-*, and in **c** again (as in vs. 44) *tāsāṁ*.

47. Three verily are the kinds of cow: the *viliptī́*, she that has given birth to [such] a cow, the [simple] cow ⌊*vaçā́*⌋; these one should present to the priests (*brahmán*), [then] he falls not under the wrath of Prajāpati.

Ppp. once more reads *viluptīs sū-* in **b**; it is easier to conjecture a meaning for *viluptī* than for *viliptī*. Most of our *saṁhitā*-mss. accent *só 'nāv-* in **d**; our text makes the necessary correction to *sò*. The irregularities of **b** and **c** are unnoticed in the Anukr.; ⌊or rather, it lets them balance each the other⌋.

48. This, O Brahmans, is your oblation — so, when asked ⌊therefor⌋, should he think, if they should ask of him the cow, which in the house of him who has not given her is fearful.

49. The gods talked about the cow in wrath, saying: he hath not given it to us; with these verses (*ṛ́c*) [they talked about] Bheda; therefore indeed he perished.

Ppp. reads *upa* for *pari* in **a**, and, for **b**, *sa no rājata heḍitā*; and in **c** it rectifies the meter by giving *bhedasya*. The Anukr. does not heed the deficiency in our verse.

50. And Bheda gave her not, when asked by Indra for the cow ⌊*vaçā́*⌋; for that offense the gods cut him off in the contest for superiority.

Some of our mss. (Bp.E.D.K.) read *etām* (unaccented) in **a**; nearly all (not Bs.s.m.D.) accent *āgasó 'vṛçcan* in **d**. Ppp. has at the beginning *utāi 'tāṁ bh-*; its second half-verse is corrupt.

51. They who, wheedling, advise (*vad*) to the non-giving of the cow ⌊*vaçā́*⌋, the villains fall under the fury of Indra through ignorance.

Ppp. combines in **a** *vaçāyā 'dā-*, and in **c–d** *jālmā "vṛç-*.

52. They who, leading away her master, then say: do not give—they, through ignorance, go to meet the hurled missile of Rudra.

Pari yanti is rendered as if *prati y-*, for which it is perhaps a misreading. Ppp. reads *cetasas* for *acittyā*. Part of our mss. (Bp.R.K.) leave *āhus* unaccented, and all have *te* instead of *té* in **c**.

53. If as offered (*hu*) and if as unoffered one cooks the cow ⌊*vaçā́*⌋ in private (*amā́*), coming into collision with the gods accompanied by the Brahmans, he goes supine (*jihmá*) out of the world.

All the *saṁhitā*-mss. curiously read in **c** *sábrāhmaṇānn* (O. *-ṇāṁn*) *ṛtvā́*; the *pada*-text has *sá*◦*brāhmaṇān : ṛtvā́*. ⌊For *amā́*, cf. vs. 38.⌋

⌊Here ends the fourth *anuvāka*, with 1 hymn and 53 verses. The quoted Anukr. says *saptabhir ūnā tu "vaçāḥ,"* i.e. 'the cows[-hymn] is a [sixty] deficient by seven.'⌋

5. The Brahman's cow.

[*Atharvācārya.* — sapta paryāyāḥ. brahmagavīdevatāḥ.*]

⌊Partly metrical: vss. 15–17, 47–53, 55–70 are so reckoned by W. in the *Index*, p. 6.⌋ Found also in the main in Pāipp. xvi., but in the central parts with omissions and disorder of which the details are not given; ⌊vss. 58, 60, 64–73 are wanting⌋. Not quoted at all by Vāit., nor probably by Kāuç., since 'the two Brahman-cow hymns' mentioned in Kāuç. 48. 13 are doubtless v. 18, 19; although the comm. ⌊Dārila: cf. Keçava, p. 351[20]⌋ declares these ⌊v. 18, 19⌋ to constitute one of the 'two,' and xii. 5 the other. *⌊The Berlin ms. reads *prāguktarṣibrahmagavīdevatāḥ*: so also SPP's citation, Critical Notice, p. 21. This seems to mean that Kaçyapa is the *ṛṣi*; h. 4 clearly has the same "deity" as this.⌋

Translated: Muir, i². 288 (vss. 4–15); Ludwig, p. 529 (vss. 47–73); Henry, 209, 257; Griffith, ii. 127.

[**Paryāya I.** — *ṣaṭ. 1. prājāpatyā 'nuṣṭubh; 2. bhurik sāmny anuṣṭubh; 3. 4-p. svarāḍ uṣṇih; 4. āsury anuṣṭubh; 5. sāmnī pan̄kti.* ⌊For 6, see under that verse.⌋]

1. By toil, by penance [is she] created, acquired by *bráhman*, supported (*çritá*) on righteousness.

All our *saṁhitā*-mss. combine *vittá ṛté.* The appearance of meter in the verse (8 + 8) is perhaps not accidental; but there is no metrical structure elsewhere in the section.

2. Covered with truth, enclosed with fortune, enveloped with glory.

Why the verse is called *sāmnī* rather than *prājāpatyā*, like its predecessor, cannot be told. The *pada*-text does not divide *prā́vṛtā*, although, in the apparently parallel case, it divides *pári○vṛtā*.

3. Set about with *svadhā́*, surrounded with faith, guarded by consecration, standing firm in the offering, the world her post (*nidhā́na*).

The *pada*-mss. absurdly write *prátiosthitāḥ* (instead of *-tā*). The metrical description of the Anukr. is not less absurd; to make the required 30 syllables, we have to resolve *pári-ūḍhā*.

4. *Bráhman* her guide, the Brahman her over-lord.

Ppp. combines *brāhmaṇo adh-*. The *á-* needs to be restored in order to make the 13 syllables required by the definition of the Anukr.

5. Of the Kshatriya who takes to himself that Brahman-cow, who scathes the Brahman, —

6. There departs the happiness (*sūnṛ́tā*), the heroism, the good luck.

⌊The London Anukr. text reads *prathamā bhāu prājāpatyānuṣṭu pakrāmatīti* (vs. 6) *satyena* (etc., vs. 2): may be the *pratīka* of vs. 6 is misplaced and should be put before [*u*]*bhāu* (vs. 6 can be stretched to 16 syllables), or else the definition of 6 is fallen out.⌋ Ppp. reads *puṇyalakṣmī*.

[**Paryāya II.**—*pañca.* *7. sāmnī triṣṭubh; 8, 9. ārcy anuṣṭubh (8. bhurij); 10. uṣṇih;* ⌊*7–10. 1-p.:* see under vs. 11;⌋ *11. ārcī nicṛt pañkti.*]

7. Both force, and brilliancy, and power, and strength, and speech, and sense (*indriyá*), and fortune, and virtue (*dhárma*), —

8. And holiness (*bráhman*), and dominion ⌊*kṣatrám*⌋, and kingdom, and subjects (*víças*), and brightness (*tvíṣi*), and glory, and honor, and property, —

9. And life-time, and form, and name, and fame, and breath, and expiration, and sight, and hearing, —

10. And milk, and sap, and food, and food-eating, and righteousness, and truth, and sacrifice (*iṣṭá*), and bestowal (*pūrtá*), and progeny, and cattle: —

11. All these depart from the Kshatriya who takes to himself the Brahman-cow, who scathes the Brahman.

Lit. 'all these of the K.,' 'that belong to him.' Ppp. omits vs. 10, and abbreviates vs. 9 to *āyuç ca çrotraṁ ca*, and vs. 11 to *tāni sarvāṇy apa krāmanti kṣatriyasya.* All our *saṁhitā*-mss. read in vs. 10 *ca ṛtám.* The Anukr. says of vss. 7–10, *etāç catasraḥ punaḥ punaḥ pādāntareṇa padābhyāsād ekapadāḥ:* ⌊that is, they are *1-p.* because repeatedly or in each case the groups ending with *ca* have to be recited with a pāda-interval, i.e. (as Dr. Ryder suggests) because there is in each verse no main cesura⌋.

[**Paryāya III.** — *ṣoḍaça.* *12. virāḍ viṣamā gāyatrī;* *13. āsury anuṣṭubh;* *14, 26. sāmny uṣṇih;* *15. gāyatrī;* *16, 17, 19, 20. prājāpatyā 'nuṣṭubh;* *18. yājuṣī jagatī;* *21, 25 sāmny anuṣṭubh;* *22. sāmnī bṛhatī;* *23. yājuṣī triṣṭubh;* *24. āsurī gāyatrī;* *27. ārcy uṣṇih.*]

12. This same Brahman-cow [is] fearful, having deadly poison, witchcraft incarnate (*sākṣā́t*), *kū́lbaja* when covered.

Kū́lbaja occurs only here and in vs. 53 below; in the latter verse, Ppp. reads instead *pūlyājām.*

13. In her are all terrible things and all deaths.

14. In her are all cruel things, all men-killers (*puruṣavadhá*).

15. This Brahman-cow, when taken to oneself, binds the Brahman-scather, the god-reviler, in the shackle of death.

Several of the *saṁhitā*-mss. (Bs.P.M.W.E.) read *-gavy ā̀3dīyá-*, curiously enough. All our mss. have *pádv-*, and one or two *-vīñç-* or *-viñç-*. The verse admits of being read as a *gāyatrī*, probably not by accident, and might better have been printed as such.

16. Verily (*hí*) a hundred-killing weapon (*mení*) is she; verily the destruction of the Brahman-scather is she.

17. Therefore indeed is the cow of the Brahmans hard to be dared against by one who understands (*vi-jñā*).

18. [She is] a thunderbolt when running, Vāiçvānara when driven up (*údvīta*).

19. A missile when extracting (*ut-khid*) her hoofs, the great god when looking away.

20. Keen-edged (*kṣurápavi*) when looking; when bellowing, she thunders at one.

Bp. reads *vā́sya-*. Vss. 19 and 20 were perhaps intended as metrical (8 + 8). ⌊As to *mení*, vs. 16, cf. Geldner, *Festgruss an Böhtlingk*, p. 32.⌋

21. Death when uttering *hing;* the formidable god when slinging about her tail.

All the *saṁhitā*-mss. read *-tyù3gró* ⌊K. *ùg-*⌋. This verse also has 16 syllables, divisible into 8 + 8, but evidently only by accident.

22. Total scathing when twisting about her ears; king-*yákṣma* when urinating.

The Anukr. does not heed that the verse has one syllable too many for a regular *sāmnī bṛhatī.*

23. A weapon (*mení*) when being milked; headache when milked.

24. Debility when approaching (*upa-sthā*); mutual strife when felt of.

Párāmṛṣṭā might also come from root *mṛj* and mean 'rubbed off.'

25. A shaft when her mouth is being fastened up; mishap (*ṛ́ti*) when being slain.

The *pada*-text has *api◦nahyámāne*, and two or three of our *saṁhitā*-mss. (P.M.O.p.m.K.R.) retain the *e* before *ṛ́tir*.

26. Deadly poisonous when falling down; darkness when fallen down.

27. Going after him, the Brahman-cow exhausts the breaths of the Brahman-scather.

[**Paryāya IV.** — *ekādaça.* *28. āsurī gāyatrī; 29, 37. āsury anuṣṭubh; 30. sāmny anuṣṭubh; 31. yājuṣī triṣṭubh; 32. sāmnī gāyatrī; 33, 34. sāmnī bṛhatī; 35. bhurik sāmny anuṣṭubh; 36. sāmny uṣṇih; 38. pratiṣṭhā gāyatrī.*]

28. [She is] hostility when being cut up, the eating of one's children when being shared out.

Two of the *pada*-texts (D.Kp.) read *pāútra◦ādyam.* It is so difficult in most mss. to distinguish *dy* and *gh*, that the reading *pāútrāgham* (cf. *pāútram aghám*, xii. 3. 14), which Pet. Lex. conjectures as an emendation, might possibly be intended here.

29. A gods' missile when being taken, failure when taken.

The participles, especially the present passive ones, in these verses, are very much bungled over by the mss. For *hriyámāṇā* here are read *hriy-*, *hrīy-*, *hṛy-*, *hiy-*; and Bp. has *ṛtā́* for *hṛtā́*. It is necessary to make the awkward renderings with 'being,' to distinguish present participle from past. The definition of the Anukr. implies the resolution *vi-ṛd-*.

30. Evil when being set on, harshness when being set down.

31. Poison when heating (? *pra-yas*), *takmán* when heated.

All the mss. read *práyastā*, but Bp. has *pra◦yáñchantī*, Bs. *-yachantī*, emended to *-yasy-*, P.M.W. *-yásyañchantī* (M. emended to *-yasy-* ⌊?⌋).

32. Evil (*aghá*) when being cooked, bad dreaming when cooked.

The description of the Anukr. implies the resolution *-pni-am.*

33. Uprooting when being turned about (? *pari-ā-kṛ*), destruction when turned about.

The participles are rendered according to the Pet. Lexx. The Anukr. expects us to resolve *pari-ā-* once, but not both times. Bp. reads *-ākrīyá-*.

34. Discord by smell; pain (*çúc*) when being taken up, a poison-snake when taken up.

The *pada*-text leaves both participles undivided, as prescribed by Prāt. iv. 62. 'Taken up,' doubtless in preparation for being served up as food. Bp. reads *udhrīyá-*.

35. Non-prosperity when being served up, disaster when served up.

The mss. again fluctuate between *-hriyá-*, *-hrīyá-*, *-hiyá-*, and, at the end, between *-hṛtā*, *-hatā* (P.M.p.m.W.), and *-hūtā* (D.). The Anukr. notices this time that the verse is *bhurij.*

36. Çarva angered when being dressed (*piç*), Çimidā when dressed.

37. Ruin when being partaken of, perdition when partaken of.

38. When partaken of, the Brahman-cow cuts off the Brahman-scather from the world, from both this one and the one yonder.

Bp. appears to read *lokā́n*, and M.R.T. correspondingly *-ā́ṅ ch-*; O. ⌊D.Kp.⌋ have *-ā́t ch-*; the rest *-ā́ ch-*, which means *-ā́c ch-*, since *ch* and *cch* are equivalent and exchangeable. The metrical definition of the Anukr. is ambiguous.

[**Paryāya V.** — *aṣṭa. 39. sāmnī pañkti; 40. yājuṣy anuṣṭubh; 41, 46. bhurik sāmny anuṣṭubh; 42. āsurī bṛhatī; 43. sāmnī bṛhatī; 44. pipīlikamadhyā 'nuṣṭubh; 45. ārcī bṛhatī.*]

39. The slaying of her is witchcraft, her cutting up (*āçásana*) is a weapon (*mení*), the contents of her bowels a secret charm.

All of these, of course, understood as directed against the offender. Ppp. combines *tasyā "han-*.

40. [She is] homelessness when hidden (?*pari-hnu*).

The Pet. Lexx. conjecture *pari-hnu* (not found elsewhere) to mean 'disavow, disown.'

41. The Brahman-cow, having become the flesh-eating Agni, entering into the Brahman-scather, eats him.

42. All his limbs, joints, roots, she cuts off (*vraçc*).

43. She severs (*chid*) his paternal connection, makes perish his maternal connection.

44. All the marriages, acquaintances of the Brahman-scather does the Brahman-cow scorch (?*api-kṣā*), when not given back by a Kshatriya.

Some of our mss. (O.D.T.R.) accent *-dīyámānā*, although part of them (O.T.R.) have accented *-trī́yeṇā́ 'pun-*. The description of the passage (7 + 6 : 8 + 10 = 31) by the Anukr. is very strange, and valueless.

45. Without abode, without home, without progeny, she makes him; he becomes without succession (?); he is destroyed:—

The translation of *aparāoparaṇá* (so the *pada*-text) is according to the conjecture of the Pet. Lexx. The metrical definition of the Anukr. implies reading *karoti ap-*.

46. Whatever Kshatriya takes to himself the cow of a Brahman who knoweth thus.

[**Paryāya VI.** — *pañcadaça. 47, 49, 51–53, 57–59, 61 (?). prājāpatyā 'nuṣṭubh; 48. ārṣy anuṣṭubh; 50. sāmnī bṛhatī; 54, 55. prājāpatyo 'ṣṇih; 56. āsurī gāyatrī; 60. gāyatrī.*]

47. Quickly, indeed, at his killing the vultures make a din (*āilabá*).

Ppp. reads at the end *kurvatāi 'lavaṁ*. The text of the Anukr. seems defective here. All that is said about the nine verses of 16 syllables is as follows: *ādyā skandhogrīvīs tvayā pramūrṇam* ⌊vs. 61⌋ *prājāpatyānuṣṭubhaḥ*. All the verses not of this measure are regularly described. Ludwig translates this whole section ⌊and the next⌋, p. 529.

48. Quickly, indeed, about his place of burning dance the long-haired women, beating on the breast with the hand, making an evil din.

The mss. write no *avasāna*-mark between the two halves of the verse. Ppp. again reads *āilavam*. Prāt. iii. 92 notes the non-lingualization of *nṛt* after *pari*. ⌊Bloomfield discusses the vs., AJP. xi. 339 or JAOS. xv., p. xlv.⌋

49. Quickly, indeed, in his abodes do the wolves make a din.

Ppp. reads, after *vāstuṣu*, *gan̄gānaṁ kurvate 'pa vṛṣāt*.

50. Quickly, indeed, they ask about him: what that was, is this now that?

We should expect rather *kíṁ tád āsī3t* ⌊instead of *yát tád* etc.⌋, since without a question there is no good reason for the protracted *ī*. Ludwig translates as if that were the reading. O.D.R. accent *ā́sī3d*, as is the rule in the Brāhmaṇas. Ppp. reads, after *pṛchanti*, *etad āsīd ataṁ nu dā*.

51. Cut thou, cut on, cut forth, scorch, burn (*kṣā*).

52. O daughter of An̄giras, exhaust thou the Brahman-scather, that takes to himself [the cow].

Ppp. reads *ādadhānam*.

53. For thou art called belonging to all the gods, witchcraft, *kū́lbaja* when covered.

Cf. vs. 12 above. Ppp. reads (as there noted) *pūlyājām*.

54. Burning (*uṣ*), consuming, thunderbolt of the *bráhman*.

55. Having become a keen-edged death, run thou out.

Ppp. reads *vibhāvasuḥ* instead of *vi dhāva tvam*; the latter reading probably carries on the figure implied in *kṣurapavi*, which applies especially to the armed wheels of a battle-chariot.

56. Thou takest to thyself the honor of the scathers, their sacrifice and bestowal, their expectations.

Iṣṭám pūrtáṁ ca: i.e., as later, the fruits of these good works. The Anukr. would have done much better to accept the resolution *ca āç-*, and reckon the verse as 16 syllables.

57. Taking to thyself what is scathed for him who is scathed, thou presentest [it to him] in yonder world.

58. O inviolable one, become thou the guide of the Brahman out of imprecation.

The translation implies emendation of *abhíçastyā* to *-tyāḥ*. The verse is wanting in Ppp.

59. Become thou a weapon (*mení*), a shaft; become thou deadly poisonous from evil (*aghá*).

60. O inviolable one, smite forth the head of the Brahman-scather that has committed offense, of the god-reviler, the ungenerous.

This verse also is wanting in Ppp. ⌊Pādas **b**, **c** recur below, vs. 65.⌋

61. Let Agni burn the malevolent one, slaughtered, crushed (*mṛd*) by thee.

Ppp. reads *tayā pravṛkṇo rucitam agnir dahatu duṣkṛtam.*

[**Paryāya VII.** — *dvādaçakaḥ. 62–64, 66, 68–70. prājāpatyā 'nuṣṭubh ; 65. gāyatrī ; 67. prājāpatyā gāyatrī ; 71. āsurī pañkti ; 72. prājāpatyā triṣṭubh ; 73. āsury uṣṇih.*]

62. Cut (*vraçc*) thou, cut off, cut up; burn thou, burn off, burn up.

63. The Brahman-scather, O divine inviolable one, do thou burn up all the way from the root.

Or 'to the root.' Bs.P.M. read *mūlān*. In Ppp., ⌊vss. 62–63 are somewhat altered and⌋ the remaining vss. are wanting.

64. That he may go from Yama's seat to evil worlds, to the distances.

65. So do thou, O divine inviolable one, of the Brahman-scather that has committed offense, of the god-reviler, the ungenerous, —

66. With a thunderbolt hundred-jointed, sharp, razor-pronged, —

67. Smite forth the shoulder-bones, forth the head.

68. His hairs (*lóman*) do thou cut up (*sam-chid*); his skin strip off; —

69. His flesh cut in pieces; his sinews wrench off; —

70. His bones distress (*pīḍ*); his marrow smite out; —

71. All his limbs, [his] joints unloosen.

72. Let the flesh-eating Agni thrust him from the earth, burn (*uṣ*) up; let Vāyu [do so] from the atmosphere, the great expanse (*varimán*); —

73. Let the sun thrust him forth from the sky, burn him down.

The Anukr. accepts the resolution *ní osatu.*

⌊The quotations from the Old Anukr. for the seven *paryāyas* may here be given together: I. *vacanāni ca ṣaṭ;* II. *pañca;* III. *ṣoḍaça;* IV. *ekādaça;* V. *aṣṭa ca;* VI. *brahmagavyām pañcadaça;* VII. *tasmād dvādaçakaḥ paraḥ.* The sum is 73. — As is readily seen, these quotations together make an *anuṣṭubh çloka;* and they are printed in metrical form by SPP., vol. i., p. 21 (Critical Notice). For *vacanāni*, see above, p. 472.⌋

⌊Here ends the fifth *anuvāka*, with 1 hymn (or 7 *paryāyas*) and 73 *vacanas* or *vacana-avasānarcas.*⌋

⌊By some mss. the book is summed up as of 4 *artha-sūktas* [their vss. number 231] and 7 *paryāya-sūktas* [73 "verses"], or as of "11 *sūktas* of both kinds," with a total of 304 verses.⌋

⌊The twenty-seventh *prapāṭhaka* ends here.⌋

Book XIII.

⌊Hymns to the Ruddy Sun or Rohita.⌋

⌊We come now to the third grand division of the text, books xiii.–xviii. In the first division (books i.–vii.) we had the short hymns of miscellaneous subjects, and in the second (books viii.–xii.) we had the long hymns of miscellaneous subjects. In the third, the principle governing the arrangement and division of the material is in the main clearly that of unity of subject (compare the General Introduction and the Table of Contents): thus book xiii. consists of hymns to the Ruddy Sun or Rohita; xiv. consists of wedding verses; xv. is the book about the Vrātya; and xviii. consists of hymns for the dead. Accordingly, it is perhaps worthy of note that the Old Anukramaṇī does not describe the length of any hymn in book xiii. by reference to a certain length assumed as a norm. The whole book has been translated by Victor Henry, *Les hymnes Rohitas. Livre XIII de l'Atharva-véda traduit et commenté*, Paris, 1891. Henry's work was made the subject of a detailed review by Bloomfield in the *American Journal of Philology* (xii. 429–443) for 1891. Then, at Paris in 1892, appeared *Le mythe de Rohita, traduction raisonnée du 13e livre de l'Atharva-véda*, by Paul Regnaud. As appears below, Ludwig's translation covers the first three of the four hymns of the book; Deussen's, the first and third; and Bloomfield's, the first. For books xii.–xvi. inclusive, the *bhāṣya* is wanting.⌋

⌊**Paryāya-hymns**: for details respecting them, see pages 471–2. The fourth or last hymn of this book is a *paryāya-sūkta* with 6 *paryāyas*. For the discrepancy of numeration as between the two editions, see page 611.⌋

⌊The *anuvāka*-division of the book is into four *anuvākas* of one hymn each, and is thus (like the *anuvāka*-division of book xii.) coincident with the hymn-division. A conspectus for book xiii. follows:

Anuvākas	1	2	3	4
Hymns	1	2	3	4
Verses	60	46	26	56¶
Decad-division	6 tens	4 tens + 6	2 tens + 6	6 P

Here ¶ means "paragraph of a *paryāya*" (such as is numbered as a "verse" in the Berlin edition) and P means "*paryāya*." Of the "decads," *anuvākas* 1, 2, and 3 contain respectively 6, 5, and 3 (in all, 14 "decads"); while *anuvāka* 4 has 6 *paryāyas*. The sum is 14 "decad"-*sūktas* and 6 *paryāya-sūktas* or 20 *sūktas* (cf. p. 737).⌋

---

1. To Rohita (the sun, as ruddy one).

[*Brahman.* — *ādhyātmam ; rohitādityadevatyam* (*3. mārutī ; 28–31. āgneyyaḥ ; 31. bahudevatyā*). *trāiṣṭubham : 3–5, 9, 12, 15. jagatī* (*15. atijāgatagarbhā*); *8. bhurij ;* [*16. ? ;*] *17. 5-p. kakummatī jagatī ; 13. atiçākvaragarbhā 'tijagatī* ; 14. 3-p. purahparaçākvarā viparītapādalakṣmyā pañkti ; 18, 19. 5-p. kakummaty atijagatī* (*18. paraçākvarā bhurij ; 19. parātijāgatā*) *; 21. ārṣī nicṛd gāyatrī ; 22, 23, 27. prākṛtā ; 26. virāṭ paroṣṇih ; 28–30* (*28. bhurij*), *32, 39, 40, 45–50 and 51–56* [*and 57–58*]. *anuṣṭubh* (*52, 55. pathyāpañkti ; 55. kakummatī bṛhatīgarbhā ; 57. kakummatī*) † *; 31. 5-p. kakummatī çākvaragarbhā jagatī ; 35. upariṣṭādbṛhatī ; 36. nicṛn mahābṛhatī ; 37. paraçākvarā virāḍ atijagatī ; 42. virāḍ jagatī ; 43. virāṇ mahābṛhatī ; 44. paroṣṇih ; 59, 60. gāyatrī.*]

Found also in Pāipp. xviii. ⌊with vs. 30 after 31; vss. 56–57, 59–60 are lacking; vs. 58 is lacking in Pāipp. xviii., but is found in Pāipp. xx.⌋. A number of the verses are used in various parts of Kāuç., and several (four) in Vāit. *⌊So the Berlin ms. (against *jagatī* of the London ms.): and *atijagatī* more nearly fits the vs.⌋ †⌊Here the Anukr. text looks as if in disorder: it seems as if *yaṁ vāta* (vs. 51) *iti ṣaḍ anuṣṭubhaḥ* ought to refer to the 6 vss. 51, 53–54, 56–58.⌋

Translated: Muir, v. 395 (parts); Ludwig, p. 536; Scherman, p. 73 (parts); Henry, 1, 21; Deussen, *Geschichte*, i. 1. 218 (cf. his introduction, p. 212 ff.); Griffith, ii. 133; Bloomfield, 207, 661. — Furthermore, Bloomfield, in his review (AJP. xii. 429–443) of Henry, discusses a considerable number of passages from this hymn. These discussions will be briefly cited by reference to "AJP. xii." He considers that the hymn is secondarily "an allegorical exaltation of a king and his queen."

1. Rise up, O powerful one (? *vājín*) that [art] within the waters, enter into this kingdom [that is] full of pleasantness; the ruddy one (*róhita*) that generated this all — let him bear thee, well-borne, unto kingdom.

Róhita is evidently a name or form of the sun; and the *vājin* (Henry, 'conqueror of booty') addressed is also the sun. The verse ⌊with faulty accents⌋ is found also in TB. (ii. 5. 2[1]), which reads ⌊*asi* after *yó* in **a**⌋, *ā́ viça* in **b**, and, for **d**, *sá no rāṣṭréṣu súdhitāṁ dadhātu*, which seems better, as removing the difficulty of the sun establishing the sun. Ppp. reads *viçvabhṛtaṁ* for *viçvaṁ idam* in **c**; and it has *pipartu* for *bibhartu* at the end; ⌊we had the converse at xi. 5. 4⌋. The resolution *ud-ā́-ihi* is required to fill out the meter of **a**. All the four hymns of the book (under the name *rohitās*) are prescribed in Kāuç. 99. 4 to be used in case of a darkening (eclipse) of the sun. The first half-verse is, according to Kāuç. 49. 18, to be used in the witchcraft ceremony of the 'water-thunderbolts' (see x. 5) 'when the boat sinks.' ⌊Cf. AJP. xii. 431.⌋

2. Up hath arisen the power (? *vā́ja*) that is within the waters; mount (*ā-ruh*) thou the clans (*víç*) that are sprung from thee (*tvádyoni*); assuming (*dhā*) the soma, the waters, the herbs, the kine, make thou the four-footed, the two-footed ones to enter here.

In **b** begins the play of words upon the root *ruh* 'ascend, mount, grow,' and its compounds and derivatives; this play is suggested by the at least apparent relationship between *ruh* and *rohita*, ⌊and is found with considerable elaboration throughout⌋ these hymns. Here it doubtless signifies 'have supremacy over.' Ppp. combines in **b** *viçā "roha*, in **c** *dadhānā 'po 'ṣadh-*, and in **d** *dvipadā "veç-*; and this last we have to accept in order to make a *triṣṭubh* pāda. In **a** the resolution of *ā́ agan*, and in **b** that of *tuád-*, make the meter right. The Anukr. takes no notice of any irregularity in the verse.

3. Do ye [who are] formidable, O Maruts, sons of the spotted mother, with Indra as ally, slaughter our foes; the ruddy one shall listen to you, ye liberal ones (*sudā́nu*), ye thrice seven Maruts that enjoy sweets together.

The first half-verse occurred above as v. 21. 11 **a**, **b**. We can hardly help emending *triṣaptā́so* to *trísaptāso*. Ppp. reads instead *triṣaptā*. The verse is found also in TB. (ii. 5. 2[3]), which reads in **a** *ugrā* (which is better), in **b** *sayújā prá ṇītha* (corrupt), in **c** *açṛṇod abhidyavaḥ*, and in **d** (with the desired accent) *trísaptāso*. The verse lacks a syllable (in **b**) of being a proper *jagatī*.

4. The ruddy one ascended (*ruh*), mounted the ascents (*rúh*); [he,] the embryo of the wives, [mounted] the lap of births; him, taken hold of by them (f.), the six wide [spaces] discovered; seeing in advance the track, he hath brought (*ā-hṛ*) hither the kingdom.

The verse is found also in TB. (ii. 5. 2[1]), which reads in **a** (much better) *róhaṁ-rohaṁ* (for *rúho ruroha*), at the beginning of **b** *prajā́bhir vṛ́ddhim*, and in **c** *sáṁrabdho avidat*. Such variations are of interest especially as showing how little connected sense was recognized in these verses by those who established the texts. This verse has no right to the name of *jagatī*, since all its pādas have a trochaic close; the two redundant syllables in **a** and **c** are removed by the TB. readings. ⌊For *ā́hāḥ*, see Prāt. ii. 46.⌋ ⌊With regard to the transition-sound between *-dan* and *ṣád*, see Prāt. ii. 9, note.⌋

5. The ruddy one hath brought hither thy kingdom; the scorners have scattered; fearlessness hath become thine; unto thee, being such, let heaven-and-earth, by the *revátīs*, yield (*duh*) here thy desire by the *çákvarīs*.

Our mss. are divided in **d** between *duhāthām* and *-tām*: the majority give *-thām* (so Bs.s.m.Bp.O.D.R.T.K.); while P.M.W.E.p.m. have *-tām*; ⌊and so has Ppp.⌋. Kp. reads *āsthat* in **b**, the other *pada*-mss. *-an*; if *-at* is accepted, it will mean 'he has scattered the scorners'; the form may best be viewed, probably, as coming from *sthā*, like *ādat* from *dā* and *ādhat* from *dhā* ⌊see *Skt. Gram.* § 847⌋; a root *asth* is extremely improbable; ⌊it is discussed at AJP. xii. 439 and IF. v. 388, where references to previous discussions are given; to these add KZ. xxxii. 435; cf. also note to vii. 76. 3 above⌋. The verse occurs also in TB. (ii. 5. 2[1]), which has very different readings: *ā́hārṣīd rāṣṭrám ihá róhito mṛdho vy àsthad ábhayaṁ no astu: asmábhyaṁ dyāvāpṛthivī çákvarībhī rāṣṭráṁ duhāthām ihá revátībhiḥ*. The verse is no *jagatī*; by the frequent and permissible contraction to *-pṛthvī* in **c** it becomes a fairly good *triṣṭubh* (badly constructed in **a**). It is reckoned as belonging to the *abhaya gaṇa*: see note to Kāuç. 16. 8. ⌊Ppp., like TB., puts *mṛdho* before *vy ā-* in **b**.⌋ ⌊For vss. 4–5, see AJP. xii. 432.⌋

6. The ruddy one generated heaven-and-earth; there the most exalted one stretched the line (*tántu*); there was supported (*çri*) the one-footed goat (?*ajá*); by strength he made firm (*dṛh*) heaven-and-earth.

Ppp. reads in **c** *ekapād yo.* The verse occurs in TB. (ii. 5. 2[3]), with only slight variants: *tásmin* for *tátra* in **b** and **c**, and *ékapāt* in **c**. ⌊Cf. AJP. xii. 443.⌋

7. The ruddy one made firm heaven-and-earth; by him was established the sky (*svàr*), by him the firmament (*nā́ka*); by him the atmosphere, the spaces (*rájas*) were measured out; by him the gods discovered immortality (*amṛ́ta*).

The verse is found in TB. (ib.), the second half-verse reading quite differently: *só antárikṣe rájaso vimā́nas téna devā́ḥ súvar ánv avindan.* Ppp. combines and reads in **d** *devā 'mṛtatvam.*

8. The ruddy one examined (*vi-mṛç*) the all-formed, collecting to himself the fore-ascents and the ascents; having ascended the sky with great greatness, let him anoint (*sam-añj*) thy kingdom with milk, with ghee.

The TB. version (ii. 5. 2[2]) has, for **a**, *ví mamarça róhito viçvárūpaḥ;* in **b**, *samācakrāṇáḥ;* in **c**, *gatvā́ya* (for *rūḍhvā́* ⌊improving the meter⌋); for **d**, *ví no rāṣṭrám unattu páyasā svéna.* Ppp. combines in **a** *-to 'mṛçat*, and reads in **b** *samākṛṇvānaṣ.*

9. What ascents, fore-ascents thou hast, what on-ascents (*ārúh*) thou hast, with which thou fillest the sky, the atmosphere, with the *bráhman*, with the milk of them increasing, do thou watch over the people (*víç*) in the kingdom of the ruddy one.

Though the first three pādas count 12 syllables each, only **a** is *jagatī* in structure. With **a**, **b** compare xviii. 2. 9 **a**, **b**. ⌊For vss. 8–9, see AJP. xii. 433.⌋

10. What clans (*víç*) of thine came into being out of ardor (*tápas*), those have come hither after the young (*vatsá*), the *gāyatrī́;* let them enter (*ā-viç*) into thee with propitious mind; let the ruddy young with its mother go against [them].

Or (in **a**) 'what clans came into being out of thy heat.' In **b**, the *pada*-text has *ihá : ā́ : aguḥ.* In **d**, *sámmātā* means more probably 'having a common mother,' but the sense is too obscure to allow of much confidence in any translation. The TB. version (ii. 5. 2[2]) reads in **a** *tápasā* (better); for **b**, *gāyatrám vatsám ánu tā́s ta ā́ 'guḥ;* in **c**, *máhasā svéna;* in **d**, *putró* (for *vatsó*). The Anukr. does not heed that the last pāda is *jagatī.* Ppp. combines in **d** *vatso 'bhy.*

11. The ruddy one hath stood aloft upon the firmament (*nā́ka*), generating all forms, [he,] young, poet; Agni shineth forth with keen light; in the third space (*rájas*) he hath done dear things.

Ppp. reads *bhāsi* in **c**. The Anukr. again passes without notice the *jagatī* pāda **b**. ⌊W. suggests by interlineation as alternative, 'hath made for himself dear forms.'⌋

12. The thousand-horned bull Jātavedas, offered to with ghee, soma-backed, having good heroes — let him not abandon me; let me not, a

suppliant, abandon thee *; assign thou to me both prosperity in kine and prosperity in heroes.

The verse is found also in TB. (iii. 7. 27), K. (xxxv. 18), and Āp. ⌊ix. 3. 1⌋. TB. (with which Āp. ⌊substantially⌋ agrees throughout) has, for **b**, *stómapṛṣṭho ghṛtávānt suprátīkaḥ;* and, for **c**, **d**, *mā́ no hāsīn metthitó nét tvā jáhāma gopoṣáṁ no vīrapoṣáṁ ca yaccha.* Ppp. reads in **b** *ghṛtāhutis so-*. The irregular verse (12 + 11 : 12 + 12, but with *triṣṭubh* cadences throughout) is very ill described by the Anukr. as simply a *jagatī.* *⌊All the translators, with W., seem to overlook the accent of *jáhāni: nét* can hardly mean aught else than 'lest.'⌋

13. The ruddy one is generator and mouth of the sacrifice; to the ruddy one I make oblation with speech, with hearing, with mind; to the ruddy one go the gods with favoring mind; let him cause me to ascend with ascensions (*róha*) of meeting (*sāmityá*).

The *pada*-texts read blunderingly in **d** *sāmoityāt* (instead of *-yāṭḥ*). Henry emends to *samityāt* 'in order to union with him'; but *sámiti* has the well-established sense of 'meeting, gathering, assembly'; hence Ludwig (for *rohāiḥ s-*) 'with abundant success in the *samiti*.' ⌊See AJP. xii. 434.⌋ Ppp. reads at the end *rohayāti.* The verse is kindred with ii. 35. 5 in general expression. Its metrical structure (12 + 15 : 13 + 11 = 51) is wholly irregular; the definition of the Anukr. ⌊52 syllables⌋ ⌊nearly⌋ fits it mechanically.

14. The ruddy one disposed the sacrifice for Viçvakarman; therefrom have these brilliancies come unto me; may I speak thy navel (*nā́bhi*) upon the range (*majmán*) of existence.

The last pāda is repeated below as vs. 37 **d**. Ppp. reads in **a** *vi dadhāt.* The metrical definition implies the resolution *vi ad-*, and two resolutions in **b** (*-si úpa* and *mā im-*, doubtless), to make a *pan̄kti* (14 + 12 : 14 = 40).

15. Unto thee ascended *bṛhatī́* and *pan̄ktí*, unto [thee], O Jātavedas, *kakúbh* with honor; unto thee ascended the *uṣṇíhā* syllable, the *váṣaṭ*-utterance; unto thee ascended the ruddy one along with seed.

Or *uṣṇihāoakṣaráḥ* (so p.) is, in spite of its accent, an adjective to *vaṣaṭkāraḥ* (so Henry). Read in **a** *bṛhaty ùtá;* though all our mss. except ⌊O.⌋ K. happen to agree here in lengthening the *ù*. *Saha* at the end is, of course, a misprint for *sahá*. Ppp. reads *at* for *uta* in **a**, and *viçvavedaḥ* in **b**. ⌊The Anukr. appears to count the syllables as 11 + 10 : 13 + 13 = 47.⌋ The metrical irregularities in this book exceed the ordinary measure. ⌊For vss. 15, 17–20, cf. AJP. xii. 434.⌋

16. This one clothes himself in the embryo (womb?) of the earth; this one clothes himself in the sky, the atmosphere; this one, on the summit of the reddish one, has penetrated the heaven (*svàr*), the worlds.

Ppp. reads *viṣṭapas sv-* in **c**–**d**, and *sam ānaçe* in **d**. The verse (9 + 9 : 8 + 8 = 34) seems to be overlooked in the Anukr., or its definition has dropped out of the mss. Verses 16–20 are prescribed in Kāuç. 54. 10 to accompany, in the *godāna*-ceremony, the dressing of the child in a new garment. They are much better suited to that use than to their surroundings here.

17. O lord of speech, [be] earth pleasant to us; [be] the lair (*yóni*) pleasant, [be] our couch very propitious; just here be breath in our companionship; thee here, O most exalted one, let Agni surround with life-time, with honor.

Henry understands *sakhyé* as dat. of *sákhi*, against the accent. The Anukr. apparently views the verse as ⌊10 + 10 : 10 + 12 + 6 = 48⌋. The verse (with the two following?) is included among the *vācaspatiliñgās*, used in Kāuç. 41.15 in a ceremony for good luck. Ppp. reads at the end *-ṣṭhi pary ahaṁ varcasā dadhāmi.*

18. O lord of speech, the five seasons that are ours, that came forth into being as Viçvakarman's — just here be breath in our companionship; thee here, O most exalted one, let the ruddy one surround with life-time, with honor.

The mss. read in **a** *yé nāu* (but I.R. *yó nāu* ⌊*yónāu*⌋); ⌊SPP's text and most of his authorities have *yé nāu:* but two have *yónāu;*⌋ the edition makes the apparently necessary correction to *yé no.* ⌊The Anukr. seems to scan as 11 + 12 : 10 + 14 + 6 = 53.⌋ Ppp. omits *ye nāu* (or *no*) in **a**, and *saṁ-* in **b**, and *āyuṣā* near the end.

19. O lord of speech, [generate] well-willing and mind; generate kine in our stall (*goṣṭhá*), progeny in our wombs (*yóni*); just here be breath in our companionship; thee here, O most exalted one, I surround with life-time, with honor.

Ppp. reads in **b** *prajām*, and in **d** *avahaṁ* (for *aham*), omitting, as before, *āyuṣā*, ⌊and having again *dadhātu* at the end, repeated unintelligently from the preceding⌋.

20. May Savitar, god Agni, surround thee [with honor]; with honor may Mitra-and-Varuṇa deck (*abhi*[+ *dhā*]) thee; striding down all niggards come thou; thou hast made this kingdom full of pleasantness.

The shift from *pári* in **a** to *abhí* in **b** makes a mixed and difficult construction. Ppp. combines *devo 'gnir* in **a** and *sarvā 'rātīr* in **c**, and reads (better) *kṛṇuhi* in **d**.

21. Thou whom the spotted one (f.), the side-horse, draws (*vah*) in the chariot, O ruddy one, thou goest with brightness (*çúbh*), making flow the waters.

This verse corresponds to RV. viii. 7. 28, which, however, has considerable variants: for **a**, *yád eṣām pṛ́ṣatī* (p. *-tīḥ*) *ráthe;* in **b**, *róhitaḥ;* in **c**, *yā́nti çubhrā́* (p. *-rā́ḥ*). As is usual in such cases, some of our mss. read *pṛ́ṣṭis* in **b**, and *ṛṇán* in **c**. And most read *rohitaḥ* ⌊unaccented⌋ at end of **b** (only Bs.R.K. *-ta*), as if under influence of the RV. version. ⌊SPP. adopts in his text *rohita*, but reports six of his mss. as giving *rohitaḥ*, without accent.⌋ Ppp. adds at the end *tene 'maṁ brahmaṇaspate ruhaṁ rohayo 'ttamam.* The verse is quoted in a ceremony for prosperity by Kāuç. (24.42), which volunteers the added explanation *dyāuḥ pṛṣaty āditya rohitaḥ;* and it is also included among the *puṣṭika mantras:* see note to Kāuç. 19.1. Kāuç. 24.43 states further that a spotted cow is given (as sacrificial fee); and the comm. appears to direct that vss. 21–26 accompany the gift.

22. She that is ruddy (*róhiṇī*) is submissive to the ruddy one, being liberal (*sūrí*), of beautiful color, vast (*bṛhatī́*), very splendid; by her may we conquer booty (? *vā́jān*) of all forms; by her may we overcome all fighters.

Róhiṇī, doubtless the dawn. Our *pada*-mss. read in **c** *-rūpām*, by a blundering misapprehension of the assimilated nasal in the combination *-pāṅ ja-* ⌊Prāt. ii. 11⌋. M.p.m. ⌊and SPP's C.⌋ read at end *syāma;* the passage is quoted as an instance of *sy-* in the comm. to Prāt. ii. 107. Ppp. reads *sūryas suv-* in **b**, and combines *pṛtanā 'bhi* in **d**. In the Anukr. (by an exceptional usage hardly met with elsewhere) this verse and the next, and a little later vs. 27, are specified as *prākṛta* ⌊mss. *prakṛta*⌋: i.e., as following the established norm of the hymn, which is *triṣṭubh*.

23. Here the seat (*sádas*), she that is ruddy, of the ruddy one; yonder the road by which the spotted one (f.) goes; her the Gandharvas, the Kaçyapas, lead up; her the poets defend unremittingly.

All the mss. except O.D. (and these differ perhaps only by accident) read in **c** *gandharvāḥ*, as if vocative.

24. The sun's yellow (*hári*) bright (*ketumánt*) horses, immortal, constantly draw the easy-running chariot; the ghee-drinking ruddy one, shining (*bhrā́j*), the god, entered the spotted sky.

Bs.E. combine in **b** *amṛtās su-*. The Anukr. does not heed the *jagatī* pāda **b**.

25. The ruddy one, the sharp-horned bull, who encompassed Agni, the sun, who props asunder (*vi-stabh*) the earth and the heaven — out of him do the gods create creations.

Ppp. begins with *ayaṁ roh-*. The curious reading of O. in **c**, *ṣṭab-h-nāti* (the *b* and *h* two different letters), was noted above, under xii. 4. 4. ⌊"Encompassed": Bloomfield, "became superior to," AJP. xii. 443.⌋ Kāuç. 18. 25 gives the verse, in company with several others, as to be used in the so-called *citrākarman* (ceremony concerning the asterism *citrā*) to accompany the partaking of a milk rice-dish; and the Paddhati includes both it and the following verse in the *salila gaṇa*.

26. The ruddy one mounted the sky, out of the great sea (*arṇavá*); the ruddy one ascended all ascents.

That the verse is reckoned as belonging to the *salila gaṇa* was noted under the preceding verse.

27. Measure thou out (*vi-mā*) the milk-giving, ghee-dripping (*ghṛtā́ñc*) [cow]; this is the unresisting milch-cow of the gods. Let Indra drink the soma; let there be comfort (*kṣéma*); let Agni commence praising; do thou thrust away the scorners.

Ppp. reads *eṣām* at end of **b**. With the verse is to be compared Āp. xi. 4. 14: *vi mime tvā payasvatīṁ devānāṁ dhenuṁ sudughām anapasphurantīm: indraḥ somam pibatu kṣemo astu naḥ*, which accompanies the measuring out of a *vedi* in shape of a cow. In Vāit. 15. 7; 28. 23, it is used in a like manner; and so also in Kāuç. 137. 10, in preparing for the *ājyatantra;* ⌊cf. also note to 137. 4⌋.

28. Agni, kindled, being kindled, increased with ghee, offered to with ghee — let the overpowering, all-overpowering Agni slay them who are my rivals.

This verse (though there are others having the same *pratīka*) is doubtless the one quoted (next after vs. 1) in Kāuç. 49. 19, to accompany the laying of bonds upon the "boat" there treated of; ⌊rather, the laying of sticks with strings on them upon the fire: Caland, p. 173⌋. The description of the Anukr. strangely forbids us to make the elision *-dho 'gnīḥ* in **a**.

29. Let him slay them, burn [them] away, — the enemy (*ári*) who fights us; by the flesh-eating fire do we burn away our rivals.

Ppp. reads in **a** *enāṁ;* we require *enaṁ*, as antecedent to **b**, which, as the verse now stands, seems to describe the subject of the verbs in **a**. Ppp. has also *agnis* for *aris* in **b**.

30. Do thou, O Indra, having arms, smite them down downward with the thunderbolt; then my rivals have I taken to myself with Agni's brightnesses (*téjas*).

Ppp. puts the verse after our 31, and reads at the end *ā dadhe.* ⌊Or *ā́diṣi* may be referred to *dā* 'cut' + *ā:* so W. in a ms. note to his *Index*, and so BR. But BR's forms from vi. 104 are referred by W. to *dā* 'tie.'⌋

31. O Agni, make our rivals fall below us; stagger the truculent (*utpípāna*) fellow, O Brihaspati; O Indra-and-Agni, O Mitra-and-Varuṇa, let them fall below [us], impotent in their fury.

Lit. 'not making their fury effective against' us. The Anukr. apparently understands the structure of the verse as 12 + 14 : 8 + 6 + 8 = 48; but there is no good reason for dividing the last redundant pāda into two. Ppp. reads *utapidānaṁ* (for *utpipānam* ⌊discussed AJP. xii. 441⌋) in **b**.

32. Do thou, O heavenly sun, arising, smite down my rivals; smite them down with the stone; let them go to lowest darkness.

Ppp. appears to read *avāi 'nāṁ raçmibhir jahi rātrīṇāṁ tamasā vadhīs taṁ hantv adhamaṁ tamaḥ.* ⌊We had our **d** at x. 3. 9 **d**.⌋

33. The young (*vatsá*) of the *virā́j*, the bull of prayers (*matí*), mounted, bright-backed, the atmosphere; with ghee they sing (*arc*) the song (*arká*) unto the young; him, being *bráhman*, they increase with *bráhman*.

Ppp. combines in **b** *-pṛṣṭho ant-*. TB. (ii. 8. 89) has a corresponding verse, but with numerous variants: *pitā́ virā́jām ṛṣabhó rayīṇā́m antárikṣaṁ viçvárūpa ā́ viveça: tám arkāír abhy àrcanti vatsám bráhma sántam bráhmaṇā vardháyantaḥ.* ⌊Bloomfield, AJP. xii. 441, would emend *arkám* to *aktám;* but the TB. variant is very much against it.⌋ Our verse is quoted in Kāuç. 12. 4, at the end of a charm for securing one's wishes.

34. Both ascend thou to heaven and ascend to earth; both ascend to kingdom and ascend to property; both ascend to progeny and ascend to immortality; make thyself contiguous with the ruddy one.

The verse is quoted in Vāit. 13. 5 to accompany the leading up of the cow that is to be exchanged for the soma-plant.

35. The kingdom-bearing gods who go to surround (*abhítas*) the sun — in concord with them let the ruddy one, with favoring mind, assign kingdom to thee.

The combination *tāís ṭe* is quoted as example under Prāt. ii. 84. The verse (7 + 8 : 9 + 11 : or 8 in **a**, if we resolve *deva-ā́* or *rāṣṭr-a-*) is far too irregular to be defined simply as an *upariṣṭādbṛhatī*.

36. Sacrifices purified by *bráhman* carry thee up; yellow (*hári*) roadsters draw (*vah*) thee; thou shinest over (*ati-ruc*) across the ocean, the sea.

The verse might better be called *virāj* than *nicṛt* (11 + 11 : 12). Ppp. reads in **b** *abhyaktuṁ* (for *adhvagato*); and in **c** *-se arṇavam*, as do some of our mss. (O.R.T.K.). ⌊Pādas **a** and **b** recur below, vs. 43.⌋

37. On the ruddy one are set (*çritá*) heaven-and-earth, on the goods-conquering, kine-conquering, booty-conquering one, of whom the births are a thousand and seven; may I speak thy navel on the range of existence.

Ppp. reads for **b** *vasujid gojit saṁdhanājiti*, and in **c** *draviṇāni saptatir*. The obscure last pāda is identical with vs. 14 **c**.

38. Glorious thou goest to the directions and quarters, glorious of cattle and of people (*carṣaṇí*); glorious in the lap of earth, of Aditi, may I become pleasant (*cā́ru*) like Savitar.

Ppp. reads *nu* instead of *ca* in **a**, and *asmi* instead of *bhūyāsam* in **d**; and it combines *pṛthivyā 'di-* in **c**. There is a deficiency of a syllable, unnoticed in the Anukr., in **a**, unless we resolve *ya-āsi*.

39. Being yonder, thou knowest here; being on this side, thou seest those things; from this side they see the shining space (*rócana*), the inspired sun in the sky.

Ppp. begins **c** with *yataṣ paç-*.

40. Thou, a god, molestest (*mṛc*) the gods; thou goest about within the sea (*arṇavá*); they kindle the same fire; it the high (*pára*) poets know.

'It,' i.e. 'the fire' (*tám*). Ppp. reads *marcayati* and *carati*. ⌊Bloomfield, AJP. xii. 437, emends to *devám arcayasi;* but Ppp., and the antithesis of **a** and **b**, admirably suggested by Deussen's *dennoch*, are in favor of *marc-*.⌋

41. Below the distant, thus beyond the lower, bearing her calf with her foot, the cow hath stood up; whitherwards, to what quarter, hath she forsooth gone away? where giveth she birth? for [it is] not in this herd.

This is a repetition of ix. 9. 17, and, as there are two successive verses beginning with *avā́ḥ páreṇa*, this one is quoted here in the mss. with the unusual expression *avā́ḥ párenẹ́ 'ti pū́rvā.* ⌊The Anukr. doubtless balances the extra syllable in **a** by counting *kúa* as one syllable in **d**.⌋

42. One-footed, two-footed [is] she, four-footed; having become eight-footed, nine-footed, thousand-syllabled, a series of existence; out from her flow apart the oceans.

This verse is the pādas **b–e** of ix. 10. 21 (RV. i. 164. 41 **b–d**, 42 **a**) ⌊see under ix. 10. 21 for variants⌋. It and the preceding are very little in place in our hymn. ⌊With **d** cf. 3. 2 **b**, below.⌋

43. Mounting the sky, immortal, do thou favor my words; sacrifices purified by *bráhman* carry thee up; yellow roadsters draw thee.

Pādas **b** and **c** are identical with 36 **a, b**. Instead of *adhvagatas*, Ppp. reads *ghṛtaṁ pibantaṁ*. Bp. accents *prá : áva*.

44. I know that of thine, O immortal one, namely (*yát*) thy climb (*ākrámaṇa*) in the sky, thy station (*sadhástha*) in the highest firmament.

Vyòmani would make a more regular *paroṣṇih*, but the Anukr. takes no notice of the deficiency.

45. The sun overlooks (*ati-paç*) the sky, the sun the earth, the sun the waters; the sun, the one eye of what exists, hath mounted the great sky.

The verse is made in Vāit. 16. 11 to accompany the *antaryāmahoma* after sunrise.

46. The wide ones (*urvī́*) were the enclosures; the earth took shape as sacrificial hearth; there the ruddy one set (*ā-dhā*) these two fires, cold and heat.

47. Having set cold and heat, having made the mountains sacrificial posts (*yūpa*), having rain as sacrificial butter, the two fires of the sky-finding ruddy one performed sacrifice (*yaj*).

The Anukr. appears to ratify the resolution *kṛtu-ā́* in **b**. Ppp., in this verse as later, combines *agnī "jāte*. ⌊For 46, Hillebrandt, *Ved. Mythol.* i. 179, cites ÇB. i. 2. 57.⌋

48. The fire of the sky-finding ruddy one is kindled with *bráhman;* therefrom heat, therefrom cold, therefrom the sacrifice was born.

The majority of mss. read correctly *yajñò 'jāy-* at the end; the rest vary between *-ñó aj-* and *-ñò aj-*. Ppp. reads *-ño aj-*; and, in **b**, *samāhitaḥ* for *sam idhyate*.

49. The two fires [are] increasing by *bráhman*, increased with *bráhman*, offered to with *bráhman:* kindled with *bráhman*, the two fires of the sky-finding ruddy one performed sacrifice.

Ppp. reads for **a** *brahmaṇā 'gnis saṁvidāno*, and in **b** *-ddho*, *-hutaḥ*, and again combines in **c** *agnī "jāte*. With **b** compare vs. 28 **b**.

50. The one is all set in truth, the other is kindled in the waters: kindled with etc. etc.

Ppp. reads in **b** *samāhitas* ⌊again: cf. 48⌋ for *sam idhyate*, and adds another pāda: *satye adbhis samāhitaḥ*.

51. What one the wind adorns about, or what one Indra, Brahmaṇaspati: kindled with etc. etc.

Ppp. omits *vā* in **b**.

52. Having shaped (*kḷp*) the earth as sacrificial hearth, having made the sky sacrificial fee, then having made heat his fire, the ruddy one made all that has soul, with rain as sacrificial butter.

53. Rain as sacrificial butter, heat as fire, earth as sacrificial hearth took shape; there, with songs (*gír*), the fire shaped these mountains aloft.

Ppp. reads *'gnir* in **a**, and some of our mss. (P.M.p.m.W.) give the same. P.M.W. also have in common the blunder *bhūmipr ak-* in **b**. It is doubtless by a loss of part of its text that the Anukr. does not define vss. ⌊57–58⌋ as *anuṣṭubh*, although it describes a minor feature of vs. 57, taken as an *anuṣṭubh*. ⌊With 52, cf. vs. 46.⌋

54. Having shaped [them] aloft by songs, the ruddy one said to the earth: in thee let this all be born, what is (*bhūtá*) or what is to be.

Ppp. reads at the end *bhavyam*.

55. That first sacrifice was born [as] the one that is, that is to be; from that was born this all, whatsoever shines out (*vi-ruc*) here, brought (*ā-bhṛ*) by the ruddy one [as] seer.

Ppp. ends the hymn with this verse, although vs. 58 is found in another place. It combines *jajñe 'daṁ*, as we are doubtless to read, though not with the sanction of the Anukr., which calls the pāda *bṛhatī*. ⌊Cf. iv. 23. 7.⌋

56. Whoever both kicks a cow with the foot and urinates in face of the sun — of such a one I hew off (*vraçc*) thy root; thou shalt not further cast (*kṛ*) shadow.

⌊Cf. the note on the vs. concerning posture in urination at vii. 102: and add that Buddhaghosa, in his comment on the description of the Acelakas, at Dīgha Nikāya, viii. 14 (as reported by Davids, Translation, p. 227), speaks of the standing posture as wrong. — As to making water with face towards the sun, cf. MBh. xiii. 104. 75 (5029), and note to Manu iv. 48 in my *Reader*, p. 349, and the references there given, especially the reference to Jolly's Viṣṇu, SBE. vii. 194 f. — As for the loss of the shadow, cf. the Peter Schlemihl story; also Jātaka, i. 102[9]; vi. 337[11].⌋

The character of this and the following verses shows that Ppp. has reason for not making them a part of the hymn. This verse makes its appearance in Kāuç. 49. 26, at the conclusion of a series of witchcraft ceremonies. ⌊For the theoretical *k* of *pratyáñk*, see note to vi. 51. 1.⌋

57. Thou that goest past me shading me, and between me and the fire, I hew off thy root; thou shalt not further cast shadow.

The connection appears to demand this pregnant rendering of *abhichāyám* 'so as to cast thy shadow on' (so also Ludwig). It is easy to read **b** as a regular *anuṣṭubh* pāda, though the Anukr. allows it only six syllables.

58. Whoso this day, O heavenly sun, shall go between both thee and me — on him we wipe off evil-dreaming, pollution, and difficulties.

This verse is found in Ppp. xx., which reads for **c** *tasmin duṣvapnyaṁ sarvaṁ*.

59. Let us not go forth from the road, nor, O Indra, from the sacrifice with soma; let not the niggards stand between us.

That is, between us and something else, so as to cut us off from our desire or object. The verse is, without variant, RV. x. 57. 1, and found also in JB. iii. 168. It is used once in Vāit. (18. 8), and several times in Kāuç. (54. 18; 82. 6; 89. 11; also by the schol. under 42. 15; 58. 17).

60. What line, accomplisher of the sacrifice, is stretched clear to the gods, that, sacrificed unto, may we attain.

The verse is RV. x. 57. 2, which reads at the end *naçīmahi*. It is used by the schol. to Kāuç. 58. 17, with vs. 59, in the ceremony of name-giving.

⌊Here ends the first *anuvāka*, 1 hymn and 60 verses. The quoted Anukr. says *ṣaṣṭiḥ*.⌋

2. To the sun.

[(*Brahman.* — *ādhyātmam; rohitādityadevatyam. trāiṣṭubham:*) *1, 12–15, 39–41. anuṣṭubh; 2, 3, 8, 43. jagatī; 10. āstārapañkti; 11. bṛhatīgarbhā; 16–24. ārṣī gāyatrī; 25. kakummaty āstārapañkti; 26. purodvyatijāgatā bhurig jagatī; 27. virāḍ jagatī; 29. bārhatagarbhā 'nuṣṭubh; 30. 5-p. uṣṇigbṛhatīgarbhā 'tijagatī; 34. ārṣī pañkti; 37. 5-p. virāḍgarbhā jagatī; 44, 45. jagatī (44. 4-p. purahçākvarā bhurij; 45. atijāgatagarbhā).*]

Found also in Pāipp. xviii. Only twice (vs. 1) quoted in Kāuç., but several times (eight different verses) by Vāit.

Translated: Ludwig, p. 540; Henry, 8, 36; Griffith, ii. 143. — In this hymn, the sun is mentioned by the name *róhita* only in vss. 25 and 39–41. Verses 39–41 are translated also by Muir, v. 396; Scherman, p. 75 (with vss. 25–26); Deussen, *Geschichte*, i. 1. 213 (also vss. 25–26 at p. 226). — The verses 16–24, which are RV. i. 50. 1–9, are translated by the RV. translators, and are commented and in part translated by me in *Skt. Reader*, p. 362–3.

1. The bright (*çukrá*) shining lights (*ketú*) of him go up in the sky — of the men-watching Āditya, him of great courses (*-vratá*), liberal (*mīḍhváṅs*).

Ppp. reads in **d** *mahīvr-*. Kāuç. 58. 22 prescribes the use apparently of the whole hymn (with xvi. 3 and xvii.) in an act of worship to the rising sun, in a ceremony for long life; also (with the same and other hymns, and xiii. 1. 25) in 18. 25, in the *citrākarman:* see the note to 1. 25 above. Vāit. 9. 16 uses it in the *cāturmāsya* ceremony when turning toward the sun in the east.

2. [Him,] shining (*svar*) with the brightness (*arcís*) of the foreknowing quarters, well-winged, flying swift in the ocean (*arṇavá*) — we would praise the sun, the shepherd of existence, who with his rays shines unto all the quarters.

The Pet. Lex. (followed by Henry) emends *prajñānām* to *prajñā́nam*, with much plausibility; yet it is opposed by x. 7. 34, *díço yáç cakré prajñā́nīḥ*. Ppp. reads *prajñānaṁ svadayanto arc-*; and it combines in **d** *diçā "bhāti.* The verse lacks two syllables of being a proper *jagatī.*

3. In that thou goest swiftly eastward, westward, at will (*svadháyā*), makest by magic (*māyā́*) the two days of diverse form — that, O Āditya, [is] great, that thy great fame (*çrávas*), that thou alone art born about the whole world (*bhū́man*).

'The two days,' i.e. 'day and night.' The first pāda is *triṣṭubh.*

4. The inspired, hasting (*taráṇi*), shining one, whom seven numerous (*bahú*) yellow steeds (*harít*) draw, whom out of the liquid (? *srutá*) Atri conducted up the sky — thee here they see going around upon thy race.

Half of our mss. appear plainly to read *stutā́t* in **c**, but the apparent distinction is of no value; *sr* and *st* are virtually one in ms. use. Ppp. helps to establish *sru-*, by reading, for **c**, **d**, *çrutād divam atri divam anyanāya taṁ tvā paçyema paryantim ājim.* GB. i. 2. 17 has **c** (the published text reads *stutād*), with vs. 12 **a**, **b**, as if a verse. ⌊As for the Atri story, cf. my essay on RV. v. 40 in *Festgruss an Roth*, p. 187. For the construction of *ājím*, see *Ved. Stud.* ii. 261.⌋

5. Let them not damage thee going around upon thy race; happily do thou cross the difficulties quickly; when, O sun, thou goest to both sky and divine earth, measuring out day-and-night.

Or, 'sky' and 'earth' may be joint objects of 'measuring' (so Henry, and apparently Ludwig). Ppp. reads *paryantam* in **a**, and *sugena durgam* in **b**. We have to make the, in its situation, awkward resolution *tu-ā* in **a** in order to fill out the meter; ⌊or *-yāantam*?⌋.

6. Well-being, O sun, [be] to thy chariot for its moving, wherewith thou goest at once about both borders (*ánta*) — which thy yellow steeds, of excellent draught, draw: a hundred horses, or else seven, numerous.

'At once' (*sadyás*), doubtless 'on one and the same day'; 'borders,' i.e. 'horizons.' Half the mss. read *báhiṣṭhās*, both in this and in the next verse. Ppp. has in **a** *carato rathāsi*, and in **b** *paryāsi*;* and for **d**, instead of repeating 7 **d**, it gives *tam ā roha sukham āsy açvam.* ⌊"Numerous" is fem.; and we may think of "horses" as fem.⌋ *⌊For the relation of *pariyāsi* to *paryāsi*, cf. that of *-āni yasya* to *-āñsy asya*, above, x. 7. 20, and see *Gram.* § 233 a.⌋

7. Mount (*adhi-sthā*), O sun, thine easy-running chariot, rich in rays, pleasant, well-horsed, powerful (? *vājín*), which thy yellow steeds, of excellent draught, draw: a hundred horses, or else seven, numerous.

All our mss. accent *sū́rya* in **a**; our edition emends to *sūrya.* Ppp. has in **b** *syonosyavahnim.* The Anukr. perhaps regards the redundant syllable in **b** as balanced by the deficiency in **a**. ⌊Cf. 6 **c**, **d**.⌋

8. The sun hath yoked in his chariot, in order to go, his seven great yellow steeds, golden-skinned; the bright one hath been freed from the dimness (? *rájas*) in the distance; shaking away the darkness, the god hath mounted the sky.

Ppp. reads *çūras* for *sūryas* in **a**, and *çakras* for *çukras* in **c**, and apparently *ayuñkta* in **b**. The verse is very ill defined as simple *jagatī;* the true reading in **b** would seem to be *hiraṇyatvacas*.

9. The god hath come up with great show (*ketú*); he hath wasted away the darkness, hath set up (*abhi-çri*) the light; that hero, heavenly eagle, son of Aditi, hath looked abroad unto all beings.

Abhi-çri, more literally, 'affix, fasten on' (to the sky). ⌊For the form *açrāit*, see *Gram.* § 889 a, and note to vi. 32. 2. For *avṛk*, *Gram.* § 832 a.⌋ Ppp. reads in **c** *sthaviras* for *sa vīras*, and has a curious **d**: *ādityāṣ putraṁ nāthagām abhayām atītā*.

10. Rising, thou extendest thy rays; thou adornest thyself with all forms; thou illuminest (*vi-bhā*) with might (?*krátu*) both oceans, encompassing all worlds, shining.

Ppp. has an altogether different **b**: *prajās sarvā vi paçyasi.* ⌊It may be that "adornest" is a slip on W's part. Cf. Henry's note, p. 37–38.⌋

11. They two move on one after the other by magic; two playing young ones go about the ocean; the one looks abroad upon all beings; yellow steeds draw the other with golden [trappings?].

The first three pādas are identical with vii. 81. 1 **a–c** (repeated at xiv. 1. 23), and are found in other texts: see the note to that verse; the last pāda is peculiar, and, as applying only to the sun, spoils the description of the pair of luminaries, sun and moon, which the verse sets out to make. Henry regards the daily and the nightly sun as intended, and the *hāiraṇyas* as the stars, by means of which the latter finds his way back to the eastern horizon. It would have been better to read *yāto 'rṇavám* here, as in vii. 81. 1, since the majority of our *saṁhitā*-mss. (all save Bs.E.) give it in this place also.

12. Atri maintained thee in the sky, O sun, to make the month; thou goest well-maintained, heating, looking down upon all things that exist.

All our mss. read in **b** *sū́ryā*, as if we had here the compound *sūryāmāsā́;* the *pada*-mss. have *sū́ryā : mā́sāya;* the correction to *sū́rya* seems unavoidable. GB., which has the first two pādas (see note to vs. 4), also gives *sūryā-*; Ppp. also has it; and, for **d**, *svar bhūtā viçākaçat* ⌊so Roth: perhaps a slip for *vicāk-*⌋.

13. Thou rushest alike (?*sam-ṛṣ*) to both borders, as a calf to two joint mothers; surely (*nanú*), that *bráhman* yon gods have long known.

A naïve extension of the usual naïve figure of the calf: as if he had two mothers, to each of which he showed equal attachment. *Bráhman*, apparently 'sacred mystery' (so Henry). In **d**, lit. 'know of old from now.'

14. What is set (*çritá*) along the ocean, that the sun desires to gain (*san*); great is stretched out his road, which is both eastern and western.

The *pada*-text has in **b** *sisāsati* ⌊misprinted and corrected by SPP.⌋, and the passage is quoted as an example under Prāt. ii. 91; iv. 29, 82. Ppp. reads *adhi* for *anu* in **a**.

15. That one he attains completely (*sam-āp*) with his swiftnesses; that he desires not to neglect (?*apa-cikits*); by that [men] do not appropriate the gods' draught of immortality (*amṛta*).

Apa-cikits, lit. 'desire to think away from,' with abl.; the expression is found only here. The logic of **d** is not obvious; Henry supplies 'the demons' as subject of *áva rundhate;* Ludwig renders it as a singular. Ppp. reads *jigitsati* in **b**; and, in **c** etc., *bhakṣaṇaṁ devānān naṁ va ru-*; *bhakṣaṇam* is an improvement; the meter of **c** halts badly without it.

16. This heavenly Jātavedas the lights (*ketú*) draw (*vah*) up, for every one to see the sun.

Or *sū́ryam* may be in apposition with *jātávedasam*. 'Draw,' i.e. as horses do. This verse, with the eight that follow, constitute RV. i. 50. 1–9, in the same order of verses, and with few variants; they are also all found in one or more other Vedic texts: this one in SV. (i. 31), VS. (7. 41; 8. 41; 33. 31), TS. (i. 2. 8²; 4. 43¹), and MS. (i. 3. 37) — in all, without a variant. The whole hymn ⌊i.e. vss. 16–24⌋ is repeated further in xx. 47. 13–21. This verse is used three times in Vāit.: at 21. 23; at 33. 5 (with the following five verses); and at 39. 16 (with the following two verses). ⌊The *pratīka* is cited at MGS. i. 2. 4. The frequency of the citation or occurrence of the verse may be judged by consulting MGS. Index, p. 148.⌋

17. Away go, like thieves, these asterisms with their rays (*aktú*), for the all-beholding sun.

Or **c** may possibly mean 'for all to behold the sun.' The remaining verses (17–24) of the RV. hymn ⌊i.e. i. 50. 1–9⌋ are found in SV. only in the Nāigeya appendix to the first book; this one (i. 634) has no variant. Henry renders *aktúbhis* 'with the night.'

18. The lights (*ketú*), the rays of him have been seen abroad among the peoples, like shining fires.

Of the other texts, only VS. (viii. 40) follows RV. in reading at the beginning *ádṛçram;* the others (SV. i. 635; MS. i. 3. 33) agree with our text.

19. Speedy, conspicuous to all, light-making art thou, O sun; thou shinest unto everything, O bright space (*rocaná*).

All our mss. read at the end *rocana*, save Bs., which has *rocanam*, and M., *rocanám*, and the translation follows them, although the word is a senseless variant of *rocanám*, which is given by RV., and by all the other texts: SV. (i. 636), VS. (xxxiii. 36), TS. (i. 4. 31¹), TA. (iii. 16. 1), and MS. (iv. 10. 6). Ppp. has *rocanā*.

20. In front of the clans of the gods, in front of those of men thou risest; in front of every one, for seeing the sky (*svàr*).

RV. reads at end of **b** *mā́nuṣān*, and SV. (i. 637) has the same.

21. With whom [as] eye thou, O purifying Varuṇa, seest him that busies himself among the people (*jánān*).

SV. (i. 638) reads at the beginning *yéna;* VS. (xxxiii. 32) agrees with RV. and our text.

22. Thou goest through the sky, the broad welkin (*rájas*), fashioning (*mā*) the day with [thy] rays, seeing the generations (*jánman*), O sun.

RV. reads *áhā* in **b**. SV. (i. 639) has the same, and also *úd* for *ví* at the beginning, and *rájaḥ p-*. Henry again renders *aktúbhis* 'with the night.'

23. Seven yellow steeds, O heavenly sun, draw in the chariot thee the flame-haired, the out-looking.

RV. reads at the end *vicakṣaṇa*, and SV. (i. 641) and TS. (ii. 4. 14[4]) agree with it. MS. (iv. 10. 6) has instead *purupriya*, and, in the preceding word, *çocíṣk-*.

24. The sun hath yoked the seven neat (*çundhyú*) daughters of the chariot; with them, [who are] self-yoked, he goeth.

SV. (i. 640) reads in **b** *naptryàḥ*, and TB. (ii. 4. 5[4]), according to its commentary, has ⌊*naptriyaḥ*⌋, although *ná príyaḥ* is printed instead in the text ⌊of Calcutta, and *naptrīyaḥ* in the Poona text, p. 518⌋. So also in **c**, ⌊in the Calc. ed.⌋ the printed text has *yāsi*, but the comm. *yāti*; ⌊while in the Poona ed. both text and comm. give *yāti*⌋.

25. The ruddy one hath mounted the sky with penance, [he] rich in penance; he comes to the womb (*yóni*), he is born again; he hath become over-lord of the gods.

Ppp. reads in **a** *ā 'kramīt*. The Anukr. regards the verse as one of four pādas (8 + 6 : 12 + 11); but the first two are plainly one *triṣṭubh* pāda, with *tápasā* intruded into it. *Rohita* appears here for the first time in this second hymn, instead of simply the sun; nor do we meet him elsewhere, save in vss. 39–41.

26. He who belongs to all men (*-carṣaṇí*) and has faces on all sides, who has hands on all sides and palms on all sides — he brings together with his (two) arms, together with his wings (pl.), generating heaven-and-earth, sole god.

The verse is, with considerable variations, RV. x. 81. 3, found also in VS. (xvii. 19: same text as RV.), TS. (iv. 6. 2[4]), TA. (x. 1. 3), and MS. (ii. 10. 2). None of the other texts has *yás* in **b**, and only MS. in **a**; they begin *viçvátaçcakṣur* (but MS. *yó viçvácakṣur*); in **b**, RV.VS. begin with *viçvátobāhur*, TS.TA.MS. *-hasta*, and all end with *viçvátaspāt*; in **c**, for *bhárati*, RV. (and VS.) has *dhámati*, TS.TA. *námati*, MS. *ádhamat*; in **d**, RV.VS.MS. give *dyā́vābhū́mī*. Ppp. agrees with RV. in **b–d**. The meter, fairly regular in RV., is distorted greatly in our text (13 + 13 : 11 + 12 = 49); the Anukr. gives an acceptable definition of it. The sense also is much defaced in the first line as we have it. Vāit. 29. 14 uses the verse to accompany a certain *graha* in the building of the fire-altar.

27. The one-footed strode out more than the two-footed; the two-footed falls upon (*abhi-i*) the three-footed from behind; the two-footed strode out more than the six-footed; they sit together [about] the body of the one-footed.

Sam-ās has no good right to an accusative object; and one of our mss. (D.) reads *tanvàm*, loc., which would be grammatically an acceptable emendation; as regards the sense, that is too obscure for us to derive any help from it. Pādas **b** and **c** are wanting in Ppp., probably by accident. The first half-verse nearly agrees with RV. x. 117.8 **a**, **b**, which (whole) verse corresponds to ⌊the first half of⌋ our 3.25 below: see the note there. It is only here and in 3.25 that we find the accentuation *dvípāt* and *trípāt*. ⌊The *pratīka* is quoted by GB. ii. 9, p. 28, l. 19.⌋ The description of the Anukr. implies an unfounded rejection of one of the resolutions *abhí eti* or *tanú-am*.

28. When, about to go unwearied, he hath approached (*ā-sthā*) his yellow steeds, he, shining (*ruc*), makes for himself two forms; rising rich in lights (*ketú-*), overpowering the dim spaces (*rájas*), thou illuminest (*vi-bhā*), O Āditya, all the advances.

Ppp. has for **b** *divi rūpaṁ* ⌊*kṛṇuṣe;* it further combines *viçvā "ditya* in **d**⌋. ⌊Pāda **b** is identical with 42 **b**.⌋ ⌊Pischel translates the vs., *Ved. Stud.* ii. 76.⌋

29. Verily (*báṭ*), great art thou, O sun; verily, O Āditya, great art thou; great is the greatness of thee the great one; thou, O Āditya, art great.

This verse is RV. viii. 90 (or 101). 11, and is found also in VS. (xxxiii. 39) and SV. (i. 276; ii. 1138), while its *pratīka* is given by TB. (i. 4. 5³: very strange, since the whole verse occurs in no Tāittirīya text). RV. and VS. read, for **c**, **d**, *mahás te sató mahimā́ panasyate 'ddhā́ deva mahā́ṅ asi;* ⌊the vs. is repeated in RV. form at xx. 58. 3;⌋ and SV. the same, except *paniṣṭama mahnā́* for *panasyate 'ddhā́*.

30. Thou shinest (*ruc*) in the sky, thou shinest in the atmosphere, O flying one; on the earth thou shinest, thou shinest within the waters; both oceans thou hast penetrated (*vi-āp*) with thy sheen (*rúci*); a god, O god, art thou, a heaven-conquering bull (*mahiṣá*).

Ppp. reads at the end *svarvit*. The Anukr. understands the structure of the verse as 12 + 9 + 7 : 12 + 11 = 51; but it is plainly a mixed *triṣṭubh-jagatī*, rather, with *pataṅga* intruded at the end of **a**, and possibly one *rócase* in **b**. All the mss. accent *pátaṅga*, because they reckon it, with the Anukr., as first word in a pāda; it should properly be *pataṅga*.

31. Hitherward from afar, extended (*pra-yam*) in mid-route, swift, inspired, flying, he the flying one, perceived (?*vícitta*) [as] Vishṇu, surpassing (*adhi-sthā*) with strength — he overpowers with his show (*ketú*) all that stirs.

Ppp. reads at the beginning *arvāk*. ⌊'Perceived as Viṣṇu': cf. note to xiii. 4. 46.⌋

32. Wondrous, understanding (*cikitvā́ṅs*), a bull (*mahiṣá*), an eagle, making to shine the two firmaments (*ródasī*), the atmosphere — day-and-night, clothing themselves about with the sun, lengthen out all his heroisms.

The adjectives in **a**, **b** are nom. masc. sing., and the shift of construction in the second half-verse is a notable one. Ppp. combines *suparṇā "roc-*, and reads *rodasīm* in **b**. The verse is used in Vāit. 33. 8 in a sacrificial session, with the remaining verses to the end of the hymn. Ppp. puts our vs. 33 before this. ⌊The first pāda is nearly the same as 42 **c**.⌋ ⌊Henry discusses the vs. in *Mém. de la Soc. de linguistique*, x. 86.⌋

33. Keen (*tigmá*), shining out (*vi-bhrāj*), sharpening himself, granting the helpful (?*araṁgamá*) advances, a winged one full of light, a vigor-bestowing bull (*mahiṣá*), he hath approached (*ā-sthā*) all the directions, arranging (*kl̥p*).

Ppp. reads in **a–b** *tanvaç çiçāno 'raṁgamāsun dhravato rarāṇāḥ*, and in **d** combines *viçvā "sthāt*. ⌊Pischel translates the vs., *Ved. Stud.* ii. 75–6.⌋ ⌊See my discussion of accusatives pl. fem. in *-āsas* and of this passage in *Noun-Inflection*, p. 363.⌋

34. Wondrous front [and] show (*ketú*) of the gods, the sun, full of light, going up the directions (*pradíç*), the day-maker, bright (*çukrá*), hath overpassed with brightnesses (*dyumná*) the glooms (*támas*) [and] all difficulties.

This verse and the next are repeated as xx. 107. 13, 14. The definition of this one by the Anukr. ⌊as 40 syllables is right from its point of view; but the verse⌋ is evidently meant for a *triṣṭubh*, and can easily be read into a respectable one, according to the low standard of AV. *triṣṭubhs*, by a few judicious resolutions. The harshness and obscurity of the constructions in **a, b** are indications of a corrupted text; Henry renders *pradíças* by 'toward the celestial regions,' Ludwig by 'from the horizon'; the translation above simply adheres to the usual sense of the word. Verses 34–36 are directed in Vāit. 39. 16 to be used alternatively in the praise of the sun; in 21. 23, the *pratīka*, namely *citraṁ devānām* (quoted with vs. 16), might apply either to this verse or to the next.

35. The wondrous front of the gods hath arisen, the eye of Mitra, of Varuṇa, of Agni; he hath filled heaven-and-earth, the atmosphere; the sun is the soul of the moving creation (*jágat*) and of the stationary (*tasthivā́ṅs*).

The verse is RV. i. 115. 1 (only variant *ā́ : aprāḥ* in **c**), and it is found almost everywhere else: thus, in SV. (i. 630: Nāigeya appendix), VS. (vii. 42; xiii. 46), TS. (i. 4. 43[1]; ii. 4. 14[4]), TB. (ii. 8. 7[3]), TA. (i. 7. 6; ii. 13. 1), MS. (i. 3. 37), AA. (iii. 2. 3); all have the same text as RV.; and so, apparently, has Ppp., ⌊combining, however, *āprādyā-*⌋. ⌊Deussen, *Geschichte*, i. 1. 213, interprets the vs.⌋ The quotation in Vāit. 33. 6 evidently applies to the verse as AV. xx. 107. 14. ⌊In **d**, *jágas tas-* is a misprint for *jágatas tas-*: an interesting instance of most modern haplography.⌋

36. Flying on high (*uccā́*), the red eagle, in the midst of the sky hasting, shining — may we see thee, whom men call the impeller (*savitŕ̥*), the unfailing light which Atri found.

Ppp. has the better reading *paçyema* in **c**. ⌊Restore the lost accent-mark under the *ṇim* of *taráṇim*.⌋

37. To the eagle running on the back of the sky, to the son of Aditi, I, frightened, approach (*upa-yā*), desiring refuge; do thou, O sun, lengthen out for us a long life-time; may we take no harm; may we be in thy favor.

The verse is obviously a regular *triṣṭubh*, with *nāthákāmas* intruded in **b**: its description by the Anukr. ⌊gives the verse 48 syllables; but how *pañcapadā virāḍgarbhā* is to be understood is not clear⌋. ⌊The verse is quoted in Vāit. 18. 7, in the *agniṣṭoma*.⌋

38. A thousand days' journey are expanded the wings of him, of the yellow swan flying to heaven; he, putting all the gods in his breast, goes viewing together all existences.

We had the verse above as x. 8. 18, and it is repeated again below as 3. 14. Ppp. reads in **c** *sa viçvān devān.*

39. The ruddy one became time, the ruddy one in the beginning Prajāpati; the ruddy one [is] face (mouth?) of the sacrifices; the ruddy one brought the bright sky (*svàr*).

Ppp. reads in **a** *loko 'bhavat* (our 40 **a**), and, for **d**, *rohito jyotir ucyate.*

40. The ruddy one became the world; the ruddy one overheated the sky; the ruddy one with his rays goes about over the earth, the ocean.

Or (**b**) 'went heating across the sky' (so Henry). Ppp. reads in **a** *bhūto 'bhavat,* omits **b**, and has *bhūmyaṁ* in **c** ⌊cf. its *nāryaṁ* for *nārīm*, xiv. 1. 59, note⌋.

41. All the quarters did the ruddy one, over-lord of the sky, go about upon; the sky, the ocean, also the earth — all that exists doth he defend.

Ppp. has in **a** (better) *saṁ carati;* in **b** it combines *rohito adh-*; in **c** it has again *bhūmyaṁ;* in **d**, *sarvalokān vi.*

42. He, mounting, glowing [and] unwearied, the great [spaces], makes for himself, shining (*ruc*), two forms; wondrous, understanding, ⌊bull,⌋ wind-going (??), when he shines out (*vi-bhā*) upon as many worlds [as there are].

That is, 'upon all existing worlds.' The second pāda is 28 **b** above; the third, nearly 32 **a**. The rendering of *vātamāyās* (p. *vā́tam-āyāḥ*) in **c** is purely to fill up the text. Henry emends to *vā́tam ā́pas;* Ludwig renders 'possessing wind-magic.' The Anukr. passes without notice the redundant syllable in **c**. Ppp. has a quite different version of much of the verse: *ārohaṅ chakro vṛhatīr yuṁktor amartyāṣ kṛṇuṣe vīryāṇi: divyas suparṇo muhiṣaṁ vātaraṅhāya: sarvāṅl lokāṅ abhi* etc. This would suggest *vāta-raṅhās* 'wind-swift' as emendation of *vātamāyās.*

43. The one he falls upon (*abhi-i*), the other he casts about — the bull, arranging with day-and-night; we, imploring, call upon the track-finding sun, dwelling in the welkin (*rájas*).

In the very obscure first half-verse, the two *anyat's* may be subjects instead (so Ludwig and Henry), *asyate* being taken as passive — which would seem more natural, save that then the nominative in **b** is left without construction. Ppp. reads in **a–b** *eti sadyo 'yaṁ vasāvam aho-*, and in **d** *nāthamānāḥ.* The verse (12 + 12 : 11 + 12 = 47) is a very irregular "*jagatī.*"

44. The earth-filling bull (*mahiṣá*), track of the implorer, of undamaged sight, hath encompassed the all; beholding (*sam-paç*) the all, beneficent, reverend, let him hear this which I say.

'Track' (in **b**), i.e. facilitation or facilitator of progress. *Mahiṣas* is an evident intrusion, and the verse is strictly a *triṣṭubh* with redundant syllables. Ppp. reads in **a** *pṛthivipro m. bādhamānasya;* for **b**, *adbhutacakṣuṣ pari saṁ babhūva;* and, for **d**, *çivāyā nas tanvā çarma yacchāt*, which is found nowhere in our text. All our mss. ⌊except D.⌋ agree in accenting *babhū́va*, for no discoverable reason. ⌊Five of SPP's authorities (as well as W's D.) read *babhūva* without accent.⌋

45. The greatness of him exceeds (*pári*) the earth, the ocean; shining abroad with light, it exceeds (*pári*) the sky, the atmosphere; beholding the all, beneficent, reverend, let him hear this which I say.

Ppp. again objects to our second half-verse, and gives instead: *ahorātrābhyām̐ saha sam̐vasānā uṣā nīyus pratarād aviṣṭam.* The "*jagatī*" is again a very rough one ⌊as the Anukr. in part admits⌋. ⌊W. interlines "encompasses" as an alternative to "exceeds."⌋

46. Agni hath been awakened by the kindling of men to meet the dawn coming like a milch-cow; like young (*yahvá*) [birds?] rising forth to a branch, the lights (*bhānú*) go forth unto the firmament (*nā́ka*).

Ppp. reads in **d** *sasṛje.* The verse is RV. v. 1. 1, and is found also in other texts: SV. (i. 73; ii. 1096), VS. (xv. 24), TS. (iv. 4. 4[1]), and MS. (ii. 13. 7), everywhere without a variant. ⌊SV. (both occurrences) reads *sasrate* in **d**; TS. accents *achá* at the end.⌋ It is quoted in Vāit. 29. 8, apparently in connection with the verses that follow it in RV. (*iti trāiṣṭubhīḥ*).

⌊Here ends the second *anuvāka*, with 1 hymn and 46 verses. The quoted Anukr. says *ṣaṭ catvārin̄çat.*⌋

3. To the sun (with imprecation on the evil-doer).

[(*Brahman.—ādhyātmam; rohitādityadevatyam. trāiṣṭubham.*) *1. 4-av. 8-p. ākṛti; 2–4. 3-av. 6-p.* (*2, 3. aṣṭi, 2. bhurij; 4. atiçākvaragarbhā dhṛti*); *5–7. 4-av. 7-p.* (*5, 6. çākvarātiçākvaragarbhā prakṛti; 7. anuṣṭubgarbhā 'tidhṛti*); *8. 3-av. 6-p. atyaṣṭi; 9–19. 4-av.* (*9–12, 15, 17. 7-p. bhurig atidhṛti, 15. nicṛt, 17. kṛti; 13, 14, 16, 18, 19. 8-p., 13, 14. vikṛti, 16, 18, 19. ākṛti, 19. bhurij*); *20, 22. 3-av. 6-p. atyaṣṭi; 21, 23–25. 4-av. 8-p.* (*24. 7-p. kṛti; 21. ākṛti; 23, 25. vikṛti*).] *

Of this hymn only one verse is found in Pāipp., namely vs. 10 in iv. Vāit. makes use of no part of it; and Kāuç. ⌊49. 19⌋ only of the first verse. ⌊Caland, p. 173, understands the whole hymn to be intended at 49. 19; and takes 49. 24 and 25 as referring to vss. 6 and 7 of this hymn.⌋ *⌊The definition of vs. 26 (*anuṣṭubh*) appears to be omitted.—The individual pādas of this hymn are largely of genuine *triṣṭubh* measure and cadence, occasionally *jagatī;* and this is possibly the intention of the "*trāiṣṭubham*" of the Anukr. (for not a single verse foots up as 44 syllables): then, again, if to the verse proper in each case we add the refrain and reckon up the totals, we get the *ākṛtis* etc. of the Anukr.⌋

Translated: Ludwig, p. 543; Henry, 14, 45; Deussen, *Geschichte*, i. 1. 226; Griffith, ii. 150.

1. He who generated these two, heaven-and-earth; who clothes himself in existences, making them a garment (*drā́pi*); in whom abide the six wide directions, toward which he, the flying one, looks all abroad—against that god, angered, [is] this offense (*ā́gas*); whoso scathes a Brahman that knows thus, do thou, O ruddy one, make him quake, destroy him; fasten on the fetters of the Brahman-scather.

All the mss. agree in the accent of *drā́pi* (RV. always *drāpí*). As is their habit, they give of the refrain only the single word *tásya* except in vss. 1 and 25; and there they set the *avasāna* not before *tásya*, but after *devásya*: in our edition this perversion of the natural division is corrected. The refrain, if we contract *yá evám* to *yā́t 'vám*, is a regular *triṣṭubh;* its addition to a preceding verse makes this hymn one of especially long meters; the first verse, 8 pādas of 11 syllables each, is an exact *ākṛti*. The verse ⌊or the hymn: see introduction⌋ is (though v. 12. 9 has the same *pratīka*) doubtless the one quoted in Kāuç. 49. 19, with xiii. 1. 28 and xvi. 6. 1, to accompany the laying on of fetters; and Bloomfield suggests that the whole hymn (or *anuvāka*) is intended also in 63. 21, one does not see why.

2. From whom the winds in their season go purifying (*pū*), out of whom the oceans flow forth — against that god etc. etc.

With **b** compare 1. 42 **d**. The verse (10 + 11 : 44 = 65) has one more syllable than a regular *aṣṭi*, as the Anukr. notices. ⌊The longer grammatical equivalent of *vā́tās* would improve the rhythm.⌋

3. Who causes to die [and] causes to breathe; from whom all existences breathe — against that god etc. etc.

An exact *aṣṭi* (9 + 11 : 44 = 64).

4. Who gratifies heaven-and-earth with breath; who fills the belly of the ocean with respiration — against that god etc. etc.

The meter is correctly enough described by the Anukr. The omission of either *apānena* or *samudrasya* would rectify the meter of **b**.

5. In whom is set (*çritá*) Virāj, the most exalted one, Prajāpati, Agni Vāiçvānara with the series (*paṅktí*); who took to himself the breath of the lofty one, the brilliancy of the loftiest one — against that god etc. etc.

We had nearly the same combination of divine personages above in viii. 5. 10 **c**, **d**; and the *paṅkti* here perhaps corresponds to the 'all the seers' there. The verse, of very irregular meter (12 + 12 : 15 : 44 = 83), is very nearly a *prakṛti* (84 syll.).

6. Upon whom are set (*çritá*) the six wide [spaces], the five quarters, the four waters, the three syllables (? *akṣára*) of the sacrifice; who, angered, looked with his eye between the two firmaments (*ródasī*) — against that god etc. etc.

All our mss. read at end of **b** *akṣárā* (not *-rāḥ*), doubtless under the influence of the ordinary use of *akṣára* as neuter. The omission in **c** of *cákṣuṣā* would better both sense and meter. The verse as best read (12 + 12 : 14 : 44 = 82) lacks two syllables of a full *prakṛti*, but could easily be filled up by resolution. ⌊For the transition *-t* after *yásmin*, cf. Prāt. ii. 9 note.⌋ ⌊Caland, p. 173, understands this vs. and the following to be intended at Kāuç. 49. 24, 25, for use in the ceremony of the "water-thunderbolts": cf. introd. to x. 5.⌋

7. Who became food-eater, lord of food, and also Brahmaṇaspati (lord of worship); who is and shall be lord of existence — against that god etc. etc.

The translation implies *bhaviṣyán* instead of *-yát* in **c**; either this emendation or that of *bhūtás* to *bhūtám* (which Ludwig and Henry assume in their versions) seems unavoidable. Our *saṁhitā*-mss. are divided between *-dó ánnapatir* and *-dó 'nna-* in **a**. The verse (11 + 8 : 12 : 44 = 75) is very near a regular *atidhṛti* (76 syll.). ⌊Cf. note to vs. 6 for use by Kāuç.⌋

8. He who measures out the thirteenth month, fabricated (*vi-mā*) of days-and-nights, having thirty members — against that god etc. etc.

The verse (6 × 11 = 66) lacks two syllables of a full *atyaṣṭi* (68 syll.).

9. Black the descent, the yellow eagles, clothing themselves in waters, fly up to the sky; they have come hither from the seat of righteousness — against that god etc. etc.

The first three pādas are RV. i. 164. 47 **a–c**, found also twice above, as vi. 22. 1; ix. 10. 22. The verse (7 × 11 = 77) is accurately described by the Anukr. It, with a good part of those that follow (11–16, 18–21, 23, 25), appears to have nothing to do with the refrain.

10. What of thee, O Kaçyapa, is bright (*candrá*), full of shining (*rocanā́vant*), what that is combined (*saṁhitá*), splendid (*puṣkalá*), of wondrous light, in which seven suns are set (*ā́rpita*) together — against that god etc. etc.

One of our mss. (T.: ⌊and perhaps also M.⌋) ⌊and one of SPP's⌋ accent *púṣkalam* (like *púṣkara*) in **b**. All ⌊of W's and of SPP's⌋ agree in the anomalous and probably incorrect accent *saṁhitám*. ⌊Cf., however, *Gram.* § 1085 b. Perhaps the case of *saṁskṛtám* at xi. 1. 35 is not parallel.⌋ Ppp. has (as noticed above) this verse, reading in **a** *kaçyapo ro-*, combining in **c** *sūryā "rpitās sapta*, and ⌊without *avasāna* after *sākam*⌋ having, as was to be expected, a wholly different apodosis: *tasmin rājānam adhi vi çraye 'mam* (cf. our ix. 5. 4 **d**), for which the refrain of this hymn is a senseless substitute. The verse is found also in K. xxxvii. 9. Our Bp. omits, by accident, the division-sign of *rocanā́vat* in **a**.

11. The *bṛhát* dresses itself in him in front; the *rathaṁtará* accepts [him] behind: [both] clothing themselves always in light unremittingly — against that god etc. etc.

12. The *bṛhát* was his wing on the one side, *rathaṁtará* on the other, [both] of like strength, of like motion (? *sadhryàñc*), when the gods generated the ruddy one — against that god etc. etc.

This verse counts 77 syllables, as required, but is irregular (9 + 13 : 11 : 44).

13. This Agni becomes Varuṇa in the evening; in the morning, rising, he becomes Mitra; he, having become Savitar, goes through the atmosphere; he, having become Indra, burns (*tap*) through the midst of the sky. — Against that god etc. etc.

Or (**a**) 'he becomes Varuṇa at evening [and] Agni' (so Henry: cf. Ludwig). The verse is very irregular, but can be made to count a *vikṛti* (92 syll.).

14. A thousand days' journey are expanded the wings of him, of the yellow swan flying to heaven; he, putting all the gods in his breast, goes viewing together all existences. — Against that god etc. etc.

The verse proper here is a repetition of x. 8. 18 and xiii. 2. 38; it is written in full in all the mss., because they have no other way of indicating the attachment here of the refrain. It is properly an *ākṛti* (8 × 11 = 88 syll.).

15. This is that god within the waters, the thousand-rooted, many-powered (?) Atri; he who generated all this existence — against that god etc. etc.

Henry makes in **b** the naturally-suggested emendation to *puruçā́khas*, 'many-branched'; ⌊cf. Bloomfield, AJP. xii. 436, and, *per contra*, Deussen, p. 228, note⌋. The verse is most naturally read as (9 + 11 : 11 : 44 = 75) a *nicṛd atidhṛti*, in accordance with the description of the Anukr.

16. Swift-running yellow [horses] draw the bright one (*çukrá*), the god shining with splendor in the sky, whose lofty bodies heat the sky; hitherward with well-colored gleams (?*paṭará*) he shines forth. — Against that god etc. etc.

Our edition ought to give in **c** *tanvàs*, since that is the *pada*-reading, and it is only by accident that nearly all the *saṁhitā*-mss. (all save R.K.) unite in protracting the *à* to *ā̀*. The verse reads most naturally as a *bhurig ākṛti* (12 + 11 : 11 + 11 : 44 = 89).

17. By whom the yellow steeds draw the Ādityas together; by what sacrifice go many foreknowing; which, sole light, shines forth variously — against that god etc. etc.

Yajñéna 'sacrifice' in **b** looks as if it needed emendation, and the irregularity of the pāda suggests corruption. Our mss. read at the end *ví bhāti* and the *pada*-text has *ví॰bhāti**; our text makes a change of accent to *vibhā́ti*. The verse (11 + 14 : 11 : 44 = 80) counts up a precise *kṛti*.

*⌊A similar *pada*-reading, impossible with the accentless verb-form, we met at vi. 74. 2 (see the note thereto) and at vi. 114. 2 (see note). And here, as at vi. 74. 2, a suspicion arises that an error has come in from confusion with a similar form near by, here with the ending of vs. 16 proper, where *ví bhāti* is called for. All SPP's authorities have *ví bhāti*, except his P[2], which has *vi॰bhā́ti*. This reading he also adopts. — The rationale of the blunder at xiv. 2. 59 (see note) appears to be similar. Cf. also the accent of *sarvé* at xiii. 4. 21, and note.⌋

18. Seven harness a one-wheeled chariot; one horse, having seven names, draws [it]; of three naves [is] the wheel, unwasting, unassailed, whereon stand all these existences. — Against that god etc. etc.

We had the verse (which is RV. i. 164. 2) above as ix. 9. 2. The mss. all give it in full here (as in the case of vs. 14 above).

19. Harnessed eight-fold draws the formidable draft-horse (*váhni*), father of gods, generator of prayers (*matí*); measuring with the mind the line of righteousness, Mātariçvan goes cleansing (*pū*) to all the quarters. — Against that god etc. etc.

Or perhaps 'he goes as Mātariçvan,' identifying the action of sun and of wind. *Mimā́nas* in **c** should be emended to *mímānas*, which is read only by D. The Anukr. notices this time the redundant syllable in **a**.

20. A united (*samyáñc*) line along all the directions, within the *gāyatrī́*, the womb (embryo?) of the immortal. — Against that god etc. etc.

'Line' here is accus., as taking up and carrying on the idea of 19 **c**. The verse lacks two syllables of being a full *atyaṣṭi* (68 syll.).

21. Three settings, dawnings also three; three welkins, skies verily three: we know, O Agni, the birth-place of thee threefold; threefold the births of the gods we know. — Against that god etc. etc.

The verse is regular if *tredhā́* in **c** (not in **d**) is made, as often elsewhere, trisyllabic.

22. He who in birth (*jā́yamāna*) opened out the earth, [who] set the ocean in the atmosphere — against that god etc. etc.

The meter is the same as that of vs. 20.

23. Thou, O Agni, impelled by powers (*krátu*), by lights (*ketú*), didst shine up, a kindled song (?*arká*) in the sky; unto what did the Maruts, having the spotted one for mother, sing, when the gods generated the ruddy one? — Against that god etc. etc.

Pischel (*Ved. Stud.* i. 26) takes *arká* as 'sun'; the connection with *abhy ārcan* in **c** is strongly opposed to this. The last pāda is the same with 12 **c** above. The verse (12 + 12 : 12 + 11 : 44) counts properly 91 syllables, one short of a full *vikṛti*.

24. He who is self-giving, strength-giving, of whom all, of whom [even] the gods wait upon the direction, who is master of these bipeds, who of quadrupeds — against that god etc. etc.

The verse proper is identical with the first three pādas of iv. 2. 1 (found also in other texts: see the notes to that hymn). Bp. here reads (doubtless by accident) *asya* in **c**. Two more syllables are needed to make a full *kṛti* (80 syll.).

25. The one-footed strode out more than the two-footed; the two-footed falls upon the three-footed from behind; the four-footed acted within the call of the two-footed ones, beholding the series (*paṅtí*), drawing near (*upa-sthā*). — Against that god etc. etc.

The first two pādas are identical with 2. 27 **a**, **b**, and the whole verse corresponds to RV. x. 117. 8. RV. reads in **a** *bhū́yo dvipádo*, in **b** *dvipā́t tripā́dam*, in **c** *eti* (for *cakre*) *dvipádām*, in **d** *paṅktī́r up-*. The accentuation *dvípāt* and *trípāt* (only in these verses) was noticed under 2. 27. Here we lack two syllables of a full *vikṛti*.

26. The white son of the black [mother], the young of night, was born; he ascends upon the sky; the ruddy one ascended the ascents.

⌊Here ends the third *anuvāka*, with 1 hymn and 26 verses. The quoted Anukr. says *ṣaḍviṅçat* (*ṣaḍviṅça?*).⌋

4. Extolling the sun.

[(*Brahman.* — *ādhyātmam ; rohitādityadevatyam. trāiṣṭubham.**) *ṣaṭ paryāyāḥ. mantrokta devatyāḥ.*]

⌊Partly prose, and vss. 14–15, 22–26, and 46–56 are so designated in W's Index, p. 6.⌋ This hymn is not found in Pāipp., nor noticed either in Kāuç. or in Vāit. *⌊Here, indeed (but cf. introd. to hymn 3), the general definition for the whole *kāṇḍa* as "*trāiṣṭubham*" does not seem to apply.⌋

Translated: Henry, 17, 51 ; Griffith, ii. 154.

[**Paryāya I.** — *trayodaça. 1–11. prājāpatyā 'nuṣṭubh ; 12. virāḍ gāyatrī ; 13. āsury uṣṇih.*]

1. He goes [as] impeller (Savitar) to the heaven (*svàr*), looking down upon the back of the sky.

2. To the cloud-mass (*nábhas*) brought by rays he goes [as] great Indra, covered.

3. He [is] the Creator (*dhātṛ́*), he the disposer, he Vāyu, the upraised (*ut-çri*) cloud-mass.

A syllable is lacking, unless we make harsh resolution, in **a**.

4. He [is] Aryaman, he Varuṇa, he Rudra, he the great god.

5. He [is] Agni, he also the Sun, he indeed great Yama.

Parts of this verse are quoted as examples under Prāt. ii. 21, 24 ; iii. 35, 36 ; iv. 116.

6. On him wait (*upa-sthā*) young ones (*vatsá*), ten, united, having one head.

Henry acutely suggests emendation in **b** to *-no 'yútā dáça* 'ten myriads' — i.e. of rays, all heading in the sun itself. It seems probable that the original text had *ékaçīrṣās :* cf. *dáçaçīrṣas*, iv. 6. 1 ; the verse as it stands is redundant.

7. From behind they stretch on forward ; when he rises, he shines forth.

Vibhā́sati would seem a better reading at the end.

8. His is this troop of Maruts ; he goes sling-made.

That is (?), 'as if hung in slings' ⌊OB. 'an Schnüre gehängt'⌋. Henry makes a venturesome and unacceptable emendation, and regards the adjective as referring to the 'troop' — which is not impossible.

9. To the cloud-mass brought by rays he goes [as] great Indra, covered.

This is a repetition of vs. 2 ; all the mss. give it in full.

10. His are these nine vessels (*kóça*), the props set nine-fold.

The *pada*-text reads *viṣṭambhā́ḥ*, undivided.

11. He looks abroad for living creatures (*prajā́*), both what breathes and what does not.

Cf. vs. 19, below : 'for,' apparently 'for the advantage of.'

12. Into him is entered (*ni-gam*) this power; he himself is one, single (*ekavṛ́t*), one only.

The verse lacks four syllables of the *gāyatrī* number, instead of two, as the Anukr. counts.

13. These gods in him become single.

The Anukr. counts fourteen syllables in the verse; one does not see where it finds more than thirteen.

[**Paryāya II.** — *aṣṭāu. 14. bhurik sāmnī triṣṭubh; 15. āsurī pañkti; 16, 19. prājāpatyā 'nuṣṭubh; 17, 18. āsurī gāyatrī.*]

14. Both fame and glory and water (?*ámbhas*) and cloud-mass and Brahman-splendor and food and food-eating.

The Pet. Lex. regards *nábhaç ca* as intruded here, and *ámbhas* as having the sense of 'might.'

15. He who knows this single god —

16. Not second, not third, also not fourth is he called.

17. Not fifth, not sixth, also not seventh is he called.

18. Not eighth, not ninth, also not tenth is he called.

19. He looks abroad for everything, both what breathes and what does not.

20. Into him is entered this power; he himself is one, single, one only.

21. All the gods in him become single.

The last three verses are nearly identical with 11–13 above. Of the last two the Anukr. does not define the meter, perhaps by an omission in the ms. (or else because they were defined just above). All our mss. save one (D.) ⌊and all SPP's authorities, except P²⌋ accent *sarvé* in 21, as if because of *eté* in 13. ⌊Both editions emend to *sárve.*⌋

[**Paryāya III.** — *sapta. 22. bhurik prājāpatyā triṣṭubh; 23. ārcī gāyatrī; 25. 1-p. āsurī gāyatrī; 26. ārcy anuṣṭubh; 27, 28. prājāpatyā 'nuṣṭubh.*]

22. Both worship (*bráhman*) and penance and fame and glory and water and cloud-mass and Brahman-splendor and food and food-eating —

This is vs. 14 over again, with two more items prefixed.

23. And what is and what shall be and faith and sheen and heaven (*svargá*) and *svadhā́*.

The mss. vary between *bhavyàm* (Bp.), *bhávyam* (Bs.p.m.D.), and *bhavyám* (Bs.s.m., and all the rest). ⌊SPP's authorities show a similar disagreement. He reads *bhávyam;* and the same reading⌋ in our text is evidently called for.

24. He who knows this single god —

This verse is identical with vs. 15 above, and is accordingly not separately described by the Anukr.

25. He verily [is] death, he immortality (*amṛ́ta*), he the monster (*abhvà*), he the demon.

The verse is probably quoted under Prāt. iii. 65 (see the note there). In order to make out the fifteen syllables of the Anukr., we have to read *só amṛ́taṁ só abhvàm.*

26. He [is] Rudra, winner of good, in the giving of good; in the expression of homage, [he is] the utterance *váṣaṭ*, put together after.

The connection here is very doubtful. Henry understands it as above; Muir (iv. 338) quite differently. The verse is very peculiarly treated by the Anukr.; first it is quoted in its proper place thus: *sa rudra ity ārṣī* (so the Berlin ms., but the London ms. has *āsurī*) *gāyatrī;* and then, after the definition of vss. 27, 28, the London ms. says again *sa rudro vasuvanir ārcy anuṣṭup.* The descriptions *ārṣī gāyatrī* and *ārcy anuṣṭubh* (each implying 24 syllables) both apply equally well, if we restore *-kāró ánu.*

27. All these familiar demons (*yātú*) wait upon his direction (*praçís*).

28. In his control are all yon asterisms, together with the moon.

[**Paryāya IV.** —*saptadaça. 29, 33, 39, 40, 45. āsurī gāyatrī; 30, 32, 35, 36, 42. prājāpatyā 'nuṣṭubh; 31. virāḍ gāyatrī; 34, 37, 38. sāmny uṣṇih; 41. sāmnī bṛhatī; 43. ārṣī gāyatrī; 44. sāmny anuṣṭubh.*]

29. He verily was born of the day; of him the day was born.

The Anukr. unaccountably ratifies the elision *áhno 'j-*, instead of restoring *aj-* and recognizing the pāda for what it is, eight syllables.

30. He verily was born of the night; of him the night was born.

31. He verily was born of the atmosphere; of him the atmosphere was born.

The verse lacks four syllables, instead of two, of the twenty-four that make a *gāyatrī.*

32. He verily was born of Vāyu (wind); of him Vāyu was born.

33. He verily was born of the sky; out of him the sky was born.

Here again the Anukr. requires us to read *divò 'j-.*

34. He verily was born of the quarters; of him the quarters were born.

Here we are to make both elisions, in **a** and **b**.

35. He verily was born of the earth; of him the earth was born.

Nearly all our mss. (all save Bp.D.R.) accent *bhūmés* and *bhūmís.*

36. He verily was born of fire; of him fire was born.

37. He verily was born of the waters; of him the waters were born.

The metrical description is the same as that of vs. 34, and with the same lack of good reason (the mss. read *sa vā adbhya ṛgbhyaḥ sāmnyuṣṇiganuṣṭubhāu*, which is senseless, and should doubtless be emended to *-uṣṇihāu*).

38. He verily was born of the verses (*ṛ́c*); of him the verses were born.

As to the meter, see the note to the preceding verse.

39. He verily was born of the sacrifice; of him the sacrifice was born.

The Anukr., as above, forces the elision *yajñò 'j-*.

40. He is the sacrifice; his is the sacrifice; he [is] made the head of the sacrifice.

41. He thunders; he lightens; he indeed hurls the stone.

That is, the thunderbolt. The second pāda is one of the examples under Prāt. iii. 36.

42. Either for the evil [man] or for the excellent; for man or for Asura.

'For,' i.e. 'at,' ⌊taking the verse as a continuation of 41⌋.

43. Either when thou makest the herbs, or when thou rainest excellently, or when thou hast increased him of the people (? *janyá*).

This appears to be the only example known of the accent *janyá* instead of *jánya*, and how little authoritative it is may be inferred from the fact that all our mss. leave *avīvṛdhas* unaccented after it. Our text makes the necessary emendation to *áv-*. ⌊All SPP's authorities, however, agree in reading not only *janyám* but also *avīvṛdhas*. The latter he also emends to *áv-*.⌋

44. Such, O bountiful one, is thy greatness; and thine, too (*úpa*), are a hundred bodies.

There is no difficulty in counting the verse into 16 syllables, as required by the Anukr. ⌊It reads naturally as 9 + 8.⌋

45. Thine, too, are two billions, [many] billions (?); or else thou art a hundred million.

The translation implies the readings *bádve bádvāni*, which, on account of the accent, seem probably meant by the mss., which vary between *bádhv-*, *báddh-*, *báddhv-*; K. reads *baddhve vádvāni*, D. *báddhe baddhā́ni*. ⌊SPP's authorities also exhibit very wide disagreements, which reflect a corresponding uncertainty of the tradition.⌋ The word is just such a one as the mss. might be expected to boggle and blunder over, both they and we being left without help from the sense. Henry, who accepts the same emendation, understands *bádve* as locative, which is perhaps better, and at any rate favored by the fact that the *pada*-text does not read *bádve íti*.

[**Paryāya V.** — *ṣaṭ. 46. āsurī gāyatrī; 47. yavamadhyā gāyatrī; 48. sāmny uṣṇih; 49. nicṛt sāmnī bṛhatī; 50. prājāpatyā 'nuṣṭubh; 51. virāḍ gāyatrī.*]

46. More is Indra than non-dying (??); more art thou, O Indra, than the deaths.

'Non-dying' is the conjecture of the Pet. Lexx. for *namurá*, which occurs nowhere else; it is adopted here, simply for lack of anything better, although in itself of a high degree of implausibility. ⌊Henry also adopts it; but see his note, p. 54.⌋ It is surprising to find Indra brought in here at the end for address, instead of the sun; there is nothing to show that the two remaining *paryāyas* are not for him. ⌊Note, however, the praise of the sun under the names of Indra and Viṣṇu, so prominent in book xvii., below: see page 805. Perhaps we have here a similar identification.⌋

47. More than the niggard, lord of strength (*çácī*) art thou, O Indra; as called mighty, prevailing, do we worship (*upa-ās*) thee.

Prāt. ii. 71 expressly forbids the combination *çácyās p-*, which we should have expected here. The verse (9 + 8 : 8 = 25) is strangely defined by the Anukr.

48. Homage be to thee, O conspicuous one (*paçyata*); see ⌊*páçya*⌋ me, O conspicuous one.

Paçyata is an anomalous and forced substitute for *darçata*, made in this passage only, for assonance with *paçya*. The Anukr. ratifies the combination *te astu*.

49. With food-eating, with glory, with brilliancy (*téjas*), with Brahman-splendor;

50. As called water (?*ámbhas*), force (*áma*), greatness, power, do we worship thee.

The Anukr. ratifies the combination *ámbho ámo*. ' By a usage that is rare, all the mss. omit in this verse ⌊what follows⌋ after *íti*, although the repetition is not of the end of the next preceding verse, but of vs. 47. Then, of course, the following verses are written in the same curtailed way until vs. 54, which is filled out to the end.

51. As called water (*ámbhas*), red, silvery (*rajatá*), welkin (*rájas*), power, do we worship thee.

Again ⌊as at vs. 31⌋ we have a verse called *virāḍ gāyatrī* which lacks four syllables of being 24.

[**Paryāya VI.** —*pañca. 52, 53. prājāpatyā 'nuṣṭubh; 54. 2-p. ārṣī gāyatrī.*]

52. As called wide, broad, happy (*subhū́*), earths (?*bhúvas*), do we worship thee.

Bhúvas is here rendered literally, in the only sense which the word has elsewhere in AV. If it is a first appearance of the *vyāhṛti* common later, its meaning is wholly obscure in this connection. ⌊Aufrecht, KZ. xxxiv. 458, makes some observations about the relations of the noun-forms and adjective-forms in vss. 52–53.⌋

53. As called breadth, width, expanse, world, do we worship thee.

54. As called one of arising good, of increasing (??) good, of gathering good, of coming good, do we worship thee.

The translation implies the heroic substitution of *vṛdhádvasu* for the wholly senseless *idádvasu*. The Pet. Lexx., to be sure, conjecture for the latter the meaning 'rich in this and that' (which Henry follows); but, besides the fact that *idát* = *idám* is not less heroic than *idát* = *vṛdhát*, the signification given does not belong rightly to the compound, nor has it any application here. Our rendering has at least concinnity — unless, indeed, in a text of this character, that be an argument against its acceptance. All the compounds are evidently possessive.

55. Homage be to thee, O conspicuous one; see me, O conspicuous one.

56. With food-eating, with glory, with brilliancy, with Brahman-splendor.

These two verses are identical with vss. 48, 49, above ⌊and are therefore not defined by the Anukr.⌋.

⌊The quotations from the Old Anukr., given piecemeal for this *paryāya-sūkta* at the end of each *paryāya*, may here be given together: I. *trayodaça;* II. *aṣṭāu ca;* III. *tataḥ paraḥ sapta;* IV. *saptadaça;* V. *ṣaṭ ca bodhyāḥ;* VI. *ṣaṣṭhaḥ pañcaka ucyate.*— They are given by SPP. in his "Critical Notice," vol. i., p. 21, with the introductory words, *caturthasyā 'vasānāni vakṣyamāṇāni tāni çṛṇu.*⌋

⌊In *paryāya* V., vss. 47, 50, and 51 have the refrain; and in VI., vss. 52, 53, and 54 have it: these verses are styled *gaṇāvasānarcaḥ*, and the rest *avasānarcaḥ* (as was already noted above, p. 472). But since none of the former is divided in two by an *avasāna*-mark, the distinction does not affect the sums of the "*ṛcaḥ* of both kinds," which are (as just stated) 3 + 3 for V. and 3 + 2 for VI.⌋

⌊Here ends the fourth *anuvāka*, consisting of 1 *paryāya-sūkta* with 6 *paryāyas* and 56 verses.⌋

⌊Some mss. reckon up the hymns as 20 (that is 14 of the decad-divisions of our hymns 1–3, plus 6 *paryāyas* of our hymn 4) and the verses as 188.⌋

⌊Here ends the twenty-eighth *prapāṭhaka*.⌋

Book XIV.

⌊Nuptial Hymns.⌋

⌊Nuptial ceremonies. — This fourteenth book is the second of the six books (xiii.–xviii.) that form the third grand division of the Atharvan collection, and shows very clearly that unity of subject which is the distinguishing characteristic of the books of that division. The book has been translated by Weber, *Indische Studien*, vol. v. (1862), pages 178–217; and the parts peculiar to our text by Ludwig in his *Der Rigveda*, vol. iii. (*Die Mantra-litteratur*), pages 470–476. The *bhāṣya* is again lacking.⌋

⌊The subject of the book has been often treated: thus, by that great scholar, Colebrooke, in 1801, in vol. vii. of the *Asiatic Researches* (the paper is reprinted in Cowell's edition of H. T. Colebrooke's *Essays*, vol. i., pages 217–238); by E. Haas, in the volume of Weber's *Studien*, just cited, pages 267–412, *Die Heirathsgebräuche der alten Inder, nach den Gṛihyasūtra;* and latterly by Dr. M. Winternitz, in the *Denkschriften* of the Vienna Academy for 1892, vol. xl., *Das altindische Hochzeitsrituell nach dem Āpastambīya-gṛihyasūtra* etc., with a detailed comparison of the nuptial ceremonies prevailing among the other Indo-European peoples. Then, some five years later (in 1897), in the *Anecdota Oxoniensia*, Dr. Winternitz published *The Mantra-pāṭha or the Prayer Book of the Āpastambins*, which contains very many of the *mantras* cited in the editor's *Hochzeitsrituell;* and for this reason the citations of those *mantras* are given below in duplicate, in order that they may be easily found in either work. — Here may be mentioned also the elaborate comments given in my *Sanskrit Reader*, pages 398–401, upon chapters 5, 7, and 8 of Āçvalāyana's Gṛhyasūtra, book i., which treat of the wedding customs and the wedding-service.⌋

⌊**Division into anuvākas.** — This book is divided into two *anuvākas*, the first with 64 verses, and the second with 75. This division is confirmed by the Old Anukr. or *Pañcapaṭalikā* (as quoted at the end of each *anuvāka*), which says *ādyaḥ sāuryaç catuḥṣaṣṭiḥ* and *pañcasaptatir uttaraḥ*. Here *ādyaḥ* and *uttaraḥ* doubtless refer to *anuvākaḥ* understood. It is also confirmed by AV. xix. 23. 24.⌋

⌊**The decad-division** is shown in the mss. as usual: thus hymn 1 is divided into 6 "decad"-*sūktas* (5 tens and 1 "decad" of 14 vss.), and hymn 2 is divided into 8 "decad"-*sūktas* (7 tens and 1 "decad" of 5 vss.). The sum is 14 "decad"-*sūktas*.⌋

⌊**Division into hymns.** — This seems to be a matter more or less questionable. By the Berlin edition, and also by that of SPP., the book is in fact divided into two hymns, each of which coincides with an *anuvāka*, as is the case with books xii. and xiii. The Old Anukr. seems to offer no evidence either for or against the division into hymns.⌋

⌊The mss. seem to support the division of the book into two hymns: thus, at the end of *anuvāka* 1, several mss. say *anuvāke arthasūkta 1; ṛcā* (!) *64;* [supply presumably *daçatayaḥ*] *6.* And, at the end of the second, they say *anuvāke arthasūkta 1; ṛcā 75.* Moreover, as noted on page 768, some mss. sum up the book as of two hymns.⌋

⌊The Major Anukr., on the other hand, seems rather to indicate that the book should not be divided into two hymns: 1. by its mingling the verses of the whole book together (see the next paragraph, which is by Mr. Whitney) in its metrical and other definitions; and 2. by its expression *çatatamyā* [*ṛcā*] 'hundredth verse,' which implies a continuous counting from the beginning of the book beyond the limits of the first *anuvāka* (or hymn?), which contains only 64 verses. *Per contra*, this method of designating a verse by any ordinal higher than the first few ordinals is very unusual, and (so far as I have noted) unexampled, save by the expression *trayoviṅçatikayā* in the next clause and by the ordinals of Kāuç. 49. 24, 25 (see note to x. 5. 6).⌋

The descriptions of meter etc. are ⌊by the Major Anukr.⌋ given together for the whole book; they are here separated for the two recognized divisions (*anuvākas*, treated as hymns) in accordance with the method elsewhere followed. The order of verses is so much disregarded in the metrical etc. descriptions as to make one wonder whether the arrangement contemplated by the Anukr. was the same with that which we have ⌊cf. p. 740, top⌋; yet minor deviations from the order are not very rare elsewhere. Other special points are mentioned in the notes to the verses.

⌊The Major Anukr. begins its treatment of the book as follows: *satyene 'ti* (xiv. 1. 1) *sāikonacatvāriṅçachataṁ dvayānuvākakāṇḍam. Sāvitrī Sūryā. ātmadāivatam. ānuṣṭubham. prathamābhiḥ pañcabhiḥ* (xiv. 1. 1–5) *somam astāut; parābhiḥ* (xiv. 1. 6–?) *svavivāham; çatatamyā* [?] (xiv. 2. 36) *devān; trayoviṅçatikayā* (xiv. 1. 23) *somārkāu; parayā* (xiv. 1. 24) *candramasam.*⌋

⌊That is to say: 'The double-*anuvāka*-book (the expression *dvaya* is a little strange: the phrase would fit also books xv. and xvi.) that begins with *satyena* has [verses] a-hundred-and-forty-save-one (64 + 75 = 139). [The seer is] Sūryā,[1] daughter of Savitar (cf. AV. vi. 82. 2; xiv. 2. 30; Bergaigne, *Rel. Véd.* ii. 486 f.). The deity is the same. The meter, *anuṣṭubh.* With the first five verses she praised (or mentioned, *laudavit:* see note to i. 7. 1) Soma; with the next verses (does this mean the verses from 6 to the end of the book? or to the end of the Sūryā-hymn proper, vss. 6–16?), her own wedding; with the hundredth verse (100 = 64 [vss. of h. 1] + 36 [vss. of h. 2]: hence xiv. 2. 36), the gods[2]; with the twenty-third verse (xiv. 1. 23), moon and sun; with the next (xiv. 1. 24), the moon.'⌋

[1] ⌊The RV. Anukr. also ascribes the corresponding RV. hymn (x. 85) to Sūryā Sāvitrī.⌋

[2] ⌊This statement does not fit xiv. 2. 36. On the other hand, Dr. Ryder points out that it does fit xiv. 2. 46 and that the RV. Anukr. makes *devāḥ* the deity of RV. x. 85. 17 (which = AV. xiv. 2. 46): and he accordingly offers the suggestion that *çatatamyā* may be a text-error for *daça-çatatamyā.*⌋

⌊The Major Anukr. continues: *parā* [?] (xiv. 1. 25–?) *nṛṇāṁ vivāhamantrāçiṣaḥ. parā dehy* (xiv. 1. 25) *açlīlā tanūr* (xiv. 1. 27) *iti dve vadhūvāsaḥsaṁsparçamocanyāu. ye vadhva* (xiv. 2. 10) *iti yakṣmanāçanī. parā* (xiv. 2. 11) *dampatyoḥ paripanthināçanī.*⌋

⌊The statements of the RV. Anukr. as to "deity" correspond quite closely with those just given, but with some differences: thus it says *-nindā* for *-mocanyāu*; etc. In particular, the description *nṛṇāṁ vivāhamantrā āçiṣaç ca* is applied by the RV. Anukr. to RV. x. 85. 20–28. All these 9 RV. verses have more or less close correspondents in AV. xiv.: they are, respectively, AV. xiv. 1. 61; 2. 33 (cf. RV. vss. 21 and 22); 1. 34; 1. 19, 18, 20, 21, 26. All this, it seems, fails to square with the *parāḥ* of the text of our Anukr., and reinforces Mr. Whitney's suspicion (above, p. 739) that the arrangement of the verses contemplated by that text may have been different from that which appears in the Berlin edition. — In connection with this suspicion should be considered also the fact that the Anukr. adds at the end the *pratīkas* iii. 30. 1, ii. 36. 1, and xx. 126. 1: see below, p. 768.⌋

⌊In the Major Anukr., moreover, a curious addition is inserted after the definition of xiv. 1. 60, as follows: (the text of its beginning is uncertain: *ity?* or *parāviny?*) *edhiṣīmahīti vyāghrādiṣv avagantavyaḥ*. Cf. the introduction to xi. 1 and especially the note to xv. 5. 7.⌋

---

1. Marriage ceremonies.

[*Sāvitrī Sūryā. — ātmadāivatam (1–5. somam astāut; 6–⌊?⌋. svavivāham; 23. somārkāu; 24. candramasam; — 25⌊?⌋–[?]. nṛṇāṁ vivāhamantrāçiṣaḥ; 25, 27. vadhūvāsaḥsaṁsparçamocanyāu).* ⌊As to the foregoing, see above, p. 739.⌋ *ānuṣṭubham: 14. virāṭ prastārapañkti; 15. āstārapañkti; 19, 20, 23, 24, 31–33, 37, 39, 40, 45, 47, 49, 50, 53, 56, 57, [58, 59, 61]. triṣṭubh (23, 31, 45. bṛhatīgarbhā); 21, 46, 54, 64. jagatī (54, 64. bhurik triṣṭubh); 29, 55. purastādbṛhatī; 34. prastārapañkti; 38. purobṛhatī 3-p. paroṣṇih; [48. pathyāpañkti;] 60. parānuṣṭubh.*]

The hymn (except vss. 4, 62, which are wanting altogether, and 41, 42, which occur in other books) is found also in Pāipp. xviii., with petty differences of order, noted under the verses. A large part of the *anuvāka* or hymn corresponds to the wedding hymn (x. 85) in the Rig-Veda. The Vāit. does not treat the marriage ceremony, and only four or five of the verses of the book are quoted by it; but a large part of them are used in the sections (75–79) of the Kāuç. which deal with the subject.

Translated: in so far as it corresponds to RV. verses, by the RV. translators; further, the parts that are peculiar to our text, by Ludwig, p. 470; and, as AV. hymn, all of it, by Weber, *Ind. Stud.* v. 195–204 (see 178 ff.); Griffith, ii. 159. — A large part of the wedding-hymn is given in my *Sanskrit Reader*, pages 89–90: the notes thereon (at pages 389–390) may be consulted, and also the notes at pages 398–401.

1. By truth is the earth established (*ut-stabh*); by the sun is the sky established; by righteousness the Ādityas stand; Soma is set (*çritá*) upon the sky.

The verse is RV. x. 85. 1, without variant. The *pada*-text also reads *úttabhitā*, by Prāt. iv. 62, the *s* being omitted by ii. 18. Kāuç. directs vss. 1 and 23 to be used in preparing the sacrificial fire, at the beginning of the chapter on the marriage-rites (75. 6: according to the comm., vss. 1–16 are meant, and 23–24); and again, near the end of the chapter (79. 16), the whole book is directed to be so used. ⌊Ppp. has *satvena* for *satyena* at the beginning.⌋ ⌊Cf. MP. i. 6. 1, and Wint., p. 66.⌋

2. By Soma are the Ādityas strong; by Soma is the earth great; likewise in the lap of these asterisms is Soma placed (*ā-dhā*).

Is RV. x. 85. 2, without variant. ⌊Cf. MP. i. 9. 2; Wint., p. 74; MGS. i. 14. 8 and p. 157.⌋

3. One thinks himself to have drunk Soma when they crush up an herb; what Soma the priests (*brahmán*) know, of that no earthly man partakes.

RV. (x. 85. 3) reads at the end *káç caná* for *pā́rthivas*. In **b**, Bs.P.M.W.T. read *-piṣanti*, D. *-pīṣanti*; Ppp. has *-piçanti*. The *pratīka* is quoted in GB. i. 2. 9 ⌊printed 8⌋.

4. When, O Soma, they drink thee ⌊up⌋, then thou fillest thyself up again; Vāyu is Soma's defender; the month is norm (*ā́kṛti*) of the years (*sámā*).

RV. (x. 85. 5) reads *deva* for *soma* in **a**. The verse (as noted above) is wanting in Ppp.

5. Guarded by covering-arrangements, defended by watchmen (?? *bā́rhata*), O Soma, thou standest hearing the pressing-stones; no earthly one partakes of thee.

Is RV. x. 85. 4, without variant. All this talk about the moon as identical with Soma at the beginning of the *Sūryā*-hymn seems very meaningless unless Sūryā is really the moon, who every month "goes to" her spouse the sun.

6. Intention (*cítti*) was the pillow, sight was the ointment, heaven [and] earth were the coffer (*kóça*), when Sūryā went to her husband.

Is RV. x. 85. 7, without variant.

7. The *rā́ibhī* was the parting [song] (?? *anudéyī*), the *nārāçaṅsī́* was the welcoming one (? *nyócanī*); Sūryā's garment verily was excellent; she goes adorned with song (*gā́thā*).

Is RV. x. 85. 6, which reads at the end *páriṣkṛtam* (p. *pári॰kṛtam*) for *páriṣkṛtā* (which our p. and s. both have). The translation given ventures new conjectures for *anudéyī* (lit. 'to be given after') and *nyócanī* (lit. 'making wonted *or* at home'); the Pet. Lexx. say 'dowry' ⌊so BR. iii. 569, OB. i. 52: but cf. BR. i. 205 and v. 987⌋ and 'ornament'; Ludwig 'vom Hause mitgegeben' and '[ins neue Haus] einführend'; Weber, 'train' and 'hand-maid.'

8. The laudations (*stóma*) were the cross-pieces (?? *pratidhí*); meter was the *kurī́ra*, the *opaçá*; of Sūryā the Açvins were the wooers, Agni was the forerunner.

Is RV. x. 85. 8, without variant. For *kurī́ra* and *opaçá*, women's head-dresses or parts of such, compare vi. 138. In this connection the commentators' explanation of *pratidhí* "cross-pieces on the chariot-pole" is extremely unlikely; it must rather be some article of a woman's dress. Ppp. reads and combines *paridhayaṣ k-*.

9. Soma was the bride-seeker; both Açvins were wooers, when Savitar gave to her husband Sūryā, praising (*çaṅs*) with her mind.

Is RV. x. 85. 9, without variant, save that our *pada*-mss. falsely leave *adadāt* unaccented. 'Praising,' apparently 'assenting gladly.' Ppp. reads at end '*dadhāt*.

10. Mind was her cart; heaven also was [its] canopy; the two draft-oxen were white (*çukrá*), when Sūryā went to her husband.

RV. (x. 85. 10) has at end *gr̥hám* instead of *pátim*.

11. Haltered with verse (*ŕc*) and chant (*sáman*), thy two oxen went peaceful (?*sāmaná*); ears were thy (two) wheels; in the sky the wandering track.

Abhíhita seems to be the correlative to *abhidhānī*. Our 'ears' (p. *çrótre íti*) is a bad variant to RV. (x. 85. 11) *çrótram*, 'hearing.' RV. also has in **b** *itas* for *āitām*. We have to gain in **c** a syllable by harsh resolution in order to make a full pāda. Ppp. reads in **a** *upahitāu*.

12. Clean were the (two) wheels of thee as thou wentest; out-breathing (*vyāná*) was the inserted axle; a cart made of mind did Sūryā ascend when going forth to her husband.

Is RV. x. 85. 12, without variant. The *pada*-reading *manasmayam* in **c** is by Prāt. iv. 24. ⌊Here Roth's Collation says "*çacī* wie Vulgata"!⌋

13. The bridal (*vahatú*) of Sūryā, which Savitar sent off (*ava-sr̥j*), has gone forth; in the Maghās are slain the kine; in the Phalgunīs is the wedding.

RV. (x. 85. 13) reads in **c** *aghā́su* * ⌊Ppp. has the same⌋, and *hanyante* without the antithetical accent which all our mss. give, and which our text ought to read, and, for **d**, *árjunyoḥ páry uhyate*. The Maghā stars are what we call the Sickle, in the neck of Leo; the Phalgunī stars are the rectangle β, θ, δ, 93 Leonis; *arjunī* = *phalgunī*; the moon is in the latter either one or two days after it is in the former.† From such utterly indefinite data the attempt to extract a date is wasted labor. 'Is the wedding': *vy ùhyate* is the verb corresponding to *vivāha* 'wedding,' lit. 'driving away'; Ppp. reads instead *vi havyate*. The second half-verse is quoted in Kāuç. 75. 5, in the general definition of the time for wedding. ⌊With reference to this much-discussed verse, see: Weber, in *Abh. der Berliner Ak.* for 1861 (Nakṣatra-essay), p. 364, and in *Sb.* for 1894, p. 804; Jacobi, *Festgruss an Roth*, p. 69; Wint., p. 32.⌋

*⌊Weber discusses the readings *aghā́su* and *maghā́su*, and deems the RV. reading to be in this case the secondary one: *Sb.* 1894, p. 807.⌋ †⌊Concerning these asterisms (no's 10, and 11, 12) see Whitney, JAOS. vi. 332–4, or *Oriental and Linguistic Studies*, ii. 352–3. It is not impertinent to note that the regents of the Phalgunīs are Bhaga and Aryaman, and that those of the Maghās are the Manes. For the latter, cf. TB. iii. 1. 4[8]: *só 'tra juhoti: pitŕbhyaḥ svā́hā, maghā́bhyaḥ svā́hā, 'naghā́bhyaḥ svā́hā, gadā́bhyaḥ svā́hā, 'rundhatī́bhyaḥ svā́he, 'ti;* but better TS. iv. 4. 10.⌋

14. When, O Açvins, ye went asking, with your three-wheeled [chariot], to Sūryā's bridal, where was one wheel of yours? where stood ye for pointing out?

The verse corresponds, without variant, to RV. x. 85. 14 **a**, **b** and 15 **c**, **d**. The sense of the questions is wholly obscure.

15. When ye went, O lords of beauty, unto the wooing of Sūryā, all the gods assented to that [deed] of yours; Pūshan as son chose a father.

This verse, again, corresponds to parts of two in the RV., namely x. 85. 15 **a**, **b** and 14 **c**, **d**; the only variant is that RV. reads *pitárāu* for *-ram* in **d**, and Ppp. *pitarā 'vr-*, which doubtless means the same. Metrically the verse is as much *virāj* as vs. 14.

16. The two wheels of thee, O Sūryā, the priests (*brahmán*) know seasonably; further, the one wheel that is in secret — that, verily, the enlightened (*addhātí*) know.

Is RV. x. 85. 16. All our mss. accent in **a** *sū́rye* and in **d** ⌊all save D.⌋ *vidúḥ;* our edition corrects both words to accordance with RV. Close correspondence with RV. x. 85 ceases with vs. 16, at the end of the Sūryā-hymn proper. ⌊SPP. reads *sū́rye* with all his authorities, and *vidúḥ* with nearly all. He adds: "the correction to *viduḥ* is not inevitable." But I do not see how the accented form is to be rendered.⌋

17. We make offering to Aryaman of good connections, husband-finder; like a gourd from its bond, from here I release, not from yonder.

This verse is found as RV. vii. 59. 12, a late and ungenuine appendage to that hymn, and having no *pada*-text; its reading is very different, namely: *tryàmbakaṁ yajāmahe sugándhim puṣṭivárdhanam : urvārukám iva bándhanān mṛtyór mukṣīya mā́ 'mṛ́tāt;* and with this agree TS. (i. 8. 6²) and MS. (i. 10. 4), except that they accent *sugandhím* in **b**; VS. (iii. 60) has *tryàmbakam* in **a**; for **b**, *sugandhím pativédanam;* for **d**, *itó mukṣīya mā́ 'mútaḥ*. Ppp. has at end *muñca mā 'mutaḥ*. Vāit. 9. 19 quotes the RV. verse in the *cāturmāsya* ceremony, giving the text in full; Kāuç. 75. 22 makes our verse accompany an oblation offered when the wooer comes in. The Anukr. takes no notice of the redundant syllable in **c** (read *-kám 'va*). ⌊For 17, 18, cf. MP. i. 5. 7, and Wint., p. 56.⌋

18. I release [her] from here, not from yonder; I make her well-bound yonder, that she, O gracious Indra, may be rich in sons, well-portioned.

Is RV. x. 85. 25, without variant ⌊save that our text does not give *muñcā́mi* the antithetical accent⌋. Prāt. ii. 65 teaches the combination *-tas karam*. Ppp. begins *pre 'to muñcata mā 'mutaḥ*. The *mantrapāṭha* ⌊MP. i. 4. 5⌋ of the Āpastamba Gṛhya-Sūtra (see Winternitz, *Altind. Hochzeitsrituell* etc., p. 54) has a varying version, reading in **a** *muñcā́ti mā́* ⌊Oxford text *ná*⌋, and in **b** *karat*.

19. I release thee from Varuṇa's fetter, with which the very propitious Savitar bound thee; in the lair (*yóni*) of righteousness, in the world of the well-done, be it pleasant for thee accompanied by the wooer (*-sambhalá*).

The first three pādas are the same with RV. x. 85. 24 **a–c**, the only RV. variant being *suçévaḥ* at end of **b**; for **d**, RV. has *áriṣṭāṁ tvā sahá pátyā dadhāmi*. TS. (i. 1. 10²; iii. 5. 6¹) has a nearly corresponding verse: *imáṁ ví ṣyāmi váruṇasya pā́çaṁ yám ábadhnīta savitā́ sukétaḥ : dhātúç ca yónāu sukṛtásya loké syonám me sahá pátyā karomi*. Our first half-verse is repeated below as 58 **a**, **b**; and the *pratīka* quoted in Vāit. 4. 11 doubtless belongs to the latter, and not to this verse as assigned by the editor. On the other hand, the *pratīka* quoted in Kāuç. 75. 23, used in connection with loosing the scarf (*veṣṭa*) tied about the bride, doubtless belongs here. The Āpastamba-text (Winternitz, p. 63) gives two slightly differing versions of the verse ⌊MP. i. 5. 16⌋.

Ppp. puts the verse next after our vs. 16; ⌊but further it makes our 19 **c**, **d** change place with our 58 **c**, **d**, reading, however, *'stu sahapatnī vadhū* for our *astu sahásambhalāyāi*⌋.

20. Let Bhaga lead thee hence, grasping thy hand; let the Açvins carry thee forth by a chariot; go to the houses, that thou mayest be housewife; thou, having control, shalt speak unto the council.

RV. (x. 85. 26) begins with *pūṣā́* instead of *bhágas*. In Kāuç. (76. 10) the verse accompanies the leading of the bride out of her house.

21. Let what is dear succeed (*sam-ṛdh*) here for thy progeny; watch thou over this house in order to housewife-ship; mingle thy self (*tanū́*) with this husband; then shalt thou in advanced age speak to the council.

RV. (x. 85. 27) reads in **a** *prajáyā* (as does also Ppp.), and in **c–d** *sṛjasvā́ 'dhā jívrī vidátham ā́ vadāthaḥ*. Our **d** is the same with viii. 1. 6 **d** above, and our mss. here also read *jírvis* (except Bs.I., *jívis*), which ought to have been adopted in our text. The Āpastamba text (Winternitz, p. 74 ⌊MP. i. 9. 4⌋) has *jīvrī*. The verse, with several others, is quoted in Kāuç. 77. 20 in connection with the bride's entering her new abode. The verse lacks two syllables of being a full *jagatī*. ⌊Vs. discussed by Bloomfield, JAOS. xix.[2] 14; cf. Baunack, KZ. xxxv. 495, 499.⌋

22. Be ye (two) just here; be not separated; attain your whole life-time, sporting with sons [and] grandsons, rejoicing, well-homed.

RV. (x. 85. 42) reads *své gṛhé* instead of *svastakāú*, and Ppp. has the same. Ppp. also has *dīrgham* for *viçvam* in **b**. ⌊Cf. MP. i. 8. 8 and note.⌋

23. These two move on one after the other by magic; two sporting young ones go about the ocean; the one looks abroad upon all beings; thou, the other, disposing the seasons art born new.

24. Ever new art thou, being born; sign of the days, thou goest to the apex of the dawns; thou disposest to the gods their share as thou comest; thou extendest, O moon, a long life-time.

These two verses are repeated here from vii. 81. 1, 2; ⌊see the notes to those verses: also the Anukr. extracts at p. 739, ¶ 4, which refer vs. 23 to sun and moon and vs. 24 to the moon⌋. Most of verse 23 we had also as xiii. 2. 11. In order to make sure that the two right ones are reproduced, all our mss. read here *pūrvāparáṁ návonavaḥ* (instead of, as usual, *pūrvāparám íti dvé*). They are RV. x. 85. 18, 19, and are found also in other texts, as to which and the various readings see the notes to vii. 81. 1, 2. Ppp. has in 23 **d** (with RV.) *jāyate punaḥ*, and in 24 (also with RV.) *bhavati*, *eti*, and *dadhāti* (but apparently *tirase*). In Kāuç. 75. 6, vs. 23 (according to the comm., both 23 and 24) is used with vs. 1; in 79. 28, vs. 64 is allowed instead of vs. 24, in case the latter is not known.

25. Give thou away the *çāmulyà*; share out goods to the priests (*brahmán*); it, becoming a walking (*padvánt*) witchcraft, enters the husband [as] a wife.

RV. (x. 85. 29) differs only by reading *bhūtví* in **c**; our *pada*-text has *bhūtvā́ : ā́ : j-*. According to Kāuç. 79. 20, the verse accompanies the giving away of the bride's undergarment, which is regarded as extremely ill-omened if not so disposed of and expiated by gifts to the Brahmans. ⌊Cf. the Anukr. extracts, p. 739, end.⌋ *Çāmulyà* is defined in the Pet. Lexx. as "a woolen shirt," as identical with *çāmūla*, which is so defined by the comm. to LÇS. ix. 4. 7. The Āpastamba text (Winternitz, p. 100 ⌊MP. i. 17. 7⌋) reads instead *çābalyà*.

26. It becomes blue-red; [as] witchcraft, infection, it is driven away (?); her relations (*jñātí*) thrive; her husband is bound in bonds.

Is RV. x. 85. 28, without variant. *Vy àjyate* is translated as coming from root *aj* instead of *añj*, 'is smeared.' Pāda **a** perhaps refers to the bloody discoloration of the garment; **d** to its ill effects if not duly expiated. The Āp.-text (Wint., p. 67 ⌊MP. i. 6. 8⌋) has for **a** *nīlalohité bhavataḥ*, as if the garments were two. RV. and AV. *pada*-texts have *āsaktíḥ* undivided.

27. Unlovely becomes [his] body, glistening in that evil way, when the husband wraps his own member with the bride's garment.

RV. (x. 85. 30) reads at the beginning *açrīrā́*, and at the end *-dhítsate*; Ppp. also has *açrīrā;* ⌊and *tanus* for *tanū́s*⌋. Most of our mss. (all save P.M.W.) give *vā́sasas* in **c**, and this is accordingly more probably to be regarded as the AV. reading. ⌊So SPP. with all his authorities.⌋ ⌊The Berlin ed. has *vā́sasā*, to accord with the RV.⌋ *Añga* might mean 'body' (so the translators). ⌊For vss. 27, 28, 29, cf. respectively MP. i. 17. 8, 10, 9, and see Wint., p. 100.⌋

28. Carving on, carving open, also cutting over apart; see the forms of Sūryā; them also the priest (*brahmán*) cleans (*çumbh*).

RV. (x. 85. 35) reads at the end *tú çundhati* ⌊cf. BR. vii. 261, top⌋. Weber ⌊p. 190⌋ sees in the verse a comparison of the blood on the bride's garment with that from the sacrificial victim when dismembered, the priest having power to cleanse both stains away.

29. Harsh is that, sharp, barbed, poisoned; that is not to be eaten; what priest (*brahmán*) knows Sūryā, he indeed deserves the bride's [garment].

RV. (x. 85. 34) inserts another *etát* after *kátukam*, and reads *vidyā́t* for *v'da* in **c**. The omission of *káṭukam* (with, in RV., *etát*) would rectify the meter of **a**; as it stands, it is an extremely poor "*bṛhatī*" pāda. *Áttave* 'to be eaten' is very strange here. Sūryā in **c** is generally understood to mean 'the Sūryā-hymn.'

The following four verses are found in no other text.

30. That priest verily takes this garment, pleasant, well-omened, who goes over the expiation, by whom the wife takes no harm.

The *pada*-text reads *prā́yaçcittim*, undivided; if we had *-ttam*, *yéna* would apply to it, instead of to *brahmā́*. Ppp. reads, for **a**, **b**: *sa vāi taṁ syono harati brahma vāsas sumañgalan*.

31. Do ye (two) bring together a successful (*sáṁṛddha*) portion, speaking right in right-speakings; O Brahmaṇaspati, make the husband shine (*ruc*) for her; let the wooer (*saṁbhalá*) speak this speech agreeably (*cā́ru*).

According to Kāuç. 75. 8, 9, this verse is addressed to the wooer and his companion, when they are sent out to win the bride; the second half-verse to the priest (who is one of them?). 'Make shine,' doubtless 'set in a favorable light.' The verse ⌊scanned by the Anukr. as 11 + 9: 12 + 12 = 44⌋ may best be read as 11 + 11 : 12 + 12; ⌊but **d** has a bad cadence⌋. Ppp. reads *mṛtyodyena* at end of **b**, and *ṣumbhalo* in **d**.

32. May ye be just here; may ye not go away; may ye, O kine, increase this man with progeny; going in beauty, ruddy, with soma-splendor — may all the gods turn (*kṛ*) your minds hither.

In Kāuç. 79. 17 this verse (according to the commentators, this and the next) seems to be directed to accompany the paying (in kine) the price demanded for the bride; but surely that cannot have been its original sense. The first pāda is identical with iii. 8. 4 **a**; **c** has a redundant syllable. The *pada*-text writes *çúbham : yatīḥ*, but the expression is, so far as accent is concerned, treated as if a compound: compare 2. 52 below. No reason is discoverable for the accent of *krán* in **d**.

33. May ye, O kine, enter this man together with progeny; this man minisheth (*mī*) not the share of the gods; for this man shall Pūshan, and all the Maruts, for this man shall Dhātar, Savitar quicken (*sū*) you.

Ppp. reads *viçadhvam* at end of **a**. This verse indicates distinctly that the preceding one is meant as a wish for prosperity in respect to kine.

34. Free from thorns, straight, let the roads be by which [our] comrades go a-wooing for us; together with Bhaga, together with Aryaman — let Dhātar unite [us] with splendor.

The first half-verse is RV. x. 85. 23 **a**, **b**, which, however, reads ⌊with MP.⌋ *pánthās* for ⌊our metrically bad⌋ *-thānas*; the second half goes on: *sám aryamā́ sám bhágo no ninīyāt* etc. ⌊cf. MP. i. 1. 2⌋; our text is a foolish and inconsistent substitute. Kāuç. 77. 3 gives the verse, with 2. 11, as to be used when the bridal train starts off home; in 75. 12 it ⌊according to Daça Kar., only the first half-verse⌋ is made to accompany the sending out of a guard for the bride. ⌊Cf. Wint., p. 40.⌋

35. Both what splendor is placed in dice, and what in strong drink — what splendor, O Açvins, is in kine, with that splendor favor (*av*) ye this woman.

All our mss. accent *açvínā* in **c**; our edition makes the necessary correction to *açvinā*. ⌊SPP. adopts and defends the reading *açvínā.*⌋ Ppp. puts the verse after our vs. 36. The Anukr. does not heed that the first pāda lacks a syllable. According to Kāuç. 75. 27, this verse, with 43 below, is used in connection with pouring of water on the bride; and again, in 139. 15, this and the next, with several others from different books, accompany a libation ⌊in the fire⌋ in the ceremony of initiation into Vedic study; both also (35, 36) are reckoned as belonging to the *varcasya gaṇa* (see note to Kāuç. 13. 1). ⌊Cf. ix. 1. 18; vi. 69. 1.⌋

36. With what [splendor] the backsides of the courtezan (*mahānagnī́*), O Açvins, or with what the strong drink, with what the dice were flooded (*abhi-sic*), with that splendor favor ye this woman.

That is, apparently, give her all the attractions which these various seductive things are known to possess. 'Courtezan,' lit. 'great naked woman,' emending to *-nagnyā́s:* ⌊but all authorities, both SPP's and W's, have *-naghnyā́s*⌋. The verse has a distant likeness to one in PGS. ii. 6. 12. The *ṣ* of *aṣicyanta* is by Prāt. ii. 92, where this example is quoted in the commentary. The redundant syllable in the first pāda passes unheeded by the Anukr. For the use of the verse in Kāuç. see the note to the preceding verse. Ppp. puts the verse before our 35 as noted above, and the ms. reads for **a**: *yan mā nagnā jaghnam.*

37. He who shines (*dī*) without fuel within the waters, whom the devout (*vípra*) praise at the sacrifices (*adhvará*) — O child of the waters, mayest thou give waters rich in honey, with which Indra increased, full of heroism.

The verse is RV. x. 30. 4, which accents *dī́dayat*, and reads at the end *vīryā̀ya.* Ppp. combines in **a** *yo 'nidhmo.* Kāuç. 75. 14 makes the verse accompany the piercing (*pra-vyadh*) of a stick of wood (*loga*) in the water.

38. Now do I remove (*apa-ūh*) the glistening seizer (*grābhá*), body-spoiling; what sheen is excellent, that I draw up (*ud-ac*).

Ppp. reads in the first half-verse *tanūdūṣim athi nudāmi.* For its second half it has *yaç çivo bhadro rocanas tena tvām api nudāmi*, making a fair half-*anuṣṭubh.* According to Kāuç. 75. 15, 16, the thing (the pierced piece of wood) is removed with the first two pādas; and with the third water is drawn up (*anvīpam* 'in the direction of the current') and is then presented with vs. 39. The verse (9 + 8 : 11 = 28) is described by the Anukr. with mechanical correctness.

39. Let the Brahmans take for her [water] for bathing; let them draw up (?) waters that slay not a hero; let her go about the fire of Aryaman, O Pūshan; father-in-law and brother-in-law are looking on (*prati-īkṣ*).

The translation implies the obvious emendation of *ajantu* to *acantu* in **b**. ⌊Cf. the MP. reading *acantu*, and also xi. 1. 2, where *vā́cam* answers to the RV. reading *vā́jam.*⌋ There is also something wrong about **d**, where a plural verb is made to agree with two singular subjects. The Āpast. *mantra*-text (Wint., p. 43 ⌊MP. i. 1. 7–8⌋) has in both pādas (as well as in other respects) better readings: *ā́ 'syāi brāhmaṇā́ḥ snápanaṁ harantu: ávīraghnīr úd acantv ā́paḥ*: aryamṇó agním pári yantu kṣiprám prátī "kṣantāṁ çvaçrúvo devárāç ca.* Ppp. reads in **a–b** *ā 'smāi harantu snapanaṁ brahmaṇā 'vīr-*; and in **c**, *'gniṁ pary eti kṣipraṁ.* ⌊The *kṣipram* of Ppp. and MP. suggests that⌋ our *pūṣan* in **c** may be a corruption for *oṣám;* ⌊cf. also vii. 73. 6 **a**⌋. The use of the verse by Kāuç. 75. 17 was noticed in the preceding note; in 76. 20, the second half-verse accompanies the leading of the bride thrice about the fire (in Āpast. the laying of a ring of *darbha*-grass upon her head). The Anukr. does not heed the lack of a syllable in **b**. *⌊Oxford text *āpaḥ:* misprint?⌋

40. Weal be to thee gold, and weal be waters; weal be the post (*methí*), weal the perforation (*tárdman*) of the yoke; weal be for thee the waters having a hundred cleansers (*-pavítra*); for weal, too, mingle thyself with thy husband.

Ppp. is much corrupted in this verse, but can be seen to read *metis* for *methis* in **b**; in **c** it combines *tā "paḥ*, and in **d** it omits *u*. In Kāuç. 76. 12, the verse is muttered (according to the *paddhati*, it and the following verse) while the bride is bound to the right yoke-pole and the left yoke-hole, and a piece of gold is fastened to her forehead. Purification by the yoke-hole (apparently growing out of the occurrence of the next verse in RV.) plays a part in various versions of the marriage-rites; ⌊cf. note to vs. 41⌋. Āpast. (Wint., p. 44 ⌊MP. i. 1. 10⌋) has this same verse with unimportant variations (*medhī* in **b**, etc). ⌊Cf. Wint., p. 46.⌋ The verse (11 + 12 : 11 + 11 = 45) is slightly irregular ⌊but has *triṣṭubh*-cadences throughout⌋.

41. In the hole of the chariot, in the hole of the cart, in the hole of the yoke, O thou of a hundred activities, having thrice purified Apālā, O Indra, thou didst make her sun-skinned.

The verse is RV. viii. 80 (91). 7, which has for sole variant *pūtvī́* in **c**. Prāt. ii. 64 prescribes the combination *triṣ p-*, but part of our mss. (O.R.K.) read *triḥ*. The Āpast. version (Wint., p. 43 ⌊MP. i. 1. 9⌋) is quite corrupt. ⌊Cf. MGS. i. 8. 11 and p. 149.⌋ In Ppp. the verse is not found among the marriage verses, but in book iv., ⌊and without variant⌋. ⌊For a careful treatment of the Apālā story, see H. Oertel, in JAOS. xviii.[1] 26.⌋ ⌊The MP. version of this verse furnishes Böhtlingk occasion for sôme interesting general critical remarks, *Berichte der sächsischen Gesellschaft*, Feb. 5, 1898, p. 4.⌋

42. Hoping for well-willing, offspring, good-fortune, wealth, becoming obedient (*ánuvrata*) to thy husband, gird thyself in order to immortality.

This verse also is found in Ppp. away from the rest, in book xx., and with much difference of text: thus, **b–d**, *praco bahur atho balam : indrāṇy anuvratā san nahye amṛtāya kam*. In Kāuç. 76. 7, the verse is used, with 2. 70, when the bride is girded with a bond, a yoke-rope (*yoktra*). The Āpast. version (Wint., p. 45 ⌊MP. i. 2. 7⌋) has *tanū́m* for *rayím* in **b**, *agnér* for *pátyur* in **c**, and, for **d**, *sám nahye sukṛtā́ya kám*. Vāit. 2. 6, again, makes it accompany the girding of the sacrificer's wife at the sacrifice. ⌊In the Berlin ed., correct *kam* to *kám*.⌋

43. As the ⌊mighty (?*vṛṣā*)⌋ river (*síndhu*) won (?*sū*) the supremacy of the streams (*nadī́*), so be thou supreme (*samrā́jñī*), having gone away to thy husband's home.

Perhaps *síndhu* should be rendered 'Indus' (so Zimmer, p. 317; Weber, p. 199). *Suṣuve*, lit. 'impelled for one's self,' is employed here in an unusual sense; the word is quoted as example under Prāt. ii. 91; iv. 82. Ppp. reads *sūṣuve vṛkāt*. By Kāuç. 75. 27, the verse accompanies the emergence of the bride from the bath (with vs. 35, above).

44. Be thou supreme among fathers-in-law, supreme also among brothers-in-law; be thou supreme over sister-in-law, supreme also over mother-in-law.

The verse is RV. x. 85. 46, which, however, reads for **a**, *s. çváçure bhava;* for **b**, *s. çvaçrvā́m bhava;* for **c**, *nánāndari s. bhava;* for **d**, *s. ádhi devṛ́ṣu;* and MB. (i. 2. 20) agrees throughout with RV. (*çvaçryām* in **b** must be a blunder). ⌊MP. i. 6. 6 follows RV., but with *çvaçruvā́m* in **b**: cf. Wint., p. 66.⌋

45. They (f.) who spun, wove, and who stretched [the web], what divine ones (f.) gave the ends about, let them wrap thee in order to old age; [as] one long-lived put about thee this garment.

Ppp. combines in **a** *yā 'kṛntan*. The verse is found also in PGS. (i. 4. 13), HGS. (i. 4. 2), MB. (i. 1. 5). All end **a** with *yā atanvata;* in **b**, all insert *ca* after *yās;* and PGS. reads *tantūn abhito* * *tatantha*, and MB. *devyo antān abhito tatantha;* for **c**, they have *tās tvā devīr* (MB. *devyo*) *jarasā* (PGS. *-se*) *saṁvyayantv* (PGS. *-yasva*); in **d**, only HGS. has *āyuṣmān*. ⌊Cf. MP. ii. 2. 5, and Wint., p. 47, and MGS. i. 10. 8 and p. 154.⌋ The verse has an extra syllable in **a** which the Anukr. does not notice. In Kāuç. 76. 4, this and vs. 53 accompany the putting of a hitherto unused garment upon the bride. ⌊The same two vss. are referred to by the name *paridhāpanīye* at 79. 13: so the schol.⌋ *⌊This sandhi is of course not to be laid at the door of the accurate Stenzler: it is doubtless the true reading of PGS., and occurs (not only in MB., but also) in Bhavadeva's Paddhati, as Stenzler observes in his Transl., p. 12.⌋

⌊The corruption of *abhito 'dadanta* (so AV.) to *abhito tatantha* (PGS. MB. Bhavadeva) is of peculiar text-critical interest, not merely because it is a senseless and unintelligent perversion, but because it is revealed as a corruption by the ignorant failure of the persons responsible for it to change their sandhi in such a way (*abhitas tatantha*) as to fit their blunder. — This interest is heightened by the fact that we can see the probable occasion of the perversion, to wit, the occurrence in the preceding pāda of the words for 'spun,' 'wove,' 'stretched web' (root *tan*). These technical terms of cloth-making lend a semblance of appropriateness to the introduction of *tantūn tan* 'stretch the warp' in pāda **b**. — Roth had already booked *tatantha* among the cases of exchange between sonants and surds at ZDMG. xlviii. 108.⌋

46. They bewail the living one (m.); they lead away the sacrifice (*adhvará*); the men sent their thoughts after ⌊root *dhī* . . . *ánu*⌋ a long reach (*prásiti*); what is lovely (*vāmá*) for the Fathers who came together here; joy to the husbands for embracing the wife.

This is a literal version of this extremely obscure verse. RV. (x. 40. 10) reads in **a** *vi mayante adhvaré;* in **b**, the equivalent *dīdhiyus* ⌊so also Ppp.⌋; in **c**, the equivalent *sameriré;* in **d**, *jánayas* (for our *janáye*, which might better have been emended in the edition to *jánaye*); ⌊Ppp. reads and combines *janayaṣ*⌋. The Āpast. text (Wint., p. 42 ⌊MP. i. 1. 6⌋) reads at the beginning *jīvām*. The verse is used, with 2. 59, in Kāuç. 79. 30, simply to accompany a libation, at the very close of the marriage rites. In two Sūtras (AGS. ⌊i. 8. 4⌋ and ÇGS. ⌊i. 15. 2⌋) it is directed to be used when the bride, on the journey to her new home, wails or cries; this is plainly only on account of the word 'bewail' (*rudanti*) at the beginning. ⌊Cf. Lanman's *Skt. Reader*, p. 387; Winternitz, p. 42; and Bloomfield, who devotes 9 pages to the stanza in AJP. xxi. 411–9.⌋

47. I maintain for thee, in order to progeny, a pleasant, firm (*dhruvá*) stone in the lap of the divine earth; stand thou on that, one to be exulted after, of excellent glory; let Savitar make for thee a long life-time.

Ppp. puts *syonam* after *dhruvam* in **a**, reads *pṛthivyām* in **b**, and *tam ā rohā 'numadyā suvīrā* for **c**, and *tvā* for *te* in **d** ⌊i.e., it has *tvāyus* for *ta āyus*⌋. In Kāuç. 76. 15, the first half-verse accompanies the setting of a stone in a lump of dung, and in 76. 16 the second accompanies the stepping of the bride upon it: this at the bride's home; and the same is repeated (Kāuç. 77. 17, 19) in the new home of the pair after their arrival there. Pāda **a** has 12 syllables, unnoticed by the Anukr.

48. Wherewith Agni grasped the right hand of this earth, therewith grasp I thy hand; do not stagger in company with me, with both progeny and riches.

The last pāda ⌊*prajayā* etc.⌋ is wanting in Ppp., ⌊which puts the vs. after 50⌋. The verse accompanies in Kāuç. 76. 19 the seizing of the bride's hand to lead her about the fire. The Anukr. seems to overlook the vs.; though, if the last pāda were omitted, it would fall under the general definition of the hymn, as an *anuṣṭubh*. ⌊As to vss. 48–51, cf. Wint., p. 48 f. For the *pāṇigrahaṇa*, he cites Rāmāyaṇa, i. 75 (Gorresio: or i. 73 Schlegel).⌋

49. Let god Savitar grasp thy hand; let king Soma make thee to have good offspring; let Agni, Jātavedas, make the spouse well-portioned, long-lived, for her husband.

Ppp. has this verse next after our vs. 47, by removing ⌊as noted⌋ 48 to after 50. The Anukr. takes no notice of the deficiency of two syllables in **c**.

50. I grasp thy hand in order to good-fortune, that with me as husband thou mayest be long-lived; Bhaga, Aryaman, Savitar, Purandhi ⌊*púraṁdhi*⌋ — the gods have given thee to me in order to housewifeship.

The verse is RV. x. 85. 36, which varies only by reading at the beginning *gṛbhṇā́mi*. MB. (i. 2. 16) has precisely the RV. form of the verse; HGS. (i. 20. 1) and Āpast. (Wint., p. 49 ⌊MP. i. 3. 3⌋) read in **a** *suprajāstvāya*, and HGS. has also *gṛhṇāmi* and (at end of **b**) *asat*. ⌊Cf. MGS. i. 10. 15 a, and p. 150.⌋ ⌊As to *puraṁdhi*, cf. WZKM. iii. 268; and Pischel, *Ved. Stud.* i. 202–216.⌋

51. Bhaga hath grasped thy hand; Savitar hath grasped thy hand; thou art [my] spouse by ordinance (*dhárman*), I thy house-lord.

Ppp. reads *dhātā* for *bhagas* in **a**, inserts *te* before *hastam* in **b**, and adds after **b** two pādas: *bhagas te h. a.* and *aryamā te h. a.*, ⌊then finishing with our **c**, **d**⌋. One of the subsidiary treatises (see note to Kāuç. 76. 10) substitutes the verse for vs. 20 above (see note there).

52. Be this woman mine, bringing prosperity (*póṣya*); Brihaspati hath given thee to me; in company with me ⌊as husband⌋ do thou live, rich in offspring, a hundred autumns.

Bp. and Bs.p.m. give in **c** (as does Ppp.) *prajā́vatī*, and I.K. *prajā́vati*; *prajā́vatī* is evidently the preferable reading; ⌊and is implied in the translation⌋. ⌊Of SPP's authorities, 4 have *prajā́vatī* against 6 with *prajāvati* (which latter he adopts): but not less than 7 have (like W's I.K.) the impossible *prajā́vati*, which supports both readings or neither!⌋ The verse is found also in PGS. i. 8. 19, and in a *khila* to RV. x. 85 (Aufrecht[2], p. 682); both have *prajāvatī*; in **a**, both have *dhruvāi 'dhi poṣye* (RV. *-ṣyā*) *mayi*. ⌊See also MP. i. 8. 9: that also has *prajā́vatī*.⌋

53. Tvashṭar disposed (*vi-dhā*) the garment for beauty, by direction of Brihaspati, of the poets; therewith let Savitar and Bhaga envelop this woman, like Sūryā, with progeny.

In Kāuç. 76. 4, this verse is used with vs. 45, above ⌊which see⌋, with dressing the bride in a new garment ⌊cf. Wint., p. 47⌋; and the same is repeated in Kāuç. 79. 13 at another point in the ceremonies. The full number of syllables is to be obtained in **b** only by a harsh resolution. Ppp. has in **c** *nāryaṁ* ⌊cf. note to vs. 59⌋, and at the end the decidedly better reading *prajāyāi*.

54. Let Indra-and-Agni, heaven-and-earth, Mātariçvan, Mitra-and-Varuṇa, Bhaga, both Açvins, Brihaspati, the Maruts, the *bráhman*, Soma, increase this woman with progeny.

Ppp. has again *nāryaṁ* in **d**. Only **a** is a real *jagatī* pāda, even by number of syllables (and doubtless we are to read *-pṛthvī*); the second definition of it in the Anukr. notices this.

55. Brihaspati first prepared (*klp*) the hairs on the head of Sūryā; with this, O Açvins, do we thoroughly adorn (*çubh*) this woman for her husband.

It looks as if *prathamás* were an intrusion in **a**. ⌊In **c**, Ppp. has for a third time *nāryaṁ*.⌋ In Kāuç. 79. 14 the verse is made to accompany the parting of the bride's hair with a blade of *darbha*-grass; according to the *paddhati*, this verse and the next are used together for the purpose.

56. This [is] that form in which the young woman (*yóṣā*) dressed herself; I desire to know with [my] mind the wife (*jāyā́*) moving about; I will go after her with nine-fold (?*návagva*) comrades: who, knowing, unloosened (*vi-cṛt*) these fetters?

This obscure verse gets no light from Ppp., the other texts, or the *sūtras*. The *pada*-text reads in **c** *ánu : artiṣye;* doubtless it is only a contraction for *ánu vartiṣye*.

57. I loosen (*vi-sā*) in me the form of her; he verily shall know, seeing the nest of mind; I eat not stolenly; I was freed (*ud-muc*) by mind, myself untying (*çrath*) the fetters of Varuṇa.

Ppp. reads at the end *pāçam*. This verse and doubtless the next (its *pratīka*, which is *pra tvā muñcāmi*, would also designate vs. 19 above) are used, with vii. 78. 1, by Vāit. 4. 11, to accompany the ungirding of the sacrificer's wife. Both are used also by Kāuç. 76. 28 with the ungirding of the bride.

58. I release thee from Varuṇa's fetter, with which the very propitious Savitar bound thee; wide space (*loká*), an easy road here, do I make for thee, O bride (*vadhū́*), with thy husband.

The first half-verse is identical with vs. 19 **a**, **b**, and corresponds with RV. x. 85. 24 **a**, **b** (which reads at end *suçévaḥ*). Ppp. reads for **a–b** *imāṁ vi ṣyāmi varuṇasya pāçaṁ tena tvā* etc.; ⌊cf. the TS. version of our 19 **a**⌋. ⌊As noted under vs. 19, Ppp. makes our 58 **c**, **d** change place with our 19 **c**, **d**, reading, however, *sūgam itra* for our *sugáṁ átra* and *sahapatnī vadhūḥ* for our *sahápatnyāi vadhu.*⌋ Vss. 58, 59, 61 appear to be overlooked by the Anukr., probably by a loss of something out of the text: this (11 + 11 : 10 + 12 = 44) is an irregular *triṣṭubh;* ⌊the longer form *pánthānam* would relieve the difficulty: cf. vs. 34, where, as between the longer and shorter equivalent forms, our text is most clearly at fault⌋.

59. Raise ye [your weapons]; may ye smite away the demon; set this woman in what is well done; inspired Dhātar found for her a husband; let king Bhaga go in front, foreknowing.

⌊Ppp. combines **a–b** thus: *hanāthe imāṁ;* and that is followed by⌋ *nāryaṁ* ⌊for *nārīm*, as in 53, 54, 55*⌋ in **b**. Kāuç. 76. 32 uses vss. 59, 60, 62 at the setting out of the bride for her new home. This verse also is an irregular *triṣṭubh* (11 + 10 : 12 + 11 = 44). *⌊Cf. the Ppp. variant *bhūmyaṁ* for *bhū́mim*, xiii. 2. 40, 41.⌋

60. Bhaga fashioned the four feet; Bhaga fashioned the four framepieces (?*úṣyala*); Tvashṭar adorned (*piç*) the straps (?*várdhra*) along in the middle; let her be to us of excellent omen.

Kāuç. uses the verse not only as stated in the preceding note, but also (76. 25), more properly, with 2. 31, when the bride mounts the couch (*talpa*). Ppp. reads in **a** *padas;* in **b**, *catvāry aṣpadāni;* in **c**, *madhyato varadhrāṁ.* ⌊For *úṣyala*, cf. note to vi. 139. 3.⌋ ⌊For the addition to the Anukr. at this point, see above, p. 740, ¶ 2, and especially the note to xv. 5. 7.⌋

61. The well-flowered (*sukiṅçuká*), all-formed bridal-car (*vahatú*), golden-colored, well-rolling, well-wheeled, do thou mount, O Sūryā, to the world of the immortal; make thou a bridal-car pleasant to husbands.

The verse is RV. x. 85. 20, which reads *çalmalī́m* in **a** for *vahatúm*, and in **d** *pátye* for *pátibhyas*, and *kṛṇuṣva* for *kṛṇu tvám.* MB. (i. 3. 11) also has *çalmalim*, *patye*, and *kṛṇuṣva*, but further in **b** *suvarṇavarṇaṁ sukṛtam*, and in **c** *nābhim* for *lokam.* ⌊Cf. MP. i. 6. 4; MGS. i. 13. 6 and p. 157.⌋ Kāuç. 77. 1 combines it with 2. 30, as used when the bride is made to mount the vehicle that takes her to her new home. Ppp. has in **c** *sukṛtasya loke.* The verse is a good *triṣṭubh.*

62. Her, not brother-slaying, O Varuṇa; not cattle-slaying, O Brihaspati; not husband-slaying, possessing sons, O Indra — bring [her] for us, O Savitar.

The Āpast. text (Wint., p. 41 ⌊MP. i. 1. 3⌋) has a corresponding but quite different verse: reading *ápatighnīm* in **b**, and, for **c**, **d**, *índrā́ 'putraghnīṁ lakṣmyàṁ tā́m asyāi savitaḥ suva.* The Anukr. does not heed the deficiency of a syllable in **a**. For the use of the verse in Kāuç. (76. 32), see the note to vs. 59. It is wanting (as above noticed) in Ppp.

63. Injure ye not the maiden (*kumārī́*), ye (two) pillars, on the god-made road; the door of the divine house we make pleasant, a road for the bride.

Or, 'we make a pleasant road' etc. In Kāuç. 77. 20, the verses 2. 26; 1. 21, 63, 64, in this order, are used to accompany the bride's stepping forward into the house. ⌊Cf. Wint., p. 72, top.⌋

64. Let the *bráhman* be yoked after, the *bráhman* before, the *bráhman* at the end, in the middle, the *bráhman* everywhere; going forward to an impenetrable stronghold of the gods, do thou (f.), propitious, pleasant, bear rule in thy husband's world.

Besides the use of the verse in Kāuç. 77. 20, as noticed just above, it is quoted, with 2. 8, in 77. 2, when the bride sets out, with a Brahman in front. In 79. 28, it is allowed to be substituted for vs. 23; and in that case (? 79. 32) the ceremony is called *brāhmya* instead of *sāurya*.

⌊Here ends the first *anuvāka*, with 1 hymn (but see page 739, top) and 64 verses. The quoted Anukr. says *ādyaḥ sāuryaç catuḥṣaṣṭiḥ* (see p. 738).⌋

2. Marriage ceremonies (continued).

[*Sāvitrī Sūryā.* — *ātmadāivatam* (*10. yakṣmanāçanī; 11. dampatyoḥ paripanthināçanī; 36* ⌊*?*⌋. *devān astāut*). ⌊As to the foregoing statements, see above, page 739, ¶'s 8, 4, 5.⌋ *ānuṣṭubham: 5, 6, 12, 31, 37, 39, 40. jagatī* (*37, 39. bhurik triṣṭubh*); *9. 3-av. 6-p. virāḍ atyaṣṭi; 13, 14, 17–19,* [*34, 36, 38,*] *41, 42, 49, 61, 70, 74, 75. triṣṭubh; 15, 51. bhurij; 20. purastādbṛhatī; 13* ⌊*!*⌋, *24, 25, 32, 33* ⌊*!*⌋. *purobṛhatī;* [*26. 3-p. virāṇ nāma gāyatrī;*] *33. virāḍ āstārapañkti; 35. purobṛhatī triṣṭubh; 43. triṣṭubgarbhā pañkti; 44. prastārapañkti;* [*47. pathyābṛhatī;*] *48. sataḥpañkti* ⌊see under the verse⌋; [*50. upariṣṭādbṛhatī nicṛt;*] *52. virāṭ paroṣṇih; 59, 60, 62. pathyāpañkti;* [*68. pura-uṣṇih;*] *69. 3-av. 6-p. atiçakvarī; 71. bṛhatī.*]

The Anukramaṇī, as we have it, omits the description of several of the verses (26, 34, 36, 38, 47, 50, 68); ⌊and, on the other hand, it defines verses 13 and 33 each twice, each once right and once wrong;⌋ and it mixes the order of others ⌊compare Whitney's remarks, above, page 739, ¶ 3, and mine, page 740, top⌋.

The verses (except 50, 58) of this *anuvāka* or hymn are found also in Pāipp. xviii. (for slight differences of order, see under the verses). ⌊About a dozen verses of this *anuvāka* or hymn also occur in the RV. wedding-hymn, x. 85.⌋ Only one verse (47) is used by Vāit., but nearly all by Kāuç.

Translated: parts, of course, by the RV. translators; and the parts peculiar to our text by Ludwig, p. 472; and, as AV. hymn, by Weber (as above), *Ind. Stud.* v. 204–217. For vss. 59–62, see Bloomfield, AJP. xi. 336–341, or JAOS. xv., p. xliv, = PAOS. for Oct. 1890.

1. For thee in the beginning they carried about Sūryā, together with the bridal-car; mayest thou, O Agni, give to us husbands the wife, together with progeny.

The verse is RV. x. 85. 38, RV. reading *púnaḥ* for *sá naḥ* in **c**. All our mss. accent in **d** *ágne*, but it has been emended to *agne* in our edition. Ppp. agrees with RV. in having in **c** *punaṣ pat-*. ⌊Cf. PGS. i. 7. 3; MP. i. 5. 3; MGS. i. 11. 12 b, and p. 150.⌋ Kāuç. 78. 10 quotes this verse with 45 below, both preceded by vi. 78. 1, and followed by a long prose-passage, when the pair approach the priest to receive a sort of baptism.

2. Agni hath given back the spouse, together with life-time, with splendor; of long life-time, may he who is the husband of her live a hundred autumns.

Is RV. x. 85. 39, without variant. ⌊Cf. MP. i. 5. 4; MGS. i. 11. 12 c, and p. 152.⌋ The combination *yáḥ pátiḥ* in **c** is assured by Prāt. ii. 70.

3. Soma's wife first; the Gandharva thy next husband; Agni thy third husband; thy fourth, one of human birth.

The verse is RV. x. 85. 40, which, however, has for **a**, **b** *sómaḥ prathamó vivide gandharvó vivida úttaraḥ.* It is found also in PGS. (i. 4. 16) and HGS. (i. 20. 2); the former agrees entirely with RV.; the latter deviates from it only in **d**, where it gives *turīyo 'ham man-*: Ppp. combines in **b** *aparaṣ p-*. ⌊Cf. MP. i. 3. 1.⌋

4. Soma gave to the Gandharva; the Gandharva gave to Agni; both wealth and sons hath Agni given to me, likewise this woman.

Is RV. x. 85. 41, without variant. Found also in MB. (i. 1. 7) and HGS. (i. 20. 2): in the latter, with very different readings: *somo 'dadād gandharvāya gandharvo 'gnaye 'dadāt: paçūṅç ca mahyam putrāṅç cā 'gnir dadāty atho tvām.* ⌊Cf. MP. i. 3. 2; MGS. i. 10. 10 a, and p. 157; also Wint., p. 48.⌋

5. Your favor hath come, O ye (two) of abundant good things (?*vājínīvasu*); [our] desires have rested in [your] hearts, O Açvins; ye have been twin keepers, O lords of beauty; may we, being dear, attain favorers (*aryamán*) of our homes (?*dúrya*).

The verse is RV. x. 40. 12, RV., however, reading *ayaṅsata* at end of **b**. ⌊MP. i. 7. 11 follows the RV. text, but with *kāmāṅ* for *kāmās*: cf. Wint., p. 70.⌋ More points than one in the translation are doubtful.

6. Do thou (f.), rejoicing with propitious mind, assign wealth having all heroes, to be extolled; an easy crossing (*tīrthá*), well provided with drink, O lords (du.) of beauty; do ye smite away the pillar standing in the road, [namely] disfavor.

This verse is altered from RV. x. 40. 13 in a strange and senseless manner. RV. reads for **a**, **b** *tā́ mandasānā́ mánuṣo duroṇá ā́ dhattáṁ rayíṁ sahávīraṁ vacasyáve*, thus making the verse concern the Açvins throughout; who is our 'thou' (*sā́*) does not appear. In **c** the sense is destroyed by altering the RV. verb *kṛtám* (as if it were misunderstood for a participle) to *sugám*; and in **d** *patheṣṭhā́m* (p. *pathe⁀sthā́m*) is turned to *páthiṣṭhām* (p. *páthi⁀sthām*) and accented as if it were a superlative; ⌊cf. the confusion at vi. 28. 1⌋. The verse is used also in the Āpast. sūtra (Wint., p. 68 ⌊MP. i. 6. 12⌋), with *daçavīram* in **b** as its only variant from RV. Ppp. appears to read with our text. The verse lacks two syllables of being a real *jagatī*. In Kāuç. 77. 8 the verse is directed to be used on arriving at a ford or river-crossing on the bridal journey.

7. What hérbs [there are], what streams, what fields, what forests — let these, O bride, defend from the demon thee, possessing progeny, for thy husband.

The Āpast. text (Wint., p. 70 ⌊MP. i. 7. 9⌋) has the same verse, but with different readings: for **b**, *yā́ni dhánvāni yé vánāḥ* ⌊Oxford text *vánā*⌋; in **c**, *té* for *tā́s*; for **d**, *prá tvé muñcantv áṅhasaḥ.* Kāuç. 77. 11 uses it on the bridal journey 'under the circumstances mentioned in the verse.'

8. We have mounted this road, easy, bringing welfare, on which a hero takes no harm, [but] finds others' goods.

The Āpast. text (Wint., p. 67 ⌊MP. i. 6. 11⌋) has the same verse, but with *sugám pánthānam ā́ 'rukṣam áriṣṭaṁ svas-* in **a**, **b**. Kāuç. uses it in 77. 2, with 1. 64: see the note to 1. 64. ⌊For *yásmin* in **c** Ppp. has the sense-equivalent *yatra:* cf. its *oṣam* for our *kṣiprám* at xii. 1. 35; etc.⌋

9. Pray hear ye now of me, O men, by what blessing (*āçís*) the two spouses attain what is agreeable (*vāmá*): what Gandharvas [there are] and heavenly Apsarases, who stand upon these forest trees (*vānaspatyá*), let them be pleasant unto this bride; let them not injure the bridal-car as it is driven.

The last four pādas form a verse also in the Āpast. text (Wint., p. 70 ⌊MP. i. 7. 8⌋), where for our **d** is read *eṣú vṛkṣéṣu vānaspatyéṣv ā́sate*, further *çivā́s* (for *syonā́s*) and *vadhvāì* in **e**, and *ūhyámānām* in **f**. In TS. iii. 2. 8⁴ is found the phrase *yám āçírā dámpatī vāmám açnutáḥ*, and *āçīrdāyā́ dámpatī vāmám açnutām*. The verse is to be used, according to Kāuç. 77. 9, when the bridal train passes great trees. The Anukr. ⌊appears to scan as 9 + 12 : 11 + 12 : 11 + 11 = 66; but pāda **a** is essentially defective⌋. All our mss. ⌊and SPP's authorities⌋ read in **e** *te*, which our edition emends to *té;* ⌊but SPP. reads *te*, construing **a–d** together, and **e–f** separately: 'unto thee, the bride here'; which seems hard⌋. Ppp. combines in **c** *gandharvā 'ps-*.

10. What *yákṣmas* go to the bride's brilliant (*candrá*) car among the people, let the worshipful gods conduct those back whence they came.

The verse is RV. x. 85. 31; RV. reads in **b** *jánād ánu*. The Āpast. text (Wint., p. 67 ⌊MP. i. 6. 9⌋) has the same verse. ⌊The Anukr. calls the vs. *yakṣmanāçanī*.⌋

11. Let not the waylayers who pursue (*ā-sad*) [them] find the two spouses; let them go over what is difficult by an easy [road]; let the niggards run away.

Is RV. x. 85. 32, whose only variant is *sugébhis* in **c**. We had **a** as xii. 1. 32 **d**, and **d** as vi. 129. 1–3 **d**. MB. (i. 3. 12) and Āpast. (Wint., p. 67 ⌊MP. i. 6. 10⌋) have the RV. reading. The verse is used (Kāuç. 77. 3), with 1. 34, when the bridal train starts. ⌊The Anukr. calls the vs. *dampatyoḥ paripanthināçanī*.⌋

12. I cause the bridal-car to be viewed by the houses with worship (*bráhman*), with a friendly, not terrible eye; what of all forms is fastened on about, let Savitar make that pleasant for the husbands.

Ppp. reads at the end *kṛṇotu tat*. According to Kāuç. 77. 14, the verse is uttered when the train comes in sight of the house. Āpast. vi. 6 (Wint., p. 70 ⌊MP. i. 7. 10⌋) has the same verse, with the variants *māitreṇa* in **b**, *asyā́m* for *ásti* in **c**, and (like Ppp.) *kṛṇotu tát* at the end. The comm. to Āpast. understands **c** of the ornaments worn by the bride, as indicated by the reading *asyā́m*. The verse (13 + 11 : 11 + 12 = 47) is but a poor *jagatī*.

13. Propitious hath this woman come to the home; Dhātar appointed this world (sphere) to her; her let Aryaman, Bhaga, both Açvins, Prajāpati, increase with progeny.

The Anukr. takes no notice of the irregularities of the meter (9 + 11 : 10 + 11 = 41). ⌊It defines the verse twice, first as *triṣṭubh*, then as *purobṛhatī* (cf. vi. 126. 3). Pādas **b** and **d** are good *triṣṭubh* pādas; and **a** and **c** will pass if we resolve *naārī iyam* and *taām*.⌋

14. [As] a soulful cultivated field hath this woman come; in her here, O men, scatter ye seed; she shall give birth to progeny for you from her belly (*vakṣáṇās*), bearing the exuded (*dugdhá*) sperm of the male (*ṛṣabhá*).

A couple of our mss. (⌊E.⌋D.) read *asyā̆m* in **c**. The first pāda is capable of being compressed into 11 syllables, but with violence. Ppp. has for **b** *yasyān naro vapanta bījam asyāḥ*, and in **c** *janayāt*.

⌊The likening of the woman to the field is very familiar later: cf. Manu ix. 33 f. Cf. also the ματρὸς ἄρουραν of Aeschylus (Septem, 753); Sophocles' ἀρώσιμοι γὰρ χἀτέρων εἰσὶν γύαι (Ant., 569); Eurip. Phoen. 18; etc. My colleague, Professor George F. Moore, calls my attention to Koran ii. 22, "Your women are your plow-land," in Arabic, *ḥarth*. — Griffith's (not very close) version suggests a different interpretation: he takes *dugdhám* as 'milk' of the maternal breast. Perhaps after all we should (with W.) join it with *rétas*, and in the sense of 'milked'; but with this difference, that it refers to the *rétas* which is "milked" as a result of the action implied in *páso ní galgalīti dhā̆rakā* at VS. xxiii. 22. Mahīdhara says *vīryaṁ kṣarati* (cf. *kṣīram*). — This interpretation is fortified by the use of *dhayati* at RV. i. 179. 4, *Lópāmudrā vṛ́ṣaṇaṁ* (*nadáṁ*) *dhayati çvasántam*.⌋

15. Stand firm; *virā́j* art thou; as it were, Vishṇu here, O Sarasvatī; O Sinīvālī, let her have progeny; may she be in the favor of Bhaga.

Kāuç. 76. 33 uses the verse to accompany the act of making the bride stand firm after rising from the couch. The Anukr. forbids us to abbreviate to *'va* in **b**. In Ppp. a considerable part of the verse is lost. The second half-verse appears again below as 21 **c**, **d**.

16. Let your wave smite up the pegs; O waters, release the yoke-ropes (*yóktra*); let not the two inviolable [kine], not evil-doing, free from guilt, come upon what is unpropitious (? *áçuna*).

The verse is RV. iii. 33. 13, which, however, reads *çū́nam* for *áçunam* in **d**, and *vyènasā* for *-sāu* in **d**; and Ppp. agrees with RV. ⌊W's "[kine]" seems to overlook the gender of *aghnyā́u*: see Griffith's note, p. 174.⌋ Kāuç. 77. 15 makes the verse accompany the sprinkling of the car and unyoking of the oxen at the end of the bridal journey.

17. With an eye not terrible, not husband-slaying, pleasant, helpful (*çagmá*), very propitious, of easy control (*suyáma*) for the houses, hero-bearing, loving brothers-in-law (?), with favoring mind — may we thrive together with thee.

The concluding word is here rendered as the text gives it, but there is little question that it ought to be emended (with Ppp.) to *-mānāḥ*, as qualifying 'we.' This verse and the next are a sort of duplication and variation of RV. x. 85. 44; our **a** here is nearly the same with the first pāda of that verse, which, however, reads *edhi* for our *syonā*. Ppp. makes our 17 **c**, **d** and 18 **c**, **d** change places, reading for the former *vīrasū́r devakāmā syonāṁ tvedhiṣīmahi sumanasyamānāḥ*. Our mss. are divided in **c** between *devṛ́kāmā* and *devák-*, the majority (not Bp.Bs.p.m.E.O.D.) having, with RV. and Ppp., the latter, which is therefore more probably the true reading. Ppp. has in **a** (like RV.) *edhi* but with *syonā* after it ⌊a "blend-reading" such as the Vulgate shows at vs. 18?⌋; and, in **b**, *sūyamā gṛheṣu*. ⌊Cf. MP. i. 1. 4; MGS. i. 10. 6, and

p. 146.⌋ The verse accompanies in Kāuç. 77. 22 the leading of the bride thrice about the fire. PGS. i. 4. 16 and HGS. i. 20. 2 have it in its RV. form, with slight variants in HGS. Our verse (11 + 11 : 7 + 13 = 42) is metrically much too irregular to be set down as simply a *triṣṭubh.*

18. Not brother-in-law-slaying, not husband-slaying be thou here, propitious to the cattle, of easy control, very splendid, having progeny, hero-bearing, loving brothers-in-law(?), pleasant, do thou worship (*sapary*) this householder's fire.

Our mss. differ, as in the preceding verse, between *devṛ́kāmā* and *devák-* in **c**. The first three pādas agree nearly with RV. x. 85. 44 **a–c**, but the latter begins **a** with *ághora-cakṣus* (like our 17 **a**) ⌊and omits *ihá*⌋, reads *sumánās* instead of *suyámā* in **b**, and in **c** omits *prajā́vatī* and gives *devákāmā ;* its fourth pāda is the commonplace phrase *çáṁ no bhava dvipáde çáṁ cátuṣpade.* Ppp. reads for **a**, **b** : *adevaraghni patiraghny edhi syonaṣ paçubhyas sumanas suvīraḥ ;* and, for **c**, **d** (given, as noted above, as second half of the preceding verse) : *prajāvatī vīrasūr devṛkāme 'mam agn-* etc. ; it thus gets rid of the *syonā* whose apparent intrusion spoils the *triṣṭubh*-character of our **c**, **d**. ⌊The ms. reckons *syonā́* to **d** (by placing the mark of pāda-division before it) ; but the integrity of *imám* etc. as a pāda (without *syonā́*) is palpable. Likely our text represents a blend of two readings : *vīrasū́ur devákāmā sionā́* (RV.), and *prajā́vatī vīrasū́r devṛ́kāmā* (Ppp.) : cf. under vs. 17. — Perhaps the corruption at xviii. 1. 39 below is in part due to a confused blending of two readings.⌋

19. Stand up from here ; desiring what hast thou (f.) come hither? I [am] thine overcomer, O Iḍā, out of [my] own house ; thou that hast come hither, O perdition, seeking the empty — stand up, O niggard ; fly forth ; rest not here.

This exorcism accompanies, according to Kāuç. 77. 16, a complete sprinkling of her new home by the bride. All our mss. ⌊and all SPP's authorities⌋ have at end of **c** *ājagándha ;* our edition ⌊not SPP's⌋ makes the, as it seems, necessary emendation to *-ntha*, which Ppp. also appears to have. ⌊See Roth, ZDMG. xlviii. 108.⌋ Ppp. further reads in **a** *-ṭhā 'daṣ kim*, combines *ā 'gā 'haṁ*, and begins **c** with *açūnyeṣī.* In **b** the translation assumes the *pada*-reading *iḍe* — not *īḍe*, as previous translators prefer to understand ; it is hard to tell which word is more out of place. The verse is once more a very poor sort of *triṣṭubh.* ⌊It may be counted as 44 syllables. Pādas **a**, **b**, **c** scan easily as 11 + 12 : 11 ; but the good *triṣṭubh* cadence of **d** casts suspicion on the integrity of its prior part.⌋

20. When this bride hath worshiped the householder's, the former (*pū́rva*) fire, then, O woman, do thou pay homage to Sarasvatī and to the Fathers.

Ppp. (which not rarely substitutes *āi* for *ī*) seems to agree with all our mss. in reading *asaparyāit* ⌊see the note to vi. 32. 2⌋. Prāt. ii. 65 prescribes the combination *námas k-* in **d**. The first pāda (10 syll.) is both irregular and defective. By Kāuç. 77. 23, the verse, with vs. 46 below, is to accompany the homage paid by the bride to the deities mentioned.

21. Take this protection, defense, to spread under this woman ; O Sinīvālī, let her have progeny ; may she be in the favor of Bhaga.

The second half-verse is the same with 15 **c**, **d** above. The rendering implies ⌊after *náryāi* in **b**⌋ an emendation to *upastíre* (infinitive), which is the reading of Ppp. The Āpast. text (Wint., p. 71 ⌊MP. i. 8. 1⌋) also has it; further, in **a** it has *idám á bhara*, and, in **d**, *iyám* inserted before *bhágasya*. In Kāuç. 78. 1, the verse is directed to be uttered while he (the bridegroom?) brings the hide of a red ox.

22. What rushes (*bálbaja*) ye cast down, and [what] hide ye spread under, that let the girl (*kanyà*) of good progeny mount, who finds a husband.

Balbaja is the *Eleusine indica*, a coarse rush-like grass. In Ppp., the parts of vss. 22 and 23, and of 24 and 25, are more or less exchanged. In Kāuç. 78, the second pāda is first quoted (in 2), after our vs. 21; then follows (in 3) **a**, then (in 4) the first part of vs. 23, then (in 5) our **c**, then (in 6) the second half of vs. 23, all accompanying the corresponding acts of preparing a seat for the bride, that she may take a Brahman-boy into her lap, to encourage the obtainment of male progeny. It may be that Ppp. follows with its changed order the succession of the acts as given in Kāuç.

23. Spread under the rushes upon the red hide; sitting down upon it, of good progeny, let her worship this fire.

Bp.E. ⌊and SPP's C.⌋ read at the end *saparyata*. For the use in Kāuç., see the preceding note. The second half-verse is used again in 79. 5, when the bride sits down on the nuptial bed.

24. Mount the hide; sit by the fire; this god slays all the demons; here give birth to progeny for this husband; may this son of thine be of good primogeniture.

The last pāda is used by Kāuç. 78. 8 as the boy is seated in the bride's lap, though unsuited to the purpose unless forced out of its natural meaning. ⌊Cf. Wint., p. 75.⌋ There must be some error in the Anukr. text relating to this verse and vs. 25 (which are *triṣṭubh*) and vs. 32 (see below).

25. Let there come forth (*vi-sthā*) from the lap of this mother animals (*paçú*) of various forms, being born; as one of excellent omen, sit thou by this fire; with thy husband (*sámpatnī*), be thou serviceable to the gods here.

In Kāuç. 78. 9 this verse accompanies the removal of the boy again from the bride's lap. The verse is a pure *triṣṭubh*. ⌊W. pencils the note "cf. K. xxxix. 10."⌋

26. Of excellent omen, extender (*pratáraṇa*) of the houses, very propitious to thy husband, wealful to thy father-in-law, pleasant to thy mother-in-law, do thou enter these houses.

The comm. to Prāt. iii. 60 notes the accent of *çvaçrvāí*. The verse seems to be overlooked altogether in the Anukr. as we have it; it should be called a *3-p. virāṇ nāma gāyatrī* (11 + 11 : 11 = 33). It is used in Kāuç. 77. 20 as the bride enters her new abode.

27. Be thou pleasant to fathers-in-law, pleasant to husband, to houses, pleasant to all this clan; pleasant unto their prosperity (*puṣṭá*) be thou.

Ppp. puts this verse at the end of the book.

28. Of excellent omen is this bride; come together, see her; having given unto her good-fortune, go asunder and away with ill-fortunes.

The verse is RV. x. 85. 33, which, however, has a different ending: *asyāi dattvā́yā 'thā́ 'staṁ ví páre 'tana;* and this is read also by PGS. (i. 8. 9) and MB. (i. 2. 14). ⌊Cf. MP. i. 9. 5; Wint., p. 74; MGS. i. 12. 1, and p. 157.⌋ According to Kāuç. 77. 10, it is to be addressed to women who come to look at the bride on her journey. Ppp. reads in **d** *dāurbhāgyena par-*. Our edition should read *dattvā́*.

29. What evil-hearted young women, and likewise what old ones, [are] here — do ye all ⌊*sám*⌋ now give splendor to her; then go asunder and away home.

The last pāda is nearly identical with RV. x. 85. 33 **d**: see the preceding note. All our mss. ⌊and SPP's⌋ read in **b** *jaratīs*, as if vocative; our edition ⌊not SPP's⌋ emends to *jár-*, as seems unavoidable.

30. The gold-cushioned (?*-prastaraṇa*) vehicle, bearing all forms, did Sūryā, Savitar's daughter, mount, in order to great good-fortune.

⌊Nearly⌋ all our mss. ⌊and four of SPP's⌋ accent *rukmáprást-* (p. *rukmá°prást-*) in **a**; our edition emends to *rukmápra-*. ⌊SPP., with 13 of his authorities, reads *rukmaprá-*.⌋ The verse is used with 1. 61 (Kāuç. 77. 1), when the bride mounts the car. ⌊Note *bíbhratam* joined with *vahyám*, neuter! is the case like those of *cakrám āçúm, rátnam bṛhántam, gotráṁ hariçríyam* of RV.? cf. my *Noun-inflection*, p. 600, *s.v. Genders.*⌋

31. Mount the couch with favoring mind; here give birth to progeny for this husband; like Indrāṇī, waking with good awakening, mayest thou watch to meet dawns tipped with light.

Ppp. reads in **c** *suptā* for *subúdhā*, of which the stem and sense are questionable (it occurs elsewhere only in vs. 75, below); at the end it has *cākaraḥ* (for *jāgaraḥ*). ⌊Cf. Wint., p. 92.⌋ The excess of syllables in **d** is a very poor reason for calling the verse (11 + 11 : 11 + 13 = 46) a *jagatī*. In Kāuç. 76. 25 the verse is used, with 1. 60, when the bride mounts the couch; and again, 79. 4, when she ascends the nuptial bed (vs. 23 immediately follows: see above).

32. The gods in the beginning lay with (*ni-pad*) their spouses; they embraced (*sam-spṛç*) bodies with bodies; like Sūryā, O woman, all-formed, with greatness, having progeny, unite (*sam-bhū*) here with thy husband.

Ppp. combines at the beginning *devā 'gre*. The verse (11 + 11 : 12 + 11 = 45) is almost a good *triṣṭubh*, in spite of the Anukr. ⌊It would be a perfect *triṣṭubh* in cadence and otherwise if we had the right to excise *nāri*, the intrusive character of which is very likely.⌋ It is used in Kāuç. 79. 6 when the bride enters the nuptial bed; and also, in 75. 11, vss. 32–36 are strangely made to accompany the strewing of grasses by the wooers who have gone out to arrange for the bridal.

33. Stand up from here, O Viçvāvasu; with homage do we praise thee; seek thou a sister (*jāmí*) sitting among the Fathers, inserted (?*nyàktām*); that is thy portion by right of birth; know thou that.

This verse corresponds to RV. x. 85. 22 **a**, **b** and 21 **c**, **d**; but RV. reads at the beginning *úd īrṣvā́ 'to viç-*; and in **c** *anyā́m* for *jāmím*, and *vyàktām* for *nyàktām*, which seems a mere ignorant substitution for it. Our mss. are divided between *nyàktam* and *-tām;* I.E.p.m.O.s.m.R.T.D.K. give *-tām*, which ending is doubtless to be accepted as the true reading. Ppp. reads with RV. at the beginning, but goes on independently: *ud īrṣvā 'taṣ patī hy eṣāṁ viçvāvasuṁ namasā gīrbhir īḍe.* The Āpast. text (Wint., p. 89 ⌊MP. i. 10. 1–2⌋) reads *vittām* for *vyaktām*. Compare Hillebrandt also in ZDMG. xl. 711; he renders *vyàktām* simply by 'bride,' one does not see why. ⌊Cf. also *Ved. Mythol.* i. 435.⌋ ⌊For the metrical definitions of the Anukr., see above.⌋

34. The Apsarases revel a joint reveling, between the oblation-holder and the sun; they are thy birthplace; go away to them; homage I pay thee with the Gandharva-season.

The first half-verse is identical with vii. 109. 3 **a**, **b**. The verse, a fairly good *triṣṭubh*, appears, with vss. 36 and 38, to be passed over by the ⌊London⌋ Anukr. ⌊The Berlin ms. gives the three *pratīkas*, followed, without *iti*, by *agastatakṣe* (!).⌋ Ppp. begins the verse with *yā 'psarasas s-* (for *yā́ aps-*), and in **b** puts *antara* (for *-rā*) before *havirdhānam.*

35. Homage to the Gandharva's mind (?), and homage to his terrible (*bhā́ma*) eye we pay; O Viçvāvasu, homage [be] to thee with worship (*bráhman*); go away unto thy wives, the Apsarases.

The translation implies the naturally suggested emendation in **a** of *námase* to *mánase*, which Ppp. supports, reading *manaso.* Ppp. has further *bhāsāya* for *bhāmāya* in **b**; and, for **c**, *viçvāvaso namo brahmaṇā te kṛṇomi*, and, in **d**, combines *jāyā 'ps-*. The addition of *'stu* at the end of our **c** would rectify the meter of the pāda and make the definition of the Anukr. exact.

36. With wealth may we be well-willing; we have made the Gandharva go (*vṛt*) up from here; that god hath gone to the highest station (*sadhástha*); we have gone where they lengthen out [their] life-time.

The prefix *ā́* in **b** seems out of place. The last pāda appears twice in RV. (i. 113. 16 **d**; viii. 48. 11 **d**). The definition of the verse (as noted under vs. 34) appears to be omitted in the Anukr. For the application made in Kāuç. of this and the preceding verses, see under vs. 32; it does not seem at all suitable. Ppp. has in **d** for *yatra* the variant *vayam* ⌊implying, perhaps, that the Kashmir Vāidikas understood *pratiránta* (p. *pra°tiránte*) as *pratirántas*⌋. ⌊With regard to an Anukr. statement that seems to concern this verse, see above, p. 739, ¶'s 4, 5, 7.⌋ ⌊Cf. xviii. 2. 29 n.⌋

37. Unite (*sam-sṛj*), O ye (two) parents (*pitṛ́*), the (two) things that are seasonable; ye shall be mother and father of seed; as a male (*márya*) a female (*yóṣā*), do thou mount her; make ye (two) progeny; here enjoy (*puṣ*) wealth.

⌊For "mount her," W. suggests in pencil "make her mount"; but I suspect that the full expression would be *ádhi rohaya çépa enām.*⌋ In **a**, *ṛ́tviye* is regarded by the *pada*-text as dual, and is translated accordingly; it probably means the respective contributions of the two to the embryo. Ppp. reads instead (*-rā*) *vṛddhaye*, a welcome emendation. Further, in **b**, it puts *pitā* before *mātā* and has *ja* for *ca* and ends **b** with *bhavātha;* ⌊and it makes our 37 **d** and 39 **c** change place, but with *puṣyatu no* for our *puṣyatam*⌋. ⌊Pronounce *máryeva* in **c**: the verse then scans easily as 11 + 11 : 11 + 12, if we accept the resolution *ṛtuiye* in **a**.⌋ According to Kāuç. 79. 8, it is used in the act of coition. ⌊Concerning the matter as an essential element of the ritual, see Winternitz, p. 92.⌋ Ppp. arranges this and the following six verses in the order 37, 40, 38, 39, 42, 41, 43.

38. Send, O Pūshan, her, most propitious, in whom men scatter seed (*bīja*); who, eager, shall part our thighs; in whom we, eager, may insert the member.

The verse is RV. x. 85. 37, which, however, reads at end of **c** (with Ppp.) *-çrayāte* ⌊'who, eager, shall part her thighs for us'⌋, and of **d** *-hárāma çépam*. All our mss. accent *pū́ṣan* in **a**; Bp. begins **c** with *yā́ḥ : naḥ*. The same verse is found in HGS. i. 20. 2, with *nas* after *tām* in **a**, *visrayātāi* in **c**, and *-harema çepam* in **d**. PGS. (i. 4. 16) has a corresponding, but quite different, text: *sā naḥ pūṣā çivatamām e "raya sā na ūrū uçatī vi hara: yasyām uçantaḥ praharāma çepaṁ yasyām u kāmā bahavo niviṣṭyāi.* The Āpast. text (Wint., p. 90 ⌊MP. i. 11. 6⌋) has the RV. version, except *-çráyātāi* at end of **c**. ⌊Barring the bad cesura in **a**, the verse is a good *triṣṭubh;* but the definition (as noted under vs. 34) is omitted by the Anukr.⌋

39. Mount thou the thigh; apply the hand; embrace thy wife with well-willing mind; make ye (two) progeny here, enjoying; let Savitar make for you a long life-time.

The first half-verse is found also in the Āpast. text (Wint., p. 90 ⌊MP. i. 11. 7⌋), with the variant (after *ūrúm*) *úpa barhasva bāhúm*. ⌊Ppp., as just noted, makes our 37 **d** change place with our 39 **c**, reading, however, *rodamānāu* for *mod-*; and in its **d** it has *tu* for *vām*, combining *tv āyus sav-*.⌋ The verse is ill defined as a *jagatī* or *bhurik triṣṭubh;* it is properly a *svarāṭ triṣṭubh*.

40. Let Prajāpati generate progeny for you (two); let Aryaman unite (*saṃ-añj*) [you] with days-and-nights; not ill-omened, enter thou this world of thy husband; be weal to our bipeds, weal to [our] quadrupeds.

The verse is RV. x. 85. 43, which, however, begins **a** with *ā́ naḥ pr-*, **b** with *ājarasā́ya*, and **c** with *ádurmañgalīḥ p-*. Ppp. also reads the latter (*-līs p-*); and, in **d**, *astu* for *bhava*. RV. further omits *imám* in **c**. ⌊MB. at i. 2. 18 follows RV.⌋ The Āpast. text (Wint., p. 90 ⌊MP. i. 11. 5⌋) has precisely the RV. version. MS. (ii. 13. 23) has pāda **a** only. The verse is almost a good *jagatī*, only a little damaged by the intrusion of *imam* in **c**; ⌊and a perfect *jagatī*, if (with RV. MB. MP.) we omit *imam*⌋.

41. This bridal garment and bride's dress, given by the gods together with Manu, whoso gives to a knowing (*cikitvā́ṅs*) priest (*brahmán*), he verily slays the demons of the couch (?).

The translation implies at the end the emendation (suggested also by Weber, p. 211) of *tálpāni* to *tálpyāni*, as required by both sense and meter, and supported by the Ppp. reading *tṛpyāni*. For **b**, Ppp. gives *vādhūyaṁ baddho* (*vadhvo?*) *vāso 'syāḥ*, which, though metrically awkward, is not redundant in expression. In Kāuç. 79. 21, the verse accompanies the priest's acceptance of the bridal garment, given him with 1. 25. The verse is a good *triṣṭubh*, if emended as proposed in **d**. ⌊Cf. vii. 37. 1 n.⌋

42. What priest's portion they (dual) give to me the bride-seeker (*vadhūyú*), the bridal garment and bride's dress, do ye, O Brihaspati and Indra, assenting, together give it to the priest (*brahmán*).

The anomalous accent *dattám* at the end is read by all our ⌊and SPP's⌋ authorities. Ppp. varies considerably: *yan no 'diti brahmabhāgaṁ vadhūyor vāso vadhvaç ca vastram;* and *dhattām* at the end.

43. Awaking out of a pleasant lair (*yóni*), mightily enjoying yourselves, merry, having good kine, good sons, good houses, may ye, living, pass the outshining dawns.

Ppp. reads in **c**, **d** *subhāu suputrāu sukṛtāu carātāu jīvā uṣ-*; our P.M.W. have *carātho*. To accent *tárāthas*, counting it to **d** instead of **c**, would be an improvement. The verse (which scans 11 + 11 : 8 + 11 or 11 + 8 = 41) is very ill described by the Anukr. According to Kāuç. 79. 12, it accompanies the rising from the nuptial bed.

44. Clothing myself anew, fragrant, well-dressed, I have risen alive unto the outshining dawns; as a bird from the egg, I have been released out of all sin.

Ppp. combines **a**–**b** *suvāso 'dā-*. According to Kāuç. 79. 27, the verse is used when the priest comes back after washing the bridal garment.

45. Beautiful [are] heaven-and-earth, pleasant near by, of great courses seven divine waters have flowed; let them free us from distress.

This verse is a repetition of vii. 112. 1. Ppp. reads in **b** *yantusumne*, and, for **c**, *āpaḥ sapta sravantīs* (*tā* etc.). The redundant syllable in **c** is not noticed by the Anukr here, although it was so at the other occurrence. The verse is used by Kāuç. 78. 10 with vs. 1 (see the note to that verse), and again in 78. 13 it accompanies the pouring of water into the folded hands of the pair; and yet again, in 79. 25, the pouring of water on the bridal garment; this use is evidently the one which gives the verse its place here.

46. Unto Sūryā, unto the gods, unto Mitra and Varuṇa, unto them who are forethoughtful of that which exists, have I paid this homage.

The verse is RV. x. 85. 17, with a differently ordered **d**, *idáṁ tébhyo 'karaṁ námaḥ*, by which is avoided the redundancy of a syllable — which the Anukr. passes unheeded. ⌊Ppp. avoids it in yet another way by reading *tebhyo 'ham akaraṁ namaḥ.*⌋ Kāuç. uses it twice in 77; once in 5, on the wedding-journey; and again in 23, on arrival at the new home. ⌊As to the "deity" of the verse, see above, p. 739, ¶'s 4, 5, 7.⌋

47. He who, without a clamp (?*abhiçrís*), before the piercing of the neck-ropes (?*jatrú*), combines (*sam-dhā*) a combination — he the bountiful, the one of much good — removes again what is spoiled (*víhruta*).

⌊Or 'joins a joining' and 'mends again what is damaged,' as W. suggests in pencil.⌋ This obscure verse is RV. viii. 1. 12, and is found also in several other texts, as SV (i. 244), MS. (iv. 9. 12), TA. (iv. 20. 1), PB. (ix. 10. 1), KÇS. xxv. 5. 30. The RV. text differs from ours only by having in **d** *íṣkartā* for *níṣk-*; KÇS. alone agrees with RV. in this; SV. is throughout as AV.; PB. begins *yakṣate cid*, and has *vihṛtam* in **d**; TA begins *yád ṛté*, has *jartṝbhyas* in **b**, *purovásus* in **c**, ⌊and *vṛhṛtam* in **d** in the Calcutta ed.: the Poona ed., p. 327, prints it *vṛhrutam*, with a *virāma* after the *h*!⌋. MS. has a very corrupt text for **a**, **b** (*jári cétid* etc.), and *saṁdhís* and *puruv-* in **c**; and the Āpast. text (Wint., p. 69 ⌊MP. i. 7. 1⌋) agrees throughout with TA. Ppp. writes *ārdaḥ* for *ātṛdaḥ*. The needed description of the verse as a *pathyābṛhatī* is omitted by our Anukr. Vāit. 12. 7 has the verse used as expiation when anything is broken during the sacrifice; Kāuç. 77. 7, when anything on the bridal car needs mending; and also, 57. 7, when a student's staff is broken.

48. Away from us let the darkness shine (*vas*), that is deep blue, brown (*piçáñga*), also red; she who is consuming, spotted, her I fasten (*ā-saj*) on this pillar.

The latter half-verse is corrupt in Ppp. beyond intelligibility. ⌊The definition *sataḥ-pañkti* (cf. my note to vi. 20. 3 and *Ind. Stud.* viii. 45) presumably means 9 + 11 : 9 + 11. If we could dispense with the *yā́* in **c**, the verse would be excellent so far as rhythm and cadence go (8 + 11 : 8 + 11).⌋ It is used in Kāuç. 79. 22 in connection with taking away the bridal garment to cleanse it. The 'she' is perhaps the female demon supposed to belong to the defiled article.

49. How many witchcrafts in the outer garment (?*upàvā́sana*), how many fetters of king Varuṇa, what failures, what non-successes — them I cause to sit upon this pillar.

Ppp. has *paçcācāne* in **a** for *upavāsane;* and, for **d**, *asmin tā stāno muñcāmi sarvām*. Our P.M.W. read in **d** *tā́ṁ sth-*; the rest, *tā́ḥ sth-*. In Kāuç. 79. 23 the verse is used immediately after the preceding. The lack of a syllable in **a** is disregarded by the Anukr.

50. What is my dearest self (*tanū́*), that of me is afraid of the garment; of it do thou, O forest-lord, make first (*ágre*) for thyself an inner wrap (*nīví*); let us not suffer harm.

This verse is used in Kāuç. 79. 24 next after the two preceding, the person who has the garment in charge wrapping a tree with it. The Anukr. contains no definition of the meter (8 + 8 : 8 + 11 = 35). The verse, as noted above, is wanting in Ppp.

51. What ends [there are], how many edges (*síc*), what webs, and what lines; what garment woven by the spouses — may that touch us pleasantly.

More lit., '[as] a pleasant one.' With this verse, according to Kāuç. 79. 26, the new possessor of the garment puts it on, then coming back with vs. 44. The Anukr. notices this time the redundant syllable in **b** (we are doubtless to contract to *yāú 'tavo*). Ppp. reads, for **c**, **d**, *vāso yat patnībhṛtaṁ tanvā syonam upa spṛçaḥ*.

52. Eager, these young girls, going to a husband from the father's world, have let go the consecration: hail!

All our mss. ⌊and SPP's authorities⌋ leave *yatīḥ* in **b** unaccented, as in I. 32 **c**, as if *pátiṁ yatīḥ* were a sort of compound word, ⌊although the *pada*-text treats them as separate words!⌋. ⌊Cf. MP. i. 4. 4, and Wint., p. 54, vs. 4, p. 55 n. 1.⌋ The Anukr. counts in *svā́hā* at the end as a metrical part of the verse. According to Kāuç. 75. 24, this verse is uttered as the bride lays fuel on the fire; then ⌊75. 25⌋, with seven verses, (apparently, this and the six that follow ⌊so schol.⌋), the prepared water is heated, and with vs. 65 below, the bride is bathed.

53. Her, let go by Brihaspati, all the gods maintained; what splendor is entered into the kine, with that do we unite this woman.

⌊Cf. Böhtlingk, ZDMG. liv. 614.⌋ Besides the use of vss. 53–58 made by Kāuç. 75. 25, as noticed in the preceding note, they are again applied in 76. 31, when at the end of the wedding ceremony the bride is sprinkled with fragrant powders. The connection of *ávasr̥ṣṭām* with *ávā 'sr̥kṣata* in vs. 52 **c**, suggests *dīkṣām* as the word to be supplied in the first lines of these verses; and so Ludwig translates.

54. Her, let go etc. etc.; what brilliancy (*téjas*) is entered etc. etc.

55. Her, let go etc. etc.; what fortune (*bhága*) is entered etc. etc.

56. Her, let go etc. etc.; what glory is entered etc. etc.

57. Her, let go etc. etc.; what milk (*páyas*) is entered etc. etc.

58. Her, let go etc. etc.; what sap is entered etc. etc.

Of these six verses, differing from one another only in one word, Ppp. omits one (58), and puts 55 after 56.

59. If these hairy people have danced together in thy house, doing evil with wailing — from that sin let Agni and Savitar release thee.

This and the three following verses are discussed by Bloomfield in AJP. xi. 336 ff. ⌊or JAOS. xv., p. xliv. = PAOS. for Oct. 1890⌋. They evidently have no connection originally with marriage ceremonies, but rather with wailings for the dead, which are regarded as ill-omened and requiring expiation.* ⌊Cf. the following verses.⌋ Kāuç. quotes only this one (79. 30), and for no definite purpose, combining it with 1. 46 (see note to the latter). Ppp. reads in **a** *yad amī* for *yadī 'me*, and in **c** *kr̥ṇvatīs*. The false accent *kr̥ṇvantás* (which our edition has not corrected) is read by all our mss. save one (D.).

⌊The case is nearly the same with the authorities of SPP., who says, "This reading [*kr̥ṇvantó*] appears ancient, traditional, and general." A note in my copy of AV. suggests that the blunder may have crept in from vs. 61; and I find my surmise confirmed not only by SPP. (who, however, attributes the wrong accent and *kampa* to vs. 60; see his note), but also by the fact of similar occurrences elsewhere: cf., for example, the curious *avagraha* of *sám◦jñapayāmi* at vi. 74. 2 (and my note); the impossible *vi◦bhāti* at xiii. 3. 17, and note; etc.⌋

*⌊Cf. Francis James Child, *The English and Scottish Popular Ballads*, part x., p. 498, under the heading "Tears destroy the peace of the dead," and the citation from MBh. xi. 1. 42–43 given on p. 294 of the same part: "For they [the tears], like sparks, 'tis said, do burn those men [for whom they're shed]."⌋ ⌊See Lüders, ZDMG. lviii. 507.⌋

60. If this daughter of thine has wailed with loosened hair (*vikeçá*) in thy house, doing evil with wailing — from that sin etc. etc.

Ppp. has a very different text: *yad āsāu* ⌊! *yadā 'sāu ?*⌋ *duhitā tava vikreṣv arujat: bahu rodhena kr̥ṇvaty agham.*

61. If (*yát*) sisters (*jāmí*), if young women, have danced together in thy house, doing evil with wailing — from that sin etc. etc.

Because of the redundant syllable ⌊the second *yád*, intrusion?⌋ in **a**, the Anukr. absurdly separates this verse from the others here, and calls it a *triṣṭubh*.

62. If in thy progeny, in thy cattle, or in thy houses is settled (*ni-sthā*) any evil done by the evil-doers — from that sin etc. etc.

63. This woman, scattering shrivelled grains (*pū́lya*) appeals: be my husband long-lived; may he live a hundred autumns.

Ppp. reads in **b** *pūlpāni* ⌊instead of our *pū́lyāni*. For the distinction between *lpa* and *lya* (note to vi. 127. 1), *nāgarī* mss. are of course not to be trusted. All but one of SPP's read *pū́lpāni* and his two then living *çrotriyas* recited *pū́lpāni*. But in view of the Prākrit *pulla* etc. he reads *pū́lyāni*.⌋ Instead of our **d**, Ppp. reads *edhantāṁ pitaro mama*. The same verse is found in several Sūtras: PGS. (i. 6. 2), HGS. (i. 20. 4), MB. (i. 2. 2), and the Āpast. text (Wint., p. 56 ⌊MP. i. 5. 2⌋); but with sundry various readings in **b** and **d**: for *pūlyāni*, the Āpast. text has *gúlpāni* ⌊Oxford ed. *kúlpāni*⌋, and PGS. *lājān*, while HGS. and MB. give for the whole pāda '*gnāu lājān āvapantī;* in **d** the Āpast. text reads *jī́vātu*, and the other three (nearly agreeing with Ppp.) for the whole pāda *edhantāṁ jñātayo mama;* MB., moreover, inserts between **c** and **d** *çataṁ varṣāṇi jīvatu*. ⌊PGS. has in **c** *āyuṣmān* for *dīrghā́yus*.⌋ ⌊Cf. MGS. i. 11. 12 d, and p. 148.⌋ According to Kāuç. 76. 17, the verse is repeated while the bride stands firm upon the stone and scatters the grains. ⌊For *āvapantikā́*, cf. ii. 3. 1; iv. 37. 10; v. 13. 9 and notes.⌋

64. Here, O Indra, do thou push together these two spouses like two *cakravākás;* let them, with [their] progeny, well-homed, live out all their life-time.

Ppp. has in **c** the better reading *prajāvantāu sv-*, and, in **d**, *dīrgham* for *viçvam*. Some of our mss. (Bp.E.T.K.) ⌊and three of SPP's⌋ read at the end *-nutam*. The Kāuç. (79. 9), on account of the verb *sam-nud*, has the verse used to accompany the act of coition.

65. What is done on the chair (*āsandī́*), on the cushion (*upadhā́na*), or what on the covering (*upavā́sana*); what witchcraft they have made at the wedding (*vivāhá*) — that do we deposit in the bath.

Ppp. reads in **a** *āsandhyā up-*. By Kāuç. 75. 26, the verse is used at the bride's bath, next after vss. 52–58, and before 1. 35, 43. ⌊Griffith would seem to take *yád* as virtually equivalent to *yā́ṁ kṛtyā́m*.⌋

⌊The *āsandī́* appears to be now a throne (cf. AB. viii. 5, 6, 12), and now something between a lounging chair and a bed, 'a long reclining chair' such as Anglo-Indians use today with more comfort than elegance. That it was usable also as a bier carried by four bearers appears from Dīgha Nikāya, ii. 23, and Buddhaghosa's scholion. Compare also the description below, AV. xv. 3. 3 ff. — In Hāla's Saptaçataka, *āsandiā* is glossed by *khaṭvā* (no. 112, ed. 1870) or *paryañkikā* (no. 700, ed. 1881).⌋

66. What ill deed, what pollution at the wedding, and what on the bridal car — that difficulty do we wipe off on the dress (*kambalá*) of the wooer.

Ppp. reads in **c** *sambharasya.* Kāuç. 76. 1 makes the verse accompany the rubbing of the bride dry after the bath with a garment, which is then carried to the woods and fastened to a tree.

67. Having settled the defilement on the wooer, the difficulty on the dress, we have become worshipful, cleansed (*çudh*); may he extend our life-times.

Ppp. also has this time *sambhale* in **a**; in **d**, it combines *nā "yūnṣi* and reads *tāriṣam.* ⌊Here, as at iv. 10. 6 and ii. 4. 6: see notes,⌋ part of our mss. (Bs.E.O.D.) read *tārṣat.* With the verse compare xii. 2. 20 above. The Anukr. passes without notice the extra syllable in **a**.

68. The artificial hundred-toothed comb (?) that is here shall scratch away the defilement of the hair of her, away that of her head.

The majority of our mss. (all but Bs.s.m.P.R.) read *káṇṭakas* 'thorn' in **a**. Ppp. has *kañkadas.* The Kāuç. text, 76. 5, with the subsidiary texts (see note to that rule), gives *kañkata*, with our edition. There is little to choose between the two readings. Ppp. reads in **b** *apā 'syāt k-.* The verse, which is a *purauṣṇih*, is not defined by the Anukr. Kāuç. 76. 5 makes it accompany the combing of the bride's hair after she has been bathed and (with 1. 45, 53) clothed in a new garment.

69. Away from every limb of her do we deposit the *yákṣma;* let that not attain (*pra-āp*) the earth nor the gods; let it not attain the heaven, the wide atmosphere; let that defilement not attain the waters, O Agni; let it not attain Yama and all the Fathers.

Ppp. reads in **a**, **b** *yo 'yam asyām upa yakṣmaṁ ni dhatta naḥ.* Kāuç. 76. 14 uses the verse to accompany the purifying of the bride. The metrical structure (8 + 8 : 11 + 11 : 11 + 11 = 60) is described as well as the Anukr. knows how.

70. I gird thee with the milk of the earth; I gird thee with the milk of the herbs; I gird thee with progeny, with riches; do thou, being girded, win (*ā-san*) this strength (?*vā́ja*).

TS. (iii. 5. 6[1]) has a corresponding verse, of which this seems an artificial variation: *sáṁ tvā nahyāmi páyasā ghṛténa s. t. n. apá óṣadhībhiḥ : s. t. n. prajáyā 'hám adyá sā́ dīkṣitā́ sanavo vā́jam asmé.* ⌊Cf. MGS. i. 11. 6 (with *adbhís* for *apás*), and p. 156.⌋ Kāuç. 76. 7 uses the verse (with 1. 42) at the girding of the bride.

71. He am I, she thou; chant am I, verse thou; heaven I, earth thou; let us (two) come together here; let us generate progeny.

The verse (8 + 8 + 8 : 7 + 8 = 39) is strangely called a *bṛhatī* by the Anukr. It is found, with more or less variation, in a host of other texts: AB. (viii. 27. 4), TB. (iii. 7. 1[9]), K. (xxxv. 18), ÇB. (xiv. 9. 4[19]), AGS. (i. 7. 6), PGS. (i. 6. 3), HGS. (i. 20. 2), Āp. (ix. 2. 3). In the first pāda, TB. (with which HGS. and Āp. agree throughout) has the unintelligent reading *ámūhám;* AB. has *sa* for *sā*, which seems also a mere blunder. After this, AB.ÇB.AGS.PGS. add the same, inverted: *sā́* (AB. *sa* again) *tvám asy ámo 'hám* (ÇB. PGS. *ahám*). As regards our third pāda, there is no variant in reading, but AB.TB.AGS.HGS.Āp. put it before our second. In our second pāda, the same texts omit the *asmi;* the whole pāda is wanting in Ppp. For our **d**, AB. has *tāv eha saṁ vahāvahāi*, and ends there; TB. etc. give as ending to the verse *tā́v é 'hi sáṁ bhavāva* *sahá réto dadhāvahāi puṁsé putrā́ya véttavāi;* ÇB. nearly the same, but with *saṁrabhā́vahāi, dadhā́vahāi*, and *víttaye;* AGS. instead *tāv e 'hi vi vahāvahāi prajām pra janayāvahāi;* PGS. spins out the longest ending: *tāv e 'hi vi vahāvahāi saha reto dadhāvahāi prajām pra janayāvahāi putrān vindāvahāi bahūn te santu jaradaṣṭayaḥ.* ⌊Cf. MP. i. 3. 14, and Wint., p. 52; also MGS. i. 10. 15 d, and p. 146, and i. 10. 15 e, and p. 150, s.v. *tā;* also GB. ii. 3. 20; JUB. i. 54.⌋ Kāuç. 79. 10 uses the verse, with i. 34. 1, after the consummation of the union.

72. The unmarried of us seek a wife, the liberal seek a son; may we (two), with uninjured life-breath, be companions (*sac*), in order to what is great, to winning of strength (? *vā́ja-*).

'Of us' in **a** is dual (*nāu*) in the text, but requires, doubtless, emendation to *nas* or to *nú*. The corresponding half-verse in RV. (vii. 96. 4 **a, b**) has *nú;* it reads *janīyánto nv ágravaḥ putrīyántaḥ s-*. That our denominatives have a right to their short *i* is further vouched for by their quotation as examples for it under Prāt. iii. 18. Whether one should emend in **d** to *bṛhatyāi*, or translate as is done above, may be made a question; it seems most likely to be a mixed construction, meaning virtually 'in order to the gaining of great *vāja*.' *Vā́jasātaye* is never joined with an adjective in RV. Ppp. reads with our text throughout.

73. What bride-beholding Fathers have come to this bridal-car, let them bestow on this bride, with her husband, protection accompanied with progeny.

The *pada*-text has the bad reading *ā́ : agaman*, instead of *ā॰ágaman*. Part of our mss. (Bp.P.M.W.O.) read in **c** *sámpatyāi*, but doubtless only by the scribes' oversight. According to Kāuç. 77. 12, the verse is to be used when the bridal train passes by a burial-place.

74. She who hath come hither before, girdling herself (?), having given to this woman here progeny and property — her let them carry along the road of what is not gone; this one, a *virā́j*, having good progeny, hath conquered.

This obscure verse is not made clear by Kāuç. 77. 4; though the latter perhaps means it to be used if another bridal procession goes athwart the track at a cross-roads. The *pada*-text in **a** divides without any reason *raçanā॰yámānā*. Perhaps, too, we ought to resolve *pū́rvā́gan* into *pū́rvā : ā॰ágan*, instead of *pū́rvā : ágan*, as the p. does. The third pāda is perhaps a mere ill-wish with contempt: 'she may go to grass.' Ppp. reads in **b** *dhattām*, in **c** *abhi* for *anu*, and combines in **d** *suprajā 'ty-*. ⌊For consistency, the Berlin text should have *dattvā́*.⌋

75. Continue thou awake, waking with good awakening, unto length of life of a hundred autumns; go to the houses that thou mayest be house-mistress; let Savitar make for thee a long life-time.

Ppp. reads for **c** *gṛhān pre 'hi sumanasyamānā*, and combines in **d** *tā "yus sav-*. We had ⌊part of **a**, above, in 31 **c**⌋; **c** above as 1. 20 **c**; and **d** as 1. 47 **d** ⌊nearly = ⌋ 2. 39 **d**. According to Kāuç. 77. 13, the verse is to be used if the bride falls asleep on the road.

The Anukr. is not content with this length of hymn, but adds three more pieces from other parts of the Veda to fill up the "wedding of Sūryā": *sahṛdayam* (iii. 30. 1) *ity atharvā sāumyam* ⌊*sāmmanasyam?*⌋ *ānuṣṭubham ā no agna* (ii. 36. 1) *iti pativedanaḥ sāumyaṁ trāiṣṭubhaṁ vi hī* (xx. 126. 1) *'ti tryadhikāi "ndro* ⌊*tryadhikam āindro?*⌋ *vṛṣākapir indrāṇī 'ndraç ca* (mss. *-drasya*) *samūdire pāñktam ity eṣa sāuryavivāha iti.*

⌊Here ends the second *anuvāka*, with 1 hymn (but see pages 738–9) and 75 verses. The quoted Anukr. says *pañcasaptatir uttaraḥ* (see p. 738).⌋

⌊Some mss. sum up the book as of 2 hymns and 139 verses (see p. 739).⌋

⌊Here ends the twenty-ninth *prapāṭhaka.*⌋

Book XV.

⌊The Vrātya.⌋

⌊This fifteenth book is the third book of the third grand division (books xiii.–xviii.) of the Atharvan collection; and (like books xiii. and xiv.) it clearly shows that unity of subject which is the distinguishing characteristic of the books of the division. Books xv. and xvi. are unlike all the others in that they consist exclusively of *paryāya-sūktas*, the former of 18, and the latter of 9. The book has, I believe, the distinction of being the first book of the Atharva-veda ever translated into an Occidental language: not only a translation of it, but also the original text, was published by Theodor Aufrecht, in the very first part of the first volume of the *Indische Studien*, pages 121–140, in August, 1849 (title-page, 1850: but see ZDMG. iii., pages 484, 482), some five or six years before the first part of the Berlin edition, the provisional preface of which is dated February, 1855. The *bhāṣya* is again lacking.⌋

⌊The word *vrā́tya* is defined by BR. as 'belonging to a roving band (*vrā́ta*), vagrant; member of a fellowship that stood without the Brahmanical pale.' It is further applied to the son of an uninitiated man (Bāudhāyana, i. [8.] 16[16]: cf. Manu, x. 20), or also to one who has let the proper time for the sacrament of initiation slip by (Manu, ii. 39). And the MBh., at v. 35. 46 = 1227, classes the *vrātya* with the offscourings of society, such as incendiaries, poisoners, pimps, adulterers, abortionists, drunkards, and so on.— In the St. Petersburg Lexicon, vi. 1503, BR. express the opinion that the praise of the *vrātya* in this book is an idealization of the pious vagrant or wandering religious mendicant. In this connection, Weber's *History of Indian Lit.*, p. 112, may be consulted; also Bloomfield's more recent paragraph in his contribution to Bühler-Kielhorn's *Grundriss*, entitled *The Atharvaveda*, p. 94.⌋

⌊The Anukr., in its statements as to the "deity" of the book, says *adhyātmakam* (see p. 773); and the Cūlikā Upanishad (see Deussen's *Upanishads*, pages 637, 640) reckons the *vrātya* as one among the many forms in which Bráhman is celebrated in the AV., mentioning in the same verse with *vrātya* (celebrated in AV. xv.) also the *brahmacārin* and the *skambha* and the *palita* (celebrated respectively at AV. xi. 5 and x. 7, 8 and ix. 9), etc.—And this view accords well with the penultimate verse of the fifth *prapāṭhaka* of the Chāndogya Upanishad (v. 24. 4), where it is said of the sacrificial remnant that, if it be offered even to an outcaste, it is as good as if offered to the omnipresent All-soul, provided only it be done with the right knowledge. And a similar idea is perhaps meant to be expressed by our text here, AV. xv. 13. 8, 9.⌋

⌊In spite of its puerility and surface-obscurity, the book is not unworthy of a searching investigation. That investigation should be one of much wider scope than I can now make; but I presume that the principal passages of the literature which would here come into consideration are those that treat of the *vrātya-stomas* (ceremonies by which *vrātyas* gain admission to the Brahmanical order), namely the seventeenth *adhyāya* of the PB. (parts 1–4) and the eighth *prapāṭhaka* of LÇS. (part 6). — Excerpts from these passages were given by Weber (1849), *Ind. Stud.* i. 33, 52; and, more recently, the main points were reported by Hillebrandt, *Ritual-litteratur*, p. 139. And the whole matter has been made the subject of an article by Rājārām Rāmkrishṇa Bhāgavat, in the *Journal of the Bombay Branch of the RAS.*, vol. xix., pages 357–364. He regards the *vrātyas* as non-Aryans. It is noteworthy that a number of the articles of the outfit of a *vrātya* as rehearsed by these two texts are found also in our AV. text: so, for example, the turban, the goad, the *vipatha.*⌋

⌊**The divisions of the book.** — To begin with, the division into two *anuvākas* or 'lessons,' the first of 7 and the second of 11 *paryāyas*, is clearly avouched by the Old Anukr. (see next ¶ but one); and it is also proved by AV. xix. 23. 25, where the *vrā́tya*-book is mentioned as a dual, the text reading *vrātyā́bhyāṁ* [accent!: sc. *anuvākā́bhyām ?*] *svā́hā*, 'to the *anuvākas* about the *vrā́tya* hail!' — The decad-division is wanting.⌋

⌊In the foregoing books, the Berlin edition has grouped together for the purposes of numeration the combinable *paryāyas* (see pages 471–2) so as to form the groups which it numbers as viii. 10 (with 6 *paryāyas*); ix. 6 (with 6); [ix. 7 has but 1;] xi. 3 (with 3); xii. 5 (with 7); and xiii. 4 (with 6). For theoretical consistency, the same procedure should have been followed in this book and the next: but the practical difference would have amounted to little (we should have had to cite, for example, xv. 1. 18¹ instead of xv. 18. 1, or xvi. 1. 9¹ instead of xvi. 9. 1); moreover, the procedure of the Berlin edition is questionable and has not been followed by the Bombay edition. For an account of the discrepancies thus arising, see pages 610–611; and for SPP's detailed defense of his procedure, see the Critical Notice in his first volume, pages 21–22, where he prints the pertinent text of the Old Anukr. in full and that of the Major Anukr. in large part. — A comparison of the two texts shows that the later work has quoted the precise words of its predecessor throughout.⌋

⌊The quotations from the Old Anukr. are given piecemeal at the end of the *anuvāka* or *paryāya* or group of *paryāyas* to which they severally refer. They may here be given in metrical form. Of the first line, the prior half refers to the first *anuvāka* as a whole, and the latter half to the second. Lines 2–4 refer to the *paryāyas* of the first *anuvāka;* and lines 5–10 refer to those of the second. The numbers in parentheses refer to the *paryāyas* as counted from the beginning of the *anuvāka;* and those in brackets refer to the *paryāyas* as counted from the beginning of the book.

vrātyādyāḥ sapta paryāyā ekādaça paro bhavet:

aṣṭāu (i. 1) *dvyūnā tatas triṅçad* (i. 2) *ekādaça paro bhavet* (i. 3).

dvyūnā tu viṅçatis turyaḥ (i. 4) *pañcamaḥ ṣoḍaça smṛtaḥ* (i. 5):

viṅçatiḥ ṣaṭ ca ṣaṣṭhaç ca (i. 6) *saptamaḥ pañcaka ucyate* (i. 7).

ekādaçakās trayo 'tra bodhyā (ii. 3, 4, 5) [10, 11, 12]
dvāv ādyāv atha niçcitāu trikāu tāu (ii. 1, 2): [8, 9]
ṣaṣṭhaṁ [*tu*] *caturdaçā 'tra vidyād* (ii. 6) [13]
daça daçamaṁ (ii. 10) *navamas tu saptakaḥ syāt* (ii. 9). [17, 16]
catvāri viṅçatiç cāi 'va saptamo vacanāni tu (ii. 7): [14]
aṣṭamaṁ navakaṁ vidyāt (ii. 8) *pañcako daçamāt paraḥ* (ii. 11). [15, 18]⌋

⌊A conspectus of the divisions in tabular form follows. In each of the two tables, the first line gives the number of the *anuvāka*, and that of the *paryāya* as counted from the beginning of the *anuvāka*; the second line gives the number of the *paryāya* as counted from the beginning of the book; the third gives the number of such divisions (*gaṇas*: p. 472) of a *paryāya* as show minor subdivisions; and these subdivisions are shown in the fourth line of the first table and in the fourth and fifth lines of the second table (the subdivisions of the fourteenth *paryāya* being called *vacanāni*: p. 472). In each table, the last line gives the number of divisions of a *paryāya* which are not further subdivided. — Observe that the statements of the two tables are all contained in the text of the Old Anukr., excepting those concerning the number of *gaṇas* (the third line in each table), which statements are taken from the summations noted by some mss. at the end of the *gaṇa-paryāyas*, and excepting the "sums" in the last column, and excepting the distribution of the *avasānarcas* of *paryāyas* 13 and 11 into 2 categories (as explained in the fourth paragraph of the next page).

								Sums
Pary.-no in anuv.	i. 1	i. 2	i. 3	i. 4	i. 5	i. 6	i. 7	
" " book	1	2	3	4	5	6	7	
Gaṇas		4		6	7	9		
Gaṇāvasānarcas		28		18	16	26		88
Paryāyāvasānarcas	8		11				5	24
								112

												Sums
Pary.-no in anuv.	ii. 1	ii. 2	ii. 3	ii. 4	ii. 5	ii. 6	ii. 7	ii. 8	ii. 9	ii. 10	ii. 11	
" " book	8	9	10	11	12	13	14	15	16	17	18	
Gaṇas				3		5	12					
Gaṇāvasānarcas				6		10						16
Vacanāni							24					24
Paryāyāvasānarcas	3	3	11	5	11	4		9	7	10	5	68
												108

Note that the "fourteen" and "eleven" assigned respectively to *paryāyas* ii. 6 (or 13) and ii. 4 (or 11) represent non-coördinate divisions, as explained below, p. 772. — Some mss. sum up the *avasānarcas* of the first *anuvāka* as 112. This agrees with the Old Anukr. (and the table). At the end of the second, we find the summation: *gaṇas*, 20; *gaṇa-avasānarcas*, 16; *vacana-avasānarcas*, 24; *paryāya-avasānarcas*, 71; in all, 16 + 24 + 71 = 111. This agrees with the table except in the last item, 71, which exceeds the 68 of the table by 3; and the sum for the whole book, (112 + 111 =) 223, shows the same excess.⌋ ⌊See pp. clxi, cxxx end, cxxxvii top, clx.⌋

⌊**Differences between the two editions in the divisions of the paryāyas.** There are no differences between them in the *paryāyas* proper (as distinguished from the *gaṇa-paryāyas*), i.e. in those eleven *paryāyas* which have no subdivided divisions, to wit, *paryāyas* 1, 3, 7, 8, 9, 10, 12, 15, 16, 17, 18. But for 15 and 16 and 17, this statement needs to be modified by rehearsal of the fact that SPP. prefixes to the *yò 'sya* of each of the *avasānarcas* of the Berlin ed. from 15. 3 to 17. 7, and also to the 3 remaining *avasānarcas* of 17, the words *tásya vrā́tyasya* with an *avasāna*-mark, but nevertheless makes his numbering as does the Berlin ed.⌋

⌊The differences accordingly are confined to the remaining seven *paryāyas* (those which have subdivided divisions), that is, to the *gaṇa-paryāyas* 2, 4, 5, 6, 11, 13, 14.— In *paryāya* 14, each of the 12 numbered divisions of the Berlin ed. is really a *gaṇa* and is subdivided (alike in both editions, by a mark just after *kṛtvā́*) into 2 *vacanas:* but the *vacanas* are numbered as 24 only by SPP.—A similar statement applies to *paryāya* 4, save that here the subdivision is each time into 3: thus the 6 divisions of the Berlin ed. become 18 with SPP.—We should expect the case of *paryāya* 6 to be just like that of 4: namely that the 9 *gaṇas* of the Berlin ed. would become (9 × 3 =) 27 *gaṇa-avasānarcas* in the Bombay ed.; but in fact the mss. divide one *gaṇa* (the eighth: see note thereon) into only 2 subdivisions; so that the sum is only 26. Note here especially that the anomalous division is supported by the Old Anukr. and that the two editions do not differ in the marking of the subdivisions, but only in the numbering.⌋

⌊With *paryāyas* 5 and 2, the case is as explained on pages 628–629: in a sequence of refrains or *anuṣaṅgas*, the refrain is given in full and counted as a separate *avasāna* only for its first and last occurrence in that sequence.— In *paryāya* 5 (see note), there are 7 *gaṇas*, each with 3 subdivisions (the first ending with *akurvan* and the second with *īçānaḥ*): therefore we have 2 *gaṇas* (the first and last), each with 3 subdivisions, making 6; and the remaining 5, each with 2 (**a** and **b–c**), making 10; and so, in all, 16.— In *paryāya* 2 (for minor differences, see notes), we have the first and last, each with 8 subdivisions, making 16; and the remaining 2, each with 6 (**a**, **b**, **c**, **d**, **e**, and **f–h**), making 12; and so, in all, 28.⌋

⌊Finally, in the case of *paryāyas* 13 and 11, we have divisions which are not coördinate. In 13, each of the first 5 divisions as numbered in the Berlin ed. is really a *gaṇa* with 2 subdivisions (the prior one ending with *vásati*); and each of the remaining 4 is undivided: SPP. therefore numbers them as (5 × 2 =) 10 *gaṇa-avasānarcas* and 4 *paryāya-avasānarcas*, thus making "14 *avasānarcas* of both kinds," as required by the Old Anukr.— In the case of *paryāya* 11, the Old Anukr. requires the division into 11 *avasānarcas*, and this is the division of both editions. The requirement of the non-coördinate subdivisions, namely into 5 + (3 × 2 =) 6 = 11, is made only by the summations of the mss., and only by some of them, not all. This division, if made at all, is doubtless to be made by taking the first 5 as *paryāya-avasānarcas* and the last 6 as *gaṇa-avasānarcas* (3 *gaṇas* of 2 each).⌋

⌊Of this book we find in Pāipp. (in xviii.) only the first *paryāya* and a phrase from the second.* Moreover, neither Kāuç. nor Vāit. make any citations from the book; but it may be noted that xv. 5. 1 is reckoned to the *rāudra gaṇa* by the schol. to Kāuç. 50. 13. In respect of contents and style, the book is quite like the Brāhmaṇas, and it is all in prose. Occasional sequences of words are rhythmical (so the first phrase of 17. 8 and the relative clauses of 15 and 16 and 17); but these are doubtless mere casual lapses into meter (cf. p. 869).⌋

*⌊See p. 1016.⌋

⌊Whitney's ms. appears to indicate that he intended to give to each *paryāya-sūkta* a heading (in **Clarendon type**, as before); and I have thought it well, for the sake of convenience and typographical clearness, to carry out his apparent intent.— Moreover, to facilitate reference to the Bombay edition, I have added, in ell-brackets (⌊ ⌋), the numbers of SPP's minor divisions, wherever the latter differ from those of the Berlin edition.⌋

⌊The excerpts from the Major Anukr. which concern the *kāṇḍa* as a whole may first be given.⌋

[*aṣṭādaça paryāyāḥ. adhyātmakam; mantroktadevatyā uta vrātyadāivatam.*]

---

1. Paryāya the first.

[*aṣṭāu. 1. sāmnī pañkti; 2. 2-p. sāmnī bṛhatī; 3. 1-p. yajurbrāhmy anuṣṭubh; 4. 1-p. virāḍ gāyatrī; 5. sāmny anuṣṭubh; 6. 3-p. prājāpatyā bṛhatī; 7. āsurī pañkti; 8. 3-p. anuṣṭubh.*]

Translated: Aufrecht, *Ind. Stud.* i. 130; Griffith, ii. 185.

1. A Vrātya there was, just going about; he stirred up Prajāpati.

Ppp. reads: *vrātyo vā ida agra āsīt.* The verse lacks one syllable of a full *sāmnī pañkti* (20 syll.).

2. He, Prajāpati, saw in himself gold (*suvárṇa*); he generated that.

For *suvarṇam ātmann*, Ppp. reads: *ātmanas suparṇam.*

3. That became one; that became star-marked (*lalā́ma*); that became great; that became chief; that became *bráhman*; that became fervor; that became truth; therewith he had progeny.

Ppp. has the same text with slight differences of order. The verse counts the required 48 syllables if we restore the elided *a* in *tápo abhavat.*

4. He increased; he became great; he became the great god (*mahādevá*).

In this verse both elided initial *a*'s have to be restored, making 19 syllables.

5. He compassed the lordship of the gods; he became the Lord (*īçāna*).

We need to read *pári āit* and *-no abhavat* to make 16 syllables. ⌊Of this verse, Ppp. has only the last three words.⌋

6. He became the sole Vrātya; he took to himself a bow; that was Indra's bow.

Ppp. inserts *devānām* before *ekavr-*, and reads *tad indradhanur abhavat.* To read *abhavat*, again, fills out the 20 syllables.

7. Blue its belly, red [its] back.

That is, apparently, of the bow (the rainbow); though 'its' (*asya*) might equally well be 'his.'

8. With the blue he envelops (*pra-vṛ*) a hostile cousin, with the red he pierces one hating him [— he who knows thus]: so say the theologians (*brahmavādín*).

If we read *-ti íti*, the syllables are 32; but to call the passage an *anuṣṭubh* is absurd. It can hardly be questioned that the addition in brackets is called for by the sense.

2. Paryāya the second.

[*dvyūnā triṅçat.* **a** *of 1–4, 1* **f**, *4* **f**. *sāmny anuṣṭubh ;* **b** *of 1, 3, 4. sāmnī triṣṭubh ; 1* **c**. *2-p. ārṣī paṅkti ;* **d** *of 1, 3, 4. 2-p. brāhmī gāyatrī ;* **e** *of 1–4. 2-p. ārcī jagatī ; 2* **f**. *sāmnī paṅkti ; 3* **f**. *āsurī gāyatrī ;* **g** *of 1–4. padapaṅkti ;* **h** *of 1–4. 3-p. prājāpatyā triṣṭubh ; 2* **b**. *1-p. uṣṇih ; 2* **c**. *2-p. ārṣī bhurik triṣṭubh ; 2* **d**. *ārṣī parānuṣṭubh ; 3* **c**. *2-p. virāḍ ārṣī paṅkti ; 4* **c**. *nicṛd ārṣī paṅkti.*]

The Anukr. professes to count 28 divisions in this *paryāya ;* but its metrical definitions are of 32 divisions, 8 in each ; in the translation they are marked by introduced letters. ⌊The reckoning is explained above, at page 772, ¶ 3.⌋

Translated : Aufrecht, *Ind. Stud.* i. 130 ; Griffith, ii. 186.

1. **a.** ⌊1.⌋ He arose ; he moved out (*vi-cal*) toward the eastern quarter ; **b.** ⌊2.⌋ after him moved out both the *bṛhát* and the *rathaṁtará* and the Ādityas and all the gods ; **c.** ⌊3.⌋ against both the *bṛhát* and the *rathaṁtará* and the Ādityas and all the gods doth he offend (*ā-vraçc*) who reviléth a thus-knowing Vrātya ; **d.** ⌊4.⌋ of both the *bṛhát* and the *rathaṁtará* and of the Ādityas and of all the gods doth he become the dear abode (*dhā́man*) [who knoweth thus]. Of him in the eastern quarter **e.** ⌊5.⌋ faith is the harlot, Mitrá the *māgadhá* (bard?), discernment the garment, day the turban, night the hair, yellow the two *pravartás, kalmalí* the jewel (*maṇí*), **f.** ⌊6.⌋ both what is and what is to be the two footmen (*pariṣkandá*), mind the rough vehicle (*vipathá*), **g.** ⌊7.⌋ Mātariçvan and Pavamāna (the 'cleansing' wind) the two drawers (*-vāhá*) of the rough vehicle, the wind the charioteer, the whirlwind the goad, **h.** ⌊8.⌋ both fame and glory the two forerunners : to him cometh fame, cometh glory, who knoweth thus.

The natural division of the matter of this and the following verses is in the latter half strangely violated by the tradition. Division **d** should most certainly have at its end *yá evám véda*, as is shown by the requirements of the sense and by the occurrence of these words in the same connection in 6. 1–9, 8. 3, and 9. 3 ; but the phrase is wanting in all the mss. ; we have introduced it in our text, and the translation gives it (in brackets). Then the mss. most senselessly reckon to **d** the words which really introduce **e**–**h**, or the second half of the verse ; i.e., they set no *avasāna* before *tásya*, but have one after *diçí ;* and the Anukr. follows the same method ; it is corrected in our text ⌊although the division by letters in the translation follows the mss.⌋ ; the analogy of the verses of hymns 4 and 5 is a sufficient justification for so doing. In the second half, the only natural division is after *puraḥsarāú ;* very strangely, however, the mss. and Anukr. set no *avasāna* here, but one, altogether out of place, after *pratodás*, and two that are uncalled for after *maṇís* and *vipathám* respectively ; of these two we have retained only that after *maṇís* (as it denoted a certain change of subject), while we have shifted forward to its proper place the one after *pratodás*. The metrical definitions of the Anukr. are evidently applicable, with the usual degree of exactness, to the divisions as made by the mss.

The translation follows the mss. in reading in **e** *mitró* (but all save Bs.s.m.D.R. accent *mítro*) *māgadhó*. ⌊Correct the Berlin ed. from *mántro* to *mitró*.⌋ The Pet.

Lex. conjectures *pravarta* to signify a rounded ornament. ⌊As for turban, goad, etc., see p. 770, ¶ 2.⌋ ⌊Ppp. has *sa prācīṁ diçam anuvyacalat;* the remainder of the book is wanting.⌋

2. **a.** ⌊9.⌋ He arose; he moved out toward the southern quarter; **b.** ⌊10.⌋ after him moved out both the *yajñāyajñíya* and the *vāmadevyá* and the sacrifice and the sacrificer and the cattle; **c.** ⌊11.⌋ against both the *yajñāyajñíya* and the *vāmadevyá* and the sacrifice and the sacrificer and the cattle doth he offend who revileth a thus-knowing Vrātya; **d.** ⌊12.⌋ of both the *yajñāyajñíya* and the *vāmadevyá* and the sacrifice and the sacrificer and the cattle doth he become the dear abode [who knoweth thus]. Of him in the southern quarter **e.** ⌊13.⌋ dawn is the harlot, the *mántra* the *māgadhá*, discernment the garment, day the turban, night the hair, yellow the two *pravartás*, *kalmalí* the jewel, **f.** ⌊14.⌋ both new moon and full moon the two footmen, mind the etc. etc.

All the mss. have in **e** *mántro;* ⌊so also SPP.: correct the Berlin ed.⌋; in our text it and the *mitró* of 1 **e** have been made to change places, for the sake of better adaptation to the surroundings. Why 2 **d** (44 syllables) should be called by the Anukr. an *ārṣī parānuṣṭubh* is obscure; perhaps *triṣṭubh* is to be added (or implied from the next preceding definition). ⌊For *paçavas*, perhaps 'victims' would suit the connection better than 'cattle,' here and below.⌋

3. **a.** ⌊15.⌋ He arose; he moved out toward the western quarter; **b.** ⌊16.⌋ after him moved out both the *vāirūpá* and the *vāirājá* and the waters and king Varuṇa; **c.** ⌊17.⌋ against both the *vāirūpá* and the *vāirājá* and the waters and king Varuṇa doth he offend who revileth a thus-knowing Vrātya; **d.** ⌊18.⌋ of both the *vāirūpá* and the *vāirājá* and the waters and king Varuṇa doth he become the dear abode [who knoweth thus]. Of him in the western quarter **e.** ⌊19.⌋ cheer is the harlot, laughter the *māgadhá*, discernment the garment, day the turban, night the hair, yellow the two *pravartás*, *kalmalí* the jewel, **f.** ⌊20.⌋ both day and night the two footmen, mind the etc. etc.

All our earlier mss. accent *irā̂* in **e**, and our edition followed them, but some of the later ones (O.D.R.s.m.K.) have correctly *írā*, and the text should be emended accordingly. ⌊SPP., p. 322, maintains that the mss. showing *írā* are influenced by the RV. accentuation of the word, and holds that *irā̂* is the true AV. reading.⌋ Some mss. (Bs.R.s.m.D.) accent *hasás*.

4. **a.** ⌊21.⌋ He arose; he moved out toward the northern quarter; **b.** ⌊22.⌋ after him moved out both the *çyāitá* and the *nāudhasá* and the seven seers and king Soma; **c.** ⌊23.⌋ against both the *çyāitá* and the *nāudhasá* and the seven seers and king Soma doth he offend who revileth a thus-knowing Vrātya; **d.** ⌊24.⌋ of both the *çyāitá* and the *nāudhasá* and the seven seers and king Soma doth he become the dear abode [who knoweth thus]. Of him in the northern quarter **e.** ⌊25.⌋ lightning is the

harlot, thunder the *māgadhá*, discernment the garment, day the turban, night the hair, yellow the two *pravartás*, *kalmalí* the jewel, f. ⌊26.⌋ both what is heard and what is heard abroad the two footmen, mind the ⌊rough vehicle, g. 27. Mātariçvan and Pavamāna the two drawers of the rough vehicle, the wind the charioteer, the whirlwind the goad, h. 28. both fame and glory the two forerunners: to him cometh fame, cometh glory, who knoweth thus.⌋

The majority of our mss. read *çāitá* in b, c, d; *çyāitá* is given by I.O.D.R.K. In b, I.O.K. have *saptarṣ-*; in c, d they agree with the rest in *saptarṣ-*. ⌊The *çyāita* and *nāudhasa* are mentioned together at KBU. i. 5.⌋

3. Paryāya the third.

[*ekādaça. 1. pipīlikamadhyā gāyatrī; 2. sāmny uṣṇih; 3. yājuṣī jagatī; 4. 2-p. ārcy uṣṇih; 5. ārcī bṛhatī; 6. āsury anuṣṭubh; 7. sāmnī gāyatrī; 8. āsurī pañkti; 9. āsurī jagatī; 10. prājāpatyā triṣṭubh; 11. virāḍ gāyatrī.*]

Translated: Aufrecht, *Ind. Stud.* i. 131; Griffith, ii. 188.— In part also by Zimmer, p. 155.

1. He stood a year erect; the gods said to him: Vrātya, why now standest thou?

One ms. (O.) accents *ūrdhvó 't-*. The Anukr. apparently reads *-vó at-* and scans as 10 + 6 + 8 = 24.

2. He said: Let them bring together a settle ⌊*āsandí*⌋ for me.

The Anukr. implies *só ab-* and *-tu íti*.

3. For that Vrātya they brought together a settle.

The Anukr. implies *-yāya ās-*. With the description that follows compare that of a similar structure in KBU. i. 5, and JB. ii. 24, ⌊AB. viii. 12, and my note to xiv. 2. 65⌋.

4. Of it, both summer and spring were two feet, both autumn and the rains [were] two.

5. Both *bṛhát* and *rathaṁtará* were the two length-wise [pieces], both *yajñāyajñíya* and *vāmadevyá* the two cross[-pieces].

Nearly all our mss. (not Bp., which has *-cye íti*) give *anūcyè;* ⌊and SPP. so reads without note of variant⌋. At the end, the majority have *tiraçcé* or else *-çcè* (E.O.K. have *-çcè*: but Bp. has *-çce íti*); and this accent ⌊the *svarita*⌋ points distinctly toward *tiraçcyè*, which is doubtless the true reading; it is given by R.T., and I. has *-çcyé*, with wrong accent; our text is to be emended accordingly to *tiraçcyè* (cf. *adharācyà*, *anūcyà*, *apīcyà*, *udīcyà*, *pratīcyà*, *prācyà*). ⌊SPP. reads *tiraçcyè* with no less than six of his authorities; and these are supported, *pro tanto*, by nine others that read *-çcè*.⌋

6. The verses (*ṛ́c*) the forward cords (*tántu*), the sacrificial formulas (*yájus*) the cross ones.

The descriptions in KBU. and JB. have *ātāna* instead of *tantu*.

7. The Veda the cushion (*āstáraṇa*), the *bráhman* the pillow (*upabárhaṇa*).

8. The chant (*sā́man*) the seat, the *udgīthá* the support (?).

The translation implies that *udgīthò 'paçrayáḥ* at the end (p. *-tháḥ : apa○çrayáḥ*) is a corruption for *-thá upaçrayáḥ*, this being favored by *udgītha upaçrīḥ* ⌊so the Poona ed., p. "114–13," top⌋ in KBU.; the Pet. Lexx. conjecture 'cushion' (*Polster*) for *apaçrayá*, but one does not see how the word should get any such sense; Aufrecht conjectures 'coverlet,' as does M. Müller ⌊SBE. i. 278⌋ for *upaçrī:* but the latter should be something that leans against or is leaned against.

9. That settle the Vrātya ascended.

10. Of him the god-folk were the footmen, resolves (*saṁkalpá*) the messengers (*prahāyyà*), all beings the waiters (*upasád*).

The mss. vary considerably in their readings of *prahāyyàs;* Bp.O. ⌊and five of SPP's authorities⌋ have *-āryy-*, R.p.m. *-āry-*, R.s.m. *-āy-*, E. *-āyyà v-*, P.M.W. *-āyyàn.* ⌊SPP. reads *prahāyyàḥ* with twelve of his authorities.⌋

11. All beings become his waiters who knoweth thus.

R. is the only ms. that has the last two words.

4. Paryāya the fourth.

[*dvyūnā viñçati.* **a** *of 1, 5, 6. dāivī jagatī;* **a** *of 2, 3, 4. prājāpatyā gāyatrī; 1* **b**, *3* **b**. *ārcy anuṣṭubh; 1* **c**, *4* **c**. *2-p. prājāpatyā jagatī; 2* **b**. *prājāpatyā pañkti; 2* **c**. *ārcī jagatī; 3* **c**. *bhāumārcī* ⌊*?*⌋ *triṣṭubh; 4* **b**. *sāmnī triṣṭubh; 5* **b**. *prājāpatyā bṛhatī; 5* **c**, *6* **c**. *2-p. ārcī pañkti; 6* **b**. *ārcy uṣṇih.*]

Translated: Aufrecht, *Ind. Stud.* i. 131; Griffith, ii. 188.—For a table of the seasons and months, see the Introduction to my translation of the *Karpūra-mañjarī* (ed. Konow), p. 214.

1. ⌊1.⌋ For him, from the eastern quarter, ⌊2.⌋ they made the two spring months guardians, and *bṛhát* and *rathaṁtará* attendants. ⌊3.⌋ The two spring months guard from the eastern quarter, and *bṛhát* and *rathaṁtará* attend (*anu-sthā*), him who knoweth thus.

The subdivisions of verses ⌊see page 772, ¶ 2 above⌋ acknowledged by the Anukr. in this hymn are those marked by the mss. and edition; 1 **a** has one syllable less than belongs to it by the definition (and so also 1 **b**, but there is no name * for a division containing 23 syllables). In **b** is to be read in all the verses *ákurvan*, with the mss. The Pet. Lexx. render *anuṣṭhātṛ́* by 'accomplisher,' which does not suit well with *anu-sthā* in **c**. *⌊That is, no express name: *gāyatrī nicṛt* is a description by reference to another metrical unity.⌋

2. ⌊4.⌋ For him, from the southern quarter, ⌊5.⌋ they made the two summer months guardians, and *yajñāyajñī́ya* and *vāmadevyá* attendants. ⌊6.⌋ The two summer months guard from the southern quarter, and *yajñāyajñī́ya* and *vāmadevyá* attend, him who knoweth thus.

3. ⌊7.⌋ For him, from the western quarter, ⌊8.⌋ they made the two rainy months guardians, and *vāirūpá* and *vāirājá* attendants. ⌊9.⌋ The

two rainy months guard from the western quarter, and *vāirūpá* and *vāirājá* attend, him who knoweth thus.

The Anukr. implies in **a** *pratīci-ās*. For **c**, the definition *bhāumārcī* ⌊so the Berlin ms. and SPP's excerpts in his Critical Notice, p. 224⌋ is elsewhere unknown, and appears to be equivalent to simple *ārcī*.

4. ⌊10.⌋ For him, from the northern quarter, ⌊11.⌋ they made the two autumn months guardians, and *çyāitá* and *nāudhasá* attendants. ⌊12.⌋ The two autumn months guard from the northern quarter, and *çyāitá* and *nāudhasá* attend, him who knoweth thus.

Here again (as in 2. 4), the mss. vary between *çyāitá* and *çāitá* in **b** and **c**, but Bp. this time has *çyāi-*.

5. ⌊13.⌋ For him, from the fixed quarter, ⌊14.⌋ they made the two winter months guardians, and earth and fire attendants. ⌊15.⌋ The two winter months guard from the fixed quarter, and earth and fire attend, him who knoweth thus.

6. ⌊16.⌋ For him, from the upward quarter, ⌊17.⌋ they made the two cool months guardians, and heaven and Āditya attendants. ⌊18.⌋ The two cool months guard from the upward quarter, and heaven and Āditya attend, him who knoweth thus.

5. Paryāya the fifth.

[*ṣoḍaça. mantroktarudradevatyāḥ. 1* **a**. *3-p. samaviṣamā gāyatrī; 1* **b**. *3-p. bhurig ārcī triṣṭubh;* **c** *of 1–7. 2-p. prājāpatyā 'nuṣṭubh; 2* **a**. *3-p. svarāṭ prājāpatyā pañkti;* **b** *of 2–4, 6. 3-p. brāhmī gāyatrī;* **a** *of 3, 4, 6. 3-p. kakubh;* **a** *of 5, 7. bhurig viṣamā gāyatrī; 5* **b**. *nicṛd brāhmī gāyatrī; 7* **b**. *virāj.*]

In this hymn, again, the division made by the mss. and the Anukr. is very strange and obviously opposed to the sense. Sixteen subdivisions ⌊the reckoning is explained above at p. 772, ¶ 3⌋ are made by reckoning the last 16 syllables ⌊following *īçānaḥ* and⌋ (beginning with *ná 'sya*) as belonging only to verses 1 and 7; and the mss. set no *avasāna*-mark after *tiṣṭhati*, where alone it has reason, but, in vss. 1, 7, introduce it after *īçānaḥ*, in the middle of a sentence. Rather than put it in so out of place, we have omitted it in our text. One ms. (R.), it may be noticed, fills out to *tiṣṭhati°: ná 'sya paçū́n ná sa-°*, showing that it understands vss. 2–6 to be carried out in full, like 1 and 7; the other mss. stop at *diçáḥ*, ⌊but at *anuṣṭhātā́* in vs. 6⌋.

Translated: Aufrecht, *Ind. Stud.* i. 132; Muir, iv.² 338; Griffith, ii. 189.

1. ⌊1.⌋ For him, from the intermediate direction of the eastern quarter, they made the archer (*iṣvāsá*) Bhava attendant. ⌊2.⌋ The archer Bhava attends him [as] attendant from the intermediate direction of the eastern quarter; not Çarva, not Bhava, not Īçāna ('the lord') ⌊3.⌋ injures him nor his cattle nor his fellows who knoweth thus.

A resolution is needed in **a** to make 24 syllables (10 + 6 + 8), also in **b** to make the meter *bhurij*. ⌊This paragraph is reckoned to the *rāudra gaṇa;* see note to Kāuç. 50. 13.⌋ ⌊The word "him" after "injures" is part of the second *avasāna*.⌋

2. ⌊4.⌋ For him, from the intermediate direction of the southern quarter, they made the archer Çarva attendant. ⌊5.⌋ The archer Çarva attends him as attendant from the intermediate direction of the southern quarter; not Çarva etc. etc.

3. ⌊6.⌋ For him, from the intermediate direction of the western quarter, they made the archer Paçupati ('lord of cattle') attendant. ⌊7.⌋ The archer Paçupati attends him as attendant from the intermediate direction of the western quarter; not Çarva etc. etc.

4. ⌊8.⌋ For him, from the intermediate direction of the northern quarter, they made the archer, the formidable god, attendant. ⌊9.⌋ The archer, the formidable god, attends him as attendant from the intermediate direction of the northern quarter; not Çarva etc. etc.

At the beginning, read in our text *tásmā* for *tásmāi.*

5. ⌊10.⌋ For him, from the intermediate direction of the fixed quarter, they made the archer Rudra attendant. ⌊11.⌋ The archer Rudra attends him as attendant from the intermediate direction of the fixed quarter; not Çarva etc. etc.

6. ⌊12.⌋ For him, from the intermediate direction of the upward quarter, they made the archer Mahādeva ('great god') attendant. ⌊13.⌋ The archer Mahādeva attends him as attendant from the intermediate direction of the upward quarter; not Çarva etc. etc.

7. ⌊14.⌋ For him, from all the intermediate directions, they made the archer Īçāna attendant. ⌊15.⌋ The archer Īçāna as attendant attends him from all the intermediate directions; not Çarva, ⌊not Bhava, not Īçāna, 16. injures him nor his cattle nor his fellows who knoweth thus⌋.

The mss. vary in **a** and **b** between *sárvebhyo ant-* and *-bhyo 'nt-*; in **a**, only P.M.W.E. have *-bhyo 'nt-*; in **b**, ⌊at least two, E. and⌋ Bs. Probably our text ought to give in both places *-bhyo ant-*; ⌊so SPP. with all but two of his authorities⌋.

After the definition of the **c** of 1–7 the Anukr. adds: *hinasti vyāghrādiṣv avagantavyaḥ;* which apparently means that in 2–6 is to be understood the verb *hinasti*, which is expressed only in 1 **c** and 7 **c**; *vyāghrādiṣu* is probably a corruption.

⌊After its metrical definition of xi. 1. 36, the Anukr. inserts the words *vyāghrādiṣv avagantavyā;* and after that of xiv. 1. 60 occur the words (see p. 740) *ity*, or *parāviny, edhiṣīmahīti vyāghrādiṣv avagantavyaḥ.* — One ritual use of xiv. 1. 60 is as a prayer for the safety of the bride as she sets out for her new home. In that connection, a specification of the safety as "in respect of tigers and so forth" would be entirely appropriate. And it is also appropriate here, at xv. 5. — The verse xi. 1. 36 is used in the ritual (Kāuç. 63. 9) with iv. 14. 5 in the *sava* offering: the former, as a prayer for safety on the road to heaven (*ágne patháḥ kalpaya devayā́nān*); the latter, somewhat similarly (*svàr yantu yájamānāḥ svastí*). Although tigers more frequently accelerate than retard a Hindu's transit to heaven, the verses may nevertheless be conceived as used secondarily for safety on terrestrial paths. — Accordingly the remark of the Anukr is perhaps intended as exegetical, but it is at any rate most unexpected. — The vs. AV. xii. 1. 49 furnishes testimony (quite superfluous) to the familiarity of the ancient Hindus with "man-eaters." ⌋

6. Paryāya the sixth.

[*ṣaḍviṅçati.* *1* a, *2* a. *āsurī pañkti;* a *of 3–6, 9. āsurī bṛhatī; 8* a. *paroṣṇih; 1* b, *6* b. *ārcī pañkti; 7* a. *ārcy uṣṇih; 2* b, *4* b. *sāmnī triṣṭubh; 3* b. *sāmnī pañkti; 5* b, *8* b. *ārcī triṣṭubh; 7* b. *sāmny anuṣṭubh; 9* b. *ārcy anuṣṭubh; 1* c. *ārṣī pañkti; 2* c, *4* c. *nicṛd bṛhatī; 3* c. *prājāpatyā triṣṭubh; 5* c, *6* c. *virāḍ jagatī; 7* c. *ārcī bṛhatī; 9* c. *virāḍ bṛhatī.*]

In this *paryāya*, the division of the Anukr. and of the mss. suits (except in vs. 8, which see) the sense, and has therefore been retained unchanged in our text.

Translated: Aufrecht, *Ind. Stud.* i. 132; Griffith, ii. 190.

1. ⌊1.⌋ He moved out toward the fixed quarter; ⌊2.⌋ after him moved out both earth and fire and herbs and forest trees and they of forest trees and plants. ⌊3.⌋ Verily both of earth and of fire and of herbs and of forest trees and of them of forest trees and of plants doth he become the dear abode who knoweth thus.

To make the metrical descriptions fit closely the subdivisions, we need to read *vi-acal-* in a and b, and *só ag-* in c: and so more or less throughout the hymn.

2. ⌊4.⌋ He moved out toward the upward quarter; ⌊5.⌋ after him moved out both right and truth and sun and moon and asterisms. ⌊6.⌋ Verily both of right and of truth and of sun and of moon and of asterisms doth he become the dear abode who knoweth thus.

In c, *ca* is to be inserted after *ṛtásya*.

3. ⌊7.⌋ He moved out toward the highest quarter; ⌊8.⌋ after him moved out both the verses and the chants and the sacrificial formulas and the *bráhman*. ⌊9.⌋ Verily both of the verses and of the chants and of the sacrificial formulas and of the *bráhman* doth he become the dear abode who knoweth thus.

4. ⌊10.⌋ He moved out toward the great quarter; ⌊11.⌋ after him moved out both the *itihāsá* ('narrative') and the *purāṇá* ('story of eld') and the *gā́thās* ('songs') and the *nārāçaṅsī́s* ('eulogies'). ⌊12.⌋ Verily both of the *itihāsá* and of the *purāṇá* and of the *gā́thās* and of the *nārāçaṅsī́s* doth he become the dear abode who knoweth thus.

5. ⌊13.⌋ He moved out toward the most distant quarter; ⌊14.⌋ after him moved out both the fire of offering and the householder's fire and the southern fire and the sacrifice and the sacrificer and the cattle. ⌊15.⌋ Verily both of the fire of offering and of the householder's fire and of the southern fire and of the sacrifice and of the sacrificer and of the cattle doth he become the dear abode who knoweth thus.

6. ⌊16.⌋ He moved out toward an unindicated quarter; ⌊17.⌋ after him moved out both the seasons and they of the seasons and the worlds and they of the worlds and the months and the half-months and day-and-night. ⌊18.⌋ Verily both of the seasons and of them of the seasons and of the worlds and of them of the worlds and of the months and of the half-months and of day-and-night doth he become the dear abode who knoweth thus.

Most of the mss. accent *lóka* in both **b** and **c** (R.s.m.K.D. have *lokā́s;* only R.s.m. has *lokā́nām*); our text makes the needed correction. ⌊With the almost unanimous support of his authorities, SPP. prints *lókās*, *lókānām*, which accentuation (albeit so isolated) he takes in this case to be "the genuine Atharvan accent": see his notes, p. 330 f.⌋

7. ⌊19.⌋ He moved out toward an unreturned quarter; from it he thought not that he should return; ⌊20.⌋ after him moved out both Diti and Aditi and Iḍā and Indrāṇī. ⌊21.⌋ Verily both of Diti and of Aditi and of Iḍā and of Indrāṇī doth he become the dear abode who knoweth thus.

Ánāvṛtta in **a** is obscure: the Pet. Lexx. render 'untrodden,' and Aufrecht, 'unvisited'; but both against the analogy of *nā́ "vartsyán* (also of *ánāvṛt* and *anāvartin;* perhaps the true reading is *anāvṛtyā́m* 'not to be returned from.' Bp. reads *avartsyán*, the other *pada*-mss. *ā°vartsyán*. I. accents *indrāṇyā̀ç*.

8. ⌊22.⌋ He moved out toward the quarters; ⌊no *avasāna!*⌋ after him moved out the *virā́j* and all the gods and all the deities. ⌊23.⌋ Verily both of *virā́j* and of all the gods and of all the deities doth he become the dear abode who knoweth thus.

There seems to be no good reason why this verse should not be divided, like all the rest, into three parts; but the Anukr. does not so prescribe, nor do the mss. set an *avasāna*-mark after the first *vy àcalat:* ⌊compare above, p. 772, ¶ 2⌋. The mss. all agree in accenting the second *ánu*.

9. ⌊24.⌋ He moved out toward all the intermediate directions; ⌊25.⌋ after him moved out both Prajāpati and the most exalted one and the father and the grandfather. ⌊26.⌋ Verily both of Prajāpati and of the most exalted one and of the father and of the grandfather doth he become the dear abode who knoweth thus.

7. Paryāya the seventh.

[*pañcaka. 1. 3-p. nicṛd gāyatrī; 2. 1-p. virāḍ bṛhatī; 3. virāḍ uṣṇih; 4. 1-p. gāyatrī; 5. pañkti.*]

Translated: Aufrecht, *Ind. Stud.* i. 133; Griffith, ii. 191.

1. That greatness, becoming sessile (?*sádru*), went to the end of the earth; it became ocean.

⌊Or, 'He, becoming a sessile greatness, went' etc.: so W. suggests in a pencilled note.⌋ Aufrecht and the Pet. Lexx. suspect a play of words between *sádru* and *samudrá*, but the likeness is too slight to make the matter certain. Aufrecht renders *sádrur bhūtvā́* by "setting itself in motion," as if *sa* + *dru*, and the Pet. Lexx. seem to favor the same etymology as had in view by the writer, but it is hardly to be credited. Aufrecht reads in the third pāda *sa samudro;* I have noted *sá* only as inserted *sec. manu* in one ms. (O.); if read, it would make the verse answer better the metrical description. ⌊SPP. does in fact read *sá samudró*, with the support of all his authorities.⌋*

2. After it, turned out both Prajāpati and the most exalted one and the father and the grandfather and the waters and faith, becoming rain.

3. To him come waters, to him cometh faith, to him cometh rain, who knoweth thus.

All our mss. read *gachati* after *ā́pas;* ⌊and so all of SPP's authorities⌋.

4. Unto it turned about both faith and sacrifice and world and food and food-eating, coming into being (*bhūtvā́*).

5. To him cometh faith, to him cometh sacrifice, to him cometh a world, to him cometh food, to him cometh food-eating, who knoweth thus.

⌊Here ends the first *anuvāka* with 7 *paryāyas:* see above, p. 770, end. For the summation of *avasānarcas* (112), see p. 771, near end.⌋

8. Paryāya the eighth.

[*trika. 1. sāmny uṣṇih ; 2. prājāpatyā 'nuṣṭubh ; 3. ārcī pan̄kti.*]

Translated: Aufrecht, *Ind. Stud.* i. 134; Griffith, ii. 192.

1. He became impassioned (*raj*); thence was born the noble (*rājanyà*).

Both elided initial *a*'s need to be restored in order to fill out the metrical description of the Anukr.

2. He arose toward (*abhi°*) the tribes (*víç*), the kinsmen, food, food-eating.

Half the mss. (Bp.Bs.p.m.E.O.D.K.) omit *ánnam;* the metrical definition of the Anukr. implies its presence.

3. Verily both of the tribes and of the kinsmen and of food and of food-eating doth he become the dear abode who knoweth thus.

---

*⌊Upon the margin of his ms., opposite this passage, Whitney has pencilled the memorandum "? Ask Weber and Rost and Roth." He evidently intended to ask them to examine upon this point the Berlin and London and Tübingen mss. respectively and to tell him whether any of them did in fact read *sa samudro.* In the brief interval since that query was noted, all those three distinguished men of learning have passed away, and likewise he who would have asked them. Meantime, the question has been cleared up (*vyākṛta*) by the edition of that admirable Hindu scholar, S. P. Pandit, and he too, alas, is no more here!

prastavyāḥ prastukāmaç ca te sarve svargam āsthitāḥ |
āihikānityatām paçya na vyākartā 'pi jīvati || ⌋

9. Paryāya the ninth.

[*trika. 1. āsurī jagatī; 2. ārcī gāyatrī; 3. ārcī pañkti.*]

Translated: Aufrecht, *Ind. Stud.* i. 134; Griffith, ii. 192. — Cf. Zimmer, p. 194.

1. He moved out toward the tribes.

2. After him moved out both the assembly and the gathering and the army and strong drink.

3. Verily both of the assembly and of the gathering and of the army and of strong drink doth he become the dear abode who knoweth thus.

10. Paryāya the tenth.

[*ekādaçaka. 1. 2-p. sāmnī bṛhatī; 2. 3-p. ārcī pañkti; 3. 2-p. prājāpatyā pañkti; 4. 3-p. vardhamānā gāyatrī; 5. 3-p. sāmnī bṛhatī; 6, 8, 10. 2-p. āsurī gāyatrī; 7, 9. sāmny uṣṇih; 11. āsurī bṛhatī.*]

Translated: Aufrecht, *Ind. Stud.* i. 134; Griffith, ii. 192.

1. So then, to the houses of whatever king a thus-knowing Vrātya may come as guest, —

2. He should esteem him better than himself; so does he not offend (*ā-vraçc*) against dominion; so does he not offend against royalty.

⌊That is, 'he [the king] should esteem him [the Vrātya] better,' etc.⌋ The Berlin mss. read, as the sense requires, *mānayet táthā*, nor was any deviation from this noted in the mss. collated before publication; those compared later, however, all give *mānaye táthā*; ⌊and so do all of SPP's authorities, including his then living reciters, but excepting his ms. C^{p}, which has *mānayet táthā*, secunda manu, and *mānaye t-*, prima manu. — Compare the case of *yame dīrgham*, *yamed dīrgham*, at xviii. 2. 3.⌋

3. Thence verily arose both sanctity (*bráhman*) and dominion; they said: Whom shall we enter?

'Thence' (*átas*) Aufrecht understands to mean "out of him (the Vrātya)" — which is possible, but doubtful: compare *átas* in vs. 5.

4. Let sanctity enter Brihaspati [and] dominion Indra; thus verily: it was said (*íti*).

Or the *iti* means 'he (the Vrātya) said'; Aufrecht so understands it. The mss. make very bad work over the verb in this verse: Bp. reads *pra°viçatu*, Bs.P.M.O.T.K. *prāviçatu*, all without accent; E. has *prā́ viçatu*, R. *prāviçátu*, D. *pra°viçátu*. The true reading is doubtless *praviçátu*, and our text should be emended to this; the situation is one in which an accent on the verb-form is called for. There is no reason for understanding *pra-ā*, and the prolongation of simple *pra* to *prā* is wholly unsuited to this book. ⌊SPP's authorities show a fairly bewildering variety of differences, in respect to *bráhma praviçátu*: see his note, p. 334.⌋ The metrical definition of the Anukr. ⌊6 + 7 + 8: *Ind. Stud.* viii. 129⌋ does not fit at all.

5. Thence (*átas*) verily sanctity entered Brihaspati [and] dominion Indra.

For *prā́viçat* the *pada*-text has *prá : aviçat*; doubtless it should be *pra°áviçat*.

6. This earth verily is Prajāpati, the sky is Indra.

7. This fire verily is sanctity, yonder Āditya is dominion.

8. To him comes sanctity, he becomes possessed of the splendor of sanctity (*brahmavarcasín*), —

9. Who knows earth as Brihaspati, fire as sanctity.

10. To him comes Indra's quality, he becomes possessed of Indra's quality, —

11. Who knows Āditya as dominion, the sky as Indra.

11. Paryāya the eleventh.

[*ekādaçaka. 1. dāivī pan̄kti; 2. 2-p. pūrvātriṣṭub atiçakvarī; 3–6, 8, 10. 3-p. ārcī bṛhatī (10. bhurij); 7, 9. 2-p. prājāpatyā bṛhatī; 11. 2-p. ārcy anuṣṭubh.*]

⌊As for the minor divisions of this *paryāya*, see page 772, ¶ 4, above.⌋

Translated: Aufrecht, *Ind. Stud.* i. 134; Griffith, ii. 193. — Griffith here cites most appositely the parallel passages of the Āpastambīya Dharma-sūtra; and I have thought it good to give them in the sequel.

⌊For convenience of comparison, the passage from Āp. Dharma-sūtra, ii. 3. 7, parallel to our vss. 1–2, may here be given: *āhitāgniṁ ced atithir abhyāgacchet, svayam enam abhyudetya brūyāt: vrātya kvā 'vātsīr iti: vrātya udakam iti: vrātya tarpayan̄stv* (!) *iti.* 13. *purā 'gnihotrasya homād upān̄çu japet: vrātya yathā te manas tathā 'stv iti: vrātya yathā te vaças tathā 'stv iti: vrātya yathā te priyaṁ tathā 'stv iti: vrātya yathā te nikāmas tathā 'stv iti.* 14.⌋

1. So then, to whosesoever houses a thus-knowing Vrātya may come as guest, —

All that the mss. give for this verse is the two words *vrā́tyó 'tithiḥ.* But this is obviously in virtue of their usual abbreviation in case of repeated matter; the verse is the same with 10. 1 except for the omission of *rā́jñas* between *vrā́tyas* and *átithis.* The abbreviation is continued in 12. 1 and in 13. 1–4, and then 13. 5 reads in full *tád yásyāi 'vám vidvā́n vrā́tyaḥ*, because it is the last case of occurrence of the phrase. All this admits of no real question, and the verses are all thus filled up by Aufrecht in his translation, although he leaves the Sanskrit text in its abbreviated form; it is worth so many words here only because the Anukr. commits the blunder of regarding *vrā́tyó 'tithiḥ* as the whole verse, and defines it as one of five syllables (restoring the elided *a*). He has never committed the same blunder in the numerous, but less striking, cases of the same kind that we have had hitherto.

2. Himself coming up toward him, he should say: Vrātya, where hast thou abode (*vas*)? Vrātya, [here is] water; Vrātya, let them gratify [thee]; Vrātya, be it so as is dear to thee; Vrātya, be it so as is thy will (*váça*); Vrātya, be it so as is thy desire (*nikāmá*).

3. In that he says to him: Vrātya, where hast thou abode? he thereby gains possession of the roads that the gods travel.

4. In that he says to him: Vrātya, [here is] water, he thereby gains possession of the waters.

R. is the only ms. that writes out at the beginning of this verse and the next *yád enam āha*. It seems a blunder of the Anukr. to include this verse with 3, 5, 6, 8, 10 in one definition, as it is shorter than they by some six syllables; one of the mss. does in fact omit it here, but gives no definition of it elsewhere. ⌊At AB. viii. 24 is a passage bearing some similarity to this.⌋

5. In that he says to him: Vrātya, let them gratify [thee], he thereby makes his breath (*prāṇá*) longer.

⌊We had the last clause above at ix. 6. 19.⌋

6. In that he says to him: Vrātya, be it so as is dear to thee, he thereby gains possession of what is dear.

7. To him cometh what is dear, he becometh dear to his dear one (m.), who knoweth thus.

8. In that he says to him: Vrātya, be it so as is thy will, he thereby gains possession of [his] will.

Here again all the mss. save one (R.) omit the first four or five words, because they occur again in vs. 10. The majority of mss. (except E.D.R.s.m.K.) accent *vaçám*, though all have *váças*. ⌊Eight or nine of SPP's have *vaçám*.⌋

9. Unto him cometh [his] will, a will-possessor of will-possessors becometh he who knoweth thus.

Most of the mss. (except D.R.s.m.) again accent *vaçás*; ⌊and so twelve of SPP's, but not his *çrotriyas*⌋; O. has *vaçī́nām*. Read at the beginning in our text *āí 'nam* (an accent-sign slipped out of place).

10. In that he says to him: Vrātya, be it so as is thy desire, he thereby gains possession of [his] desire.

11. To him cometh [his] desire, he cometh to be (*bhū*) in the desire of desire, who knoweth thus.

One would like to emend *nikāmé* to *-mī́*.

12. Paryāya the twelfth.

[*ekādaçaka. 1. 3-p. gāyatrī; 2. prājāpatyā bṛhatī; 3, 4. bhurik prājāpatyā 'nuṣṭubh (4. sāmnī); 5, 6, 9, 10. āsurī gāyatrī; 8. virāḍ gāyatrī; 7, 11. 3-p. prājāpatyā triṣṭubh.*]

Translated: Aufrecht, *Ind. Stud.* i. 135; Griffith, ii. 194.

⌊The passage from Āp. Dharma-sūtra, ii. 3. 7 (see introd. to *paryāya* 11), parallel to our vss. 1–3, may here be given: *yasyo 'ddhṛteṣv ahuteṣv agniṣv atithir abhyāgacchet svayam enam abhyudetya brūyāt: vrātya atisṛja hoṣyāmi: ity atisṛṣṭena hotavyam: anatisṛṣṭaç cej juhuyād doṣam brāhmaṇam āha.* 15.⌋

1. Now then, to whosesoever houses a thus-knowing Vrātya may come as guest when the fires are taken up and the fire-offering (*agnihotrá*) set on, —

Not one of the mss. writes the first four words of the verse, they being viewed as repeated from 10. 1; and here also (compare note to 11. 1) the Anukr. reckons them as not belonging to the verse. Bp.O.Kp. write *údhṛteṣu* (the compound being inseparable by Prāt. iv. 62). Bp. further has *ádhi°çṛte.*

2. Himself coming up toward him, he should say: Vrātya, give permission; I am about to make oblation.

3. If he should permit, he may make oblation; if he should not permit, he may not make oblation.

4. He who, being permitted by a thus-knowing Vrātya, makes oblation,—

Prājāpatyā and *sāmny anuṣṭubh* are each of sixteen syllables; what the Anukr. means by its use of both terms in regard to this verse and not in regard to vs. 3 is difficult to see. ⌊His words are . . . *iti dve prājāpatyānuṣṭubhāu; dvitīyā sāmnī; tatho 'bhe bhurijāu.* He appears to set up a class of two vss. (3 and 4) of 17 syllables (16 + 1) each: from which he then proceeds to except one vs. (4) by saying that it is *sāmnī* or has only 16. He might have expressed himself much less awkwardly by writing (instead of the last two clauses) *pūrvā bhurik.*⌋

5. He foreknows the road that the Fathers go, the road that the gods go.

A couple of the mss. (D.R.) accent *jānā́ti*, which is better; ⌊and so do seven or eight of SPP's authorities⌋.

6. He does not offend against the gods; his oblation is [duly] made.

7. There is left over in this world a support (*āyátana*) for him who, being permitted by a thus-knowing Vrātya, makes oblation.

8. Now then, he who, being unpermitted by a thus-knowing Vrātya, makes oblation, —

9. He knows not the road that the Fathers go, nor the road that the gods go.

The same mss. accent *jānā́ti* here as in vs. 5.

10. He offends against the gods; his oblation is not [duly] made.

The majority of mss. (except Bs.E.) read *vṛçcate ah-*, which is therefore probably the true text; ⌊and so SPP. reads with all but two of his authorities⌋. The accent *ahutám* (for *áhutam*) is probably an error.

11. There is left in this world no support for him who, being unpermitted by a thus-knowing Vrātya, makes oblation.

13. Paryāya the thirteenth.

[*caturdaça. 1* a. *sámny uṣṇih; 1* b, *3* b. *prájāpatyá 'nuṣṭubh;* a *of 2–4. āsurī gáyatrī; 2* b, *4* b. *sámnī bṛhatī; 5* a. *3-p. nicṛd gāyatrī; 5* b. *2-p. virāḍ gāyatrī; 6. prājāpatyā pañkti; 7. āsurī jagatī; 8. satahpañkti; 9. akṣarapañkti.*]

⌊As to the minor divisions of this *paryāya*, see page 772, ¶ 4, above.⌋
Translated: Aufrecht, *Ind. Stud.* i. 135; Griffith, ii. 195.

⌊The passage from Āp. Dharma-sūtra, ii. 3. 7 (see introd. to *paryāya* 11), parallel to our vss. 1–5, may here be given: *ekarātraṁ ced atithīn vāsayet pārthivāṅl lokān abhijayati, dvitīyayā 'ntarikṣyāṅs, tṛtīyayā divyāṅç, caturthyā parāvato lokān, aparimitābhir aparimitāṅl lokān abhijayatī 'ti vijñāyate.* 16.⌋

1. ⌊1.⌋ Now in whosesoever house a thus-knowing Vrātya abides one night as guest, ⌊2.⌋ he thereby gains possession of those pure (*púṇya*) worlds that are on the earth.

Here again, and in the following verses through 4, the Anukr. fails to make any account of the first four words, *tád yásyāi 'vám̐ vidvā́n*, omitted by the mss. on account of repetition (see note to 11. 1); they are restored in our text.

2. ⌊3.⌋ Now in whosesoever house a thus-knowing Vrātya abides a second night as guest, ⌊4.⌋ he thereby gains possession of those pure worlds that are in the atmosphere.

Part of the mss. (I.O.R.T.), ⌊with nine of SPP's authorities⌋, read *yé ant-* at beginning of **b**.

3. ⌊5.⌋ Now in whosesoever house a thus-knowing Vrātya abides a third night as guest, ⌊6.⌋ he thereby gains possession of those pure worlds that are in the sky.

4. ⌊7.⌋ Now in whosesoever house a thus-knowing Vrātya abides a fourth night as guest, ⌊8.⌋ he thereby gains possession of those worlds that are pure of the pure.

That is, doubtless, that are especially pure. In **a**, read *vidvā́n* (an accent-mark slipped out of place).

5. ⌊9.⌋ Now in whosesoever house a thus-knowing Vrātya abides unlimited nights as guest, ⌊10.⌋ he thereby gains possession of those pure worlds that are unlimited.

In **a**, read again *vidvā́n* (same error). ⌊Instead of the *tripadā* of our mss. of the Anukr. in the description of 5 **a**, SPP. prints *dvipadā*, Critical Notice, p. 22[17].⌋

6. ⌊11.⌋ Now to whosesoever houses may come as guest a non-Vrātya, calling himself a Vrātya, bearing the name [only], —

Nāma◦bibhratí (so in p.) is so anomalous a formation that we can hardly regard it as otherwise than corrupt, perhaps for *nā́ma bíbhrat* or *nāmabibhrát*.

7. ⌊12.⌋ He may draw him, and he may not draw him.

That is, apparently, whether he invite him urgently or not. But the Pet. Lex. takes the verb as meaning 'treat with violence, punish'—which is unacceptable, as the entertainer is not supposed to be certain whether his guest is a real Vrātya or not. Aufrecht leaves the verse untranslated. There is ⌊with this interpretation⌋ no perceptible reason why the second *kárṣet* should be accented. Another interpretation, however, may be suggested as possible: that *kárṣed enam* is apodosis to the preceding verse: 'he may tousle (maltreat) him'; and the rest, protasis to vs. 8: 'if he do not tousle him' (because he is not sufficiently certain of his real character), then he may pay him honors under protest, as stated in vs. 8. But then we should expect vs. 7 to be divided into two pādas, which is done neither by the *pada*-mss. nor by the Anukr.

8. ⌊13.⌋ For this deity I ask water; this deity I cause to abide; this, this deity I wait upon—with this thought he should wait upon him.

That is, my attentions are meant for the deity whom a Vrātya represents, and not for this particular individual. ⌊See above, p. 770, top.⌋ The repetition *imā́m imā́m* is very strange, and seems unmotived. The *pada*-text sets its *avasāna*-mark, as if denoting a *pāda*-division, both times between *imā́m* and *devátām*, in palpable violation of the sense.

9. ⌊14.⌋ In that deity doth that become [duly] offered of him who knoweth thus.

14. Paryāya the fourteenth.

[*catvāri viṅçatiç ca* ⌊sc. *vacanāni*.⌋. *1* a. *3-p. anuṣṭubh ;* b *of 1–12. 2-p. āsurī gāyatrī* (b *of 6–9. bhurik prājāpatyā 'nuṣṭubh*); *2* a, *5* a. *purauṣṇih ; 3* a. *anuṣṭubh ; 4* a. *prastārapañkti ; 6* a. *svarāḍ gāyatrī ; 7* a, *8* a. *ārcī pañkti ; 10* a. *bhuriñ nāgī gāyatrī ; 11* a. *prājāpatyā triṣṭubh.*]

⌊Respecting the subdivisions of the *paryāya*, see page 772, top.⌋
Translated: Aufrecht, *Ind. Stud.* i. 136; Griffith, ii. 195.

1. ⌊1.⌋ As he moved out toward the eastern quarter, the troop (*çárdhas*) of Maruts, coming into being (*bhūtvā́*), moved out after, making mind [their] food-eater; ⌊2.⌋ with mind as food-eater doth he eat food who knoweth thus.

Aufrecht understands the meaning to be as just given, and takes it correspondingly in the verses below. But it would be admissible also to render thus: 'when he moved out toward the eastern quarter, he moved out toward [it] after becoming the troop of Maruts' — and correspondingly in all the other verses. It is possible, by due resolution, to read the first subdivision as 32 syllables and the second as 15 — and so in general in the other verses; no remark will be made upon them unless the cases are especially difficult.

2. ⌊3.⌋ As he moved out toward the southern quarter, Indra, coming into being, moved out after, making strength [his] food-eater; ⌊4.⌋ with strength as food-eater doth he eat food who knoweth thus.

3. ⌊5.⌋ As he moved out toward the western quarter, king Varuṇa, coming into being, moved out after, making the waters [his] food-eaters; ⌊6.⌋ with the waters as food-eaters doth he eat food who knoweth thus.

Most of the mss. accent *apó 'nnādī́ḥ* (but Bs. has *-ó*). One or two (I.K.) combine *-dī́ṣ kṛtvā́*.

4. ⌊7.⌋ As he moved out toward the northern quarter, king Soma, coming into being, moved out after, making the offering (*ā́huti*) in what is offered by the seven seers [his] food-eater; ⌊8.⌋ with the offering as food-eater doth he eat food who knoweth thus.

5. ⌊9.⌋ As he moved out toward the fixed quarter, Vishṇu, coming into being, moved out after, making *virā́j* [his] food-eater; ⌊10.⌋ with *virā́j* as food-eater doth he eat food who knoweth thus.

6. ⌊11.⌋ As he moved out toward the cattle, Rudra, coming into being, moved out after, making the herbs [his] food-eaters; ⌊12.⌋ with the herbs as food-eaters doth he eat food who knoweth thus.

7. ⌊13.⌋ As he moved out toward the Fathers, king Yama, coming into being, moved out after, making the call *svadhā́* [his] food-eater; ⌊14.⌋ with the call *svadhā́* as food-eater doth he eat food who knoweth thus.

8. ⌊15.⌋ As he moved out toward men (*manuṣyà*), Agni, coming into being, moved out after, making the cry *svā́hā* ('hail') [his] food-eater; ⌊16.⌋ with the cry *svā́hā* as food-eater doth he eat food who knoweth thus.

9. ⌊17.⌋ As he moved out toward the upward quarter, Brihaspati, coming into being, moved out after, making the cry *vā́ṣaṭ* [his] food-eater; ⌊18.⌋ with the cry *vā́ṣaṭ* as food-eater doth he eat food who knoweth thus.

The first pāda is not metrically defined by the Anukr.

10. ⌊19.⌋ As he moved out toward the gods, Īçāna ('the lord'), coming into being, moved out after, making fury [his] food-eater; ⌊20.⌋ with fury as food-eater doth he eat food who knoweth thus.

If *nāgī gāyatrī* means 9 + 9 + 6 (Colebrooke, *Miscellaneous Essays*, ii. 136, as cited by BR.), the first subdivision here comes so near it as to be capable of being read as 9 + 9 + 7 (being *bhurij*).

11. ⌊21.⌋ As he moved out toward progeny, Prajāpati ('lord of progeny'), coming into being, moved out after, making breath [his] food-eater; ⌊22.⌋ with breath as food-eater doth he eat food who knoweth thus.

12. ⌊23.⌋ As he moved out toward all the intermediate directions, the most exalted one, coming into being, moved out after, making the *bráhman* [his] food-eater; ⌊24.⌋ with the *bráhman* as food-eater doth he eat food who knoweth thus.

The metrical definition of the first subdivision is wanting in the Anukr.

15. Paryāya the fifteenth.

[*navaka.* *1. dāivī paṅkti; 2. āsurī bṛhatī; 3, 4, 7, 8. prājāpatyā 'nuṣṭubh (4, 7, 8. bhurij)*; 5, 6. 2-p. sāmnī bṛhatī; 9. virāḍ gāyatrī.*]

*⌊The Anukr. counts 'sya as asya in vss. 3, 4, 7, and 8, and thus makes them count as 16, 17, 17, and 17 syllables respectively. The text says simply *tisro bhurijas*; but vss. 4, 7, and 8 must be meant.⌋

Translated: Aufrecht, *Ind. Stud.* i. 137; Griffith, ii. 197.

1. Of that Vrātya —

Bp. combines this verse and the following into one, reckoning only eight verses in the hymn. And one ms. (R.) regards every verse* in hymns 15, 16, 17 as beginning with *tásya vrā́tyasya* ⌊followed by an *avasāna*-mark, as, in fact, SPP. prints them: see my statement at page 771, end⌋; this, which is opposed to the Anukr., seems also quite uncalled for and wrong. ⌊But, for our vss. 3 and 4 at least, SPP. notes that his procedure is in accord with all his authorities.⌋ *⌊Except 15. 2, which, however, ought properly to form one verse with 15. 1, as it does in fact in Bp.⌋

2. [There are] seven breaths, seven expirations (*apānā́*), seven out-breathings (*vyānā́*).

3. His breath that is first, upward by name, that is this fire.

4. His breath that is second, preferred (?*prāū́ḍha*) by name, that is yon sun (*ādityā́*).

The *pada*-mss. accent, doubtless falsely, *pra॰ū́ḍhaḥ* (instead of *prā́॰ūḍhaḥ*); Bs. and O.p.m. read *próḍh-*: see Prāt. iii. 45, note.

5. His breath that is third, inferred (?*abhyū́ḍha*) by name, that is yon moon.

Some mss. ⌊of W's and of SPP's also⌋ accent *'bhyū́ḍho*, and Bp. has accordingly *abhi॰ū́ḍhaḥ* (but D. *abhí॰ū-*); our text makes the necessary correction to *abhyū́-*; ⌊and so SPP.⌋.

6. His breath that is fourth, mighty (*vibhū́*) by name, that is this cleansing one (*pávamāna*).

That is, doubtless, the wind, and not soma.

7. His breath that is fifth, womb (?*yóni*) by name, that is these waters.

8. His breath that is sixth, dear by name, that is these cattle.

9. His breath that is seventh, unlimited by name, that is these creatures (*prajā́*).

16. Paryāya the sixteenth.

[*saptaka. 1, 3. sāmny uṣṇih; 2, 4, 5. prājāpatyo 'ṣṇih; 6. yājuṣī triṣṭubh; 7. āsurī gāyatrī.*]

⌊The metrical definitions of the Anukr. imply in every verse the inclusion of the words *yo 'sya* (pronounced as *yo asya*), and the reading of *apānaḥ* as 3 syllables. — As noted at p. 771, end, SPP. puts each time before *yo 'sya* the words *tásya vrā́tyasya* with an *avasāna*-mark.⌋

In this hymn, the mss. in general omit at the beginning both *yó* and *asya*, while in 15 and 17 they omit only *yó*. Some, however, have *asya* here also (so K.; R. *yó asya* throughout).

Translated: Aufrecht, *Ind. Stud.* i. 137; Griffith, ii. 198.

1. His expiration that is first, that is the day of full moon.

2. His expiration that is second, that is the day of the moon's quarter (*áṣṭakā*).

3. His expiration that is third, that is the day of new moon.

4. His expiration that is fourth, that is faith.

5. His expiration that is fifth, that is consecration.

6. His expiration that is sixth, that is sacrifice.

7. His expiration that is seventh, that is these sacrificial gifts.

⌊Bloomfield, AJP. xvii. 411, makes some observations on the word *çraddhā*, vs. 4.⌋

17. Paryāya the seventeenth.

[*daça. 1, 5. prājāpatyo 'ṣṇih ; 2, 7. āsury anuṣṭubh ; 3. yājuṣī pañkti ; 4. sāmny uṣṇih ; 6. yājuṣī triṣṭubh ; 8. 3-p. pratiṣṭhā "rcī pañkti ; 9. 2-p. sāmnī triṣṭubh ; 10. sāmny anuṣṭubh.*]

Translated: Aufrecht, *Ind. Stud.* i. 137 ; Griffith, ii. 198.

1. His out-breathing that is first, that is this earth.

2. His out-breathing that is second, that is the atmosphere.

3. His out-breathing that is third, that is the sky.

4. His out-breathing that is fourth, that is the asterisms.

5. His out-breathing that is fifth, that is the seasons.

6. His out-breathing that is sixth, that is they of the seasons.

7. His out-breathing that is seventh, that is the year.

8. The gods go about the same purpose (*ártha*) ; thus (*etát*) verily the seasons go about after the year and the Vrātya.

One ms. (R.) prefixes *tásya vrā́tyasya* also to this and the two following verses. ⌊In the Bombay ed., each verse begins with *tásya vrā́tyasya* and an *avasāna*-mark : see p. 771, end.⌋ The sense of the three is obscure ; Aufrecht leaves them untranslated.

9. As they enter together into the sun (*ādityá*), just so [do they] also into new-moon day and full-moon day.

The great majority of the mss. (all save Bs.D.K.) accent *amāvāsyā́m.*

10. One [is] that immortality of theirs : to this effect (*íti*) [is] the offering.

Except two (D.R.), all the mss. accent *éṣām.*

18. Paryāya the eighteenth.

[*pañcaka. 1. dāivī pañkti ; 2, 3. ārcī bṛhatī ; 4. ārcy anuṣṭubh ; 5. sāmny uṣṇih.*]

Translated: Aufrecht, *Ind. Stud.* i. 138 ; Griffith, ii. 199.

1. Of that Vrātya —

2. As for (*yát*) his right eye, that is yonder sun (*ādityá*) ; as for his left eye, that is yonder moon.

3. As for his right ear, that is this fire ; as for his left ear, that is this cleansing one ('wind').

4. Day-and-night [are his] two nostrils ; Diti and Aditi [his] two skull-halves ; the year [his] head.

5. With the day [is] the Vrātya westward, with the night eastward : homage to the Vrātya.

⌊Here ends the second *anuvāka*, with 11 *paryāyas* : see above, p. 770. For the summations of *avasānarcas* (questionable), see p. 771.⌋

⌊Here ends the thirtieth *prapāṭhaka.*⌋

Book XVI.

⌊Unity of subject not apparent.⌋

⌊This is the fourth book of the third grand division (books xiii.–xviii.) of the Atharvan collection. By what warrant it has found a place among the books whose distinctive feature is their unity of subject it is hard to say; and the same is in a measure true of the next book, book xvii.: but see Whitney's General Introduction; also Bloomfield's contribution to the Bühler-Kielhorn *Grundriss*, p. 94. The study of the ritual applications of the book distinctly fails, in my opinion, to reveal any pervading concinnity of purpose or of use.⌋

⌊In the *Indische Studien*, xiii. 185, Weber has suggested that parts of the book are evening prayers, to be recited before going to rest, and especially for the warding off of evil dreams (see 1. 11; 5; 6; 7. 8–11); and 9. 3–4, at the end of the book, may well be taken as the words of them "that watch [have watched] for the morning" and as expressing the "joy" that "cometh in the morning," and are accordingly placed, as is usual and appropriate, at the end of the *mantras* concerned, in order to indicate the successful accomplishment of the purpose of those *mantras*. One is half tempted to give to the book the title "Against the 'terror by night'?"⌋

⌊Laying apart book vi., which has received great attention from the translators (see p. 281), it may be noted that this is the first book of the Atharvan *saṁhita* of which no translation has as yet been published by the translators of single books. Here again the *bhāṣya* is lacking.⌋ ⌊☞ For "Paritta" as title of book, see p. 1045.⌋

The ⌊Major⌋ Anukr. calls the whole book *prājāpatya: prājāpatyasya nava paryāyāḥ;* and both of its two *anuvākas* are evidently called by the same name ⌊*prājāpatyābhyām*⌋ in xix. 23. 26; whether this means to ascribe the authorship of the book to Prajāpati is not certain.—⌊On the other hand, the Old Anukr. seems rather to imply by its

prājāpatyo ha catuṣkaḥ; pañcaparyāya uttaraḥ

that the name *prājāpatya* pertains only to the first *anuvāka*, 'the one of four *paryāyas*.' It may, however, be added that the *prājāpatyasya* in the first line of the printed extract below may mean the whole book or else only the first *anuvāka*.⌋

⌊Quotations from the Old Anukr. are given piecemeal through the mss. of the book. They may here be given in connected form as printed by SPP. in his Critical Notice, p. 23.—Line 1 refers to the 'prior' and the 'last' (that is the 'latter') of the two *anuvākas* of the 'prājāpatyan' book: unless indeed the relation of the first two words is appositive ('of the prior, the prājāpatyan' [*anuvāka*]: see the preceding paragraph). — At the end of the first *anuvāka*, 8 of W's mss. say *prājāpatyo ha catuṣkaḥ;* and at the end of the second is read *pañcaparyāya uttaraḥ:* the two quotations make a half-çloka which we may expect to find in the text of the Old Anukr., standing between lines 1 and 2 of our extract. — Line 2 refers to the *paryāyas* of the first *anuvāka;* and lines 3–6 refer to those of the second. — The numbers in parentheses refer to the *paryāyas* as counted from the beginning of the *anuvāka;* and those in brackets refer to the *paryāyas* as counted from the beginning of the book.

prājāpatyasya pūrvasya paramasya punaḥ çṛṇu:
trayodaçā "dyaṁ (i. 1) *vijānīyād, dvāu* (i. 2, 3) *ṣaṭkāu, saptakaḥ paraḥ* (i. 4).

ādyaṁ (ii. 1) *daçakaṁ, hy* (?) *ekādaçakaṁ* (ii. 2) [5, 6]
tasmāc ca paraṁ (ii. 3) *dvyadhikaṁ vihitam:* [7]
ekādaça vāi triguṇāny aparaç (ii. 4) [8]
catvāri vāi vacanāni paraḥ (ii. 5). [9]

The quoted bit of the Old Anukr. at the end of *paryāya* 6 (or ii. 2) is *hyekādaçakam* (or *hyāu-*): the fact that the verse is so divided by piecemeal quotation as to bring *hi* at the beginning of its fragment seems to oppugn the correctness of the reading *hi;* and the word, as noted below, is not incorporated into the Major Anukr., the Berlin ms. of which, moreover, boggles at this point. — A comparison of the text of the Old Anukr. (above) with that of the Major Anukr. shows that the later text has quoted every word of lines 2–6 of the older, excepting *tasmāc ca param* and *aparaḥ* and the questionable *hi.*⌋

⌊A conspectus of the divisions of the book in tabular form follows. The explanations given on page 771 (which see: in book xv.), apply for the most part also to this table.

Pary.-no in anuv.	i. 1	i. 2	i. 3	i. 4	ii. 1	ii. 2	ii. 3	ii. 4	ii. 5	Sums
" " book	1	2	3	4	5	6	7	8	9	
Gaṇas					2			2		
Gaṇāvasānarcas					6			8		14
Vacanāni									4	4
Paryāyāvasānarcas	13	6	6	7	4	11	13	25		53

Note that the "ten" (6 + 4) and the "thrice eleven" (8 + 25) assigned by the Old Anukr. to *paryāyas* 5 (or ii. 1) and 8 (or ii. 4) represent non-coördinate divisions, as noticed and explained above, p. 771, and p. 772, ¶ 4. — Some mss. sum up the *avasānarcas* of the first *anuvāka* as 32 (correctly). Those of the second are summed up as follows: *paryāya-avasānarcas*, 53 (correctly); *gaṇa-avasānarcas*, 14 (correctly); *avasānarcas* "of both kinds," 68 (! but by D. correctly as 67). The 67 with the 4 *vacanas* make 71 (so Bs. correctly). And 71 + 32 make 103 for the whole book, and so one ms. at least sums them up.⌋

⌊Since the book consists wholly of *paryāya-sūktas*, there is no difference between the two editions in respect to the hymn-numbers: compare pages 611 and 770. — The division into decads is wanting.⌋ ⌊See pp. clxi, cxxx end, cxxxvii top, clx.⌋

⌊**Differences between the two editions in the division of the paryāyas.** The differences occur (as above, p. 771) only in the *gaṇa-paryāyas* 5 (or ii. 1) and 8 (or ii. 4). In these, SPP. has, as the Old Anukr. requires, 10 and 33 divisions respectively (as against 6 and 27 of the Berlin edition). The explanation is as on pages 628–629 and on page 772: namely, that, in a sequence of refrains, the refrain is given in full and counted as a separate *avasāna* only for its first and last occurrence in that sequence. — In *paryāya* 5 there are properly 6 *gaṇas*, each with 3 subdivisions: therefore we have 2 *gaṇas* (the first and last), each with 3 subdivisions, making 6; while in each of the remaining 4, the refrains (**b**, **c**) are counted as one with **a** (thus **a–b–c**), making 4; and so, in all, we have 10. — In like manner, in *paryāya* 8, there are properly 27 *gaṇas*, each with 4 subdivisions: therefore we have 2 *gaṇas* (the first and last), each with 4 subdivisions, making 8; and (27—2=) 25, each counted as one (**a–b–c–d**), making 25; and so, in all, we have 33.⌋

⌊The book is mainly prose: Whitney, *Index*, p. 5, excepts verses 1. 10, 12, 13; 4. 2, 6; 6. 1–4, 11; 9. 1, 2.⌋

In Pāipp. (xviii.) are found only fragments of the book, namely 1. 1–3; 4. 7 (beginning with *mo 'pa*), the first words of 5. 1, then 8. 1, and finally 9. 4, the concluding verse. This looks as if the whole book were acknowledged as part of the text, but its complete presentation deliberately declined for some reason. ⌊The fragments in question follow immediately the fragment of book xv. cited in the note to xv. 2. 1.⌋ ⌊☞ See pages 1015–6.⌋

⌊In the Vāit., the book is noticed only twice: see under 2. 6 and 9. 3. And in the Kāuç., it is noticed only about a dozen times: see under 1. 1; 2. 1, 6; 3. 1; 4. 1; 5. 1; 6. 1; 9. 3, 4.⌋

---

1. Paryāya the first.

[*Prajāpati* (?). — *trayodaça. 1, 3. 2-p. sāmnī bṛhatī; 2, 10. yājuṣī triṣṭubh; 4. āsurī gāyatrī; 5, 8. sāmnī pañkti (5. 2-p.); 6. sāmny anuṣṭubh; 7. nicṛd virāḍgāyatrī; 9. āsurī pañkti; 11. sāmny uṣṇih; 12, 13. ārcy anuṣṭubh.*]

Translated: Griffith, ii. 201.

1. Let go [is] the bull of the waters; let go [are] the heavenly fires.

The verse, or the hymn (*paryāya*), is quoted in Kāuç. 9. 9, in the process of preparing holy water (*çāntyudaka*); with it one "lets go the waters," and then follow question and answer respecting the preparation. In Ppp. the initial *a* of *atisṛṣṭās* is not elided.

2. Breaking, breaking about, killing, slaughtering; —

3. Dimming ⌊*mroká*⌋, mind-slaying, digging, out-burning, self-spoiling, body-spoiling.

All these epithets are nom. sing. masc.; as *mroká* and *nirdāhá* are found together in v. 31. 9 as epithets of the flesh-eating fire, they are probably names of the fires mentioned in vs. 1: cf. also vs. 7, below; Ppp. combines *-dāhā "tma-*. ⌊Weber (*Ind. Stud.* xiii. 185), discussing *mroká* as it occurs above at ii. 24. 3 in the long string of epithets, takes our *paryāya* here as an evening prayer (see p. 792), and notes the names of the ten Agnis here rehearsed in vss. 2, 3.⌋

4. That one now I let go; that one let me not wash down against myself; —

5. That one do we let go against him who hates us, whom we hate.

These two verses form a part of vss. 15–21 in the water-thunderbolt (*udavajra*) hymn, above, x. 5 ⌊see my note⌋; and fragments of the same hymn are found further on in this *paryāya* and in 7. 6, 13, indicating some connection of application with that hymn, though Kāuç. suggests such connection only for xvi. 2. 1.

6. Thou art tip (*ágra*) of the waters; I let you go down unto the ocean.

With the second part compare the opening words of x. 5. 23.

7. The fire that is in the waters, it do I let go, the dimming, digging, body-spoiling one.

With this verse compare PGS. ii. 6. 10, used in the ceremonies commemorating the end of Vedic study. ⌊The definition of the Anukr. seems to be wide of the mark.⌋

8. The fire that entered into you, O waters, this is that; what of you is terrible, this is that.

9. May [it] pour upon you with Indra's Indra-power (*indriyá*).

10. Free from defilement (*-riprá*) [are] the waters; let them [carry] away from us defilement;—

11. Let them carry forth from us sin; let them carry forth evil-dreaming.

With the last two verses compare parts of x. 5. 24.

12. With propitious eye look at me, O waters; with propitious body touch my skin.

We had this verse above as i. 33. 4 **a, b**.

13. We call the propitious fires that sit in the waters. Put in me dominion [and] splendor, O divine [waters].

2. Paryāya the second.

[*ṣaṭka. vāgdevatya. 1. āsury anuṣṭubh; 2. āsury uṣṇih; 3. sāmny uṣṇih; 4. 3-p. sāmnī bṛhatī; 5. ārcy anuṣṭubh; 6. nicṛd virāḍgāyatrī.*]

Translated: Griffith, ii. 202.

1. Out of evil-eating (?) with refreshment [comes] speech rich in honey.

The translation implies the change of *durarmaṇyàs* to *duradmanyàs*, as proposed by the Pet. Lexx. (add TB. iii. 3. 9[9] as a reference for *duradmaní*). The reading of the mss. is, however, assured by its quotation in the Prāt. (4. II. 16 ⌊i.e. Add'l Note, p. 592⌋), and three times in the Kāuç.: namely, in 49. 27, at the very end of the chapter of witchcraft ceremonies, after use of x. 5. 6, 7 and xiii. 1. 56, with the direction *iti saṁdhāvyā 'bhimṛçati;* and again, twice (58. 6, 12) in the ceremony for long life after initiation to Vedic study, once with the direction *iti saṁdhāvya*, and once with a smearing with fragrant powders. The word *ūrjā́* in our text might also be nominative, and 'comes' is of course doubtful. The metrical definition implies the resolution *-ṇi-a*.

2. Rich in honey are ye; may I speak speech rich in honey.

'Ye': i.e., the waters, the adjective being feminine. ⌊We had a phrase like to our second clause at iii. 20. 10: cf. *Gram.* § 738 a.⌋

3. Invoked of me [is] the guardian (*gopā́*); invoked [is] guardianship.

The different metrical designation of these two 14-syllabled verses is apparently wholly arbitrary.

4. Well-hearing ears, ears hearing what is excellent; may I hear excellent encomium (*çlóka*).

'Ears' is both times dual; we might fill out to 'well-hearing are my ears' etc.

5. Let both well-hearing and listening (*úpaçruti*) not desert me — eagle-like sight, unfailing light.

⌊For the *mā* . . . *mā́*, cf. below, 3. 2, etc.⌋

6. Spread (*prastará*) of the seers art thou; homage be to the spread of the divine ones (*dāíva*).

The verse is used twice in Kāuç. (2. 18; 137. 33), and once in Vāit. (2. 9). In the former, it accompanies the taking up of part of the *darbha*-grass provided, and making a seat for the *brahman*-priest south of the fire, once at the *parvan* sacrifice and once in the *ājyatantra* ceremony. In the latter, it accompanies the making of such a spread in the *parvan* ceremonies. In all the three cases, it is evidently taken because of its specific meaning, and not because of any connection of those ceremonies with the one implied here.

3. Paryāya the third.

[*Brahman.* — *ṣaṭka. ādityadevatya. 1. āsurī gāyatrī; 2, 3. ārcy anuṣṭubh; 4. prājāpatyā triṣṭubh; 5. sāmny uṣṇih; 6. 2-p. sāmnī triṣṭubh.*]

Translated: Griffith, ii. 202.

1. May I be the head (*mūrdhán*) of riches, the head of my equals.

Or, perhaps, 'I am the head of the one, may I be so of the other.' The verse (or the *paryāya*) is quoted twice in Kāuç., once (18. 25) in the *citrā* ceremony, together with a whole series of other hymns or verses, in partaking of a milk-rice-dish; and once (58. 22), in the ceremony of giving food to a young child (*annaprāçana*), with a part of the same hymns.

2. Let both breaking (?*rujá*) and longing (*vená*) not desert me; let both the head (*mūrdhán*) and the distributer (?*vídharman*) not desert me.

The nouns in this and the following verses are in part of obscure meaning and reference.

3. Let both the kettle (?) and the cup (*camasá*) not desert me; let both the maintainer (*dhartṛ́*) and the supporter (*dharúṇa*) not desert me.

The translation follows the suggestion of the Pet. Lexx., to emend *urvá* at the beginning to *ukhá*.

4. Let both the releaser (*vimoká*) and the wet-rimmed one not desert me; let both him of wet drops (*-dā́nu*) and Mātariçvan not desert me.

5. Brihaspati my soul, manly-minded by name, hearty (*hṛ́dya*).

6. Free from torment my heart, a wide pasture, an ocean am I by extent (*vídharman*).

4. Paryāya the fourth.

[*Brahman.* — *saptaka. ādityadevatya. 1, 3. sāmny anuṣṭubh; 2. sāmny uṣṇih; 4. 3-p. anuṣṭubh; 5. āsurī gāyatrī; 6. ārcy uṣṇih; 7. 3-p. virāḍgarbhā 'nuṣṭubh.*]

Translated: Griffith, ii. 203.

1. May I be the navel of riches, the navel of my equals.

The scholiast (*pariçiṣṭa*) adds this verse (or *paryāya*) to 3. 1 under Kāuç. 18. 25. ⌊Cf. note to 3. 1.⌋

2. Of good seat (?*svāsát*) art thou, of good dawns, an immortal among mortals.

The adjectives are sing. masculine. The *pada*-text reads *su○āsát* and *su○uṣā́ḥ*.

3. Let not breath quit me; nor let expiration, deserting me, go away.

⌊For 'deserting me' one might perhaps say 'leaving me low.' For the combination with *párā gā*, cf. TS. v. 7. 9[1].⌋ Most of our mss. (all except D.R.) leave *mā́m* unaccented; ⌊the curious blunder is made also by nine of SPP's mss., as against five mss. and two reciters that gave *mā́m*⌋. All our mss. save one (R.) combine *apānó 'va-* ⌊instead of *-nò*⌋. The verse is ⌊almost⌋ identical with vii. 53. 4 **a, b** ⌊which has *me 'mám* for *mā́ mā́m*⌋.

4. Let the sun protect me from the sky, Agni from the earth, Vāyu from the atmosphere, Yama from men (*manuṣyà*), Sarasvatī from them of the earth.

The verse can be read into 32 syllables, but the metrical definition of the Anukr. is altogether absurd. ⌊Griffith gives *ahnás* its usual meaning: possibly W's "sky" is not intentional, but a mere slip. Cf., however, 7. 6, below.⌋

5. O breath-and-expiration, do not desert me; let me not perish (*pra-mī*) among the people (*jána*).

6. With well-being today, O waters, may I, whole [and] with my whole train (*-gaṇá*), attain dawns and evenings.

The verse is really composed of two *triṣṭubh* pādas.

7. Puissant (*çákvarī*) are ye; may cattle approach me; let Mitra-and-Varuṇa [assign] me breath-and-expiration; let Agni assign me dexterity.

Nearly all our mss. (not T.s.m.R.) give *stheṣu* instead of *stheṣus;* ⌊and so do three of SPP's⌋. ⌊For the form, see *Gram.* § 894 c.⌋

⌊Here ends the first *anuvāka*, with 4 *paryāyas* and 32 *avasānarcas:* see the summations at page 793, above. The piece here quoted from the Old Anukr. is *prājāpatyo ha catuṣkaḥ:* see p. 792.⌋

5. Paryāya the fifth.

[*Yama.* — *daçaka. duḥsvapnanāçanadevatya.* a *of 1–6. virāḍ gāyatrī* (*5* a. *bhurij; 6* a. *svarāj*)*; 1* b, *6* b. *prājāpatyā gāyatrī; 1* c, *6* c. *2-p. sāmnī bṛhatī.*]

⌊Both the Anukramaṇīs reckon the *paryāya* as of 10 *avasānas:* that is, they count the *anuṣaṅgas* (b–c) only in their first and last occurrences, as explained at p. 793, end (cf. pages 628–9, 772).⌋ One or two of the mss. (W.R.) indicate by fragments of b and c given also with verses 2–5 that they regard all the six verses ⌊or *gaṇas*, rather⌋ as of equal length. ⌊It is true that the summations (see p. 793 and table) number the *gaṇas* as 2 and call the *avasānarcas* of the remaining 4 by the name of *paryāya-avasānarcas;* but it is not apparent why the *gaṇas* should not be counted as 6, just as those of the second *paryāya* of xi. 3 are counted as 18 (p. 632, top, p. 628, ¶ 10). — The numbers of the *avasānas* as given by SPP. in accord with the Anukr. are added by me in ell-brackets.⌋

Translated: Ludwig, p. 468; Griffith, ii. 203.

1. ⌊1.⌋ We know thy place of birth (*janítra*), O sleep; thou art son of seizure (*grā́hi*), agent of Yama; ⌊2.⌋ ender art thou, death art thou; ⌊3.⌋ so, O sleep, do we comprehend thee here; do thou, O sleep, protect us from evil-dreaming.

The verses of this hymn are nearly ⌊vs. 6 exactly⌋ identical with vi. 46. 2; and whether they or it are quoted in Kāuç. 46. 9, 13, it is impossible, and wholly unimportant, to determine ⌊cf. introd. to vi. 46⌋.

2. ⌊4.⌋ We know thy place of birth, O sleep; thou art son of perdition, agent etc. etc.

3. ⌊5.⌋ We know thy place of birth, O sleep; thou art son of ill-success (*ábhūti*), agent etc. etc.

4. ⌊6.⌋ We know thy place of birth, O sleep; thou art son of extermination (*nírbhūti*), agent etc. etc.

5. ⌊7.⌋ We know thy place of birth, O sleep; thou art son of calamity (*párābhūti*), agent etc. etc.

6. ⌊8.⌋ We know thy place of birth, O sleep; thou art son of the wives (*-jāmí*) of the gods, agent of Yama; ⌊9.⌋ ender art thou, death art thou; ⌊10.⌋ so, O sleep, do we comprehend thee here; do thou, O sleep, protect us from evil-dreaming.

This verse agrees ⌊precisely⌋ with vi. 46. 2, and the ⌊words *dévānām patnīnāṁ garbha yámasya kara* (the readings are not quite certain)⌋ appear in xix. 57. 3; the other verses are therefore most probably varied repetitions of this one.

6. Paryāya the sixth.

[*Yama.* — *ekādaça. duḥsvapnanāçanadevatya; uṣodevatya. 1–4. prājāpatyā 'nuṣṭubh; 5. sāmnī paṅkti; 6. nicṛd ārcī bṛhatī; 7. 2-p. sāmnī bṛhatī; 8. āsurī jagatī; 9. āsurī bṛhatī; 10. ārcy uṣṇih; 11. 3-p. yavamadhyā gāyatrī vā "rcy anuṣṭubh* (see under vs. 11).]

Translated: Griffith, ii. 204.

1. We have conquered today, we have won today; we have become guiltless.

The verse corresponds to the first two pādas of RV. viii. 47. 18, which differ only by reading *ca* in place of the second *adyá*. It and its two successors (or also vs. 4) are really metrical, half *anuṣṭubhs*. The verse, or the *paryāya*, is used in Kāuç. 49. 19, nearly at the end of the *abhicāra* or witchcraft chapter, with xiii. 1. 28 and 3. 1, to accompany the putting on of *adhipāças* (conjectured 'gag' in the minor Pet. Lex.).

2. O dawn, of what evil-dreaming we have been afraid, let that fade away (*apa-vas*).

The verse ⌊cf. note to vs. 1⌋ is, without variant, RV. viii. 47. 18 **c**, **d**.

3. Carry that away to him that hates; carry that away to him that curses.

4. Whom we hate, and who hates us, to him we make it go.

Our *yás* (in *yáç ca no*) is an emendation for *yát*, which all the mss. read. ⌊SPP. reads *yát* with all his authorities.⌋

5. Heavenly dawn, in concord with speech; heavenly speech, in concord with dawn; —

Part of the mss. read in **b** *devy ùṣásā*.

6. The lord of dawn, in concord with the lord of speech; the lord of speech, in concord with the lord of dawn :—

The Anukr. mss. read *ārṣī* instead of *ārcī* in their definition of the meter of this verse.

7. Let them carry away for yon man the niggards (*aráya*), the ill-named ones, the *sadā́nvās*, —

8. The *kumbhīkās*, the spoilers (*dūṣīkā*), the revilers (*pīyaka*), —

9. Waking evil-dreaming, sleeping evil-dreaming.

Literally 'of one waking' and 'in sleep.' The *pada*-text reads *°dusvapnyám* both times. The Anukr. twice resolves *-ni-am*.

10. Boons that will not come, plans of non-acquisition, fetters of hatred that does not release : —

That is, probably, plans or desires that issue in failure. ⌊Griffith takes *drúh* here and at ii. 10 as a female fiend.⌋

11. That, O Agni, let the gods carry away for yon man, that he may be impotent (*vádhri*), faltering, not good (*sādhú*).

'For him,' here and in vs. 7, is plainly equivalent to 'to him,' or that they may be his. All the mss. accent *vìthuras;* ⌊so SPP. reads with all his authorities⌋. As *gāyatrī* and *ārcy anuṣṭubh* both imply 24 syllables, the Anukr. seems willing to give us our choice between them.

⌊Perhaps we should understand the definition *3-p. yavamadhyā gāyatrīvārcy anuṣṭup* as an '*anuṣṭubh* of 24 syllables, like (*iva:* not *vā*) a *3-p. yavamadhyā gāyatrī*'

(7 + 10 + 7: *Ind. Stud.* viii. 129): only this one divides rather as 8 + 10 + 6. — One is tempted to deem *agne* an intrusion and to regard the verse as a couple of simple *triṣṭubh* pādas: and the temptation is strengthened by the fact that the sole mark of pāda-division in W's Collation Book comes after *vahantu*.⌋

7. Paryāya the seventh.

[*Yama.* — *dvyadhikaṁ vihitam. duḥsvapnanāçanadevatya. 1. pañkti; 2. sāmny anuṣṭubh; 3. āsury uṣṇih; 4. prājāpatyā gāyatrī; 5. ārcy uṣṇih; 6, 9, 11. sāmnī bṛhatī; 7. yājuṣī gāyatrī; 8. prājāpatyā bṛhatī; 10. sāmnī gāyatrī; 12. bhurik prājāpatyā 'nuṣṭubh; 13. āsurī triṣṭubh.*]

The definition of number of verses in the *paryāya* is taken by the Anukr. verbatim from the Old Anukr. (cf. p. 793, line 12), and appears to mean that the number of verses exceeds by two that of the preceding *paryāya.*

Translated: Griffith, ii. 205.

1. With that I pierce him; with ill-success I pierce him; with extermination I pierce him; with calamity I pierce him; with seizure I pierce him; with darkness I pierce him.

The 'that' of the first clause doubtless refers to 6. 11.

2. I demand against him with the terrible, cruel demands (*prāiṣá*) of the gods.

The word *prāiṣá* seems here to be used, not in its ritual sense which is common later, but rather in a sense suggested by its etymology.

3. I set him in the two tusks of Vāiçvānara.

⌊This seems to be an unmetrical version of iv. 36. 2 **c**, **d**.⌋

4. So, not so, may she swallow down.

The *pada*-text reads *evá : áneva : áva*, and the translation follows it. The text is probably corrupt; the 'she' (*sā́*) seems unmotived. Neither Pet. Lex. contains *áneva* ⌊in its main part; but the word is given in a supplement to the minor Lex., iii. 250 c⌋.

5. Whoso hates us, him let [his] self (*ātmán*) hate; whomso we hate, let him hate [his] self.

6. Let us disportion our hater from heaven, from earth, from atmosphere.

Compare x. 5. 25 etc.; we should expect *bhajāmas* here as there.

7. O thou of good ways (*suyāman*), of sight (*cākṣuṣá*).

Both the words may be proper names. Our P.M. read *cākṣuṣaḥ*, accentless.

8. Now (*idám*) do I wipe off evil-dreaming on him of such-and-such lineage, son of such-and-such a mother.

9. What I went at on such-and-such an occasion, what at evening, what in early night; —

The translation follows our emendation, *abhyágacham;* all the mss. read *-chan* (one or two in *pada* perhaps *-chat*); the true sense is very doubtful. ⌊SPP. reads *-chan* with all his authorities: see his note, vol. iii., p. 352.⌋

10. What when awake, what when asleep, what by day, what by night; —

11. What day by day I go at, from that do I cut him off (*ava-day*).

12. Him do thou smite, with him amuse thyself (?*mand*), his ribs do thou crush in.

13. Let him not live; him let breath quit.

This verse also forms a part of x. 5. 25 etc.

8. Paryāya the eighth.

[*ekādaça vāi triguṇāni.* **a** *of 1–27. 1-p. yajur brāhmy anuṣṭubh;* **b** *of 1–27. 3-p. nicṛd gāyatrī; 1* **c.** *prājāpatyā gāyatrī;* **d** *of 1–27. 3-p. prājāpatyā triṣṭubh;* **c** *of 2–4, 9, 17, 19, 24. āsurī jagatī;* **c** *of 5, 7, 8, 10, 11, 13, 18. āsurī triṣṭubh;* **c** *of 6, 12, 14–16, 20–23, 27. āsurī pañkti;* **c** *of 25, 26. āsurī bṛhatī.*]

⌊The discrepancy in the numeration of the subdivisions of the *paryāya*, as between the Bombay edition (which follows the Old Anukr.) and the Berlin edition, is of the same kind as in *paryāya* 5, above, and the explanation given above (p. 794, top) may be consulted. The numbers of the *avasānas* as given by SPP. are added by me in ell-brackets.⌋

Translated: Griffith, ii. 206.

1. ⌊1.⌋ Ours [is] what is conquered, ours what has shot up, ours right (*ṛtá*), ours brilliancy, ours *bráhman*, ours heaven (*svàr*), ours the sacrifice, ours cattle, ours progeny, ours heroes. ⌊2.⌋ From that we disportion him yonder: so-and-so, of such-and-such lineage, son of such-and-such mother, who is yonder; ⌊3.⌋ let him not be released from the fetter of seizure. ⌊4.⌋ Of him now (*idám*) I involve the splendor, brilliancy, breath, life-time; now I make him fall downward.

Here is again a partial correspondence with x. 5. 36. Compare also Āpast. iv. 15. 3. The addition *yajus* to the name *brāhmy anuṣṭubh* (48 syllables) in the Anukr. seems, ⌊in the light of the corresponding expression at xvii. 1. 22, 23, intended to inform us that subdivision **a** is a *yajus;* but it is not apparent why the author should give this bit of information, which is (of its kind) so isolated: cf. third note to xv. 5. 7⌋.

2. ⌊5.⌋ Ours is etc. etc.; let him not be released from the fetter of perdition. Of him now etc. etc.

3. ⌊6.⌋ Ours is etc. etc.; let him not be released from the fetter of ill-success. Of him now etc. etc.

4. ⌊7.⌋ Ours is etc. etc.; let him not be released from the fetter of extermination. Of him now etc. etc.

5. ⌊8.⌋ Ours is etc. etc.; let him not be released from the fetter of calamity. Of him now etc. etc.

6. ⌊9.⌋ Ours is etc. etc.; let him not be released from the fetter of the wives of the gods. Of him now etc. etc.

7. ⌊10.⌋ Ours is etc. etc.; let him not be released from the fetter of Brihaspati. Of him now etc. etc.

8. ⌊11.⌋ Ours is etc. etc.; let him not be released from the fetter of Prajāpati. Of him now etc. etc.

9. ⌊12.⌋ Ours is etc. etc.; let him not be released from the fetter of the seers. Of him now etc. etc.

All our mss. except one (D.) accent *ṛṣīṇā́m;* our text emends to *ṛ́ṣīṇām.* ⌊In like manner, SPP. reads *ṛ́ṣīṇām* with four or three of his authorities, against twelve or thirteen that have *ṛṣīṇā́m.*⌋

10. ⌊13.⌋ Ours is etc. etc.; let him not be released from the fetter of them of the seers. Of him now etc. etc.

11. ⌊14.⌋ Ours is etc. etc.; let him not be released from the fetter of the Angirases. Of him now etc. etc.

12. ⌊15.⌋ Ours is etc. etc.; let him not be released from the fetter of them of the Angirases. Of him now etc. etc.

13. ⌊16.⌋ Ours is etc. etc.; let him not be released from the fetter of the Atharvans. Of him now etc. etc.

14. ⌊17.⌋ Ours is etc. etc.; let him not be released from the fetter of them of the Atharvans. Of him now etc. etc.

15. ⌊18.⌋ Ours is etc. etc.; let him not be released from the fetter of the forest trees. Of him now etc. etc.

16. ⌊19.⌋ Ours is etc. etc.; let him not be released from the fetter of them of the forest trees. Of him now etc. etc.

17. ⌊20.⌋ Ours is etc. etc.; let him not be released from the fetter of the seasons. Of him now etc. etc.

18. ⌊21.⌋ Ours is etc. etc.; let him not be released from the fetter of them of the seasons. Of him now etc. etc.

19. ⌊22.⌋ Ours is etc. etc.; let him not be released from the fetter of the months. Of him now etc. etc.

20. ⌊23.⌋ Ours is etc. etc.; let him not be released from the fetter of the half-months. Of him now etc. etc.

21. ⌊24.⌋ Ours is etc. etc.; let him not be released from the fetter of day-and-night. Of him now etc. etc.

22. ⌊25.⌋ Ours is etc. etc.; let him not be released from the fetter of the two congruent (*sam-yánt*) days. Of him now etc. etc.

There is nothing elsewhere in the text to show what these two days are. Perhaps they are day and night over again, viewed as each a form or aspect of a day. ⌊The use of the obscure *saṁyánt* (with *ṛtú* and *çrī́*) at ix. 5. 33 should here be noted.⌋

23. ⌊26.⌋ Ours is etc. etc.; let him not be released from the fetter of heaven-and-earth. Of him now etc. etc.

24. ⌊27.⌋ Ours is etc. etc.; let him not be released from the fetter of Indra-and-Agni. Of him now etc. etc.

25. ⌊28.⌋ Ours is etc. etc.; let him not be released from the fetter of Mitra-and-Varuṇa. Of him now etc. etc.

26. ⌊29.⌋ Ours is etc. etc.; let him not be released from the fetter of king Varuṇa. Of him now etc. etc.

27. ⌊30.⌋ Ours [is] what is conquered, ours what has shot up, ours right, ours brilliancy, ours *bráhman*, ours heaven, ours the sacrifice, ours cattle, ours progeny, ours heroes. ⌊31.⌋ From that we disportion him yonder: so-and-so, of such-and-such lineage, son of such-and-such mother, who is yonder; ⌊32.⌋ let him not be released from the fetter, the shackle of death. ⌊33.⌋ Of him now I involve the splendor, brilliancy, breath, life-time; now I make him fall downward.

Some of the mss. read *páḍvin̄çāt* or *páḍvīn̄çāt.* ⌊There should be an *avasāna*-mark in vs. 26 of the Berlin ed. after the second circle indicating omission.⌋

9. Paryāya the ninth.

[*catvāri vāi vacanāni. 1. prājāpatyā; 2. mantroktabahudevatyā; 3, 4. sāurye. 1. ārcy anuṣṭubh; 2. ārcy uṣṇih; 3. sāmnī pan̄kti; 4. paroṣṇih.*]

Translated: Griffith, ii. 208.

1. Ours [is] what is conquered, ours what has shot up; I have withstood all fighters, niggards.

The verse is identical with the first part of x. 5. 36; and its second part, with vs. 2, is found in MS. i. 5. 3 (reading *abhy àsthām*).

2. That Agni says; that, too, Soma says: may Pūshan set me in the world of the well-done.

The two pādas are second and fourth pādas of a verse in MS. i. 5. 3 (which rectifies the meter by reading *na ā́ dhāt* in place of *mā dhāt:* our own text probably ought to read *mā́*, i.e. *mā ā́*). With either of these readings, we have two faultless *triṣṭubh* pādas; but the Anukr. sanctions only 21 syllables. The first pāda is also found as viii. 5. 5 **a** and xix. 24. 8 **c**.

3. We have gone to heaven (*svàr*); to heaven have we gone; we have united (*sam-gam*) with the sun's light;—

The first half is the beginning also of TS. i. 6. 6. In Kāuç. 6. 16, the verse is used in the *parvan* ceremonies, while one looks at the sun; but according to Dārila, this verse with the next is to be so used: ⌊and his view is accepted by SPP. (iii. 350[16]) and is supported by the suspension of the sense (see note to vs. 4)⌋. In Vāit. 24. 5, it is used, together with a RV. verse, to accompany the coming up from the bath in the *agniṣṭoma* ceremony. ⌊For the general import of this vs., see p. 792, ¶ 2.⌋

4. In order to becoming better (*vásyas-*). Rich in good (*vásu-*) [is] the sacrifice; good may I win (*van*); rich in good may I be; good put thou in me.

The first word seems to belong in sense rather to the preceding verse; ⌊see note thereon⌋. All the mss. read *vañçiṣīya*, and the edition follows them; but we ought unquestionably to have emended to *vañsiṣīya*. There is even probably a play on words intended between *vásu* and *vañs-*. ⌊Yet SPP. reads *vañçiṣīya* without note of variant: as to the form, see *Gram.* § 914 b.⌋ ⌊For use by Kāuç., see under vs. 3.⌋

⌊Here ends the second *anuvāka*, with 5 *paryāyas* and 71 *avasānarcas*: but see the summations at p. 793 and cf. p. 798 and p. 801. The piece here quoted from the Old Anukr. is *pañcaparyāya uttaraḥ*: see p. 792.⌋

⌊Here ends the thirty-first *prapāṭhaka*.⌋

Book XVII.

⌊Prayer to the Sun, identified with Indra and with Vishṇu.⌋

⌊This is the fifth book of the third grand division (books xiii.–xviii.) of the Atharvan collection, and its unity of subject (as indicated by the title, above, which is slightly modified from Whitney's, p. 806) is sufficiently apparent. It is the only book of the entire collection that consists of a single *anuvāka.* At xix. 23. 27, it is called the Viṣāsahi (*viṣāsahyāí svā́hā:* note the singular number); and the Old Anukr., as noted below at page 812, gives it the same designation. As was true of the preceding book (see page 792), no translation of this book has been published by the translators of single books; but from here on to the end of xx. 37 we have the *bhāṣya.*⌋

⌊The Atharvaṇīya-paddhati, in a chapter on *veda-vratas* (note to Kāuç. 57. 32), nominates a *viṣāsahi-vrata;* and the same *vrata* is mentioned by Keçava, in his note to Kāuç. 42. 12, p. 344[24], together with the *çiro-vrata*, which latter is known as a necessary preliminary to the study of the "Shaveling Upanishad" (see Muṇḍaka, iii. 2. 10). "Doubtless this hymn figured prominently in it" [the *viṣāsahi-vrata*], says Bloomfield, in his part of the *Grundriss*, p. 95.⌋

⌊The hymn consists of just 30 verses: and so again we find the decad-division, — here into three precise decads. This, however, is a mechanical division. Structurally, the hymn is composed of five parts, as follows.⌋

⌊**Part I., verses 1–5.** — This is a sequence of 5 verses of 6 pādas each and of the scheme 8 + 8 : 8 + 12 : 8 + 8 = 52. All 5 verses are identical in the first 5 pādas, which are made up mostly of words containing the roots *sah* 'overpower' and *ji* 'win by conquest'; and they differ only in the sixth pāda, which is characterized by the phrase 'may I be' (*bhūyāsam*), with an *ūha* which makes vs. 1 fall short of the full tale of syllables and makes an overplus for vs. 5.⌋

⌊**Part II., verses 6–19.** — This is a sequence of 14 verses characterized by the refrain 'Thine, O Vishṇu' (*távéd viṣṇo*). It is a curious fact that the mss. do not separate this refrain from the stock of the verse by an *avasāna*-mark; and herein they are supported by the Anukr. (see below), which describes verses [1–8: that is, 1–5 of Part I. and] 6–8, 10–13, 16, 18–19, and 24 as *try-avasāna.* In all the *taved viṣṇo* verses (6–19, and 24), the Bombay ed. follows the mss.: the Berlin ed., on the other hand, inserts an *avasāna*-mark before the *taved;* and, so far as the sense and structure go, it is imperatively demanded. — All the vss. of this part are of 7 pādas except 9, 14–15, and 17, which are of 5 each, and except 10, which is of 8.⌋

⌊**Part III., verses 20–23.** — This consists of 4 bits of prose. The verses contain: praise and prayer to the Sun (20–21: 'brilliant art thou; may I be brilliant'); and homage to the Sun, rising, setting, etc. (22–23: *namas*).⌋

⌊**Part IV., verses 24–26.** — These are 3 perfectly regular *anuṣṭubh* verses, to the first of which is added the *anuṣaṅga* that is characteristic of Part II. The 3 verses are closely related and are addressed to the Sun as Āditya or Sūrya, the first and last being appropriate for use at sunrise, and the second for use at sundown. — It may be noted that of the Pāli *paritta* verses (Jātaka, ii. p. 33–35) cited in the introduction to iii. 26, one set is used at sunrise and the other at sundown.⌋

⌊**Part V., verses 27–30.** — These (if we disregard the palpably intrusive *bráhmaṇā* of 27 **a**) are 4 perfectly regular stanzas, of which all the pādas are *triṣṭubh* except 30 **a** and 30 **c**, which are *jagatī* in count and cadence. We might call them *paritta*-verses, charms for defense and protection; they show various derivatives of the roots *vṛ* and *gup*, and references to Kaçyapa (see note to iv. 20. 7).⌋

---

1. Prayer and praise to Indra and the Sun.

[*Brahman. — ṛcas triṅçat.*[1] *ādityadevatyās. 1. jagatī; 1–8. try-avasāna;*[4] *1–4* ⌊*intending 2–5?*⌋*. atijagatī;*[2] *6, 7, 19. atyaṣṭi;*[3] *8, 11, 16. atidhṛti; 9. 5-p. çakvarī; 10–13, 16, 18–19, 24. try-avasāna;*[4] *10. 8-p. dhṛti; 12. kṛti; 13. prakṛti; 14–15. 5-p. çakvarī; 17. 5-p. virāḍ atiçakvarī; 18. bhurig aṣṭi; 24. virāḍ atyaṣṭi; 1–8* ⌊*intending 1–5?*⌋*. 6-p.;* ⌊*6–8,*⌋ *11–13, 16, 18–19, 24. 7-p.*[5] *20. kakubh; 21. 4-p. upariṣṭādbṛhatī; 22. anuṣṭubh; 23. nicṛd bṛhatī (22–23. yajuṣī dve;*[6] *2-p.); 25, 26. anuṣṭubh; 27, 30. jagatī; 28, 29. triṣṭubh.*]

The Anukr. has some bad readings and confusions in its account of the book, but they do not concern things of much consequence. ⌊So Whitney, in a note to vs. 5, which note I have transposed hither. He had altered (as often, for brevity) the order of his excerpts from the Anukr.: but I have restored them in this case to the order of the original. Moreover, there are several trifling items which he has omitted or misapprehended: and these I have added or tried to set right without marking them with the usual ell-brackets.⌋

⌊**Notes to the Anukramaṇī-excerpts.**⌋ [1]⌊The text begins, *viṣāsahir ṛcas triṅçat*, which is taken from the Old Anukr.: see p. 812.⌋ [2]⌊As to the structure and count of vss. 1–5, see page 805, ¶ 4.⌋ [3]⌊Text reads simply *udihīti dve asati sad atyaṣṭayaḥ:* read *ity aṣṭayaḥ?* or, perhaps, *ity atyaṣṭayaḥ?* but see note to verse 7.⌋ [4]⌊The statements concerning the *try-avasāna* verses are given in two instalments and are entirely correct, although the Berlin edition makes them seem partially incorrect: vss. 1–5 are 3-*av.* in both ed's; 6–8 and 10–13, 16, 18–19, 24 are 3-*av.* in the mss. and the Bombay ed. and are 4-*av.* in the Berlin ed.: see page 805, ¶ 5, above.⌋ [5]⌊The text says *aṣṭāu* [should be *pañca*] *ṣaṭpadāḥ, çeṣāḥ saptapadāḥ:* 'the rest' (*çeṣāḥ*) are those that remain after taking out from the verses thus far discussed those verses (1–8[5], 9–10, 14–15, 17) the number of whose pādas has been already stated: and the Anukr. therefore means (after emending *aṣṭāu* to *pañca*), 'verses 1–5 are of 6 pādas, while the rest, — namely verses [6–8,] 11–13, 16, 18–19, 24, — are of 7 pādas'; and this is quite correct.⌋ [6]⌊See note to vs. 22 and cf. note to xvi. 8. 1.⌋

⌊Partly prose — verses 20–23: see ¶ 1, on this page.⌋

The hymn, or *anuvāka*, or book, occurs (except vss. 13, 14, 24) also in Pāipp. xviii., following immediately upon what represents our xvi.

A few of the later verses (18, 21–23) are used in Vāit. The hymn (or the first verses of it) is reckoned to the *salila gaṇa*, according to Kāuç. (18. 25); and the Pariçiṣṭa ⌊given under Kāuç. 54. 11⌋ reckons it also to an *āyuṣya gaṇa*. It is used (with i. 30; iii. 8; etc.) in the ceremony of reception of a Vedic student (Kāuç. 55. 17); and (with iii. 31; iv. 13; etc.) in the following ceremony for long life (58. 3, 11); and in the *anna-prāçana* rite (58. 22); further, in a solar eclipse (the whole hymn or *sūkta*: 99. 3; and Keçava, in his note to 100. 3, p. 372[5], adds it also for use in a lunar eclipse). ⌊Vss. 1–5 are quoted by the schol. to Kāuç. 7. 21. As to the use of the hymn in the *viṣāsahi-vrata*, see above, p. 805, ¶ 2.⌋

Translated: Griffith, ii. 209. — Perhaps the Sun is elsewhere variously identified: thus at xiii. 4. 46 (see note) with Indra; and at xiii. 2. 31 with Viṣṇu.

1. Indra of mighty power, overpowering, having overpowered, very powerful, overpowering, power-winning (*saho-jít*), heaven-winning, kine-winning, booty-winning, to be praised (*īḍ*), by name, do I call: may I be long-lived.

2. Indra of mighty power etc. etc. do I call: may I be dear to the gods.

3. Indra of mighty power etc. etc. do I call: may I be dear to living beings (*prajā́*).

4. Indra of mighty power etc. etc. do I call: may I be dear to cattle.

5. Indra of mighty power etc. etc. do I call: may I be dear to my equals (*samānā́*).

Ppp. reads ⌊in the above 5 verses⌋ every time *viṣāsahyam*; and, for **c–f**, *s. s. viçva-jitaṁ svarjitam abhijitaṁ vasujitaṁ gojitaṁ saṁjitaṁ saṁdhanājitam: īdyaṁ nāma bhūyā indram āyuṣmān priyā bhūyāsam*; in the repetitions, *hūya* (in place of its previous *bhūyā*), and *indra devānāṁ priyo bhūyāsam*. Here, and everywhere else in the hymn, the comm. insists that by *indra* is intended the sun, and not Indra, quoting in proof of it TS. i. 7. 6[3]: *asāú vā ādityá índraḥ*. ⌊For the structure and count of the vss., see above, p. 805, ¶ 4.⌋

6. Arise, arise, O sun; arise upon me with splendor; both let my hater be subject to me, and let not me be subject to my hater. — Thine, O Vishṇu, are heroisms manifold; do thou fill us with cattle of all forms; set me in comfort in the highest firmament (*vyòman*).

Ppp. reads in the concluding pāda of the refrain *svadhāyāṁ no dh-*; the comm. also has *svadhāyām*. The mss. commit the absurdity throughout of setting no *avasāna* between the verse proper and the refrain; we have, as required by the sense, introduced it in our text; ⌊the matter is further discussed above, p. 805, ¶ 5⌋. The refrain is, as usual, represented in vss. 7–18 only by the word *táva* in the mss. (except in R., which fills it out a little further). ⌊With reference to the main stock of the verse, the comm. cites most appositely TB. iii. 7. 6[23], *úd agād ayám ādityó víçvena sáhasā sahá: dviṣán-tam máma randháyan mó aháṁ dviṣató radham*, although it does not appear why he did not cite rather our verse 24 **a–d**, below, which see.⌋

⌊The refrain seems to count as 11 : 12 + 11 = 34 syllables with the Anukr.; but the true *triṣṭubh* cadences (*viçvárūpāiḥ*, *vioman*) of its second and third pādas suggest the suspicion of metrical disorder in the prior part of each of those pādas. One is tempted to think of *pṛṇīhi* as an ill-considered modernization of *pūrdhi;* and to wish that *mā* (before *dhehi*) might be excised, as superfluous in meter and in sense and as making a harsh change from plural (*nas*) to singular. — The change from singular to plural as between the main stock and the refrain, considering the looseness of their connection, is not to be called harsh.⌋

7. Arise, arise, O sun; arise upon me with splendor; both those whom I see and those whom I do not — among them make thou favor for me. Thine, O Vishṇu etc. etc.

We should expect *me* for *mā* in **d**; and the comm., on account of *mā*, takes *sumatim* as an adjective (= *çobhanabuddhiyuktam*) — which is not grammatically impossible, but against all Vedic usage. Verses 6 and 7, ⌊if the main stock of each verse be read rhythmically,⌋ are undoubtedly to be counted as 66 syllables, two less than a true *atyaṣṭi* (68), ⌊but also, on the other hand, two more than a true *aṣṭi* (64); but the **a** and the **b** of each can be read as 7 so as to make totals of just 64: see above, page 806, ¶ 6, note 3⌋. ⌊Concerning the refrain, see notes to vs. 6.⌋

8. Let them not damage thee in the sea, within the waters — they who approach there having fetters; quitting imprecation, thou hast ascended that sky; be thou then gracious to us; may we be in thy favor. — Thine, O Vishṇu etc. etc.

Ppp. reads in **b** *pāçinam*, and in **c** *ā ruha etān*. The verse counts most naturally 78 syllables (11 × 4 : 34); a proper *atidhṛti* has 76. Bp. reads in **d** *ā́ : rukṣaḥ;* D.Kp. and all SPP's authorities have *ā́ : ar-*, which is doubtless the true *pada*-text.

9. Do thou, O Indra, in order to great good-fortune, protect us about with unharmed rays. — Thine, O Vishṇu etc. etc.

The comm. takes *aktúbhis* in its sense of 'night.' Ppp. reads *adabdhāiṣ pari* in **b**.

10. Do thou, O Indra, with propitious aids, be most wealful to us — ascending to the triple heaven of the heaven (*dív*), besung unto soma drinking, having a dear abode (*-dhā́man*) unto well-being. — Thine, O Vishṇu etc. etc.

Ppp. reads in **a** *indro adbhiç* (*ç-*). The comm. gives us our choice between *-sthāna* and *-tejas* as meanings of *-dhāman* in **e**. The verse has two syllables too many for a regular *dhṛti* (72); ⌊it reads properly as 5 × 8 and 34; but pāda **a** may be read as 6⌋.

11. Thou, O Indra, art all-conquering, all-gaining (*sarva-víd*); much invoked [art] thou, O Indra; do thou, O Indra, send onward this well-invoking praise; be thou gracious to us; may we be in thy favor. — Thine, O Vishṇu etc. etc.

Ppp. reads in **a** *viçvavit;* and instead of our **d** (= 8 **d**) it has *çivābhis tanubhir abhi nas sajasva*. The verse is a true *atidhṛti* by number of syllables, but very irregular in structure (8 + 10 : 13 + 11 : 34 = 76).

12. Unharmed in the heaven (*dív*), also on earth, art thou; they have not attained thy greatness in the atmosphere; increasing with unharmed

worship (*bráhman*), do thou there, O Indra, being in the heaven (*dív*), bestow protection (*çárman*) on us. — Thine, O Vishṇu etc. etc.

Ppp. reads *divaṣ p-* in **a**. ⌊In **d**, all of SPP's authorities give *ṣáṅ* or *sán:* and W's Collation Book notes nothing to the contrary; but⌋ the comm. omits the word, as the meter plainly requires. The verse (11 + 12 : 11 + 12 : 34 = 80) is by number of syllables an exact *kṛti*.

13. What body of thine, O Indra, is in the waters, what on the earth, what within the fire; what of thine, O Indra, is in the heaven-gaining (*svarvíd*) purifying one (*pávamāna*); with what body, O Indra, thou didst permeate (*vi-āp*) the atmosphere — with that body, O Indra, bestow thou protection upon us. — Thine, O Vishṇu etc. etc.

In nearly all our mss. (all save D. and R.p.m.) *vyāpitha* (p. *vi○āpitha*) is most strangely left unaccented, and the reading was in our text emended to *vyā̆pitha*, in accordance with the invariable accentuation of such forms in RV. and AV. elsewhere. But a minority of SPP's authorities are reported by him as accenting *vyāpithá*, and he accordingly prints *vyāpithá* in his edition (our D.R.p.m. have the same). The 'purifying one' is doubtless here the wind (*vāyu:* so comm.). The verse (12 + 16 : 12 + 12 : 34 = 86) counts two more syllables than a proper *prakṛti*.

14. Increasing thee, O Indra, with worship (*bráhman*), the imploring seers have sat down [for] the session (*sattrá*). — Thine, O Vishṇu etc. etc.

The verse (11 + 12 : 34 = 57) has one more syllable than a regular *çakvarī*. ⌊Verses 13 and 14, as was noted above, are wanting in Ppp.⌋

15. Thou goest about Tṛita (?), thou about the fountain of a thousand streams, the heaven-gaining council. — Thine, O Vishṇu etc. etc.

All the mss., and hence both editions, read *tṛtám* in **a**; but the ms. of the comm. has *tritam*, and we cannot well believe that the latter is not the true reading; though the sense of the whole verse is extremely obscure. The comm. explains *tritam* mysteriously, as either *vistīrṇam antarikṣam* or *meghāir āvṛtam udakam*. *Vidatha*, he says, = *yajña*. The verse is capable of being read as 56 syllables. Ppp. puts it after our verse 17.

16. Thou defendest the four directions; thou shinest abroad with brightness (*çocís*) unto the two firmaments (*nábhas*); thou pursuest (*anu-sthā*) all these beings; thou, knowing, followest (*anu-i*) the way of righteousness. — Thine, O Vishṇu etc. etc.

The *saṁhitā*-mss. read *vidvā̆ṅs távé 'd* between verse and refrain. The whole (11 + 11 : 12 + 11 : 34 = 79) reads naturally as three more syllables than belong to an *atidhṛti*.

17. With five thou heatest upward (*párāṅ*), with one hitherward; thou goest driving off the imprecation in good weather (*sudína*). — Thine, O Vishṇu etc. etc.

The comm. supplies, as is natural, *dīdhiti* or *marīci* 'ray' for the missing noun, and explains the five as required in order to illuminate so many worlds beyond the sun.

But Ppp. reads instead *saptabhiṣ p-* 'with seven.' ⌊With reference to the rays, Griffith (note to xi. 1. 36) cites Mahīdhara as quoted by Eggeling on ÇB. i. 9. 3[16].⌋ The comm. has the bad reading *nādhamānas* for *bādh-*. We have to resolve a *saṁdhi* in **a** in order to make 58 syllables in the verse.

18. Thou art Indra, thou great Indra, thou the world, thou Prajāpati; for thee the sacrifice is extended; to thee the offerers make oblation.— Thine, O Vishṇu etc. etc.

Ppp. reads *viṣṇus* for *lokas* in **b**, and, in **c**, *yajāyate* for *vi tāyate*. Our Bp.P.M.W. T.R.p.m. also have *jāyate* for *tāyate*. To make the verse only *bhurig aṣṭi* (65 syll.), we have to read the first pāda as seven syllables, though it easily makes eight. In Vāit. 3. 3 the verse, with vi. 5. 2, is made to accompany a *sāṁnāyya* offering to Indra, in the *darçapūrṇamāsa* ceremony. In our edition, the *ṁ* of *tváṁ* before *lokás* is lost in printing.

19. In the non-existent is the existent made firm; in the existent is being (*bhūtá*) made firm; being is set in what is to be; what is to be is made firm in being. Thine, O Vishṇu etc. etc.

Ppp. combines *bhavyā "hitam* ⌊double sandhi after *-e* as at ix. 1. 14⌋ in **c**, and has *samāhitam* for *pratiṣṭhitam* in **d**. The verse, like 6 and 7, lacks two syllables of a full *atyaṣṭi;* ⌊but see note to vs. 7 and p. 806, ¶ 6, note 3, above⌋.

20. Brilliant (*çukrá*) art thou; shiny art thou; as thou art shiny by the shining one (*bhrā́jant*), so may I by the shining one shine.

The Ppp. text of this verse is in confusion. Our P.M.I.T. combine (second time) *bhrājò 'si*, as if we had here, as the first time, *asi* (instead of *ási*). The first pāda is the same with the beginning of ii. 11. 5. MS. iv. 9. 5 has passages resembling this verse and the next. This prose bit is a queer *kakubh:* ⌊the *kakubh* calls for 8 + 12 + 8 = 28; and this may be read as 8 + 11 + 9⌋.

21. Brightness art thou, bright art thou; as thou by brightness art bright, so may I by both cattle and Brahman-splendor be bright (*ruc*).

Our P.M.T. have again (second time) *rocò 'si;* ⌊and one of SPP's *pada*-mss. has correspondingly *asi* without accent⌋. The MS. version is in some respects better: *rucir asi rucò* (or *rocyò*) *'si sá yáthā tváṁ rucyā̆ rócasa evám aháṁ rucyā̆ rociṣīya.* Ppp. also gives *rociṣīya.* ⌊For *ruciṣīya* or *roc-*, see *Gram.* § 907.⌋ The metrical definition of the Anukr. is absurd, the "verse" being prose, and having only three possible divisions; it can be made 36 syllables by reading *roco asi* either in **a** or in **b**. It is used in Vāit. 14. 2, in the *agniṣṭoma* ceremony.

22. To the rising one be obeisance; to the one coming up be obeisance; to the arisen one be obeisance; to the wide ruler (*virā́j*) be obeisance; to the self-ruler (*svarā́j*) be obeisance; to the universal ruler (*samrā́j*) be obeisance.

We should expect, by the analogy of the next verse, *udeṣyaté* for *udāyaté*. The comm. explains the latter by *ūrdhvam īṣad gacchate.* In Vāit. 11. 16, the verse accompanies worship of the rising sun in the *agniṣṭoma* ceremony. It is so far an *anuṣṭubh* that it contains 32 syllables. ⌊The Anukr. informs us that this verse is a *yajus;* and so of the next. A similarly isolated bit of information we had concerning xvi. 8. 1 **a**.⌋

23. To the setting one be obeisance; to the one about to set be obeisance; to the one that has set be obeisance; to the wide ruler be obeisance; to the self-ruler be obeisance; to the universal ruler be obeisance.

In Vāit. 11. 13, the verse accompanies worship of the setting sun in the *agniṣṭoma* ceremony. The Anukr. restores both the elided initial *a*'s in the first half-verse, thus counting 35 syllables.

24. This Āditya hath arisen, together with all ardor (*tápas*), making subject to me my rivals; and let me not be subject to my hater. — Thine, O Vishṇu etc. etc.

We have repeated here once more the refrain of vss. 6–19. The verse is wanting in Ppp. Pādas **c**, **d** are nearly identical with our 6 **c**, **d** above. ⌊The main stock of the vs., without the refrain, corresponds to⌋ RV. i. 50. 13, which reads *sáhasā* in **b**, and *dviṣántam* (for *sapátnān*) in **c**; also *mó* for *mā́ ca* in **d**; ⌊and it is also TB. iii. 7. 6[23], quoted above in full under vs. 6, which reads like RV., save that it has *máma* for *máhyam* in **c**, and *dviṣató* for *dviṣaté* in **d**. — In the Calcutta ed. of TB., *sáhasā* is misprinted *máhasā* in the text, but is given aright in the comm. (p. 504), and aright in the Poona ed., p. 1105.⌋

25. O Āditya, thou hast ascended a boat of a hundred oars in order to well-being; thou hast made me to pass over the day, make thou me likewise (*satrā́*) to pass over the night.

The comm. explains *satrā́* by *sahāi 'va, ahnā saha;* he gives also as admissible alternative explanation "I have ascended thee as a boat" etc., understanding the second person to be used as a first! Ppp. reads, in fact, *ā 'ruham;* and, in **c**, *ahar ṇo 'ty.*

26. O sun, thou hast ascended a boat of a hundred oars in order to well-being; thou hast made me to pass over the night, make thou me likewise to pass over the day.

Passages analogous and in part accordant with the two preceding verses are found in MB. ii. 5. 13, 14. Ppp. reads in **a** *ā 'rikṣam;* and, in **c**, *rātrī ṇo 'ty.*

27. With Prajāpati's worship (*bráhman*) [as] defense am I covered, with Kaçyapa's light and splendor; long-lived, of finished heroism, vigorous (? *víhāyas*), having a thousand life-times, well-made, may I go about.

⌊Or, to bring out the connection between *varman* and *āvṛta*, one may render, 'with P's defense am I defended,' 'with P's covering am I covered.'⌋ It is plain that *bráhmaṇā*, which is metrically redundant, has slipped in here out of 28 **a**; but it appears to be found also in Ppp., as in the text of the comm. The latter explains *vihāyās* by *vividhagamanaḥ, sarvatrā 'pratibaddhagatiḥ;* ⌊cf. Bergaigne, *Rel. Véd.* iii. 287⌋. The verse (14 + 11 : 11 + 10[or 11?] = 46) has nothing of a *jagatī* character; ⌊but, if we excise *bráhmaṇā*, it is a perfectly good *triṣṭubh*⌋.

28. Encompassed with worship [as] defense am I, with Kaçyapa's light and splendor; let not the arrows that are the gods' attain me, nor those of men, let loose in order to slay (*vadhā́ya*).

SPP. reports his *pada*-mss. as reading *yā́* instead of *yā́ḥ* at end of **c**; I have not observed the blunder in ours. All, both his and ours, give *ávao-sṛṣṭā* instead of *-ṭāḥ* in **d**. The comm. adds the *visarga* in both words. A part of the verse is wanting in Ppp.

29. Guarded by righteousness and by all the seasons, guarded by what is and by what is to be am I; let not evil attain me, nor death; I interpose with a sea of speech.

That is, I set my uttered charms like a sea between me and them.

30. Let Agni [as] guardian protect me all about; let the sun, rising, thrust [away] the fetters of death; out-shining dawns, firm mountains—let a thousand breaths abide (*ā-yat*) in me.

Ppp. reads in **a** *gopaṣ pari*, transposes pādas **b** and **c** (corrupting to *vicchantīr*, and combining *uṣasaṣ p-*), and ends **d** with *mayu te ramantām;* and it then adds our xviii. 4. 49. The connection of our **c** is obscure; the comm. understands *mṛtyupāçān nudantām* or else *mām anugṛhṇantu:* the former is possible. ⌊The verse is to be read as 12 + 11 : 12 + 11.⌋

⌊Here ends the first and sole *anuvāka*, with 1 hymn and 30 verses. The words *prathamo 'nuvākaḥ* are not printed here in either edition, but are found in several of W's mss. The quotation from the Old Anukr. is *ity etat samanukrāntam ṛcas triñçad "viṣāsahiḥ."*⌋

⌊Here ends also the thirty-second *prapāṭhaka.*⌋

Book XVIII.

⌊**Funeral verses.**⌋

⌊Funeral ceremonies. — This eighteenth book is the sixth and last book of the third grand division (books xiii.–xviii.) of the Atharvan collection, and shows very clearly that general unity of subject which is the distinguishing characteristic of the books of that division. In particular, however, the verses of the book do not show an orderliness of arrangement corresponding with that unity of subject. In large part, the verses of this book appear also in the Rigveda and in book vi. of the Tāittirīya Āraṇyaka, and the readings of these two texts are wont to agree together rather than with those of the Atharvaveda. As appears from the excerpts below, p. 814, the *Pañcapaṭalikā* seems to have a special name for this book, 'The Yamas' or 'Yama-hymns.' The book has been translated by Weber in the *Sitzungsberichte der königlich Preussischen Akademie der Wissenschaften zu Berlin* (cited below as "*Sb.*") for 1895 and 1896. The *bhāṣya* is not wanting.⌋

⌊The funeral ceremonies of the ancient Hindus (like their nuptial ceremonies — see p. 738) have been often treated: thus, as early as 1801, by Colebrooke, in vol. vii. of the *Asiatic Researches* (the paper is reprinted by Cowell in his edition of H. T. Colebrooke's *Essays*, vol. i.: see pages 172–206); by H. H. Wilson, *Works*, ii. 270 f.; by R. Roth, ZDMG. viii. 467–475; by Max Muller, ZDMG. ix., appendix, pages i–lxxxii; by Monier-Williams in his *Religious Thought and Life in India*, chapter xi.; and by H. Oldenberg, *Religion des Veda*, pages 570–591. Closely akin in subject is Whitney's essay on *The Vedic doctrine of a future life*, reprinted in his *Oriental and Linguistic Studies*, i. 46–63. — See also my notes upon the customs and ritual of cremation and burial (AGS. iv. 1–6) in my *Sanskrit Reader*, pages 401–405, and my notes on RV. x. 18 etc., *Reader*, pages 382–386: in both places I have given many pertinent bibliographical references. — The sixth *prapāṭhaka* of the Tāittirīya Āraṇyaka is devoted to the funeral rites, and contains much of the material of this book of the AV. Rājendralāla Mitra's analysis of the *prapāṭhaka* (pages 41–48 of the "Contents" prefixed to his text-edition) may well be consulted, and also pages 33–58 of his Introduction. — The most comprehensive treatment of the subject has been given by Dr. W. Caland, under the title *Die Altindischen Todten- und Bestattungsgebräuche mit Benutzung handschriftlicher Quellen dargestellt*, Verhandelingen der Koninklijke Akademie van Wetenschappen te Amsterdam, Afdeeling Letterkunde, Deel I. No 6, Amsterdam, 1896, pages xiv + 193.⌋

⌊Hymns (or *anuvākas*) 1 and 2 are treated by Weber (as above) in the *Sitzungsberichte* for 1895, pages 815–866; and hymns (or *anuvākas*) 3 and 4, in the *Sitzungsberichte* for 1896, pages 253–294. — Weber's essays give first a general introduction for the whole book (*Sb.*, 1895, pages 815–819); and then, for each *anuvāka*, a special introduction followed by a translation with running comment. Each special introduction treats of the ritual uses of the *anuvāka* concerned and of the provenience of the various verses or groups of verses which enter into its composition and also of some general matters relating to that *anuvāka.*⌋

⌊**Divisions of the book.** — The material of this book is divided by our text into 4 *anuvākas* and this division coincides with the division into 4 hymns. (Compare the *anuvāka*-division of books xii. and xiii. and xiv.) A conspectus for book xviii. follows:

Anuvākas	1	2	3	4
Hymns	1	2	3	4
Verses	61	60	73	89
Decad-division	5 tens + 11	6 tens	6 tens + 13	8 tens + 9

Of the "decads," *anuvākas* 1, 2, 3, and 4 contain respectively 6, 6, 7, and 9. The sum is 28 "decad"-*sūktas*. These 4 *anuvākas* and 28 *sūktas* are recognized by the Major Anukr., as noted below, next ¶. The sum of verses is 283, as is also stated by the same treatise, if we disregard an apparent misreading, *ibidem.*⌋

⌊**The Major Anukr.** begins its treatment of the book thus: *o cit sakhāyam* (xviii. 1. 1) *iti caturanuvākam aṣṭāviṅçatisūktakaṁ tryaçītidviçatanavatyarcaṁ* (? read *-dviçatarcam*) *yamadevatyaṁ trāiṣṭubhaṁ kāṇḍam atharvā mantroktabahudevatyaṁ ca.*⌋

⌊That is to say: 'The book that begins with *o cit sakhāyam* has four *anuvākas* and twenty-eight *sūktas* and two-hundred-and-eighty-three verses and is in *triṣṭubh* meter; the seer is Atharvan; and the deities are Yama and many others mentioned in its *mantras*.'⌋

⌊**The Pañcapaṭalikā.** — The excerpts from the Old Anukr. are given piecemeal at the end of each *anuvāka* and may here be reconstructed into a metrical couplet:

ekaṣaṣṭiç ca ṣaṣṭiç ca saptatis tryadhikā paraḥ:
ekonanavatiç cāi 'va yameṣu vihitā ṛcaḥ.

That is to say: 'Sixty-one; and sixty; the next [*anuvāka*] three-over-seventy; and ninety-less-one: are the verses disposed among the Yama-hymns.' These excerpts are quoted in part and verbatim by the Major Anukr.⌋

⌊It would thus appear from the Old Anukr. that the division into *anuvākas* is indeed of considerable antiquity. On the other hand, we cannot claim much intrinsic significance for the coincident division into hymns: at all events, the fact that a ritual sequence runs over the division-line between hymns 1 and 2 (see my note to 1.49) makes against such significance; and my suggestion (p. 848) as to a possible misdivision between hymns 3 and 4 points the same way.⌋ ⌊See p. clx, near end.⌋

The whole book is wanting in Pāipp., although a very few of the verses (namely, 1.46; 2.13, 17; 3.56; 4.49) are found here and there in its text. In the Vāit., which has no chapter devoted to funeral rites, only fifteen scattered passages ⌊covering about a score of verses⌋ are used; but in the Kāuç., most of the verses from 1.40 on to the end of the book are quoted, solely in the chapter (*adhyāya* xi.: sections or *kaṇḍikās* 80–89) which deals with funeral rites and rites to the Fathers or Manes. ⌊See p. 1016.⌋

1. ⌊Funeral verses.⌋

[*Atharvan.—ekaṣaṣṭi. yamadevatyam mantroktabahudevatyaṁ ca (41–43. sarasvatīdevatyās; 40. rāudrī; 44–46. mantroktapitṛdevatyās; 51, 52. pitrye). trāiṣṭubham: 8, 15. ārṣī pañkti; 14, 49, 50. bhurij; 18–20, 21–23. jagatī; 37, 38. paroṣṇih; 56, 57, 61. anuṣṭubh; 59. purābṛhatī.*]

⌊Only one verse (46) is found in Pāipp., and that in book ii. Only four *sūtras* of the Vāit. cite verses from this hymn, and those verses are 44–46, 51, and 55. In the Kāuç., as already noted by Whitney, p. 814, nearly all the verses from 1.40 to the end of the book have their uses in the ritual. That Parts I. and II. and III. of the hymn as divided below are utterly impertinent to the proper subject of the book and therefore without ritual application, is a fact on which Weber, *Sb.* 1895, p. 819, has already animadverted.⌋

⌊A clear synoptic statement of the provenience of the different groups of verses, or of the single verses, that enter into the composition of this hymn appears so desirable for the critical study thereof, that I subjoin the following:

Part I., verses 1–16.—This is the hymn of Yama and Yamī, RV. x. 10, of 14 vss., but covering 16 in our text by reason of the strange insertion of RV. i. 84. 16 between the RV. vss. 5 and 6 (our 5 and 7) and the expansion of the RV. vs. 12 to two (our 13 and 14).—See Weber, *Sb.* 1895, p. 819.

Part II., verses 17–26.—This is the Agni-hymn, RV. x. 11, of 9 vss. The order of the last two is inverted, and to the whole part is prefixed a vs. (our 17) not found in other texts.—See Weber, *Sb.* 1895, p. 828.

Part III., verses 27–36.—This is the Agni-hymn, RV. x. 12, of 9 vss., with the order of vss. 3 and 4 inverted and with its last vs., 9, which we had above as our vs. 25, not repeated. To the whole is prefixed (as our 27, 28) a repetition of the Agni-vss., AV. vii. 82. 4, 5: perhaps vs. 5 (our 28: of which all four pādas begin with *práti*) is put here as a parallel to our 29 (on account of its *pratyáñ*); in that case, vs. 4 (our 27) might be regarded as a mere variation of vs. 5, with *ánu* four times for *práti*, etc.—See Weber, *Sb.* 1895, p. 830.

Part IV., verses 37, 38.—To Indra, RV. viii. 24. 1, 2. See Weber, l.c., p. 819 n.

Part V., verse 39.—Corresponds to RV. x. 31. 9.

Part VI., verse 40.—Here begin the vss. used in the ritual.—To Rudra, RV. ii. 33. 11.

Part VII., verses 41–43.—To Sarasvatī with the Fathers, RV. x. 17. 7–9.

Part VIII., verses 44–46.—To the Fathers, RV. x. 15. 1, 3, 2.

Part IX., verse 47.—To the Fathers, RV. x. 14. 3.

Part X., verse 48.—To Soma, RV. vi. 47. 1.

Part XI., verses 49, 50.—To Yama, RV. x. 14. 1, 2.

Part XII., verses 51, 52.—To the Fathers, RV. x. 15. 4, 6.

Part XIII., verse 53.—*Tvaṣṭā duhitre* etc., RV. x. 17. 1.

Part XIV. a, verse 54.—To the dead man, RV. x. 14. 7.

Part XIV. b, verse 55.—Averruncatio, RV. x. 14. 9.

Part XV., verses 56, 57.—Fire-kindling, RV. x. 16. 12 and variation.

Part XVI., verses 58–60.—To Yama and the Fathers, RV. x. 14. 6, 5, 4.

Part XVII., verse 61.—To the Fathers (?), SV. i. 92.⌋

⌊It thus appears that every verse of our hymn has its correspondent in the RV. save four (or five, if one wishes to count vs. 57): to wit, vs. 17, which is not found to my knowledge in any other text; vss. 27, 28, repeated from AV. vii. (see above); and vs. 61, found in SV.⌋

Translated: as AV. hymn, by Weber, as already noted, *Sb.* 1895, pages 825–842; Griffith, ii. 215.—Translated, furthermore, in so far as it corresponds to RV. material (see above), by the RV. translators, Wilson, Ludwig, Grassmann; 8 of the 14 verses 47 to 60 are from RV. x. 14, which has been translated by Geldner, *Siebenzig Lieder des Rigveda*, p. 146. In particular, Part I. (RV. x. 10), "Yama and Yamī," has been rendered by Muir, v. 288–291; Geldner, l.c., p. 142; Ludwig, in his *Rigveda*, vol. ii., no. 989, with comment in vol. v., p. 510. With reference to this same Part I., J. Ehni, *Die ursprüngliche Gottheit des vedischen Yama*, Leipzig, 1896, pages 139–141, may be consulted. Most important is Geldner's article in the *Gurupūjākaumudī*, pages 19–22, in which he subjects his older views concerning RV. x. 10 to a critical revision in the light of Sāyaṇa's interpretation.

1. Unto a friend would I turn with friendship; having gone through much ocean, may the pious one take a grandson of [his] father, considering further onward upon the earth (*kṣám*).

That is, 'making thoughtful provision for the future.' The verse is, without variant, RV. x. 10. 1. Our Bs.E. have *purú* in *saṁhitā*. The verse is also SV. i. 340, which has a considerably different text: for **a**, *ā́ tvā sákhāyaḥ sakhyā́ vavṛtyus;* in **b**, *arṇavā́n jagamyāḥ;* for **d**, *asmín kṣáye pratarā́ṁ dī́dyānaḥ*. The comm. takes *vavṛtyām* as of causative value, = *vartayāmi: dīdhyānas* he explains first (as if it were *dī́dyānas*) by *dīpyamānas*, 'becoming illustrious over the whole earth'; but also, alternatively, by "thinking [upon a means of impregnating me]."—The word *sakhyā́* he takes as instr. of *sakhyá* 'friendship' ⌊so Lanman, *Noun-Inflection*, JAOS. x. 336⌋, and renders by *sakhitvena;* but also alternatively as instr. of *sakhī*, 'by means of a female friend,' a go-between!

⌊An oxytone feminine stem *sakhī́* corresponding (cf. JAOS. x. 368) to a barytone masculine *sákhi* should accent its instr. *sakhyā̀* (JAOS. x. 368, top, 381), not *sakhyā́*.⌋ ⌊Aufrecht, *Festgruss an Böhtlingk*, 1888, page 1, took *sakhyā́* as a dative of *sakhyá;* and Pischel, *Ved. Stud.* i. 65 (title-page dated 1889), made a cogent and interesting argument against my view and came (independently, without doubt) to the same conclusion as Aufrecht.—For Geldner's interpretation of the whole verse, see *Gurupūjākaumudī*, p. 19–20.⌋

2. Thy friend wants (*vaç*) not that friendship of thine, that she of like sign should become of diverse form; the sons of the great Asura, heroes, sustainers of the sky (*dív*), look widely about.

That is, Varuṇa's spies are on the watch against such unpermitted acts. Our Bp.Bs. read in **b** *sálakṣmyā*. The comm. understands *salakṣmā* as *ekodaratvalakṣaṇaṁ yasyāḥ* 'marked as from the same womb,' and *viṣurūpā* as "changing from sister to wife." The same expression occurs below in 1. 34, and variations of it in TS. i. 3. 10¹ (quoted further at vi. 3. 11²) and MS. i. 2. 17 (a passage corresponding to, but different from, that in TS.); also VS. vi. 20 **b** (do.). It seems to have a kind of proverbial currency, as applied to things that change from one character to another. The comm. renders *pari khyan* by *pari vadanti* or *nirākariṣyanti*. The verse is RV. x. 10. 2.

3. Truly those immortals want that—posterity (? *tyajás*) of the one mortal; may thy mind be set in our mind; mayest thou enter [as] husband a wife's body.

The verse shows no variant from RV. x. 10. 3. Bs.E. read in **d** *tanvàm*. The comm. explains *tyajásam* by *tyāgam, garbhān nirgamanam, utpattim.* ⌊Cf. Weber, *Sb.*, p. 824.⌋

4. What we (pl.) did not do formerly, why [do that] now? speaking righteousness, should we prate unrighteousness? The Gandharva in the waters and the watery woman (*yóṣā*) — that is our (du.) union (*nā́bhi*), that our ⌊du.⌋ highest relation (*jāmí*).

RV. x. 10. 4 reads *ṛtā́* in **b**, and *sā́ no n-* in **d**, but *nāu* at the end. ⌊The inconcinnity of number as between *no* and *nāu* tempts one to think that here at least the text of the AV. has scored a point against that of the RV.⌋ *Ánṛta* seems to be used here, as hardly elsewhere, in the directly opposed sense to *ṛtá*. The comm. explains *rapema* by *spaṣṭam brūmaḥ*. ⌊Cf. Weber, *Sb.*, p. 825.⌋

5. Verily, the generator made us (du.) in the womb man and spouse — god Tvashṭar, Savitar of all forms; none overthrow (*pra-mī*) his ordinances (*vratá*); earth knows us ⌊two⌋ as such, also heaven.

RV. x. 10. 5 has no variants. The treatment of *pṛthivī́* in **d** as *pragṛhya* is noticed in Prāt. iii. 34 c. ⌊Presumably, W's literal version of **d** would be 'earth is cognizant of that [fact] of us two, also heaven.'⌋

6. Who yokes to the pole today the kine of righteousness, the diligent, the bright, the slow to wrath (?*durhṛṇāyú*), that have arrows in the mouth, that shoot at the heart, amiable ones? whoso shall prosper their burden, he shall live.

This strangely intruded verse ⌊cf. Weber, *Sb.* 1895, p. 819 n.⌋ is RV. i. 84. 16 (also found in TS. iv. 2. 11[3]; MS. iii. 16. 4), without variant ⌊save that TS. accents *dúr-hṛṇāyūn*⌋. SV. has it at i. 341 (next after our verse 1), with the bad variants *āsánn eṣam apsuvā́haḥ* in **c**. ⌊Cf. Aufrecht's *Rigveda*², vol. i., preface, p. xliv.⌋ The comm. understands *bhṛtyā́m ṛṇádhat* in **d** as here translated; also *durhṛṇāyū́n* ⌊alternatively⌋ in **b**.

7. Who knows of that first day? who saw it? who shall proclaim it here? Great is the ordinance (*dhā́man*) of Mitra, of Varuṇa; why, O lustful one, wilt thou speak to men with deceit (?*vī́ci*)?

RV. x. 10. 6 has no variants. The comm. blunderingly attributes the verse to Yamī; he also takes *vī́cyā* ⌊p. *vī́cyā*⌋ as for *vī́cyās*, an adj. meaning *vividham añcanto gacchantaḥ saṁcarantaḥ*, and qualifying *nṝ́n*, which is used as nominative, = *narās!* ⌊See Geldner, *Gurupūjākaumudī*, p. 21–22.⌋

8. Desire of Yama hath come unto me Yamī, in order to lying together in the same lair (*yóni*); I would fain yield (*ric*) my body, as wife to husband; may we whirl off, like two chariot wheels.

That is, probably, like the wheels of two chariots interlocked with each other in battle. RV. x. 10. 7 has no variants from our text. The comm. makes *vi vṛheva* mean *saṁçleṣaṁ karavāva*, adding *itaretarayoḥ saṁçleṣo vivarhā;* and his first explanation of *rathyā* is as = *rathyayā* 'on the carriage road'! Our P.M.I. accent *vṛhéva*. The metrical definition of the Anukr. as *pañkti* is very strange, though the verse can be reduced to 40 syllables by refusing to make ordinary resolutions.

9. They stand not, they wink not, those spies of the gods who go about here; with another than me, O lustful one, go quickly; with him whirl off like two chariot wheels.

The verse is RV. x. 10. 8, without variant. The comm. reads *eke* at end of **a**; he explains *tū́yam* in **c** by *tūrṇam*, and supplies *ramasva*: 'hasten to enjoy thyself.'

10. By nights, by days one may pay reverence (*daçasy*) to him; the sun's eye may open (? *ún mimīyāt*) for a moment; with heaven, with earth paired, of near connection; — Yamī must bear the unbrotherly (*ájāmi*) [conduct] of Yama.

RV. x. 10. 9 differs from our text only by reading in **d** *bibhṛyāt*; and this reading the translation implies, *vivṛhāt* seeming unexplainable save as a corruption, suggested by the forms of *vi-vṛh* in the two preceding verses. The connection of the verse is very loose, and the sense of **b** especially doubtful. One is tempted to emend to *mimīlyāt*; but *ā́ mimīyāt* is found in TB. iii. 6. 13 ⌊2d *prāiṣa*⌋, explained by its commentary as meaning *āgatya praviçeyuḥ*. Our comm. explains *ún m-* as *ūrdhvaṁ gacchet* (the RV. comm. as *ud etu*). Our comm. further reads at the end *ajāmis*, and understands it of Yamī. The adjectives in **c** are dual; the comm. supplies "earth with heaven and heaven with earth." ⌊Cf. Weber, *Sb.*, p. 823.⌋

11. Verily there shall come those later ages (*yugá*) in which next of kin (*jāmí*) shall do what is unkinly ⌊*ájāmi*⌋. Put thine arm underneath a hero (*vṛṣabhá*); seek, O fortunate one, another husband than me.

The verse is, without variant, RV. x. 10. 10. *Upa barbṛhi* in **c** means 'make an *upabárhaṇa* (cushion, pillow) of.' Our comm. regards the anomalous *barbṛhi* ⌊*Gram.* § 1011 a⌋ as *barbṛ* + *hi*, *-bṛ-* being for *-bṛh-* by Vedic license.

12. What should brother be when there is no protector? or what sister, when destruction impends (*ni-gam*)? Impelled by desire, I prate thus much; mingle thou thy body with my body.

The first half-verse apparently means that the matter of near kindred is overborne in importance by the consideration of her loneliness and of the necessity for continuing their race. The verse agrees throughout with RV. x. 10. 11. The comm. renders *-mūtā* in **c** by *mūrchitā*.

13. I am not thy protector here, O Yamī; I may not mingle my body with thy body; with another than me do thou prepare enjoyments; thy brother wants not that, O fortunate one.

All our mss. save Op.K. accent *yámi* in **a**; SPP. reports only one of his as doing so. RV. x. 10. 12 is in our text expanded into two verses, its second half being our **c**, **d**, without variant. The comm. reads *nūnam* for *tanūm* in **b**; he explains *nāthám* in **a** by *abhimatārthasampādakas*.

14. Verily, I may not mingle my body with thy body; they call him wicked (*pāpá*) who should approach his sister. That is not consonant

(?*asaṁyát*) with my mind [and] heart, that I, a brother, should lie in a sister's bed (*çáyana*).

The first half-verse ⌊cf. vs. 13⌋ is RV. x. 10. 12 **a**, **b**, which latter, however, reads in **a** *te tanvā̀ tanvàṁ sám*. All the mss. leave *çayīya* at the end unaccented, and both editions read accordingly; we ought in ours to have made the necessary emendation to *çáyīya*. The mss. vary in **c** between *ásaṁyat*, *asaṁyát*, *ásaṁyát*, and *asaṁyat;* SPP. gives in his text *ásaṁyat*, which is better than our *asaṁyát;* the *pada*-text divides *asam∘yat*. The comm. reads instead *asuṁ yat*, and supplies a verb, *apaharet*, to govern *asum*.

15. A weakling (?*batá*), alas, art thou, O Yama; we have not found mind and heart thine; verily, another woman shall embrace thee, as a girth a harnessed [horse], as a twining plant (*líbujā*) a tree.

RV. x. 10. 13 varies from this only by reading (as also our Bp.) in **d** *ṣvajāte*. The translation given of *kakṣyè 'va yuktám* agrees with the comm. (also the comm. to RV.), which renders *yuktam* by *svasambaddham açvam*. Pāda **b** evidently alludes to 14 **c**, where Yama talks of his mind and heart. If *batás* is a genuine word (the metrical disarray intimates corruption), it looks like being the noun of which the common exclamation *bata* is by origin the vocative. The RV. Anukr. takes no notice of the defective meter; ours requires the verse to be read as only 40 syllables, which is possible (10 + 9 : 10 + 11 = 40); ⌊**c** and **d** are good *triṣṭubh* pādas and **b** has a *triṣṭubh* cadence⌋.

16. Another man, truly, O Yamī, another man shall embrace thee, as a twining plant a tree; either do thou seek his mind or he thine; then make for thyself very excellent concord (*saṁvíd*).

RV. x. 10. 14 has for **a** the much better version *anyám ū ṣú tvám yamy anyá u tvā́m*, and in **b** again *ṣvajāte*. Our D., and a single ms. of SPP's (with the comm.), also have *anyam* ⌊at the beginning⌋, and SPP. accordingly admits *anyám* into his text, in spite of the absence of *tvám*. But the comment on the Prāt. three times (under ii. 97; iii. 4; iv. 98) reads *anya ū ṣu*, and it cannot well be questioned that this is the true text of our AV. Our P.M.E. accent again *yámi*. The Anukr. takes no notice of the lacking syllable in **a**; ⌊perhaps it balances **c** against **a**⌋.

17. Three meters the poets extended (?*vi-yat*) — the many-formed one, the admirable, the all-beholding; waters, winds, herbs — these are set (*árpita*) in one being (*bhúvana*).

The verse is extremely obscure, in meaning and in connection. The mss. vary much as regards the accent of *pururūpam;* two of ours (O.D.) and several of SPP's accent *-rū́p-*, which, as it is found in other texts, the latter has very properly admitted in his edition. The comm. renders *vi yetire* by *yatnaṁ kṛtavantaḥ*. The Anukr. takes no notice of the irregularity of the meter. ⌊Concerning this *prakṣipta*-verse, "glossenartige Parallelstelle," see Weber, *Sb.* 1895, p. 819 note, and p. 828.⌋

18. The bull yieldeth (*duh*) milks for the bull with the milking of the sky (*dív*), he the unharmable son (?*yahvá*) of Aditi; everything knoweth he, like Varuṇa, by thought (*dhī́*); he, sharing the sacrifice (*yajñíya*), sacrificeth to the seasons that share the sacrifice.

The verse is RV. x. 11. 1, whose only variant is *yajatu* for *-ti* in **d**. The comm. explains *vṛ́ṣā* as Agni, and *vṛ́ṣṇe* as the sacrificer, *dóhasā* as = *dohanasādhanena yajñādinā*, *yahvás* as *mahān* and qualifying *vṛ́ṣā* together with *ádābhyas*, while *ádites* means "indivisible" and qualifies *diváḥ*, which is ablative: the general sense being that the god procures rain for his worshiper. His understanding of **c** agrees with the translation given above. Compare Pischel's version of the verse and general explanation of the RV. hymn in *Ved. Stud.* i. 183 ff.; his exposition is excessively ingenious and extremely unsatisfactory.

19. Prateth the Gandharvī and watery woman; in the noise of the noisy one (*nadá*) let [her] protect our mind; let Aditi set us in the midst of what is desired (?*iṣṭá*); our oldest brother shall first speak out.

RV. x. 11. 2 has for sole variant *me* for *nas* in **b**. The comm. to the first half-verse appears to be defective; but it certainly understands the goddesses Bhāratī and Sarasvatī to be intended in **a**; *iṣṭasya* is either *phalasya* or *yāgasya*; the "brother" is Agni. ⌊Pischel discusses the RV. verse at *Ved. Stud.* i. 183.⌋

20. She now, the excellent, rich in food, full of glory — the dawn hath shone for man (*mánu*), full of light (*svàr-*); since they have generated for the council [as] *hótṛ* Agni, the eager one, after the will (*krátu*) of the eager ones.

This is RV. x. 11. 3, without variant. The comm. renders *kṣumátī* in **a** by *mantrarūpaçabdavatī*, and *vidáthāya* (of course) by *yajñāya*, and understands *ánu krátum* as "for each several ceremony."

21. Then that mighty (*vibhū́*) conspicuous drop did the bird, the lively falcon, bring at the sacrifice; if the Aryan tribes (*víç*) choose the wondrous one, Agni, [as] *hótṛ*, then prayer (*dhī́*) was born.

RV. x. 11. 4 differs only by reading *iṣitás* in **b**. The comm. makes a couple of references, to TB. iii. 2. 1[1] and TS. vi. 1. 6[1], where the legends of the bringing of soma from heaven by the falcon are given. Prāt. iii. 25 notes the short final of *ádha* in **a** and **d**.

22. Ever art thou pleasant (*raṇvá*), as pastures to him that enjoys (*puṣ*) them, being, O Agni, well sacrificed to with the offerings of man (*mánus*); or when, active, praiseworthy, having won the strength (*vā́ja*) of the inspired one (*vípra*), thou approachest with very many.

RV. x. 11. 5 differs only by reading *ukthyàṁ* at end of **c**. The construction and meaning of the second half-verse are difficult and obscure. The comm. explains *çaçamānas* by *çaṅsan yajamānam praçaṅsan* (similarly the comm. to RV.); and *bhūribhis* as "accompanied by many desires or else by many gods" (RV. comm. only the latter).

23. Send thou up the (two) fathers, [as] a lover, unto enjoyment (*bhága*). The welcome one (*haryatá*) desires to sacrifice; he sends from the heart; the bearer (*váhni*) speaks out; the merry one (?*makhá*) does a good work; the Asura shows might (*taviṣy*); he trembles with purpose (?*matī́*).

The verse is RV. x. 11. 6, without variant. It is extremely obscure, and the general sense, as well as the meaning of several words, is in a high degree doubtful; the translation given is no more than mechanical. ⌊Cf. Weber, p. 829.⌋ The 'two fathers' (parents) are declared by the comm., probably rightly, to be heaven and earth; *jāras* is explained as *ādityas*, and *ā* as = *iva*. Or, alternatively, *jāras* is "praiser," coming from *jarā* "praise," and to *ā* is to be supplied *hvayati*. The *iṣyati* is made = *icchati;* *vahni* is Agni; *makhas* is *makhasādhano manhanīyo vā; taviṣyate* is *vardhiṣyate*. All this is of interest only as showing that no help is to be obtained from the native exegetes.

24. Whatever mortal hath seen thy favor, O Agni, son of power, he is renowned exceedingly; acquiring (*dhā*) food (*íṣ*), borne by horses, he, lightful, vigorous, passes (?*ā-bhūṣ*) the days (*dív*).

RV. x. 11. 7 reads in a *ákṣat*, of which our *ákhyat* is doubtless only a corruption. Our Bp. and one of SPP's authorities have *akṣat*. The comm. renders *ā bhūṣati* by *ābhavati;* ⌊he adds alternatively : *bhūṣati* = *bubhūṣati, dyumān . . . bhavitum icchati* ⌋. In **b** he reads *abhi* instead of *ati*.

25. Hear us, O Agni, in thy seat, thy station; harness the speedy chariot of the immortal (*amŕ̥ta*); bring to us the two firmaments (*ródasī*), parents of the gods; be thou of the gods never (*mā́kis*) away; mayest thou be here.

The verse is RV. x. 11. 9 (and 12. 9), without variant. The comm. comfortably supplies *saṁghe* in **d** to govern the genitive *devānām*. Then, as alternative explanation, he understands *bhūs* and *syās* as third persons, and *mā́kis* as "no one."

26. That, O Agni, this meeting may take place (*bhū*), divine, among the gods, worshipful, thou reverend one, and that thou mayest share out treasures, O self-ruling one, do thou enjoy here our portion filled with good things.

The verse is, without variant, RV. x. 11. 8 (also found in MS. iv. 14. 15).

27. Agni hath looked after the apex of the dawns, after the days, [he] first, Jātavedas; a sun, after the dawns, after the rays; after heaven-and-earth he entered.

28. Agni hath looked forth to meet the apex of the dawns, to meet the days, [he] first, Jātavedas, and to meet the rays of the sun in many places; to meet heaven-and-earth he stretched out.

These two verses we had above as vii. 82. 4, 5. They are here again written out in full by two of our mss. (O.R.). ⌊Cf. my introduction, above, p. 815.⌋

29. Heaven and earth, first by right, truth-speaking, are within hearing, when the god, making mortals to sacrifice, sits as *hótr̥*, going to meet his own being (*ásu*).

The verse is RV. x. 12. 1, without variant. Some of our mss. (Bp.Bs.Op.) read *abhisrāvé* in **b**. The comm. explains the word by *stotuḥ çravaṇayogye*.

30. A god, encompassing the gods with right, carry thou first our offering, understanding [it]; smoke-bannered by the fuel, light-beaming, a pleasant, constant *hótr̥*, skilled sacrificer with speech.

The verse is RV. x. 12. 2, without variant. The majority of SPP's mss., with one of ours (Op.), read *bhā́rcīko* in **c**. Neither our Anukr. nor that of the RV. notes the deficiency of a syllable in **a**.

31. I praise (*arc*) your (du.) work unto increase, ye ghee-surfaced ones; O heaven-and-earth, hear me, ye two firmaments (*ródasī*); when days, O gods, went to the other life (*ásunīti*), let the two parents (*pitárā*) sharpen us here with honey.

The rendering is only mechanical, the obscurity of the verse being unresolved. It is RV. x. 12. 4, which, however, reads for **c** *áhā yád dyā́vó 'sunītim áyan*. Our mss. and the authorities of SPP. vary in **c** between *devā́s*, *dévās*, and *devās;* SPP. reads *devā́s*, with ⌊at least⌋ two of his; our *dévās* is not defensible; the translation implies *devā́s*. The comm. makes the word the subject of *ā́yan*, taking *áhā* (p. *áhā*) as for *ahaḥsu;* he explains *devās* by *stotāras* or *r̥tvijas*. Our Bp. is the only *pada*-ms. that reads (with the RV. *pada*) *ápaḥ* in **a**; the others have *ā́paḥ;* but, as the comm. gives the former, SPP. adopts it in his text. A majority of SPP's mss. accent *ghr̥tásnū*, but only one of ours (O.) does so.

32. If the god's immortality (*amŕ̥ta*) is easy to appropriate for the cow, thence those who are born maintain themselves on the broad [earth]; all the gods go after that sacrificial formula of thine, when the hind yields (*duh*) the ghee, heavenly liquor (*vā́r*).

The verse is RV. x. 12. 3, without variant. It is all extremely obscure, especially the first pāda, which admits of being rendered in half-a-dozen different ways; the translation given is purely tentative. The comm. gives little help. The *pada*-text does not divide or otherwise change *svā́vr̥k*, which indicates that its makers did not see in the word the formation *su-ā-vr̥j*, which is plausibly seen in it by western scholars and by our comm. The latter takes *urvī́* (p. *urvī́ íti*) as dual, but in the Prāt. it is quoted by the comment (to i. 74) as example of a locative in *ī*, which it doubtless is. Our comm. derives *yájus* first from root *yuj* and makes it = *karman;* *devās* is again, as above (vs. 31), *stotāras*, *r̥tvijas*. ⌊With the expression *divyáṁ vā́ḥ*, applied to ghee, compare the expression at x. 4. 3, *vā́r ugrám*, applied to snake-venom, which may well be called a 'terrible fluid': but see note to x. 4. 3.⌋

33. Why forsooth hath the king seized (*grah*) us? what have we done in transgression of (*áti*) his ordinance (*vratá*)? who discerns [it]? for even Mitra, swerving the gods, like a song of praise (*çlóka*), is the might also of them that go.

The verse is RV. x. 12. 5, without variant. The second half-verse, especially the last pāda, is bafflingly obscure. The accent of *ásti*, as well as the absence of other construction for *mitrás*, strongly indicates that the whole of the second half-verse forms one sentence; in which case *vā́jas* is perhaps most probably a corruption. The comm. understands *rā́jā* in **a** as Yama, and *jagr̥he* as signifying his "acceptance" of offerings — which is very ill guessed; doubtless it is Varuṇa (so Ludwig; the RV. comm. makes it

Agni). He then renders *juhurāṇás* most absurdly by *āhvayan*, ⌊saying that "the root *hvṛ* 'crook' is here used in the sense of root *hū* 'call'"⌋. He reads in **d** (as do some of the mss., including our O.Op.R.) *yātān*, as accus. of the pple *yāta*, qualifying *devān* understood, rendering *devān abhigacchato no 'smān rakṣitum!* and so on. The version of the line given above is of course mechanical only.

34. Hard to reverence (?*durmántu*) here is the name of the immortal, that she of like sign should become of diverse form; whoso shall reverence Yama with proper reverence (?*sumántu*), him, O Agni, exalted one, do thou protect, unremitting.

This verse is found also as RV. x. 12. 6, without variant, but the RV. comm. passes it without notice, as if recognizing it as not genuine. It is very strange to find repeated here as **b** vs. 2 **b**, above, as the connection this time does not explain the feminine words in it. The comm. first explains (like Grassmann) the pāda as quoted from the other verse; but goes on to add other interpretations. He defines *durmántu* by *durmananaṁ durvacam.*

35. In whom the gods revel at the council, maintain themselves in Vivasvant's seat — they placed light in the sun, rays in the moon: the two, unfailing, wait upon (*pari-car*) the brightness (*dyotaní*).

The verse is x. 12. 7, without variant. The comm. separates *yásmin* from *vidáthe*, supplying *agnāu* for the former to qualify (the RV. comm. does the same); perhaps rather *manmani* is to be inferred from the following verse. ⌊W. suggests by a note to his ms. as an alternative for **a**, 'In what council the gods revel.'⌋ Our comm. also explains, in **d**, *dyotanīm* by *dyotamānam agnim*, and it reads *ajasram*, understanding it adverbially; *aktūn* in **c** is either *raçmīn* or *rātrīs*. ⌊This vs. and the next are discussed by Foy, KZ. xxxiv. 228.⌋

36. In what secret (*apīcyà*) devotion (*mánman*) the gods go about (*sam-car*) — we know it not; may Mitra, may Aditi, may god Savitar declare us here guiltless to Varuṇa.

The verse is RV. x. 12. 8, without variant. Our comm. explains *mánmani* by *mantavye sthāne varuṇākhye.*

37. O companions, we would supplicate (*ā-çās*) worship (*bráhman*) for Indra, possessor of the thunderbolt, to praise, indeed, the most manly, the daring.

The verse is RV. viii. 24. 1 (also SV. i. 390), which reads in **a** *çiṣāmahi* (SV. *-he*), and inserts in **c** *vas* after *ū ṣú*, as required by the meter. The comm's text (but not his exposition) also has the *vas*. Our Anukr. takes no notice of the lack of a syllable in the pāda. The comm. explains *ā́ çiṣāmahe* by *āçāsmahe*, and supplies *kartum;* he renders *stuṣé* by either *stāumi* or *stotum*. The particles *ū ṣú* are included in the prescriptions of Prāt. ii. 97; iii. 4; iv. 98. ⌊Weber, *Sb.* 1895, p. 819 n., can assign no reason why vss. 37–38 should appear here.⌋

38. For thou art famed for might (*çávas*), for Vṛitra-slaying, a Vṛitra-slayer; thou out-bestowest the bounteous with thy bounties, O hero.

The verse is RV. viii. 24. 2, and without variant, if, with SPP., we read *çrutás* at end of **a**. Our text has *çritás*, with a part of the mss.; they vary between *çrutás* (our

O.Op.D.R., and half of SPP's; also the comm.), *çritás* (our P.M.T., and two of SPP's), and *çr̥tás* (our Bp.Bs.E.I.K.Kp., and three or four of SPP's authorities) — which last is doubtless only a careless variant of *çritás*. The translation given above implies *çrutás*. The comm. perhaps reads in **b** *vr̥trahatye 'va*.

39. Thou goest over the earth as a *stegá* over the ground; let winds blow here on the great earth (*bhū́mi*) for us; Mitra for us there (*átra*), Varuṇa, being joined, hath let loose heat (*çóka*), as fire does in the forest.

RV. x. 31. 9 corresponds, but has very considerable differences of reading: in **a**, *eti pr̥thvī́m;* for **b**, *mī́haṁ ná vā́to ví ha vāti bhū́ma;* in **c**, *yátra* (for *no átra*) and *ajyámānas* (for *yuj-*); in **d**, *'gnír v-*. Part of the AV. mss. also have *'gnír v-* (our O.R., and nearly half of SPP's), which accordingly might well be adopted in the text; but SPP., like our edition, reads *agnír v-*. One or two of our mss. (Op.R.s.m.) read in **d** *asr̥ṣṭa* (*vyàs-*), and so do a minority of SPP's; and the latter gives in his *saṁhitā*-text *vyásr̥ṣṭa*, but (apparently by an oversight) in his *pada*-text *ví : asr̥ṣṭa;* one sees no reason at all for the accentuation of the verb ⌊in the AV. text, with its *átra*⌋.* Our text is plainly an unintelligent corruption of an unintelligible verse. The RV. comm. guesses *raçmisaṁghāty ādityaḥ* to be the meaning of the ⌊very rare⌋ *stegá*, but only on the ground of a worthless etymology. Our comm. is defective here, but the lacuna is filled up by the editor, who makes it signify "a frog"! ⌊a meaning possibly suggested by the passage at TS. v. 7. 11 (which is parallel to VS. xxv. 1)⌋. Ludwig conjectures "a plowshare" ⌊and Weber follows him⌋. Our *pada*-text reads in **b** *mahī́ íti*, and the case is quoted under Prāt. i. 74 as that of a locative in *ī;* our comm. renders it ⌊alternatively⌋ by *mahatīm;* he also renders *vyásr̥ṣṭa* by *nāçayatu!* The *ṁ* of *pr̥thivī́ṁ* is ⌊almost or quite illegible⌋ in our text. The Anukr. takes no notice of the metrical irregularities of the verse (10 + 11 : 12 + 11 = 44).

*⌊The RV. reads *vy ásr̥ṣṭa*, and has the difficult *pada*-reading *ví : ásr̥ṣṭa:* here the RV's accentuation of *ásr̥ṣṭa* is accounted for by the RV's *yátra;* and the accent of *ví* is to be put with the remarkable cases (some thirty) mentioned by W., *Gram.* § 1084 a, whether we regard it as a blunder helped by the wavering tradition as to *átra*, *yátra*, or not. (Cf. what is said about "blend-readings" under xiv. 2. 18 and, just below, under xviii. 1. 42.) Whitney's Bp. follows the RV. in giving *ví : ásr̥ṣṭa* and his Bs. has *vyásr̥ṣṭa:* cf. the *ví : ádadhus* of xix. 6. 5 **a**.⌋

40. Praise thou the famed sitter on the hollow of men (*jána*), the terrible king, formidable assailant (?*upahatnú*); being praised, O Rudra, be gracious to the singer; let thine army (?*sényа*) lay low (*ni-vap*) another than us.

The verse corresponds to RV. ii. 33. 11 (also found in TS. iv. 5. 10³, without variant from RV.), which reads in **a–b** *-sádaṁ yúvānam mr̥gáṁ ná bh-*, and, for **d**, *'nyáṁ te asmán ní vapantu sénāḥ*. The substitution in our text of *sényam* for *sénās* at the end throws into confusion sense and construction. The comm. first takes it as = *senās*, and then as accus. qualifying *anyám* and signifying *tava senārham*, in the latter case supplying *senās* as subject of the verb. *Gartasádam* he takes first in the Nirukta sense of *çmaçānasaṁcaya*, and then in its "ordinary" (*prasiddha*) meaning, adding *tasyā 'raṇye saṁcārād gartasadanaṁ yujyate*. The Kāuç. (85. 19) uses the verse in connection with the digging of a hollow (*garta*) in the middle of the measured space at the *piṇḍapitr̥yajña*, and the scattering into it of a number of heterogeneous substances.

Our comm., by some rare and strange oversight, makes no mention of this *viniyoga*, and so does not take it into account in the explanation of the verse. Apparently it is only the occurrence of *gartasad* in the verse that suggests the use; of real applicability to the situation there is none.

41. On Sarasvatī do the pious call; on Sarasvatī, while the sacrifice is being extended; on Sarasvatī do the well-doers call: may Sarasvatī give what is desirable to the worshiper (*dāçvā́ṅs*).

RV. x. 17. 7 is the same verse, but makes better meter by having *ahvayanta* for *havante* in **c**; and the comm. agrees with it. Verses 41–43, with others to Sarasvatī (vii. 68. 1–2; also xviii. 3. 25), are used by Kāuç. (81. 39) in the *pitṛmedha* ceremony, accompanying offerings to Sarasvatī. ⌊And they recur below, as noted under vs. 43.⌋ The Anukr. takes no notice of the deficiency of a syllable in 41 **c**, and 42 **a**, nor of the excess of two syllables in 43 **a**.

42. On Sarasvatī do the Fathers call, arriving at the sacrifice on the south; sitting on this *barhís* do ye revel; assign thou to us food (*íṣas*) free from disease.

Here again the RV. version (x. 17. 9 **a**, **b**, 8 **c**, **d**) makes the meter good by inserting ⌊or rather (cf. vs. 59), by not omitting⌋ *yā́m* in **a** before *pitáras* (and hence accenting *hávante* *); it also accents *dakṣiṇā́* in **b**, as other texts do; two of our mss. (O.s.m.Op.) do the same, with the majority of SPP's, whence the latter adopts *dakṣiṇā́* in his edition; it is undoubtedly the correct reading ⌊as is explicitly stated also by the comm. to xix. 13. 9, page 325[21]⌋. RV. also avoids the change of subject in the second line by reading *mādayasva* in **c**. *⌊It is interesting to note that SPP's C^p accents *hávante*, as if the missing *yā́m* were not missing: cf. my note about "blend-readings" under xiv. 2. 18, and the end of my note under xviii. 1. 39; also note to 4. 57.⌋

43. O Sarasvatī, that wentest in company (*sarátham*) with the songs (*ukthá*), with the *svadhā́s*, O goddess, reveling with the Fathers, assign thou to the sacrificer here a portion of refreshment (*íḍ*) of thousandfold value, abundance of wealth.

Here, once more, the AV. disturbs the meter by the intrusion into **a** of *ukthā́ts*, which is wanting in the RV. version (x. 17. 8 **a**, **b**, 9 **c**, **d**). ⌊RV. reads *yájamāneṣu* in **d**.⌋ The three Sarasvatī verses are repeated below as xviii. 4. 45–47. The comm. gives *annasya* as equivalent of *iḍā́s*.

44. Let the lower, let the higher, let the midmost Fathers, the soma-drinking (?*somyá*), go up; they who went to life (*ásu*), unharmed (*avṛká*), right-knowing — let those Fathers aid us at our calls.

The verse is found, without variant, as RV. x. 15. 1, VS. xix. 49, and in TS. ii. 6. 12[3], MS. iv. 10. 6. It is used twice by Kāuç. in the funeral book: once (80. 43) at the piling of the funeral pile, and once (87. 14), in the *piṇḍapitṛyajña*, at the digging of a pit for receiving certain offerings. Verses 44–46 appear together (87. 29) in the latter ceremony with the bringing in of certain water-pots ⌊i.e. the pouring in (of their contents)?⌋. In Vāit. (30. 14), vss. 44 and 45, with 51, and 3. 44, 45, are prescribed to be repeated after the pouring of *surā* into a perforated vessel, in the *sāutrāmaṇī* ceremony; and again, vss. 44–46 accompany (37. 23) the binding of a victim to the sacrificial post in the *puruṣamedha*.

45. I have won hither (*ā-vid*) the beneficent Fathers, both the grandson and the wide-striding of Vishṇu; they who, sitting on the *barhís*, partake of the pressed drink with *svadhā́* — they come especially hither.

The verse is, without variant, RV. x. 15. 3, VS. xix. 56, and found in TS. ii. 6. 12³ and MS. iv. 10. 6 (MS. puts *yé* after *svadhā́yā* in **c**). Our comm. is uncertain from which root *vid* to make *avitsi*, and casts no light on the obscure second pāda; he renders *āgamiṣṭhās* either by *āgamaya* or *āgacchantu*. The abbreviated form *barhiṣádas* (p. *barhiosádaḥ*) is one of those quoted by the Prāt. comment as aimed at by rules ii. 59; iv. 100. For the use of the verse by Kāuç. and Vāit., see under vs. 44.

46. Be this homage today to the Fathers, who went first, who went after, who are seated in the space (*rájas*) of earth, or who are now in regions (*díç*) having good abodes (*suvṛjána*).

The verse is RV. x. 15. 2, which, however, reads in **b** *úparāsas*, and in **d** *vikṣú;* and with it in both respects read the corresponding verses in TS. ii. 6. 12⁴ and MS. iv. 10. 6; also VS. xix. 68 (but this, with our E., has *námo 'stu* in **a**). Ppp. also gives the verse in book ii., reading in **b** *ye parāsaṣ pareyuḥ*, and in **d** *suvṛjināsu vikṣu*. Some of our mss. (P.M.I.R.T.), and one of SPP's, agree with RV. in reading *úparāsas;* the comm. divides *u parāsas;* and our E. has *vikṣú*, while P.M. give *divikṣú*, and I. *prikṣú*. For the use of the verse in Kāuç. and Vāit. with vss. 44–45, see under 44; it also (or else, more probably, 4. 51: see under that verse) is prescribed alone (80. 51) to accompany the scattering of *darbha*-grass in preparing the funeral pile.

47. Mātalī with the *kavyás*, Yama with the Angirases, Brihaspati increasing with the *ṛkvans* ('praisers'); both they whom the gods increased and who [increased] the gods — let those Fathers aid us at our calls.

RV. x. 14. 3 has the first three pādas, but, instead of repeating our 44 **d**, reads for the fourth *svā́hā 'nyé svadhā́yā 'nyé madanti;* and TS. (ii. 6. 12⁵) and MS. (iv. 14. 16) agree with it in so doing.

48. Sweet verily is this [*sóma*], and full of honey is this; strong (*tīvrá*) verily is this, and full of sap is this; and no one soever overpowers in conflicts (*āhavá*) Indra, having now drunk of it.

The verse is RV. vi. 47. 1, without real variant; its applicability in the funeral book is not apparent, and neither Kāuç. nor Vāit. uses it. Part of our mss. (O.R.K.), with nearly all SPP's, combine at the beginning *svādúṣ k-*, which RV. also has; and SPP., with good reason, adopts this in his text.

49. Him that went away to the advances called great, spying out the road for many, Vivasvant's son, gatherer of people, king Yama, honor (*sapary*) ye with oblation.

The verse is RV. x. 14. 1, which, however, reads *ánu* for *íti* at end of **a**, and *duvasya* for *saparyata* in **d**. A verse in MS. iv. 14. 16 has the RV. version throughout. TA. (in vi. 1. 1) gives at the end the genuine variant *duvasyata*, but also in **a** and **b** the incredible blunders *pare yuvā́nsam* and *anapaspaçā́nám;* ⌊so even the Poona ed., p. 405⌋. With the first half-verse is to be compared our vi. 28. 3 **a**, **b**. The *íti* of our version, at end of **a**, seems a worthless corruption (SPP. thinks it certainly "a mistake for *áti*"; but that is not very plausible, though our I., doubtless by an accidental slip, has *áti*, and P.M. have *ata*); the comm. reads *anu*, with the other texts. ⌊With this vs. and the next, cf. 3. 13 below: the second half of 3. 13 is identical with the second half of this vs.⌋ In Kāuç. (81. 34), recital of the verse accompanies offerings to Yama at the lighting of the funeral pile. Metrically, it is *svarāj* (12 + 11 : 11 + 12 = 46) rather than *bhurij*.

⌊Caland, *Todtengebräuche*, p. 65, observes that "Kāuç. 81. 34–36 [meaning 34–37] form one single whole." They indicate the eleven verses (translated by C., p. 64) that are to be used to accompany the eleven oblations to Yama (*yāmān homān*), offered in the *pitṛmedha*, after the lighting of the fire. The vss. are: xviii. 1. 49, 50, for the first two oblations; xviii. 1. 58, 59, 60, 61 (the last vs. of the hymn) and xviii. 2. 1, 2, 3, for the next seven; and xviii. 3. 13 and 2. 49, for the last two: in all, eleven, *ity ekādaça*. Whereupon follow the oblations to Sarasvatī. — It should be noted that the group 1. 58 to 2. 3 (Kāuç.: *iti saṁhitāḥ sapta*) disregards the existing division of the book into *anuvāka*-hymns.⌋

50. Yama first found for us a track (*gātú*); that is not a pasture to be borne away; where our former Fathers went forth, there (*enā́*) [go] those born [of them], along their own roads.

The corresponding RV. verse (x. 14. 2) reads *pareyús* at end of **c**, and MS. (in iv. 14. 16) agrees with it. The comm. has *yena* instead of *enā* in **d**. The verse (with vs. 51?) is used by Kāuç. (81. 35) next after the preceding one, in the same ceremony.

51. Ye *barhís*-seated Fathers, hitherward with aid! these offerings have we made for you; enjoy [them]! do ye come with most wealful aid; then assign to us weal [and] profit, free from evil.

The corresponding RV. verse (x. 15. 4) has *áthā* at beginning of **d**. VS. (xix. 55) agrees throughout with RV.; TS. (in ii. 6. 12[2]) spoils the meter of **d** by changing *nas* to *asmábhyam*; MS. (in iv. 10. 6) has at the end *dadhātana*; | so has W's Op.⌋. The comm. also reads *atha*. The verse is used by Kāuç. (87. 27), along with 3. 44–46 and 4. 68, to accompany the untying and strewing of the *barhis* in the *piṇḍapitṛyajña*. In Vāit. 30. 14, it appears with 1. 44, 45 etc. (see under 1. 44); and again (9. 8), in the *cāturmāsya* sacrifice, accompanying (with 3. 44, 45 and 4. 71) a libation to Soma and the Fathers.

52. Bending the knee, sitting down on the right, let all assent to (*abhi-gṛ*) this libation of ours; injure us not, O Fathers, by reason of any offense (*ā́gas*) which we may do to you through humanity.

That is, through human frailty. The corresponding RV. verse (x. 15. 6) reads for **b** *imáṁ yajñám abhí gṛṇīta víçve;* and VS. (xix. 62) agrees with RV.; the comm., too, so far as to have *gṛṇīta*. In Kāuç. (83. 28), the verse accompanies the arranging of the bone relics of the deceased at their place of burial (repeated, with two other verses, in the *piṇḍapitṛyajña*, 87. 28). The Anukr. takes no notice of the redundant syllable in **b**.

53. Tvashṭar makes a wedding-car for his daughter; by reason of this, all this creation comes together; the mother of Yama, wife of great Vivasvant, being drawn about, disappeared.

The corresponding RV. verse (x. 17. 1) has *íti* for *téna* at beginning of **b**; and the comm. also reads *iti*. With the first half-verse compare iii. 31. 5 **a**, **b**, which is a sort of travesty of it. The second verse of the curious and obscure and much discussed (see Bloomfield in JAOS. xv. 172 ff.) bit of legend is found below, as 2. 33, as much out of all connection with its surroundings as this one here. Neither of the two is used by Kāuç. or Vāit. The comm. quotes a passage of eight verses from the Bṛhaddevatā in explanation of the legend.

54. Go thou forth, go forth by roads that go to the stronghold (*pūryā́ṇa*), as (*yénā*) thy Fathers of old went forth; both kings, reveling with *svadhā́*, shalt thou see, Yama and god Varuṇa.

Or *svadhā́yā* may be 'at their pleasure' or 'according to their wont.' The corresponding RV. verse (x. 14. 7) has in **a–b** *pathíbhiḥ pūrvyébhir yátrā naḥ pū́rve pitáraḥ pareyúḥ*, and, in **c**, *rā́jānā* and *mádantā*; and MS. (in iv. 14. 16) agrees with it except in reading, with our text, *páretās* ⌊in **b**, and in having *pūrvébhis* in **a**⌋. Our comm. reads *rājānā* in **c**. Prāt. iii. 83 prescribes the *ṇ* in *pūryā́ṇāis* (p. *pūḥ॰yā́nāiḥ*); the comm. absurdly explains the word as = *pumā́ṅso yena . . . yānti!* for the *pūr*, compare x. 2. 28 ff.; xix. 17 and 19. The Anukr. takes no notice of the metrical irregularity in the verse. ⌊It is due to the displacement of *pūrviébhis* by *pūryā́ṇāis*: the secondary character of the latter (occurring elsewhere only at 4. 63 below) is palpable in more ways than one.⌋ Kāuç. does not quote the verse; but our comm. declares it to accompany the laying of the dead body on the cart (for transportation to the funeral pile).

55. Go ye away, go asunder, and creep apart from here; for this man the Fathers have made this world; adorned with days, with waters, with rays (*aktú*), a rest (*avasā́na*) Yama gives to him.

The verse is RV. x. 14. 9, without variant; and TA. (in i. 27. 5; vi. 6. 1) has the first, third, and fourth pādas; while VS. (xii. 45) and TS. (in iv. 2. 4[1]), TB. (i. 2. 1[16]), and MS. (ii. 7. 11), have only the first (agreeing with TA. in the second). TA., however, reads *dadātv av-* in **d**, and that is found also in our P.M.I. The comm. has for **b** the pāda of the other texts: *ye 'tra stha purāṇā ye ca nūtanāḥ*. ⌊My discussion of the verse in *Skt. Reader*, p. 378, may be consulted.⌋ The verse, with 2. 37, accompanies in Kāuç. (80. 42) the sprinkling of the place of cremation with holy water; in Vāit. (28. 24), the sweeping of the site for the householder's fire, in the *agnicayana* ceremony. ⌊Weber, *Sb.* 1895, p. 839, takes the verse as a call, addressed to all creatures (whether animals or demons) that may infest the resting-place of the dead man, to quit the same (averruncatio).⌋

⌊Böhtlingk, in his paper *Ueber esha lokaḥ*, discusses this verse at *Ber. der sächsischen Gesell.* for 1893, xlv. 131. — He would read *vī́ta*, not *vīta*, referring to Whitney's *Grammar*[2] § 128, and suggesting that *divī̀va* is perhaps the only example for the circumflex; but I have noted *vī̀ndra*, RV. x. 32. 2, *vī̀va*, vii. 55. 2, *nī̀ta*, AV. iii. 11. 2, and *bhindhī̀dám*, vii. 18. 1, and suspect that Whitney has collected all the *prāçliṣṭa svaritas* from AV. (nearly a score) in his note to the Prāt. iii. 56.⌋

56. Eager (*uçánt*) would we light thee, eager would we kindle; do thou, eager, bring the eager Fathers to eat the oblation.

The corresponding verse in RV. (x. 16. 12; also VS. xix. 70) has *ní dhīmahi* for *idh-* in **a**; TS. (in ii. 6. 12[1]) and MS. (in i. 10. 18) read instead *havāmahe*, and with these our comm. agrees. Used in Kāuç. (87. 19: the comm. says, with vs. 57 also) to accompany, in the *piṇḍapitṛyajña*, the lighting of two pieces of wood. ⌊The next vs. is a variation of this.⌋

57. Lightful (*dyumánt*) would we light thee, lightful would we kindle; do thou, lightful, bring the lightful Fathers to eat the oblation.

More than half the mss. (including all ours except O.Op.T.K. ⌊which have *dyumatá*, p. *dyu°matáḥ*⌋) read *dyumantás* in **c**, which we accordingly adopted in our text, though the form is of course ungrammatical; SPP. reads correctly *dyumatás*. ⌊Cf. my *Noun-Inflection*, p. 521.⌋ ⌊This vs. is a mere variation of the preceding, with *dyumánt*-forms in place of *uçánt*-forms. Perhaps in this connection the fact is noteworthy that W's codex I. does not accent the vs. Here again the comm. reads *havāmahe* for *idhīmahi.*⌋

58. The Añgirases, our *návagva* Fathers, the Atharvans, the Bhṛigus, soma-drinkers (*somyá*) — may we be in the favor of those worshipful ones, likewise in their excellent well-willing.

The verse is RV. x. 14. 6, also VS. xix. 50, and in TS. ii. 6. 12[6], all without variant; the second half is met with further at AV. vi. 55. 3 ⌊reading as here⌋; and in other verses of RV. and AV.: ⌊namely, RV. iii. 1. 21; vi. 47. 13; x. 131. 7; AV. vii. 92. 1: but with *tásya yajñíyasya* instead of our plural⌋. It is used by Kāuç. (81. 36) in the cremation service ⌊with vss. 59–61 and 2. 1–3: see note to vs. 49⌋.

59. Come thou hither with the worshipful Añgirases; revel here, O Yama, with the Vāirūpas — I call Vivasvant, who is thy father — sitting down upon this *barhís*.

The verse is found as RV. x. 14. 5, and in TS. ii. 6. 12[6] and MS. iv. 14. 16. All these rectify the meter by inserting ⌊or rather (cf. vs. 42), by not omitting⌋ *yajñé* after *asmín* in **d**, and they have in **a** the equivalent reading *áñgirobhir á gahi yajñíyebhiḥ*. The AV. version is *bṛhatī* ⌊possibly because one can count its **d** as 9 syllables: *purā-bṛhatī* does not seem to occur elsewhere and perhaps it is wrong⌋.

60. Ascend thou, O Yama, this cushion (*prastará*), in concord with the Añgiras Fathers; let the sacred utterances (*mántra*) made in praise by the poets bring thee; then (*ená*), O king, revel thou in the oblation.

This verse also is found as RV. x. 14. 4, and in TS. ii. 6. 12[6] and MS. iv. 14. 16, all of which have *sída* for *róha* in **a**, and *haviṣā* for *-ṣas* in **d**. The comm., too, reads *sīda*. The only one of our mss. that accents *róha* is Op., and our reading the word with an accent was an emendation; SPP. gives the same, on the authority of most of his mss. ⌊The comm. calls *hí* an expletive.⌋ Kāuç. 84. 2 uses the verse with an offering to Yama in the ceremony of interment of the bones; and the comment appears to quote the same rule under 45. 14, in the *vaçāçamana* rite.

61. These ascended up from here; they ascended the backs of the sky (*dív*); the Añgirases have gone forth to heaven (*dív*), like *bhūrjís*, by the road.

The verse is found in SV. (i. 92), which combines in **b** *diváḥ pṛ-*, accents *bhūrjáyas* in **c**, and inserts *úd* before *dyám* and leaves *yayus* unaccented in **d**. It also accents *udā́ruhan* in **a**, as does our edition; but the mss. decidedly favor *úd ā́ 'ruhan* (p. *út : ā́ : aruhan*), and SPP. rightly adopts this reading. The comm. reads *etad* instead of *ete* in **a**; it makes *bhūrjáyas* (p. *bhūḥ॰jáyaḥ;* SV. p. *bhū́ḥ : jáyaḥ*, this *pada*-text dividing compound words without any hyphen or its equivalent between the parts) an epithet of the Aṅgirases, rendering it by *bharaṇavanto bhuvaṁ jitavanto vā*, and justifies the accent of *yayús* by treating *yáthā* as = *yādṛçena* "by what road the *bhūrjis* went" etc. SPP. accents *bhūrjáyas* on the authority of a single one of his mss.; all ours leave it without accent (in our text the accent-mark under its final syllable has become lost in printing); both Pet. Lexx. ignore the word entirely; its real meaning is wholly obscure, as it seems to have been to the makers of the *pada*-text; for their suggested etymology is plainly valueless. The verse is used by Kāuç. (80. 35), with 2. 48, 53; 3. 8, 9; 4. 44, in preparing for taking the body of the deceased person to the funeral pile; the six verses are called *hariṇīs*, and are repeatedly employed in other parts of the funeral and ancestral rites (82. 31; 83. 20, 23; 84. 13); also by Vāit. (37. 24), in a like connection.

⌊Here ends the first *anuvāka*, with 1 hymn and 61 verses. The quoted Anukr. says *ekaṣaṣṭiç ca.*⌋

2. ⌊Funeral verses.⌋

[*Atharvan.—ṣaṣṭi. yamadevatyam mantroktabahudevatyaṁ ca* (*4, 34. āgneyyāu; 5. jātavedasī; 29. pitryā*). *trāiṣṭubham : 1–3, 6, 14–18, 20, 22, 23, 25, 30, 34, 36, 46, 48, 50–52, 56. anuṣṭubh;* [*4,*] *7, 9, 13. jagatī; 5, 26, 49, 57. bhurij; 19. 3-p. ārṣī gāyatrī; 24. 3-p. samaviṣamā* "*ṛṣī gāyatrī; 37. virāḍ jagatī; 38–44. ārṣī gāyatrī* (*40, 42–44. bhurij*)*; 45. kakummaty anuṣṭubh.*]

⌊Of the eight "measuring-verses," 38–45, the first (vs. 38) is a true *gāyatrī;* the next six (39–44) are mere repetitions of vs. 38, with an *ūha* in the first pāda which sometimes spoils the meter; and the last (vs. 45) agrees in its last two pādas with the rest, but has a prior half which is true prose.⌋

⌊Of this hymn, only vs. 13 **a**, **b** and vs. 17 are found in Pāipp., in books xix. and xx. respectively. The ritual uses by Vāit. are naturally very meagre: namely, we find vss. 19–20 used once, and that in the *puruṣamedha*. On the contrary, all but about 18 of the 60 vss. are cited by Kāuç. (see under the verses). Bloomfield's Index may be corrected on page 410 by the insertion of vss. 1–3 (see under vs. 1). Verses 1–3 and 49 constitute, with verses from hymns 1 and 3, parts of an important ritual sequence of 11 verses, as noted under 1. 49. And verses 4–18, the *anuṣṭhānīs*, constitute (with the exception of vs. 10) another such sequence.⌋

⌊**The provenience of the material of this hymn.**— Whereas nearly all of the preceding hymn (all but 4 or 5 out of 61 verses) is found also in the RV., of this hymn, on the other hand, but little more than a third part (hardly 25 vss. out of 60) is RV. material. As elsewhere noted, the hymn begins with 3 vss. which form part of a ritual sequence (of 11 vss.) continuous with the last verses of the preceding hymn.

Part I., verses 1–13. — These are two groups of verses from RV. x. 14 (to wit: our vss. 1–3, which sub-group we may call **I. a**, and which equals RV. x. 14. 13, 15, 14: and our vss. 11–13, which sub-group we may call **I. b**, and which equals RV. x. 14. 10, 11, 12), between which are interposed the first 5 vss. of RV. x. 16, our vss. 4–5 and 7–8 and 10, which sub-group we may call **I. c**. — Again, between the second and third verses of **I. c** (our vss. 5 and 7) is interposed the single verse, RV. x. 14. 16 (our 6); and between the fourth and fifth verses of **I. c** (our vss. 8 and 10) is interposed a single verse (our 9) which appears to be a parallel to our 8, but is not found in other texts to my knowledge, though its prior half resembles that of xiii. 1. 9.

Part II., verses 14–18. — The Yama-verses of RV. x. 154, in the order 1, 4, 2, 3, 5.

The "measuring-verses," 38–45, form a sequence by themselves, and do not recur elsewhere, so far as I know. Compare Caland's *Todtengebräuche*, p. 145.

For the rest, RV. verses occur only sporadically:

our 19	= RV. i. 22. 15	our 54	= RV. x. 17. 3
our 33	= RV. x. 17. 2	our 55	= RV. x. 17. 4
{ our 35 **ab**	= RV. x. 15. 14 **ab**	our 58	= RV. x. 16. 7
{ our 35 **cd**	= RV. x. 15. 13 **cd**	our 59 **cd**	= RV. x. 18. 9 **cd** }
our 50 **cd**	= RV. x. 18. 11 **cd**	our 60 **ab**	= RV. x. 18. 9 **ab** }

It may be added that a considerable part of the material of the hymn is naturally found in the *pitṛmedhaprapāṭhaka* (vi.) of the TA.: that is to say, all the RV. verses of Part I. or all of it save our vs. 9; and 3 verses of Part II., our 14, 17, 16 = RV. verses 1, 3, 2; and, besides, our vs. 25 and about 8 of the last 11 verses. Of the verses last mentioned, vs. 25 and vss. 56 and 57 seem to be peculiar to AV. and TA. — Finally, several fragments (9 **ab**, 26 **ab**, 49 **ab**) recur elsewhere in the AV.; and 33 is properly inseparable from 1. 53. — The TA. readings correspond more nearly with those of RV. than with those of AV. — Verse 51 is a variation of 50: compare the relation of 1. 57 and 56.⌋

Translated: by Weber, *Sb.* 1895, pages 842–866; Griffith, ii. 227; — verses 9 and 20–59, by Ludwig, pages 482–484 (for vss. 32–33, see p. 332); a considerable number also by Muir, v. 293–296, 304; and the RV. verses, of course, by the RV. translators. — For an analysis of the hymn with reference to its contents, see Weber, p. 843.

1. For Yama the soma purifies itself; for Yama is made the oblation; to Yama goes the sacrifice, messengered by Agni, made satisfactory.

The verse corresponds to RV. x. 14. 13, which, however, in **a** reads *sómaṁ sunuta*, and in **b** *juhutā* (for *kriyate*). TA. (vi. 5. 1) agrees with RV. in both points, but has *gachatu* in **c**. The comm. reads at the end *alaṁkṛtas*.

⌊Verses 1, 2, and 3 of this hymn are used (Kāuç. 81. 36) in one continuous sequence with the last four of the preceding hymn (*iti saṁhitāḥ sapta!*), to accompany the oblations to Yama in the cremation ceremony: for details, see my note to xviii. 1. 49.⌋

2. Offer ye to Yama what is most honeyed, and stand forth; this homage to the former-born, the former, the path-making seers.

This verse and the next correspond to RV. x. 14. 15 and 14, save that RV. makes our 2 **b** and 3 **b** change places* and they become respectively its 14 **b** and 15 **b**, the double inversion thus leaving our 2 **b** and 3 **b** in the same relative position in both texts. TA. (in vi. 5. 1) agrees throughout with RV., both in this verse and the next. Our 2 **b** agrees also with RV. i. 15. 9 **b**. But RV. in both places has, like TA., *juhóta* for our *juhótā*.

*⌊The case is interesting as showing how easily the component elements of many of these verses may be shuffled about without detriment to what we may, out of politeness to the Rishis, call the "sequence of thought." The result of the transpositions is best shown by parallel columns, thus:

RV. x. 14. 14 **ab**.	AV. xviii. 2. 3 **ab**.
yamā́ya ghṛtávad dhavír	*yamā́ya ghṛtávat páyo*
juhóta prá ca tiṣṭhata.	*rā́jñe havír juhotana.*
RV. x. 14. 15 **ab**.	AV. xviii. 2. 2 **ab**.
yamā́ya mádhumattamaṁ	*yamā́ya mádhumattamaṁ*
rā́jñe havyáṁ juhotana.	*juhótā prá ca tiṣṭhata.*

Roth has beautifully illustrated the matter by shuffling together verses from Schiller's Riddles ("Von Perlen baut sich eine Brücke" and "Es steht ein gross geräumig Haus"): see ZDMG. xxxvii. 109. — Cf. notes to xviii. 2. 35; 3. 47.⌋

3. Unto Yama the king offer ye an oblation, milk rich in ghee; he furnishes (*ā-yam*) to us among the living a long life-time, for living on.

The verse is RV. x. 14. 14 (found also in TA. vi. 5. 1), except that **b** is 15 **b**: ⌊see note to the preceding verse⌋. ⌊TA. agrees with RV.⌋ For *páyas* in **a**, RV. reads *havís;* for *havís* in **b**, *havyám;* and in **c**, **d**, it has *devéṣv ā́ yamad dīr-*. SPP. reads in **c–d** *yamed dīr-* ⌊so also Caland, *Todtengebräuche*, note 243⌋, which is certainly better than *yame dīr-*: half his authorities give the former; but of our mss. only Op. has *yamet*, while D. has *yamat*, like RV. ⌊TA. and the comm.⌋. ⌊The case is strikingly like that of *mānaye tathā*, *mānayet tathā*, at xv. 10. 2.⌋ — The Prāt. (ii. 76) distinctly requires *ā́yuṣ prá* to be read in **d**, but of our mss. only O.s.m. (in margin) gives it; nearly half of SPP's *saṁhitā*-mss., however, have it, and it ought to be received as the true AV. text, though both editions read *ā́yuḥ*. These three verses make no appearance in Kāuç. ⌊This last statement now appears to be wrong: see note to vs. 1.⌋

⌊Considering the exaggerated nicety of the theory of the Hindus respecting consonant groups (cf. Whitney, AV. Prāt., p. 584–90), and in particular their doctrine of the *varṇa-krama* ("At the end of a word, a consonant is pronounced double," *padānte vyañjanaṁ dviḥ*, Prāt. iii. 26), it is strange that the mss. sometimes fail to come up even to the simple requirements of orthography as set by grammar and sense. On the other hand, it can hardly be said that the mss. in the cases of these shortcomings are a less truthful representation of the actual connected utterance of the text than would be for instance the graphical representation of the English *some more* by the words *some ore*. — I have thought it worth while to assemble a few notable cases where the one of two needed double letters is omitted. Thus besides *yame[d] dīrghám* and *mānaye[t] táthā*, just mentioned, we have: at xviii. 3. 3, *jīvā́m [m]ṛtébhyas* (a most striking example: there is abundant ms. authority for the false *ṛtébhyas*, which is yet shown beyond all peradventure to be a blunder by the *mṛtā́ya jīvā́m* of TA.); at xviii. 4. 40, *juṣantām | ā́sīnām ū́rjam úpa yé sácante*, shown to be a gross corruption by HGS., which reads *juṣantām | māsī 'mām ūrjam* etc.; at xix. 31. 2, *sá[m] mā sṛjatu puṣṭyā́*, where Ppp. has in fact *sam mā*, and where *sám* is supported by the parallelism of our vi. 5. 2; and, at xix. 7. 3, *áriṣṭa[m] mū́lam*, where all authorities agree in omitting the *-m*. — On the other hand, a superfluous double is sometimes written. Thus we find: at xix. 42. 3, *sumatím [m]āvṛṇānáḥ*, where the *pada*-text reveals its modernity and lack of insight by reading unaccented *mā* and *vṛṇānáḥ* instead of *ā°vṛṇānáḥ;* and at xix. 58. 4, *púraḥ kṛṇudhvam [m]ā́yasīḥ*. At xix. 46. 6, the *ghṛtā́d dúrluptas* or *úrluptas* of some authorities, instead of *-ā́d úllup-*, is a blunder of similar origin. Cf. *sā́danā[t] te*, xviii. 3. 52, note. The well-known *sám [m]ahema* of RV. i. 94. 1, as taken by BR. at vii. 1609, i. 567, would belong in this category; but Grassmann manages to refer it to root *mah*.⌋

4. Do not, O Agni, burn him up; do not be hot upon (*abhi-çuc*) him; do not warp (*kṣip*) his skin, nor his body; when thou shalt make him done, O Jātavedas, then send him forward unto the Fathers.

This verse and the next are RV. x. 16. 1 and 2, but RV. makes our 4 **c** and 5 **a** change places (cf. note to our vs. 2). RV., however, reads *çocas* for *çūçucas* in **a**, and at the end *pitṛ́bhyas* ⌊as in our 5 **b**⌋ for *pitṝ́nr úpa*. In **d**, SPP. reads, with RV., *áthe "m enam*, alleging for his reading three out of eight authorities, as against two or three that have *imám*. The comm. appears to read *īm*. Of our mss., all save O.Op.R. give *áthe 'mám enam* (and O. is corrected once to this, but the correction struck out again), as our edition reads; this is so bad a corruption that the authority for the other should be regarded as sufficient. TA. (in vi. 1. 4) agrees with RV. except in having *karávas* in its **c** ⌊our 5 **a**⌋. The text of the comm. agrees with RV. and TA. in having *pitṛbhyas* for *pitṝ́nr upa*, while the comm. quotes *pitṛbhyas* and then adds and explains *upa* ⌊constructively a blend-reading⌋. Our Bp. appears to give in **a** *çuçucaḥ*, as it ⌊apparently⌋ ought to do according to Prāt. iv. 86, though the example is not quoted in the comment on that rule; but the other *pada*-mss. ⌊and SPP.⌋ have *çūçucaḥ*. The Anukr. is questionable in its reading as to the verse, whether *triṣṭubh* or *jagatī:* the RV. version is pure *triṣṭubh;* the AV. one is mixed (12 + 11 : 11 + 12). Kāuç. (81. 33) prescribes this verse to be used, with 2. 36; 3. 71, and ii. 34. 5, when the youngest son lights the funeral pile, some of the schol. declaring vss. 4–7 to be intended instead ⌊cf. the comm., page 86[20]⌋; then, in 81. 44, vss. 4–9 and 11–18 are called *anuṣṭhānīs*, and are to be repeated by the *anuṣṭhātṛ* during the cremation. ⌊Root *kṣip* properly means 'warp' in its obsolete sense 'cast *or* throw.' If, as I think, W. is right in rendering the causative here by 'warp' = 'twist out of shape, contort,' the cases present an interesting semantic parallel. BR. render by 'platzen machen.' Different is the sense of *ava-kṣip* at 4. 12: see my note.⌋

5. When thou shalt make him done, O Jātavedas, then commit him to the Fathers; when he shall go to that other life (*ásunīti*), then shall he become a controller (?*vaçanī́*) of the gods.

The verse is RV. x. 16. 2, but RV. makes our 5 **a** and 4 **c** change places: see note to vs. 4. RV. has *yadā́* ⌊for our *yadó* = *yadā́ u*⌋ at beginning of **c**, and *áthā* at beginning of **d**. TA. (in vi. 1. 4) agrees throughout with RV. save in accenting *karási* in **a**. Both, of course, read *áthe "m enam* in **b**; but this time the AV. mss. are as good as unanimous in the corruption of *īm* to *imám*, and both the published texts are compelled to read it; the Anukr., too, seems to ratify it, by calling the verse *bhurij;* the comm. has instead *idam*, and one or two of SPP's authorities follow it. The comm. explains *asunīti* by *asūn prāṇān nayati lokāntaram*, and hence *prāṇāpahartrī devatā;* and *devānām* by *svakīyānām indriyāṇām;* while *vaçanīs* is (*cakṣurādīndriyāṇāṁ*) *sūryādidevatāprāpakaḥ!* ⌊Weber deems the idea of getting the gods under your control to be an indication of lateness or possibly of Buddhistic influence: *Sb.* 1895, p. 845, and 1897, p. 597.⌋

6. With the *tríkadrukas* it purifies itself; six wide ones, verily one great one; *triṣṭúbh*, *gāyatrī́*, the meters: all those [are] set in Yama.

RV. x. 14. 16, the corresponding verse, has in **a** *patati*, and at the end *ā́hitā;* TA. (in vi. 5. 3) agrees with it, but transposes *triṣṭúbh* and *gāyatrī́* in **c**. The sense of the verse is wholly obscure. According to our comm., the *trikadrukas* are the *jyotiṣṭoma*, *goṣṭoma*, and *āyuṣṭoma;* the "six wide ones" (f.) are heaven and earth and day and night and waters and herbs; "the great one" (n.) is taken ⌊alternatively⌋ as applying to Yama (m.): *mahāntaṁ yamam uddiçyāi 'va pravartante!* The commentator's ignorance is as great as our own; only he has no mind to acknowledge it. ⌊Hillebrandt cites passages akin with this, *Ved. Mythol.* i. 500.⌋

7. Go thou to the sun with thine eye, to the wind with thy soul (*ātmán*); go both to heaven and to earth with [their] due shares (?*dhármán*); or go to the waters, if there it is acceptable (*hitá*) to thee; in the herbs stand firm with thy bodies.

In the corresponding RV. verse (x. 16. 3) is read in **a** *cákṣur gachatu* and *ātmā́*; in **b**, *dyā́m* and *dhármaṇā*; TA. (vi. 1. 4: cf. 9. 2) has the same, but also inserts *te* in **a** after *sū́ryam*, and accents *gácha*, Brāhmaṇa-wise, in **b**—as does also SPP. in his text, with a minority of his authorities (and our Op.): there is the same reason (but no authority) for *gácha* in **a** also, but none in **c**, where, nevertheless, our Op. and R.s.m. have *gácha*. The verse lacks a syllable of being a full *jagatī*. ⌊Cf. the note to this vs. in my *Reader*, p. 379.⌋

8. The goat is the share of the heat (*tápas*); heat thou that; that let thine ardor (*çocís*) heat, that thy flame (*arcís*); what propitious bodies (*tanū́*) are thine, O Jātavedas, with them carry him to the world of the well-doing.

The RV. version of this verse has (x. 16. 4) *tápasā* in **a**; in this case, as seldom, the AV. reading is better. TA. (in vi. 1. 4) also gives *tápasā*, and it ends differently: *vahe 'mám sukṛ́tām yátra lokā́ḥ*; ⌊and it reads *ajó 'bhāgás*, which is explained by its comm. as *bhāgarahitaḥ*⌋. The comm. also has *tapasā*. Kāuç. (81. 29) directs the verse, with 2. 22 (some mss. say, with 2. 57), to be repeated while "binding a goat on the south," the *anustaraṇī* (as which, nevertheless, the goat is here meant) having been already laid, as a cow, on the body to be burned. ⌊But see Weber's treatment of the vs., *Sb.* 1895, p. 847.⌋

9. What ardors (*çocí*), swiftnesses (*rán̐hi*) are thine, O Jātavedas, with which thou fillest the sky, the atmosphere, let them collect (*sam-ṛ*) after the goat as he goes; then with other most propitious ones make him propitious.

With the first half-verse is to be compared xiii. 1. 9 **a**, **b**. SPP. reads in **d** *çṛtám* for *çivám*, with the decided majority of his authorities; of our mss., only O.Op.R.K. have *çṛtám*. The comm. has *çṛtam*; and further, in **b**, *prīṇāsi*, rendering it by either *pūrayasi* or *tarpayasi*. He takes *ran̐háyas* as an adj., = *vegavatyas*, which is not unacceptable. The verse is no proper *jagatī*, either in movement or in number of syllables (12 + 12 : 11 + 14 = 49). ⌊The comm. has *çivatarābhiḥ* in **d**.⌋

10. Release again, O Agni, to the Fathers him who goes (*car*) offered to thee, with *svadhā́*; clothing himself in life (*ā́yus*), let him go unto [his] posterity (?*çéṣas*); let him be united with a body, very splendid.

The corresponding verse in RV. (x. 16. 5) reads at end of **b** *svadhā́bhis*, in **c** *vetu* for *yātu*, and at end *jātavedaḥ* (for *suvárcāḥ*); TA. (in vi. 4. 2) also has *svadhā́bhis* and *jātavedas*, but in **c** gives *úpa yātu çéṣam*. ⌊The last pāda, **d**, recurs below at 3. 58.⌋ The third pāda is of doubtful meaning, but perhaps relates to the return of the deceased, after due installation among the Manes, to receive the ancestral offerings. The comm. explains *çéṣas* ⌊which he takes as *çeṣa-s*, masc.⌋ simply as *apatyanāman*. ⌊Kāuç. 81. 44 excepts this verse from the sequence of 14 *anuṣṭhānī* verses (4–18): see under vs. 4.⌋ In Kāuç. (82. 28) the verse is used in the ceremonies of the third day after cremation, in connection with sprinkling and collecting the bones. The Anukr. takes no notice of the deficiency of a syllable in **d**. ⌊As to *çeṣas*, see my note on this vs., *Reader*, p. 379–380: W's interpretation seems to me much better than either of those there noted.⌋

11. Run thou past the two four-eyed, brindled dogs of Saramā, by a happy (*sādhú*) road; then go unto the beneficent Fathers, who revel in common revelry with Yama.

The corresponding verse in RV. is x. 14. 10. RV. puts *sārameyāú* before *çvā́nāu*: ⌊and with this order (but not with that of AV.), the resolution to *çuā́nāu* is effective in giving a normal rhythm⌋. RV. reads in **c** *áthā* for *ádhā*, and *úpa* for *ápi;* TA. (in vi. 3. 1) has *ápī 'hi*, but agrees otherwise with RV. The comm. gives instead *ape 'hi;* and it explains this difficult reading by either taking *apa* as used in the sense of *upa*, or else understanding it to mean "go away [from the dogs]"! The Anukr. pays no attention to the redundant syllable in **b**, ⌊unless it assumes a deficiency in **a** to balance it⌋. The verse (according to the comm., vss. 11–13) is used (Kāuç. 81. 22) when the two kidneys of the accompanying sacrificed animal are (by way of a "sop to Cerberus") put into the hands of the dead man on the funeral pile. Then verses 11–18 are (Kāuç. 80. 35) mentioned and used with the *hariṇīs* (see under 1. 61); and by the schol. ⌊see note to Kāuç. 82. 31⌋ and the comm. they are reckoned themselves as *hariṇīs*. The comm. further prescribes them as accompanying the transfer of the dead body to the place of cremation.

12. What two defending dogs thou hast, O Yama, four-eyed, sitting by the road, men-watching, with them, O king, do thou surround him; assign to him well-being and freedom from disease.

The verse is RV. x. 14. 11, which in **b** reads *pathirákṣī nṛcákṣasāu*, and for **c** *tā́bhyām enam pári dehi rājan* (our *dhehi* is a corruption), and in **d** inserts *ca* after *svasti*. TA. (in vi. 3. 1) agrees with RV. except in having *-cákṣasā*, and in placing *rājan* and *enam* in **c** as does AV. The comm. makes a compound of *yamarakṣitārāu* in **a**; and it declares *pari dhehi* in **c** to = *paridehi*.

13. Broad-nosed, feeding on lives (?*asutṛ́p*), copper-colored, Yama's two messengers go about after men (*jána*); let them give us back here today excellent life (*ásu*), to see the sun.

The corresponding verse in RV. (x. 14. 12) differs only by combining in **a** *-tṛ́pā ud-* (p. *-tṛ́pāu : ud-*). TA. has the verse in vi. 3. 2: it reads in **a** *-pāv ulumbalāú* ⌊which seems to answer phonetically to a form beginning *uḍum-* and is glossed by *prabhūta-balayuktāu*, as if *ulum-** were = *urum-*?⌋; in **b**, instead of *jánān*, it reads *'váçān* ⌊i.e. *avá́çān:* glossed by *asvādhīnān prāṇinaḥ*⌋; and in **d**, for *dātām*, it has *dattāv* ⌊accentless, and glossed by *prayacchatām!*⌋. Ppp. has the first half-verse, in book xix., reading *udumbarāu* and *caratāu*. *⌊For the confusion between the sounds of *ḍ* and *ḷ* and *d* and *l*, see Kuhn's *Pāli-gram.*, p. 37, and cf. below, at 3. 1, *-pāláyantī*, *-pād-*.⌋

14. Soma purifies itself for some; some wait upon (*upa-ās*) ghee; for whom honey runs forward (?), unto them do thou go.

The 'go' in these verses is *gachatāt*, imperative of remoter or after action. The translation implies restoration in **c** of the RV. (x. 154. 1) reading *pradhā́vati*, of which our *pradhā́v* (p. *pra∘dhāú*) *ádhi* seems only a blundering and unintelligible corruption. Some of our mss. (and one of SPP's) accent *pradhā́vadhi*. The comm. agrees with RV., and SPP. is not to be blamed for adopting, though against all the authorities save the comm., *pradhā́vati* in his text. TA. (which has our vss. 14, 17, and 16 following immediately after our 11–13, little as the two sets appear to have to do with each other) reads (in vi. 3. 2) with RV. ⌊See p. xcii.⌋

15. They who of old were won by right, born of right, increasers of right — to the seers rich in fervor (*tápas-*), born of fervor, O Yama, do thou go.

The corresponding RV. verse (x. 154. 4) reads in **a**, **b** *pū́rva ṛtasā́pa ṛtā́vānaḥ*, in **c** *pitṝ́n*, in **d** *tā́ñç cid evá* (as in our vss. 14, 16, 17). The comm. explains *yama* here to mean *yamavan niyata*, or *yamena nīyamāna preta*, which is probably not far from correct; it is the deceased person who is addressed.

16. They who by fervor are unassailable, who by fervor have gone to heaven (*svàr*), who made fervor their greatness, unto them do thou go.

The corresponding RV. verse (x. 154. 2) has no variant; in TA. (vi. 3. 2), however, we find *gatā́s* for *yayús* in **b**, and *mahát* for *máhas* in **c**: this latter reading the comm. appears to have in mind when he explains *mahas* as signifying *mahat*.

17. They who fight in the contests (*pradhána*), who are self-sacrificing (*tanūtyáj*) heroes, or who give thousand-fold sacrificial gifts, unto them do thou go.

The corresponding RV. verse (x. 154. 3) has no variant; TA. (in vi. 3. 2) has *tanuty-* in **b**. Ppp. has the verse, in book xx., and reads for **c**, *tās tvaṁ sahasradakṣiṇāḥ*, and in **d** *gachatām*.

18. Poets (*kaví*) of a thousand lays (*-nīthá*), who guard the sun — to the seers rich in fervor, born of fervor, O Yama, do thou go.

The verse is RV. x. 154. 5, without variant. The comm. adds this time to its explanation of *yama* (cf. under vs. 15) *niyata çakaṭe baddha vā*.

19. Be pleasant to him, O earth, a thornless resting-place; furnish him broad refuge.

RV. has a corresponding verse (i. 22. 15), but reads for **a** *syonā́ pṛthivi bhava*; and in **c** it reads *nas* for *asmāi*, and *sapráthas* for *-thās* ⌊see my *Noun-Inflection*, p. 560⌋; VS. (xxxv. 21) has nearly the same, but inserts *nas* after *pṛthivi*, and ends with *-thās*, like our text; MB. (ii. 2. 7) agrees with VS. except in having *-thas*, like RV.; it also adds a fourth pāda. ⌊MP. ii. 15. 2 agrees with RV. save that it combines *naç çárma* and ends with *-thās*. Cf. the *pratīka* in MGS. i. 10. 5, and the Index, p. 158.⌋ The comm. explains *anṛkṣarā* by *anādhikā*. In Kāuç. (80. 3) this verse (according to the comm., vss. 19–21) is to be used when the man threatened with death is laid on the floor on *darbha*-grass; and again (80. 38), when the dead body is taken down from the cart at the funeral pile; and once more (82. 33), when the jar containing the bones is deposited in (or on) the earth. In Vāit. 37. 25, vss. 19 and 20 accompany the knocking-down of the animal-victim in the *puruṣamedha* sacrifice.

20. In the unoppressive wide space (*loká*) of earth be thou deposited; what *svadhā́s* thou didst make when living, be they dripping with honey for thee.

Most of the *pada*-texts (except our Op. and one of SPP's) read *svadhā́* instead of *svadhā́ḥ* in **c**. ⌊SPP. gives as *pada*-reading *svadhā́ḥ*, and so the comm. interprets.⌋ At end of **c**, the authorities are bothered by a confusion of *jī́van* and *jīvám*. The *pada*-mss. read *jīván* (two of SPP's ⌊P. and P.², which are unaccented in this book⌋ have *jīvan*): the *saṁhitā*-mss. have either *jīváṅs t-* (most of our mss.), or else *jīváṁ t-* (our O. and most of SPP's authorities), or else *jīvā́n t-* (one or two of SPP's). SPP. reads in his text *jī́van t-*, and says "the emendation is mine," not noticing that we had made it (the necessity of it being perfectly obvious) before him. The comm., too, has *jīvan*. The comm., with four or two of SPP's mss., makes the common blunder of reading at the end *-çcyutaḥ*. In Kāuç. (82. 21) the second half-verse is quoted in full to accompany the pouring a pot-offering into the fire on the second day after cremation (here, too, only one ms. reads *jīvaṅs t-*, and most of the rest *jīvaṁ t-*).

21. I call thy mind hither with mind; come unto these houses, enjoying [them]; unite thyself with the Fathers, with Yama; let pleasant, helpful (?*çagmá*) winds blow thee unto [them].

Excepting K., all our mss. read *imā́m* (or *imā́ṁ*) in **b**; SPP. records the reading as given only by two of his *pada*-mss. ⌊Pāda **c** is RV. x. 14. 8 **a**.⌋ The comm. glosses *çagmās* with *sukhakarās*. The Anukr. does not heed the redundant syllable in **b**.

22. Let the water-carrying, water-floating Maruts carry thee up, making [thee] cool by the goat, let them sprinkle [thee] with rain, splash!

Some of the authorities (our O.Op.R.D., and near half of SPP's, with the comm.) have in **b** *udaplútas*. For the use of the verse by Kāuç., see under vs. 8 above. ⌊Cf. the use of *bā́l* in i. 3. 1.⌋

23. I have called up life-time unto life-time, unto ability (*krátu*), unto dexterity, unto life; let thy mind go to its own ⌊pl.⌋; then run unto the Fathers.

The majority of our mss. (except Bs.s.m.R.Op.K. ⌊which have *svā́n*⌋; T. has *svā́ṁn*), and two of SPP's, read *svā́m* at beginning of **c**, as does also the comm., which supplies *tanum* for it to qualify. SPP. gives in **c–d** *máno ádhā*, and claims that all his authorities without exception read thus; our Bs. has *'dhā*, and if any of the other *saṁhitā*-mss. ⌊except O., which has *máno ádhā*⌋ do not agree with this, I have failed to note it.

24. Let nothing whatever of thy mind, nor of thy life (*ásu*), nor of thy members, nor of thy sap, nor of thy body, be left here.

The translation implies emendation of *mánas* to *mánasas*, as called for by the connection and by the meter. The Anukr. scans the verse as 6 + 8 : 10 = 24. Bs.E. have *tanvàḥ* in **c**. This verse, with 26 below, is used by Kāuç. (82. 29) in connection with gathering up the bones after cremation; with the same, and further with 3. 25–37, in connection (85. 26) with their interment. ⌊For its general purport, see Weber, *Sb.* 1894, p. 775, note 2.⌋

25. Let not the tree oppress thee, nor the great divine earth; having found a place (*loká*) among the Fathers, thrive (*edh*) thou among those whose king is Yama.

Only about half the mss. have at the end the true reading *yamárājasu* (which both editions give, as was proper); some of our *saṁhitā*-mss. (P.M.T.) accent *yama-rā́jasu*, and most of the *pada*-mss. have correspondingly, as two independent words, *yama : rā́ja∘su* (namely Bp.D.Kp., and two of SPP's); one (I.) has *yamárā́j-*. One or two (including our O.) give *bādhiṣṭhe* in **a**. TA. (in vi. 7. 2) has two corresponding verses: *mā́ tvā vṛkṣāú sám bādhiṣṭām mā́ mātā́ pṛthivi tvám : pitṝ́n hy átra gácchāsy édhāsaṁ yamarā́jye*, and *mā́ tvā vṛkṣāú sám bādhethām mā́ mātā́ pṛthivī́ mahī́ : vāivasvatáṁ hí gácchāsi yamarā́jye ví rājasi :* both are partly corrupt. According to Kāuç. (82. 32), the verse accompanies the deposit of the collected bone-relics "at the root of a tree." ⌊Baunack, ZDMG. l. 281, 284, understands *vánaspáti* at RV. v. 78. 5 and AV. xviii. 3. 70, as meaning, like *vṛkṣá* here, a tree used after the manner of a coffin. Curiously enough, *peṭikā* (Sāyaṇa's gloss for *vanaspati*) usually means κόφινος.⌋ ⌊For consistency, the Berlin ed. should read *vittvā́t-*.⌋

26. What limb of thine is put over at a distance, and what expiration [or] breath has gone forth upon the wind (?), let the associated (*sánīḍa*) Fathers, assembling, make that enter thee again, bit (*ghāsá*) from bit.

With the first half-verse is to be compared vii. 53. 3 **a**, **b**. All the *saṁhitā*-mss. in **b** accent *vā́te*, save one of SPP's, *sec. manu*; and all our *pada*-mss. divide *vā́ : te*, as if, after all, they thought *vā : te* intended. SPP's *pada*-mss. also divide *vā́ : te* (only one of them is accented); he adopts *vā te*, on the authority of the one altered ms. ⌊and the comm.⌋. To me *vā́te* seems rather the preferable reading, though there is not much to choose between the two. Our O. and two or three of SPP's authorities give *páretāḥ* ⌊plural: but no *pada*-ms. has *yé* to correspond⌋. Several of our mss., and the decided majority of SPP's authorities (except the *pada*-authorities: which, as he fails to report them, presumably have *-ḍāḥ*) read *sánīḍād gh-*; but of our *pada*-mss., all but one ⌊Op.s.m.⌋ give *sá∘nīḍāḥ*, and this SPP. adopts in his text, as do we. The comm. has *sanīlās*; in **b**, he reads *ye . . . paretāḥ*. The use of the verse with vs. 24 in Kāuç. was stated under vs. 24.

27. The living have excluded this man from their houses; carry ye him out, forth from this village; death was the kindly messenger of Yama; he made his life-breaths (*ásu*) go to the Fathers.

The verse is used in Kāuç. (80. 18) with an oblation to the fires, when preparing the body of the deceased for cremation. ⌊Note that the "messengers" or "men" of death or of Yama play a rôle in the Buddhist literature: see Aṅguttara Nikāya, iii. 4 (35: p. 138), Devadūta Vagga; Jātaka, i., p. 138[24], and scholion; Journal of the Pāli Text Society, 1885, p. 62.⌋

28. What barbarians (*dásyu*), having entered among the Fathers, having faces of acquaintances, go about, eating what is not sacrificed, who bear *parāpúr* [and] *nipúr*— Agni shall blast (*dham*) them forth from this sacrifice.

Similar verses are found in VS. (ii. 30), ÇÇS. (iv. 4. 2), AÇS. (ii. 6. 2), MB. (ii. 3. 4), and Āp. (three varying versions at i. 8. 7). Āp. has in its first version for **a**, **b** *apa yantv asurāḥ pitṛrūpā ye rūpāṇi pratimucyā 'caranti*, a close analogue to our first half-verse; the rest ⌊including of Āp. only the second version⌋ have, without variant, *yé rūpā́ṇi pratimuñcámānā ásurāḥ sántaḥ svadháyā cáranti*, which is not quite so near. ⌊The third version in Āp. is *ye jñātīnām pratirūpāḥ pitṝn māyayā 'surāḥ praviṣṭāḥ*.⌋ In **c**, all the texts ⌊including the three versions in Āp.⌋ agree with ours. For **d**, all the texts ⌊including the first two versions in Āp.⌋ have *agníṣ ṭā́n lokā́t prá ṇudāty* (AÇS. *-dātv*, MB. *-datv*) *asmā́t;* ⌊while the third version in Āp. reads *agne tān asmāt praṇudasva lokāt*⌋. The comm. to VS. explains *parāpúras* as *sthūladehān* and *nipúras* as *sūkṣmadehān*, which is, of course, the purest nonsense; that to MB. divides *parā puro ni puro ye bharanti*, and connects the prepositions with the verb, rendering the first *puras* by "our enemies' houses" and the second by "our kindred's houses"—quite as bad. Our comm., finally, explains *parāpúras* (through *parā pṛṇanti*) as *piṇḍadātāraḥ putrāḥ*, and *nipúras* (through *niprṇanti* ⌊cf. his remark about *ni-pṛ* reported at the end of note to vs. 30⌋) as *pāutrāḥ*—if possible, worse than either of the others. All we can see clearly is that the native exegetes are quite as much in the dark as we with regard to the value of these obscure words. Except O.R., all our mss. have the false accent *dasyávas* in **a**; of SPP's, only two do so. Of the mss. in our hands at the time of printing of the text, only I. accented *jñātimukhās* at all (two of SPP's also leave it accentless), and we accordingly emended to *jñātímukhās*, according to the usual rule for such a compound; but I.O.Op.R.K., with the majority of SPP's authorities, read *jñātimukhā́s*, which SPP. has therefore properly adopted in his edition. By Kāuç. (87. 30) the verse is prescribed to be repeated while a lighted brand is carried three times about and then flung away.

29. Let there enter together (*sam-viç*) here our own Fathers, doing what is pleasant, lengthening [our] life-time; may we be able to reach them with oblation, living long for numerous autumns.

The translation implies in **a** the *pada*-reading *svā́ḥ : naḥ*, which SPP. gives by emendation, all the *pada*-mss. save Bp. (which has *svā́ : naḥ*) having *svā́naḥ;* again, it implies in **b** *pra°tiránta̱ḥ*, while all read *pra°tiránte* ⌊or *-ate*⌋; here also SPP. emends to *-ntaḥ*. The comm. reads *-nte*, and glosses it by *pravardhayantu!* ⌊A similar uncertainty (as between the Vulgate and Ppp.) concerning the understanding of the combination *pratiranta āyuḥ* was noted by me under xiv. 2. 36.⌋ The verse is used, according to Kāuç. (83. 29), next after the use of I. 52, in arranging the bones for burial; and it is repeated, like the latter, in the *piṇḍapitryajña* (87. 28); *sam-viç*, as here applied, perhaps has its secondary sense of 'turn in, lie down.' The comm. reads *dakṣamāṇās* in **c**, explaining it by *vardhamānās*. The Anukr. does not notice the redundant syllable in **c** ⌊or perhaps assumes a deficiency in **d** to balance it. The word *nakṣ-* demands an accusative: so that both meter and syntax combine to cast suspicion on *tebhyas*⌋.

30. What milch-cow I set down (*ni-pṛ*) for thee, and what rice-dish for thee in milk (*kṣīrá*)—with that mayest thou be the supporter of the person (*jána*) who is there (*átra*) without a living.

That is, 'without the means of sustaining life.' Our Bp.E. read *ajīvanas*, unaccented; the normal accent would be *ajīvanás*. The comm. remarks that *ni-pṛ* is used distinctively of a gift for the Fathers (*pitrye dāne vartate*).

31. Pass forward [over a stream] rich in horses, which is very propitious, or, further on, an *ṛkṣáka*, more new; he who slew thee, be he one to be killed; let him not find any other portion.

The first half-verse is extremely obscure, and its translation only mechanical; we may conjecture that its text is corrupt. Such a combination as *-vā : ṛkṣ-* (so all the *pada*-texts read) into *-vā ṛkṣ-* is contrary to grammatical rule, unauthorized by the Prāt., and unsupported, so far as I know, by any second case. Part of our *saṁhitā*-mss. (P.M.E.I.) have *-vā ṛkṣ-*, but that is equally abnormal; SPP. makes no mention of any such reading among his authorities. "Stream" is supplied to *açvāvatīm* because Kāuç. (82. 10) prescribes the verse to be used, in the ceremonies of the first day after cremation, on crossing a stream, and *prá tara* naturally suggests it. *Ā́çvāvatīm* is unquestionably the AV. text; it is quoted as an example of long *ā* in such a position under Prāt. iii. 17. One may conjecture as a plausible emendation *áçmanvatīm prá tarayā suçévām* (cf. for *áçmanvatī* xii. 2. 26, 27; and our comm. reads here *taraya* for *tara yā́*). Then *ṛkṣā́ka* might possibly be a region or road ⌊beyond the river⌋ 'infested by bears' (*ṛ́kṣa :* so the comm.); the word *ṛkṣā́ka* is ignored by both Pet. Lexx. ⌊save in so far as this vs. is cited by the Major Lex. under *ṛkṣī́kā*⌋. ⌊Weber takes it as 'the milky way': *Festgruss an Roth*, p. 138.⌋ But it is of little use to speculate in such a case. SPP. reads in **c** *vadhyas*, with (as he reports) all his authorities save two; we also have both *va-* and *ba-* among our mss., but I cannot specify all that favor the one reading or the other. The lacking syllable in **b**, not noticed by the Anukr., helps in its degree to indicate corruption of text.

32. Yama beyond, below Vivasvant — beyond that do I see nothing whatever; into Yama has entered my sacrifice; Vivasvant stretched after the worlds (*bhū́*).

SPP. accents *páras* in **a**, and *vívasvān* in **a** and **d**, though the majority of his authorities have *parás*, and, in **a**, *vivásvān;* of our mss., only Op. has *páras* and in **a** *vívasvān;* but O.Op.R.T.K. have *vívasvān* in **d**. The Anukr. takes no notice of the metrical irregularities (10 + 12 : 11 + 11 = 44).

33. They hid away the immortal one (f.) from mortals; having made one of like color, they gave her to Vivasvant; what that was carried also the two Açvins; and Saraṇyū deserted two twins.

Whether 'two pairs of twins' is meant is not altogether certain; but that would be strictly *dvé mithuné;* ⌊but see BR. v. 777, line 3⌋. The verb *abharat* does not mean 'bore,' in the sense of 'gave birth to,' though it might mean 'carried [in her womb],' and so might have a nearly equivalent value; our comm. renders it by *samabharat* or *udapādayat*. The third pāda means 'that substitute, whatever it really was,' though the usual version "when that was" (for *yát tád ā́sīt*) is not altogether impossible. The verse is RV. x. 17. 2, which differs only by reading in **b** *kṛtvī́* and *adadus* (for which our *-dhus* is a common corruption). It is properly inseparable from 1. 53 above; ⌊for bibliographical references, see under that vs.⌋. Kāuç. and Vāit. pass it unused, as they did 1. 53. ⌊The comm., with one or two of SPP's mss., reads *amṛtān* in **a**.⌋

34. They that are buried, and they that are scattered (*vap*) away, they that are burned and they that are set up (*úddhita*) — all those Fathers, O Agni, bring thou to eat the oblation.

Āp. (in i. 8. 7) has a verse analogous with this; the divisions there are ⌊*ye garbhe mamrus,*⌋ *parāstās, uddhatās*, and *nikhātās*. The comm. explains *paroptās* by *dūradeçe kāṣṭhavat parityaktāḥ;* but *uddhitās* by *saṁskārottarakālam ūrdhvadeçe pitṛloke sthitāḥ!* it evidently refers to exposure on something elevated, such as is practised by many peoples. The *pada*-text reads *úddhitāḥ*, undivided, by Prāt. iv. 63. The verse (according to Kāuç. 87. 22) is used, with 3. 47, 48 and 4. 41, in the *piṇḍapitṛyajña* ceremony, to accompany the setting up of one of two lighted sticks (cf. under 1. 56) and piling fuel around it.

35. They who, burned with fire, [and] who, not burned with fire, revel on *svadhā́* in the midst of heaven — them thou knowest, if thine, O Jātavedas; let them enjoy with *svadhā́* the sacrifice, the *svádhiti*.

The verse corresponds to RV. x. 15. 14 **a**, **b** and 13 **c**, **d** (and to VS. xix. 60 **a**, **b** and 67 **c**, **d**). In the first half, AV. and RV. agree (two of our mss., O.R., combine *yé 'nag-*); VS. has *-ṣvāttās* both times for *-dagdhās*. For **c**, RV. and VS. read *tvám vettha yáti té jāt-* 'thou knowest how many they are,' and of this our text is doubtless a corruption. Nearly half the mss. have *te* (both editions, with the remaining mss., including our O.R.T.K., *té*); the translation implies *te*. HGS. (ii. 11. 1) has *agne tān vettha yadi te jātavedaḥ*. For **d**, RV. and VS. have *svadhā́bhir yajñám súkṛtaṁ juṣasva;* and here again our text seems only a corruption; *svádhitim* (p. *svá○dhitim*) must be meant as *nomen actionis* to *svadhā́*, I think, = 'the giving of *svadhā́*' — a false formation. The comm. reads *svadhāyās* and *svadhitam*, explaining the latter as *svadhā saṁjātā yasya*. According to the comm., this verse and the preceding are used in the *piṇḍapitṛyajña* "on laying two pieces of fuel."

36. Burn (*tap*) thou propitiously (*çám*); do not burn overmuch; O Agni, do not burn the body; be thy vehemence (*çúṣma*) in the woods; on the earth be what is thy violence (*háras*).

Two of our mss. (R.s.m.Op.), and one of SPP's reciters, leave *tapas* at end of **b** unaccented; and this is, of course, more correct. For the application of the verse according to Kāuç., see under 2. 4, with which it is closely akin in sense. ⌊The comm. reads *tanvas* in **b**.⌋

37. I give this release to him who hath thus come and hath become mine here — thus replies the knowing Yama — let this one approach (*upa-sthā*) my wealth here.

The translation implies that *rāyá* before *úpa* in **d** means *rāyás* (accus. pl.), and not *rāyé*, as understood by the *pada*-text; the comm. understands *rāyas*. Also, that *céd* in **b** admits of being taken as *ca íd* ⌊the *pada*-text always reads *ca : ít*, even when the meaning is 'if'⌋ with individual meaning, and not as the compound particle, = 'if.' ⌊There is a gap in the commentary just after the explanation of *etat:* but the commentator's text of the AV.⌋ reads *yát* for *yás* at beginning of **b**. For the Kāuç. use of the verse with 1. 55, see under the latter. This verse also accompanies (with 3. 73: Kāuç. 85. 24) the deposition of the bones in the hole in the ceremony of interment.

38. This measure do we measure, so that one may not measure further; in a hundred autumns, not before.

That is, that there be no more such measuring for any of us till his hundred years of life are full. The comm. understands *yáthā ná mā́sātāi* ⌊*Gram.* § 893 a⌋ as *yathā mā*

⌊= *mām*⌋ *nā "sātāi, nā "sīta, na prāpnuyāt!* Kāuç. uses the verse twice (85. 3, 12 — unless in the *ce 'mām* of sūtra three is disguised the beginning of vs. 39 or 41) in connection with the elaborate measuring out of the place of interment of the bone-relics. ⌊See Caland, *Todtengebräuche*, p. 145 and note 534.⌋

39. This measure do we measure forth, so that etc. etc.
40. This measure do we measure off, so that etc. etc.
41. This measure do we measure apart, so that etc. etc.
42. This measure do we measure out, so that etc. etc.
43. This measure do we measure up, so that etc. etc.
44. This measure do we measure together, so that etc. etc.

The comm. regards all these *paryāya*-variations of vs. 38 as to be used with it where it is prescribed; the Kāuç. says nothing of this. The comm. also gives artificial and absurd interpretations of the altered prepositions at the beginnings of the verses. ⌊Some of the alterations spoil the meter (p. 830, ¶ 4).⌋

45. I have measured the measure, I have gone to heaven (*svàr*); may I be long-lived; so that etc. etc.

⌊The prior half of the verse appears to be prose.⌋ The Anukr. scans 8 + 6 : 8 + 8 = 30 syllables. This verse (according to the comm., vss. 45–47) follows the process of measurement (Kāuç. 85. 17).

46. Breath, expiration, through-breathing (*vyānā́*), life-time, an eye to see the sun: by a road not beset with enemies (*-pára*) go thou to the Fathers whose king is Yama.

The comm. explains: *mukhanāsikābhyām bahir niḥsaran vāyuḥ prāṇaḥ: antargacchann apānaḥ: madhyasthaḥ sann açitapītādikaṁ vividham āniti kṛtsnadehaṁ vyāpayatī 'ti vyānaḥ.* It foolishly understands *yamárājñas* in **d** as gen. sing.: (the road) "of king Yama." The Pet. Lexx. render *áparipara* by 'not roundabout,' as if the final *para* were somehow also a *pari;* the comm. understands the word nearly as above translated; ⌊and the translation is supported by VS. iv. 34⌋. The Prāt. (iv. 39 c) notes the division *vi°ānáḥ* in *pada*-text, while *prāṇá* and *apāná* are always undivided.

47. They that departed unmarried [but] assiduous, abandoning hatreds, having no progeny — they, going up to heaven (*dív*), have found a place (*loká*), ⌊they,⌋ shining (?*dī́dhyāna*) upon the back of the firmament.

The comm. commits the absurdity of glossing *agru* by *agragāmin*, and *çaçamāná* ('assiduous': i.e. having faithfully performed their religious duties) by *çaṅsamāna* or else (from root *çaç* 'leap') *plutagamanaçīla!* It seems hardly possible to avoid taking *dīdhyāna* in **d** as meant for *dīdyāna;* the comm. renders by *dīpyamāna*. The mss. vary between *agrávas* and *ágravas*, none of ours that were collated before publication having the latter, which is the true accent ⌊correct the Berlin ed.⌋, and is adopted by SPP. on the authority of a majority of his authorities (with which our O.Op.R.T. agree).

48. Watery is the lowest heaven (*dív*), full of stars (?*pīlu-*) is called the midmost; the third is called the fore-heaven (*pradív*), in which the Fathers sit.

Rather than leave *pīlu-* in **b** untranslated, we set in our version the comm's worthless etymological guess (*pālayantī 'ti pīlavaḥ : grahanakṣatrādayaḥ*). SPP. has at the beginning the better accent *udanvátī*, as read by half his authorities (and by our O.Op.R. among those collated after publication). Our Bp.D. accent also *pīlumatī́;* O. reads *pītúmatī*, doubtless an accidental blunder, yet suggesting the emendation *pitumátī* 'rich in nourishment.' For the use of the verse prescribed by Kāuç., see under I. 61; the comm. says simply that with this verse and another one (*iti dvābhyām*) the body is raised in order to being laid on the cart or litter (for transportation to the funeral pile); a schol. (note to Kāuç. 82. 31) uses it also in connection with the interment of the bone-relics.

49. They that are our father's fathers, that are [his] grandfathers, that entered the wide atmosphere, they that dwell upon earth and heaven (*dív*) — to those Fathers would we pay worship with homage.

The first half-verse is found again below as 3. 59 **a**, **b**. The verse is used (Kāuç. 81. 37) ⌊as the last one of eleven verses (see my note to xviii. I. 49) which accompany the oblations offered to Yama and poured upon the corpse (comm., vol. iv., p. 115[17]: he says *iti dvābhyām*) in the cremation ceremony after the fire is lighted⌋.

50. This time, verily, not further (*áparam*), seest thou the sun in the heaven (*dív*); as a mother her son with her hem (*síc*), do thou cover him, O earth.

The last half-verse is RV. x. 18. 11 **c**, **d**, without variant (TA., in vi. 7. 1, has at the end *bhūmi vṛṇu*), and is also found below as 3. 50 **c**, **d**. Kāuç. (86. 10) applies the verse, with 3. 49 and 4. 66, in raising a pile over the interred bones; according to the comm. ⌊vol. iv., p. 115⌋, the pile is of an uneven number of sticks (*çalākā*) or bricks, and vss. 50–52 are to be used. ⌊Over "hem" W. interlines "skirt." "Border of the garment" says our comm., *celāñcalena.*⌋ ⌊As to this beautiful verse, see Weber, *Sb.* 1895, p. 861, and cf. the epilogue to the Īça Upanishad, especially vss. 15, 16.⌋

51. This time, verily; not further; in old age another further than this; as a wife her husband with her garment, do thou cover him, O earth (*bhū́mi*).

The first half-verse is very obscure, and the second pāda perhaps corrupt. The comm. takes *jarási* with the first pāda, and explains that "what food etc. has been enjoyed in old age, this verily, left over, not anything else [further], is to be enjoyed"; and then "than this place of interment, any other place is not found for him": all of which is simply silly. The Anukr. pays no attention to the redundant syllable (unless we pronounce *patim 'va*) in **c**.

52. I cover thee excellently with the garment of mother earth; what is excellent among the living, that with me; *svadhā́* among the Fathers, that with thee.

The comm. does not scruple to take *bhadráyā* as used for *bhadrāyās*, and qualifying *pṛthivyā́s*. ⌊He treats *tā́n máyi* etc. as at xi. 7. 5, 12, 14: cf. note to xi. 7. 12. Weber thinks this vs. is spoken by the heir of the dead man.⌋

53. O Agni-and-Soma, makers of roads, ye have distributed (*vi-dhā*) to the gods a pleasant treasure [and] world; send ye unto [us] Pūshan, who shall carry by goat-traveled roads him that goes thither.

The translation implies emendation at the end of *gachatam* to *gáchantam*, which seems necessary in order to make sense; the corruption to the former may have been made because it better suits the meter.—⌊The translation also implies the reading *préṣyatam*, which is given in the Berlin text and is supported by⌋ our Op. (*prá : iṣyatam*), by SPP's ⌊Cp. (*prá : īṣyatam*) and by his⌋ Dc. secunda manu: all the rest read *préṣyantam* (p. *prá : iṣ-* or *prá : īṣ-*), which SPP. accordingly adopts in his *saṁhitā*-text; ⌊but in his *pada*-text he prints *prá : īṣyantam*, and he mentions the accent in his note⌋. The comm. glosses *preṣyantam* with *pragacchantam* in his usual loose and easy way.—Nearly all our mss. also have *ajoyā̀nāis* (p. *ajaḥ॰y-*) in **d**; we followed Bs. in giving *ajay-* (which the translation implies). ⌊Weber also accepts the reading *ajay-* and interprets it as 'traveled by man's unborn (*a-ja*) or immortal part, i.e. his spirit': *Festgruss an Roth*, p. 138 and note 5.⌋ On the authority of a single ms., SPP. accepts as his reading *añjoyā̀nāis*; ⌊as to this matter, see my note marked with a * in the next paragraph⌋. The reading *añjoyā̀nāis* had already been conjectured by the Pet. Lexx.; ⌊so BR. v. 959, with the meaning 'leading straight to the goal': cf. OB. i. 18 b⌋. The reading *añjay-* is given by two or three of SPP's mss.; among them is that of the comm., who explains by *añjasā, ārjavena yānti . . . ebhiḥ*. The "goat-traveled" roads, of course, are those to which Pūṣan's team of goats are wonted.—Two of SPP's authorities give *dadhatus* in **b**; the comm. reads *dadhatus* in one of two alternative explanations, and *-thus* in the other.—Possibly *ví* before *lokám* is to be taken as belonging to this word alone: 'ye have assigned to the gods a pleasant treasure.' ⌊I do not see what W. means by the last sentence.⌋—For the use of the verse by Kāuç. etc., see under 1. 61 and 2. 48; the comm. includes with it vss. 54 and 55. It exceeds a proper *triṣṭubh* by two syllables.

* ⌊In reading *añjoyā̀nāis*, SPP. is supported in fact by three or four of his mss. (B.C.R.Dc.p.m.) and presumably also by at least three of his *pada*-mss., since he reports nothing to the contrary. Moreover, he thinks that further support is given him by the reading *añjāy-* of two of his authorities (Dc. sec. manu, and the reciter V.), which reading, as he says, may represent an ill-corrected reading *añjoy-*; and perhaps the *ajāuy-* of the reciter K. points in the same direction, to *añjoy-*. As between the readings *añjoy-* and *ajay-*, even Whitney's mss. point decidedly to *añjoy-*.—Leaving the mss. of this passage out of account, however, the word *añjoyā̀na* is well supported by its exact synonym *añjasā̀yana*, p. *añjasā॰dyana*, used four times of the paths (*srutí*) by which one goes to the heavenly world (TS. vii. 2. 1[2]; 3. 5[3]; 4. 1[3]: also AB. iv. 17, here as the exact opposite of a 'roundabout road' *mahāpathaḥ paryāṇaḥ*), and also by the doubtless precisely equivalent *añjasī̀nām* (*srutím*) of the Rigveda (x. 32. 7).—This last phrase Sāyaṇa explains alternatively by *ṛjum akuṭilam mārgam*; cf. his similar explanation of *pathó devatrā̀ 'ñjase 'va yā̀nān* at x. 73. 7; cf. also *añjasāyano*, used in the Dīgha Nikāya, xiii. 4 ff., as a synonym of *uju-maggo*: all of which is in most perfect accord with the above-mentioned *ārjavena* etc. of our comm., whose testimony therefore is decidedly in favor of the reading *añjoyā̀nāis*.—If *añjoy-* is the true reading and *ajay-* the corrupt one, the corruption is a very natural one, considering that Pūṣan's team (see RV. vi. 55. 6, 4; 57. 3; x. 26. 8; and the occurrences of *ajā̀çva*) consists of goats.⌋

54. Let Pūshan, knowing, urge thee forth from here — he, the shepherd of creation (*bhúvana*) who loses no cattle; may he commit thee to those Fathers, [and] Agni to the beneficent gods.

The RV. has a corresponding verse (x. 17. 3), without variant. TA. (in vi. 1. 1) has in **c** *dadāt* (as has our comm.), and at the end *suvidátrebhyas*. The mss. are somewhat equally divided in **c–d** between *-bhyo 'gnír* and *-bhyo agnír;* our text adopts the latter; SPP., better, the former, with RV. and TA.

55. May life-time, having all life-time, protect thee about; let Pūshan protect thee in front on the forward road; where sit the well-doers, whither they have gone, there let god Savitar set thee.

RV., in the corresponding verse (x. 17. 4), reads *pāsati* in **a**, and *té yayús* at end of **c**, ⌊thus rectifying the meter in both places⌋; and TA. (in vi. 1. 2) agrees with it both times; the comm. also has *pāsati.* The verse is metrically irregular (10 + 11 : 12 + 11 = 44); ⌊but perfectly good in its RV. form (11 + 11 : 12 + 11)⌋.

56. I yoke for thee these two conveyers ⌊*váhni*⌋, to convey (*vah*) thee to the other life; with them to Yama's seat and to the assemblies go thou down (*áva*).

Ava, in **d**, is so strange that we can only regard it as a corruption for *ápi*, which TA. reads in the corresponding verse (in vi. 1. 1). TA. also has the better reading *-nīthāya* in **b** ⌊so both editions⌋, as has also the comm., though its explanation seems rather to imply *-nītāya*. TA. further has the bad accent *vahnī́* in **a**, and gives in **c** *yā́bhyām*, and in **d** (for *sámitīs*) *sukṛ́tām*. The comm. has *sam iti*, taking *sam* as joint prefix with *ava*, and *iti* as *anena prakāreṇa;* our Bp.E. read *sámitī ca;* possibly the comm's error is akin with this. According to Kāuç. (80. 34), the verse is used when two draft-oxen, or two men, are harnessed to draw the body to the funeral pile.

57. This garment hath now come first to thee; remove (*apa-ūh*) that one which thou didst wear here before; knowing, do thou follow along with what is offered and bestowed, where it is given thee variously among them of various connection (?*víbandhu*).

TA. (in vi. 1. 1) has a corresponding verse, but with sundry variants: at the beginning, *idáṁ* (which is better) *tvā vástram;* in **c**, **d**, *ánu sáṁ paçya dákṣiṇāṁ yáthā te*. *Te dattám* is perhaps better 'given by thee' — thy former deeds of religion and charity, now to be enjoyed in their fruit; and *víbandhu* 'to those not thine own connections.' The Pet. Lexx. explain *víbandhuṣu* as 'destitute of connections or relatives.' The comm., with its customary regardlessness of accent, understands the word as two words, *vi bandhuṣu*, and connects *vi* (= *viçeṣeṇa*) with *dattam*. According to Kāuç. 80. 17, the verse is used, with 4. 31, in connection with dressing the body for cremation; in 81. 29, some of the mss. substitute it for vs. 22 above. Some of the schol. (note to Kāuç. 80. 52) use it and 4. 31 when the body is laid on the funeral pile. The verse, as a *triṣṭubh*, is rather *svarāj* than *bhurij* (11 + 12 : 11 + 12 = 46).

58. Wrap about thee of kine a protection from the fire; cover thyself up with grease and fatness, lest the bold one, exulting with violence (*háras*), shake thee strongly (*dadṛ́h*) about, intending to consume thee.

The corresponding RV. verse is x. 16. 7; in **b** it transposes *médasā* and *pī́vasā*, and in **d** it has *vidhakṣyán paryañkháyāte*, which is decidedly better. TA. (in vi. 1. 4) reads *dádhad vidhakṣyán paryañkháyātāi*. Our *vidhakṣán*, though read by both editions, is only another example of the not infrequent careless omission of *y* after a *ṣ* or *ç*; only one of our mss. (Op.) reads *-kṣyán*, but five of SPP's authorities give *-kṣyan* (as against six with *-kṣan*), and it is much to be wondered at that he has not adopted it in his text; the comm. seems to read *-kṣan*, but explains as if *-kṣyan* (*viçeṣeṇa dagdhum icchan*). At the end we ought to read *parīñkháyātāi*, and SPP. gives that, with the majority of his mss., the rest having, with our text, *párīñkhay-*; of our mss., only two of the later collated ones (O.Op.) have the proper accent; Bp. has *pári॰īñkhayātāi*, which is absurd *; the comm. treats *pari* as an independent word (as if the reading were *párī "ñkháyātāi*). The comm. glosses *dadhṛ́k* by *pragalbhas;* ⌊cf. my *Noun-Inflection*, JAOS. x. 498⌋. By Kāuç. (81. 25) the verse is taught to be used when the dead man's face is covered with the omentum of the *anustaraṇī* cow (hence 'of kine') on the pile; the omentum is to be pierced with seven holes. *⌊Cf. the impossible *pada*-reading *vi॰bhāti* at xiii. 3. 17, and the other similar ones cited in the note to that verse.⌋

59. Taking the staff from the hand of the deceased man (*gatásu*), together with hearing, splendor, strength — thou just there, here may we, rich in heroes, conquer all scorners [and] evil plotters.

60. Taking the bow from the hand of the dead man, together with authority (*kṣatrá*), splendor, strength — take thou hold upon much prosperous good; come thou hitherward unto the world of the living.

The two verses together correspond to RV. x. 18. 9, our 60 **a, b** most nearly to 9 **a, b**, and our 59 **c, d** to 9 **c, d**. But RV. has for its **b** *asmé kṣatrā́ya várcase bálāya*, and in its **d** *spṛ́dhas* for *mṛ́dhas*. TA. (in vi. 1. 3) has three verses, with **a–b** respectively as follows: *suvárṇaṁ hástād ādádānā mṛtásya çriyāí bráhmaṇe téjase bálāya; dhánur hástād ādádānā mṛtásya çriyāí kṣatrā́yāú 'jase bálāya;* and *máṇiṁ hástād ādádānā mṛtásya çriyāí viçé púṣṭyāi bálāya;* their common second half agrees with RV. except in having *suçévās* for *suvī́rās;* they are addressed to Brahman, Kshatriya and Vāiçya respectively, as our two are addressed to Brahman and Kshatriya, and that of RV. to Kshatriya only. 'Hearing' in our 59 **b** has a special meaning, the hearing or inspired reception of the sacred word ⌊cf. i. 1. 2, and note⌋. Kāuç. 80. 48, 49 explains the two verses as uttered while staff or bow is taken from the dead hand, as the body lies on the pile ready for cremation; and 80. 50 implies a third verse addressed to a Vāiçya, on taking from him a goad (*aṣṭrām*). Our 60 **c, d** is evidently addressed to the person (the son) who removes the article. The comm. reads in 59 **c** (with TA.) *suçevās*.

⌊Here ends the second *anuvāka*, with 1 hymn and 60 verses. The quoted Anukr. says *ṣaṣṭiç ca:* cf. page 814, ¶ 5.⌋

⌊Here ends also the thirty-third *prapāṭhaka*.⌋

3. ⌊Funeral verses.⌋

[*Atharvan.— saptatis tryadhikā. yamadevatyam mantroktabahudevatyaṁ ca* (*5, 6. āgneyyāu; 44, 46. mantroktadevatye; 50. bhāumī; 54. āindavī; 56. āpyā*). *trāiṣṭubham: 4, 8, 11, 23. satahpañkti; 5. 3-p. nicṛd gāyatrī; 6, 56, 68, 70, 72. anuṣṭubh; 18, 25–29, 44, 46. jagatī* (*18. bhurij; 29. virāj*)*; *30. 5-p. atijagatī; 31. virāṭ çakvarī; 32–35, 47, 49, 52. bhurij; 36. 1-av. āsury anuṣṭubh; 37. 1-av. āsurī gāyatrī; 39. parātriṣṭup pañkti; 50. prastārapañkti; 54. puro'nuṣṭubh; 58. virāj; 60. 3-av. 6-p. jagatī; 64. bhurik pathyāpañkty ārṣī; 67. pathyā bṛhatī; 69, 71. upariṣṭādbṛhatī.*]

*⌊The Anukr. (the text of which is perhaps in disorder at this point) reads *añjate vyañjata* (vs. 18) *indro mā marutvān iti pañca* (vss. 25–29) *jagatyas: tatrāi 'kādhikā* (?) *bhurig antyā* (vs. 29) *virāṭ*. See under vss. 18 and 29.⌋

⌊The prose parts are the first pādas (the *ūha*-pādas) of vss. 25–28 and 30–35, and the *yajurmantras*, vss. 36–37: see Part III., below.⌋

⌊In Pāipp. (in xx.) is found of this hymn only verse 56.⌋

⌊Ritual uses. — Only eight verses (2, 5, 18, 25, 38, 39, 44, 45: the last two together twice, and both times in the order 45, 44) are used in Vāit., and, of course, in rites other than funeral rites: see under the verses. In Kāuç., about three quarters of the hymn (all but 21 vss.) are used, and used in the chapter (xi.: as noted by Whitney, page 814) on funeral rites: see under the verses. It is of critical interest that two blocks of verses (Parts II. and IV., as divided below, where see) which find no use in the funeral ritual, form each a nearly corresponding block in RV.⌋

⌊**The provenience of the material of this hymn.** — In this hymn, as compared with hymn 2 (see p. 830), the proportional part of material recurring in the RV. rises again, and is about 33 verses out of 73, or nearly one half. — The "Parts" into which the hymn is here divided are primarily for the convenience of the discussion, although some of them (as II., III., IV., V., VI.) have also a critical significance.

Part I., verses 1–20. — This part contains only 3 verses (2, 6, 13) from the funeral hymns of the RV., and only 2 others (7, 18) from other parts thereof, parts widely separated. Of the last 7 vss. of this part, only vss. 17 and 18 find use in the Kāuçikan ritual.

Part II., verses 21–24. — This block of verses corresponds, without changes of order, to the last *varga* of the second Vāmadeva hymn, more precisely to RV. iv. 2. 16, 17, 18, and 19 **a**, **b**, to which is then appended the last half-verse of RV. ii. 23, with the Gṛtsamada refrain. Neither ritual makes any use whatever of any verse or pāda of this part.

Part III., verses 25–37. — This part consists of two six-membered sequences, **a** and **b** (**a** = the five verses, 25–29: **b** = the six verses, 30–35), each sequence with one member for each of the "six directions" (E., S., W., N., fixed, and upward); the whole followed by two *yajurmantras* (vss. 36–37: comm., p. 1584). — All the 11 verses of sequences **a** and **b** have the refrain *lokakṛtas* etc. (a *jagatī-triṣṭubh* half-verse) in common. Moreover, all those 11 verses (except one, namely vs. 29) have as their second pāda the obscure *jagatī*-pāda, *bāhucyútā pṛthivī́ dyā́m ivo 'pári;* and for their first pāda an *ūha*-pāda applying in turn to one or another of the six directions. — In the excepted verse (vs. 29: see my note below), it would seem as if two directions had been crowded into one verse, the 'fixed' into pāda **a** and the 'upward' into pāda **b**: if so, it is this condensation that has reduced sequence **a** from 6 verses to 5, and effected the displacement of the pāda *bāhucyútā* etc. — Thus the refrains of this part are all metrical (smooth *jagatī* or *triṣṭubh* pādas), as is also the first half of vs. 29; while the *ūha*-pādas are prose, as are also the *yajurmantras*. — Parts III. **a** and III. **b** look to me like antiphonal sequences (cf. the introduction to ii. 5), the verses of **a** containing the prayers that are worded as if uttered by the suppliant dead man, and the verses of **b** containing the responses* of his helper, very likely the dead man's eldest son (see my note to vs. 25: but just how they were used, of course, I cannot say). If I am right, vs. 34, reinforced by the first two clauses of 36, would answer to 29 **a**; and vs. 35 would answer to 29 **b**. But against my view is the fact that we have *tvā* in 29 **a** where we should expect *mā*. — *[After writing the above, I find that Weber, *Sb.* p. 265, had expressed a similar view as to the responsive structure, and had proposed to emend *tvā* to *mā*.]

Part IV., verses 38–41. — This again is a real unity in the RV., being the entire hymn RV. x. 13 except its last verse, the fifth, and except its vs. 1 **d**. The verses of this part, again like those of part II., find no use in the funeral ritual (although, indeed, Vāit. uses two of them in the *agniṣṭoma*). For the curious dislocation and misdivision of the material by AV., see p. 858, ¶ 10, and cf. ¶ 8 of this page.

Part V., verses 42–48. — Verses from the principal RV. hymn to the Fathers, x. 15, namely its vss. 12, 7, 11, 5, 8, 9, and 10, with much derangement of the RV. order.

Part VI., verses 49–52. — Burial-verses from RV. x. 18, to wit, vss. 10, 11, 12, 13, in strict RV. sequence.

Part VII., verses 53–60. — Eight verses, of which seven are from five of the RV. funeral hymns, x. 14, 15, 16, 17, 18 (represented in the order 16, 16, 17, 18 : 14, 15, 16), and of which the remaining one (our vs. 54) is without ritual use and plainly intrusive and doubtless put after our 53 on account of its striking surface-resemblances to our 53. Our vs. 60 is widely separated from its fellow, our vs. 6, as is noted under the verses.

Part VIII., verses 61–64. — Verses not elsewhere found, save, in part, in AV.ÇÇS.MB.

Part IX., verses 65–67. — Found in RV. outside the limits, x. 10 and x. 18, between which the funeral verses are massed, to wit, as RV. x. 8. 1 ; x. 123. 6 ; and vii. 32. 26.

Part X., verses 68–72. — This is an *anuṣṭubh* sequence, peculiar to our AV. text, and with only a couple of longer pādas (namely 69 **d**, *jagatī ;* 71 **d**, *triṣṭubh*).

Part XI., verse 73. — This is a *triṣṭubh* which looks as if it had been put here on account of superficial likenesses to its next following companion, vs. 1 of hymn 4. If this surmise is correct, we are to assume here a misdivision of their material by the makers of the *anuvāka*-divisions somewhat similar to that seen at RV. vii. 55. 1. Cf. the cases at AV. i. 20 (vs. 4) and 21, vi. 63 (vs. 4) and 64 : also at iv. 15. 11 and 12.⌋

Translated : Weber, *Sb.* 1896, pages 253–277 (with analysis, etc.) ; Griffith, ii. 236 ; verses not taken from the RV. are rendered by Ludwig, pages 484–487. — The RV. verses are translated, of course, by the RV. translators : the verses from RV. x. 18, in particular, by Whitney, *Oriental and Linguistic Studies*, i. 54, 53 (vs. 44 at p. 60 : and so on) ; RV. x. 18 also by Roth, in *Siebenzig Lieder des RV.*, p. 150.

1\. This woman, choosing her husband's world, lies down (*ni-pad*) by thee that art departed, O mortal, continuing to keep [her] ancient duty (*dhárma*) ; to her assign thou here progeny and property.

Verses 1–4 are translated and interpreted (I think, incorrectly) by Hillebrandt in ZDMG. xl. 708 ff. Kāuç. (80. 44) and the comm. declare that with this verse the wife is made to lie down beside her dead husband on the funeral pile. The comm. glosses *dharmam* with *sukṛtam*, and understands the sense of the pāda as it is translated above. The sense of **d** alone seems to indicate that the woman's action is nothing more than a show, expected to be followed by that of the next verse, since "progeny and property" are rewards for this life, not for the other. The comm. says it is meant for her next birth. TA. also has the verse (in vi. 1. 3), but reads for **c** *viçvam purāṇám ánu pāláyantī* — a very inferior text. Some of our mss. (O.Op.D.R.K.), and even the majority of SPP's, have in **c** *-pādáyantī*, but SPP. rightly accepts *-pālá-* ; ⌊cf. the phonetic relation of *udumbara* and *ulumbala*, above, 2. 13⌋.

2\. Go up, O woman, to the world of the living ; thou liest by (*upa-çī*) this one who is deceased : come ! to him who grasps thy hand, thy second spouse (*didhiṣú*), thou hast now entered into the relation of wife to husband.

The verse is RV. x. 18. 8, whose text differs only by reading in **c** *didhiṣós*, and this is given also by two of our mss. (R.D.) and the majority of SPP's, so that it certainly ought to be accepted as the true reading, *dadh-* being only a corruption. TA. (in vi. 1. 3) has *didhiṣós*, but after it *tvám etát*, and in **b** *itā́sum*, in neither case making any important change in the sense. ⌊TA., both text and comm. in both ed's, reads *abhí sámbabhūva:* the comm. renders by *ābhimukhyena samyak prāpnuhi!* which procedure gives a shock even to one who is wonted to the Hindu laxity of ideas about *vāiyadhikaraṇya.*⌋ The meaning given to *abhí sám-bhū* in the translation is decidedly the only admissible one; nor need one hesitate to render *didhiṣú* according to its later accepted meaning. The woman cannot be left free and independent; she can only be relieved of her former wifehood by taking up a new one (even if this be, as is probable enough, nominal only); he who grasps her hand to lead her down from the pile becomes, at least for the nonce, her husband. The direction of Kāuç. (80. 45) in connection with the verse is simply "one makes her rise"; the comm. ⌊vol. iv., p. 129, end⌋ specifies that this is done "if she desires to live in this world again"; neither tells who is to take her hand — as, for example, Āçvalāyana does (AGS. iv. 2. 18): "her husband's brother, a representative of her husband, a pupil [of her husband], or an aged servant." ⌊Whether the *levir* and the "representative" are the same person or two different ones does not appear from the translation nor from the original of AGS.⌋ Vāit. (38. 3) uses the verse in the *puruṣamedha.*

3. I saw the maiden being led, being led about, alive, for the dead; as she was enclosed with blind darkness, then I led her off-ward (*ápācī*) from in front (*prāktás*).

The translation of **b** implies, ⌊not the *jīvā́m ṛtébhyas* of the Berlin text, but rather⌋ the reading *jīvā́m mṛtébhyas:* this is accepted by SPP. and is supported by the majority of his authorities ⌊including two reciters⌋ and by the comm. and by some of our mss. collated later (O.Op.R.T.), ⌊and especially by the variant of TA., below⌋. ⌊Compare the cases of *yame dīrgham*, etc., discussed in the note to xviii. 2. 3.⌋ The version in TA. (vi. 12. 1) is better than ours in **a**, **b**: *ápaçyāma yuvatím ācárantīm mṛtā́ya jīvā́m pariṇīyámānām;* but not so good in **c**, **d**: *andhéna yā́ támasā prā́vṛtā́ 'si prā́cīm ávācīm áva yánn áriṣṭyāi.* According to Kāuç. (81. 20), vss. 3 and 4 are used as the cow (to serve as *anustaraṇī*) is led, at the funeral pile, around (the fires) leftwise; the comm. gives a corresponding explanation; and the comment to TA. also understands it of such a cow (*rājagavī*); ⌊cf. Caland, *Todtengebräuche*, p. 40⌋. It is very difficult to believe that this was the original meaning of the verse, and that it did not rather refer to some rescue from immolation of a young wife. The comm. paraphrases pāda **d** by *enāṁ gām pūrvadeçāt çavasamīpād apāñmukhīṁ çavāt parāñmukhīm asmadabhimukhīm prāpayāmi:* this is of no authority. Pāda **a** can be made full only by the unacceptable resolution *ápaçiam;* the TA. reading of the word would remove the difficulty.

4. Foreknowing, O inviolable one, the world of the living, moving together [with him] upon the road of the gods — this is thy herdsman (*gópati*); enjoy him; make him ascend to the heavenly (*svargá*) world.

There is no difficulty in understanding this of the *anustaraṇī* cow, with the *sūtras* and commentaries, although we should expect rather *pitṛlokám* in **a**, and *joṣaya* in **c**. ⌊By "*sūtras*" I suppose W. means *sūtra* 20 of Kāuç. 81 (cited under vs. 3) and *sūtra* 37 of Kāuç. 80 (cited under this vs.); and by "commentaries," the AV. comm. to vss. 3–4 (vol. iv., p. 1313) and the comm. to the TA. correspondent in vi. 12. 1 (Poona ed., p. 449) of our vs. 3.⌋ Besides the use of the verse with the one preceding, as explained under the latter, it again (Kāuç. 80. 37) accompanies the leading of a cow around fuel and fire; and the schol. (note to 81. 33) employ it further at the kindling of the pile. The verse lacks only one syllable of being a regular *triṣṭubh* (11 + 11 : 10 + 11 = 43).

5. Unto sky (*dív*), unto reed, more helpful of streams; O Agni, gall of the waters art thou.

The translation of **a** and **b** is purely mechanical. Other texts have a quite different version of them. VS. (xvii. 6 **a–c**) reads *úpa jmánn úpa vetasé 'vatara nadíṣv ā́;* MS. (in ii. 10. 1; but p. *ávataram*) the same (and the editor reports K. and Kap.S. as agreeing); TS. (in iv. 6. 1²) the same except *ávattaram;* VS. and MS. admit a much more intelligible rendering ('close to earth, close to reeds, descend thou in the streams'). In all the other texts, the verse is preceded by our vi. 106. 3 **a**, **b** and other similar addresses to Agni, in the *agnicayana* ceremony; and so also in Vāit. (29. 13), where the verses accompany the drawing of a frog, of the water-plant *avakā*, and of reeds, across the fire-site in all directions. In Kāuç. (82. 26), this verse and 3. 60 are used in the ceremony of gathering the bone-relics on the third day after cremation, with the direction *iti mantroktāny avadāya.* ⌊The authorities differ as to the day: Caland, *Todtengebräuche*, p. 99.⌋ The comm. explains ⌊vol. iv., p. 132¹⁵, p. 169²⁰⌋ that vss. 5 and 6 ⌊(cf. Ath. Paddhati cited in note to Kāuç. 82. 26)⌋ ⌊and 60⌋ are addressed to the plants mentioned in those verses ⌊and gives a list of plants: cf. SPP's note with extract from Keçava, and Bloomfield's note to 82. 26⌋. The comm. adds that the plants are used by the performer in besprinkling a Brahman's bones with milk. Under this verse the comm. makes *dyām* mean *avakām*, because this rises above the water without touching earth! The verse does not need to be scanned as *nicṛt.*

6. Whom thou, O Agni, didst consume, him do thou extinguish again; let there grow here the *kyā́mbū*, the *çāṇḍadūrvā́*, the *vyàlkaçā.*

RV. (x. 16. 13) has the same verse, but calls two of the plants *kiyā́mbu* and *pāka-dūrvā́*. *Vyàlkaçā* (p. *vi॰alkaçā*) might well be an adjective, 'free from *alkaça*' or the like, if we only knew what *alkaça* meant. ⌊W's Op.R. accent *vyalkaçā́:* and so five of SPP's authorities, against four with *vyàl-*.⌋ TA. disagrees with both AV. and RV. in reading at vi. 4. 1 *kyāmbū́s* ⌊both ed's⌋, but agrees with RV. in having *pākadūrvā́*, ⌊and with both ed's of AV. in accenting *vyàlkaçā*⌋; it reads *jāyatām* for *rohatu* in **c**, and *tvám* for *tám* in **b**. — The comm. explains *çāṇḍadūrvā* as *dūrvā* ('millet') that springs up near water, having egg-shaped roots, or that has long joints, and adds that it is called "big millet" (*bṛhaddūrvā*); but this is probably without authority. With as little reason he glosses *alka* by *çākhā* 'branch,' and declares *vyalkaça* to mean "furnished with various (*vividha*) branches"; ⌊so also the comm. on RV. and on TA.⌋. The verse is not directly quoted by Kāuç., but (as was pointed out above) it is regarded by the comm. ⌊and the Paddhati⌋ as included with vss. 5 and 60 in 82. 26, and probably with justice. — This verse and its successor in RV. and TA. (strangely removed to be 3. 60 in AV.) are both plainly intended as remedial and expiatory for the cruel office of Agni in burning a corpse; the fire is not only to be extinguished, but to be followed by its antithesis, the growth of water-plants and the appearance of their attendant frogs: compare Bloomfield in AJP. xi. 342–350 ⌊or JAOS. xv., p. xxxix⌋. ⌊This expiatory and remedial rite is avouched for antiquity by MBh. viii. 20. 50 = 819: *Pāṇḍyaḥ . . . svadhām* (= *pretaçarīrarūpaṁ haviḥ*) *ivā* "*pya jvalanaḥ pitṛpriyas* (= *çmaçānāgniḥ*) *tataḥ praçāntaḥ salilapravāhataḥ;* and a note to the P. C. Roy version of this passage, p. 65, says that it persists even to this day in India.⌋

7. Here is one for thee, beyond is one for thee; enter thou into union with the third light; at entrance be thou fair (*cā́ru*) with [thy] body, loved of the gods in the highest station.

The verse is RV. x. 56. 1, which reads in **c** *tanvàs*, and in **d** *janítre* (for *sadhásthe*). It is also found in SV. (i. 65), TB. (in iii. 7. 13), TA. (vi. 3. 1; 4. 2), and Āp. (ix. 1. 17); in **a**, TB.Āp. have *u* (for *ū* before *te*); in **c**, all have *saṁvéçanas*, while SV. gives *tanvè* and the others *tanúvāi;* in **d**, TB.Āp. read *priyé*, and SV.TB.Āp. agree with RV. in *janítre.* According to Kāuç. (80. 36), the verse accompanies the carrying of the fire at the head of the procession to the funeral pile; as the comm. states it, carrying the three fires, in the case of one who has established sacrificial fires. The three "lights" are thus understood to be the three sacrificial fires; but they are probably, in the original meaning of the verse, rather three regions of light, to the highest of which the deceased is to be translated.

8. Rise thou, go forth, run forth; make thee a home (*ókas*) in the sea [as] station; there do thou, in concord with the Fathers, revel with soma, with the *svadhā́s*.

The first half-verse is found also in TA. (in vi. 4. 2) which has the easier ending *paramé vyòman;* the second half of the TA. verse is our vi. 63. 3 **c**, **d**. The majority of our *saṁhitā*-mss. combine *dravó 'kaḥ* in **a–b**, but SPP. reports nothing of the kind from his authorities. The verse can be forced down to forty syllables (as a *pañkti*) by violence in **c**; ⌊its natural scansion is as 8 + 11 : 11 + 11⌋. It is one of the *utthāpanī* or 'uplifting' verses, which, with the *hariṇīs* or 'taking' verses, are used more than once in Kāuç., and are cited in Vāit. (37. 23–24) and elsewhere, in connection with lifting and moving the corpse etc. This one accompanies (Kāuç. 80. 31) the raising of the corpse to carry it to the funeral pile, and later (80. 35), with 1. 61 and 3. 9 and others, the lifting on to the cart and removing; and yet later (82. 31) the gathering up and carrying away the bone-relics.

9. Start (*cyu*) forward, collect (*sam-bhṛ*) thy body; let not thy limbs (*gā́tra*) nor thy frame (*çárīra*) be left out; enter together after thy mind that has entered; wherever in the world thou enjoyest, thither go.

The first half-verse and the last pāda are found also, as parts of different verses, in TA. vi. 4. 2; which, however, reads *út tiṣṭhā́ 'tas tanúvaṁ sám bharasva mé 'há gā́tram áva hā mā́ çárīram*, and *yátra bhū́myāi vṛṇáse tátra gaccha.* Some of our mss. (P.M.O.R.T.K.) accent *ánu* in **c**; and some (all except O.Op.R.K., also two of SPP's) have *bhū́me* in **d**; the comm. reads *bhū́māu.* According to Kāuç. (80. 32), the dead body, after being raised (*utthāpay-*) with the preceding verse, is made three times to set forth (? *saṁhāpay-*; *sam-hā* means usually simply 'get up': it is added, "as many times as it is raised") with this one; and this verse is used again, with the preceding verse (under which see) and others, in 80. 35 and 82. 31.

10. Let the soma-drinking (*somyá*) Fathers anoint me with splendor, the gods with honey, with ghee; making me pass further on unto sight, let them increase me, attaining old age, unto old age.

Some of the mss. (including our D.R.p.m.T.) read *ájantu* in **b**; possibly it is their way of emending the false accent of *áñjantu;* doubtless we ought to change this to *añjántu* rather than to admit the modulated stem *áñja.* The *pratīka* (*varcasā mām*) applies either to this verse or to the next, or probably is used to include both; whatever it applies to is used, according to Kāuç. (81.47; 87.4), in connection with rinsing the mouth at the end of the cremation ceremony and at the beginning of the *piṇḍapitṛyajña;* and also (86.17), with 3.61–67, in the ceremony of interring the bones, in connection with supporting the *dhruvanas** on the north-west of the fire. The comm. takes notice of only the first of these three applications. *⌊Caland, WZKM. viii. 369, would read *dhuvanāny upayachante* at 86.16: I suppose he would render, 'they offer fannings [to the relics].' But are we sure that 86.17 goes with 86.16 and forms a part of the *dhuvana* ceremony? — Cf. my note to vs. 17 below. — The non-lingualization of the first *n* gives the strongest possible support for *dhuvanāni* as against *dhru-*.⌋

11. Let Agni anoint me completely with splendor; let Vishṇu anoint wisdom into my mouth; let all the gods fix wealth upon me; let pleasant waters purify me with purifiers.

The verse is, with resolution of *mā-am*, a regular *triṣṭubh*, and no *pañkti.* As to its ritual application, see under the preceding verse; the comm. regards it as sharing with that verse.

12. Mitra-and-Varuṇa have enclosed (*pari-dhā*) me; let the sacrificial posts of Aditi increase me; let Indra anoint splendor into my hands; let Savitar make me one attaining old age.

Most of our mss. (all except Op.R.), and half of SPP's, read at the beginning *mitrā-varuṇā* (Bp. *-ṇāu*), vocative, which might stand if we altered *adhātām* to *-thām;* both editions give *mitrā̆várunā*, ours by emendation. A variant for *svāravas* in **b** would be very welcome; the comm. gets rid of the difficulty in its characteristic way, by making the word an adjective to *ādityās*, and signifying either "making a pleasant sound" or "making a distress directed at our enemies"! The third pāda, if properly read, has a redundant syllable; but the Anukr. would apparently have us read *nyanaktu* in three syllables, as written. The Kāuç. uses the verse with washing the hands, at the end of the cremation ceremony (81.46), and at the beginning of the *piṇḍapitṛyajña* (87.3); the comm. notices only the latter of the two uses.

13. Him who died first of mortals, who went forth first to that world, Vivasvant's son, assembler of people, king Yama honor ye with oblation.

The second half-verse is identical with 1.49 **c**, **d**, and the first half is analogous with the same, **a**, **b** (= RV. x. 14. 1 etc.: see under 1.49). The verse is redundant by a syllable in ⌊the perfectly good *jagatī* pāda⌋ **d**. For its use by Kāuç., with 2.49, see under the latter; ⌊and especially my note to i. 49⌋. ⌊The verse is discussed by Hillebrandt, *Ved. Mythol.* i. 491.⌋

14. Go away, ye Fathers, and come; this sacrifice is all anointed with honey for you; both give to us here excellent property, and assign to us wealth having all heroes.

The second half-verse is found also in AÇS. (ii. 7.9) and MB. (ii. 3.5); both read at the end *ni yacchata*, and at the beginning MB. has *dattā 'sm-*, and AÇS. strangely *dattāyā 'sm-*. ⌊Our *pada*-texts read *dattó* (= *dattá u*) *íti:* see Prāt. i. 80.⌋ The translation implies that *drávine 'há* is for *drávinam ihá* (p. *drávinā : ihá*); the comm. glosses *drávinā* by *dravinam;* ⌊cf. my *Noun-Inflection*, p. 331, ¶ 4⌋. The comm. also understands the first pāda to signify that the Fathers are to go to their own world, and then to return when invoked to their own sacrifice; and this is probably the sense.

15. Let Kaṇva, Kakshīvant, Purumīḍha, Agastya, Çyāvāçva, Sobharī, Archanānas, Viçvāmitra, Jamadagni here, Atri, Kaçyapa, Vāmadeva, aid us.

The comm. amuses himself with giving etymologies for all these names, only passing over Agastya and Sobharī as "evident" (*prasiddha*).

16. O Viçvāmitra, Jamadagni, Vasishṭha, Bharadvāja, Gotama, Vāmadeva — Atri hath taken (*grabh*) our *çardís* with obeisances; ye Fathers of good report, be gracious to us.

The translation implies in **d** emendation of *sú-saṁçāsas* to *suçaṅsasas* ⌊so W's ms.! it must certainly be a double slip for *súçaṅsāsas*⌋, for which it seems most probably a corruption, and which is read by the comm. ⌊he reads in fact *suçaṅsāsas*, and understands it as W. does⌋; the only variants in the mss. are *súçaṅçāsas* ⌊with palatal *ç* twice⌋ in some of ours (P.M.I.) and one (C.) of SPP's, and the accentuation on the second syllable, *-sáṁç-*, in a few (including our O.R.T.).* *Pítaras* in **b** ought properly to be without accent. ⌊As to what precedes, see the next ¶.⌋ Some of the mss. read *çárdir* or *çárdīr*. The comm. first identifies the word with *chardis*, and pronounces it a name for 'house'; then, as alternative, he gets it from root *çard* and makes *çardayati* signify *balayati;* ⌊and, as a final alternative, he regards the word as the name of a Rishi⌋. Neither Kāuç. nor Vāit. makes any use of these two verses. ⌊Weber, *Episches im vedischen Ritual*, *Sb.* 1891, p. 787, suggests a special connection of this book xviii. with the Kāuçikan Viçvāmitras.⌋

*⌊The decision here lies between the well-authenticated *su-çáṅsa* ('of good wishes, kindly': root *çaṅs*) and the doubtful *su-saṁçās* ('kindly admonishing,' presumably oxytone: root *çās* with *sam*). The former occurs five times in RV. and also at AV. xix. 10. 6. The latter occurs nowhere, unless here, nor does it seem to be apposite in meaning: yet the authority of the mss. and of the *çrotriya* V. is decidedly in favor of it. No ms. soever actually gives *súçaṅsāsas;* but the mss. that have the impossible *súçaṅçāsas* may well be regarded as intending *súçaṅsāsas*. — Moreover, if the two vocatives stood in the order *pítaraḥ su-*, I should leave the second one unaccented (*Gram.* § 314 d), as W. suggests; but with the order *sú- pít-*, the second seems distinctly more independent of the first (*Gram.* § 314 e) and may properly be accented. I would therefore read *súçaṅsāsaḥ pítaraḥ*, and render 'O ye kindly ones, ye Fathers!' As for the meaning of *suçáṅsa:* note that *çáṅsa* means 'a wish, good *or* evil,' i.e. not only 'curse,' but also 'blessing,' and is used in these two opposite senses in two contiguous RV. verses, vii. 25. 2, 3; and that, in its good sense, it is pertinent to the Fathers, as at RV. x. 78. 3, *pitṝṇā́ṁ ná çáṅsāḥ surātáyaḥ*. Note further that 'kindly' accords well with the character of the Fathers as described in RV. x. 15: they bless and help (vss. 5 **d**, 4 **c**), and are harmless (1 **c**, 6 **c**) and gracious (3 **a**, 9 **c**). — That, in such a "pestilent congregation of" sibilants as *súçaṅsāsas*, a blunder of the tradition is rather to be expected than not, is my opinion: whoso doubts it, let him attempt "with moderate haste" to repeat aloud three times the simple English sentence "she sells sea-shells."⌋

17. They overpass defilement (*riprá*), wiping [it] off in the metal bowl (? *kasyá*), assuming further on newer life-time, filling themselves up with progeny and riches; then may we be of good odor in the houses.

⌊Pāda **c** = RV. x. 18. 2 **c**.⌋ The translation boldly assumes that *kasyá* is a corruption of, or equivalent to, *kan̄sá*; the Pet. Lexx. pass the word without notice; the comm. says that *kasa* means *kīkasa* 'vertebra,' the *kī* being dropped by Vedic license (!), and that *kasya*, as an adjective derived from it, means "the place of cremation"! All authorities read *kasyé* without variation, ⌊save that SPP's *çrotriya* K., whose memory of this book was not perfect, recited *kásye*⌋. ⌊See note *, below.⌋ The authorities are divided, however, between *mṛjā́nās* and *mṛ́jānās* (among those having the latter are our O.R.); both editions give the former, though it is an isolated accentuation; *mṛjāná* is regular (and occurs in RV.), while *mṛ́jāna* is supported (*Gram.* § 619 d) by the analogy of several other such participles; ⌊cf. note to vs. 73⌋. Two of our three *pada*-mss. (Bp.Kp.) have *āyuḥ*∘*dádhānās* in **b** as compound, and most of our *saṁhitā*-mss. (all save O.R.) accent accordingly *āyur d-*; but SPP. acknowledges the reading in only a single ms. (*pada*), and of course gives in his text (as we in ours by emendation) *ā́yur d-*. The comm. regards *surabháyas* in **d** as figurative, for *çlāghyaguṇayuktās*. In Kāuç. (84. 10) the verse is directed to be used as the women go three times round (the relics of the funeral pile) leftwise, with disheveled hair and beating the right thigh.

*⌊According to Caland, WZKM. viii. 369, the passage in Kāuç. 84. 8–11 describes the curious rite named *dhuvana* or 'fanning' of the bone-relics: see his *Todtengebräuche*, pages 138–9, and cf. my note to vs. 10, above. The *dhuvana* is part of the procedure called *nidhāna* or 'laying to rest' (ibidem, p. 129). According to the *sūtra* next preceding 84. 10, an empty pot, *rikta-kumbha*, is set down, and beaten with an old shoe. According to our AV. comm. (p. 143[17]: but see SPP's note 5), our verse is repeated by the one who breaks the empty jar, *rikta-kalaça*, on the night of the day of cremation, that is, at a time a good deal earlier than the *nidhāna!*—However that may be, it does seem as if our *kasyé* might well mean the same thing as the *kumbha* or *kalaça* of the ritual authorities.⌋

18. They anoint, they anoint out (*ví*), they anoint together (*sám*); they lick the rite (? *krátu*), they smear (*abhi-añj*) with honey; the bull (*ukṣán*) flying in the upheaving of the river, the victim (*paçú*) do the gold-purifiers seize (*gṛh*) in them ⌊f.⌋.

The verse is RV. ix. 86. 43, the only variant in which is *gṛbhṇate* at the end (and our I. also has this; also the comm.). SV. (i. 564; ii. 964) has it also and agrees with RV. in this word, but also has before it *apsú* instead of *āsu*, and in **b** *mádhvā*. The comm. understands *sthālīṣu* to be intended by the pronoun *āsu*. The verse is one of the wild utterances of the soma-purifiers in RV., and seems to be introduced here without any proper connection with the funeral ceremonies, simply because there is so much "anoint" in it. In Kāuç. (88. 16), it accompanies an anointing in the *piṇḍapitṛyajña*; and in Vāit. (10. 4), a smearing of the sacrificial post with butter in the *paçubandha*. ⌊Pādas **b**, **c**, **d** are good *jagatī*: but **a** has no *jagatī* character whatever, and by count it is *virāj* rather than *bhurij*; but perhaps the Anukr. (see note to the excerpts from Anukr.) does not mean to call it *bhurij*.⌋

19. What of you is joyous, O Fathers, and delectable (*somyá*), therewith be at hand (*sac*), for ye are of own splendor; do ye, rapid (? *árvan*) poets, listen, beneficent, invoked at the council.

Nearly all our mss. (save Op.R.s.m.) accent *pitáras* in **a**; SPP. reports only a single *pada*-ms. as doing so, and of course reads *pitaras*, as does our text by emendation. Nearly all the authorities, again, give *bhūtám* at end of **b**; ⌊but Whitney's Op. has *bhūtā́;* and his⌋ K. has *bhūtá*, as have three of SPP's, who reads *bhūtá*. ⌊The word itself is lost from the comm., but glossed by *bhavatha.*⌋ We ought to have emended to *bhūtá*. Once more, all the authorities without exception accent *suvidatrā́s*, which SPP. accordingly retains, while we have made the necessary emendation to *-dátrās*. One is tempted to change *arvāṇas* in **c** to *arvāñcas*. The extra syllable in **b** suggests corruption; ⌊and so, perhaps, does the fact that in O.R. the *avasāna* is before *bhūtám*, not after it⌋.

20. Ye who are Atris, Añgirases, Navagvas, having sacrificed, attached to giving (? *rātiṣác*), bestowers (*dádhāna*), and who are rich in sacrificial fees, well-doing — do ye revel, sitting on this *barhís*.

The meaning of some of these epithets is not altogether clear. No use is made of the verse in the *sūtras*.

21. So then as our distant Fathers, the ancient ones, O Agni, sharpening the rite: they went to the bright, they shone,* ⌊*should be* shining⌋, praising with song; splitting the ground, they uncovered the ruddy ones.

The verse corresponds to RV. iv. 2. 16, found also in VS. (xix. 69) and TS. (in ii. 6. 12[4]) which read precisely with RV. The variants of our text are no better than corruptions; the others have at end of **b** *āçuṣāṇā́s* ⌊p. *āçuṣāṇā́ḥ*⌋, and in **c** *dī́dhitim*. The translation follows our text.* The comm. takes *āçaçānā́s* (p. *ā○çaç-*) from root *aç*, and glosses it with *vyāpnuvantas!* The "ruddy ones" are in its opinion the dawns ⌊or else the stolen cows which the Añgirases got back from the Paṇis⌋. — * ⌊Whitney's ms. reads "they shone": this is probably an oversight and should be "shining"; his Bp., to be sure, but Bp. alone, has *dī́dhyata*, not *-taḥ.*⌋

22. Of good actions, well-shining, pious, heavenly ones (*devá*), forging the generations as [smiths forge] metal, brightening Agni, increasing Indra, they have made for us a wide conclave (*pariṣád*), rich in kine.

The corresponding verse in RV. (iv. 2. 17) combines in **a–b** *devayánto 'yo*, has in **c** *vavṛdh-*, and for **d** *ūrvám̐ gávyam pariṣádanto agman;* its *pada*-text in **b** reads ⌊*jánima* like ours⌋. ⌊Weber, *Sb.* 1896, p. 263–64, takes *devā́* (*jánimā*) as = *devā́nām* and the whole verse as a parallel to vs. 23, where the phrase *devā́nām̐ jánimā* occurs in full.⌋

23. As herds at food (*kṣúm*), the formidable one hath looked over ⌊*áti*⌋ the cattle, the births of the gods, near by; mortals have lamented the *urváçīs*, unto the increase of the pious, of the next man.

The translation is purely mechanical, and sundry of the words in it are extremely questionable. The verse corresponds to RV. iv. 2. 18, which, however, reads in **a** *kṣumáti* as one word (p. *kṣu○máti;* our p. *kṣúm : áti*), makes good meter in **b** by inserting *yát* after *devā́nām*, and reads in **c** *mártānām*. SPP. reads, with RV. and with the comm., *kṣumáti;* this is against nearly all his and our authorities; ⌊they have *kṣúm áti*⌋; but our O.R. have *kṣumáti* and Op. has ⌊the impossible⌋ *kṣum : áti* ⌊with accentless *kṣum*⌋. The translation implies at the end of **b** *ugrás*, which SPP. reads, with about half his authorities and the comm.; of ours, most of the later ones have it also

(Op.D. *ugráḥ;* O.R.K. *ugraḥ* ⌊accentless!⌋). The comm. renders **a, b** thus: "the mighty one, Agni, looks near by upon the birth of the gods, Indra etc., as in a noisy (*kṣumati* = *çabdavati*) herd (*yūthā* being = *yūthe*) of kine a master sees his own cattle (*paçvas*)": or, he says, it is the consuming fire that is addressed: "O Agni, this sacrificer who is being consumed by thee, mighty by thy favor, in a noisy cattle-crowd, looks upon the birth of the gods as upon herds of cattle (*paçvas*); the sense being that the gods come to light in the neighborhood of him who has gone to the world of the gods." This is the kind of help that the commentator gives in a difficult passage. *Urváçīs* is to him the Apsarases, Urvaçī etc.; and *akṛpran* = *akalpayan*, which means *upabhoktuṁ samarthā bhavanti*. *Aryás* = *svāmī*. The verse can be forced into the compass of forty syllables (11 + 8 : 10 + 11 = 40), as the Anukr. estimates it.

*⌊The RV. verse has been discussed by Bloomfield, JAOS. xx.[1], p. 183. He renders **c, d** thus: "Even for mortal men Urvaçīs were fashioned for the production of the noble lower Āyu." He takes *akṛpran* as 'there were formed,' aor. pass. of *kṛp* = *kḷp*: cf. the *akalpayan* of our comm. and the *kḷptās* of Sāyaṇa on RV. He explains: Just as Urvaçī, the goddess Cloud, produces the celestial fire, so the fire-drills (called *urváçīs*) produce for mortals the terrestrial sacrificial fire (*úpara āyú*).⌋

24. We have made [sacrifices] for thee; we have been very active; the illuminating (*vi-bhā*) dawns have shone upon [our] rite (*ṛtá*); all that is excellent which the gods favor; may we talk big at the council, having good heroes.

The first half-verse is, without variant, RV. iv. 2. 19 **a, b**; the second half is, also without variant, RV. ii. 23. 19 **c, d** (and VS. xxxiv. 58 **c, d**). Many of the mss., however, (including our Bs.O.K.) combine in **a–b** to *abhūma ṛtám*. The comm. has in **b** the strange reading *avasvan* (voc.: = *avanavan* or *pālaka*).

25. Let Indra with the Maruts protect me from the eastern quarter; arm-moved [is] the earth, as it were to the sky above; to the world-makers, the road-makers, do we sacrifice, whoever of you are here, sharing in the oblation of the gods.

⌊As for this whole passage, vss. 25–37, see my introductory notes, p. 847, ¶ 8, and Caland's orientation of it in his *Todtengebräuche*, p. 154.⌋ This is a very curious and obscure refrain (its last two pādas occur again as refrain of 4. 16–24). In **b**, *bāhucyútā* (which ought to mean 'by a mover, or a moving, of arms') is rendered as if it were *bāhúcyutā;* ⌊Weber proposes to emend to *-tām;*⌋ the comm. also takes *-cyutā* as past pass. pple., glossing it by *vinirgatā*, or, in an alternative explanation, by *prāptā:* either "proceeded out from the arms of the givers" or "arrived in the arms of the receivers"; the allusion being to the giving of land to Brahmans: "as land given protects in the future (*upári*) the heavenly world which is to be enjoyed by both parties"! The use by the *sūtras* casts no light upon the meaning. Vāit. (22. 3) prescribes the verse for use with an offering to the Maruts in the *agniṣṭoma* ceremony ⌊doubtless on account of the word *marutvān*⌋. In Kāuç. (81. 39), this verse alone, so far as appears ⌊but the comm., p. 1525, says vss. 25–29⌋, is combined with 1. 41–43 etc. to accompany the offerings to Sarasvatī at the funeral pile; again (85. 26), vss. 25–37 (the comm. says, 25–35) are used with 2. 24, 26, etc. in connection with the interment of the bone-relics.

⌊This last use does indeed perhaps cast light on the passage. The previous *sūtra*, 85. 25, with Caland's emendation (l.c., p. 154), reads: *edaṁ barhir* [xviii. 4. 52] *ity asthitas tanuṁ yathāparu saṁcinoti.* I think his emendation receives support from the AV. comm., who says, at vol. iv., p. 224[6], *edam barhir ity ṛcā kule jyeṣṭho 'sthīni yathāparu saṁcinuyāt.* If we take *sam-ci* in the sense of 'assemble' as used in the phrase 'assemble the interchangeable parts of a bicycle or a Waltham watch,' our *sūtra* would then mean, 'while repeating xviii. 4. 52, he (the dead man's eldest son) assembles a human figure (*tanum*), limb by limb, from the bones (*asthi-tas*), *i.e.* he makes such a figure out of the bones by assembling them.' — If this be right, then we probably have to infer from the AV. text and from the next *sūtra*, 85. 26, that the eldest son addresses the deities with vss. 25–29, and does so as spokesman of his dead father, represented by the prostrate figure of bones; and that, while uttering vss. 30–35, he addresses his dead father, but does so as speaking for himself. — As to forming a human figure (*puruṣākṛti*) with the bones, cf. further Bāudhāyana's *Pitṛmedhasūtra*, i. 10, especially lines 5, 7, 10, 13 of p. 15, ed. Caland.⌋

26. Let Dhātar protect me from perdition from the southern quarter; arm-moved etc. etc.

27. Let Aditi with the Ādityas protect me from the western quarter; arm-moved etc. etc.

28. Let Soma with all the gods protect me from the northern quarter; arm-moved etc. etc.

29. Dhartar the maintainer shall maintain thee aloft, as Savitar the light (*bhānú*) to the sky above; to the world-makers etc. etc.

The translation follows the comm. in connecting *ūrdhvám* with what precedes, instead of (as the meter suggests, and as is perhaps rather to be preferred) with what follows it.* The definition by the Anukr. of the meter of these five verses is not very acceptable; the refrain of 25–28 has 35 syllables (12 : 12 + 11); the prefixed variable part varies from 12 to 14; 28 has 46 syllables (11 + 12 : 12 + 11). ⌊Cf. note to excerpts from Anukr., above, p. 847, top.⌋

*⌊There is a clear play of words in *dhartā dharuṇo dhārayātāi*, not without conscious reminiscence, perhaps, of the familiar plays in *varaṇo vārayātāi* at x. 3. 5 and vi. 85. 1, and in *vār idaṁ vārayātāi varaṇāvatyām adhi* at iv. 7. 1.† Moreover, I think that these derivatives of root *dhṛ* make clear reference to *dhruvā diç*, the 'fixed direction' or 'steadfast region,' and that *ūrdhvam* makes similar reference to the 'upward region.' Render perhaps: 'Let the Steadier, steadying, steady thee [in the steadfast region], as aloft [that is, in the upward region] Savitar [steadieth *or* maintaineth] the light, the sky above.' Cf. my note, p. 847, ¶ 8. — † Cf. xix. 36. 6 **d.**⌋

30. In the eastern quarter, away from approach (?), do I set thee in *svadhā́*; arm-moved etc. etc.

The phrase *purā́ saṁvṛ́taḥ* is very doubtful; perhaps it means rather, with the more literal sense of *purā́* and taking *-vṛt* as from root *vṛ*, 'before covering up' ⌊so Caland takes it: *Todtengebräuche*, p. 154–5⌋; the comm., with his ordinary heedlessness of accent, makes it a pple. (as if *sáṁvṛtas*), rendering it "formerly covered up" (*pūrvaṁ saṁchāditaḥ*); or else, he says, *purā́* is instr. of *pur* = *çarīra* 'body,' and it means "along with thy body" (*saçarīra eva san*). Kāuç. (80. 53) uses the verse (doubtless with the five that follow it) in fixing the body in place on the funeral pile; but he adds in the next rule that Uparibabhrava prohibits it. The comm. takes no notice of any such application.

31. In the southern quarter, away etc. etc.
32. In the western quarter, away etc. etc.
33. In the northern quarter, away etc. etc.
34. In the fixed quarter, away etc. etc.
35. In the upward quarter, away etc. etc.

These six verses, 30–35, have the same refrain of 35 syllables as vss. 25–28; and the prefixed part, variable only in its first word, ranges from 17 to 19 syllables; the definition of the Anukr. is approximately accurate.

36. Dhartar ('maintainer') art thou; maintaining art thou; bull (*váṅsaga*) art thou.

37. Water-purifying art thou; honey-purifying art thou; wind-purifying art thou.

The comm. regards both these prose verses (*yajurmantra*) as addressed to Agni, quoting RV. iv. 58. 3 and vi. 16. 39 to prove the applicability to him of the epithets in 36. The *sūtras* make no use of them save by their inclusion in the series 25–37 in Kāuç. 85. 26: see above, under vs. 25. The Anukr., in counting the syllables of 36, restores both the elided initial *a*'s.

⌊**Verses 38 and 39** are addressed to the oblation-carts. The rearrangement of the RV. pādas in the AV. text is of such critical interest that it is worth a little space to exhibit the method to the eye. — The *yuje vām* etc. of the RV. seems to be clearly prefatory, and probably few will deny that the RV. order is the more nearly original, and that the AV. order and readings are secondary.

RV. x. 13. 1 and 2.	AV. xviii. 3. 38 and 39.
yujé vām bráhma pūrvyáṁ námobhir	
ví çlóka etu pathyè̀va sūréḥ |	
çṛṇvántu víçve amṛ́tasya putrā́	
ā́ yé dhā́māni divyā́ni tasthúḥ ‖ 1	*itáç ca mā amútaç cāvatām* [*mā ?*]
yamé iva yátamāne yád āitam	*yamé iva yátamāne yád āitám* |
prá vām bharan mā́nuṣā devayántaḥ |	*prá vām bharan mā́nuṣā devayánta*
ā́ sīdataṁ svám u lokáṁ vídāne	*ā́ sīdataṁ svám u lokáṁ vídāne* ‖ 38
svāsasthé bhavatam índave naḥ ‖ 2	*svā́sasthe bhavatam índave no*
	yujé vām bráhma pūrvyáṁ námobhiḥ |
	ví çlóka eti pathyè̀va sūríḥ
	çṛṇvántu víçve amṛ́tāsa etát ‖ 39 ⌋

38. Both from here and from yonder let them (du.) aid me.

As ye (du.) ⌊neut.⌋ went pressing on (root *yat*) like two twins, god-loving men (*mā́nuṣa*) bring you forward; sit ye, [each] on thine own place, knowing [it]; —

⌊See my added note just preceding the translation of verse 38.⌋

In this and the three following verses we have the ⌊entire⌋ RV. hymn x. 13, ⌊except its last verse, the fifth, and⌋ except its vs. 1 **d**. ⌊See introduction, page 848, top.⌋ This verse is its 2 **a**, **b**, **c** ⌊its **d** follows at the beginning of our next verse⌋, with a pāda prefixed as our **a** that forms no part of the RV. hymn. The first two verses are addressed to the two *havirdhānas*, or vehicles or vessels in which the soma-stalks are brought to the place of pressing; ⌊cf. our comm., p. 158, and Sāyaṇa on RV.⌋. The reason of the introduction of the hymn here is altogether obscure (unless it be the occurrence of the word *yama* in 38 **b**), and Kāuç. has no use for it. In **a**, our mss., so far as noted, accent *mā́*, but SPP. mentions ⌊only one⌋ among his ⌊as reading *mā́*⌋; and both editions give *mā*, as is undoubtedly correct. RV., in **b**, accents *ā́ttam*, which, of course, is alone grammatically possible; but both AV. editions have *āitám*, with all the mss. TA. (in vi. 5. 1) also has the verse, and differs from RV. only in having *étam:* ⌊so, indeed, the Calc. ed., text and comm.! *étam* (not *etám*, pron.) can only be an imperative: but the Poona ed., text and comm., has *ā́ttam*, like RV.⌋. Our text has *sīdatam* in **d**, with RV. and a part of our mss. (not O.Op.R.D.K. ⌊which read badly *-tām*⌋); but SPP. admits *-tām*, in spite of its inappropriateness, because ⌊*-tam* is supported by⌋ only one of his authorities and the comm. ⌊Is the consentaneousness of the mss. in the blundering *-tām* possibly due to a reminiscence of the correct *ā́sīdatām* of the immediately preceding context in TA.? cf. the case at x. 6. 17, and note.⌋ *Vídāne* might be from *vid* 'find'; the comm. glosses it with *jānatī*. One might conjecture that *ā́ttam* in **b** is for *ā○āttam* 'came,' but neither *pada*-text views it in that way. The verse cannot be made a full *triṣṭubh* without violent resolutions in the first pāda — which is, of course, properly prose. ⌊Considering the textual inaccuracies in the tradition of this passage, perhaps it is not too bold to suggest the query whether a *mā* has been lost: *itáç ca mā amútaç cāvatām mā* would be a perfect *triṣṭubh* pāda.⌋ Vāit. (15. 11) makes vss. 38 and 39 accompany in the *agniṣṭoma* ceremony the driving up of the two *havirdhānas*.

39. Be ye comfortable (? *svā́sastha*) for our soma.
I yoke for you ancient worship (*bráhman*) with obeisances; the song (*çlóka*) goes forth like a patron (*sūrí*) on his road; let all the immortals hear that.

⌊See my added note just preceding the translation of verse 38.⌋

The verse is pāda **d** of the RV. vs. x. 13. 2 ⌊of which pādas **a**, **b**, **c** immediately precede in our AV. text⌋, followed by pādas **a**, **b**, **c** of the RV. vs. 1. RV. accents in **a** *svāsasthé;* ⌊the AV. accent seems wrong;⌋ both *pada*-texts divide *su○ās-*. RV. further reads in ⌊its **b**, our⌋ **c**, *etu* and *sūrés*, and at the end *amṛ́tasya putrā́ḥ*. The RV. verse is found also in VS. (xi. 5) and MS. (in ii. 7. 1) with the same readings throughout as in RV.; and in TS. (iv. 1. 1²), which reads for our **c** *ví çlókā yanti pathyè 'va sū́rāḥ*, and in **d** varies from RV. etc. only by having *çṛṇvánti*. The comm. glosses *svā́sasthe* with *sukhāsanasthe;* he takes *yujé* as 1st sing., as it is translated above; the form might, of course, be 3d sing., like *duhé*, *çáye*, etc. ⌊In **d**, *çṛṇváttu* is a misprint for *çṛṇvántu*.⌋

40. Three steps the form (?) ascended, it went (?) after the four-footed one (f.) with its course (*vratá*); it matches the song (*arká*) with the syllable; in the navel of right it purifies.

The translation is purely mechanical, the verse being highly obscure, and its AV. version evidently corrupt. RV. (x. 13. 3) reads in **a** *páñca* (for *trī́ṇi*) and *aroham*, in **b** *emi* for the absurd *āitat* (apparently a blundering extension * of *āit*), at end of **c** *mima etā́m*, and in **d** *ádhi* (our *abhí* has to be omitted in translation) *sám punāmi*. It also has in **a** *rupás*, which SPP. admits in his text on the authority of the majority of his mss. and of the comm. (the latter takes it from root *rup*, and makes it mean *mṛtaḥ* *puruṣaḥ*); some of our later mss. (O.Op.R.D.) also give it, and it is to be regarded as the preferable reading, if there is such a thing in this case. In **b**, SPP. strangely reads in his *saṁhitā*-text *āitad vr-* and in his *pada*-text *etat*, his *pada*-mss. having *etat* or *āit* — both, doubtless, by accidental misreadings*; the comm., however, gives *etat*, and makes it qualify *vratena*, being itself = *etena!* For *nābhāu* in **d** the comm. has *yonāu*.

*⌊If *āitat* is a "blundering extension of *āit*," one does not see why W. calls the *pada*-reading *āit* "an accidental misreading." — Meantime, in Oertel's edition of JUB., published in JAOS. xvi., we find (i. 48, p. 125–6) *sa hāi 'vaṁ ṣoḍaçadhā "tmānaṁ vikṛtya, sārdhaṁ samāit. tad yat sārdhaṁ samāitat, tat sāmnas sāmatvam;* and (iii. 38, p. 197) *tā ṛcaç çarīreṇa mṛtyur anvāitat. tad yat* etc. On p. 234, Oertel suggests that we might regard *samāitat* and *anvāitat* as due to dittography of the following *tat*, "were it not for AV. xviii. 3. 40, *anvāitat*, which is protected by the meter." Cf. also Henry, *Revue Critique*, 1894, no's 39–40, p. 146. — See also SPP's full critical notes upon the verse, p. 160. It may be added that W's O. gives *-padīmáṁnvāitád*, and his Op. *ánu : āitát.*⌋

41. For the gods he chose death; for his progeny did he not choose immortality (*amṛ́ta*)? Brihaspati [as] seer extended the sacrifice; Yama left (*ā-ric*) his dear self (?).

Or, 'the dear body (*tanū́*).' Here too the variations from the RV. version (x. 13. 4) seem to be corruptions only. RV. has *kám* in **b**, correlative to that in **a**; for **c** it gives *bṛ́haspátiṁ yajñám akṛṇvata ṛ́ṣim*, and at the end *prā́ 'rirecīt*. The comm. explains *ā rireca* by *samantād riktaṁ niḥsāram mṛtaṁ kṛtavān*. ⌊See Ludwig's discussion of the verse, *Ueber die kritik des RV.-textes*, Abh. der k. bohmischen Gesellschaft der Wiss., 1889, no. 5, p. 46.⌋

42. Thou, O Agni, Jātavedas, being praised, hast carried the offerings, having made them fragrant; thou hast given to the Fathers; they have eaten after their wont (? *svadháyā*); eat thou, O god, the presented oblations.

The verse corresponds to RV. x. 15. 12, found also in VS. (xix. 66) and TS. (in ii. 6. 12[5]). ⌊Disregarding *īḷitó*,⌋ RV. differs only by reading *kṛtvī́* at end of **b**; and VS. agrees with it in this, but has *kavyavāhana* for *jātavedas* in **a**; ⌊TS. agrees with AV. throughout⌋. Āp. (in i. 10. 14) and MB. (ii. 3. 17) have a verse that agrees with this in **b** and **c**, save that MB. has *prā 'dāt* for *prā 'dās* in **c**: but their **a** is *abhūn no dūto haviṣo jātavedāḥ;* and for **d**, Āp. has *prajānann agne punar apy ehi devān*, while MB. reads *p. a. p. ehi yonim.* The second half-verse occurs again below as 4. 65 **c**, **d**. Kāuç. (89. 13) makes the verse, with 4. 88, and with two verses not found elsewhere, accompany the feeding of the fire at the end of the *piṇḍapitṛyajña*. ⌊The forms *ávāṭ* and *akṣan* are treated, *Gram.* § 890 a and § 833 a. As for the sandhi *ḍhḍh* of the mss., see note to Prāt. i. 94.⌋

43. Sitting in the lap of the ruddy ones (f.), assign ye wealth to your mortal worshiper (*dāçvā́ṅs*); of that good, O Fathers, present ye to your sons; do ye bestow (*dhā*) refreshment here.

The verse is found, without variant, as RV. x. 15. 7 and VS. xix. 63. The comm. glosses *aruṇīnām* in **a** as *aruṇavarṇānām mātṝṇām*, without further explanation. Kāuç. does not quote the verse.

44. Ye fire-sweetened Fathers, come hither; sit on each seat, well-conducting ones; eat on the *barhís* the presented oblations, and assign to us wealth having all heroes.

The verse is RV. x. 15. 11 through three pādas, RV. having for **d**: *áthā rayíṁ sárvavīraṁ dadhātana;* it also reads *attá* ⌊p. *attá*⌋ in **c**; and three other texts (VS. xix. 59; TS. in ii. 6. 12[2]; MS. in iv. 10. 6) agree throughout with it. The comm., too, gives *atta* and *dadhātana*. The Anukr. does not heed that we need at the end *dadhātana* to make a full *jagatī*. For the use of the verse by Kāuç., with 45 and 46 and other verses, see under i. 51; for its use by Vāit., with 45 and other verses, see under i. 44 and 51.

45. Called unto [are] our delectable (*somyá*) Fathers, to dear deposits on the *barhís;* let them come; let them listen here; let them bless, let them aid us.

The verse is RV. x. 15. 5, which differs only by omitting the meter-disturbing *nas* in **a**. Other texts (VS. xix. 57; TS. ii. 6. 12[3]; MS. iv. 10. 6) agree with RV.; but TS. combines *té avantu* in **d**. ⌊Our **d** recurs at TB. ii. 6. 16[2].⌋ The use of the verse in Kāuç. and Vāit. is the same as that of vs. 44. The comm. glosses *nidhíṣu* by *nidhīyamāneṣu haviḥṣu*.

46. They who, our father's fathers, who [his] grandfathers, followed after (? *anu-hā*) the soma-drinking, best ones — with them let Yama, sharing his gift of oblations, he eager with them eager, eat at pleasure.

The verse is RV. x. 15. 8 (and VS. xix. 51, which has the same text with RV.); this, however, reads for **a**: *yé naḥ pū́rve pitáraḥ somyā́saḥ*. In **b** our text gives, with RV. VS. *anūhiré* (RV. p. *anu॰ūhiré*), but it is by emendation, for all our mss. have *anujahiré* or *anūjahiré*, p. *anu॰jahiré;* ⌊the actual details seem to be as follows: *anujahiré* is given by Bp.P.D., while O.Op.R. have *anujahīré;* and *anūjahiré* is given by Bs.M.T., while K. has *anūjahīré.*⌋ ⌊SPP's authorities show the same four varying forms of the word:⌋ he reads *anūjahiré*, p. *anu॰jahiré*, although the majority ⌊five⌋ of his *saṁhitā*-authorities and the comm. have the preferable *anujah-* ⌊as against three with *anūjah-*⌋. Our translation implies the manuscript reading, though it is plainly a corruption of what RV. gives. ⌊Whether we read *anujahiré* (from *anu-hā*) or *anūhiré* (from *anu-vah*: Sāyaṇa, *ānupūrvyeṇa . . . dattavantaḥ;* Mahīdhara, *anuvahanti;* Weber, 'welche nachgezogen sind'), in either case the sense is about the same.⌋ The comm. treats the word as if it came from root *hṛ*: *anukrameṇa haranty ātmasāt kurvanti.* It looks a little as if the text-makers had in mind the root *jeh*, found in the next verse. The use of the verse with its two predecessors in Kāuç. was noted under vs. 44. It is very unsuitably reckoned by the Anukr. a *jagatī*, having only one real *jagatī* pāda; ⌊it scans perfectly as 12 + 11 : 11 + 11; the corruption *anujahire* gives **b** 12 syllables, but no true *jagatī* character⌋. ⌊W's version of **c** accords with Geldner's at *Ved. Stud.* i. 170 note.⌋

47. They who thirsted panting among the gods, knowers of offering, praise-fashioned, with songs (*arká*) — come, O Agni, with the thousand god-revering true poets, seers sitting at the *gharmá*.

⌊This verse and the next correspond to RV. x. 15. 9 and 10; but AV. makes the third pāda of 9 change place with the third pāda of 10: cf. the shuffling at xviii. 2. 2 and note.⌋ The RV. verse occurs also in TB. ii. 6. 16[2] and MS. iv. 10. 6. All these read in **d** *kavyāḥ pitṛ́bhis* after *satyā́s;* and TB. has in **a** *tā́tṛpús*, and in **b** *hotrāvṛ́dhas*. Nearly all our mss., but, according to his account, only one of SPP's, accent *ṛṣíbhis* in **d**.* The comm. glosses *jéhamānās* with *prayatamānās;* his explanation of the strange compound *stómataṣṭa* is in part lost; he understands by *gharma* the *pravargya* soma-offering; and he paraphrases *sahasram* by *aparimitaṁ dhanaṁ yathā bhavati*. This verse and the next are used by Kāuç. (87. 22) as explained under 2. 34. *⌊SPP. plausibly suggests that the *madhyodātta* of *ṛṣíbhis* in this vs. and the next is to be accounted for by the *madhyodātta* of the corresponding word in RV., to wit, *pitṛ́bhis*. If he is right, the case is very probably similar to that of *ṛṣíbhyas* at xix. 22. 14 (cf. the *çiṣíbhyas* of many mss. in the next vs.!) and to those noted under xiv. 2. 59: other cases at xix. 22. 9, 10; 38. 1 **d**.⌋

48. The true, oblation-eating, oblation-drinking ⌊ones⌋, that [go] in alliance (*sarátham*) with the gods, with strong (*turá*) Indra — come hitherward, O Agni, with the beneficent, exalted (*pára*), ancient seers, sitting at the *gharmá*.

The RV., in the corresponding verse (x. 15. 10 **a**, **b**, **d**, 9 **c**) ⌊see under our vs. 47⌋, reads *dádhānās* in **b** for *turéṇa*, and *pitṛ́bhis* in **d** for *ṛṣibhis* — which again all our mss. save one (Op.), but of SPP's only one, accent *ṛṣíbhis* (as in 47 **d**) ⌊see my note marked with a * under 47⌋. In **c** (see under vs. 47), MS. reads *arvā́k* (but its *pada*-ms. *arvā́n̄*), ⌊while TB. (ii. 6. 16[2]) reads as AV. RV.⌋. The verse is used in Kāuç. only with its predecessor, which see.

49. Approach (*upa-sṛp*) thou this mother earth (*bhū́mi*), the wide-expanded earth (*pṛthivī́*), the very propitious; the earth (*pṛthivī́*) [is] soft as wool to him who has sacrificial gifts; let her protect thee on the forward road in front.

The RV., in the corresponding verse (x. 18. 10), reads *yuvatís* for the repetitious *pṛthivī́* in **c**, and, at the end of **d**, *nírṛter upásthāt;* and TA. (in vi. 7. 1) agrees in general with RV., but substitutes the ⌊modernized⌋ equivalent form *nírṛtyās;* it also has the real variants *dákṣiṇāvatī* in **c** ⌊and *upásthe* in **d**⌋. SPP. makes no remark on *ū́rṇamradās*, but three of our *pada*-mss. ⌊Bp.D.Kp.⌋ have the blundering division *ū́rṇamoṁradāḥ*, and nearly all our *saṁhitā*-mss. (not R.) correspondingly *ū́rṇaṁmradās:* the blunder grows, of course, out of the equivalence in grammatical theory of *mr* and *mmr*. The verse (according to the comm., vss. 49–51) is used ⌊Kāuç. 86. 10⌋ with 2. 50 (see under that verse) in covering the bones.

50. Swell thou up, O earth; do not press down; be to him easy of access, easy of approach; as a mother her son with her skirt (*síc*), do thou, O earth (*bhū́mi*), cover him.

The corresponding verse in RV. (x. 18. 11) has at end of **b** *sūpavañcanā́*. TA. (in vi. 7. 1) has in **a** *úchmañcasva* and *ví bādhithās*, in **b** *-vañcanā́*, and at end of **d** *bhūmi vṛṇu*. We had the latter half-verse above, as 2. 50 **c**, **d**. The comm. paraphrases *uchvañcasva* with *ucchūnāvayavā pulakitā bhava*. ⌊W. appears to follow the comm. in rendering *úc chvañcasva* by 'swell thou up.' I do not see why he quit his old version, 'open thyself.' In my *Reader*, p. 385, I said "Note the meaning of *çvañc* ['open itself; receive in open arms (as a maid her lover)'] and its concinnity with the metaphor of *yuvatí*" [of the vs. which precedes alike in RV. and AV.]. At RV. x. 142. 6,

Ludwig renders *úc chv-* by 'gäne empor': cf. Eggeling's version of *ucchvañka* and the context at ÇB. v. 4. 19. In neither RV. passage does Sāyaṇa seem convincing.⌋

51. Let the earth kindly remain swelling up, for let a thousand props support (*upa-çri*) it; let these houses, dripping with ghee, pleasant, be forever a refuge for him there (*átra*).

⌊As to *uchváñc-*, see note to vs. 50.⌋ The verse is RV. x. 18. 12, which in **c** reads *bhavantu* for *syonā́s*. TA. (in vi. 7. 1) has in **a** *úchmáñc-* ⌊so Calc. ed.: Poona has *ucchmáñc-*⌋ and *hí* ⌊*tíṣṭhasi*⌋ for *sú* ⌊*tiṣṭhatu*⌋; in **b** it leaves *çrayantām* unaccented (if it be not a misprint); ⌊so Calc.: Poona has it rightly *çráy-*;⌋ in **c** it ⌊has *madhu-çcúto* for *ghṛtaçcúto*, and⌋ omits *syonā́s* (or *bhavantu*); ⌊and begins **d** with *viçvā́hā:* so accented in both ed's, as if it were two words, as in RV. i. 52. 11; 130. 2 (*áhā viçvā*); iii. 54. 22⌋. The comm. reads in **b** *mithas*, but explains it as if *mitas* (*mīyamānā oṣadhayaḥ*). The Anukr. takes no notice of the extra syllable in **a**.

52. I brace up (*ut-stabh*) the earth from about thee; setting down this clod (? *logá*), let me take no harm; this pillar do the Fathers maintain for thee; let Yama there make seats for thee.

The corresponding RV. verse (x. 18. 13) reads in **c–d** *dhārayantu té 'trā* ⌊p. *te átra*⌋, and ends with *minotu*. The TA. (in vi. 7. 1) reads *tabhnomi* in **a** ⌊despite the interposition of *te:* an interesting variant; cf. *Gram.* § 185 c, *aty aṣṭhāt* etc.⌋; in **b**, it substitutes, as do two or three mss. (including our O.) and the comm., *lokám* ⌊surd⌋ for *logám* ⌊sonant: cf. note to ii. 13. 3⌋; at the juncture of **c** and **d** it agrees with RV. ⌊*-yantu té 'trā*⌋; and ends with *sā́danāt te minotu*. ⌊As to *sā́danāt te*, cf. the contrary blunders at xv. 10. 2; xviii. 2. 3, note.⌋ Nearly all the mss. (all save our R. and one of SPP's) have *riṣan* at end of **b**; but both editions emend to *riṣam* ⌊as RV. reads⌋. Our mss. vary in accent between *sthūṇā́m* and *sthū́ṇām;* in explanation of *etāṁ sthūṇām*, the comm. says *etām prasiddhāṁ sthūṇāṁ tava gṛhanirmāṇāya*. As a *triṣṭubh*, the verse has really three syllables in excess instead of one. Kāuç. quotes it (86. 8) in the ceremony of interment of the bones, with the direction *logān yathāparu*, doubtless '[laying] clods for each several joint'; the comm. does not notice this.

53. This bowl, O Agni, do not warp (*vi-hvṛ*); [it is] dear to the gods and the delectable [Fathers]; this bowl here for the gods to drink from — in it let the immortal gods revel.

The RV. has in the corresponding verse (x. 16. 8) *eṣá* for *ayám* in **c**, and at the end *mādayante;* TA. (in vi. 1. 4) reads in **a** *jīhvaras*, and, like RV., *eṣá* in **c**. The Kāuç. (81. 9) makes it accompany the laying of the *iḍā*-bowl on the head of the corpse on the funeral pile, when the deceased's sacrificial implements are disposed about him to be burned with him. The irregularity of the verse (12 + 11 : 10 + 11 = 44) is unnoticed by the Anukr.

54. The bowl that Atharvan bore full to Indra the vigorous, in that he makes a draught of what is well done; in that, soma (*índu*) ever purifies itself.

The comm. supplies *yajñasya* to *sukṛtasya*, and, as subject of *kṛṇoti*, *ṛtvijāṁ gaṇaḥ*. ⌊The verse scans as 8 + 12 : 11 + 11.⌋—⌊See my note on Part VII., above, p. 848.⌋

55. What of thee the black bird (*çakuná*) thrust at, the ant, the serpent, or also the beast of prey (*çvā́pada*), let the all-eating ⌊*viçva-ád*⌋ Agni make that free from disease, and the soma that hath entered the Brahmans.

The verse is RV. x. 16. 6 without variant. TA. has it also, in vi. 4. 2. TA. reads in **c** ⌊for *viçvā́d* ('all-consuming') *agadám*, the curiously perverted⌋ *viçvā́d* ('from every') *anṛṇám* ⌊which is glossed by *sarvasmād upadravād ṛṇarahitam upadravarahitam*⌋. In **d** it has *brāhmaṇám* (also, in the printed ⌊Calc.⌋ text, *āviviçeṣa*; but its comm. ⌊Calc.⌋ explains *brāhmaṇe* and *āviveça*); ⌊in the Poona ed. the comm. seems to show an alternative reading, either *brāhmaṇe* or *brāhmaṇam*, glossed by *etadīye brāhmaṇaçarīre*; and it reads of course *āviveça*⌋. ⌊Our *pratīka* is cited by Keçava, p. 368[10], as *yat te kṛṣṇaḥ çakunīty ṛcā*: is *çakunī* a blunder? cf. *idáṁ yát kṛṣṇáḥ çakúnis*, vii. 64. 1, 2.⌋

In Kāuç. the verse is used (80. 5) in the very introduction of the *adhyāya*, before the handling of the corpse begins; and Keçava says it is in case the man dies of the bite of a crow or ant or the like; the comm. makes the same condition, and adds that the wounded place is to be burned with fire; this is then probably the meaning of Kāuçika's direction *ity avadīpayati*. The verse appears again (83. 20) in connection with the strewing and covering of the bone-relics.

56. Rich in milk are the herbs; rich in milk is my milk; what is the milk of the milk of the waters, therewith let one beautify (*çubh*) me.

⌊The translation implies (instead of the *çumbhantu* of the Berlin text) the reading *çumbhatu*, which is read by most of SPP's authorities and some of W's and adopted by SPP. Two or three of SPP's, and W's Op., have *çumbhata* (a blend of AV. *çumbhatu* and RV. *çundhata*?). For the misuse of *çumbh* for *çundh*, see note to vi. 115. 3.⌋ The corresponding verse in RV. is x. 17. 14, which has *vácas* instead of *páyas* at end of **b**; for **c**, the less repetitious *apā́m páyasvad ít páyaḥ*, and at the end *çundhata*. TS. (in i. 5. 10[2]) and TB. (in iii. 7. 4[7]) have again a quite different version: namely, for **b**, *páyasvad vīrúdhām páyaḥ*; for **c**, our **c**; for **d**, *téna mā́m indra sáṁ sṛja*. Ppp. also has the verse ⌊in xx.⌋ with *vacas* in **b**. Its former half appeared above, as iii. 24. 1 **a**, **b**, likewise with *vácas*. In Kāuç. (82. 9), it is used in the ceremonies of the first day after cremation, with strewing tufts of *kuça*-grass; the comm., however, says instead that it accompanies a bath taken immediately after the cremation of the dead body. The comm. supplies Varuṇa, as god of the waters, for subject of the concluding verb.

57. Let these women, not widows, well-spoused, touch themselves with ointment, with butter; tearless, without disease, with good treasures, let the wives ascend first to the place of union.

This verse (= RV. x. 18. 7; TA. vi. 10. 2) was found above, as xii. 2. 31, where see: it is not used by Kāuç. in the book of funeral and ancestral ceremonies.

58. Unite thyself (*sam-gam*) with the Fathers, with Yama, with thy sacred and charitable works in the highest firmament; abandoning what is reproachful, come again home; — let him unite himself with a body, very splendid.

The corresponding verse in RV. (x. 14. 8) reads in **c** *hitvā́ya*, and in **d** *gachasva*, continuing the general construction of the verse. The first half is found also in TA. (in vi. 4. 2), which has *svadhā́bhis* for *yaména*, and adds after it another *sám*. We had the last pāda above, as 2. 10 **d**. The mss. are divided between *ávadyam* and *avadyám* in **c**; both editions give *avadyám* ⌊with RV.⌋.

59. They that are our father's fathers, that are [his] grandfathers, that entered the wide atmosphere — for them may the autocratic (*svarā́j*) second life today shape our bodies as he will.

The first half-verse we had above as 2. 49 **a, b** ⌊and its prior pāda also at 3. 46⌋; the second half-verse corresponds to the second half of RV. x. 15. 14 (and VS. xix. 60), but is much corrupted, even to unintelligibility, so that the translation is only mechanical. RV. reads *tébhiḥ svarā́ḍ ásunītim etā́ṁ yathāvaçáṁ tanvàṁ kalpayasva;* VS. has *tébhyas* and *kalpayāti*, but the rest like RV. The last pāda is identical with vii. 104. 1 **d** above.

60. Let the mist be weal for thee; let the frost fall down [as] weal for thee; O cool one, possessing cool ones; O refreshing one, possessing refreshing ones; mayest thou be with weal a she-frog in the waters; kindly pacify thou this fire.

Or, 'this Agni.' — Of the ritual use of this verse, the comm. simply says that with it one is to sprinkle the bones of a Brahman with the plants referred to, dipped in water and milk; Kāuç. (82. 26) combines it with 3. 5 ⌊doubtless rather 3. 5 and 6: see under 3. 5⌋, in the manner explained under that verse. ⌊Partly because W. overlooked some TA. variants, it seemed necessary for me to rewrite the next paragraph; but I could not easily indicate my changes and additions by the usual ell-brackets.⌋

The main stock of this verse (pādas **c–f**) is RV. x. 16. 14 and is the third verse of TA. vi. 4. 1: in both these texts it stands next after the verse which corresponds to our 3. 6 above, namely after RV. x. 16. 13 = TA. vi. 4. 1[2]: see note to 3. 6. Considering how closely it is connected with our 3. 6 in sense and in position in those texts, it is strange that it should be so removed from 3. 6 in AV. — In **d** part of the mss. (including our Bp.P.M.I.: also the comm.) read *hlā́dake hlā́dak-*; TA. has *hlā́duke hlā́duk-*. For **e**, RV. has *maṇḍūkyà sú sáṁ gamaḥ* (of which our version, p. *maṇḍūkí́ : apᵒsú : çám : bhuvaḥ*, is no better than a corruption), and TA., again differently, *maṇḍūkyàsu* (as an adjective, supplying *apsu*) *saṁgamáya;* and the comm., finally, *maṇḍūkyā 'sya çam bhava:* moreover, for the *çám* of both ed's, some of our mss. (O.Op.R.) and one of SPP's have *sám*. In **e**, at the end, RV. has *harṣaya* and TA. *çamáya:* our *çamaya* is better than either. — To the main stock of the AV. verse are prefixed two pādas which agree nearly with the second half of the next verse but one in TA. (vs. 5: interposed as vs. 4 is matter that corresponds to our i. 6. 4 and xix. 2. 1, 2): but for our *bhavatu* the TA. has *varṣatu;* and for our *çáṁ te pruṣvā́*, it has *çám u pṛ́ṣṭhā* (so Calc.: the Poona ed. accepts *pṛ́ṣvā* but gives *pṛṣṭhā* as variant): the comm. glosses *pṛṣvā* with *jala-binduḥ*. — For Bloomfield's discussion, see under vs. 6. Bergaigne comments on the verse, *Rel. Véd.* i. 84, note, ii. 472.

61. Let Vivasvant make for us freedom from fear, he who is well-preserving, quick-giving (? *-dā́nu*), well-giving; let these heroes be many here; let there be in me prosperity (*puṣṭá*) rich in kine, rich in horses.

About half of SPP's mss., and one of ours (Op.), accent at the beginning *vívasvān*. The comm. explains *jīrádānus* alternatively by *jīvanasya kartā* and *vayohāner* (as if from *jṛ* 'waste away') *dātā*. ⌊Pāda **a** is found (with metrical rectification) as noted under vs. 62.⌋ The third pāda is identical with xii. 2. 21 **d**. By Kāuç. 81. 48 the verse is used at the end of the cremation ceremony with an oblation on the north; and again (82. 36), vss. 61 and 62 accompany each ⌊separately: see the comm., p. 176[13]⌋ a *sthālīpāka* offering to Vivasvant at the gathering of the bone-relics, while a third offering is made with them both together ⌊82. 37⌋. And further (86. 17), vss. 61–67 are used with 3. 10 in the interment of the bones (see under the latter verse); the comm. describes it thus: "in the ceremony of gathering at the cemetery, the manager and all the relatives, standing in the western part of the cemetery, should approach the departed." The comm. adds one or two more minor applications. ⌊Verses 61 and 62 are translated by Hillebrandt, *Ved. Mythol.* i. 489.⌋

62. Let Vivasvant set us in immortality; let death go away; let what is immortal come to us; let [him] defend these men until old age; let not their life-breaths (*ásu*) go to Yama.

In ÇÇS. iv. 16. 5, and MB. i. 1. 15 are found as the first two pādas of a verse our 62 **b** and 61 **a**. ⌊For the *na ātu* of our 62 **b**, both texts have *ma ā gāt* (the *me* is incongruent with the following *nas*); and for the *vivasvān* of our 61 **a**, both have *vāivasvato*,⌋ thus rectifying the meter. The mss. accent *vivasvān* as in 61 **a**. We need to resolve *mó* to *mā́ u* in **d** to make a good *triṣṭubh* pāda; but the Anukr. would apparently read *mo* and balance the lack of a syllable by the redundancy of one in **c**. Possibly *ā́* is intrusive in **c**, and the meaning was 'defend from growing old.' The ritual use of the verse was explained above, under vs. 61.

63. He who maintains himself by his might, like [birds?] in the atmosphere, poet of the Fathers, favorer (? *prámati*) of prayers (*matí*)—him praise ye, all-befriended, with oblations; may that Yama give (*dhā*) us to live further on.

The reading in the first pāda is doubtful; our text has *antárikṣeṇa*, but the other edition *-kṣe ná*. Bp. and Op. read *antárikṣe : ná*, and so, apparently, SPP's *pada*-mss.; but our D.K. have *-kṣeṇa*, and with it agree our P.M.I., while O.R.T., though they give *na*, do not accent it; SPP's mss. are somewhat similarly at variance. The commentator's interpretation is an interpretation of *antarikṣeṇa;* but his text (according to SPP.) reads *-kṣe na*. Only the sense can decide, and that is quite doubtful; the translation ventured above implies *-kṣe ná*. The second half-verse occurs again below as 4. 54 **c**, **d**. One is tempted to understand *viçvámitrās* ⌊so accented in both ed's with all the authorities⌋ in **c** as 'O Viçvāmitras'; but this is so decidedly opposed by the accent and by the short vowel of the second syllable (which is authenticated by the *pada*-reading *viçváॱmitrāḥ*, while *viçvā́mitra* is never divided: see Prāt. iii. 9 and note) that I have not dared to assume it; ⌊but the comm., ignoring these considerations, takes it as voc. For the verse in general,⌋ the comm., as usual in a trying case, gives no help whatever; he glosses *pramati* with *prakṛṣṭabuddhi*, and *mati* with *mantṛ* or *stotṛ*, in apposition with *pitṝṇām;* and he makes *antarikṣeṇa dadhre* mean (*pitṝn*) *antarā kṣāntena lokena dhārayati*.

64. Ascend ye to the highest heaven; O seers, be not afraid; ye soma-drinkers, soma-drenchers, this oblation is made to you; we have gone to the highest light.

Encouraged by the comm. (*anyān api yajamānān somam pāyayanti*), the translation mends the repetition in **c** by violently taking *-pāyin* as causative to *-pā*.

65. Agni shines forth with great show (*ketú*); the bull roars loudly unto the two firmaments (*ródasī*); ⌊even⌋ from the end of heaven he hath attained unto me (?); in the lap of the waters the buffalo increased.

The verse corresponds to RV. x. 8. 1, and is also found as SV. i. 71 and in TA. vi. 3. 1. RV. and SV. read in **a** *yāti;* in **b** ⌊which occurs again as RV. vi. 73. 1 **d** also⌋, TA. has *āvir víçvāni* (for *ā́ ródasī*); in **c**, RV. has the far more acceptable reading *ántān upamā́n*, while SV. gives *ántād upamā́m* and TA. *ántād úpa mā́m;* ⌊moreover, TA. accents *udā́naḍ*⌋. The AV. mss. are at variance in **c**; all read *ántāt* save our K., which gives *ántām;* the *saṁhitā*-mss. generally have *upamā́m* (K. *-mā́n*), and Bp. *upa॰mā́m;* but some (Op.D., also T.) and two of SPP's *pada*-mss. have *úpa : mā́m*, with TA., and with the comm.; and this last is implied by the translation, though both editions adopt *upamā́m*, with SV. ⌊Pischel, *Göttingische Gelehrte Anzeigen*, 1897, p. 811, renders the verse.⌋

66. As, longing with the heart, they looked upon thee, flying up* [as] an eagle in the firmament (*nā́ka*), golden-winged messenger of Varuṇa, busy (*bhuraṇyú*) bird (*çakuná*) in the lair of Yama.

The RV. has the verse (x. 123. 6), and it is found also in SV. (i. 320 and ii. 1196), TB. (in ii. 5. 8[5]), and TA. (vi. 3. 1); all read alike throughout, save that the RV. (not the SV.) *pada*-text has the bad division and accent *abhí : ácakṣata*. Our P.M.O. have at the end *bhuraṇyám*. It is noteworthy that vss. 65 and 66, which have no apparent connection with funeral rites, and are not used by Kāuç. save in the group 61–67, are found almost together (separated only by our 3. 7) also in the funeral collection of TA. *⌊W's "up" for *úpa* may be an oversight: render perhaps 'they looked upon thee, flying onward (*úpa*) [as] an eagle'? Our comm., taking 'thee' as the dead man, construes, 'flying unto the eagle'; but is not the verse addressed rather to Agni? cf. Griffith and comm. on TA.—Sāyaṇa, commenting on the RV. vs., says *he vena;* but in his comm. on TB. he says *he pravargyasvāmin:* an interesting diversity of opinion! Perhaps RV. ix. 85. 11 may throw light on our verse.⌋

67. O Indra, bring us ability (*krátu*), as a father to his sons; help (*çikṣ*) us in this course (*yā́man*), O much-invoked one; may we, living, attain to light.

The verse is RV. vii. 32. 26, found also as SV. i. 259; ii. 806, and TS. vii. 5. 7[4]; the only variant anywhere is that TS. has *no as-*, unlingualized, in **c**. The comm. glosses *yā́mani* with *saṁsāragamane*, and *çíkṣa* by *anuçādhi*.

68. What vessels covered (*api-dhā́*) with cakes the gods maintained for thee, be they for thee rich in *svadhā́*, rich in honey, dripping with ghee.

The verse is repeated below as 4. 25. Only one of our mss. and one of SPP's accent *ádhārayan;* ⌊but one of SPP's at 4. 25 also accents *ádhā-*⌋.

69. What grains I scatter along for thee, mixed with sesame, rich in *svadhā́*, be they for thee abundant (*vibhú*), prevailing; them let king Yama approve for thee.

According to the comm., the grains are roasted barley; and *anu manyatām* means 'assent to thine enjoying'; ⌊at 4. 26 he says *tā dhānās tava bhogāya . . . anujānātu.* It depends on Yama's favor, says Weber, *Sb.*, 1896, p. 276, whether the dead man may have the benefit of his viaticum, or not.⌋ The verse is nearly identical with 4. 26, and is precisely identical with 4. 43. Its meter is (9 + 8 : 8 + 10 = 35) rather irregular, and lacks a syllable of being full measure. ⌊With an easy double sandhi in **a** (*dhānānu-*) and the resolutions *taās* and *rājā anu* in **d**, it scans very well as 8 + 8 : 8 + 12.⌋ Kāuç. (85. 27) directs that grains be scattered 'with verses that have the sign (*saliñga*)'; and Keçava states these verses to be the two that begin *yās te dhānās* (doubtless 3. 69 ⌊= 4. 43⌋ and 4. 26, since 3. 70 is evidently not *saliñga*), also 4. 32 and 33, and another not found in the text; the comm. says that such grains are to be put upon the bones with the two vss. that begin with *yās te dhānās*, ⌊by which he seems to mean 3. 69 (= 4. 43) and 4. 26 rather than 3. 69 and 70: at any rate, he immediately cites 3. 70 for another use⌋.

⌊It is hardly doubtful that the black variety of sesame (*kṛṣṇatila*) is meant here, and that it is used, like the black rice and black victim, on account of its color: Pischel, GGA., 1897, p. 813. Pischel's view is confirmed by the fact that, if an offering to the Manes is performed apropos of some joyful occurrence in the family, barley is substituted for sesame: so Çrāddhakalpa, iv. 5, as cited by Caland, *Totenverehrung*, p. 37.⌋

70. Give back, O forest tree, him who is deposited here with thee, that in Yama's seat he may sit speaking counsels.

Two of our *pada*-mss. (Bp.Kp.) read *vidátha* in **d**. The verse is repeated, according to Kāuç. (83. 19), when the bone-relics are removed from the root of a tree, at which they had been for some time deposited: the comm. adds "provided they have been previously so deposited." It reads more as if it were originally addressed to the (hollowed) tree in which a corpse is buried (in which case, *tváyi* ought to be rendered 'in thee'). ⌊With regard to *vanaspate*, see my note to 2. 25, above: and as to *vidáthā*, see Geldner, ZDMG. lii. 735.⌋

71. Take hold, O Jātavedas; let thy seizure (*háras*) be with sharpness (*téjas-*); his body do thou consume; then set him in the world of the well-doing.

Or (in **b**) 'let thy flame be brilliant.' The verse is used ⌊Kāuç. 81. 33⌋ with 2. 4 and others (see under 2. 4) at the lighting of the funeral pile.

72. What Fathers of thine went away earlier and what later, for them let there go a brook of ghee, hundred-streamed, overflowing.

The second half of the verse is nearly identical with 4. 57 **c**, **d** below. The mss. are not agreed about *kulyāì 'tu* ⌊so both ed's⌋: some (including our R. and ⌊one or⌋ two of SPP's) read *kulyè 'tu*. Our Bp. has *kulyà : etu;* but Op. accents *-yā́*, and Kp. has *kulyaoetu*. The noun is elsewhere accented *kulyā́*, and hence our text ought doubtless to be *kulyāí 'tu* ⌊so SPP's B.⌋. The verse is twice used with 4. 57 in Kāuç.: once (86. 2) in the ceremony of interment of the bones, on filling a dish (*caru*) with butter and honey and depositing it by the head ⌊see note to 4. 16⌋; and again (88. 17), in the *piṇḍapitṛyajña*, on smearing the *piṇḍas* with sacrificial butter.

73. Ascend thou this, gaining (*ud-mṛj*) vigor (*váyas*); thine own [people] shine here greatly; go forth, unto [them], — be not left behind midway — unto the world of the Fathers that is first there.

Nearly all the mss. (all save our I.O.R., and one or two of SPP's) accent in **a** *unmṛjā́nas*, which our edition accordingly reads; SPP. makes the proper emendation to *-jānás* (cf. *mṛjānā́s*, vs. 17, note). The comm. glosses *vā́yas* with *antarikṣam*, because *viyanti gacchanty asmin!* and then of course makes it the object of *ā roha*, explaining *unmṛjānas* as *çarīrād utkramaṇena svātmānaṁ çodhayan*. For the use of the verse in Kāuç. 85. 24, with 2. 37, see under the latter. ⌊Cf. p. 848, ¶ 8.⌋

⌊Here ends the third *anuvāka*, with 1 hymn and 73 verses. The quoted Anukr. says *saptatis tryadhikā paraḥ*: cf. page 814.⌋

4. ⌊Funeral verses.⌋

[*Atharvan.* — *ekonanavati.*[1] *yamadevatyam mantroktabahudevatyaṁ ca* (*81. pitṛdevatyam*;[2] *88. āgneyī*; *89. cāndramasī*). *trāiṣṭubham*: *1, 4, 7, 14, 36, 60. bhurij*; *2, 5, 11, 29, 50, 51, 58. jagatī*; *3. 5-p. bhurig atijagatī*; *6, 9, 13. 5-p. çakvarī* (*9. bhurij*; *13. 3-av.*); *8. 5-p. atiçakvarī*; *12. mahābṛhatī*; *16–24. 3-p. bhurin̄ mahābṛhatī*; *26, 33*, [*43*]. *upariṣṭād-bṛhatī*[3] (*26. virāj*); *27. yājuṣī gāyatrī*; [*25*], *31, 32, 38, 41, 42, 55–57, 59, 61. anuṣṭubh*[3] (*56. kakummatī*); *39, 62, 63. āstārapan̄kti* (*39. purovirāj*; *62. bhurij*; *63. svarāj*); *49. anuṣṭubgarbhā triṣṭubh*; *53. purovirāṭ satahpan̄kti*; *66. 3-p. svarāḍ gāyatrī*; *67. 2-p. ārcy anuṣṭubh*; *68, 71. āsury anuṣṭubh*; *72–74, 79. āsurī pan̄kti*; *75. āsurī gāyatrī*; *76. āsury uṣṇih*; *77. dāivī jagatī*; *78. āsurī triṣṭubh*; *80. āsurī jagatī*; *81. prājāpatyā 'nuṣṭubh*; *82. sāmnī bṛhatī*; *83, 84. sāmnī triṣṭubh*; *85. āsurī bṛhatī* (*67–68, 71–86. 1-av.*)[4]; *86, 87. 4-p. uṣṇih* (*86. kakummatī*; *87. çan̄kumatī*); *88. 3-av. pathyāpan̄kti*; *89. 5-p. pathyāpan̄kti.*]

⌊**Notes to the Anukramaṇī-excerpts.**⌋ [1]⌊In giving this item, the Anukr. repeats the half-çloka from the Old Anukr., given at p. 814.⌋ [2]⌊The mss. read *namo vaḥ pitara iti pitṛdevatyam*: *ādyā* (vs. 81) *prājāpatyānuṣṭup* etc. By using the neuter *-devatyam*, perhaps the Anukr. means the whole decad-*sūkta* (the 28th), except vss. 88 and 89.⌋ [3]⌊Verses 43 and 25 were defined by the Anukr. under 3. 69 and 3. 68, and the definitions are not repeated here.⌋ [4]⌊In stating that vss. 71–86 are *1-av.*, the Anukr. uses the ... *itiprabhṛti* ... *ityātas* that appears at Kāuç. 81. 44: cf. 85. 26 and 86. 17, where also we have the strange *ityātas*.⌋

⌊Parts of the hymn are **prose**: vss. 27, 67–68, 71–74, and 76–87: so Whitney, Index, p. 6. As to vs. 75, it is hard to say whether the fact that it scans easily is significant or not. Perhaps we have here a mere casual lapse into meter (cf. p. 772, ¶ 5); or it may be that the *mantra*, as the first of the sequence to which it belongs, is intentionally metrical, while the *ūhas* of vss. 76 and 77 destroy the rhythm of those vss. The comm., p. 240[20], lumps the whole decad-*sūkta*, vss. 71–80, together, and says *etat sūktaṁ sarvaṁ yajurmantrātmakam*.⌋

⌊Only one verse (49) is found in Pāipp. As to the significance of the occurrence, see under vs. 49.⌋

⌊**Ritual uses.** — The Vāitāna naturally makes few citations from this hymn: vs. 59 is used in the *agnyādheya*; and vss. 28 and 75–77 in the *agniṣṭoma*. But in the *sākamedha*, particularly in the offering to the manes (Vāit. 9. 8) in one of the seasonal sacrifices, vs. 71 finds application; as also, I suspect, vss. 72 and 73, though the latter are not so recognized by Garbe. Something like two thirds of the verses find use in Kāuç., and those uses are all in the eleventh *adhyāya*, the *pitṛmedha* and *piṇḍapitṛyajña*, as noted above, p. 814, end. Verse 48 constitutes no real exception. For all ritual uses, see under the verses.⌋

⌊**The provenience of the material of this hymn.** — Whereas in the preceding three hymns a very large or a large part of the verses are found also in RV., in this hymn only a small part, to wit 12 verses out of 89, are so found. However much or little weight is to be laid on the fact that these 89 verses are called a "hymn," the hymn is, at any rate, the longest in the AV. In general, the collection looks as if it were made of after-gleanings from the stock material of tradition (cf. Weber, *Sb.* 1896, p. 278); although indeed some parts of it appear to be the reflex of what we may well regard as very ancient elements in the ritual: such are the giving of the viaticum to the dead (vss. 16 ff.) and the invocation of the ancestors (vss. 75–77) and so on. The relation of the order of occurrence in the AV. text to the order of use in the ritual is obscure and in part indeterminable. But a reason for the arrangement is sometimes to be found: thus the practices that go with vss. 51 and 52 are separated in the ritual; but the vss. are set together in the text because of several notable surface-resemblances between them. — The RV. verses are as follows:

our 28 = RV. x. 17. 11	our 59 = RV. vi. 2. 6
our 29 = RV. x. 107. 4	our 60 = RV. ix. 86. 16
our 45 = RV. x. 17. 7	our 61 = RV. i. 82. 2
our 46 = RV. x. 17. 9 **ab** 8 **cd**	our 69 = RV. i. 24. 15
our 47 = RV. x. 17. 8 **ab** 9 **cd**	our 88 = RV. v. 6. 4
our 58 = RV. ix. 86. 19	our 89 = RV. i. 105. 1

The verses that recur in the sixth *prapāṭhaka* of the TA. (if we count those in TA. vi. 8 as five: see note to vs. 16) also number about a dozen: to wit, 16 ff., 28, 30, 34, 35, 51, 55, 57.⌋

⌊For the purpose of the following discussion, the hymn may be divided into Parts; of which only some, not all, are of critical significance.

Part I., verses 1–15. — Refers in general to the *ignis rogalis* and its belongings and is treated as a ritual unit by Kāuç. 81. 45.

Part II., verses 16–27, and 28. — Offering of the viaticum for the dead: cakes, with milk, etc. etc.; then sesame. — The unity of vss. 16–24 is sufficiently marked by their external form alone. Verse 28 seems to me to belong to this part, and to be appended for use as an expiation in case of any spilling of the liquids of the foregoing libations: cf. TA. comm., *vikṣarantam abhimantrayate* etc.

Part III., verses 29–44. — This seems to me to be in general essentially a continuation of Part II., but with certain disturbing elements. The water poured on the bones (29–30, but also 36), the garment (31), the black sesame (32–34, but also 43), and the *vānyā̆* cow's milk (35) may well be taken as parts of the dead man's viaticum. If vs. 42 be part of the *dhuvana* (Caland), it is not far in time from the viaticum ceremony, I suppose. But the ritual use of 44 (corpse on cart) certainly precedes the cremation; while that of vss. 38–41, if rightly reckoned to the *piṇḍa* ceremony (so comm.), may well follow it by a long interval. As for vs. 37, see under the verse.

Part IV., verses 45–47. — To Sarasvatī with the Fathers, RV. x. 17. 7–9, recurring as Part VII. of hymn 1. The *tṛca* is a ritual unit, used (so comm.) immediately after the cremation.

Part V., verses 48–70. — Verse 48 and the group 58–60 and vs. 67 and vs. 70 find no use in Kāuç. The comm. assigns a use to 48, but only by a blunder; and the group he perhaps considers as a part of the *pitṛmedha* ritual; and in reporting the use of 66, he groups with it 67. — Vss. 49 and 50 stand side by side in Kāuç.: with 49 the liturge takes the two bullocks that drew the hearse, and with 50 he accepts his fee. Vs. 51 goes with the strewing of *darbha* on the pyre: and 52 would seem (see under 52) to belong with it, but is put to a use quite different and later in natural order, the forming of a human figure with the bones (Kāuç. 85.25). If the latter use be the correct one, then the acts that go with vss. 53 and 54 (covering bones with *palāça* and stones) form a reasonable sequel to it; although, to be sure, they also form a sequel to vs. 36 (besprinkling of the bones), both naturally and in the text of Kāuç. If I am right in understanding vs. 55 to accompany the patting of the grave-mound (see under 55), then the piling thereof (with vss. 66 and 67) must intervene between 54 and 55. Vs. 56, a symbolical taking of his hereditament by the oldest son, must belong to an earlier stage of the proceedings. One use of 57 is in the viaticum ceremony (described under vs. 16); the other is in the much later *piṇḍa* or cake ceremony. Here too, if anywhere (but see under 58), belongs the group 58–60; and the group 61–65, with 68, seems to belong also to the same cake ceremony (61, cake-sprinkling; 68, strewing the *barhis* to receive the cakes; 62, strewing of sesame on that *barhis;* 63, dismissal of the Fathers; 64, offering of grains with the pot-offering noticed below under Part VI.; 65, the "withdrawal of the fires," apparently the ultimate act in this connection). Vss. 66 and 67 (mound-piling) were mentioned above; and so was 68, which clearly suits the action immediately preceding that of 62. Vs. 69 accompanies a much earlier act, the expiatory bath taken just after the cremation. Vs. 70, which has no use in Kāuç., seems to me to be put here because, like 69, it contains a prayer for release from the bonds of Varuṇa.

Part VI., verses 71–87. — All this passage of unbroken prose (but see p. 869, ¶ 5) belongs to the *piṇḍapitṛyajña*. The comm., p. 2419, aptly notes that offerings to the gods are announced with *svā́hā* and *váṣaṭ* and those to the Fathers with *svadhā́* and *námas*. This Part falls naturally into 5 subdivisions, each with its own manifest unity:

subdivision 1 = verses 71, 72, 73, 74; subdivision 2 = verses 75, 76, 77;
subdivision 3 = verses 78, 79, 80; subdivision 4 = verses 81, 82, 83, 84, 85;
subdivision 5 = verses 86, 87.

Subdivisions 1 and 3 accompany the ceremony of strewing three handfuls [of grain? *trīn adhomuṣṭīn*, Keç.], and they dovetail each into the other in such wise that they are used (Kāuç. 87.8) thus: 71, with 78; 72, with 73 or 79; 74, with 80. Thus the second handful is strewn while the liturge repeats *idaṁ* "*somāya pitṛmate svadhā*" (72) either with *pitṛbhyaḥ somavadbhyaḥ* (73) or else with *pitṛbhyo antarikṣasadbhyaḥ* (79). The appropriateness of the linkage in each of the three cases is palpable. The second use of the *mantras* of subdivisions 1 and 3 is with the pot-offering (Kāuç. 88.1–4). — Then comes (88.11) the offering of the cakes with subdivision 2 (*piṇḍapradānamantrā evam āmnāyante:* comm.). These first three subdivisions are clearly triplets; and their symmetry is marred only by vs. 73, which is simply an alternative of vs. 79, awkwardly interjected after vs. 72 for lack of a better place. — Subdivision 4 consists of doublets (5 in all): to wit, 8 ascriptions of homage to the Fathers' various attributes, 4 expressed by nouns and 4 by substantival relative clauses, and a final doublet (85) with *námas* and *svadhā́*. — Subdivision 5 consists of 2 entirely symmetrical 4-membered *mantras*, the prior one relating to yonder world, the latter to this.

Part VII., verses 88 and 89. — Verse 88 accompanies the laying on of fuel just before the final withdrawal of the fires (explained under 65). Why the Tritaverse, 89, should be here, is, as Whitney observes, very obscure.⌋

Translated: as AV. hymn, by Ludwig, pages 488–493; Weber, *Sb.* 1896, pages 277–294; Griffith, ii. 247–258; also the occasional RV. verses by the RV. translators. — Weber's analysis etc., p. 277–8, may be consulted.

1. Ascend to [your] generatrix, ye Jātavedases; by [roads] that the Fathers travel I make you ascend together; the offering-carrier, sent out, hath carried the offerings; united (*yuktá*), set ye him who hath sacrificed in the world of the well-doing.

The translation implies emendation in **a** to *jātavedasas*, though all the mss., and hence both editions, read *jātáv-*; all, also, accent in **c** *havyavā́has*, and SPP. has that in his text; our edition makes the obviously necessary emendation to *-vāhás* ⌊cf. the opposite error in vs. 10⌋. All our *saṁhitā*-mss. ⌊see Prāt. i. 94, note⌋ make in **c** the false combination *ávāḍh ḍh-*; SPP. says nothing of his, and both editions have correctly *ávāḍ ḍh-*. Our O.Op.R., and one of SPP's mss., read in **c** *iṣitā́*; the comm. also has it, explaining it with *iṣitāny iṣṭāni*. The comm. also understands *jātavedasas* as vocative (probably, after his manner, simply disregarding the accent); he explains *janitrīm* as *svotpādikām araṇim*; and the Kāuç. (80. 23) takes the same view: *iti pṛthag araṇīṣv agnīn samāropayanti*; but its correctness as original sense of the verse may be strongly questioned. The comm. explains *ā rohata* by *çaktyātmanā praviçata*; and describes the *samāropaṇa* as taking place "because of the absence of any further ceremonies to be performed by him, being now dead, by help of the fires." In the comm's *viniyoga* he says simply *araṇidvayam agnāu pratāpayet*. All this is in the case of a person who has died away from home. But vss. 1–15 are also used nearly at the end of the cremation ceremony (Kāuç. 81. 45), with the direction *ity āhitāgnim* (Keç. adds *upatiṣṭhate*), ⌊and the comm. fills out the direction thus: *citistham āhitāgnim pretam upatiṣṭheta*⌋. The verse, as a *triṣṭubh*, is redundant by a syllable ⌊in **a**, which is thus a good *jagatī*-pāda: and also by one in **d**, which, however, by reason of its *triṣṭubh* cadence, is neither one thing nor the other⌋.

2. The gods, the seasons, arrange the sacrifice, the oblation, the sacrificial cake, the ladles (*srúc*), the implements (*-ā́yudha*) of sacrifice; with them go thou by roads that the gods travel, by which they that have sacrificed go to the heavenly (*svargá*) world.

The word *srucás* in **b** is shown by the meter to be probably an intrusion, and it is superfluous as regards the sense. ⌊The excision of *havís* would give a better cesura.⌋ The verse is, of course, in no way a real *jagatī*. Kāuç. (81. 10) directs it to be used as a sacrificial cake is laid on the breast of the corpse on the funeral pile; the comm. takes no notice of this.

3. Look thou happily (*sādhú*) along the road of righteousness, by which go the Añgirases, well-doers; by those roads go thou to heaven (*svargá*), where the Ādityas feed on honey; spread thou out upon the third firmament.

The last pāda we had above as ix. 5. 8 **d**. Our O.Op.R., and one or two of SPP's mss., read *tébhyas* at beginning of **c**. The comm. explains *víçrayasva* in **e** by *viçritaḥ pratiṣṭhito bhava*. The metrical description of the Anukr. fits the verse, if we ⌊decline to make two of the three easy resolutions (in **c** and **d**) by which the verse reads as five good *triṣṭubh* pādas⌋.

4. Three eagles (*suparṇá*) . . . upon the back of the firmament (*nā́ka*), at the summit (? *viṣṭáp*) are set (*çritá*); let the heavenly (*svargá*) worlds, filled (?) with *amṛ́ta*, yield (*duh*) food, refreshment to the sacrificer.

The *pada*-text reads in **a** *mā̀yú íti*, which is, I presume, intended to mark the word as a locative: see Prāt. i. 74 and note upon it. The comm., however, understands it as dual, and explains it as meaning *māyumantāu çabdakāriṇāu vāyuparjanyāu*, because Vāyu and Parjanya are noisy in connection with clouds; for *upara*, by Nirukta 2. 21, means 'a cloud'; and the three eagles are Agni, Sūrya, and Soma! the general sense being that Vāyu and Parjanya are set over the world of the atmosphere, and the other three over the heavenly world! In **c**, the translation follows the comm. ⌊and Whitney's P.M.I. and one of SPP's mss.⌋ in reading *viṣṭā́s* instead of *viṣṭhā́s* (p. *vi॰sthā́ḥ*); it is glossed with *vyāptāḥ pūrṇāḥ*. Neither this verse nor the preceding is quoted by Kāuç., nor has either a *viniyoga* indicated in the comm.

5. The sacrificial spoon (*juhū́*) sustains the sky, the offering spoon (*upabhṛ́t*) the atmosphere; the ladle (*dhruvā́*) sustains ⌊*dhṛ*⌋ the earth, the support (*pratiṣṭhā́*); unto me (?) let the worlds, ghee-backed, heavenly (*svargá*), yield every desire for the sacrificer.

The reading and sense at the beginning of **c** are very doubtful; the *pada*-mss. all give *prati॰mā́m*, as if it were accusative of *pratimā́*; most of the *saṁhitā*-mss. have *pratī́mā́m* (our Bs. has *pratī́mā́m* ⌊!⌋, and P.M. *pratimā́m*; T. has *pratī́mā́m*), and it is quoted in the comment to the Prāt. (ii. 35: so the ms.) as the same ⌊that is, I presume, in the form *pratī́mām*⌋. SPP. emends to *práti 'mā́m*, since, with his usual disregard of the accent, the comm. so reads, explaining *imām* as referring to *pṛthivīm*; our edition has *pratimā́m*, with the majority of our earlier mss. The translation implies *práti mā́m*, simply on account of superior intelligibility; doubtless the true AV. reading is *pratī́mā́m*. Simply *práti* would rectify the meter, and give a yet better sense. The verse (13 + 11 : 12 (11?) + 11 = 47) is, of course, no proper *jagatī*. This and the verse next following are used, according to Kāuç. 81. 7, as the sacrificial utensils are laid about and upon the body, to be burned with it.

6. O ladle, ascend the all-nourishing earth; stride, O offering spoon, unto the atmosphere; O sacrificial spoon, go to the sky (*dív*) in company with the sacrificer; with the little spoon (*sruvá*) [as] calf, milk thou all the teeming, unirritated quarters.

The mss. in general strangely accent the two vocatives in **a** and **b** on the final syllable; all ours (save Op.s.m.), and all but one or two of SPP's, have *dhruvé* (*-vá* in *saṁhitā*); all ours (save Op.), and nearly all SPP's, have *upabhṛ́t*; all ours ⌊save Bs.⌋ and most of SPP's, however, accent *júhu* correctly in **c** (but P.I. have *juhū́*, and M. has *júhū*); both editions make the necessary corrections. At the end, SPP. gives in his text *áhṛṇīyamānaḥ*, with the great majority of his authorities, and with the comm.* Of our mss., only O.s.m.Op.D.R.p.m. give *-naḥ*, while O.p.m.R.s.m. have *-nāḥ*; the reading *-nāḥ* is, in my opinion, decidedly the preferable one; it is the quarters that kindly make no resistance to being milked. According to the comm., the *adhvaryu*, at time of sacrifice, holds the *upabhṛt* in his left hand, and makes oblation with the *juhū* in his right. The verse (13 + 11 : 12 + 11 + 9 = 56) counts as the Anukr. describes it. Its ritual use was given under the preceding verse. *⌊The comm. assumes a very harsh change to the direct address and applies *ahṛṇ-* to the sacrificer: *atha pratyakṣavad uktiḥ: evaṁ srugbhir lokatrayam prāpito yajamānas tvam ahṛṇīyamānaḥ.*⌋

7. By fords they cross the advances (*pravát*) called the great ones, by what [road] the sacrifice-makers, the well-doers, go; there did they set a

world for the sacrificer, when they arranged the quarters, the creatures (*bhūtá*).

⌊Or, 'By crossings (*tīrthá*) they cross (*tṛ*).'⌋ The comm. explains *pravâto mahīr íti* by *prakṛṣṭā mahatīr āpadaḥ . . . evam;* it also makes *díças* and *bhūtā́ni* in **d** the joint subject of *ákalpayanta*, having before taken *adadhus* as an imperative (*vidadhatu*)! Though the verse is obscure, the probabilities are doubtless in favor of the translation as given. ⌊Pāda **a** seems to be a reminiscence of 1. 49, above, or RV. x. 14. 1. Pischel renders the vs., *Ved. Stud.* ii. 74.⌋

8. The track (*áyana*) of the Añgirases is the eastern fire; the Ādityas' track is the householder's fire; the track of the sacrificial gifts is the southern fire; do thou, with thy limbs, whole (*sárva*), powerful (?*çagmá*), go unto the greatness of Agni [as] disposed by *bráhman*.

Both in this verse and in the next, most of our mss. accent falsely *dákṣiṇāgnis;* SPP. reports it of only one of his, and only in vs. 9. The comm. glosses *çagma* with *sukhita*. The verse (11 + 11 + 11 : 13 + 11 = 57) counts short of what the Anukr. describes it (*atiçakvarī* = 60 syll.).

9. Let the eastern fire burn (*tap*) thee happily (*çám*) in front; let the householder's fire burn happily behind; let the southern fire burn refuge, defense for thee; from the north, from the midst, from the atmosphere, from each quarter, O Agni, protect him round about from what is terrible.

⌊Cf. vs. 11.⌋ As to the accent of *dakṣiṇāgnis* in **c**, see under vs. 8. The funeral pile is separately, but simultaneously, kindled from each of the sacrificial fires. To make the verse *bhurij*, we have to commit the violence of scanning *agne* instead of *'gne* in the last pāda (so 12 + 10 : 12 + 11 + 12 = 57). ⌊The *a* of *agnís* in **a** and that of *agne* in **e** are of course to be elided. The insertion of another *tvā* in **b** after *çám paçcā́t* rectifies the meter. In **c** we have perhaps to tolerate 5 pre-cesural syllables; but with this reservation and the rectification in **b**, all 5 pādas are faultless *triṣṭubhs*.⌋

10. Ye, O Agni, having become back-carrying (?*pṛṣṭiváh*) horses, shall with most healthful forms (*tanū́*) carry him that has sacrificed unto the heavenly (*svargá*) world, where they revel in common revelry with the gods.

The doubtful word in this verse is *pṛṣṭivā́has* (as both editions read). All our mss. save one (Op.), and the majority of SPP's, accent *pṛṣṭivāhás*, as if nom. sing. of *-vāhá*, apparently by an error the opposite of that committed in vs. 1. Two of our later collated mss. (Op.R.), and one of SPP's by correction ⌊as if to correspond with *-vāhás*⌋, have *áçvas* before it; and the comm. also reads *açvas*, with *praṣṭivāhas*, explaining that *praṣṭi* is a chariot of the gods, harnessed with three horses, of which one is in front and two behind; and a *praṣṭivāha* horse is, of course, one that draws such a chariot. ⌊Cf. vi. 102. 2 and note.⌋ ⌊Four⌋ of our mss. ⌊Bs.M.I.T.⌋, but only one of SPP's, leave *madanti* unaccented at the end; ⌊Whitney's Bp.O.Op.R.K. accent it, as it should be⌋; the comm. reads instead *madema*. The Anukr. passes without notice the deficiency of a syllable in **b**.

11. Burn (*tap*), O Agni, happily behind, happily in front; burn him happily above, happily below; being one, O Jātavedas, triply disposed, set him collectedly (*samyák*) in the world of the well-doers.

⌊Cf. vs. 9.⌋ The adverbs translated 'behind' etc. might with at least equal propriety be rendered 'on the west,' 'on the east,' 'on the north,' and 'on the south.' Nearly all our mss. (not Bs.I.), and half of SPP's ⌊have the impossible⌋ accent *jātávedas* in **c**; and a few (including our O.R.) have at the end *lokám*. ⌊Although *samyág enaṁ* must pass for the true AV. reading, one cannot forbear to query whether it has not displaced an original *samyák táṁ*.⌋

12. Let the fires, kindled, take hold happily; let the Jātavedases, making done (*çṛtá*) here him that is Prajāpati's [and] sacrificial, not throw him down.

The verse (11 + 12 : 12) lacks a syllable of counting as a full *bṛhatī*. Two of our mss. (O.R.) read in **b** *jātavedaḥ* (without accent). The comm. reads *sam* instead of *çam* at the beginning. ⌊Cf. vs. 13.⌋

⌊The verse reminds us strongly of 2.4 (which see), where *cikṣipas* without *ava* has quite a different meaning. Here, *cikṣipan* with *ava* means 'let them [the fires, not] throw [any part of the dead man] down'; that is, Agni (in his kindly forms, *çivā́s tanvàs*) is to treat the dead man kindly and not let a foot, the head, or a hand fall off from the funeral pile, but is to consume him completely: cf. the comm., who aptly says, *yathā niravaçeṣaṁ dahyate tathā*. The importance, in Hindu belief, of having every member of the body carried by Agni to the other world for use in the next life is abundantly shown by the hymns: see especially AV. xviii. 3. 9 **ab**; 2. 24 **c**; 4. 64; iv. 34. 2: and Whitney, *Oriental and Linguistic Studies*, i. 56–57.—When, as often happens, the pile of wood is too short for the corpse, the feet will naturally overhang and drop off from the pyre. In my journal of a visit at Benares, under date of Feb. 25, 1889, I find the following: "Saw a cremation, at the Burning Ghat. One foot of the corpse fell off the pyre (which was none too long), and a man tried to put it back on the fire with a bamboo. But failing, he took it by the toe with thumb and fingers and chucked it back." An allusion to an occurrence of this kind is clearly made by the Chāndogya Upanishad at vii. 15. 3: *atha yady apy enān utkrāntaprāṇāñ cchūlena* [cf. the bamboo, above] *samāsaṁ vyatisaṁdahet: nāi 'vāi 'nam brūyuḥ pitṛhā 'sī 'ti* etc.⌋

13. The sacrifice goes, extended, adapting itself (?*kḷp*), [taking] him who hath sacrificed, unto the heavenly (*svargá*) world; let the fires enjoy it, made a whole oblation; let the Jātavedases, making done here him that is Prajāpati's [and] sacrificial, not throw him down.

⌊Cf. vs. 12.⌋ 'Sacrifice' and 'whole oblation' ⌊and 'it,' that is *tám* in **c**,⌋ all refer, of course, to the deceased himself. ⌊Cf. Whitney, *Oriental and Linguistic Studies*, i. 56: "To burn the body of a deceased person was accordingly an act of solemn sacrifice, which made Agni its bearer to the other world, the future dwelling of its former possessor."—Cf. also Caland's most apposite citation from Bāudhāyana, *jātasaṁskāreṇe 'maṁ lokam abhijayati; mṛtasaṁskāreṇā 'muṁ lokam*, in his *Todtengebräuche*, pages 174, 178.⌋ The defective meter and incomplete construction of **b** make it altogether probable that the text is corrupt: *ījānā́nām* would help both. The comm. makes no difficulty of taking *abhi . . eti* causatively, = *abhigamayati*. He paraphrases *kalpamānas* by *iṣṭam pradeçam prāpayituṁ samarthaḥ*. The mss. vary between *kalpámānas*, *kálpamānas*, and *kalpamā́nas*; all of ours that were collated before printing had *kalpá-*, which we accordingly admitted in our text; but we ought to have emended to *kálpa-*, which SPP. reads. Two of our mss. (O.R.), and one of SPP's, also have *jātavedasaḥ* at end of **d**. The verse counts just a full *atiçakvarī* (11 + 10 : 11 + 12 : 12 = 56)

14. He that hath sacrificed hath ascended the piled fire, about to fly up to heaven (*dív*) from the back of the firmament (*nā́ka*); for him, the well-doer, shines forth from the welkin (*nábhas*), full of light, the heavenly road, traveled by the gods.

The mss. vary in **a** between *citám* and *cittám;* our text reads the latter; SPP's the former, which is doubtless correct, and which is implied by the translation. The comm. notes that *agni* is used to mean *iṣṭakacitaḥ pradeçaḥ*, quoting Āpast. 25. 4 as authority. According to Kāuç. (80. 52), the verse (the comm. says, vss. 14–15) accompanies the laying of the body supine on the pile; it comes next after 1. 46.

15. Agni thine invoker, Brihaspati thine officiating priest, be Indra on the right thy supervising priest (*brahmán*); this offered sacrifice, being completed (*sáṁsthita*), goeth where is the ancient track of those offered.

Both editions read in **c**, with nearly all the mss. (all ours save R.s.m., and half of SPP's), *hutó 'yám*, but both are wrong, the emendation to *hutò 'yám* being a matter of simple necessity (see note to Prāt. iii. 55). The verse is the last of the long passage that is used (by Kāuç. 81. 45) at the end of the cremation ceremony (see under vs. 1). It is far from being a regular *triṣṭubh;* ⌊after resolving *hotā adh-* in **a** and restoring in **c** the elided vowel, pādas **a** and **b** and **c** scan with smooth cadences as 12 + 11 : 11; there remains pāda **d**, with one syllable missing before the cesura: it would be a faultless *triṣṭubh* if we dared to insert *ásti* (*yátrā́sti*): the comm. understands the equivalent *vidyate*⌋.

16. Rich in cakes, rich in milk (*kṣīrá-*) let the dish (*carú*) take seat here; to the world-makers, the road-makers, do we sacrifice, whoever of you are here, sharing in the oblation of the gods.

⌊The definition of verses 16–24 as 14 : 12 + 11 = 37 is right by mechanical count; but the metrical character of what precedes the first *avasāna* is wholly misprized by the Anukr.: *carúr ā́ ihá sīdatu* is doubtless an *anuṣṭubh* pāda; and I am strongly tempted to suspect the loss (by haplography again: cf. iv. 5. 5, note) of a *ca* before *caru*, poor as the resulting cadence may be, so that instead of 14 we should have 8 + 8.⌋

We had the same refrain above, in 3. 25–35. ⌊Cf. my introduction to hymn 3, p. 847, ¶ 8.⌋ According to Kāuç. (86. 3), the verses beginning with *apūpavān* (16–24) are used as, in each case, what is specified in the verse (*mantroktam*) is deposited in the quarters and intermediate quarters (*dikṣv aṣṭamadeçeṣu*); this is in the ceremony of interment of the bone-relics, next after the use of 4. 57 and 3. 72 (see under the latter). ⌊At this point Whitney compares TA. vi. 8 and cites part of it. The TA. leaves out the depositions in the intermediate directions, SE. etc., and so has only 5 deposition-*mantras* instead of 9. The matter is treated more fully just below.⌋ According to the comm., *caru* means specifically the contents of the dish here: *kumbhyām pakva odanaḥ;* and *ihá* signifies: *asmin saṁcayanakarmaṇy asthnāṁ samīpe paçcimadigbhāge;* the others are set in the remaining half-directions, and one in the middle. ⌊Observe that the AV. begins the depositions with the west (so the comm., at p. 197[8], and at 201[16] just cited), while the TA. begins, as noted below, with the east.⌋

⌊As part of the requisites for performing the *pitṛnidhāna*, Kāuç. (83. 2) prescribes eleven dishes (*carūn*). According to Kāuç. 86. 2, two dishes (*carū* *) are to be deposited, with our 4. 57 and 3. 72, near the head of the human figure formed with the bones (note to 3. 25); next, eight more (Kāuç. 86. 3) in the eight directions, with 8 vss. of our present sequence, that is, 4. 16–23; and then the eleventh and last dish in the center with our 4. 24, according to Kāuç. 86. 4, where we are to read (see under vs. 24) *madhye 'pavantam* (for *pacantam*), 'in the center [a dish] with water.'⌋ *⌊So we must read, with three of Bloomfield's mss., as Caland suggests, *Todtengebräuche*, p. 152, and as the AV. comm. makes plain at 224[19] (*carudvayam*), though not at 176[23].⌋

⌊TA. vi. 8 reads thus: *apūpávān ghṛtávāñç carúr é 'há sīdatū 'ttabhnuván pṛthivī́ṁ dyā́m utó 'pári: yonikṛ́taḥ pathikṛ́taḥ saparyata yé devā́nāṁ ghṛtábhāgā ihá sthá: eṣā́ te yamasā́dane svadhā́ nī dhīyate gṛhè 'sāu: dáçākṣarā* [:] *tā́ṁ rakṣasva* etc. etc.— This set of *mantras* is metrical as far as *gṛhé* inclusive, 7 (8?) + 8 + 12 : 12 + 11 : 8 + 8; then prose. It accompanies the deposition of the cakes with a dish of ghee to the east of the bone-relics, and is followed by four other sets, which are not given in full in TA., but may, with the help of Sāyaṇa, be reconstructed as *ūhas* of this set. The order of deposition is (strangely) *pradakṣiṇa*, that is, from E. to S. to W. to N. and center. In the first set (used at the east) the words to be replaced are *ghṛtávān*, *ghṛtábhāgās*, and *dáçākṣarā;* and they are replaced in the second set (south) by *çṛtávān*, *çṛtábhāgās*, and *çatā́kṣarā* respectively; in the third set (west), by *kṣīrávān*, *kṣīrábhāgās*, and *sahásrākṣarā;* in the fourth set (north), by *dádhivān*, *dádhibhāgās*, and *ayútākṣarā;* and in the fifth set (center), by *mádhumān*, *mádhubhāgās*, and *ácyutākṣarā*. Thus the *mantra* of the last set would begin *apūpávān mádhumān* etc., for the deposition of cakes is common to that of all the dishes (so AV. comm., p. 202[5]: *apūpasāhityaṁ sarveṣāṁ carūṇāṁ sādhāraṇam*).⌋

17. Rich in cakes, rich in curds (*dádhi-*), let the dish etc. etc.

18. Rich in cakes, rich in drops (*drapsá-*), let the dish etc. etc.

Our O. reads *drápsa-*, ⌊and so does one of SPP's mss.⌋. According to the comm., *drapsa* signifies "particles of curds" (*dadhikaṇās*).

19. Rich in cakes, rich in ghee, let the dish etc. etc.

20. Rich in cakes, rich in flesh (*mā́ṅsá-*), let the dish etc. etc.

21. Rich in cakes, rich in food, let the dish etc. etc.

22. Rich in cakes, rich in honey, let the dish etc. etc.

23. Rich in cakes, rich in sap, let the dish etc. etc.

24. Rich in cakes, rich in water (*ápa-*), let the dish etc. etc.

Instead of *apavant* in this verse, the comm. has a second time *apūpavant*, explaining that it means cakes of a different material. In the five dishes of TA. (vi. 8) are contained respectively (besides the cakes), ghee, boiled flesh (*çṛtá*), milk, curds, and honey. ⌊Caland's suggestion of *'pavantam* for *pacantam* at Kāuç. 86. 4 (see WZKM. viii. 369) brings the text of Kāuç. into harmony with *ápavāñs* of this vs.: cf. ¶ 3 of the notes to vs. 16.⌋

25. What vessels covered with cakes the gods maintained for thee, be they for thee rich in *svadhā́*, rich in honey, dripping with ghee.

This is a ⌊precise⌋ repetition of 3. 68 above. While most of the mss. quote it, as usual, by the first words with *íty ékā* added, two (O.R.) write it in full. According to the comm., the verse follows the deposition of the nine dishes; and it adds: "one should put on mixed grains"; the Kāuç. makes no mention of it.

26. What grains I scatter along for thee, mixed with sesame, rich in *svadhā́*, be they for thee uprising (*udbhū́*), prevailing; them let king Yama approve for thee.

This verse, differing from 3. 69 and 4. 43 by a single word (*udbhvī́s* instead of *vibhvī́s*), is written out in full by all the mss. The comm. has, instead of *udbhvīs*, *abhvīs*, glossing it with *mahatyas*. ⌊For a possible ritual use of the verse, see under 3. 69.⌋

27. A more abundant inexhaustibleness.

The comm. adds this to the preceding verse as a part of it; but the Anukr. and the mss. reckon it as an independent verse.

28. The drop leaped (*skand*) toward the earth, the sky (*dív*), toward both this lair (*yóni*) and the one that was of old; of the drop that goes about toward the same lair do I make oblation, after seven invocations (*hótrā*).

The verse is RV. x. 17. 11, and found also in several other texts: VS. (xiii. 5), TS. (iv. 2. 8², 9⁵), TA. (vi. 6. 1), MS. (ii. 5. 10), ÇB. (vii. 4. 1²⁰). RV. differs from our text by reading in **a** *prathamā́ṅ ánu dyū́n;* all the rest agree throughout with AV., save that TS.TA. have *tṛtī́yam* for *samānám* in **c**. ⌊In MS. this verse stands between our ix. 4. 5 and 4. 4, as already noted under ix. 4. 5.⌋ Kāuç. does not apply the verse, but it is found (as above) in the funeral ceremony of TA., next after our 4. 35 below, being addressed to any overflow of the offered dish of curds and honey. The comm. explains *drapsa* by *somarasasthitodakakaṇa*, and teaches that such a drop, or the soma itself, is here praised, in view of the enjoyment of the fruit of their soma-sacrifices by the Fathers in heaven; it also points out that in ÇB. (vii. 4. 1²⁰) this drop is praised as the sun (*āditya*). In Vāit. (16. 17) the verse (with RV. x. 17. 12, 13 and one or two others) is used in the *agniṣṭoma* ceremony, with offerings to the soma-drops (*vāipruṣa*), on occasion of the overflow of soma.

29. A hundred-streamed Vāyu, a heaven-finding sun (?*arká*), wealth, do those men-beholders look upon; whoso bestow (*pṛ*) and present (*prayam*) always, they milk a sacrificial gift having seven mothers.

The verse corresponds to RV. x. 107. 4, which differs by reading *havís* at end of **b**, ⌊and *saṁgamé* at end of **c**⌋; it also reads *duhate* in **d** and puts the word after *dákṣiṇām;* the RV. hymn is one in praise of generous givers. *Nṛcákṣasas* in **b** might of course be gen. sing. (so Grassmann); both translators ⌊Grassmann and Ludwig⌋ take *saptámātaram* as 'mother of seven,' which is against the accent; the comm. takes it properly as possessive, but gives three different guesses at its value. The comm. takes *té* in **b** as 'for thy sake,' against the accent. Kāuç. does not quote the verse; the comm. says that it and the next are used together on watering the bone-relics with water falling from a vessel with a hundred holes; and these hundred holes it regards as referred to by the first word of the verse.

30. They milk a receptacle (*kóça*), a jar with four orifices, *íḍā* [as] milch-cow rich in honey, in order to well-being; reveling refreshment, Aditi among the people, injure thou not, O Agni, in the highest firmament (*vyòman*).

The first half-verse is found also in TB. iii. 7. 4[16] and Āp. i. 13. 1, both of which read *útsam* for *kóçam*, *devī́m* for *dhenúm*, and *suvarvídam* for *svastáye*. The second half occurs in VS. (xiii. 49 **c, d**), TS. (in iv. 2. 10[2]), ⌊MS., in ii. 7. 17, page 102[15]⌋, and TA. (in vi. 6. 1); they all agree in reading for **c** *ghṛtáṁ dúhānām áditiṁ jánāya*, for which our text is a corruption, capable of only mechanical translation. The comm., in **a**, still thinks of four of the holes in the hundred-holed vessel; *iḍā* is either the earth or the name of a certain cow. In the funeral ceremony of TA. (as above), our **c, d**, with ⌊the correspondent of⌋ our 36 **a, b** below as first half, is used next after our vs. 28, and for the same purpose. The Anukr. does not heed that the first two pādas are *jagatī*.

31. This garment god Savitar gives thee to wear (*bhṛ*); putting on that, which is *tārpyà*, do thou go about in Yama's realm.

Some of the mss. (including our O.Op.R.) read *dadātu* in **b**. Our Op. accents *tā́rpyam*, and the word is variously accented by half of SPP's authorities. The comm. first explains the word as *tarpaṇārham prītikaram*, and then adds: 'or, made of a kind of grass called *tṛpā*, [and] anointed with ghee.' For the ritual use of the verse, in company with 2. 57, see under the latter verse. The comm. says only that it is addressed to the garment when the dead man is wrapped up.

32. The grains became a milch-cow; the sesame became her calf; upon her, unexhausted, one lives in Yama's realm.

The mss. are a little at variance as to the accent of *tilo 'bhavat*; but the majority give *tilò*, which is accepted in both editions. The comm. reads at the end *jīvāti*. The ritual application of this verse and its successor was given with that of 3. 69 above; the comm. says here that with vss. 32–34 grains mingled with sesame are put upon the bones. The first pāda is one syllable short.

33. Be these, O so-and-so, thy milch-kine that yield what is desired; variegated, white, of like form, of different form, with sesame as calf, let them wait upon (*upa-sthā*) thee there.

One of our mss. (Op.), and three or four of SPP's authorities, accent *tílavatsās* in **d**. The comm. has *bhavanti* in **b**. The verse (8 + 7 : 11 + 11 = 37) is not at all an *upariṣṭādbṛhatī*, but rather an irregular *āstārapañkti*.

34. Grains variegated, yellow, white, grains black, red, [be] thy milch-kine here; with sesame as calf, yielding (*duh*) him refreshment, be they ever unresisting.

The verse is found also in TA. (in vi. 7. 1), with its first half abbreviated to *éṇīr dhānā́ háriṇīr árjunīḥ santu dhenávaḥ*; and it accents *tíla-* in **c** (with our Op. and one or two of SPP's mss.). Our O. ⌊and apparently also P.I.⌋, with ⌊one or⌋ two of SPP's mss., also accent *enī́s*. Only a minority of the mss. (including our Bs.p.m. and Op.) have at the end *-ntīḥ*, the rest *-ntī*. Here and in vs. 36, most of the mss. accent *anapasphúr-*, and accordingly both edited texts accept it; but the readings ought unquestionably to be emended to *ánapasphur-* (which is given here by ⌊TA., Poona ed.,⌋ our O.R., ⌊and one or two of SPP's mss.⌋; in 36, by none); the accentuation in this part of the text is more than usually faulty. The comm. stupidly declares *apasphuraṇa* = *nāça*, and the participle therefore = ⌊*avinaçvaryaḥ* or⌋ *akṣīṇāḥ*. ⌊As alternative rendering, W. suggests 'not refractory.'⌋ ⌊W's 'here' seems to be meant as (the hardly licit) version of the accentless *asya:* Weber notices the wild incongruity (absent in the TA. version) between *asya* in **a**, *te* in **b**, and *asmāt* in **c**.⌋

35. In Vāiçvānara I offer this oblation, a thousand-fold, hundred-streamed fountain (*útsa*); it supports (*bhṛ*) [our] father, grandfathers; [our] great-grandfathers it supports, swelling.

That is, with fatness or abundance (*pinv*). The verse is found also at the beginning of TA. vi. 6; but this rectifies the meter of **b** by reading *sāhasrám útsaṁ çatádhāram etám;* and its **c**, **d** are not less different: *tásminn eṣá pitáram pitāmahám prápitāmaham bibharat pínvamāne.* One of our mss. (Op.) also accents *prápitāmahān.* In TA. (as noticed above) the verse is next followed by our 4. 28, in the relic-interment ceremony; according to Kāuç. (82. 22), it is used on the second day after cremation, with an oblation on the back of a *vānyavatsā* * cow, after causing her to be milked on the site of the funeral pile. The comm. ⌊p. 209[18]⌋ calls the cow *anyavatsā* (only by an error of the editor?). ⌊If error, it is an easy one, for the comm's words as combined are *dahanasthānasaṁnidhāv anyavatsāyāḥ:* but *anyavatsā* occurs in the comm. to AB. vii. 2, mentioned below.⌋ The verse (11 + 9 : 11 + 12 = 43) is hardly fit to be reckoned a *triṣṭubh.*

*⌊Primarily, *vānyà*, *abhivānyà*, *apivānyà*, *nivānyà*, as gerundives of *van*, mean 'to be won over to *or* wonted to': *abhivānyavatsá* is 'a calf that has to be wonted to' its new or adoptive mother. Such a word as the last, with *bahuvrīhi* accent, means '(a cow) possessing such a calf,' and by inference, 'a cow that has lost her own calf': so *abhivānyàvatsā*, AB. vii. 2, and Hiraṇyakeçi-sūtra, in Caland's Pitṛmedha-sūtras, p. 58[8]; *apivānyàvatsā*, Kāuç., twice?, see below; *nivānyàvatsā*, ÇB. xii. 5. 1[4].— These possessives are then abbreviated, and we find *abhivānyā̀* at TB. i. 6. 8[4] and four times in the Pitṛmedhasūtras (see Caland's Index), and *nivānyā̀* at ÇB. ii. 6. 1[6], both words with the same meaning as *abhivānyàvatsā*, but coming to it secondarily; and also *vānyā̀* at TB. ii. 6. 16[2], p. 676 Poona, glossed by *mṛtavatsā dhenuḥ*, and ĀpÇS. viii. 15. 17, as equivalent of the not quotable *vānyàvatsā.*—After putting to paper the explanations just given I find them confirmed by Nārāyaṇa, to whom I was brought by Aufrecht's valuable note upon his excerpt from Sāyaṇa's comment on AB. vii. 2 (p. 377): Nārāyaṇa, in his comm. on AÇS. iii. 10. 17 says *abhivānyavatsā nāmā 'nyavatsena dohanīyā: abhivānyo vatso yasyāḥ sā 'bhivānyavatsā: abhivānyo 'bhivananīya ity arthaḥ.*—In Kāuç. 82. 22 there can be little doubt (cf. BR. i. 347) that we have to read *apivānyavatsām* after *ādahane ca;* and in like manner, at 80. 25, *apivānyavatsāyās:* with the latter passage is to be compared ÇB. ii. 6. 1[6], which describes the same ceremony; see also Caland, *Todtengebräuche*, p. 151. The use of the milk of a cow whose calf is dead is in keeping with the use of cows that are old, ugly, barren, etc.: cf. ÇB. xii. 5. 1[4] (dead man's *agnihotra*) and Caland, l.c., p. 173, p. 20.⌋

36. A thousand-streamed, hundred-streamed fountain, unexhausted, expanded upon the back of the sea, yielding refreshment, unresisting, do the Fathers wait on at their will (?*svadhā́bhis*).

The first half-verse stands in VS. ⌊xiii. 49⌋ TS. ⌊iv. 2. 10[2]⌋ TA. ⌊vi. 6. 1⌋ MS. ⌊ii. 7. 17, p. 102[14]⌋ as the first two pādas of a verse of which our 30 **c**, **d** above is second half; in all, the first word is *imám* followed in VS.MS. by *sāhasrám*, in TS.TA. by *samudrám*, before *çatádh-*; all of course omit the evidently intruded *ákṣitam**, and end **b** with *mádhye*, VS. having before it *sarirásya*, and TS.TA. *bhúvanasya.* Some of the mss. (including our O.⌊?⌋Op.R.K.) have in **d** the false accent *upā́sate*. The verse exceeds the proper measure of a *triṣṭubh* by the amount of *ákṣitam* in **a**. By Kāuç. (86. 5), it accompanies a sprinkling with water; ⌊Keç. says that it is the bones that are so sprinkled; so also the comm., who adds that it is done with a very leaky old dish (*sahasracchidra-pātra*): cf. Caland, l.c., p. 173. The sprinkling is part of the *dhuvana* ceremony, l.c., p. 137.⌋ *⌊The rationale of the intrusion becomes clear, I think, if we compare with our **a**, **b** the first pāda of iv. 27. 2, *útsam ákṣitaṁ viácanti yé sádā.*⌋

37. This funeral pile (?*kásāmbu*) [is] piled with piling; come, ye [his] fellows, look down at it; this mortal goeth to immortality; make ye houses for him according to his kindred.

A number of the mss. (including our P.M.I.) read in **a** *cittám*, as in 14 **a** above. The *pada*-text at end of **b** is *paçyata : ā́ : ita*. Some of the mss. make a blundering insertion of signs of *kampa* in *mártyo 'yám* in **c**. O. has at the end *-sámbudham*. The comm. shows its usual skill in explaining *kasāmbu;* it means *kasāç cā 'mbūni ca*, *kasa* being by abbreviation from *kīkasa*, and = *asthi!* Kāuç. (86.11) has the verse accompany the viewing of the bone-relics ⌊which are now in the trench, says Keç.⌋ by the 'fellows' of the deceased; the comm. says that either the relatives or all are to look at them as deposited in the hollow, while the manager recites the verse. The meter of the last pāda is redundant, and suggests emendation of the closing word. ⌊The vs., with its *cayanena citam* and *gṛhān* (cf. ÇB. as cited below under vs. 55), seems clearly to refer to a grave-mound; but the ritual use, with its trench, is in flat contradiction with such reference.⌋

38. Be thou just here, winning riches, with thought here, with ability here; be thou here, very heroic, vigor-bestowing, not smitten away.

The comm. understands *iha citta iha kratuḥ* as four independent words. According to Kāuç. (87. 21), the verse is made to accompany the taking of one of two lighted sticks of wood (see under 1. 56), and setting it up in the dirt (see under 2. 34). That this was its original office may be questioned; perhaps it is rather an invocation of the ancestor for help to his descendants.

39. These waters, rich in honey, satisfying (*abhi-tṛp*) son [and] grandson, yielding to the Fathers *svadhā́* [and] *amṛ́ta* — let the heavenly waters gratify both sides.

That is, the Fathers on the one side, and their living descendants on the other. Some of the mss. (including our O.R.) accent *abhí* in **a**. The *abhi* could extremely well be spared, and its omission would make the verse a good *āstārapañkti* ⌊with *triṣṭubh* close in **c** and **d**⌋. According to Kāuç., the next verse is used in the *piṇḍapitṛyajña* while pouring water on the fire (88. 23), after the presentation of the *piṇḍas*, and this one while then rinsing the mouth (88. 24).

⌊As to vs. 40, see p. xcvii, note.⌋

40. O waters, send forth (*pra-hi*) Agni unto the Fathers; this sacrifice of mine let the Fathers enjoy; they who attach themselves unto a sitting refreshment, may they confirm to us wealth having all heroes.

A corresponding verse is found in HGS. (in ii. 10. 6), reading thus: *āpo devīḥ pra hiṇutā 'gnim etaṁ yajñam pitaro no juṣantām : māsī 'mām ūrjam uta ye bhajante te no rayiṁ sarvavīraṁ ni yacchantu;* and the comparison appears to convict our unintelligible third pāda of being a very gross corruption. ⌊Observe that the word preceding *āsīnām* ends in *m*, and cf. the cases assembled under xviii. 2. 3.⌋ The comm. has no difficulty in explaining 'a sitting refreshment' as "a *piṇḍa* set upon the *barhis*." Both editions read at the end *yachān*, but all the mss. save one of SPP's read *yachāt;* the comm. has *-ān*. The Anukr. does not heed that the first pāda is *jagatī*. For the ritual application, see under the preceding verse. ⌊With **a**, cf. 2. 4 **d**, above.⌋

41. They kindle the immortal one, oblation-carrying, ghee-loving; he knoweth the deposited deposits, the Fathers that are gone away to the distances.

The comm., with his usual disregard of the accent, takes *ghṛtaprīyam* as from *ghṛtá* + *priyá* ⌊*prītikaram ājyaṁ yasya*⌋. For the ritual use as prescribed by Kāuç. 87. 22, see under 2. 34, one of the verses that accompanies it. But the verse is used also, by Kāuç. 86. 18, at the end of the ceremony of interment on "making the devouring (*saṁkasuka*) fire blaze up"; this the comm. does not report in his statement of *viniyoga*. ⌊Caland appears to be right in thinking that the *pratīka samindhate* means *samindhate saṁkasukam*, xii. 2. 11, and not our verse here. See under xii. 2. 11 and note the free use of vss. from xii. 2. in the *sūtras* immediately following 86. 18.⌋

42. What stirabout for thee, what rice-dish, what flesh I offer (*ni-pṛ*) to thee, be they for thee rich in *svadhā́*, rich in honey, dripping with ghee.

The second half-verse is identical with 3. 68 **c**, **d**, above. Nearly all the mss. (of ours, all save Op.) accent *mántham* in **a**; both editions read *manthám*. The comm. again ⌊see under 2. 30⌋ notes the technical sense of *ni-pṛ*: *niparaṇaṁ nāma pitryopavītinā parācīnapāṇinā pitrarthaṁ coditadravyasya prakṣepaḥ*. By Kāuç. 84. 6, the verse accompanies an offering of the articles mentioned, in the hut (*vimita*) in the preparation for interment of the relics; the comm. overlooks this. ⌊For the ceremony, cf. Caland, *Todtengebräuche*, p. 137.⌋

43. What grains I scatter along for thee, mixed with sesame, rich in *svadhā́*, be they for thee abundant, prevailing; them let king Yama approve for thee.

This is a repetition of 3. 69, being distinguished as such (and not of 4. 26) by the words *íti pū́rvā*, instead of *íty ékā*, after the *pratīka* in most of the mss. Nevertheless, the two *saṁhitā*-mss. of ours (O.R.) which give it in full, read *udbhvī́s* in **c**, the word in 4. 26, instead of *vibhvī́s*, that in 3. 69; and the comm. also states the repetition to be of 4. 26; and SPP's text reads accordingly. ⌊For the ritual, see under 3. 69.⌋

44. This [is] the former, the after down-track, by which thy former Fathers went away; they who are the forerunners, the followers (? *abhiṣác*) of it, they carry thee to the world of the well-doing.

Our reading *abhiṣā́cas* is an emendation, almost every ms. giving *abhiçā́cas* (our Op. has *abhi॰sā́caḥ*, and also one ⌊or two⌋ of SPP's authorities); *-ṣā́c-* is of course intended, and the comm. gives it. SPP's text follows the mss. The comm. explains *niyāna* as the wagon (*çakaṭa*) on which the corpse is carried to the funeral pile; and the 'forerunners' and 'followers' as the oxen that draw it, in front and on all sides: which is doubtless not at all the true sense; he also reads *vahantu* in **d**. The verse is one of the *hariṇīs* ⌊Kāuç. 80.35; 82.31 note⌋: see under i.61. It lacks (in **a**) a syllable of being a full *triṣṭubh*. Its second pāda is identical with i.54 **b**.

45. On Sarasvatī do the pious call; on Sarasvatī, while the sacrifice is being extended; on Sarasvatī do the well-doers call; may Sarasvatī give what is desirable to the worshiper.

46. On Sarasvatī do the Fathers call, arriving at the sacrifice on the south; sitting on this *barhís*, do ye revel; assign thou to us food free from disease.

47. O Sarasvatī, that wentest in company with the songs, with the *svadhā́s*, O goddess, reveling with the Fathers, assign thou to the sacrificer here a portion of refreshment of thousand-fold value, abundance of wealth.

These three verses are a repetition of i.41–43 ⌊see notes thereon⌋, quoted by *íti tisráḥ* in most mss., but written out by our O.R. (both accenting *dakṣiṇā́* in 46 **b**).

48. Thee, being earth, I make enter into earth; may god Dhātar lengthen out our life-time; let him that goeth very far away be a finder of good for you; then may the dead (pl.) come to be (*sam-bhū*) among the Fathers.

The first pāda is identical with that of xii. 3. 22, and hence the comm. here makes the blunder of reporting this verse as quoted by Kāuç. 61.30,* whereas it is evidently the other; and he explains the meaning to be that earth is smeared upon the vessel ⌊porridge-pot⌋, which is entirely out of place in this connection, the analogy being with our own phrase "earth to earth." The problematic *párāparāitā* ⌊p. *párā°parāitā*⌋ in **c** is rendered strictly according to its form, as if composed of *párā-parā* + *etṛ*; the Pet. Lexx. render it as "one who departs after another or in due order"; but I cannot see how this meaning is arrived at. The comm. reads *parāparetās* (our O. gives *-retas*), and explains it as *dūradeçam parāñmukham ito gataḥ*. The comm. also, against *pada*-text and accent, understands *adhā 'mṛtās* in **d**. *⌊Cf. p. 869, ¶ 7.⌋

49. Start ye (du.) forward hither, wipe off that which the portents (?*abhibhā́*) have said there of you; from that come ye, inviolable ones, to this which is better, being bestowers here on me, a giver to the Fathers.

This is highly obscure, and the second half-verse, especially, is rendered only mechanically, and even then with substitution of *vásīyas* where nearly all the mss. have *váçīyas* or *vaçīyas* (our M.I.D., and one of SPP's, *vaçāyas*, which our text, quite unsuccessfully, emends to *vaçā́ya*); SPP. admits *váçīyas* in his text; the comm. has *vásīyas*. According to Kāuç. (82.40), the verse is addressed to the two kine (the comm. says, the two that have drawn the hearse): the direction is *iti gāvāv upayachati*; it is perhaps intended as a purification of them after the ill-omened service which they have performed. In **c** the vocative, *aghnyāu*, is an emendation, SPP. reading with the mss. *aghnyā́u*; but the accentuation of the mss. is here very unauthoritative; the comm. also takes the word as vocative. Nearly all our mss. (all save O.Op.R.) leave *ūcus* in **b** without accent. The comm. is not ashamed to derive *abhibhās* formally from *abhi-bhū*, and to explain it by *abhibhāvakās* or *dūṣakās*; his general explication of the pāda, as intimating a reproach brought against the pair for having been engaged in such business, is doubtless good. The defective meter suggests a corruption of the text. The comm. takes *iha* and *bhojanāu* in **d** as two independent words, and renders *bhojanāu* by *bhojayitārāu* or *pālayitārāu*. Two of SPP's mss. also accent the words separately. ⌊On his margin Whitney pencilled the memorandum, "Recast this note."⌋ ⌊In Ppp., immediately after our xvii. 1. 30, comes this verse. Its appearance in that place is possibly to be interpreted as a hint at the existence in Ppp. of our book xviii., of which, however, there are no other traces in Ppp. save the straggling verses 1. 46 (in ii.), 2. 13 (in xix.), 2. 17 and 3. 56 (in xx.).⌋ ⌊☞ Last addition misplaced: see p. 1016.⌋

50. This sacrificial gift hath come excellently to us, given by him, well-milking, vigor-bestowing; old age, coming close to (?*upa-pṛc*) them living in youth, shall lead these away together unto the Fathers.

According to Kāuç. (82. 41, the next rule to that which quotes the preceding verse), the verse accompanies the giving ⌊or receiving: comm.⌋ of a *dakṣiṇā* or sacrificial gift of at least ten kine ⌊the comm. says one⌋, at the close of the after-cremation ceremonies. But this gives no clew to the meaning of the second half-verse, whose connection with the first remains very obscure. The two editions agree in their text throughout, but *upapṛ́ñcatī* is obviously an inadmissible accentuation, requiring emendation to *upa-pṛñcatī́*; and it is against all rule to accent any but the last of two or more prefixes to the same verb: hence *upasampárāṇayāt* — which accent is given by ⌊two or⌋ three of SPP's authorities, and which he therefore had good reason for adopting (it is also given by our O.Op.R., all collated after our publication). ⌊If I understand the Collation Book, O.R. accent *upasám párā-*.⌋ Three of our *pada*-mss. (Bp.Kp.D., but D. not accented) make the anomalous division *upa॰sám : parānayāt*; the other (Op.) has *upa॰sampárānayāt*, which is the regular and proper form: see Prāt. iv. 2 and note, and iv. 7. In **c**, our Bp.D. (but D. without accent) have the strange reading *yāú : váne*, and Op. *yāuvánesu*; while Bs. ⌊O.K.⌋ also accent *yāú váne*, as do two of SPP's mss. (three others *yāuváne*, and only two, with our M.T.R.s.m., *yāúvane*).

51. This *barhís* I bring forward for the Fathers; a living, higher one I strew for the gods; that do thou ascend, O man, becoming sacrificial; let the Fathers acknowledge thee who art departed.

A corresponding verse is found in TA. (in vi. 7. 2), which reads in **a** *bharema*, for **b** *devébhyo jī́vanta úttaram bharema*, for **c**, **d** *táttvam ārohā́so médhyo bháva* ⌊Poona ed. *bhávam**⌋ *yaména tvám yamyā́ saṁvidānā́ḥ*: its text is plainly in part corrupt. *Bhávan* in **c** is an emendation, all our mss. save one (Op.), and the majority of SPP's, reading *bhavan*, as if mixing the word up with *bhava*, imperative. The comm. reads in **b** *jīvan*. Neither this verse nor its predecessor is to be called with any reason a *jagatī*; ⌊but 50 **c**, **d** and 51 **c** have *jagatī* cadences⌋. This has the same *pratīka*, so far as concerns the first two words, as 1. 46, and it is impossible to tell which of the two verses is quoted by Kāuç.; but the comm. declares the first half of this one to be used as *darbha*-grass is strewn upon the wood of the funeral pile, and the second half as the corpse is laid supine upon the grass thus strewn: that is to say, this verse is intended in Kāuç. 80. 51; ⌊so also Caland, WZKM. viii. 368⌋. *⌊The mss. vary between *bhavaṁ* and *bhava* and the TA. comm. understands *bhava*.⌋

52. Thou hast sat upon this *barhís*, thou hast become sacrificial; let the Fathers acknowledge thee who art departed; collect thy body according to its joints; I arrange thy members with *bráhman*.

The reading *yathāparú* in **c** is an emendation, made alike by both editions;* the comm. has it, but all the mss. give *yathāpurú* — which is perhaps not altogether untranslatable: 'according to its muchness.' We should expect in **b** rather *jānan* than another *jānantu* (51 **d**). The verse evidently belongs with its predecessor ⌊used at 80. 51⌋, but is entirely separated from it in ritual use, accompanying, according to Kāuç. 85. 25, ⌊the assembling of the bones so as to form a human figure, as explained under 3. 25⌋; next after it are quoted 2. 24, 26 and 3. 25–37. Pāda **b** has an extra syllable. ⌊With regard to the place of the vs., see p. 870, ¶ 1, and p. 870, end.⌋

*⌊In support of the emendation, SPP. adduces ix. 5. 4, with its *yathāparú* and *paruçás*. I think that *yathāparú* (as against *yathāpurú*) is strongly supported by the sense (much less so by the mss.) of the two Kāuçikan passages which give the ritual for ix. 5. 4 and for this vs. respectively, to wit, 64. 10 and 85. 25. In the latter passage the mss. have *yathāparuḥ saṁcinoti* (one, *-puru*), and Keçava says *yathāparu*, and Bloomfield emends to *yathāparu;* but I am not quite sure that it is necessary, for *yathāparus* may not be bad Sanskrit.⌋

53. King leaf is the cover of the dishes; the strength of refreshment, the power, vigor, hath come to us, dispensing (*vi-dhā*) life-time to the living (pl.), in order to length of life for a hundred autumns.

The comm. reads in **a**, against the *pada*-text and the metrical requirement, the later abbreviated *pidhānam*. It understands by *parṇa* ('leaf') the tree so called, or the *palāça*-tree; and this may be correct; this tree, it says, owing to its sacrificial quality, is the overlord of trees. ⌊Cf. the synonyms *brahmapādapa* (in Hemacandra) and *yājñika*, *viprapriyā* (in Rājanighaṇṭu): cf. also *brahma vāi palāçaḥ*, ÇB. xiii. 8. 4[1].⌋ It takes *ūrjás* as a nominative, which makes a decidedly easier reading, but is unsupported by Vedic usage elsewhere. Only two or three mss. (including our Op.) read in **c** *vidádhat*, the rest *vídadhat* (and the *pada*-mss. *ví°dadhat*, which is absurd ⌊cf. note to xiii. 3. 17⌋, but rather indicates that the word was correctly viewed as a participle); and SPP. accepts *vídadhat*, p. *ví°dadhat*, because the comm. supports the majority of the mss. by understanding *ví dadhat*. The true reading is, beyond all reasonable question, *vidádhat*, as our text gives it. The meter seems to be viewed by the Anukr. as 10 + 11 : 8 + 11 = 40; it is rather too irregular to merit a name. Its use* in Kāuç. (86. 6) follows that of vs. 36 above; it accompanies the laying of middle-foliage (? *madhyamapalāçās*) down upon the offering dishes: the comm. says, more explicitly, upon the nine dishes spoken of in vss. 16–24, and also upon the perforated plates (*madhyapalāçapatrāir ācchādayet*); Keçava's explanation corresponds closely with this.

*⌊The *palāça* has ternate leaves, from 8 to 16 inches long: Roxburgh, *Flora Indica*, p. 540, Calc. ed. 1874. By *madhyama parṇa* or *palāça* is meant the middle one of any of these ternate groups; the middle one is especially fit for holy use by reason of its likeness to a sacrificial ladle: TB. i. 6. 10[3], *madhyaména parṇéna juhoti: srúg ghy èṣā́:* cf. also Sāyaṇa on TS. i. 8. 6, p. 1167, Poona. I am indebted to Caland's excellent paragraphs on this subject, ZDMG. liii. 212. — The "nine dishes" are the last nine of the eleven whose deposition is explained above, under vs. 16. The "plates" are the leaky old dishes noticed above under vs. 36.⌋

54. The share of refreshment that generated this man; — the stone attained (*gam*) the overlordship of the foods; — him praise ye, all-befriended, with oblations; may that Yama make (*dhā*) us to live further.

The second half-verse is identical with 3. 63 **c**, **d** above. The translation of the first half is purely mechanical, the sense being wholly obscure. The comm. renders *bhāgás* by *sambhaktā*, and *ūrjás* by *annasyā 'sthisamīpasthāpitacarulakṣaṇasya*, *yamas* being the implied subject; then the 'stone' is the one used to cover the same *annāni* or *caravas*. A couple of our mss. (O.R.) and one of SPP's read in **b** *áçvā́ 'nnām;* several (including our O.Op.R.) have *ádhipatyam*. Some of ours (O.R.K.) and three of SPP's leave *jagāma* without an accent, which seems better, and is implied in the translation. One of SPP's gives *bhāgám* in **a**. In Kāuç. (86. 7) the verse is used next after 53, and accompanies the covering of the same dishes with stones — or, the comm. adds, with bricks. ⌊Cf. Caland, *Todtengebräuche*, p. 157.⌋ It lacks a syllable in **a**. Our edition leaves *viçvamitrās* in this verse without accent, on the authority of two of our mss. (Bp.M.); all SPP's give *viçvámitrās*, p. *viçváॱmitrāḥ*, as in 3. 63, and he accepts this in his text. The two verses ought of course to be made to agree, but there is little reason for preferring either nominative or vocative ⌊the comm. takes the doubtful word as voc.⌋. ⌊If the Viçvāmitras be not meant here and at 3. 63, then Weber's observations reported under 3. 16 lose some of their basis.⌋

55. As the five clans (*mānavá*) scattered (*vap*) a dwelling (*harmyá*) for Yama, so do I scatter a dwelling, that there may be many of me (?).

A corresponding verse is found in TA. (in vi. 6. 2); it reads *hārmyám* in **a** and **c**, and *evám* in **c**; and for **d** *yáthā́ 'sāma jīvaloké bhū́rayas*, which, however unmetrical, is at least capable of being translated, while this can hardly be claimed for our **d**. All the mss. read at the end *ásatas*, save one of SPP's, which follows the comm. in giving *ásata*, as is read in both editions — in ours, purely as an emendation. The comm. makes no difficulty of taking *ásata* as = *syāta*, and explaining "that ye my relatives may be numerous"; but that would be *ásatha;* and *ásata* has no grammatical standing of any kind, and hence is to be rejected. The comparison with TA. at least shows that the pāda is corrupt. The comm. foolishly divides *evā́vapāmi* in **c** into *eva āvapāmi*. Three of our *pada*-mss. (not Op.) most absurdly divide *áva-pan* in **b**; it is strange that SPP. reports nothing of the kind from his authorities. By Kāuç. (86. 11) the verse is used next after 2. 50 etc., with the direction *iti saṁçritya* ('on finishing the pile'?); the comm. says that with it they are to divide (*kuṭṭay*) leftwise, with sticks or bricks, the part of the cemetery on which the pile stood: in TA. it accompanies the "placing in the jar [of relics] the drugs called *sarvāuṣadhi*" (hence, perhaps, the use of *vap* in the verse, as they are strewn in); ⌊but cf. Caland, *Todtengebräuche*, p. 149⌋.

⌊On *saṁçritya* (?) and *kuṭṭayeyus*. — Kāuç. 86. 10 reads: *idam id vā u na* (xviii. 2. 50) *upa sarpa* (3. 49) *asāu hā* (4. 66) *iti cinvanti*. Sūtra 11 continues: *yathā yamāya* (4. 55) *iti saṁçritya*. Upon 10, Keç. says: *çilābhir* (? *çalākābhir ?*) *viṣamābhir iṣṭakābhir vā prasavyaṁ cinvanti çmaçānam*. And the AV. comm., in giving the ritual for 2. 50 (p. 115) and 3. 49 (p. 161) and 4. 66 (p. 233), says: *çmaçānadeçaṁ viṣamasaṁkhyākābhiḥ çalākābhir iṣṭakābhir vā prasavyaṁ cinuyāt*, using the very same words in all three passages, save that he leaves out the second word in the second passage. Then, for 4. 55 (p. 224) he says: *çalākābhir iṣṭakābhir vā prasavyaṁ citaṁ çmaçānapradeçaṁ kuṭṭayeyuḥ*. — In all these passages, *çmaçāna* or *çmaçāna-deça* or *-pradeça* must mean the mound which they heap (*ci*) over the buried bones: cf. ÇB. xiii. 8. 1[1] *athā 'smāi çmaçānaṁ kurvanti, gṛhān vā prajñānaṁ vā* ('or as a monument'), and Harisvāmin's comment, p. 1017[15], *çmaçānam prasiddham asthi-saṁrakṣa-vāstu;* the mound is, as with us, not quite knee-high, ÇB. xiii. 8. 3[12], *adhojānu*. — The meaning of our comm. on 4. 55, accordingly, seems to be: 'after the mound has been heaped up (*citam*), they should pat (*kuṭṭay*) it with splints of wood or with bricks, [going around it, as they pat it,] to the left.' — If this be right and if *kuṭṭay* is the comm's version of the word after *iti* in *sūtra* 11, then I suspect that Bloomfield has not hit the right reading in the printed text. Whitney's 'on finishing the pile' would call for *saṁsthāpya;* but *saṁçnathya* is much nearer to the meaning of *kuṭṭay* and also to the probable intention of Bl's mss., and I would accordingly read *saṁçnathya* in place of the printed *saṁçritya*. Root *çnath* means 'thrust, push,' in their ordinary and in their obscene senses, and here, with *sam*, 'to make [the mound] compact or firm by striking or beating or patting,' as a modern gravemaker pats the mound with his spade to give it shape and firmness.⌋

56. Wear (*bhṛ*) thou this gold, which thy father wore before; of thy father, going to heaven (*svargá*), do thou wipe off the right hand.

The majority of mss. read *pitur* in **c**, some *pítur*, and hardly any (of ours, only Op.) *pitúr*. Many of ours have *mṛḍhḍhi* in **d**: see Prāt. i. 94 and note. The comm. strangely gives *pipṛhi* ⌊cf. xiii. 1. 1, note⌋ in **a** (though *abibhar* in **b**!). According to Kāuç. 80. 46, 47, the first half-verse is used as the manager takes with the right hand some gold worn by the deceased, smears it with ghee, and passes it to the eldest son; the second half-verse, as he makes him wipe off his (of course, the father's) right hand; the comm. states it thus: "with the first half he makes the oldest son heat (*ādīpayet:* as if the comm. read in Kāuç. *ādīpayati* instead of *ādāp-*) in the fire gold found in the hand of the deceased; with the other half the son should wipe the deceased's hand."

57. Both those who are living and those who are dead; those who are born and those who are worshipful — for them let there go a brook of ghee, honey-streamed, overflowing.

We had the second half-verse above as 3. 72 **c**, **d**, only with *çatádhārā* instead of *mádhudhārā*. The mss. are again at variance as to the accent of *kulyā;* and the majority also accent *madhúdhārā*, as if they had *çatádh-* in mind ⌊cf. end of note to 1. 42 above⌋. *Yajñíya* is a queer antithesis to *jātá*, and the comm. reads instead *jajñiyās*, explaining it as *jajñim utpattiṁ yānti gacchanti:* that is, *jajñi* + root *yā!* The comm. also understands in **d** *madhudhārās*, as object of *vyundati*. A corresponding verse is found in TA. (in vi. 12): it omits the first *ca* in **a**; has at end of **b** the almost acceptable reading *jántyās* (it ought to be *jántvās*); offers in **c** the curious corruption *dhārayitum* for *kulyāi 'tu;* ⌊and accents *mádhudhārā* in **d**⌋. The schol. add the verse to 56, as used by Kāuç. 80. 46; the Kāuç. uses it twice with 3. 72: see under that verse; in TA. it has an utterly different application, in the ceremony of turning loose the cow that was led with the corpse to the funeral pile.

58. There purifies itself the conspicuous bull of the prayers, the sun of days, lengthener out of dawns, of the sky (*dív*); the breath of the rivers hath made the jars to resound loudly; entering Indra's heart with skill.

This is a verse out of one of the most formidable hymns of the RV. soma-book (RV. ix. 86. 19), and occurring also twice in SV. (i. 559; ii. 171). In **b**, RV. reads *sómo áhnaḥ pratarītó 'ṣáso diváḥ;* in **c**, *krāṇā́* and *avīvaçat;* in **d**, *hā́rdi* and *manīṣíbhis;* with this SV. in general agrees, but has, with AV., *áhnām* and *uṣásām* in **b**, and *acikradat* in **c**; it is peculiar in reading *prāṇā́* (p. *pra॰ānā́*) at beginning of **c**; a corruption, doubtless, which is carried out to greater intelligibility in our *prāṇás*. The

AV. corruption, of both sense and meter, in **b**, *pratárītā uṣ-*, supported by the *pada*-reading *pra○tárītāḥ*, is very strange; of our mss., only three (O.R., supported by Op. *-tā : uṣ-*) have the correct *-to 'ṣ-*; of SPP's, according to his account, about half support *-to 'ṣ-*, and he accordingly admits that reading into his text; we ought to have done the same by emendation. ⌊For *hā́rdim āviçā́n* (p. *ā○viçā́n*) *man-*, the comm. reads *hārdima . . . aviçat . . . man-*.⌋ What right the verse has here (or vs. 60, coming from the same RV. hymn) does not appear; neither Kāuç. nor the comm. uses it in the ritual; but the latter says, as if by way of excuse, that, as the Fathers enjoy the fruit of the soma-sacrifices which they have offered, soma is praised in the ceremonies for the Fathers. He explains the 'rivers' in **c** as the *vasatīvarī* waters. ⌊He says, p. 224[23], *vṛṣā matīnām ityādīnāṁ tisṛṇām* (vss. 58, 59, 60) *pitṛmedha eva kāṇḍokto viniyogo 'nusaṁdheyaḥ*, which is not clear to me: should it be *pitṛmedhakāṇḍa evokto?*⌋

59. Let thy sparkling (? *tveṣá*) smoke cover, being in the sky, extended bright; for thou, O purifier, shinest like the sun with luster, with beauty (*kṛpā́*).

The verse is RV. vi. 2. 6 and SV. i. 83; both read *ṛṇvati* in **a**; ⌊in **b**, SV. combines *diví sáñ ch-*: cf. *diví ṣáñ ch-* at xvii. 1. 12⌋. The comm. explains *kṛpā* as = *kṛpayā* or *stutyā*. Vāit. (6. 11) uses the verse, with others, in the ceremony of establishing the fires.

60. Soma (*índu*) verily goes forward to Indra's rendezvous; the comrade does not violate (*pra-mī*) the comrade's agreements; thou rushest to join, as a male after females — soma, in the jar, by a road of a hundred tracks.

The verse corresponds to RV. ix. 86. 16, which has, however, important variants: in **a**, *pró ayāsīd índur* and *niṣkṛtám;* in **b**, *saṁgíram;* in **c**, *yuvatíbhis* and *arṣati;* in **d**, *çatáyāmnā;* SV. (i. 557; ii. 502) agrees with RV. except in the last item, having, like our text, *-yāmanā*. ⌊The meter shows that it is to be pronounced *-yāmanā*, whichever way it is written: cf. JAOS. x. 532.⌋ Our *níṣkṛtim* is hardly better than a corruption of the RV. reading; but the comm. understands it as Indra's "belly" (*jaṭharalakṣaṇaṁ sthānam*), and supports his opinion by quoting RV. iii. 35. 6. *Saṁgirás*, in **b**, is understood in the translation as *saṁgíras* (which is read by two or three mss., including our O.), the former being unintelligible; the comm. gives two explanations, both implying the accent *-gír-*, one from *sam-gṛ* 'agree,' the other from *sam-gṛ* or *-gil* 'swallow down,' thus finding in the verse another "belly" (*saṁgiras* = *saṁgiram* = *udaram*). Our text of **c** spoils both the meter and the connection, making the line render very lamely; the comm. reads *yóṣā*, and takes it as an instrumental (like *yuvatíbhis*); in **d** he has the RV.SV. reading. The metrical definition of the Anukr. is worthless. ⌊The RV. verse is a good *jagatī*, and so is this, barring **c**, where the corruptions have spoiled meter as well as sense.⌋

61. They have eaten; they have revelled ⌊surely⌋; they have shaken off (*áva*) those that are dear; having own brightness (*svábhānu*), they have praised; inspired, youngest, we implore.

The verse corresponds to RV. i. 82. 2 **a–d**, and is found also in other texts: SV. i. 415; VS. iii. 51; TS. in i. 8. 5[2]; MS. in i. 10. 3. All these agree in reading in **c** *priyā́s* for *priyā́n*, and, for **d**, *víprā návişṭhayā matī́;* and they add a fifth pāda, a refrain, having nothing to do with the meaning of the verse. A majority of the AV.

mss. (including our M.O.Op.R.K.D.) read *ávā 'priyā́n* (p. *áva : apriyā́n*), and this is perhaps the true Atharvan text (though the accent, in that case, should be *ávā́ 'priyān*), and defensible on the ground of sense; our last pāda is nothing but a senseless corruption. In Kāuç. (88. 27) the verse is used, next after vss. 81 ff.,* in the *piṇḍapitṛyajña*, with the direction *ity uttarasicam avadhūya;* the comm. paraphrases this to mean that one is to perform an additional sprinkling (? *uttarapariṣeka*) next after the worship (*upasthāna*) of the *piṇḍas*. For the application of the verse to the Fathers, compare TB. ii. 6. 3[2], *ákṣan pitáraḥ : ámīmadanta pitáraḥ*, etc.; ⌊also Sāyaṇa's comm. on TS. i. 8. 5[2], Poona ed., p. 1159⌋. *⌊It is to be noted that in the *piṇḍapitṛyajña* of the VS. (ii. 31), *amīmadanta pitaraḥ* etc. comes just before the verses corresponding to our vss. 81–85.⌋ ⌊ÇGS., i. 15, prescribes the RV. verse for use when the bride greases the axle of the wedding-car: is this because of the resemblance of *akṣam* ('axle') to *akṣan* (root *ghas*)?!⌋ ⌊See p. lxxix.⌋

62. Come ye, O Fathers, delectable, by profound roads that the Fathers travel, assigning to us lifetime and progeny; and do ye attach yourselves to us with abundances of wealth.

The last pāda was found above as ix. 4. 24 **d**. Corresponding verses are found in HGS. ii. 10. 5 and MB. ii. 3. 5. For **a**, **b**, MB. reads *eta pitaraḥ somyāso gambhīrebhiḥ pathibhiḥ pūrviṇebhiḥ;* and as second half-verse it has our 3. 14 **c**, **d**. HGS. has *ā yāta pitaraḥ somyā gambhīraḥ* (misprint for *-rāiḥ?*) *pathibhiḥ pūrvyāiḥ*, with an altogether different **c**, **d**. We should prefer *somyāsas* unaccented, both in this verse and in the next, but no ms. so reads. The comm. has in **c** *dadhata*, which he pronounces the same as *dhatta*. In Kāuç., in the *pitṛnidhāna* ceremony, the verse accompanies (83. 27) the bringing of the bone-relics, before sunset ⌊into the hut: Keç.⌋; and it is followed (83. 28, 29) by 1. 52 and 2. 29; then, in the *piṇḍapitṛyajña* (87. 28), the three are repeated; the comm. notices only the latter use, stating that with this verse one is to scatter sesame on the *barhis* spread for the purpose of giving the *piṇḍas*. In number of syllables, the verse answers to the description of the Anukr. (9 + 10 : 11 + 11 = 41). ⌊The MB. reading makes a rectification of the meter at the beginning of **b**.⌋

63. Go away, O Fathers, delectable, by profound roads that go to the stronghold (*pūryā́ṇa*); then, in a month, come ye again to our houses to eat the oblation, with good progeny, with good heroes.

All the *pada*-mss. commit the strange blunder of dividing *ā́yāta* in **c** into *ā́ : ayāta;* both editions make the necessary correction; the comm. also understands *ā yāta*. In **d**, some of the mss. make great difficulty over *áttum*, reading also ⌊*annum*,⌋ *atnum*, *antum*, *atnūn*, and the comm. gives as a compound *haviratnūn;* but our O.R.D., and the majority of SPP's authorities, have the correct reading; as does also HGS. in its corresponding verse ⌊ii. 13. 2⌋. HGS. ⌊spoils the meter of **a** by modernizing *somyā́sas* to⌋ *somyās;* reads in **b** *pūrvyāis;* ⌊and begins **c** with *atha*⌋. The first half-verse occurs also in MS. i. 10. 3 and AÇS. ii. 7. 9. MS. makes nearly good meter of it, reading *páre 'tana pitaraḥ somyāso gambhīrébhiḥ pathíbhiḥ pūrvébhiḥ* (which should evidently be emended to *pūrvyébhis*); AÇS. differs from this only by having at the end *pūrviṇebhis* (with K. and Kap.S., as pointed out by Schröder). Prāt. iii. 83 quotes the word *pūryāṇa*. Kāuç. uses the verse in the *piṇḍapitṛyajña* (88. 28), next after vs. 61, in dismissing the Fathers after their feast of *piṇḍas*. The metrical description of the Anukr. is very poor: ⌊it is probable that the verse originally was 11 + 11 : 12 + 11; but its **b** is spoiled metrically⌋.

64. What one limb of you Agni Jātavedas left when making you go to the Fathers' world, that same for you I fill up again; revel ye, O Fathers, in heaven (*svargá*) with [all] your limbs.

HGS. has (in ii. 11. 1) an analogous but quite different verse: *yad vaḥ kravyād aṅgam adahal lokān ayam praṇayañ jātavedāḥ: tad vo 'haṁ punar ā veçayāmy ariṣṭāḥ sarvāir aṅgāiḥ sam bhavata pitaraḥ.* Most of our mss. (all except O.Op.R.), but, by his account, only one of SPP's, leave *ajahāt* in **a** unaccented; on the other hand, all without exception accent in **d** *pitáras*, which SPP. accordingly admits into his text; but our emendation to *pitaras* is plainly necessary. What the comm. says is here unknown, because the manuscript shows a considerable lacuna, involving the latter half of the explanation of this verse, with the text of the next and the larger part of its exposition. Kāuç. uses the verse (88. 5) in the *piṇḍapitṛyajña*, next after vss. 74, 78, to accompany an offering of rice-grains with the stirring-stick (*sāyavana* ⌊that is, *sa-āyavana*: SPP's *sāṁyavana*, p. 233⁴, does not seem right⌋). ⌊As to completeness of limbs in the other world, see my note to 4. 12, above. This verse was translated metrically by Whitney, *O. and L. S.*, i. 57.⌋

65. Jātavedas has been the messenger sent forth, at evening, at close of day to be honored by men; — thou hast given to the Fathers; they have eaten after their wont; eat thou, O god, the presented oblations.

We had the second half-verse above as 3. 42 **c**, **d**. Part of our mss. (O.Op.R.D.), with, so far as appears, the majority of SPP's, read in **b** *upavándyas*, and the latter accordingly adopts it in his text; the root *vand* does not appear to be anywhere else combined with *upa*. The line reads like a kind of echo of RV. iv. 54. 1 ⌊TB. iii. 7. 13⁴⌋. The verse is the last one quoted in the *piṇḍapitṛyajña* by Kāuç. (89. 14), to accompany the withdrawal of the "extended" fires. ⌊By "extended" I suppose W. means the technical *praṇīta* (cf. comm., p. 233⁶). The words of Kāuç. are *agnim pratyānayati:* the ceremony seems to be the same as that prescribed by ÇB. at ii. 4. 2²⁴, *punar ulmukam api sṛjati*, and by ÇÇS. at iv. 5. 9, *ulmukam agnāu kṛtvā.*⌋

66. Thou yonder, ho! hither thy mind! as sisters (*jāmí*) a *kákutsala*, do thou cover him, O earth.

The translation implies the evidently necessary emendation to *ásāu* in **a**; both editions give *asāú*, because this is read by all the mss.; the comm. understands the word as a vocative; it also reads the interjection as *hā*, while the *pada*-text gives *hāí*. It further glosses *jāmayas* ⌊alternatively⌋ with *bhaginyas*, and reads *kakutsthalam*, explaining it as *pradhānāvayavapradeçam*, and paraphrasing with *putrādīnāṁ çiraḥ-prabhṛtīny aṅgāni çītātapavātanivāraṇāya.* The Pet. Lexx. conjecture *kakutsala* to be a pet word for a little child. We had the third pāda above as 2. 50 **d**, 51 **d**, and 3. 50 **d**. Kāuç. uses the verse (86. 10) with 2. 50 and 3. 49 in the ceremony over the bone-relics. The comm. includes with it vs. 67.

67. Let the worlds where the Fathers sit adorn themselves (*çumbh*); I make thee to sit in the world where the Fathers sit.

The first phrase is VS. v. 26 f, which, however, reads *çúndhantām;* Āp. vii. 9. 10 has *çundhatāṁ lokaḥ pitṛṣadanaḥ.* ⌊For variants as between *çundh* and *çumbh*, cf. notes to vi. 115. 3; xii. 2. 40; 3. 13, 21, 26; xviii. 3. 56.⌋

68. Thou art the *barhís* of them that are our Fathers.

The metrical description of the Anukr. implies the reading *yé asm-*. In Kāuç. (87. 27) the verse is used with i. 51 etc. (see under i. 51) in connection with the strewing of *barhis*.

69. Loosen up the uppermost fetter from us, O Varuṇa, [loosen] down the lowest, off the midmost; then may we in thy sphere, O Āditya, be guiltless unto Aditi.

The verse ⌊which is RV. i. 24. 15, etc.⌋ occurred above as vii. 83. 3 ⌊which see⌋; among our mss., only O.R. write it out in full. The comm. notices the repetition, yet goes on to give a full explication. In Kāuç. (82. 8), it is used in the ceremony of the first day after cremation (next before 3. 56), with the direction *iti jyeṣṭhaḥ*, apparently implying that "the oldest" son of the deceased pours water on the attendants; the comm. says that with this verse, immediately after the cremation, all the Brahmans should take a bath (*snānaṁ kuryuḥ*).

70. Release from us all fetters, O Varuṇa, with which one is bound crosswise, with which lengthwise; so may we live hundreds of autumns, by thee, O king, guarded, defended.

The rendering of *samāmé* and *vyāmé* in **b** is far from certain: cf. iv. 16. 8. The comm. explains: *samāmo nāma vyāmasaṁjñitapradeçāt saṁkucitapramāṇako deçaḥ: saṁnihite pradeçe dūre pradeçe ce 'ti yāvat.* Two of our mss. (O.R.) and one of SPP's read *samāné;* and two or three of the latter have *badhyate*, without accent. Nearly all, again, read *çarádam* in **c** (our O.R.p.m. ⌊and one of SPP's⌋ *-das*), and SPP. admits *çarádam* into his text; our *-dām* is an emendation, and a necessary one, unless we take instead *-das*, as in apposition with *çatā́ni*. The comm. makes no difficulty of reading *-dam*, understanding it, according to one of his convenient rules of interpretation, as a sing. used in place of a plural. Most of our mss., again (except P.O.Op.R.), but only one of SPP's, accent *rā́jan*. The comm. points out that *rákṣamāṇās* is for *rákṣya-*, which is altogether probable, considering how easily a *y* is lost after *ṣ* or *ç*. The first pāda is identical with vii. 83. 4 **a**. All the *pada*-mss. except one of SPP's read *gupitā́* instead of *-tā́ḥ*. The comm. directs the verse to be recited for good fortune evening and morning at the end of the *daçarātra* in the *pitṛmedha*.

71. To Agni, carrier of the *kavyás*, [be] *svadhā́* [and] homage.

72. To Soma with the Fathers [be] *svadhā́* [and] homage.

⌊Verses 71–87 are prose, except vs. 75, with regard to which see p. 869, ¶ 5.⌋ These verses ⌊71, 72⌋ are found, in reversed order, in AÇS. ii. 6. 12. In VS. ii. 29 a, b, are found both, but with *svā́hā* in place of *svadhā́ námaḥ*, and the same in ÇÇS. iv. 4. 1 and GGS. iv. 2. 39, except that in the latter *svāhā* precedes the datives. VS. accents *pitṛmáte*. ⌊See also under vs. 74.⌋ In Kāuç. 87. 8, vss. 71–74 are combined in alternation with vss. 78–80 to accompany in the *piṇḍapitṛyajña* the scattering downward of three handfuls of offering; and ⌊are used⌋ again, later (88. 2, 3, 4) in the same ceremony, with oblations. ⌊Verse 71 is employed by Vāit. (9. 8) in the *sākamedha*, and I suspect (see p. 869, ¶ 7) that the *sūtra* intends vss. 72 and 73 also to be thus used: cf. also ĀpÇS. viii. 13. 15, 16.⌋

73. To the Fathers with Soma, *svadhā́* [and] homage.

74. To Yama with the Fathers, *svadhā́* [and] homage.

For the ritual use of these verses see the preceding note. ⌊Parallels of our vss. 72 and 74 and 71, and in that order, recur at MGS. ii. 9. 13: cf. the *pratīkas* in Knauer's Index, and also under *pitṛbhyas*, p. 152.⌋

75. Here is *svadhā́* for thee, O great-grandfather, and for them that are after (*ánu*) thee.

76. Here is *svadhā́* for thee, O grandfather, and for them that are after thee.

77. Here is *svadhā́* for thee, O father.

Passages analogous with these three verses are found in a number of other texts: TS. i. 8. 5[1]; AÇS. ii. 6. 15; Āp. i. 9. 1 (cf. also viii. 16. 6; xiii. 12. 9); ÇÇS. iv. 4. 2; GGS. iv. 2. 35; ÇB. ii. 4. 2[19] forbids the use of *yé ca tvā́m ánu*, and KÇS. iv. 1. 12 is of the same opinion. ⌊Opposite vs. 75, W. notes K. ix. 6.⌋ In 77 all our mss. save one (Op.) read *tátas* instead of *tata;* half of SPP's do the same. In Kāuç. 88. 11 the three verses (doubtless: only the *pratīka* of 75 is quoted; the comm. says the three) are used on setting down three combined (*saṁhata*) *piṇḍas* on the *barhis;* and Vāit. (22. 22) employs them similarly in the *agniṣṭoma*. Though 75 is easily read as two *anuṣṭubh* pādas, the Anukr. allows it only 15 syllables, refusing to resolve *tu-ā́m* here, as it also refuses in 76. ⌊As to vs. 75, see p. 869, ¶ 5.⌋ ⌊Apropos of *tata* and *tāta*, the comm. cites AA. i. 3. 3; and Sāyaṇa, in his comment on that passage, gives two little tales about Prajāpati's early linguistic ventures which remind us somewhat of the beautiful βεκός story as told by Herodotus in the beginning of Euterpe.⌋

78. *Svadhā́* to the Fathers that sit upon the earth.

79. *Svadhā́* to the Fathers that sit in the atmosphere.

80. *Svadhā́* to the Fathers that sit in the sky (*dív*).

These verses are found also in Āp. i. 9. 6, and in GGS. iv. 3. 10. GGS. has *pṛthivīṣadbhyas* ⌊and *antarīkṣasadbhyas*⌋; both combine *pitṛbhyo 'ntar-*; and our O.R.K., with half of SPP's authorities, do the same; the Anukr. implies *-bhyo antar-*, but that proves nothing. For the ritual use, see under vss. 71, 72 above. Both Āp. and GGS. prescribe the verses for the case that the names of the Fathers intended are not known.

81. Homage, O Fathers, to your refreshment (*ū́rj*); homage, O Fathers, to your sap.

82. Homage, O Fathers, to your terror* (*bhā́ma*); homage, O Fathers, to your fury.

83. Homage, O Fathers, to that of yours which is terrible; homage, O Fathers, to that of yours which is cruel.

84. Homage, O Fathers, to that of yours which is propitious; homage, O Fathers, to that of yours which is pleasant.

85. Homage to you, O Fathers; *svadhā́* to you, O Fathers.

For a wonder, these formulas are written by all the mss. without variation and without error. Corresponding passages are to be found in many other texts: VS. ii. 32; TB. i. 3. 10[8]; MS. i. 10. 3; K. ix. 6; ÇÇS. iv. 5. 1; AÇS. ii. 7. 7; Āp. i. 10. 2 and xiii. 12. 10; GGS. iv. 3. 18–21; MB. ii. 3. 8–11; none of them agree closely with our text; but the details of accordance and of difference are not worth giving. In Kāuç. (88. 26) they accompany in the *piṇḍapitryajña* the reverence (*upasthāna*) paid to the Fathers, being then followed by vss. 61 and 63. *⌊That is, 'to your terror-inspiring fury.'⌋

86. They who are there, O Fathers — Fathers there are ye — [be] they after you; may ye be the best of them.

87. They who are here, O Fathers — alive here are we — [be] they after us; may we be the best of them.

The translation here implies certain emendations of the text: *pitaras* ⌊accentless⌋ in 87 and the first time in 86, and the omission of *yé* after the second *pitáras* in 86: the latter is made also in our text, while SPP. reads, with the mss., *yé 'tra pitáraḥ pitáro yé 'tra yūyáṁ sthá.* As to the accent of the *pitaraḥ pitaro* in 86, the mss. are wildly discordant, presenting every possible variation, and, considering the many accentual blunders which they commit in this part of the text, the details are not worth reporting, nor need we feel any hesitation in amending to what seems to make the best sense. The omission of *yé* is much more serious, but seems demanded by the sense, and by the analogy of 87. Similar passages are found in ⌊TS. iii. 2. 5[6],⌋ TB. i. 3. 10[8-9] ⌊like TS.⌋, and ÇÇS. iv. 5. 1 (the latter nearest like our text: *ye 'tra pitaraḥ pitaraḥ stha yūyaṁ teṣāṁ çreṣṭhā bhūyāstha: ya iha pitaro manuṣyā vayaṁ teṣāṁ çreṣṭhā bhūyāsma*); compare also MS. i. 10. 3 and AÇS. ii. 7. 7.* All our mss. save one (Op.), and most of SPP's, leave *stha* in 86 unaccented; this non-accentuation, so far as it goes, favors the omission of *yé.* *Bhūyāstha* is a grammatically impossible form, and should be emended to *-sta*, which is read by ⌊TS. and⌋ TB. in the corresponding passage; ÇÇS., as has been seen, gives *-stha.* One of SPP's mss. has *bhūyāsta.* In 87, most of the mss. insert an *avasāna* after *smaḥ*, and SPP. follows them; it is of course senseless, unless we use one also after *stha* in 86†; nor does the Anukr. appear to acknowledge it, since it notes no difference of division as between the two verses; but our ⌊printed⌋ text at any rate blunders in not reading either *smo asmā̃n* or *smo 'smā̃n* since it has omitted the *avasāna*-mark. The metrical definitions of the Anukr. are worthless, as there is no trace of meter in the two passages; they can by violence be read into the number of syllables called for.

*⌊In the second and third paragraphs below are given these passages from TB., MS., and AÇS. The TS. passage agrees with the TB. passage, save that TS. has *yè 'smíṅ loké* for the very bad *yè 'smiṅ loké* of TB.⌋

†⌊We ought, I think, in fact to read with SPP. an *avasāna*-mark after *smaḥ* in vs. 87, not only as being abundantly supported by the mss. of both editions, but also as called for by the sense and the general (quadripartite) structure of the verse. And the same applies to the reading of an *avasāna*-mark after *stha* in vs. 86; it is printed in neither edition, but appears to be well warranted by the authorities of both.⌋

⌊The TB. passage, at i. 3. 10[8-9], with the *avasānas* as printed in the Poona ed., is: *yá etásmiṅ loké sthá* (8) *yuṣmā́ṅs té 'nu | yè 'smiṅ loké | mā́ṁ té 'nu | yá etásmiṅ loké sthá | yūyáṁ téṣāṁ vásiṣṭhā bhūyāsta | yè 'smiṅ loké | aháṁ téṣāṁ vásiṣṭho bhūyāsam.*— This passage and its analogues have been discussed in two papers by Böhtlingk, *Berichte der sächsischen Gesell.*, sessions of July 8, 1893, and May 2, 1896. In the first, having the TB. passage before him, he proposed to read, in place of the first *sthá*, the word *syús*, and to begin the first apodosis with it, and to delete the second *sthá.* In the second, having our AV. verses before him, he ascribes the false ending of *bhūyāstha* of 86 to the correct preceding *stha;* and, on the other hand, the false *sma* of 87 to the correct ending of *bhūyāsma.* The false *sma*, however, is — as we have seen — to be printed *smo* or *smaḥ* (cf. *Index*, p. 41 b). Moreover, he suspects that the second *pitaras* of 86 may be a corruption of *páretās* ('mortui istic vos estis'): this would be an easy corruption in *nāgarī*, but I do not feel that *páretās* offers a better antithesis to the *jīvā́s* of 87 (ÇÇS. *manuṣyās*) than does the word *pitaras* itself; and the latter are distinctly enough other-world beings: cf. 2. 48 (but also 49), and 1. 50, 54 above, also x. 6. 32. — Apropos of the blunder *bhūyāstha*: reading Dīgha Nikāya on the day of writing the above note, I observed at ix. 7, line 5, the phrase *saññā uppajjanti* etc., 'ideas arise,' and then in the very next sentence, *ekā saññā uppajjanti*, 'a single idea arise,' with plural verb-ending, albeit the *ekā* makes the breach of common concord most manifest and some mss. indeed read *uppajjati*. For the like error, see xv. 7. 3: cf. also notes xiv. 2. 59; xviii. 3. 47.⌋

⌊The MS. passage, p. 143[6], is: *eṣā́ yuṣmā́kam pitaraḥ: imā́ asmā́kam: jīvā́ vo jīvanta[ḥ] ihá sántaḥ syāma.* — The AÇS., p. 125 end, reads: *etā yuṣmākam pitaraḥ: imā asmākam: jīvā vo jīvanta iha santaḥ syāma.* To this, Gārgya, in his *vṛtti*, adds: *itikārādhyāhāreṇa sūtracchedaḥ: santaḥ syāmeti mantraḥ paṭhitavyo vaḥkāraṁ varjayitvā.* — The *etās* and *imās* seem to refer to *svadhā́s* (cf. ÇÇS. as above: *yā atra pitaraḥ svadhā, yuṣmākaṁ sā: ya iha pitara edhatur, asmākaṁ saḥ*); and the *eṣā́* of MS. appears to require correction to *etā́* p. *etā́ḥ*.⌋

88. Thee, O Agni, would we kindle, full of light (*dyumánt*), O god, unwasting; as that very wondrous fuel of thine shall shine in the sky (*dív*), bring thou food for thy praisers.

The verse is RV. v. 6. 4, and occurs also as SV. i. 419 and ii. 372, and in TS. iv. 4. 4[6] and MS. ii. 13. 7. All these agree together throughout, reading in **a** *te agna idh-* for *tvā 'gna idh-*, and in **c** *syā́* for *sā́*. SPP. reads in **c**, with the comm., *yád gha*, and makes no note upon it, implying that his mss. have the same; ours, however, give *yád dha* (p. *yát: ha*), in accordance with the other texts. All the mss. put an *avasāna* between **d** and **e** ⌊i.e. after *dyávi*⌋, and the Anukr. supports it, whence SPP. has it in his edition; we left it out as being uncalled for, and wanting in the parallel texts. For the use of the verse in Kāuç. with 3. 42, see the note to the latter: cf. p. 871, ¶ 3.

89. The moon among the waters runs, an eagle in the sky (*dív*); they find not your track, O golden-rimmed lightnings: know me as such, O firmaments (*ródasī*).

The verse is RV. i. 105. 1 and also SV. i. 417 ⌊Trāita Sāman⌋; and its first two pādas are VS. xxxiii. 90 **a**, **b**; it is quoted by *pratīka* in GB. i. 2. 9; ⌊pāda **e** is refrain all through the RV. hymn, save in the last, the 19th, verse⌋. Both RV. and SV. read in **d** *vidyutas*, as vocative, and the AV. mss. are divided between that and *vidyútas;* SPP. has the former, which is to be preferred. The comm. repeats the story of Trita and his two brothers, as "told by the Çāṭyāyanins," in almost precisely the same words as those in which it is given in the commentator's introduction to RV. i. 105. ⌊Oertel gives a summary thereof, and also the corresponding passage, JB. i. 184, text and version, JAOS. xviii.[1] p. 18–20.⌋ ⌊The comm. quotes the verse as applied in a *mahāçānti* called *vāruṇī* in the Nakṣatra Kalpa, 18.⌋ Why the verse should be found as conclusion of this book of funeral hymns is very obscure. ⌊☞ See p. 1016.⌋

⌊Here ends the fourth *anuvāka*, with 1 hymn and 89 verses. The quoted Anukr. says *ekonanavatiç cāi 'va yameṣu vihitā ṛcaḥ*: cf. pages 814 and 869, ¶ 4, note 1.⌋

⌊Here also ends the thirty-fourth *prapāṭhaka*.⌋

Book XIX.

⌊Supplementary hymns.⌋

⌊This nineteenth book forms a supplement to the three grand divisions of the Atharvan collection, and is shown to be a later addition by a considerable variety of cumulative evidence. The evidence concerns in part the contents of the book; in part, the character of its tradition as respects both text and division and extent; and in part, the relation of its text to the ancillary Vedic treatises, the Pada-pāṭha and the Pañcapaṭalikā and the Prātiçākhya, and to the Kāuçika and Vāitāna sūtras.⌋

⌊**The contents** of book xix. resemble in large measure those of the earlier books, and wear (as W. says: see the General Introduction) the aspect of after-gleanings: cf. hymn 1 with i. 15; h. 18 with iv. 40; h. 34 with ii. 4, and especially 34. 4 with ii. 4. 6; h. 39 with v. 4; h. 44 with iv. 9; h. 57 with vi. 46. Had these hymns of book xix. been parts of the original collection, we should have expected (as W. intimates) to find them in their respective places with those of the earlier books. But more conclusive evidence could hardly be wished than is offered by hymn 23 of book xix., which hymn, under the form of "Homage to parts of the AV.," is incidentally also in some sort a table of contents to the preceding eighteen books, and presupposes their existence as a collection, and in an arrangement substantially accordant with that which they show in our text: cf. the introduction to h. 23.⌋

⌊**The general character of the tradition** in this book is strikingly inferior to that of the preceding eighteen. Such a statement can be duly verified only by a detailed study of the verses of the book, with reference to their intelligibility as they stand, and to the multiplicity or wildness of the variants presented; but a casual glance at the footnotes on pages 478, 484–5, and 539 of the Bombay edition will give some idea of their multiplicity. Many of them (like *trī́n nā́kaṅs* at 27. 4: see W's note) "are of the superficial variety of discordant readings which swarm in this book and have no real importance." Others are blunders of the grossest sort, as to which there is substantial agreement among the authorities or even complete harmony: such for example is the impossible *yásmāi . . . yacchati* at 32. 2, where not a single one has the absolutely necessary *yác-chati*: cf. W's note to 45. 5. Especially noteworthy is vs. 4 of h. 40 as illustrating "what this nineteenth book can do in the way of corruption even of a text that is intelligibly handed down elsewhere" (so Whitney: the AV. version is so utterly corrupt that he is forced to translate from the RV. version, RV. i. 46. 6). If degrees of corruption and badness are to be distinguished, perhaps we may set down 49. 2 as the worst in book xix., or possibly in books i.–xix.; in the latter case, vi. 22. 3 is surely a close second. The uncertainties of the tradition of this book as to the precise amount of material to be included in it, and as to its division and the numeration of the parts, are rehearsed in the sequel: cf. the references at p. 898, end of ¶ 2.⌋

⌊**Relation of the text of book xix. to the ancillary Vedic treatises.** — **First**, the Pada-pāṭha appears to be very modern, as it is certainly very blundering and untrustworthy:

see SPP's notes on pages 410 and 460 and especially 543, and W's note on hymn 68, and observe, for example, the wild resolution of *vármā sīvyadhvám* as *várma : asi : vi॰adhvám* at 58. 4. The corruptness of the text made Whitney doubt (in 1862: see his Prāt., p. 581) the existence of a *pada-pāṭha*. — **Second,** book xix. is entirely ignored by the Pañcapaṭalikā or Old Anukr., as is stated also by SPP. in his Critical Notice, vol. i., p. 24. — **Third,** "to the apprehension of the Prātiçākhya the Atharva-Veda comprehended only the first eighteen books of the present collection": so Whitney, Prāt., p. 581; cf. his Index of passages referred to by the AV. Prāt., p. 600 c, and especially his notes to Prāt. ii. 67 c and ii. 22.⌋

⌊**Relation of book xix. to Kāuçika.** — The sūtra-citations do not imply recognition of the text of book xix. as an integral part of the *saṁhitā*. — Bloomfield has made a critical separation of the more original *vidhāna*-matter from the *gṛhya*-matter in the text of Kāuçika, and styles the former "Atharva-sūtra" or "Vidhāna-sūtra": see his Introd. to Kāuç., p. xxviii., and his essay in *Göttingische gelehrte Anzeigen*, 1902, p. 489. His Vidhāna-sūtra comprehends the text of Kāuç. from the beginning of kaṇḍikā 7 to the end of kaṇḍikā 52, excepting perhaps most of the matter (42. 19 to 43. 20) just preceding the *vaçāçamana*, and excepting the *vaçāçamana* itself (43. 21 to 45. 19): that is, his Vidhāna-sūtra runs from 7. 1 to 42. 18 and from 46. 1 to 52. 21.* — Now it is in the first place to be noted that no verse whatever is cited in the text of the "Vidhāna-sūtra" (whether by *pratīka* or by technical designation or in *sakalapāṭha*) which is also to be found in book xix., with the single exception of *prā́ṇa prāṇám*.† In the second place, disregarding the verses cited by technical designation (the "*jīvās*-verses": see below) and those which are cited in full and by *pratīka* besides (33. 3; 52. 5; 72. 1: see below), it appears that there are in the entire text of Kāuçika only six *pratīkas* which might seem at first blush to imply the recognition of book xix. as part of the Atharvan text by Kāuçika. The six *pratīkas* cover some eleven verses. Including with them a seventh *pratīka*, *devásya tvā*, I give them in tabular form:

6. 37	*tvám agne vratapā́ asi* (xix. 59. 1–3) *kā́mas tád ágre* (xix. 52. 1 ‡)	[Dārila, in full; RV.MS.TS.VS.]
45. 17	*kā́mas tád ágre* (xix. 52. 1 ‡)	[RV.TB.TA.]
68. 29	*kā́mas tád* (xix. 52. 1 ‡)	
57. 26	*ágne samídham ā́hārṣam* (xix. 64. 1–4)	[Daç. Kar., in full; AGS.PGS. ÇGS.HGS.GGS.MB.]
66. 1	*vā́ñ ma āsán* (xix. 60. 1)	[TS.TA.PGS.]
91. 3	*áyuto 'hám* (xix. 51. 1)	[?]
	devásya tvā savitús (xix. 51. 2)	[Passim.]
139. 10	*ávyacasaç ca* (xix. 68. 1)	[Daç. Kar.; Ath. Paddh.; Keçavī.]

The place of citation in Kāuçika is given at the left; the place of occurrence in AV. is given in parentheses; and the texts, other than AV., in which the mantras occur, are noted at the right in square brackets.⌋ *⌊This delimitation of the Vidhāna-sūtra differs slightly from Bloomfield's as given in the places just cited: it has been revised with the help of a friendly note from him.⌋ †⌊The verse *prā́ṇa prāṇám* (xix. 44. 4) is cited at 47. 16, which is a part of Bloomfield's "Vidhāna-sūtra," and seems to have been overlooked by him at p. xxxi.⌋ ‡⌊Keçava (on 6. 37) and Dārila (on 45. 17) understand the whole AV. hymn of five verses as intended by *kā́mas tád*.⌋

⌊**Citations by pratīka.** — The three phrases, (1) *devásya tvā savitúḥ prasavé* and (2) *açvínor bāhúbhyām* and (3) *pūṣṇó hástābhyām*, are unvaried as between the AV. text and the citations by Kāuç. (in full at 2. 1 and 2. 21 and 137. 18: the citation at 91. 3 is by *pratīka* with *áyuto 'hám*) and by Vāit. (in full at 3. 9): what follows *hástābhyām* is, at Kāuç. 2. 1, *agnáye júṣṭaṁ nír vapāmi* (as at TS. i. 1.4[2]); at 2. 21 and in Vāit., it is *prasūtaḥ praçiṣā paristṛṇāmi* (Vāit. *pratigṛhṇāmi*); and at 137. 18 it is *ā́ dade* (as at TS. i. 3. 1[1] and very often); while AV. xix. differs from all these in adding *prásūta ā́ rabhe.* The phrases are of such extremely frequent occurrence (see introd. to h. 51) that they may be called a commonplace of the *sūtra*-literature; and, as W. intimates, the *pratīka*-citation by Kāuç. is not to be regarded as having any special reference to our book xix., — much less the citations in full by Kāuç. and Vāit. The case is a typical and striking one. Of the same type are the hymns *tvám agne vratapā́ asi* and *ágne samídham ā́hārṣam*, both of which, besides, are given by the scholia in *sakalapāṭha.* For the rest, so far as any necessary connection with book xix. is concerned, *vā́ñ ma āsán* and *kā́mas tád* and *ávyacasaç ca* may fairly be regarded as *kalpajā mantrās.* Only for *áyuto 'hám* am I unable to point out occurrences elsewhere than in book xix.; but it may be noted that the comm., at p. 499[4], takes *áyuto 'hám* and the immediately following *devásya tvā* as one *sūkta* of sacrificial formulas, *yajurmantrātmakaṁ sūktam.*⌋

⌊**Citations by technical designation.** — Thrice in the text of Kāuç. (at 3. 4; 58. 7; 90. 22), as also once in Vāit. (at 1. 19), we meet the prescription *jīvābhir ācamya.* The "*jīvā́s*-verses," says Dārila (on 3. 4), mean "four verses beginning with *jīvā́ stha.*" They are associated, both at Kāuç. 3. 4 and at Vāit. 1. 18, 19 as well, with other *sūtra*-material, and in particular also with the five *prapads* (which are called in Vāit. *prapadanas* and which Dārila characterizes as *kalpaja*): considering this fact, the citation may well be viewed as containing no distinct reference to our book xix., albeit indeed the verses are found there as 69. 1–4; and the entire absence of *sakalapāṭha* both in text and in scholia, if taken in connection with the mode of citation (by a technical name and so without *iti*), does not appear to be inconsistent with this view.⌋

⌊**Citations in sakalapāṭha.** — The most conclusive evidence to show that book xix. was not recognized by Kāuç. is afforded by the five verses which, although occurring in our xix., are yet cited by Kāuç. in full (*sakalapāṭha*): these are 59. 3; 33. 3 and 44. 4; and 52. 5 and 72. 1. As to the first of the five, *ā́ devā́nām ápi pánthām aganma*, cited at 5. 12, Bloomfield has already remarked in his note that the *sakalapāṭha* shows that it is regarded as coming from some other source than our book xix., and it is in fact not infrequent elsewhere (RV.MS.TS.ÇB.); moreover, it is a part of the same group as *tvám agne vratapā́ asi*, of which group, as already noted, Dārila (on 6. 37) gives the *sakalapāṭha.* The verses *tvám bhū́mim* (cited in full at 2. 1: a later citation, at 137. 32, is naturally by *pratīka*) and *prā́ṇa prāṇám* (cited in full at 47. 16) have not been found, so far as I know, except at xix. 33. 3 and 44. 4; but of the former Dārila expressly says that it is *kalpaja.* Finally, there remain the cases of *yát kāma* and *yásmāt kóçāt.* These are peculiar in that they are cited at 92. 30 and 139. 25 by *pratīka*, and immediately thereafter (at 92. 31 and 139. 26) in *sakalapāṭha:* cf. Bloomfield's Introduction, p. xxix. The verse *yát kāma* is found at xix. 52. 5, and *yásmāt kóçāt* at the end of the book, and neither elsewhere.⌋

⌊**Relation of book xix. to Vāitāna.** — Still less than Kāuçika, does Vāitāna imply by its citations a recognition of the text of book xix. as an integral part of the *saṁhitā.* — In all Vāitāna there are only seven sūtras (Garbe gives five) that cite passages occurring in book xix.: they are Vāit. 1. 18 and 19, citing the *apratiratha* hymn and the "*jīvā́s*-verses"; 3. 5 and 19. 12, citing *ā́ devā́nām;* 3. 9, citing *devásya tvā;* 28. 14, citing *yád agne yā́ni kā́ni cit;* and 37. 19, citing *sahásrabāhus.* Of these, the *devásya tvā*, the "*jīvā́s*-verses," and the *ā́ devā́nām* are cited also by Kāuç. and have already been sufficiently discussed. Of the remaining three: the *puruṣa* hymn (*sahásrabāhus:* xix. 6) appears also in RV.VS.TA.SV.; and the verse *yád agne yā́ni kā́ni cit* (xix. 64. 3) is common to RV., and to the Yajus texts, MS.K.Kap.TS.VS.; while the *apratiratha* hymn (*āçúḥ çíçānaḥ:* xix. 13. 2 ff.) is found in RV. and the Yajus texts just named and in SV. also.⌋

⌊**Divisions of the book.** — The *prapāṭhaka*-division is not found in this book, having ended with book xviii.; nor does any decad-division appear. The following statements refer to the hymns as printed, divided, and numbered in the Berlin edition. The book numbers 72 hymns, with 456 verses, and is divided into seven *anuvākas*. If the verses numbered 455, a precisely even division would give 65 to each *anuvāka*, and it appears that the division aims in general to make each *anuvāka* as nearly of that length as may be without breaking hymns: but hymn 20 is put into *anuvāka* 2 rather than 3, because it forms a subject-group with hymns 17–19; for a like reason the limit of *anuvāka* 4 is set after hymn 33 and not before it; and that of *anuvāka* 5, after hymn 45 and not before it. A tabular conspectus follows:

Anuvākas	1	2	3	4	5	6	7
Hymns	9	11	6	7	12	9	18
Verses	59	72	65	68	74	63	55

Sum, 456 verses. Several mss. sum up the verses as 457. Uncertainty of verse numeration affects hymns 16, 27, 38, 47, 54, 55, 57, and 67 (see notes to the hymns). The comm. omits hymns 60–63 and reckons 69 and 70 as one hymn (see introd. to h. 60); and some mss. insert RV. i. 99 between our 65 and 66.⌋

---

1. With an oblation for confluence.

[*Brahman.* — ⌊*tṛcam.*⌋ *yā́jñikam; cā́ndramasam. ā́nuṣṭubham: 1, 2. pathyā́bṛhatyā́u; 3. pañkti.*]

The hymn is found also in Pāipp. xix. (the order of vss. 2 and 3 being inverted). It resembles i. 15, and, as it has the same *pratīka* of the first verse, the comm. maintains that it may be used along with or instead of that hymn where the latter is quoted (Kāuç. 19. 4, and Nakṣ. K. 20). ⌊Cf. also note to Kāuç. 19. 1.⌋

Translated: Griffith, ii. 259.

1. Together, together let the rivers flow, together the winds, together the birds; increase ye this sacrifice, O songs (*gír*); I make offering with an oblation of confluence.

The first half-verse is nearly identical with i. 15. 1 **a, b**; the third pāda, nearly with i. 15. 2 **c**; the last pāda, with i. 15. 1 **d**; ii. 26. 3 **d**. The translation implies *giras*, voc., in this verse and the next; it is read by the mss. almost without exception, and so by SPP's text; also in i. 15. 2. Ppp. reads in **a** *sravanti sindhavaḥ*.

2. This sacrifice do ye aid, O offerings (*hóma*); this one, ye also that flow together: increase ye this sacrifice, O songs; I make offering with an oblation of confluence.

SPP. reads in **a** *hómās*, with all the mss., but our emendation to *homās* is evidently demanded by the sense; the comm. also understands the word as vocative. Ppp. reads *homā yajña pacate idaṁ*, and uses the last half of vs. 3 as refrain, instead of that of vs. 1.

3. Form by form, vigor (*váyas*) by vigor — taking hold together I embrace him: let the four quarters increase this sacrifice; I make offering with an oblation of confluence.

The comm. understands the sacrificer by *enam* in **b**. ⌊In **c**, *cátasraḥ* is metrically and otherwise superfluous.⌋

The metrical definitions given by the Anukr. for this hymn are of no value; the first two are inexact even as regards a mechanical count of syllables.

2. Praise and prayer to the waters.

[*Sindhudvīpa.—pañcarcam. āpyam. ānuṣṭubham.*]

Found also in Pāipp. viii. The comm. finds it used in Nakṣ. K. 20, in addressing waters brought from streams etc. for a ceremony of appeasement.

Translated: Griffith, ii. 259.

1. Weal to thee [be] the waters from the snowy mountains (*hāimavatá*), and weal be to thee those from the fountains; weal to thee the running waters, and weal to thee be those of the rain.

Our *saniṣyadā́s* in **c** is an emendation, and called for ⌊see *Skt. Gram.* § 1148. 4. k., near the end⌋; all the mss., and SPP., accent *saniṣyádās.* Many of the mss. accent *té* in **d**. The comm. omits *u* in **b**. The *pada*-mss. make the absurd division *sani॰syádāḥ*. Ppp. makes the combinations *çaṁ tā "po* and *-ṣyadā "paç ç-*.

2. Weal to thee [be] the waters of the wastes, weal be to thee those of the marshes; weal to thee the waters of the canals (*khanitríma*), weal those brought with vessels.

Ppp. has again *çaṁ tā "po dh-*; ⌊also *-trimā "paç ç-*⌋. TA. (in vi. 4. 1) has a verse and a half similar to these two, and in part accordant with them (reading corruptly *anū́kyās*): ⌊Poona ed., p. 420, rightly *anūkyā̀s*⌋ Our i. 6. 4 above is still more closely analogous.

3. Digging for themselves without shovels, keen (*vípra*), working in the deep (*gambhīrá*), more healing than the healers (*bhiṣáj*), the waters we address.

The mss. and SPP. with them, read in **b** *gambhīré apásaḥ*, which is good enough to be exempt from emendation; the comm. seems to make a compound, *gambhīreapasaḥ*. The mss. and SPP. also have in **d** *áchā vad-* (p. *ácha : vad-*); it was altered in our text to *achā́vad-* (= *acha॰ā́vad-*) because the Atharvan everywhere else ⌊except iii. 20. 2⌋ reads the latter and not the former. Ppp. reads and combines *gambhīrepsā bhiṣagbhyo bhiṣaktarā "po a-*.

4. Of the waters indeed from the sky, of the waters from the streams (*srotasyà*) — in the forth-washing indeed of the waters, ye become vigorous (*vājín*) horses.

The last pāda is very literally rendered; anything else would require some alteration of the text; it is identical with i. 4. 4 **c**. SPP. reads in **a** *divyā̀nām*, with very nearly all the mss.; the emendation of accent ⌊*divyā́-*, as in the Berlin text⌋ is unquestionably to be made. ⌊Error due to *srotasyā̀nām?*⌋

5. Weal [be] to thee the waters, propitious the waters, effecting freedom from *yákṣma* the waters; just as joy to one who thirsts, [be] they for thee healers of dislocation.

The translation follows our text, which has numerous emendations. At the beginning, the mss. and SPP. read *tā́s* for *çáṁ te* (*çāntā́s* might be better); the latter was intended to fill up both sense and meter (the Anukr. says nothing of a defective *pāda;* but this is of very little account). Then they have thrice *apás* in **a**, **b**, instead of *ā́pas;* but the comm. has *āpas* both times in **a**. In **c** they all give *tṛpyate;* Ppp. has *athāi 'va dṛçyate mayas.* For **d**, SPP. reads *tā́s ta ā́ datta bheṣajī́ḥ*, with the comm. ⌊who understands the second word as *té* or also as *te*⌋; the mss. mostly have *ād uta* (p. *āt : uta*), but they vary to *ādutta*, *ādata*, ⌊*ādatta*, *ādruta*,⌋ *āhuta*, with various accentuation. The verse is so corrupt throughout that it offers a free field for conjectural emendation. SPP. combines in **b** *apó 'yakṣmaṁkár-*, which is inadmissible, though found in the mss.; we must change to *apò 'y-*, if not to *ā́po 'y-*. Ppp. makes in **a** its usual combinations, *tā "paç çivā "po 'y-*, and reads for **d** *tvābhyatva bheṣajīḥ.*

3. Praise to Agni.

[*Atharvāñgiras.—caturṛcam. āgneyam. trāiṣṭubham: 2. bhurij.*]

The hymn occurs also in Pāipp. xx., but only in fragments, not intelligible beyond the first half-verse. The comm. notices that the hymn has the same *pratīka* as ix. 1, and labors to point out that it ⌊xix. 3⌋ and its successor have features adapting them to the same use as the two parts of ix. 1; and that hence they may also be regarded as quoted (Kāuç. 10. 24; 12. 15; etc.) by that *pratīka:* this is, of course, a worthless bit of special pleading. Vāit. (16. 12), wishing to quote ix. 1 only, adds the specification *madhusūktena.*

Translated: Griffith, ii. 260.

1. Forth from the sky, from the earth, from the atmosphere, out of the forest trees, the herbs—whithersoever borne, O Jātavedas, come thou, enjoying, thence to us.

The translation implies emendation to *jātavedas*, voc., in **c**. SPP. reads in **d** *táta stutó j-*, with nearly all the mss.; one or two read *tátas-tato j-*; ⌊this report coincides virtually with the *Index*, p. 124 b: but, if I understand the Collation Book, P. and M., which Whitney here intends, read *tátas tató j-*, which is neither one thing nor the other, but a confusion between the *āmreḍita* and *tátas + stutó;*⌋ and the comm. has *tatas-tataḥ.* The mss. also, almost without exception, give *bíbhṛtas* or *bíbhratas* in **c**; here SPP's text agrees with ours, and with the comm. Ppp. has for **b** *vātā paçubhyo ay oṣadhībhyaḥ*, evidently intending the text which TB. has in a corresponding verse (in i. 2. 1²²), *vā́tāt paçúbhyo ádhy óṣadhībhyaḥ.* For **c**, **d** TB. has *yátra-yatra jātavedaḥ sambabhū́va* ⌊so Calc. ed., text, p. 32, comm., p. 91; but Poona ed. has aright *sambabhū́tha*, text and comm., p. 83⌋ *táto no agne juṣámāṇa é 'hi;* Āp. (in v. 13. 4) agrees with TB. ⌊precisely: reading *sambabhūtha*⌋.

2. What thy greatness is in the waters, what in the woods, what in the herbs, in the cattle, within the waters—all thy bodies (*tanū́*), O Agni, grasp together; with them come to us, a giver of property, unfailing.

Two or three of our mss., ⌊and (six) half⌋ of SPP's, read *tanvā̀ḥ* in **c**, and some of ours have *bharasva* instead of *rabhasva*, probably as an only accidental variation, though *bharasva* would be a very good reading. A little emendation would rid us of the otiose repetition of *apsú* in the first line. ⌊In **d** we have to pronounce *nā́t 'hi*, with double sandhi (as often in Ppp.).⌋

3. What thy heavenly (*svargá*) greatness is, among the gods, what body of thine entered into the Fathers, what prosperity of thine was spread among men (*manuṣyà*) — therewith, O Agni, assign wealth to us.

The translation implies at end of **a** *svargás* ⌊so SPP.⌋; our text has *-gé* on the authority of only a single ms., and against the comm. ⌊*svargaḥ*⌋ and the parallel texts ⌊*suvargáḥ*⌋ as found in TB. (in i. 2. 1²¹⁻²) and Āp. (in v. 13. 4). Both these read further, for **b**, *yás ta ātmā́ paçúṣu právistaḥ*, and, for **d**, *táyā no agne juṣámāṇa é'hi;* while TB. has in **c** *prathé* for *paprathé* ⌊so Calc. ed., text and comm.: but Poona aright, *paprathé*⌋. The Anukr. takes no notice of the redundant syllable in **c**.

4. To him of hearing ears, the poet, worthy to be known, I apply for gifts (*rātí*) with words, with speeches; whence [there is] fear, be there no fear for us; pacify (*ava-yaj*), O Agni, the wrath (*héḍas*) of the gods.

The verse is found also in Āp. xiv. 17. 1, but with very different **b**: *namobhir nākam upa yāmi çan̄san;* with *tat kṛdhī naḥ* at end of **c**; and, for **d**, *'gne devānām ava heḍa iyakṣva:* cf. also Āp. v. 5. 8, which is far more different. ⌊In **c**, *asty* is a misprint for *astv.*⌋

4. To various divinities.

[*Atharvān̄giras. — caturṛcam. āgneyam* ⌊*2. mantroktadevatyā*⌋. *trāiṣṭubham: 1. 5-p. virāḍ atijagatī; 2. jagatī.*]

The second, third, and fourth verses are found in Pāipp. xix.
Translated: Griffith, ii. 261.

1. What oblation (*ā́huti*) Atharvan sacrificed first, with what one Jātavedas made an offering, that same do I first call loudly for thee; gratified with that, let Agni carry the offering: hail to Agni.

This version represents neither of the edited texts, nor the mss., nor the comm., but is a pure make-shift. SPP. reads in **a–b** *átharvā yā́ jātā́ yā́ h-*, and at beginning of **d** *tā́bhi ṣtuptó v-* (p. *tā́bhiḥ: stuptáḥ;* so all the *pada*-mss. ⌊but Op. and L. have *sruptáḥ*⌋; what *stuptáḥ* ⌊or *sruptáḥ*, for that matter⌋ should be supposed to be is a complete mystery). The comm. reads in **a–b** *atharvā yā jātāya havyām*, and in **d** *tābhi stutaḥ;* he explains that Atharvan means the *paramātman*, who at the beginning of creation made an oblation to please the gods whom he had created; pāda **b** signifies this: "what (*yā* being used instead of *yām*) oblation, given by Atharvan, Jātavedas made worthy to be offered for his progeny ⌊the progeny of Atharvan in the rôle of *paramātman*?⌋: that is, for the crowd of gods made manifest by him." Our *āyejé* in **a** is indefensible, but the translation implies *ejé* (*ā-ījé*) or something equivalent; in **d** it implies *táyā tṛptó v-*; all the mss. have *-pto*, except one of ours s.m., which favors the comm. *Johavīmi* possibly comes from root *hu* (so BR.) instead of *hū*. We ought to have in **a** *ā́kūtim*, as in the following verses, but it is not easy to reconstruct the verse so as to match that emendation.

2. Heavenly fortunate design (*ā́kūti*) do I put forward (*puro-dhā*); let the mother of intent (*cittá*) be easy of invocation for us; to what expectation I go, be it entirely mine; may I find it entered into [my] mind.

Half the mss. accent in **b** *cíttasya*; in **c** and **d**, all have *emi* and ⌊nearly all⌋ *vídeyam*, which SPP. accordingly admits into his text; our *émi* and *vidéyam* are necessary emendations: in such a condition of text as is offered in this book, it is useless to be governed by the tradition when it is certainly and palpably wrong. The verse is found also in TB. (in ii. 5. 3[2]), which reads in **a** *mánasas* for *subhágām*, in **b** ⌊*yajñásya* for *cittásya* and⌋ *me* for *nas*, and for **c**, **d** *yád icchā́mi mánasā sákāmo vidéyam enad dhṛ́daye níviṣṭam*. Ppp. reads *devyām* in **a**, and *me 'stu* in **b** ⌊? or **c**?⌋. The first pāda is the only *jagatī* element in the verse.

3. With design to us, O Brihaspati, with design come thou unto us; then assign to us of fortune (*bhága*); then be easy of invocation for us.

The comm. has in **c** *dehi*. The definition of the verse as an *anuṣṭubh* has apparently dropped out of the Anukr. Ppp. reads in **d** *subhagas*.

4. Let Brihaspati acknowledge my design, the son of Añgiras this [my] speech; of whom the gods, the deities, came into being, let that desire (*kā́ma*), well-conducting, go after us.

Kā́mas in **d** is shown both by meter and by sense to be intrusive; also the omission of *vā́cam* in **b** would improve the verse in both respects, making it easier to understand *āñgirasás* as simply epithet of Bṛhaspati. The mss. differ in their accent of *sambabhūvus*; ⌊of SPP's authorities, about seven accent *sám-*, and four accent *-vúḥ*⌋. All read in **d** *suprá ṇītās*, which SPP. accepts in his text. Ppp. gives *tasya devā devatā saṁbabhūva çiçupraṇīha*, which is too corrupt to give any help. Ppp. also combines in **a** *mā "kūtiṁ*. The comm. has *abhy etu* in **d**. The omission of metrical definition by the Anukr. seems due to a lacuna. ⌊If the suspicions resting on *vācam* and *kāmas* are justified, the vs. would scan smoothly as 8 + 11 : 11 + 11.⌋

5. Praise and prayer to Indra.

[*Atharvāñgiras* (?). — *ekarcam. āindram. trāiṣṭubham.*]

The verse is RV. vii. 27. 3, without variation, and is found also, with the same text, in Pāipp. xx. The comm. gives as its *viniyoga* that one who desires riches may worship Indra with it.

Translated: Griffith, ii. 261; also by the RV. translators.

1. Indra [is] king of the moving creation (*jágat*), of human beings (*carṣaṇí*), whatever of various form is upon the earth (*kṣám*); thence he gives good things to his worshiper (*dāçvā́ṅs*); may he, whenever praised, urge (*cud*) hitherward bestowal (*rā́dhas*).

6. Purusha and his sacrifice.

[*Nārāyaṇa.* — *ṣoḍaçarcam. puruṣadevatyam. ānuṣṭubham.*]

This is the familiar *puruṣa*-hymn of the Rig-Veda ⌊x. 90⌋ with considerable variation in the order of the verses, but comparatively little in the readings. The RV. verses are found here in the following order: 1, 4, 3, 2, 11–14, 5–7, 10, 9, 8, 15. The same hymn occurs in VS. xxxi. (in the order of RV. verses 1–5, 8–10, 7, 11–14, 6, 15) and in TA. iii. 12 (in the order of RV. verses 1–6, 15, 7–14); also the first five RV. verses in the 7th or Nāigeya chapter of SV. ⌊Nāigeya 33–37 = SV. i. 618–622⌋ (in the order of RV. verses 1, 4, 2ab3cd, 3ab2cd, 5). The verses (except our 7 and 8) occur also in Pāipp. ix. In Vāit. (37. 19), the hymn is cited, with x. 2, in the *puruṣamedha*, accompanying the release of the human victim; and the comm. finds it used in the Çāntikalpa xv., and in Pariçiṣṭa x. 1. — ⌊The Bombay ed. makes two hymns of this hymn: see note at end of the *anuvāka*, p. 915.⌋

⌊In the WZKM., xii. 277–280, von Schroeder reports the existence of the Purusha hymn in two recensions in the *ṛcaka* of the Kaṭhas, and observes that the passage may come from a Kaṭha Brāhmaṇa or Āraṇyaka. The first recension accords with that of RV.: the second also agrees in general with that of RV., except for the variants which I have reported below under verses 1, 2, 3, 5, 7 (the most important), 9, 12, 14; and, further, it agrees with RV. in the order of the verses from 1 to 15. For brevity, I refer to the source of these variants as the KaṭhaB.⌋

Translated: Griffith, ii. 262–265; and, as RV. hymn, very often: so by Colebrooke (1798), in *Misc. Essays*², i. 183; by Burnouf (1840), in the Preface to his great folio ed. of the Bhāgavata Purāṇa (see pages cxiv to cxxiv); by Muir, v. 367; Ludwig, *Der Rigveda*, ii., p. 574, notes in v., p. 437; Grassmann, *Rig-Veda*, ii., p. 486; Zimmer, p. 217; Scherman, *Philosophische Hymnen*, pages 11–23 (with ample notes); Henry W. Wallis, *Cosmology of the RV.*, p. 87; P. Peterson, *Hymns from the RV.*, p. 289; Deussen, *Geschichte*, i. 1. 150–158 (repeated in his *Sechzig Upanishads*, p. 830). — Finally, as VS. hymn, it was translated by Weber (apropos of Anquetil du Perron's Upanishads), in *Indische Studien*, ix. 5, with instructive notes and introduction and a tabular view (p. 4) of the sequence of the verses in RV., TA., VS., and AV.; and also by Griffith, in *The Texts of the White Yajurveda*, p. 260. — It may be added that the text of the hymn with Sāyaṇa's comment was published as a separate work as no. 3 of the Ānanda Āçrama Series. — Burnouf cited and translated the hymn for the purpose of comparison with the corresponding passage in the Purāṇa, ii. 5. 35–6. 29, pages 235–241. Note the multum-in-parvo half of vs. 35, *sahasro-"rv-an̄ghri-bāhv-akṣaḥ sahasrā-"nana-çīrṣavān*. — Especial attention is called to Deussen's elaborate introduction to his translation in his *Geschichte*, as cited above, p. 150–156.

1. Thousand-armed is Purusha, thousand-eyed, thousand-footed; he, covering the earth entirely, exceeded it by ten fingers' breadth.

⌊The verse is RV. x. 90. 1; VS. xxxi. 1; SV. i. 618; TA. iii. 12. 1.⌋ All the other texts begin with *sahásraçīrṣā* (SV. *-rṣāḥ*); SV.VS. ⌊KaṭhaB.⌋ have in c *sarvátas*, and VS. after it *spṛtvā́*; ⌊von Schroeder reports the KaṭhaB. reading as *smṛtvā́*: but perhaps the intention of his mss. is rather *spṛtvā́*⌋. The comm. gives very long expositions of most of the verses, but casts no light upon them. ⌊Deussen, p. 150, calls the substitution of *-bāhuḥ* for *-çīrṣā* a "rationalizing variant: because, if Purusha has 1000 eyes, he ought to have only 500 heads"! But even the AV. comm. glosses *sahasrākṣaḥ* by *bahubhir akṣibhir upetaḥ*.⌋

2. With three feet he ascended the sky; a foot of him, again, was here; so he strode out asunder, after eating and non-eating.

⌊RV. x. 90. 4; VS. xxxi. 4; SV. i. 619; TA. iii. 12. 2.⌋ RV. has a quite different text: *tripā́d ūrdhvá úd āit púruṣaḥ pā́do 'sye 'hā́ 'bhavat púnaḥ: táto víṣvan̄ vy àkrāmat sāçanānaçané abhí;* VS. agrees with this throughout; ⌊and so does KaṭhaB., except that it has *bhū́mim* for *víṣvañ*⌋; TA. differs only by reading in **b** *'hā́ "bhavāt* ⌊i.e. *'há : ā́ : bhavāt?*⌋ (doubtless, however, a misprint); ⌊but *ā́bhavāt* is read by both Calc. and Poona ed's in the text; while both ed's have *ābhavat* in the comm.⌋; SV. differs (and agrees with AV.) by *táthā* in **c** and *açan-* in **d**. The comm. has in **a** *ā 'rohat*, and in **b** (with RV. etc.) *pā́do 'sya;* two or three of SPP's authorities agree with the comm. in both points. The *pada*-mss. give in **b** *pā́dasya;* ⌊but SPP. accepts *pā́t : asya* in his *pada*-text⌋. No *saṁhitā*-ms. has *víṣvañň a-*, and accordingly SPP., against all rule and usage, admits *víṣvañ a-* in his text; but he accents *açanānaçané* with us, though almost all the mss. have *açanā́naçané.* The comm. gives an absurd array of discordant explanations of this compound: *açanā* is "men, animals, etc.," and *anaçanā* "gods, trees, etc."; then *(adhyātmapakṣe)*, the two are "the immovable and movable creation," or else "the intelligent *(cetana)* and unintelligent creation."

3. So many are his greatnesses; and Purusha is superior *(jyā́yān)* to that; a foot of him is all beings *(bhūtá)*; three feet of him are what is immortal in the sky.

⌊RV. x. 90. 3; VS. xxxi. 3; SV. i. 621; TA. iii. 12. 1; ChU. iii. 12. 6.⌋ RV. reads in **a**, **b**: *etā́vān asya mahimā́ 'to jy-*; VS.TA. agree with RV. (but TA. ⌊in the Calc. ed. only⌋ shortens the *ū* of *pū́ruṣaḥ* in **b**). ⌊SV. makes up its vss. 620 and 621 thus: 620 = RV. 2 **a**, **b** (our 4 **a**, **b**) + RV. 3 **c**, **d** (our 3 **c**, **d**); 621 = RV. 3 **a**, **b** (our 3 **a**, **b**) + RV. 2 **c**, **d** (our 4 **c**, **d**); that is, between the two halves of our vs. 4, it interjects the two halves of our vs. 3 in inverted order.⌋ SV. has for our **a**, **b**, *tā́vān asya mahimā́ táto jy-* etc.; and, for the *víçvā* of our **c**, it has *sárvā;* ⌊and so has KaṭhaB.⌋. Ppp. omits *asya* in **a** and has *pād asya* in **c**. 'Foot,' of course, in this and in the next verse, = 'quarter.' ⌊ChU. agrees with SV., except that it does not dislocate the two halves of our vs. As to the vs. in ChU., cf. Böhtlingk, *Berichte der sächs. Gesell.*, July 10, 1897, p. 82; in his edition, he emends the vs. to conformity with the RV. readings.⌋

4. Purusha is just this all, what is and what is to be; also [is he] lord *(īçvará)* of immortality, which was together with another.

⌊RV. x. 90. 2; VS. xxxi. 2; SV. i. 620; TA. iii. 12. 1.⌋ The wholly obscure last pāda is doubtless a mere corruption, all the other texts reading instead *yád ánnenā 'tiróhati* (which is itself obscure enough). In **c**, all of them give *ī́çānas;* and in **b**, RV.TA. ⌊and Ppp. and KaṭhaB.⌋ have *bhávyam*, SV. *bhā́vyam*, VS. *bhāvyàm;* this last should be the reading of our text also, as all the mss. have it; ⌊rather: all of W's and seven of SPP's ten authorities;⌋ SPP. accepts it; the comm. has *bhavyam*, and, in **d**, *annena.* Some of the mss. accent *ányena;* ⌊that is, they have the spelling of *anyéna* and the accent of *ánnena*⌋. ⌊Pāda **b** is nearly = xiii. 1. 54 **d**.⌋

5. When they separated *(vi-dhā)* Purusha, in how many parts did they distribute *(vi-kḷp)* him? what was his face? what his (two) arms? what are called his (two) thighs [and] feet?

⌊RV. x. 90. 11; VS. xxxi. 10; TA. iii. 12. 5.⌋ The mss. vary between *vyádadhus* and *vy àdadhus;* the *pada*-mss., between *ví : ad-* and *ví : ád-*: the latter is (without any good reason: cf. my *Skt. Gr.*[2] § 1084 a) ⌊and note to xviii. 1. 39⌋ the reading of the RV. *pada*-text. ⌊In **b**, KaṭhaB. has *enam* for our *ví.*⌋ In **c**, **d**, VS. agrees with our text, save that it wantonly defaces the meter by intruding an unnecessary *āsīt* after *asya;*

RV.TA. have for *kím* (except the first time) *kāú;* and RV. combines *kā́ ū-* and *pā́dā uc-* ⌊AV. and RV. *pada*-texts, *pā́dāu*⌋, while TA. has *kā́v* and *pā́dāv;* Ppp. has *pādāv ucyate:* cf. Prāt. ii. 22 and note; ⌊also my *Noun-Inflection*, p. 341⌋. ⌊KaṭhaB. agrees with VS. in showing the intrusive *āsīt*, and with Ppp. in reading the ungrammatical *ucyate.*⌋

6. The Brahman was his face; the Kshatriya (*rājanyà*) became his (two) arms; the Vāiçya [was] his middle; from his (two) feet was born the Çūdra.

⌊RV. x. 90. 12; VS. xxxi. 11; TA. iii. 12. 5.⌋ The other three texts read in **b** *rājanyàḥ kṛtáḥ*, and in **c** *ūrū́* (for *mádhyam*).

7. The moon [is] born from his mind; from his eye the sun was born; from his mouth both Indra and Agni; from his breath Vāyu was born.

⌊RV. x. 90. 13; VS. xxxi. 12; TA. iii. 12. 6.⌋ RV.TA. have no variant from our text; VS. reads for the second line *çrótrād vāyúç ca prāṇáç ca múkhād agnír ajāyata.* ⌊KaṭhaB. has for **b** the much better *cákṣuṣor ádhi sū́ryaḥ* (avoiding the undesirable *cákṣos:* see *Noun-Inflection*, p. 569 top, p. 410 top); and in **c**, **d** it agrees with VS., except that it substitutes *násor* for *çrótrād.*⌋

8. From his navel was the atmosphere; from his head the sky came into being (*sam-vṛt*); from his (two) feet the earth, the quarters from his ear (*çrótra*): so shaped they the worlds.

⌊RV. x. 90. 14; VS. xxxi. 13; TA. iii. 12. 6.⌋ The three other texts agree with ours throughout.

9. Virāj in the beginning came into being (*sam-bhū*); out of Virāj, Purusha; it, when born, exceeded the earth behind, also in front.

⌊RV. x. 90. 5; VS. xxxi. 5; SV. i. 622; TA. iii. 12. 2.⌋ RV.TA. read, for **a**, *tásmād virā́ḍ ajāyata;* SV.VS. ⌊and KaṭhaB. read⌋ the same, save *tátas* for *tásmāt.* Ppp. reads in **b** *pāuruṣāt*, and in **d** *purā.* ⌊For *puraḥ* in the Berlin ed., read *puráḥ.*⌋

10. When, with Purusha as oblation, the gods extended the sacrifice, spring was its sacrificial butter, summer its fuel, autumn its oblation.

⌊RV. x. 90. 6; VS. xxxi. 14; TA. iii. 12. 3.⌋ ⌊The first half-verse is our vii. 5. 4 **a**, **b**, where, however, *devā́s* follows *yajñám.*⌋ Of the other three texts, the only variant is *vasantò 'sy-* in VS.

11. They sprinkled with the early rain (*prāvṝ́ṣ*) that sacrifice, Purusha, born in the beginning; therewith the gods sacrificed, the Perfectibles (*sādhyá*) and they that are Vasus.

⌊RV. x. 90. 7; VS. xxxi. 9; TA. iii. 12. 3.⌋ The other three texts agree in reading in **a** *barhíṣi* (for *prāvṝ́ṣā*), in **b** *agratás*, in **d** *ṝ́ṣayas* (for *vásavas*). Ppp. has in **d** *sādhyā ca.* One or two of our mss. give *agratás* (like RV. etc.); about half SPP's authorities accent *áyajanta* ⌊as does also TA.⌋.

12. From that were born horses, and whatever [animals] have teeth in both jaws; kine were born from that; from that [are] born goats and sheep.

⌊RV. x. 90. 10; VS. xxxi. 8; TA. iii. 12. 5.⌋ The other three texts ⌊but not KaṭhaB.⌋ omit *ca* after *yé* in **b**.

13. From that all-sacrificing sacrifice were born the verses (*ṛ́c*), the chants (*sā́man*); meter ⌊sic!⌋ were born from that; sacrificial formula was born from that.

⌊RV. x. 90. 9; VS. xxxi. 7; TA. iii. 12. 4.⌋ The other texts have at beginning of **c** *chándāṅsi*, and our edition gives the same; but the mss., except one of ours p. m. and two of SPP's, read instead *chándo ha*, and SPP. follows them; this, though an ungrammatical corruption (as shown in the translation), has the best right to figure as Atharvan text. ⌊See p. xcvii.⌋

14. From that all-sacrificing sacrifice was collected the speckled butter (*pṛṣadājyá*); it made those cattle belonging to Vāyu — those that are of the forest and of the village.

That is, the wild and the tame. ⌊The verse is RV. x. 90. 8; VS. xxxi. 6; TA. iii. 12. 4.⌋ RV. alone combines in **c** *paçū́n tā́-*; in **d**, RV. and TA. read *āraṇyā́n*. SPP. unaccountably accents at end of **b** *pṛṣadājyàm*, against the majority of his mss., all of ours, and the usage everywhere else. The mss. vary between *vāyavyā́n* and *vāyavyàn*. Ppp. has in **c** *cakrire;* ⌊and so has KaṭhaB.⌋.

15. Seven were made its enclosing sticks (*paridhí*), thrice seven its pieces of fuel, when the gods, extending the sacrifice, bound Purusha as victim.

⌊RV. x. 90. 15; VS. xxxi. 15; TA. iii. 12. 3.⌋ The other three texts offer no variant. In connection with the 'seven,' the comm. of course thinks of the meters; of the 'twenty-one' he gives more than one explanation, sufficient to show that he is merely guessing.

16. Seven times seventy rays (*aṅçú*) were born from the head of the great god, of king Soma, when born out of Purusha.

This verse is found nowhere else. The RV. has also a 16th verse, an appendage to the hymn in a different meter, which was earlier found as RV. i. 164. 50, and is our vii. 5. 1, besides occurring in a number of other texts — in VS. ⌊xxxi. 16⌋ and TA. ⌊iii. 12. 7⌋, in connection with the rest of the Purusha-hymn. The comm. refers to the double character of soma, as plant and as moon, and notes that, while the sun's rays are a thousand, those of the moon are four hundred and ninety.

7. To the lunar asterisms: for blessings.

[*Gārgya.* — *pañca. mantroktanakṣatradevatyam. trāiṣṭubham: 4. bhurij.*]

The hymn is wanting in Pāipp. The comm. finds it used three times (in 1, 6, and 12) in the Nakṣatra Kalpa.

⌊Regarding the asterisms in general, the reader may consult Whitney's *Oriental and Linguistic Studies*, ii., pages 351–356, 377, and 421 and the chart following it, or else Whitney in JAOS., vi. 414, 468, and chart; further, Weber's essays, *Die vedischen Nachrichten von den naxatra*, *Abh. der Berliner Ak.*, 1860 and 1861.* A list of the asterisms is given in my translation of the Karpūra-mañjarī, appended to Konow's ed.,

p. 214. Especially important are the *nakṣatra*-passages, TS. iv. 4. 10 and TB. i. 5. 2 and iii. 1. 1–2: cf. references to asterisms in AV. vi. 110 and notes, ii. 8, xiv. 1. 13, etc. — Note, on the one hand, that our series begins, as does that in TS., with the old beginning in Taurus, to wit, with the Kṛttikās or Pleiades, and not (as later: see Whitney, *O. and L. S.*, ii. 421), two asterisms further to the west, in Aries, with *açvayujāu* or *açvinī* (β and γ Arietis). Note also, on the other hand, that our series, unlike the series in TS., by including *abhijit* or Vega, far to the north of the ecliptic, comprises 28 asterisms, as is expressly stated below, at 8. 2 **a**: but whether 28 or 27 is the original Hindu number is a moot point carefully discussed by Whitney, l.c., pages 409–411. — The names of the asterisms in our hymn differ from those in TS. in a number of minor and major points: most notable among the latter is the TS. name *tiṣyà* for the 6th (or 8th) asterism, our *puṣyá*; and TS. has *çroṇā́* for the 21st (or 23d), our *çrávaṇa*. — Bloomfield, in his part of the *Grundriss*, p. 35, observes that this hymn and the next are repeated in full in Nakṣatra Kalpa 10 and 26; and he infers that the date of the incorporation of these hymns into the text of the Vulgata is posterior to the time of the Nakṣatra Kalpa, because, in the contrary case, they would have been quoted by their *pratīkas*.⌋ *⌊See especially the second essay, pages 300, 303, 315: at p. 300, Weber gives the deities of the several asterisms.⌋

Translated: Griffith, ii. 265.

1. Seeking favor of the twenty-eight-fold (?) wondrous ones, shining in the sky together, ever-moving, hasting in the creation (*bhúvana*), I worship (*sapary*) with songs the days, the firmament (*nā́ka*).

The translation implies our conjectural emendation of *turmíçam* ⌊two of W's mss., *-mich-*⌋ in **c** to *aṣṭāviṅçám* (or *-çā́*). ⌊This is supported by the textually unimpeachable *aṣṭāviṅçā́ni* of 8. 2 **a**, and the fact that the series in this hymn is actually of 28 members, as noted in the introduction.⌋ The comm. has *turmiçām*, and gives for it a double etymology and explanation: either it is *turmi* + *çā*, or it is *tur* + *miçā*; in the former case, *turmi* is from root *turv*, and means "injuring" (*hiṅsaka*), and *çā* is the root *çā* 'sharpen,' hence "make thin"; in the latter case, *tur* is ⌊a root-stem from⌋ root *turv*, and *miçā* is by Vedic license for *miṣā*, from root *miṣ* "contend" (*spardhāyām*); in either case, the compound means "putting down oppressors," and is adjective qualifying *sumatím*! All the mss. accent *saparyā́mi*, and SPP. admits it in his text; the accent is defensible, and would be required by Brāhmaṇa usage. Our emendation in **c** helps the meter as well as the sense; but no stress can be laid upon the circumstance that the Anukr. appears to regard the verse as a full *triṣṭubh*.

2. Easy of invocation for me [be] the Kṛittikās and Rohiṇī; be Mṛigaçiras excellent, [and] Ārdrā healthful (*çám*); be the two Punarvasus pleasantness, Pushya what is agreeable, the Āçleshās light (*bhānú*), the Maghās progress (*áyana*) ⌊for me⌋.

The translation again implies in **a** the emendation *me* for *agne*, made in our text, for the improvement both of sense and of meter; SPP. reads *agne*; and the comm. points out that Agni is invoked here because he is the deity of Kṛttikās, and that the deities also of the other asterisms are to be regarded as included in their invocations — which is quite ingenious. The mss. in **b** are divided between *çám* and *sám*; in **c**, between *púṣyas* and *puṣyàs*; SPP. gives *púṣyas*, with, as he reports, nearly all his authorities; and this is doubtless the better supported reading. There seems to be no good reason for imagining that *áyana* in **d** contains any hidden reference to the solstice (in later astronomical language, *ayana*, by abbreviation for *ayanānta* 'end of a [northern or southern] progress of the sun') as occurring in Maghās.

3. Be the former Phalgunīs and Hasta here auspicious (*púṇyam*); be Chitrā propitious, and Svāti easy (*sukhá*) for me; be the two Viçākhās bestowal (*rā́dhas*), Anurādhā easy of invocation, Jyeshṭhā a good asterism, Mūla uninjured.

There are sundry difficulties in this verse, in part attempted to be removed by emendation in our edition. It is very strange to find in **a** the former Phalgunīs distinctly mentioned, and the latter (*uttara*) as distinctly left out; it would be easy to put the *dvayā́* of 5 **b** in place of *pū́rvā* here;* or one wonders whether *uttara* is not somehow hidden in the awkwardly redundant *átra*. All the mss. (both *saṁh.* and *pada*) agree in the ungrammatical ⌊ending *-ti* of⌋ *svāti*, and SPP. accordingly admits *svāti* into his text: ours emends to *svātis*: *svātī́* would have been equally acceptable, and is supported by two of SPP's çrotriyas ⌊V. and K.⌋ and by the comm. The masc. *sukhás* (p. *su∘kháḥ*) can hardly be tolerated; we ought to have *sukhám*, or else, with the comm., *sukhā́*. All the mss. read in **c** *rā́dhe*, as if there were an adjective *rā́dha*; SPP. and the comm. read *rā́dhe*, the latter explaining it as another name for *viçākhe* (not a word defining the expected blessing!): this involves an anachronism,† and would be in the highest degree improbable even if it did not: *rā́dho* is a very easy and plausible improvement. Finally, all the mss. have in **d** *áriṣṭa mū́lam* ⌊cf. note to xviii. 2. 3⌋, which SPP. adopts, in spite of its utter ungrammaticalness; the comm., with his usual disregard of *pada*-text and accent, appears to understand *ariṣṭamūlam*, a compound.

*⌊Or rather to put *dvayé*? The comm. renders *pū́rvā* by *pūrve*, for which *pū́rvā* is a bad reading or a worse solecism. But the position of *ca*, too, is very suspicious.⌋

†⌊I suppose Whitney's implication is that *rādhā*, as a name for the 14th (or 16th) asterism *viçākhā*, is a later one, based on a misunderstanding of the name of the 15th (or 17th) asterism, *anurādhā*, which word simply means 'success' (cf. *ánv eṣām arātsmé 'ti: tád anūrādhā́ḥ*, TB. i. 5. 2[8]), but was thought of as meaning the one 'after (*anu*) or following *rādhā*.'⌋

4. Let the former Ashāḍhās give me food; let the latter ones bring refreshment; let Abhijit give me what is auspicious; let Çravaṇa [and] the Çravishṭhās make good prosperity.

Here are more bad readings: in **a**, the mss. give *pū́rvā rāsatām*, and SPP. accepts the reading, as if *rāsatām* could be 3d du. act., which, in view of all the circumstances, is absurd; our emendation to *-ntām* is unavoidable.* In **b**, the mss. vary between *dehy útt-* ⌊all of Whitney's and most of SPP's⌋ and *devy útt-*, and SPP. adopts the latter, because the comm. has it; but then the comm. makes no difficulty of understanding it as = *devyas*; it is merely, in his opinion, a Vedic substitution of sing. for pl.; and it is to be hoped that no modern scholar would follow him in that. The emendation of our text to *yé hy úttare*,† considering that all our mss. (and all but two of SPP's authorities) have *úttare* (p. *út∘tare*), was a naturally suggested and easy one; but we need instead *yā́ hy úttarā ā́*, feminine words, like the *pū́rvās* ⌊the *pada*-mss. and the Anukr. read *pū́rvā*⌋ in **a**; SPP. reads *úttarās*, with the comm. and two of his reciters. The meter of **d** would be better if we had *çróṇas* for *çrávaṇas*; but the Anukr. acknowledges the redundancy of the verse.

*⌊SPP. seems rather to view *rāsatām* in **a** as of the plural number, 3d person imperative middle, = *dadatu* (the ms. of the comm. has in fact *dadātu*, singular): and plural 3d it might be (from the *s*-aorist tense-stem *rās*, used as a secondary root: *Gram.* § 896), thus conforming in number with *vahantu*. On the other hand, we cannot take *rāsatām* in **c** otherwise than as of the singular number, 3d person imperative middle of the *a*-conjugation, present-stem *rāsa*: and the identical form in **a** ought, one would think, to be of the same value. If we take it as singular, and read *aṣāḍhā́* as fem. and sing. so as to conform with *pū́rvā* (p. *pū́rvā*), then pāda **b** is intolerably out of congruity with **a** in the matters of gender and number. —I offer the following suggestions for what they may be worth. First, in spite of the (unauthoritative) *pada*-reading *út◦tare*, I would take the *úttarā ā́* of the living reciters K.V. as representing a correct metrical utterance of *úttarā́* (= *út◦tarā : ā́*). Secondly, for *vahantu* I would read *vahātu* (cf. *svadātu*, *nudātu*, *muñcātu*): this seems to me better than a possible *vahāti*, and does as little violence to the tradition as the *rāsantām* and *yé hy úttare* suggested above. If our *vahantu* is a corruption, it may well be a faulty assimilation (cf. end of ¶ 4 of note on xviii. 4. 87) of *vahātu* to the ending of vs. 5 **d**. — My text then would be as follows: *ánnam pū́rvā* (p. *-vā*) *rāsatām* (as 3d sing.) *me aṣāḍhórjam* (p. *-ḍhā́ : ū́r-*) *devy úttarā́ vahātu* (p. *devī́ : úttarā : ā́ : vahātu*): 'may the Former Ashāḍhā give me food; may the Latter, the divine one, bring refreshment.'⌋ †⌊It appears from the Collation Book that RW. meant in fact to print *yé hy útta-*: but the Berlin ed. has actually *yé hy ùtta-*, an accent-mark having perhaps slipped to the left, over *hyu* from over *tta*.⌋

5. Let Çatabhishaj [bring] to me what is great widely; let the double Proshṭhapadās [bring] to me good protection (*suçárman*); let Revatī and the two Açvayuj [bring] fortune to me; let the Bharaṇīs bring to me wealth.

There are no difficulties or variants in this verse.

8. For well-being: to the asterisms etc.

⌊*Gārgya.* — *sapta.* *mantroktanakṣatradevatyam* (*6. brāhmaṇaspatyā*). *trāiṣṭubham: 1. virāḍ jagatī; 6. 3-av. 6-p. atijagatī.*]

Verses 4–6 are found in Pāipp. xx. The same *viniyoga* is pointed out by the comm. for this as for the preceding hymn.

⌊As to the asterisms, and as to the inclusion of the full text of this hymn in the Nakṣatra Kalpa, see introduction to hymn 7.⌋

Translated: Griffith, ii. 267.

1. What asterisms are in the sky, in the atmosphere, in the waters, on the earth, what ones in the mountains, in the quarters, what ones the moon goes on preparing (*pra-kḷp*), let all those be propitious to me.

The mss., and so SPP., have the incorrect accent *prákalpayan* in **c**; it is emended in our text. It is possible, but not natural, to count in the verse 46 syllables, with the Anukr.

2. Let them of the series of twenty-eight, propitious, helpful, together allot to me acquisition (*yóga*); I go forward to acquisition and possession (*kṣéma*); I go forward to possession and acquisition; homage be to day-and-night.

In **b**, the comm. reads *sahá yógam* as a compound, *sahayogam*. He explains, after the usual fashion, *yoga* as *alabdhavastuprāpti* (his ms., *alabhya-*), and *kṣema* as *labdhavastuparipālana*, and the translation follows him. The verse (11 + 8 : 8 + 8 + 8 = 43) is quite improperly let pass as simply a *triṣṭubh*. ⌊As for the twenty-eight, see introduction to hymn 7.⌋

3. Be it for me well at sunset (?), well in early morning, well at evening, well by day; be it for me well with beasts, well with birds; with easy invocation, O Agni, having gone with well-being to a mortal, come thou again enjoying.

In **a** the translation follows our conjectural emendation of *svástitam* (or *svastí tám*, or *svastítam*, as some of the mss. variously read; the *pada*-texts have *svastí : tám* or *svástitam;* ⌊one ms. and two çrotriyas of SPP. and⌋ the comm. give *svastí tát*) to *svastamitám*, which is bold, but not implausible. For *sudivám* the comm. has the better supported *sudinam*. The mss. ⌊except D. and L., which read *suçakunám*⌋ and SPP. accent *suçakúnam*, which may be correct. The translation of the second half-verse is only a makeshift; the line appears to be thoroughly corrupt; implied is the reading *svastyā́ mártyaṁ gatvā́;* SPP. reads, with nearly all the mss., *svasty àmártyaṁ gatvā́*, against the proper accent *ámartyam*. SPP's *pada*-mss. read at the end *ā́ya : abhiºnándan* (one has *ā́yā*); both our mss. are imperfect, one reading simply *ā́*, the other perhaps *ā́yā* with the *y* erased; if the word is to be accepted at all, it should apparently be *ā́ : aya*. The repetition of *martya* in our text is doubtless too daring, considering how unsatisfactory a result it yields after all.

4. Detraction, evil gossip, reproach, sneezing about (?)—them, O Savitar, drive (*suva*) away for me empty-handed (?), with all.

The translation implies the text of the mss., which is also read by SPP., in the second half-verse: *sárvāir me riktakumbhā́n párā* ⌊most mss. *parā* or *yarā*⌋ *tā́nt savitaḥ suva;* we might alter *sárvāis* to *sarvátas*, so as to fill out the meter and give a much better sense; the comm. understands it to mean "allied with all the deities of the asterisms"; *riktakumbha* he simply glosses with *çūnyakalaça*, adding no further explanation; the Pet. Lexx. conjecture "perhaps idle talk (lit. emptypottedness)"; the translation implies their going away 'with empty vessels'—that is, carrying off no result or advantage. The comm. explains *anuhavá* as a calling out ⌊inauspiciously⌋ to a person from behind, and *parihavá* as the same from both sides; *parivādá* is "harsh talk" (*paruṣabhāṣaṇa*); *parikṣavá* is ⌊alternatively⌋ *sarvataḥ kṣutam*. Some of the mss. read *parichavám* in **b** ⌊cf. note * and vs. 5⌋. Ppp. has for **b** *parīvādaṁ parikṣayam;* and for **c**, **d**, *savyāimaviriktakumbhyāṁ parā tāṁ savitus savaḥ*. The comm. appears to read *suvaḥ* at the end, but glosses it with *parākuru*, as if *suva*.

⌊The AV. comm. begins his remarks on this vs. virtually as follows: If a man sets out on business under a lucky asterism, and some one from behind him calls his name or does something of that sort [probably scolding, sneezing, and coughing are meant], those things are of ill-omen as tending to thwart the business in hand; and this verse contains a prayer for warding off the ill effects of those omens. (In this connection, we may note the cries and slaps by which the woodpecker deters the hunter just as he sets out, Jātaka, ii. 153^{22}, 154^{3}.)—It almost seems as if our comm. were acquainted with ĀpGS. 9. 2, which prescribes an expiation in case some one sneezes or coughs near one who is setting out on business: *arthaprādhvasya parikṣave parikāsane cāpa upaspr̥çyo 'ttare yathāliñgaṁ japet* (cf. ed. of Winternitz, p. 12 and p. 61). Winternitz, *Hoch-*

zeitsrituell, p. 95 (cf. p. 26), gives the verses that are to be repeated: I give them as he has printed them at MP. i. 13. 5–6: *anuhavám parihavám parīvādám parikṣapám : dúsvapnaṁ* (should be *-niaṁ*) *dúruditaṁ tád dviṣádbhyo diçāmy ahám : ánuhūtaṁ párihūtaṁ çakúnāir yád açākunám : mṛgásya sṛtám akṣṇáyā tád* etc. This passage and AV. x. 3. 6 stand in close rapport with our vss. 3–4 here.⌋

*⌊As for the readings *parichavam* and *chavam* as against *parikṣavam* and *kṣavam* (4 **b**, 5 **a**, **b**), the former are avouched by a large minority of SPP's authorities and they prevail also in the mss. first collated by Whitney: and so Ppp. has *paricchava* for *parikṣava* of our x. 3. 6. The forms with *ch* appear to be allowable Prākritisms, like *uchantu* = *ukṣantu* at iii. 12. 4: cf. *ṛchara* = *ṛtsara* at x. 9. 23 and my note; and *uccase* = *ucyase* at xii. 4. 4. — For sneezing as an omen, see Henry C. Warren, On superstitious customs connected with sneezing, JAOS. xiii. = PAOS. May, 1885, p. xvii–xx. He quotes Jātaka, ii., p. 15 ff. etc., and Whitney adds JB. ii. 155.⌋

5. [Drive] away evil sneezing about; may we enjoy (*bhaj*) propitious (*púṇya*) sneezing; let the evil-nosed jackal and the *púṇyaga* urinate upon [it] for thee.

Part of the mss. read in **a**, **b** *parichavam* and *chavam:* ⌊see note * to vs. 4⌋. All the mss., and so SPP., have at the beginning *apapāpám;* the comm., with us, *ápa pāpám*. Again, all the mss. and SPP. accent *bhakṣīmáhi*. Ppp. reads *āpa māpa parikṣapaṁ puṇyaṁ bhakṣīmahi kṣapam*, which gives no help. For **c**, **d**, SPP. reads *çivā́ te pāpa nā́sikām púṇyagaç cā 'bhí mehatām* (the *pada* being *púṇya*○*gaḥ : ca : abhí : me : hatām*); the comm., *çivā te pāpanāçikā paṇḍakaç cā 'bhi medhatām*. The comm. explains *çivā* as a name for jackal (so adopted in the translation above); *pāpanāçikā* is, of course, destroying evil; *abhi medhatām* = *protsāhayatu:* the general sense being that, whereas the sight or hearing of a jackal, or the sight of a eunuch, is a bad omen, they are in virtue of the spell of this verse to have a totally opposite influence. How SPP. would render his text ⌊of **a**, in particular?⌋ it is impossible to see. The version given here lays no claim to being of any value. Ppp. reads *çivā te pāpanāçakā* (in this word favoring the comm.) *ṣaṇṇagusyā 'bhimehataḥ*, which does not seem to help us. The reading of the line in our edition is not to be praised.

6. These (fem.), O Brahmaṇaspati, that go dispersing upon the wind — do thou, O Indra, making them come together, make them most propitious for me.

The *pada*-mss. give in **b** *vā́taḥ* instead of *vā́te*, which latter is evidently the true reading. The comm. also understands *vātas*, which compels him to take *īrate* as = *īrte*, and to translate it as if causative. The comm. understands the quarters (*diças*) as intended, and points it out as well-known that in a violent wind these are confounded, one of them being taken for another. This is hardly better than silly; but what is really the subject of the verse is very hard to see. The Anukr. omits any definition of these three *anuṣṭubh* verses*; and, what is much more strange, although it describes the hymn as of seven verses, and the mss. and the comm. so number, it combines 6 and 7 together into one verse as 8 + 8 : 8 + 8 : 11 + 9 = 52. ⌊Ppp. has, for **b**, *viṣūcer vāca īyate*, and at end of **d** *-tamaṣ kṛdhi.*⌋

*⌊No: see p. 912, line 9.⌋

7. Let well-being be ours; let fearlessness be ours; homage be to day-and-night.

The verse is wanting in Ppp.

9. For appeasement and weal: to various divinities.

[*Brahman* (*çāntikāmaḥ*). — *caturdaça. sāumyam. trāiṣṭubham: 1. virāḍ urobṛhatī; 5. 5-p. pathyāpañkti; 9. 5-p. kakummatī; 12. 3-av. 7-p. aṣṭi; 14. 4-p. saṁkṛti.*] ⌊The Anukr. adds: *çeṣāḥ* (that is vss. 2–4, 6–8, 10–11, 13) *kāṇḍapratīkatvenā* * '*nuṣṭubhaḥ*. There thus remains not a single vs. that is not excepted from the definition *trāiṣṭubham!* — The Berlin ms., in its treatment of hymns 9–12, after *ekarcam* (h. 12), adds: *vāsiṣṭhaṁ vāiçvadevaṁ çantātīyaṁ trāiṣṭubham* (these four words apply well to hymns 10–11) *ādyam* (hymn 9) *mantroktabahudevatyam*. W. follows the London ms.⌋ *⌊At the beginning of its treatment of the *kāṇḍa*, the Anukr. says *brahmakāṇḍam ānuṣṭubham*.⌋

The hymn is not found in Pāipp. The comm. finds it used in Pariçiṣṭa 4. 5 ("muttering this, one should conduct a king to his dwelling-house") and 6. 5 (in the *piṣṭarātrikalpa*), and in Nakṣ. K. 18, as a hymn belonging to the *çānti gaṇa* (cf. note to Kāuç. 9. 7). Translated: Griffith, ii. 268.

1. Appeased (*çāntá*) be heaven (*dyú*), appeased be earth, appeased be this wide atmosphere, appeased the waters rich in moisture (*udanvánt*), appeased be the herbs for us.

⌊With **a**, **b**, cf. AGS. ii. 4. 14; PGS. iii. 3. 6; MGS. ii. 8. 6 b.⌋

2. Appeased be the foretokens, appeased for us be the-done-and-undone, appeased both what is and what is to be: be just everything weal for us.

The comm. explains *pūrvarūpāṇi* first as *kāryāpekṣayā kāraṇāvasthāpannāni vastūni*, and again as "former births, the fruit of evil deeds." Instead of *nas* in **b** it reads *me;* and it points out that 'the done' means what is done that should not be done, and 'the undone' what was left undone that should have been done — which is far from necessary or certain.

3. This speech that is most exalted, divine, sharpened by *bráhman*, by which is produced (*sṛj*) what is terrible — by that be there appeasement for us.

4. Or (?) this mind that is most exalted, sharpened by *bráhman*, by which is produced what is terrible — by that be there appeasement for us.

All the mss. read in **b** *vām* instead of *vā*, and SPP's text follows them. The comm. makes no mention of either in its exposition of the verse; but its text (so SPP. reports) reads *vā*, as does ours by emendation.

5. These five senses, with mind as sixth, that are in my heart, sharpened by *bráhman*, by which is produced what is terrible — by them be there appeasement for us.

The mss. read *mánaḥ ṣaṣṭhā́ni* (p. *mánaḥ : ṣaṣṭhā́ni*), but SPP., as well as our text, emends to *-ṭhāni*, and this the comm. also understands. In all the verses 3–5, some of the mss. leave *sasṛje* unaccented. This verse (10 + 8 + 7 : 8 + 8 = 41) is ill defined by the Anukr.

6. Weal for us be Mitra, weal Varuṇa, weal Vishṇu, weal Prajāpati, weal for us Indra, Bṛihaspati, weal for us be Aryaman.

This verse corresponds nearly to RV. i. 90. 9 and VS. xxxvi. 9; both these, however, put the pādas in the order **a**, **d**, **c**, **b**, and they read for our **b** *çáṁ no víṣṇur urukramáḥ.*

7. Weal for us be Mitra, weal Varuṇa, weal Vivasvant, weal the destroyer (*ántaka*), [weal] the portents from earth and from atmosphere, weal for us the planets (?) moving in the sky.

The mss. vary between *utpā́tās* and *utpātā́s*, the great majority favoring the former. SPP. reads *pā́rthivā "ntárikṣās*, giving in *pada*-text *-vā : ánt-*, while the *pada*-mss. read *-vā : ant-*; but his reading is palpably wrong and impossible, while a very slight emendation would have given *pārthivāntarikṣā́s* (implying the *pada*-text *pārthiva○āntarikṣā́ḥ*), which is implied in the translation above. The comm. explains as if he had *pārthivās* and *āntarikṣās* as two separate words; but, according to SPP., his text reads *pārthivāntarikṣāḥ.* Half the *saṁhitā*-mss. or more combine *-ikṣāchā́ṁ no*, as if the word had ended in *-kṣāt;* and, as these included all known to us down to the time of printing, our text reflects them. The comm. of course makes no question of explaining *grahās* at the end as "Mars and the rest"; and perhaps there is no sufficient reason for questioning that interpretation. The Anukr. does not remark the redundancy of a syllable in 7 **c**.

8. Weal for us be the quaking (*vip*) earth, and weal what is meteor-smitten; weal be the red-milked kine, weal the earth when cleaving down.

All the mss. accent *vepyamānā́* in **a**, and nearly all (including the *pada*-mss.) end it as a nom. pl. *-mānā́ḥ;* SPP. emends by dropping the blundering *visarga*, but does not venture to alter the equally blundering accent; of course, it must be made *vepyámānā*, as pres. pass. pple of the causative, unless we emend further to *vépamānā*, as our text reads, and as is decidedly better. The comm. reads *vepyamānā*, and explains it once by *kampamānā* and once by *kampyamānā.* ⌊Most⌋ mss., and SPP., read in **b** *ulkā́ nírh-*; ⌊but Whitney's I. and three of SPP's authorities give *ni-* for *nir-*⌋; the comm. ⌊reads *-ni-* and⌋ understands the two words to form a compound, as it is made to be in our text by simply removing the accent of *-nir-*; one does not see the applicability of the prefix *nis-*. In **c**, some of the mss. read *lóhitaḥ*, and some accent *kṣīrā́ḥ;* 'red-milked' would be with equal propriety rendered 'bloody-milked'; and the two things are of course equivalent. In **d**, the comm. has *avadīryatī*, glossing it with *avadīryamāṇā*, and this reading has been gratefully adopted in the translation. All the mss. give *ávatīryatī́s*, and all the *pada*-mss. divide it *ávatīḥ : yatī́ḥ;* SPP. emends to *áva tīryatī́ḥ*, by which nothing at all is gained; we emended to *avatī́ryatī*, which is at least grammatical, though hardly intelligible; *avadīryatī* is both; ⌊one of SPP's reciters gives *áva dīryatī́*⌋.

9. Be the meteor-smitten asterism weal for us; weal for us the enchantments and weal be the witchcrafts; weal for us the buried spells (*valagá*), weal the meteors; and weal be for us the land-plagues.

Literally, 'the afflictions (*upasarga*) of a region.' All the mss. read in **a** *ulkā́bhīh-* (p. *ulkā́ : abhí○h-*), which SPP. accordingly adopts; the comm. again (as in 8 **b**) regards it as a compound, which it is unquestionably meant to be, and which our text gives by emendation; the prefix *abhi* suits the situation, as *nir* (8 **b**) did not. In **c**, SPP. has the better accent *níkhātās*, with a large minority of his mss.; none of ours give it, and we accepted *nikhātā́s*, since it is not without support elsewhere. Our *valagā́s* was an emendation for *valgā́s;* but our two *pada*-mss. ⌊D.s.m. L.⌋ compared later, have *valagā́ḥ*, as does one of SPP's; the latter, however, adopts *valgā́s*, against meter and sense, and against the comm. The *pada*-mss. all have *ulkā́* in **c**, an evident blunder for *-kā́ḥ*, which SPP. this time ventures to read by emendation: it is extremely difficult to understand his selection of the cases where he is willing to emend. The metrical definition of the verse (really 12 + 11 : 11 + 11 = 45) by the Anukr. is as bad as possible.

10. Weal for us be the planets belonging to the moon, and weal the sun (*ādityá*) with Rāhu; weal for us smoke-bannered death, weal the Rudras of keen brightness.

The translation follows in **b** the text of the comm. *ādityaç ca rāhuṇā*, as is read also by SPP., who follows the comm. and three or four authorities. Most of the mss. have *-tyaḥ çarāhuṇā* (p. also *çarāhuṇā*), but two or three *çaṁ rāhuṇā*. Those that accent *-rāhuṇā* or *rāhuṇā* at all accent it on the final, *-huṇā́*, and this accent SPP. has not dared to change, although it is against all rule and practice. In connection with *dhūmaketu* the comm. quotes Kāuç. 127. 1, where the word is used; it seems to me extremely unlikely that it signifies a comet; ⌊does it not refer rather to the smoke that rises from the pyre?⌋.

11. Weal [for us be] the Rudras, weal the Vasus, weal the Ādityas, weal the fires; weal for us the divine great seers, weal the gods, weal Bṛihaspati.

In **c**, SPP. reads *maharṣáyas*, against most of his authorities (although he gives *saptarṣáyas* in the two following verses). Some of the mss. leave *devās* in **c** unaccented; and two of SPP's treat the word in the same manner in **d**. Our emendation in **d** to *devī́s* is probably too venturesome, although it seems strange to have 'the gods' mentioned as a body in connection with the mention of so many of them separately.

12. The *bráhman*, Prajāpati, Dhātar, the worlds, the Vedas, the seven seers, the fires — by them happy progress (*svastyáyana*) is made for me: let Indra grant (*yam*) me refuge; let Brahmán grant me refuge; let all the gods grant me refuge; let the gods all grant me refuge.

The Anukr., the comm., and a better connection are here followed, by adding to this verse the two pādas which in our edition are printed as 13 **a**, **b**, in accordance with the numbering of our mss. (8 + 10 : 8 + 8 + 8 : 10 + 10 = 62, two syllables short of a full *aṣṭi*); SPP. makes the same division. Some of SPP's mss. read in **b** *devā́s* instead of *vedā́s*: the accent *vedā́s* seems to be modeled on *devā́s*, for 'the Vedas' should be *védās*, and the word ought doubtless to be so emended; ⌊O.D. actually have *védās*, and the comm. says the four Vedas are intended⌋. We should expect at the beginning *brahmā́*. ⌊With **c**, cf. 16. 1 **b**.⌋

13. Whatsoever things that are appeased in the world the seven seers know, be they all weal for me; let weal be mine, let fearlessness be mine.

Many of the mss. accent in **b** *lóke* and *saptárṣayo*. ⌊In **d** *asty* is a misprint for *astv*.⌋

14. [Be] earth appeasement, atmosphere appeasement, sky appeasement, waters appeasement, herbs appeasement, forest trees appeasement; [be] all the gods appeasement for me, the gods all appeasement for me,

appeasement with appeasements; by those appeasements all-appeasing do I appease what here is terrible, what here is cruel, what here is evil; [be] that appeased, [be] that propitious; be just everything weal for us.

With a large minority of his authorities, and with the comm., SPP. adds one more *çāntiḥ* before *çā̆ntibhis* at the end of the first division; in the second division, he follows the mss. slavishly in reading *sárva çā̆ntibhiḥ;* the comm. apparently (it is defective here) agrees with our emendation to *sarvaçāntíbhis.* After this word, the mss. all have *çamayāmoham,* accenting either *çámayā̆mohám* or *çámayāmohám;* the *pada*-mss. divide it absurdly *çámaya : mohám;* the comm. understands it as *çamayāmo 'ham,* with substitution of *aham* for *vayam* by Vedic license (a mere exchange of plural and singular); SPP. unaccountably gives *çámayāmohám* with the *pada*-text *çám : ayāmaḥ : ahám;* our emendation to *çamayāmy ahám* is evidently necessary. Similar passages occur in VS. xxxvi. 17; TA. iv. 42 (28); MS. iv. 9. 27 ⌊p. 138[12]⌋; but it is not worth while to quote them in detail; TA. (29) contains the compound *sarvaçāntí* and MS. has *sárva-çānti.* The "verse" is the only one in the whole work that is called a *saṁkṛti* (96 syllables); it counts naturally 94 syllables.

⌊Here ends the first *anuvāka,* with 9 hymns and 59 verses. The comm. (not SPP.) divides the Purusha-*sūkta* (our hymn 6) into two hymns, so that our vss. 1–5 make his hymn 6 and our vss. 6–16 make his hymn 7: thus his first *anuvāka* consists of 10 hymns. — There are of course no further quotations from the Old Anukr. or *Pañcapaṭalikā:* cf. p. 896, line 4.⌋

10. For well-being.

[*Brahman* (*çā̆ntikāmaḥ*). — *daça. sāumyam. trāiṣṭubham.*]

This hymn and the one following it are together RV. vii. 35, this one being vss. 1–10 of the latter, in unchanged order, and without a variant except in 8 **b**. Both are found together in Pāipp. xiii. ⌊For the quotation of the hymn in the *çānti gaṇa,* see note to Kāuç. 9. 7.⌋

Translated: Griffith, ii. 270; and also, of course, by the RV. translators.

1. Weal for us be Indra-and-Agni, with their aids; weal for us Indra-and-Varuṇa, on whom offerings are bestowed; weal Indra-and-Soma, for welfare, weal [and] profit (*yós*); weal for us Indra-and-Pūshan in booty-winning.

This verse is found also in VS. xxxvi. 11, which inverts the order of pādas **c** and **d**. The comm. takes *indrāgnī* in **a** as vocative ⌊and says so expressly; but⌋ apparently out of mere carelessness, as he does not make any change in the 3d du. verb *bhavatām.*

2. Weal for us be Bhaga, and weal for us Çaṅsa; weal for us Purandhi, and weal be wealths; weal for us the tribute (*çáṅsa*) of well-ordered (*suyáma*) truth; weal for us be the much-born Aryaman.

About half the mss. read in **c** *suyámas tu* (p. *suºyámastu*). Pādas **b** and **c** have dropped out of Ppp. The comm. takes *çaṅsas* in **a** to be by abbreviation for *narāçaṅsas.*

3. Weal for us be Dhātar, and weal for us Dhartar; weal for us be the wide-spreading one (*urūcī*) with her powers (?*svadhā́*); weal the two

great firmaments (*ródasī*), weal for us the rock (*ádri*); weal for us be the successful invocations of the gods.

The mss. write in **b** *urūcī́*, *urucī́*, and *ūrūcī́*; the comm. explains it as the earth, *dhartṛ* as Varuṇa, separator (*vidhārayitṛ*) of the good and bad, and *svadhā* as *anna*; *adri* he simply glosses by *parvata*.

4. Weal for us be Agni with front of light, weal for us Mitra-and-Varuṇa, weal the two Açvins; weal for us be the things well done of the well-doers; weal let the lively (*iṣirá*) wind blow upon us.

Ppp. has in **b** *-ṇā açvinā*.

5. Weal for us be heaven-and-earth in our early invocation; the atmosphere be weal for us to see; weal for us be the herbs, the trees (*vanín*), weal for us be the conquering lord of the welkin (*rájas*).

The comm. regards Indra as intended in the last pāda.

6. Weal for us be god Indra with the Vasus; weal Varuṇa of excellent praise ⌊*su-çáṅsa*⌋ with the Ādityas; weal for us healing (*jálāṣa*) Rudra with the Rudras; unto weal for us let Tvashṭar listen here with his spouses (*gná*).

The comm. declares *jalāṣa* a *sukhanāman*. All the *pada*-mss. have in **d** *tváṣṭā : agnā́bhiḥ!* SPP. emends to *gnā́bhiḥ*; the comm. of course has *gnābhis* and glosses it with *devapatnībhis*. ⌊As to *suçáṅsa*, cf. note to xviii. 3. 16.⌋

7. Weal for us be soma, weal for us the *bráhman*; weal for us the pressing-stones, and weal be the sacrifices; weal for us be the settings of the sacrificial posts; weal for us the sprouts (*prasū́*), and weal be the sacrificial hearth (*védi*).

The sprouts, namely, of sacrificial grass. The comm. declares *svaru* used in the sense of *yūpa* as the thing possessed for the possessor. ⌊The last pāda has dropped out of Ppp.⌋

8. With weal for us let the wide-looking sun arise; weal for us be the four directions; weal for us be the firm mountains; weal for us the rivers, and weal be the waters.

The RV. order of words in **b** ⌊cf. introd.⌋ is this: *çáṁ naç cátasraḥ pradíço bhavantu*. ⌊The first pāda has dropped out of Ppp.⌋

9. Weal for us be Aditi with her courses (*vratá*); weal for us be the tuneful (*svarká*) Maruts; weal for us Vishṇu, and weal be for us Pūshan; weal for us the place of being (?*bhavítra*), and weal be Vāyu.

The comm. glosses *vratebhis* with *karmabhiḥ sārdham*, and *bhavitram* by *bhuvanam udakam antarikṣaṁ vā*. ⌊Ppp. also reads *bhavitram*.⌋

10. Weal for us be the rescuing god Savitar; weal for us be the out-shining dawns; weal for us be Parjanya for our progeny; weal for us be the wealful lord of the field (*kṣétra*).

The comm. quotes a verse to the effect that some regard Rudra, and some Agni, as 'lord of the field.'

11. For well-being.

[*Brahman* (*çāntikāmaḥ*). — *ṣaṭ. sāumyam. trāiṣṭubham.*]

The hymn is made up of the remaining verses of RV. vii. 35, ⌊vss. 11–15,⌋ with another RV. verse (v. 47. 7) added. Among the former the differences of order and reading are very slight. ⌊The hymn is found, as noted under hymn 10, in Pāipp. xiii.⌋
Translated: Griffith, ii. 272; and also, of course, by the RV. translators.

1. Weal for us be the lords of truth; weal for us the coursers and weal be the kine; weal for us the Ṛibhus, well-doers, having good hands; weal for us be the Fathers at our invocations.

This verse and the following one are found in RV. in inverted order (as vss. 12 and 11). The comm. quotes sundry RV. verses illustrating the character of the Ṛibhus, and is uncertain whether *háva* at the end comes from root *hū* or from *hu*.

2. Weal for us be the gods, the all-gods; weal be Sarasvatī with the prayers (*dhī*); weal the followers (?*abhiṣác*) and weal the gift-following (?*rātiṣác*); weal for us they of the sky, they of the earth, weal for us they of the waters.

This verse is found, without variant, also in TB. ii. 8. 6³ and MS. iv. 14. 11. The comm. declares *devā́ viçvádevās* to mean *bahustotrakā indrādayaḥ; abhiṣā́cas, yajñam abhitaḥ samavayanto devāḥ;* and *rātiṣā́cas, dānārthaṁ saṁgacchamānā devāḥ* — these two epithets belonging to the *viçve devāḥ*. Ppp. reads at the end *āpyāḥ*.

3. Weal for us be the divine (*devá*) one-footed goat (*ajá ékapad*), weal the bottom snake (*áhi budhnyà*), weal the ocean; weal for us be Peru, grandson of the waters (*apā́ṁ nápāt*); weal for us be the spotted one (*pṛ́çni*), guarded by the gods.

The RV. version reads in **b** *çáṁ nó 'hir b-*, and at the end *-gopāḥ* ⌊Müller's 2d quarto ed. and Aufrecht's 2d ed. have *-gopā:* as for the form, see my *Noun-Inflection*, p. 445⌋; Ppp. agrees with RV. in **b**, and has *-gopāḥ* at the end. The comm. explains *perús* as *pārayitā duḥkhebhyaḥ*, and *pṛçni* as mother of the Maruts. The omission of *nas* in our **b** makes the meter defective, but the Anukr. takes no notice of it.

4. Let the Ādityas, the Rudras, the Vasus enjoy this very new worship (*bráhman*) as it is performed; let there hear us them of the sky, them of the earth, also the kine-born, who are worshipful.

The RV. version ⌊vs. 14⌋ reads at end of **a** *juṣanta*. The comm. explains *gojātās* as the Maruts, born of Pṛçni.

5. They who are the worshipful priests (*ṛtvíj*) of the gods, to be worshiped of man (*mánu*), immortal, right-knowing — let them bestow on us today wide passage (*urugāyá*): do ye protect us ever with blessings.

RV. reads in **a** *devā́nāṁ yajñíyā yajñíyānām*. The comm. apparently takes *-gāya* as from *gā* 'sing,' as he glosses *urugāyám* with *prabhūtāṁ kīrtim*, and does not even, as is his wont in such cases, give an alternative explanation implying *gā* 'go.'

6. Be it so, O Mitra-and-Varuṇa, so, O Agni: weal [and] profit for us be this praise (*çastá*); may we reach sounding (*gādhá*) and firm standing; homage to the great sky, [our] seat.

The verse is found, without variant, as RV. v. 47. 7. The comm. takes *çastam* in **b** as adjective to *çaṁ yos*, which is perhaps better; also it connects *bṛhate* with *sādanāya*, and understands by this the earth. Ppp. reads in **c** *gātum* for *gādham*, and in **d** *sādhanāya*.

12. For success and long life.

[*Brahman* (*çāntikāmaḥ*). — *ekarcam. sāumyam. trāiṣṭubham.*]

The hymn, or verse, is wanting in Pāipp. Its first half is identical with RV. x. 172. 4; its second half, with RV. vi. 17. 15 (also SV. i. 454). It is reckoned as a *çānti*-hymn, and used as such in company with the hymns that precede it ⌊see note to Kāuç. 9. 7⌋.

Translated: Griffith, ii. 273; and by the RV. translators.

1. The dawn, with nobleness, makes the darkness roll together [and] away on her sister's track; therewith may we win the prize (*vā́ja*) set by the gods; may we revel, living a hundred winters, rich in heroes.

The sense of the first half-verse is difficult and doubtful. *Ápa* in **a** is really an emendation ⌊following RV.⌋, all our mss. ⌊save B., which has *áṣaḥ*⌋, and very nearly all SPP's (only one has *ápa* ⌊and one, *apá*⌋) reading instead *ápaḥ*; the comm. has *apa*. Half ⌊of SPP's authorities, and one or two of W's⌋ give in **b** *suyātátā*. The comm. amuses himself with etymologizing *svasṛ* as *svayam eva sāriṇī*.

13. For success in war: ⌊Apratiratha hymn⌋.

[*Apratiratha. — ekādaça. āindram. trāiṣṭubham: 3–6, 11. bhurij.*]

The hymn is, with slight variations, identical for the most part with the familiar Apratiratha hymn of the Rig-Veda (x. 103), found also in other texts: VS. xvii. 33 ff.; SV. ii. 1199 ff.; TS. iv. 6. 4; MS. ii. 10. 4. ⌊The readings of VS. and SV. agree with those of RV., as noted under vs. 2.⌋ Our first verse is peculiar, being found elsewhere only in SV. (ii. 1219); and vss. 10, 12, 13 of the RV. hymn are here wanting. ⌊The RV. vss. here occur in the order 1–3, 5–7, 4, 8–9, 11.⌋ The hymn occurs also in Pāipp. vii. In Vāit. 1. 18, the selected brahman-priest is directed to recite the Apratiratha hymn; this probably means our hymn; GB. (ii. 1. 18) quotes the *pratīka* of our vs. 1 as the *apratiratha*. ⌊Varāhamihira's Yogayātrā (8. 6) prescribes the hymn for use by a king just about to march forth to war: *Ind. Stud.* xv. 170.⌋

Translated: Griffith, ii. 273; and by the RV. translators. — Cf. also Oldenberg, *Die Hymnen des RV.*, i. 247.

1. Indra's two arms [are] stout, virile (*vṛ́ṣan*), these two wondrous successful bulls; them will I first yoke when the conjuncture (*yóga*) arrives — they by which was conquered the heaven (*svàr*) that is the Asuras'.

The SV. text (ii. 1219) is considerably different: in **a**, **b**, *yúvānāv anādhṛṣyāú supratīkā́v asahyāú*; in **c**, *tāú yuñjīta prathamāú*; at the end, *sáho mahát*. *Vṛ́ṣāṇāu* (instead of the regular *vṛ́ṣaṇāu*) is read also by Ppp., and the meter demands it ⌊cf. *Noun-Inflection*, p. 537, 523⌋. The combination *citrā́ imā́ vṛṣ-*, if representing, as the sense clearly requires, *citrāú : imāú : vṛṣ-*, is anomalous in AV., though regular for some of the other Vedic texts (cf. Prāt. ii. 22 note); and the *pada*-text shows a sense of this, by reading *citrā́ḥ : imā́ : vṛṣ-*. SPP. gives as his *pada*-text *citrā́ : imā́*, which leaves the *saṁhitā* reading unaccounted for; the comm. assumes *citrāu* and *imā*. In **c**, all the mss. (whence also SPP.) read *yokṣe*, for which our *yokṣye* is an emendation, plainly demanded by both sense and meter; it is one of the common cases of a *y* lost after *ṣ*; Ppp., too, has *yokṣye* (before it, *ta* for *tāu*); the comm. has the senseless *yakṣe*. All the mss., again, read *prathamás* (*-mó yó-*), and the comm. likewise, with, of course, SPP.; our emendation to *-māú* (with SV.) is an improvement, but not a necessity. The comm. foolishly declares *āgate* = *kṣeme*, in order to bring about the ordinary combination of *yoga* and *kṣema*, here quite out of place. He also takes *svàr yát*, against accent and *pada*-text, as one word ⌊cf. 15. 4, note⌋, and explains *-yat* as a participle, = *gacchat!* Ppp. reads and combines in **c** *prathamayogā "gate*.

2. Swift, sharp, terrible like a bull, greatly smiting, disturber of men (*carṣaṇí*), roaring, unwinking, sole hero, Indra conquered a hundred armies together.

This verse ⌊RV. vs. 1⌋ agrees throughout with the RV. text; SV. and VS. show no variants from RV. through the whole hymn; TS.MS. read here in **a** *yudhmás* for *bhīmás*, and MS. has also *kṣóbhanas*. The mss. also vary in this last word between *-ṇas* and *-nas*; SPP. adopts *-ṇas*, as does our text.

3. With the roaring, unwinking, conquering, invincible, immovable, bold one — with Indra thus conquer, thus overpower the fighters, O men, with the arrow-armed bull (*vṛ́ṣan*).

RV. ⌊vs. 2⌋ begins **b** with *yutkāréṇa*, and all the other texts agree with it. The comm. carelessly reads *yodhyena* instead of *ay-*, explaining it by *yuddhasaṁsaktena;* he takes *yúdhas* in **d** as vocative = *yoddhāras;* with *tát* (twice) in **c** he supplies *jetavyam* ⌊and *abhibhavanīyam*⌋.

4. He with the arrow-armed, he with the quiver-hung, [is] controller; he, Indra with his train, brings together the fighters — [he,] conquering those brought together, soma-drinker, defiant with his arms, of formidable bow, shooting with fitted [arrows].

⌊Vs. 3 in RV.⌋ TS.MS. read in **d** *ūrdhvádhanvā;* and MS. has a very different **b**, *sáṁsṛṣṭāsu yutsv índro gaṇéṣu*. Many of the mss. (as often in such words) read in **b** *sáṁsṛṣṭā;* some (as also elsewhere) lengthen the *u* in *kampa* at beginning of **d**; all have at the end *ástāt* — which, however, even SPP. emends to *ástā*, with the comm. The *pada*-mss. give in **c** *soma॰pā́* (RV. *-pā́ḥ*). ⌊The comm. notes as an alternative that *yudhas* in **b** (both ed's, *yúdhas*) may be taken as *yudhás*, oxytone and abl. sing. (he cites Pāṇini, vi. 1. 168) — which is a regard for the accent (cf. note to vs. 9) that is unusual with him.⌋ ⌊For *prátihitā* used pregnantly of an arrow, cf. the citations under vi. 65. 1.⌋

5. To be known by his strength, stout, foremost hero, powerful, vigorous (*vājín*), overpowering, formidable, excelling heroes, excelling warriors, conquering with power — mount, O Indra, the victorious kine-winning chariot.

The fourth verse of the RV. hymn is transposed ⌊in the AV. text so as⌋ to follow our vs. 7, and vs. 5 AV. is vs. 5 RV. The other texts ⌊RV. etc.⌋ all read at the end *govít;* and all except MS. have in **c** *sahojā́s*. SPP. retains in **a** the *visarga* before *stháv-*, with the majority of the mss.; he also accepts in **c** *abhíṣatvā*, with half the mss., but against all the parallel texts, apparently because the comm. has *ṣ*. Ppp. reads for **d** *jāitrāyāi ā ratham ā tiṣṭha kovidam*. ⌊The *govídam* of the Berlin text seems to be an emendation. Nearly all the authorities of W. and of SPP., and SPP's text as well, and the comm., have *govídan;* but one or two have *govít*, with RV. etc.⌋

6. Be ye excited after this formidable hero; take hold, O companions, after Indra, the troop-conqueror, kine-conqueror, thunderbolt-armed, conquering in the race, slaughtering with force.

We had this verse ⌊which is RV. vs. 6⌋ above, as vi. 97. 3; the reversal in the other texts of the order of the two lines, and the other variants, were there noticed. TS. and MS. alter a little the order of verses: RV. 4 is followed in TS. by RV. 6, 5, 7, and in MS. by RV. 7, 5, 6. The Anukr. reckons vss. 3–6 alike as *bhurij*, although 3 is redundant by two syllables. ⌊Ppp. reads *satvānas* for *sakhāyas* in **b**.⌋

7. Plunging with power into the cow-stalls, Indra, pitiless, formidable, of hundred-fold fury, immovable, overpowering fighters, invincible — let him favor our armies in the fights.

The stalls, namely, in which the kine are shut up by the Asuras. All the *saṁhitā*-mss. read *'dāyá ugráḥ* at beginning of **b**, but all the *pada*-mss. (except one of SPP's) give *adayáḥ*, and one of ours puts after it the sign that is wont to be used when a word shows an anomalous change in *saṁhitā*. RV.⌊vs. 7⌋SV.VS. (also K.Kap.: see Schröder's note to MS.) read *adayás*, and our text follows their authority; but TS. has *adāyás* (of which the Pet. Lexx. take no notice), and MS. has *ādāyás;* the comm. reads *adāyas*, but explains it by *nirdayas*, as if it were *adayás*. *Adāyás* is doubtless the established AV. reading. All the other texts have after it *vīrás* instead of *ugrás*. In **c**, all the others except MS. have *ayudhyás*. Most of the *pada*-mss. accent *ayodhyàḥ*, ⌊and so the *pada*-reading of MS.⌋. The first pāda is *bhurij* ⌊read *gotrā́* ?⌋.

8. O Bṛihaspati, fly about with thy chariot, demon-slaying, forcing away our enemies; breaking up our foes, slaughtering our enemies, be thou the helper of ourselves.

Or, 'of our bodies (*tanū́*).' This verse corresponds to vs. 4 of all the other texts; and they read in concert for **c** *prabhañjánt sénāḥ pramṛṇó yudhā́ jáyann*, and at the end *ráthānām*. The *pada*-mss. commit the blunder of reading *mítrān* ⌊or *mitrā́n*⌋ in **b**; SPP. emends to *amítrān*, which the comm. also gives. A number of SPP's *saṁhitā*-mss. have (after the fashion of MS.) *-mitráṅ* or *-mítraṅ;* ⌊cf. note to 27. 4, below⌋.

9. Indra [be] their leader; let Bṛihaspati, the sacrificial gift, the sacrifice, soma, go in front; in the midst of the smashing conquering armies of the gods let the Maruts go.

⌊RV. vs. 8.⌋ The text of MS. agrees throughout with ours; the others read *āsām* in **a**, and *ágram* (for *mádhye*) in **d** ⌊but TS. *ágre*⌋. The comm. does here a thing which is hardly paralleled elsewhere in his work: he points out that some explain *dakṣiṇā* in **b** as meaning "on the south," but that, as the word would in that case have to be accented *dakṣiṇā́*, as shown by xviii. 1. 42, it must signify here rather 'sacrificial gift' (*yajñe dīyamānā gorūpā dakṣiṇā*). A like attention to the element of accent elsewhere would notably improve the character of his lucubrations. ⌊Cf. note to vs. 4.⌋

10. Of Indra the bull (*vṛ́ṣan*), of king Varuṇa, of the Ādityas, of the Maruts, the spirit (*çárdhas*) [is] formidable; the noise of the great-minded, creation-stirring, conquering gods hath arisen.

⌊RV. vs. 9.⌋ All the other texts agree with ours throughout.

11. Indra [is] ours when the banners meet [in conflict]; let the arrows that are ours conquer; let our heroes be superior; us, O gods, aid ye at the invocations.

All the other texts read in **d** *asmā́ṅ u devās;* and MS. has the peculiar ending *bhā́reṣv ā́*. The verse is vs. 11 of the RV. hymn, RV. vs. 10 being omitted in the Atharvan (save as it is found in part as iii. 19. 6); RV. vs. 10 is omitted also by MS., which ends its hymn with 11; in TS., RV. vs. 10 is put after 11, and 13 follows, only 12 being omitted; in the Atharvan, RV. vs. 12 occurs as iii. 2. 5, and 13 in part at iii. 19. 7.

14. For safety.

[*Atharvan.* — *ekarcam. dyāvāpṛthivīyam. trāiṣṭubham.*]

This hymn is not found in Pāipp. It and the one following are included in the *abhaya gaṇa* (note to Kāuç. 16. 8).

Translated: Griffith, ii. 274. Griffith calls it a "hymn after victory" and refers *tvā* to the conquered enemy.

1. Here have I come up to a better stop (*avasā́na*); heaven-and-earth have been propitious to me; let the directions be for me free from rivals; we verily hate thee not; be there fearlessness for us.

The mss. read in **a** *uchréyas* (p. *ut∘çréyaḥ*); very possibly the true reading would be *u çréyas*. The *pada*-mss. fail to divide *avasā́nam* (it should be *ava∘sā́nam*, and this SPP. reads by emendation). Some mss. read *te* for *me* in **b**. Some of ours combine at the end *no 'stu*. Āp. vi. 29. 1 has a corresponding passage: *idaṁ çreyo 'vasānaṁ yad āgāṁ syone me dyāvāpṛthivī abhūtām: anamīvāḥ pradiçaḥ santu mahyam: gomad . . . svāhe 'ty avasite juhoti:* cf. also Āp. xiii. 25. 3.

15. For safety and success.

[*Atharvan.* — *ṣaḍṛcam. 1–4. āindram; 5, 6. mantroktabahudevatyam. 1. pathyābṛhatī; 2, 5. 4-p. jagatī; 3. virāṭ pathyāpañkti; 4, 6. triṣṭubh.*]

The hymn is found also in Pāipp. iii. As noted under the preceding, it belongs to the *abhaya gaṇa;* and the comm. points out sundry uses of the *gaṇa* (Çānti K. 16; Nakṣ. K. 18; Pariçiṣṭa 5. 3).

Translated: Ludwig, p. 513; Griffith, ii. 275.

1. What we fear, O Indra, make thou fearlessness for us of it; O bounteous one, help (*çak*) that for us by thy aids; smite away haters, away scorners.

The verse is RV. viii. 50 (61). 13, without variant; also SV. i. 274; ii. 671, which reads *ūtáye* in **c**. Most of the mss. give *tvám* instead of *tát* in **c**, but two of ours (P.M.) have *tán na ū-*, and on the authority of these and of RV.SV. our text gives the same; SPP. reads *tvám*, and so does the comm., and it is probably to be regarded as the true Atharvan version.

2. Indra the success-giver do we invoke; may we be successful with biped, with quadruped; let not the niggardly armies come upon us; make the haters (*drúh*) disperse and disappear.

The translation is defective in making no account of the prefix *anu* (twice), which ought to have an appreciable value, although it is very difficult to see what; the comm. paraphrases *anurādham* by *anukrameṇa pūjanīyam*, and he quotes RV. iv. 25. 8 in illustration of how various classes in succession invoke Indra. Ppp. preserves the *a* of *anu* in **b**. SPP. reads in **d**, with all the mss., *druhás;* there was no good reason for its alteration in our text to *drúhas*.

3. Indra [is] rescuer and Vṛitra-slayer, our desirable far-and-wide protector (?); be he our defender at the extremities, he in the middle, he behind, he in front.

In **b** the translation follows the comm., who explains *paraspā* (*-pāḥ*) *no v-*; all the mss. (save one or two s.m.) * have *parasphā̆no v-* (p. *parasphā̆naḥ*, without division), and this is doubtless the true Atharvan text, though an unintelligible corruption, of which our *gayasphāna* is an only partially successful emendation. *⌊In fact, W's O. and three of SPP's mss. have *-sphā-*, p.m., and *-spā-*, s.m.; and SPP's reciter K. gave *-sphā-*, while his reciter V. gave *-spā-*.⌋ Ppp. reads *parampāno* (*paraspā no?*). The *pada*-mss. unintelligently divide *ca : ramatáḥ* in **c**; some of our mss. have *-matá sá*. The verse (8 + 8 : 12 + 10 = 38) is poorly described by the Anukr.

4. Do thou, knowing, lead us toward broad space (*loká*), light that is heavenly (*svàr*), fearlessness, well-being; may we dwell under the formidable arms of thee the stout one, O Indra, [those two] great refuges.

The verse is RV. vi. 47. 8, found also in TB. (in ii. 7. 13³); both these texts read in **b** *svàrvaj jy-*, at beginning of **c** *ṛṣvā́*, and in **d** *stheyāma*. The comm. gives *svaryat*, but explains the *-yat* as *-gacchat* (as above, 13. 1); Ppp. agrees with RV.TB. ⌊in reading *svàrvaj*⌋; ⌊Ppp. abbreviates the consonant group *-j jy-* to *-jy-*; and so does TB., ed. Calc., reading *súvarva jy-*⌋. In **d**, the comm. has the better reading *kṣiyema*.

5. May the atmosphere make for us fearlessness; fearlessness both heaven-and-earth here; fearlessness from behind, fearlessness from in front; from above, from below be there fearlessness for us.

The comm. prefers to take the words of direction in **c**, **d** in their other admissible sense of points of compass, pointing out that *adhara* gets the value 'south' by antithesis to *uttara* 'north.' The verse (11 + 12 : 11 + 11 [?] = 45) is no sort of a *jagatī*.

6. Fearlessness from friend, fearlessness from enemy, fearlessness from one known, fearlessness [from one] that is away; fearlessness for us by night, fearlessness by day; be all places my friend.

At the beginning of **b**, all the mss. read *ábhaye*, but even SPP. emends to *-yam*, having the comm. with him. At the end of the same pāda, all ⌊so also Ppp.⌋ give *puró yáḥ* (p. *puráḥ : yáḥ*), which SPP. retains; the comm. reads *paro yaḥ*, but understands it as if *páro yáḥ*, explaining as *jñātād anyaḥ* or *aparijñātaḥ*. Our emendation to *parókṣāt* is defensible; but the translation implies *paró yáḥ*, as a less alteration. ⌊In **d**, Ppp. combines *sarvā* "*çā* and omits *máma*.⌋ ⌊"Save me from my friends:" cf. ii. 28. 1 **d** and note; also RV. iv. 55. 5, where the antithesis between *jányam áṅhas* and *mitríyam áṅhas* is most instructive.⌋

16. For safety and protection.

[*Atharvan.—tṛcam.* mantroktabahudevatyam. 1. anuṣṭubh; 2. 3-av. 7-p. bṛhatīgarbhā 'tiçakvarī.*] *⌊So the London ms.; the Berlin ms. says in fact *dvyṛcam:* see under vs. 2.⌋

This and the following hymns, to 23 inclusive, are wanting in Pāipp. The comm. has 16–19 used in the night, in a ceremony to be performed by the *purohita*, on the entrance of a king into his sleeping-house (according to Pariçiṣṭa iv. 5). The hymn is repeated below as 27. 14, 15.

Translated: Griffith, ii. 276.

1. Freedom from rivals in front, behind us [is] fearlessness made; Savitar [protect] me on the south, the lord of Çachī me on the north.

The comm. takes *kṛtám* in **b** as 2d du. impv., = *kurutam*, in spite of the accent, trying to find a dual subject in the two gods mentioned in **c**, **d**; and SPP., in obedience to this, even reads *kṛtam*, although twelve of his thirteen authorities (with all of ours) have *kṛtám*, the thirteenth evidently disagreeing with the rest purely by the accidental omission of an accent-mark.* It would not be impossible to take *mā* in **c** and **d** as object of *dakṣiṇatás* and *úttarāt*. *⌊For the use of *kṛtám* (the participle), cf. *tāír me kṛtáṁ svastyáyanam*, above, 9. 12 **c**. — In his Collation Book, W. refers to RV. *khila*, 3. 4, which reads *asapatnám purástān naḥ çiváṁ dakṣiṇataḥ kṛdhi: abháyaṁ sátatam paçcā́d bhadrám uttarató gṛhé.*⌋

2. From the sky let the Ādityas defend me; from the earth let the fires defend; let Indra-and-Agni defend me in front; let the Açvins yield (*yam*) refuge round about; crosswise let the inviolable [cow], let Jātavedas, defend [me]; let the being-makers be my defense (*várman*) on all sides.

In **e** the mss. all read *tiraçcīnaghnyā́*, which the *pada*-text resolves into *tiraçcīn : aghnyā́*, and this SPP. retains, though *tiraçcīn* is not a possible word. Our emendation to *-cīnā 'ghnyā́* is a very simple one (implying *-cīnā : aghnyā́*); the translation is founded on it; but a more radical alteration of the pāda would be acceptable: something like, for instance, *tiryák cā 'gnī́ rakṣatu jātávedāḥ;* the *jātávedās* leads naturally to the suspicion that *agnís* is somehow hidden in the *'ghnyā́;* the comm. indeed reads *tiraçcīn agnī r-*; but he is able to regard *tiraçcīn* as a masc. accus., implying *asmān;* or else as by Vedic license for *-cīs*, and this for *-cībhyas*, implying *digbhyas* (!); and such assumptions are forbidden us. The *pada*-mss. all read *rakṣantu* in **e**.

The Anukr. in its metrical definition treats this all as one verse, and the same treatment is implied by the summation at the end of the *anuvāka* (see p. 928); but the comm. and one of our mss. make what follows the second *avasāna* into a separate or third verse; ⌊a like contradiction obtains as between the Anukr. and the comm. in the repeated passage, below, 27. 14, 15 (see the note); here, moreover, as noted above, the mss. of the Anukr. are at variance as to whether the hymn is to be reckoned as of 2 vss. or of 3⌋. The addition of *bṛhatīgarbhā* to the metrical definition is quite uncalled-for; ⌊doubtless because pāda **b** scans better as 8 syllables than as 9: no less uncalled-for is the addition of *saptapadā*, unless, dividing what follows the second *avasāna* into 3 pādas, we begin the seventh with an enclitic⌋.

⌊I suspect that our text consists of 6 pādas (8 + 8 : 11 + 11 : 11 + 11 = 60, "*atiçakvarī*"), call them 1 vs. or 2, as you will. Pādas **c** and **e** and **f** have good *triṣṭubh* cadences: **c** is good *triṣṭubh* if we resolve *indraagnī;* so is **e**, with W's *tiryák cā 'gnī́ r-*; the presence of *me* in **f** is all that spoils **f**; and the absence of *me* after *yachatām* is all that spoils the cadence of **d**, if, substituting the grammatical equivalent, we pronounce *açvínā 'bhítaḥ* at the beginning.⌋

17. For protection: to various gods.

[*Atharvan.—daçakam. pratyṛcam mantroktadevatyam. jāgatam: 5, 7, 10. atijagatī; 6. bhurij; 9. 5-p. atiçakvarī.*]

⌊Prose.⌋ ⌊Not found in Pāipp.⌋ This hymn and the next are used, the comm. points out, in the same ceremony as 16, with other hymns, as detailed in Pariçiṣṭa 4. 4; both are also prescribed in Par. 19. 1 (see note to Kāuç. 140. 9), in a ceremony against danger from the various quarters. ⌊See introd. to next hymn.⌋ ⌊Note that the vss. of this hymn group themselves in 5 dyads (comm., *paryāya-dvayas*), one for each cardinal point and a fifth for the 'fixed and upward points'; and that those of h. 18 do likewise and are so grouped by the comm. also.⌋

Translated: Griffith, ii. 276.

1. Let Agni with the Vasus protect me on the east: in him I step, in him I take refuge (*çri*), to that stronghold I go forward; let him defend me, let him guard me; to him I commit myself: hail!

The comm. first understands and explains *krame* and *çraye* as nouns in the locative, qualified by *tasmin!* then he again makes them verbs, quoting from vs. 6 *tāsu krame tāsu çraye*, to support this understanding of them; no one less superficial and blundering could possibly suggest the former explanation, against the accent and the sense.

2. Let Vāyu with the atmosphere protect me from that quarter: in him I etc. etc.

3. Let Soma with the Rudras protect me from the southern quarter: in him I etc. etc.

4. Let Varuṇa with the Ādityas protect me from that quarter: in him I etc. etc.

The comm. quotes AÇS. ii. 11. 12 to show that elsewhere also Soma is associated with the Rudras and Varuṇa with the Ādityas.

5. Let the sun with heaven-and-earth protect me from the western quarter: in him I etc. etc.

6. Let the waters with (*-mant*) the herbs protect me from that quarter: in them I . . .; let them defend . . .; to them I etc. etc.

7. Let Viçvakarman with the seven seers protect me from the northern quarter: in him I etc. etc.

8. Let Indra with (*-vant*) the Maruts protect me from that quarter: in him I etc. etc.

The comm. quotes Bhagavad-Gītā x. 6 (rather futilely) to support the association of the seven seers with Viçvakarman as highest self (*paramātman*), and (most superfluously) RV. viii. 85 (96). 7 and AB. iii. 20. 1 (part) to show that Indra and the Maruts go together.

9. Let Prajāpati, possessing generative powers (*prajánanavant*), together with firm support (*pratiṣṭhā́*), protect me from the fixed quarter: in him I etc. etc.

Many of the mss. give various other accents to *prajánanavān;* all read *pratiṣṭhā́yā* (p. *°sthā́yāḥ*), which SPP. accordingly retains,* although it is a palpable corruption; the comm. makes no difficulty of it, viewing it simply as a case of the substitution of genitive for instrumental; he adds, however, another interpretation, supplying *prajananena* for *sahá* to govern, and making *pratiṣṭhā́yās* an adjective qualifying *diçás*. *⌊W's B. and all of SPP's authorities appear to accent *pratíṣṭhāyā*, p. *pratí°sthāyāḥ*, and this is in fact the accentuation and reading in SPP's text, although I do not see what is to be made of it.⌋

10. Let Bṛihaspati with all the gods protect me from the upward quarter: in him I etc. etc.

The comm. calls these prose "verses" and those of the next hymn *paryāyas;* and the metrical definitions of the Anukr. are of course worthless, although it is possible to read out something like the numbers of syllables required by that treatise.

18. For protection: to various gods.

[*Atharvan.—daçakam. pratyṛcam mantroktadevatyam. dvāipadam: 1, 8. sāmnī triṣṭubh; 2–6. ārcy anuṣṭubh (5. samrāj* ⌊intending *svarāj?*⌋); *7, 9, 10. prājāpatyā triṣṭubh.*]

⌊Prose.⌋ ⌊Not found in Pāipp.⌋ See note to the preceding hymn ⌊for ritual uses⌋. The gods etc. are throughout the same as in that hymn. ⌊The two hymns are closely accordant in general and special peculiarities of structure.⌋ ⌊A similar passage is found at MS. i. 5. 4, p. 71⁹⁻¹⁵, as W. notes in the Collation Book: he also says "cf. K. vii. 2." AV. v. 10 presents some analogies with our hymn, and iv. 40 still more.⌋

Translated: Griffith, ii. 277.

1. Let those malignants (*aghāyú*) who shall attack (*abhi-dās*) me from the eastern quarter come upon (*ṛch*) Agni with (*-vant*) the Vasus.

The comm. has the more regular *vasumantam.* All the mss., and the comm., have at the end of all the verses *'bhidā́sāt*, which SPP. accordingly retains; our edition makes the absolutely necessary emendation to *-sān.* ⌊Is *-dā́sāt* a faulty reminiscence of AV. v. 10?⌋ Most of the *saṁhitā*-mss. also accent *diçó 'bhi-*. Some of the mss. leave *té* unaccented. 'With' is represented throughout the hymn by *-vant* or *-mant*, not by the instrumental case. As usual, *ṛch* signifies a coming into hostile or detrimental contact or collision. ⌊W. interlines "run against" as alternative for "come upon."⌋

2. Let those malignants who shall attack me from that quarter come upon Vāyu with the atmosphere.

3. Let those malignants who shall attack me from the southern quarter come upon Soma with the Rudras.

4. Let those malignants who shall attack me from that quarter come upon Varuṇa with the Ādityas.

The Anukr. ought properly to call this verse *bhurij*.

5. Let those malignants who shall attack me from the western quarter come upon the sun with heaven-and-earth.

⌊The accent of *dyā́vā-* is noted by W., *Skt. Gram.* § 94 b.⌋

6. Let those malignants who shall attack me from that quarter come upon the waters with the herbs.

7. Let those malignants who shall attack me from the northern quarter come upon Viçvakarman with the seven seers.

In our text there has dropped out an accent-sign under *va* before *údīcyā*.

8. Let those malignants who shall attack me from that quarter come upon Indra with the Maruts.

9. Let those malignants who shall attack me from the fixed quarter come upon Prajāpati with generative qualities.

10. Let those malignants who shall attack me from the upward quarter come upon Bṛihaspati with all the gods.

Verse 8 is properly *bhurij* (23 syllables). Verses 9 and 10 are each properly of 27 syllables; but by restoring elided initial *a* here and there (with regard to which the Anukr. appears to acknowledge no rule) the meters as defined can be made out.

19. For protection by various gods.

[*Atharvan.* — *ekādaçakam. cāndramasam uta mantroktadevatyam. pāñktam: 1, 3, 9. bhurig bṛhatī; 10. svarāj; 2, 4–8, 11. anuṣṭubgarbhā.*]

⌊Prose.⌋ ⌊Not found in Pāipp.⌋ The comm. says that, besides the uses stated in connection with preceding hymns, the *purohita* is to accompany with this the entrance of the king in the night into his sleeping-house; and that it also appears in the ceremony of a king's entrance into his city.

Translated: Griffith, ii. 278.

1. Mitra ascended with the earth: to that stronghold I lead you forward; that enter ye into; that enter ye; let that yield (*yam*) you both refuge and defense.

The comm. declares that Mitra here means Agni.

2. Vāyu ascended with the atmosphere: to that stronghold etc. etc.

3. The sun ascended with the sky: to that stronghold etc. etc.

4. The moon ascended with the asterisms: to that stronghold etc. etc.

5. Soma ascended with the herbs: to that stronghold etc. etc.

6. The sacrifice ascended with the sacrificial gifts: to that stronghold etc. etc.

7. The ocean ascended with the streams: to that stronghold etc. etc.

8. The *bráhman* ascended with the Vedic students: to that stronghold etc. etc.

The comm. says that *bráhman* here means the Veda with the *an̄gas*.

9. Indra ascended with heroism: to that stronghold etc. etc.

10. The gods ascended with the immortal (*amṛ́ta*): to that stronghold etc. etc.

11. Prajāpati ascended with progeny: to that stronghold etc. etc.

The comm. explains *ud akrāmat* by *yām puraṁ rakṣitum utkrāntavān*, as antecedent of *tām puram* etc. The metrical definitions of the Anukr. are not worth comparing in detail.

20. For protection by various gods.

[*Atharvan.* — *bahudevatyam. trāiṣṭubham: 2. jagatī; 3. purastādbṛhatī; 4. anuṣṭubh.*]

⌊Not found in Pāipp.⌋ The comm. says, purely on his own authority, that with this hymn the *purohita* arms with a breastplate a king going to battle. ⌊For the reference to vs. 4 in Kāuç. 25. 36 note, see above, introd. to viii. 5.⌋

Translated: Griffith, ii. 279. ⌊In Anukr. we miss *caturṛcam*.⌋

1. Have set down apart the human deadly weapon Indra-and-Agni, Dhātar, Savitar, Bṛihaspati, king Soma, Varuṇa, the Açvins, Yama; let Pūshan protect us round about from death.

It is quite as likely that 'Soma' etc. in the second half-verse should be viewed as coördinate with Pūshan. The translation omits *yám* in **a**; it seems probable that **a** is deeply corrupt. ⌊Caland, KZ. xxxiv. 456, citing Avestan usage, takes *pāúruṣeyaṁ vadháṁ yám* as accusative of the crystallized combination *pāúruṣeyo vadhó yáḥ* which we had at i. 30. 1: see note to xii. 2. 19. But W's suspicion is weighty.⌋ All the mss. accent *nyádhus* (the *pada*-mss. having, against all rule and practice, *nyádhuḥ*, instead of *ni॰ádhuḥ* or *ní: adhuḥ*), and SPP. follows them (in p. also); our *nyàdhus* is an emendation, apparently a necessary one — unless we can construe, with the comm., **b–d** as together constituting the apodosis: 'what means of death for men [our enemies] have fixed in secret — from [that] death let Indra-and-Agni etc. etc. protect us.' ⌊Griffith: 'May Soma etc. guard us from Mṛityu — death caused by men, which Indra etc. appointed.'⌋ The verse is far too irregular (11 + 12 : 12 + 9 = 44) to be called simply a *triṣṭubh*.

2. What [defenses] he who is lord of creation, Prajāpati, Mātariçvan, made for his creatures (*prajā́*), what ones the directions and the quarters put on (*vas*) — let those defenses (*várman*) be abundant (*bahulá*) for me.

The mss. accent *vasaté* ⌊except several that have *vasate*⌋; our emendation to *vasáte* is unquestionably called for, even though there are a few cases in RV. of such accent as *vasaté* ⌊*Gram.* § 613⌋. The comm. etymologizes *mātariçvan* as *antarikṣe çvasitī* '*ti*. ⌊The verse is properly 12 + 11 : 11 + 11 : for **d** has *triṣṭubh* cadence, and there are three possibilities of excising a syllable from its prior half.⌋

3. What [defense] those gods fastened on themselves, when fighting for overlordship, what defense Indra made for himself, let that protect us on all sides.

Pāda **b** is altogether corrupt; the translation implies the reading *ádhirājyāya yodhínaḥ*, which differs a little from the emendation in our text, but which the Pet. Lex. assumes under *ādhirājya*. The mss. give (*devā́*) '*dhirājayódhehinaḥ*, which the *pada*-text analyzes into (*deva* :) *ádhi°rāja* : *yáḥ* : *dhehi* : *naḥ* (SPP. reports his *pada*-mss. as giving at the beginning *devā*, apparently by an oversight, as *devā* is no form*). The comm. has (*devāḥ*) *dyurājayo* (implying p. *dyu°r-*) *dehinaḥ*, and this SPP. accepts, despite its unsatisfactory character; the comm. explains *dyurājayas* as *divi dyuloke rājamānās*, which is absurd, and adds that, since the wearing of armor implies a body (*deha*), the gods were embodied (*dehinas*), which is silly. The *pada*-mss. (and one of SPP's *saṁhitā*-mss.) strangely read *sarvátas* at the end instead of *viçvátas*; the comm. and both editions accept the latter; ⌊and since W. notes nothing to the contrary, his D. presumably has *viçvátaḥ*⌋. The text, with **b** as translated, and with *ca-kṛ-e* in **c** ⌊making 11 + 8 : 8 + 8⌋, answers excellently to the definition of the Anukr. *⌊W. means, I take it, no form which is usable in this connection.⌋

4. Defense for me may heaven-and-earth, defense may day, defense may the sun, defense for me may all the gods make; let not the affrontress (?*pratīcikā́*) reach me.

Some of the mss. leave *pratīcikā* accentless, and nearly all accent *krán*; both editions have *kran* and *-kā́*. The comm. seems to read *agnis* instead of *áhas* in **b**, and *mo* for *mā́* in **d**. The comm. paraphrases *pratīcikā* as *çatrusenā 'jñātapratikūlāñcanā* (*ka* being added to *pratīcī* "*ajñātārthe*"); the ⌊minor⌋ Pet. Lex. conjectures 'discomfort' (*Ungemach*); the translation above is of course only tentative. To be compared with the verse is viii. 5. 18 above; found also in AÇS. i. 2. 1, which has our **a**, **b** (but reading *agnis* with our comm.), and, for third pāda, *varma me santu tiraççikāḥ*; and in Āp. xiv. 26. 1, with *agnis* in **b**, and, for **c**, **d**, *varma me brahmaṇaspatir mā mā prāpad ato bhayam*.

⌊Here ends the second *anuvāka*, with 11 hymns and 72 verses. If we counted hymn 16 as of 3 verses, there would be 73. Some mss. sum up the verses as 72, and thus support the numeration of hymn 16 as given by both editions (see p. 923).⌋

21. The meters.

[*Brahman*. — *ekarcam*. *chāndasam*. *1-av*. *2-p*. *sāmnī bṛhatī*.]

⌊Prose.⌋ ⌊Not found in Pāipp.⌋ The comm. finds the verse quoted by the appellation *chandogaṇa* in Nakṣatra Kalpa 18. — ⌊The Anukr. says: *idam Brahmā chandonukrāntivijñānāyā 'paçyat*. — The meters are arranged, according to the number of their syllables, in an arithmetical progression ascending by a difference of 4. In VS. xxiii. 33, all these and *kakúbh* are mentioned.⌋

Translated: Griffith, ii. 279.

1. Gāyatrī, uṣṇih, anuṣṭubh, bṛhatī, pañkti, triṣṭubh-and-jagatī.

The mss. are at variance as to the use of any *kampa*-sign between the first two words. ⌊The metrical definition (18 syllables) calls for the resolution *gāyatrī uṣ-*.⌋

SPP's authorities appear all (except one *pada*-ms., *-tī*) to read at the end *jágatyāi;* ours vary between *-tī*, *-tye*, *-tyāi*, and *-tyāu*. The text of the comm. reads *pañkti* (instead of *-tis*), and, either with reason or on account of his usual disregard of accent, he takes the whole verse as a single compound word in the dative case, explaining it to mean *gāyatryāi svāhā*, *uṣṇihe svāhā*, etc., and declaring it thus to contain seven *mantras;* and SPP. thinks this to be "doubtless" the original character of the line; it would be safer to say "perhaps," or "possibly," since the separate accentuation, the nominative form *pañktís*, and the division by the Anukr. into two pādas (in the *pada*-mss., after *anuṣṭúp*) all speak against it. The mss. accent *triṣṭúb jágatyāi.*

22. Homage to parts of the Atharva-Veda.

[*Añgiras.—ekaviñçati. mantroktadevatyam. 1. sāmny uṣṇih; 3, 19. prājāpatyā gāyatrī; 4, 7, 11, 17. dāivī jagatī; 5, 12, 13. dāivī triṣṭubh; 2, 6, 14–16, 20. dāivī pañkti; 8–10. āsurī jagatī; 18. āsury anuṣṭubh (1–20. 1-av.); 21. 4-p. triṣṭubh.*]

⌊Verses 1–20, prose.⌋ ⌊Not found in Pāipp.⌋ The comm. quotes from Nakṣatra Kalpa, 17, 18, to the effect that this hymn and the following (together called *samāsa*) are to be used in the great appeasement-ceremony called *āñgirasī*, by one who seeks success as practising or suffering witchcraft. ⌊Cf. introd. to next hymn.⌋

Translated: Griffith, ii. 279; vs. 21 also by Ludwig, p. 219.

1. With the first five *anuvākás* of the Āñgirasas, hail!

It is very strange that the instrumental case is used here, instead of the dative, which is used everywhere else through this hymn and the next. ⌊Conversely, note the use of the abl.-dat. form *mādbhyás*, below, 27. 2 **c**, where we expect the instrumental, as in the other pādas.⌋

2. To the sixth, hail!
3. To the seventh-and-eighth, hail!
4. To the black claws, hail!
5. To the green ones, hail!

Two of our mss. (O.D.) accent with our text *háritebhyas;* SPP. reads *haritébhyas*, with (apparently) all his authorities and nearly all of ours.

6. To the petty ones, hail!
7. To them of the *paryāyas*, hail!
8. To the first conchs, hail!
9. To the second conchs, hail!
10. To the third conchs, hail!

In 9 and 10, SPP. accents, with all the mss., *dvitīyébhyas* and *tṛtīyébhyas;* we have not hesitated to make the necessary emendations to *-tī́ye-*. ⌊The false accent is perhaps a blundering assimilation to that of *prathamébhyas:* cf. notes to vss. 13 and 14, and especially to xviii. 3. 47.—Two of W's later collated mss., D.L., have rightly *-tī́ye-*.⌋

11. To the next to the last ones, hail!
12. To the last ones, hail!
13. To the further ones, hail!

SPP. again follows the mss. in accenting *uttarébhyas;* ⌊again a blundering assimilation to the accent of *uttamébhyas*, vs. 12⌋.

14. To the seers, hail!

Here also we emended the accent ⌊to *ṛ́ṣibhyas*, which W's D.L. indeed give⌋; but SPP. has, with the mss., *ṛṣíbhyas*. ⌊For the rationale of the blunder (due to *çiṣíbhyas*, vs. 15), cf. notes to vss. 10 and 13 and note to xviii. 3. 47.⌋

15. To the peaked ones (?*çikhín*), hail!

Here the mss. vary between *çikhíbhyas* and *çiṣíbhyas*.

16. To the *gaṇás*, hail!

17. To the great *gaṇás*, hail!

18. To all the *gaṇá*-knowing (??) Añgirases, hail!

It is altogether likely that *vidagaṇá* either never meant anything or is a corrupt reading; the translation is given merely in order not to leave the word untranslated.

19. To the two thousands severally, hail!

20. To the *bráhman* (?), hail!

SPP. reads *brahmáṇe*, and mentions no disagreement among his authorities; all but one or two of ours have the same, and our text might probably have been better left to read so; but the accentuation of the mss. is wholly unauthoritative, and the distinction here also of no manner of importance. The comm. understands *brahmáṇe*. ⌊I think *bráhmaṇe* is to be preferred for the reason given at p. 932, line 7.⌋ The numbers of syllables in the verses agree throughout with those demanded by the definitions of the Anukr.

It is a great disappointment to find that the designations given in this hymn to the various parts or elements of the Atharvan text are just as much a puzzle to the commentator as they are to us, so that he does not even venture to conjecture a meaning for them. He understands the authors rather than the *mantras* to be meant as the recipients of the homage. His whole comment follows: *atra viṅçatikāṇḍātmikāyām asyāṁ çākhāyāṁ vidyamānānuvākasūktagaṇaviçeṣādisaṁjñārūpāiḥ çabdāir anuvākādidraṣṭāra etannāmāna ṛṣayaḥ pratipādyante: nīlanakhādisūktaviçeṣāṇām prasiddhatvāt tāni viçeṣato na pradarçitāni:* **brahmane svāhe** *'ti brahmaçabdena viṅçatikāṇḍātmakavedavācakena tasya draṣṭā brahmākhya ṛṣiḥ pratipādyate: anyat sarvaṁ nigadavyākhyātam.* It sounds like a bad joke that he calls *nīlanakha* etc. 'familiarly known.' That *anuvāka* is used in vs. 1 in the same sense as in the present division of the text seems very unlikely.

21. Heroisms [were] gathered with the *bráhman* as chief; the *bráhman* as chief in the beginning stretched the sky; the Brahmán was born as first of creatures; therefore (*téna*) who is fit to contend with the Brahmán?

Or (in **d**) 'with that (*téna*) Brahmán.' SPP's text of the verse agrees with ours save that he accents in **d** *bráhmaṇā* with the mss., and has in **c** *prathamó 'tá* (p. *-máḥ: utá*, though the *pada*-mss. read *-mā́ : utá*); the text of the comm. has *-mo 'ta* here, but *-mo 'tha* in the verse repeated as 23. 30; the emendation in our text to *-mó ha* is plainly the easiest way out of the difficulty. The *pada*-mss. divide at the beginning, with remarkable absence of intelligence, *bráhma : jyeṣṭhā*, or *jyeṣṭhā́*; half the *saṁhitā*-mss. also accent *jyeṣṭhā́*; finally, the *pada*-mss., with incredible folly, divide at the end *spárddhi : tuṁkáḥ!* SPP. holds that the verse must have originally had *brahmán* throughout (four times), and gives in his note a text of it in that form (but with *prathamó 'tha* in **c**); but it is far from improbable that *bráhman* was used in the first half-verse and *brahmáṅ* in the second, as in our text. Indeed, in a corresponding verse in TB. (ii. 4. 7[10]), *bráhman* ⌊more appropriately, it would seem, if I am right in supposing that vss. 29 and 30 of hymn 23 refer to the Brahmaveda: cf. p. 932, l. 3⌋ is used every time: *bráhmajyeṣṭhā* (its commentary takes this as vocative) *vīryā̀ sámbhṛtāni bráhmā́ 'gre jyéṣṭham dívam ā́ tatāna: ṛtásya bráhma prathamó 'tá* (! its comment paraphrases by simply *prathamám*) *jajñe ténā 'rhati bráhmaṇā spárdhituṁ káḥ.* Our comm. gives a second explanation of *brahmajyeṣṭhā* as = *brahmaṇā jyeṣṭhena*, the case-ending of the former word being omitted, as well as the *in* part of that of the second!

23. Homage to parts of the Atharva-Veda.

[*Atharvan.—triṅçat. mantroktadevatyam uta cāndramasam. 1. āsurī bṛhatī; 2–7, 20, 23, 27. dāivī triṣṭubh; 8, 10–12, 14–16. prājāpatyā gāyatrī; 17, 19, 21, 24, 25, 29. dāivī pañkti; 9, 13, 18, 22, 26, 28. dāivī jagatī; (1–29. 1-av.).*]

⌊Verses 1–29, prose.⌋ ⌊Not found in Pāipp.⌋ The application of the hymn, as defined by the comm., was given with the one preceding.

As in the case of the preceding hymn, the comm. to all the verses is given together at the end. Its main parts are given below under the separate verses. It further declares that by the words *ekarca* to *daçarca* are designated the *ṛṣis* named Atharvan, and by those from *ekādaçarca* to *viṅçati* are designated the *ārṣeyas* named Ātharvaṇa; and it quotes as authority the beginning of i. 1. 5 of the Gopatha Brāhmaṇa.

⌊With regard to this hymn in general, and leaving books xix. and xx. out of account in the statements that follow: in the **first** place it is clear that the books of the **third grand division** of the AV., books xiii.–xviii. (see p. 708), are intended by verses 23–28 respectively (see under the verses below and see the introductions to the several books).⌋

⌊In the **second** place it is clear that the hymns of the books (but not the books themselves severally) of the **first grand division** of the AV., books i.–vii. (see p. 388), are intended to be covered by verses 1–15 and 19 and 20 (between 19 and 20 we miss the *dvyṛcebhyaḥ* which the commentator's text has). In this connection it is significant that vs. 1 begins with homage "to them of four verses," which is the norm of our first book, and not with homage "to them of one verse"—see the first table on p. 388. Moreover, as appears from the table on p. cxliv, the first grand division contains a hymn or hymns of every number of verses from 4 verses to 18 verses (mostly in books i.–v.) and from 1 verse to 3 verses (exclusively in books vi. and vii.). Again, while there is in the first grand division (and only there) one hymn or more of every number of verses from 1 verse to 18 verses, it is interesting to note that there is, in the whole AV. (books i.–xviii. or even i.–xix.), not one hymn of 19 verses, nor yet one of 20 verses (cf. p. 471 top): and of this fact account seems to be taken in so far as the form of our verses 16 and 17 differs from that of the 15 preceding.⌋

⌊**Thirdly**, the books of the **second grand division** of the AV. (books viii.–xii.) consist of hymns of over 20 verses (p. 471, top). There is, therefore, in all our present hymn, no special reference to this division, unless it be in verse 18, which may accordingly mean 'To the division (*kāṇḍa*) of great (*mahant*) [hymns], hail,' and refer to books viii.–xii. It is not impossible that a Hindu might use *kāṇḍa* to signify a 'division' comprising several books and tantamount to one of our so-called "grand divisions" (see my note to vs. 18). Against my view, I might well object that *dīrgha* would be a more appropriate adjective than *mahant* for the 'long' individual hymns of which the division consists; but, per contra, if the difference between *mahadguṇa* and *mahāguṇa* be a valid parallel, the text ought, if it means 'great book,' to read *mahākāṇḍāya*. A graver objection to my view, perhaps, is the position of vs. 18, which, if I were or am right, ought to come between verse 20 and verse 23.⌋

⌊**Fourthly,** verses 29 and 30 doubtless refer to this **Veda as a whole,** to the Brahmaveda, or to the incantations (*bráhman*) which form its subject-matter. After writing this, I note that Bloomfield in the *Grundriss*, p. 40, note 7, expresses an opinion similar, but much less specific. If I am right, *bráhman* is to be preferred to *brahmán* in these two verses, as also in vss. 20–21 of the preceding hymn: cf. the TB. vs. cited under 21. 21. On the other hand, I ought not to pass in silence the fact that the Anukr., at the beginning of its treatment of book xix., seems to call book xix. the *brahmakāṇḍa*.⌋

⌊**Finally,** therefore, aside from verse 18, just discussed, and assuming that verses 16 and 17 were added (in genuine Hindu fashion) merely for schematic completeness, we have only to note that all the verses of the hymn are reasonably accounted for, save only verses 21 and 22.⌋ ⌊☞See pages cl, clvii, clix.⌋

Translated: Griffith, ii. 280.

1. To them of four verses of the Ātharvaṇas, hail!
2. To them of five verses, hail!
3. To them of six verses, hail!

All the *saṁhitā*-mss. read *ṣaḍarc-*, and two of SPP's *pada*-mss. *ṣaḍá°ṛc-*; both editions *ṣaḍṛc-*, with the comm. and three *pada*-mss. The Gop.Br. has *ṣaḍarc-* in i. 1. 5.

4. To them of seven verses, hail!
5. To them of eight verses, hail!
6. To them of nine verses, hail!
7. To them of ten verses, hail!
8. To them of eleven verses, hail!
9. To them of twelve verses, hail!
10. To them of thirteen verses, hail!
11. To them of fourteen verses, hail!
12. To them of fifteen verses, hail!
13. To them of sixteen verses, hail!
14. To them of seventeen verses, hail!
15. To them of eighteen verses, hail!
16. Nineteen: hail!
17. Twenty: hail!

In these two verses, some of the mss. read *-çatí sv-*; the text of the comm. has *-çatyāí*, which would be an improvement; and two of SPP's reciters give the same. ⌊But cf. p. 931, ¶ 6, end.⌋

18. To the great book (*mahat-kāṇḍá*), hail!

⌊All of W's and of SPP's mss., and the reciters as well, give *mahat-*, not *mahā-*; but the comm. appears to read *mahā-*, and to say that it means the 'entire Veda of twenty books': *mahākāṇḍāye 'ti çabdena viṅçatikāṇḍātmakakṛtsnavedavācinā;* and this seems to support my suggestion that a Hindu might use *kāṇḍa* of a group of *kāṇḍas:* cf. ¶ 5 of introduction, above. Weber suggested at *Ind. Stud.* iv. 433 that *mahatkāṇḍa* might mean book xx.; but in a later volume (xviii. 154), that book v. might be intended.⌋

⌊See pages clvii–viii.⌋

19. To them of three verses, hail!

Between this verse and the next, the commentator's text inserts *dvyṛcebhyaḥ svāhā.*

20. To them of one verse, hail!

21. To the petty ones, hail! ⌊See page clviii top.⌋

This is a repetition of 22.6 above, and after it the commentator's text adds 22. 7.

22. To them of a half-verse, hail!

All the mss., and the comm., have here *ekānṛcébhyas* (p. *eka○anṛc-*), and SPP. follows them. Our *ekadvyṛcébhyas* (misprinted *ekadvṛc-*) was meant as an emendation, but is hardly successful. What *ekānṛc-* should mean does not appear; the translation simply follows the comm., for lack of anything better.

23. To the ruddy ones (*rohita*), hail!

The mss. ⌊except W's O.D., which have *róh-*⌋, and hence also SPP., accent here *rohitébhyas.* The comm. remarks that in this and the following verses the books intended are clear. This, of course, means book xiii. ⌊which is designated by *rohitāis* at Kāuç. 99. 4⌋.

24. To the two Sūryās, hail!

That is, to the two parts (*anuvākas*) of the book beginning with the Sūryā-hymn (xiv.).

25. To the two Vrātyas, hail!

Again the two *anuvākas* of the Vrātya-book (xv.). ⌊Both ed's read *vrātyā́bhyām*, with all the authorities, save W's D.L., which have *vrā́tyā-*. The minor Pet. Lex., vi. 189, notes *vrātyá* as an adj. to *vrā́tya:* hence, rather, 'To the two [*anuvākas*] about the *vrā́tya*, hail!' See my note, p. 770, ¶ 3.⌋

26. To the two of Prajāpati, hail!

The two *anuvākas* of book xvi. are evidently intended, though why they are called *prājāpatya* is difficult to say. ⌊The Major Anukr. calls the whole book *prājāpatya*, as noted p. 792, ¶ 4.⌋ The Old Anukr. quoted in the endings says at the end of xvi. 4 *prājāpatyo ha catuṣkaḥ*, ⌊· · · ·⌋ *saptakaḥ paraḥ:* i.e. 'the [first] Prajāpati-*anuvāka* has four hymns ⌊or *paryāyas*⌋; the [*paryāya*] next after [2 and 3: i.e. *paryāya* 4] is one of seven verses.' ⌊For the probable relative position and the significance of these extracts, see p. 792 (¶ 5) –793.⌋

27. To the *viṣāsahí*, hail!

The seventeenth book begins with the word *viṣāsahím;* and this time the comm. takes the trouble to specify that "the seventeenth *kāṇḍa*" is intended. ⌊Cf. p. 805, ¶ 1.⌋

28. To them of good omen (*mañgaliká*), hail!

This, from its position, ought to signify book xviii.; the comm. says nothing about it; his text reads *māñg-*. ⌊That the funeral book is held to be most inauspicious appears from SPP's preface to his ed., vol. i., p. 4, p. 5, and especially p. 2. To call the book auspicious is a euphemism such as is familiar in the case of the dreadful god Çiva.⌋

One of our mss. (I.) inserts after this verse five others which do not appear to occur elsewhere, as SPP. does not mention them: *nákṣatrakalpāya svā́hā.* 29. *vāitānakalpāya svā́hā.* 30. *çāntikalpāya svā́hā.* 31. *añgirasakalpāya svā́hā.* 32. *sā́ṁhitāvidhaye svā̂hāṁ*. 33. Our 29 then follows, in the form *tulibrahmáṇe svā̂hā*, and our 30 as given in all the mss.: *bráhmajyeṣṭhé 'ty ékā*. ⌊The foregoing are the readings of the Collation Book: apart from the accents, they require correction, I suppose, to *ā̃ñgirasa-* and *saṁhitā-*.⌋

29. To the *bráhman*, hail!

See above, 22. 20, with which this is identical. This time, two of our mss. ⌊and three of SPP's⌋ have *bráhmaṇe;* the others, and SPP's text, read *brahmáṇe*. ⌊As to the meaning, see introduction, p. 932, ¶ 2.⌋

30. Heroisms were gathered with the *bráhman* as chief; the *bráhman* as chief in the beginning stretched the sky; the Brahmán was born as first of creatures; therefore who is fit to contend with the Brahmán?

This is a repetition of 22. 21 above; the commentator's text apparently gives it in full, as SPP. notes that (doubtless only by an accident) it reads this time in **c** *prathamo 'tha*.

24. For prosperity: with a certain garment.

[*Atharvan.—aṣṭāu. mantroktabahudevatyam uta brāhmaṇaspatyam. ānuṣṭubham: 4–6, 8. triṣṭubh; 7. 3-p. ārṣī gāyatrī.*]

The hymn, except vs. 2, is found also in Pāipp. xv. The comm. points out that it is prescribed by Nakṣatra Kalpa 17–18 to be used in a *mahāçānti* ceremony called *tvāṣṭrī*, on occasion of the loss (*kṣaya*) of a garment.

Translated: Ludwig, p. 458; Griffith, ii. 281.

1. With what [garment] the gods caused to wrap god Savitar, with that, O Brahmaṇaspati, do ye wrap this man in order to royalty.

The translation implies emendation in **b** of *ádhārayan* to *ádhāpayan;* this, obviously suggested by the whole sense of the hymn (and proposed in the Pet. Lex.), is supported by the Ppp. text, which reads *devā 'diyāpayan*. The comm. reads *-dhār-*, but explains it as if it were *-dhāp-*: *paritaḥ sarvata ācchādayan*. Many of the mss. have *adhārayan*, unaccented. The comm. quotes TS. vi. 1. 14, to the effect that "this same garment belongs to all the gods," to explain why the verb in the second half-verse is plural.

2. Wrap ye this man [as] Indra in order to life-time, to great dominion, that [it] may conduct him unto old age; may he long watch over dominion.

All the mss., both here and in the next verse, read at end of **c** *nayā̂m*, which SPP. therefore accepts, although both form and accent are indefensible; the comm. has both times *naya;* the translation implies our emendation to *náyāt*, the propriety of which can hardly be questioned, especially as it is supported by a corresponding verse three times repeated, with variations, in HGS. i. 4. 8: *parī 'mam indra brahmaṇe mahe çrotrāya* (or *rāṣṭrāya*, or *poṣāya*) *dadhmasi: athāi 'naṁ jarimā ṇayej jyok çrotre* (or *rāṣṭre*, or *poṣe*) *adhi jāgarat:* of these three forms, the first is intended for a Brahman, the second for a Kṣatriya, the third for a Vāiçya: compare our next verse. The comm., ⌊in 2 **a** and 3 **a**, appears to have had before him *indramāyuṣe* and *somamāyuṣe*, whatever his accentuation and *pada*-text may have been: this he understands as *indra mā* *"yuṣe* and *soma mā "yuṣe*, his vocative *indra*⌋ agreeing with HGS. and giving an easier and better text; ⌊his *mā* goes easily as an appositive with *imám*, but the following *enam* is quite out of joint with it⌋.

3. Wrap ye this man [as] Soma in order to life-time, to great instruction (*çrótra*), that [it] may conduct him unto old age; may he long watch over instruction.

It is perhaps only by an accident that vs. 2 is omitted in Ppp.; at any rate, this verse shows what would have been read for verse 2 by it: it has *somam*, not *soma*, in **a**;* and *naya*, with the comm., in **c**; further, in **a** it gives *pare 'maṁ*. *⌊Strictly speaking, it has *somamāyuṣe*, with a possibility for the same objectionable division as appears under vs. 2, which see.⌋

4. Wrap, set ye him for us with splendor; make him one to die of old age; [make] long life-time; Bṛihaspati furnished (*pra-yam*) this garment to king Soma for wrapping himself.

This is a repetition of ii. 13. 2, above. The comm. mentions that the verse has been already explained where it first occurred, but adds: "the sense, however, is compendiously this," and proceeds to give the same exposition over again, word for word (unless, indeed, the editor is responsible for the repetition). For the parallel passages etc., see the note to ii. 13. 2.

5. Go thou safely (*sú*) unto old age; wrap thyself in the garment; become thou protector of the people (?) against imprecation; and live thou a hundred numerous autumns; and wrap further about (*upa-sam-vyā*) thee abundance of wealth.

⌊The verse is found in PGS. (i. 4. 12), HGS. (i. 4. 2), and MP. (ii. 2. 7). In **a**, PGS. omits *sú*, while HGS.MP. have *jarā́ṁ gacchāsi;* in **b**, all three texts read *kṛṣṭīnā́m* and *abhiçastipā́vā;* all three end **c** with *suvarcās;* and PGS. has for **d** *rayiṁ ca putrān anu saṁvyayasva*, adding *āyuṣmatī 'dam paridhatsva vāsaḥ.*⌋ In **b**, the translation follows Ppp. ⌊and the three texts just cited⌋ in reading *kṛṣṭīnā́m* 'people' instead of the absurd *gṛṣṭīnā́m* 'heifers,' which is given by all the mss. and the comm., both here and in the nearly accordant verse ii. 13. 3: see note to ii. 13. 3 ⌊and cf. Roth, ZDMG. xlviii. 110⌋. The comm. is driven by the reading *gṛṣ-* into taking *abhiçasti-* from *ças* 'cut': *abhito viçasanaṁ hiṅsā*. ⌊Our *abhiçastipā́ u*, at the end of **b** in vss. 5 and 6, would seem, in view of the *-pā́vā* of the other texts, to be a faulty assimilation to the end of **d** in vs. 4, *páridhātavā́ u*, such as may be found elsewhere.⌋

6. Thou hast wrapped thyself in this garment in order to well-being; thou hast become protector of thine allies (?) against imprecation; and live thou a hundred numerous autumns; living, pleasant (*cā́ru*), thou shalt share out good things.

The translation implies in **b** *ábhūr āpīnā́m* ⌊see below⌋, or else an analysis of the ms. reading *vāpīnā́m* ⌊misprinted *vap-* in foot-note of Berlin ed.⌋ into *u* and *āpīnā́m* (the *pada*-mss. have *ábhūḥ : vāpīnā́m*). The *vaçā́nām* of our text* is a conjecture provoked by the *gṛṣṭīnā́m* of vs. 5; as that is got rid of, this naturally falls away also. The comm. has again *gṛṣṭīnām*, and this time interprets *abhiçasti-* as a fear on the part of the 'heifers' of losing their skins (*tvagādānabhīti* ⌊cf. note to ii. 13. 3⌋)! The Ppp.

text appears to give us no variants. The HGS. has a corresponding verse (in i. 4. 3), reading in **a**, **b** *adhi dhāḥ* ⌊one ms. correctly '*dhithāḥ*⌋ *svastaye* '*bhūr āpīṇām*† *abhiçasti-pāvā:* and, for **d**, *vasūni cāyyo vi bhajā sa jīvan;* the variant to *cārus*, taken in connection with the small appropriateness of *cārus*, makes its genuineness suspicious. ⌊MP., at ii. 2. 8, also has *āpīnā́m*: and it agrees otherwise with HGS., save that it has *dhā* for *dhāḥ*, *cāryó* for *cāyyo*, and *ví bhajāsi* (agreeing with AV.). Kirste, in his note to HGS., p. 8, mentions as further variants *cāyo* and *cārye*. MB., at i. 1. 6, has **c**, ending with *suvarcās*, and **d**, reading *cārye*.⌋ *⌊Misprinted *vaçānā́m*.⌋ †⌊One ms. correctly *āpīnām*.⌋ ⌊See page xxxvi, note.⌋

7. We, companions, call to aid Indra the very mighty at every conjuncture, in every contest (? *vā́ja*).

This verse is, without variant, RV. i. 30. 7; also found in SV. (i. 163; ii. 93), VS. (xi. 14), TS. (in iv. 1. 2[1]), MS. (in ii. 7. 2), ⌊MP. i. 6. 3⌋. *Sákhāyas*, in **c**, which might be either nominative or vocative, the comm. prefers to take as nominative.

8. Of golden color, unaging, of excellent heroes, having old age as death, do thou enter into union (*sam-viç*) with progeny: this Agni says, and this Soma says, this Bṛihaspati, Savitar, Indra.

The second half-verse we had above as viii. 5. 5 **a**, **b** ⌊which see; and pāda **c** occurred at xvi. 9. 2⌋; the comm. does not notice the repetition. He explains *saṁ viça* as used in the sense of *nirviça* 'enjoy'; or else, he says, of *praviça* = *svagṛham adhitiṣṭha*. Ppp. reads in **a** *ajayas suv-*.

25. To a horse.

[*Gopatha.—ekarcam. vājidevatyam. ānuṣṭubham.*]

The verse is not found in Pāipp. The comm. finds it quoted in Nakṣ. K. 17–18, in a *mahāçānti* ceremony called *gāndharvī*, on occasion of the loss (*kṣaya*) of a horse.
Translated: Griffith, ii. 282.

1. I harness (*yuj*) thee with the mind of one that is unwearied and that is first; be thou an up-carrier uphill; having carried up, then run thou back.

The real sense of the hymn is very obscure; neither the *viniyoga* nor the comm. casts any light upon it. ⌊SPP. regards the comm. as taking *utkūlamudvaho* as one word;⌋ the comm. reads *bhavas* for *bhava:* and he explains the phrase simply by *atidṛpto bhava*. Instead of *uduhya*, the comm. has *duhīya* (= *çatrujayalakṣaṇāni phalāni labheya*). SPP. accents *útkūlam*, with all the mss.; our alteration to *utkū́lam* is not sufficiently motived; the minor Pet. Lex. has *utkūlám*, which is more in accordance with general analogies. Fully half the mss. accent *úduhya*. In our text, *bháva* (in **c**) is a misprint for *bhava* (an accent-mark fallen out).

26. For long life etc.: with something golden.

[*Atharvan.—caturṛcam. āgneyam; hāiraṇyam. trāiṣṭubham: 3. anuṣṭubh; 4. pathyāpañkti.*]

Of this hymn only vs. 4 is found in Pāipp. (in xx.). The comm. finds it used in Nakṣ. K. 17, 19, in a *mahāçānti* ceremony called *āgneyī*, on occasion of danger from fire, with the insertion of a golden earring; further, in Pariç. 11. 1, in a *tulāpuruṣa* ceremony.
Translated: Grill, 49, 192; Griffith, ii. 283; Bloomfield, 63, 668.

1. The gold that, born out of the fire, immortal, maintains itself over mortals — whoso knows it, he verily merits (*arh*) it; one that dies of old age becomes he who wears (*bhṛ*) it.

SPP. accents at the end *bibhárti*, with the great majority of the mss. (the same also in 2 **d**); our preference for *bíbharti* was because only this accent is found elsewhere in AV. Most of the mss. accent *énad* in **c**. The masculine *enam* in **c** is surprising, as no hint of anything masculine is met with elsewhere in the hymn; the comm. explains it as *anvādiṣṭaṁ hiraṇyarūpam padārtham*. In a corresponding verse (6) found in a *khila* of the RV. (to x. 128) is read instead *enad* (one ms. *vedam*), which is more likely to be the true text. The same has in **b** *jajñe* for *dadhre*. The Anukr. takes no notice of the redundant syllable in **c**.

2. The gold, of beauteous color by the sun, that men (*mánu*) of old with their progeny sought — that, shining (*candrá*), shall unite thee with splendor; of long life becomes he who wears it.

Very nearly all the mss. read *iṣiré* at end of **b**; but both editions, and the comm., give *īṣiré*. The majority of mss. also accent *pūrvé*. SPP. reads at end of **c** *sṛjati*, with all the authorities (save his P., which has *sṛjāti*) *; both sense and meter so plainly call for *sṛjāti* that we adopted it as an emendation in our text; the comm. reads *sṛjatu*. As to *bibharti* at the end, see note to vs. 1. *⌊W's P.M. have *sṛjasvā "yu-*.⌋

3. For life-time thee, for splendor thee, and for force and for strength — that with brilliancy of gold thou mayest shine out among the people.

The comm. reads in **c** *hiraṇyaṁ tej-*. The comm. supplies in **a**, **b** *saṁ sṛjatu* to each noun, as if they were in the instrumental case, which is plainly wrong. Probably the 'thee' of the first line is different from the 'thou' of the second, being addressed to the article of gold itself.

⌊The comm. (as noted) and the text of the comm. have *hiraṇyaṁ tejasā;* but all the other authorities are agreed as to the accentuation *hiraṇyatéjasā;* which, however, is inherently improbable (*Gram.* § 1267 b), if, with the *pada*-text, we take the combination as one compound word. Both mss. and comm. and accent all point the other way, and we have doubtless to assume as *pada*-reading *hiraṇya : téjasā*, as two words, of which the first is vocative; and, but for our blundering *pada-kāra*, this is just what our *saṁhitā*-reading would naturally be taken to mean. The comm. understands 'thee' as referring to the man who wears the gold amulet; but the whole verse gains in concinnity, if we refer 'thee' (with W.) to the amulet itself, and supply with the first half the verb *badhnāmi* (as at i. 35. 1 **c**; iv. 10. 7 **c**; xix. 46. 1 **c**, **d**), and take the second half also as addressed to the amulet.⌋

4. What king Varuṇa knows, [what] divine Bṛihaspati knows, what Indra the Vṛitra-slayer knows, — may that be for thee life-giving, may that be for thee splendor-giving.

Next after the verse already quoted (under vs. 1) from the RV. *khila*, occurs another corresponding to this, but having for **b** *yad u devī sarasvatī*, and for **d** *tan me varcasa āyuṣe*, and lacking a fifth pāda. Ppp. has in **b** *yad u divo bṛh-*, puts *yad* before *indras* in **c**, and has for **d**, and for end of the verse, *tac cittaṁ cittam arhaṇam*.

⌊Here ends the third *anuvāka*, with 6 hymns and 65 verses.⌋

27. For protection etc.: with a triple amulet.

[*Bhṛgvañgiras.* —*pañcadaçakam. trivṛddevatyam uta cāndramasam. ānuṣṭubham: 3, 9. triṣṭubh; 10. jagatī* ⌊? see under the verse⌋; *11. ārcy uṣṇih; 12. ārcy anuṣṭubh; 13. sāmnī triṣṭubh* (*11–13. 1-av.*).]

Found (except verses 12 and 13) also in Pāipp. x. The comm. quotes from the Nakṣ. K. (17, 19) its use, in a *mahāçānti* called *prājāpatyā*, by one desiring progeny and cattle, and in case of the loss of progeny, with the binding on of an amulet made of three metals, gold and silver and copper.

Translated: Griffith, ii. 283.

1. Let the bull (*ṛṣabhá*) protect thee with the kine; let the virile one (*vṛ́ṣan*) protect thee with the vigorous ones (*vājín*); let Vāyu protect thee with *bráhman*; let Indra protect thee with Indra's powers (? *indriyá*).

The comm. reads in **a** *vṛṣabhas.** In **b**, he naturally understands horses as intended, and connects *vājin* with the root *vij* (*vājibhir vejanavadbhiḥ çīghragatibhir açvāiḥ*). Of *bráhman* he gives three different and equally worthless explanations. To *indriya* he says *indriyāṇy atre 'ndrasṛṣṭānī 'ndrajuṣṭāni vā*, which gives us no help. *⌊But the text of the comm. has *pātv ṛṣabhas.*⌋

2. Let Soma protect thee with the herbs; let the sun protect with the asterisms; [let] the moon, Vṛitra-slayer, [protect] ⌊thee⌋ from the months; let the wind defend with breath.

All the mss. without exception read in **c** *mādbhyás*, instead of the *mādbhís* which we should have expected, and which the comm. has. It seems like a blundering confusion of the two cases (the reverse of that in 22. 1, above). The comm. makes *nakṣatra* here refer to the planets, most unnecessarily; he reads in **d** *rakṣati*, but glosses it with *rakṣatu*.

3. They call the heavens (*dív*) three, the earths three, the atmospheres three, the oceans four, the song of praise (*stóma*) triple, the waters triple: let these triple ones defend thee with the triple ones.

In Ppp., **b** and **c** have apparently dropped out, and **d** is made to end with *trivṛtās trivṛttibhiḥ*. The mss. vary between *trivṛ́tā* (which both editions read), *trivṛ́tās*, and *trivṛ́tāt;* the translation implies *trivṛ́tas*, which the comm. has, and which is pretty evidently the intent of the verse; ⌊cf. vs. 9 **d**, below⌋. The mss. to a great extent read *trv-* instead of *triv-*, as in other like cases. In **a** in our text, emend to *tisráḥ*. We need to combine *trivṛtā "pa ā-* in **c** to make a good *triṣṭubh*. ⌊I doubt if it is a *triṣṭubh*. To reckon *trī́ṇi* to pāda **a** is very harsh. I suspect we have to pronounce *pṛthvī́s* in **a**, and to read and pronounce *trī́ṇy antárikṣā* in **b**. Thus the verse scans as 8 + 11 : 11 + 11.⌋

4. The three firmaments (*nā́ka*), the three oceans, the three bright ones (*bradhná*), the three at the summit (? *vāiṣṭapá*), the three Mātariçvans, the three suns, do I arrange (*kḷp*) as thy guardians.

Nearly all the mss. read in **a** *nā́kāṅs*, and a part also *bradhnā́ṅs.** The comm. has *badhnān*, and ⌊some of⌋ our mss. also *badh-*, although SPP. strangely appears to find no *badh-* among his authorities. The *pada*-mss. give *nā́kam* and ⌊some of them⌋ *bradhnán*.

Some mss. accent *mātáriç-* in **c**, and read *goptrī́n* in **d**. All these are of the superficial variety of discordant readings which swarm in this book, and have no real importance. The comm. explains his *badhnān* thus: *trīn badhnān badhnaḥ sarvasya bandha ādhāra-bhūta ādityaḥ*, in which he shows himself equal to the occasion after precisely his own fashion. The Anukr. takes no notice of the metrical irregularity (7 + 7 : 9 + 7 = 30). ⌊Roth notes expressly that Ppp. reads *vāiṣṭapān.*⌋ *⌊Cf. note to 13. 8 above, and to 28. 2; also Müller's 1st quarto ed. of RV., vol. i., preface, p. xii; and Pischel, *Gram. der Prakrit-sprachen*, § 83.⌋

5. With ghee do I sprinkle thee all over, O Agni, increasing thee with sacrificial butter; of fire, of moon, of sun, let not the wily ones damage the breath.

The comm. takes the liberty of filling out **c**, **d** so as to mean "by the favor of the fire etc. . . . thy breath, O man that wearest the threefold amulet." Some of SPP's mss. read in **a** *ukhyāmi* and *ukṣyāmi.*

6. Let not the wily ones damage your breath, nor your expiration nor flame (? *háras*); shining, all-possessing, run ye, O gods, with what is of the gods.

The translation implies emendation of *devā́s* in **d** to *dévās;* the comm. understands *dévās*, but doubtless only by his customary disregard of the accent. He understands *vas* in **a** ⌊alternatively⌋ as *plur. majest.* of the king on whom the amulet is bound, and *haras* in **b** as *çatrubalāpahārakaṁ tejas*. To *dāivyena* in **d** he supplies *rathādinā sādhanena vegena vā*. We are tempted to emend at the end to *dāívyenā́ 'dhāvata;* Ppp. reads *māvata* for *dhāvata*.

7. One unites Agni with breath; the wind is combined with breath; with breath the gods generated the sun that faces all ways. ⌊See p. xxxvi, n.⌋

All the mss. (save one of SPP's, which has *-jāti*) read *sṛjati* in **a**, and, as the meter favors it, it might better stand (our text emended to *-anti*). Ppp. gives for **a** *prāṇenā 'gniṁ saṁ dadhata*, and ⌊reads and⌋ combines at the end ⌊*sūryaṁ*⌋ *devā 'janayan*.

8. Live thou with the life-time of the life-time-makers; live as one long-lived; do not die; live with the breath of the soulful (*ātmanvánt*); do not come under the control of death.

Nearly all the mss. read in **a** *āyuḥkṛ́tām*, and SPP. follows them, although the comm. gives *-uṣk-*. In **c**, both the editions emend to *ātmanvátām*, all the mss. having *ātmat-vátām* (p. *ātma°tvátām!*); the comm. appears to imply *-nvatām* in his explanation, though (according to SPP.) his text also has *-tvatām*. Nearly all ⌊SPP's authorities⌋ accent after it *jīvá;* both editions read *jīva*, ⌊SPP.⌋ on very slender authority. Our *úpa gās* in **d** is an emendation, for the *úd agās* of the mss., SPP., and the comm.; the change was demanded by the requirements both of grammar and of the sense; and Ppp. supports it, reading *upa gā v-*.

9. The treasured (*ni-dhā*) treasure of the gods that Indra discovered by roads that the gods travel — the gold did the waters guard with triple ones; let those triple ones defend thee with the triple ones.

The last pāda is a repetition of 3 **d**, and has the same readings as there in mss.,* editions, and comm. Instead of *índro 'nv-* in **a**, **b** the mss. give *indrā 'nv-* (p. *indra : anu-*); but this time SPP. also, as well as we, emends to the former reading, which is that of the comm. ⌊*Nidhíṁ devā́nāṁ níhitaṁ yáṁ índraḥ* would be good rhythm.⌋ *⌊Or nearly so: but *trivṛ́tā* of 3 is here *tṛvátā*.⌋

10. Thirty-three deities and three heroisms guarded [it] within the waters, holding [it] dear; what gold there is upon this shining one (?*candrá*), therewith shall this man do heroisms.

All the mss. read in **b** *priyā́yamā́ṇā* (p. *priyā́ya : mā́ṇā !*); but here again SPP. has the courage to follow us in emending to *priyāyámāṇās* (p. *priya॰yámāṇāḥ*), since the comm. so understands it; it is only a question whether in *pada*-text *-māṇā* should not rather be read, as agreeing with the nearer of the two nouns; the comm. takes it as fem. (*priyam ivā "carantyaḥ*). The Anukr. is curiously confused here; after correctly defining the verse *devānāṁ nihitaṁ nidhim* as a *triṣṭubh*, it proceeds to define *āpo hiraṇyaṁ jugupuḥ* as a *jagatī*, and takes no note of *trayastriñçad devatāḥ* as a *pratīka*. Probably there is a *quid pro quo* here, by a slip of memory; but one does not see how this highly irregular* verse (13 + 11 : 10 + 11 = 45) should be called simply a *jagatī*. ⌊With **a**, cf. 37. 1 **c**, below.⌋ *⌊Possibly we have to substitute the older grammatical equivalent in **a**, *trī́ ca vīryā̀* (cf. 3 **b**); a *'sti* before *ádhi* would mend **c**.⌋

11. Ye, O gods, that are eleven in the sky, do ye, O gods, enjoy this oblation.

12. Ye, O gods, that are eleven in the atmosphere, do ye, O gods, enjoy this oblation.

13. Ye, O gods, that are eleven on the earth, do ye, O gods, enjoy this oblation.

With these three verses corresponds RV. i. 139. 11: *yé devāso divy ékādaça sthá pṛthivyā́m ádhy ékādaça sthá : apsukṣíto mahinā́ 'kādaça sthá té devāso yajñám imáṁ juṣadhvam;* VS. vii. 19 precisely agrees with this; MS. (in i. 3. 13) reads *devās* in **a**; TS. (in i. 4. 10) reads *devās* in both **a** and **d** ⌊and *apsuṣádo* in **c**⌋. The comm's text inserts in vs. 11 *divyās* after *devās*.

14. Freedom from rivals in front, behind us [is] fearlessness made; Savitar [protect] me on the south, the lord of Çachī me on the north.

15. From the sky let the Ādityas defend me, from the earth let the fires defend; let Indra-and-Agni defend me in front; let the Açvins yield refuge round about; crosswise let the inviolable [cow], let Jātavedas, defend [me]; let the being-makers be my defense on all sides.

These two verses are a repetition of 16. 1, 2 above, and in our mss., as usual, are read simply thus: *asapatnám purástād íti dvé*. The Anukr. does not repeat its definition of their meter; inasmuch as it reckons the hymn as of fifteen verses, it plainly takes the addition here as of two verses only; the comm., however, again counts three, making of ⌊our 15 **a**, **b**⌋ a separate verse*; ⌊cf. notes to 16. 2⌋. In general, the comm. does not comment for the second time a repeated passage; here, however, he gives a full explanation, as if it were the first appearance of the verses; and in 14 **b** (perhaps merely by an oversight?) he reads *me* instead of *nas*. *⌊The comm. in fact takes our vss. 11–13 as one vs., his 11; our 14 as his 12; our 15 **ab** as his 13; and our 15 **c–f** as his 14. Or, he says, we may take our 14 with 15 **ab** as one *mantra*. He reads *agnis* again in our **e** as in 16. 2 **e**.⌋

28. For various blessings: with an amulet of darbhá.

[*Brahman* (*sapatnakṣayakāmaḥ*). — *daçakam*. *mantroktadarbhamaṇidevatyam*. *ānuṣṭubham*.]

The hymn is found also in Pāipp. xiii., with very few variants. The comm. finds it ⌊or rather the whole triad of hymns, 28, 29, 30⌋ used by the Nakṣ. K. ⌊17, 19⌋ in a *mahāçānti* ceremony called *āindrī*, with binding on of a *darbha* amulet, by one desiring victory and the like.

Translated: Griffith, ii. 285.

1. I bind for thee this amulet, in order to long life, to brilliancy — the *darbhá*, damager of rivals, burner (*tápana*) of the heart of the hater.

Nearly all the mss. accent *dárbham*. Ppp. reads in **b** *varcase*, and in **c** *-jambhanā*.

2. Burner of the heart of the hater, causing to burn the mind of foes, do thou, O *darbhá*, burn together like heat (*gharmá*) against all the evil-hearted.

The mss., and hence SPP., read for **a** *dviṣatás tāpáyan hṛdáḥ*, as if *hṛdás* could be an accus. sing.; and the comm. has the same, and glosses *hṛdas* with *hṛdayam*. ⌊By some oversight, SPP. says on p. 384, note 3, that the text of the comm. reads *sarvaṅs tvaṁ;* and on p. 385, note 1, "Sāyaṇa's text too has *sarvaṁ*."⌋ The comm. explains as if the ⌊questionable⌋ word were simply *sarvam*, 'the evil-hearted one's everything.' In **d**, the mss. and SPP. read *ivā 'bhī́nt saṁtāpáyan* (one of ours *abhī́t*, another *abhāút:* mere accidental variations), the *pada*-text presenting *abhī́n : sam°*; the comm. has the same, and explains thus: *abhīn abhayān saṁtāpayan bhinddhi* ⌊*iti sambandhaḥ* : connecting the phrase with the *bhinddhi* of vss. 3, 4, 5⌋. Our *abhisáṁtāpaya* is heroic surgery, but very plausible; *abhī́'t s-* (i.e. *abhí : ít : s-*) would save a little more of the original, and *ít* is elsewhere added to reinforce *abhí:* cf. viii. 4. 21; xi. 1. 6; Ppp. has very nearly this reading, namely, *gharme 'vā 'bhī 't saṁtāpayaṁ*. The comm. glosses *gharmas* first with *ādityas*, then (on authority of TA. v. 1. 5) with *pravargyas*. The Anukr. takes no notice of the redundancies caused in 2 **d** and 3 **a** and **d** and 4 **c** if *iva* is not abbreviated to *'va;* in at least two of the cases, 2 **d** and 3 **d**, Ppp. combines to suit the meter, *gharme 'va*, *indrāi 'va*. ⌊The first pāda is wanting in Ppp.⌋

3. Burning against [them] like heat, O *darbhá*, burning down the haters, O amulet, split thou our rivals to the heart, like Indra breaking apart Vala.

The translation implies emendation in **d** to *valám*, as made in our edition; SPP. follows the mss. and comm. in accepting *balám*, in spite of its false accent. Nearly all the mss. read *virujám* (p. *vi°rujám*), but the comm. *-jan*, which, of course, is alone admissible; SPP. very strangely compromises by reading *virujáṁ* in *saṁhitā*, but *vi°ruján* in *pada!* In **c**, SPP. gives, with ⌊five of his authorities⌋, *-dáḥ sapátnānām bhinddhi;* even the *pada*-mss. vary between *sa°pátnān : ā́ : bh-* and *sa°pátnānām : bh-*; the comm. has *-nānām*, and so has Ppp.; the translation above implies *-nān ā́*,* in spite of the separation of *ā́* from *hṛdás*. ⌊Ppp. gives *indrāi 'va* in **d**, as noted under vs. 2.⌋

* ⌊This reading is given by eight of SPP's mss. and one of W's. In *sapátnānām* we may have a case of faulty assimilation from 4 **a**: SPP's Dc., which is usually carefully corrected, here carries the blunder half way prima manu, giving *sapátnānā́m* (accents! so perhaps also W's O.D.L.), and completes it secunda manu, giving *sapátnānām*.⌋

4. Split, O *darbhá*, the heart of our rivals, of our haters, O amulet; make their head fly apart, as the rising [sun] does the skin of the earth.

The comm. reads and explains *ni pātaya* in **d** (though the ms. gives *vi p-*). The obscure and perhaps corrupt third pāda is thus explained: *udyann ūrdhvaṁ gacchan bhujādipradeçam adhitiṣṭhan tvam bhūmyās tvacam [iva] tṛṇagulmāuṣadhyādy-adhiṣṭhānabhūtāṁ yathā takṣaṇena nipātayati gṛhādinirmāṇārthaṁ loke.*

5. Split, O *darbhá*, my rivals; split those that fight against me; split all my enemies (*durhā́rd*); split my haters, O amulet.

In the following fourteen verses, of this hymn and the one that follows it, only the verb in each pāda is changed. In **c**, Ppp. blunderingly reads *chindhi*, anticipating the next verse.

6. Sever, O *darbhá*, my rivals; sever those etc. etc.

7. Hew down (*vraçc*), O *darbhá*, my rivals; hew down those etc. etc.

8. Cut, O *darbhá*, my rivals; cut those etc. etc.

In verses 6, 8, 9, 10 of this hymn, also in 29. 2 below, a part of the mss. read *durhā́rdān* instead of *-das* in **c**; and SPP. strangely follows them in 28. 6, 8.

9. Carve (?), O *darbhá*, my rivals; carve those etc. etc.

The Pet. Lex. (under root *piṣ*) proposes to emend in this verse *piñçá* to *piṅṣá*. As, however, we have root *piṣ* below in 29. 6, there seems to be no sufficient reason for substituting it here. One of SPP's mss. reads here *pīṅṣá* p.m. ⌊*piñçá* s.m.⌋.

10. Pierce, O *darbhá*, my rivals; pierce those etc. etc.

The mss. vary here between *vídhya* and *vidhyá*. ⌊Ppp. reads *viddhi*.⌋

29. Continuation of the foregoing.

[*As 28. navakam.*]

This is a mere continuation of the preceding hymn, and it is hard to see why they are divided. They are found together in Pāipp. xiii. ⌊Ritual use under 28.⌋

Translated: Griffith, ii. 286.

1. Gore, O *darbhá*, my rivals; gore those that fight against me; gore all my enemies; gore my haters, O amulet.

Half the mss. accent in this verse *nikṣá*. The comm. follows the *dhātupāṭha* in interpreting it to mean *cumba* 'kiss'! ⌊He intends rather the root *cumb* 'harm,' *hiṅsāyām*, not *cumb*, *vaktrasaṁyoge*.⌋

2. Bore, O *darbhá*, my rivals; bore those etc. etc.

The comm. glosses the verb with *nāçaya*.

3. Obstruct, O *darbhá*, my rivals; obstruct those etc. etc.

The comm. glosses the verb (after the *dhātupāṭha*) with *āvṛṇu nirodhaṁ kuru.* The Pet. Lex. ⌊s.v. 3 *ru* 'zerschlagen'⌋ suggests reading instead *rudhi* "according to mss."; but *rudhi* is found in only one ms., in **a**, while the same ms. has *rundhi* in **b**, **c**, **d**; *rudhi* is accordingly only a careless misreading. Ppp. has *bhaṅkti.*

4. Kill, O *darbhá*, my rivals; kill those etc. etc.

5. Grind, O *darbhá*, my rivals; grind those etc. etc.

About half the mss. accent *manthá*. The comm. gives, as if from the *dhātupāṭha*, *mantha loḍane* (Westergaard and Böhtlingk *viloḍane*).

6. Crush (*piṣ*), O *darbhá*, my rivals; crush those etc. etc.

Ppp. reads *piṇḍi.*

7. Scorch (*uṣ*), O *darbhá*, my rivals; scorch those etc. etc.

The majority of mss. combine in **a–b** *me óṣa*, and SPP. follows them.

8. Burn, O *darbhá*, my rivals; burn those etc. etc.

The decided majority of mss. accent *dahá.*

9. Slay, O *darbhá*, my rivals; slay those etc. etc.

30. For protection etc.: with an amulet of darbhá.

[*As 28. pañcakam.*]

Found also in Pāipp. xiii., with the two preceding, and, according to the comm., associated with them in use.

Translated: Griffith, ii. 287. ⌊☞ See p. 1045.⌋

1. What thou hast that brings death in old age, O *darbhá*, that has hundred-fold defense, good defense, therewith having made this man defended (*varmín*), smite thou my rivals by thy heroisms.

The translation implies *jarā́mṛtyu çatávarma suvárma te*, which is the text of neither edition, nor of the mss., nor of the comm., but simply what makes best sense with least departure from the mss. The mss. all give *-tyuḥ çatáṁ vármasu* ⌊W's B. *varmasu*⌋ (p. *várma°su*) *várma te;* the comm. has *jarāmṛtyuçatam marmasu* (explaining *jarasām mṛtyūnāṁ ca çataṁ granthiṣu!*). The *te* in **b** had to be omitted in translating.

2. A hundred are thy defenses, O *darbhá*, a thousand thy heroisms; as such, all the gods have given thee to this man to wear, in order to [attain] old age.

Ppp. has at the end *dadus.* The comm. (with two of SPP's mss.) again reads in **a** *marmāṇi.* The decided majority of mss. have *tvám* at beginning of **c**; none of ours collated before publication had *tám*, which is doubtless the true text, and is read ⌊by W's O. and⌋ by SPP. and by the comm.

3. Thee they call the gods' defense, thee, O *darbhá*, Brahmaṇaspati; thee they call Indra's defense; thou defendest kingdoms.

The majority of mss. leave *devavarma* unaccented. We are tempted to emend to *-páteḥ* in **b**. Ppp. reads ⌊presumably in **c**⌋ *tvām indrād devavarmā "hus.*

4. A destroyer of our rivals, O *darbhá*, burner of the heart of our hater — an amulet, increaser of dominion, protector of thy body, I make for thee.

Emendation to *darbhám* in **a** would relieve the anacoluthon of the verse. The comm., to get rid of it, first explains *te* as = *tvā;* but then secondly connects the whole verse into one sentence leaving *darbha* out. ⌊I am not quite clear as to whether he means to leave it out. He says: *atha vā rakṣākāmaḥ puruṣaḥ sambodhyate: he rājan darbhamaṇiṁ sapatnakṣayaṇādisāmarthyopetaṁ te tubhyaṁ kṣatrasya vardhanaṁ tanūpānaṁ ca kṛṇomī 'ti sambandhanīyam.*⌋

5. What the ocean roared (*krand*) against, [and] Parjanya with the lightning, therefrom was born the golden drop (*bindú*), therefrom the *darbhá*.

Our edition emends in **a** to *samudré*, which is doubtless an improvement, but not necessary. ⌊The translation follows the mss., SPP., and comm., which have *samudró:* Ppp. *samudro 'bhya-*.⌋ The comm. derives the word (as many times elsewhere) from *sam-ud-dravanti*, and makes it an epithet of *parjanyas*, which he explains as meaning *meghas*. Most of the mss. accent *bíndus*. The comm. makes the second *tatas* refer to *bindu*, but gives no opinion as to the meaning of the latter. ⌊Ppp. reads *vindus* in **c**.⌋ ⌊Cf. Pischel, ZDMG. xxxvi. 135, who thinks the "drop" refers to pearl: cf. introduction to iv. 10.⌋

31. For various blessings: with an amulet of udumbára.

[*Savitṛ* (*puṣṭikāmaḥ*). — *caturdaça. mantroktāudumbaramaṇidevatyam. ānuṣṭubham: 5, 12. triṣṭubh; 6. virāṭ prastārapañkti; 11, 13. 5-p. çakvarī; 14. virāḍ āstārapañkti.*]

⌊Partly prose, vs. 12 (?).⌋ Found also in Pāipp. x. The comm. finds it used in Nakṣ. K. 17, 19, by one desiring wealth, or in the case of loss of wealth, in a *mahāçānti* ceremony called *kāuberī*, with binding on of an amulet of *udumbara*.

Translated: Griffith, ii. 287.

1. With an amulet of *udumbára*, for the pious one desiring prosperity: may Savitar make in my cow-stall fatness (*sphātí*) of all cattle.

The translation implies in **b** emendation to *vedháse*, which seems hardly avoidable. The comm. gives two explanations of *vedhasā: vidhātrā purā prayogaḥ kṛtaḥ;* and *puṣṭyādividhātrā kartrā maṇinā*. Nearly all the mss. accent *paçūnām* (one of ours has *-çūnā́m*), and SPP. passes the anomaly without remark.

2. Whatever householder's fire of ours may be overlord of cattle: let the virile (*vṛ́ṣan*) amulet of *udumbára* unite me with prosperity.

The connection of the parts of the verse is obscure. The comm. makes **b** apodosis to **a**, supplying *asti* in **a**, and taking *ásat* optatively — which is extremely implausible. In **d** the mss. read *sá mā* (p. *sáḥ : mā*); the comm. divides *sam ā*, with his usual disregard of accent (*ā* = *sarvataḥ*); our *sám mā* is an obvious and unquestionable emendation, and is also read by Ppp. ⌊See my note to xviii. 2. 3, where this case and similar ones are put together, and cf. vi. 5. 2.⌋ The mss. further vary between *púṣṭyā* and *puṣṭyā́*, the decided majority having the latter.

3. Rich in manure, rich in fruit, *svadhā́* and cheer (*írā*) in our house — prosperity let Dhātar assign to me through the keenness (*téjas*) of the [amulet] of *udumbára.*

A few of the mss. again accent *pū́ṣṭim.* Ppp. reads in **a** *karīṣiṇaṁ phalāvatīṁ.* The comm. explains *irā* first as = *bhūmi,* and then as = *ilā gāuḥ* = *gāvaḥ.*

4. Both what [is] two-footed and what four-footed, what foods [there are], what savors (*rása*) — I seize (*grah*) the abundance of them, wearing the amulet of *udumbára.*

Some of the mss. read *rásā* at end of **b**. In **c**, our *téṣām* is an obviously called-for emendation; most mss. read *tvéṣām* or *tveṣām* (p. *tú : éṣām* or *tú : eṣām*); SPP. strangely gives *tvéṣām* in *saṁhitā* and *tú : eṣām* in *pada,* the two not agreeing together; the comm. either reads *eṣām* simply or overlooks the *tu* in his exposition. Ppp. gives *gṛhṇīyāṁ teṣāṁ bhāumānaṁ.*

5. I have seized all (*pári-*) the prosperity of cattle, of quadrupeds, of bipeds, and what grain [there is]; the milk of cattle, the sap (*rása*) of herbs, may Bṛihaspati, may Savitar confirm to me.

Nearly all the mss. accent this time *puṣṭím.*

6. Let me be the over-ruler of cattle; let the lord of prosperity (*puṣṭá-*) assign to me prosperity; let the amulet of *udumbára* confirm to me possessions (*dráviṇa*).

SPP. leaves *asāni* in **a** unaccented, though every ms. but one (doubtless an accidental exception) accents it, and defensibly, on the ground of antithesis.

7. Unto me the amulet of *udumbára,* with both progeny and riches: the amulet quickened by Indra hath come to me together with splendor.

Either Ppp. lacks 6 **d** and 7 **a–c**, or so much of its text is lost in the manuscript. Our *jinvitás* in **c** was an emendation, all the mss. (SPP's as well as ours) giving *jinvátas,* and Ppp. likewise; but the comm. has *jinvitas,* and SPP. accordingly adopts it also in his text. Some of the mss. leave *upa* at the beginning unaccented.

8. The heavenly amulet, rival-slaying, riches-winning, in order to the winning of riches: let it confirm [to me] abundance of cattle, of food, [and] fatness of kine.

Nearly all the mss. read in **d** *sphā́tir ní;* ⌊disregarding the accent, five of SPP's authorities show *sphātim*⌋; SPP's text agrees with ours ⌊*sphātím*⌋, the comm. having the same. Ppp. again has *bhāumānaṁ* in **c**.

9. As in the beginning thou, O forest tree, wast born together with prosperity, so let Sarasvatī assign to me fatness of riches.

Some of the mss. accent *pū́ṣṭyā,* and all ⌊but four⌋ leave *jajñiṣe* unaccented. The majority accent *sphā́tim* in **c**. Ppp. reads in **d** *ā dadāti* ⌊*sarasvatīm* (or *-tī?*)⌋.

10. Riches, fatness of milk, and grain shall Sarasvatī, shall Sinīvālī, and this amulet of *udumbára* bring to me.

Both our *pada*-mss. divide in **b** *páyaḥ॰phātim*, but SPP. reports no such reading among his three, and gives correctly *páyaḥ॰sph-* (the accent is probably false). Our text emends, perhaps unnecessarily, to *gáy-*. In **c**, the *pada*-mss. make the blundering analysis of *úpāvahāt* into *úpa : avahāt;* SPP. gives, by emendation, *úpa : vahāt;* our text emends further to *upā́vahāt* (i.e. *upa॰ā́vahāt*); it is uncertain which the comm. favors, but probably the latter: the sole ms. has ⌊twice *upāvahāt* and once⌋ *upa vahāt* (probably misreading for *upāvahāt*) *upāvahatu*. Ppp. has *upāvahat;* in **b**, it agrees with the mss. in reading *payasph-*.

11\. Thou art the virile (*vṛ́ṣan*) over-ruler of amulets; in thee the lord of prosperity generated prosperity; in thee [are] these powers (*vā́ja*), [are] all possessions; do thou here, O [amulet] of *udumbára*, force (*sah*) far away from us the niggard, misery, and hunger.

In **a** the comm. reads *adhipas*. In **b** Ppp. gives *puṣṭipatis*. At beginning of **c**, the comm. has *tvayā me*, which is not bad. In **c**, the *pada*-mss. have *vājā*. At beginning of **d**, all the mss. present *āúdumbaras*, and SPP. does not emend to *-ra* with us, although the comm. has it and the sense demands it. But in **e**, where all the mss. read *amṛ́tam*, he ventures to follow the comm. in substituting *ámatim*, which is better than our conjecture *ávartim* (misprinted *avártim*). ⌊Ppp. has, for **e**, *ārād arātim abhitikṣayaṁ ca.*⌋ The verse scans naturally as $5 \times 11 = 55$: it is easy, but needless, to make up the full count of a *çakvarī*, 56, by resolution.

12\. Troop-leader art thou, arising a troop-leader; being anointed (*abhi-sic*), do thou anoint me with splendor; brilliancy art thou, brilliancy maintain thou upon me; wealth art thou, wealth assign thou to me.

The reading of **a** is probably corrupt; for *utthā́ya*, which both editions give (with two or three mss.), the mss. in general have *ukthyāya* or *utthyāya* or *ucchyāya*, with *ā̀* or *ā́*. According to SPP., the comm's text has *grāmaṇī chāyā*, and Ppp. strangely gives the same; what he attempts to explain is very doubtful: *ato 'smākam api grāmaṇīr bhava . . . atha vā mām api çreṣṭhaṁ kuru*. SPP. divides *grāma॰nīḥ* in his *pada*-text, but without authority from the mss., and against his practice in iii. 5. 7. In **b**, some of the mss. read *ṣiñca*. On the ground of meter, SPP. suggests that *rayís* in **d** may be for *ádhi-rayis*, one of the two successive *adhi*'s being lost; this would be more acceptable if the word *adhirayi*, or anything closely analogous with it, anywhere occurred. The comm. makes an *adhirayis* (explaining it as *adhigatarayis* or *prāptadhanas*) by stealing for it the *ádhi* of **c**, with his usual disregard of *pada*-division and accent (neither of which, to be sure, is of much account in this book). ⌊The *Index* calls this vs. prose; but with *ádhi* at the end of **c** and *ádhirayis* in **d** it might scan as 11 + 12 : 11 + 11.⌋

13\. Prosperity art thou, with prosperity anoint (*añj*) thou me completely; being house-sacrificer, make thou me householder; O [amulet] of *udumbára*, do thou here put in us and confirm to us wealth having all heroes; I fasten thee on in order to abundance of wealth.

The comm., against the Anukr. and the natural division, adds **e** to verse 14. Part of the mss. again accent *púṣṭi* in **a**. Some, including all the *pada*-mss., have *indhi* for *añdhi;* Ppp. *agdhi*. SPP. again fails to follow us, the comm., Ppp., and one of our mss., in reading *āúdumbara* (instead of *-ras*) in **c**; some of his mss. leave *tvam* without accent. ⌊The non-elision of *a* in *ahám* justifies the count as *çakvarī*, but hurts the meter, which is none too good if we scan the vs. as 5 × 11.⌋

14. This amulet of *udumbára* is bound, a hero, to a hero; let it make for us a winning rich in honey, and may it confirm to us wealth having all heroes.

Some of the mss. accent *sánim* in **c**. Ppp. reads *ucyate* for *badhyate* in **b**.

32. For long life etc.: with an amulet of darbhá.

[*Bhṛgu* (*sarvakāmaḥ. āyuṣe*).—*daçakam. mantroktadevatyam. ānuṣṭubham: 8. purastād-bṛhatī; 9. triṣṭubh; 10. jagatī.*]

Found also in Pāipp. xii. The comm. finds the hymn quoted in Nakṣ. K. 19, as used in a *mahāçānti* ceremony called *yāmī*, with the binding on of an amulet of *darbha*, in case of fear of Yama (*yamabhaye*).

Translated: Griffith, ii. 289; vs. 8 also by Zimmer, p. 205, with comment.

1. Hundred-jointed, hard to be stirred, thousand-leaved, uplifting (?) —the *darbhá* that is a formidable herb, that I bind on thee in order to [prolonged] life-time.

Some of the mss., as usual, read *duçcav-* in **a**. Very nearly all read *uttirás* in **b** (p. *ut°tiráḥ*), and SPP. follows them; and this the translation implies, since it is acceptable enough ⌊cf., for the formation, *uttudás*, iii. 25. 1, and, for the meaning, *uttirán*, vi. 36. 2⌋, and appears in Ppp. (with *-ṛṇam* before it); but the comm. has *úttaras*, as our text by conjectural emendation. Some mss. have *tát* for *tám* in **d**; the comm., *tena* for *taṁ te*. ⌊Ppp. combines *yograoṣadhis* in **c**, which is susceptible of more than one interpretation.⌋ ⌊The gender of *ugrás* would seem to call for some remark.⌋

2. His hair they scatter not forth, they smite not blows on their breast [for him], to whom one yields refuge by the *darbhá* of uncut leaves.

The expression in **a** is a good example for the real identity of roots *vap* 'strew' and *vap* 'shear.' Many of the mss. accent *urási* in **b**. All the mss. leave *yachati* in **d** unaccented, and both editions commit the error of refraining from emendation to *yáchati*, which is of course necessary. Ppp. has at end of **b** *ghnatī*, and combines in **c** *yasmā 'cch-*. Bloomfield translates and comments on the verse in AJP. xi. 339 ⌊or JAOS. xv., p. xlv⌋. The comm. supplies in the first line as subject *mṛtyudūtā rakṣaḥpiçācādyā vā*, renders *pra vapanti* by *ākarṣanti*, and combines *urasitāḍam* into a compound—all very bad.

3. In the sky is thy tuft, O herb; in the earth art thou set (*ni-sthā*); with thee, that hast a thousand joints, do we increase further our life-time.

The translation follows the mss., the comm., SPP., and Ppp., all of which read *tū́lam* in **a**. ⌊Cf. ii. 7. 3, which perhaps suggested the wrong emendation of the Berlin text.⌋ In **b**, the comm. has *viṣṭhitas* ⌊and Ppp. *niṣṭhitā*⌋.

4. Thou didst bore through the three skies, also these three earths; by thee do I bore into my enemy's (*durhárd*) tongue [and] utterances (*vácas*).

In **a**, SPP. reads more correctly *divás*, with nearly all the mss. The comm. reads *atṛṇas;* he explains *aty atṛṇas* by *atikramya gatavān asi* or *veṣṭitavān asi*, and *ni tṛṇadmi* by *veṣṭayāmi*, both very unsuitably. The meter clearly calls for *ca* at the end, and Ppp. has it; whether the comm. means to acknowledge it as part of the text is doubtful; his text, according to SPP., does not present it. ⌊None of the other authorities has *ca*, but the Berlin ed. gives *ca* by emendation.⌋ Ppp. reads in **b** *tisro dyāṁ pṛth-*.

5. Thou art overpowering; I am full of power; may we, both of us, becoming full of power, overpower our rivals.

The comm. reads in **a** *sahamānā;* Ppp. in **a–b**, *-no aham.* To be compared is iii. 18. 5 (RV. x. 145. 5), which ends grammatically with a dual, *sahāvahāi.* Our *sahiṣīvahi* ⌊*Skt. Gram.* § 907⌋ was an emendation, but is given also by Ppp.; the mss., SPP., and the comm., have *-mahi.*

6. Do thou overpower our hostile plotter, overpower those that fight us; overpower all enemies (*durhárd*); make for me many friends (*suhárd*).

Most of the mss. read in **d** *bahúm;* Ppp. and the comm. and two of SPP's authorities and one of ours have *bahūn.* Ppp. combines and reads in **a**, **b** *no 'bhimātihaṁ sahasvā pṛ-*.

7. With the *darbhá*, god-born, constantly sky-propping—with it I have constantly won and shall win men (*jána*).

In **a** most of the mss. read *devajāténa;* SPP. with us. In **b**, SPP. follows the mss. in giving *diví ṣṭambhéna* (p. *diví : stambhéna*); our emendation to *diviṣṭambhéna* is obviously required, and is assumed by the comm. In **c**, our *jánāṅ* was an emendation for the *jánās* of the mss.; but two of SPP's mss. read *jánāṅ*, and it is accepted also in SPP's text. The comm. supports it by giving *janān;* ⌊and his text has *janān asanam*⌋. ⌊Ppp. also has *janān*, as noted below.⌋ In **d**, nearly all the authorities read *ásanām* (three of them have *ásanānt s-*), but SPP. finds among his, two that agree with the ⌊text of the⌋ comm. in presenting *ásanam*, which he adopts, and which is undoubtedly the true text; the aorist is the tense that best suits the connection. ⌊This remark seems to involve the implication that *asanām* might be an imperfect of the *nā*-class; but that can hardly have been Whitney's intention.⌋ Ppp. reads *janān asanāṁ*, ⌊and, in **b**, *divaṣṭambhena*⌋.

8. Make me, O *darbhá*, dear to Brahman-and-Kshatriya, both to Çūdra and to Āryan, and to whomsoever we desire, and to every one that looks abroad.

That is, 'every one that has eyes to see.' ⌊Cf. 62. 1, below, and VS. xviii. 48.⌋ A few authorities have the more proper accent *-nyā̀bhyām*, but VS. xxvi. 2 (which has this and the following four words together) likewise accents *-nyā̀-*, as does SPP. Our *çūdrā̀ya* was an emendation, all our mss. ⌊collated at time of publication⌋ having *sūryā̀ya*, as do nearly all SPP's; but one of our later ones, with two or three of SPP's, the comm., and Ppp., give *çūdrā̀ya.* All the mss. mis-accent *vipáçyate*, most having *vipaçyaté*, others *vípaçyate* or *vipaçyate;* SPP. this time ventures to follow us in emending to ⌊*vipáçyate*⌋ the true reading. The Anukr. regards *brahmarājanyā̀bhyām* as belonging to the first pāda, and does not heed that the pāda has 13 syllables, one too many for a *purastādbṛhatī.*

9. He that, being born, made firm the earth, that propped (*stabh*) the atmosphere and the sky, whose wearer evil hath not found out — that *darbhá* here [is] our supporter [and] blessing.

Or, 'be our supporter.' Here at the end, the translation follows the very acceptable reading of Ppp., *dharuṇo 'dhivākaḥ*. All the mss. give *vā́ruṇo* ⌊one, *vā́ruṇó!*⌋ *divā́ kaḥ* (the comm. *divā 'kaḥ*), which was plainly corrupt, but which SPP. (justifiably, from his point of view) retains without question. Roth's emendation, as read in our text, to *vā́raṇo 'dhivākā́ḥ* hit very near the mark. All the mss. (except, doubtless by accident, one of ours) have in **c** *viveda*, without accent, and this SPP. admits in his text, though emendation (to *vivéda*, as made in our edition) is as obviously necessary as in vs. 8. All the mss. ⌊but O. *tanú*⌋, and Ppp., read in **c** *nanú;* ⌊and so does SPP.;⌋ our emendation to *nā́ 'nu* is acceptable, but not necessary. The comm. explains quite prosaically the plant's 'making firm the earth'; its roots keep the ground from being dissolved by water! The last words he understands thus: *varuṇa* (as coming from *vṛ*) means a keeper off (*nivāraka*) of darkness; and *divā 'kaḥ* signifies *prakāçaṁ karotu*. ⌊Ppp. begins **b** with *so 'stabh-*.⌋

10. Rival-slaying, hundred-jointed, powerful, came into being the first of plants; let that *darbhá* here protect us all about; by it may I overpower fighters, them that fight [against me].

In **a–b** the mss. read *sáhasvanāú 'ṣadh-* (p. *-svanā : óṣ-*), but SPP. emends, as we had done, to *-vān óṣadh-*, as is read ⌊by one of his *pada*-mss., p.m.,⌋ by the comm., and also by Ppp. It is a naturally suggested conjecture that at some time *-āno-* as written in the Bengālī fashion may have been misread into *-anāu-*, and SPP. puts this forward; the lateness and unscholarly character of the *pada*-text to this book make the assumption of such an error far from implausible; we are surprised only at finding the comm's text antecedent to it. In **d** a few of the mss. accent *pṛtanyátas*. The verse is *jagatī* only in its second half. ⌊Pāda **c** is identical with 33. 1 **c**.⌋

33. For various blessings: with an amulet of darbhá.

[*As 32. — pañcakam. 1. jagatī; 2, 5. triṣṭubh; 3. ārṣī paṅkti; 4. āstārapaṅkti.*]

Found in Pāipp. xii., following our hymn 32. Used with the latter in the same ceremony, according to the comm. ⌊For citations by Kāuç., see under vs. 3.⌋

Translated: Griffith, ii. 290.

1. Of thousand-fold worth, hundred-jointed, rich in milk, fire of the waters, consecration (*rājasūya*) of plants — let this *darbhá* here protect us all about; may the divine amulet unite us with [prolonged] life-time.

SPP. accents in **a** *sahasrārghás*, with the minority of mss.; Ppp. has *-ghyas*. The comm. reads *sahasvān* (for *pay-*), and renders *sahasrārghas* by *bahumūlyas*. Ppp. reads in **d** *dāivas* and *sṛjātu*.* The verse is a *jagatī* only in the second half. ⌊Pāda **c** is identical with 32. 10 **c**.⌋ *⌊Other forms like *sṛjātu* under 7. 4.⌋

2. Snatched out of ghee, rich in honey, rich in milk, earth-establishing, unstirred, stirring [other things], thrusting away and putting down rivals — ascend thou, O *darbhá*, with the energy (*indriyá*) of the great ones.

There are no variants in this verse except of a few mss. on one and another point of no consequence. Ppp. has at the end *mahatā mahendriyeṇa*. The verse is a sort of variation of v. 28. 14, above; ⌊and **a** recurs below, 46. 6 **a**⌋.

3. Thou goest across the earth with force; thou sittest beauteous (*cā́ru*) on the sacrificial hearth at the sacrifice; the seers bore thee [as] purifier; do thou purify us from difficulties.

Literally, 'purify (remove, strain out) difficulties from us.' ⌊As to **a**, Griffith notes appositely that "the [darbha] grass spreads with great rapidity, re-rooting itself continually."⌋ In **c**, the translation follows the text of SPP., who emends *bhárantas* of all the mss. ⌊save one⌋ and of our edition to *abharanta* on the authority of the comm. alone. Ppp. reads *bhūmig ady eṣy oj-*. The comm. quotes TB. i. 3. 7[1] to prove that *darbha* is properly called a 'purifier' or 'strainer.' There is not a bit of *pañkti*-character in the verse; ⌊with the ordinary resolutions, and that of *bhuumim* besides, it scans easily as 12 + 12 : 11 + 11;⌋ of course it can be scanned down to 40 syllables by neglecting easy and natural resolutions. ⌊The verse is quoted by Kāuç. in full at 2. 1 and by *pratīka* at 137. 32: cf. p. 897, ¶ 3, and see Bloomfield's notes to the passages of Kāuç.⌋

4. A keen (*tīkṣṇá*) king, of mighty power, demon-slaying, belonging to all men (*-carṣaṇí*), force of the gods, formidable strength [is] that; I bind it on thee in order to old age, to well-being.

Ppp. reads in **c** *tejas* for *ojas*, and in **d** *tat* for *tam*.

5. With the *darbhá* thou shalt do heroic deeds; wearing the *darbhá*, do thou not stagger by thyself; excelling (*ati-sthā*) over others with splendor, shine thou like the sun unto the four quarters.

Our *kṛṇávas* is an emendation; all the mss., and SPP., give *kṛṇávat* or *kṛṇavat*, which the comm. also reads ⌊and renders by *kuryās*⌋ (without spending a word of explanation on the grammatical anomaly; it simply falls under his general rule that in the Veda one form may be used in place of another); Ppp. has *kṛṇu*. In **c** SPP. reads, with the comm. ⌊but the ms. *atha*⌋, *ádha* instead of our *ádhi* (*várcasā́ 'dhā 'nyā́nt s-*); the mss. have *várcasāidhyányāṁ* (also *-sāiṅdhyá-*, *-sāidhá-*, *-sāiṅdhá-*, *-sīdha-*; and the comm's text *-sāudha-*), in *pada*-text *várcasā : āidhi* (or *eddhi*) *: ányām* (or *anyā́m*), or (in our *pada*-mss., and one of SPP's s.m.) *várcasā : edhányām*. Our emendation affords better sense, and accounts for the *y** that appears in the majority of mss. after *dh*. Ppp. also supports it, reading *atiṣṭhāpo varcase 'dhy anyā sūryāi 'vā bhāhi*. ⌊In **b**, Ppp. reads *bibhratā "tmanā*.⌋ ⌊The comm. has *adhiṣṭhāya* in **c**.⌋ *⌊But SPP. points out that *dhya* and *dhā* look very much alike in most old mss.⌋

⌊Here ends the fourth *anuvāka*, with 7 hymns and 68 verses. If you reckoned 27. 14–15 as 3 verses, the sum would be 69.⌋

34. With a jañgiḍá-amulet: for protection etc.

[*Añgiras.* — *daçakam. mantroktadevatyam uta vānaspatyam. ānuṣṭubham.*]

Found also in Pāipp. xi. The comm. quotes it as used by Nakṣ. K. 19, in a *mahāçānti* ceremony called *vāyavyā*, with the binding on of an amulet from the *jañgiḍa* tree. Hymn 35 is used in company with it.

Translated: Bloomfield, 38, 669; Griffith, ii. 291; verses 1 and 7 **ab** also by Grohmann, *Ind. Stud.* ix. 417–18.

1. *Jañgiḍá* art thou, *jañgiḍá;* defender art thou, *jañgiḍá;* what of ours is two-footed, four-footed — let *jañgiḍá* defend it all.

Our emendation at the beginning to *áñgirā asi* ⌊suggested by vs. 6?⌋ is to be disapproved and withdrawn; it is not even necessary to change to vocative the *jañgiḍás* at the end of **a** and **b** (though in the translation they may be understood as either nom. or voc.); but the comm. reads *jañgiḍa* at end of **b**; ⌊the text of the comm. has *jañgiḍo 'si jañgiḍo rakṣitā 'si jañgiḍa*⌋. Compare iv. 12. 1; ix. 5. 16; RV. i. 191. 1 for similar repetitions, in part of nominatives where we should think it more natural to change in part to vocative. SPP. reads ⌊in **a** and **b**⌋, with all the mss., *jañgiḍás* three times. Ppp. has at the beginning the corrupt *jañgiḍisi*, but in both other instances ⌊in **a** and **b**⌋ *-ḍas.* Compare the hymn ii. 4, where alone this plant appears further. The comm. amuses himself (and us) with a number of his ludicrous derivations for *jañgiḍa* — from roots *jā* or *jan* or *ji* with *gir* 'swallow'; or from *jañgam*, intensive.

2. The witchcrafts that are thrice fifty, and the witchcraft-makers that are a hundred — may the *jañgiḍá* make them all of vanished brilliancy (*-téjas*) [and] sapless.

The first pāda is corrupt in the mss., and very doubtful; the translation implies *yā́ḥ kṛtyā́ḥ*, which is most naturally suggested by the connection, and takes *tripañcāçī́s* as an indefinite large number (like *tisráḥ pañcāçátaḥ*, RV. i. 133. 4), and as formed like *triṣaptá*, *triṇavá*, etc., in spite of the important objection that none of these make a fem. in *ī*, and that the word most naturally means 'fifty-three, composed of fifty-three,' or the like. ⌊W's conjecture, *yā́ḥ kṛtyā́ḥ*, nearly coincides with that of Geldner (KZ. xxvii. 218), *yā́ç ca kṛtyā́ḥ.* Geldner's is metrically better; and he takes *trip-* as an indefinitely large number (cardinal), as does W.⌋ It was this word *tripañcāçá*, applied to the set of dice in RV. ⌊x. 34. 8⌋ (but perhaps meaning 'thrice fifty'), that suggested the not very happy emendation in our edition to *akṣa-kṛtyā́s.* The mss. read mostly *jāgṛtsyas tr-* (with various accent, most often on *-syás:* p. *jāgṛtsyáḥ : tripañca*° *āçī́ḥ !*), also *jyā-*, *yyā*, and (two of SPP's) *yāgṛtsyás;* this last the comm. also has, and understands it as *yā(ḥ) gṛtsyas*, explaining the latter as = *gardhanaçīlās* ⌊SPP's *pada*-text accordingly, *yā́ḥ : gṛ́tsyaḥ*⌋, and *tripañcāçīs* as *tryadhikapañcāçatsaṁkhyākās*, both as epithets of *kṛtyās* (understood). ⌊With this reading, we can take *gṛ́tsyas* as nom. pl. fem. to *gṛ́tsa* and render 'what fifty-three clever *or* sly [witchcrafts there are]'; but *gṛ́tsa*, in such an application and with such sinister meaning, has rather slender support, to wit, VS. xvi. 25, as cited by BR. ii. 778.⌋ Ppp. gives *yā kṛcchrā tripañcāçīç ch-*, which, while it is itself (emended to *yāḥ kṛcchrās*) not wholly unacceptable, also favors our *yā́ḥ kṛtyā́s;* there is insufficient reason for the feminine words if *kṛtyās* be not expressed. ⌊I cannot here attach much value to the evidence of Ppp.: on the one hand, it confuses surd and sonant very often (*kovidam* for *govidam*, xix. 13. 5: cf. xi. 5. 4, note); and, on the other, the relation of its *cch* to *ts* may be somewhat like that discussed under x. 9. 23 (*ṛchára*, *ṛtsára*, etc.). The mss. are decidedly in favor of *gṛtsyas* as against *kṛtyās;* but Whitney's objection as to the omission of *kṛtyās* seems to me a weighty argument in favor of his conjecture.⌋ Our *vínaṣṭatejasas* in **c** was an emendation, which, now that the comm. also reads it, may be regarded as sufficiently established; the mss. mostly *vinaktatéjasas* (also *vinaktu t-*, *viniṣṭat-*, *bhanakti t-*, *minaktu t-* ⌊etc.⌋: *pada*-readings, *vinaktu* [as independent word or as compounded with *téjasaḥ*] or also *vinakta*°*t-*). SPP. strangely contents himself with *vinaktu téjasas*, which certainly he would be unable to translate into anything even simulating sense.

Ppp. is corrupt, and brings no help; it has *sarva vyunaktu tej-*. ⌊Did not SPP. understand his reading thus: 'Let the amulet separate them all from their *téjas* (ablative)'? The instrum. *téjasā*, which good authorities give, would also be a proper construction with root *vic*: 'Let the amulet part them all with their efficiency (*téjas*),' i.e. rob the wizards of their power to make their witchcrafts efficacious against us. Whitney's reading and rendering are wholly satisfactory in themselves: but *vinaktu téjasas* or *-sā* seems to me no less so; and it has much stronger support (directly or indirectly) from the mss., and even from Ppp., than has RW's *vínaṣṭatejasas*. — After writing the above, I notice that Bloomfield, p. 672, interprets SPP's reading quite differently: the way in which he construes *vic* does not seem to me admissible.⌋

3. Sapless the artificial noise, sapless the seven that fall apart; away from here, O *jan̄giḍá*, make fall (*çat*) misery, as an archer (*ástṛ*) an arrow.

The first half-verse is perhaps corrupt, as it is certainly unintelligible. The *pada*-text makes in **a** the astonishing division *kṛtrím : anna*○*adám*; many of the *saṁhitā*-mss. read *kṛtṛ́m-*. All the mss. accent *vísrasas*, and SPP. with them; our text emends to *visrásas*. The minor Pet. Lex. suggests that the *saptá visrúhas* of RV. vi. 7. 6 may be meant: ingenious, but not comforting, as no one has any idea what the latter signifies. The comm's guess is this: *mūrdhaniṣṭheṣu ... saptasu cchidreṣv abhicarato 'tpāditāḥ sapta niṣyandāḥ*. In **a**, **b**, the reading of Ppp. is *rasaṁ kṛtrimaṁ nādam arasas s-*. In **c** the mss. have much unimportant variation of accent. At the end, Ppp. gives *sādhayā*. The translation gives to *çātaya* the meaning ascribed to it by the Hindu grammarians, since it suits the connection; the comm. renders the word by *tanūkuru*, of which it is hard to see the reason or sense.

4. A spoiler of witchcraft verily is this, likewise a spoiler of niggardry; likewise may the powerful *jan̄giḍá* lengthen out our life-times.

The majority of mss. leave *ayám* in **a** unaccented; and they divide pretty evenly between *tāriṣat* and *tārṣat* at the end; ⌊cf. under iv. 10. 6⌋. Ppp. reads *kṛtyādūṣaṇa vāyam atho 'rāt-*. With the verse compare ii. 4. 6, which is nearly the same.

5. Let that greatness of the *jan̄giḍá* protect us all about, wherewith [it] overpowered the *víṣkandha* with force, [being] a counteracting force (?).

Sáṁskandha occurs nowhere else, and is in the translation assumed to be a word made as the opposite and contrary of *víṣkandha*; it may, of course, be only a variation of the latter, another evil of the same sort, as understood by the Pet. Lexx. and the comm. (*yena rogeṇa skandhaḥ saṁnataḥ saṁlagno bhavati sa rogaḥ saṁskandhaḥ*). The majority of the mss. read in **c** *sāsáha* (p. *sasaha* ⌊with various accent⌋); but *sāsahé* (as in our text) is in accordance with the nearly invariable use of the root in AV. as middle, ⌊and is read by one of SPP's mss.⌋. Ppp. reads *sāsahā*, and combines in **d** *ojo 'jasā*. The comm. reads and explains in **c** *viṣkandham ojasā saha* (favoring *sāsaha*).

6. Thrice the gods generated thee that art settled (*ni-sthā*) upon the earth; and Brahmans of old know thee thus as An̄giras by name.

All the mss. read at the beginning *tṛṣṭvā́* (p. the same); but even SPP. emends to *trís ṭvā*, as we had done; the comm. has the latter. Ppp. gives *niṣ ṭvā*. The comm. reads *tiṣṭhantam* in **b** instead of *niṣṭhitam*. Some of the mss. are discordant as to the accent of *an̄girās* in **c**.

7. Not the former herbs surpass thee, not thee the recent; a formidable dispeller [is] the *jan̄giḍá*, a protector round about, of good omen.

Some of SPP's mss. read *návā* at end of **b**. The comm. has *jan̄giḍa* in **c**; ⌊in both text and comment of the comm., the *ḍa*-sound is, naturally enough, spelled with a *la*⌋. Our *pada*-mss. read in **d** *paripā́naḥ*, without division.

8. So then when thou didst come into being, O *jan̄giḍá*, ⌊O thou⌋ of unmeasured heroism, Indra of old, O formidable one, ⌊in the beginning (*agratás*)⌋, gave unto thee heroism.

The translation follows our text, which, however, is more thoroughly altered from that of the mss. than in any instance thus far; and, of course, in a manner open to question. At the beginning, all the *saṁhitā*-mss. give *áthopadā́nábhagavo* ⌊one, *bhá-*⌋, which the *pada*-mss. divide thus: *átho íti : padā́ : ná : bhagavaḥ* ⌊one, *-váḥ*⌋; but the comm. understands it as *átho 'padāna bh-*, and SPP. follows him (p. *átha : upadāna : bh-*); the comm. explains *upadāna* by *upādīyate svīkriyate kṛtyānirharaṇādivyāpāreṣu* — which is utterly implausible. Ppp. gives no help, giving *açvayopadāni bh-*. For **c**, the mss. read *purā́ ta ugrā́ grasata* (*úp-*), p. *purā́ : te : ugrā́ : grasate : úpa :* etc.; and SPP. emends only by changing *ugrā́* to *ugrā́ḥ* ⌊in p.⌋, as the comm. understands. The latter explains it to mean: "Indra, perceiving that formidable creatures will devour (*purā grasate = bhakṣayiṣyanti!*) thee, O *jan̄giḍa*, gave" etc. Ppp. has a text for **c–d** that would make good sense: *purā ta ugrāya sato 'pendro* (i.e., by the usual double combination, *sate : upa*) 'to thee, being before formidable, Indra added further heroic quality.'

9. To thee, O forest tree, the formidable Indra imparted (*ā-dhā*) formidableness; expelling all diseases (*ámīvā*), do thou smite the demons, O herb.

With the first half-verse compare iv. 19. 8 **d**. For this verse there are no variants of any consequence, and the two editions agree throughout with one another and with the comm. Ppp. reads in **a–b** *vanaspataya indro 'j-*, and, for **c**, *amīvās sarvā rakṣāṅsi*.

10. The crusher, the burster, the *balā́sa*, the side-ache, the *takmán* of every autumn, may the *jan̄giḍá* make sapless.

The two names in **a** are found nowhere else; the comm. regards them as names of specific diseases, the one meaning 'wholly injurious,' the other 'especially injurious.' The root *çr* has not been found with *ā* as prefix ⌊except, as noted by OB. vi. 209, at GB. i. 2. 18⌋. The words might of course also be epithets. The only variants concern the accent of *pṛṣṭyāmayam*; the majority of mss. agree with the editions; some have *pṛṣṭyā̀mayam*. Ppp. reads at the beginning *āçarīraṁ*, and in **d** *arasaṁ*.

35. The same.

[*As 34. — pañcakam. 3. pathyāpan̄kti; 4. nicṛt triṣṭubh.*]

This hymn is found with the preceding in Pāipp. (in xi.), and it has the same *viniyoga*. Translated: Grohmann, *Ind. Stud.* ix. 419; Zimmer, p. 65; Bloomfield, 39, 674; Griffith, ii. 293.

1. Taking (*grah*) the name of Indra, the seers gave the *jan̄giḍá*, which the gods in the beginning made a remedy, spoiler of the *víṣkandha*.

The comm. (apparently by an oversight) explains at the end *viṣkandhabheṣajam*, while his text, according to SPP., agrees with ours.

2. Let that *jan̄giḍá* defend us, as a protector of riches his riches; which ⌊*jan̄giḍá*⌋ the gods, the Brahmans, made a protector round about, slayer of niggards.

The *pada*-mss. read at end of **b** *dhánaoiva;* ⌊SPP. emends to *dhánāoiva*, which the translation implies;⌋ Ppp. gives *dhanāi 'va*.

3. The enemy of terrible aspect (*-cákṣus*), the evil-doer that has come — them do thou, O thousand-eyed one, make to vanish by thy watchfulness (?*pratībodhá*); thou art *jan̄giḍá* that protects round about.

The translation implies in **a** emendation to *durhā́rdaṁ ghorácakṣuṣam*, which is venturesome, but something has to be done to make sense. SPP. reads, with ⌊most of⌋ the mss. and the comm., *durhā́rdaḥ sáṁghoraṁ* (= *atyantakrūram*, comm.) *cákṣus;* the comm. ⌊joins *cakṣus* with⌋ *nāçaya*. Ppp. gives no help; its text (*dūhārda saṁghora cakṣuṁ*) apparently is meant for the same with ours. In **b** is implied, instead of the *ā́ 'gamam* of the mss. and both editions, *ā́gatam*, which may be confidently accepted on the authority of both Ppp. and the comm. ⌊But *ā́dabhan* is read by W's O., by two of SPP's mss., and by a third,* s.m.⌋ Our text emends at the end to *jan̄giḍa;* as all the authorities, including Ppp., give *-ḍaḥ*, this is retained in the translation. In **d** the comm. appears to have *pratib-*, but it is very probably an oversight of the ms. The Anukr. takes no notice of the deficiency of a syllable in **c**. *⌊The carefully corrected Dc.⌋

4. Me from the sky, me from the earth, from the atmosphere, me from the plants, me from what is, and me from what is to be — from every direction let the *jan̄giḍá* protect us about.

The majority of mss. accent in **c** *mó 'tá bhavyā́t*. One of the mss. of the Anukr. calls the verse a *jagatī;* for this there is no ground, but also as little for calling it *nicṛt* as a *triṣṭubh*.

5. What [witchcraft-]workers are made by the gods, and also what from mortals — all those may the all-healing *jan̄giḍá* make sapless.

The translation follows our text, which deviates widely from that of the mss. in **a**, **b**. All these have, without exception, *yáḥ kṛṣṇávo;* all further *devakṛtā* (p. *devaokṛtāḥ*), but with differences of accent; ⌊of SPP's authorities, 6 give correctly *-vá-*, and 8 give *-tā́ḥ;*⌋ then they vary in **b** between *yá* and *ya* (all the *pada*-mss. *yā́ḥ*); all have *utó* (p. *utó íti*); ⌊but W's B. seems to read *yā́tó;*⌋ finally, they vary between *vabhṛtenyàḥ* (the majority), *-tenyáḥ*, *-thenyàḥ*, *-tyenyàḥ* (the *pada*-mss., *vabhṛtenyàḥ*, or *-ténya̱ḥ*). SPP's text has *yá* (p. *yé*) *ṛṣṇávo devákṛtā* (p. *-tāḥ*) *yá* (p. *yā́ḥ*) *utó vavṛté 'nyáḥ* (p. *vavṛté : anyáḥ :* but this would give for *saṁhitā*-text *vavṛtè 'nyáḥ*), which, apart from the added accents, is the text of the comm., as SPP. reports; the comm., however, assumes in his explanation *ye . . . anye* in **b** instead of *yáḥ . . . anyáḥ*, and declares *vavṛte* = *vavṛtire*. Ppp., finally, gives *ye ṛṣṇavo devakṛtā yo co bibhṛthebhyā*. The case is evidently a rather desperate one. The word *ṛṣṇavas*, found in both Ppp. and comm., occurs nowhere else; the comm. gives for it one of his usual artificial and wholly worthless explanations, *gantāro hiṅsakāḥ puruṣāḥ;* **b** he makes to mean "also what other oppressors (*bādhakās*) go about."

36. With a çatávāra-amulet: for protection etc.

[*Brahman.* — *ṣaḍṛcam.* *çatavāradāivatam.* *ānuṣṭubham.*]

Found also ⌊except 4 **c**, **d**, 5 **a**, **b**⌋ in Pāipp. ii. The comm. quotes its use from Nakṣ.K. 19, in the *mahāçānti* ceremony called *saṁtati*, performed for a failure of family, with the *çatavāra* amulet.

Translated: Griffith, ii. 294.

1. The *çatávāra* hath by its keenness (*téjas*) made to vanish the *yákṣmas*, the demons, mounting together with splendor, an amulet that expels the ill-named.

Our *maṇís* in **d** was an emendation, all the mss. having *maṇím;* SPP. also has *-ís*, on the authority of the comm.; Ppp. reads *-ṇiṁ* and *-çātanam*. What *çatávāra* really means is very questionable; the Pet. Lexx. conjecture "consisting of a hundred hairs," which does not seem probable; the comm. says "having a hundred roots, or awns"; and he further adds, on the authority of vs. 6, where the accordance with *vāraya-* is played upon, "warding off a hundred diseases"; moreover, there is no reason apparent why it should not signify 'bringing a hundred choice things' (cf. *viçvávāra*). The comm. declares 'ill-named' to denote a skin-disease. ⌊"Mounting": i.e. being raised up to the neck of the person on whom it is "bound" — so Griffith.⌋

2. With its two horns it thrusts away the demon, with its root the sorceresses; with its middle it drives off (*bādh*) the *yákṣma;* no evil overpasses it.

All the mss., the comm., and Ppp., read at the end *tatrati*, which we emended to *tarati*, as the other seems an inconceivable 3d sing.; the comm. glosses it with *atikrāmati*, and explains the form by *çluḥ çaç ce 'ti vikaraṇadvayam*. The comm. explains the 'two horns' as "the two parts of its apex, set on like horns." The mention of a "root" is, of course, an indication (though not a certain one) that a plant is intended.

3. The *yákṣmas* that are petty, and they that are great, noisy — all of them the *çatávāra* amulet, slayer of the ill-named, hath made vanish.

Ppp. reads in **b** *çapathinas*. The Anukr. takes no notice of the deficiency of a syllable in **a**.

4. A hundred heroes it generated; a hundred *yákṣmas* it scattered away; having slain all the ill-named ones, it shakes down the demons.

The mss. (both s. and p.) vary in **a** between *vīrā́s* and *vīrā́n*, the decided majority of SPP's giving the latter; of ours, none save one or two of those collated since publication; SPP. reads *vīrān aj-*. Ppp. has *çataṁ vīrāṇi janayac ch-*, which, with emendation to *vīryāṇi janayañ*, is perhaps the true reading. About half, indeed, of the mss. read *-nayan*, which also makes a possible text (*çatáṁ vīrā́ ajanayan*).

5. A golden-horned bull [is] this amulet of *çatávāra;* having shattered (*tṛh*) all the ill-named ones, it hath trodden down the demons.

A few of the authorities ⌊some confusing the primary with the *vṛddhi*-derivative⌋ read in **b** *çatávāras* or *çatavārás* or *çātávāras*. In **c**, all the mss. ⌊save perhaps W's B.⌋ read *tṛdhvā́*, which SPP. mistakenly emends to *tṛḍḍhvā́* (as if one were to emend the *ḍhvā* of *rūḍhvā* and *līḍhvā* to *-ḍḍhvā*). Ppp. is corrupt, giving *durṇās tris sarvās triḍhvā apa rakṣāṅsy apa kramīm.* The second half of vs. 4 and the first half of vs. 5 are wanting in Ppp.

6. With the *çatávāra* I ward off (*vāraya-*) a hundred of the ill-named ones (f.), a hundred of the Gandharvas-and-Apsarases, and a hundred of the doglike ones (f.).

Some of the mss. accent in **b** *gandharvā́psarásām.* All ⌊save W's B.⌋ have in **c** *çatáṁ çaçvanvátīnām* (varying to *çaçcatv-*: p. *çaçvan°vátīnām*); our *çatáṁ ca çvánva-* is an emendation, and, as it seems, an easy and necessary one, supported by Ppp., which reads *çataṁ ca çunvatīnāṁ* ⌊Griffith renders by 'dog-mated nymphs,' referring it to the Apsarases, and citing most appositely xi. 9. 15 and iv. 37. 11⌋. The comm. reads with the mss., and furnishes one of his characteristic absurd explanations: the word comes from *çaçvat* 'constantly,' with *n* substituted for *d* in the combination, and means *muhur-muhuḥ pīḍārtham āgantryo grahāpasmārādyā vyādhayaḥ!* He declares the fem. *durṇāmnī* to be used in **a** ⌊with reference to⌋ *vyādhi*, forgetting that *vyādhi* is masculine. ⌊For the play in **d**, cf. my note to xviii. 3. 29.⌋

37. With an amulet: for various blessings.

[*Atharvan. — caturṛcam. āgneyam. trāiṣṭubham: 2. āstārapañkti; 3. 3-p. mahābṛhatī; 4. purauṣṇih.*]

Not found in Pāipp. The comm. neither quotes nor devises a *viniyoga*, but SPP. finds it used in Nakṣ.K. 19, in the *mahāçānti* ceremony called *tvāṣṭrī*, with a threefold amulet, on occasion of the loss of a garment.

Translated: Griffith, ii. 295.

1. This splendor hath come, given by Agni, brightness (*bhárga*), glory, power, force, vigor (*váyas*), strength; and the heroisms that are thirty-three — those let Agni give forth to me.

Most of the mss. accent *balám* at end of **b**. The first half-verse corresponds to a first half-verse in TB. (ii. 5. 7[1]), MS. (ii. 3. 4), and AÇS. (vi. 12. 2); all these read at end of **a** *ā́ 'gāt*, and AÇS. has *rādhas* instead of *várcas;* then, in **b**, TB. and AÇS. give *yáço bhárgaḥ sáha ójo bálaṁ ca*, MS. *máhi rā́dhaḥ sáha ójo bálaṁ yát*, all making a good *triṣṭubh* pāda; the verse is too irregular to be called simply a *triṣṭubh.* ⌊With **c**, cf. 27. 10 **a**, above.⌋

2. Splendor set thou in my body (*tanū́*), power, force, vigor, strength; unto Indra-like action, unto heroism, unto [life] of a hundred autumns, do I accept thee.

The majority of mss. again accent *balám*. In **a**, SPP. has the better reading *tanvàm*, with the comm. and a single ms. (accidental?). ⌊The transition-form ought probably to be oxytone, *tanvā́m:* see my *Noun-Inflection*, p. 412, near top.⌋ ⌊With our second half-verse cf. the second half of the verse just cited from TB.MS.AÇS.: apart from two or three misprints, it reads *dīrghāyutvā́ya çatáçāradāya práti gṛhṇāmi* (MS. *gṛbhṇāmi:* AÇS. *gṛbhnāmi*, cf. *Grammar* § 195 a) *mahaté vīryàya* (MS. *-tá indriyā́ya*) — a confused blending of tags: cf. xi. 1. 3, 7, and so on.⌋ ⌊The comm. takes **a**, **b** as addressed to Agni.⌋ Under 2 **c**, **d** and vss. 3 and 4, he speaks of the thing addressed simply as a *padārtha*, 'a substance,' not presuming to define what it is: an unusual restraint on his part.

3. Unto refreshment thee, unto strength thee, unto force, unto power thee, unto superiority thee do I carry about, unto the wearing of royalty for a hundred autumns.

Very likely the last word is best rendered as a noun; the comm. so takes it. The mss. all accent *rāṣṭrábhṛt-*, which SPP. retains; our text makes the necessary emendation to *-ṭrabhṛ́t-* ⌊cf. *Gram.* § 1213 c⌋. ⌊Even though *3-p. mahābṛhatī* be taken (*Ind. Stud.* viii. 243) as 12 : 12 : 12,⌋ the definition of the Anukr. is bad: the verse is just as much an *āstārapañkti* as vs. 2; ⌊both are doubtless to be scanned as 8 + 8 : 11 + 11⌋.

4. Thee with the seasons, with them of the seasons; thee unto lifetime, unto splendor; with the brilliancy of the year — with that we make [thee] cheek by jowl.

⌊All the mss. give here *ṛtúbhiṣ ṭvé 'ty ékā* (= v. 28. 13), except W's O. and SPP's careful Dc., which have, disregarding the accents, *ṛtubhyaṣ ṭve 'ty ekā* (= iii. 10. 10). The metrical definition of the Anukr. as *purauṣṇih*, coinciding with its definition of v. 28. 13 (not with that of iii. 10. 10), supports the mss. in the implication that a repetition of v. 28. 13 is here intended; and so does the *pratīka* given by the Anukr., which is *ṛtubhaṣ ṭvā "rtavāiḥ* (not the *"rtavebhyaḥ* of iii. 10. 10). The Berlin ed., accordingly, here repeats v. 28. 13: SPP., on the other hand, repeats iii. 10. 10;⌋ in this he follows the comm., who gives at this point, curiously, iii. 10. 10 in full, and makes an entirely new commentary upon it, taking no notice of its having occurred before. The mss. appear to have confounded the two *pratīkas* in a measure: ⌊and this probably accounts for the false lingualization of *-bhyaṣ ṭvā* — see note to iii. 10. 10, and observe that both mss. of the Anukr. here have *ṛtubhaṣ ṭv-*, which is neither one thing nor the other!⌋ ⌊For *sáṁhanu*, W's 'cheek by jowl' is perhaps a better version than the one which he gave at v. 28. 13, 'of closed jaw, free from involuntary opening of the jaws.' A third version is given by Griffith: 'we fasten thee [the amulet] about the neck.' Dīgha Nikāya, ii. 61, suggests still a fourth interpretation, 'affected with lock-jaw,' not applicable here: cf. viii. 1. 16.⌋

38. With gúggulu: against disease.

[*Atharvan. — tṛcam. mantroktagulguludevatākam. ānuṣṭubham. 2* **a–d**. *4-p. uṣṇih; 2* **e–f**. *1-av. prājāpatyā 'nuṣṭubh.*]

Found also in Pāipp. xix. Used, according to the comm. (together with hymn 39), by Pariç. 4. 4, in the ceremony of a king's entrance into his sleeping-house, to the accompaniment of incense of *kuṣṭha* and *guggulu*.

⌊With regard to the name of the latter substance, there is a question as to its spelling, whether with *-lg-* or with *-gg-*; and a second as to its accent, whether on the first syllable or on the last. As to the first question, the mss. are here, as elsewhere, quite at variance: see below. As to the second, the proper accent seems to be proparoxytone: so TS. at vi. 2. 8[6], *gúlgulu*, nominative; and above, at ii. 36. 7, where the word is nom., both W's and SPP's authorities agree in accenting the first syllable. In this hymn, however, all of W's and of SPP's authorities agree in vs. 1 in accenting the last syllable,

-gulós, and so both editions print: in vs. 2, again, all (save W's P.M.W., *-ló*) agree in having *-lú;* and the Bombay ed. has *-lú* (as nom.), while the Berlin ed. and the *Index* have *guggulu* (as voc.); whether the comm. intends *guggulo* (voc.) or *guggulus* (nom., with the later gender), I am not sure. If we read *guggulu* (as voc.), it may be noted that no other voc. sing. neuter from stems in *u* or *i* is registered in my *Noun-Inflection* (see p. 413, 390).⌋

Translated: Grill, 39, 193; Bloomfield, 40, 675; Griffith, ii. 295.

1. *Yákṣmas* obstruct him not, a curse attains him not, whom the agreeable odor of the healing *gúggulu* attains.

All the mss., and SPP., read in **a** *árundhate*, which our text emends to *ar-*; but the form is obviously false; *ā́ rundhate* would be the simplest and easiest change. Ppp. has *yakṣmā ru-* ⌊i.e. *yakṣmāru-*: which may of course mean *yakṣmās ā ru-* as well⌋; and, at end of **b**, *-tho 'çnute*. As everywhere, the mss. vary between *gugg-* and *gulg-* in **c**; SPP. adopts the latter; the comm. agrees with our text in giving the former; Ppp. has always *gulg-*. At the end of **d**, all the mss. have *açnute*, but this time SPP. follows us in making the necessary emendation to *açnuté*. ⌊Again, as often (cf. note to xviii. 3. 47), the accent-blunder is due to a faulty assimilation,—in this case, with the accent of *açnute* at the end of the preceding half-verse.⌋

2. From him the *yákṣmas* scatter away, like antelopes from a wild beast. If, O *gúggulu*, thou art from the river, or if also from the ocean, the name of both have I taken (*grah*), that this man may be uninjured.

There is discordance among the authorities as to the division and numbering of the verses of this hymn. The Anukr. makes three verses, reckoning the last two pādas as third verse, and SPP. follows it, although this division is wholly opposed to the sense, as breaking a sentence in two. The comm. reckons only the first of the three lines as vs. 2, noting that it may also be explained as belonging to vs. 1, being connected in sense with that; the other two lines he makes vs. 3. Our division followed the majority of our mss., with which agree the minority of SPP's. The choice between the three modes of division is difficult, and fortunately the matter is of no importance. ⌊Grill, p. 193, suggests that 1 **a**, **b** is the foreign element, a prefixed fragment about *yakṣma*. That leaves 1 **c**, **d** and 2 **a**, **b** for our first vs., and 2 **c–f** for our second.⌋ The mss. all read in **b** *mṛgā́ áçvā iva*,* which is obviously wrong and unintelligible, though the comm., after his fashion, gives two equally worthless interpretations, once taking *áçvās* as an adjective (= *āçugāminas*) to *mṛgā́s*, and once supplying a second *iva:* "like deer [or] like horses." The translation follows our emendation, which is certainly plausible to an acceptable degree. Ppp. is corrupt: *yakṣmād mṛgāyaṣāya vedhase*. The *pada*-mss. blunderingly read *irate* at end of **a**; even SPP. allows himself to emend to *īrate*. In **c** he again gives *gulgulú* ⌊not *gugg-*⌋, with the majority of his mss.: our *guggulu* is in respect to accent ⌊as voc.⌋ an emendation (our mss. read *-lú* or *-ló*), but one called for by the following *ási;* ⌊this reason does not seem to me cogent: reading the nom. *-lú* (with SPP.: see introd.), we may render, 'whether thou art *guggulú* from the river or [*guggulú*] from the ocean'⌋. In **d**, the mss. give either *yádvāpyási* or *yádvā́pyā́si* (p. *yát : vā : ápi : ā°ási*); SPP. accepts in his *saṁhitā*-text *vā́ 'py ā́si*, but in his *pada*-text changes *ā°ási* to *ási*, thus making the two texts discordant; if he had courage for the latter alteration, he should also have had it for emending *ā́si* in *saṁhitā* to *ási*, as we had done, and as is plainly required. ⌊The text of the comm. has *'py asi.*⌋ *⌊But W's P.M.W., *mṛgā́ṁ.*⌋

39. With kúṣṭha: against diseases.

[*Bhṛgvañgiras. — daçakam. mantroktakuṣṭhadevatyam. ānuṣṭubham: 2, 3. pathyāpañkti; 4. 6-p. jagatī (2–4. 3-av.); 5. 7-p. çakvarī; 6–8. aṣṭi (5–8. 4-av.).*]

Found also in Pāipp. vii. The *viniyoga* is the same with that of the preceding hymn. ⌊Whitney, note to Prāt. ii. 67, speaks of the critical bearing of the fact that vs. 1 is cited by the comm. to the Prāt.: see above, p. 896, ¶ 1.⌋

Translated: Grohmann, *Ind. Stud.* ix. 392, 420–422 (parts); Ludwig, p. 198; Bloomfield, 5, 676; Griffith, ii. 295. — Hillebrandt, *Ved. Mythol.*, i. 65–66, discussing the connection of *kuṣṭha* and *soma*, cites part of the hymn. Cf. v. 4 and vi. 95.

1. Let the heavenly rescuing *kúṣṭha* come hither from off the snowy [mountain]; do thou make vanish all *takmán* and all the sorceresses.

Of course, *himávant* may also be rendered 'Himālaya.' ⌊For *-tas pari*, cf. note to Prāt. ii. 67.⌋ Emendation in **c** to *nāçáyan* is suggested as acceptable; ⌊and *nāçayaṁ* is the reading of Ppp., both here and in 5 **f**⌋. Some of the mss. read at the beginning *étu;* the *pada*-mss. have blunderingly *āitu* instead of *ā́ : etu;* SPP. emends to the latter.

2. Three names are thine, O *kúṣṭha:* by-no-means-killing, by-no-means-harming: — by no means may this man take harm, for whom I bespeak (*pari-brū*) thee, at evening and in the morning, likewise by day.

In **a**, part of the mss. accent *kúṣṭha.* In **b**, **c**, SPP. reads *nadyamāró nadyā́riṣaḥ: nádyā 'yám* etc. There is hardly any ms. that distinguishes *dya* and *gha* in such a manner that confidence can be placed in its testimony as between the two; so that, although SPP. reports *nadya-* from all his mss., it is really of no account. But the comm. shows that he reads *nadya-* by his explanation: *nadya*, he says, means "being in a stream (*nadī*)," and by "stream" is meant the waters (*udakāni*) in a stream; and the virtual sense is "diseases that originate in faults of water"; or else, he sagely adds (betraying that his expositions are, as usual, the merest guesses of a skilless etymologist), *nadya* means *nadanīya* or *çabdanīya:* i.e., *atyantaduṣpariharatvena çabdyamāna;* and the two epithets mean "killing" or "harming" such *nadyas;* while the third name is *nadya* simply, since a killer (*māraka*) of *nadyas* is himself called *nadya.* We had the second of the two epithets above, at viii. 2. 6 and 7. 6, and in the former passage the comm. explained (falsely) and read *nagha-*. It seems hardly doubtful that our readings ⌊with *gh*, not *dy*⌋ and the translation founded on them are the true ones here, though that implies that the comm. worked from mss. only, and not from oral representatives of the text. ⌊Weber, *Sb.* 1896, p. 681, discusses *na gha.*⌋ Ppp. agrees precisely with our text in **b** and **c** (in **d** it has *asmāi* and in **e** *divaḥ*). In **b**, all the mss. read (assuming, here and later, that the character is *dya*, and not *gha*) *nadyá māro* (p. *nadyá : mā́raḥ*); nearly all follow it with *nadyā́yuṣo* or *-ṣaḥ* (p. *nadyá : ā́yuṣaḥ*); but two of SPP's, and two others p.m., give *nadyā́riṣo* ⌊the comm. *nadyariṣo*⌋. In **c** the general reading is *nadyā́yámpúruṣoriṣat*, but one or two fail to accent *'yam*, and a few have *-ṣo rṣat* (all the *pada*-mss. *ṛṣat*). The comm. treats *nadya* in **c** as a vocative, and SPP. accordingly changes the accent to *nádyā 'yám;* in **b** he alters the *pada*-text to *nadya°mārā́ḥ: nadyá°riṣaḥ.* The Anukr. pronounces this verse, as well as the two following, *tryavasāna*, but nearly all the mss. omit here the sign of interpunction before *na ghā 'yam puruṣo riṣat*, although they introduce it both times later; in this verse, our edition follows the mss., but SPP's the Anukr. In **d**, all the mss. give *pári bra-*; SPP. follows us in emending the accent to *paribrávīmi*. The comm. repeats *nadyā 'yam puruṣo riṣat* a second time.

3. "Lively" by name is thy mother; "living" by name is thy father:—by no means may etc. etc.

All the mss., the comm., and Ppp., read in **b** *jīvantás*, and so of course SPP.; there was doubtless no sufficient reason for altering to *jīvalás* in our text. Ppp. adds further, after *pitā, mārṣa nāma te svasā*. With **a**, **b** compare i. 24. 3 **a**, **b**.

4. Thou art the highest (*uttamá*) of herbs, as the draft-ox of moving creatures (*jágat*), as the tiger of beasts of prey:—by no means may etc. etc.

⌊Pādas **a–c** are repeated from viii. 5. 11: see note.⌋ Ppp. combines *uttamo 'sy oṣ-*. It repeats in the refrain its readings *asmāi* and *divaḥ* (see note to vs. 2).

5. Thrice from the Çāmbus, from the Añgirases, thrice from the Ādityas, thrice from the All-Gods art thou born; this all-healing *kúṣṭha* stands along with soma; do thou make vanish all the *takmán* and all the sorceresses.

All the authorities ⌊save Ppp.⌋ agree in *çámbubhyas*, and our alteration to *bhṛ́gubhyas* is not to be approved. All our *saṁhitā*-mss., and the majority of SPP's *saṁhitā*-authorities, with the text of the comm., read after it *áñgireyebhyas* (one or two *-raye-*), and the comm. takes the word as adjective (= *añgirasām apatyabhūtebhyaḥ*) qualifying *çámbubhyas*. SPP. adopts *áñgirebhyas*, with the rest of the mss.; our emendation to *-robhyas* is a very simple and plausible one, when dealing with a text in the condition of this. Ppp. is very corrupt: *tiṣyāmividyogirayebhyas;* in **d**, further, it has *-bheṣaja*, in **e** *tiṣṭhasi*, in **f** *nāçayaṁ* (as in 1 **c**). SPP., probably by an oversight, inserts a stroke of interpunction between **d** and **e**; it is against the Anukr., and our mss. do not have it.

6. The *açvatthá*, seat of the gods, in the third heaven from here: there [is] the sight (*cákṣaṇa*) of immortality; thence was born the *kúṣṭha*.

This verse and the next correspond nearly with v. 4. 3, 4 (repeated as vi. 95. 1, 2). Most of the mss. accent in **d** *kuṣṭhás*. SPP. adds to this verse and the next the last four pādas of vs. 5, as a refrain continued from that verse; and this is evidently the understanding of the Anukr., and the comm. ratifies it. Whether SPP. makes the addition on the authority of these two alone, or whether some of his mss. also intimate it, he does not state; not one of our mss. gives any sign of it. ⌊Ppp. has *jayatāt saḥ:* presumably answering to the end of pāda **d** of the Berlin ed.; but Roth's Collation is not quite clear.⌋

7. A golden ship, of golden tackle, moved about in the sky; there [is] the sight etc. etc.

As to the correspondence and the extent of this verse, see the note to vs. 6. Ppp. reads *hiraṇyena nāur* ⌊and omits **c**, **d**⌋.

8. Where there is no falling downward (?), where the head of the snowy [mountain], there is the sight of immortality; thence was born the *kúṣṭha:*—this all-healing *kúṣṭha* etc. etc. (as vs. 5).

The mss. all ⌊save SPP's D., which has *nā́vaḥ:* cf. the *navaṣ* of Ppp.⌋ read in **a** *nā́ 'va prabhráñçanam* (p. *ná : áva : pra∘bhr-*), and the comm. so understands it (*yatra dyuloke tatrasthānāṁ sukṛtināṁ avāñmukhaprabhrañço nā 'sti*); and considering this (if there were such a place-name, it is just the sort of thing that we might fairly expect the comm. to know and report), and that *nāva* nowhere appears as combination-form of *nāu*, and that *pra-bhrañç* is not used of the sliding down of a boat or ship on a mountain, and appears wholly unadapted to that use, it must be pronounced an excessively daring and not less questionable proceeding to emend to *nāvaprabhráñçanam*, translate it by the "descent of the ship," and connect it with the more modern Brāhmaṇa-legend of Manu's flood — as is done in our text, by Weber in his notes to *Die Fluthsage* (*Ind. Streifen* i. 11), and by others elsewhere ⌊cf. Griffith's note⌋. Ppp. reads ⌊*sa*⌋ *yatra navaṣ paribhraçanaṁ*.

9. Thou whom Ikshvāku of old knew, or thou whom Kushṭhakāmya [knew], whom Vāyasa, whom Mātsya — thereby art thou all-healing.

There is almost nothing here that is not very questionable. Only the comm. has *ikṣvākus* in **a**; the majority of mss. give *iṣvākas*, but some (which SPP. follows) *ikṣvākas*. In **b** the *pada*-mss. divide *kuṣṭha : kāmyàḥ*, and the comm. so understands it (*kāmya* = *kāmaputra*); SPP. follows them; though here our emendation to *kuṣṭha-kāmyàs* seems plainly called for. In **c**, the mss. have *yáṁ vā váso* (or *vā́so:* SPP. *váso*) *yám ā́tsyas t-*; the text of the comm., *yaṁ vā vaso yamāsyas* (explained as "having a mouth like Yama's"!); here emendation is a rather desperate undertaking; the translation follows the conjectures of our text ⌊but with *ikṣvākur* in **a**⌋. Ppp. reads, in **a–c**, *pūrvakṣvāko yaṁ vā tvā kuṣṭikāç ca ahiçyāvaso anusāricchas tenā-* etc. — too corrupt to give any help.

10. The head-paining, the tertian, ⌊and⌋ that which is constant, is hibernal — the *takmán*, O thou of power in every direction, do thou impel (*sū*) away downward.

The last half-verse is identical with v. 22. 3 **c**, **d**, above. The mss. read in **a** *çīrṣa-lokám* (p. *-ṣa∘lo-*); and the comm. understands it as two words, *çīrṣa lokam*, translating "they call thy head the third world (i.e. the sky, which is third world in respect to earth)"! Ppp. has *çīrṣālākaṁ*. The comm. reads in **c** *-vīryam*, with his customary disregard of accent; ⌊some mss. accent *viçvádhā*, thus suggesting *viçvádhāvīryam* (epithet of *takmā́nam*) as a possible, if inferior, variant⌋. Only two or three of the mss. give the accent *tṛ́tīyakam*, found elsewhere in the text (i. 25. 4: v. 22. 13), and SPP. follows the majority and adopts *tṛtī́-*. SPP. is also inconsistent in writing in *pada*-text *sadam∘dih* but in *saṁhitā*-text *sadandír;* Ppp. has instead *sadantī*.

40. To various divinities: for various blessings.

[*Brahman. — caturṛcam. bārhaspatyam uta vāiçvadevam. ānuṣṭubham: 1. parānuṣṭup triṣṭubh; 2. purahkakummaty upariṣṭādbṛhatī; 3. bṛhatīgarbhā; 4. 3-p. ārṣī gāyatrī.*]

Of this hymn only the first verse occurs in Pāipp. (in xix.). The comm. reports no *viniyoga*, but SPP. supplies one, finding it quoted in Pariç. 37. 4, in a ceremony of expiation for the loss (*nāça*) of a strainer; ⌊and again, in 37. 14, for use in case a certain earthen vessel (*upayāma*) falls from the hand⌋.

Translated: Griffith, ii. 297.

1. What that is defective (*chidrá*) of my mind, and what of my voice hath found (?*jagā́ma*) Sarasvatī enraged, let Bṛihaspati, in concord with all the gods, mend (*sam-dhā*) that.

The meaning of **b** is extremely doubtful. SPP. reads *sárasvatī* against the large majority of his authorities and all of ours, which have *-tīm*. Our *hárasvantam* was a conjecture, and perhaps not a particularly successful one. The translation given (tentatively) above implies *-tīm manyumatī́m*, while all the mss., the comm., and SPP., have *-mántam*. Ppp. reads *sarasvatī : manvavittaṁ jagāma*. Hardly a ms. gives an accent to *jagāma* (one of SPP's, probably by accident, and another, p.m.). Ppp. reads in **d** *sandadātu*. There are corresponding verses in VS. (xxxvi. 2) and Āp. (xiv. 16. 1), but they cast no light on **b**: VS. reads *yán me chidráṁ cákṣuṣo hṛ́dayasya mánaso vā́ 'titṛṇṇam bṛ́haspátir me tád dadhātu;* and Āp., *yan me manasaç chidraṁ yad vāco yac ca me hṛdaḥ : ayaṁ devo bṛhaspatiḥ saṁ tat siñcatu rādhasā.*

2. Do not ye, O waters, devastate (*pra-math*) our wisdom nor our *bráhman;* come ye flowing with easy flow, being invoked; [be] I of good wisdom, having splendor.

All the mss. accent *ā́pas* in **a**, and SPP. refuses to follow us in the obvious emendation to *āpas*, although the comm. also takes the word as vocative. At the end of **b**, the comm., followed by three of SPP's authorities, has *mathiṣṭa naḥ*. In **c**, the mss. read *çuṣyadā́* (p. the same), and the comm. understands it as *çuṣyat : ā;* SPP. emends by conjecture to *suṣyadā́s* (p. *su॰syadā́ḥ*), which is decidedly more successful than our *çuṣmadā́s*. The translation, however, ventures to emend yet further, to *suṣyádā́* (p. *su॰syádā : ā́*). Most of the mss. give *syannadhvam;* ⌊W's O. and SPP's carefully corrected Dc., s.m.,⌋ join with the comm. in *syanda-*, which stands in both printed texts. The translation, finally, implies our reading *úpahūtās*, against the mss., SPP., and the comm., which give *-tas* (*-to 'ham*); against, also, the Anukr.,* but making much better meter than if **c** is ended with *syandadhvam*. The mss. and SPP. have *sumédhās* (the *p.*-mss. wrongly *su॰médhā*); ⌊in the edition⌋ we ⌊should have⌋ rectified the accent ⌊so as to read⌋ *sumedhā́s*. *⌊The Anukr. would scan as 6 + 8 : 8 + 12; the Berlin text as 6 + 8 : 12 + 8.⌋

3. Do not ye injure our wisdom, nor our consecration, nor what ardor (*tápas*) is ours; be they propitious to us in order to [prolonged] life-time; let them become [our] propitious mothers.

The mss. have in **b** *hiṅsiṣṭam*, and SPP. does not follow our obviously acceptable emendation to *-ṣṭa*. The comm., too, has *-ṣṭam*, and explains it by calling ⌊into service⌋ that everlasting pair *dyāvāpṛthivī;* but, as alternative, he apparently goes on to anticipate the pair of Açvins from vs. 4; there is, however, a lacuna in the sole manuscript, cutting off this explanation almost at the beginning. In **c**, the mss. all have *sáṁsvanta ā́y-* (p. *sám॰svantaḥ !*), but the comm. *çaṅsantu*, explaining it as = *stuvantu;* ⌊SPP. reports that the text of the comm. is *çaṁsantu* and that the sole ms. of the commentary has actually *santu;*⌋ SPP. takes this, and alters it to *çáṁ santu;* our emendation to simple *santu*, suiting both sense and meter, is obviously to be accepted. The *pada*-mss. in general give *çivā́* in **c**; ⌊but one of W's and one of SPP's, each s.m., have *çivā́ḥ;*⌋ they all ⌊except perhaps W's L.⌋ have *çivā́ḥ* in **d**. There is no good reason why the Anukr. should call the verse *bṛhatīgarbhā*, since **c** can be read as eight syllables in either form.

4. That food (?*íṣ*), O Açvins, which, full of light, shall make us pass through the darkness, may ye give (*rā*) to us.

The verse corresponds to RV. i. 46. 6, and is translated from the RV. text, the AV. version being utterly corrupt, and offering a very noteworthy measure of what this nineteenth book can do in the way of corruption even of a text that is intelligibly handed down elsewhere. The ms. reading is *mā́ naḥ píparid açvinā jyótiṣmatī támas tiráḥ: tā́m asmāt rāsatām íṣum.* Our text differs from that of RV. only by reading *píparid* (which is an oversight for the *píparad* ⌊*Grammar* § 869 c⌋ of the RV.) and *rāsathām* (which is bad); ⌊RV. has *rāsāthām*, to be taken as augmentless *s*-aorist, 2d person dual middle⌋. The comm. differs from RV. by giving *mā́* at the beginning; ⌊his text, furthermore, has *rāsātām;* but his comment has *rāsāthān*, like RV.⌋; he understands *açvinā* correctly as vocative. SPP. clings to *rāsatām*, and thinks to make it answer by accenting *açvínā* (on the authority, ⌊probably⌋ accidental, of a single ms.). ⌊I suppose Whitney means to imply that, if SPP. intends to make *rāsatām* a 3d person dual imperative middle of the *s*-aorist, but from an *a*-stem, as explained at *Grammar* § 896, the form ought to be *rāsetām*, corresponding to the 3d singular *rāsatām* there noticed.⌋ There is really no way but to adopt the RV. text throughout; any attempt at compromise simply spoils the verse. The comm. takes *mā pīparat* as *pāram mā gamayatu*, and **b** as its antithesis, supplying *karotu* to *tiras;* and he refers at the end to *yā* as read *çākhāntare* (i.e., in RV.).

41. For some one's welfare.

[*Brahman.* — *ekarcam. mantroktatapodevatyam. trāiṣṭubham.*]

Not found in Pāipp. No *viniyoga.*
Translated: Griffith, ii. 298.

1. Desiring what is excellent, the heaven-finding seers in the beginning sat down in attendance upon (*upa-ni-sad*) ardor [and] consecration; thence [is] born royalty, strength, and force; let the gods make that submissive to this man.

Asmé 'to us' would be an acceptable emendation in **d**; ⌊but TS. has *asmāi*⌋. The comm. glosses *upaníṣedus* simply by *prāptās;* in his explanation of **c**, **d** there is a considerable lacuna. A corresponding verse is found in TS. (in v. 7. 4[3]; repeated without variation in TA. iii. 11. 9): *bhadrám páçyanta úpa sedur ágre tápo dīkṣā́m ṛ́ṣayaḥ suvarvídaḥ: tátaḥ kṣatrám bálam ójaç ca jātáṁ tád asmāi devā́ abhí sáṁ namantu.*

42. Extolling the bráhman etc.

[*Brahman.* — *catasras. mantroktabrahmadevatyam. 1. anuṣṭubh; 2. 3-av. kakummatī pathyāpañkti; 3. triṣṭubh; 4. jagatī.*]

Only fragments of this hymn are found in Pāipp.; ⌊Roth's Collation says that the hymn probably stood somewhere near the beginning⌋. No *viniyoga* is given.
Translated: Griffith, ii. 298.

1. The *bráhman* is invoker (*hótṛ*); the *bráhman* is the sacrifice; by the *bráhman* the sacrificial posts are set up; the officiating priest (*adhvaryú*) is born from the *bráhman;* within the *bráhman* is put the oblation.

In **a** all the authorities ⌊and so SPP.⌋ read *yajñā́s*, which might better have been left unchanged. In **b** the authorities have mostly *svā́ravāmitā́* (also *svā̀ravāmitā́*, and *sā́r-* or *sā̀ravāmitā́*), *pada*-text *svā̀ḥ : avāmitā́ ;* the comm., *svaragāmitā*, for which he gives a labored and worthless explanation; *svā́ravo mitā́ḥ* was our emendation, which is made certain by its occurrence in TB. ii. 4. 7[10] (in a verse otherwise corresponding with our vs. 2); and even SPP. follows it. In **d** the comm. has *brahmaṇi*, which suits better with *antar;* but the same sense is perhaps possible with *-ṇas*,* which is the universal reading. Then the mss. give *antárhite* (p. *antáḥ॰hite*); our edition emends to *antár hitám;* SPP. agrees so far as to give *antárhitam;* the comm. has either the one or the other (the absence of accent makes it impossible to say which); if *bráhmaṇas* is not altered to *-ṇi*, *antárhitam* is as good as necessary; otherwise, each is about equally acceptable. *⌊W. seems to have in mind such a construction as *tád antár asya sárvasya*, at Īçā Upanishad, vs. 5. If so, I do not see why he says that, if we read *bráhmaṇas*, we must also read *antárhitam.*⌋

2. The *bráhman* is the sacrificial spoons filled with ghee; by the *bráhman* is the sacrificial hearth set up (*ud-dhā*); and the *bráhman* is the essence (*tattvá*) of the sacrifice — the priests that are oblation-makers: ⌊to the slaughtered [victim] hail!⌋

To the verse corresponds one in TB. ii. 4. 7[10], which, however, has for **b** our 1 **b** (as noted above), and in **c** *yajñásya tántavaḥ*, and lacks the addition after **d**. In our text is left in **a** inadvertently *srucás*, which most of the mss. give; SPP. has the correct *srúcas* (so TB.). In **b**, our *pada*-mss. have *út॰hitā*, ⌊a word-division⌋ which is contrary to Prāt. iv. 63 and to the usage of the AV. hitherto; SPP. reads in his *pada*-text *úddhitā*, and makes no note upon the matter; ⌊he had in fact a note stating that his P.P.[2]J. also read *út॰hitā :* but, as appears from his "Corrections" to vol. iv., p. 446, his note was disordered in printing;⌋ the comm. has instead *uddhṛtā*. In **c** all the authorities give *yajñásya táttvaṁ ca* ⌊but W's P. *tánvaṁ*⌋, and SPP. retains *táttvaṁ*, without even making the necessary emendation of accent to *tattvám;* the comm. also supports it, and it is implied in the translation given above; our alteration to *yajñáç ca sattráṁ ca* is probably more venturesome than is called for. ⌊The place of the accent in the ms.-reading *táttvaṁ ca*, the Paris reading *tán-*, the un-Vedic look of *tattvam*, the *ṛ́caḥ prā́ñcas tántavas* of AV. xv. 3. 6, and the TB. parallel, all join in suggesting that the true reading is *yajñásya tántavas.*⌋ In the appendix to the verse, the comm. reads *sammitāya*.

3. To him who frees from distress I bring forward my devotion (*manīṣā́*), unto him who rescues well, choosing to myself his favor; accept, O Indra, this oblation; let the desires of the sacrificer be realized.

Or (at the end) 'come true.' A corresponding verse is found in TS. (in i. 6. 12[3]) and in MS. (in iv. 12. 3). In **a** both read *bharemā* ⌊p. *-ma*⌋ *manīṣā́m*, thus rectifying the meter; and Ppp. does the same; for **b**, TS. gives *oṣiṣṭhadā́vne sumatíṁ gṛṇānā́ḥ* ⌊good grammar (plural *-nā́s*) and good meter⌋; MS. *bhū́yiṣṭhadā́vne sumatím āvṛṇānáḥ* ⌊bad in both respects⌋. Very nearly all the AV. authorities give in **b** *-tím mā vṛṇānā́ḥ;* ⌊per contra, cf. note to xviii. 2. 3⌋. One would like to get rid of the superfluous *ā́* at the beginning of **b** by emending to *āçutrā́vṇe* ⌊*āçu-* would accord closely in sense with the *oṣiṣṭha-* of TS.⌋. ⌊Our *bhare* is evidently a corruption due to haplography, which has brought in its train the further corruption of *āvṛṇānā́ḥ* to *-náḥ.*⌋ In **c**, **d**, TS.MS.

agree throughout* with AV. ⌊save that MS. has *juṣasva* for *gṛbhāya*⌋. In **c**, Ppp. has *havyā;* only parts of the verse are left in its text; ⌊Roth says the first word is lost⌋. The comm. reads *sutrāmṇe* in **a**, *-tiṅ gṛṇānaḥ* (like TS.) in **b**, and *havyā* (like Ppp.) in **c**. *⌊In **c**, the *idám* of the Berlin text is an emendation, since all the mss. collated by W. before publication have *imám;* and it is confirmed by TS.MS., which give *idám*, and by W's subsequently collated O., and apparently also by his L. But SPP. prints *imám* without note of variant; and the comm. has *imam*, which he makes = *idam* in the sense of *idānīm!*⌋

4. Him who frees from distress, the bull of the worshipful, him that shines forth (*vi-rāj*), the first of the sacrifices (*adhvará*), the child of the waters, O Açvins, I call with prayer (*dhī*); do ye with Indra give me Indra-like force.

A corresponding verse in TS. (in i. 6. 12[3]) reads thus: *prá samrā́jam prathamám adhvarā́ṇām aṅhomúcaṁ vṛṣabháṁ yajñíyānām: apā́ṁ nápātam açvinā háyantam asmín nara indriyáṁ dhattam ójaḥ.* It helps us least in the critical part of our verse, where the mss. all read *açvínā huvé* ⌊*huve, havé*⌋ *dhíya* (p. *dhíyaḥ*) *indriyéṇa ta* (p. *te*) *indr-*. The translation follows our emendation (*açvinā*, with TS.; *dhiyé 'ndreṇa ma indr-*). SPP. follows the mss. Ppp. nearly agrees with them: *açvināu huve dhiya indriyeṇa na indriyaṁ dhattam ojaḥ.* The comm. has *dhiyam* and *dhattām* (but his text, according to SPP., reads *dhattam*).

43. To various gods: for attaining heaven.

[*Brahman.—aṣṭāu. bahudevatyam uta brahmadevatyam. 1–8. 3-av. çaṅkumatī pathyāpaṅkti.*]

Not found in Pāipp. No *viniyoga*.
Translated: Griffith, ii. 299.

1. Whither the *brahman*-knowers go, along with consecration, with ardor—thither let Agni conduct me; let Agni impart (*dhā*) to me wisdom: to Agni hail!

SPP. strangely prefers to read *medhā́ da-* in **d**, with a mere majority of his authorities, but with the comm. ⌊who gives *medhās*⌋; our mss. also are divided between *-dhā́* and *-dhā́ṁ*. In the *pada*-text, SPP. emends to *-dhā́ḥ;* the *pada*-mss. have *-dhā́* or *-dhā́ṁ*.

2. Whither the etc. etc.—thither let Vāyu conduct me; let Vāyu impart to me breaths: to Vāyu hail!

3. Whither the etc. etc.—thither let the sun conduct me; let the sun impart to me sight: to the sun hail!

4. Whither the etc. etc.—thither let the moon (*candrá*) conduct me; let the moon impart to me mind: to the moon hail!

5. Whither the etc. etc.—thither let Soma conduct me; let Soma impart to me milk: to Soma hail!

The comm. has a *lacuna* including all the explanations of verse 4, and part of the text of verse 4 and of this.

6. Whither the etc. etc. — thither let Indra conduct me; let Indra impart to me strength: to Indra hail!

7. Whither the etc. etc. — thither let the waters conduct me; let immortality (*amṛ́ta*) approach (*upa-sthā*) me: to the waters hail!

Our *nayantu* in **c** is the obviously necessary emendation of *nayatu* of all the mss., which SPP., after his manner, retains. The comm. does not have occasion to quote the word; but his text also, according to SPP., reads *nayatu.* ⌊The faulty assimilation of the original *nayantu* to the *nayatu* which obtains throughout all the other verses of the sequence, is precisely paralleled by the *gachati* (so all authorities) after *ā́pas* at xv. 7. 3.⌋

8. Whither the etc. etc. — thither let Brahmán conduct me; let Brahmán impart to me *bráhman:* to Brahmán hail!

The comm. explains *brahmán* by *jagatsraṣṭā hiraṇyagarbhaḥ*, and *bráhman* by *svasvarūpabhūtaṁ çrutādhyayanajanyaṁ tejo vā.*

44. With an ointment: against diseases etc.

[*Bhṛgu.—daça. mantroktāñjanadevatyam. (8, 9. vāruṇe.) ānuṣṭubham: 4. 4-p. çaṅkumaty uṣṇih; 5. 3-p. nicṛd viṣamā gāyatrī.*]

⌊Partly prose: verses 4 and 5.⌋ Found also in Pāipp. xv. Used, according to the comm., with an ointment amulet, by Nakṣ.K. 19, in a *mahāçānti* ceremony called *nāirṛtī*, when one is seized by *nirṛti* (destruction). ⌊Verse 4 is quoted in *sakalapāṭha* by Kāuç. at 47. 16, to accompany the taking of a staff in a witchcraft ceremony.⌋

Translated: Griffith, ii. 300. — He very pertinently notes that this hymn closely resembles in parts iv. 9. See W's notes thereon.

1. Thou art an extender of life-time; all-healing art thou called; so, O ointment, do thou [make] wealfulness; make, O ye waters, weal [and] fearlessness.

The translation follows our text, which is variously emended. In **b**, the mss. and comm. and SPP. read *vipram bheṣajám;* the comm. explains *vipram* as *prīṇayitṛ* (as if it were somehow *priyam*) *vipravac chuddhaṁ vā.* Ppp. gives *vipre.* In **c**, all have *çaṁtāte*, glossed by the comm. with *çaṁrūpa* ⌊the ms. of the comm. actually has *-pam*⌋. In **d**, all accent *ā́pas*, and also (with one accidental exception) *kṛtám;* but one of our mss. (probably also by accident) gives *kṛtá*, which we adopted, with emendation to *kṛta;* ⌊if I understand W's Collation Book, his B. has *kṛta*, without accent;⌋ SPP. is satisfied with emending to *kṛtam*, as if *āñjana* and *āpas* could somehow be construed together as a dual subject. Part of the mss. have *ucyate* at end of **b**. The *pada*-mss. read *çaṁtāte* without division. Ppp. has for second half-verse *yad āñjani draṁ çaṁtāte açināyo bhavaṁ kṛtam*, which is too corrupt to be of any assistance.

2. What the jaundice is, the *jāyányа*, the limb-splitter, the *visálpaka* — all *yákṣma* from thy limbs let the ointment expel (*nir-han*) out.

The mss. make very bad work with the last pāda, nearly all (the variations are of no account) giving *barhir nirahantv* (p. *barhiḥ : niḥ : ahantu*); SPP. makes the same emendation that we had made; and ⌊it is confirmed by⌋ Ppp. and the comm., ⌊which⌋ have the same. ⌊Three or four of SPP's authorities, including two reciters, gave *bahis.*⌋

In **a**, the comm. strangely reads and explains *jyāyān yaḥ;* Ppp. presents *jāyāṁyo.* For *visalpakas* (which SPP. reads here also, as in vi. 127 and ix. 8), the comm. gives *visarpakas*, explaining it as *vividhaṁ saraṇaçīlo vraṇaviçeṣaḥ;* Ppp. has *viçalyakas.*

3. The ointment, born on the earth, excellent, giving life to men — let it make [me] unperishing, of chariot-swiftness, free from offense.

Ppp. reads in **d** *rathajūtam.* The comm. thinks the word may mean either *rathavadvegagāminam* or *rathavantam.*

4. O breath, rescue thou breath; O life-breath (*ásu*), be gracious to life-breath; O destruction, free us from the fetters of destruction.

⌊Prose.⌋ The comm. follows a different division in verses 4–7, making of them but three verses,* and of the whole hymn but nine. The method of the mss. and the Anukr. is plainly decidedly preferable; it is followed also by SPP. One does not see any justification for the division by the Anukr. of the last five words of this verse into two pādas, with five syllables (*çañku-*) in the closing one. ⌊It counts 7 + 7 : 7 + 5.⌋ Ppp. reads *trāyasva aso 'save.* The comm. has *mām* instead of *nas.* About half the authorities give at the beginning *prā́ṇas.* ⌊For the citation of the vs. by Kāuç., see introd. to this hymn, and cf. especially p. 897, ¶ 3.⌋ *⌊Our 4,5**ab** = his 4; our 5**cd**,6**ab** = his 5; our 6**cd**,7 = his 6.⌋

5. Embryo of the river art thou, flower of the lightnings; the wind [thy] breath, the sun [thine] eye, from the sky [thy] milk.

⌊Prose.⌋ SPP. and the comm. read *púṣpam*, and all the mss. probably are to be regarded as having it; *ṣpa* and *ṣya* are practically indistinguishable in the mss. Ppp. also gives *puṣpam.* At the beginning all the mss. have *síndho* (p. *síndho íti*); even SPP. emends to *síndhos*, the comm. giving it. The comm. curiously explains *vidyutām puṣpam* by *vṛṣṭyudakam:* one can hardly help suspecting a misreading. The Anukr. scans the "verse" (restoring the *a* of *asi*) as 6 + 5 : 12 = 23; its definition is far from acceptable. ⌊Bloomfield discusses the vs., AJP. xvii. 405.⌋

6. O divine ointment, thou from the three-peaked [mountain], do thou protect me all about; the herbs do not surpass (*tṛ*) thee — those from abroad and those from the mountains.

All the mss. ⌊save one of SPP's⌋ read *dévāñjanam* (p. *déva∘āñj-*) *trāίkakudam;* SPP. emends the former to *-na*, but not the latter to *-da*, although this is as indisputably vocative as the other; the comm. ⌊with one of SPP's mss.⌋ makes the same difference, though he regards *trāikakudam* as vocative (*he trāik-*). Ppp. reads *devāñjani trāikakuda.* ⌊As to the rarity of neuter vocatives, see my *Noun-Inflection*, p. 339.⌋ The great majority of mss. accent *bāhyā́s;* SPP. reads *bā́hyās.* The comm. understands the word as meaning "from other localities than the mountains." Our emendation to *bāṭyā́s*, supported by an article ⌊2. *vāṭyá* 'cultivated'⌋ in the major Pet. Lex. ⌊vi. 903⌋ is withdrawn by the omission of that article in the minor Lex. Ppp. reads corruptly *bāhyaṁ parvatyā.*

7. The demon-slayer, disease-expeller, hath crept down over the middle here, expelling all diseases, making portents vanish from here.

The change to masculine here in **b** is obscure and questionable; emendation to *-cā́tanam* is desirable; it would allow *idám* to be understood as 'this [ointment],' which is easier and more natural. Ppp., too, has *-cātanaṁ*, which gives the emendation sufficient support.* Ppp. has for **a** *vīraṁ madhyam avāsṛjat.* The *pada*-mss. commit the egregious inconsistency of reading *cātáyan : nāçáyat* in **c**, **d**; SPP. emends in *pada*-text to *cātáyat.** Ppp. has in **d** *nāçayatam ivāhitā.* ⌊In **c** of the Berlin ed., correct *sárvaç* to *sárvāç.*⌋

*⌊Both editions print *rakṣohā́mīvacā́tanaḥ*, and the *pada*-reading is *rakṣaḥ॰hā́ : amīva॰cā́tanaḥ.* Whitney, doubtless by oversight, neglects to say how he would emend *rakṣohā́* to make a corresponding neuter of it, and the question is a very troublesome one (for details, see *Noun-Inflection*, p. 478 end, p. 479). The neuter form would properly be *-hắ';* but none such is quotable, so far as I know, unless here. May it be that we have here that very form, *-hắ'* (neuter), concealed in the combination *-hā́mīva-*, and that the misunderstanding of it as *-hā́* (masculine) *amīva-* led to a corruption of an original *-cā́tanam* into *-cā́tanaḥ* and also of an original *pada*-reading *cātáyat* into *cātáyan?* If so, all would be in harmony.⌋

8. Much untruth, O king Varuṇa, doth man (*pū́ruṣa*) say here; from that sin (*áṅhas*) do thou free us, O thou of thousand-fold heroism.

The mss. vary between *rā́jan* and *rājan*, and between *ánṛtam*, *anṛ́tam*, and *ánṛ́tam.* The great majority accent at the end *páryaṅhasaḥ*, and all the *pada*-mss. have *pári॰ aṅhasaḥ.* SPP. reads at the beginning *bahv ìdám*, after the manner of the Sāma-Veda; we emended to *ìdám*, because that is the Atharvan practice (cf. note to Prāt. iii. 65, p. 499), against which the concurrence even of all the mss. ⌊save W's I.⌋, as here, ought not to count. Ppp. reads in **b** *puruṣaḥ.*

9. In that we have said O waters, O inviolable [kine], O Varuṇa, from that sin do thou free us, O thou of thousand-fold heroism.

That is, if we have called these divinities to witness an untruth: cf. the nearly equivalent vii. 83. 2 **c–e**. The translation implies emendation to *ághnyās; váruṇa*, which can be only vocative, proves each of its predecessors such; the comm. understands all the three as vocative, and paraphrases [*he*] *āpo yūyaṁ jānīdhve, he aghnyā yūyam mama cittaṁ jānīdhve*, etc. Ppp. reads in **b** *varuṇena yad.* Our mss. read again *páryaṅh-* (p. *pári॰aṅhasaḥ*), and so apparently do SPP's, although he does not distinctly say so; ⌊his note to vs. 8 (note 2, p. 455) perhaps makes such an implication⌋.

10. Both Mitra and Varuṇa went forth after thee, O ointment; they, having gone far after thee, brought thee back for enjoyment (*bhogá*).

All the authorities ⌊save W's E. and one of SPP's reciters⌋, and Ppp. also, give at the end *púnar ohatu;* but the *pada*-mss. give *púnaḥ : rohatu*, which is a blunder, since the corresponding *saṁhitā* would be *púnā rohatu* ⌊which W's E. in fact has⌋. SPP. emends to *púnar ó "hatuḥ* (p. *púnaḥ : ā́ : ūhatuḥ*), and the translation follows this, rather than our own nearly equivalent and equally acceptable emendation to *púnar ó "hatām.* ⌊Whitney here overlooks the lack of accent on the *oh-*: the Berlin text, the text of W's Collation Book, and his *Index*, under 1 *ūh*, all give *ohatām* without accent. Root 1 *ūh* does not appear to be quotable with *ā́*, and it would seem that SPP's emendation (root *vah* with *ā́*) must of need be preferred.⌋ The comm., ⌊with his text, and with SPP's reciter V., who accented *púnar āhatuḥ*,⌋ gives *punar āhatuḥ* (= *punar āgantavyam ity ūcatuḥ!*). ⌊We might better render *bhogāya* by 'for our use.'⌋ Half the mss. accent with us *ánu préy-* in **b**; SPP. gives *anu*, with the *pada*-text (*anu॰préyatuḥ*).

45. With an ointment etc.: for various objects.

[*Bhṛgu.* — *daça.* *1–5. āñjanadevatyam; 6–10. mantroktadevatyam. 1, 2. anuṣṭubh; 3–5. triṣṭubh; 6–10. 1-av. mahābṛhatī* (*6. virāj; 7–10. nicṛt*).]

⌊Prose in part, vss. 6–10.⌋ Found (except vs. 9) also in Pāipp. xv., next after our 44. The practical use is, according to the comm., the same with that of 44.

Translated: Griffith, ii. 301.

1. Bringing together witchcraft to the house of the witchcraft-maker, as it were debt from debt, do thou, O ointment, crush in the ribs of the hostile eye-conjurer.

With the second half-verse compare ii. 7. 5 **c**, **d**. The first half seems to mean "paying back or returning . . . as debt upon debt, or repeated debt"; this is, except for the sense given to the ablative *ṛṇāt* (which he explains by *ṛṇāt . . . bhītaḥ*, or, alternatively, *ṛṇadātur uttamarṇāt:* both wrongly), the understanding of the comm. ⌊Griffith says: "*As debt from debt:* as a man returns to his creditor a part of what he owes him."⌋ Many of the authorities give *riṇā́d riṇám* (Ppp. has *ṛṇ-*); and some accent the first syllable, *ri-* or *ṛ-*. At the end of **a**, nearly all have *saṁnayám* (p. *sam॰nayám*), but the comm. *saṁnayan*, which SPP. adopts (*saṁnáyan*) and which is followed in the translation above, as being a smaller alteration of the original than our emendation *sáṁ naya*, and at least equally acceptable in point of sense. In **c** the comm. has the bad reading *cakṣur mitrasya*. Ppp. ends **d** with *āñjanam*.

2. What evil-dreaming [is] in us, what in [our] kine, and what in our house, also the . . . of one hostile, let him that is unfriendly take upon himself (*prati-muc*).

Both sense and meter require the emendation in **d** of *priyás* to *ápriyas*, and the comm. has the latter, but all the authorities,* and Ppp. (*durhārdaṣ priya pra-*), and SPP. give the former. In **c**, the general reading of the mss. is *ánāmagas tvám* (p. *ánāmagaḥ : tvám*); for *tváṁ ca* is found *tvā́ṁ ca, táṁ ca, táṁta,* ⌊*tvác ca, tá ca, tac ca*⌋. SPP. accepts *ánāmagas tám*, but what sense he can possibly attach to the words does not appear. Ppp. gives *māmagatasya dur-*. The comm. reads *anāmakas tac ca*, which is equally impossible; and he makes a senseless explanation of *anāmakas: īdṛṅnāmā tādṛṅnāme 'ty evaṁ nāmarahitaḥ;* and he falsely regards *durhārdas* as a nom. sing. qualified by *anāmakas*. Our conjecture, *anāmayatváṁ ca d-*, is very unsatisfactory, in regard both to meter and to sense; *anāgastvám* 'guiltlessness' would make a good *anuṣṭubh* pāda, and be very near to the reading of the mss.; but it would be, equally with *anāmayatvam*, discordant with *duṣvápnyam*, and would require *priyás* in **d**. ⌊Ppp. reads *muñcatā* at the end.⌋

*⌊The reciter V., curiously, has as an alternative, *durhā́rdo 'priyás*, which (the accent being wrong) is neither one thing nor the other, but may well be taken as supporting the comm's reading *ápriyas*, as against *priyás;* the true *saṁhitā*-reading would then be *durhā́rdó 'priyaḥ*.⌋

⌊The solution of this desperate passage seems to me to be suggested by 57. 5 below, of which the first part is identical with our **a**, **b** here, and of which the second part begins with *anāsmākás tád* and ends (nearly like v. 14. 3 **d**) with *niṣkám iva* (pronounce *niṣkéva*) *práti muñcatām*. In our **c**, **d** I would read *anāsmākás tád durhā́rdó 'priyaḥ práti muñcatām* (*pada*-reading *duḥ॰hā́rdaḥ : ápriyaḥ*), and render 'that let him who is not of us, the evil-hearted, the unfriendly, put upon himself.' The *tád* is supported by the comm., and in a measure by SPP's D.V. and Cs.; the *ápriyas*, by the comm. and V. (as above) and the meter; and *anāsmākás* comes near to the ms.-readings, and, indeed, considering the *ánāmakas* of the living reciter V. and of the comm., is not ill supported.⌋

⌊It remains to note that no valid objection can be taken against making a nom. sing. of *durhā́rda-s:* its use as such is a natural way of avoiding the form from the consonantal stem (which was as much of a stumbling-block to the ancient Hindu as it is to the modern tyro in Sanskrit), and is entirely analogous to the use of *hṛ́dayam* rather than *hṛ́d* (cf. my *Noun-Inflection*, p. 471). The comm. is accordingly right in saying here *durhārdo duṣṭacittaḥ*, as he was also in glossing the *suhā́rt* of ii. 7. 5 by *çobhanahārdaḥ sumanaskaḥ*. The nom. *durhā́rda-s* is a form of transition to the *a*-declension, with *durhā́rd-am* (so viii. 3. 25) as its point of departure (cf. *durhā́rdān* of the mss. at xix. 28. 8); just so the later *pā́da-s* (from *pā́d-am*) replaces the older *pā́t* (*Noun-Inflection*, p. 471).⌋

⌊Of the older nom. sing. masc. or fem., however, the true form is *suhā́r*, p. *su°hā́ḥ*, of which traces, albeit scanty, are found in the Veda: one is at MS. iv. 2. 5, p. 26[19], *priyā́ naḥ suhā́r ṇaḥ;* and another is at AV. ii. 7. 5, where both ed's read *yáḥ suhā́rt téna naḥ sahá*. Here the *saṁhitā*-authorities taken together are divided between *suhā́rt téna* (so 11) and *suhā́t téna* (so 6); but the *pada*-authorities (7 out of 8) give *su°hā́t*, the notable exception being the *çrotriya* K., who recited the true form *su°hā́ḥ*. The *saṁhitā*-form for this ought to be *suhā́s* (*téna*), and possibly this form is concealed in the reading *suhā́tténa* of Sm. etc. If not, then (since *rtt* = *rt: Gram.* § 232) we may regard the combination *suhā́rt t-* as representing *suhā́r t-*, nom. *suhā́r*, with breach of the rule of sandhi requiring the change of *suhā́r* to *suhā́s* before *t-*. The motive for this breach was perhaps to avoid disguising still further the form *suhā́r*, itself extremely rare and none too easily recognized; and the motive is perhaps as clear as it is in the case of *aves avet*, *ajāis ajāit*, etc., cited by W., *Gram.* § 555 a.—The nom. *suhā́rt* seems to be grammatical and not intolerable in the texts, and to be unparalleled (cf. *Noun-Inflection*, p. 472).⌋ ⌊☞ See p. 1046.⌋

3. Increasing from the force of the refreshment of the waters, born out of Agni Jātavedas — may the ointment that is four-heroed, that is of the mountains, make the quarters, the directions, propitious to thee.

In **a**, *ūrjás* might, of course, be ablative, coördinate with *ójasas;* the whole expression is too obscure to help the construction by the sense. The comm. reads *ūrjam;* Ppp. combines *ūrjo 'jaso*, and has in **c** *parvataṁ*. The Anukr. does not heed the redundant syllable in **c**.

4. The four-heroed ointment is bound to thee; be all the quarters free from fear for thee; firm shalt thou stand, like Savitar desirable; let these people (*víças*) render thee tribute.

In **a**, **b** Ppp. combines *badhyatā "ñj-*, *diço 'bhayās*. In **c**, the mss. ⌊with one or two exceptions⌋ read *cā́ryà i-* (p. *ca : āryàḥ*); SPP. alters the accent to *cā́rya* (p. *ca : ā́ryaḥ*); our emendation to *vā́ryas* ⌊W's B. has *vāryà i-*⌋ is not absolutely necessary, yet certainly a plausible improvement; and it is in a certain measure supported by Ppp., which gives *vāri imā;* the translation above implies it. The comm. understands *arya*, vocative, rendering it by *svāmin*. In **d** all the mss. have *víças* ⌊but W's E. seems to have *díças*⌋, and our substitution of *díças* was hardly called for; but Ppp. favors it, reading *diço bhriyante.* The comm. gives two explanations for the strange epithet *caturvīra*, showing that he is merely guessing what its sense might possibly be. We have in **d** again an extra syllable of which the Anukr. takes no notice.

5. Use thou one as ointment; make one an amulet; bathe with one; drink one of them; let the four-heroed one protect us about from the four destructive bonds of seizure (*gráhi*).

All the mss.* have at the beginning *ā́kṣva*, which the *pada*-text leaves undivided; SPP. goes so far as to emend the latter to *ā́ : akṣva*, but is unwilling to follow us in reading *ā́ 'ñkṣva*, although *akṣva* is no possible form, and the comm. agrees with our emendation. Ppp. reads *ākṣakaṁ maṇ-*. In **b** the mss. give *ékenā́pivātkam*, and the *pada*-mss. resolve it into *ékena : ápi : vā : ékam.* Our emendation to *ékena píbāt 'kam* is evidently just what is required; but SPP. chooses to retain *ékenā́*, and so reads ⌊in *pada*-text⌋ *ékena : ā́ : piba*, remarking that "if RW. had discerned the *ā́* after *ékena*, their very correct emendation would have been free from the defect of unnecessarily changing the ancient accent of the *saṁhitā*-text." This reads like a joke, considering how the text of book xix. (not to speak of previous books) abounds in gross errors of accentuation, and how often we and he have been compelled to emend it — for example, in the preceding verse, where the "ancient accent" *cāryà* was changed by him to *cā́rya.* ⌊Apart from this passage,⌋ the compound *ā* + *pā* does not occur in the Atharvan, and, although it is not unknown, it would be distinctly out of place here. The version of the pāda in Ppp. is totally corrupt: *çvāçīkenapavīkam eṣām.* The comm. reads *ekenā 'vivekam eṣām*, and labors, with his usual ill-success, to devise an explanation of *avivekam.* To *ekam* etc. he supplies *āñjanam;* as his reading gets rid of the fourth, he connects the first three with the "three-peaked mountain" from which the ointment is derived: *triṣu parvatakakutsū 'tpannāni!* Apparently the fourfold-ness is related in some way or other to the "four-heroed"-ness. In **d**, the comm. commits the extraordinary blunder of taking *grāhyās* as gerundive: *grahītavyā āñjanamayā oṣadhayaḥ!* and this compels him to change *pātu* to *pāntu.* The *pada*-mss. (except one of SPP's, p.m.) have *grā́hyā*, they also failing to recognize the not uncommon noun *grā́hi;* SPP. makes the necessary emendation to *-hyāḥ.* *⌊But SPP's Sm., *ākṣvā́ikam.*⌋

6. Let Agni favor (*av*) me with fire (? *agní*), in order to breath, to expiration, to life-time, to splendor, to force, to brilliancy, to well-being, to welfare: hail!

The comm. is uncertain whether by the second *agni* (*agninā*) is meant *agnitvadharmeṇa*, or *pāvakādiguṇakena svamūrtyantareṇā 'gninā sahitaḥ.* All the mss. accent *subhūtáye* here, ⌊but *súbhūtyā* at iii. 14. 1 (cf. *Grammar* § 1288 e): SPP. accents here *-táye*, with the mss.; but the Berlin text *sú-* here, in conformity with both editions and the mss. at iii. 14. 1⌋. Ppp. reads *mā agninā.*

7. Let Indra favor me with what is Indra's (*indriyá*), in order to breath etc. etc.

The comm. gives a double interpretation of *indriya.* Ppp. again has *mā indriy-.*

8. Let Soma favor me with what is Soma's (*sāúmya*), in order to breath etc. etc.

The comm. explains *sāúmyena* as *somatvasampādakena dharmeṇa jagadāpyāyanakāritvādidharmeṇa.*

9. Let Bhaga favor me with fortune (*bhága*), in order to breath etc. etc.

The comm. has here a lacuna, embracing the commentary to this verse and the text of the next. ⌊The verse is wanting in Ppp., as noted above.⌋

10. Let the Maruts favor me with troops, in order to breath etc. etc.

Ppp. reads this time *suprabhūtaye*. It is possible to make out of these prose "verses" the number of syllables demanded by the Anukr. Perhaps the modification *nicṛt* belongs only to vss. 7–9 (the manuscripts are discordant and unclear).

⌊Here ends the fifth *anuvāka*, with 12 hymns and 74 verses.⌋

46. With and to an amulet called ástṛta 'unsubdued.'

[*Prajāpati.* — *saptakam. astṛtamaṇidāivatam. trāiṣṭubham: 1. 5-p. madhyejyotiṣmatī triṣṭubh; 2. 6-p. bhurik çakvarī; 3, 7. 5-p. pathyāpañkti; 4. 4-p.**; *5. 5-p. atijagatī; 6. 5-p. uṣṇiggarbhā virāḍ jagatī.*] *⌊The Anukr. says: *indrāya tvā* (vs. 4) *catuṣpadā: asminmaṇāv* (vs. 5) *iti pañcapadā jagatī* (Berlin ms., *atijagatī*): most unsatisfactory; and why should vs. 4 be defined as *4-p.*?⌋

Found also in Pāipp. iv. (in the verse-order 1, 2, 6, 5, 3, 4, 7). Used, according to the comm., by one desiring strength, in a *mahāçānti* ceremony called *mārudgaṇī*, with a threefold amulet named *astṛta*, being so prescribed by Nakṣ.K. 19.

Translated: Ludwig, p. 462; Griffith, ii. 302. — See also Bergaigne-Henry, *Manuel*, p. 165.

1. Prajāpati bound thee first [as] unsubdued (*ástṛta*), in order to heroism; it do I bind for thee in order to life-time, to splendor, and to force and to strength: let the unsubdued one defend thee.

Astṛta is literally 'not laid low.' In the two occurrences above (i. 20. 4: v. 9. 7) it is accented on the final; but, as *ástṛta* would be the normal accent, it is left here unchanged in our text, as well as in SPP's. The *pada*-texts read in **a** *badhnāt*, but that is no reason why we should not understand it as *abadhnāt*, and our text (not SPP's) so prints it. Our text further emends at the beginning of **c** the *tát* of the mss. to *táṁ*, as required by the gender of *astṛtas*. The omission of *badhnāt* in **a**, and of *várcase* in the second half-verse, would make an *anuṣṭubh* (apart from the refrain); but the meter throughout the hymn is unusually careless of regularity, and Ppp. has both words, reading in **a**, **b** *badhnātu prathama saṁbhṛtaṁ*, and in **d**, **e** combining *varcaso 'jase* and *ca astṛtas*. ⌊With **c**, **d**, cf. iv. 10. 7 **c**, **d**.⌋

2. Standing upright, defend thou this man unremittingly, O unsubdued one; let not the Paṇis, the sorcerers, damage thee; as Indra the barbarians, [so] do thou shake down them that fight [us]; overpower and scatter (*ví*) all our rivals: let the unsubdued one defend thee.

All the mss. ⌊with unimportant variants⌋ read in **a** *tiṣṭhanta;* SPP. emends to *tiṣṭhatu*, because the comm. reads the latter; our *tíṣṭhan* suits the connection decidedly better. ⌊The vocative *astṛta* and the *tvā* are⌋ perhaps sufficient reasons for our altering the *rákṣann* of the mss. (also of the comm. and Ppp.) into *rakṣa*, and the translation follows ⌊the printed text of Berlin⌋. To humor his *tiṣṭhatu*, SPP. changes the following *ástṛta* (mss. *ástṛte 'mám;* p. *ástṛta : imám*) to *ástṛtas* ⌊but only in the *pada*-text, so that his *saṁhitā* does not agree therewith⌋; our text simply emends to *astṛta* ⌊accentless⌋; the comm. also regards the word as vocative. Ppp. has instead *saṁbhṛta*, ⌊and, if I understand Roth's Collation, combines it with a following corrupt *imanu*, so as to read *saṁbhṛte 'manu*⌋; and, in **c**, Ppp. has *indrī 'va*. The majority of mss. accent *pṛtanyátas*. The Anukr. apparently means us to scan thus: 11 + 4 + 11 : 15 + 8 + 8 = 57.

3. Whom even a hundred, hurling (*pra-hṛ*), smiting down, have not subdued (*stṛ*), to him Indra committed sight, breath, also strength: let the unsubdued one defend thee.

In **a**, the *pada*-mss. wrongly divide *ca : ná*, and SPP. follows them. In **b**, about a third of SPP's authorities read *vighnántas;* Ppp. has *bhijanto*. The *yám* that follows it is our emendation, plainly suggested by the meter, the requirement of the sense, and the accent of the verb; but the comm. and Ppp. agree with the mss. in lacking it. At the end of **b** our *tastriré* is an emendation (now supported by Ppp., which has the same reading) for the *tastiré* of the mss. (one or two have *tasthiré*), the comm. ⌊but the ms. has *nirastire*⌋, and SPP.; the comm. explains it as = *tastarire*, with Vedic omission of part of the ending: this is of his usual degree of insight; what SPP. would do with his *tastiré* is hard to see; the emendation to *tastriré* is obvious and unquestionable. For *tásmin* in **c** Ppp. gives *yasmin*. The mss. in general read *páryadanta* (p. *pári : adanta*), but two or three of ours, with the comm's text (SPP.), *-ntaḥ cá-*; our emendation to *páry adatta*, now ratified by Ppp., is accepted by SPP. The comm's explanation implies *pari yad antaç ca-*; and he takes the *yat* as a form of root *i* (*pari yat paryagamayat paripūritavān*)! With the insertion of *yám* in **b**, the verse is a good *pañkti*, as defined by the Anukr.

4. With Indra's defense (*várman*) we surround thee, who became over-king of the gods; let all the gods lead thee forward again; let the unsubdued one defend thee.

A part of the verse ⌊pāda b, it would seem?⌋ has fallen out in Ppp.; ⌊this has *dhāmāi* for *dhāpayāmo*⌋. The meter is insufficiently defined by the Anukr. (13 + 11 : 11 + 8 = 43): ⌊see introduction, above⌋.

5. In this amulet [are] a hundred and one heroisms; a thousand breaths in this unsubdued one; a tiger, do thou attack (*abhi-sthā*) all [our] rivals; whoso shall fight against thee, be he inferior (*ádhara*): let the unsubdued one defend thee.

SPP. reads in **b** *asmin;* our *asmín* is given by a small minority of the mss.; the majority have *ásmin*, some *asmin*, one *asmìn*. ⌊The vs. (11 + 10 : 11 + 11 + 8 = 51) is a *triṣṭubh* (defective in **b**), with the refrain added: see introd.⌋

6. Snatched out of ghee, rich in honey, rich in milk, thousand-breathed, hundred-wombed (?*-yóni*), vigor-imparting, both wealful and delightful, both rich in refreshment and rich in milk — let the unsubdued one defend thee.

⌊We had **a** at 33. 2 **a**, above: cf. v. 28. 14.⌋ Ppp. reads at the beginning *ullabdhas;* one or two of SPP's mss. have *dúrluptas* ⌊cf. note to xviii. 2. 3⌋, *úrluptas*. In **b**, all the authorities (save one or two) give *sahásram prāṇás* or *sahásra prāṇáḥ*

(p. *sahásram : prāṇáḥ*); * but the comm. implies (perhaps only by his usual neglect of accent) *sahásraprāṇas*, and SPP. reports one of his mss. as giving the same; and he accordingly follows us in adopting it; Ppp. reads with the mss. ⌊*sahasraṁ prāṇaḥ*⌋. The comm. gives an extraordinary explanation of *-yoni* in **b**: *yoniçabdena çatrusaṁgamananimittaṁ çatruviyojanasādhanaṁ vā balaṁ vivakṣyate*: that is, without any regard to the established meanings of *yoni*, he takes it here as a mere representative of the radical sense of the root *yu* 'unite' or of the root *yu* 'separate'—he does not venture to decide which! The metrical description of the Anukr. is fairly correct (11 + 12 : 7 + 8 + 8 = 46). *⌊These corruptions of the true *sahásraprāṇas* are noteworthy as examples of faulty half-way assimilation of a reading to something similar in the immediate context: here the cause of the confusion is plainly the *sahásram prāṇā́ḥ* of vs. 5 **b**.⌋

7. That thou mayest be superior, free from rivals, rival-slaying—mayest be controler of thy fellows—so may Savitar make thee: let the unsubdued one defend thee.

The mss., and SPP., read in **a** *uttarás* (p. *ut°taráḥ*); our text makes the necessary emendation to *úttaras*. In **c**, the same read *asat;* we emended to *asas*, and ought to have gone a step further and accented *ásas*, since the following *táthā* shows that the three preceding pādas are all alike under the government of *yáthā;* Ppp. has in **c**, with us, *asas*. Ppp. further combines *'so 'sapatnaḥ* in **a–b**, and reads *tvā abhi* in **e**.

47. To night: for protection.

[*Gopatha.—navakam. mantroktarātridevatyam. ānuṣṭubham: 1. pathyābṛhatī; 2. 5-p. anuṣṭubgarbhā parātijagatī; 6. purastādbṛhatī; 7. 3-av. 6-p. jagatī.*]

Found also in Pāipp. vi. According to the comm., hymns 47 and 48 form a single "sense-hymn" (*arthasūkta*), and 49 and 50 another; and their use is prescribed in Pariç. 4. 3–5, as of two hymns, in a ceremony of worship of night.

Translated: Ludwig, p. 467; Zimmer, p. 179; Griffith, ii. 303.

1. O night, the earthly space (*rájas*) hath been filled with the father's orderings (*dhā́man*); great, thou spreadest thyself (*vi-sthā*) to the seats of the sky; bright darkness comes on (*ā-vṛt*).

The verse is VS. xxxiv. 32, and is also found as first verse of a *khila* (Aufr., p. 682) to RV. x. 127, in both places without variant. ⌊It is quoted in Nirukta, Dāivatakāṇḍa iii. 29.⌋ Ppp. reads in **b** *pitaraṣ prāyu dh-*, and in **c** *sudhāṅsi*. The comm. holds 'the father' in **b** to designate the "skyey world" (*dyuloka*), quoting the commonplace *dyāuḥ pitā pṛthivī mātā* in support of it; *dhāmabhis* he glosses with *sthānāiḥ saha*, and *tveṣam* with *dīpyamānam*. ⌊For *dhā́mabhis* we might perhaps better say 'by *or* in accordance with the orderings'; but Griffith understands it as 'wondrous works.'⌋

2. She of whom the further limit is not seen, nor what separates; in her everything that stirs goes to rest (*ni-viç*); uninjured may we, O wide darksome night, attain thy further limit—may we, O excellent one, attain thy further limit.

In **a**, SPP. accents *dádṛçe*, without adding any note as to ms.-readings; it is perhaps merely an oversight, as all our mss. save one have plainly *dadṛçé*, and this is the Atharvan accent (cf. x. 8. 8), against RV. *dádṛçe*, which is wholly anomalous. Ppp. reads *yoyavad*, and, in **b**, *ni miṣate rejati;* its **c** is wholly corrupt. The comm. connects *na yoyuvat* with what follows, and explains it thus: *na vibhajamānaṁ vibhaktaṁ nā 'sīt kiṁ tu viçvaṁ ekākāram evā 'bhūt.* The RV. *khila*, in vs. 4, has pāda **e**, twice repeated.

3. The men-watching lookers that are thine, O night, ninety [and] nine — eighty are they [and] eight, also seven [and] seventy of thine;—

In **b**, SPP's *pada*-mss. have *navatīḥ.* In **c**, the decided majority accent *áçītis*, and all *santi*, which SPP. emends to *sánti*, thus changing "the ancient accent," and without sufficient reason, since *santi* is defensible, 3 **c** to 5 **b** inclusive being of the nature of a parenthesis, extending the *navatír náva* of 3 **b**. The *khila* ⌊vs. 2⌋ to RV. x. 127 has a corresponding verse ⌊as also has ÇÇS. at ix. 28. 10⌋, with *yuktā́sas* for *draṣṭā́ras*, with *santu* in **c**, and ⌊so the *khila*, at least⌋ the accent *saptá* in **d**. The Atharvan mss. vary between *sápta* and *saptá;* our text gives the former, SPP. the latter, which is better, as being the usual Atharvan accent, and having ⌊about⌋ half the mss. in its favor. The comm. explains the *draṣṭā́ras* as "troop-gods" (*gaṇadevās*), and does not so much as hint at any connection with the stars, which nevertheless we cannot well question to be meant, in their various and manifold groupings. A *ca* after *aṣṭāú* in **c** would be a welcome addition to both meter and sense.

4. And sixty and six, O wealthy one; fifty [and] five, O pleasant one; four and forty, three and thirty, O mighty (*vājín*) one;—

Ppp. has in **b** *naçaṁnihi*, in **d** *vādini.*

5. And two of thine and twenty of thine, O night; eleven the least (*avamá*) — with those protectors today do thou protect us, O daughter of the sky.

At beginning of **d** all the authorities ⌊with one unimportant variant⌋ read *ná*, which seems impossible. We emended it to *nú* (cf. *nú pāti* in ix. 10. 23); SPP., following that blind guide the comm., reads *nú;* this is entirely unacceptable, both on account of the sense, and because *nú* cannot stand at the beginning of a pāda: cf. note to v. 6. 5. The authorities are much at odds as to the accent of *duhitar divas*, the majority having *duhitár divás.* Ppp. reads in **b** *rātrī ek-.*

6. Let no demon, [no] mischief-plotter master us; let no evil-plotter master us; let no thief today master our kine, nor a wolf our sheep;—

The mss. have at the beginning *rákṣā* (p. *rákṣa*), as 2d sing. imperative, and pāda **d** of RV. vi. 71. 3 (the verse is found also in VS. ⌊xxxiii. 69⌋ TS. ⌊i. 4. 24^1⌋ TB. ⌊ii. 4. 4^7⌋ MS. ⌊i. 3. 27⌋) gives the same, ⌊as does RV. vi. 75. 10 **d**⌋. The translation follows our conjectured emendation, which, in view of the implausibility of the impv. *rákṣa* standing so alone, has a right to consideration. Ppp. reads *mākir ṇo a-.*

The comm. reckons our 6 **a**, **b** as a whole verse ⌊his 6⌋; our 6 **c**, **d** and 7 **a**, **b** as his vs. 7; our 7 **c**, **d** and 8 **a**, **b** as his vs. 8; our 8 **c**, **d** and 9 **a**, **b** as his vs. 9; and our 9 **c**, **d** and 10 as his vs. 10; thus making the sixth verse instead of the tenth to consist of two pādas only, while yet counting ten verses in the hymn. SPP., on the other hand ⌊see his Critical Notice in vol. i., p. 24⌋, counts vs. 6 as our edition does, but adds our 8 **a**, **b** to our vs. 7 to form his vs. 7, thus making it of six pādas; and then counts our 8 **c**, **d** and 9 **a**, **b** as his vs. 8, and our 9 **c**, **d** and 10 as his vs. 9. This is in accordance with the Anukr. ⌊in that it gives six pādas to vs. 7 and makes a total of 9 vss.⌋, and is a decidedly preferable division to that in our text, which was founded on the numbering of our first mss., and it will be followed in translating here. The sense, however, would be still better suited by making vs. 6 of three lines, instead of vs. 7. ⌊In what follows, I give first the numeration of the Berlin edition, and then, in parenthesis, SPP's numeration.⌋

7, 8 **a, b.** (7.) Nor a robber our horses, O excellent one; nor the sorceresses our men.

By the most distant roads let the thief, the robber, run; by a distant one let the toothed rope, by a distant one let the malignant hasten (*ṛṣ*).

As to the division, see under the preceding verse. In the fourth pāda, part of the mss. accent *taskarás*. In the first, there is discordance among them as to the accent of *bhadre*. The 'rope with teeth' is of course the snake, as the comm. also has sense to see (*rajjuvad āyataḥ sarpādiḥ*). Our 8 **a, b** is identical with iv. 3. 2 **c, d**; and our 7 **c, d** resembles **a, b** of the same verse. ⌊For *yātudhānyàs* the comm. reads the masculine, *-nās*.⌋

8 **c, d,** 9 **a, b.** (8.) Do thou, O night, make the snake blind, harsh-smoked(?), headless; grind up the two jaws of the wolf; cast (*ā-han*) the thief into the snare.

⌊Apart from the variation in **c**, the verse is identical with 50. 1, below: see note thereon.⌋ All the mss. (except, by accident, one of SPP's) at the beginning have *ándha;* SPP. reads *ádha*, with one ms. and the comm.; but *ádha* is plainly out of place, and *andham*, as emended in our text (it should have been accented *andhám;* ⌊correct the misprint⌋), a very plausible correction. Our rendering of *tṛṣṭadhūma* is mechanically accurate; probably the word is corrupt; Ppp. reads the pāda *andho rātri tiṣṭadhūmam*. The comm. explains as *ārtikārī dhūmo viṣajvālādhūmo ni-* (ms. *vi-*) *çvāsadhūmo vā yasya;* the translators understand *-dhūma* as "breath" or "odor"; ⌊Griffith renders 'with pungent breath'⌋. In **c, d** the mss. have *jambháyāsténa táṁ drupadé jahi* (but many of them have *-bhā́-*). SPP. follows them and prints *jambháyās téna táṁ dr-*: from this our text makes a bold departure* ⌊implying as its *pada*-reading *jambhaya : ā́ : stenám : drupadé : jahi*⌋; but something had to be done to make sense; any one is invited to do better if he can. The comm. reads with the mss., and forces through a meaningless version. Ppp. has a different and corrupt text: *hano vṛkasya jambhayādvāinaṁ nṛpate jahi* ⌊cf. end of note to 50. 1⌋.

*⌊The assumption of an *ā́* (*ā́ . . . jahi*) after *jambhaya* is supported by *nirjahyāsténa . . . jahi* at 50. 1 **c, d**, below, where the collocation is almost unequivocal (see the note); for although *jahyās* (as given by the *pada*-mss.) is a good optative of *hā*, the combination of *hā* with *nis* is hardly Vedic, and we must there assume the division *nir jahy ā ste-*, the locative *drupadé* fitting well with *ā jahi* (cf. i. 11. 4; x. 8. 4 **c**). The rationale of the corruption here is not hard to see: the hiatus between **c** and **d** being once covered by the fusion of the final of *jambhaya* with the *ā́* of *ā́ stenám*, nothing was easier than to see a form *jambhayās* in the first part of the combination, and then to substitute *téna* for the vastly less common *stenám* or for the meaningless *tenám* (which might be read out of the combination: see Prāt. ii. 40 note); the exigency of the meter occasioned by the blunder with *jambhayās* then made the insertion of *tám* easy. With the Berlin solution of the corruption, the meter is in perfect order. The interesting parallel from the Avesta, *hām zanva zembayadhwem*, Yasht i. 27, adduced by Geldner, KZ. xxx. 514, may here be noted.⌋

9 **c, d,** 10. (9.) With thee, O night, we stay; we shall sleep, do thou watch; yield refuge to our kine, horses, men (*púruṣa*).

'Stay' (*vas*) means specifically 'spend the night.' In **b** the *pada*-mss. commit the incredible blunder of dividing *svapiṣyā́m : ási* (or *asi*); some of the *saṁhitā*-mss. accent *svápiṣyā́-*; and all either *jāgṛhi* or *jā́gṛhi;* SPP. follows us in violating the "ancient accent" and emending to *jāgṛhí.* In **c**, Ppp. has *yachād aç-*.

48. To night: for protection.

[*As 47.—ṣaṭ. ānuṣṭubham: 1. 3-p. ārṣī gāyatrī; 2. 3-p. virāḍ anuṣṭubh; 3. bṛhatīgarbhā; 5. pathyāpañkti.*]

Found also in Pāipp. vi., in connection with hymn 47, with which it also shares its liturgical application.

Translated: Griffith, ii. 305.

1. Now then what things we note, or what things are within the box, those things we commit to thee.

The first pāda here differs widely from the traditional text, which instead of *cáyāmahe* has *ca yásmā* (p. *yásmāi*) *āha*, or (a minority) *yásmāha;* the comm's text (according to SPP.) gives *ca yasmā ha*, but his explanation implies instead *yasmāi* (explained as $=$*yasya*); and SPP. accordingly reads in *saṁhitā*-text *ca yásmā ha*, and in *pada*-text *ca : yásmāi : ha*, which is altogether to be condemned, since the two texts must correspond, and *yásmā* is also no word. SPP. in a note proposes further emendation of our *cáyāmahe* to *ca yā́mahe* ($=$ *īmahe* or *yācāmahe*), which seems entirely unacceptable, as regards both form and sense. The whole verse is so obscure in meaning that we get little help from this element in reconstruction of the text; yet it is plain that we do not commit to another that which we do not possess, but are only wishing for. Ppp. also fails us; its reading of **a, b** is *atho yāni tamassahe yāni cā 'ntaṣ pareṇihi.* The *yā́nivāntáḥ* of **b** is by the *pada*-mss. strangely resolved into *yā́n°iva : antáḥ* (but one of SPP's has p.m. *yā́ni . vā : antáḥ*). It is also strange that SPP. emends to *cā 'ntáḥ*, on the sole authority of the comm., though as regards the sense there is nothing to choose between *ca* and *vā.* All the mss. accent *párīṇahi* (except our *pada*-mss., which have *pariṇáhi;* and one of SPP's has s.m. *pári : ṇahi*); but SPP. follows our emendation *parīṇáhi.* Nearly half the mss. have at the end *dadhmasi*, and Ppp. agrees with them. The comm. in his explanation connects the verse closely with 47. 9: there one's ⌊domestic⌋ animals were spoken of, here one's very numerous house-articles (*bahiṣṭhāni gṛhavartīni . . . vastūni*); and in two classes: those out in open sight (*anāvṛtadeçe*), and those inside an enclosed house or the like (*parito naddhe pariçrite gṛhādāu*).

2. O night! mother! commit thou us to the dawn; let the dawn commit us to the day, the day to thee, O shining one (*vibhāvarī*).

Compare 50. 7, below*; also MB. i. 5. 15, where more such commitments are given. The comm. reckons the first division of the verse to vs. 1. The metrical definition of the Anukr. is mere arithmetic ($12 + 10 + 8 = 30$). The *pada*-text, both here and below, leaves *vibhāvari* undivided (RV. *vibhā°vari*). *⌊Also vi. 107. 1–4.⌋

3. Whatsoever flies here, whatsoever that is crawling (*sarīsṛpá*) is here, whatsoever creature is on the mountain—from that do thou, O night, protect us.

The third pāda is wholly corrupt. All the mss. read *parvatāyāsatvam* (p. *pár-vatāya : sáḥ : tvám*), with some differences of accent (*-yāsátvam*, or *-yāsátvám*, or *-yā́sátvám*); and the comm. and SPP. (in *saṁhitā*) follow them (SPP. *-yāsátvam*; but in p., by emendation, *-tāya : asátvam*, since the comm. so understands). Our text emends to *párvaṇy ā́saktam* 'what has fastened on the joint,' which seems extremely unsatisfactory. The translation above is perhaps hardly better, but it implies a text much closer to the mss. —*párvata* (i.e. *-te*, hence *-tay*) *ā́ sattvám*; and so it may pass for what it is worth; it is by no means proposed as a definite solution of the difficulty. Ppp. has *padvad āsunvan*, which gives no help. Ppp. also reads *yadi kim* three times.

4. Do thou protect behind, thou in front, thou from above and from below; do thou guard us, O shining one; here we are, thy praisers.

5. They who follow (*anu-sthā*) the night, and who watch over beings, who defend all cattle — they watch over our selves (*ātmán*), they watch over our cattle.

The mss. accent *jā́grati** in **d** and **e**, and in **d** the accent might well enough be retained, on the principle of antithesis; SPP. gives *jāgrati*, like us. Emendation to *jāgratu* would be decidedly welcome in both pādas. Ppp. has considerable variations: for **b**, *yeṣu bhūteṣu jāgrabhi*,† and, for **d**, **e**, *tenā tvam asi jāgratu te naṣ paçubhir jāgratu*: corrupt, but supporting our proposed *jāgratu*. *⌊It is very reasonable to suppose that in *jā́grati* at end of **d** and **e** we have two cases of assimilation of an original *jāgratu* to the *jā́grati* which stands correctly at the end of **b** (cf. note to xix. 43. 7), each case being doubly faulty, in respect, namely, of accent and of ending.⌋ †⌊In Roth's Collation there is a note which perhaps means that Ppp. reads *jāgrati* for *rákṣanti* at end of **c**; but I am not at all sure.⌋

6. Verily I know thy name, O night; thou art "ghee-dripping" (*ghṛtā́cī*) by name; as such Bharadvāja knows thee; do thou watch over our property.

In **b**, Ppp. combines *vā 'si*; in **c** and **d** it reads, with our edition, *tvā* and *jāgṛhi*, while SPP. gives *tvā́m* and *jāgrati*, the latter for *jā́grati*, as all the mss. ⌊save one⌋ read; our emendation was a perfectly obvious one, and should have been followed by SPP. The comm., to be sure, reads *-rati*, but, by the simple application of his general rule, that any verb-form can be used for any other, he is able to declare it = *jāgartu* — which SPP. has too much knowledge and conscience to do. The *pada*-mss. have *tvā́m*, *tvām*, and *tvám*; our *tvā* was an emendation, called for after *tā́m*. More than half of the mss. accent *bharadvājás*. In our text, the accent-sign printed over *jā* in **d** should be shifted to over *dhi*: it is a misprint.

49. Praise and prayer to night.

[*As 47.** — *daçakam. ānuṣṭubham: 1–5, 8. triṣṭubh; 6. āstārapaṅkti; 7. pathyāpaṅkti; 10. 3-av. 6-p. jagatī.*] *⌊The Anukr. adds *bharadvājaç ca* (or *bhārad-*), apparently meaning that Gopatha and Bharadvāja were jointly the seers in the case of this hymn.⌋

This hymn and the following occur together also in Pāipp. xiv. Their *viniyoga* is the same with that of the two preceding hymns (see under hymn 47). They are translated together (but in reversed order) by Ludwig.

Translated: Ludwig, p. 466; Griffith, ii. 306.

1. The lively woman, household maiden, night, of god Savitar, of Bhaga, all-expanded, of easy invocation, of assembled fortune (?-*çrí*), hath filled heaven-and-earth with greatness.

In **a**, the *pada*-mss. read *dámūnā;* SPP. emends to *-nāḥ*. In **c**, all the mss., with the comm. and SPP., read *açvakṣabhā́* (p. *açva○kṣabhā́*), which, as being unintelligible, our edition emends at a venture to *viçvávyacās*, and the translation follows the latter, for lack of anything better. The comm. gives two explanations: *açu* (= *āçu*) + *akṣa* + *bhā* (= *abhibhavati* or *tiraskaroti*), meaning *çīghrapravṛtticakṣurādinirodhikā;* or, alternatively, by analogy with vs. 4 **c**, *açvakṣā* (= *açvān kṣāyati* or *kṣapayati*) *bhā* (= *dīptiḥ*) *yasyāḥ sā:* both as absurd as possible. Ppp. reads *açvakṣarā*. Many of the mss. read *sámbhṛtaḥçrīr*, and the *pada*-mss. divide falsely *sám○bhṛtaçrīḥ* instead of *sámbhṛta○çrīḥ;* SPP. follows them. Ppp. reads *saṁbhṛtaḥçīr ā*.

2. The profound one hath surmounted all things; the most mighty one hath ascended to the loftiest sky; the eager night spreads toward me like a friend with excellent *svadhā́s*.

The translation follows our text of the verse, which, however, is full of emendations, and by no means satisfactory. Nearly every ms. reads at the beginning *ávi* (one *áviṁ*, and one authority ⌊SPP's reciter V., with impossible accent⌋ *ábhi*), while Ppp. has *abhi*, which is also, except for the accent, an easier emendation for *ávi*. The comm. has *ati*. Nearly all authorities, again, have for verb in **a** *áruhat* (the accent is perfectly defensible as an antithetical one, and might well have been left in our text); but the reciter V. gives (*ábhi*) *árhat*, thus agreeing in part with the (*ati*) *arhat* of the text of the comm.; ⌊and one of W's mss. has *ásahat*⌋. The explanation of the comm. reads *atyarhati*, which he glosses by *atikramya vyāpya vartate*, which is wholly without authority, since even the Dhātupāṭha gives only *pūjāyām* as the sense of *arh*. Ppp. has *aruhat*. SPP. goes half way with the comm., adopting *áti . . . aruhat* (unnecessarily abandoning the "ancient accent" of the verb). All authorities have *víçvāni* (but Ppp. only *viçvā ar-*); and all ⌊save Ppp. again⌋ have *gambhīró*, p. *-ráḥ*, ⌊but one of W's *pada*-mss. gives *-rā*, p.m.⌋, although the comm., against his own text (according to SPP.), explains *gambhīrā*. Here perhaps Ppp. brings help, reading *gabhīro 'd varṣ-*; this is better than our *-rā́* = *rā́ : ā́*. ⌊The *gabhīrā́* of the Berlin ed. seems to be a misprint for *gambhīrā́*, if we judge by the Collation Book and the Index Verborum: but it may be intended as an emendation, as it certainly is a metrical improvement.⌋ SPP. reads *gambhīró vá-*, although *gambhīrás* is simply unusable, and the change to *-rā́* as easy as possible. Nearly all, including Ppp., read *várṣiṣṭham*, ⌊save three of SPP's authorities and one of W's, which have *-ṣiṣṭam*⌋. Then follows in nearly all *aruhántas*, p. *aruhántaḥ;* but *-háta* is found in one, *-hánta* in two, and *arháti* is given by a reciter, with the comm.; the comm. has *arhati*, and explains it precisely as he did his *ati . . . arhati* above; SPP. emends to *aruhanta;* our ⌊*ā́ . . .*⌋ *dyā́m aruhat* is very bold, but the case was a desperate one. Ppp. reads *aruhad açraviṣṭhā*, and this, with emendation to *áçramiṣṭhā* (cf. RV. iv. 4. 12), makes acceptable sense. One of SPP's mss. has *çramiṣṭhā́*, but doubtless only by accident; all the other authorities, including the comm., have ⌊apart from some unimportant details⌋ *çraviṣṭhā́*, which SPP. emends to *çráviṣṭhāḥ*. There was probably no sufficient reason for our changing *çrav-* to *çáv-* in our text. The fairly acceptable and least altered version of the line would be this: *abhí víçvāny áruhad gambhīró 'd várṣiṣṭham aruhad áçramiṣṭhā*. The third pāda is in equally bad condition. All the authorities ⌊with unimportant variants⌋, including

Ppp., have at the beginning *uçatī́ rā́try (a-)*, but the *pada*-mss. give *rā́tri* instead of *rā́trī*, as they should give, and as SPP's *pada*-text reads by emendation. What follows it the *pada*-mss. offer as *ánu॰sāma : drā́him* (or *drāhím*); in the *saṁhitā*-mss. the first word appears as *ánusāma* (once *ánusama*) or (accentless, and so making one word with *-drā́him* or *-drā́hi*) *anusāma-* or *aṁnusāma-*; and the second appears as *-drā́him*, *-drā́hi, drā́him, drā́hím, drāhí, drā́vi, prā́him.* The rest of the half-verse, *tiṣṭhate mitrá iva svadhā́bhiḥ*, is the same in all, including the comm. and Ppp. SPP. emends to *ánu sā́ bhadrā́ 'bhí ti-*, which appears to be modeled on our *ánu mā bhadrā́bhir ví ti-*, but is defective both in sense and in meter. The comm. gives *anukṣaṇaṁ vi ti-*, cutting loose entirely from the ms.-reading; his own text, according to SPP., has *anusāmadrā vi ti-*. Ppp., finally, has *avasāna bhadrād vi ti-*, which suggests the emendation *uçatī́ rā́try ávasā no bhadrā́ ví tiṣṭhate* etc. Our *ví tiṣṭhate*, at any rate, is by the support of Ppp. and the comm. put nearly beyond question.

⌊I have made some modifications in the above paragraph which I could not well indicate by the ell-brackets. — For those who do not have the Bombay ed., it may be well to give SPP's reconstructions of the verse : first, the text of the comm. : *ati viçvāny arhad gambhīro varṣiṣṭham arhati çraviṣṭhā : uçatī rātry anusāmadrā vi tiṣṭhate mitra iva svadhābhiḥ ;* second, the text which the comm. actually explains : *ati viçvāny arhati gambhīrā varṣiṣṭham arhati çraviṣṭhā : uçatī rātry anukṣaṇaṁ vi tiṣṭhate mitra iva svadhābhiḥ ;* third, SPP's reading : *áti víçvāny aruhad gambhīró várṣiṣṭham aruhanta çráviṣṭhāḥ : uçatī́ rā́try* (p. *rā́trī*) *ánu sā́ bhadrā́ 'bhí tiṣṭhate mitrá iva svadhā́bhiḥ.*⌋

3. O desirable, welcome, well-portioned, well-born one! thou didst come, O night; mayest thou be well-willing here; save thou for us the things that are produced (*jātá*) for men, likewise what [are] for cattle, by prosperity ⌊*puṣṭyā́*⌋.

⌊Or, '[and] prosperous,' if we read *puṣṭā́.*⌋ The mss. all read in **a** *várye*, which we need not have altered to *vā́rye*, as *várya* is found elsewhere as early as TB.; Ppp. has *niryāi.* Three of SPP's authorities and one of ours have *vándye*, ⌊one has *véde*⌋, the rest with Ppp., *vánde;* the comm. *vade* (= *sarvāir abhiṣṭūyamāne*). Ppp. has *svajātā.* In **b**, most of the mss. begin with *ā́jāgan* (one *ájāgan;* p. *ā́ : jā́ : agan*), and the true reading is in all probability *ā́ 'jāgan*, impf. intensive of *gam;* or, if left as "pluperfect," as in our edition, it should at any rate be *ā́ 'jagan*, as SPP., with the comm., reads. *Rātri* is our (evidently called-for) emendation for *rā́tri* of the mss., which SPP. follows. *Syās*, at the end of **b**, is also for *syām* of the mss., the comm., and SPP.; it is an obvious improvement, though not quite necessary ⌊and receiving no support from Ppp. : see below⌋. Ppp. has a peculiar (and corrupt) version : *ā* (if *svajātā*, as quoted above, is for *svajāta ā*) *cāgni rātri sumanā hy asyām.* In **c**, the translation implies emendation of *asmā́ṅs* to *asmé*, against all the authorities, including Ppp. and the comm. The *pada*-mss. read *jātā́ḥ*, their natural inference from the rare and anomalous combination *jātā́ átho;* SPP. emends to *jātā́.* In **d**, Ppp. reads *çriyā* instead of *atho*, and at the end *puṣṭyā*, with all the mss. (they vary only as to its accent), and with SPP.; our conjectural emendation *puṣṭā́* is supported only by the comm. ⌊text and explanation⌋.

4. The eager night has taken to herself the splendor of the lion, of the stag, of the tiger, of the leopard, the horse's bottom, man's (*púruṣa*) roar (? *māyú*); many forms thou makest for thyself, shining out.

The *saṁhitā*-mss. accent *rātry uçatī́* (p. *rātri : uçatī́*); SPP. emends, with us, to *rā́try uçatī́;* the comm. also understands *rā́trī.* The mss. all ⌊with trifling variations⌋

read *pīṣásya* or *pīn̈ṣásya* (or *ṣīṣásya*); SPP. accepts *pīn̈ṣásya;* the comm. gives *piṣasya*, which is doubtless only a bad spelling of our *piçásya;* ⌊lion and stag are mentioned by these names together at RV. i. 64. 8;⌋ Ppp. has *nipasya;* and, at end of **b**, *varcādhe*. In **c**, all the authorities, including Ppp. ⌊but not the comm.⌋, offer *bradhnám;* the translation implies correction to *budhnám*,* which is the reading of the commentator (he explains it as = *mūlam*) ⌊and adds, *açvavīryasya vego hi mūlam*⌋; in vi. 38. 4 we had the horse's *vā́ja* and man's *māyú* combined; and TB. (ii. 7. 7[1]) in the corresponding passage reads *krándye* for *vā́je*. The comm. explains *māyúm* as *çabdam āhvānādilakṣaṇam*. Ppp. has *kṛnuṣī* for *-ṣe*. ⌊The majority of the authorities read *vibhātīḥ* at the end.⌋ *⌊Cf. *áçvabudhna*, RV. x. 8. 3; and Aufrecht on *áçvabudhya*, ZDMG. xxiv. 206.⌋

5. Propitious to me [be] night and [the time] after sunrise; be the mother of cold (*himá*) easy of invocation for us; notice, O well-portioned one, this song of praise, with which I greet thee in all the quarters.

The translation implies in **a** a new conjectural reading: *çivā́ me rā́try anūtsūryáṁ ca;* an accusative is opposed by the connection, and the meter needs another syllable. *Anūtsūryá* is venturesome, but we had *otsūryám*, p. *ā॰utsūryám*, above, at iv. 5. 7. At any rate, neither our text nor that of SPP. (*çivā́ṁ rā́trim anusū́ryaṁ ca*) seems to give any sense. Ppp. supports the mss.: *çivāṁ rātrim ahni sūryaṁ ca;* the majority of the *saṁhitā*-mss. have *çivā́ṁ rā́trim ahi sū́-*, others *anu* for *ahi* (p. *çivā́m : rā́trim : anu॰sū́ryam : ca*); the comm. has *rātrimahi*, and understands it as *rātri* (voc.) *mahi* (= *mahāntam*, and qualifying *sūryam!*). ⌊SPP. suggests *çivā́ rā́trī mahī́ sū́ryaç ca.*⌋ In **b**, Ppp. has *yamasya*. In **c**, nearly all the mss. read *açvá* (or *áçva*) for *asyá;* and the *pada*-mss. treat it as an independent word; SPP. has *asyá*, with us. In **d**, a few mss. have *vándye* or *vádye*. Ppp. reads at the end *vikṣu*.

6. Our song of praise, O shining (*vibhā́van*) night, like a king thou enjoyest; may we be having all heroes, may we become having all possessions, through (*ánu*) the out shining dawns.

The mss. read at the end *anūṣásaḥ* (p. *anu॰uṣásaḥ*); SPP. emends as we had done. Ppp., in **b**, **c**, **d**, has *joṣasī yathā nas sarvavīrā bh-*. The verse is very ill described by the Anukr.; it is a good *pan̄kti* with one syllable wanting in **c**.

7. Pleasant names thou assumest: — whoso desire to damage my riches, them, O night, do thou burn continually, so that no thief be found, so that he be not found again.

The translation follows our text, which is considerably altered from that of the mss. All of them, with the comm. and SPP., have at the beginning *çámyā*, for which our *rāmyā́* is, so far as the written form is concerned, a very easy emendation. The comm. explains: "thou wearest the name *çamyā* = *çatruçamanasamarthā*": one of his usual absurdities. Ppp. reads for **a**, **b** *çramyā ha nāma taruṣe vimṛcchantī yo janāṅ*. There seems to be no good reason why *dadhiṣé* should be accented. Nearly all the mss. give *dhánāḥ* at end of **b**; the comm. understands *dhanā*, and SPP. reads it. For **c** the *pada*-text is *rā́trī : hitā́* ⌊or *hi : tā́*⌋ *: naḥ : suta॰pā́!* The comm. understands instead *rā́trī 'hī tā́n asutapā́*, and SPP. follows him, making a new *pada*-text to correspond (*rā́tri : ihī : tā́n : asu॰tapā́*). The comm. explains *asutapā* as either "burning their life-breaths" (*asu-tapa*) or "badly burning" (*a-su-tapa*). Ppp. gives no help, reading ⌊for our **c**,

d, e: it is not clear just how much of the reading is to be assigned to **c**⌋ *rātri hīrcāna sadamātasteno anvavidyate.* Our emendation is fairly acceptable; but the *hī* ⌊which, with the imperative, hardly needs a separate word in translation⌋ requires that we accent *anutápa.* For our *yáthā*, in **d** and **e**, the mss. and SPP. give the first time *yás* and the second time *yát;* the comm. both times *yas;* the meter and sense alike call for our emendation. Ppp. has for both pādas only *ta steno anv avidyate,* ⌊which might (see above) be understood as *atas steno* etc.⌋.

8. Excellent art thou, O night, like a decorated bowl; thou bearest [as] maiden the whole form of kine; full of eyes, eager, [thou showest] me wondrous forms; thou hast put on (*prati-muc*) the stars of heaven (*divyá*).

Of this verse also the translation is a make-shift, following in part the mss. and in part our conjectural emendations. In **a** the only point of question is the last word, which the mss. read as *ṣiṣṭás* (so the majority) or *çiṣṭás* or *viṣṭás* ⌊etc.⌋; the comm. has *viṣṭas* (= *bhojanārtham pariviṣṭas*). Ppp. gives the whole pāda as *bhadrā 'si rātris tapaso nu viṣṭo.* In **b**, nearly all the mss. give *víçvaṁ górūpaṁ yuvatír* ⌊several have *-tīm*⌋ *bibharṣi* (one has *bíbh-*), and this the translation follows, alterations not seeming to supply a better sense. SPP., however, follows the comm. in offering *víṣvañ* for *víçvam* (in *saṁhitā* he prints it incorrectly *víṣvaṁ gó-*, as if there were an assimilated final in the case); ⌊but in his Corrections at the end of vol. iv. he duly notes the error;⌋ he would hardly accept the comm's interpretation, = *viṣūcī* (one gender for another); but how he would render it, it is hard to see. Ppp. reads *viçvaṁ gorūpaṁ yuvatid vibharṣi,* but another hand has written above *-tir bibha-.* In **c**, nearly all the mss. (including the comm's text, as stated by SPP.) leave *me* unchanged before *uçatí*, and SPP. accepts it in his text, though against all rule and practice; two of our mss. have *ma.* ⌊All the authorities give *cákṣuṣmatī*, and this is followed by the comm. and SPP., and also by W. in the translation, therein departing from the emendation ('to me having eyes') of the Berlin ed.⌋ Ppp. has for the pāda *cakṣuṣmatī ve yuvatī 'va rūpaḥ.* The translation supplies a verb, as seems necessary unless the text be still further altered. For **d** the general ms.-reading is *práti tyā́ṁ divyā́ tákmā amukthāḥ* (also *tvám* and *tvā́* for *tyā́m*, and *takmā́:* p. *takmàḥ* or *-mā́ḥ*); but the comm. offers *práti tvā́ṁ divyā́ ná kṣā́m amukthāḥ*, and this SPP. accepts ⌊accenting thus⌋ and prints. Ppp. has *pratyāṁ dityāṁ divyām arukṣam amugdhaḥ.* The comm's version of the text is senseless, and his attempt to put meaning into it very absurd; it might suggest *práti tvā́ṁ divyā́ nákṣatrāṇy amukthāḥ.* Our text ought to accent *tā́rakā am-*, if the reading is admitted.

9. What thief shall come today, [what] malicious mortal villain, may night, going to meet him, smite away the neck, ⌊away⌋ the head of him; —

The two following pādas ⌊10 **a, b**⌋ evidently belong to this verse rather than to verse 10; but our division is that of the mss. and the Anukr., and so is adopted also by SPP. The comm. inserts another line after our 9 **a, b**: *yo mama rātri surūpa āyati sa sampiṣṭo apāyati;* and then he divides the four lines that follow into two verses of four pādas each, giving eleven verses to the whole hymn. The majority of mss. accent *martyás* in **b**. The comm. reads *harat* for *hanat* at the end. Ppp. has *yu dya stenā yutv aghāyu mṛtyo ripuḥ;* and, in **d**, *pra gīyasva pra.* Pāda **a** is the **a** of iv. 3. 5, ⌊of which the **b** recurs here as the second pāda of the comm's inserted line and also as the fourth pāda of our vs. 10⌋.

10. ⌊Away⌋ his feet, that he may not go; ⌊away⌋ his hands, that he may not harm.

What marauder shall approach, may he go away all crushed; may he go away, may he go well away; may he go away in a dry place (?).

At the end of **b**, the majority of mss. read *yáthā́çiṣaḥ*, which all the *pada*-mss. resolve into *yáthā : áçiṣaḥ;* ⌊most of⌋ the rest, and SPP., give *yáthā́ 'çiṣat;* the comm. *yathā "çliṣat* (= *saṁçleṣayet*). Ppp. offers *pra pādāu na yat āhataṣ pra hastāu na yanāçiṣat.* In **e**, the *pada*-mss. compound *su॰ápāyati*, doubtless wrongly; ⌊read as *pada*-text *sú : ápa : ayati*⌋. All the mss., the comm., and SPP., give in **f** *sthāṇāú*, and the comm. explains it as = *çākhopaçākhārahitavṛkṣamūla āçraye.* After it, the mss. have *apā́yataḥ* (p. *apa॰áyataḥ*), but the comm. agrees with us in *ápā 'yati*, and SPP. accordingly also adopts it. The translation follows throughout the emendations of our text; perhaps, in **f**, *sthā́ne* would be better than *sthalé*, as more closely resembling the ms.-reading. We are deprived of the help of Ppp. upon the point, as it skips from *apāyati* in **e** to *tṛṣṭadhūmam* in 50. 1 **a**; for **c**, **d**, it had *yo mulalaṁ sulapāyati sa saṁpiṣṭyo upāyati.* We had **d** above as iv. 3. 5 **b**; ⌊cf. the end of the note to vs. 9⌋.

50. To night: for protection.

[*As 47. — saptakam.*]

Follows also in Pāipp. xiv. our hymn 49. Has the same liturgical use as hymn 49. Translated: Ludwig, p. 465; Griffith, ii. 307.

1. Do thou, O night, make the snake blind, harsh-smoked, headless; smite out the eyes of the wolf; cast the thief into the snare.

This verse is nearly identical with that translated as 47. 8 above (8 **c**, **d** and 9 **a**, **b** of the printed text). As there, the mss. have at the beginning *ándha*, which SPP., with the comm., changes to *ádha;* and all, in **c**, **d**, have *nír jahyās téna* táṁ* ⌊or *tváṁ*⌋ *drupadé jahi* in a manner analogous with the reading there. ⌊The translation implies the division *nír jahy ā́ . . . jahi:* cf. my note to 47. 8.⌋ ⌊Apart from some less important variants,⌋ the mss. are divided, as often in such cases, between *akṣāú* and *akṣyāú*, and SPP. chooses the worse, *akṣāú;* our *akṣyāú* is alone defensible. Ppp. omits (see note to 49. 10) the first two words, and reads, as at 47. 8, *tiṣṭadhūmam;* ⌊it begins the second line with *hano vṛkasya* and ends it (as above) with *nṛpate jahi;* what the intervening words are is not clear from Roth's Collation⌋. ⌊Meantime Bloomfield kindly informs me that Ppp. reads the line thus: *hano vṛkasya nir jahy ā tvāinaṁ nṛpate jahi:* this gives no support for a *jahyās* (see note to 47. 8); but the *tvāinaṁ* obviously stands in some relation to the *dvāinaṁ* of the Ppp. reading at 47. 8, which is *jambhayādvāinaṁ.*⌋ *⌊The *pada*-reading is *níḥ : jahyāḥ : téna.*⌋

2. What draft-oxen thou hast, O night, sharp-horned, very swift, with them do thou today pass us always (*viçváhā*) over difficulties.

SPP. follows the mss. in the false accent *tī́kṣṇa-* in **b**. In **c**, **d**, he reads *pārayā́ 'ti* with us and with the comm. (also with Ppp.), ⌊but against the mss., most of which⌋ have *pārayaty áti.* In **b**, Ppp. gives *-çṛṅgyāçvāsavaḥ.*

3. May we pass (*tṛ*) night after night receiving no harm with ourselves (*tanvā̀*); may the niggards fail to pass [it], as men without boats a deep [water].

Or *tanvā* belongs to *tarema*. The comm., against the accent and the sense, takes *ádriṣyantas* as a future participle (=*gamiṣyantas*)! Ppp. reads in **c**, **d** *apravāyuṣaṁ na tarehur ar-*.

4. As the millet-seed, flying forth, blowing away, is not found, so, O night, make him fly forth who is malicious against us.

The mss. read in **a** mostly *çāmyā́kas* (so the comm. and SPP.), also *çyāmyā́kas* and *çyāmā́kas;* and have *prapátan* or *prápatan*, with other chance variations; and in **b**, *apavā́n* (p. *apa॰vā́n*) or *-vā́ṁ;* in respect to this word, the translation ⌊taking it as present participle of *apa-vā*⌋ follows them rather than our emendation *aparám*. None of the mss. accent *na*, but SPP. ventures ⌊with the Berlin ed.⌋ to emend the reading. At the beginning of **c**, the mss. all have *etā́v ā́* ⌊several *ā*⌋ (p. *etāú : ā́*); the comm. and SPP. (also Ppp.) agree with our *evā́*. The majority of mss. have at the end *-yánti*. Ppp. has in **a**, **b** *sānyākaṣ prapatante divāṁ nā 'nu-*; in **d** it combines *yo 'smāṅ*.

5. Thou didst make the thief stay away, and the kine-driving robber, also him who, haltering the courser's head, tries to lead it [away].

The *pada*-mss. strangely read at the beginning *apáḥ;* the rest ⌊save one of SPP's, p.m., which has *ápa*⌋ accent *apá;* SPP., as well as our text, emends to *ápa*, which the comm. also understands. All the mss. have *vā́sas*, and the comm., and SPP.; our *avāsayas* is a bold emendation, but makes both good meter and good sense. Ppp. gives no help: *apa stedaṁ vāsamathaṁ*. In **b**, SPP. follows the comm. in reading *goajám;* most of the mss. give *gór ájam*, but a part *górájas* (p. *górájaḥ!* but one ms. *gó 'jaḥ* ⌊or *gó॰jaḥ:* that is *gó* and *jaḥ* with *avagraha*-sign between⌋, corrected to *gódjaḥ*). ⌊Ppp. reads *gotham.*⌋ The comm. absurdly takes *goajám* as a copulative compound, =*gā ajāñç ca*, and makes it and *vā́sas* objects of *nínīṣati*. The translation implies rather SPP's text than ours ⌊that is *goajám* rather than *gór ájam*, I suppose⌋. ⌊At the end, the *nínesati* of the Berlin text is doubtless to be corrected to *nínīṣati* (cf. the stems in W's *Roots, Verb-forms*, etc., p. 233–4): *nínīṣati* is read by Ppp., by W's O.D.I., and (since he reports nothing to the contrary) by all of SPP's authorities. From the *Index Verborum* and from the *Roots* (p. 91) it would appear that W's later judgment rejected the *nínesati* of the text and some mss., though he has overlooked the matter here. The desiderative⌋ so distinctly calls for a prefix that one is tempted further to emend *átho* in **c** to *ápa*.

6. When, O well-portioned night, thou comest today, sharing out what is good, ⌊then⌋ make us to enjoy that, that it go not away.

The translation follows our text, which is very different from that of the mss. and SPP. Our *adyā́* in **a** implies *adyá ā́* (*ā́ . . . áyas*), which all the *pada*-mss. have, while SPP., with the comm., treats it as only *adyá* with the final lengthened by the usual Vedic license. In **b** all the mss. accent *ví bhajanti* ⌊p. *ví : bhajanti*⌋; SPP. emends to *vi-bhájanti*, while our text means *vibhájantī*. The comm. understands *-nti* ⌊supplying *çatravas* as subject⌋, and takes *áyas* after it as the noun, 'metal' (*ayomayaṁ vastu*); to us *áyas* is verb. ⌊Ppp. has *vasuḥ* at end of **b**.⌋ In **c** the mss., the comm., and SPP., begin with *yád;* we have emended it to *tád*. For **d**, most mss. have *yáthe 'dáṁ nā́ 'nupāyási* (p. *anu॰pāyási*); but one *-yáti*, one *-dányā́nu-*; SPP. follows the comm. and prints *yáthé 'd anyā́n upā́yasi* (p. *upa॰áyasi*), but in a note conjectures *yáthé 'd anyā́n nó 'pā́yati* 'that it go not unto others,' which is very acceptable, as giving a good sense with less alteration of the original text than our version requires. Ppp. is wholly corrupt: *yathed yasmā nitājaya yathed anyān upāyatī;* but the last pāda favors SPP's conjecture.

7. Unto the dawn, O night, do thou commit us all, free from guilt; may the dawn bestow (*ā-bhaj*) us on the day, the day on thee, O shining one.

The comm., two of SPP's reciters, and Ppp., read in **c** *bhajat.* Compare the verse 48. 2, above ⌊and MB. i. 5. 15, there cited⌋.

51. Accompanying acceptance (?).

[*Brahman.— dve. 1. ātmadevatyā; 2. sāvitrī. 1. 1-p. brāhmy anuṣṭubh; 2. 3-p. yavamadhyo 'ṣṇih (1, 2. 1-av.).*]

⌊Prose.⌋ Both the "verses" of this hymn are quoted in Kāuç. 91. 3, in the *madhuparka* ceremony, accompanying acceptance (*prati-grah*) of the offering. The second verse contains a formula very often used in the liturgical literature,* and this formula, as far as *hastābhyām*, occurs several times in Kāuç., given in full, and not to be regarded as having anything to do with the verse here; the same is the case with the use of the formula in Vāit. 3. 9. There is nothing to correspond to the hymn in Pāipp. *⌊An idea of its frequency may be gained from the array of citations (fourscore or more) given by Knauer in his Index to MGS., p. 151 a. See the table on p. 896, and cf. p. 896, end.⌋

Translated: Griffith, ii. 308.

1. Unrepelled (?*áyuta*) am I, unrepelled my soul, unrepelled my sight, unrepelled my hearing, unrepelled my breath, unrepelled my expiration, unrepelled my out-breathing, unrepelled the whole of me.

We unfortunately lack the comm's interpretation of *áyuta*, there being a lacuna in the ms. at this point; SPP. supplies *sampūrṇa*, it does not appear on what authority, but certainly without the least particle of plausibility. ⌊The count of the Anukr. (48 syllables) implies restoration of all the elided *a*'s.⌋

2. In the impulse of the heavenly impeller (*savitṛ́*), with the arms of the Açvins, with the hands of Pūshan, I, impelled, take hold of thee.

To render (in the first clause) 'of god Savitar' would hide the word-play between *prasava* and *savitṛ.* The syllables (if the *a* of *açvinos* is restored) count 10 + 11 + 6 = 27: a pretty poor *uṣṇih.*

52. Of and to desire (kā́ma).

[*Brahman.—pañcakam. mantroktakāmadāivatam. trāiṣṭubham. 3. 4-p. uṣṇih; 5. upariṣṭād-bṛhatī.*]

Found also in Pāipp. i. Used* in Kāuç. 6. 37, with xix. 59, at the very end of the sections on the *parvan*-ceremony (hence perhaps a later addition?), to appease the fuel, in case there has been an omission of the due ceremony; again, in 45. 17 (with iii. 29. 7; vi. 71; vii. 67), after the end of the *vaçāçamana* ceremony (also here a later addition?), to accompany the acceptance of something; once more, in 68. 29, in the *savayajñas*, with the acceptance of the sacrificial gifts (?*sadakṣiṇam*); and the Paddhati (note to

Kāuç. 79. 28) adds it at the end of the chapter of marriage ceremonies. The comm. notes the Kāuç. uses, but not the Paddh. one; and he adds one application, from Pariç. 10. 1, of this hymn with the two following and xix. 6 (the *puruṣasūkta*), in the rite of presenting a golden image of the earth. *⌊See table on p. 896.⌋

Translated: Griffith, ii. 309. — Cf. ix. 2, above.

1. Desire here came into being (*sam-vṛt*) in the beginning, which was the first seed of mind; O desire, being of one origin with great desire, do thou impart abundance of wealth to the sacrificer.

The first half-verse is nearly identical with RV. x. 129. 4 **a**, **b** ⌊TB. ii. 4. 1[10]; 8. 9[4]; TA. i. 23. 1⌋, which differ only by adding *ádhi* at end of **a**; the word is missed in our verse both for sense and for meter. Our text omits * at beginning of **c** a *sá* (*sá kāma*) that is in both these respects superfluous; it is found, however, also in Ppp. The comm. explains *kā́mena bṛhatā́* to mean *mahatā deçakālavastuparicchedarahitena kāmayitrā parameçvareṇa*. The last pāda is xviii. 1. 43 **d**. *⌊And so accents *kā́ma*.⌋

2. Thou, O desire, art set firm with power, mighty, shining (*vibhā́van*), companion for him who seeks a companion; do thou, formidable, overpowering in fights, impart power [and] force to the sacrificer.

The second pāda nearly corresponds with RV. x. 91. 1 **d**, which, however, reads *suṣákhā sakhīyaté*. The authorities give *sakha ā́ sakhīyaté* (or *-te*); and the *pada*-mss. make the very blundering division *vi°bhā́u : ā°sakhe : ā́ : sakh-*. ⌊The comm. understands *sakhīyate* (not as dative pple, but) as finite verb-form (3d sing., which would have to be accentless: he says *bhavacchabdādhyāhāreṇa prathamapuruṣaḥ*.⌋ SPP. follows the comm. in reading *vibhā́vā sakha ā́* ⌊SPP's *pada*-text is *vibhā́°vā : sakhe : ā́*⌋; but he disagrees with the comm. by ⌊making a participle of⌋ *sakhīyaté*, which he accents. The translation implies *sákhā́*, i.e. *sákhā ā́*. ⌊We have *ā́* with the denominative *çravasyāt* at RV. v. 37. 3; but with the pple, *ā́* seems very strange; nor do I see how W. meant to take it. One is tempted to fall back on the RV. reading *suṣákhā*: the more so, inasmuch as⌋ Ppp. presents the RV. reading *suṣakhā*. In **d**, Ppp. has *soho 'jo yaj-*.

3. To him that desired from afar, that trembled on at the inexhaustible — the places (*ā́çā*) listen to him; by desire they generated heaven.

It is of no consequence how this verse, especially the first half, is rendered; it is nothing but corrupt nonsense. The degree of its corruption may be seen by comparing it with the corresponding verse in TA. iii. 15. 1: *sadyáç cakamānā́ya pravepanā́ya* ⌊Poona ed., *-vepān-*⌋ *mṛtyáve : prā́ 'smā ā́çā açṛṇvan kā́menā 'janayan púnaḥ*; neither version is translatable. The majority of authorities read in **b** *pravipāṇā́yākṣayé* ⌊or *-ā́kṣaye*⌋ (the *pada*-readings are, for the first part, *pravi°pāṇā́ya*, and, for the second, *ā°kṣayé* or *ā́°kṣaye* or *ā°kṣaye*); but some have *pratipāṇā́ya* ⌊the lingual *ṇ* of which seems to betray the *ti* as a corruption for *vi*⌋ and *praripāṇā́ya*. The comm. understands *pratipāṇāya* and *akṣaye*, and SPP. follows him, accenting *pratipāṇā́ya* and *ákṣaye*, and reading in *pada*-text *prati°pānā́ya* (as if that would or could become in *saṁhitā*-text *-pāṇ-*!); with his usual carelessness, the comm. takes *-pāṇāya*, in spite of its *ṇ*, from root *pā* (= *sarvatorakṣaṇāyā 'bhimataphalaprāpaṇāya*: the latter equivalent looks as if he also saw something of *pra-āp* in it!). Ppp. has in **b** *pratipāṇāyākṣe*, in **c** *āsmā 'çṛṇvann*, and in **d** *-janayat saha*. The translation implies in **b** *pravipāṇā́yā́ 'kṣaye*. The Anukr. apparently scans the verse as 7 + 7 : 7 + 7 = 28.

4. By desire hath desire come to me, out of heart to heart; the mind that is theirs yonder, let that come unto me here.

In TA. (iii. 15. 2) a corresponding verse follows the one quoted under vs. 3: *kā́mena me kā́ma ā́ 'gād dhṛ́dayād dhṛ́dayam mṛtyóḥ: yád amī́ṣām adáḥ priyáṁ tád ai 'tú 'pa mā́m abhí.* SPP. has the same text as we, both deviating in **d** from the mss., which leave *upa* unaccented (p. *upa॰mā́m*); ⌊but SPP's R. has *úpa mā́m* and the comm. also takes *upa mām* as two words⌋. Ppp. combines *kāmā "gan* in **a**.

5. Desiring what, O desire, we make to thee this oblation, let that all succeed with us; then eat (*vī*) thou of this oblation: hail!

The verse is found, ⌊cited by *pratīka* at Kāuç. 92. 30, and⌋ written in full ⌊*sakala-pāṭha*⌋ at 92. 31, prescribed for use at the end of the *madhuparka* ceremony.* SPP. gives the same text as we; the mss. leave *kṛṇmási* unaccented in **b**, and most of them accent *té* after it. At the beginning, all the *pada*-mss. ⌊except possibly L., of which no note is made⌋ very strangely read *yát॰kāmaḥ*, though no *saṁhitā*-mss. have *kāmaḥ*; ⌊with the support of the latter, as also of the comm. and of Ppp., both ed's read *yát kāma*⌋. *⌊See p. 897, ¶ 3.⌋

53. Praise of time (kālá).

[*Bhṛgu. — daçakam. mantroktasarvātmakakāladevatyam. ānuṣṭubham: 1–4. triṣṭubh; 5. nicṛt purastādbṛhatī.*]

This hymn and the following, which (as even the Anukr. ⌊cf. introd. to h. 56⌋ points out) are only two divided parts of one hymn, occur also in Pāipp. xiv. and xii. (53. 1–6 in xiv.; 53. 7 to 54. 6 in xii.). They are translated together by Muir, Ludwig, Scherman, and Bloomfield. As *kālasūkta*, they are used by Pariç. 10. 1 in connection with the preceding hymn (*kāmasūkta*): see under that hymn.

Translated: Muir, v. 407; Ludwig, p. 191; Scherman, *Philosophische Hymnen*, p. 78; Grill, 73, 193; Deussen, *Geschichte*, i. 1. 210; Griffith, ii. 309; Bloomfield, 224, 681. — Cf. also Monier-Williams, *Indian Wisdom*3, p. 25; Hillebrandt, *Veda-Chrestomathie*, p. 41. — The epic *kāla*-verses are in rather a different vein: cf. Böhtlingk, *Ind. Sprüche*, 1688–1709, 3193–6; Hopkins, in AJP. xx. 25, etc.

1. Time (*kālá*) drives (*vah*) [as] a horse with seven reins, thousand-eyed, unaging, possessing much seed; him the inspired poets mount; his wheels are all beings (*bhúvana*).

The 'wheels' in **d** show that the 'mounting' in **c** is not on the back of the horse, but on the chariot drawn by him. Ppp. combines in **a** *kālo 'çvo v-*, and reads in **b** *akṣaras*, and in **c** *vipaçyatas*. There is nothing at all noteworthy in the exposition of the comm. ⌊In **d**, read *cakrā́ṇi?*⌋

2. Seven wheels doth this time drive; seven [are] his naves, immortality (*amṛ́ta*) forsooth [his] axle; he, time, including (?) all these beings, goes on as first god.

The principal difficulty is here in the third pāda, where our *arvā́ñ* (though accepted by all the translators without any heed to the ms.-readings given at the foot of the page) is a very bold and questionable emendation, most of the mss. (with the comm. ⌊the ms. has *añjan**⌋ and SPP.) giving instead *añjat*, a few *añját*, and some of ours *anyat* or *ayat* (evidently accidental and unimportant variations); Ppp. has *añjaṅ* ⌊i.e. *bhuvanānyañjaṅ*⌋; *arvā̃n* is not to be accepted as at all satisfactory, much less authoritative; it is no proper antithesis to *pratyáñ*† in 3 **c**, nor construable with the accusative. The translation, for a venture, implies *bhúvanā nyañján*, evolving a sense for *nyañján* out of *nyàkta* 'inherent'; it may pass for what it is worth. All the mss., and SPP., read in **a** *cakrā̃n* ⌊and so does Ppp.⌋; the comm. has *cakrā 'nu vahati*. The redundancy of syllables in **d** could be easily remedied either by omitting the superfluous *sá* (left out in the translation) or by reading *īrte* for *īyate* ⌊or by reading *sé "yate* with double *saṁdhi* as Ppp. suggests⌋. Ppp. reads *kāle sāiyyate*. The comm. has in **b** *amṛtaṁ tanv akṣaḥ*. ⌊For the *nú* of **d**, the ms. of the comm. has in fact *u*.⌋ *⌊The comm. has in one place *añjat*, explained as *añjan;* and, in another, the ms. of the comm. has (as noted) *añjan*, which SPP. prints as *añjat = prerayan!*⌋

†⌊It is a curious fact that Whitney here anticipates and parries the very argument in favor of the Roth-Whitney emendation *arvā̃n* which Bloomfield later adduces, SBE. xlii. 684. W. may have written this in 1893 or thereabouts. Bl's translation appeared in 1897.⌋

3. A full vessel is set upon time; we indeed see it, being now manifoldly; it [is] in front of all these beings; it call they time in the highest firmament (*vyòman*).

⌊For '[is] in front of' W. interlines the alternative 'faces toward.'⌋ All the mss. ⌊save W's P.: *santúḥ*⌋ read at end of **b** *santás*, and SPP. retains it, without even changing its false accent; the comm. glosses it with *satpuruṣās*, or, in an alternative explanation, with *sadrūpabrahmopāsakās*. Our emendation to *sántam* is supported by Ppp., which gives *ni santaṁ*. We also emend the *páçyāmas* of the mss. (and SPP.) to *paçy-*. Ppp. combines in **a** to *adhi kālā "hitas*, and reads in **c** *pratyaṁ*. The highly obscure 'full vessel' is thus illuminated (?) by the comm.: *pūrṇaḥ sarvatra vyāptaḥ kumbhaḥ kumbhavat kumbho 'horātramāsartusaṁvatsarādirūpo 'vacchinno janyaḥ kālaḥ*.

4. He indeed together brought beings; he indeed together went about (*pari-i*) beings; being father, he became son of them; than him verily there is no other brilliancy that is higher (*pára*).

The position of *sám* in **a** and in **b** is so strange that we are tempted to emend both times to *sán* 'being';* one *pada*-ms. reads *sán* in **a**, but this can count for nothing. The comm's exposition omits *sám* in **a** ⌊there seems to be a gap in the ms.⌋, but duly treats it (*samyak parigacchati*) in **b**. Ppp. reads in **b** *sa yava saṁ parīyāiḥ*. ⌊With **c** (*pitā̃ . . . putrás*), cf. the note to 54. 3 **a**.⌋ The Anukr. takes no notice of the metrical irregularities. *⌊In that case, perhaps we might render *sá evá* by 'the same.'⌋

5. Time generated yonder sky, time also these earths; what is and what is to be stands out sent forth by time.

SPP. reads in **a** *amū̃m* with a small minority of the authorities, and with the comm.; Ppp. also has it, ⌊combining *'mūm*⌋. For **b**, Ppp. gives *kālāi 'māṁ pṛthivīm uta*. In **c**, our *kāléna* was an emendation, for the *kālé ha** of the mss. (which SPP. follows); we find the former now supported by Ppp. In **d**, the mss. have *havis* (p. *haviḥ*) for *ha vi;* the text of SPP. follows us in emending to the latter, which the comm. also gives; Ppp. reads (*ca*) *eṣataṁ ha vi ti-*. The metrical definition of the Anukr. is not to be approved. *⌊Probably a faulty assimilation to the reading of vs. 6 **c**.⌋

6. Time created the earth; in time burns (*tap*) the sun; in time [are] all existences; in time the eye looks abroad.

Our *bhū́mim* in **a** is an emendation for the *bhūtím* of the mss.: SPP. accepts *bhūtím;* the comm. explains it as = *bhavanavaj jagat.* Ppp. reads *bhūtam asṛjat;* it also omits *ha* in **c**.

7. In time is mind, in time is breath, in time is name collected (*sam-ā-dhā*); by time, when arrived, all these creatures (*prajā́*) are glad (*nand*).

This and the remaining three verses of the hymn are found in Ppp. xii., with the following hymn, without any ⌊real⌋ variants in the four verses.

8. In time is fervor, in time is what is chief, in time is the *bráhman* collected; time is the lord (*īçvará*) of all, who was father of Prajāpati.

All the *pada*-mss. except one, resolve *pitā́sīt* in **d** into *pitā́ : āsīt;* SPP. reads *ā́sīt.* In spite of the repetition of *kālé* between, *jyéṣṭham* and *bráhma* may be conjectured to belong together: cf. x. 7. 24, 32–34; xi. 5. 5, 23. ⌊Note that the usual RV. accent is *jyéṣṭha*, and that the usual AV. accent is *jyeṣṭhá;* and that AV. has the RV. accent only in books xix. and xx. and in a RV. passage, at v. 2. 1.⌋

9. Sent by it, born by it, in it is this (*tát*) set firm; time, becoming the *bráhman*, bears the most exalted one.

We should expect *janitam* 'generated' in **a**. The comm. understands *iṣitam* as *iṣṭam* or *kāmitam.*

10. Time generated progeny, time in the beginning Prajāpati; the self-existent Kaçyapa from time, fervor from time was born.

The comm. identifies *Kaçyapa* with the eighth sun as taught in TA. i. 7. 1. ⌊Cf. Bloomfield's remarks, at AJP. xvii. 403, on the *kaçyapaḥ paçyako bhavati* of TA. i. 8. 8.⌋ Ppp. combines in **b** *kālo 'gre.*

54. Praise of time.

[*Bhṛgu etc.* (*as 53*). —*pañcakam.* *2. 3-p. ārṣī gāyatrī; 5* ⌊*5 and 6 of the Berlin ed.*⌋. *3-av. 6-p. virāḍ aṣṭi.*]

Properly a part of the same hymn with the preceding, and found with vss. 7–10 of the latter in Pāipp. xii. See under hymn 53.

Translated: Muir, v. 409; Ludwig, p. 191; Scherman, *Philosophische Hymnen*, p. 80; Deussen, *Geschichte*, i. 1. 212; Griffith, ii. 311; Bloomfield, 225, 687.—As to the verse-division, see under vss. 2 and 5, and SPP's Critical Notice, vol. i., p. 24.

1. From time came into being the waters; from time [came] the *bráhman*, fervor, the quarters; by time the sun rises; in time he goes to rest (*ni-viç*) again.

All the mss. save two ⌊of SPP's⌋ read *abhavat* at end of **a**; SPP. also ⌊as well as the Berlin ed.⌋ gives *-an*, with the comm., and with Ppp. In **b**, the comm. reads *vrata-tapas* for *bráhma tápas.*

2. ⌊Comm's 2 **a**, **b**, **c**.⌋ By time the wind cleanses (*pavate*); by time the earth [is] great; the great sky in time [is] set.

A part of the verse is lost in Ppp. The comm. adds the first two pādas of our vs. 3 to this one, and makes then the three remaining verses of four pādas each. This makes a decidedly better division, so far as the sense is concerned; but the mss., the Anukr., and SPP. agree in the division given in our text (except as regards vs. 6), and it is accordingly retained here.

3. ⌊Comm's 2 **d**, **e**.⌋ Time, [their] son, generated of old what is and what is to be. ⌊Comm's 3 **a**, **b**.⌋ From time the verses (*ṛ́c*) came into being; the sacrificial formula (*yájus*) was born from time;—

In the first half-verse, the translation follows the mss. ⌊they read *kāló* and *putró*⌋, rather than our emendations ⌊*kālé** and *mántro*⌋, which seem more venturesome than there is reason for; and departs from them only in assuming at the end *purā́*, instead of *púras*, as the mss. in general read (*purā́* is accepted by both editions, and is supported apparently by Ppp., and to a certain degree by one of SPP's mss. which has *púrā*). Perhaps *púnaḥ* ⌊which Whitney's I. actually has⌋ is a yet more plausible substitute for *púraḥ*. Ppp. has *kālena bhūtaṁ janayat:* ⌊so Roth's Collation: I take it to mean "*kālena bhūtaṁ* in **a** and *'janayat* in **b**"⌋; and the comm. also has at the beginning *kālena* ⌊which he glosses with *pitrā prerakeṇa*: cf. his *putras* in **b**, and cf. 53. 4 **c**⌋; and at the end of **b** he seems to have read *puras* ⌊the word does not actually appear⌋, since he gives *purastāt* for explanation. In **c**, part of the mss. have *abhavat*. *⌊As *kāló* is given by all the mss. collated by W. before publication, *kālé* was indeed an emendation; but some of SPP's authorities do have *kālé*.⌋

4. ⌊Comm's 3 **c**, **d**.⌋ Time set in motion (*sam-īr*) the sacrifice, an unexhausted portion for the gods. ⌊Comm's 4 **a**, **b**.⌋ In time are set firm the Gandharvas-and-Apsarases; in time the worlds;—

In **a**, the translation implies *kālás*, with all the authorities, but *āirayat*, against nearly all of them; the comm. gives *āirayat* and SPP. accepts it; ⌊and it is supported by his ms. P. (which has *āirayan*, p.m., corrected to *āirayat*) and by Ppp's *īrayat*⌋. Ppp. reads *kālo yajño sam īrayat*, and has at the end *samāhitāḥ*.

⌊5 and 6 of Berlin ed. = 5 of Bombay ed.⌋ ⌊Comm's 4 **c**, **d**.⌋ Upon time stand this heavenly Añgiras and Atharvan. ⌊Comm's 5 **a**, **b**.⌋ Both this world and the highest world, and the pure (*púṇya*) worlds and the pure separations —⌊6 of Berlin ed.: Comm's 5 **c**, **d**.⌋ all worlds by the *bráhman* having conquered, this time goes on as highest god.

Verses 5 and 6 of our edition are here combined into one, on the authority of the Anukr. and part of the mss., and in accordance with SPP. Of the mss. compared by us before printing, all made a sixth verse of the last two pādas. In **a**, the mss. read *kāléyám* ⌊W's O. has *kāleyám*⌋ (p. *kāleyám* or *kāléyam*) ⌊SPP's *pada*-ms. Cp., here unaccented, has *kāleyam*⌋; SPP. emends the *pada*-text to *kālé : ayám*, but strangely presents a *saṁhitā*-text inconsistent with this, namely *kālé 'yám*, instead of *kālè 'yám*, as our edition reads. All the mss. read *divó 'th-* in **a**–**b** (p. *diváḥ*), but SPP., on authority of the comm., emends to *devó 'th-*, and the translation follows this; Ppp. also reads *devo 'th-*. ⌊At the end of **b**, the comm. reads *tiṣṭhati*.⌋ In **d** a number of the mss. give *vídhṛtīñç ca;* the obscure word is passed over lightly by the comm., who simply glosses it with *lokadhārakān*. The last pāda is identical with 53. 2 **d**, ⌊save that it has *paramó* where 53. 2 **d** has *prathamó*⌋, and Ppp. combines, as there, *sāiyyate*. The most natural count of syllables (8 + 8 : 11 + 11 : 11 + 12 = 61) comes three short of a full *aṣṭi:* ⌊the *jagatī* cadence of **e** suggests that something is missing (read *sárvāñç ca lo-*?) in that pāda; and **f** is to be read (like 53. 2 **d**, with Ppp. double *saṁdhi*) as 11 syllables⌋.

⌊Here ends the sixth *anuvāka*, with 9 hymns, and with 63 verses as they are numbered by the Berlin text and summed up by certain mss.; but the Anukr. counts 9 and 5 verses (instead of 10 and 6) in hymns 47 and 54 respectively, which makes the sum 61 instead of 63.⌋

55. To Agni.

[*Bhṛgu.* — *ṣaḍṛcam. āgneyam. trāiṣṭubham: 2. āstārapañkti; 5* ⌊*i.e. 5 and 6* **a, b** *of the Berlin ed.*⌋. *3-av. 5-p. purastājjyotiṣmatī.*] ⌊*Of 6* (= *6* **c, d**, *7* **a, b** *of Berlin ed.*), *the definition is lacking: see my note to vs. 6.*⌋

Only the first verse is found in Pāipp. (in xx.). The comm. points out that the hymn is plainly meant to be used in the early morning worship of Agni, but quotes no authority. ⌊As to a seventh verse, see SPP's Critical Notice, vol. i., p. 24, and see under vss. 5 and 7.⌋

Translated: Ludwig, p. 363; Griffith, ii. 312.

1. Night after night bringing to him without mixture, as fodder to a horse that stands, let not us, O Agni, thy neighbors, receive harm, reveling with abundance of wealth, with food (*íṣ*).

The verse corresponds nearly with VS. xi. 75, also with a verse in TS. iv. 1. 10[1] and MS. ii. 7. 7. VS. begins **a** with *áhar-ahar* (but ÇB. vi. 6. 4[1] ⌊like KÇS. xvi. 6. 2⌋ gives a *pratīka* with *rā́trīṁ-rātrīm* instead), TS. reads with us, and MS. has *rā́trīṁ-rātrīm* ⌊and repeats the *pratīka* at iii. 1. 9, p. 12[12]⌋. At end of **b**, all have *asmāi* unaccented. In **d**, all put *ágne* at the beginning, *'gne mā́ te práti-*. In **a**, all the authorities have *áprayātam* ⌊an isolated *-tum* counts for nothing⌋, and so has the text of the comm., according to SPP., who prints *áprayātam*. But the comm. in his explanation has *aprayāvam*, which he glosses by *apracchidya* or *sāṁtatyena* ⌊which harmonizes well with the *sádam ít* of iii. 15. 8 **a**⌋; ⌊the six Yajus texts just cited (both verses and *pratīkas*) all read *áprayāvam*, on which the Berlin emendation* rests⌋. ⌊Weber, *Ind. Stud.* xvii. 251, cites K. xvi. 7 as reading *rātrīṁ-rātrīm*, with the rest as in VS.; and Knauer, Index to MGS., p. 155, adds K. xix. 10 and Kap. S. xxx. 8.⌋ The second half of our iii. 15. 8 above agrees precisely with our **c, d** here; the first half differs a good deal, ⌊having for **a** *viçvā́hā te sádam íd bharema*, and ending **b** with *jātavedaḥ* instead of *ghāsám asmā́i*⌋. Ppp. has in **a** *aprayāmaṁ*, at end of **b** *agne* for *asmāi* (as in our vs. 7), and in **d** *'gnāi mā te pr-* (intending the same as the Yajus texts).

*⌊Griffith's version of *áprayāvam* is 'with care unceasing' (AV.VS.); and Eggeling's is 'unremittingly' (ÇB.); so also W. at iii. 5. 1 (see the note); and in his *Roots* he connects *-yāvam* only with root *yu* 'separate'; one does not see why he departs from that here: nevertheless, the sense 'mix' is well avouched for the root *yu* 'unite' with *pra* by JUB. i. 8, *yathā madhunā lājān prayuyād evam* (see JAOS. xvi. 88 and 228). — I may add in the proof that even the Anukr. reads *aprayātam*, but that the Yajus readings, and the *sádam ít* (W. 'constantly') of iii. 15. 8, seem to place the Berlin emendation beyond doubt: and that the Ppp. reading *aprayucchan* at iii. 5. 1 helps to establish for the Vulgate not only the form *áprayāvam* as gerund, but also the meaning 'without being careless' or 'unremittingly' as against 'without mixing.'⌋

2. Of thee that art good what arrow [is] in the wind, this is that of thine; therewith be gracious to us. Let not us, O Agni, thy neighbors, receive harm, reveling with abundance of wealth, with food.

The translation follows the text of the mss. rather than our emendations, as the latter afford no more satisfactory sense than does the former. Several authorities, however, read *yā́ta* instead of *vā́ta* (one has *vā́ca;* one *ī́ṣuḥ*, two *éṣuḥ;* ⌊and so on⌋): the *pada*-mss. divide *vā́taḥ : ī́ṣuḥ : sā́.* The comm's text has *iṣa;* but how his explanation is related to the text is hard to see: *he agne vāsakasya tava yā 'nugrahabuddhir anna-pradasya yā cā 'nugrahabuddhis tayā 'smān sukhaya;* that is all.

3. Evening after evening [is] Agni our house-lord; morning after morning [is he] giver of well-willing; be thou giver of good to us of every kind; may we, kindling thee, adorn (*puṣ*) ourselves.

The third pāda is literally 'of good thing after good thing be thou giver of good.' The *pada*-mss. divide *vasu°dā́naḥ : edhi* instead of *vasu°dā́ḥ : naḥ : edhi*, as is implied by our text; the meter makes us suspect that the true original reading was *vasudā́no na edhi.* The fourth pāda is v. 3. 1 **b** etc. (see under that verse). ⌊Cf. vs. 4.⌋

4. Morning after morning [is] Agni our house-lord; evening after evening [is he] giver of well-willing; be thou giver of good to us of every kind; kindling thee, may we thrive (*ṛdh*) a hundred winters.

In **d** the mss. read *çatáṁhimās* (p. *çatáṁ°himāḥ*); the comm. takes it as two words, *çataṁ himās*, ⌊ignoring the accent⌋. ⌊With pāda **d**, cf. RV. i. 64. 14 **d.**⌋ ⌊Cf. vs. 3.⌋

5. May I be one not falling short of food; to the food-eating lord of food, to Agni [as] Rudra be homage.

Here also there is discordance as to the verse-division; the Anukr. ⌊and comm.⌋ further add to vs. 5 what in our edition is 6 **a**, **b**, and then make one verse of what remains of the hymn; and SPP. follows them. The translation adheres to our text (which represents all the mss. till that time known to us), especially because its division seems better suited to the sense. At the beginning, all the authorities, and SPP., have *ápaçcādag-dhā́nnasya*, divided by the *pada*-text into *ápaçcā : dagdhá°annasya* (or *-gdha°án-*); ⌊but Whitney's W. has *daghānt-*; his M. has *dagdhvānn-*; and his P. has *dagghvānt-* or possibly *dagdhvānt-*, it is not clear which: at any rate, in P. and M. there is a *v* before the *ā;*⌋ the comm. understands *apaçcādagdhā 'nnasya*, and solemnly explains it as meaning: *annasyā 'paçcā[dagdhā] paçcādbhāge 'dagdhā sthālīpṛṣṭhabhāge dagdhānnara-hitaḥ!* The correctness of our conjectural emendation to *ápaçcādaghvā́ 'nnasya* is put beyond question by the occurrence of a corresponding phrase, *ápaçcāddaghvā́ 'nnam bhūyāsam*, in MS. iii. 9. 4, p. 120[17], and also in Āp. vii. 28. 2.* Part of the mss. accent *bhūyāsám.* In **b**, all SPP's authorities ⌊save one⌋, and most of ours, give *annādayo 'nn-* (variously accented: p. *anna°adáyaḥ*), apparently a case of misunderstanding of *āyā* as *yo* after the Bengālī method of writing *o;*† but two of our mss., P.M., have *annādā́yā́ 'nn-*, which is the reading of our text; the comm. likewise understands *-dāya*, and SPP. also accepts it in his text.

*⌊The phrase *á-paçcād-daghvane náre* occurs at RV. vi. 42. 1; TB. iii. 7. 10[6]; Āp. xiv. 29. 2; compare *apaçcā-daghvane naraḥ* at SV. i. 352, ii. 790. It may be worth noting that the comm. to TB. brings the epithet into connection with food, explaining the phrase as 'a man devoid of brightness (i.e. dull) after his meal, unable to digest what he has

eaten,' *paçcād bhakṣottarakālaṁ dīptirahitāya, bhakṣitaṁ jarayitum asamarthāya.* He seems to connect *a- . . -daghvan* (= *dīptirahita*) with *dah;* but BR. and W., with Sāyaṇa on RV., derive it from *dagh:* cf. RV. i. 123. 5 **c**; vii. 56. 21 **b**.⌋ †⌊Cf. SPP's notes to xviii. 4. 48; xix. 32. 10; 48. 1; 56. 3.⌋

6. O thou of the assembly, protect my assembly (*sabhā́*), and [them] who are of the assembly, sitters in the assembly; having much invoked thee, O Indra, may they attain their whole life-time.

The translation is to be taken simply for what it is worth, as it does not follow the mss., nor either printed text. At the beginning, the mss. ⌊except several of W's, which have the impossible *sabhyá*⌋, SPP., and the comm., read *sabhyás*, which might well enough have been left by us unchanged, save for accent (viii. 10. 5 *sábhyas*). But the mss. read *sabhyás* again later ⌊save two of W's, which have *sabhyā́s*⌋; this time SPP. emends to *sabhyā́s* (should be *sábhyās*, with us?), since the comm. has this. In **c**, the mss. in general give *tvám indrā* (or *índrā*) *puruhūtya* (p. *puru°hūtya*); the comm's text offers *tvām* ⌊his exposition: *tvam*⌋ *indra puruhūta;* and SPP. adopts *tvám indrā* (p. *indra*) *puruhūta;* our conjecture, *tváyé 'd gā́ḥ puruhūta*, seems too violent, and the translation implies *tvā́m indra puruhū́ya*, with *açnavan* at the end, while the mss., and SPP., have *açnavat* (the comm. has the same, unblushingly explaining it as = *prāpaya*, a mere substitution of one person for another!), and our text emended to *-vam*, an ungrammatical but not wholly unprecedented form. ⌊The London ms. of the Anukr. adds as the *pratīka* of its vs. 6 *tvam indrā puruhūtye 'ti* (our 6 **c**: note the reading), but gives no metrical definition: the Berlin ms. does not even give the *pratīka.*⌋

7. Day after day taking tribute to thee, O Agni, as fodder to a horse that stands [, let not us, O Agni, thy neighbors, receive harm, reveling with abundance of wealth, with food (*íṣ*)].

None of the mss. have the second half-verse; it was added because it seemed called for by the first half, as in vss. 1 and 2. That the comm. and part of the mss., and so also SPP., in agreement with the Anukr., make only six verses in the hymn, was explained above under vs. 5. A majority of the mss. accent *bálim* in **a** (including all those used by us before publication), and so the error has got into our text; SPP. has correctly *balím;* some leave *hárantas* without accent; the comm. and a ms. or two have *ítye* for *ít te* (= *prāptavye gṛhe vartamānāyā 'gnaye*, comm.). All the mss. have in **b** *jātám* instead of *ghāsám;* but the comm. has the latter, and it is therefore read in SPP's text as well as in ours.

56. To sleep (or dream).

[*Yama.* — *ṣaṭkam. dāuṣvapnyam. trāiṣṭubham.*]

Found also in Pāipp. iii. The comm. quotes no authority as to the *viniyoga*, but points out that the hymn is shown by its content to belong to the ceremony for getting rid of *duḥsvapna* 'evil-dreaming.' He holds, namely, throughout the hymn, that *svápna* means *duḥsvapna* (in the Atharvan always *duṣvápnya*); and the language is too obscure to show clearly whether he is right or not; the probability is certainly against him, because elsewhere (e.g. in the next hymn), when evil-dreaming is intended, its own name is freely used, and in xvi. 5 *svapna* is contrasted with *duṣvapnya.* ⌊As in the case of hymns 53 and 54, the Anukr. suggests that the hymns 56 and 57 are only two divided parts of one group of 11 verses; and the suggestion is reinforced by the juxtaposition in the RV. text (viii. 47. 15 and 17) of matter corresponding to our 56. 4 and 57. 1 (see under those verses); and hymns 56 and 57 are translated together by Ludwig.⌋

Translated: Ludwig, p. 467; Griffith, ii. 313.

1. Out of Yama's world hast thou come hither (*ā-bhū*); with mirth (?) dost thou, wise, make use of (*pra-yuj*) mortals; knowing, thou goest in alliance (*sarátham*) with the solitary one, fashioning (*mā*) sleep in the lair (*yóni*) of the Asura.

If *prámadā* (p. *prá○madā*) is to be rendered as above, it must have its accent changed to *pramádā;* the comm., against the *pada*-text, understands it as *pramadās* = *striyas*, joint object with *mártyān* of *prá yunakṣi.* One or two mss. read *mártān* in **b**. The comm. renders *dhīras* by *dhṛṣṭas.* ⌊Apart from W's P.M.W., which have *svā́pnam*,⌋ all the mss., the comm., and SPP., read *svápnam* in **d**, and the translation follows this rather than our *svápna*, willing, in so obscure a matter, to stick as closely to the authorities as possible. Ppp., to be sure, gives *svapna mi-*, but this counts for very little. The comm. understands the verse to be addressed to the demon of ill-dreaming (*he duḥsvapnābhimānin krūra piçāca*); but his explanations through the whole hymn are worthless, being only the etymologizing guesses of one to whom the real sense is precisely as obscure as it is to us: *asura* is *prāṇavant ātman;* the 'lonely one' is the man who is dying of the effect of evil-dreaming, having abandoned son, wife, relatives, etc.; *yāsi* means *yamalokam prāpayasi;* and so on, and so on. ⌊Griffith cites "Death and his brother Sleep" of Shelley's Queen Mab (it is found also at Iliad xiv. 231) and "the twins, Sleep and Death," Il. xvi. 682.⌋

2. The all-vigorous bond saw thee in the beginning, in the one day before the birth of night; from thence, O sleep, didst thou come (*ā-bhū*) hither, hiding thy form from the physicians.

In this verse also, for the reason given above, the translation follows the mss. more closely than does our text. Nearly all authorities have at the beginning *bandhás;* a couple ⌊the reciters, K. and V.⌋, with the comm., *bandhús* (wrong accent ⌊as in vs. 5⌋); Ppp. reads *baṁbhas.* All have *viçvácayās* (p. *viçvá○cayāḥ*), though in some of them the *c* could be read as *v;* the comm. is able to make a sense for it: *sarvasya cetā, saṁcetā, sraṣṭā;* the translation implies *viçvávayās*, as the smallest possible intelligible change; Ppp. presents *viçvavathāv* ⌊and *apaçyan*⌋. The *pada*-mss. divide in **b** *rā́tryā : jánitaḥ : réke;* the comm. understands, with us, *rā́tryāḥ : jánitoḥ : éke;* and SPP. substitutes this in his *pada*-text. *Eke ahni* ⌊which Ppp. combines to *eke 'hni*⌋ might, of course, also be understood as locative absolute. Our *tátas* at beginning of **c** was an emendation for *táva* of the mss.; the comm. has it (also Ppp.), and SPP. accordingly also adopts it in his text. The whole pāda reads in Ppp.: *tatas svapnena madhyā ca bhāyatha.* In **d** all the mss. have *bhiṣágbhya r-*, and the *pada*-mss. *bhiṣágbhya○rūpam* (!); only one or two give an accent to *rūpám;* the comm. understands *bhiṣágbhyo rūpám*, and SPP. reads this; the translation follows it. There is much discordance as to the accent of *apagūhamānas.* Ppp. reads *bhiṣajña rūpam apigūh-.* The comm. is a grammarian of such sort that he does not accept *éke* as used here for the more regular *ékasmin;* but he does accept *ahni* as used, by the ordinary license to put one case in place of another, for *ahnas*, coördinate in construction with *rātryās;* and *eke* means *mānasaprajāpatyādayas*, and is subject of *apaçyan* understood! The evil-dreaming hid itself away from the medicine-men, says the comm., lest they should meet it with an efficacious remedy; and something like that is possibly the real meaning.

3. He of great kine (?) turned unto the gods away from the Asuras, seeking greatness; to that sleep the three-and-thirty ones, having attained the sky, imparted over-lordship.

At the beginning, the *saṁhitā*-mss. in general read *bṛhád gā́vā* (p. *bṛhát : gā́vā* or *grā́vā*); Ppp. has *vṛhaṁgrāvā* ⌊combining *-vāsurebhyo*⌋; the comm. gives *bṛhadgāvā*, as nom. of *-gāvan*, deriving it from *gā* 'go'; and SPP. accepts this (*bṛhadgā́vā*, p. *bṛhat॰gā́vā*), while at the same time suggesting that *-gavó* may be meant, by such a confusion of the two modes of writing *o* as we have already more than once ⌊cf. 55. 5 **b** and the note⌋ had occasion to conjecture. Ppp. reads *'bhi* instead of *'dhi*. There is discordance among the mss. as to the accent of *upā 'vartata*. Ppp. reads at end of **b** *ṛcchan*. The majority of mss. have in **d** *tráyastriṅçāsá sv-*; and part of the *pada*-mss. divide *tráyaḥ॰triṅçā́ḥ : sáḥ : sv-;* SPP. gives *trayastriṅçā́saḥ sv-*, as do we.

4. Not the Fathers, and not the gods, know it, whose (pl.) murmur goes about within here; in Trita Āptya did the men (*nṛ́*), the Ādityas, taught by Varuṇa, set sleep.

The mss. read at the beginning *nā́t 'tā́m* ⌊and so SPP.⌋, the *etā́m* 'it' apparently being viewed as relating to *jálpis;* the comm. makes the relation plainer by giving in **b** *yāi 'ṣām;* but this latter SPP. rejects. At end of **b**, the mss. vary between *antarétā́m* and *antaré 'dā́m* (p. *antarā́ : idā́m*); the comm. gives the latter, and SPP. accepts it; Ppp. also has it; ⌊and it is implied in the translation⌋. The mss., as always, vary between *tṛté* and *trité;* the great majority here give the former. *Váruṇena* in **d** was our emendation for *ár-*; it is read also by the comm., and by one of SPP's mss., and is found in Ppp.; SPP. also adopts it in his text. The mss. all accent *ā́dityāsas*, and SPP. does not emend, as we do, to *ādityā́sas*. Ppp. reads in **b** *jalpyaç c-*, and has for **c** *trite svapnam arididṛhā prate narā* (*ādit-*). With **c**, compare RV. viii. 47. 13–17 and especially 15 **c**, **d**. The comm. tells a tale of how *duḥsvapna*, having received overlordship from the gods, waxed topping, and seized on the Ādityas; the latter applied for relief to Varuṇa, and, duly instructed by him, put off the *duḥsvapna* upon the great seer (*maharṣi*) Trita, son of the waters: this is pretty plainly no tradition, but an account devised by the comm. to fit the immediate case.

5. Of whom the evil-doers shared ⌊*bhaj*⌋ the cruelty, the well-doers, by non-sleep, [shared] the pure (*púṇya*) life-time — thou revelest in the sky (*svàr*) with the highest relative; thou wast born out of the mind of one practising fervor.

The translation is a merely literal rendering, and does not pretend to be an intelligent one. It implies in **a**, with SPP., a majority of his mss., and the comm., *ábhajanta* (the other readings are *apacanta*, *abhacanta*, *aṣacanta;* and there are varieties of accent); in **b**, all the *saṁhitā*-mss. combine *duṣkṛ́to sv-*, implying *asvápnena;* but ⌊SPP's⌋ *pada*-mss. ⌊and W's *pada*-ms. D., p.m.⌋ read *svápnena;* ⌊W's D. seems to be corrected to *asváp-* and his L. also seems to have *asváp-*;⌋ SPP. accepts *asváp-*, with the comm. Ppp. gives no help; its text is *vy asya krūram abhijanta duṣkṛṇe sv-*; and *āpuḥ* for *āyuḥ* at the end of **b**. In **c**, *bandhúnā* (read by both editions, with the mss.) ought to have been emended ⌊cf. vs. 2 **a**⌋ to *bándhunā*, as both texts emend to *tapyá-* from *tápya-*, which appears in most of the mss. At the end, SPP. has the correct *jajñiṣe*, with about ⌊half of his authorities, including the carefully corrected Dc.⌋ (and with one of our later ones); our *jajñiṣé* represents the rest, but has no reason. Ppp. has in **c** *svarasajasi*.

The comm. renders *abhajanta* by *prāpnuvanti*, and *asvapnena* by *duḥsvapnadarçanābhāvena*; he regards *duḥsvapna* as addressed in the second half-verse, and explains *svàr* as equivalent to a locative (as rendered above) ⌊cf. *Noun-Inflection*, p. 488⌋, and *bandhunā* (cf. 2 a) as *sṛṣṭeḥ prākkāle tvāṁ dṛṣṭavatā vidhātrā saha.*

6. We know all thine attendants (?) in front; we know, O sleep, who is thine over-ruler here; protect us here with the glory of the glorious one; go thou away far off with poisons.

In b, the *pada*-mss. give blunderingly *svapna∘yáḥ*. Ppp. reads *yo 'dhipā hyo te*. Of course, *yaçasvinas* in c may be accus. pl., 'us who are glorious'; the comm. takes it so, and explains that the glory comes from our wonderful knowledge as set forth in the first half-verse. ⌊Ppp. reads *yaçaso hi* for *yáçase 'há.*⌋ In d, the *saṁhitā*-mss. (also Ppp.) give *ārā́dviṣ-*, which is equivalent to *ārā́ddviṣ-*; and the *pada*-mss. assume the latter, dividing *ārā́t : dviṣébhiḥ*; since a derivative *dviṣá* is as good as unknown, and of a very unusual formation, we preferred to read *viṣébhis*; ⌊the comm., text and exposition, has *dviṣobhis*;⌋ SPP. has *dviṣébhis*. In a the translation of *parijā́s* is that of the comm. (= *parijanān*), which seems more probable than the conjecture of the Pet. Lexx., "perhaps places of origin."

57. Against evil-dreaming.

[*Yama.—pañcakam. dāuṣvapnyam. trāiṣṭubham: 1. anuṣṭubh; 3* ⌊of Anukr.: = *3 and 4* a (to *mukham*) of Berlin ed'n⌋. *3-av. 4-p. triṣṭubh; 4* ⌊of Anukr.: = *4* b *to 5* b of Berlin ed'n, that is *taṁ tvā svapna* to *gṛhe*⌋. *6-p. uṣṇigbṛhatīgarbhā virāṭçakvarī; 5* ⌊of Anukr.: = *5* c *to 6* of Berlin ed'n, that is *anāsmākas tad* to end of hymn⌋. *3-av. 5-p. paraçākvarā 'tijagatī.*]

⌊Partly prose — verses 2, 3, 4, and 6.⌋ Pāipp. has only the first verse (in ii.). The comm. quotes from a Pariçiṣṭa (SPP. is unable to identify the passage) a direction for using it (with vi. 45, 46) to a king who sees bad dreams. ⌊As to the connection of the material of this hymn with that of h. 56, see introd. to h. 56.⌋ ⌊As to the differences of division, see under vss. 3, 4, and 5, and cf. SPP's Critical Notice, vol. i., p. 24.⌋

Translated: Ludwig, p. 468; Griffith, ii. 314.

1. As a sixteenth, as an eighth, as a [whole] debt they bring together, so do we bring together all evil-dreaming on one who is offensive (*ápriya*).

The verse is nearly identical with vi. 46. 3, differing only by substituting *ápriye* in d for *dviṣaté*. *Apriye* comes near to the *āptyé* of RV. viii. 47. 17, with which both verses correspond: see note to vi. 46. 3. The comm., in fact, reads *āptye*.

2. Kings have gathered (*sam-gā*), debts have gathered, *kuṣṭhás* have gathered, sixteenths have gathered; all evil-dreaming that is in us — let us impel away evil-dreaming to him that hates us.

The *pada*-mss. read *sáḥ : mṛṇā́ni* for *sám : ṛṇā́ni*, and *sáḥ : kalā́ḥ* (the *saṁhitā*-mss. also *sá kalā́ ag-*) for *sám : kalā́ḥ*; SPP. follows us in emending in both places to *sám*, which the comm. also has. At the beginning of the second division, we have emended *sám* of the mss. and comm. (which SPP. follows) to *sárvam*. For *yát* (after *asmā́su*) the *saṁhitā*-mss. read *yáta*, and the *pada*-mss. *yátaḥ*; our *yát* is supported by the comm., and SPP. adopts it. The comm. says that *kuṣṭha* is a skin-disease, symptomatic of various maladies; and, when one of these remains unhealed, boils and sores etc. (? *piṭakavraṇādīni*) show themselves. Also, that *kalās* are *anupādeyāvayavopalakṣaṇa*, and worthless parts of cattle etc. are collected in old pits. And in like manner collected ill-dreaming is made over to an enemy. That is his idea, and a wholly unacceptable one, of the general meaning of the verse. ⌊The verse is prose, no *triṣṭubh;* but may be stretched so as to count as 43 syllables.⌋

3. Embryo of the wives of the gods, instrument of Yama, excellent dream; the evil [dream] that is mine, that do we send forth to him that hates us.

The mss. all read *devā́nām pā́tnīnām̐ gā́rbha* (one *pada*-ms. *-bham*) *yamā́sya kā́rayo bhadrā́svapnaḥ;* the translation implies no further emendation than to *gā́rbho* and *kā́raṇo;* ⌊the minor Pet. Lex., iv. 249, accepts *bhadrā́svapna* as a descriptive compound, although the accent (*Gram.* § 1280 c) is very exceptional;⌋ SPP., following the comm., changes to *devā́nām patnīnām̐ garbha yā́masya kara yó bhadrā́ḥ svapna*. Our *devā́patnīnām* and *kā́raṇas* were suggested especially by the *devajā́mīnā́m* and *kā́raṇas* of vi. 46. 2 and xvi. 5. 6, of which neither the comm. nor SPP. take any notice. In the second division of the verse the two editions agree, save that ours emends *tā́t* of the mss. (which SPP follows) to *tā́m;* and the latter is supported by our P.M., and by the comm. But the mss. have at the beginning *samā́mayaḥ*, and the *pada*-mss. resolve it into *samā́m : ayaḥ*. The Anukr. and comm. and SPP. add to this verse what in our text is the first division of vs. 4; our division is that of our first mss., and is preferable on the ground of the sense. ⌊The prose verse, according to the division of the Anukr., may be made to count (8 + 10 : 13 : 13 ?) as 44 syllables.⌋

4. Thee that art "harsh" by name, mouth of the black bird (*-çakúni*) — thee, O sleep, we thus know completely; do thou, O sleep, as a horse a halter, as a horse a girth, scatter him who is not of us, the god-reviler, the mocker.

⌊Prose.⌋ The translation here is of no authority, including various venturesome emendations of the text; it follows our text except at the end, where, instead of *badhāna*, it implies the (unsatisfactory) *vapa* of the comm. and SPP.; all the mss. read *vā́pus* ⌊or *vápu*⌋. At the beginning, the *pada*-mss. give *mā́tr̥ṣṭā : nāma : asi : kr̥ṣṇaoçakune : múkham;* and the *saṁhitā*-mss. agree with them, with worthless variations of accent ⌊and some slight differences besides⌋, and with *-kuner* in one or two. SPP. reads, however, *mā́ tr̥ṣṭā́nām asi kr̥ṣṇaçakunér múkham*, won, as he claims, by adding accents to the comm's text; but this differs from the mss. only by ⌊the word-division and⌋ by *-nāmasi* and *-ner;* how the comm. divides and understands *mātr̥ṣṭānāmasi* is unknown, as his explanation of the words is wanting (though SPP. notes no lacuna). So much (to *múkham*) is, as was noted above, added to vs. 3 by Anukr., comm., and SPP. In the next division of the verse, for *kakṣyā̀m*, the mss., the comm., and SPP., give *kāyám*, which might mean 'body'; the comm. is apparently imperfect here, reading *açvo yathā svakīyaṁ rajodhūsaraṁ* [*kāyaṁ*] *dhunoti yathā cā 'çvo nīnāham palyāṇakavacādikam avakirati:* with *kāyam* is perhaps omitted also *çarīram*, its gloss. Our mss. end vs. 4 with *nīnāhā́m*, and it was our emendation to add the next clause; but this the comm. does also, ending with *vapa*, while SPP. goes on to *gr̥he* without making a verse-division; the sense (so far as we can be said to understand it) favors our division and the comm's. The latter reads *avā 'smākam*, finding thus an *ava* . . . *vapa*, which he explains by *tiraskuru*. All the mss. give *pípāruṁ* ⌊P.M.: *píy-*⌋ *vápur* ⌊or *vápu*⌋ *yád* etc., with not even a pāda-division after *vápus;* such a division was due in our text, however, after *nīnāhám*. ⌊The Anukr. seems to intend to count the verse (*taṁ tvā* to *gṛhe*) as 9 + 9 + 7 + 13 (reading *vapa*): 8 + 8 = 54.⌋

5. What evil-dreaming is in us, what in our kine, and what in our house, that let him who is not of us, the god-reviler, the mocker, put on like a necklace (*niṣká*).

⌊Pādas **a** and **b** are identical with 45. 2 **a**, **b**, above; and the rest of the verse seems to throw much light on 45. 2 **c**, **d**: see my note to that verse. In his Collation-Book, Whitney here made a note of this important parallel, but seems to have overlooked his note when working out his commentary.⌋ The mss. again all read *pípārus* ⌊P.M.: *píy-*⌋; and the comm. again *avā 'smākam*, supplying a *gamaya* to the *ava* in his explanation. The omission of *devapīyús* would make a fair *anuṣṭubh* of this verse ⌊and a faultless one, if we pronounce *niṣkéva*⌋; it is evidently metrical, and a verse by itself ⌊cf. 45. 2⌋ as it stands in our text; the Anukr. and SPP., with part of the mss., end vs. 4 with *gṛhé*, and throw all the rest of the hymn together as vs. 5; the comm. agrees with us as to vss. 5 and 6. ⌊The Anukr. seems to intend to count its verse 5 (*anāsmākás tád* to end of hymn) as 12 + 9 : 9 + 7 [:] 14 = 51, and to put its second *avasāna*, with some of the mss., after *pári*, as does SPP.⌋

6. Having measured off nine cubits, forth from that do we divide off to him who hates us all our evil-dreaming.

⌊Prose.⌋ Instead of our *apamáya*, the mss., the comm., and SPP. read *ápamayā* (p. *ápa॰mayāḥ*); how the comm. (or SPP.) would explain it does not appear, as he gives only the general sense of the expression: *asmākaṁ sambandhi duṣvapnyaṁ navāratniparyantam apasāraya*. He reads at the end *apriye saṁ nayāmasi* (= 1 **d**).

58. For various blessings.

[*Brahman.—ṣaḍṛcam. mantroktabahudevatyam uta yājñikam. trāiṣṭubham: 2. puro'nuṣṭubh; 3. 4-p. atiçakvarī; 5. bhurij.*]

The first four verses occur also in Pāipp. i.; ⌊Roth's Collation, strictly interpreted, means that the whole hymn is found there⌋. The comm. quotes vs. 5 as used in Kāuç. 3. 16; but the verse there intended is evidently ii. 35. 5, of which vs. 5 here is a repetition. At the beginning of his exposition of vs. 1 he says: *asmin sūkte manasā nirvartyo yajñaḥ stūyate*.

Translated: Griffith, ii. 315.

1. The swiftness of ghee evenly always increasing the year with oblation — be our hearing, sight, breath unsevered; unsevered be we from life-time, from splendor.

The translation implies in **a** *samanā́ sadā́t 'vá*. ⌊This last may be a slip for *sádāivá*, p. *sádā : evá;* the Berlin text and the *Index* imply *sádeva*, p. *sádā॰iva*.⌋ Five authorities give *samanā́* (so in p.); five or six, *samanā́ḥ;* the rest *samanāḥ* or *sámanāḥ*, or else *samā́nāḥ* or *samā́nā* or finally *sámanā;* SPP. accepts the last, from only two mss.; the comm. reads *samanāḥ*, and explains it as *samānamanaskā*. After it the mss. read *sádevāḥ* (p. *sá॰devāḥ*), but the comm. and his text *sadevā*, and SPP. follows these, accenting *sádevā*. Ppp. has *yūtis sumanās sudevās* (*s-*). The comm. says that, since all words signifying 'motion' also signify 'knowledge,' *jūti* here means *sarvatra prasṛtaṁ jñānam!* Ppp. combines in **c** *prāṇa ach-*. In **d**, the *pada*-mss. read *áchinnā* instead of *-nāḥ*. The connection of the two half-verses is perhaps this: it is prayed that the prospering flow of the libations of sacred butter be uninterrupted, carrying as a consequence the continuance of physical blessings.

2. Let breath call unto us; we call unto breath; the earth, the atmosphere hath seized (*grah*) splendor; splendor [also] Soma, Bṛihaspati, the maintainer.

Some mss. (including most of the *pada*-mss.) begin **b** with *úpa hvayám*. In **c**, one of SPP's mss. and Ppp. combine *pṛthivy ānt-*. At the end, the *pada*-mss. have correctly *dhartā́;* the *saṁhitā*-mss. vary between this and *dhattā́*, *dhattā́m*, and *dhattā́t;* and the reciter K. gave *vidhartā́*. The comm's text (SPP.) has *vidhattām*, but his explanation reads *vidhattā* (misreading for *-arttā?*) *viçeṣeṇa dhartā 'gniḥ sūryo vā;* and SPP. most strangely adopts the senseless *vidhattā́* (it is read also by one ms.). Ppp. gives instead *bibhartu*, which is not bad. Furthermore, Ppp. begins **a** with *apa*, but **b** with *upa*. The seizing of splendor by these various divinities is, according to the comm., for the purpose of giving it to us. Pādas **b** and **d** lack each a syllable. ⌊A similar antithesis with *upahū* occurred at i. 1. 4, and others were pointed out there.⌋

3. Heaven-and-earth have become joint-seizers of splendor; seizing splendor may we go about upon the earth; with glory the kine, coming, wait upon (*upa-sthā*) the lord of kine; seizing glory may we go about upon the earth.

⌊The verse is by no means one of 4 pādas, but rather one of 6 (**a–f**: so designated below): in fact, it is a regular *anuṣṭubh*, to each half of which is added in prose an *ūha*-refrain (*varco* etc., *yaço* etc.) of 14 syllables.⌋ The mss. read in **b** *babhūváthus*, accenting also *dyā́vāpṛthivī́;* the translation implies the simpler and more probable emendation to *-vatus;* ⌊and of course the retention of the ms.-accentuation of *dyā́vāpṛthivī́:* correct the Berlin ed. accordingly;⌋ SPP. leaves both words unchanged, without heeding their irreconcilable character; that the comm. takes *dyā́vāpṛthivī́* as vocative is simply in accord with his usual disregard of the accent. In **c** and **f**, the mss. vary between *ánu-sam* ⌊so most⌋, *anu-sám*, and *ánu sám* (the *pada*-mss. have *anu॰sáṁcarema:* but one has *ánu॰saṁcarema!*); SPP. adopts *ánu sám* ⌊cf. note to Prāt. iv. 3⌋, against our *anu-sám;* there is little choice between the two. In **d**, the mss. in general begin with *yaçásām* ⌊some with *yáçasām*⌋, two or three having *yáçasam* or *yaçásam;* SPP. adopts the last, we *yáçasā;* here, again, there is little to choose; the comm. explains *yaçasā*, though his text (SPP.) gives *yaçasām*. The comm. foolishly takes *āyatī́s* in **e** as, jointly with *yáças*, object of *gṛhītvā́* in **f**, supplying *dhenū́s* for it to qualify. The verse counts (16 + 14 : 16 + 14 = 60) as a full *atiçakvarī;* ⌊but see beginning of this paragraph⌋.

4. Make ye a pen (*vrajá*), for that is men-protecting for you; sew ye coats-of-mail (*várman*), abundant, broad; make ye strongholds of metal, unattackable (*ádhṛṣṭā*); let not your bowl leak (*sru*); make it strong.

The verse is RV. x. 101. 8, with slight variation: RV. has *várma* in *saṁhitā* as well as in *pada* in **b**; the mss., too, leave *dṛ́ṅhatā* in **d** without accent, and SPP. does not correct their error. ⌊Roth notes that Ppp. reads *varmā:* cf. *Noun-Inflection*, p. 540 top,

539 end.⌋ But the *pada*-text exhibits its skill in blundering: in **b** it reads *várma : asi : vi°adhvám* (and nearly all the *saṁhitā*-mss. accent *sīvyadhvám*), and in **c** *kṛṇudhvam : mā́ : ā́yasīḥ* (or *ayasīḥ*) *: ádhṛṣṭā* (and the *saṁhitā*-mss. accordingly read *-dhvaṁmāy-*). The comm. gives three distinct interpretations of the verse: as concerned respectively with the senses, with officiating priests, and with soldiers (*indriyaparatvena ṛtvikparatvena yoddhṛparatvena*). ⌊As to *-dhvam mā-*, cf. note to xviii. 2. 3.⌋

5. Of the sacrifice the eye, beginning, and face; with voice, with hearing, with mind do I make oblation; to this sacrifice, extended by the all-working one, let the gods come ⌊*ā-i*⌋, with favoring minds.

We had this verse above, as ii. 35. 5 ⌊see note thereon⌋. Our mss. cite it by the whole first pāda: *yajñásya cákṣuḥ prábhṛtir múkhaṁ cé 'ty ékā.* ⌊The Anukr. does not ignore the *ā́* at the beginning of **d**.⌋

6. They that are priests (*ṛtvíj*) of the gods, and that are worshipful, for whom the oblation (*havyá*) is made the portion — coming to this sacrifice together with their spouses, let the gods, as many as they are (*yā́vant*), revel on the oblation.

In **b**, the mss. have also *kriyate, kṛyate,* ⌊*kṛyáte,*⌋ and *kṛṇute.* In **c**, the *pada*-mss. read *sahá°patnībhiḥ*, and nearly all the *saṁhitā*-mss. agree with them; SPP. also emends to *pát-*. In **d**, all the mss. have *tavíṣā* or *táviṣā* (p. *-ṣā*); SPP. reads, with the comm., *taviṣā́s* (= *mahāntaḥ*, comm.); the translation implies *havíṣā*, instead of our emendation *sám iṣā́*. The verse ⌊12 + 11 : 11 + 12⌋ has two more syllables than a regular *triṣṭubh;* ⌊the cadences of **a**, **b**, **c** accord with the number of syllables: but **d**, with 12, has a *triṣṭubh* cadence; this casts still further suspicion on *taviṣā*, in place of which we should expect only two syllables⌋.

59. For successful sacrifice.

[*Brahman.—tṛcam. āgneyam. trāiṣṭubham : 1. gāyatrī.*]

Hymns 59–64 are not found in Pāipp. For the practical use of 59 with 52, see under the latter. ⌊Other uses under vs. 3.⌋ Verses 1 and 2, it will be noticed, are put together also in TS., and vs. 3 is not far off ⌊preceding 1 and 2⌋. In MS., on the other hand, vss. 2 and 3 have the same sequence as here; ⌊but in RV. their sequence is inverted⌋. ⌊As for the ritual use, cf. p. 896 and the table.⌋

Translated: Griffith, ii. 317.

1. Thou, O Agni, art protector of vows among gods (?), among mortals; thou art to be praised at the sacrifices.

The verse is RV. viii. 11. 1, and found also in VS. iv. 16; TS. i. 1. 14⁴; 2. 3¹, and MS. i. 2. 3, everywhere without variant, except as the AV. mss. in general read in **b** *devā́ ā́ m-* ⌊three have *devā́ ām-*⌋; ⌊Whitney's P. and M. and SPP's Sᵐ. and his Dᶜ., p.m., have *devá ā́ m-*;⌋ the *pada*-mss. give *devā́ḥ* (two of SPP's, after it, *ā°mártyeṣu*). The RV. *pada*-text has *deváḥ;* ⌊so also TS. *pada*-text: see Weber's note in his ed., p. 13;⌋ the translation implies *devé*, in the sense of *devéṣu*. The comm. understands *devás*, and SPP. also reads it by emendation.

⌊Roth, *Ueber gewisse Kürzungen des Wortendes im Veda*, p. 3, treats the RV. verse, with report of the comm. on RV.VS.TS.: he assumes *devé : ā́* as *pada*-reading and understands *devé* as = *devéṣu*. Cf. *daça* (= *daçabhis*) *dvādaçabhir vā 'pi*,

MBh. xii. 307 (or 306). 10 = xii. 11377, as cited by Hopkins, JAOS. xxiii. 111; cf. also English *inside and out* (*out = outside*); Goethe's *Jeden Nachklang fühlt mein Herz froh-* (*= froher*) *und trüber Zeit*; etc.⌋

2. If we, O gods, detract from (*pra-mī*) your [ordained] courses — we that are very unknowing, of you that are knowing — let Agni the all-devouring fill that up, knowing, and the soma that has entered the Brahmans.

The first three pādas are RV. x. 2. 4 **a–c**, found also in TS. i. 1. 14[4] and MS. iv. 10. 2. All these read in **c** *viçvam ā́ pṛṇāti*; our *viçvā́d* (p. *viçva°át*) can only be regarded as a corruption; the translation, however, follows it, as being the real Atharvan reading; SPP. adopts it in his text, against the comm., who reads and explains *viçvam*. The comm. agrees with RV. etc. further in giving *pṛṇāti*. As for the last pāda, we had it above as **d** of xviii. 3. 55; it is also a RV. phrase, and found elsewhere: see under that verse.

3. We have come unto the road of the gods, to convey (*vah*) along forward what we may be able; Agni [is] knowing; he shall make offering; he verily is *hótar*; he shall arrange the sacrifices (*adhvará*), he the seasons.

The verse is RV. x. 2. 3, and found also in TS. i. 1. 14[3], MS. iv. 10. 2, and ÇB. xii. 4. 4[1]. These texts read in **c**, **d** *sé 'd u hótā só adhv-*, and all save ÇB. accent *ánu* in **b**. The comm's text also has the RV. reading *se 'd u hotā*. The verse, with the Atharvan readings in **c**, **d**, is found in full in Kāuç. 5. 12, in the *parvan*-ceremonies. In the same ceremonies it accompanies in Vāit. 3. 5 an offering to Agni *sviṣṭakṛt*; and again, in Vāit. 19. 12, an after-offering to various gods. ⌊As for the critical significance of the citation of the vs. in *sakalapāṭha*, see p. 897, ¶ 3.⌋

60. For physical abilities.

[*Brahman.—dvyṛcam. mantroktavāgādidāivatam. 1. pathyābṛhatī; 2. kakummatī purauṣṇih.*]

⌊Prose.⌋ As was noticed above, the hymn is wanting in Pāipp. Hymns 60–63, both text and explication, are lacking in the comm. The comm., at p. 517[5], assigns only fourteen hymns to this the final *anuvāka*; ⌊but at p. 552[9] he numbers the last hymn as the thirteenth, having combined hymns 69 and 70 of the Berlin ed. into one of 5 vss. (*pañcamantrātmakaṁ sūktam*, p. 548[1]): both numbers are at variance with the⌋ eighteen of the mss. ⌊in general: but see under h. 65⌋ and of the Anukr. The hymn is quoted in Kāuç. 66. 1 in the *savayajña* chapter ⌊see table on p. 896⌋; the mss. of Kāuç. read *āsyan* ⌊like the AV. mss.⌋.

Translated: Griffith, ii. 317.

1. Speech in my mouth, breath in my nostrils, sight in my eyes, hearing in my ears, my hair not gray, my teeth not broken, much strength in my arms.

A similar enumeration is found in TS. (in v. 5. 9[2]), TA. (x. 72, in supplement: ⌊p. 887 of Poona ed.⌋), and PGS. (in i. 3. 25): *vā́n ma āsán* (PGS. *āsye*) *nasóḥ prāṇó 'kṣyóç cákṣuḥ kárṇayoḥ çrótram bāhuvór bálam ūruvór ójó 'riṣṭā víçvāny áñgāni* (PGS. *'riṣṭāni me 'ñgāni*) *tanū́s tanúvā me sahá*; it covers both verses of our hymn and the beginning of the next. ⌊MGS. i. 4. 4 may be compared.⌋ Nearly all the *saṁhitā*-mss. read *āsyán* ⌊like those of Kāuç.⌋ *násoḥ;* ⌊and the *pada*-reading is *āsyám : násoḥ*⌋. Further on, the mss. read *akṣóḥ* or *akṣyóḥ* (one of ours and one of SPP's give *akṣṇóḥ;* our text gives *akṣṇóḥ*, but it should be *akṣyóḥ*, as everywhere else in the Atharvan, and as in the parallel texts); yet further, *ápalitā kéçā* ⌊or *keçā́*⌋ *çóṇaditā báha* (or *váha*) *bā́hvor bálam.* SPP. follows our emendations (even *akṣṇós*) throughout; except that he very properly corrects our *bāhvòs* to *bāhvós*. Instead of *áçoṇā dántāḥ* the minor Pet. Lex. suggests *áçīrṇā d-*, which is decidedly preferable, and is implied in the translation.

2. Force in my thighs, speed in my calves, firm standing in my feet, all things of mine uninjured, myself not down-fallen.

⌊Passing in silence some minor details of variation,⌋ the mss. read *ója* instead of *ójas* ⌊but *ójaḥ* is found in two or three *pada*-mss.⌋; ⌊about ten authorities⌋ leave *jañghayos* unaccented; they accent *jávas* or *javás*, and *pā́dayos* or *pādáyos;* some insert a blundering *avasāna* between *pā́dayoḥ* and *pratiṣṭhā́;* ⌊all accent *ariṣṭā́ni* instead of *ár-*;⌋ and end with *sárvān mā́ 'tiprṣṭhāḥ* or *-ṣṭhā* (p. *áti॰prṣṭhā* or *-āḥ*). SPP. follows our emendations quite closely: but he corrects to *jáñghayos;* accents *javás* (which is rather to be preferred *); ⌊accents correctly *pā́dayos:* the accent of the Berlin ed. should be amended accordingly;⌋ leaves the *avasāna* after *pā́dayoḥ;* and forgets in *saṁhitā*-text to combine *pratiṣṭhā́* and *áriṣṭāni* into *pratiṣṭhā́ 'riṣ-*; the mss., however, commit the same oversight, although the *pada*-text reads *prati॰sthā́* (not *-ā́ḥ*). The blunder arises possibly from the transference of the *avasāna*-sign from its proper place after *pratiṣṭhā́* (to which our text restores it) to the place before that word. The metrical definitions of the Anukr. for these two bits of prose are naturally worthless, and the extensive emendations in our text make them still more inapplicable. *⌊In RV. the masc. *javá* is oxytone, and the neuter *jávas* is paroxytone; but at iii. 50. 2 and iv. 27. 1 we have the adjective stem *javás:* cf. *Gram.* § 1151. 2. e.⌋

61. For length of life etc.

[*Brahman.—ekarcam. brāhmaṇaspatyam. virāṭ pathyābṛhatī.*]

Wanting, as already pointed out, in the comm. and in Pāipp.
Translated: Griffith, ii. 317.

1. A body together with my body. ⌊. . .⌋ May I attain all my life-time. Sit thou on what is pleasant; fill thyself full, cleansing thyself in heaven (*svargá*).

The verse is utterly obscure and disconnected, and we might long for the comm., if we had found that he ever gave any help in such a case. The first clause is translated as corresponding with that in TS. etc. (see under 60. 1); what is inserted between it and the following clause is omitted as unintelligible. The mss. read *sahe* (with varying accent), and *dántāḥ* (so all the *pada*-mss. and some others) or *datáḥ*, or *rádátāḥ* ⌊or *radántāḥ*⌋; SPP. adopts *sahe datáḥ*, to which he might be puzzled to give any meaning. In the second division, SPP. reads with the mss. *syonáṁ me s-*, and *purúḥ pṛ-*.

62. For popularity.

[*Brahman* (*etc., as 61*). — *anuṣṭubh.*]

Wanting in Pāipp. and in the comm.
Translated: Zimmer, p. 205; Griffith, ii. 318.

1. Make thou me dear to the gods, make me dear to kings, dear to everything that sees, both to Çūdra and to Āryan.

A nearly corresponding verse is found in the supplement to RV. x. 128 (Aufr.², p. 685), and in HGS. i. 10. 6, ⌊and in *Kaṭha-hss.*, p. 36⌋. In the first half-verse, RV. differs only by reading both times *kuru;* its **c** is *priyaṁ viçveṣu gotreṣu*, and its **d** entirely different from ours. HGS. also has *kuru*, with *mā brahmaṇi* for *rājasu mā* in **b**, and the second half-verse reads *priyaṁ viçyeṣu çūdreṣu* ⌊cf. *rúcaṁ víçyeṣu çūdréṣu*, VS. xviii. 48⌋ *priyam mā kuru rājasu*. The mss. read in **c–d** ⌊with varying accent⌋ *paçyato 'ta* (p. *paçyata : uta*); ⌊but one of SPP's *pada*-mss. has *paçyatáḥ*, p.m.⌋; and a part of the mss. (including ⌊so far as noted⌋ all the *pada*-mss.) have *çūdrám* in **d**. SPP's text agrees throughout with ours. ⌊With this verse Zimmer compares 32. 8, above, and VS. xviii. 48 etc. With the **d** of the Berlin text, cf. the **d** of iv. 20. 4 and 8. Zimmer rightly notes that the "gods" of **a** are the Brahmans, and aptly cites ÇB. ii. 2. 2⁶, with 32. 8 etc. as just mentioned.⌋

63. To Bṛihaspati: for sundry blessings.

[*Brahman* (*etc., as 61*). — *virāḍ upariṣṭādbṛhatī.*]

Wanting in Pāipp. and in the comm.
Translated: Griffith, ii. 318.

1. Arise, O Brahmaṇaspati; awaken the gods with the sacrifice; increase [his] life-time, breath, progeny, cattle, fame, and the sacrificer ⌊himself⌋.

The mss. vary between *paçúm* and *paçū́n* in the second half-verse. *Kīrtím* is pretty evidently intruded, spoiling the ⌊otherwise good *anuṣṭubh*⌋ meter; the Anukr. reckons it to the fourth pāda. The *paddhati* uses the verse (see note to Kāuç. 6. 21) in the course of the *darçapūrṇamāsa* ceremony.

64. To Agni: with fuel.

[*Brahman.* — *caturṛcam. āgneyam. ānuṣṭubham.*]

Not found in Pāipp. Used in Kāuç. (57. 26) in the ceremony of initiation of a Vedic student, to accompany the laying of four sticks of fuel on the fire — the schol. say, one at each verse. ⌊With regard to the ritual use, see the table on p. 896, and p. 897, l. 9.⌋
Translated: Griffith, ii. 318; vs. 1 also by Ludwig, p. 265.

1. O Agni, I have taken fuel for the great Jātavedas; let that Jātavedas extend to me both faith and wisdom.

The whole verse is found in ÇGS. ii. 10, the only variant being *agnaye* at the beginning; ⌊Oldenberg's text (cf. his note, p. 139) should read *āhārṣam*, with his codex F.⌋; the first half-verse occurs in several other Sūtras (AGS. i. 21. 1; PGS. ii. 4. 3; HGS.

i. 7. 2; MB. i. 6. 32), with a very different latter half, but all reading *agnaye;* ⌊and we find *agnáye* at MP. ii. 6. 2; and again at GGS. ii. 10. 46, where the *pratīka* is cited⌋. The comm. also has *agnaye*, with one of SPP's reciters. The Atharvan reading is plainly *ágne*, apparently a metrical emendation, and the translation follows it, rather than our unnecessary conjecture, *ágre*. ⌊In this case, as the meter clearly shows, we must allow that the AV. has the better reading *ágne* as against the *agnaye* of a whole series of Sūtra-texts. Their inferior reading is of course not to be changed; but still less should the AV. be changed to *agnáye*, as Oldenberg, note to ÇGS., p. 139, overlooking the meter, suggests.⌋

2. With firing, O Jātavedas, with fuel do we increase thee; so do thou increase us, both with progeny and with riches.

The ⌊text and explanation of the⌋ comm. add ⌊as does the Daça Karmāṇi: see Kāuç. 57. 26 note⌋ the further pāda *dīrgham āyuḥ kṛṇotu me*, and two or three of SPP's authorities give it or have traces of it.

3. In that, O Agni, we put on for thee any pieces of wood whatever, be all that propitious to me; enjoy thou that, O youngest one.

The first two pādas and the fourth are RV. viii. 91 (or 102). 20, which reads *kā́ni kā́ni cid* in **a** ⌊and *tā́* for the *tád* of our **d**⌋. The Yajus-texts, VS. xi. 73, MS. (in ii. 7. 7), TS. (in iv. 1. 10¹), all have the inserted pāda **c**: VS.MS. end it with *te ghṛtám* instead of our *me çivám*, while TS. makes it read *tád astu túbhyam íd ghṛtám*. VS. reads **a** as does RV., but TS.MS. have *yā́ni kā́ni ca*. Nearly all the authorities have *dā́ruṇi* ⌊only W's P.M. have *dā́rūṇi*⌋; and all have *dadhmasi*, without accent: SPP. emends both words to accordance with RV., as we had done. Part of the mss. ⌊and the comm.⌋ have in **d** *yaviṣṭha*. The verse is used by Vāit. (28. 14) in the *agnicayana* ceremony. ⌊Cf. p. 898, line 1.⌋

4. These pieces of fuel are for thee, O Agni; with them, O burning one, become thou united; put in us [long] life-time; put immortality in the Āryan.

The second and fourth pādas are wholly corrupt; the translation follows in part our emended text. ⌊For **b**, the translation implies *tā́bhir dhakṣo* (cf. RV. x. 115. 4; ii. 4. 4, where the *saṁhitā* has *dákṣoḥ;* RV. Prāt. iv. 41 end) *sám íd bhava;*⌋ and for **d**, it implies *amṛtatváṁ cā́ "rye*. For **b**, the general reading of the authorities is *tvā́m íd dhaṅsó* (p. *haṅsáḥ*) *samíd* (p. *sam॰ít*) *bhava;* one or two have *dhaso* or *vāṅso*, one *tvā́v íd dhaṅsó*, three *bhavaḥ*. SPP. conjectures that the original reading may have been *tā́bhir vaso samíd bhava;* he adopts as his text, from the comm., *tvám iddháḥ samíd bhava*. In **c**, the *ā́* before *dhehi* is not found in the mss.; a less correction, with better meter, would have been *dhehy ā́*. For **d**, the mss., the comm., and SPP., give *amṛtatvám ācāryā̀ya* (p. *amṛta॰tvám : ā॰cāryā̀ya*).

⌊The Daç. Kar., as reported by Bloomfield on Kāuç. 57. 26, also gives *ācāryāya;* moreover, the passage in PGS. (ii. 4. 3), which treats of the ceremony of initiation to which (see introd., above) these verses belong, contains in fact a prayer of the student on behalf of his teacher or initiator: *jīvaputro mamā "cāryo medhāvy aham asāni* etc.; and the AV. comm. explains *ācāryāya* accordingly by *upanayanakartre gāyatrīpradātre* etc. This all makes against W's *cā́ "rye* and in favor of the ms.-reading *ācāryā̀ya:* this dative, no less than the locative *asmā́su*, goes easily with *dhehy ā́*⌋.

65. Praise of the sun.

[*Brahman.—ekarcam. jātavedasam; sāuryam. jāgatam.*]

Found also in Pāipp. xvi. The comm. says that hymns 65–67 are shown by their contents to belong to the worship of Sūrya.

Translated: Griffith, ii. 319.

1. A yellow eagle, thou hast ascended unto heaven (*dív*) with radiance (*arcís*); whoso (pl.) would injure thee flying up to heaven, them smite thou down with flame (*háras*), O Jātavedas, unfearing; ascend unto heaven, O sun, formidable, with radiance.

By metrical evidence, *jātavedas* in **c** is an intrusion ⌊although obviously older than the Anukr.⌋, besides being at least superfluous in sense. The mss. read *bíbhyad ugro 'rc-* (p. *bíbhyat : ugraḥ*); but SPP. emends to *ábibhyat : ugráḥ*, as we had done ⌊but neglects the necessary *abhinihita svarita*⌋; the comm. so understands the words. Ppp. reads *ugro arciṣā* in **d**.

After this hymn, three of our mss. (P.M.W.) insert as next hymn, numbering it 66, the one-versed RV. i. 99, without variant.

66. To Agni: for aid.

[*Brahman.—ekarcam. jātavedasam; sāuryam; vajradevatyam. atijāgatam.*]

Found also in Pāipp. xvi. The comm. connects it in use with the preceding hymn.

Translated: Griffith, ii. 319.

1. The trickish Asuras that go about, having metal nets, hooking with fetters of metal, them I make subject to thee with flame, O Jātavedas; go thou, a thousand-barbed thunderbolt, slaughtering our rivals.

Ppp. combines in **a** *-jālā 'surā*, and reads in **b** *ayasmāi p-*; in **c** it seems to give *harase*, which would be an acceptable emendation. Our *sahásrabhṛṣṭis* in **d** is for the *-hṛṣṭis* (the majority) or *-dṛṣṭis* ⌊two⌋ or *-hraṣṭis* ⌊two or three⌋ or ⌊*-haṣṭis* or *-hraṣṭi* or⌋ *-hruṣṭis* or *-riṣṭis* or *-bhṛṣṭis* (all these, one each) of the authorities; SPP. reads, with the comm., *-ṛṣṭis*. SPP. also follows the comm. in adopting *pāhi*, against the majority of his authorities (though in such a case their reading, whether *pā-* or *yā-*, is extremely doubtful); ⌊here the testimony of his oral reciters is of especial weight, and they (his K. and V.) gave *yāhi*⌋.

67. For long life and prosperity.

[*Brahman.—aṣṭāu. sāuryam. prājāpatyā gāyatrī.*]

Not found in Pāipp. According to the comm., it is used in the same manner as the two preceding hymns. ⌊Cf. *khila* to RV. i. 50.⌋

Translated: Griffith, ii. 319.

1. May we see a hundred autumns.
2. May we live a hundred autumns.
3. May we wake a hundred autumns.

4. May we ascend (*ruh*) a hundred autumns.
5. May we prosper a hundred autumns.
6. May we be a hundred autumns.
7. May we adorn a hundred autumns.
8. More autumns than a hundred.

The comm.* reckons the hymn as only one verse; the Anukr. and all the mss. ⌊see SPP's ed., p. 543, note 1⌋ count eight verses, and SPP. also adopts this. The first two verses are the last two pādas of RV. vii. 66. 16; they are found also in GGS. iii. 8. 5; a third verse, with *çṛṇuyāma*, is added in PGS. i. 6. 3; ⌊MS., at iv. 9. 20, has four pādas, with *çṛṇuyā́ma* pushed to the fourth place by the insertion of *prábravāma* (ed. *prábruv-*) in the third;⌋ and the series is carried further in VS. xxxvi. 24, which, beginning as does PGS., has five pādas, ⌊with *prábravāma* in the fourth, and *ádīnāḥ syāma* in the fifth, and⌋ with the added ending *bhū́yaç ca çarádaḥ çatā́t*, which needs emendation. ⌊MGS., at i. 22. 11, agrees with VS.⌋ In TA. iv. 42. 5 and in HGS. i. 7. 10 ⌊the series is carried to eight pādas⌋: these agree from 1 to 7 ⌊with *páçyema, jī́vema, nándāma, módāma, bhávāma, çṛṇávāma, prábravāma*⌋, and differ only in the eighth, where TA. has *ájītāḥ syāma* against *ajitāḥ syāma* of HGS.; and both have the added ending *jyók ca sū́ryaṁ dṛçé*. In none of the other versions is there anything to help us with the doubtful forms in the Atharvan. In vs. 3, most of the mss. read *búddhema* (some *búdhema*); our emendation *búdhyema* is given also by the comm., and SPP. adopts it. In vs. 5, on the other hand, the mss., the comm., and SPP., give the wholly anomalous *pū́ṣema* (=*puṣṭiṁ labhemahi*, comm.); SPP. ought to have emended to *púṣyema*, as we had done. *Bhū́yema* (= *bhūyāsma*, comm.) in vs. 7 is another impossibility retained by SPP. In vs. 8 all the mss. have *bhū́yasī* ⌊or *-āsī*⌋; but the comm. has *-sīs*, and so SPP. has the courage to adopt and read it, as we had done before. *⌊At p. 543⁹.⌋

68. With ceremonial performance.

[*Brahman.—ekarcam. mantroktakarmamātradevatyam. ānuṣṭubham.*]

Found in Pāipp. xix. Quoted once in the text of Kāuç. (139. 10), in the ceremony of introduction to Vedic study, as to be murmured prior to pronouncing, by pādas, the Gāyatrī (RV. iii. 62. 10), and the Atharvan verses iv. 1. 1 and i. 1. 1 (or 1–4). But the various schol. (the Paddhati, Daç. Kar., Keçavī) make frequent mention and use of it: thus (see note to Kāuç. 25. 36), it is reckoned to a *svastivācana*; it is used in the *sīmantonnayana* (to 35. 20) and *godāna* (to 53. 2) ceremonies; it is added (note to 57. 22) to vii. 33. 1 in the ceremony of restoring lost fire, in the initiation of a Vedic student; it is used in the *vedavratāni* (to 57. 32), in the *annaprāçana* (to 58. 19), and the preparation for the marriage ceremonies (to 75. 1), and for the *ājyatantra* (to 137. 4), and in the introduction to the *rājakarmāṇi* of § 14 (p. 315, l. 2). In all this is very probably to be seen only the influence of the occurrence of *védam* and of *kármāṇi kṛṇmahe* in the second half-verse; it need not imply any real comprehension of the obscure verse, with recognition of its appropriateness to all these various situations. ⌊As to the critical bearing of the uses of the vs. in the ritual, cf. the table on p. 896, and see p. 897, line 12.⌋

Translated: Griffith, ii. 319.

1. Of non-expansion and of expansion do I untie the aperture with magic; by those two having taken up the Veda, we then perform acts.

That is, doubtless, 'conduct sacred ceremonies.' All the mss.* have at the beginning *ávyasas* (p. *ávi॰asaḥ*), and so have Ppp., the Anukr., Kāuç. and all its scholiasts, and the comm.; whence of course also SPP.; it is unquestionably the Atharvan reading. Yet even the comm. can only say for it that it is the same as *avyacasas*, a syllable being omitted by Vedic license; and the analysis of the *pada*-text appears to be one of those wild and senseless guesses of which in this book it presents not a few examples. ⌊The important thing to observe in the pāda *avya[ca]saç ca vyacasaç ca* is the recurrence of so many confusingly similar syllables: the corruption is a case of haplography (cf. note to iv. 5. 5, and Bloomfield in AJP. xvii. 418); but one would expect *avyacaso vyacasaç ca*.⌋ The *pada*-mss. ⌊save SPP's J.⌋ have *víṣyāmi* in b as an integral word; but the comm. understands *ví: syāmi*, and SPP., as well as our text, so reads; many of the mss. have *bí* instead of *ví*. One accents in c *vedám*, ⌊and one has *vedam*, without accent; Griffith's 'bunch of grass' implies the reading *vedám* here and at 72. 1⌋; we might conjecture *védim* as a better reading; *véda* is not to be expected in the Atharvan. ⌊The *Index* gives for books i.–xviii. three occurrences of *véda*, namely at iv. 35. 6; x. 8. 17; xv. 3. 7 : at x. 8. 17 W. suggests that it is perhaps to be rendered simply by 'knowledge'; but in iv. and xv. it can hardly be aught else than 'Veda.'⌋ Some of the mss. accent *kṛṇmáhe*. There was no sufficient reason for altering the accent of *vyácasas* in our text to *vyacásas*; SPP. reads *vyác-* with the majority of his authorities. The comm. has no notion of what the verse really means: he gives two different expositions — one explaining *ávyacas* and *vyácas* to mean the two varieties of breathing, *prāṇa* and *vyāna*, the *bila* to be the *mūlādhāra*, and *veda* 'the Veda' (*akṣarātmakamantrasaṁgha*); the other taking the first two to be the *paramātman* and *jīvātman*, the *bila* the heart, and *veda* 'knowledge' (*cikīrṣitakarmaviṣayaṁ jñānam*). *⌊If I understand the Collation Book, W's P. actually begins with *avyacásaç cá vyácasáç ca*, which, apart from the wild accents, is worth noting.⌋

In Ppp., this hymn is immediately followed by our hymn 72.

69. To the waters: for long life.

[*Brahman. satasraḥ. mantroktābdevatyāḥ.* *1. āsury anuṣṭubh; 2. sāmny anuṣṭubh; 3. āsurī gāyatrī; 4. sāmny uṣṇih (1–4. 1-av.).*]

⌊Prose.⌋ Found also in Pāipp. xix. The four verses of this hymn are called in Kāuç. and Vāit. *jīvās*, and are prescribed to accompany the rinsing of the mouth with water in the *parvan* ceremony (Kāuç. 3. 4; Vāit. 1. 19, misunderstood by the editor), in a rite for long life at the reception of a Vedic student (Kāuç. 58. 7), and in the *madhuparka* ceremony (Kāuç. 90. 22); of these the comm. takes notice only of Kāuç. 58. 7. With this use is doubtless connected the attribution of the hymn in the Anukr. to the waters as divinity. ⌊As to the citation by technical designation, and especially as to the ritual uses, see p. 897, ¶ 2.⌋

Translated: Griffith, ii. 320.

1. Living are ye; may I live; may I live my whole life-time.

2. Living on are ye; may I live on; may I live my whole life-time.

3. Living together are ye; may I live together; may I live my whole life-time.

4. Lively are ye; may I live; may I live my whole life-time.

The comm. adds our hymn 70 as fifth verse to this hymn, and then commits the blunder of understanding Indra etc., there spoken of, as addressed with "living are ye" etc.; it is, of course, the waters that are meant, as the liturgical use plainly shows. In vs. 2 all authorities give *úpa jīvā́ stha* (p. *úpa : jīvā́ḥ : stha*); ⌊both editions give *upajīvā́s*⌋. In vs. 3 they have *saṁjīvā́s* (though with considerable variety of accent); most, too, accent *saṁjīvyā́sam*. The comm. reads *upajīvyās* and *saṁjīvyās*, which make the decidedly easier sense, 'fit to be lived on and with'; then the following clauses would mean 'may I live on you and with you.' Ppp. reads throughout *stu* instead of *stha*.

70. For long life.

[*Brahman. — ekarcam. sāuryam. 3-p. gāyatrī.*]

⌊Prose.⌋ Not found in Pāipp. ⌊See note to 69. 4.⌋
Translated: Griffith, ii. 320.

1. Live, O Indra; live, O Sūrya; live ye, O gods; may I live; may I live my whole life-time.

The mss. read *jī́vās* after *dévās*, and SPP. retains it, false accent and all. The comm. explains it by adding a *bhavata*.

71. For various blessings.

[*Brahman. — ekarcam. gāyatrīdāivatam. 3-av. 5-p. atijagatī.*]

Wanting in Pāipp. The comm. is unable to quote any authority as to its use; but he declares it to belong to the worship of the Veda that one has studied, or of the *gāyatrī*.
Translated: Zimmer, p. 204; Griffith, ii. 320.

1. Praised by me [is] the boon-giving Veda-mother. Let them urge on the soma-hymn of the twice-born. Having given to me life-time, breath, progeny, cattle, fame, property, Vedic splendor, go ye to the *brahma*-world.

A corresponding verse is found in the supplement (p. 915 of the Calc. ed.) ⌊p. 855 of the Poona ed.⌋ to TA. x. 36, reading thus: *stuto mayā varadā vedamātā pracodayantī pavane dvijātā: āyuḥ pṛthivyāṁ draviṇam brahmavarcasam mahyaṁ datvā prajātum brahmalokam* (the accentuation is only partial, and worthless); its variants hardly help the interpretation of our verse. The translation given above makes no pretense to being an intelligent one; it merely endeavors to make what sense it can, with least divergence from the manuscript readings. For **a** it implies *stutā́ máyā varadā́ vedamātā́*, which agrees throughout with the mss., save that they accent *vedamātā* in several different ways; the *pada*-mss. give *varadā* without division. For **b** is implied *prá codayantām pāvamānī́ṁ dvijā́nām* (with our edition); the mss. accent *pracodáyantām;* and ⌊excepting W's P.M.W., which give *pāvamānī́m*⌋ they read *pāvamānī́*, which SPP. adopts. In the second division, SPP. reads *paçúm*, with ⌊about⌋ half the authorities, and with the comm.; the remaining authorities favor our *paçū́n*, giving that or *paçū́ṁ*. The comm. explains *varadā* by *iṣṭakāmapradātrī*, and *vedamātā* by *vedasya ṛgādirūpasya mātā*, signifying the *sāvitrī*, and standing as subject to *pra codayantām*, which is *pluralis majestaticus*, as is also *vrajata*. ⌊Weber discusses *varadā* and the TA. passage at *Ind. Stud.* ii. 194 (as Whitney notes in the margin), and resolves *stuto* into *stutā u*.⌋

72. For the favor of the gods.

[*Bhṛgvañgiras Brahman.—ekarcam. paramātmadāivatam. trāiṣṭubham.*]

Follows in Pāipp. directly after hymn 68. It is given in full* in the Kāuç. text (139. 26), at the end of the ceremony of commencement of Vedic study; ⌊and the *pratīka* is cited at 139. 25;⌋ and the scholiasts add its use at the end of the *parvan* ceremonies (Keç. to section 6; p. 310, l. 5), and of the *piṇḍapitṛyajña* (Keç. to 89. 17; p. 371, l. 12), and to the *snānavrata* (note to 42. 18). *⌊As to the citation in *sakala-pāṭha*, cf. p. 897, ¶ 3.⌋

Translated: Griffith, ii. 320.

1. Out of what receptacle we bore up the Veda, within that do we set it down; what is performed [and] sacrificed by the heroic might of the *bráhman*, with that fervor, O gods, favor ye me here.

Some of the mss. accent variously *abharāma* and *vedam;* ⌊Griffith renders by 'bunch of grass,' again (as at 68. 1) implying the accent *vedám:* but this accent is given only by SPP's Sm.;⌋ two or three of SPP's have *ṛtám* instead of *kṛtám* in **c**; the version in Kāuç. 139. 26 gives in place of either *adhītam.* Ppp. reads in **a**, **b** *udbharāmi veda tasminn antar va dudhmay enam.*

⌊Here ends the seventh and last *anuvāka*, with 18 hymns (or 14 or 13: see introd. to hymn 60, above); and with 55 verses, if we count them as they are numbered in the Berlin text. They are summed up as 55 verses by certain mss.—No mention of the ending of a *prapāṭhaka* is made in the colophon.⌋

⌊Pāippalāda excerpts concerning book xx.⌋

⌊Roth, at the end of his Collation, adds the Ppp. variants for verses 12 and 16 and 17 of AV. xx. 34; the hymn appears in Ppp. xiii. and corresponds to the *sá janāsa índraḥ* hymn, RV. ii. 12.⌋

⌊Verse 12. In **a**, Ppp. has *paryacarakṣac* instead of *paribhávaṁ;* its **b** is *yo vārgakasya vāpibat sutam;* its **c** reads *yajamānaṁ bahuṁ janaṁ;* and in **d**, it has *āmorucakṣat* for *ámūrchat.*⌋

⌊Verse 16. In **a**, Ppp. has *vyakṣat putror up-* for *vyàktaḥ pitrór up-*; its **b** is simply *bhuvana veda janitaḥ;* its **c** is *parasyā bhaviṣyamāṇo hrojokṣad.*⌋

⌊Verse 17. In **a**, Ppp. has *haryasyaçur* for *háryaçva āsutér.*⌋

⌊Then follows a note to the effect that nothing of the Kuntāpa hymns appears in Ppp.⌋

⌊Roth's Collation closes with the words:

"explicit feliciter 25. Juni 1884."⌋

INDEXES AND OTHER AUXILIARY MATTER

1. List of Non-metrical Passages of the Atharvan Saṁhitā

⌊Whitney gives a compact list of the prose passages in his *Index Verborum*, p. 5. It may be repeated here in different form and with slight revision. It is to be understood that the whole hymn is prose, except when otherwise specified, as by the giving of the verses.⌋

i. none
ii. 11; 16–24
iii. 26; 27; 29. 7
iv. 39. 1–8
v. 6. 4 e, 9–14; 9; 10; 14. 8 a; 16; 21. 11 cd, 12; 24; 26 (parts); 27 (do.); 28. 1 cd
vi. 10; 16. 4; 44. 3; 46. 1–2; 48; 79. 3; 83. 4; 99. 3; 123. 3–4
vii. 81. 4–5; 88; 89. 4; 97. 5–8
viii. 1. 14; 8. 22–24; 10
ix. 1. 14 a, 21–24; 2. 13; 3. 25–31; 5. 16, 20–22, 23–30 (parts), 31–36; 6 (except verses 1–2); 7; 10. 24
x. 5 (except verses 22–24, 42–43, 45–50, and parts of 7–14, 36–41)
xi. 1. 35; 3 (except verses 19–22)
xii. 2. 42, 44; 3. 55–60 (parts); 5 (except verses 15–17, 47–53, 55–70)
xiii. 4. 14–15, 22–26, 46–56
xiv. none
xv. all
xvi. all (except 1. 10, 12, 13; 4. 2, 6; 6. 1–4, 11; 9. 1–2)
xvii. 1. 20–23
xviii. 2. 45 ab; 3. 25–28 (parts), 30–35 (do.), 36–37; 4. 27, 67–68, 71–74, 76–87
xix. 9. 14; 17–19; 21; 22 (all but last verse); 23 (do.); 31. 12?; 44. 4–5; 45. 6–10; 51; 57. 2–4, 6; 60; 61; 69; 70

2. List of Hymns ignored by the Kāuçika-Sūtra

⌊In his copy of the Kāuçika, Whitney has noted the hymns in question. I have modified his list; but it can hardly be drawn with entire precision and certainty. Thus if we accept the statements of the scholiasts as to what hymns or verses are included in certain *gaṇas* or meant by certain terms (like *brahmagavyāu* at 48. 13 or *vṛṣaliṅgāḥ* at 29. 15) or *pratīkas*, all the hymns under book v. and some others (like vi. 95) may be struck from the list. At 36. 13, *rathajitām* should mean vi. 130; but Dārila and Keçava both understand 130–132 to be intended. For some hymns as to which the reader, seeing an asterisk or a blank in Bloomfield's Index, might be in doubt, a few words may be said: iv. 4 is textually cited at 40. 14, and so is ix. 9 at 18. 25; for ii. 20–23, see introd. to ii. 19; and for iv. 7, see introd. to iv. 7. Hymns iii. 26–27 are really cited under the name *digyukte* at 14. 25; iv. 23–29, as the *mṛgāra*-hymns, at 27. 34; and vi. 35–36 as the *vāiçvānarīye* at 31. 5. Hymn vii. 81 is cited as the *dārçī*-verses at 24. 18. Certain pairs have the same *pratīka* and so give rise to questions: thus vii. 59. 1 and vi. 37. 3; vii. 73. 11 and ix. 10. 20; vii. 75. 1 and iv. 21. 7; xvi. 5. 1 and vi. 46. 2. Hymns vi. 94, vii. 92, and vii. 93 are perhaps doubtful. As to book xix., see p. 896. The table follows according to the three grand divisions.⌋

i. none	viii. 4, 9, 10	xiii. 4
ii. none	ix. 6, 10	xiv. none
iii. none	x. 2, 7, 8	xv. all
iv. none	xi. 3, 5, 7, 8	xvi. P's 4, 5, 7, 8
v. 4, 5, 16, 18, 19	xii. 5	xvii. none
vi. 47, 95, 120, 131, 132		xviii. none
vii. 5, 23, 27, 28, 40, 47–49, 58, 59, 94		xix. all but 51, 52, 59, 60, 64, 68
		xx. all

3. Concordance of two Methods of citing the Kāuçika-Sūtra

⌊The references to this treatise in the commentary as printed in the Bombay edition are made by *adhyāya*, and by *kaṇḍikā* as numbered from the beginning of each *adhyāya*, but without giving the individual *sūtra*. Bloomfield and Whitney cite by *kaṇḍikā* as numbered from the beginning of the treatise, and by *sūtra*. The addition of the *sūtra* makes the reference more precise and convenient; but both methods are at fault. The citations should be by *adhyāya*, by *kaṇḍikā* as numbered from the beginning of the *adhyāya*, and by *sūtra*. For the convenience of those who wish to study the Kāuçika as cited by the comm., the following concordance is given. The Roman numerals with the smaller Arabic figures (at the left and middle of each column) show the citations according to the method of the Bombay edition; the larger Arabic figures show the *kaṇḍikās* as numbered by Bloomfield. A better way to harmonize the two methods than by the use of this table is to write on the upper outside corner of each odd page of Bloomfield's text-edition the *adhyāya* with a Roman numeral, and the *kaṇḍikā* as numbered from the beginning of the *adhyāya* with an Arabic numeral.

i.	1	1	iii.	4	21	v.	5	41	viii.	2	61	xi.	2	81	xiii.	9	101	xiii.	29	121
	2	2		5	22		6	42		3	62		3	82		10	102		30	122
	3	3		6	23		7	43		4	63		4	83		11	103		31	123
	4	4		7	24		8	44		5	64		5	84		12	104		32	124
	5	5	iv.	1	25		9	45		6	65		6	85		13	105		33	125
	6	6		2	26		10	46		7	66		7	86		14	106		34	126
	7	7		3	27	vi.	1	47		8	67		8	87		15	107		35	127
	8	8		4	28		2	48		9	68		9	88		16	108		36	128
	9	9		5	29		3	49	ix.	1	69		10	89		17	109		37	129
ii.	1	10		6	30	vii.	1	50		2	70	xii.	1	90		18	110		38	130
	2	11		7	31		2	51		3	71		2	91		19	111		39	131
	3	12		8	32		3	52		4	72		3	92		20	112		40	132
	4	13		9	33		4	53		5	73	xiii.	1	93		21	113		41	133
	5	14		10	34		5	54		6	74		2	94		22	114		42	134
	6	15		11	35		6	55	x.	1	75		3	95		23	115		43	135
	7	16		12	36		7	56		2	76		4	96		24	116		44	136
	8	17	v.	1	37		8	57		3	77		5	97		25	117	xiv.	1	137
iii.	1	18		2	38		9	58		4	78		6	98		26	118		2	138
	2	19		3	39		10	59		5	79		7	99		27	119		3	139
	3	20		4	40	viii.	1	60	xi.	1	80		8	100		28	120		4-5	140–1⌋

4. Concordance of Berlin and Bombay Hymn-numbers

⌊The discrepancies between the two editions have been duly explained in the proper places, and are discussed in vol. VII., p. cxxxiv, where all needed references to those explanations may be found.

Hymns of the Bombay ed.	The underwritten hymns or parts of hymns of the Berlin edition correspond to the hymns of the Bombay edition as numbered in either margin.					Hymns of the Bombay ed.
	Book viii.	Book ix.	Book xi.	Book xii.	Book xiii.	
1	1	1	1	1	1	1
2	2	2	2	2	2	2
3	3	3	3.1-31	3	3	3
4	4	4	3.32-49	4	4.1-13	4
5	5	5	3.50-56	5.1-6	4.14-21	5
6	6	6.1-17	4	5.7-11	4.22-28	6
7	7	6.18-30	5	5.12-27	4.29-45	7
8	8	6.31-39	6	5.28-38	4.46-51	8
9	9	6.40-44	7	5.39-46	4.52-56	9
10	10.1-7	6.45-48	8	5.47-61		10
11	10.8-17	6.49-62	9	5.62-73		11
12	10.18-21	7.1-26	10			12
13	10.22-25	8				13
14	10.26-29	9				14
15	10.30-33	10				15⌋

5. Pāippalāda Passages corresponding to Passages of the Vulgate

⌊**Primary use of the table, its genesis and character.**—Its primary use is for finding in the facsimile the Pāipp. parallel of a given Vulgate passage. For the genesis of the table, the reader will please consult pages lxxxv–lxxxvi. It is a provisional table; but it will be, as I hope, a very useful one, pending the appearance of the transliteration of the Kashmirian text with marginal references and index as explained at p. lxxxvii. The pencilled numbers described at p. lxxxv I have used with care in making the table; but since I have not verified the table from the facsimile, I do not warrant its accuracy, nor can I vouch for its completeness.⌋

⌊**Incidental uses of the table.**—It is of no small critical interest as giving a bird's-eye view of the mutual relations of the Vulgate and Pāippalāda material as respects general arrangement. Thus the cases in which hymns of a given Vulgate book correspond to hymns of the same book in Pāipp. are noticeably frequent in books i., ii., iii., and iv.; while Vulgate book vi. appears largely in book xix. of Pāipp. The fact that the hymns of book vii. appear mostly in the very last book of Pāipp. (in xx.) agrees remarkably with our conclusions respecting the character of that book as a supplement to the nucleus of the first grand division. So, again, the fact that the material of the second grand division is massed in

Pāipp. in its books xvi. and xvii. is a striking confirmation of the view that the Vulgate books viii.–xii. constitute a distinct unity subordinate to that of the whole saṁhitā. Even yet more striking is the fact that the material of the third grand division of the Vulgate, books xiii.–xviii., has been grouped by the Pāippalāda text-makers into a single book, their xviii. The fact has already been noted above (p. clix) in its proper connection; and the details of the correspondence are given below, in the next paragraph. It will be noticed that while nearly all of the *paryāya* material of division II. appears in Pāipp., nearly all of that of division III. is no less noticeably lacking, although it is probably recognized in the case of books xv. and xvi. as a part of the text. Once more, the table shows interesting examples of the breaking up in Pāipp. of material which, although treated as a hymn-unit in the Vulgate (cf. vi. 28), is devoid of internal connection. As was noted above (pages cli and cliv), the put-together character of some of the hymns in vii. appears plainly here; and the added verse by which the Vulgate hymn in vi. transcends the norm is conspicuously absent in Pāipp. — I may add that the table gives a conspectus of the number of the verses of the individual hymns which will sometimes prove useful. In vii., although retaining the Berlin numbering, I have made shift to take account of the true division of the material into hymns (cf. the table at vii. 6, 45, 54, 68, 72, 76).⌋

⌊**Vulgate grand division III. and Pāippalāda book xviii.** — This book fills just a trifle less than a dozen of the birch-bark leaves, namely leaves 228–239: its first verse (= first vs. of Vulgate xiv.) begins on the very last line of folio 227 b, and its last (= last vs. of Vulgate xviii.) ends on line 8 of folio 239 b with the vīpsā of Vulgate xviii. 4. 89 d, *oṁ vittam me asya rodasī.* The Pāipp. book falls between 313 a and 330 b of Roth's Kashmirian nāgarī transcript (p. lxxxi); but, in the citations which follow in this paragraph, reference is made, not to that transcript, but rather to the leaves of the birch-bark original as given in the facsimile, and the side of the leaf, recto or verso, is indicated by a or b, and the line by a number. The relations of Vulgate division III. to Pāipp. xviii. are obscured in the table on p. 1023 by the straggling verses of which account is there made; I therefore subjoin (p. 1015) a tabular statement designed expressly to make those relations clear. It will be observed, in the first place, that, on the one hand, the Vulgate books xiv. (wedding verses) and xvii. (Vishṇu sun-hymn), and the first half of xiii. (Rohita sun-hymns) are given substantially in full in Pāipp.; and that, on the other, the *paryāya*-books xv. (Vrātya) and xvi. (Paritta) and book xviii. (funeral verses) are not textually given, but are merely acknowledged as a part of the text by the citation of a few representative passages; and that, moreover, so far as Pāipp. xviii. is concerned, the *paryāya*-hymn xiii. 4 and the hymn xiii. 3

Conspectus of the Contents of Pāippalāda book xviii.

Vulgate			Birch-bark leaf side	line
xiv. 1.	1a	*satyenottabhitā bhūmis* (then substantially the whole hymn: 5 pages)	227b	20
	64d	*çivā syonāṣ patiloke vi rāja* (end of hymn)	230a	12
		Colophon of anuvāka 1		13
2.	1a	*tubhyam agre pary avahan* (then substantially the whole hymn: 6 pp.)		13
	75d	*dīrghan tāyus savitā kṛṇotu* (end of hymn and book)	233a	11
		Colophon of anuvāka 2		15
xiii. 1.	1a	*udīhi vājin yo 'psv antar* (then substantially the whole hymn: 4 pp.)		15
		Colophon of anuvāka 3 (to be expected 6 lines later)	235a	14
	55e	*rohitena riṣaṇābhṛtam* (end of hymn: vss. 56–60 wanting)		20
2.	1a	*ud asya ketavo divi* (then substantially the whole hymn: 4 pp.)		20
	46d	*pra bhānavas sasṛje nā[kam a]cha* (end of hymn: not of book)	237b	1
		Colophon of anuvāka 4		16
		Vulgate xiii. 3 and paryāya-hymn xiii. 4 are wanting		
xv. 1.	1	*vrādyāu vā ida agra āsīt* (with most of paryāya 1: 7 lines)		16
	8	to *iti brahmavādino vadanti* (end of paryāya 1)	238a	1
2.	1	then *sa prācīn diçam anu vy acalat* (and no more of xv.)		2
xvi. 1.	1	*atisṛṣṭo apāṁ vṛṣabho* (then 3 or 4 verses of paryāya 1: 3 lines)		2
4.	7	*agnir me dakṣaṁ dadhātu* (end of Vulgate anuvāka 1)		6
5.	1	*vidma te svapna janitram* (beginning of Vulgate anuvāka 2)		6
9.	1	*jitam asmākam udbhin[n]am asmākam* (beginning of last paryāya, namely 9 [not 8], of Vulgate anuvāka 2): then 4 lines		6
	4	ending with *vasumān bhūyāsam* (end of Vulgate anuvāka 2)		11
		Colophon of anuvāka 5		12
xvii. 1.	1a	*viṣāsahyaṁ sahamānam* (then substantially the whole hymn, namely 2 or 3 pages, ending)		12
	30d	*sahasraṁ prāṇā mayu te ramantām* (end of hymn and book)	239b	6
		Then follows, without a syllable intervening,		
xviii. 4.	89	*candramā apsv antar ā* (the entire last verse of hymn and book)		6
		Colophon of Pāippalāda book xviii.		9
vi. 1.	1	*doṣo gāya bṛhad gāya* (as beginning of Pāipp. xix.)		11

are ignored entirely. —It appears, secondly, that the order of Vulgate xiii. and xiv. is inverted in Pāipp.; but that the order of the remaining four books is the same for both recensions. —It appears, thirdly, that Pāipp. xviii. consists of 6 anuvākas, and that these anuvākas correspond in the main to certain Vulgate anuvākas: anuvākas 1 and 2 of Pāipp. to the two long anuvāka-hymns which make up Vulgate xiv.; 3 and 4 of Pāipp. to the first two anuvāka-hymns of Vulgate xiii.; and anuvāka 6 of

Pāipp.[1] to the Vulgate anuvāka-hymn, or book, xvii., and the representative verse of Vulgate xviii. — It appears, finally, that anuvāka 5, containing the representative citations from Vulgate books xv. and xvi., consists of hardly 16 lines. The fact that so brief a passage should figure in the text as an anuvāka (it is expressly so called in its colophon: 238 a 12) must, I think, be interpreted as indicating that these books were acknowledged as a part of the text by the text-makers (so Roth and Whitney: cf. p. 794). — The colophon of anuvāka 3, we may add, appears to be somewhat misplaced: another case of misdivision (cf. p. 814).⌋

⌊By way of correction to p. 794, line 10, we may add that Roth errs in saying that xvi. 8. 1 is given in Pāipp.; its pratīka is like that of 9. 1, but the facsimile actually shows 9. 1 and not 8. 1. This is in accord with the general method of scribal abbreviation (cf. p. cxx), for 9. 1 is the last paryāya, and the abbreviated book thus appears to be represented, as it should be, by the beginning and end of each of its two anuvākas. — A similar error has arisen at p. 884, in my second addition to the note on xviii. 4. 49, where this verse is said to come immediately after the end of Vulgate xvii. in Pāipp. The error is due to a slip of Roth's, who, in his Collation, had written xviii. 4. 49 where he should have written xviii. 4. 89. The latter is the last verse of xviii., and is therefore the one that we should expect as representative verse. The addition should be transposed from p. 884 to p. 894.⌋

⌊**Explanation of the table.** — The table follows the sequence of the hymns of the Vulgate, book by book. At the left of each column is the number of the hymn. Then follows the word "has," with the number of verses of which the hymn consists and a colon. If the hymn is lacking in Pāipp., the colon and all else is omitted. Otherwise, after the colon comes the word "at" and then the number of the leaf of Roth's Kashmirian nāgarī transcript (p. lxxxi) on which the beginning of the correspondent of the Vulgate passage concerned occurs, with the recto or verso of the leaf indicated by *a* or *b*. At the right is added in Roman numerals, immediately after the word "in," the book of the Kashmirian recension to which the passage concerned belongs. It is to be understood that the Vulgate passage includes the whole hymn unless the contrary is indicated by the specification of the verses of the hymn between the colon and the word "at." The number specifying the verses is to be understood as an ordinal throughout division I. and the Supplement (the short hymns). Elsewhere (that is, throughout divisions II. and III., the hymns of many verses) it is to be understood as a cardinal, and the abbreviation vss. or vs. is added. To find which verses of a given hymn are meant and the

⌊[1] There is no special colophon for this anuvāka, its place being taken by the colophon for the whole book.⌋

details of their order, the reader will have to consult the introduction to that hymn (cf. the introduction to ix. 3 or 4 or x. 2 or xi. 6).⌋

⌊**Manner of using the table.** — Example: to find in the facsimile of the birch-bark ms. the Pāippalāda passage corresponding to Vulgate xix. 50. 5. First find in the table the number of the leaf of Roth's Kashmirian nāgarī transcript, which is 196 b. Then find in the facsimile the number 196 b, noted in the margin in Roth's hand. Between that and 197 a will be found the beginning of the passage required, which in this case will be at line 1 of birch-bark folio 158 b, on plate 286, and in the Second Part. The passage belongs to book xiv. of the Kashmirian recension.⌋

⌊Users of the table will find it convenient to note clearly in pencil on the margin of each plate of the facsimile the number of the leaf of the transcript opposite the place where Roth has written it on the birch-bark original, since, by reason of repairs to the original or otherwise, Roth's numbers are sometimes hard to make out when taken singly. When taken together in their regular sequence, they can usually be identified with ease. Thus the 197 a on plate 286 (just cited) is very faint indeed; but the 197 b (some five inches lower down) is so plain that it enables us to identify the 197 a. Of the references to Roth's Kashmirian nāgarī transcript on the first 42 plates, only a few can be made out easily (6 a, 6 b, 7 a, 8 a, 11 b, 12 a, 12 b, 13 b, 14 a, 15 b, 16 a); but beginning with 19 a, on plate 43, there is usually little difficulty.⌋

⌊**Tabular Concordance.** — The table now follows on the next six pages. It is made up into pages in such a way as to give incidentally a good idea of the structure of the Vulgate text; and the same purpose I have endeavored to subserve also in the arrangement of the Table of Hymn-titles (pages 1024–1037): see especially pages 1034 and 1035.⌋

[FIRST GRAND DIVISION: BOOKS I.–VII.

Vulgate, Book I.

(Norm: 4 verses)

Hymn		
1	has 4:	at 3 a in i.
2	has 4:	at 1?
3	has 9:	7, 8 at 346 b in xix.
4	has 4	
5	has 4:	1–3 at 368 a in xix.
6	has 4:	at 1?
7	has 7:	at 67 a in iv.
8	has 4:	1–3 at 67 a in iv.
9	has 4:	at 6 b in i.
10	has 4:	at 3 b in i.
11	has 6:	2–4 at 2 b in i.
		5 at ? in xx.
		6 at ? in xx.
12	has 4:	at 6 a in i.
13	has 4:	2–4 at 332 b in xix.
		1 at ? in xix.
		1 at 205 b in xv.
14	has 4:	at 5 b in i.
15	has 4:	at 8 a in i.
		? at 367 a in xix.
16	has 4:	at 4 a in i.
17	has 4:	at 333 b in xix.
18	has 4:	1, 3 at 387 a in xx.
		2 at ? in xx.
19	has 4:	at 7 a in i.
20	has 4:	1–3 at 342 b in xix.
		4 at 48 a in ii.
21	has 4:	at 48 a in ii.
22	has 4:	at 9 a in i.
23	has 4:	at 6 a in i.
24	has 4:	at 8 b in i.
25	has 4:	at 10 a in i.
26	has 4:	1, 2 at 332 b in xix.
		3, 4 at ? in xix.
27	has 4:	at 356 a in xix.
28	has 4	
29	has 6:	1–3, 5, 6 at 4 a in i.
30	has 4:	at 5 a in i.
31	has 4:	at 7 b in i.
32	has 4:	at 8 a in i.
33	has 4:	at 8 b in i.
34	has 5:	1, 2, 5 at 27 a in ii.
		3 at ? in vi.
		4 at 139 a in viii.
35	has 4	

Vulgate, Book II.

(Norm: 5 verses)

Hymn		
1	has 5:	at 26 a in ii.
2	has 5:	at 3 a in i.
3	has 6:	1, 2, 4, 5 at 3 b in i.
4	has 6:	1–5 at 27 b in ii.
5	has 7:	1, 3, 4 at 26 b in ii.
		5–7 at ? in xiii.
6	has 5:	at 61 b in iii.
7	has 5	
8	has 5:	1 at 21 a in i.
9	has 5:	at 27 b in ii.
10	has 8:	at 24 b in ii.
11	has 5	
12	has 8:	at 26 a in ii.
13	has 5:	1, 4, 5 at 199 b in xv.
14	has 6:	1, 5, 6, 2, 3 at 25 b in ii.
		4 at ? in v.
15	has 6:	at 107 b in vi.
16	has 5:	1–4 at 38 b in ii.
17	has 7:	at ? in ii.
18	has 5:	at ? in ii.
19	has 5:	at ? in ii.
20	has 5	
21	has 5	
22	has 5	
23	has 5	
24	has 8:	1–6 at 38 a in ii.
25	has 5:	at 70 b in iv.
26	has 5:	at 28 a in ii.
27	has 7:	at 29 a in ii.
28	has 5:	1–4 at 4 b in i.
		5 at ? in xv.
29	has 7:	1–3 at 344 a in xix.
		4–7 at 5 a in i.
30	has 5:	at 29 b in ii.
31	has 5:	at 28 b in ii.
32	has 6:	at 28 b in ii.
33	has 7:	at 68 a in iv.
34	has 5:	at 61 a in iii.
35	has 5:	1–4 at 18 a in i.
36	has 8:	1–5, 7 at 31 b in ii.

Vulgate, Book III.

(Norm: 6 verses)

Hymn		
1	has 6:	at 51 a in iii.
2	has 6:	at 50 b in iii.
3	has 6:	at 45 a in ii.
4	has 7:	at 49 a in iii.
5	has 8:	1–7 at 54 a in iii.
6	has 8:	1–5, 7, 8 at 50 a in iii.
7	has 7:	at 49 b in iii.
8	has 6:	1–4 at 6 b in i.
		5 = vi. 94.1 in xix.
9	has 6:	at 51 b in iii.
10	has 13:	1–8, 10–12 at 22 a in i.
11	has 8:	1–4 at 14 a in i.
12	has 9:	1–5, 7 at 56 a in iii.
		6 at 389 b in xx.
		8 at 308 a in xvii.
13	has 7:	1–6 at 50 b in iii.
14	has 6:	1–4, 6 at 28 b in ii.
15	has 8:	1, 2, 4, 6 at 370 b in xix.
		4 at 12 b in i.
16	has 7:	at 78 a in iv.
17	has 9:	2, 1, 5, 4 at 32 a in ii.
		3 at ? in xix.
		6 at ? in xix.
		6 at ? in xii.
18	has 6:	1, 2, 4, at 124 a in vii.
19	has 8:	at 55 b in iii.
20	has 10:	1–9 at 62 a in iii.
21	has 10:	1–9 at 53 a in iii.
		10 at 123 b in vii.
22	has 6:	1–5 at 55 a in iii.
23	has 6:	at 54 a in iii.
24	has 7:	1–6 at 97 a in v.
25	has 6	
26	has 6:	1, 3–5 at 53 a in iii.
27	has 6:	1, 2, 4–6 at 57 a in iii.
28	has 6	
29	has 8	
30	has 7:	at 93 a in v.
31	has 11	

Vulgate, Book IV.

(Norm: 7 verses)

Hymn

1 has 7: at 83 b in v.
2 has 8: at 83 b ? in iv.
3 has 7: 1–4, 6, 7, at 27 a in ii.
4 has 8: 1–6, 8, at 67 b in iv.
  ? at 340 a in xix.
5 has 7: at 68 a in iv.
6 has 8: 2–8 at 87 a in v.
7 has 7: 1 at 87 b in v.
  2–6 at 24 b in ii.
  7 at 110 b in vi.
8 has 7: at 65 a in iv.
9 has 10: 2–10 at 129 a in viii.
10 has 7: 1–4, 6, 7 at 75 b in iv.
11 has 12: at 58 a in iii.
12 has 7: at 71 b in iv.
13 has 7: at 92 b in v.
14 has 9: 1–6 at 64 a in iii.
  7–9 at ? in xvi.
15 has 16: 1, 3–14, 16 at 86 a in v.
16 has 9: 2, 3, 5, 7, 8 at 100 a in v.
  4, 6 at 98 a in v.
17 has 8: 1–6 at 95 a in v.
  8 at 33 b in ii.
18 has 8: at 95 a in v.
19 has 8: at 96 a in v.
20 has 9: at 130 a in viii.
21 has 7
22 has 7: at 56 b in iii.
23 has 7: at 79 a in iv.
24 has 7: at 82 a in iv.
25 has 7: at 79 b in iv.
26 has 7: at 80 b in iv.
27 has 7: at 80 a in iv.
28 has 7: at 81 a in iv.
29 has 7: at 81 b in iv.
30 has 8
31 has 7: at 70 a in iv.
32 has 7: at 78 b in iv.
33 has 8: at 77 b in iv.
34 has 8: at 115 b in vi.
35 has 7
36 has 10
37 has 12: 1–8, 10–12 at 178 a in xiii.
38 has 7
39 has 10: 9 at 185 a in xiii.
40 has 8

Vulgate, Book V.

(Norm: 8 verses)

Hymn

1 has 9: at 105 b in vi.
2 has 9: at 105 a in v.
3 has 11: at 84 b in v.
4 has 10: 1–3 at 336 b in xix.
  5–7 at 338 b in xix.
  8–10 at 30 a in ii.
5 has 9: at 107 a in vi.
6 has 14: 1–5, 8–14 at 110 b in vi.
7 has 10
8 has 9: 1–6, 8, 9 at 126 b in vii.
9 has 8
10 has 8
11 has 11: at 128 a in viii.
12 has 11
13 has 11: 2–11 at 128 b in viii.
  ? at 11 b in i.
14 has 13: 1, 2, 4, 6–8, 10–12 at 117 a in vii.
  9, 13 at 37 a in ii.
15 has 11: at ? in viii.
16 has 11: at 130 a in viii.
17 has 18: 1–7, 9–11 at 148 a in ix.
  18 at ? in ix.
18 has 15: 1–6, 8–15 at 149 b in ix.
19 has 15: 1–4, 7, 8, 10, 12 at 150 b in ix.
  15 at ? in ix.
20 has 12: at 156 a in ix.
21 has 12
22 has 14: 1, 3–10, 12, 14, at 176 a in xiii.
  ? at 94 a in v.
  13 at 10 a in i.
23 has 13: 1–9, 13 at 117 b in vii.
24 has 17: 1, 2, 4, 7–12, 14, 15, 17 at 200 b in xv.
25 has 13: 1, 3–13 at 176 b in xiii.
26 has 12: at 140 b in ix.
27 has 12: at 140 a in ix.
28 has 14: 1, 3–11 at 42 a in ii.
29 has 15: 1–9, 12–15 at 185 a in xiii.
30 has 17: at 147 a in ix.
31 has 12: 12 at 11 a in i.

Vulgate, Book VI.

(Norm: 3 verses)

Hymn

1 has 3: at 330 b in xix.
2 has 3: at 331 a in xix.
3 has 3: at 331 a in xix.
4 has 3: at 331 b in xix.
5 has 3: at 332 b in xix.
6 has 3: at 332 b in xix.
7 has 3: at ? in xix.
8 has 3
9 has 3: at ? in ii.
10 has 3
11 has 3: at 339 a in xix.
12 has 3: at 333 a in xix.
13 has 3: at 333 b in xix.
14 has 3: at 340 a in xix.
15 has 3: at 334 a in xix.
16 has 4: 1–3 at 334 a in xix.
17 has 4: 2–4 at 333 a in xix.
18 has 3: at 335 b in xix.
19 has 3: at 335 b in xix.
20 has 3: 3 at ? in xiii.
21 has 3: at 10 a in i.
22 has 3: at 348 b in xix.
23 has 3: at 333 b in xix.
24 has 3: at 335 b in xix.
  ? at 55 b in iii.
25 has 3: at 334 a in xix.
26 has 3: at 345 a in xix.
27 has 3: at 340 a in xix.
28 has 3: 1 at 340 b in xix.
  2 at 158 b in x.
  3 at 353 a in xix.
29 has 3
30 has 3: at 350 a in xix.
31 has 3: at 368 a in xix.
32 has 3: 1, 2 at 338 b in xix.
33 has 3: at 353 a in xix.
34 has 5: 1, 3, 4 at 368 a in xix.
35 has 3: at 337 a in xix.
36 has 3: at 333 a in xix.
37 has 3: at 385 b in xx.
38 has 4: at 29 b in ii.
39 has 3: ? at 336 a in xix.
  ? at 338 a in xix.
40 has 3: 1, 2, at plate 14 in i.
41 has 3
42 has 3: at 336 b in xix.
43 has 3: at 358 a in xix.
44 has 3: 1 ab at 65 a in iii.
  1 cd, 2 at 395 a in xix.

FIRST GRAND DIVISION: BOOKS I.–VII. (*Continued*)

Vulgate, Book VI. (*Continued*)

(Norm : 3 verses)

Hymn

45 has 3: at ? in xix.
46 has 3: 1, 3 at ? in xix.
3 at 36 b in ii.
47 has 3: at 366 b in xix.
48 has 3
49 has 3: at 356 b in xix.
50 has 3: 2 at 346 a in xix.
51 has 3: at 366 b in xix.
? at 106 a in vi.
52 has 3: at 335 b in xix.
? at 24 a in i.
53 has 3: at 336 a in xix.
? at 66 b in iv.
54 has 3: at 336 a in xix.
55 has 3
56 has 3: at 337 b in xix.
57 has 3: at 337 b in xix.
58 has 3: 1, 2 at 337 b in xix.
59 has 3: at 341 a in xix.
60 has 3: at 341 a in xix.
61 has 3: at 341 a in xix.
62 has 3: at 355 a in xix.
63 has 4: 1, 2 at 338 b in xix.
4 at 335 a in xix.
64 has 3: 1, 2 at 379 a in xix.
65 has 3: 1, 2 **ab**, 3 **cd** at 339 a in xix.
66 has 3: at 339 a in xix.
67 has 3
68 has 3: at 344 a in xix.
69 has 3: 1 at 36 a in ii.
2 at 357 b in xix.
70 has 3
71 has 3: at 34 a in ii.
1 at 384 a in xx.
72 has 3: at 384 a ? in xx.
73 has 3: at 338 a in xix.
74 has 3: at 342 a in xix.
75 has 3: at 342 a in xix.
76 has 4: at 342 a in xix.
77 has 3: at 342 b in xix.
78 has 3: at 343 a in xix.
79 has 3: at 343 b in xix.
80 has 3: at 343 a in xix.
81 has 3: at 343 b in xix.
82 has 3: at 343 b in xix.
83 has 4: 1–3 at 7 b in i.
84 has 4

Vulgate, Book VI. (*Continued*)

(Norm : 3 verses)

Hymn

85 has 3: at 334 b in xix.
86 has 3: at 335 a in xix.
87 has 3: at 334 b in xix.
88 has 3
89 has 3
90 has 3: at 344 b in xix.
91 has 3: at 344 b in xix.
92 has 3: at 359 a in xix.
93 has 3: at 341 b in xix.
94 has 3: 1 at 341 b in xix
95 has 3
96 has 3: at 339 a in xix.
97 has 3: at 339 b in xix.
98 has 3: at 339 b in xix.
99 has 3: at 340 a in xix.
100 has 3: at 340 a in xix.
101 has 3
102 has 3: at 341 a in xix.
103 has 3: at 345 a in xix.
104 has 3: at 371 b in xix.
105 has 3: 2 **ab** at 349 b in xix.
106 has 3: at 358 a in xix.
107 has 4: at 367 a in xix.
108 has 5: 1, 2, 5 at 344 a in xix.
109 has 3: at 352 b in xix.
110 has 3
111 has 4
112 has 3: 1, 2 at 347 b in xix.
3 at ? in i.
113 has 3: 1 **ab** at ? in i.
114 has 3: at 233 b in xvi.
115 has 3: at 234 a in xvi.
116 has 3: at 234 a in xvi.
117 has 3: at 234 a in xvi.
118 has 3: at 234 b in xvi.
119 has 3: at 234 b in xvi.
120 has 3: at 235 a in xvi.
121 has 4: 1 **ab**, 2 **ab**, 3, 4 at 235 a in xvi.
122 has 5: 2, 3 at 235 b in xvi.
123 has 5
124 has 3
125 has 3: at 252 b in xv.
126 has 3: at 122 b in vii.
127 has 3
128 has 4: 1, 2, 4 at 350 b in xix.

Vulgate, Book VI. (*Concluded*)

(Norm : 3 verses)

Hymn

129 has 3: at 356 b in xix.
130 has 4
131 has 3
132 has 5
133 has 5: at 100 b in v.
134 has 3: at 100 b in v.
135 has 3: at 100 b in v.
136 has 3
137 has 3: 2 at 16 a in i.
138 has 5: 1–4 at ? in i.
139 has 5
140 has 3: at ? in xix.
141 has 3: at 348 a in xix.
142 has 3

Vulgate, Book VII.

(Norm: 1 verse)
(*According to Berlin numbering*)

Hymn
1 has 2: at 376 a in xx.
2 has 1: at 376 b in xx.
3 has 1: at 377 a in xx.
4 has 1: at 377 a in xx.
5 has 5: 1, 2 at 377 a in xx.
6 has 2: at 376 b in xx.
and 2: at 376 b in xx.
7 has 1: at 376 b in xx.
8 has 1: at 377 b in xx.
9 has 4: 4 at ? in xx.
10 has 1
11 has 1
12 has 4: 1, 2 at 388 b in xx.
13 has 2: at 347 a in xix.
14 has 4: 3, 4 at 377 b in xx.
15 has 1: at 377 b in xx.
16 has 1
17 has 4: 1 at 11 a in i.
2–4 at 377 a in xx.
18 has 2: at ? in xx.
19 has 1: at 348 b in xix.
20 has 6: at 378 a in xx.
21 has 1: at 378 b in xx.
22 has 2: at 378 b in xx.
23 has 1 (cf. iv. 17. 5)
24 has 1
25 has 2: at 384 b in xx.
26 has 8: 1–3 at 379 b in xx.
27 has 1
28 has 1: at ? in xx.
29 has 2: at 379 b in xx.
30 has 1
31 has 1
32 has 1: at ? in xx.
33 has 1: at 114 a in vi.
34 has 1: at ? in xx.
35 has 3: 1 at ? in xx.
2 at 393 b in xx.
36 has 1: at ? in xx.
37 has 1
38 has 5: 1, 2 at ? in xx.
3–5 at 60 a in iii.
39 has 1: at 381 b in xx.
40 has 2: at 381 b in xx.
41 has 2: at 381 b in xx.
42 has 2: at 23 b in i.
43 has 1
44 has 1: at 384 b in xx.
45 has 1: at 383 b in xx.
and 1: at 383 b in xx.

Vulgate, Book VII. (*Continued*)

(Norm: 1 verse)

Hymn
46 has 3: at 383 b, 382 b in xx.
47 has 2: at 379 a in xx.
48 has 2: at 382 a in xx.
49 has 2
50 has 9: 1, 2, 5 at 337 a in xx.
3 at ? in xx.
7 at 308 a in xvii.
8, 9 at 12 a in i.
51 has 1: at ? in xv.
52 has 2
53 has 7: 1 at 379 a in xx.
2–4 at 382 a in xx.
7 at 86 a in v.
54.1 is 1: at 390 b in xx.
54.2 at 405 b in xx.
55.1
(54.2 and 55.1 make 1 hymn)
56 has 8: 1–4 at 384 a in xx.
8 at ? in ?
57 has 2: 1 at ? in xx.
2 at ? in xx.
58 has 2: at 379 b in xx.
59 has 1 (cf. vi. 37. 3)
60 has 7: 1–6 at 59 a in iii.
61 has 2: 1 cd at 353 b in xx.
62 has 1: at ? in xx.
63 has 1: at 394 b in xx.
64 has 2: at ? in xx.
65 has 3
66 has 1: at 394 b in xx.
67 has 1
68.1–2 are 2
.3 is 1
69 has 1: at ? in xx.
70 has 5: 1, 2 at 352 a in xix.
71 has 1: at 352 b in xix.
72.1–2 are 2
.3 is 1
73 has 11: 1–6 at 382 b in xx.
10, 11 at 381 a in xx.
74 has 4
75 has 2
76.1–4 are 4: 1 at 7 b in i.
3, 4 ab at 363 b in xix.
xix. [xix.
.5–6 are 2: 5 cd at 363 b in
6 at ? in xx.
77 has 3: 2, 3 at 394 a in xx.
78 has 2: at 321 a in xx.
79 has 4: 1 at ? in xx.
2, 3 at 22 a in i.

Vulgate, Book VII. (*Concluded*)

(Norm: 1 verse)

Hymn
80 has 4: 1, 4 at 21 b in i.
81 has 6
82 has 6: 2, 6 at 394 a in xx.
3 at 61 b in iii.
83 has 4: 1, 2 at 394 b in xx.
84 has 3: 1 at 62 a in iii.
85 has 1
86 has 1
87 has 1: at ? in xx.
88 has 1: at ? in xx.
89 has 4: 1–3 at 10 b in i.
90 has 3: at 393 a in xx.
91 has 1
92 has 1
93 has 1
94 has 1: at 334 b in xix.
95 has 3
96 has 1: at ? in xx.
97 has 8: at 395 a in xx.
? at 383 a in xx.
98 has 1: at 395 b in xx.
99 has 1
100 has 1: at 396 a in xx.
101 has 1: at 396 a in xx.
102 has 1
103 has 1: at ? in xx.
104 has 1: at 378 a in xx.
105 has 1: at 380 a in xx.
106 has 1: at 386 a in xx.
107 has 1
108 has 2
109 has 7: at 69 a in iv.
110 has 3: 1, 2 at ? in xx.
3 at ? in xx.
111 has 1: at 381 b in xx.
112 has 2
113 has 2: at 385 a in xx.
114 has 2: 1 at 385 a in xx.
115 has 4: 1, 2 at 385 b in xx.
116 has 2
117 has 1
118 has 1

SECOND GRAND DIVISION: BOOKS VIII.–XII.

Vulgate, Book VIII.

(Paryāya-hymn: 10)

Hymn

1 has 21: at 207 b in xvi.
2 has 28: 27 vss. at 209 a in xvi.
3 has 26: at 211 a in xvi.
4 has 25: at 213 a in xvi.
5 has 22: 21 vss. at 223 a in xvi.
6 has 26: at 250 b in xvi.
7 has 28: at 215 a in xvi.
8 has 24: at 224 b in xvi.
9 has 26: 24 vss. at 218 b in xvi.
P 10 has 33: 30 vss. at 274 b in xvi.

Vulgate, Book IX.

(Paryāya-hymns: 6 and 7)

1 has 24: at 226 a in xvi.
? at 108 a
? at 69 b
(see p. 517, last ¶)
2 has 25: 24 vss. at 248 b in xvi.
3 has 31: at 229 a in xvi.
4 has 24: at 221 b in xvi.
5 has 38: 20 vss. at 259 a in xvi.
9 vss. at ? in xvi.
3 vss. at 64 b in iii.
2 vss. at 139 a in viii.
(see p. 533, ¶ 2)
P 6 has 62: 59 vss. at ? in xvi.
P 7 has 26: 24 vss. at ? in xvi.
8 has 22: 21 vss. at 247 b in xvi.
9 has 22: at 242 a in xvi.
10 has 28: 23 vss. at 242 a in xvi.

Vulgate, Book X.

(Partly prose: hymn 5)

Hymn

1 has 32: at 227 a in xvi.
2 has 33: 29 vss. at 238 b in xvi.
3 has 25: 23 vss. at 240 b in xvi.
4 has 26: at 217 a in xvi.
5 has 50: 41 vss. at 272 b in xvi.
4 vss. at 15 a in i.
6 has 35: 25 vss. at 231 a in xvi.
7 has 44: 40 vss. at 290 b in xvii.
8 has 44: 25 vss. at 262 b, at 261 b, and at 263 in xvi.
9 has 27: at 275 b in xvi.
10 has 34: 33 vss. at 265 a in xvi.

Vulgate, Book XI.

(Paryāya-hymn: 3)

1 has 37: at 255 b in xvi.
2 has 31: at 263 b in xvi.
P 3 has 56: ? vss. at 236 a in xvi.
(see p. 625, ¶ 7)
4 has 26: at 220 a in xvi.
5 has 26: at 283 b in xvi.
6 has 23: 20 vss. at ? in xv.
7 has 27: 26 vss. at 252 a in xvi.
8 has 34: 32 vss. at 253 b in xvi.
9 has 26: bits of 15–17 at ? in xvii.
10 has 27

Vulgate, Book XII.

(Paryāya-hymn: 5)

Hymn

1 has 63: 61 vss. at 285 b in xvii.
? at 373 b in xix. ?
2 has 55: 53 vss. at 304 b in xvii.
? at 395 a in xx. ?
3 has 60: 59 vss. at 308 a in xvii.
4 has 53: at 295 b in xvii.
P 5 has 73: 61 vss. at 278 b in xvi.

THIRD GRAND DIVISION: BOOKS XIII.–XVIII : SEE P. 1014

Vulgate, Book XIII.

(Rohita sun-hymns)

(Paryāya-hymn: 4)

Hymn [xviii.

1 has 60: 55 vss. at 321 b in
1 vs. at ? in xx.
2 has 46: at 324 b in xviii.
3 has 26: 1 vs. at 66 a in iv.
P 4 has 56

Vulgate, Book XIV.

(Wedding verses)

1 has 64: 60 vss. at 313 a in xviii.
1 vs. at 76 a in iv.
1 vs. at 395 b in xx.
2 has 75: 73 vss. at 316 b in xviii.

Vulgate, Book XV.

(Vrātya-book)

(Consists of 7 + 11 paryāyas)

Hymn

P 1 has 8: at 328 a in xviii.
P 2 has 4: 1 phrase at 328 a in xviii.
The rest (P 3–P 18) is lacking

Vulgate, Book XVI.

(Paritta)

(Consists of 4 + 5 paryāyas)

The beginning and the end of each of its two anuvākas are given at 328 ab in xviii. See p. 1016.

Vulgate, Book XVII.

(Vishṇu sun-hymn)

Hymn

1 has 30: 27 vss. at 328 b in xviii.

Vulgate, Book XVIII.

(Funeral verses)

1 has 61: 1 vs. at 34 a in ii.
2 has 60: 1 vs. at 373 b in xix.
1 vs. at 398 a in xx.
3 has 73: 1 vs. at 383 b in xx.
4 has 89: 1 vs. at 330 b in xviii.
See pp. 814, 1016.

SUPPLEMENT: BOOK XIX.

Vulgate, Book XIX.

(After-gleanings)

1 has 3: at 367 a in xix.
2 has 5: at 131 b in viii.
3 has 4: at 388 a in xx.
4 has 4: 2–4 at 350 a in xix.
5 has 1: at 386 a in xx.
6 has 16: 1–6, 9–16 at 142 a in ix.
7 has 5
8 has 7: 4–6 at 400 a in xx.
9 has 14
10 has 10: at 183 a in xiii.
11 has 6: at 183 b in xiii.
12 has 1
13 has 11: at 118 b in vii.
14 has 1
15 has 6: at 62 b in iii.
16 has 2
17 has 10
18 has 10
19 has 11
20 has 4
21 has 1
22 has 21
23 has 30
24 has 8: 1, 3–8 at 200 b in xv.
25 has 1

Vulgate, Book XIX.

(*Continued*)

26 has 4: 4 at 403 a in xx.
27 has 15: 1–11, 14, 15 at 162 a in x.
28 has 10: at 187 a in xiii.
29 has 9: at 187 b in xiii.
30 has 5: at 187 b in xiii.
31 has 14: at 160 b in x.
32 has 10: at 172 b in xii.
? at 65 a
33 has 5: at 173 a in xii.
34 has 10: at 168 b in xi.
35 has 5: at 168 b in xi.
36 has 6: at 33 b in ii.
37 has 4
38 has 2: at 349 b in xix.
39 has 10: at 122 b in vii.
40 has 4: 1 at 362 a in xix.
41 has 1
42 has 4: bits at ? in ?
43 has 8
44 has 10: at 198 b in xv. [xv.
45 has 10: 1–8, 10 at 199 a in
? at 60 b in iii.
46 has 7: at 74 b in iv.
47 has 10: at 114 b in vi.
48 has 6: at 115 a in vi.

Vulgate, Book XIX.

(*Concluded*)

49 has 10: at 196 a in xiv.
50 has 7: at 196 b in xiv.
51 has 2
52 has 5: at 9 b in i.
53 has 10: 1–6 at 189 a in xiv.
7–10 at 171 a in xii.
54 has 6: at 171 a in xii.
55 has 7: 1 at 401 a in xx.
56 has 6: at 52 a in iii.
57 has 6(5): 1 at 36 b in ii.
58 has 6: 1–4 at 24 a in i.
59 has 3
60 has 2
61 has 1
62 has 1
63 has 1
64 has 4
65 has 1: at 281 b in xvi.
66 has 1: at 281 b in xvi.
67 has 8
68 has 1: at 359 b in xix.
69 has 4: at ? in xix. ?
70 has 1
71 has 1
72 has 1: at 359 b in xix.]

6. Whitney's English Captions to his Hymn-translations

⌊**These captions form an important element in his interpretation of this Veda.** — Upon this subject I have already spoken in the proper place, above, p. xcv, which see. I would merely repeat the statement that these captions or hymn-titles have been formulated with much care and deliberation by the author, and give briefly his view of the general purport of each hymn. The absence of a positive view in them is often to be taken as indicating that he could not accept the view of his predecessors. Such titles of individual hymns as are not from Whitney's hand are enclosed in ell-brackets; but the headings to the Grand Divisions and to the books of division III. and to the *paryāyas* of books xv. and xvi., although not bracketed, are from the editor's hand.⌋

⌊**In tabular form, they give a useful conspectus of the subject-matter of this Veda.** — While this fact is obvious, it is perhaps not so obvious that the giving of this table as a part of the Table of Contents in volume VII., beginning on p. xv, would have detracted much from the perspicuity of that table as a guide to this work as a whole. Moreover, such a table as this is more naturally sought near the end of the work, and the balance of the two volumes is better maintained by putting these pages in volume VIII.⌋

HYMN-NUMBER

First Grand Division. — Books I.–VII.

PAGE

Seven books of short hymns (433) of miscellaneous subjects

I. Book the first

1	For the retention of sacred learning	1
2	Against injury and disease: with a reed	2
3	Against obstruction of urine: with a reed	3
4	To the waters: for blessings	4
5	To the waters: for blessings	5
6	To the waters: for blessings	6
7	To Agni: for the discovery of sorcerers	7
8	To Agni and other gods: for the discovery of sorcerers	8
9	For some one's advancement and success	9
10	For some one's release from Varuṇa's wrath	10
11	For successful childbirth	11
12	Against various ailments (as results of lightning?)	12
13	Deterrent homage to lightning	14
14	Imprecation of spinsterhood on a woman	15
15	With an oblation: for confluence of wealth	16
16	Against demons: with an amulet of lead	17
17	To stop the vessels of the body	18
18	Against unlucky marks	19
19	Against enemies	20
20	Against enemies and their weapons	21

21 Against enemies . . . 22
22 Against yellowness (jaundice) . . . 22
23 Against leprosy: with a healing herb . . . 23
24 Against leprosy . . . 24
25 Against fever (*takmán*) . . . 25
26 For protection from the wrath of the gods . . . 26
27 Against various evils . . . 27
28 Against sorcerers and witches . . . 28
29 For a chief's success: with an amulet . . . 29
30 For protection: to all the gods . . . 30
31 To the divine guardians of the quarters . . . 31
32 Cosmogonic . . . 32
33 To the waters: for blessings . . . 33
34 A love-spell: with a sweet herb . . . 34
35 For long life etc.: with a gold amulet . . . 35

II. Book the second

1 Mystic . . . 37
2 To Gandharvas and Apsarases . . . 39
3 For relief from flux: with a certain remedy . . . 40
4 Against various evils: with a *jañgiḍá* amulet . . . 42
5 Praise and prayer to Indra . . . 43
6 Praise and prayer to Agni . . . 45
7 Against curses and cursers: with a plant . . . 47
8 Against the disease *kṣetriyá*: with a plant . . . 48
9 Against possession by demons: with an amulet . . . 50
10 For release from evils, and for welfare . . . 51
11 To counteract witchcraft: with an amulet . . . 53
12 ⌊Against such as would thwart my incantations⌋ . . . 53
13 For welfare and long life of an infant . . . 56
14 Against *sadā̃nvās* . . . 57
15 Against fear . . . 59
16 For protection . . . 60
17 For various gifts . . . 61
18 For release from demons and foes . . . 61
19 Against enemies: to Agni (fire) . . . 62
20 The same: to Vāyu (wind) . . . 63
21 The same: to Sūrya (sun) . . . 63
22 The same: to the moon . . . 63
23 The same: to water . . . 63
24 Against *kimīdíns*, male and female . . . 63
25 Against *káṇvas*: with a plant . . . 64
26 For safety and increase of kine . . . 66
27 For victory in disputation: with a plant . . . 67
28 For long life for a certain person (child?) . . . 68
29 For some one's long life and other blessings . . . 70
30 To secure a woman's love . . . 72
31 Against worms . . . 73
32 Against worms . . . 74
33 For expulsion of *yákṣma* from all parts of the body . . . 76
34 Accompanying the sacrifice of an animal . . . 77
35 To expiate errors in the sacrifice: to Viçvakarman . . . 79
36 To get a husband for a woman . . . 81

III. Book the third

1 Against enemies . . . 84
2 Against enemies . . . 86
3 For the restoration of a king . . . 87
4 To establish a king . . . 89
5 For prosperity: with a *parṇá*-amulet . . . 91
6 Against enemies: with *açvatthá* . . . 92
7 Against the disease *kṣetriyá* . . . 94
8 For authority . . . 96
9 Against *víṣkandha* and other evils . . . 98
10 To the *ekāṣṭaká* (day of moon's last quarter) . . . 99
11 For relief from disease, and for long life . . . 103
12 Accompanying the building of a house . . . 104
13 To the waters . . . 107
14 A blessing on the kine . . . 109
15 For success in trade . . . 111
16 Morning invocation to various gods, especially Bhaga . . . 113
17 For successful agriculture . . . 114
18 Against a rival wife: with a plant . . . 117
19 To help friends against enemies . . . 119
20 To Agni and other gods: for various blessings . . . 121
21 With oblation to the various forms of fire or Agni . . . 123
22 To the gods: for splendor (*várcas*) . . . 126
23 For fecundity . . . 127
24 For abundance of grain . . . 129
25 To command a woman's love . . . 130
26 Homage to the gods of the quarters etc. ⌊snake charms?⌋ . . . 131
27 The same: with imprecation on enemies . . . 133
28 To avert the ill omen of a twinning animal . . . 134
29 With the offering of a white-footed sheep . . . 135
30 For concord . . . 137
31 For welfare and long life . . . 139

IV. Book the fourth

1 Mystic . . . 142
2 To the unknown god . . . 145
3 Against wild beasts and thieves . . . 148
4 For recovery of virility: with a plant . . . 149
5 An incantation to put to sleep . . . 151
6 Against the poison of a poisoned arrow . . . 152
7 Against poison . . . 154
8 Accompanying the consecration of a king . . . 156
9 For protection etc.: with a certain ointment . . . 158
10 Against evils: with a pearl-shell amulet . . . 161
11 In praise of the draft-ox . . . 163
12 To heal serious wounds: with an herb . . . 166
13 For healing . . . 168
14 With the sacrifice of a goat . . . 169
15 For abundant rain . . . 172
16 The power of the gods . . . 176
17 Against various evils: with a plant . . . 179
18 Against witchcraft: with a plant . . . 181
19 Against enemies: with a plant . . . 182
20 To discover sorcerers: with an herb . . . 184

21 Praise of the kine . . . 186
22 For the success and prosperity of a king . . . 188
23 Praise and prayer to Agni . . . 190
24 Praise and prayer to Indra . . . 191
25 Praise and prayer to Vāyu and Savitar . . . 193
26 Praise and prayer to heaven and earth . . . 194
27 Praise and prayer to the Maruts . . . 196
28 Praise and prayer to Bhava and Çarva . . . 197
29 Praise and prayer to Mitra and Varuṇa . . . 198
30 Self-laudation of Speech (?) . . . 200
31 Praise and prayer to fury (*manyú*) . . . 201
32 Praise and prayer to fury (*manyú*) . . . 203
33 To Agni: for release from evil . . . 205
34 Extolling a certain rice-mess offering . . . 206
35 Extolling a rice-mess offering . . . 208
36 Against demons and other enemies . . . 209
37 Against various superhuman foes: with an herb . . . 211
38 For luck in gambling: by aid of an Apsaras . . . 214
39 For various blessings . . . 216
40 Against enemies from the different quarters . . . 218

V. Book the fifth

1 Mystic . . . 220
2 Mystic . . . 223
3 To various gods: for protection and blessings . . . 224
4 To the plant *kúṣṭha:* against *takmán* ⌊fever⌋ . . . 227
5 To a healing plant, *lākṣā* . . . 228
6 ? ⌊Disconnected verses⌋ . . . 230
7 Against niggardliness and its effects . . . 232
8 Against enemies: to Indra and other gods . . . 233
9 For protection: to various gods . . . 235
10 For defense from all quarters . . . 236
11 ⌊Dialogue between⌋ Varuṇa and Atharvan . . . 236
12 Āprī-hymn: to various divinities . . . 239
13 Against snakes' poison . . . 242
14 Against witchcraft: with a plant . . . 244
15 For exorcism: to a plant . . . 246
16 Exorcism . . . 247
17 The Brahman's wife . . . 247
18 The Brahman's cow . . . 250
19 The Brahman's cow . . . 252
20 To the war-drum . . . 254
21 To the war-drum . . . 257
22 Against fever (*takmán*) . . . 259
23 Against worms . . . 261
24 To various gods as overlords . . . 263
25 For successful conception . . . 265
26 Accompanying a sacrifice . . . 267
27 Āprī-hymn: to various divinities . . . 269
28 With an amulet of three metals: for safety etc. . . . 272
29 To Agni: against demons . . . 274
30 To lengthen out some one's life . . . 276
31 Against witchcraft . . . 278

VI. Book the sixth

1 Praise to Savitar . . . 281
2 Praise and prayer to Indra . . . 283
3 To various divinities: for protection . . . 283
4 To various divinities: for protection . . . 284
5 For some one's exaltation . . . 285
6 Against enemies . . . 286
7 For blessings . . . 286
8 To win a woman's love . . . 287
9 To win a woman's love . . . 287
10 Greeting to divinities etc. of the three spheres . . . 288
11 For birth of sons . . . 288
12 Against the poison of snakes . . . 289
13 To the instruments and ministers of death . . . 290
14 Against the *balā́sa* . . . 290
15 For superiority . . . 291
16 To various plants (?) . . . 292
17 Against premature birth . . . 293
18 Against jealousy . . . 293
19 For ceremonial purification . . . 294
20 Against fever (*takmán*) . . . 295
21 To healing plants . . . 295
22 To the Maruts . . . 296
23 To the waters: for blessings . . . 297
24 To the waters: for blessings . . . 298
25 For relief from pains (?) in neck and shoulders . . . 298
26 Against evil . . . 299
27 Against birds of ill omen . . . 299
28 Against birds of ill omen etc. . . . 300
29 Against birds of ill omen . . . 301
30 To the *çamī́* plant: for benefit to the hair . . . 302
31 At rising of the sun (or moon) . . . 303
32 Against demons . . . 304
33 Praise to Indra . . . 305
34 Praise and prayer to Agni . . . 306
35 Prayer to Agni Vāiçvānara . . . 306
36 In praise of Agni . . . 307
37 Against curses . . . 308
38 For brilliance . . . 309
39 For glory . . . 309
40 For freedom from fear . . . 310
41 To various divinities . . . 311
42 To remove wrath . . . 311
43 To assuage wrath . . . 312
44 For cessation of a disease . . . 312
45 In atonement of offenses . . . 313
46 Against evil dreams . . . 314
47 For blessings: at the three daily libations . . . 315
48 To the deities of the three daily libations . . . 316
49 To Agni etc. . . . 316
50 Against petty destroyers of grain . . . 317
51 For various blessings . . . 318
52 For deliverance from unseen pests . . . 319
53 For protection: to various gods . . . 320

54 To secure and increase some one's superiority 321
55 For various blessings 322
56 For protection from serpents 323
57 With a certain remedy against disease 323
58 For glory 324
59 For protection to cattle 325
60 For winning a spouse 325
61 Prayer and boasts 326
62 Vāiçvānara etc.: for purification 327
63 For some one's release from perdition (*nírṛti*) 328
64 For concord 329
65 For success against enemies 330
66 For success against enemies 330
67 For success against enemies 331
68 To accompany the act of shaving 332
69 For glory etc. 332
70 To attach a cow to her calf 333
71 Against harm from improper food 334
72 For virile power 335
73 To assure supremacy 335
74 For harmony 336
75 To eject a rival 337
76 For a *kṣatríya's* security from death 338
77 For recovery and retention of what is lost 338
78 For matrimonial happiness 339
79 For abundance at home 340
80 The heavenly dog and the *kālakāñjás* 340
81 For successful pregnancy: with an amulet 341
82 To obtain a wife 342
83 To remove *apacíts* 342
84 For release from perdition 343
85 For relief from *yákṣma* 344
86 For supremacy 345
87 To establish some one in sovereignty 345
88 To establish a sovereign 346
89 To win affection 347
90 For safety from Rudra's arrow 347
91 For remedy from disease 348
92 For success of a horse 348
93 For protection: to many gods 349
94 For harmony 350
95 For relief from disease: with *kúṣṭha* 350
96 For relief from sin and distress 351
97 For victory 351
98 To Indra: for victory 352
99 For safety: to Indra 353
100 Against poison 354
101 For virile power 354
102 To win a woman 355
103 To tie up enemies 356
104 Against enemies 356
105 To get rid of cough 357
106 Against fire in the house 357
107 For protection: to various divinities 358

108 For wisdom . . . 358
109 For healing: with *pippalī* . . . 359
110 For a child born at an unlucky time . . . 360
111 For relief from insanity . . . 361
112 For expiation of overslaughing . . . 362
113 For release from seizure (*gráhi*) . . . 362
114 Against disability in sacrifice . . . 363
115 For relief from sin . . . 364
116 For relief from guilt . . . 365
117 For relief from guilt or debt . . . 366
118 For relief from guilt . . . 367
119 For relief from guilt or obligation . . . 368
120 To reach heaven . . . 369
121 For release from evil . . . 370
122 With an offering for offspring . . . 371
123 For the success of an offering . . . 372
124 Against evil influence of a sky-drop . . . 373
125 To the war-chariot: for its success . . . 374
126 To the drum: for success against the foe . . . 375
127 Against various diseases: with a wooden amulet . . . 376
128 For auspicious time: with dung-smoke . . . 377
129 For good-fortune: with a *çiṅçápā* amulet . . . 378
130 To win a man's love . . . 379
131 To win a man's love . . . 379
132 To compel a man's love . . . 380
133 To a girdle: for long life etc. . . . 380
134 To crush an enemy with a thunderbolt . . . 381
135 To crush an enemy . . . 382
136 To fasten and increase the hair . . . 383
137 To fasten and increase the hair . . . 383
138 To make a certain man impotent . . . 384
139 To compel a woman's love . . . 384
140 With the first two upper teeth of a child . . . 385
141 With marking of cattle's ears . . . 386
142 For increase of barley . . . 387

VII. Book the seventh

1 Mystic . . . 389
2 Of Atharvan . . . 390
3 Mystic . . . 390
4 To the wind-god with his steeds . . . 391
5 Mystic: on the offering or sacrifice . . . 391
6 Praise of Aditi . . . 392
7 Praise of the Ādityas . . . 394
8 For some one's success . . . 394
9 Praise and prayer to Pūshan . . . 395
10 To Sarasvatī . . . 395
11 Against injury to the grain by lightning . . . 396
12 For success in the assembly . . . 396
13 Against one's foes . . . 397
14 Prayer and praise to Savitar . . . 398
15 Prayer to Savitar . . . 399
16 Prayer to Savitar (or Brihaspati) . . . 399
17 Prayer to Dhātar for blessings . . . 399

18 For rain, etc. . . . 400
19 For progeny, etc. . . . 401
20 Praise and prayer to Anumati . . . 402
21 In praise of the sun . . . 403
22 To the sun (?) . . . 403
23 Against ill conditions and beings . . . 404
24 To various gods . . . 404
25 Praise to Vishṇu and Varuṇa . . . 404
26 Praise and prayer to Vishṇu . . . 405
27 Prayer and praise to Iḍā . . . 407
28 Of the instruments of offering . . . 407
29 To Agni and Vishṇu . . . 408
30 For successful anointing . . . 409
31 To Indra: for aid . . . 409
32 Homage to Soma (?) . . . 409
33 For blessings: to various gods . . . 410
34 To Agni: against enemies . . . 410
35 Against a rival (woman) . . . 411
36 Husband and wife to one another . . . 411
37 The wife to the husband . . . 412
38 To win and fix a man's love: with a plant . . . 412
39 In praise of Sarasvant (?) . . . 414
40 Prayer and praise to Sarasvant . . . 414
41 To the heavenly falcon (the sun) . . . 415
42 To Soma and Rudra . . . 415
43 Of speech (?) . . . 416
44 Extolling Indra and Vishṇu . . . 416
45 To cure jealousy . . . 416
46 To Sinīvālī (goddess of the new moon) . . . 417
47 To Kuhū (goddess of the new moon) . . . 418
48 To Rākā (goddess of the full moon) . . . 418
49 To the spouses of the gods . . . 419
50 For success with dice . . . 419
51 For protection by Brihaspati and Indra . . . 421
52 For harmony . . . 422
53 For some one's health and long life . . . 423
54 Extolling verse and chant . . . 424
55 To Indra (?) . . . 425
56 Against poison of snakes and insects . . . 425
57 Prayer to Sarasvatī etc. . . . 427
58 Invitation to Indra and Varuṇa . . . 427
59 Against cursers . . . 428
60 To the home: on returning or leaving . . . 428
61 For success of penance . . . 430
62 To Agni: against enemies . . . 430
63 To Agni: for aid . . . 431
64 Against evil influence of a black bird . . . 431
65 To the plant *apāmārgá*: for cleansing . . . 432
66 For recovery of sacred knowledge (*bráhmaṇa*) . . . 432
67 For recovery of sense, etc. . . . 433
68 Praise and prayer to Sarasvatī . . . 433
69 Prayer for good fortune . . . 434
70 Against an enemy's sacrifice . . . 434
71 To Agni: for protection . . . 435

VII. Book the seventh: continued

72 With an oblation to Indra . . . 436
73 With a heated offering to the Açvins . . . 437
74 Against *apacits*: against jealousy: to Agni . . . 439
75 Praise and prayer to the kine . . . 440
76 Against *apacíts* and *jāyā́nya*: etc. . . . 441
77 To the Maruts . . . 443
78 To Agni: in favor of some one . . . 444
79 To Amāvāsyā (night or goddess of new moon) . . . 444
80 To the night or goddess of full moon (*pā́urṇamāsī́*) . . . 445
81 To the sun and moon . . . 446
82 Praise and prayer to Agni . . . 448
83 For release from Varuṇa's fetters . . . 449
84 To Agni: and to Indra . . . 451
85 Invocation of Tārkshya . . . 452
86 Invocation of Indra . . . 452
87 Homage to Rudra . . . 452
88 Against poison . . . 453
89 To Agni and the waters . . . 453
90 To destroy some one's virile power . . . 454
91 To Indra: for aid . . . 455
92 To Indra: for aid . . . 456
93 For Indra's aid . . . 456
94 For Indra's help to unanimity . . . 456
95 A spell against some one . . . 457
96 For quiet kidneys (?) . . . 457
97 Accompanying an offering . . . 458
98 With an oblation to Indra . . . 460
99 When bestrewing the *védi* . . . 460
100 Against bad dreams . . . 461
101 As to food enjoyed in a dream . . . 461
102 Accompanying self-relief . . . 461
103 For betterment . . . 462
104 Concerning Atharvan's cow . . . 462
105 An exhortation to holy life . . . 462
106 Deprecation for offenses . . . 463
107 To relieve a stinging pain . . . 463
108 Against enemies: to Agni . . . 463
109 ⌊For success with the dice⌋ . . . 464
110 To Indra and Agni: for help . . . 466
111 To a soma-vessel . . . 467
112 For release from guilt and distress . . . 467
113 Against a (woman) rival: with a plant . . . 467
114 Against enemies . . . 468
115 Against ill luck . . . 468
116 Against intermittent fever . . . 469
117 Invitation to Indra . . . 470
118 When arming a warrior . . . 470

⌊**Note on the division of this work into two separately bound volumes.** — With reference to this subject, the reader is asked to consult the paragraphs entitled "External form of this work," volume VII., pages xxiv–xxv. In order to arrange the following matter so that Division II. should face Division III. (pages 1034–5), it was necessary to leave this page blank. The blank may be utilized in part to show clearly that the break between volume VII. and volume VIII. corresponds with the break in the text between the first grand division on the one hand, and the second and third grand divisions on the other. In using this work, it will be convenient, as it is also easy, to remember that

Volume VII. ends with book vii., page 470,

and that

Volume VIII. begins with book viii., page 471.⌋

Second Grand Division. — Books VIII.–XII.

Five books of long hymns (45) of miscellaneous subjects

VIII. Book the eighth

1 For some one's continued life 472
2 To prolong some one's life 476
3 To Agni: against sorcerers and demons 481
4 Against sorcerers and demons: to Indra and Soma 486
5 Against withcraft etc.: with an amulet 490
6 To guard a pregnant woman from demons 493
7 To the plants: for some one's restoration to health 498
8 To conquer enemies 502
9 Mystic: extolling the *virā́j* 507
10 Extolling the *virā́j* (first *paryāya*-hymn, with 6 *paryāyas*) 511

IX. Book the ninth

1 To the honey-whip etc. 517
2 To Kāma: for various blessings 521
3 To accompany the releasing of a house 525
4 Accompanying the gift of a bull 529
5 With the offering of a goat and five rice-dishes 533
6 Exalting the entertainment of guests (second *paryāya*-hymn, with 6 *paryāyas*) . 539
7 Extolling the ox (third *paryāya*-hymn, with 1 *paryāya*) 547
8 Against various diseases 549
9 Mystic 552
10 Mystic 556

X. Book the tenth

1 Against witchcraft and its practisers 562
2 The wonderful structure of man 567
3 With an amulet of *varaṇá* 572
4 Against snakes and their poison 575
5 Preparation and use of water-thunderbolts (largely prose) 579
6 With an amulet 585
7 Mystic: on the *skambhá* or frame of creation 589
8 Mystic 595
9 With the offering of a cow and a hundred rice-dishes 602
10 Extolling the cow (*vaçā́*) 605

XI. Book the eleventh

1 Accompanying a rice-dish offering 612
2 To Rudra, especially as Bhava and Çarva 620
3 Extolling the rice-dish (*odaná*) (fourth *paryāya*-hymn, with 3 *paryāyas*) . . . 625
4 Extolling the breath (*prāṇá*) 632
5 Extolling the Vedic student (*brahmacārín*) 636
6 To many different gods: for relief 640
7 Extolling the remnant (*úcchiṣṭa*) of the offering 643
8 Mystic: especially on the constitution of man 647
9 To conquer enemies: to Arbudi 651
10 To conquer enemies: to Trishandhi 655

XII. Book the twelfth

1 To the earth 660
2 The flesh-eating and the householder's fires 672
3 Cremation as a sacrifice 682
4 The cow (*vaçā́*) as belonging exclusively to the Brahmans 693
5 The Brahman's cow (fifth *paryāya*-hymn, with 7 *paryāyas*) 701

Third Grand Division. — Books XIII.–XVIII.

Six books of long hymns (15), the books showing unity of subject

Book XIII. — Hymns to the Ruddy Sun or Rohita. Seer: Brahman

1 To Rohita (the sun, as ruddy one) . . . 709
2 To the sun . . . 719
3 To the sun (with imprecation on the evil-doer) . . . 727
4 Extolling the sun (*paryāya*-hymn, with 6 *paryāyas*) . . . 732

Book XIV. — Wedding Verses. Seer: Sāvitrī Sūryā

1 Marriage ceremonies . . . 740
2 Marriage ceremonies (continued) . . . 753

Book XV. — The Vrātya. Seer: —

1 Paryāya the first or xv. 1. 1 . . . 773
Paryāya the second or xv. 1. 2 . . . 774
Paryāya the third or xv. 1. 3 . . . 776
Paryāya the fourth or xv. 1. 4 . . . 777
Paryāya the fifth or xv. 1. 5 . . . 778
Paryāya the sixth or xv. 1. 6 . . . 780
Paryāya the seventh or xv. 1. 7 . . . 781
2 Paryāya the eighth or xv. 2. 1 . . . 782
Paryāya the ninth or xv. 2. 2 . . . 783
Paryāya the tenth or xv. 2. 3 . . . 783
Paryāya the eleventh or xv. 2. 4 . . . 784
Paryāya the twelfth or xv. 2. 5 . . . 785
Paryāya the thirteenth or xv. 2. 6 . . . 786
Paryāya the fourteenth or xv. 2. 7 . . . 788
Paryāya the fifteenth or xv. 2. 8 . . . 789
Paryāya the sixteenth or xv. 2. 9 . . . 790
Paryāya the seventeenth or xv. 2. 10 . . . 791
Paryāya the eighteenth or xv. 2. 11 . . . 791

Book XVI. — Paritta. Seer: Prajāpati [?]

1 Paryāya the first or xvi. 1. 1 . . . 794
Paryāya the second or xvi. 1. 2 . . . 795
Paryāya the third or xvi. 1. 3 . . . 796
Paryāya the fourth or xvi. 1. 4 . . . 797
2 Paryāya the fifth or xvi. 2. 1 . . . 798
Paryāya the sixth or xvi. 2. 2 . . . 798
Paryāya the seventh or xvi. 2. 3 . . . 800
Paryāya the eighth or xvi. 2. 4 . . . 801
Paryāya the ninth or xvi. 2. 5 . . . 803

Book XVII. — Prayer to the Sun as Indra and Vishṇu. Seer: Brahman

1 Prayer and praise to Indra and the Sun . . . 809

Book XVIII. — Funeral Verses. Seer: Atharvan

1 ⌊Funeral verses⌋ . . . 815
2 ⌊Funeral verses⌋ . . . 830
3 ⌊Funeral verses⌋ . . . 846
4 ⌊Funeral verses⌋ . . . 869

Supplement. — Book XIX.

After-gleanings (72 hymns), chiefly from the traditional sources of division I.

Book XIX. — Supplementary Hymns

1 With an oblation for confluence 898
2 Praise and prayer to the waters 899
3 Praise to Agni 900
4 To various divinities 901
5 Praise and prayer to Indra 902
6 Purusha and his sacrifice 902
7 To the lunar asterisms: for blessings 906
8 For well-being: to the asterisms etc. 909
9 For appeasement and weal: to various divinities 912
10 For well-being 915
11 For well-being 917
12 For success and long life 918
13 For success in war: ⌊Apratiratha hymn⌋ 918
14 For safety 921
15 For safety and success 921
16 For safety and protection 923
17 For protection: to various gods 924
18 For protection: to various gods 925
19 For protection by various gods 926
20 For protection by various gods 927
21 The meters 928
22 Homage to parts of the Atharva-Veda 929
23 Homage to parts of the Atharva-Veda 931
24 For prosperity: with a certain garment 934
25 To a horse 936
26 For long life etc.: with something golden 936
27 For protection etc.: with a triple amulet 938
28 For various blessings: with an amulet of *darbhá* 941
29 Continuation of the foregoing 942
30 For protection etc.: with an amulet of *darbhá* 943
31 For various blessings: with an amulet of *udumbára* 944
32 For long life etc.: with an amulet of *darbhá* 947
33 For various blessings: with an amulet of *darbhá* 949
34 With a *jan̄giḍá*-amulet: for protection etc. 950
35 The same 953
36 With a *çatávāra*-amulet: for protection etc. 955
37 With an amulet: for various blessings 956
38 With *gúggulu:* against disease 957
39 With *kúṣṭha:* against diseases 959
40 To various divinities: for various blessings 961
41 For some one's welfare 963
42 Extolling the *bráhman* etc. 963
43 To various gods: for attaining heaven 965
44 With an ointment: against diseases etc. 966
45 With an ointment etc.: for various objects 969
46 With and to an amulet called *ástṛta* 'unsubdued' 972
47 To night: for protection 974
48 To night: for protection 977
49 Praise and prayer to night 978

50 To night: for protection 983
51 Accompanying acceptance (?) 985
52 Of and to desire (*kā́ma*) 985
53 Praise of time (*kālá*) 987
54 Praise of time 989
55 To Agni 991
56 To sleep (or dream) 993
57 Against evil-dreaming 996
58 For various blessings 998
59 For successful sacrifice 1000
60 For physical abilities 1001
61 For length of life etc. 1002
62 For popularity 1003
63 To Brihaspati: for sundry blessings 1003
64 To Agni: with fuel 1003
65 Praise of the sun 1005
66 To Agni: for aid 1005
67 For long life and prosperity 1005
68 With ceremonial performance 1006
69 To the waters: for long life 1007
70 For long life 1008
71 For various blessings 1008
72 For the favor of the gods 1009

7. The Names of the Seers of the Hymns, as given by the Anukramaṇī

⌊**Whitney's exploitation of the Major Anukramaṇī.** — In his Excerpts from the Anukramaṇī, Whitney has given most of the material of value to be found in that treatise, but of course without attempting to settle all doubtful points in such a way as might properly be expected of a critical editor of its text. One of the uses of the following Index will be to make the deficiencies of this part of his work more readily apparent. The Excerpts and Index together will make the task of producing a critical edition relatively easy.⌋

⌊**Doubtful points.** — In some cases, this Index does not tally perfectly with the Excerpts. Thus vi. 46 and 47, as well as 45, seem to be ascribed to "Aṅgiras Pracetas, with Yama": cf. the Excerpts. Again, *mantroktarṣi* of the Excerpt for vi. 48 may perhaps mean "Agni and Ṛbhu and Indra"; but I have not entered those names for this hymn in the Index. Whitney seems to have had a doubt as to vii. 27–29, whether they should not be ascribed rather to Bhṛgvaṅgiras than to Medhātithi; and as to vii. 31, whether it should not be ascribed rather to Brahman than to Bhṛgv-aṅgiras; and as to vii. 33. What the Anukr. means to say about vi. 63 is not wholly clear.⌋

⌊**Entire books of division III. ascribed each to a single seer.** — It will be noticed that four entire books (all belonging to the third grand division: see p. 1035) are ascribed by the Major Anukramanī each to a single seer: books xiii. and xvii., each addressed to the Sun, are ascribed to Brahman as seer; the wedding verses, book xiv., most appropriately to Sāvitrī Sūryā; and the funeral verses, book xviii., to Atharvan (the Old Anukr. most appropriately calls them the Yama-hymns: p. 814). Further, so far as quasi-authorship goes, the Vrātya book, xv., is treated as a unit in that no seer is named for the whole nor for any part of it. As for book xvi., which puzzles us in more ways than one, there is good reason to think that tradition ascribes it to Prajāpati (see p. 792, ¶ 4); on the other hand, this is not wholly certain (p. 792, ¶ 5), and the Excerpts actually assign 3–4 to Brahman and 5–7 to Yama, and leave 2 and 8 and 9 without express assignment, unless indeed we are to assume that the statements for 1 and for 7 hold good respectively for 2 and for 8 and 9.⌋

⌊**Value of these ascriptions of quasi-authorship.** — The facts just cited would appear to be of some moment as differentiating the third grand division from the other two; but otherwise and in general, how much value, if any, is to be attached to these ascriptions is matter for special study. It would be interesting to compare the ascriptions of the AV. Anukr. with those of the RV. Anukr. and to see how far the two treatises agree as to hymns or verses common to both saṁhitās. The Puruṣa-hymn (xix. 6 = RV. x. 90) is ascribed by both treatises alike to Nārāyaṇa; and the Apratiratha-hymn (xix. 13 = RV. x. 103) similarly to Apratiratha. In this connection, cf. Dr. Ryder's pertinent observation at p. 739, ¶ 7.⌋

⌊**Prominence of Atharvan and Brahman as seers.** — The most prominent names among the "seers" are Atharvan and Brahman. To the former are ascribed 175 hymns or parts of hymns; and to the latter, 100. Then comes Atharvāñgiras with 17, and Añgiras with 16. The preponderance of ascriptions to Atharvan and Brahman may have something to do with the designation of the text as "Atharva-Veda" and "Brahma-Veda" (*brahman* suggests both Brahmán = 'God Brahm' and *bráhman* = 'incantation': cf. p. 931, top). It is perhaps matter for surprise that more hymns are not ascribed to the "dreadful Añgirases" (RV. x. 108. 10: cf. x. 14. 3 a).⌋

⌊**Question of contrast between hymns of Atharvan and hymns of Añgiras.** — Bloomfield, discussing at SBE. xlii., p. xviii, the name Atharvāñgiras as name of this Veda, opines that atharvan refers to the auspicious practices and añgiras to the practices of hostile sorcery (*yātú, abhicārá*) of this Veda. Similarly Victor Henry, in his *La magie dans l'Inde*, p. 22. This opinion is not in the least degree supported by the general character of the hymns ascribed respectively to Atharvan and to Añgiras. Of those ascribed to Atharvan, nearly all are indeed intended for use in working good, and the infrequent exceptions (like iii. 18; vii. 35 and 70; vi. 138, a charm to make a man impotent) do not count for much. Of those ascribed to Añgiras, on the other hand, hardly more than one (vii. 90: this also is for destroying a man's virility) may be said to be for use in working evil. It is licit, however, to adjudge the facts last rehearsed as making rather against the critical value of the Anukramaṇī's ascriptions than against the acceptability of the opinion of Bloomfield and Henry.⌋

⌊**Consistency in the ascriptions.** — Consistency does nevertheless characterize these ascriptions to a certain degree. Thus the frequency with which each of the hymns of a related pair or of a larger group (e.g. the Mṛgāra hymns) is ascribed to the same seer is significant. Significant also are such facts as follow. Of the seven hymns ascribed to Garutman, every one is an incantation to be used against poison: v. 13 and vi. 12 and x. 4, in particular, against snake-poison. Each of the three hymns ascribed to Kāṇva is an incantation against worms. Each of Jamadagni's three has for its purpose to win a woman's love. Of those ascribed to Yama or to Yama with Añgiras (disregarding xvi. 8 and 9, they number 13), all but one refer either to "Death" or to "his brother Sleep" (cf. p. 994, ¶ 4). Thus ten, as appears from the *duḥsvapna* etc. of the Excerpts, refer to evil dreams; and one (vii. 64) to the omen of a "black bird" as Yama's "messenger of death"; and one (xii. 3) to cremation of the dead. Verse 13 of this last also makes reference to the black bird, and so does xix. 57. Of the four ascribed to Bādarāyaṇi,* two (iv. 38; vii. 109) are for success in gambling.⌋

* ⌊Weber suspected that the author of the Anukr. may have been a Vedantist, and that it was thus not unnatural that the name of Bādarāyaṇi should appear among his ascriptions (see above, p. 218, top). Weber derived his suspicion from a remark by the author of the Anukr. on the last verse of book iv., *Brahmāṇaṁ sarvatra Jātavedābhimukhyenāstāut.* If the author bases his remark upon the letter of our text (which has *bráhma*, neuter), let us hope that his philosophical acumen was more penetrant than his philological.⌋

⌊**Palpably fabricated ascriptions.** — Not a few of the ascriptions are palpably fabricated from a word in the text. Of this kind are Up-heater and Forth-heater (Ucchocana and Praçocana) as seers of vi. 103 and 104, and Deliverance and Release (Unmocana and Pramocana) as seers of vi. 105 and 106. Strangely enough, none of these four words (or "names") occurs in any of these four hymns, but rather (the first two) in vii. 95 and (the second two) in v. 30, which latter furthermore is also ascribed to Unmocana.⌋

⌊**Alphabetical index of seer-names and of passages ascribed to them.** — This Index was made by Whitney, but was carefully revised by Dr. Ryder and again by me.⌋

Agastya vi. 133

Añgiras ii. 3; 35. iv. 39. 1–8. v. 12. vi. 83–84. vii. 50–51; 77; 90. xix. 22; 34–35. See also Atharvāñgiras and Pratyañgirasa and Bhṛgvañgiras

Añgiras Pracetas, with Yama, vi. 45–47

Atharvan i. 1–3; 9–11; 15; 20–21; 23; 27; 30; 34–35. ii. 4; 7; 13; 19–23; 29; 34. iii. 1–5; 8; 10; 15–16; 18; 26–27; 30. iv. 3–4; 10; 15; 22 (? or Vasiṣṭha ?); 30; 34. v. 5–6; 7–8 (?); 11; 24; 28. vi. 1–7; 13; 17–18; 32. 3; 36–40; 50; 58–62; 64–69; 73–74; 78–80; 85–90; 92; 97–99; 109–113; 124–126; 138–140. vii. 1–7; 13–14; 18; 34–38; 45. 2; 46–49; 52; 56; 61; 70–73; 76; 78–81; 85–87; 91–92; 94; 97–99; 105–106. viii. 7; 9. ix. 1–2. x. 3; 7; 9. xi. 2–3; 7. xii. 1. xviii. 1–4 (the whole book). xix. 14–20; 23–24; 26; 37–38. See also Bṛhaddiva Atharvan; also Sindhudvīpa Atharvākṛti

Atharvan Vītahavya vi. 136–137

Atharvāñgiras iv. 8. vi. 72; 94; 101; 128–132. vii. 74; 115–118. xix. 3–4; 5 (?). Cf. Añgiras

Atharvācārya viii. 10. Cf. xii. 5 (Kaçyapa)

Apratiratha xix. 13

Ātharvaṇa: cf. Bhṛgu Ātharvaṇa

Ucchocana vi. 103

Uddālaka iii. 29. vi. 15

Unmocana v. 30. vi. 105

Uparibabhrava vi. 30–31. vii. 8–9; 75

Ṛbhu iv. 12

Kapiñjala ii. 27. vii. 95–96

Kabandha vi. 75–77

Kaçyapa x. 10. xii. 4–5

Kaçyapa Mārīca vii. 62–63

Kāñkāyana vi. 70. xi. 9

Kāṇva ii. 31–32. v. 23

Kutsa x. 8

Kāurupathi vii. 58. xi. 8

Kāuçika vi. 35; 117–121. x. 5. 25–35

Garutman (so ! not -mant) iv. 6–7. v. 13. vi. 12; 100. vii. 88. x. 4

Gārgya vi. 49. xix. 7–8

Gopatha xix. 25 ; 47–48 ; 50
Gopatha, with Bharadvāja, xix. 49 (?)
Cātana i. 7–8 ; 16 ; 28. ii. 14 ; 18 ; 25. iv. 36. v. 29. vi. 32. 1–2 ; 34. viii. 3–4
Jagadbījampuruṣa iii. 6
Jamadagni vi. 8–9 ; 102
Jāṭikāyana vi. 33 ; 116
Tvaṣṭṛ vi. 81
Draviṇodas i. 18
Druhvaṇa (?) vi. 63
Nārāyaṇa x. 2. xix. 6
Pativedana ii. 36
Prajāpati ii. 30. iv. 35. vi. 11. vii. 102. xvi. 1 (but see p. 792, ¶ 4) ; 2 (?). xix. 46
Pratyañgirasa x. 1. Cf. Añgiras
Pramocana vi. 106
Praçocana vi. 104
Praskaṇva vii. 39–44 ; 45. 1
Babhrupiñgala vi. 14
Bādarāyaṇi iv. 37–38. vii. 59 ; 109
Bṛhacchukra vi. 53. Cf. Çukra
Bṛhaddiva Atharvan v. 1–3. Cf. Atharvan
Bṛhaspati x. 6
Brahman i. 17 ; 19 ; 22 ; 24 ; 26 ; 31–32. ii. 15–17 ; 24 ; 33. iii. 12 ; 14 ; 23 ; 28 ; 31. iv. 5 ; 16 ; 21 ; 33 ; 39. 9–10. v. 9–10 ; 20–21 ; 25–27. vi. 26 ; 41 ; 54–55 ; 71 ; 114–115. vii. 19–22 ; 24 ; 32 ; 33 (?) ; 53 ; 54. 1 ; 60 ; 66–67 ; 103–104 ; 111. viii. 1–2. ix. 4 ; 6–7 ; 9–10. x. 5. 37–41. xi. 1 ; 5. xiii. 1–4 (the whole book). xvi. 3–4. xvii. 1 (the whole book). xix. 1 ; 9–12 ; 21 ; 28–30 ; 36 ; 40–43 ; 51–52 ; 58–71
Brahman, with Bhṛgvañgiras, iii. 11
Brahmāskanda iv. 31–32
Bhaga vi. 82
Bharadvāja ii. 12
Bharadvāja, with Gopatha, xix. 49 (?)
Bhāgali vi. 52
Bhārgava vii. 113–114
Bhārgava Vāidarbhi xi. 4
Bhṛgu iii. 13 ; 24–25. iv. 9 ; 14. vi. 27–29 ; 122–123. vii. 15–17 ; 54. 2 ; 55 ; 84 ; 107–108 ; 110. ix. 5. xii. 2. xix. 32–33 ; 44–45 ; 53–55
Bhṛgu Ātharvaṇa ii. 5
Bhṛgvañgiras i. 12–14 ; 25. ii. 8–10. iii. 7. iv. 11. v. 4 ; 22. vi. 20 ; 42–43 ; 91 ; 95–96 ; 127. vii. 30–31 ; 93. viii. 8. ix. 3 ; 8. xi. 10. xix. 27 ; 39. Cf. Añgiras ; and see introduction to this Index
Bhṛgvañgiras Brahman xix. 72
Bhṛgvañgiras, with Brahman, iii. 11
Mayobhū v. 17–19
Mātṛnāman ii. 2. iv. 20. viii. 6
Mārīca : cf. Kaçyapa Mārīca. See p. 579, ¶ 5
Mṛgāra iv. 23–29
Medhātithi vii. 25–29 (but see introduction to this Index)
Yama vii. 23 ; 64 ; 100–101. xii. 3. xvi. 5–7 ; 8–9 (?). xix. 56–57
Yama, with Añgiras Pracetas, vi. 45–47
Varuṇa vii. 112
Vasiṣṭha i. 29. iii. 19–22. iv. 22 (? or Atharvan ?)
Vāmadeva iii. 9. vii. 57
Viçvāmitra iii. 17. v. 15–16. vi. 44 ; 141–142
Vihavya x. 5. 42–50
Vītahavya : cf. Atharvan
Vena ii. 1. iv. 1–2
Çamtāti i. 33. iv. 13. vi. 10 ; 19 ; 21–24 ; 51 ; 56–57 ; 93 ; 107. vii. 68–69. xi. 6
Çambhū ii. 28
Çukra ii. 11. iv. 17–19 ; 40. v. 14 ; 31. vi. 134–135. vii. 65. viii. 5. Cf. Bṛhacchukra
Çunahçepa vi. 25. vii. 83
Çāunaka ii. 6. vi. 16 ; 108. vii. 10–12 ; 82
Savitṛ ii. 26. xix. 31
Sāvitrī Sūryā xiv. 1–2 (the whole book). See p. 739, ¶ 5
Sindhudvīpa i. 4–5. vii. 89. x. 5. 1–24. xix. 2
Sindhudvīpa Atharvākṛti i. 6. Cf. Atharvan

8. Brief Index of Names and Things and Words and Places

⌊**An elaborate index uncalled for here.** — The existence of Whitney's complete and accurate *Index Verborum* to the AV. makes needless a full index of Sanskrit words for this work. Again, since the whole text is treated, each place or passage in its natural order, an index of places is also unnecessary. Moreover, an excellent English index of names and things is furnished by Griffith in his Translation. The following index, therefore, may legitimately be kept within very narrow limits. Its purpose is merely to aid in finding a few matters which are not to be found by the help of Whitney or Griffith. On the other hand, it is obvious that it would be possible and most useful to make for this work an exceedingly detailed index, giving, for example, under the heading *Surd and sonant interchanged*, every case of that kind to be found by careful comparison of the Atharvan text with the variants reported in this work. Such an index would be practically a collection of brief essays upon the subjects named in its headings, and would involve (see p. xxxvii, ¶ 2) a variety of special investigations which are too large to be undertaken here and must be left for another occasion. I hope that the student of this work will find the arrangement of the matter of the General Introduction so clear, and the analytical table of contents so thorough and perspicuous, that the absence of a detailed index to the matter of the Introduction will not be felt.⌋

⌊Arabic numerals by themselves refer to the pages of the main body of this work, the "Translation and Notes"; Roman numerals by themselves refer to the pages of volume VII. which precede the "Translation and Notes." Numerals in groups refer to book and hymn and verse, or rather to the notes thereon.⌋

⌊Abbreviations explained, xcix
Accent heeded by the commentator, xix. 13. 9
Antigone, cited, i. 14. 1
Antiphonal responses, ii. 5, introduction
Asterisms, regents of, xiv. 1. 13; in general, xix. 7 and 8
Athenæum Press, xl
Auditory errors, xcii
Barth, on Griffith's translations, xcv, note
Βεκός story of Herodotus, xviii. 4. 77
Benares, cremation at, xviii. 4. 12
Black sesame for mournful occasion, xviii. 3. 69
Blend-readings, xciii, xiv. 2. 18; xviii. 1. 39, 42; 4. 57
Bloomfield's argument in favor of RW's emendation anticipated and parried by W., xix. 53. 2; his Vedic Concordance, xxxvii, xc, xci; works on the ritual, lxxv, ci
Brahma-jāla-sutta, the name, x. 5. 1
"Brought nearer to completion," meaning of the phrase, xxxiv, xl
Caland, works of, on ritual, lxxv, ci
Cappeller, Carl, xl
Chāndogya Upanishad, vii. 15[3] discussed at xviii. 4. 12
Cremation at Benares, xviii. 4. 12
Death and Sleep, xix. 56. 1
Decad-sūktas, cxxxii
Dedication of this work, motif of the, xxxix

Delbrück, B., lxxvii, note
Diarrhœa caused by fear, iii. 2. 5
Eleven dishes, deposition of, xviii. 4. 16
Ell-brackets, use of, explained, xxviii, c
Endings, of words, abbreviated, xix. 59. 1
Errors, remarkable series of, xxxvi, note. See *Auditory errors* and *Visual errors*
Faulty assimilation of endings, xviii. 4. 87 [cf. Album-Kern, p. 303]
Garbe, Richard, xl, xliv, note, lxxxii
Geldner, Karl F., xliv, note, 816, etc.
Genders, confused?, xiv. 2. 30
Glosses, hypermetric, xciii
Grierson, George A., xl, v. 13. 5
Griffith's translations, Barth on, xcv, note
Hadley, James, xlix, xliii
Halévy, J., on hrūḍu, i. 25. 2
Haplography, cases of, lxxxiii, xciii, iv. 5. 5; xv. 7. 1
Henri d'Orléans, Prince, on a symbolic practice, vii. 38. 5
Henry, Victor, on hrūḍu, i. 25. 2
Hopkins, E. W., xl, xlviii, xii. 1. 51
Index Verborum in fuller form, Whitney's unpublished MS. thereof, xxv, note
Infelicities of expression in the translation, xxxvii, xcviii
Integer vitae, lxxviii
Jacobi, Hermann, xl
Kaegi, Adolf, xliv, note
Karait, venomous little snake, v. 13. 5
Lindner, Bruno, xliv, note
Mahā-bhārata, possible reminiscence of AV. in the, x. 4. 9; verse in AV. resembling adages of, v. 19. 9
Māitrāyaṇī, peculiar orthography of, disregarded, xc
Manuscript D. confused with Op., lxv
Manuscripts, designations of, explained, cix
Messengers of Yama, xviii. 2. 27
Milky Way, vi. 128. 4.
Misdivision between hymns, clx, near end, i. 20. 4 and introd. to i. 21, 1016
Mixed construction, xiv. 2. 72
Moore, George F., xl, xiv. 2. 14
Morgan, Morris H., xl
One hundred and one, i. 30. 3; iii. 11. 5; viii. 2. 27; xi. 6. 16
Pada-pāṭha, blunders of, lxix, xiii. 3. 17; xix. 26. 3; etc.
Paritta, as name for sixteenth book, clviii, note, xv, cxlv, 792, 1023, 1035; as name for the hymn iii. 26, introduction to iii. 26
Pearls formed from rain-drops, introd. to iv. 10
Pischel, Richard, xci, xviii. 1. 1; etc.
Play of words, xviii. 3. 29
Prākritism in orthography, iii. 12. 4; x. 9. 23; xix. 8. 4 [cf. Album-Kern, p. 302]
Protests: against issue of works in confusing subdivisions, xxv, note; against separate pagination of reprints, xcix, note
Rain-drops become pearls, introd. to iv. 10
Reprints, see *Protests*
Ryder, A. W., xxxix, lxxxvi, 420, 515, 579, 663, 664, 702, 739, 1039, 1040
Salisbury, Edward E., xliii, xliv, note, xlix, l
Sense-equivalent variants, lxxx, xviii. 2. 16
Seventh book, exceptional character of, cli; one verse its norm, cxlix
Shadow, loss of, xiii. 1. 56
Shuffling of pādas, xviii. 2. 2; 3. 38; 3. 47
Sleep and Death, xix. 56. 1
Smith, Theobald, xl, v. 13. 4
Snake-poison, autotoxic action of, v. 13. 4; vii. 88. 1; x. 4. 26
Suggestions for future work relating to the AV.: in general, xxxvii, ¶ 2, 1042; edition of Pañcapaṭalikā, lxxii; edition of Major Anukramaṇī, lxxii, 1038; edition of Kashmirian text, lxxxvi; sifting of various interpretations, xxxi; criticism of the Pada-pāṭha, lxix; comparison of grouping of mantras in the ritual and in the saṁhitā, lxxv; critical study of hymns that exceed the normal length, cliii and note; question of identity of Sāyaṇa of RV. with "Sāyaṇa" of AV., lxviii; publication of Roth's exegetical notes, xcvi
Suggestions for future work relating to the RV., xxxvii, xxxviii
Suggestions of Roth for future work, xxxviii, note
Surd and sonant confused, lxxxiii, xcii, ii. 13. 3; xiv. 1. 45; xviii. 2. 14; 1045
Tears destroy peace of the dead, xiv. 2. 59

Translation, infelicities of expression in, xxxvii, xcviii
Twin-consonant wrongly inserted or omitted, lxxxiv, xcii, xviii. 2. 3
Ūha-pādas in the saṁhitā, 503, 847 [cf. Album-Kern, p. 301]
Urination, posture in, vii. 102. 1; xiii. 1. 56
Visual errors, xciii
Wales Professorship of Sanskrit at Harvard, xliv, note
Warren, Henry Clarke, vii, xxiv, xxxviii, xxxix
Whitney, Mrs. W. D., xxxix, xlvi
Whitney, Miss Maria, xl
Women likened to field, xiv. 2. 14
Word-endings abbreviated, xix. 59. 1
Word-play, xviii. 3. 29
Yama's messengers, xviii. 2. 27

akṛpran, xviii. 3. 23
ajayānāis, xviii. 2. 53
añjoyānāis, xviii. 2. 53
a-paçcād-daghvan, xix. 55. 5
abhito taṭantha, interesting corruption, xiv. 1. 45
arir mitram arer etc., iv. 9. 4
artha-sūktas, cxxxiii
ahighnyo, x. 4. 7
āsandī, xiv. 2. 65
índra-çatru and *indra-çatrú*, lxviii
āitat, xviii. 3. 40
-ka, as added to stems of participles, ii. 3. 1; iv. 37. 10; v. 13. 9; v. 23. 7; xiv. 2. 63; JAOS. xx. 25
kuṭṭayeyus, xviii. 4. 55
gúggulu, orthography and accent, 957
tu, sole occurrence of, in AV., iv. 18. 6
dhuvana, xviii. 3. 10, 17
nāvaprabhrañçana, xix. 39. 8
nicṛt, lxxiv, note
pada-nī, xi. 2. 13
paryāya-sūktas, cxxxiii
palāça, xviii. 4. 53
pitṛnidhāna (eleven dishes), xviii. 4. 16
peṭikā = κόφινος, xviii. 2. 25
prastavyā ityādi, 782, foot-note
prāçliṣṭa svarita, xviii. 1. 55
bhurij, lxxiv, note
rakṣohā̆ (?), neuter, xix. 44. 7
vānya, *abhivānya*, etc., xviii. 4. 35
virāj, lxxiv, note
viṣāṇā, etymology, iii. 7. 1; vi. 44. 3; vi. 121. 1
vāiyadhikaraṇya, xviii. 3. 2
vyāghrādiṣu etc. of Anukr., xv. 5. 7
saṁçritya, xviii. 4. 55
su-çañsa, xviii. 3. 16
suhār, *suhārt*, xix. 45. 2, 1046
svarāj, lxxiv, note
hariṇīs or 'taking' verses, xviii. 3. 8

ii. 13. 1, lxxiii
iii. 10. 12, lxiv
iii. 12. 1, lxxxiii
iv. 10. 6, lxx
iv. 19. 6, lxvii, lxx
iv. 28. 3, lxvii, lxx
iv. 32. 3, lxxiv
vi. 1. 3, lxix, note
vi. 32. 3, xcii
vi. 70. 3, xcii
vii. 57. 2, xcvii
x. 2. 24, lxxxix
x. 3. 18, 21, 22, lxxxiii
xii. 3. 36, lxxxviii
xiv. 1. 9, lxix
xiv. 2. 18, xciii
xviii. 1. 50, xciv
xviii. 2. 46, lxviii
xviii. 3. 3, xcii
xviii. 4. 40, xcvii
xviii. 4. 61, lxxix
xix. 23, cl, clvii, clix
xix. 50. 5, 7, lxxxiii

9. Additions and Corrections

⌊**Omissions and errors not easy to rectify in the electrotype plates.** — Of the omissions and errors, the minor ones have been made good in the plates; the more considerable ones are rectified here, and to these rectifications special attention is called at the proper places by a hand (☞) inserted in the plate and pointing to the number of this page or the following.

PAGE

lxxxii, paragraph 2, and lxxxv, top: I seem to be in error in supposing that Roth made his autograph nāgarī transcript directly from the birch-bark original. Garbe writes me, April 27, 1905, that Roth's autograph nāgarī transcript consists of two quarto volumes, that it was made from Roth's Kashmirian nāgarī transcript (see p. lxxxi), and that it has been collated with the birch-bark original at the beginning, not very far, the variants being noted in red ink. I can hardly see what Roth's purpose was in making a new transcript from anything else than the birch-bark original, unless it be that the new transcript was to serve merely as a convenient hand-copy on which to note the variants of the birch-bark leaves, which could thus be collated in their proper order without injury.

57 (ii. 13. 3): Confusion of surd and sonant, aspirate and non-aspirate. This is shown by the variants of the following passages which I have noted: AV. vi. 3. 3; 28. 1; 29. 3; ix. 9. 17; x. 4. 13, 23 (*sarvebhyo*); 7. 43; xi. 1. 2; 5. 1; xii. 2. 23; 3. 2, 55; 4. 29; xiii. 1. 1; 2. 15, 43; xiv. 2. 31, 37 (*vṛddhaye*), 68; xviii. 1. 30; 2. 14, 35, 47; 3. 52; 4. 63; xix. 9. 8; 11. 6; 13. 5; 24. 6 (*adhi dhās*); 33. 3; 34. 2, 3; 36. 3; 38. 1 (*gantho*); 39. 10; 56. 4, 5. Roth discusses these matters, ZDMG. xlviii. 106–111. Cf. above, p. 1043, Index, s.v. *Surd;* also J. Hertel, Tantra-ākhyāyika, 1904, p. xvi; and Bloomfield's Vedic Concordance, passim (e.g., under *atha* and *adha*).

58 (ii. 14, introd.): See Ludwig, Sb. der Böhmischen Ges. der Wiss., 1898, no. 10, p. 11.

94 (iii. 7. 1): As to *viṣāṇā*, see references in Index, s.v., p. 1044.

197 (iv. 27. 6): Neither von Schröder nor I can find the MS. citation.

266 (v. 25. 8): ÇGS. reads *abhi kranda vīlayasva.*

327 (vi. 61. 3): Add: ⌊Here ends the sixth *anuvāka*, 10 hymns with 30 verses; the Anukr. quotation is [*pañcama-*]*ṣaṣṭhāu triṅçatkāu* (read *triṅçakāu*?).⌋

455 (vii. 90. 3): The Old Anukr. says [*dvitīya-*]*aṣṭamāu nava.* The *dvitīya-* was not given at p. 404, but refers to *anuvāka* 2, with its 9 hymns.

461 (vii. 101. 1): The hymn is treated at length by Pischel, Album-Kern, 115–7.

547 (ix. 7, introd., line 10): The an-uktapāda verses are rather *all except* 7, 18, 19, 22, 23.

601 (x. 8. 43): Garbe, in his Sāṁkhya-tattva-kāumudī, Abh. der Bayerischen Ak. der Wiss., xix., p. 529, reports previous views as to this verse, renders **b** by "mit drei Schnüren (d. i. dreifach) umhüllt," and takes "triply covered" as referring to skin and nails and hair.

792 (book xvi., introd.): It occurred to me as an afterthought (p. clviii, note) that the Pāli term Paritta, 'protection, defense' (cf. Sanskrit *paritrāṇa*), might be an acceptable equivalent in a single word for 'a prayer against the terror by night.' See Index, p. 1043, s.v. Paritta, and compare the use of the term in the Jātaka, ii. 34^{16}, 35^{22}, and especially at 148^{9}. The Mora-jātaka contains a Paritta to be used at sunrise (ii. 33^{19}; iv. 334^{4}) and one to be used at sunset (ii. 35^{11}; iv. 334^{7}).

943 (xix. 30): It is of interest to note that a part of this hymn was translated by Sir William Jones in a botanical essay published by him in the Asiatick Researches, Calcutta, 1795, vol. iv., p. 257. In the London reprint of 1798, it may be found at

iv. 253; and in that of 1801, at iv. 243. I do not remember meeting any earlier translation into English of a part of this Veda.

970 (xix. 45. 2): Whitney cites doubtfully, at Grammar, § 194, the MS. combination *suhā́rṇ ṇaḥ*. At § 150 b he records instances of retention of radical non-nasal mute after *r*: thus, *ū́rk*, *várk*, *avart*, *ámārṭ*, *suhā́rt;* compare Kielhorn's Grammar, § 14 of either edition, German or English.⌋